Major Conservation and Recreation Areas

Orkney
Shetland Islands
National Parks (Regional Parks in Scotland)
Forest Parks and Forest Recreation Areas
Community Forests (England)
Areas of Outstanding Natural Beauty (National Scenic Areas in Scotland)
Heritage Coasts (England and Wales)
National Trails (Long Distance Routes in Scotland)
World Heritage Sites
SCOTLAND
Speyside Way
West Highland Way
Loch Lomond
Fife
Clyde Muirshiel
Pentland Hills
Southern Upland Way
Northumberland
Hadrian's Wall Path
NORTHERN IRELAND
Proposed
North York Moors
Cleveland Way
Lake District
Yorkshire Dales
Wolds Way
Pennine Bridleway
Pennine Way
Peak District
Snowdonia
Offa's Dyke Path
The Broads
(Special protected area)
Peddars Way and Norfolk Coast Path
WALES
ENGLAND
Pembrokeshire Coast
Pembrokeshire Coast Path
Brecon Beacons
Cotswold Way
Ridgeway
Thames Path
North Downs Way
South Downs Way
Exmoor
South West Coast Path
Dartmoor
South West Coast Path
New Forest Heritage Area
0 40 80 120 km
0 20 40 60 80 miles
World Heritage Sites
1. Canterbury Cathedral
2. Maritime Greenwich
3. Palace of Westminster, etc.
4. Tower of London
5. Stonehenge and Avebury
6. City of Bath
7. Blenheim Palace
8. Blaenavon Industrial Landscape
9. Ironbridge Gorge
10. Castles of Edward I
11. Studley Royal Gardens and Fountains Abbey
12. Durham Cathedral and Castle
13. Hadrian's Wall
14. Edinburgh Old and New Towns
15. Giant's Causeway
16. St Kilda
17. The Heart of Neolithic Orkney

Physical Features

Orkney Islands
Shetland Islands
Land over 400 metres
Land 100–399 metres
Land 0–99 metres
Peaks
Rivers
National borders
Cape Wrath
Dunnet Head
Lewis
Ben Hope 927 m
Clisham 799 m
Morven 705 m
Ben More Assynt 998 m
St Kilda
Outer Hebrides
Harris
Hebrides
Skye
Ben Dearg 1081 m
Moray Firth
Ben Wyvis 1045 m
R. Spey
Cuillin Hills 1009 m
Càrn Eige 1182 m
Loch Ness
Cairn Gorm 1245 m
Ben Macdhui 1311 m
R. Dee
Inner
Loch Morar
Ben Nevis 1343 m
Lochnagar 1154 m
Grampians
Schiehallion 1081 m
Mull
Ben Lawers 1014 m
Ben More 966 m
Firth of Tay
R. Tay
Loch Lomond
Atlantic Ocean
R. Forth
Firth of Forth
Islay
Bute
SCOTLAND
Holy I.
R. Clyde
R. Tweed
Goat Fell 874 m
NORTHERN IRELAND
Arran
Southern Uplands
The Cheviot 816 m
Mountains of Antrim
North Channel
R. Foyle
R. Bann
Trostan 554 m
Merrick 843 m
North Sea
R. Tyne
Sperrin Mountains
Sawel 683 m
Lough Neagh
R. Eden
Cross Fell 893 m
Solway Firth
Cumbrian
Lower Lough Erne
R. Lagan
Strangford Lough
Isle of Man
Scafell Pikes 978 m
R. Tees
Upper Lough Erne
Mourne Mountains
Mountains
North Yorkshire Moors 454 m
Slieve Donard 852 m
Snaefell 620 m
Whernside 737 m
Flamborough Head
R. Swale
R. Derwent
Yorkshire Wolds
Morecambe Bay
REPUBLIC
R. Wharfe
R. Ribble
Irish Sea
R. Aire
Lough Ree
Spurn Head
R. Don
Anglesey
The Peak 636 m
Lincolnshire Wolds
OF
R. Mersey
Pennines
Cheshire Plain
The Wash
Snowdon 1085 m
R. Dee
R. Trent
Lough Derg
Cader Idris 892 m
Cambrian Mountains
The Fens
IRELAND
R. Welland
The Broads
Cardigan Bay
R. Nene
Plynlimon 752 m
ENGLAND
R. Severn
R. Avon
R. Ouse
East Anglia
St. George's Channel
WALES
Gog Magog Hills
R. Wye
Cleeve Cloud 330 m
Cotswolds
Brecon Beacons 886 m
Chiltern Hills
R. Lea
R. Thames
Berkshire Downs
R. Thames
North Foreland
Celtic Sea
Lundy I.
Bristol Channel
R. Avon
R. Kennet
North Downs
Mendip Hills
Hampshire Downs
Strait of Dover
Hartland Point
Exmoor
Dunkery Beacon 520 m
Salisbury Plain
R. Medway
R. Parrett
R. Wey
The Weald
High Willhays 621 m
R. Avon
South Downs
R. Exe
North Dorset Downs
Beachy Head
Brown Willy 419 m
Dartmoor
R. Tamar
Bodmin Moor
Lyme Bay
Portland Bill
Isle of Wight
English Channel
Greenwich Meridian 0° longitude
Land's End
Lizard Point
Scilly Isles
0 40 80 120 km
0 20 40 60 80 miles
Channel Islands
FRANCE
R. Seine

Prepared by the Office for National Statistics

While every attempt has been made to ensure that the information in this yearbook is up to date at the time of publication, the publisher cannot accept responsibility for any inaccuracies.

First published 2001

ISBN 0 11 621457 0

the Stationery Office

Published by The Stationery Office and available from:

The Stationery Office
(mail, telephone and fax orders only)
PO Box 29, Norwich NR3 1GN
Telephone orders/General enquiries 0870 600 5522
Fax orders 0870 600 5533

www.thestationeryoffice.com

The Stationery Office Bookshops
123 Kingsway, London WC2B 6PQ
020 7242 6393 Fax 020 7242 6394
68–69 Bull Street, Birmingham B4 6AD
0121 236 9696 Fax 0121 236 9699
33 Wine Street, Bristol BS1 2BQ
0117 926 4306 Fax 0117 929 4515
9–21 Princess Street, Manchester M60 8AS
0161 834 7201 Fax 0161 833 0634
16 Arthur Street, Belfast BT1 4GD
028 9023 8457 Fax 028 9023 5401
The Stationery Office Oriel Bookshop
18–19 High Street, Cardiff CF1 2BZ
029 2039 5548 Fax 029 2038 4347
71 Lothian Road, Edinburgh EH3 9AZ
0870 606 5566 Fax 0870 606 5588

The Stationery Office's Accredited Agents
(see Yellow Pages)

and through good booksellers

Printed in the UK for The Stationery Office.

J4797 C119 11/01

Contents

Page

Foreword v

PART ONE *Britain and its People*
1 Introduction 1
2 England 7
3 Northern Ireland 13
4 Scotland 22
5 Wales 28
Essay: Census 2001: 'count me in' 34

PART TWO *Government and Foreign Affairs*
6 Government 37
7 Overseas Relations 75
8 Defence 99

PART THREE *Social and Cultural Affairs*
9 The Social Framework 108
10 Education and Training 126
11 The Labour Market 148
12 Social Protection 164
13 Health 184
14 Criminal and Civil Justice 213
15 Religion 237
16 Culture 247
17 Media and Communications 269
18 Sport and Active Recreation 289
Essay: Design 311

PART FOUR *The Environment and Transport*
19 Environmental Protection 312
20 Planning, Housing and Regeneration 340
21 Transport 359
Essay: Sustainable Development 378

PART FIVE *Economic Affairs*
22 The Economy 379
23 Public Finance 399
24 International Trade and Investment 410
25 Science, Engineering and Technology 423
26 Agriculture, Fishing and Forestry 446
27 Manufacturing and Construction 468
28 Energy and Natural Resources 490
29 Finance and Other Service Industries 509
Essay: E-commerce 536

Appendix 1: Government Departments and Agencies 537
Appendix 2: Obituaries 547
Appendix 3: Principal Abbreviations 552
Appendix 4: Public Holidays, 2002 555

Index 556

Maps

The Waterways Network in the UK
Major Conservation and Recreation Areas
Physical Features
Gas and Oil Production in the UK
Passenger Railway Network in the UK
Motorways and Major Roads
} *endpapers*
England: Counties and Unitary Authorities 8
The Regions of England Covered by the GOs and RDAs 10
Northern Ireland: Districts 15
Scotland: Council Areas 23
Wales: Unitary Authorities 30
The European Union 77
The Commonwealth 78
Some Minerals Produced in Britain 505

Photographs

Credits for the photographs appear within the colour sections.

Census 2001 between pp. 10 and 11
General Election 2001 between pp. 42 and 43
Leisure and Volunteering between pp. 106 and 107
Visual Arts between pp. 202 and 203
Archaeology in the Landscape between pp. 266 and 267
Sport and Fitness for All between pp. 298 and 299
Development Cooperation Overseas between pp. 330 and 331
Science and Technology between pp. 426 and 427
Exhibitions in the UK between pp. 522 and 523

Cover Photographs

Foreword

UK 2002, formerly known as the *Britain Yearbook*, is the 53rd edition of an official annual reference book that was first published in the 1940s. Since 1997 it has been produced by the Office for National Statistics (ONS). Drawing on a wide range of official and other authoritative sources, *UK 2002* provides a factual and up-to-date overview of the United Kingdom, and also describes the main aspects of current government policy. It is a widely used work of reference, both in the United Kingdom itself, and overseas, where it is an important element of the information service provided by British diplomatic posts.

The 53rd edition has been fully updated and revised. Every effort is made to ensure that the information given in *UK 2002* is accurate at the time of going to press. The text is generally based on information available up to the end of August 2001. More website addresses have been included this year: these were also current in August 2001. Information about particular companies has been taken from company reports and news releases, or from other publicly available sources. No information about individual companies has been taken from returns submitted in response to ONS statistical inquiries, which remain entirely confidential.

Acknowledgments

UK 2002 has been researched, written and edited by a combination of in-house authors and freelances and compiled with the cooperation of around 250 organisations, including other government departments and agencies. The editors would like to thank all the people from these organisations who have taken so much time and care to ensure that the book's high standards of accuracy have been maintained. Their contributions and comments have been extremely valuable.

Editors	Jil Matheson, Nigel Pearce, Henry Langley, Jill Barelli
Chapter authors	Nigel Pearce (1); Derek Tomlin (2, 3, 4, 5, 6, 12, 14); Richard German (7,17); Oliver Metcalf (8); Carol Summerfield (9); Anthony Osley (10), Dave Sharp (11); Shaun Flanagan (12); Mike Short (13); Conor Shipsey (14, 15, 16); Henry Langley (17, 18, 22, 23, 29); Christine Lillistone (19); Nina Mill (20); Ben Bradford (21); David Harper (22, 24, 26, 27, 29), John King (25), John Collis (28)
Index	Richard German
Production assistants	Sharon Adhikari, John Chrzczonowicz, Sunita Dedi, Steve Howell
Proof readers	Jole Cosgrove, Rosemary Hamilton, Jane Howard, Jeff Probst
Cover design	Frances Riddelle, Richard Birch
Picture research and design of the colour sections	Frances Riddelle
Layout of colour sections/design of charts and maps	Ray Martin
Additional black and white maps	Alistair Dent/Nick Richardson

Conventions

- In this book, 1 billion means 1,000 million.
- Figures given in tables and charts may not always sum to the total because of rounding.
- In tables, 'n.a.' means not available.
- The full title of the UK is 'the United Kingdom of Great Britain and Northern Ireland'. 'Great Britain' comprises England, Wales and Scotland. The adjectives 'British' and 'UK' are often used interchangeably and 'Britain' is sometimes used as an alternative to 'UK'.
- As far as possible, the book applies to the UK as a whole. However, data are not always available on a comparable basis, so some information is given for one or more of the component parts of the UK. Geographical coverage is clearly indicated.

Note On National Accounts Revisions

The ONS has completed a major programme resulting in significant long run revisions to the national accounts and associated indicators. This programme includes new data sources and improvements to methodologies. The results were included in the National Accounts dataset release on 25 September and in the 2001 editions of *United Kingdom National Accounts—the Blue Book* and *United Kingdom Balance of Payments—the Pink Book*. The majority of figures in *UK 2002* were compiled before these new data were available.

About the Office for National Statistics

The Office for National Statistics (ONS) is the government agency responsible for compiling, analysing and disseminating many of the United Kingdom's economic, social and demographic statistics, including the retail prices index, trade figures and labour market data, as well as the periodic census of the population and health statistics. It is also the agency that administers the statutory registration of births, marriages and deaths. The Director of ONS is the National Statistician and the Registrar General for England and Wales.

A National Statistics publication

National Statistics are produced to high professional standards set out in the National Statistics Code of Practice. They undergo regular quality assurance reviews to ensure that they meet customer needs. They are produced free from any political interference.

Readers' Comments

We welcome readers' comments and suggestions. These should be sent to: The Editor, *UK Yearbook*, Room B5/02, Office for National Statistics, 1 Drummond Gate, London SW1V 2QQ, UK. E-mail: Britain.Yearbook@ons.gov.uk

1 Introduction

Physical Features	1	Population	3
Channel Islands and Isle of Man	1	City Status	4
Climate	2	Historical Outline	4

The establishment in 1999 of the Scottish Parliament, the National Assembly for Wales and the Northern Ireland Assembly was the most significant change in the constitution in the United Kingdom since its formation in 1801.[1] In July 2000 the Greater London Authority assumed its responsibilities, the first of a possible nine regional assemblies in England to be set up over the next few years.

Physical Features

The United Kingdom (UK) constitutes the greater part of the British Isles. The largest of the islands is Great Britain, which comprises England, Scotland and Wales. The next largest is Ireland, comprising Northern Ireland, which is part of the UK, and the Irish Republic. Western Scotland is fringed by the large island chains known as the Inner and Outer Hebrides, and to the north of the Scottish mainland are the Orkney and Shetland Islands. All these, along with the Isle of Wight, Anglesey and the Isles of Scilly, have administrative ties with the mainland, but the Isle of Man in the Irish Sea and the Channel Islands between Great Britain and France are largely self-governing, and are not part of the UK. The UK is one of the 15 Member States of the European Union (EU).

With an area of about 243,000 sq km (93,000 sq miles), excluding inland water, the UK is just under 1,000 km (about 600 miles) from the south coast to the extreme north of the Scottish mainland and just under 500 km (around 300 miles) across at the widest point.

Channel Islands and Isle of Man

Although the Channel Islands and the Isle of Man are not part of the United Kingdom, they have a special relationship with it. The Channel Islands were part of the Duchy of Normandy in the 10th and 11th centuries and remained subject to the English Crown after the loss of mainland Normandy to the French in 1204. The Isle of Man was under the nominal sovereignty of Norway until 1266, and eventually came under the direct administration of the British Crown in 1765, when it was bought for £70,000. Its parliament, 'Tynwald', was established more than 1,000 years ago and is the oldest legislature in continuous existence in the world. Today the territories have their own legislative assemblies and systems of law, and their own taxation systems. The British Government is responsible for their international relations and external defence.

[1] When the UK was the United Kingdom of Great Britain and *Ireland*. The Irish Free State (now the Irish Republic) was created in 1922, leaving Northern Ireland in the Union. The devolution of political power is discussed in greater detail in chapters 2, 3, 4, 5 and 6.

- Highest mountain: Ben Nevis, in the Highlands of Scotland, 1,343 m (4,406 ft)
- Longest river: the Severn, 322 km (200 miles) long, which rises in central Wales and flows through Shrewsbury, Worcester and Gloucester in England to the Bristol Channel
- Largest lake: Lough Neagh, Northern Ireland, 396 sq km (153 sq miles)
- Deepest lake: Loch Morar in the Highlands of Scotland, 310 m (1,017 ft) deep
- Highest waterfall: Eas a'Chual Aluinn, from Glas Bheinn, also in the Highlands of Scotland, with a drop of 200 m (660 ft)
- Deepest cave: Ogof Ffynnon Ddu, Powys, Wales, 308 m (1,010 ft) deep
- Most northerly point on the British mainland: Dunnet Head, north-east Scotland
- Most southerly point on the British mainland: Lizard Point, Cornwall
- Most easterly town in England: Lowestoft, Suffolk
- The Channel Tunnel, near Dover in Kent, links England and France. It is 48 km (30 miles) long, of which nearly 37 km (23 miles) are actually under the English Channel (*La Manche*).

The Channel Islands and Isle of Man are neither EU Member States nor part of the UK Member State. Broadly speaking, EU rules on the free movement of goods and the Common Agricultural Policy apply to the Islands, but not those on the free movement of services or persons. Islanders benefit from the provision for free movement of persons only if they have close ties with the UK.

Climate

The climate in the United Kingdom is generally mild and temperate. Prevailing weather systems move in from the Atlantic, and the weather is mainly influenced by depressions and their associated fronts moving eastwards, punctuated by settled, fine, anticyclonic periods lasting from a few days to several weeks. There are few extremes of temperature, which rarely rises above 32°C (90°F) or falls below –10°C (14°F).

Rainfall is greatest in western and upland parts of the country, where the annual average exceeds 1,100 mm (43 inches); the higher mountain areas receive more than 2,000 mm. Over much of lowland central England, annual rainfall ranges from 700 to 850 mm, although parts of East Anglia and the South East receive just 550 mm. Rain is fairly well distributed throughout the year, with late winter/spring (February to March) the driest period and autumn/winter (October to January) the wettest. During May, June and July (the months of longest daylight) the mean daily duration of sunshine varies from five hours in northern Scotland to eight hours in the Isle of Wight. During the months of shortest daylight (November, December and January) sunshine is at a minimum, with an average of an hour a day in northern Scotland and two hours a day on the south coast of England.

Climate Change and Flooding

It is said that the British are always talking about the weather. During 2000 they had good reason to do so. The year began with the sunniest winter over England and Wales since 1909, followed by the wettest April since records began in 1766. Parts of Scotland and Northern Ireland then had the driest July since 1927, before October saw rainfall records broken throughout the UK. The autumn of 2000 turned out to be the wettest for England and Wales since 1766, and the wet weather continued into spring 2001, breaking the record again for the 12 months to March. However, 2000 was also the fifteenth warmest year in Central England in a series going back to 1659, although the winter of 2000–01 has provisionally been classified as cold.

Unusual weather is not just a recent phenomenon in the UK. On 21 January 1661 Samuel Pepys recorded in his diary: 'It is strange what weather we have had all this

Table 1.1: UK Population, 2000

	England	Wales	Scotland	Northern Ireland	United Kingdom
Population (thousands)	49,997	2,946	5,115	1,698	59,756
Per cent of population aged:					
under 5	*6.0*	*5.7*	*5.6*	*7.0*	*6.0*
5–15	*14.2*	*14.4*	*13.9*	*17.0*	*14.2*
16 to pension age[1]	*61.8*	*60.0*	*62.4*	*60.7*	*61.7*
above pension age[1]	*18.0*	*19.9*	*18.1*	*15.2*	*18.1*
Area (sq km)	130,422	20,779	78,133	13,576	242,910
Population density (people per sq km)	383	142	65	125	246
Per cent population change 1981 to 2000	6.8	4.7	−1.3	10.0	6.0
Live births per 1,000 population	11.5	10.6	10.4	12.7	11.4
Deaths per 1,000 population	10.1	11.4	11.3	8.8	10.3

[1] Pension age is 65 for males and 60 for females.
Sources: Office for National Statistics, National Assembly for Wales, General Register Office for Scotland and Northern Ireland Statistics and Research Agency

winter; no cold at all, but the ways are dusty, and the flyes fly up and down, and the rose-bushes are full of leaves, such a time of the year as was never known in this world before here.'[2] Even so, the increased incidence of extreme events in the UK and worldwide appears to add substance to the predicted impact of human activity on climate variability—although the evidence from historical records indicates that recent extremes are not unprecedented.

The floods in Britain in autumn 2000 were among the worst in living memory, setting a benchmark for severe flooding along with 1998 (river), 1953 (coastal) and 1947 (snowmelt). The severe weather caused the flooding of over 10,000 properties, and 11,000 people had to be evacuated from their homes. By the following spring some had still not been able to return. Conditions were so extreme in some parts of England and Wales that properties were flooded up to three times between October and November. Farmland was also widely affected. However, the successful operation of flood defences and warning systems, and the coordinated efforts of the Environment Agency, emergency services and local authorities, prevented long-term damage to a further 300,000 or so properties.

[2] The Pepys diary entry continues: 'This day many of the Fifth Monarchy men were hanged.' No hanging has taken place in the UK since 1965.

With nearly 2 million homes and businesses at risk of flooding from rivers and the sea in England and Wales, the Government has redoubled its efforts to prepare for unusual levels of flooding in the future, while announcing extra assistance (for example, £11.6 million in January 2001) for immediate repairs to damaged flood defences.

A Climate Change Model for Scotland

In one scenario in a study carried out for the Scottish Executive by the Tyndall Centre for Climate Change Research, and published in February 2001, average annual rainfall in Scotland could increase by around 20% if there were an annual average warming of between 2°C and 3°C. Furthermore, intense precipitation, expected every two years, would increase by up to 15% for every 1°C of warming. In other words, although Scotland would have milder winters, it would also suffer from wetter, stormier days with an increased threat of flooding.

Population

The population of the UK increased from 38.2 million in 1901 to 59.8 million in 2000 (see Table 1.1). Official projections, based on mid-1999 population estimates, forecast that the population will reach nearly 61.8 million by 2011.

City Status

In December 2000, to mark the Millennium, three towns in Britain were granted city status: Brighton & Hove and Wolverhampton in England, and Inverness in Scotland. There are now 61 cities in the UK: 49 in England, five in Scotland, four in Wales and three in Northern Ireland. City status is a mark of distinction granted by the personal Command of the Sovereign, on the advice of his or her Ministers. The last towns to achieve city status before 2000 were St David's in Wales and Armagh in Northern Ireland, both in 1994, and Sunderland in England in 1992.[3]

Historical Outline

The name 'Britain' derives from Greek and Latin names which probably stem from a Celtic original. Although in the prehistoric timescale the Celts were relatively late arrivals in the British Isles, only with them does Britain emerge into recorded history. The term 'Celtic' is often used rather generally to distinguish the early inhabitants of the British Isles from the later Anglo-Saxon invaders.

After two expeditions by Julius Caesar in 55 and 54 BC, contact between Britain and the Roman world grew, culminating in the Roman invasion of AD 43. Roman rule was gradually extended from south-east England to include Wales and, for a time, the lowlands of Scotland. The final Roman withdrawal around 409 followed a period of increasing disorder during which the island began to be raided by Angles, Saxons and Jutes from northern Europe. It is from the Angles that the name 'England' derives. The raids turned into settlement and a number of small English kingdoms were established. The Britons maintained an independent existence in the areas now known as Wales and Cornwall, while in Scotland the Picts were neighbours and rivals of the Scots, who had migrated there from Ireland. Among the Anglo-Saxon kingdoms more powerful ones emerged, claiming overlordship of the whole of England, first in the north (Northumbria), then in the midlands (Mercia) and finally in the south (Wessex). However, further raids and settlement by the Vikings from Scandinavia occurred, although in the 10th century the Wessex dynasty defeated the invading Danes and established a wide-ranging authority in England. In 1066 England was invaded by the Normans (see p. 7), who then settled along with others from France.

Dates of some of the main events in Britain's history are given below. The early histories of England, Wales, Scotland and Northern Ireland are included in chapters 2 to 5.

[3] The other cities are: England—Bath, Birmingham, Bradford, Bristol, Cambridge, Canterbury, Carlisle, Chester, Chichester, Coventry, Derby, Durham, Ely, Exeter, Gloucester, Hereford, Kingston upon Hull, Lancaster, Leeds, Leicester, Lichfield, Lincoln, Liverpool, London, Manchester, Newcastle upon Tyne, Norwich, Nottingham, Oxford, Peterborough, Plymouth, Portsmouth, Ripon, Salford, Salisbury, Sheffield, Southampton, St Albans, Stoke-on-Trent, Truro, Wakefield, Wells, Westminster, Winchester, Worcester and York; Scotland—Aberdeen, Dundee, Edinburgh and Glasgow; Wales—Bangor, Cardiff and Swansea; Northern Ireland—Belfast and Londonderry/Derry.

Significant Dates

55 and 54 BC: Julius Caesar's expeditions to Britain
AD 43: Roman conquest begins under Claudius
122–38: Hadrian's Wall built
c.409: Roman army withdraws from Britain
450s onwards: foundation of the Anglo-Saxon kingdoms
597: arrival of St Augustine to preach Christianity to the Anglo-Saxons
664: Synod of Whitby opts for Roman Catholic rather than Celtic church
789–95: first Viking raids
832–60: Scots and Picts merge under Kenneth Macalpin to form what is to become the kingdom of Scotland
860s: Danes overrun East Anglia, Northumbria and eastern Mercia
871–99: reign of Alfred the Great in Wessex

1066: William the Conqueror defeats Harold Godwinson at Hastings and takes the throne
1086: *Domesday Book* completed: a survey of English landholdings undertaken on the orders of William I
1215: King John signs Magna Carta to protect feudal rights against royal abuse
13th century: first Oxford and Cambridge colleges founded
1301: Edward of Caernarvon (later Edward II) created Prince of Wales
1314: Battle of Bannockburn ensures survival of separate Scottish kingdom
1337: Hundred Years War between England and France begins
1348–49: Black Death (bubonic plague) wipes out a third of England's population
1381: Peasants' Revolt in England, the most significant popular rebellion in English history
c.1387–c.1394: Geoffrey Chaucer writes *The Canterbury Tales*
1400–c.1406: Owain Glyndŵr (Owen Glendower) leads the last major Welsh revolt against English rule
1411: St Andrews University founded, the first university in Scotland
1455–87: Wars of the Roses between Yorkists and Lancastrians
1477: first book to be printed in England, by William Caxton
1534–40: English Reformation; Henry VIII breaks with the Papacy
1536–42: Acts of Union integrate England and Wales administratively and legally and give Wales representation in Parliament
1547–53: Protestantism becomes official religion in England under Edward VI
1553–58: Catholic reaction under Mary I
1558: loss of Calais, last English possession in France
1588: defeat of Spanish Armada
1558–1603: reign of Elizabeth I; moderate Protestantism established
c.1590–c.1613: plays of Shakespeare written
1603: union of the crowns of Scotland and England under James VI of Scotland
1642–51: Civil Wars between King and Parliament
1649: execution of Charles I
1653–58: Oliver Cromwell rules as Lord Protector
1660: monarchy restored under Charles II
1660: founding of the Royal Society for the Promotion of Natural Knowledge
1663: John Milton finishes *Paradise Lost*
1665: the Great Plague, the last major epidemic of plague in England
1666: the Great Fire of London
1686: Isaac Newton sets out his laws of motion and the idea of universal gravitation
1688: Glorious Revolution; accession of William and Mary
1707: Acts of Union unite the English and Scottish Parliaments
1721–42: Robert Walpole, first British Prime Minister
1745–46: Bonnie Prince Charlie's failed attempt to retake the British throne for the Stuarts
c.1760s–c.1830s: Industrial Revolution
1761: opening of the Bridgewater Canal ushers in Canal Age
1775–83: American War of Independence leads to loss of the Thirteen Colonies
1801: Act of Union unites Great Britain and Ireland
1805: Battle of Trafalgar, the decisive naval battle of the Napoleonic Wars
1815: Battle of Waterloo, the final defeat of Napoleon
1825: opening of the Stockton and Darlington Railway, the world's first passenger railway
1829: Catholic emancipation
1832: first Reform Act extends the franchise (increasing the number of those entitled to vote by about 50%)
1833: abolition of slavery in the British Empire (the slave *trade* having been abolished in 1807)
1836–70: Charles Dickens writes his novels
1837–1901: reign of Queen Victoria
1859: Charles Darwin publishes *On the Origin of Species by Means of Natural Selection*
1868: founding of the Trades Union Congress (TUC)
1907: Henry Royce and C.S. Rolls build and sell their first Rolls-Royce (the Silver Ghost)

1910–36: during the reign of George V, the British Empire reaches its territorial zenith
1914–18: First World War
1918: the vote given to women over 30
1921: Anglo-Irish Treaty establishes the Irish Free State; Northern Ireland remains part of the United Kingdom
1926: John Logie Baird gives the first practical demonstration of television
1928: voting age for women reduced to 21, on equal terms with men
1928: Alexander Fleming discovers penicillin
1936: Jarrow Crusade, the most famous of the hunger marches in the 1930s
1939–45: Second World War
1943: Max Newman, Donald Michie, Tommy Flowers and Alan Turing build the first electronic computer, Colossus I, which was used for breaking enemy communications codes in the Second World War
1947: independence for India and Pakistan: Britain begins to dismantle its imperial structure
1948: the National Health Service comes into operation, offering free medical care to the whole population
1952: accession of Elizabeth II
1953: Francis Crick and his colleague James Watson of the United States discover the structure of DNA
1965: first commercial natural gas discovery in the North Sea
1969: first notable discovery of offshore oil in the North Sea
1973: the UK enters the European Community (now the European Union)
1979–90: Margaret Thatcher is the UK's first woman Prime Minister
1994: Channel Tunnel opened to rail traffic
1999: Scottish Parliament, National Assembly for Wales and Northern Ireland Assembly assume their devolved powers

Further Reading

The Office for National Statistics issues a number of statistical publications, many of which are used in compiling this *Yearbook*, including: *Annual Abstract of Statistics*, *Economic Trends*, *Family Spending*, *Labour Market Trends*, *Living in Britain: Results from the General Household Survey*, *Monthly Digest of Statistics*, *Population Trends*, *Regional Trends*, *Social Trends*, *Travel Trends*, *United Kingdom Balance of Payments—the Pink Book* and *United Kingdom National Accounts—the Blue Book*. Details of these can be found on the National Statistics website (*www.statistics.gov.uk*) or by contacting The National Statistics Customer Enquiry Centre, Room 1.015, ONS, Government Buildings, Cardiff Road, Newport NP10 8XG. Tel: 0845 601 3034 (UK), +44 (0)1633 812973 (overseas). Fax: +44 (0) 1633 652747. E-mail: info@statistics.gov.uk

Websites

The Met Office: www.metoffice.com

The Environment Agency for England and Wales (including advice on flooding): www.environment-agency.gov.uk

2 England

Early History	7	Rural Areas	11
Government	9	The Environment	11
London	9	Culture	12
The Regions of England	10		

More than four-fifths of the total population of the United Kingdom live in England, with the greatest concentrations in London and the South East, South and West Yorkshire, Greater Manchester and Merseyside, the West Midlands, and adjoining towns in the North East on the rivers Tyne, Wear and Tees. Between 1851 and the end of the 20th century, the population of England almost trebled and the rise is expected to continue from 50.2 million people in 2001 to 53.7 million in 2021.

England is a country of mostly low hills and plains with a 3,200-km (2,000-mile) coastline cut into by bays, coves and estuaries. Upland regions in the north include the Pennine Chain, splitting northern England into north-western and north-eastern sectors; the Cumbrian mountains, home of the Lake District, with the highest point in England, Scafell Pike at 978 metres (3,209 ft); and the rugged landscape of the Yorkshire moors. The South West's highest point is on Dartmoor (rising to 621 metres, 2,038 ft), but there are other upland areas, such as Exmoor (520 metres, 1,706 ft), Bodmin Moor (420 metres, 1,378 ft), and the Mendip Hills (325 metres, 1,066 ft).

Early History

When the Romans finally withdrew from Britain in 409, the lowland regions were invaded and settled by Angles, Saxons and Jutes (tribes from what is now north-western Germany). England takes its name from the first of these. To begin with, the Anglo-Saxon kingdoms were fairly small and numerous, but as time went on they formed themselves into fewer but larger areas of control. Eventually the southern kingdom of Wessex came to dominate, mainly because it played a leading role in resisting the Danish invasions of the 9th century. Athelstan (who reigned from 924 to 939) used the title of 'King of all Britain', and from 954 there was a single Kingdom of England.[1]

In 1066 the last successful invasion of England took place. Duke William of Normandy defeated the English at the Battle of Hastings and became King William I, known as 'William the Conqueror'. Many Normans and others from France came to settle; French became the language of the

[1] The present Royal Family is descended from the old royal house of Wessex and, in recognition of this, the Queen's youngest son, Prince Edward, was created Earl of Wessex on his marriage in June 1999.

England[1]: Counties and Unitary Authorities

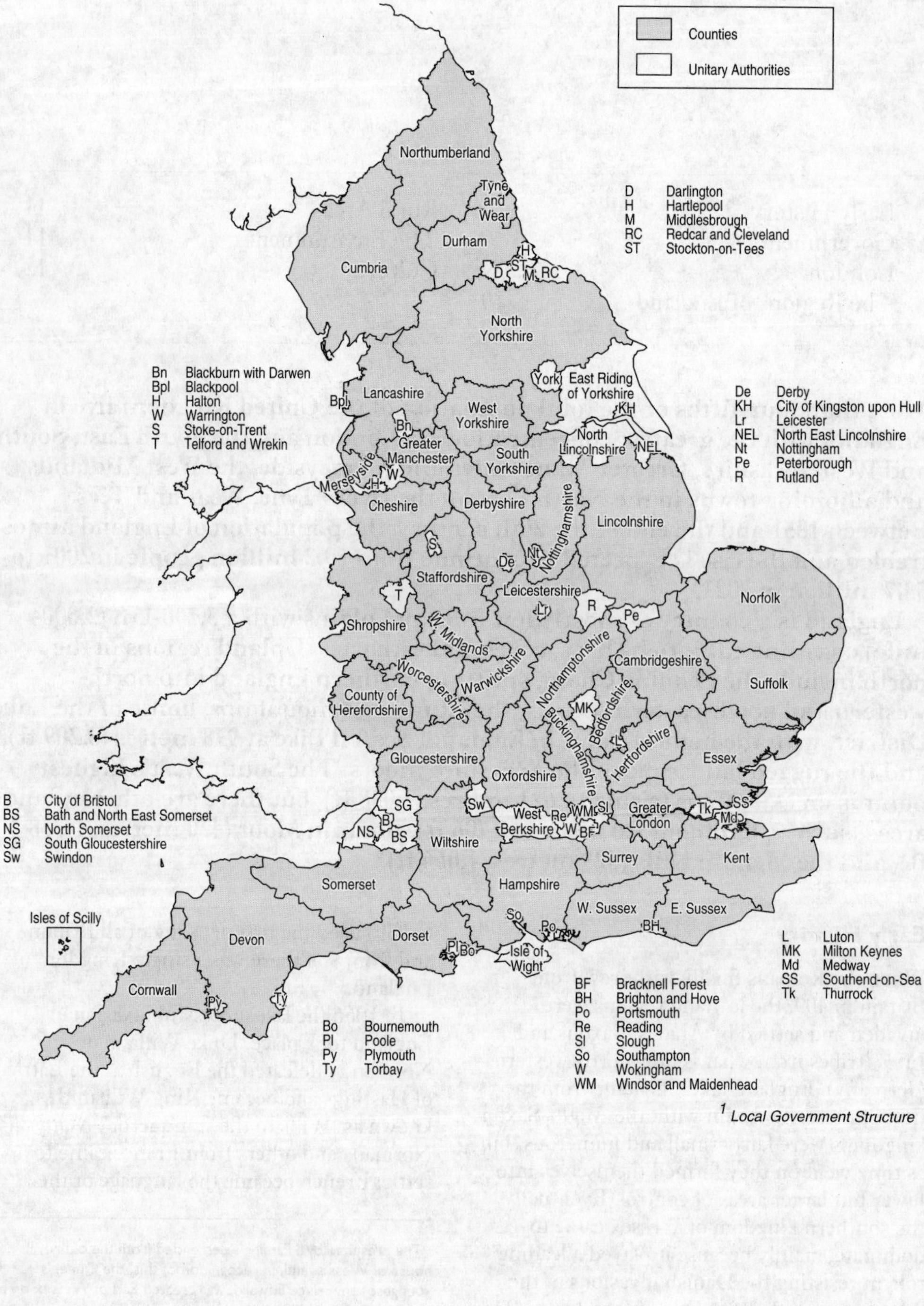
Counties
Unitary Authorities
Northumberland
Tyne and Wear
Durham
Cumbria
D Darlington
H Hartlepool
M Middlesbrough
RC Redcar and Cleveland
ST Stockton-on-Tees
North Yorkshire
York
East Riding of Yorkshire
KH
Bn Blackburn with Darwen
Bpl Blackpool
H Halton
W Warrington
S Stoke-on-Trent
T Telford and Wrekin
Lancashire
West Yorkshire
Greater Manchester
Merseyside
South Yorkshire
North Lincolnshire
NEL
De Derby
KH City of Kingston upon Hull
Lr Leicester
NEL North East Lincolnshire
Nt Nottingham
Pe Peterborough
R Rutland
Cheshire
Derbyshire
Nottinghamshire
Lincolnshire
Staffordshire
Leicestershire
Norfolk
Shropshire
W. Midlands
Warwickshire
Northamptonshire
Cambridgeshire
Suffolk
Worcestershire
County of Herefordshire
Bedfordshire
Buckinghamshire
Hertfordshire
Essex
Gloucestershire
Oxfordshire
B City of Bristol
BS Bath and North East Somerset
NS North Somerset
SG South Gloucestershire
Sw Swindon
West Berkshire
Greater London
Wiltshire
Surrey
Kent
Somerset
Hampshire
W. Sussex
E. Sussex
Isles of Scilly
Devon
Dorset
Isle of Wight
Cornwall
L Luton
MK Milton Keynes
Md Medway
SS Southend-on-Sea
Tk Thurrock
BF Bracknell Forest
BH Brighton and Hove
Po Portsmouth
Re Reading
Sl Slough
So Southampton
W Wokingham
WM Windsor and Maidenhead
Bo Bournemouth
Pl Poole
Py Plymouth
Ty Torbay

[1] *Local Government Structure*

ruling classes for the next three centuries; and the legal and social structures were influenced by those in force across the Channel.

When Henry II, originally from Anjou, was king (1154–89), his 'Angevin empire' stretched from the river Tweed on the Scottish border, through much of France to the Pyrenees. However, almost all the English Crown's possessions in France, after alternating periods of expansion and contraction, were finally lost during the late Middle Ages.

England and Wales were brought together administratively and legally in 1536–42 during the reign of Henry VIII, and the union of England and Scotland took place in 1707, when Queen Anne was Sovereign.

Government

In contrast to Wales, Scotland and Northern Ireland, England has no separate elected national body exclusively responsible for its central administration. Instead a number of government departments look after England's day-to-day administrative affairs (see Appendix 1) and a network of nine Government Offices for the Regions (GOs—see p. 11) is responsible for carrying out a number of government programmes regionally.

There are 529 English parliamentary constituencies represented in the House of Commons. After the General Election of June 2001, England had 323 Labour Members of Parliament (MPs), 165 Conservative, 40 Liberal Democrat and one independent. Conservative support tends to be strongest in suburban and rural areas, and the party has a large number of parliamentary seats in the southern half of England. The Labour Party's key support comes mainly from the big cities and areas associated with traditional industry, but it also holds many seats which had in the past been considered safe Conservative constituencies. The Liberal Democrats, who are traditionally strong in the South West, now have nearly 40% (15) of their English seats in Greater London and the South East.

In many areas a two-tier system of county and district councils is responsible for government at the local level. However, there are also a number of single-tier, or unitary, authorities—especially in the larger cities. Since July 2000 the strategic government of London has been the responsibility of the Greater London Authority (see below).

England elects 71 representatives (MEPs) to the European Parliament (see p. 73). In the June 1999 election, the Conservatives won 33 seats, Labour 24, the Liberal Democrats 9, the UK Independence Party 3 and the Green Party 2.

The English legal system is made up of 'common law' (based on ancient custom and rulings made earlier in similar cases), 'statute law' (parliamentary and European Community legislation) and 'equity' (general principles of justice correcting or adding to common or statute law).

The official religion of England—the Established Church—is the Church of England, which broke away from the Roman Catholic Church during the Reformation in the early 16th century. The Sovereign is head of the Church of England and appoints its two archbishops and 42 diocesan bishops (see p. 241).

London

In May 2000 Londoners voted for a directly elected Mayor for the capital, and a separately elected Assembly of 25 members[2] (see p. 10). Subsequent elections will take place every four years. The Mayor and Assembly form the Greater London Authority (GLA), the first elected London-wide body since the Greater London Council was abolished in 1986. When the GLA took up its powers in July 2000, four other administrative bodies for which it is responsible also came into being. These are the Metropolitan Police Authority; the London Fire and Emergency Planning Authority; Transport for London; and the London Development Agency, one of nine regional agencies covering the whole of England (see p. 10).

---

[2] The new arrangements do not affect the continuance of the separate post of Lord Mayor of London (first established in 1191), whose role is restricted to the City of London—the financial 'Square Mile' at the heart of the capital.

New Greater London Authority Building

A new home for the Greater London Authority is being built on a site between London Bridge and Tower Bridge on the south bank of the river Thames. Work is expected to be finished in spring 2002 and the building occupied in the summer.

This new landmark for the capital takes the form of a geometrically modified glass sphere standing 50 metres high with 21,700 square metres of floor space on ten storeys. In conventional terms the building has no front or back. It uses its radical shape to minimise its surface area—approximately 25% less than an equivalent rectangular building—and high-performance glass facing to ensure the best energy efficiency. A further 'green' feature is the use of cold ground water to air condition the building.

Mayor

Elections for London's Mayor are held under the supplementary vote system, in which voters mark both their first and second choices. If, in the first round, no candidate receives more than 50% of the total votes cast, the second choices for just the two leading candidates are added to their initial scores to decide the overall winner. By this method, Ken Livingstone was elected Mayor for London in 2000 with a total of 776,427 votes (58%). From an electorate of 5,093,464 the turnout was 1,714,162 (33.7%).

Table 2.1: Election Results for the Greater London Assembly by Party, May 2000

Party	*Number of constituency seats*	*Number of top-up seats*	*Total*
Labour	6	3	9
Conservative	8	1	9
Liberal Democrats	—	4	4
Green	—	3	3

Assembly

For Assembly elections, London is divided into 14 constituencies whose members are elected using the 'first-past-the-post' system. A further 11 London-wide seats are allocated on a 'top-up' basis, whereby votes are counted across London and shared among the political parties in proportion to the votes each party receives. Table 2.1 shows the election results for the first London Assembly.

The Regions of England

Regional Development Agencies (RDAs) were launched in eight English regions in April 1999. The ninth, in London, followed in July 2000 after the GLA elections. RDAs aim to provide coordinated regional economic development and regeneration, reduce the economic imbalances which exist within and between regions and enable the English regions to improve their competitiveness.

RDAs are accountable through ministers to Parliament. Each RDA has a board of 13 or 14 members, including the chairman, and on each board members have business experience. The boards also include local councillors, and members with expertise in education, rural affairs, the voluntary sector and trade union issues. RDAs have been allocated some £1.5 billion of programme spending for 2001–02; this is scheduled to rise to £1.7 billion by 2003–04. They are also expected to attract private finance for their work.

The Regions of England Covered by the GOs and RDAs

CENSUS 2001 LAUNCH WITH TV CHEF AINSLEY HARRIOTT

COI Communications

A Gigantic Exercise

Census 2001

Census Office, Northern Irel
Statistics and Research Ager

PA Photos

Crown Copyright: GROS

Crown Copyright: ONS

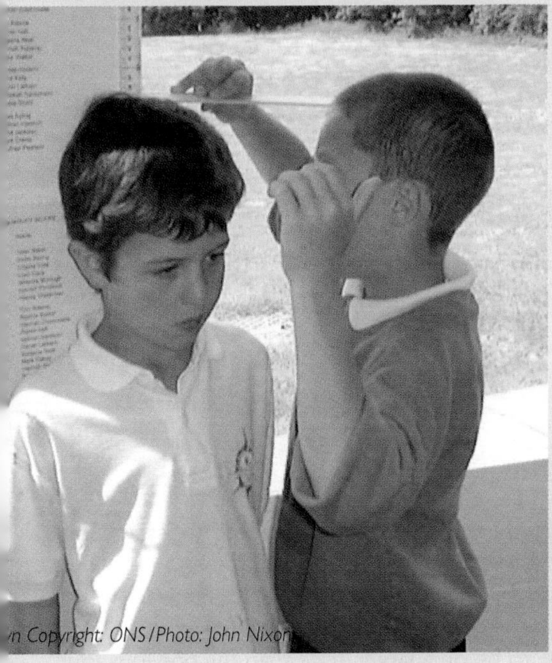

Crown Copyright: ONS / Photo: John Nixon

Crown Copyright: ONS

Clockwise from top left: Graham Jones, Director, Census 2001 in England and Wales, recruiting team leaders and enumerators in London, January 2001; John Randall, Registrar General in Scotland, who had overall responsibility for Scotland's census in 2001; enumerating in inner cities; the census-taking operation complied with special movement restrictions enforced during the foot and mouth crisis; a machine operator sorts census envelopes at a south London mail centre–forms were delivered to over 25 million households throughout the UK; pupils in Northern Ireland taking part in 'Census in School' aimed at the UK's younger population; gathering information at a Hampshire school for the on-line schools' census–over 59,000 pupils took part.

The picture shows part of the 1841 census form on which the author Charlotte Brontë's name appears. Her occupation is listed as 'Governess' (she was a Governess at Upperwood House at the time–an experience which she later drew on for her portrayal of Jane Eyre in the novel of the same name). Charlotte's age is recorded as 20.

A hundred years later, just before the issue of the 1951 census form, the question of a lady's age–at that time deemed to be too personal–brought a flood of queries in newspaper problem pages from women fearful that their true age would become public knowledge. As census information is kept closed to the public for 100 years, they need not have worried.

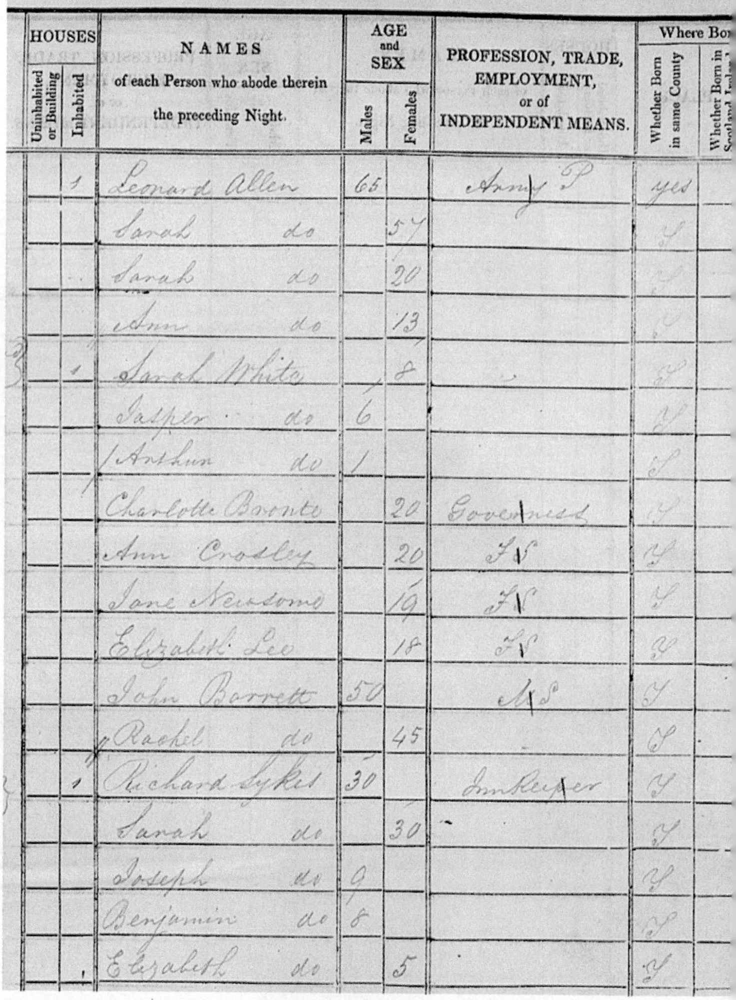

HOUSES		NAMES of each Person who abode therein the preceding Night.	AGE and SEX		PROFESSION, TRADE, EMPLOYMENT, or of INDEPENDENT MEANS.	Where Born	
Uninhabited or Building	Inhabited		Males	Females		Whether Born in same County	Whether Born in Scotland, Ireland
	1	Leonard Allen	65		Army P	yes	
		Sarah do		57		Y	
		Sarah do		20		Y	
		Ann do		13		Y	
	1	Sarah White		8		Y	
		Jasper do	6			Y	
		Arthur do	1			Y	
		Charlotte Bronte		20	Governess	Y	
		Ann Crosley		20	F S	Y	
		Jane Newsome		19	F S	Y	
		Elizabeth Lee		18	F S	Y	
		John Barrett	50		M S	Y	
		Rachel do		45		Y	
	1	Richard Sykes	30		Innkeeper	Y	
		Sarah do		30		Y	
		Joseph do	9			Y	
		Benjamin do	8			Y	
		Elizabeth do		5		Y	

Crown Copyright: Public Record Office HO 107/1313

Crown copyright: ONS

Before being appointed as the first Registrar General for England and Wales in 1836, Thomas Henry Lister was known as a romantic novelist. He was given the responsibility for organising the 1841 census, which was to be on a larger scale than the previous four. For the first time, every individual was to be named on the household schedule, which some thought intrusive and resulted in police protection in a few urban areas for the specially employed enumerators.

The 1841 census introduced self-completion forms which people were legally obliged to complete. The administration of the forms throughout the census process took place at the newly established General Register Office in Somerset House, London. This 'new' census system was to remain largely unaltered until 1911.

In April 2000 the Government set up a Regional Co-ordination Unit, bringing together the regional interests of a range of central departments. The main functions of the Unit are to:

- coordinate the delivery of central government's regional initiatives, including those affecting local areas;
- promote the use of Government Offices for the Regions (GOs) by Whitehall departments;
- encourage better working between the GOs and other regional and local partners; and
- manage the shared functions of the GOs.

In the longer term, the Government has said that it is committed to moving to directly elected regional government for England where support for this is demonstrated in referendums. No decisions have yet been taken on the form of the proposals which might be the subject of such referendums or when they might be held.

Economic Performance

The economic performance of the nine English regions (see map on p. 10), and sub-regions within them, varies quite considerably. For example, Inner London has had the highest level of Gross Domestic Product (GDP) per head in the European Union (EU) for a number of years, even though it also contains some of the worst pockets of deprivation in the UK. Under the new Objective 1 status for EU funding that came into force in January 2000 (see p. 393), three areas of England—Merseyside, South Yorkshire, and Cornwall and the Isles of Scilly—qualified for funding from 2000 to 2006. According to the latest figures, household disposable income per head in 1999 was above the England average in London (by 18%) and in the South East and East (both by 10%), and the same three regions had the highest gross hourly earnings for full-time employees in 2000. The North East had the lowest household disposable income and GDP per head in 1999, as well as the lowest average hourly earnings in 2000.

Among the consequences of economic success in the wealthier English regions are higher residential and industrial property prices, higher rental costs for offices and higher volumes of traffic. As people working in London tend to live further away from their workplaces than those in other cities, average journey times to work are longer in London than elsewhere, ranging from 31 minutes in Outer London to 56 minutes in Central London, compared with an average in Great Britain of just 25 minutes. In autumn 1999 the number of people entering Central London between 7.00 a.m. and 10.00 a.m. on each working day was nearly 1.1 million, a 1% increase on the previous year. Public transport is used by 79% of those working in Central London, compared with the average of 14% for Great Britain as a whole.

In terms of tourism, England accounts for some 85% of all overseas visitors to the UK (estimated at over 25 million in 2000) and around 90% of overseas visitors' spending (estimated at £12.75 billion in 2000).

Rural Areas

According to the Countryside Agency, there are over 16,500 rural towns, villages and hamlets in England with populations of 10,000 or fewer. By this definition, one in five people live in a rural area. Over three-quarters of rural settlements have populations of under 500.

Car ownership is greater in rural households (83%) than nationally (70%), but the countryside often does not have services which people living in urban areas take for granted. The closures of many rural post offices and banks in recent years are notable examples. Another is the comparative lack of public transport serving country areas. In 1998 the Government allocated an extra £150 million over three years to improve rural transport in the UK as a whole. A further £10 million a year for the next two years was announced in the 1999 Budget. This extra funding has led to the creation of 1,800 new or improved rural bus services in England.

The Environment

Despite its high population density and degree of urbanisation, England has many unspoilt rural and coastal areas. There are eight

National Parks (including the Norfolk and Suffolk Broads), nine forest parks, 37 designated Areas of Outstanding Natural Beauty, 22 Environmentally Sensitive Areas, over 200 country parks recognised by the Countryside Agency, and more than 1,057 km (657 miles) of designated heritage coastline. At the end of March 2001, there were 208 National Nature Reserves, 670 Local Nature Reserves and 4,115 Sites of Special Scientific Interest (see also chapter 19).

Culture

London and other large English towns and cities have many cultural attractions, including art galleries, museums, theatres, ballet and opera houses, and concert halls.

National, London-based theatre, dance and opera companies frequently tour the country giving performances at venues in the English regions. Popular culture also thrives: there are numerous kinds of pop music, theatre styles (such as pantomime and musicals), jazz and folk festivals and comedy shows (see chapter 16).

Many regions and towns are associated with great English writers, artists and musicians. These include Stratford-upon-Avon (William Shakespeare), the Lake District (William Wordsworth), Stoke-on-Trent (Arnold Bennett), Haworth (the Brontë sisters) and Dorset (Thomas Hardy); Essex and Suffolk (John Constable) and Salford (L. S. Lowry); and Worcestershire (Edward Elgar), Aldeburgh (Benjamin Britten) and Liverpool (The Beatles).

Table 2.2: England Population and Population Density, by Region,[1] 2000

	Population (thousands)	Population density (people per sq km)	Change in population 1981–2000 (%)
North East	2,577	300	–2.2
North West	6,894	487	–0.7
Yorkshire and the Humber	5,058	328	2.8
East Midlands	4,208	269	9.2
West Midlands	5,335	410	2.9
East	5,460	286	12.5
London	7,375	4,668	8.4
South East	8,115	425	12.0
South West	4,975	209	13.6
England	**49,997**	**383**	**6.8**

[1] The region in England covered by each regional Government Office.
Source: Office for National Statistics

Further Reading

Regional Trends (annual publication), Office for National Statistics. The Stationery Office.

Social Trends (annual publication), Office for National Statistics. The Stationery Office.

Websites

Countryside Agency: www.countryside.gov.uk

Department for Environment, Food and Rural Affairs: www.defra.gov.uk

Department for Transport, Local Government and the Regions: www.dtlr.gov.uk

Department of Trade and Industry: www.dti.gov.uk

Greater London Authority: www.london.gov.uk

Office for National Statistics: www.statistics.gov.uk

3 Northern Ireland

History	13	Security Policy	19
Political Change	16	The Economy	20
Government	17	The Irish Language	21
Intergovernmental Dialogue	18	Culture and the Arts	21
Human Rights and Equality	19		

At its nearest point, Northern Ireland's north-eastern coast is separated from Scotland by a stretch of water—the North Channel—only 21 km (13 miles) wide. It has a 488-km (303-mile) border with the Irish Republic, forming the UK's only land boundary with another Member State of the European Union. About half of Northern Ireland's 1.7 million population live in the eastern coastal region, at the centre of which is the capital, Belfast.

In December 1999 the Westminster Parliament devolved power to the Northern Ireland Assembly and its Executive Committee of Ministers to run most of Northern Ireland's domestic affairs. It did so following a referendum held in May 1998 which endorsed the Belfast (Good Friday) Agreement.

Policing in Northern Ireland has undergone a number of changes as a result of provisions in the Police (Northern Ireland) Act 2000. These include a fundamental restructuring of the Royal Ulster Constabulary (RUC) and renaming it the 'Police Service of Northern Ireland (incorporating the Royal Ulster Constabulary)'.

In the late 1990s the Northern Ireland Continuous Household Survey (CHS)[1] reported that 54% of the population regarded themselves as Protestants and 42% as Roman Catholics. (The 2001 Census in Northern Ireland asked what religion, religious denomination or body people living there belonged to or were brought up in. Analysis of the responses will not be available until 2002.) Most of the Protestants are descendants of Scots or English settlers. Northern Ireland today has a younger population, with proportionately more children and fewer pensioners, than any other region in the UK.

[1] Northern Ireland Statistics and Research Agency: CHS sample 1995–96 to 1997–98.

History

The Vikings ruled Ireland from the 10th century until Henry II of England invaded in 1169. He had been made the country's overlord by the English Pope Adrian IV, who wanted the Irish Church to be fully obedient to Rome. Although Anglo-Norman noblemen controlled a large part of the country during the Middle Ages, little direct authority came from England.

Table 3.1: Northern Ireland Population and Population Density, by Board[1] and District, 2000

	Population (thousands)	Population density (people per sq km)	Change in population 1981–2000 (%)
Eastern	673	385	5.0
Ards	72	190	24.7
Belfast	283	2,577	–10.7
Castlereagh	67	788	10.0
Down	64	99	19.0
Lisburn	112	250	31.1
North Down	76	937	13.3
Northern	431	105	14.3
Antrim	51	122	11.3
Ballymena	60	95	8.4
Ballymoney	26	63	14.1
Carrickfergus	39	476	34.0
Coleraine	56	115	19.2
Cookstown	32	61	11.1
Larne	31	92	6.5
Magherafelt	39	70	20.0
Moyle	15	31	6.6
Newtonabbey	82	543	12.9
Southern	312	101	13.7
Armagh	55	81	10.8
Banbridge	41	90	34.7
Craigavon	81	286	9.5
Dungannon	49	63	10.4
Newry and Mourne	88	98	13.3
Western	282	61	12.5
Derry	107	281	18.6
Fermanagh	58	34	10.6
Limavady	32	54	16.6
Omagh	48	42	6.8
Strabane	38	44	4.1
Northern Ireland	**1,698**	**125**	**10.0**

[1] Health and Social Services Board areas.

Sources: Office for National Statistics and Northern Ireland Statistics and Research Agency

The Tudor monarchs tended to intervene in Ireland far more, and during the reign of Elizabeth I there were several attempts to deal with rebellion. The northern province of Ulster was particularly subject to unrest, but in 1607, after the resistance leaders had been defeated and had fled, Protestant immigrants came to settle there from Scotland and England.

The English civil wars (1642–51) led to further uprisings in Ireland, which Oliver Cromwell suppressed. More fighting took place after the overthrow of King James II, a Roman Catholic, in 1688. At the Battle of the Boyne (1690) the Protestant William of Orange (later King William III) defeated the forces of James II who was trying to regain the English throne from his power-base in Ireland.

Northern Ireland: Districts

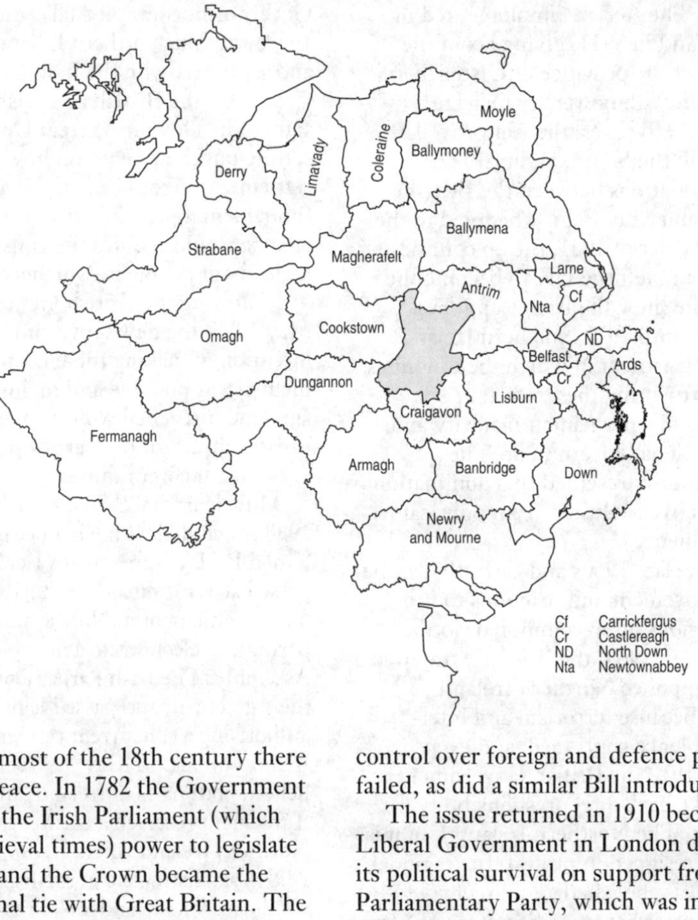

Throughout most of the 18th century there was an uneasy peace. In 1782 the Government in London gave the Irish Parliament (which dated from medieval times) power to legislate on Irish affairs, and the Crown became the only constitutional tie with Great Britain. The Parliament, however, represented only the privileged Anglo-Irish minority; the Roman Catholic majority was excluded. Following the unsuccessful rebellion led by Wolfe Tone's United Irishmen movement in 1798, Great Britain took back control of Ireland under the 1800 Act of Union. The Irish Parliament was abolished in 1801 and Irish interests were represented by members sitting in both Houses of the Westminster Parliament.

The 'Irish Question' was one of the major issues of British politics during the 19th century. In 1886 the Liberal Government introduced a Home Rule Bill to give a new Irish Parliament devolved authority over most internal matters with Great Britain keeping control over foreign and defence policy. This failed, as did a similar Bill introduced in 1893.

The issue returned in 1910 because the Liberal Government in London depended for its political survival on support from the Irish Parliamentary Party, which was in favour of Home Rule. The controversy deepened as unionists and nationalists in Ireland formed private armies and in 1914 Home Rule was approved in the Government of Ireland Act. The outbreak of the First World War, however, suspended its implementation.

In 1916 a nationalist uprising in Dublin was put down and its leaders executed. Two years later the nationalist Sinn Féin party won a large majority of the Irish seats in the General Election to the Westminster Parliament. Its members refused to attend the House of Commons and instead formed their own assembly—the Dáil Éireann—in Dublin. A nationalist guerrilla force called the Irish Republican Army (IRA) began operations against the British administration in 1919.

In 1920 the Government of Ireland Act provided for separate Parliaments in Northern and Southern Ireland, subordinate to Westminster. The Act was implemented in Northern Ireland in 1921, giving six of the nine counties of the province of Ulster their own Parliament with powers to manage internal affairs. However, the Act proved unacceptable in the South, and in 1922, following negotiations between the British Government and Sinn Féin, which led to the Anglo-Irish Treaty of 1921, the 26 counties of Southern Ireland left the UK to become the Irish Free State (now the Irish Republic).

From 1921 until 1972 Northern Ireland had its own Parliament in which the unionists, primarily representing the Protestant community, held a permanent majority and formed the regional government. The nationalist minority resented this domination and their effective exclusion from political office and influence.

Between the late 1960s and early 1970s, the civil rights movement and reactions to it resulted in serious inter-communal rioting. Consequently, in 1969, the British Army was sent in to help police Northern Ireland.

However, because terrorism and inter-communal violence continued, and even worsened, in 1972 the British Government decided to take back direct responsibility for law and order. The Northern Ireland Unionist Government resigned in protest, the regional government was abolished and direct rule from Westminster began. A Secretary of State was appointed with a seat in the UK Cabinet and he was given overall responsibility for Northern Ireland's government.

Political Change

It was never intended to make direct rule permanent. Over the years, successive British and Irish Governments have worked closely together to try to bring lasting peace to Northern Ireland, recognising the need for new political arrangements acceptable to both sides of the community.

In 1985 an Anglo-Irish Agreement provided a new basis for relations between the UK and the Irish Republic, creating an Intergovernmental Conference in which to discuss issues of mutual interest such as improved cross-border cooperation and security. Within this framework, the British Government continued talks during the early 1990s with the Northern Ireland political parties and separately with the Irish Government.

In 1993 the British and Irish Governments signed the Downing Street Declaration, setting out their views on how a future settlement might be achieved and restating the fundamental principle that any constitutional change would require the consent of a majority of people in Northern Ireland.

Following the British General Election in May 1997, the new Government confirmed its intention of making the talks process as inclusive as possible and maintained that any agreement reached would have to have the broad support of the parties representing each of the main communities.

Multi-party talks held in Belfast in April 1998 concluded with what became known as the 'Good Friday Agreement'. Legislation was passed at Westminster authorising a referendum on the settlement in Northern Ireland and permitting elections to a new Northern Ireland Assembly. The Irish Parliament also considered the Agreement and passed legislation authorising a concurrent referendum in the Irish Republic. In May 1998 referendums were held in both parts of Ireland, and the Agreement received a clear endorsement. Northern Ireland voted 71.1% in favour and 28.8% against, while in the Irish Republic the result was 94.3% and 5.6% respectively.

A new Northern Ireland Assembly of 108 members was elected by proportional representation (single transferable vote) in June 1998 and met for the first time the following month (see p. 17). The Westminster Parliament subsequently implemented the whole settlement and formally instituted devolved administrative powers in the Northern Ireland Act 1998.

In December 1999 power was devolved to the Assembly and its Executive Committee of Ministers. At the same time the North/South Ministerial Council, North/South Implementation Bodies, British-Irish Council and a new British-Irish Intergovernmental Conference became fully functioning institutions. However, in February 2000 the Secretary of State for Northern Ireland suspended the operation of the devolved administration, owing to a lack of substantive progress being made on decommissioning of illegally held arms—a condition necessary for the complete fulfilment of the Belfast (Good Friday) Agreement by 2001. After further talks, a political settlement was reached and devolved powers were restored to the Assembly and Executive in May 2000. Nevertheless, arms decommissioning has remained a contentious issue, prompting the resignation of the Ulster Unionist First Minister on 1 July 2001 and the appointment of an acting successor.

Government

Following devolution, the Secretary of State for Northern Ireland remains responsible for Northern Ireland Office matters not devolved to the Assembly. These include policing, security policy, prisons and criminal justice. The Secretary of State represents Northern Ireland interests in the UK Cabinet and is tasked with ensuring that the devolution settlement works satisfactorily.

Northern Ireland elects 18 Members of Parliament (MPs) to the House of Commons and, by proportional representation, three of the 87 UK representatives to the European Parliament (MEPs).

Northern Ireland's 26 local government district councils have limited executive functions. They nominate locally elected representatives to sit as members of the various statutory bodies dealing with, for example, education and libraries, health and personal social services, drainage and fire services.

Northern Ireland Assembly

The Assembly meets in Parliament Buildings at Stormont, Belfast, and is the prime source of authority for all devolved responsibilities. It has full legislative and executive powers within this framework, which means it can make laws and take decisions on all the functions of the Northern Ireland departments (see **p. 18**).

At its first meeting in July 1998, the Assembly elected, on a cross-community basis, a First Minister and a Deputy First Minister and appointed ten ministers with responsibility for each of the Northern Ireland departments, which together form the Executive. These 12 ministers make up the Executive Committee, which meets to discuss and agree on those issues which cut across the responsibilities of two or more ministers. Its role is to prioritise executive business and recommend a common position where necessary.

The Executive's main function is to plan each year, and review as necessary, a

Table 3.2: Northern Ireland Electoral Representation

House of Commons (June 2001 General Election) *Party*	*Seats*	Northern Ireland Assembly (as at May 2001) *Party*	*Seats*
Ulster Unionist	6	Ulster Unionist	28
Social Democratic & Labour	3	Social Democratic & Labour	24
Democratic Unionist	5	Democratic Unionist	21
Sinn Féin[1]	4	Sinn Féin	18
		Alliance	6
		Northern Ireland Unionist	3
		United Unionist Assembly	3
		Progressive Unionist	2
		NI Women's Coalition	2
		United Kingdom Unionist	1
Total	**18**		**108**

[1] The Sinn Féin members have not taken their seats in the Westminster Parliament.

programme of government with an agreed budget. This is subject to approval by the Assembly, after scrutiny in Assembly Committees, on a cross-community basis. Assembly members can be on more than one Assembly Committee. The first budget was agreed in December 2000, and in March 2001 the Assembly approved the first Programme for Government which set out the Executive's plans and priorities for the three years from April 2001. The Programme identified five key areas for action to be taken by the Northern Ireland departments working together and with others: Growing as a Community; Working for a Healthier People; Investing in Education and Health; Securing a Competitive Economy; and Developing North/South, East/West and International Relations. The Programme for Government will be reviewed on an annual basis.

The Assembly has ten Statutory Committees. Membership of Committees is in broad proportion to party strengths in the Assembly to ensure that the opportunity of Committee places is available to all Members. Each Committee has a scrutiny, policy development and consultation role in relation to its department and a role in the initiation of legislation.

The Northern Ireland Departments

The Office of the First Minister and Deputy First Minister (OFMDFM) is responsible, among other things, for coordinating and developing a coherent policy direction on the work of the Executive Committee, and the response of the Northern Ireland administration to external relationships. The departments which, together with the OFMDFM, comprise the Executive Committee are: Agriculture and Rural Development (DARD); Culture, Arts and Leisure (DCAL); Education (DEd); Employment and Learning (DEL); Enterprise, Trade and Investment (DETI); Environment (DOE); Finance and Personnel (DFP); Health, Social Services and Public Safety (DHSSPS); Regional Development (DRD); and Social Development (DSD). (For functions and contact details, see Appendix 1, pp. 537–546.)

A 60-member Civic Forum was established in October 2000, representing the business, trade union, voluntary and other sectors of the Northern Ireland community. It has a chairperson appointed by the First Minister and Deputy First Minister and acts as a consultative mechanism on social, economic and cultural matters.

> **The Northern Ireland Assembly Emblem**
>
> The Northern Ireland Assembly has adopted the linen or flax plant as its official emblem. The six flowers signify the counties of Northern Ireland, while the plant itself is a reminder of the economic importance linen has had in Northern Ireland's agricultural and manufacturing industries. The prevalence of blue in the furnishings of the Assembly Chamber reflects the colour of the flax plant's flowers, and the wall panels of damask linen represent the fibre which it produces.

Intergovernmental Dialogue

The North/South Ministerial Council is a forum for those with executive responsibilities in Northern Ireland and the Irish Government. The Council meets on a regular basis to develop consultation, cooperation and action on an all-island and cross-border basis.

The North/South Implementation Bodies, established by international agreement between the British and Irish Governments, implement the policies agreed by ministers in the North/South Ministerial Council. They deal with: waterways; food safety; trade and business development; special European Union programmes; marine matters; and language.

The British-Irish Council aims to promote and develop good relationships among all the peoples of the United Kingdom and Ireland. It has representatives from the British and Irish Governments, the devolved institutions in Northern Ireland, Scotland and Wales, and others from the Channel Islands and the Isle of Man.

The British-Irish Intergovernmental Conference's role is to promote bilateral cooperation on matters of mutual interest between the two governments.

Human Rights and Equality

The European Convention on Human Rights became part of Northern Ireland domestic law when the Human Rights Act 1998 (see p. 214) came into effect throughout the UK in October 2000.

A commitment to protect human rights and promote equality was central to the Belfast Agreement. The resulting Northern Ireland Act 1998 not only placed a statutory duty of equality on all public authorities but also established the following bodies with specific responsibilities for fostering equal opportunities and good community relations:

- *The Northern Ireland Human Rights Commission*—to give advice to the Government and the Northern Ireland Assembly on human rights issues, particularly on any need for legislation to protect human rights.
- *The Equality Commission for Northern Ireland*—to be responsible for fair employment, equal opportunities, racial equality, disability issues and enforcing the statutory duty of equality on public authorities.
- *The Parades Commission*—to help implement the Public Processions (Northern Ireland) Act 1998 covering contentious parades in Northern Ireland. The Commission imposed legally binding route conditions on 168 such parades in the year to 31 March 2001 out of a total of 3,440. The majority of parades each year are organised by the Protestant/Unionist community and most take place during the six months from around Easter to the end of September.
- *The Victims of Violence Commission*—to look at possible ways of providing support for the victims of the violence caused by inter-community unrest over the past 30 years.

Security Policy

The Government remains committed to ensuring that the security forces in Northern Ireland have available the powers they need to counter the terrorist threat. The Terrorism Act 2000 (see p. 218) therefore contains a temporary part for Northern Ireland. These provisions are limited to five years, require annual renewal, and each provision can be stopped by order at any time. Setting these temporary powers in the context of a UK-wide framework of permanent counter-terrorism measures underlines the Government's commitment to repealing the Northern Ireland specific powers as soon as it is safe to do so.

Policing and Justice

An independent Policing Commission, set up under the terms of the Belfast Agreement, reviewed the policing needs in Northern Ireland. Its report—*A New Beginning: Policing in Northern Ireland* (Patten Report)—was published in September 1999 and made recommendations which led to the Police (Northern Ireland) Act 2000. The Act contains provisions to:

- enhance the police service's accountability through a new Policing Board to be made up of ten members of the Assembly and nine independent members;
- give the Board reporting and inquiry powers and require it to monitor and assess police performance;
- create new district policing partnerships aimed at improving local accountability;
- introduce measures to redress the religious imbalance in the police service between Protestants and Catholics;
- change the name of the RUC to the 'Police Service of Northern Ireland (incorporating the Royal Ulster Constabulary)'. For operational purposes, the service will be called the 'Police Service of Northern Ireland'; and
- establish a Commissioner to oversee the implementation of changes.

In parallel with the work of the Policing Commission, the Government carried out a review of the criminal justice system in Northern Ireland in which political parties, interested bodies, organisations and individuals were consulted. Its recommendations, published in March 2000, were subject to further consultation which ended the following September. Detailed preparation of the legislation and implementation plan for the review is well advanced.

The Police (Northern Ireland) Act 1998 established the office of a Police Ombudsman to provide an independent means of impartially investigating complaints against police officers in Northern Ireland. When it is perceived to be in the public interest, the Police Ombudsman can also react to incidents, even if no individual complaint has been made. Between taking up position in November 2000 and the end of April 2001, the Police Ombudsman received 1,829 cases involving 2,349 separate complaints. Investigations or further enquiries are ongoing for about 50% of these cases; the remaining ones have been closed for a variety of reasons, such as complainant non-cooperation or the incident complained about being outside the Police Ombudsman's remit. By the end of April 2001, the Police Ombudsman had reacted to 21 public interest incidents.

The Economy

Employment in Northern Ireland grew throughout the 1990s and unemployment has declined since 1993. The Labour Force Survey for April to June 2001 showed that 67.8% of people of working age in Northern Ireland were in employment, compared with 74.8% in the UK as a whole. Comparable ILO rates for unemployment were 5.9% and 5.0% respectively.

In Northern Ireland, manufacturing industry accounted for some 19% of Gross Domestic Product (GDP) in 1998, compared with 20.3% for the UK as a whole. Agriculture, forestry and fishing accounted for 4.0% of GDP in 1998, compared with 1.3% for the UK.

In 2000, 58.5% of export trade was to the EU, similar to the UK average, but trade from the EU accounted for nearly 36% of imports, lower than the overall UK average of 48.6%. A substantial increase in new inward investment in growth industries such as computer software, telecommunications and network services contributed to the 7,145 new jobs promoted by the Industrial Development Board in 2000–01.

Northern Ireland's economic development strategy is being reviewed following the Enterprise, Trade and Investment Committee's consideration of the Strategy 2010 report, and taking into account the Executive's priorities under the Programme for Government (see p. 18). Following further consultation with the Committee, the Economic Development Forum and others, it is planned to have strategic priorities in place by March 2002.

The public expenditure allocation within the Northern Ireland Executive's responsibility for 2001–02 is £5.8 billion.

Economic Assistance

The Berlin EU summit at the end of March 1999 agreed a Special Programme for Northern Ireland in support of peace, worth about £260 million between the years 2000 and 2004. It also confirmed the renewal for three years of EU support of approximately £10 million a year for the International Fund for Ireland, set up in 1986 by the British and Irish Governments to encourage cross-border cooperation in business enterprise, tourism, community relations, urban development, agriculture and rural development. Donors include the United States, Canada, New Zealand and the European Union.

Including funding from the new Special Programme, Northern Ireland will receive around £900 million under the EU Structural Funds Programmes over the period 2000–06 (see p. 393). Within these programmes is a unique Structural Funding package working under the authority of the Northern Ireland Community Support Framework (CSF). Its priorities, which have been agreed with the European Commission, are to support peace and reconciliation; economic growth and renewal; employment, human resource development and social inclusion; balanced regional, urban and rural development; and

North/South and wider cooperation. An indicative allocation of 7.5% of the funds in the Northern Ireland CSF has been set aside for North/South cooperation.

The Irish Language

Estimates suggest that around 142,000 people in Northern Ireland have some ability to use Irish as a means of communication, either orally or in writing. A cross-border implementation body has been set up with responsibility for promoting the Irish language and facilitating and encouraging its use.

In 1998 a statutory duty was placed on the education authorities in Northern Ireland to promote Irish-medium education. In May 2001 there were 11 grant-aided schools and five units (four primary and one secondary) teaching 1,845 primary and secondary school pupils in Irish as the first language. There were also ten Irish-medium independent schools teaching a further 105 pupils.

In March 2001, the UK ratified the European Charter for Regional or Minority Languages, which commits signatory States to supporting indigenous minority languages in key areas such as education, justice, the public services, cultural policies and the media. The Charter, which came into force in July 2001, recognises as regional languages both Irish and Ulster-Scots and promotes the use of Irish in public life. These developments are compatible with the Northern Ireland Assembly's obligations under the Belfast Agreement and reinforce its commitment to help protect the linguistic diversity of the UK.

Culture and the Arts

Northern Ireland has a rich cultural heritage and its people have made a significant contribution to literature and the performing arts.

Northern Irish writers such as Keith Baker, Colin Bateman, Jack Higgins, Maurice Leitch, C. S. Lewis, Sam McAughtry, Bernard McLaverty, Robert McLiam Wilson, Brian Moore and Glenn Patterson have written about places which visitors familiar with their books enjoy coming to see.

Poets with international reputations include Ciaran Carson, John Hewitt, Derek Mahon, Medbh McGuckian, Louis MacNeice, John Montague and Paul Muldoon. Among the best known, perhaps, are Nobel Laureate Seamus Heaney and his contemporary Michael Longley, who was awarded the prestigious Queen's Gold Medal for Poetry in April 2001.

Northern Ireland has produced some fine actors among whom are Colin Blakely, Kenneth Branagh, Amanda Burton, James Ellis, Denys Hawthorne, Doreen Hepburn, Liam Neeson, James Nesbitt and Stephen Rea. The Irish dramatic tradition continues today with playwrights like Brian Friel, Marie Jones, Martin Lynch, Frank McGuinness, Stewart Parker and Graham Reid.

Music is associated with cultural and social life in Northern Ireland and there is a wide variety on offer, from live bands in local pubs to the Ulster Concert Orchestra in the prestigious Waterfront Hall. Among the famous names in music are flautist James Galway, singer/songwriter Van Morrison, pianists Phil Coulter and Barry Douglas, opera singer Kathleen Feeney, blues guitarist Ronnie Greer and pop groups Ash, The Divine Comedy and Therapy.

Further Reading

Northern Ireland Office 2001 Departmental Report. Expenditure Plans and Priorities. The Government's Expenditure Plans 2001–02 to 2003–04 and Main Estimates 2001–02. Cm 5122. The Stationery Office, 2001.

Websites

Northern Ireland Assembly: www.niassembly.gov.uk
Northern Ireland Executive: www.northernireland.gov.uk
Northern Ireland Office: www.nio.gov.uk
Northern Ireland Tourist Board: www.discovernorthernireland.com

4 Scotland

Early History	22	The Economy	25
Population	23	Legal System	26
Scottish Parliament and Executive	23	Education and Culture	27

Scotland, the most northerly of the four parts of the United Kingdom, covers about one-third of the island of Great Britain. Bounded by England to the south, the Atlantic Ocean to the west and north, and the North Sea to the east, Scotland is a country with large areas of unspoilt and wild landscape, and many of the UK's mountains, including its highest peak, Ben Nevis (1,343 m, 4,406 ft).

Just over 5 million people live in Scotland, three-quarters of them in the central lowlands where two of its largest cities are situated: Edinburgh (the capital) on the east coast and Glasgow on the west. Aberdeen and Dundee are its two other principal cities. Together these four cities and their surrounding regions account for 75% of Scotland's Gross Domestic Product (GDP).

Following devolution to the Scottish Parliament in 1999, day-to-day administration of Scottish domestic affairs is the responsibility of the Scottish Executive, headed by the First Minister.

Early History

Evidence of human settlement in what is now known as Scotland dates from around the third millennium BC. By the time the Romans invaded Britain, many tribes were living in the region, but despite a number of attempts to control them, Roman rule never permanently extended to most of Scotland. In the sixth century, the Scots, a Celtic people from Ireland, settled on the north-west coast of the island of Great Britain, giving their name to the present-day Scotland.

The kingdoms of England and Scotland were frequently at war during the Middle Ages. When King Edward I tried to impose direct English rule over Scotland in 1296, a revolt for independence broke out, which ended in 1328 when King Edward III recognised its leader, Robert the Bruce, as King Robert I of Scotland.

In 1603 Queen Elizabeth I of England, who never married and had no children of her own, was succeeded by her nearest heir, King James VI of Scotland. He became King James I of England and so united the English and Scottish crowns in one person. Politically, however, England and Scotland remained separate during the 17th century, apart from a period of union forced on them by Oliver

Scotland: Council Areas

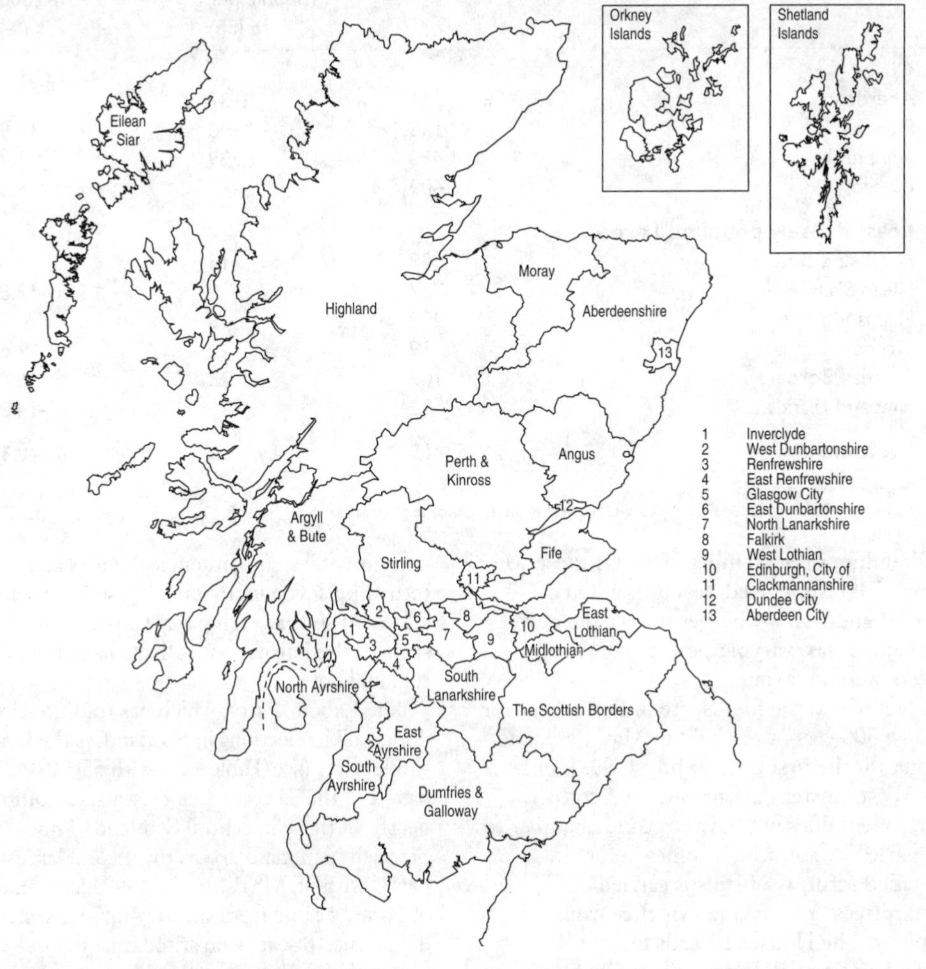

Cromwell in the 1650s. It was not until 1707 that the English and Scottish Parliaments agreed on a single Parliament for Great Britain to sit at Westminster in London.

Population

Scotland's population has changed relatively little in the last 50 years. In June 2000 the estimated population was 5.1 million (see Table 4.1), compared with 5.2 million in 1971 and 5.1 million in 1951. The population density is the lowest in the UK, averaging 65 people per sq km.

Scottish Parliament and Executive

The Scotland Act 1998 gave the necessary statutory framework to set up a Scottish Parliament and Executive, which the majority of Scottish people had endorsed in a

> Prince William, the elder of the Prince of Wales's two sons and second in line to the throne after his father, started studying at the University of St Andrews, Fife, in the autumn of 2001. He will follow a four-year course in the History of Art leading to an MA (Honours) degree.

Table 4.1: Scotland Population and Population Density, 2000

	Population (thousands)	Population density (people per sq km)	Change in population 1981–2000 (%)
Cities			
Aberdeen	211	1,137	–0.6
Dundee	143	2,190	–15.9
Edinburgh	453	1,729	1.7
Glasgow	609	3,481	–14.5
Least densely populated areas			
Argyll and Bute	89	13	–2.4
Eilean Siar[1]	27	9	–13.8
Highland	209	8	7
Orkney Islands	19	20	1.6
Scottish Borders	107	23	5.6
Shetland Islands	22	16	–14.8
Scotland	**5,115**	**65**	**–1.3**

[1]Formerly Western Isles.
Sources: Office for National Statistics and General Register Office for Scotland

referendum in September 1997. Of those who voted, 74% supported devolution. On a second question—whether to give the new Parliament tax-varying powers—64% of voters were in favour.

Elections to the first Scottish Parliament for almost 300 years were held in May 1999, and it met for the first time in July 1999. Unlike the Westminster Parliament, the Scottish Parliament does not have a second chamber to revise legislation which comes before it. Detailed scrutiny of Bills is carried out in committees or by taking evidence from outside experts. The House of Lords no longer considers Scottish legislation on devolved matters (though it remains the final court of appeal in hearing civil cases arising from the Scottish courts—see chapter 14).

The Scottish Parliament's 129 members (MSPs) are elected for a fixed four-year term. The 'additional member' system of proportional representation (PR) is used in Scottish Parliamentary elections, giving each voter two votes: one for a constituency MSP and one 'regional' vote for a registered political party or an individual independent candidate. There are 73 single-member constituency seats and 56 seats representing eight regions (based on the European parliamentary constituencies) with each returning seven members. These MSPs are allocated so that each party's overall share of seats in the Parliament reflects its share of the regional vote.

The Labour Party, which has traditionally done well in elections in Scotland, is the largest single party (see Table 4.2), with 55 MSPs. It has 52 of the 73 constituency seats, including nearly all those in central Scotland. The Scottish National Party is the second largest party, with 35 MSPs. In the 1999 election, most of its seats came from the 'top-up' PR system, as did all the 18 seats won at the time by the Conservative Party, the third largest party in the Parliament. In March 2000 the Conservatives won their first constituency seat in a by-election, taking it from the Labour Party.

Responsibilities

The Scottish Parliament's responsibilities include health; education and training; local government; housing; economic development; many aspects of home affairs and civil and criminal law; transport; the environment; agriculture, fisheries and forestry; and sport and the arts. In these areas, the Scottish Parliament is able to amend or repeal existing

Table 4.2: Electoral Representation in Scotland, July 2001

	Scottish Parliament Constituency MSPs	Additional MSPs	Total MSPs	Westminster Parliament (MPs)	European Parliament (MEPs)
Labour	52	3	55	56[1]	3
Scottish National Party	7	28	35	5	2
Conservative	1	18	19	1	2
Liberal Democrats	12	5	17	10	1
Independent	1	—	1	—	—
Scottish Socialist Party	—	1	1	—	—
Green	—	1	1	—	—
Total seats	73	56	129	72	8

[1]Including the Speaker of the House of Commons.

Acts of the UK Parliament and to pass new legislation of its own.

Responsibility for a number of other issues, including overseas affairs, defence and national security, overall economic and monetary policy, energy, employment legislation and social security, remains with the UK Government and Parliament as 'reserved' matters under Schedule 5 of the Scotland Act 1998. The Secretary of State for Scotland has a seat in the Cabinet and is responsible for representing Scottish interests within the UK Government through the Scotland Office.

The Scottish Executive—the devolved administration in Scotland—has responsibility for all public bodies whose functions and services have been devolved to it, and is accountable to the Scottish Parliament for them. It also has an input into organisations such as the Forestry Commission (see p. 466), whose work covers Scotland as well as other parts of the UK.

The Parliament currently meets at the General Assembly Hall in Edinburgh's Old Town. A new Parliament building, due for completion in the winter of 2002, is being built at Holyrood, at the lower end of the Royal Mile (a street in the historic centre of Edinburgh and the location of Parliament House, where the previous Scottish Parliament met from 1640 to 1707).

The First Minister, normally the leader of the party with most support in the Parliament, heads the Scottish Executive. Since the first elections, the Executive has been run by a partnership between Labour and the Liberal Democrats, with the latter having two seats in the Cabinet, including that of Deputy First Minister. There are 11 Cabinet positions in all.

Finance

The Scottish Parliament's budget for 2001–02 is £19.8 billion. Most of the money is allocated to it by the UK Parliament through the Secretary of State for Scotland. Once the budget has been set, the Scottish Executive can share out the resources across its expenditure programmes.

The Parliament has the power to increase or decrease the basic rate of income tax—currently 22 pence in the pound—by a maximum of 3 pence. A person is liable to pay income tax if he or she is a UK resident for tax purposes and either spends 50% or more of the tax year in Scotland or has his or her only or principal home there.

The Parliament is also responsible for deciding the form of local taxation. It may, if it wishes, alter both the council tax and business rates.

The Economy

In the last 50 years the Scottish economy has moved away from the traditional industries of coal, steel and shipbuilding. Extraction of offshore oil and gas, growth in services and, more recently, developments in high-technology industries—such as chemicals, electronic engineering and information technology—have taken their place. Manufacturing still remains important, however, and Scotland's manufacturing exports in 2000 were valued at £18.3 billion.

Key features of the Scottish economy include:

- *Electronics.* Scotland has one of the biggest concentrations of the electronics industry in Western Europe, employing about 40,600 workers in 2000. Electrical and instrument engineering exports were worth £10 billion in 2000, accounting for 56% of Scotland's manufactured exports.
- *Oil and gas.* Offshore oil and gas production has made a significant contribution to the Scottish economy in the last 30 years. Many of the UK's 115 offshore oilfields are to the east of the Isles of Shetland and Orkney or off the east coast of the mainland (see map, at the back of the book).
- *Whisky.* Whisky production continues to be important to Scotland. In 2000 the value of drinks exports, dominated by whisky, was valued at £1.3 billion. There are 90 whisky distilleries in Scotland, most of them in the north-east.
- *Tourism.* Tourism is a major industry, supporting about 193,000 jobs. In 1999 expenditure by tourists was valued at £2.5 billion and there were around 12.4 million tourist trips, including those originating in Scotland.
- *Financial services.* Funds managed by financial institutions in Scotland were worth some £351.1 billion at the end of 2000, of which £117.9 billion were in long-term life insurance and £131.1 billion in pensions. A number of financial institutions are based in Scotland, including insurance companies, fund managers, unit trusts and investment trusts. There are four Scottish-based clearing banks, which have limited rights to issue their own banknotes.
- *Forestry.* Scotland accounts for just under half of the UK's timber production. In the last ten years there has been significant international and local investment in wood-based panel production and in pulp and paper processing.
- *Fishing.* Fishing remains significant, particularly in the north-east and in the Highlands and Islands. In 2000 Scotland accounted for 70% by weight and 60% by value of the fish landed in the UK by British trawlers. Fish farming, particularly of salmon, has grown in importance; Scotland produces the largest amount of farmed salmon in the EU.

Scottish Enterprise and Highlands and Islands Enterprise (see p. 392) manage domestic support for industry and commerce, while Locate in Scotland, a joint operation between the Scottish Executive and Scottish Enterprise, encourages inward investment. In 2000–01, 102 inward investment projects were recorded, which are expected to lead to investment of £1,763 million and the creation or safeguarding of over 14,000 jobs.

The Labour Force Survey for April to June 2001 showed that 73.9% of people of working age in Scotland were in employment, compared with 74.8% in the UK as a whole. Comparable rates for ILO unemployment (see p. 148) over the same period were 6.1% and 5.0% respectively.

Legal System

The Scottish legal system (see chapter 14) differs in many respects from that of England and Wales. This is because, during the 16th century, it based itself partly on medieval church laws and partly on those borrowed from other European legal systems. The 1707 Treaty of Union allowed Scotland to keep Scots law, its own courts and legal profession. The prosecution, prison and police services are also separate from those in England and Wales.

Drug Courts

Scotland's first pilot drug court will start operating in Glasgow towards the end of 2001. This special court aims to address the problem of drug addicts committing crimes to feed their habit, being punished and then reoffending. It is part of the Scottish Executive's wider strategy to tackle drug misuse in Scotland and is expected to deal with between 150 and 200 cases a year. The court will:

- make treatment orders with immediate effect;
- review the performance of participants on treatment orders in open court on a regular basis;
- provide frequent and regular drugs tests for offenders; and
- impose penalties and sanctions for non-compliance.

If the Glasgow drug court is successful, the Scottish Executive will consider further pilots in other parts of Scotland.

Education and Culture

The Scottish education system has a number of distinctive features (see chapter 10), including a separate system of examinations and differences in the curriculum. Record numbers of students are entering post-compulsory education—around 571,000 students were enrolled in vocational, further or higher education in 1999–2000.

It is estimated that Gaelic is spoken by some 70,000 people, many of whom live in the Hebrides (the islands off Scotland's west coast). The Scottish Executive is providing £13.3 million to support Gaelic in 2001–02. Broadcasting is the largest single area, accounting for £8.5 million. In 2000–01 there were 1,862 children in Gaelic-medium education in 60 primary schools and 326 pupils in 14 secondary schools.

The annual Edinburgh Festival is one of the world's leading cultural occasions. Edinburgh Festivals bring about £120 million into the Scottish economy each year. The International Festival, Jazz Festival, Festival Fringe, Book Festival, Film Festival and Military Tattoo combine to make the Edinburgh Festival the largest arts event in the UK.

Scotland has several major collections of the fine and applied arts, such as the Burrell Collection in Glasgow, and the National Gallery of Scotland and the Scottish National Gallery of Modern Art in Edinburgh. The National Museums have built the new Museum of Scotland in Edinburgh to house the national Scottish collections and in July 2001 they opened the Museum of Scottish Country Life at Kittochside near East Kilbride, the first major national museum in the west of Scotland.

Further Reading

The Scottish Budget: Annual Expenditure Report of the Scottish Executive. Scottish Executive, 2001.
Scotland Office Departmental Report 2001: The Government's Expenditure Plans 2001–02 to 2002–03. Cm 5120. The Stationery Office, 2001.

Websites

Scotland Office: www.scottishsecretary.gov.uk
Scottish Executive: www.scotland.gov.uk
The Scottish Parliament: www.scottish.parliament.uk
Scottish Tourist Board: www.visitscotland.com

5 Wales

Early History	28	Economy	32
National Assembly for Wales	28	Environment	32
Welsh Language	32	Cultural and Social Affairs	33

Wales (or Cymru in Welsh) is a mountainous country on the western side of Great Britain. Around one-quarter of the land is above 305 m (1,000 ft) and in the north its highest peak, Snowdon (Yr Wyddfa), rises to 1,085 m (3,560 ft). The Welsh coastline stretches for 1,180 km (732 miles) and consists of many bays, beaches, peninsulas and cliffs.

About two-thirds of the population of Wales live in the south-eastern part of the country. In the 18th and 19th centuries, the Industrial Revolution had a major impact in south Wales, where the iron and steel factories and coal mines were concentrated. The capital, Cardiff, grew in the 19th century as a coal exporting port, and Swansea and Newport also depended for their prosperity on the surrounding industries and their position as ports in the Bristol Channel. In the 20th century these traditional industries fell into decline, to be replaced by those involving new technology.

Since 1999 Wales has had its own National Assembly—headed by a First Minister with a Cabinet of eight other ministers—which has powers to make secondary legislation to meet the specific needs of the Welsh people.

Early History

After the Romans finally left Britain early in the 5th century (see p. 4), Wales remained a Celtic stronghold ruled by sovereign princes under the influence of England. In 1282 King Edward I brought Wales under English rule and the castles he built in the north remain among the UK's finest historic monuments. Edward I's eldest son—later King Edward II—was born at Caernarfon in 1284 and was created the first English Prince of Wales in 1301. The eldest son of the reigning monarch continues to bear this title, Prince Charles being made Prince of Wales in 1969.

At the beginning of the 15th century, Welsh resentment of unjust English laws and administration, and widespread economic discontent, resulted in the nationalist leader Owain Glyndŵr heading an unsuccessful revolt against the English. From 1485 to 1603 the Tudor dynasty, which was of Welsh ancestry, ruled England and it was during this time that the Acts of Union (1536 and 1542) united England and Wales administratively, politically and legally.

National Assembly for Wales

In a referendum in May 1997, the Welsh people narrowly endorsed government

Table 5.1: Wales Population and Population Density, 2000

	Population (thousands)	Population density (people per sq km)	Change in population 1981–2000 (%)
Blaenau Gwent	71	654	–5.9
Bridgend (Pen-y-bont ar Ogwr)[1]	132	524	4.2
Caerphilly (Caerffili)	171	613	–0.8
Cardiff (Caerdydd)	328	2,339	14.2
Carmarthenshire (Sir Gaerfyrddin)	169	71	2.5
Ceredigion (Sir Ceredigion)	72	40	18.0
Conwy	113	100	13.9
Denbighshire (Sir Ddinbych)	92	110	6.0
Flintshire (Sir y Fflint)	148	339	7.0
Gwynedd	117	46	4.4
Isle of Anglesey (Sir Ynys Môn)	65	91	–4.7
Merthyr Tydfil (Merthyr Tudful)	56	503	–7.8
Monmouthshire (Sir Fynwy)	87	103	14.2
Neath Port Talbot (Castell-nedd Port Talbot)	138	312	–3.3
Newport (Casnewydd)	139	729	4.6
Pembrokeshire (Sir Benfro)	115	72	6.8
Powys	127	24	13.1
Rhondda, Cynon, Taff (Rhondda, Cynon, Taf)	240	565	0.6
Swansea (Abertawe)	230	609	0.4
Torfaen (Tor-faen)	90	712	–1.0
The Vale of Glamorgan (Bro Morgannwg)	123	371	8.6
Wrexham (Wrecsam)	126	249	5.5
Wales (Cymru)	**2,946**	**142**	**4.7**

[1] Welsh-language local authority names are given in parenthesis if there are differences between the English and Welsh names.

Sources: Office for National Statistics and National Assembly for Wales

Table 5.2: Electoral Representation in Wales, August 2001—Number of Seats

	National Assembly (AMs)			UK	European
	Constituency seats	Regional seats	Total seats	Parliament (MPs)	Parliament (MEPs)
Labour	*27*	*1*	28	34	2
Plaid Cymru[1]	*9*	*8*	17	4	2
Conservative	*1*	*8*	9	—	1
Liberal Democrats	*3*	*3*	6	2	—
Total seats	*40*	*20*	60	40	5

[1] The full title is Plaid Cymru—The Party of Wales.

Wales: Unitary Authorities

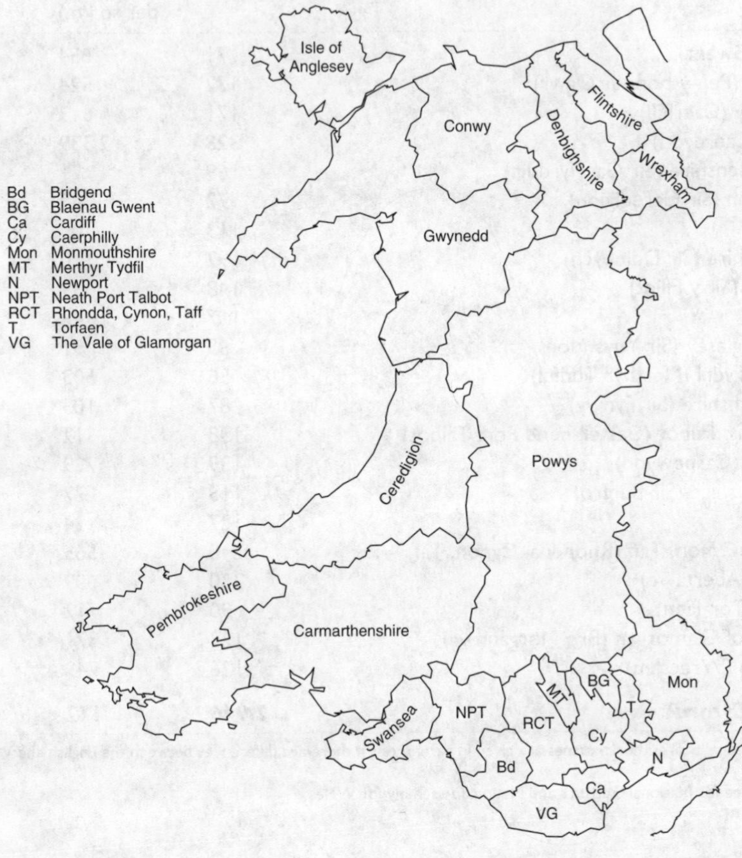

> **Welsh Emblems**
> The leek and the daffodil are two plants which have come to represent Wales, but the reasons for this are not clear. One suggestion for the leek is that St David (the patron saint of Wales) advised the Britons to wear leeks in their caps so that they could recognise one another in battle. This has become a tradition which survives today, with soldiers in Welsh regiments wearing leeks on St David's Day (1 March). A possible reason for the daffodil is that, in Welsh, the word for 'leek' is 'cenhinen' while that for 'daffodil' is 'cenhinen pedr'.

proposals to devolve certain powers and responsibilities to a National Assembly, when 50.3% of those who voted were in favour and 49.7% against. The Government of Wales Act 1998 laid down the necessary statutory framework to establish the National Assembly for Wales, which held its first elections in May 1999 and began functioning as a devolved administration two months later.

Electors have two votes in Assembly elections: one for a candidate in their local constituency and one for a party list. The Assembly comprises 60 members (AMs): 40 from local constituencies (with the same boundaries as those for Welsh seats in the House of Commons) and 20 regional members elected by the additional member system of proportional representation (four for each of the five former European parliamentary constituencies in Wales—elections to the European Parliament are now based on a single all-Wales constituency).

The Labour Party has traditionally had strong support in Wales. It has the largest number of seats in the Assembly (see Table 5.2), although it does not have an overall majority. Since October 2000 it has run the Assembly in partnership with the Liberal Democrats.

Responsibilities

The National Assembly for Wales has powers to make secondary legislation (see p. 54) to meet distinctive Welsh needs. It is responsible for: economic development; agriculture, forestry, fisheries and food; education and training; industry; local government; health and personal social services; housing; the environment; planning; transport and roads; arts, culture and the Welsh language; ancient monuments and historic buildings; and sport and recreation.

The Assembly's budget for 2001–02 to 2002–03 is £9.7 billion. In January 2000 the Assembly Cabinet published *Better Wales*—its ten-year strategy built round five key areas for improving life in Wales: opportunities for learning; a stronger economy; better health and well-being; quality of life; and better, simpler government. *Better Wales* also set out more than 100 targets for achievement by the end of the current Assembly including: no infant classes with more than 30 pupils; a 10% increase in the number of Welsh exporting companies; and the number of tourism trips to increase to 12.2 million per year.

In October 2000 the First Minister, who heads the Assembly, appointed a Cabinet of eight ministers in charge of: economic development; finance and communities; education and lifelong learning; health and social services; culture and sports; rural affairs; environment; and trefnydd (business manager).

The Assembly is also responsible for over 50 public bodies. The organisations with the largest expenditure are:

- the Higher Education Funding Council for Wales (with planned gross expenditure in 2001–02 of £318 million); and
- the Welsh Development Agency (WDA, see p. 393) (£273 million).

Local Government

The 22 Welsh unitary authorities (see map on p. 30) have collective responsibility for spending over a third of the National Assembly's budget. The Assembly sets the policy framework and makes the secondary legislation within which local government operates. It also has a responsibility to ensure that local decision-making reflects the requirements of the law and, where appropriate, priorities fixed by the Assembly. The Local Government Act 2000, which the Assembly has implemented in Wales, contained measures to modernise local authority management structures, strengthen local democracy and improve local financial accountability.

A Partnership Council has been formed, whose role is to advise the National Assembly on the various functions of local government. It comprises locally elected representatives (including those from the National Parks, police and fire authorities, and community councils) and selected members of the Assembly. It also assists the Assembly in preparing guidance and advice to local councils.

Role of the UK Government in Wales

Following devolution, the UK Government has kept responsibility in Wales for certain matters including foreign affairs, defence, taxation, overall economic policy, crime, justice and prisons, social security and broadcasting. The office of Secretary of State for Wales continues. The post holder has a seat in the UK Cabinet and is responsible for promoting the devolution settlement, bringing forward primary legislation, bidding for the Assembly's budget and ensuring that Welsh interests are properly represented and considered within the UK Government. As part of the UK, Wales retains full constituency representation in the Westminster Parliament.

Welsh Language

Estimates suggest that 20% of the population over the age of three in private households are able to speak Welsh. In much of the rural north and west, Welsh remains the first language.

Welsh is widely used for official purposes, and is treated equally with English in the work of the Assembly. It is quite extensively used in broadcasting, and most road signs are bilingual. Welsh-medium education in schools is encouraged. Since September 2000, Welsh has been taught—as a first or second language—to all pupils between the ages of 5 and 16, and other subjects are taught in Welsh to primary and secondary school children in about 500 schools.

The National Assembly is responsible for supporting Welsh culture and developing greater use of the Welsh language. The Welsh Language Act 1993 set the principle that, in public business and in the administration of justice in Wales, Welsh and English should have equal treatment. The Welsh Language Board's role is to promote the use of Welsh.

Economy

The Welsh economy, which was traditionally based on coal and steel, experienced some major changes during the 20th century. Wales now has a more varied range of manufacturing industries, including many at the forefront of technology, and a growing number involved in e-commerce. However, the steel industry remains important, and crude steel production in Wales was around 6.8 million tonnes in 1999, accounting for 42% of UK steel output.

The Labour Force Survey for April to June 2001 showed that 68.5% of people of working age in Wales were in employment, compared with 74.8% in the UK as a whole. Comparable rates for ILO unemployment were 6.2% and 5.0% respectively. As part of the *Better Wales* ten-year strategic plan (see p. 31), the National Assembly has set a target for an additional 40,000 jobs to be created in Wales before the end of its first term of office (2003).

Manufacturing accounts for 24.4% of Gross Domestic Product (GDP) in Wales, compared with 18.1% in the UK as a whole. Wales is an important centre for consumer and office electronics, automotive components, chemicals and materials, aerospace, and food and drink. There were around 35,000 employee jobs in the manufacture of optical and electrical equipment, and 11,000 in the manufacture of parts and accessories for motor vehicles and their engines in Wales, according to the 1999 Annual Business Inquiry. In the service sector, tourism and leisure services are significant—estimates indicate that about 10.9 million tourist trips were made to Wales in 1999—while call centre activity is becoming more important and widespread.

A key feature of the economy has been the volume of investment from overseas companies and from elsewhere in the UK. Since 1983, over 2,000 inward investment projects have been recorded in Wales, bringing in a total of £13.9 billion and promising the creation and safeguarding of nearly 220,000 jobs. Overseas-owned manufacturing companies in Wales employ more than 70,000 people.

The Welsh Development Agency has broad functions and powers, so that it is well placed to contribute to economic regeneration across the whole of Wales. Increased resources are being provided to support business development and promote innovation. The WDA is coordinating an Entrepreneurship Action Plan for Wales in order to develop a strong business culture.

Environment

About one-quarter of the land in Wales is designated as a National Park or Area of Outstanding Natural Beauty (see p. 315). As well as three National Parks—Snowdonia, the Brecon Beacons and the Pembrokeshire Coast—and five Areas of Outstanding Natural Beauty, there are two national trails, 36 country parks and large stretches of heritage coast. There are also 62 National Nature Reserves, over 1,000 Sites of Special Scientific Interest and a number of internationally important nature conservation sites. For example, 89 sites are proposed for designation as Special Areas of Conservation under the European Community (EC) Habitat Directive,

15 Special Protection Areas are classified under the EC Wild Birds Directive, and ten wetlands of international importance are designated under the Ramsar Convention (see p. 321). There are six Environmentally Sensitive Areas (see p. 456), representing about 25% of the land in Wales. The Tir Gofal (Land in Care) scheme, introduced in 1999–2000, aims to encourage agricultural practices that will help to protect and improve the landscape and wildlife of the Welsh countryside.

Cultural and Social Affairs

Welsh literature has a long tradition and is one of the oldest in Europe. Music is also very important to the Welsh people: Wales is particularly well-known for its choral singing, while both the Welsh National Opera and the BBC National Orchestra of Wales have international reputations. Special festivals, known as eisteddfodau, encourage both Welsh literature and music. The largest is the annual Royal National Eisteddfod, consisting of competitions in music, singing, prose and poetry entirely in Welsh. Performers from all over the world come to Llangollen in Denbighshire for the annual International Musical Eisteddfod, while the 'Cardiff Singer of the World' competition—held every two years—is recognised as one of the world's leading singing competitions.

The National Museums and Galleries of Wales include the Museum of Welsh Life at St Fagans, near Cardiff, and the recently rebuilt Welsh Slate Museum at Llanberis, Gwynedd. The main building in Cardiff contains many paintings by Welsh artists, including Augustus John, Gwen John and Kyffyn Williams as well as a representative collection of other important works. A new Industrial and Maritime Museum is to be built in Swansea. The National Library of Wales at Aberystwyth, Ceredigion, contains over 4 million books.

The media in Wales include several Welsh and English language newspapers, local radio stations and the television broadcaster, Sianel Pedwar Cymru (S4C), which has recently been transmitting programmes in Welsh for 12 hours a day on its new digital channel.

Among many sporting activities, there is particular interest in rugby union, which has come to be regarded as the Welsh national game. Association football is also popular in Wales, and in May 2001 the Football Association Cup Final was held at the Millennium Stadium in Cardiff where it will also be staged in 2002.

Further Reading

Better Wales. National Assembly for Wales, 2000.
Wales Office Departmental Report 2001: The Government's Expenditure Plans 2001–02 to 2003–04. Cm 5121. The Stationery Office, 2001.

Websites

National Assembly for Wales: www.wales.gov.uk
Office of the Secretary of State for Wales: www.walesoffice.gov.uk
Wales Tourist Board: www.visitwales.com

Census 2001: 'count me in'

A Gigantic Exercise

Sunday 29 April 2001 was Census Day in the United Kingdom. In the weeks running up to the day itself, some 72,000 'enumerators', trained and supervised by about 8,600 census managers, delivered census forms—around 36 million—to every household and communal establishment in the UK. The processing of the returned forms began in June, and the first results will be reported to Parliament in December 2002.

The 2001 Census was organised by the Office for National Statistics (ONS) in England and Wales, the General Register Office for Scotland (GROS) and the Northern Ireland Statistics and Research Agency (NISRA). The cost of the whole exercise, at about £255 million, reflects the complexity of the operation, the years of preparation needed to ensure it goes smoothly (13 years from the start of planning to when all the information is published), the painstaking statistical analyses of the results, and unexpected obstacles.[1] It is equivalent to less than £5 per person per year spread over the 13-year cycle.

The Importance of the Census

As censuses only occur at ten-year intervals, a decade of strategic planning and expenditure relies on the information each one yields. Today over £50 billion of public spending is based on census information every year. The answers to the questions on the form, mainly about what kind of people live in what type of household, are used to allocate central government funding to local authorities for the planning and delivery of local services such as education, health and transport. For example, it is vitally important to know how many older people and residents with health problems or disabilities there are in a given area, so that an adequate social support structure can be put in place for them.

Equally, a local authority needs to be aware of how many babies and children it has in its area in order to provide the right number of nursery places, schools, colleges and teachers.

The census provides highly detailed statistics at a local level. No other source does this to the same extent or so accurately. Furthermore, it is easy to make comparisons between areas because the census asks the same questions of everybody at the same time,[2] giving citizens a chance to view a single snapshot of their entire country. Nor is it just central and local government that make practical use of the information that emerges from the census. Businesses can use it for their forward planning; voluntary organisations that provide social services are as reliant on it as government; and it is a rich resource for academics. The census has developed from its comparatively simple origins into a sophisticated tool for research and policy implementation at many levels.

A Window onto the Past

As well as being itself a census year, 2001 was the bicentenary of the first 'modern' census in Britain. There had been forerunners of a sort—a Gaelic version in Scotland in the 7th century and the *Domesday Book* in England in 1086. But the census of 10 March 1801 was the first in a series that has continued every ten years to the present day, with the single exception of 1941 which was cancelled because of the Second World War.

Since 1801 the population of Great Britain has increased around sixfold, while there are now about 12 times as many households as 200

---

[1] In 2001 special arrangements applied in parts of the countryside to which access was restricted because of foot-and-mouth disease (see p. 460). In these areas forms were delivered by post or to a previously agreed point such as a farm boundary.

[2] The only exceptions in 2001 were, in Wales, a question that asked 'Can you understand, speak, read, or write Welsh?'; and, in Northern Ireland, more detailed questions on 'religious denomination or body'.

years ago. It was fears about the burgeoning population that led to the Census Bill coming before Parliament in 1800. Two years earlier, Thomas Robert Malthus had published his *Essay on the Principle of Population*, which argued that population tended to grow at a much faster rate than food supplies. A series of bad harvests at the end of the 18th century seemed to underline this gloomy thesis and the consequent need to base plans for the future on a firm statistical foundation.

The questions in successive censuses have thus often reflected the social and economic concerns of the day. Ironically, it was the *decline* in birth rates, particularly among upper and middle class families, that aroused anxiety a century later. The 1911 Census therefore included a question about the number of children born to married women. Twenty years earlier a question had been introduced on the number of rooms in each household, in response to fears of overcrowding in industrial cities. Already in the 1800s census information had enabled government statisticians to demonstrate a link between early death and certain occupational groups, such as coal miners and tailors. In 1921 the census asked about 'place of work' for the first time, as people moved out of cities to the suburbs and began to travel more by bus and train.

Over time the number of questions asked in the census has steadily increased, as has their level of detail. The 1801 Census was a simple count of the number of people and their houses, with a very broad idea of occupations. In the early 1800s *individual* occupation was an unfamiliar concept; the family was the economic unit and *family* occupation was the information sought. However, by the mid-19th century detailed information on individual occupations was available. In 1991 the value of ethnic monitoring was fully understood, and a carefully worded question on ethnicity was included for the first time in Great Britain.

The 2001 Census

The 2001 Census was the first in the UK to use the Internet. Extensive use was made for publicity purposes and to give updates on census developments; in due course, census results will be available on the ONS, GROS and NISRA websites. In other ways, too, it was a ground-breaking exercise. For the first time the main method of collection was the post-back of completed forms in postage-paid envelopes. The information is being scanned directly from the forms onto computer and stored on microfilm. The paper copies are destroyed and the paper recycled. Census questions were translated into 26 languages, from Albanian to Vietnamese, and everyone in Wales had the option of completing a Welsh language version of the form. Versions were also available in large print, Braille and on audio tape. There was a helpline with a dedicated minicom facility for people who are deaf or hard of hearing and British Sign Language interpreters were on hand if needed.

The 2001 Census included a question on time spent caring for people with a long-term physical illness or disability, people with a mental health problem, or those experiencing problems related to old age. This partly reflected concerns about the ageing population and new government initiatives designed to support carers. Householders were required to supply full details of the relationships of the various people in the household, including 'partners' and step-relations—an acknowledgement of recent changes in family units and attitudes towards divorce, separation, cohabitation and single parenthood. The ethnic group question in England, Wales and Scotland was extended to reflect user requirements for more detailed information about those from specific ethnic groups or cultural backgrounds including 'Black British', 'Asian British', 'Irish' as well as those of 'Mixed' ethnic origin. In Northern Ireland a basic question on ethnic group was included for the first time. Altogether it was the most comprehensive census yet in the UK.

Confidentiality

Census forms are kept closed for 100 years and the information they contain is rigorously protected by law. When statistical information from censuses is published, no individual can

'CensusAtSchool'

During October 2000 the largest survey of 7–16 year olds ever undertaken in the UK produced responses via the Internet, from 59,391 pupils at over 350 schools in England, Wales and Northern Ireland. Among these first findings of the 'junior census' was confirmation that Manchester United was the nation's most popular football team among this age-group, especially English girls. Art emerged as the favourite school subject (26%), followed by PE/sport (23%) and mathematics (9%). Nearly 60% of secondary pupils had their own mobile telephone and 85% had access to a home computer.[3]

be identified from it. Indeed, although the census collects information from each person and household in the country, its purpose is to produce aggregate statistics and aid research about the community as a whole and groups within it, not individuals.

Census Poem

The Poet Laureate,[4] Andrew Motion, commemorated the 2001 Census with the following poem. The opening reference to a 'field full of folk' is a quotation from the 700-year-old poem 'Piers Plowman' by William Langland.

All of Us

Who would ever think
a field full of folk
meant wet eyes and lips
smattered among rose-hips,

and bright shining faces
bobbing in silver grasses?

No, our sense of folk
comes in stadium-hulks,

with steamrollering chants
of implacable want.

But it's all the same.
As we shuttle through time

we might or might not
change skin-colour, forget

history, love God
or prefer ourselves instead.

The question of who we are
still goes on before—

A bow-wave we watch
creaming, but cannot catch.

Or so I thought, at least,
that grey day on the coast

I strode off with my Dad
Along a sand-spine made

by wind fighting waves,
him near the end of his life,

me in the middle. Our shoes
gave that definite soft kiss

of people leaving their mark,
but when I looked back

the tide had swallowed us both.
That is the truth.

Websites

Office for National Statistics (England and Wales): www.statistics.gov.uk

General Register Office for Scotland: www.gro-scotland.gov.uk

Northern Ireland Statistics and Research Agency: www.nisra.gov.uk

[3] For full results and copies of the questionnaire see *www.censusatschool.ntu.ac.uk*

[4] The title given to a poet who receives a stipend as an officer of the Royal Household and is called upon to write poems for royal and official occasions.

6 Government

The Monarchy	39	Modernising Government	63
The Privy Council	42	The Civil Service	65
Parliament	42	Local Government	67
Her Majesty's Government	58	Pressure Groups	71
Government Departments	61	The UK in the European Union	72

The United Kingdom's system of government is known as a constitutional monarchy, though its constitution is not contained in any one document; instead it has evolved over many years. Ministers of the Crown govern in the name of the Sovereign, who is both head of state and head of the government. The Queen's succession to the throne can be traced back for more than a thousand years and the Westminster Parliament is one of the oldest representative assemblies in the world.

In the General Election held in June 2001, the Labour Party was returned to office—the first time it has been elected with sufficient MPs to govern for a second full five-year period. The Government intends to take forward its long-term programme of decentralising power, opening up government and reforming Parliament.

Scotland, Wales and Northern Ireland now govern their own domestic affairs and London now has a Mayor and an elected city-wide authority. Following the General Election, a number of major departmental changes were made, aimed at giving a sharper focus to the Government's priorities and at delivering better public services.

The Constitution

The United Kingdom does not have a 'written constitution' set out in any one document. Instead, the relationship between the State and the people relies on statute law, common law and conventions.[1]

The *UK Parliament* is the legislature and the highest authority in the land. The *executive* comprises the Government (members of the Cabinet and other ministers responsible for policies); government departments and agencies, in charge of domestic matters in England and UK-wide issues such as defence and monetary policy; local authorities, which look after many local services; public corporations, charged with running certain nationalised

[1] Conventions are rules and practices which are not legally enforceable but which are regarded as indispensable to the working of government.

industries; independent bodies which regulate the privatised industries; and other bodies subject to ministerial control.

The *judiciary* (see chapter 14) determines common law and interprets statutes.

Origins of Government

Each of the countries which form the United Kingdom—England, Wales, Scotland and Northern Ireland—has its own distinct culture and history. England was united as a kingdom over a thousand years ago (see p. 7), and Wales became part of that kingdom during the reign of King Henry VIII (see p. 28). The thrones of England and Scotland were united in 1603, and in 1707 the English and Scottish Parliaments passed laws creating a single Parliament for Great Britain with ultimate authority over England, Wales and Scotland (see p. 23).

Ireland had links with the kingdom of England from the 13th century, and in 1801 the creation of the United Kingdom was completed when the Irish Parliament joined that of Great Britain (see p. 15). In 1920, the six counties of what is now Northern Ireland voted to remain within the United Kingdom and were given their own subordinate Parliament, while the 26 counties in the south of Ireland (now the Irish Republic) became, in 1922, an entirely separate and self-governing country.

Despite the recent establishment of the devolved administrations of Scotland, Wales and Northern Ireland (see below), the UK Parliament in Westminster still has an elected chamber including members from English, Scottish, Welsh and Northern Irish constituencies, and continues to have the supreme authority for government and law-making in the UK as a whole (see p. 52).

Administration of Scottish, Welsh and Northern Irish Affairs

Following devolution, the responsibilities of the Secretaries of State for Scotland, Wales and Northern Ireland changed considerably. They are responsible for ensuring that the reserved interests of the countries they represent are properly considered in central government; and for leading the presentation of government policy. When necessary, they bring forward primary legislation for their part of the UK, although in Scotland and Northern Ireland this occurs much less often than in the past as much primary legislation is dealt with in the devolved parliaments. Much of their previous administrative role is also now devolved. The main new function of these UK Cabinet members following devolution is to see that the devolution settlements work satisfactorily.

Background to Devolution

Referendums held in Scotland and Wales in 1997 backed proposals to devolve power from the Parliament at Westminster to a Scottish Parliament (see p. 24) and a National Assembly for Wales (see p. 30). Laws were passed in 1998 to set up these institutions, and elections were held in May 1999. Both bodies became fully operational in July 1999.

In Northern Ireland, the political settlement reached in April 1998 under the Belfast (Good Friday) Agreement led to a referendum endorsing its proposals, and elections to a Northern Ireland Assembly were held in June (see p. 16). The Assembly first took up its devolved powers in December 1999, although it was temporarily suspended between February and May 2000 (see p. 17).

Major differences exist in how the devolved institutions operate, reflecting the very different historical and administrative circumstances in each. The Scottish Parliament may make primary legislation for matters within its competence and it has defined and limited financial authority to vary tax revenue. It has control over most Scottish domestic matters, including health, education, justice, local transport, agriculture and the environment and scrutinises the Scottish Executive, the devolved government for Scotland. The National Assembly for Wales has secondary legislative powers and can reform and direct the Welsh public bodies for which it is responsible. It oversees a similar range of policy areas to those of the Scottish Parliament, the main difference being that policing and justice matters in Wales remain the responsibility of the UK Government. The Northern Ireland Assembly is also in charge of

Figure 6.1: Principal Members of the Royal Family from the Reign of Queen Victoria to July 2001

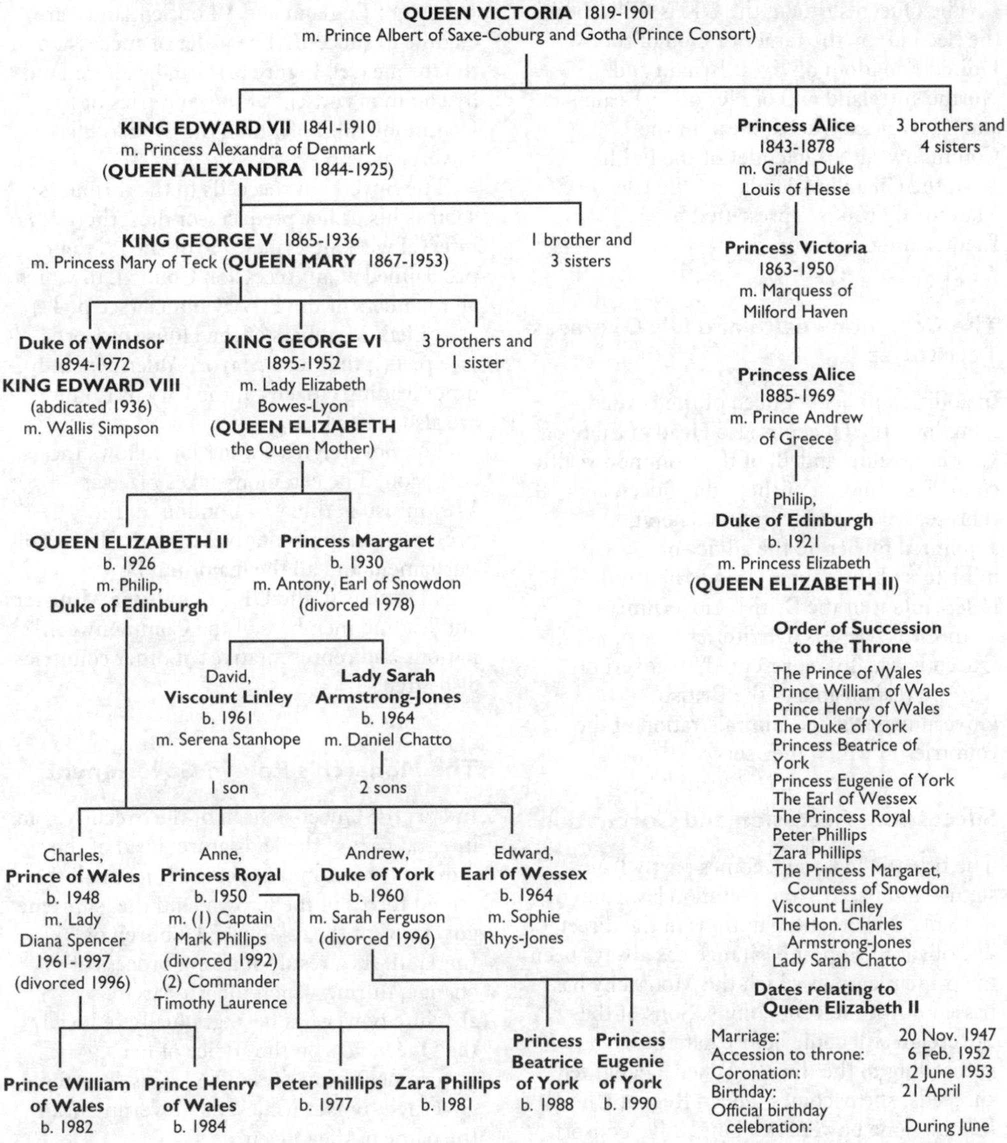

its own domestic affairs and has powers to make primary legislation, although issues of policing, internal security policy, prisons and criminal justice remain matters for the Secretary of State for Northern Ireland.

The UK Government's overall responsibility for economic and monetary policy, employment, overseas affairs, defence and national security remains unchanged.

The Monarchy

The Monarchy is the oldest institution of government. Queen Elizabeth II is directly descended from King Egbert, who united England under his rule in 829. The only interruption in the history of the Monarchy was during the short-lived republic, which lasted from 1649 to 1660.

The Queen's title in the UK is: 'Elizabeth the Second, by the Grace of God of the United Kingdom of Great Britain and Northern Ireland and of Her other Realms and Territories Queen, Head of the Commonwealth, Defender of the Faith'.

In the Channel Islands and the Isle of Man the Queen is represented by a Lieutenant-Governor.

The Commonwealth and UK Overseas Territories

In addition to being queen of the United Kingdom, the Queen is also Head of State of 15 other realms and all of the Commonwealth countries.[2] In each of these the Queen is represented by a Governor-General, appointed by her on the advice of the ministers of the country concerned and independent of the British Government.

In UK Overseas Territories (see p. 79) the Queen is usually represented by governors, who are responsible to the British Government for the administration of the countries in which they serve.

Succession, Accession and Coronation

The title to the Crown comes partly from statute and partly from common law rules of descent. Despite interruptions in the direct line of succession, inheritance has always been the principle upon which the Monarchy has passed down the generations. Sons of the Sovereign still come before daughters in succeeding to the throne. When a daughter succeeds, she becomes Queen Regnant, and has the same powers as a king. The 'consort' of a king takes her husband's rank and style, becoming Queen. The constitution does not give any special rank or privileges to the husband of a Queen Regnant.

Under the Act of Settlement of 1700, only Protestant descendants of Princess Sophia, the Electress of Hanover (a granddaughter of James I of England and VI of Scotland), are eligible to succeed. The order of succession to the throne (see Figure 6.1) can be altered only by common consent of the countries of the Commonwealth of which the Monarch is Sovereign.

The Sovereign succeeds to the throne as soon as his or her predecessor dies: there is no interval without a ruler. He or she is at once proclaimed at an Accession Council, to which all members of the Privy Council (see p. 42) are called. Members of the House of Lords (see p. 44), the Lord Mayor, Aldermen and other leading citizens of the City of London are also invited.

The Sovereign's coronation follows the accession. The ceremony takes place at Westminster Abbey in London, in the presence of representatives of both Houses of Parliament and all the major public organisations in the UK. The Prime Ministers and leading members of the Commonwealth nations and representatives of other countries also attend.

The Monarch's Role in Government

In law, the Queen is head of the executive; an integral part of the legislature; head of the judiciary; the commander-in-chief of all the armed forces of the Crown; and the 'supreme governor' of the established Church of England. As a result of a long process of change, during which the Monarchy's absolute power has been gradually reduced, the Queen acts on the advice of her government ministers. The UK is therefore governed by Her Majesty's Government in the name of the Queen.

Within this framework the Queen still takes part in some important acts of government. These include summoning, proroguing (discontinuing until the next session without dissolution) and dissolving Parliament; and giving Royal Assent to Bills passed by the UK or Scottish Parliament and the Northern Ireland Assembly. The Queen formally

[2] The other Commonwealth states of which the Queen is Sovereign are: Antigua and Barbuda; Australia; the Bahamas; Barbados; Belize; Canada; Grenada; Jamaica; New Zealand; Papua New Guinea; St Kitts and Nevis; St Lucia; St Vincent and the Grenadines; Solomon Islands; and Tuvalu.

appoints important office holders, including the Prime Minister and other government ministers (see p. 58), judges, officers in the armed forces, governors, diplomats, bishops and some other senior clergy of the Church of England. In instances where people have been wrongly convicted of crimes, she is involved in pardoning them. She also confers peerages, knighthoods and other honours.[3] In international affairs the Queen, as Head of State, has the power to declare war and make peace, to recognise foreign states, to conclude treaties and to take over or give up territory.

With very few exceptions (such as appointing the Prime Minister), acts involving the use of 'royal prerogative' powers are now performed by government ministers, who are responsible to Parliament and can be questioned about particular policies. It is not necessary to have Parliament's authority to exercise these prerogative powers, although Parliament may restrict or abolish such rights.

The Queen holds Privy Council meetings (see p. 42), gives audiences to her ministers and officials in the UK and overseas, receives accounts of Cabinet decisions, reads dispatches and signs state papers. She is consulted on many aspects of national life, and must show complete impartiality.

The law states that a regent has to be appointed to perform the royal functions if the monarch is totally incapacitated. The regent would be the Queen's eldest son, the Prince of Wales, then those aged 18 or over, in order of succession to the throne. In the event of her partial incapacity or absence abroad, the Queen may delegate certain royal functions to the Counsellors of State (her husband the Duke of Edinburgh, the four adults next in line of succession, and the Queen Mother). However, Counsellors of State may not dissolve Parliament (except on the Queen's instructions) or create peers.

Royal Income and Expenditure

Public funds (known as the 'Civil List') and government departments together meet the costs of the Queen's official duties. In 2000–01, expenditure on royal travel was £5.4 million, and £16.4 million was spent on the upkeep of the royal palaces and on media and information services.

In July 2000 a Royal Trustees' Report recommended that Civil List payments should remain at the 1991 level of £7.9 million a year for a further ten years from 2001. About three-quarters of the Queen's Civil List provision is needed to meet the cost of staff. Under the Civil List, the Queen Mother and the Duke of Edinburgh receive annual parliamentary allowances (together amounting to £1 million) to enable them to carry out their public duties. In return for the Civil List and other financial support, the Queen surrenders the income from the Crown Estate (£147.7 million in 2000–01) and other hereditary revenues to the nation. The Prince of Wales does not receive a parliamentary allowance, since as Duke of Cornwall he is entitled to the annual net revenues of the estate of the Duchy of Cornwall.

The Queen's private expenditure as Sovereign comes from the Privy Purse, which is financed mainly from the revenues of the Duchy of Lancaster;[4] her expenditure as a private individual is met from her own personal resources.

Since 1993 the Queen has voluntarily paid income tax on all personal income and on that part of the Privy Purse income which is used for private purposes. The Queen also pays tax on any realised capital gains on her private investments and on the private proportion of assets in the Privy Purse. In line with this, the Prince of Wales pays tax on the income from the Duchy of Cornwall so far as it is used for private purposes.

In July 2001 the Lord Chamberlain, the most senior member of the Queen's Household, published revised guidelines setting out how members of the Royal Family could pursue careers, including those in business, in a way which would avoid allegations of exploitation of royal status.

---

[3] Although most honours are conferred by the Queen on the advice of the Prime Minister, a few are granted by her personally—the Order of the Garter, the Order of the Thistle, the Order of Merit and the Royal Victorian Order.

[4] The Duchy of Lancaster is a landed estate which has been held in trust for the Sovereign since 1399. It is kept quite apart from his or her other possessions and is separately administered by the Chancellor of the Duchy of Lancaster.

A New Great Seal of the Realm

In February 2001, the Queen approved the commissioning of a new Great Seal of the Realm to replace the existing one which had been in service since 1953 and is showing considerable signs of wear.

The Great Seal of the Realm dates back to the 11th century, originating in the reign of Edward the Confessor who used it to prevent forgeries of his royal proclamations by rebellious barons. Today it is kept in the House of Lords in the care of the Lord Chancellor and is used on State documents such as those approving treaties, permitting general elections, proclaiming royal marriages and appointing bishops.

Previous Great Seals commissioned include those of: Victoria (1838, 1860, 1878 and 1898); Edward VII (1904); George V (1912 and 1930); and George VI (1938 and 1948).

From now on, before a member of the Royal Family takes on a new business activity, he or she must ensure that the Lord Chamberlain has been consulted, and the Lord Chamberlain would be expected to advise against accepting an invitation to an engagement which could not be kept entirely separate from any aspects of the business activities of the member of the Royal Family concerned.

The Privy Council

The Privy Council was formerly the chief source of executive power in the State; its origins go back to the King's Court, which helped the Norman monarchs run the government. As the system of Cabinet government developed in the 18th century, the Cabinet (which is still, technically, a committee of Privy Counsellors) took on much of the role of the Privy Council.

Nowadays the Privy Council is the main way in which ministers advise the Queen on the approval of Orders in Council (such as those granting Royal Charters or enacting subordinate legislation) or the issue of royal proclamations (such as the summoning or dissolving of Parliament).

At any one time there are about 500 Privy Counsellors (who may add the words 'Right Honourable' before their names). Their appointment is for life. The Privy Council consists of all members of the Cabinet, other senior politicians, senior judges and some individuals from the Commonwealth. It is only members of the government of the day, however, who play any part in its policy work. The Prime Minister recommends membership of the Privy Council to the Sovereign.

Committees of the Privy Council

There are a number of Privy Council committees, normally comprising ministers with the relevant policy interest, such as those dealing with legislation from the Channel Islands and the Isle of Man. Except for the Judicial Committee, membership is confined to members of the current administration.

The Judicial Committee of the Privy Council is the final court of appeal from courts in UK Overseas Territories and those Commonwealth countries which decided to keep this method of appeal after their independence. In addition, the Committee hears appeals from the Channel Islands and the Isle of Man, and from the disciplinary and health committees of the medical and associated professions. It is also the Supreme Court for determining cases relating to the powers and actions of the devolved administrations, and has a limited jurisdiction to hear certain ecclesiastical appeals. Members of the Judicial Committee include the Lord Chancellor, the Lords of Appeal in Ordinary, other Privy Counsellors who hold or have held high judicial office and certain judges from the Commonwealth.

The secretariat of the Privy Council is the Privy Council Office, a government department of which the President of the Council, a Cabinet minister, is in charge.

Parliament

Origins of Parliament

Medieval kings had to meet all royal expenses, private and public, out of their own income. If

PA Photos

Charles Kennedy,
Liberal Democrats

Tony Blair,
Labour Party

William Hague,
Conservative Party

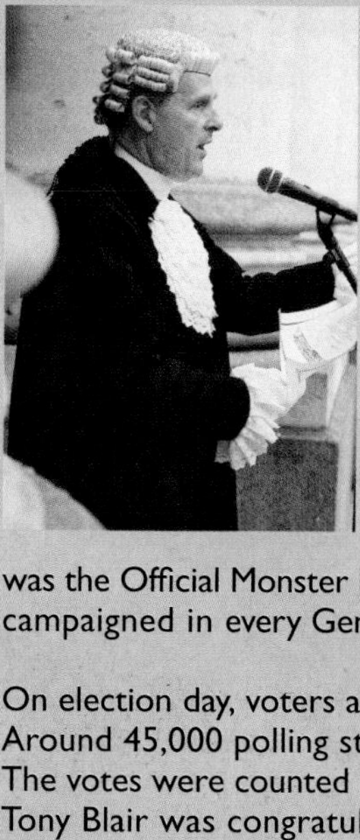

© Corporation of London

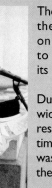

The 2001 General Election on 7 June was the 16th to be held since the end of the Second World War. Parliament was dissolved on 14 May and, in line with an ancient tradition dating back to the 15th century, this was announced in the City of London by its 'Common Cryer and Serjeant-at-Arms', Richard Martin (left).

During the election period the three main party leaders travelled widely throughout the United Kingdom, campaigning with their respective party candidates and meeting the electorate. For the first time a series of special party leader 'Question Time' election debates was broadcast on television. Each leader answered questions put by the general public (see next page).

A number of independent parties stood in the election. Among them was the Official Monster Raving Loony Party, which was established in 1983 and has campaigned in every General Election since then. Alan Hope is the party's current leader.

On election day, voters arrived at their local polling stations, some in unusual locations. Around 45,000 polling stations were open throughout the UK, each closing at 10pm. The votes were counted by hand and most results were announced during the night. Tony Blair was congratulated on his election victory in a personal telephone call on 8 June by Opposition leader William Hague. Britain's re-elected Prime Minister–the first Labour Prime Minister to win a second consecutive full term of office–travelled from his Sedgefield constituency to London. He thanked his colleagues outside the party's headquarters and addressed members of the waiting media. The new Parliament met on 13 June, when the first business was the election of the Speaker and the swearing in of its new members.

On 20 June the State Opening of Parliament took place. The Queen's Speech outlined the new Labour Government's legislative programme.

Following the election William Hague announced his resignation as leader of the Conservative Party. Iain Duncan Smith was elected as his successor in September 2001.

PA Photos

PA Photos

PA Photos

PA Photos

PA Photos

© FCO /Patrick Tsui

All photos: PA

extra resources were needed for an emergency, such as going to war, the Sovereign would try to persuade his barons in the Great Council—a gathering of leading men which met several times a year—to offer help. During the 13th century several English kings found their own private revenue, together with aid from the barons, insufficient to meet the expenses of government. They therefore called not only their land-owning barons to the Great Council but also representatives of counties, cities and towns, mainly to get them to agree to additional taxation. In this way the Great Council came to include those who were summoned by name (who, broadly speaking, were later to form the House of Lords) and those who were representatives of communities—the Commons. These two groups, together with the Sovereign, became known as 'Parliament'—a term originally meaning a meeting for *parley* or discussion.

By the middle of the 14th century the phrase 'by the Commons with the advice of the Lords Spiritual and Temporal' on enactment of a Bill signalled Parliament's agreement to the 'voting of supplies to the Crown'—that is, approval for the Government to spend money on a particular project. In 1407 Henry IV pledged that the House of Commons should approve all money grants before consideration by the Lords.

There was a similar development in the way laws were made. Originally the King's legislation needed only the agreement of his councillors, but, starting with the right of individuals to present petitions, the Commons was eventually allowed to appeal to the Crown on behalf of groups of people. During the 15th century they won the right to take part in the process of giving their requests—or 'Bills'—the form of law.

These were the foundations on which the House of Commons developed its power, while the constitutional changes of the 17th century led to Parliament gaining its position as the supreme legislative authority.

The Powers of Parliament

The three parts of Parliament—the Sovereign, the appointed House of Lords and the elected House of Commons—are based on different principles. They meet together only on occasions of symbolic significance such as the State Opening of Parliament, when the Commons is summoned by the Sovereign to the House of Lords. The agreement of all three is normally needed to pass laws, but that of the Sovereign is given as a matter of course.

Despite devolution, Parliament at Westminster can legislate for the UK as a whole and keeps powers to legislate for any parts of it separately. However, by convention it will not normally legislate on devolved matters without the agreement of the Scottish Parliament and the Welsh and Northern Irish Assemblies. It still has responsibility for certain matters (see p. 38) under the Acts of Parliament which set up these administrations. In the Channel Islands and the Isle of Man, which are Crown dependencies and not part of the UK, legislation on domestic matters normally takes the form of laws enacted by Island legislatures. However, UK laws are sometimes extended to the Islands, with their agreement, for example in areas such as immigration and broadcasting.

As there are no legal restraints imposed by a written constitution, Parliament may legislate as it pleases, as long as the UK meets its obligations as a member of the European Union (EU—see p. 72). It can make or change law, and overturn established conventions or turn them into law. It can even legislate to prolong its own life beyond the normal period without consulting the electorate.

In practice, however, Parliament does not assert itself in this way. Its members work within the common law and normally act according to precedent. The House of Commons is directly responsible to the electorate, and, increasingly during the 20th century, the House of Lords recognised the supremacy of the elected chamber.

The Functions of Parliament

The main functions of Parliament are:

- to pass laws;
- to provide (by voting for taxation) the means of carrying on the work of government;

- to scrutinise government policy and administration, including proposals for expenditure; and
- to debate the major issues of the day.

In carrying these out, Parliament helps to bring the relevant facts and issues to the attention of the electorate. By custom, Parliament is also informed before important international treaties and agreements are ratified. The making of treaties is, however, a royal prerogative carried out on the advice of the Government and does not need parliamentary approval.

The Meeting of Parliament

A Parliament has a maximum duration of five years, but not all Parliaments serve their full five-year term. The maximum life has been prolonged by legislation only in rare circumstances such as the two World Wars. The Sovereign dissolves Parliament and calls for a General Election on the advice of the Prime Minister.

The life of a Westminster Parliament is divided into sessions. Each usually lasts for one year—normally beginning and ending in October or November. There are 'adjournments' (when the House does not sit) at night, at weekends, at Christmas, Easter and the late Spring Bank Holiday, and during a long summer break usually starting in late July. The average number of 'sitting days' in a session is about 148 in the House of Commons and about 152 in the House of Lords.[5] At the start of each session the Sovereign's speech to Parliament outlines the Government's policies and proposed legislative programme. Each session is ended by the Sovereign dismissing it—called 'prorogation'. Parliament then 'stands prorogued' for a few days until the new session begins. Prorogation brings to an end nearly all parliamentary business: in particular, public Bills which have not been passed by the end of the session are lost, unless the Opposition has agreed they may be carried over.

[5] Taken over the last seven sessions. This includes two 'short' sessions in the election years of 1997 (1996–97, 79 days) and 2001 (2000–01, 83 days) and the 'long' session in 1997–98 (228 days).

The House of Lords

Reform

The Government has begun a step-by-step reform of the House of Lords aimed at making the second chamber more representative of British society at the start of the 21st century. As part of this process, in November 1999 the Government passed legislation to reduce the number of hereditary peers who had the right to sit and vote in the second chamber from over 750 to 92 (see below).

In May 2000 the Government set up the House of Lords Appointments Commission to make recommendations on the appointment of non-political peers (including 'people's peers'—see p. 46). It has taken over the role previously played by the Political Honours Scrutiny Committee. The Commission is an independent body responsible for vetting all nominations to the Sovereign for membership of the House of Lords to ensure they meet the highest standards of propriety. (Party-nominated peerages are usually given in recognition of service in politics or other walks of public life or because one of the political parties wants to have that particular person to speak in support of its policies in the House of Lords.)

After winning its second consecutive term of office in June 2001, the Government announced its intention to consult and then introduce legislation to implement the next phase of House of Lords reform which would remove the remaining hereditary peers and create a partly elected upper house.

Current Composition

The House of Lords consists of the Lords Spiritual and the Lords Temporal. The Lords Spiritual are the Archbishops of Canterbury and York, the Bishops of London, Durham and Winchester, and the 21 next most senior bishops of the Church of England. The present Lords Temporal consist of:

- 92 hereditary peers, who were selected to sit in the chamber by ballot from among the membership of the House of Lords before November 1999;

Table 6.2: Transitional House of Lords Composition by Party Strength, July 2001

Party	Lords Temporal		Lords Spiritual	Total
	Hereditary peers	*Life peers*		
Conservative	50	173		223
Labour	4	191		195
Liberal Democrats	5	56		61
Cross-bench	32	141		173
Other	—	31	26	57
Total	**91**[1]	**592**	**26**	**709**

[1]In June 2001 one of the hereditary peers was declared bankrupt and is therefore not eligible to attend the House.
Source: House of Lords

- life peers created to help carry out the judicial duties of the House (Lords of Appeal in Ordinary or 'law lords');[6] and
- all other life peers, including 15 'people's peers' created in April 2001 (see p. 46).

In July 2001 there were 114 women peers, and 28 'law lords' (created under the Appellate Jurisdiction Act 1876).

The three main political parties are represented in the House of Lords; the number of peers eligible to sit at July 2001 is shown in Table 6.2.

Members of the House of Lords receive no salary for their parliamentary work, but can claim for expenses incurred in attending the House (for which there are maximum daily rates) and certain travelling expenses. Average daily attendance is about 352 Members.

Officers of the House of Lords

The House is presided over by the Lord Chancellor, who sits on the woolsack[7] and acts as Speaker of the House. If the Lord Chancellor is not present, a nominated deputy takes his place.

As Clerk of the House of Lords, the Clerk of the Parliaments is responsible for the records of proceedings of the House of Lords and for the text of Acts of the UK Parliament. The postholder is the accounting officer for the House, and is in charge of its administrative staff, known as the Parliament Office. The Gentleman Usher of the Black Rod, usually known simply as 'Black Rod', is responsible for security, accommodation and services in the House of Lords' part of the Palace of Westminster.

The House of Commons

The House of Commons consists of 659 elected Members of Parliament (MPs). In July 2001 there were 118 women MPs and 12 MPs who had declared that they were of ethnic minority origin. Of the 659 seats, 529 represent constituencies in England, 40 in Wales, 72 in Scotland, and 18 in Northern Ireland. The Scotland Act 1998, which set up the Scottish Parliament, abolishes the statutory minimum of 71 Scottish seats, and provides that, at the next review of boundaries in Scotland, the electoral quota for England will be applied. This is expected to reduce the number of Scottish seats to around 57 to 60. The Boundary Commission for Scotland is next due to report between 2002 and 2006. It began its work on this review in June 2001.

General Elections are held after a Parliament has been dissolved and a new one summoned by the Sovereign. When an MP dies, resigns[8] or is given a peerage, a

[6] The House of Lords is the final court of appeal for civil cases in the UK and for criminal cases in England, Wales and Northern Ireland. In Scotland the High Court of Justiciary, sitting as the Scottish Court of Criminal Appeal, is the final court of appeal in criminal cases.

[7] The woolsack is a seat in the form of a large cushion stuffed with wool from several Commonwealth countries; it is a tradition dating from the medieval period, when wool was the chief source of the country's wealth.

[8] An MP who wishes to resign from the House can do so only by applying for an office under the Crown as Crown Steward or Bailiff of the Chiltern Hundreds, or Steward of the Manor of Northstead, thereby disqualifying him or herself from membership of the House of Commons.

'People's Peers'

In its first term of office, the Government announced that it wanted the House of Lords to be more representative of the country as a whole and that a small number of non-party appointments would be made from public nominees. Anyone in the UK would be able to nominate himself or herself, or nominate another person.

In September 2000, the House of Lords Appointments Commission (see p. 44) invited nominations for these 'people's peers', who would need to demonstrate that they were people with integrity and independence, and had a significant record of achievement in their chosen field or way of life.

In April 2001 the Queen announced her intention to bestow non-political life peerages on the 15 people nominated by the House of Lords Appointments Commission. They were selected from a total of 3,166 applications on the basis that they would bring considerable experience and authority to the House, adding to the range of expertise available in a number of areas, including science, social policy, housing, employment, education, business and international affairs.

by-election takes place. Members are paid an annual salary of £51,822 (from July 2001) and, under a new system that took effect from July 2001, provision for up to £70,000 for staff salaries and £18,000 for incidental expenses. (For ministers' salaries see p. 59.) All MPs are entitled to travel allowances and London members may claim a supplement for the higher cost of living in the capital. MPs from other parts of the UK may receive allowances for subsistence and for second homes nearer to the Palace of Westminster.

Officers of the House of Commons

The chief officer of the House of Commons is the Speaker, elected by MPs to preside over the House. Other officers include the Chairman of Ways and Means and two deputy chairmen, who may all act as Deputy Speakers. They are elected by the House as nominees of the Government, but may come from the Opposition as well as the government party. They, like the Speaker, neither speak nor vote except in their official capacity (that is, when deputising for the Speaker). The House of Commons Commission, a statutory body chaired by the Speaker, is responsible for the administration of the House.

Permanent officers (who are not MPs) include the Clerk of the House of Commons—the principal adviser to the Speaker on the House's privileges and procedures. The Clerk's other responsibilities relate to the conduct of the business of the House and its committees. The Clerk is also accounting officer for the House. The Serjeant at Arms, who waits upon the Speaker, carries out certain orders of the House. The postholder is also the official housekeeper of the Commons' part of the building, and is responsible for security. Other officers serve the House in the Library, the Department of the Official Report (*Hansard*), the Finance and Administration Department, and the Refreshment Department.

Parliamentary Electoral System

For electoral purposes the UK is divided into 659 constituencies, each of which returns one member to the House of Commons. To ensure that constituency electorates are kept roughly equal, four permanent Parliamentary Boundary Commissions, one each for England, Wales, Scotland and Northern Ireland, keep constituencies under review. (When the Parliamentary Boundary Commissions' latest reviews have been completed, the Commissions will be absorbed by the independent Electoral Commission—see p. 49.) They recommend any adjustment of seats that may seem necessary in the light of population movements or other changes. Reviews are conducted every 8 to 12 years. The recommendations in the Commissions' last general reviews were approved by Parliament in 1995. The Parliamentary Boundary Commissions for England and Scotland have begun general reviews and aim to produce reports by the end of 2005.

Voters

British citizens, together with citizens of other Commonwealth countries and citizens of the Irish Republic resident in the UK, may vote in parliamentary elections provided they are:

- aged 18 or over;
- included in the annual register of electors for the constituency; and
- not subject to any legal incapacity to vote.

People not entitled to vote include those under 18, members of the House of Lords, foreign nationals (other than Commonwealth citizens or citizens of the Irish Republic), some patients detained under mental health legislation, sentenced prisoners and people convicted within the previous five years of corrupt or illegal election practices. Members of the armed forces, Crown servants and staff of the British Council employed overseas (together with their wives or husbands if accompanying them) may be registered for an address in the constituency where they would live if not serving abroad. British citizens living abroad may apply to register as electors for a period of up to 20 years after they have left the UK.

Voting Procedures

Each elector may cast one vote, normally in person at a polling station. However, new measures which help to modernise voting and registration procedures for UK elections were introduced under the Representation of the People Act 2000 and implemented for the General Election held in June 2001. Provisions in the new Act include:

- the right for electors to cast their vote by post if they find that method more convenient;
- a new rolling register, updated monthly, to enable voters to register at any time of the year, replacing the one which was previously updated once a year in October and took effect the following February;
- local authority pilot schemes to evaluate innovative electoral procedures, such as electronic voting, all-postal ballots, early and weekend voting, and mobile polling stations;
- improved access and facilities for disabled voters, including a large print version of the ballot paper and a template for blind and partially sighted voters; and
- easier registration for homeless people (who were previously barred from voting because they had no fixed address), those in mental institutions (other than those who are held there because of criminal behaviour) and unconvicted or remand prisoners (if they are likely to be spending a long period in custody).

Voting is not compulsory and the simple majority system of voting is currently used for UK General Elections. Candidates are elected if they have more votes than any of the other candidates (although not necessarily an absolute majority over all other candidates). The Government is reviewing whether there should be changes to the voting system for the House of Commons.

Candidates

British citizens and citizens of other Commonwealth countries, together with citizens of the Irish Republic, may stand for election as MPs provided they are aged 21 or over and are not disqualified. Those disqualified include undischarged bankrupts; people who have been sentenced to more than one year's imprisonment; peers; and holders of certain offices listed in the House of Commons Disqualification Act 1975.

The statutory provisions which formerly barred ministers of religion from becoming MPs were repealed by the House of Commons (Removal of Clergy Disqualification) Act 2001. The new Act enables all former and serving clergy to stand for election to the House of Commons, but bishops sitting in the House of Lords as Lords Spiritual continue to be ineligible to serve as MPs because they already have a voice in the upper chamber.

A candidate's nomination for election must be proposed and seconded by two electors registered as voters in the constituency and signed by eight other electors. Candidates do not have to be backed by a political party.

A candidate must also deposit £500, which is returned if he or she receives 5% or more of the votes cast.

The maximum sum a candidate may spend on a General Election campaign is £5,483 plus 4.6 pence for each elector in a borough constituency, or 6.2 pence for each elector in a county constituency. A higher limit of £100,000 has been set for by-elections because they are often seen as tests of national opinion in the period between General Elections. A candidate may send by post an election communication to each elector in the constituency free of charge. All election expenses, apart from the candidate's personal expenses, are subject to the statutory maximum.

The Political Party System

The party system, which has existed in one form or another since the 18th century, is integral to the working of the constitution. The present system depends upon there being organised political parties, each of which presents its policies to the electorate for approval; in practice most candidates in elections, and almost all winning candidates, belong to one of the main parties. A system of voluntary registration for political parties in the UK was introduced in 1998. Registered parties contest elections to the Scottish Parliament, the National Assembly for Wales and the European Parliament (see p. 73) in their own right using 'lists' of candidates. Registration helps prevent the use of misleading descriptions on ballot papers, since only candidates representing a registered political party are permitted to have the name and emblem of the party printed alongside their names.

For the last 150 years Britain has had a predominantly two-party system. Since 1945 either the Conservative Party, whose origins go back to the 18th century, or the Labour Party, which emerged in the last decade of the 19th century, has held power. The Liberal Democrats were formed in 1988 when the Liberal Party, which also traced its origins to the 18th century, merged with the Social Democratic Party, formed in 1981. Other parties include two national parties, Plaid Cymru (founded in Wales in 1925) and the Scottish National Party (founded in 1934). Northern Ireland has a number of parties. They include the Ulster Unionist Party, formed in the early part of the 20th century; the Democratic Unionist Party, founded in 1971 by a group which broke away from the Ulster Unionists; the Social Democratic and Labour Party, founded in 1970; and Sinn Féin.[9]

Since 1945 the Conservative Party and Labour Party have each won eight General Elections.

The party which wins most seats (although not necessarily the most votes) at a General Election, or which has the support of a majority of members in the House of Commons, usually becomes the Government. By tradition, the Sovereign asks the leader of the party with the majority to form a government, about 100 of whose members in the House of Commons and the House of Lords receive ministerial appointments (including appointment to the Cabinet—see p. 59) on the advice of the Prime Minister. The largest minority party becomes the official Opposition, with its own leader and 'shadow cabinet'.

The Party System in Parliament

Leaders of the Government and Opposition sit on the front benches in the debating chamber of the House of Commons with their supporters ('the backbenchers') sitting behind them. There are similar seating arrangements for the parties in the House of Lords, but many peers do not wish to be associated with any political party, and therefore choose to sit on the 'cross-benches'.

The effectiveness of the party system in Parliament relies to a large extent on the relationship between the Government and the opposition parties. Depending on the relative strengths of the parties in the House of Commons, the Opposition may try to overthrow the Government by defeating it on a 'matter of confidence' vote. In general, however, the Opposition aims to contribute to

[9] Sinn Féin is the political wing of the IRA (see p. 15).

The General Election of 7 June 2001

The June 2001 General Election was notable in a number of ways:

- Of a total electorate of 44.4 million people, 26.4 million voted. This represented a turnout of 59.4%, compared with 72% in 1997, and was the lowest for over 80 years. The turnout for England was 59.1%, Wales 61.4%, Scotland 58.1% and Northern Ireland 68.0%.
- There was a relatively small change in seats (see Table 6.3) compared with the 1997 election. For example, only one of the 72 seats in Scotland changed hands and two of the 40 in Wales. (In Northern Ireland, however, several seats changed hands.)
- The Labour Party won its second highest number of seats (its highest being in the 1997 election). It was also the first time that it had been elected with sufficient MPs to govern for a second full five-year period.
- The Liberal Democrats improved their showing and gained their highest number of seats.
- The Conservatives restored their presence in Scotland but still have no MPs in Wales.

the formulation of policy and legislation by constructive criticism; to oppose government proposals with which it disagrees; to table amendments to Government Bills; and to put forward its own policies to improve its chances of winning the next General Election.

The Government Chief Whips in the Commons and the Lords, in consultation with their Opposition counterparts, arrange the scheduling of government business; they do so under the direction of the Prime Minister and the Leaders of the two Houses. Collectively, the Chief Whips are often referred to as 'the usual channels' when the question of finding time for a particular item of business is being discussed. The Leaders of the two Houses control the running of business in their respective parts of the Palace of Westminster.

The Chief Whips and their assistants, who are usually chosen by the party leaders, manage their parliamentary parties. Their duties include keeping members informed of forthcoming parliamentary business, maintaining the party's voting strength by ensuring members attend important debates, and passing on to the party leadership the opinions of backbench members. Party discipline tends to be not as strong in the Lords as in the Commons, since peers have less hope of high office and no need of party support in elections.

Financial Assistance to Parties

The Political Parties, Elections and Referendums Act 2000 contains provisions to make party funding more open, control spending on elections and ensure the fair conduct of referendums. It implements the recommendations in the Committee on Standards in Public Life's report *The Funding of Political Parties in the UK*, published in 1998. The Act's provisions are being introduced in stages (see below).

In November 2000 a new independent Electoral Commission was set up under the Act to supervise the financial restrictions on parties and oversee referendums. In due course it will take over the functions of the Parliamentary Boundary Commission and the Local Government Boundary Commissions (see p. 46) and has broad responsibility for electoral law.

Donations

- Since February 2001, political parties may only accept donations from 'permissible donors': individuals on the UK electoral register, registered companies incorporated in the EU which do business in the UK, registered political parties and trade unions. Any political donation of over £200 to a party must be from a permissible donor;
- all donations of over £5,000 to a political party's central organisation must be reported to the Electoral Commission on a quarterly basis—weekly during a General Election campaign;

Table 6.3: General Election Results by Party, 7 June 2001

	Votes cast	*% share of vote*	*MPs elected*	*Gains on 1997*	*Losses on 1997*	*Net change in seats*
Labour	10,724,953	40.7	412	2	8	–6
Conservative	8,357,615	31.7	166	9	8	+1
Liberal Democrats	4,814,321	18.3	52	8	2	+6
Scottish National	464,314	1.8	5	0	1	–1
Plaid Cymru	195,893	0.7	4	1	1	0
Ulster Unionist	216,839	0.8	6	1	5	–4
Democratic Unionist	181,999	0.7	5	3	0	+3
Social Democratic and Labour	169,865	0.6	3	0	0	0
Sinn Féin[1]	175,933	0.7	4	2	0	+2
Speaker	16,053	0.1	1	0	0	0
Others[2]	28,487	0.1	1	1	2	–1

[1] The Sinn Féin Members have not taken their seats.
[2] The seat in the 2001 General Election was won by the Independent Kidderminster Hospital and Health Concern candidate. The figure for votes cast is only that for his vote.
Source: House of Commons Information Office

- all donations of over £1,000 to accounting units, such as a constituency association, must be reported to the Electoral Commission; and
- individual MPs and other people elected to office, including MEPs (see p. 73), members of the devolved assemblies of Wales and Northern Ireland and the Scottish Parliament, members of local authorities and the Mayor for London, are subject to similar controls on the source of donations and have to report to the Electoral Commission any donations over £1,000.

Campaign Expenditure

- A cap on campaign spending by political parties will apply during the 365 days before a General Election. A party will have an allowance of £30,000 for each constituency contested so that a party contesting all 659 parliamentary constituencies will be able to spend nearly £20 million in total; and
- third parties at elections (such as trade unions) are also subject to expenditure limits set at 5% of the maximum for political parties.

Referendums

- The Electoral Commission will be able to comment on the wording of a referendum question to ensure that people understand it;
- the Government of the day, local authorities and all other public bodies will not be allowed to produce promotional material 28 days before a referendum; and
- there will be a sliding scale of expenditure of between £0.5 million and £5 million for a registered political party depending on the size of its vote at the previous General Election, with £0.5 million for other permitted participants.

Election Broadcasting

- Since March 2001, the broadcasting of local items during an election period has been subject to new codes of practice drawn up by the BBC and independent broadcasting authorities, taking into account the views of the Electoral Commission.

Donations to Candidates

- New, tighter controls on donations to candidates came into force in July 2001, along with other measures under the Representation of the People Act 2000 designed to clarify the controls on election expenses.

Electoral Education

- The Electoral Commission has been responsible for education about electoral and democratic systems since July 2001.

Parliamentary Procedure

Parliamentary procedure is largely based on the way things have been done in the past, partly set down by each House in a code of practice known as its 'Standing Orders'. The debating system is similar in both Houses. Every subject starts off as a proposal or 'motion' by a member. After debate, in which each member (except the person putting forward the motion) may speak only once, the motion may be withdrawn: if it is not, the Speaker or Chairman 'puts the question' whether to agree to the motion or not. The question may be decided without voting, or by a simple majority vote. The main difference between the two Houses is that in the House of Lords the Lord Chancellor, in his role as Speaker, or a deputising Chairman, does not control procedure; instead such matters are decided by the general feeling of the House, which is sometimes interpreted by its Leader.

In the Commons the Speaker has full authority to enforce the rules of the House and must uphold procedure and protect minority rights. The Speaker may or may not allow a motion to end discussion so that a matter may be put to the vote, and has powers to stop irrelevant and repetitious contributions in debate. In cases of serious disorder the Speaker can adjourn or suspend the sitting. The Speaker may order members who have broken the rules of behaviour of the House to leave the Chamber or can suspend them for a number of days.

The Speaker supervises voting in the Commons and announces the final result. If there is a tie, the Speaker gives a casting vote (usually to keep the situation as it is), without expressing an opinion on the merits of the question. Voting procedure in the House of Lords is broadly similar, although the Lord Chancellor may vote but does not have a casting vote.

Modernisation of the House of Commons

Most of the recommendations made by the Select Committee on Modernisation of the House of Commons, first set up in 1997, have now been implemented. Among them are:

- measures to improve the examination of proposed legislation, including a system for publishing Bills in draft;
- the experimental use of Westminster Hall, formerly known as the Grand Committee Room, mainly for adjournment debates and discussion of consultative documents;
- reformed procedures for examining European legislation;
- abolishing old-fashioned customs, such as that requiring a Member to remain seated and wear an opera hat to raise a point of order during a division;
- the introduction of programme motions to limit the amount of time spent in debating some Bills;
- some divisions to be deferred until the following Wednesday afternoon to reduce the need for MPs to stay at the House late into the night to vote;
- experimenting with the hours during which the House sits; and
- carrying over, in defined circumstances, Public Bills from one session to the next.

Financial Interests

The Commons has a public register of MPs' financial (and some non-financial) interests. Members with a financial interest must declare it when speaking in the House or in Committee and must indicate it when giving notice of a question or motion. In other proceedings of the House or in dealings with other members, ministers or civil servants, MPs must also disclose any relevant financial interest. MPs cannot express favourable views in the House on matters which are related to the source of any personal financial interest.

The House of Lords also has a Register of Interests, on lines similar to that for MPs. A report of the Committee of Standards in Public Life, published in November 2000, made recommendations for certain changes to the rules and procedures governing conduct in the House of Lords, including registration of financial interests (see p. 65).

Parliamentary Commissioner for Standards

The post of Parliamentary Commissioner for Standards was created in 1995, following recommendations of the Committee on Standards in Public Life (see p. 64). The Commissioner, who is independent of government, can advise MPs on matters of standards, and hold initial investigations into complaints about alleged breaches of the rules by Members. The Commissioner reports to the House of Commons Select Committee on Standards and Privileges.

Public Access to Parliamentary Proceedings

Proceedings of both Houses are normally public. The minutes and speeches (transcribed in *Hansard*, the Official Report) are published daily.

The records of the Lords from 1497 and of the Commons from 1547, together with the parliamentary and political papers of a number of former members of both Houses, are available to the public through the House of Lords Record Office. A wide range of information on all aspects of the workings of Parliament can be found on the Houses of Parliament website at *www.parliament.uk*.

The proceedings of both Houses of Parliament may be broadcast on television and radio, either live or, more usually, in recorded or edited form. Complete coverage is available on cable and satellite television and the 'webcasting' of Parliament is currently being considered.

The Law-making Process

Statute law consists of Acts of Parliament and delegated legislation (commonly known as statutory instruments) made by ministers under powers given to them by Act (see p. 54). While the *interpretation* of the law is refined constantly in the courts (see chapter 14), *changes* to statute law can only be made by Parliament.

Draft laws take the form of parliamentary Bills. Proposals for legislation affecting the powers of particular bodies (such as individual local authorities) or the rights of individuals (such as certain plans relating to railways, roads and harbours) are known as Private Bills, and are subject to a special form of parliamentary procedure. Bills which change the general law and make up the more significant part of the parliamentary legislative process are called Public Bills.

Public Bills can be introduced into either House, by a government minister or by any member or peer. Most Public Bills which become Acts of Parliament are introduced by a government minister and are known as 'Government Bills'. Bills introduced by other MPs or Lords are known as 'Private Members' Bills'. Government Bills are generally accompanied by Explanatory Notes, written by the Department which is promoting the Bill and updated when it is enacted. The notes are designed to help the reader understand more easily what the Bill seeks to achieve and how it goes about it. They also provide other background information about the legislation, but are not passed or endorsed by Parliament.

The main Bills forming the Government's legislative programme are announced in the Queen's Speech at the State Opening of Parliament, which usually takes place in November or shortly after a General Election, and the Bills themselves are introduced into one or other of the Houses over the following weeks.

Before a Government Bill is drafted, there may be consultation with professional bodies, voluntary organisations and others with an interest, including pressure groups looking to promote specific causes. 'White Papers', which are government statements of policy, often contain proposals for changes in the law; these may be debated in Parliament before a Bill is introduced. As part of the process of modernising procedures (see p. 51), some Bills are now published in draft for pre-legislative scrutiny before beginning their passage through Parliament. The aim is to allow more input from backbenchers and other interested parties at an early stage, helping to save time and reducing the number of amendments which are made during the legislative process. The Government may also publish consultation papers, sometimes called 'Green Papers', setting out proposals which are still taking shape and inviting comments from the public.

Passage of Public Bills

Public Bills must normally be passed by both Houses. Bills relating mainly to financial matters are almost always introduced in the Commons. Under the provisions of the Parliament Acts 1911 and 1949, the powers of the Lords in relation to 'money Bills' are very restricted. The Parliament Acts also make it possible for a Bill to be passed by the Commons without the consent of the Lords in certain (very rare) circumstances.

The process of passing a Public Bill is similar in each House. On presentation the Bill is considered, without debate, to have been read for a first time and is printed. After an interval, which may be between one day and several weeks, a Government Bill will receive its second reading debate, during which the general principles of the Bill are discussed.

If it gets a second reading in the Commons, a Bill will normally be passed to a standing committee (see p. 55) for detailed examination and amendment. In the Lords, the committee stage usually takes place on the floor of the House, and this procedure may also be followed in the Commons if MPs decide to do so (usually in cases where there is a need to pass the Bill quickly or where it raises matters of constitutional importance).

The committee stage is followed by the report stage ('consideration') on the floor of the House, during which further amendments may be made. In the Commons, the report stage is usually followed immediately by the third reading debate, when the Bill is reviewed in its final form; in the Lords, the third reading debate usually takes place on a different day. Substantive amendments to a Bill cannot be made at third reading.

After completing its third reading in one House, a Bill is sent to the other House, where it passes through all its stages once more and where it is, more often than not, further amended. Amendments made by the second House must be agreed by the first, or a compromise reached, before a Bill can go for Royal Assent.

In the Commons the House may vote to limit the time available for consideration of a Bill. This is done by passing a 'timetable' motion proposed by the Government, commonly known as a 'guillotine'. There are special procedures for Public Bills which bring together pieces of existing legislation.

Royal Assent

When a Bill has passed through all its parliamentary stages, it is sent to the Queen for Royal Assent, after which it becomes an Act of Parliament and is part of the law of the land. The Royal Assent has not been refused since 1707. In the 1999–2000 session 45 Public Bills were enacted.

Limitations on the Power of the Lords

The main legislative function of the non-elected House of Lords is to act as a revising chamber, complementing but not rivalling the elected House of Commons. As a result, it has some limitations on its powers.

Most Government Bills introduced and passed in the Lords go through the Commons without difficulty, but a Lords Bill unacceptable to the Commons would normally be amended before it became law. The Lords, on the other hand, do not usually prevent Bills from being enacted which the Commons are keen to pass, although they will often amend and return them to the Commons for further consideration.

The Lords pass Bills authorising taxation or national expenditure without amendment as a formality. A Bill which deals only with taxation or expenditure must become law within one month of being sent to the Lords, whether or not the Lords agrees to it, unless the Commons directs otherwise. If no agreement is reached between the two Houses on a non-financial Commons Bill, the Lords can delay the Bill for a period which, in practice, amounts to at least 13 months. Following this the Bill may be presented to the Queen for Royal Assent, provided it has been passed in the current session and previous session by the Commons. There is one important exception: any Bill to lengthen the life of a Parliament needs the full assent of both Houses.

Private Members' Bills

Early in each session backbench members of the Commons ballot (draw lots) for the chance to introduce a Bill on one of the Fridays when such Bills have precedence over government business. The first 20 members whose names are drawn win this privilege, but it does not guarantee that their Bills will pass into law. Members may also present a Bill on any day without debate, while on most Tuesdays and Wednesdays when the Commons is sitting MPs may introduce a Bill under the 'ten minute rule' which gives an opportunity for a brief speech by the member proposing the Bill (and by one who opposes it).

In most sessions some become law (six in the 1999–2000 session). Private Members' Bills do not often require public expenditure; but if they do they cannot go forward to committee stage unless the Government decides to provide the necessary money. Peers may introduce Private Members' Bills in the House of Lords at any time. A Private Member's Bill passed by one House will not proceed in the other unless taken up by a member of that House.

Private and Hybrid Bills

Private Bills are promoted by people or organisations outside Parliament (often local authorities) to give them special legal powers. They go through a similar process to Public Bills, but most of the work is done in committee, where procedures follow a semi-judicial pattern. Hybrid Bills are Public Bills which may affect private rights, for example, the Channel Tunnel Rail Link Bill, which was passed in 1996. As with Private Bills, there are special arrangements for the passage of Hybrid Bills through Parliament which allow those affected to put their case.

Delegated Legislation

To reduce unnecessary pressure on parliamentary time, primary legislation (that is the law as set out in an Act of Parliament) often gives ministers or other authorities the power to make minor, technical changes to an Act by means of secondary or 'delegated' legislation (usually in the form of 'statutory instruments'). Such powers are normally delegated only to authorities directly accountable to Parliament or to the devolved legislatures, so that the risk of undermining the authority of Parliament is kept to a minimum. Acts which allow for delegated legislation usually give Parliament the opportunity to agree to or disagree with any resulting statutory instruments, while some also require that organisations affected must be consulted before rules and orders can be made.

A joint committee of both Houses reports on the technical propriety of these 'statutory instruments'. In order to save time on the floor of the House, the Commons uses standing committees to debate the merits of instruments; actual decisions are taken by the House as a whole. In the Lords, debates on statutory instruments take place on the floor of the House. The House of Lords has appointed a delegated powers scrutiny committee which examines the appropriateness of the powers to make secondary legislation in Bills.

Parliamentary Committees

Committees of the Whole House

Either House may vote to turn itself into a 'Committee of the Whole House' in order to consider Bills in detail after their second reading. This allows unrestricted discussion: the general rule that an MP or peer may speak only once on each motion does not apply in committee.

Standing Committees

House of Commons standing committees debate and consider Public Bills at the committee stage. The committee examines the Bill clause by clause, and may amend it before reporting it back to the House. Ordinary standing committees do not have names but are called simply Standing Committee A, B, C and so on; a new set of members is appointed to them to consider each Bill. Each committee has between 16 and 50 members, with a party balance reflecting as far as possible that in the House as a whole. The standing committees currently still include two Scottish standing committees, and the Scottish, Welsh and Northern Ireland Grand Committees.

The Scottish Grand Committee comprises all 72 Scottish MPs (and may be convened anywhere in Scotland as well as at Westminster). It may consider the principle of any Scottish Bill at the second and third reading stages, where such a Bill has been referred to the Committee by the House for that purpose. It also debates other matters concerning Scotland. In addition, its business includes questions tabled for oral answer, ministerial statements and other debates, including those on statutory instruments referred to it.

The Welsh Grand Committee, consisting of all 40 Welsh MPs and up to five others who may be added from time to time, may consider Bills referred to it at second reading stage, questions tabled for oral answer, ministerial statements, and other matters relating exclusively to Wales.

The Northern Ireland Grand Committee considers Bills at the second and third reading stages, takes oral questions and ministerial statements, and debates matters relating specifically to Northern Ireland. It includes all sitting Northern Ireland MPs and up to 25 others as nominated by the committee of selection. The Belfast Agreement allows for the Northern Ireland Grand and Select Committees to scrutinise the responsibilities of the Secretary of State.

There is a Standing Committee on Regional Affairs, consisting of all Members sitting for constituencies in England, plus up to five others. It was revived in April 2000.

There are also standing committees to debate proposed European legislation, and to examine statutory instruments and draft statutory instruments brought forward by the Government.

In the Lords, various sorts of committees on Bills may be used instead of, or as well as, a Committee of the Whole House. Such committees include Public Bill Committees, Special Public Bill Committees, Grand Committees, Select Committees and Scottish Select Committees.

Select Committees

Select committees are appointed for a particular task, generally one of enquiry, investigation and scrutiny. They report their conclusions and recommendations to the House as a whole; in many cases they invite a response from the Government, which is also reported to the House. A select committee may be appointed for a Parliament, or for a session, or for as long as it takes to complete its task. Parliament is helped in controlling the executive by 15 committees, set up by the House of Commons to examine aspects of public policy, expenditure and administration across the main government departments and their associated public bodies. The Foreign Affairs Select Committee, for example, 'shadows' the work of the Foreign & Commonwealth Office. Each committee is constituted on a basis which is in approximate proportion to party strength in the House.

Other regular Commons select committees include those on Public Accounts, Standards and Privileges, and European Legislation. 'Domestic' select committees also cover the internal workings of Parliament.

Each House has a select committee to keep it informed of EU developments, and to enable it to scrutinise and debate EU policies and proposals, while three Commons standing committees debate specific European legislative proposals. Ministers also make regular statements about EU business.

In their examination of government policies, expenditure and administration, committees may question ministers, civil servants, interested bodies and individuals. Through hearings and published reports, they bring before Parliament and the public an extensive amount of fact and informed opinion on many issues, and build up considerable expertise in their subjects of inquiry.

In the House of Lords, besides the Appeal and Appellate Committees in which most of the House's judicial work is carried out, there are two major select committees: on the European Community and on Science and Technology. From time to time other committees may also be set up to consider particular issues (or, sometimes, a particular Bill), and 'domestic' committees—as in the Commons—cover the internal workings of the House.

Joint Committees

Joint committees, with a membership drawn from both Houses, are appointed in each session to deal with Consolidation Bills[10] and statutory instruments (see p. 54). The two Houses may also agree to set up joint select committees on other subjects.

Unofficial Party Committees

The Parliamentary Labour Party comprises all members of the party in both Houses. When the Labour Party is in office, a parliamentary committee, half of whose members are elected and half of whom are government representatives, acts as a channel of communication between the Government and its backbenchers in both Houses. When the party is in opposition, the Parliamentary Labour Party is organised under the direction of an elected parliamentary committee, which acts as the 'shadow cabinet'.

The Conservative and Unionist Members' Committee (the 1922 Committee) consists of the backbench membership of the party in the House of Commons. When the Conservative Party is in office, ministers attend its meetings by invitation and not by right. When the party is in opposition, the whole membership of the parliamentary party may attend meetings. The leader appoints a consultative committee, which acts as the party's 'shadow cabinet'.

Other Forms of Parliamentary Control

In addition to the scrutiny by select committees, both Houses offer a number of other opportunities for the examination of government policy by the Opposition and the Government's own backbenchers. In the House of Commons, these include:

- Question Time, when for 55 minutes on Monday, Tuesday, Wednesday and Thursday, ministers answer MPs' questions. The Prime Minister's Question Time takes place for half an hour every Wednesday when the House is sitting. Parliamentary Questions are one means of finding out about the Government's intentions. They are also a way of raising complaints brought to MPs' notice by constituents. MPs may also put questions to ministers for written answer; the questions and answers are published in *Hansard*. There are about 40,000 questions every year.
- Adjournment debates, when MPs use motions for the adjournment of the House to raise constituency cases or matters of public concern. There is a half-hour adjournment period at the end of the business of the day, and opportunities for several adjournment debates on Wednesday mornings. Since November 1999, under experimental measures to modernise and reform parliamentary procedures, a second chamber, Westminster Hall (see p. 51), has also been widely used for adjournment debates. In addition, an MP wishing to discuss a 'specific and important matter that should have urgent consideration' may, at the end of Question Time, ask for an adjournment of the House. On the very few occasions when this action is successful, the matter

[10] A Consolidation Bill brings together several existing Acts into one, with the aim of simplifying the statutes.

is debated for three hours in what is known as an emergency debate, usually on the following day.

- Early day motions (EDMs) are another way in which backbench MPs may express their views on particular issues. A number of EDMs are tabled each sitting day; they are very rarely debated but can be useful in measuring the amount of support for the topic by the number of MPs who add their signatures to the EDM.
- On 20 days in each session (sometimes divided into half-days) opposition parties choose the business to be discussed. Of these days, 17 are allocated to the Leader of the Opposition and three are at the disposal of the leader of the second largest opposition party.
- Debates on three days in each session on details of proposed government expenditure, chosen by the Liaison Committee (a select committee largely made up of select committee chairmen, which considers general matters relating to the work of select committees).
- Procedural opportunities for criticism of the Government also occur during the debate on the Queen's Speech at the beginning of each session; on motions of censure for which the Government provides time; and in debates on the Government's legislative and other proposals.

In the House of Lords, similar opportunities for criticism and examination of government policy come at daily Question Time, during debates and by means of questions for written answer.

Control of Finances

The main responsibilities of Parliament, and more particularly of the House of Commons, in overseeing the revenue of the State and public expenditure, are to authorise the raising of taxes and duties, to decide on the various areas of spending and to allocate the amount to be spent on each. Parliament also has to be sure that the sums granted are spent only for the purposes which it intended. No payment out of the central government's public funds can be made, and no taxation or loans authorised, except by Act of Parliament. However, limited interim payments can be made from the Contingencies Fund.

The Finance Act is the most important piece of annual legislation. It authorises the raising of revenue and is based on the Chancellor of the Exchequer's Budget statement (see p. 387). Scrutiny of public expenditure is carried out by House of Commons select committees (see p. 55).

Forcing the Government to Resign

As a final act of parliamentary control, the House of Commons may force the Government to resign by passing a resolution of 'no confidence'. The Government must also resign if the House rejects a proposal which the Government considers so vital to its policy that it has declared it a 'matter of confidence' or if the House refuses to vote the money required for the public service.

Parliamentary Commissioner for Administration

The Parliamentary Ombudsman—officially known as the Parliamentary Commissioner for Administration—investigates complaints from members of the public (referred to him by MPs) alleging that they have been unfairly treated through inefficiency of the system. The Ombudsman is independent of government and reports to a select committee of the House of Commons. The Ombudsman's area of authority covers central government departments and agencies, and a large number of non-departmental public bodies (NDPBs—see p. 61). He cannot investigate complaints about government policy, the content of legislation or relations with other countries.

In making investigations, the Commissioner has access to all departmental papers, and has powers to call before him those from whom he wishes to take evidence. When an investigation is completed, he sends a report with his findings to the MP who referred the complaint (with a copy for the complainant). When a complaint is upheld, the Ombudsman normally recommends that the department or other body makes some kind of compensation (which might be financial in appropriate cases). There is no appeal against the Ombudsman's decision.

The Ombudsman received 1,721 new complaints in 2000–01 (an increase of 7% over the previous year). He settled 1,787 complaints and completed 247 full investigations. Complaints against the then Department of Social Security accounted for 42% of the total received.

The Parliamentary Ombudsman also investigates complaints arising from breaches of the Code of Practice on Access to Government Information (see p. 63).

Separate arrangements for a Scottish Parliamentary Commissioner for Administration and a Welsh Administration Ombudsman have been set up to deal with complaints about the Scottish Executive, the National Assembly for Wales and devolved public bodies. Complaints to the Scottish Commissioner are referred through Members of the Scottish Parliament; complaints to the Welsh Administration Ombudsman can be made direct.

Parliamentary Privilege

To ensure that Parliament can carry out its duties without hindrance, certain rights and immunities apply collectively to each House and its staff, and individually to each member. They include freedom of speech; first call on the attendance of its members, who are therefore free from arrest in civil actions and excused from serving on juries, or being forced to attend court as witnesses; and the right of access to the Crown, which is a collective privilege of the House. Further privileges include the rights of the House to control its own proceedings (so that it is able, for instance, to keep out 'strangers'[11] if it wishes); to decide upon legal disqualifications for membership and to declare a seat vacant on such grounds; and to punish for breach of its privileges and for contempt. Parliament has the right to punish anybody, inside or outside the House, who commits a breach of privilege—that is, offends against the rights of the House. The privileges of the House of Lords are broadly similar to those of the Commons.

[11] All those who are not members or officials of either House.

Her Majesty's Government

Her Majesty's Government are those ministers responsible for the conduct of national affairs. The Queen appoints the Prime Minister, and all other ministers are appointed by the Queen on the recommendation of the Prime Minister. Most ministers are members of the Commons, although the Government is also fully represented by ministers in the Lords. The Lord Chancellor is always a member of the House of Lords.

The composition of governments can vary both in the number of ministers and in the titles of some offices. New ministerial offices may be created, others may be abolished, and functions may be transferred from one minister to another (see box on p. 62).

Prime Minister

The Prime Minister is also, by tradition, First Lord of the Treasury and Minister for the Civil Service. The Prime Minister's unique position of authority comes from majority support in the House of Commons and from the power to appoint and dismiss ministers. By modern convention, the Prime Minister always sits in the Commons.

The Prime Minister presides over the Cabinet (see p. 59), is responsible for allocating functions among ministers and, at regular meetings with the Queen, informs her of the general business of the Government.

The Prime Minister's other responsibilities include recommending a number of appointments to the Queen. These include: Church of England archbishops, bishops and certain deans and some 200 other clergy in Crown 'livings'; senior judges, such as the Lord Chief Justice; Privy Counsellors; and Lords Lieutenants. He also recommends certain civil appointments, such as Lord High Commissioner to the General Assembly of the Church of Scotland (after consultation with the First Minister of the Scottish Parliament), The Poet Laureate, The Constable of the Tower (of London), and some university posts; and appointments to several public boards and institutions, such as the BBC (British Broadcasting Corporation), as well as various royal and statutory commissions.

The Prime Minister's Office supports him in his role as head of government. This includes providing policy advice, tracking the delivery of government commitments and initiatives, and ensuring effective communications to Parliament, the media and the public. Following the 2001 General Election, several new units, including the Delivery Unit, the Forward Strategy Unit and the Office of Public Services Reform, have been set up within the Cabinet Office to assist the Prime Minister in these tasks.

Departmental Ministers

Ministers in charge of government departments are usually in the Cabinet; they are known as 'Secretary of State' or may have a special title, as in the case of the Chancellor of the Exchequer.

Non-departmental Ministers

The holders of various traditional offices, namely the President of the Council, the Chancellor of the Duchy of Lancaster, the Lord Privy Seal, the Paymaster General and, from time to time, Ministers without Portfolio, may have few or no departmental duties. They are therefore available to carry out any duties the Prime Minister may wish to give them. In the present administration, for example, the President of the Council is Leader of the House of Commons, and the Chancellor of the Duchy of Lancaster is Minister for the Cabinet Office.

Lord Chancellor and Law Officers

The Lord Chancellor holds a special position, as both a minister with departmental functions and the head of the judiciary (see p. 222). The three Law Officers of the Crown advising the UK Government are the Attorney-General and the Solicitor-General (for England and Wales) and the Advocate-General for Scotland.

Other Ministers

Ministers of State are middle-ranking ministers. They normally have specific responsibilities, and are sometimes given titles which reflect these functions, for example, 'Minister for Housing and Planning' or 'Minister for E-Commerce and Competitiveness'.

The most junior ministers are Parliamentary Under-Secretaries of State (or, where the senior minister is not a Secretary of State, simply Parliamentary Secretaries). They may be given responsibility, directly under the departmental minister, for specific aspects of the department's work.

Ministerial Salaries

The salaries of ministers in the House of Commons (from July 2001) range from £78,657 a year for junior ministers to £119,979 for Cabinet ministers (inclusive of their parliamentary salaries—see p. 46). The Prime Minister receives a salary of £165,418 and the Lord Chancellor £173,875.

Ministerial salaries in the House of Lords (as at April 2001) range from £58,961 for junior ministers to £88,562 for Cabinet ministers.

The Leader of the Opposition in the Commons receives a salary of £114,301 (inclusive of his parliamentary salary); two Opposition whips in the Commons and the Opposition Leader and Chief Whip in the Lords also receive additional salaries.

The Cabinet

About 20 ministers (the number can vary) chosen by the Prime Minister sit in the Cabinet; these may include both departmental and non-departmental ministers. The Cabinet balances ministers' individual duties with their collective responsibility as members of the Government and takes the final decisions on all government policy.

Cabinet Meetings

The Cabinet meets in private and its business is confidential, although after 30 years Cabinet papers may become available for inspection in the Public Record Office at Kew, Surrey.

Normally the Cabinet meets weekly when Parliament is sitting, and less often when it is not. Cabinet Committees take some of the pressure off the full Cabinet by settling issues among smaller groups of people or at a lower level, or at least by clarifying them and defining points of disagreement. Committees let those ministers most closely concerned come to decisions in a way which ensures that the Government as a whole can accept full responsibility for them. This delegated responsibility means that Cabinet Committee decisions have the same formal status as those taken by the full Cabinet.

Cabinet Committees include those dealing with defence and overseas policy, economic policy, home and social affairs, the environment, and local government. The membership and terms of reference of all ministerial Cabinet Committees are published. Where appropriate, the Secretary of the Cabinet and other senior Cabinet Office officials go to meetings of the Cabinet and its Committees.

The Cabinet Office

The Cabinet Office, together with HM Treasury and the Prime Minister's Office, is at the centre of UK Government.

The Secretary of the Cabinet (a senior civil servant who reports directly to the Prime Minister) manages the Cabinet Secretariats, which together serve ministers in carrying out Cabinet business and coordinating policy at the highest level. Since 1983, the Cabinet Secretary has also had the role of Head of the Home Civil Service.

A new Office of the Deputy Prime Minister has been set up in the Cabinet Office (see p. 62). This oversees the work of the Social Exclusion Unit and has responsibility for the Regional Coordination Unit and the Government Offices for the Regions (GOs—see p. 11). It also assists the Deputy Prime Minister in the role he plays in support of the Prime Minister on issues such as Northern Ireland and climate change. The current Chancellor of the Duchy of Lancaster is also Minister for the Cabinet Office and has ministerial responsibility for the Prime Minister's new Delivery Unit, regulation and e-Government (see p. 402).

The Cabinet Office is responsible for current policies to:

- modernise and simplify government so that it works more effectively for the benefit of the people;
- work with departments to improve the delivery of public services; and
- provide the central strategic management of the Civil Service.

Ministerial Responsibility

'Ministerial responsibility' refers both to the collective responsibility for government policy and actions which ministers share, and to ministers' individual responsibility for the work of their own departments.

'Collective responsibility' means that all ministers unanimously support government policy once it has been settled. The policy of departmental ministers must agree with the policy of the Government as a whole. Once the Government has decided its policy on a particular matter, each minister is expected to support it or resign. On rare occasions, ministers are allowed free votes in Parliament on important issues of principle or conscience.

Ministers are individually accountable for the work of their departments and agencies, and have a duty to Parliament to answer for their policies, decisions and actions.

Departmental ministers normally decide all matters within their responsibility. However, many issues cut across departmental boundaries and need the agreement of more than one minister. The full Cabinet or a Cabinet Committee considers proposals where the issue is one which raises major policy concerns, is likely to lead to significant public comment or criticism, or where the departmental ministers concerned have been unable to agree.

On taking up office ministers resign directorships in private and public companies, and must ensure that there is no conflict between their public duties and private interests. Detailed guidance on handling ministers' financial interests is set out in the Ministerial Code.

Government Departments

The main role of government departments and their agencies is to implement government policy and advise ministers. They are staffed by politically impartial civil servants and generally receive their funding from money provided by Parliament. They often work alongside local authorities, non-departmental public bodies, and other government-sponsored organisations.

The structure and functions of departments are sometimes reorganised if there are major changes in government policy (see box on p. 62 for new departments and responsibilities following the June 2001 General Election). A change of government, however, does not necessarily affect the functions of departments.

The work of some departments (for instance, the Ministry of Defence) covers the UK as a whole. Other departments, such as the Department for Work and Pensions, cover England, Wales and Scotland, but not Northern Ireland. Others again, such as the Department for Transport, Local Government and the Regions, are mainly concerned with affairs in England. (For changes in responsibilities associated with devolution, see chapters 3, 4 and 5.)

The Regional Co-ordination Unit is responsible for considering government initiatives with a regional or local dimension and for promoting closer links between government activity in the regions with that done centrally.

The nine Government Offices (see pp. 10–11) are the key arms of government in the English regions, responsible for the effective delivery of government programmes regionally and locally. Their staff represent seven government departments: DTI, DfES, DWP, DTLR, HO, DCMS and DEFRA. Working together and with regional partners, including local authorities and Regional Development Agencies (RDAs), the Government Offices are best placed to ensure that government policies are coordinated at a regional level.

RDAs were formally launched in eight English regions in April 1999. The ninth, in London, followed in July 2000 when the new Greater London Authority took up its full powers and responsibilities. The RDAs provide coordinated regional economic development and regeneration, and help the English regions to improve their competitiveness relative to their European counterparts.

Voluntary regional chambers have been established in each region. They provide a means through which the RDAs can consult on their proposals and give an account of their activities.

Most departments are headed by ministers. However, some are non-ministerial departments headed by a permanent office holder and ministers with other duties are accountable for them to Parliament. For example, the Secretary of State for Education and Skills accounts to Parliament for the work of the Office for Standards in Education (OFSTED). OFSTED is headed by HM Chief Inspector of Schools in England, who is largely independent of the Secretary of State.

The functions of the main government departments and agencies are set out in Appendix 1, pp. 537–546.

Non-departmental Public Bodies

A non-departmental public body (NDPB sometimes known as 'quango') is a national or regional public body, working independently of ministers to whom they are accountable. There are two main types of NDPB:

- **Executive NDPBs** are those with executive, administrative, commercial or regulatory functions. They are typically engaged in a wide variety of activities and are set up in a number of different ways. Executive NDPBs carry out set functions within a government framework but the degree of operational independence varies. Examples include the Arts Council of England, the Environment Agency and the Health and Safety Executive.
- **Advisory NDPBs** are those set up by ministers to advise them and their departments on particular matters. Examples include the Committee on Standards in Public Life and the Low

New Departments and Changes of Responsibilities after the General Election, June 2001

Cabinet Office (CO)
The Cabinet Office, which now includes a new Office of the Deputy Prime Minister, oversees the development of government policy, including at regional level, and cross-departmental matters such as social exclusion and leads the drive to improve the delivery of public services. The Social Exclusion Unit, the Regional Coordination Unit and the Government Offices for the Regions report to the Deputy Prime Minister.

Department for Culture, Media and Sport (DCMS)
Gambling, licensing, censorship, video classification and planning for the Queen's Golden Jubilee celebrations in 2002 have come to the DCMS from the Home Office.

Department for Environment, Food and Rural Affairs (DEFRA)
This new Department is in charge of promoting 'green issues' and the countryside. It has taken over responsibility for agriculture, food and fisheries from the Ministry of Agriculture, Fisheries and Food (MAFF) which now no longer exists. It has taken control of government policy for the environment, the countryside and sustainable development from the former Department of the Environment, Transport and the Regions (DETR), and animal welfare and hunting from the Home Office.

Department for Education and Skills (DfES)
This new Department has taken over the responsibilities of the former Department for Education and Employment (DfEE) for education and has a particular remit to raise standards, increase higher education participation and improve work-based training and lifelong learning.

Department of Trade and Industry (DTI)
New responsibilities taken on by the DTI following departmental reorganisation include sponsorship of the construction industry (previously under the former DETR) and the Regional Development Agencies. It has acquired a number of responsibilities from the former DfEE relating to equality, including the Race Relations Equality Advisory Service and Equality Direct, which provide policy on work-life balance and give advice to employers. Responsibility for Sunday trading, street markets and chartered fairs, and the calendar has transferred from the Home Office.

Department for Transport, Local Government and the Regions (DTLR)
In addition to taking over responsibility for the fire service and electoral law from the Home Office, this new Department is in charge of most of the policy areas of the former DETR except those dealing with environmental matters.

Department for Work and Pensions (DWP)
The welfare and pensions responsibilities of the former Department of Social Security (DSS) now come under this new Department, together with the employment and disability portfolios from the former DfEE. From October 2001, it will be responsible for a new agency, Jobcentre Plus, which will bring together the functions of the Employment Service and those parts of the Benefits Agency which provide services for people of working age.

Lord Chancellor's Department (LCD)
As part of the reorganisation of departmental responsibilities, the LCD has taken over responsibility from the Home Office for open government, including freedom of information and data protection; royal, Church and hereditary issues and Lords Lieutenants; Crown Dependencies; and human rights issues.

Ministry of Defence (MoD)
The MoD has taken over responsibility for the Security Services Group from the Cabinet Office and the War Pensions Agency from the former DSS.

Home Office (HO)
Although it has lost some of its less central responsibilities in the reorganisation (see entries above), the HO has taken control of the UK Anti-Drugs Co-ordination Unit, which previously came under the Cabinet Office. It has also taken on responsibility for the issue of work permits from the former DfEE.

Pay Commission. Some Royal Commissions are also classified as advisory NDPBs.

There are currently over 1,000 NDPBs in the UK. A list of all NDPBs is held centrally by the Cabinet Office and is issued annually in the publication *Public Bodies*. An electronic directory is available via the Cabinet Office website.

The Lobby

As press adviser to the Prime Minister, the Prime Minister's Official Spokesman and other staff in the Prime Minister's Press Office have direct contact with the parliamentary press through regular meetings with the Lobby correspondents. The Lobby correspondents are a group of political journalists with the special privilege of access to the Lobby of the House of Commons, where they can talk privately to government ministers and other members of the House. The Prime Minister's Official Spokesman is the accepted channel through which information about parliamentary business is passed to the media.

Modernising Government

The Government has taken a number of measures as part of its long-term programme to modernise and improve public services. These include:

- drawing up Public Service Agreements (PSAs) with government departments (see p. 402) to set a clear framework of policy objectives and resource allocation, and provide a way of measuring and monitoring effectiveness;
- a coherent programme for more responsive and higher quality public services, including schemes like Charter Mark to promote excellence (see p. 64);
- the establishment of the Prime Minister's Delivery Unit to drive improvements in health, education, crime reduction and transport, and the creation of the Centre for Management and Policy Studies to improve policy-making, draw on external experience and strengthen the skills of civil servants;
- making all government services available electronically by 2005 so that they are more responsive to the needs of citizens and businesses and encourage greater government efficiency. By the end of 2000, 42% of public services were online with over 70% planned to be available by 2002; and
- a reform programme to create a more open, diverse and professional Civil Service.

Freedom of Information

The Freedom of Information Act 2000 replaces a non-statutory Code of Practice on Access to Government Information and creates a statutory right of access to recorded information held across the public sector, including Parliament, government departments, and local authorities, health trusts, doctors' surgeries, publicly funded museums and other organisations.

The main features of the Act are:

- a right of wide general access to information, subject to clearly defined exemptions and conditions;
- a requirement to consider discretionary disclosure in the public interest even when an exemption applies;
- a duty to publish information; and
- powers of enforcement through an independent Information Commissioner and Information Tribunal.

National Statistics

In line with the Government's commitment to greater openness and accessibility of publicly held information, the UK's independent national statistical service makes available all its online data free of charge. National Statistics, set up in June 2000, aims to provide an accurate, up-to-date, comprehensive and meaningful picture of the UK economy and society to support the formulation and monitoring of economic and social policies by government at all levels.

The National Statistician is the Head of National Statistics, Head of the Government Statistical Service, Director of the Office for National Statistics, Registrar General for England and Wales, and the UK Government's chief professional adviser on statistical matters. He has professional responsibility for the quality of the outputs comprising National Statistics and maintains and publishes a National Statistics Code of Practice to help achieve this.

A new Statistics Commission has also been set up. It is an independent, non-executive advisory body whose role includes presenting the comments of users and suppliers on the National Statistics work programme, advising ministers of areas of widespread concern about the quality of official statistics and reviewing the need for statistical legislation. It is required to produce an annual report which is laid before Parliament.

Charter Mark

A key objective of the Government's future plans is to improve the delivery of public services with more emphasis on the consumer.

The Charter Mark scheme aims to help public service organisations become more focused on the needs of users. The scheme applies to all public services, at both national and local level. It sets out clear standards of service, ensures consultation with users, has an easy-to-use complaints procedure and works with other providers to ensure better services which are simple to use and well coordinated.

Committee on Standards in Public Life

This Committee was set up in 1994 against a background of increasing public concern about standards in many areas of public life. Its standing terms of reference are 'to examine current concerns about standards of conduct of all holders of public office, including arrangements relating to financial and commercial activities, and make recommendations as to any changes in present arrangements which might be required to ensure the highest standards of propriety in public life'.

The Committee has published seven reports. The first, in 1995, led to the appointment of a Parliamentary Commissioner for Standards and a Commissioner for Public Appointments (see p. 65).

Reports in 1996 and 1997 examined standards of conduct in local public spending bodies and conduct in local government, and called for a radical change in the ethical framework within which local government operates. A proposal was made for a new criminal offence of misuse of public office.

In 1997 the Prime Minister gave the Committee additional terms of reference to review the funding of political parties. The Committee's report, published in 1998, called for a new regulatory regime, overseen by an independent Electoral Commission, for political party funding in the UK. Provisions in the Political Parties, Elections and Referendums Act 2000 (see p. 49) have now addressed these matters.

In January 2000, the Committee published *Reinforcing Standards*, a major review of public sector ethics, which concluded that, although the process of raising standards had been a success, more still needed to be done. Its recommendations, the majority of which were accepted by the Government in July 2000, called for:

- changing the rules on the conduct of MPs and disciplinary procedures;
- amending the Ministerial Code to make it clear that a minister, having had the advice of his or her Permanent Secretary on potential conflicts of interest, must take full responsibility for any subsequent decision;
- ensuring that staff appointed on secondments or short-term contracts are alert to ethical issues within the public sector and limiting the total number of special advisers that can be appointed within Government;
- strengthening the guidance on lobbying and self-regulation by lobbyists;
- disclosing in departmental annual reports, and to the public on request, details of sponsorship of government activities by the private and voluntary sectors; and

- ➢ establishing an agreed definition of a task force, specifying, among other things, that if it ran for more than two years, it should be disbanded or reclassified as an advisory NDPB.

The Committee's latest report—*Standards of Conduct in the House of Lords*—was published in November 2000. It made a number of recommendations for changes to the rules and procedures governing conduct in the House of Lords. A working group set up by the House to consider the report unanimously accepted the recommendations for mandatory registration of all peers' relevant interests and a short code of conduct. In July 2001 the House passed a resolution to adopt a new Code of Conduct with effect from 31 March 2002.

Commissioner for Public Appointments

The Commissioner for Public Appointments is independent of government and is responsible for monitoring, regulating and auditing approximately 12,500 ministerial appointments to a range of public bodies including NDPBs, public corporations, nationalised industries, National Health Service (NHS) Trusts and utility regulators. The Commissioner has issued a Code of Practice which covers the seven principles to be applied to these appointments—ministerial responsibility, merit, independent scrutiny, equal opportunities, probity, openness and transparency, and proportionality.

Civil Service Commissioners

The Civil Service Commissioners are responsible for ensuring that recruitment to the Civil Service should be on merit and based on fair and open competition. The Commissioners, who are independent of government, produce a mandatory Recruitment Code and audit the recruitment policies and practices of departments and agencies to ensure that they comply. They also approve appointments through external recruitment to the Senior Civil Service, and hear and determine appeals in cases of concern about propriety and conscience under the Civil Service Code.

The Civil Service

The constitutional and practical role of the Civil Service is to help the Government of the United Kingdom, the Scottish Executive or the National Assembly for Wales formulate their policies, carry out decisions and administer public services for which they are responsible.

Civil servants are servants of the Crown; in effect this means the Government of the United Kingdom, the Scottish Executive and the National Assembly for Wales. The executive powers of the Crown are generally exercised by ministers of the Crown, Scottish ministers and ministers of the National Assembly for Wales, who are in turn answerable to the appropriate Parliament or Assembly. The Civil Service as such has no separate constitutional personality or responsibility. The duty of the individual civil servant is first and foremost to the minister in charge of the department in which he or she is serving. A change of minister, for whatever reason, does not involve a change of staff.

Cabinet ministers may each appoint a maximum of two special advisers. The Prime Minister approves all appointments. There are about 80 such advisers in the present administration. The advisers are paid from public funds. Their appointments come to an end when the Government's term of office finishes, or when the appointing minister leaves the Government or moves to another appointment.

The Civil Service Code, introduced in 1996, is a concise statement of the role and responsibilities of civil servants. It was revised in May 1999 to take account of devolution. The Code includes an independent line of appeal to the Civil Service Commissioners on alleged breaches of the Code.

Civil servants constitute about 2% of the working population in employment, and about 10% of all public sector employees. The number of permanent civil servants fell from 751,000 in 1976 to 478,500 in October 2000. These figures include the Senior Civil Service, which comprises around 3,000 of the most senior managers and policy advisers. Part-time working has increased over recent years with 13.4% of civil servants working part time at October 2000.

About half of all civil servants provide services to the public. These include paying benefits and pensions, running employment services, staffing prisons, issuing driving licences, and providing services to industry and agriculture. A further quarter are employed in the Ministry of Defence and its agencies. The rest are divided between central administrative and policy duties; support services; and largely financially self-supporting services, for instance, those provided by the Royal Mint. Four-fifths of civil servants work outside London. Approximately 11,000 civil servants work in the Scottish Executive and 2,700 in the National Assembly for Wales.

Northern Ireland Civil Service

The Northern Ireland Civil Service (NICS) is modelled on its counterpart in Great Britain, and has its own Civil Service Commission. There were about 24,000 civil servants in the NICS in September 2001. There is a degree of mobility between the NICS and the Home Civil Service.

The Diplomatic Service

The Diplomatic Service, a separate service of some 6,000 people, provides staff for the Foreign & Commonwealth Office (FCO—see p. 96) in London and at British diplomatic missions abroad.

Terms and conditions of service are comparable, but take into account the special demands of the Service, particularly the requirement to serve abroad. Home civil servants, members of the armed forces and individuals from the private sector may also serve in the FCO and at overseas posts on loan or attachment.

Equality and Diversity

The Civil Service aims to create a culture in which the different skills, experience and expertise that individuals bring are valued and used. Its equal opportunities policy states that there must be no unfair discrimination on the basis of age, disability, gender, marital status, sexual orientation, race, colour, nationality, ethnic or national origin or (in Northern Ireland) community background. The Civil Service is committed to achieving greater diversity, particularly at senior levels, where women, people from ethnic minorities and those with disabilities are under-represented.

In October 2000, the overall proportion of women in the Civil Service was 50%; ethnic minority representation was 6%; and at least 3.6% of staff employed were disabled. Progress is monitored and reported on regularly by the Cabinet Office.

Central Management

As Minister for the Civil Service, the Prime Minister is responsible for central coordination and management of the Civil Service. He is supported by the Head of the Home Civil Service who chairs the Civil Service Management Board. (The function of official Head of the Home Civil Service is combined with that of Secretary of the Cabinet.) The Cabinet Office oversees the central framework for management of the Civil Service. Day-to-day responsibility for a wide range of terms and conditions has been delegated to departments and agencies, the Scottish Executive and the National Assembly for Wales.

Executive Agencies

Executive agencies were introduced to deliver government services more efficiently and effectively within available resources. They are part of the Civil Service, but under the terms of individual framework documents they have greater delegation of financial, pay and personnel matters. Agencies are headed by chief executives who are normally directly accountable to ministers but are personally responsible for day-to-day operations. Abolition, privatisation, contracting-out, merger or rationalisation of a given government function are all options considered before an agency is set up. These options are reconsidered for each agency and NDPB when they are reviewed, which normally happens every five years.

Local Government

Local Authorities' Powers

Local authorities only work within the powers laid down under various Acts of Parliament. Their functions are far-reaching. Some are mandatory, which means that the authority must do what is required by law; others are discretionary, allowing an authority to provide services if it wishes. In certain cases, ministers have powers to secure uniformity in standards in order to safeguard public health or to protect the rights of individual citizens. Where local authorities exceed their statutory powers, they are regarded as acting outside the law and can be challenged in court.

The main link between local authorities and central government in England is the Department for Transport, Local Government and the Regions. However, other departments, such as the Department for Education and Skills, the Department for Work and Pensions, the Department of Health and the Home Office, are also concerned with various local government functions. In Scotland, Wales and Northern Ireland local authorities now deal mainly with the devolved Parliament and Assemblies.

Reform of Local Government Structure

A major reform of local government took place in 1974 in England and Wales and in 1975 in Scotland. This created two main tiers of local authority throughout England and Wales: counties and the smaller districts. Local government in London had been reorganised along the same lines in 1965. In Scotland functions were allocated to regions and districts on the mainland; single-tier authorities were introduced for the three Islands areas. In Northern Ireland changes were made in 1973 which replaced the two-tier county council and urban/rural council system with a single-tier district council system.

The Local Government Act 1985 abolished the Greater London Council and the six metropolitan county councils in England. Most of their functions were transferred to the London boroughs and metropolitan district councils respectively in 1986 (see below).

Further restructuring of local government later took place in non-metropolitan England and in Scotland and Wales. In 1992 the Local Government Commission was set up to review the structure, boundaries and electoral arrangements of local government in England and to carry out electoral reviews at regular intervals. In its reviews of local government in non-metropolitan England, the Commission considered whether the two-tier structure should be replaced by single-tier ('unitary') authorities in each area; for the most part it recommended keeping two-tier government, but suggested unitary authorities for some areas, especially the larger cities. Parliament approved reorganisation in 25 counties, creating a total of 46 new unitary councils (see map on p. 8). The reorganisation was completed in 1998.

In Scotland 29 new unitary councils replaced the previous system of nine regional and 53 district councils in 1996; the three Islands councils remained in being. In Wales 22 unitary authorities replaced the previous eight county councils and 37 district councils, again in 1996.

Principal Types of Local Authority

Greater London

Greater London is made up of the 32 London boroughs and the City of London, each with a council responsible for a number of key local services in its area. The Greater London Authority (GLA), led by the Mayor for London, sets key strategies on a range of London-wide issues, such as transport, economic development, strategic and spatial development and the environment (see p. 9).

English Metropolitan County Areas

The six metropolitan county areas—Tyne and Wear, West Midlands, Merseyside, Greater Manchester, West Yorkshire and South Yorkshire—have 36 district councils, but no county councils. The district councils are responsible for all services apart from those which have a statutory authority over areas wider than the individual boroughs and districts—for example, waste disposal (in certain areas); the fire services, including civil defence; and public transport. These are run by joint authorities composed of elected councillors nominated by the borough or district councils.

English Non-metropolitan Counties

Before the recent reforms, local government in England—outside Greater London and the metropolitan areas—was divided into counties and sub-divided into districts. All the counties and districts had locally elected councils with separate functions. County councils provided large-scale services, while district councils were responsible for the more local ones. These arrangements are broadly continuing in areas where two-tier local government remains.

County councils are responsible for transport, planning, highways, traffic regulation, education, consumer protection, refuse disposal, the fire service, libraries and the personal social services. District councils are responsible for environmental health, housing, decisions on most local planning applications, and collection of household waste. Both tiers of local authority have powers to provide facilities such as museums, art galleries and parks; arrangements depend on local agreement. In areas where the new unitary authorities have been set up, county and district level functions have joined together.

In addition to the two-tier local authority system in England, over 10,000 parish councils provide and manage local facilities such as allotments and village halls, and act as agents for other district council functions. They are also a forum for discussion of local issues.

Scotland, Wales and Northern Ireland

In Scotland the 32 single-tier councils are responsible for the full range of local government services. In Wales the 22 single-tier councils have similar functions, except that fire services are provided by three combined fire authorities. In addition, about 750 community councils in Wales have functions similar to those of the parish councils in England (see above); Scotland has community councils to represent the views of their local communities to local authorities and other public bodies in the area. In Northern Ireland 26 district councils are responsible for delivering services to their local communities.

Fire Services in the UK

Every part of the UK is covered by a local authority fire service. Each of the 59 fire authorities must by law provide a firefighting service and maintain a brigade to meet all normal requirements. Each fire authority appoints a Chief Fire Officer (Firemaster in Scotland) who has day-to-day control of operations. The fire services in England and Wales employ around 56,000 staff and spend about £1.5 billion each year.

Election of Councils

Local councils consist of elected councillors. In England and Wales each council elects its presiding officer annually. Some districts have the ceremonial title of borough, or city, both granted by royal authority. In boroughs and cities the presiding officer is normally known as the Mayor, or in Scotland the Provost. In the City of London and certain other large cities, he or she is known as the Lord Mayor. In Scotland the presiding officer of the council of the four longest established cities—Aberdeen, Dundee, Edinburgh and Glasgow—is called the Lord Provost.

Councillors are elected for four years. Whole council elections are held every four years in all county councils in England, borough councils in London, and about two-thirds of non-metropolitan district councils. In the remaining districts (including all metropolitan districts) one-third of the councillors are elected in each of the three years when county council elections are not held. Unitary authorities in non-metropolitan districts and London boroughs have a pattern of elections similar to that in metropolitan districts.

In Scotland whole council elections are held every three years, with the next elections due in 2002. In Wales whole council elections are held every fourth year, with the next due in 2003.

County, district and unitary authority councillors are paid a basic allowance but may be entitled to additional allowances and expenses for attending meetings or taking on special responsibilities.

Electoral Areas and Procedure

Counties in England are divided into electoral divisions, each returning one councillor. Districts in England and Northern Ireland are divided into wards, returning one or more councillors. In Scotland the unitary councils are divided into wards and in Wales into electoral divisions; each returns one councillor or more. Parishes (in England) and communities (in Wales) may be divided into wards, returning at least one councillor.

The procedure for local government voting in Great Britain is broadly similar to that for parliamentary elections. In Northern Ireland district councils are elected by proportional representation because it allows for the representation of sizeable minorities.

Eligibility rules for voters are also similar to those for parliamentary elections, except that citizens of other member states of the EU may vote. To stand for election, candidates must also either be registered as an elector or have some other close connection within the electoral area of their candidature, such as their principal place of employment.

The electoral arrangements of local authorities in England are kept under review by the Local Government Commission (see p. 67), and in Wales and Scotland by the Local Government Boundary Commissions. Electoral arrangements in England and Wales for parishes and communities can be reviewed by local councils.

Provision of Local Services

In recent years, there has been a move away from direct service provision, to a greater use of private contractors, and an increase in what is often called the 'enabling' role. Local authorities now carry out many functions in partnership with both public and private organisations.

The Government considers that councils should not be forced to put their services out to tender, but equally it sees no reason why a service should be delivered directly if more efficient means are available elsewhere. The Local Government Act 1999 therefore places a duty on local authorities to achieve best value.

The Best Value programme encourages local accountability and involves local communities in deciding the quality, level and cost of the services they receive. Local authorities are expected to set themselves challenging targets for the improvement of services following regular reviews of their performance. Local people may see how well their authority is performing through the publication of annual performance plans.

The Government of Wales Act 1998 requires the National Assembly to set up a Partnership Council to oversee relations between the Assembly and local government. A Commission to establish effective relations between local government and the new Scottish Parliament has been set up (see chapter 4).

Internal Organisation of Local Authorities

The Local Government Act 2000 requires local authorities to implement new decision-taking structures, including the possibility of a directly elected mayor. These arrangements replace the traditional committee system of decision-taking for most council functions. In most authorities the arrangements are based on one of three executive frameworks: a mayor and cabinet; a council leader and cabinet; or a mayor and council manager. Within these options local authorities have considerable flexibility to work within a constitution which reflects local circumstances. Small shire district councils with a population of fewer than 85,000 have, in addition to executive arrangements, the choice of reforming their existing committee system.

All new constitutions are required to incorporate rigorous arrangements for review and scrutiny of councils' policies and the decisions they make. Some decisions, such as the acceptance of policies and the budget, are reserved for the full council, but most of those relating to the implementation of policy are for the executive. The executive is also responsible for preparing the policies and budget to propose to the council. Decisions may be taken by the executive collectively, by individual members of the executive, by committees of the executive or by officers of the authority. The executive is also able to delegate decision-making to area committees and to enter into partnership arrangements with other authorities.

The new arrangements are designed to ensure that people know who in the council is responsible for taking decisions, how they can make their input into decision-making and how to hold decision-makers to account.

Public Access

Under the Local Government Act 2000, the public (including the press) is admitted to meetings of the executive when key decisions are being discussed. They also have access to agendas, reports and minutes of meetings and certain background papers. In addition, local authorities must publish a Forward Plan setting out the decisions which will be taken over the coming months. Local authorities may exclude the public from meetings and withhold papers only in limited circumstances.

Employees

About 2.2 million people[12] are employed by local authorities in the UK. These include school teachers, police, firefighters and other non-manual and manual workers. Education is the largest service with 1.3 million full-time equivalent jobs. Councils are individually responsible, within certain national legislative requirements, for deciding the structure of their workforces.

The elected councillors usually make senior staff appointments. More junior appointments are made by heads of departments. The Secretary of State for Education and Skills sets the pay and conditions of school teachers, after receiving recommendations from the School Teachers' Pay Review Body. Police pay is determined by a formula tied to median private sector non-manual pay settlements. Other pay and conditions of service are usually a matter for each council, although firefighters' pay increases are set by a formula linked to the upper quartile of male manual workers' earnings. For other workers, most authorities follow the scales recommended as a result of national negotiation between authorities and trade unions.

Local Authority Finance

Local government expenditure accounts for about 25% of public spending. In 2000–01 expenditure by local authorities in the UK was about £91.1 billion. Current expenditure amounted to £76.8 billion; capital expenditure, net of capital receipts, was £7.0 billion; and debt interest £3.2 billion. Local government capital expenditure is financed primarily by borrowing within limits set by central government and from capital receipts from the disposal of land and buildings.

Local authorities in Great Britain raise revenue through the council tax (see chapter 23), which meets about 25% of their revenue expenditure. Their spending is, however, financed primarily by grants from central government (the devolved administration in Scotland) and by the redistribution of revenue within each country from their national non-domestic rate, a property tax levied on businesses and other non-domestic properties.

District councils in Northern Ireland continue to raise revenue through the levying of a domestic rate and business rates.

Financial Safeguards

Local councils' annual accounts must be audited by independent auditors appointed by the Audit Commission in England and Wales, or in Scotland by the Accounts Commission for Scotland. In Northern Ireland the chief local government auditor carries out this role. Local electors have a right to inspect the accounts to be audited. They may also ask questions and lodge objections with the auditor.

[12] Full-time equivalents.

Figure 6.4:
Local Authority Expenditure and Funding in England, 2001–02

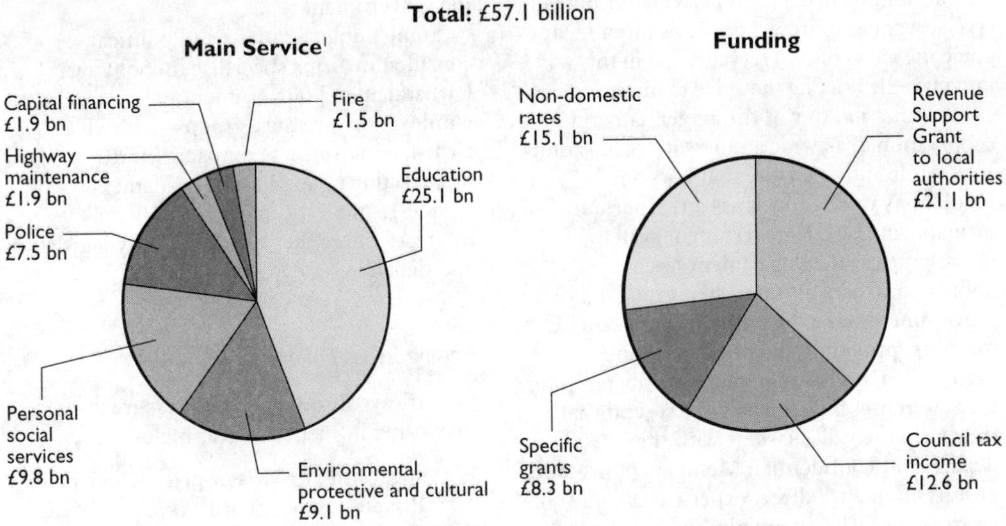

[1] Total includes £0.2 billion of unallocated expenditure.

Source: Department for Transport, Local Government and the Regions

Local Government Complaints System

Local authorities are encouraged to settle complaints through internal mechanisms, and members of the public often ask their own councillor for help in this. Local authorities must also appoint a monitoring officer, whose duties include ensuring that the local authority acts lawfully when carrying out its business.

Complaints against inefficient or badly managed local government may be investigated by independent Commissions for Local Administration, often known as 'the Local Ombudsman service'. There are three Local Government Ombudsmen in England, and one each in Wales and Scotland. A report is issued on each complaint fully investigated and, if injustice is found, the Local Ombudsman normally proposes a solution. The council must consider the report and reply to it. In 2000–01 the Local Government Ombudsmen for England received 19,179 complaints, 9% more than in 1999–2000.

In Northern Ireland a Commissioner for Complaints deals with complaints alleging injustices suffered as a result of maladministration by district councils and certain other public bodies.

Pressure Groups

Pressure groups are informal organisations which aim to influence the decision-making of Parliament and Government, to the benefit of their members and the causes they support. There is a huge range of groups, covering politics, business, employment, consumer affairs, ethnic minorities, aid to developing countries, foreign relations, education, culture, defence, religion, sport, transport, social welfare, animal welfare and the environment. Some have over a million members; others only a few. Some bring pressure to bear on a number of different issues; others are concerned with a single subject. Some have come to play a recognised role in the way the UK is governed; others attempt to influence through radical protest.

Pressure groups operating at a national level may affect how the UK is governed. Their actions may simply highlight a particular problem or their membership may point to broad representation in a specific field. Ministers have a duty to give fair consideration and due weight to informed and impartial advice from civil servants, so pressure groups often try to guide the views of civil servants and in this way influence the briefing they give to ministers.

Consultation to win the agreement and cooperation of as wide a range of organisations as possible and to ensure that laws and regulations work properly is an important principle in the UK government system.

In some cases a department has a legal obligation to consult interested groups. The Government has a duty to consult organised interests, providing the pressure groups involved have a broad enough membership for them to represent a majority view, and that they keep their discussions with the department confidential. Members of pressure groups often have direct expertise and an awareness of what is practicable, and can therefore offer useful advice to the Government in forming policy or drafting legislation. The contacts between civil servants and pressure group representatives may be relatively informal—by letter, telephone or e-mail—or more formal, through involvement in working parties or by giving evidence to committees of inquiry.

Pressure Groups and Parliament

Lobbying—which means approaching MPs or peers, persuading them to act on behalf of a cause, and helping them do so by providing advice and information—has substantially increased in recent years. A common pressure group approach is to ask members of the public to write to their MP about an issue—for example, the conditions in which certain countries hold political prisoners—in order to raise awareness and win the MP's support in Parliament.

Parliamentary Lobbyists

Many pressure groups employ full-time parliamentary workers or liaison officers, whose job is to develop contacts with MPs and peers sympathetic to their cause, and to brief them when issues affecting the group are raised in Parliament. In 1998 the Government issued guidance to civil servants who come into contact with groups and people outside the Government.

Some public relations and political consultancy firms specialise in lobbying Parliament and Government. They are employed by pressure groups—as well as by British and overseas companies and organisations—to monitor parliamentary business, and to promote their clients' interests where they are affected by legislation and debate.

Raising Issues in Parliament

Other ways through which pressure groups may bring influence to bear include:

- suggesting to MPs or peers subjects for Private Members' Bills (see p. 54); many pressure groups have ready-drafted bills waiting to be sponsored;
- approaching MPs or peers to ask Parliamentary Questions as a means of gaining information from the Government and of drawing public attention to an issue;
- suggesting to MPs subjects for Early Day Motions (see p. 57) and suggesting to peers subjects for debates; and
- organising public petitions as a form of protest against government policy, or to call for action.

The UK in the European Union

As a member of the European Union, the UK is bound by the various types of European Community (EC) legislation and wider policies (for policies, see chapter 7). Almost all UK government departments are involved in EU-wide business, and European legislation is an increasingly important element of government.

The Community enacts legislation which is binding on the national governments of the 15 member states or, in certain circumstances, on individuals and companies within those states.

British government ministers take part in the discussions and decision-making, and the final decision is taken collectively by all the member states.

The UK Representative Office (UKREP), based in Brussels, conducts most of the negotiations on behalf of the UK Government. The devolved administrations of Scotland and Wales are also represented by UKREP. In October 1999 an office specifically aimed at helping to promote Scotland's interests within the EU opened in Brussels; an office fulfilling the same role for Wales opened in May 2000. Both operate in close cooperation with UKREP.

There are three legislative bodies:

The Council of the European Union is the main decision-making body. Member states are represented by the ministers appropriate to the subject under discussion. When, for instance, education matters are being discussed, the UK's Secretary of State for Education and Skills attends with his or her European counterparts. The Presidency of the Council changes at six-monthly intervals and rotates in turn among the 15 member states of the Union.

In some cases Council decisions must be unanimous; in others taken by qualified majority voting (a qualified majority being the number of votes required for a decision to be adopted) with votes weighted according to a country's population—currently ten each for Germany, France, the United Kingdom and Italy; eight for Spain; five each for Belgium, Greece, the Netherlands and Portugal; four each for Austria and Sweden; three each for Denmark, Finland and the Irish Republic; and two for Luxembourg. The threshold for the qualified majority is set at 62 votes out of 87.

The *European Council*, which is not a legislative body and usually meets twice a year, comprises the heads of State or Government accompanied by their foreign ministers and the President of the European Commission and one other Commissioner. The Council defines general political guidelines.

The European Commission is the executive body. It implements the Council's decisions, initiates legislation and ensures that member states put it into effect. Each of the 20 Commissioners, who are drawn from all member states (there are two from the UK), is responsible for a specific policy area, for example, education, transport or agriculture. The Commissioners are entirely independent of their countries, and serve the EU as a whole.

The European Parliament, which plays an increasingly important role in the legislative process, has 626 directly elected members (MEPs), including 87 from the UK. The Parliament is consulted about major decisions and has substantial shared power with the Council of the European Union over the EC budget. In areas of legislation, its role varies between *consultation*, where it can influence but does not have the final say in the content of legislation; the *cooperation and assent* procedures, where its influence is greater; and *co-decision* (introduced by the Maastricht Treaty and extended in the Amsterdam Treaty—see chapter 7), where a proposal requires the agreement of both the Council and the European Parliament.

Elections to the Parliament take place every five years, most recently in June 1999. In the UK, these were held under a proportional voting system,[13] bringing the country in line with the other member states.

European Parliament Elections, June 1999

UK Results by Party—MEPs elected

Conservative	36
Labour	29
Liberal Democrats	10
UK Independence Party	3
Green	2
Plaid Cymru	2
Scottish National Party	2
Democratic Unionist Party	1
Ulster Unionist Party	1
Social Democratic and Labour Party	1

[13] The regional list system is used for England, Scotland and Wales, under which an elector may cast his or her vote for a party list of candidates. England is divided into nine regions while Scotland and Wales each constitute one region. These 11 regions each return between four and 11 MEPs, depending on the size of the electorate of each region. Northern Ireland, which also constitutes one region, continues to use the single transferable vote system to return its three MEPs.

The European Parliament meets in full session in Strasbourg for about one week every month, although its committee work normally takes place in Brussels.

EC legislation is issued in some areas jointly by the Council of the European Union and the European Parliament, by the Council in other areas, or by the Commission under delegated powers. It consists of Regulations, Directives and Decisions.

- *Regulations* are directly applicable in all member states, and have the force of law without the need for implementing further measures;
- *Directives* are equally binding as to the result to be achieved but allow each member state to choose the form and method of implementation; and
- *Decisions*, like Regulations, do not normally need national implementing legislation. They are binding on those to whom they are addressed.

Other EU Institutions

Each member state provides one of the judges to serve in the **European Court of Justice**, which is the final authority on all aspects of Community law. Its rulings must be applied by member states, and fines can be imposed on those failing to do so. The Court is assisted by a Court of First Instance, which handles certain cases brought by individuals and companies. The UK is also represented on the **Court of Auditors**, which examines Community revenue and expenditure, to see that it is legally received and spent.

Further Reading

The Committee on Standards in Public Life's Seventh Report: *Standards of Conduct in the House of Lords*. Cm 4903. The Stationery Office, 2000.

Cabinet Office Annual Report 2001. Cm 5119. The Stationery Office, 2001.

Department of the Environment, Transport and the Regions Annual Report 2001. Cm 5105. The Stationery Office, 2001.

Websites

The British Monarchy: www.royal.gov.uk

Cabinet Office: www.cabinet-office.gov.uk

Central government: www.ukonline.gov.uk

Department for Transport, Local Government and the Regions: www.dtlr.gov.uk

National Assembly for Wales: www.wales.gov.uk

Northern Ireland Executive: www.northernireland.gov.uk

National Statistics: www.statistics.gov.uk

Prime Minister's Office: www.number-10.gov.uk

Scottish Executive: www.scotland.gov.uk

United Kingdom Parliament: www.parliament.uk

7 Overseas Relations

International Organisations	75	Human Rights	91
Overseas Territories	79	Crime and Terrorism	92
European Union	81	Development Cooperation	93
Regional Relations	85	Administration of Foreign Policy	96
Peacekeeping	88	British Council	97
Arms Control	90		

The United Kingdom is a democratic country with global foreign policy interests and an economy heavily dependent on international trade and investment. The Government supports the maintenance of an open and stable international order. UK membership of the United Nations (UN), the European Union (EU), the Commonwealth, the North Atlantic Treaty Organisation (NATO) and other major international organisations remains central to policy to achieve this objective.

INTERNATIONAL ORGANISATIONS

United Nations

The UK is a founder member of the UN and one of the five permanent members of the Security Council, along with China, France, Russia and the United States. It supports the purposes and principles of the UN Charter, including the maintenance of international peace and security, the development of friendly relations among nations, the achievement of international cooperation on economic, social, cultural and humanitarian issues, and the protection of human rights and fundamental freedoms. The UK is the fifth largest contributor to the UN regular budget and to peacekeeping operations, and one of the biggest voluntary contributors to UN funds, programmes and agencies. In order to enhance the UN's effectiveness, the UK is advocating modernisation of the organisation, including reform of the Security Council's composition. The UK is also committed to the reinforcement of the UN's role in preventing and resolving conflicts around the world.

European Union

The UK is a member of the EU (see also pp. 72 and 81–5), which promotes social and economic progress among its members, a common foreign and security policy, European citizenship and police and judicial cooperation in criminal matters. The other 14 EU Member States are Austria, Belgium, Denmark, Finland, France, Germany, Greece, the Irish Republic, Italy, Luxembourg, the Netherlands, Portugal, Spain and Sweden.

The Commonwealth

There are 54 members of the Commonwealth, including the UK. It is a voluntary association of independent states, nearly all of which were once British territories, and includes almost one in three people in the world. The members are Antigua and Barbuda, Australia, the Bahamas, Bangladesh, Barbados, Belize, Botswana, Brunei Darussalam, Cameroon, Canada, Cyprus, Dominica, Fiji,[1] The Gambia, Ghana, Grenada, Guyana, India, Jamaica, Kenya, Kiribati, Lesotho, Malawi, Malaysia, Maldives, Malta, Mauritius, Mozambique, Namibia, Nauru, New Zealand, Nigeria, Pakistan,[2] Papua New Guinea, St Kitts and Nevis, St Lucia, St Vincent and the Grenadines, Samoa, Seychelles, Sierra Leone, Singapore, Solomon Islands, South Africa, Sri Lanka, Swaziland, Tanzania, Tonga, Trinidad and Tobago, Tuvalu, Uganda, United Kingdom, Vanuatu, Zambia and Zimbabwe.

The Queen is head of the Commonwealth and is head of state in the UK and 15 other member countries. The Commonwealth Secretariat, based in London, is the main agency for multilateral communication between member governments on matters relevant to the Commonwealth as a whole. The Secretariat promotes consultation and cooperation, disseminates information, and helps host governments to organise Heads of Government Meetings (normally held biennially), ministerial meetings and other conferences. It administers assistance programmes agreed at these meetings, including the Commonwealth Fund for Technical Cooperation, which provides advisory services and training to Commonwealth developing countries.

North Atlantic Treaty Organisation

Membership of NATO is central to UK defence policy (see p. 100). NATO's stated functions are to:

- help provide security and stability in the Euro-Atlantic area;
- provide a transatlantic forum for Member States to consult on issues of common concern;
- deter and defend against any threat to the territory of any NATO member state;
- contribute to crisis management and conflict prevention on a case-by-case basis; and
- promote partnership, cooperation and dialogue with other countries in the Euro-Atlantic area.

Each of the 19 Member States—Belgium, Canada, the Czech Republic, Denmark, France, Germany, Greece, Hungary, Iceland, Italy, Luxembourg, the Netherlands, Norway, Poland, Portugal, Spain, Turkey, the United Kingdom and the United States—has a permanent representative at NATO headquarters in Brussels. The main decision-taking body is the North Atlantic Council. It meets at least twice a year at foreign minister level, and weekly at the level of permanent representatives. Defence ministers also meet at least twice a year.

Group of Eight

The UK is one of the Group of Eight (G8) leading industrialised countries. The other members are Canada, France, Germany, Italy, Japan, Russia (included as a full member from 1998, although the other countries continue to function as the G7 for some discussions) and the United States. The G8 is an informal group with no secretariat. Its Presidency rotates each year among the members, the key meeting being an annual summit of heads of government. Originally formed in 1975 (as the G7) to discuss economic issues, the G8 agenda now includes a wide range of foreign affairs and international issues such as terrorism, nuclear safety, the environment, UN reform and development assistance. Heads of state or government agree a communiqué issued at the end of summits. The G8 summit meeting in July 2001 was hosted by the Italian Government in Genoa.

Organisation for Security and Co-operation in Europe

The UK is a member of the Organisation for Security and Co-operation in Europe (OSCE), a regional security organisation whose 55 participating states are from Europe, Central Asia and North America. All decisions are

[1] Fiji was suspended from the councils of the Commonwealth in June 2000 following a declaration of martial law by the Fiji military in response to an internal security crisis.

[2] Pakistan was suspended from the councils of the Commonwealth in October 1999 following a military coup.

The European Union

The European Union currently consists of 15 member states. Negotiations are under way to allow another 13 candidate countries to join. Cyprus, the Czech Republic, Estonia, Hungary, Poland and Slovenia are likely to be in the first wave of new entrants, followed by Bulgaria, Latvia, Lithuania, Malta, Romania and Slovakia. Turkey's candidature for membership has also been recognised.

The Commonwealth

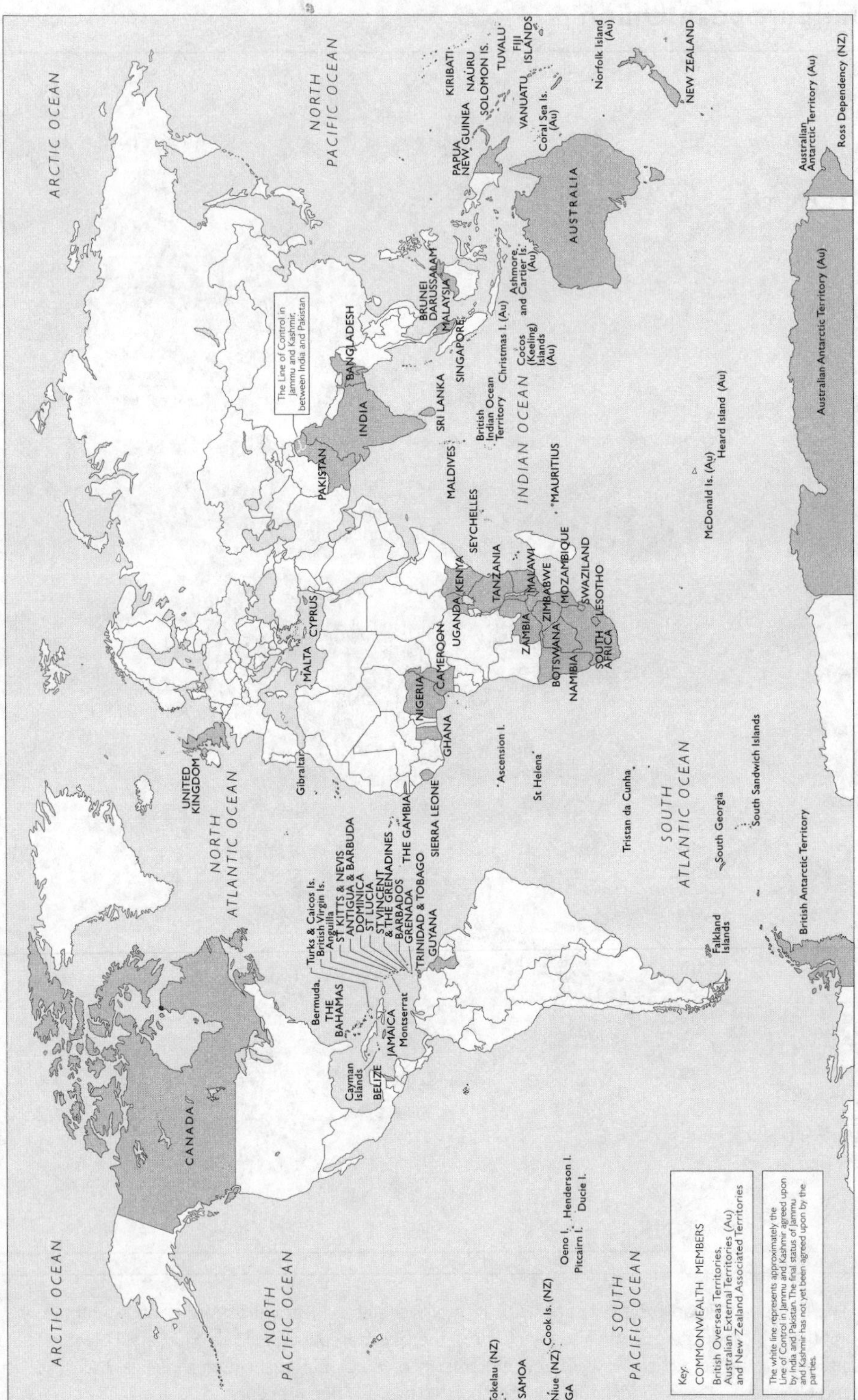

taken by consensus. The OSCE is based in Vienna, where the UK has a permanent delegation. The main areas of work are:

- early warning and prevention of potential conflicts through field missions and diplomacy and the work of the OSCE High Commissioner on National Minorities;
- observing elections and providing advice on human rights, democracy and law, and media;
- post-conflict rehabilitation, including civil society development; and
- promoting security through arms control and military confidence-building.

Council of Europe

The UK is a founding member of the Council of Europe, which is open to any European state accepting parliamentary democracy, the rule of the law and fundamental human rights. There are 43 full Member States. One of the Council's main achievements is the European Convention on Human Rights in 1950 (see p. 92).

Other International Bodies

The UK belongs to many other international bodies, including: the International Monetary Fund (IMF), which regulates the international financial system and provides credit for member countries facing balance-of-payments difficulties; the World Bank, which provides loans to finance economic and social projects in developing countries; the Organisation for Economic Co-operation and Development (OECD), which promotes economic growth, support for less developed countries and worldwide trade expansion; and the World Trade Organisation (WTO—see p. 418). Other organisations to which Britain belongs or extends support include the regional development banks in Africa, the Caribbean, Latin America and Asia, and the European Bank for Reconstruction and Development.

OVERSEAS TERRITORIES

The UK's Overseas Territories (OTs) have a combined population of nearly 180,000. The territories are listed on p. 80. Most have considerable self-government, with their own legislatures. Governors appointed by the Queen are responsible for external affairs, internal security and defence. Most domestic matters are delegated to locally elected governments and legislatures. Ultimate responsibility for government rests with the UK. The British Indian Ocean Territory, the British Antarctic Territory, and South Georgia and the South Sandwich Islands have non-resident Commissioners, not Governors. The UK aims to provide the OTs with security and political stability, ensure efficient and honest government, and help them achieve economic and social advancement. None of the Territories has expressed a desire for independence from the UK.

The UK Government is proposing to offer British citizenship to all those OT residents who do not already have it and who wish to take it up.[3] The necessary legislation is currently before Parliament.

Offshore financial service industries are of major importance in several of the Territories. The UK Government's policy is to ensure that international standards of regulation are met and that effective steps are taken to combat financial crime and regulatory abuse. An independent review of financial regulation in the Caribbean OTs and Bermuda, commissioned jointly by the OT Governments, Foreign & Commonwealth Office (FCO—see p. 96) and HM Treasury, was published in October 2000.

An OT Department within the FCO provides a single focus and direct point of contact with the UK Government, although Gibraltar, because of its EU status, is dealt with primarily by the FCO's European Departments. The Department for International Development (DFID—see pp. 93–7) also has an OT Unit, which administers aid to Anguilla, the British Virgin Islands, Montserrat, the Turks and Caicos Islands, St Helena (and Ascension Island and Tristan da Cunha) and Pitcairn. An OT

[3] The offer of right of abode is on a non-reciprocal basis, as the territories do not have the capacity to absorb uncontrolled numbers of new residents. The UK Government's decision on this follows the precedent set by Gibraltar and the Falkland Islands, whose existing right of abode is also non-reciprocal.

The Overseas Territories at a Glance

Anguilla (capital: The Valley)
Area: 96 sq km (37 sq miles) (Sombrero, 5 sq km).
Population: 12,400 (1998).
Economy: tourism, offshore banking, fishing and farming.
History: British territory since 1650.

Bermuda (capital: Hamilton)
Area: 53 sq km (21 sq miles).
Population: 60,140 (1996).
Economy: financial services and tourism.
History: first British settlers in 1609–12. Government passed to the Crown in 1684.
UN World Heritage Site: town of St George and related fortifications (from 2000).

British Antarctic Territory
Area: 1.7 million sq km (660,000 sq miles).
Population: Two permanent British Antarctic Survey stations are staffed by 40 people in winter and 150 in summer. Scientists from other Antarctic Treaty nations have bases in the Territory.
History: The British claim to the Territory dates back to 1908. The UK is one of 44 signatories to the 1961 Antarctic Treaty, which states that the continent should be used for peaceful purposes only.

British Indian Ocean Territory
Area: 54,400 sq km (21,000 sq miles) of ocean, including the Chagos Archipelago land area.
Economy: Territory used for defence purposes by the UK and United States.
History: archipelago ceded to Britain by France under the 1814 Treaty of Paris.

British Virgin Islands (capital: Road Town)
Area: 153 sq km (59 sq miles).
Population: 19,100 (1997).
Economy: tourism and financial services.
History: discovered in 1493 by Columbus and annexed by Britain in 1672.

Cayman Islands (capital: George Town)
Area: 259 sq km (100 sq miles).
Population: 38,000 (1998).
Economy: tourism and financial services.
History: the 1670 Treaty of Madrid recognised Britain's claim to the islands.

Falkland Islands (capital: Stanley)
Area: 12,173 sq km (4,700 sq miles).
Population: 2,220 (1996), plus British garrison.
Economy: fishery management and sheep farming.
History: first known landing in 1690 by British Naval Captain, John Strong. Under continuous British occupation and administration since 1833.

Gibraltar
Area: 6.5 sq km (2.5 sq miles).
Population: 27,200 (1999).
Economy: financial services, tourism, port services.
History: ceded to Britain in 1713 under the Treaty of Utrecht.

Montserrat (capital: Plymouth)
Area: 102 sq km (39 sq miles).
Population: 3,500 (1998).
Economy: agriculture and fishing.
History: colonised by English and Irish settlers in 1632.

Pitcairn, Ducie, Henderson and Oeno (capital: Adamstown)
Area: 36 sq km (14 sq miles).
Population: 54 (1999).
Economy: fishing, agriculture, postage stamp sales.
History: occupied by mutineers from the British ship *Bounty* in 1790; annexed as a British colony in 1838.
UN World Heritage Site: Henderson Island (from 1988).

St Helena (capital: Jamestown)
Area: 122 sq km (47 sq miles).
Population: 5,000 (1998).
Economy: fishing and agriculture.
History: taken over in 1661 by the British East India Company.

Ascension Island (St Helena Dependency)
Area: 88 sq km (34 sq miles).
Population: 1,050 (1999).
Economy: communications and military base.
History: the British garrison dates from Napoleon's exile on St Helena after 1815.

Tristan da Cunha (St Helena Dependency)
Area: 98 sq km (38 sq miles).
Population: 285 (1998).
Economy: fishing.
History: occupied by a British garrison in 1816.
UN World Heritage Site: Gough Island Wildlife Reserve (from 1995).

South Georgia and the South Sandwich Islands
No indigenous population. First landing by Captain Cook in 1775. Small British military detachment on South Georgia, plus British Antarctic Survey all-year research station on Bird Island.

Turks and Caicos Islands (capital: Cockburn Town)
Area: about 500 sq km (193 sq miles).
Population: 23,000 (1999).
Economy: tourism, financial services and fishing.
History: Europeans from Bermuda first occupied the islands from about 1678, then planters from southern states of America settled after the War of Independence in the late 18th century.

Consultative Council, comprising the Chief Minister or equivalent from each territory and British ministers (and chaired by the relevant FCO minister), convened its second annual meeting in October 2000.

Falkland Islands

The Falkland Islands are the subject of a territorial claim by Argentina. The UK Government does not accept the Argentine claim and is committed to defending the Islanders' right to live under a government of their own choice. This right of self-determination is enshrined in the 1985 Falkland Islands Constitution.

The UK and Argentina, while sticking to their respective positions on sovereignty, maintain diplomatic relations and continue to discuss their common interests in the South Atlantic region, such as fisheries conservation and the exploitation of oil reserves.

Gibraltar

Spain ceded Gibraltar to Britain in perpetuity under the 1713 Treaty of Utrecht but has long sought its return. However, the UK is committed to the principle, set out in the preamble to the 1969 Gibraltar Constitution, that it will never enter into arrangements under which the people of Gibraltar would pass under the sovereignty of another state against their freely and democratically expressed wishes.

Gibraltar has an elected House of Assembly, and responsibility for a range of 'defined domestic matters' is devolved to elected local ministers. The Territory is within the EU, as part of the United Kingdom Member State, although it is outside the common customs system and does not participate in the Common Agricultural or Fisheries Policies or the EU's value added tax arrangements. The people of Gibraltar have been declared UK nationals for EU purposes.

EUROPEAN UNION

The Treaties

The Union had its origins in the post-Second World War resolve by Western European nations, particularly France and Germany, to prevent further conflict and establish lasting peace and stability.

Rome Treaty

The 1957 Rome Treaty, establishing the European Community, defined its aims as the harmonious development of economic activities, a continuous and balanced economic expansion and an accelerated rise in the standard of living. These objectives were to be achieved by the creation of a common internal market, including the elimination of customs duties between Member States, free movement of goods, people, services and capital, and the elimination of distortions in competition within this market. These aims were reaffirmed by the 1986 Single European Act, which agreed measures to complete the single market (see p. 83). The UK joined the European Community in 1973.

Under the Rome Treaty, the European Commission speaks on behalf of the UK and the other Member States in international trade negotiations. The Commission negotiates on a mandate agreed by the Council of the European Union. (For further information on overseas trade, see chapter 24.)

Maastricht Treaty

The 1992 Maastricht Treaty amended the Rome Treaty and made other new commitments, including moves towards economic and monetary union (see p. 82). It established the European Union (EU), which comprises the European Community and intergovernmental arrangements for a Common Foreign and Security Policy (CFSP—see p. 84) and for increased cooperation on justice and home affairs policy issues (see p. 85). It also enshrined the principle of subsidiarity under which, in areas where the Community and Member States share competence, action should be taken at European level only if its objectives cannot be achieved by Member States acting alone and can be better achieved by the Community. In addition, the Treaty introduced the concept of EU citizenship as a supplement to national citizenship.

Amsterdam Treaty

In 1996 an intergovernmental conference considered further treaty amendments. This resulted in the Amsterdam Treaty, which entered into force in 1999. It provides for the further protection and extension of citizen's rights; integration of the social chapter (a separate protocol to the Maastricht Treaty) into the Treaty, following its adoption by the UK; new mechanisms to improve the coordination and effectiveness of the CFSP; an increase in the areas subject to co-decision between the Council of Ministers and European Parliament, and simplification of the co-decision procedure (see p. 73); and a binding protocol on subsidiarity.

Treaty Ratification

Any amendments to the Treaties must be agreed unanimously and must then be ratified by each Member State according to its own constitutional procedures. In the UK, Treaty ratifications must be approved by Parliament before they can come into force.

Economic and Monetary Union

The Maastricht Treaty envisaged the achievement of economic and monetary union in preparatory stages, culminating in the adoption on 1 January 1999 of a single currency (the euro). In May 1998 a meeting of EU heads of state and government agreed that 11 of the 15 EU Member States (excluding the UK, Denmark, Greece and Sweden) would take part in the single currency from its launch date. It also agreed the establishment of the European Central Bank (ECB) from June 1998.

On 1 January 1999 conversion rates between currencies of qualifying countries and the euro were legally fixed. The euro became the legal currency in those countries and the ECB assumed responsibility for formulating the monetary policy of the euro area. Since no euro banknotes or coins will be available until 1 January 2002, national currencies will continue to exist in parallel with the euro and national banknotes and coins will be used for all cash transactions.

Nice Treaty

This Treaty was agreed in December 2000 at the Nice European Council and signed in February 2001. Subject to ratification, it would introduce changes to the EU's institutional machinery in preparation for enlargement (see below). From 2005 the number of votes for each EU country in the Council of the European Union (see p. 73) would be altered to take account of prospective new members, the total number rising from the 87 votes for the current 15 Member States up to 342 votes for 27 Member States. The UK, Germany, France and Italy would each have 29 votes. The total needed for a qualified majority would increase from 62 to 255, and for a blocking minority from 26 to 88. Qualified majority voting would be extended to 35 more areas, including trade in some services, aspects of asylum and immigration policy, regulation of the European Court of Justice, and decisions on senior EU appointments. Also from 2005 the European Commission would be composed of one member from each country, up to 27. The Treaty would create amended arrangements for groups of countries within the EU to pursue closer cooperation on certain issues without involving every Member State.

Greece, having earlier failed the economic convergence criteria, joined the euro zone on 1 January 2001. The UK Government's policy towards joining the single currency is described in chapter 22 (see p. 385).

Enlargement

Enlargement of the EU—to include those European nations sharing its democratic values and aims, which are functioning market economies, able to compete in the EU and to take on the obligations of membership—is a key policy objective for the Union. In 1998 an accession process with the applicant states was launched, and formal negotiations started with Poland, Hungary, Slovenia, Estonia, Cyprus and the Czech Republic. Then, in 1999, the

EU agreed to invite six other countries—Bulgaria, Latvia, Lithuania, Malta, Romania and Slovakia—to open accession negotiations (which were launched in February 2000), and also confirmed Turkey's candidature for membership.

In 1999 the European Council agreed the EU's budgetary arrangements for the period 2000–06 (see below), including making financial provision for the first new Member States to join the Union in that period. Following an EU intergovernmental conference, convened in February 2000, the Treaty of Nice was negotiated, which would provide (upon its entry into force) for the institutional changes necessary for enlargement.

European Community Budget

The Community's revenue consists of levies on agricultural imports from non-member countries, customs duties, the proceeds of value added tax (VAT) receipts and contributions from Member States based on gross national product (GNP).

In 1999 the European Council agreed on budgetary amendments. The 'own resources' system for financing the EU maintains the current ceiling of 1.27% of GNP; but, progressively from 2001, more revenue will be raised from contributions linked to GNP and less from VAT receipts and customs payments. It was also agreed that the UK's annual budget rebate (in place since 1984, and without which the British net contribution would be far greater than that justified by its share of Community GNP) would remain.

Single Market

The single European market, providing for the free movement of people, goods, services and capital within the EU, came into effect in 1993 (see also p. 417). It covers, among other benefits, the removal of customs barriers, the liberalisation of capital movements, the opening of public procurement markets and the mutual recognition of professional qualifications.

Under the European Economic Area (EEA) Agreement, which came into force in 1994, most of the EU single market measures have been extended to Iceland, Norway and Liechtenstein. EEA Member States comprise the world's largest trading bloc, accounting for 40% of all global trade.

Agriculture and Fisheries

The Common Agricultural Policy (CAP) was designed to secure food supplies and to stabilise markets. It also, however, created overproduction and unwanted food surpluses, placing a burden on the Community's budget. The Common Fisheries Policy is concerned with the conservation and management of fishery resources. See chapter 26 for further details of these policies, and of the UK's support for radical CAP reform to meet the challenges posed by the WTO and by enlargement.

Regional and Infrastructure Development

The economic and social disparities within the EU are considerable, and will become more evident with further enlargement. To address the regional imbalances there are Structural Funds designed to promote economic development in underdeveloped regions and regenerate regions affected by industrial decline (see also p. 393).

Infrastructure projects and industrial investments are financed by the European Regional Development Fund. The European Social Fund supports training and employment measures for the unemployed and young people. The Guidance Section of the European Agricultural Guidance and Guarantee Fund supports agricultural restructuring and some rural development measures. The Financial Instrument of Fisheries Guidance promotes the modernisation of the fishing industry. A Cohesion Fund, set up under the Maastricht Treaty, provides financial help to reduce disparities between EU members' economies. Other initiatives promote new economic activities in regions affected by the restructuring of traditional industries, such as steel, coal and shipbuilding. There are also funds to help prepare the candidate countries for accession to the EU.

Funding levels for the Structural and Cohesion Funds in the financial period 2000–06 were agreed by the European Council in 1999. The UK will receive over £10 billion.

The European Investment Bank, a non-profit-making institution, lends at competitive interest rates to public and private capital investment projects in the EU and in candidate countries. It also provides money through the European Investment Fund for venture capital initiatives.

Economic Reform

In March 2000 the Portuguese Presidency hosted a special European Council in Lisbon on Economic Reform, Employment and Social Inclusion. Member States agreed the UK's proposal that the EU should set itself the target of becoming, by 2010, the most competitive and dynamic knowledge-based economy in the world, capable of sustainable economic growth with more and better jobs and greater social cohesion. The objectives of the programme include:

- expanding access to the Internet and e-commerce;
- improving the internal market in services, updating public procurement rules, and reducing state aids;
- improving coordination of national research and development (R&D) programmes, and adopting by the end of 2001 a Community patent;
- removing barriers to small business growth;
- promoting education, training and employability, giving higher priority to lifelong learning and basic IT skills;
- combating social exclusion and poverty through targeting specific groups (such as minorities or the disabled); and
- modernising social protection systems (in particular, pensions).

The European Council in Stockholm in March 2001 (the first of regular Council sessions reviewing economic reform to be held every spring) focused on the ten-year programme set out at Lisbon. The Council agreed, in particular, on rapid implementation of a comprehensive plan to liberalise financial services, and made a commitment to open up EU energy markets. The European Council in Gothenburg in June 2001 agreed a strategy for sustainable development to add an environmental dimension to the process of economic reform.

Common Foreign and Security Policy

The intergovernmental CFSP, dating from 1993, provides for EU Member States to agree unanimously common policies and/or joint actions on a wide range of international issues.

The Treaty of Amsterdam introduced changes to make the policy more effective, including the appointment of a High Representative to help with the formulation, preparation and presentation of CFSP policy decisions, and the establishment of a Policy Planning and Early Warning Unit in the Council Secretariat to sharpen the preparation and focus of CFSP decisions. The Amsterdam Treaty preserves the principle that all policy should be decided by unanimity, but states that decisions implementing common strategies, which are themselves agreed by unanimity, will be by qualified majority voting. A Member State may prevent a vote being taken by qualified majority voting for 'important and stated reasons of national policy'. It may also abstain and stand aside from an EU decision/action when its interests are not affected.

European Security and Defence Policy

In 1998 the UK launched an initiative to strengthen the EU's capacity to respond to crises, on the basis that, if the Union is to play a coherent and effective political role, this needs to be underpinned by a credible European military capability. Hitherto, the EU had looked to the Western European Union (WEU)[4] to carry out such military crisis management activity on its behalf.

---

[4] WEU ministers agreed in November 2000 to close down the WEU as an operational body, to be replaced by a smaller residual structure in 2001.

In support of this initiative, the European Council in December 1999 agreed to develop by 2003 the capability to deploy up to 60,000 ground troops, with naval and air support as appropriate, able to deal with the full range of crisis management tasks. At the maximum scale of operation, the UK could contribute up to 12,500 ground troops, 18 warships and 72 combat aircraft. Collective defence remains the responsibility of NATO, which will also continue to have a major role in crisis management (see also p. 100).

Justice and Home Affairs

The Maastricht Treaty established intergovernmental arrangements for increased cooperation among EU states on justice and home affairs issues. These issues include visa, asylum, immigration and other policies related to free movement of people; and police, customs and judicial cooperation in criminal matters (including cooperation through EUROPOL—see p. 93). This is a growing aspect of EU work and, since the entry into force of the Amsterdam Treaty, has both Community-based and intergovernmental-based areas of cooperation. A protocol annexed to the Amsterdam Treaty recognises the UK's right to exercise its own frontier controls.

REGIONAL RELATIONS

Central and Eastern Europe and Central Asia

European Security

In 1990 the UK and its NATO allies, together with former adversaries in the Warsaw Pact Communist bloc, set up the North Atlantic Cooperation Council to promote understanding. In 1994 NATO invited the non-Alliance states in Central and Eastern Europe and Central Asia to join a Partnership for Peace programme, a form of association which, among other things, enlists the Partners' assistance in peacekeeping operations. The Euro-Atlantic Partnership Council was set up in 1997 to develop closer political and military links between NATO countries and non-members.

The UK played a significant role in negotiations leading to:

- the 1997 Founding Act between NATO Member States and Russia, introducing new mechanisms for a permanent relationship;
- a NATO-Ukraine partnership charter, also signed in 1997; and
- the accession to NATO in 1999 of the Czech Republic, Hungary and Poland.

Economic Help

The UK and other Western countries continue to help deal with the economic problems following the fall of Communism, and to promote the development of market economies. The IMF provides support for stabilisation programmes and the World Bank finance for structural reform to nearly all countries in the region. This is further bolstered by the European Bank for Reconstruction and Development's investments and its role in facilitating additional private investment. The EU's PHARE scheme[5] is primarily devoted to aiding Central European countries in the process of reform and development of their infrastructure. A new aid programme—Community Assistance for Association, Democratisation and Stabilisation (CARDS)—is focused on countries in the Western Balkans. Countries of the former Soviet Union (excluding Estonia, Latvia and Lithuania) and Mongolia receive help through a parallel programme (TACIS),[6] which concentrates on democratisation, financial services, transport, energy (including nuclear safety) and public administration reform. The UK's Export Credits Guarantee Department (ECGD) provides insurance cover for exporters to a number of these countries.

[5] An aid programme for economic restructuring in Central Europe, which consists of many individual projects and operations to underpin the process of reform. It was initially applicable to Poland and Hungary, but has since been extended to other countries in Central Europe.
[6] An EU aid programme providing technical assistance to recipient countries.

Association and Co-operation Agreements

The EU has strengthened relations with Bulgaria, the Czech Republic, Estonia, Hungary, Latvia, Lithuania, Poland, Romania, Slovakia and Slovenia by signing Europe (Association) Agreements with them. The agreements provide an institutional framework to support the process of integration, and anticipate accession of these countries to the EU when they are able to assume the obligations of membership (see p. 82).

EU Partnership and Co-operation Agreements are in force with Russia, Ukraine, Moldova, Kazakhstan, Kyrgyzstan, Georgia, Armenia, Azerbaijan and Uzbekistan. Trade and Co-operation Agreements with Albania and Macedonia are also in force. The purpose of these agreements is to reduce trade barriers, develop wide-ranging cooperation and increase political dialogue.

The EU is promoting closer links through Stabilisation and Association Agreements (SAA) with states in south-eastern Europe, provided that they meet the EU's conditions on democracy, electoral and media reform, and respect for human rights. The first Stabilisation and Association Agreement, with Macedonia, was signed in April 2001. An SAA with Croatia was initialled in May 2001.

Middle East

Arab–Israeli Peace Process

The UK supported the breakthrough in the Middle East peace process in 1993, when Israel and the Palestine Liberation Organisation (PLO) agreed to mutual recognition and signed a declaration on interim self-government for the Palestinians in Israeli-held territories occupied since 1967. The first stage of the declaration was implemented in 1994, when the Palestinians adopted self-government in the Gaza Strip and the Jericho area. A peace treaty between Israel and Jordan was also signed in that year. The UK has continued to encourage peace talks between Israel, Syria and Lebanon.

In 1995 Israel and the PLO reached an agreement providing for a phased Israeli troop withdrawal from occupied Palestinian areas of the West Bank and for elections to a new Palestinian Council with legislative and executive powers. The UK took part in the EU-coordinated observation of the Palestinian elections in 1996.

Progress in the process since then has been far from smooth, with frequent disruptions over political and security concerns. The UK has sought to complement the mediation efforts of the United States, based on the conviction that a lasting resolution must both protect Israel's security and provide a just exchange of land for peace; and, with its EU partners, it has reaffirmed the Palestinian right to self-determination including the option of statehood.

The British Government has expressed its concern over the serious escalation of violence between Israelis and Palestinians which has continued since September 2000 and is undermining prospects for peace.

Iraq

The UK condemned Iraq's invasion of Kuwait in 1990 and supported all UN Security Council resolutions designed to force Iraqi withdrawal and restore international legality. Because of Iraq's failure to withdraw, its forces were expelled in 1991 by an international coalition led by the United States, the UK, France and Saudi Arabia, acting under a UN mandate.

UN sanctions against Iraq, imposed at that time, still remain in force (although with substantial humanitarian exemptions), because Iraq has failed to comply with the relevant Security Council resolutions, particularly those relating to the supervision of the elimination of its weapons of mass destruction. In 1999 the UK drafted and co-sponsored a further Security Council resolution creating the UN Monitoring, Verification and Inspection Commission (as the successor organisation to the former UN Special Commission on Iraq, or UNSCOM). The same resolution lifted the ceiling on Iraq's oil exports and expanded the humanitarian programme for Iraq.

In order to protect the Shia minority in southern Iraq and the Kurdish population in the north against attacks by Iraqi regime forces, UK and US warplanes continue to patrol 'no-fly' zones over southern and northern Iraq, established after the war in 1991.

Mediterranean

The UK and other EU Member States are developing, on the basis of the Barcelona Declaration of 1995, closer links with 12 Mediterranean partners with the aim of promoting peace and prosperity in the region. Libya has also been invited to sign up to the Declaration. Association Agreements covering political dialogue, free trade and cooperation in a number of areas are already in force with several Mediterranean countries. In November 2000 EU and Mediterranean ministers reaffirmed the goal of a free trade area by 2010.

Asia-Pacific Region

The UK has well-established relations with Japan, China, the Republic of Korea, many South East Asian nations, Australia and New Zealand, and has defence links with some countries in the region. British commercial activity has developed through increased trade and investment and the setting up of business councils, joint commissions or industrial cooperation agreements. The UK is also taking advantage of increased opportunities for English language teaching, cooperation in science and technology, and educational exchanges.

The Asia-Europe Meeting (ASEM) process was inaugurated in 1996. ASEM is intended to foster closer economic and political ties between EU countries and Brunei, China, Indonesia, Japan, the Republic of Korea, Malaysia, Singapore, the Philippines, Thailand and Vietnam. The third ASEM was hosted in Seoul by the Government of the Republic of Korea in October 2000.

Agreement was reached between the UK and North Korea in December 2000 to establish diplomatic relations.

The UK and its EU and G8 partners continue to encourage India and Pakistan to join international nuclear non-proliferation regimes (see p. 90) and reduce bilateral tension over the disputed territory of Kashmir.

In 1998 Britain rejoined the South Pacific Commission, having withdrawn from membership in 1995. The Commission provides technical advice and assistance to its Pacific Island members, with which the UK has long-standing and Commonwealth ties.

Hong Kong

In 1997 the UK returned Hong Kong to Chinese sovereignty under the provisions of the 1984 Sino-British Joint Declaration, which guarantees that Hong Kong's way of life, including its rights and freedoms, will remain unchanged for 50 years from the handover. As set out in the Joint Declaration, Hong Kong is a Special Administrative Region (SAR) of China. The SAR Government enjoys a high degree of autonomy, except in foreign affairs and defence, which are the responsibility of the Chinese Government in Beijing.

The UK is represented in Hong Kong by one of the largest British diplomatic posts in the world. It continues to have responsibilities towards Hong Kong and the 3.5 million British passport holders living there. Hong Kong is the UK's second largest export market in Asia.

The Americas

The British Government considers that the close transatlantic links between the UK, the United States and Canada remain essential to guarantee the security and prosperity of Europe and North America.

The UK and the US cooperate closely on nuclear, defence and intelligence matters. As founding members of NATO, Britain and the US are deeply involved in Western defence arrangements and, as permanent members of the UN Security Council, work closely together on major international issues. In addition, there are important economic links. The US is the UK's largest trading partner—UK exports of goods and services in 1999 amounted to £39.8 billion. Also, the UK and US are each other's biggest source of inward investment—in 1999 UK investment represented 18.6% of total foreign direct investment in the US, while 18.7% of total US overseas investment (36% of US investment in Europe) was in the UK.

Strong political and economic links are maintained with Canada, with which the UK shares membership of the Commonwealth, NATO and other key international organisations. The UK is the second largest investor in Canada (after the US) and Canada is the fifth largest investor in the UK.

Important British connections with Latin America date from the participation of British volunteers in the wars of independence in the early 19th century. Greater democracy and freer market economies in the region have enabled Britain to strengthen its relations with Latin America. The UK is now one of the largest investors in the region after the United States. The first summit of EU, Latin American and Caribbean heads of state and government (representing 48 countries) was held in Rio de Janeiro in 1999, with the aim of building a strategic partnership between the two regions based around a political, economic and cultural dialogue. Progress will be reviewed at the next summit in Spain in 2002.

The first UK/Caribbean Forum, held in 1998 in Nassau, Bahamas, marked the beginning of a new longer-term process of cooperation between the UK and the countries of the region. The second meeting, hosted by the British Government, in London in May 2000, agreed initiatives to encourage new investment in the Caribbean region, and to promote educational and judicial links.

Africa

The UK Government is giving political and practical support to efforts to prevent or end African conflicts; promoting trade, reducing debt and supporting development for lasting prosperity; and supporting African governments, organisations and individuals espousing the principles of democracy, accountability, the rule of law and human rights. The first EU-Africa summit was held in Cairo, Egypt, in 2000.

Since the abolition of apartheid and the election of the first African National Congress government in 1994, South Africa's relations with the UK have broadened into areas ranging from development assistance to military advice, and from sporting links to scientific cooperation. There has also been a steady flow of state and ministerial visits to and from South Africa. The UK is South Africa's largest single trading partner, and largest foreign investor. Both countries are committed to build on this relationship by promoting the further expansion of bilateral trade and investment. A trade, development and cooperation agreement between the EU and South Africa was signed in 1999, providing for the creation of a free trade area and for further substantial development assistance from the EU.

PEACEKEEPING

The UN is the principal body responsible for the maintenance of international peace and security. At the end of 2000 there were some 42,800 troops, military observers and police officers from 89 nations deployed to 16 peacekeeping operations around the world.

As the fifth largest contributor to the UN's peacekeeping budgets, meeting around 7% of the estimated US$2.5 billion costs, the UK has provided civilian police, military observers and troops for a wide range of UN missions. The UK contributes personnel to UN-led or UN-authorised operations in Bosnia, Kosovo, Iraq, Cyprus, Democratic Republic of Congo, East Timor, Georgia and Sierra Leone.

Cyprus

The UK has a contingent of 314 troops in the UN Force in Cyprus, established in 1964 to help prevent the recurrence of fighting between Greek and Turkish Cypriots. Since the hostilities of 1974, when Turkish forces occupied the northern part of the island, the Force has been responsible for monitoring the ceasefire and for control of a buffer zone between the two communities.

Iraq/Kuwait

In 1991 UN Security Council Resolution 687 established a demilitarised zone extending 10 km into Iraq and 5 km into Kuwait to deter violations of the boundary and to observe hostile or potentially hostile actions. The UK, with the other permanent members of the Security Council, contributes 11 personnel to the UN Iraq/Kuwait observer mission.

Sierra Leone

In May 2000 there was a serious deterioration in the security situation in war-torn Sierra Leone as members of the UN peacekeeping mission there were taken hostage by rebel forces. In response, the UK Government rapidly deployed to Sierra Leone around 600 British soldiers from the Parachute Regiment, supported by a Royal Navy amphibious group including 600 Royal Marines. Their objectives were to evacuate entitled personnel and to secure the main airport near the capital, Freetown, while the UN forces (UNAMSIL) were built up. Having achieved these aims, the British force was withdrawn and British training teams were deployed from June 2000 to help establish new, accountable Sierra Leone armed forces and a police force. By September 2001 around 8,500 soldiers had been trained and equipped by the UK, which continues to help the Government of Sierra Leone and UNAMSIL to regain control over the whole country and prepare for democratic elections.

Bosnia and Herzegovina

The UK supports the establishment of a peaceful, multi-ethnic and democratic Bosnia and Herzegovina, and is helping to implement the 1995 Dayton/Paris Peace Agreement. The Stabilisation Force (SFOR), around 20,000-strong in mid-2001, comprises troops from NATO nations and other contributing countries, including Russia and a number of other Partnership for Peace members (see p. 100). The UK contributes some 1,700 troops to SFOR and around 80 British police officers to the UN International Police Task Force in Bosnia.

The main task of SFOR is to ensure continuing compliance with the military aspects of the Dayton Agreement, including monitoring the actions of the armed forces within the territory and inspecting weapon sites. It also provides support to the main organisations responsible for the civil aspects of the Agreement, including the Office of the High Representative, the International Police Task Force, the UN High Commissioner for Refugees, the OSCE and the UN Mission in Bosnia and Herzegovina.

The UK is helping the International Criminal Tribunal in The Hague, which was set up to try those indicted for war crimes in the former Yugoslavia. With other SFOR contributors, British forces have detained several of those indicted. As well as contributing to the funding of the Tribunal, the UK provides staff, information and forensic science expertise.

The UK is spending over £16 million in humanitarian and reconstruction aid in 1999–2002; it also contributes through the EU, OSCE and UN.

Kosovo

From early 1998 there was increasing international concern over the deteriorating situation in the province of Kosovo in the Federal Republic of Yugoslavia (FRY—comprising Serbia and Montenegro) and its implications for regional stability in south-eastern Europe. Excessive repression by Serbian security forces against the overwhelmingly ethnic Albanian population, and terrorism by Kosovo Albanian extremists, prompted widespread condemnation and calls for a peaceful solution based on the territorial integrity of the FRY and autonomy for Kosovo.

The situation worsened at the beginning of 1999, and a peace conference broke up in mid-March with the refusal of the Yugoslav delegation to accept settlement proposals. Later that month the UK and other NATO countries began intensive air operations against targets in the FRY in pursuit of a resolution to the Kosovo crisis.

In June 1999 the Yugoslav Parliament and Government accepted peace terms presented by special EU and Russian envoys. These entailed the withdrawal of Serbian security forces from Kosovo and deployment of an international security presence (with NATO participation at its core), enabling the return of displaced persons and refugees to their homes. With the subsequent authorisation of the UN, a multinational force (KFOR—including around 10,000 British troops) deployed into Kosovo with the task of restoring peace to the province. About 3,500 UK troops were still in Kosovo in mid-2001.

The UK is also providing some 200 civilian police, specialist officers, local government administrators and judicial experts to the UN-led civilian administration, which is helping to establish self-government in the province.

Other Developments in the Balkans

The UK welcomed the overthrow of the regime of Slobodan Milosevic in the FRY in October 2000 and the establishment of an elected, democratic government. The Government pressed the new FRY administration under President Kostunica to hand Milosevic over to the International Criminal Tribunal in The Hague (p. 89) to stand trial for war crimes, and in June 2001 he was extradited.

All five states that emerged from the former Yugoslavia have now elected democratic leaders, but tensions remain. From February 2001, incursions into Macedonia from Kosovo developed into serious armed conflict between ethnic Albanian groups and the Macedonian security forces. In March 2001 EU leaders expressed support for the Government and territorial integrity of Macedonia, and condemned the Albanian insurgency. In August and September UK forces participated in a NATO deployment to collect and destroy weapons from ethnic Albanian groups. This operation, approved at the end of June 2001, took place while a framework agreement providing a lasting constitutional solution was under debate in the Macedonian Parliament.

ARMS CONTROL

Because of the global reach of modern weapons, the UK has a clear national interest in preventing proliferation of weapons of mass destruction and promoting international control.

Weapons of Mass Destruction

Nuclear Weapons

The main instrument for controlling nuclear weapons is the 1968 Treaty on the Non-Proliferation of Nuclear Weapons (NPT), to which the UK Government is committed. The UK helped secure its indefinite extension in 1995, and played an active role in the sixth review conference in 2000 (where, for the first time since 1985, all participants agreed a final document which reviewed progress on nuclear non-proliferation and disarmament over the previous five years, and set out an agenda for the next five).

The UK was also involved in the negotiations on the Comprehensive Test Ban Treaty (CTBT), which it signed in 1996 and ratified in 1998. The CTBT, with its permanent verification system, will come into force upon ratification by the remaining 13 of 44 named states. The UK Government is also pressing for the negotiation of a treaty banning the future production of fissile material for use in nuclear weapons.

While large nuclear arsenals and risks of proliferation remain, the Government considers that the UK's minimum nuclear deterrent (see p. 103) remains a necessary and continuing element of the UK's security.

Biological Weapons

The 1972 Biological Weapons Convention provides for a worldwide ban on such weapons, but there are no effective compliance mechanisms. The UK is participating in negotiations to strengthen the Convention.

Chemical Weapons

The 1993 Chemical Weapons Convention, which came into force in 1997, provides for a worldwide ban on chemical weapons. The Organisation for the Prohibition of Chemical Weapons is responsible for verification. All the necessary British legislation is in place to license the production, possession and use of the most toxic chemicals and to implement the Convention's trade controls.

Conventional Armed Forces

The UK continues to work with its NATO partners and other European countries to develop and improve agreements to enhance stability in Europe in the light of the changed security environment. The main agreements reached are:

- the Conventional Armed Forces in Europe (CFE) Treaty (signed originally in 1990 and adapted at an OSCE summit in 1999),[7] which limits the numbers of heavy weapons in the countries of NATO and the former Warsaw Pact, and includes a verification regime. The CFE Treaty is widely regarded as a linchpin of European security;
- the Vienna Document, developed under the auspices of the OSCE, which is a politically binding agreement on the promotion of stability and openness on military matters in Europe; revised in 1999, it contains confidence- and security-building measures, and verification arrangements; and
- the 1992 Open Skies Treaty, which provides for the overflight and photography of the entire territory of the 27 participating states to monitor their military capabilities and activities. Ratification by the Russian parliament in April 2001 enables the Treaty to enter into force.

The UN Register of Conventional Arms, which came into effect in 1992, is intended to allow greater transparency in international transfers of conventional arms and to help identify excessive arms build-ups in any one country or region.

Landmines

The UK signed the Ottawa Convention banning the use, production, trade, transfer and stockpiling of anti-personnel landmines in 1997. The Convention, which Britain ratified in 1998, entered into force on 1 March 1999. The UK destroyed its stockpile of anti-personnel mines by October 1999. It has a programme to support humanitarian demining activities, which is focused on helping affected countries develop the capacity to clear landmines and on improving the coordination of international demining resources.

[7] In the light of Russia's breach of CFE limits through its military action against separatists in Chechnya, ratification of the 1999 revision by the UK and its NATO allies will depend on the level of all parties' compliance with the limits that have been agreed.

Small Arms

The UK attaches great importance to international efforts to curb small arms proliferation and participated in the July 2001 UN Conference on the Illicit Trade in Small Arms and Light Weapons.

Export Controls

The UK is a founding member of all the international export control regimes which govern the export of conventional arms, technology associated with weapons of mass destruction, missiles, and 'dual-use' goods (those having a legitimate civil use as well as a potential military application).

In 1997 the UK Government issued new criteria for assessing licence applications for arms exports, one of which is that licences will not be granted if there is a clearly identifiable risk that weapons might be used for internal repression or international aggression. At the same time it banned the export of certain items for which there is clear evidence of use for torture or other abuses; it also declared its commitment to preventing British companies from manufacturing, selling or procuring such equipment and to pressing for a global ban. In 1998 EU Member States agreed on a Code of Conduct on Arms Exports, setting similar common standards to which all EU members would adhere.

HUMAN RIGHTS

The UK Government has stated its commitment to working for improvements in human rights standards across the world and, in September 2001, published its fourth annual human rights report describing the activities and initiatives pursued during the previous year. The £6.5 million Human Rights Project Fund, launched in 1998, provides flexible and direct financial assistance for grass-roots human rights projects around the world.

International Conventions

United Nations

Universal respect for human rights is an obligation under the UN Charter. Expressions of concern about human rights do not, therefore, constitute interference in the internal affairs of another state.

The UK Government promotes the standards set out in the Universal Declaration of Human Rights, which was adopted by the UN General Assembly in 1948. Since this is not a legally binding document, the General Assembly adopted two international covenants on human rights in 1966, placing legal obligations on those states ratifying or acceding to them. The covenants came into force in 1976, the UK ratifying both in the same year. One covenant deals with economic, social and cultural rights and the other with civil and political rights. Other international instruments to which the UK is a party include those on:

- the elimination of racial discrimination;
- the elimination of all forms of discrimination against women;
- the rights of the child;
- torture and other cruel, inhuman or degrading treatment or punishment;
- the prevention of genocide;
- the abolition of slavery; and
- the status of refugees.

Council of Europe

The UK is also bound by the Council of Europe's Convention for the Protection of Human Rights and Fundamental Freedoms (ECHR), which covers areas such as:

- the right to life, liberty and a fair trial;
- the right to marry and have a family;
- freedom of thought, conscience and religion;
- freedom of expression, including freedom of the press;
- freedom of peaceful assembly and association;
- the right to have a sentence reviewed by a higher tribunal; and
- the prohibition of torture and inhuman or degrading treatment.

The rights and obligations of the ECHR were enshrined in UK law upon the implementation of the Human Rights Act 1998 in October 2000 (see p. 214).

Organisation for Security and Co-operation in Europe

The OSCE's Office for Democratic Institutions and Human Rights (in Warsaw) promotes participating states' adherence to commitments on human rights, democracy and the rule of law, and takes a lead in monitoring elections within the OSCE area. The Office provides a forum for exchanges of experts on the building of democratic institutions and the holding of elections in participating states. It also provides expertise and training on human rights, constitutional and legal matters, and promotes practical measures to strengthen civil administration.

International Criminal Court

The UK has supported the establishment of an International Criminal Court to try cases of genocide, crimes against humanity and war crimes. The Government signed the Court's Statute in 1998, and parliamentary legislation to enable ratification was enacted in May 2001.

CRIME AND TERRORISM

The UK supports international efforts to combat illegal drugs, working with producer and transit countries, especially those where drug production and trafficking represent a direct threat to the UK. Over 60 drug liaison officers are stationed in UK missions in key countries, in cooperation with the host authorities. Working with its EU partners, the UK is helping Latin American, Caribbean and Central Asian states to stem the transit of drugs across their territories. It also participated in the negotiation of the EU drugs strategy for 2000–04, which was endorsed by the European Council in 1999. The UK is involved in the United Nations drug control structure, and is one of the largest contributors to the UN International Drug Control Programme.

Britain contributes to international efforts to counter financial crime, for example through its membership of the Financial Action Task Force against money laundering, and through its support for regional anti-money laundering groups.

Together with its EU partners, the UK is confronting serious and organised international crime through, for example, the European Police Office (EUROPOL) which supports investigations and operations conducted by national law enforcement agencies. EUROPOL powers and duties are set out in the EUROPOL Convention, which entered into force in 1998. EU Member States also belong to the International Criminal Police Organisation (INTERPOL). UK liaison with INTERPOL is provided by the National Criminal Intelligence Service (see p. 219).

The UK participated in the negotiation of the UN Convention Against Transnational Crime, and three protocols covering the smuggling of migrants, trafficking in human beings and illegal firearms. The Convention was signed by 120 states, including the UK, in December 2000.

The British Government has stressed its condemnation of all terrorist acts, its opposition to concessions to terrorist demands and its commitment to ensuring that terrorists do not benefit from their acts. It works bilaterally with other like-minded governments, and multilaterally through the UN, EU and G8, to promote closer international coordination against terrorism. The UK is party to a series of international counter-terrorism conventions agreed since 1963. It ratified the most recent—the International Convention for the Suppression of Financing of Terrorism—in February 2001, upon the entry into force of the Terrorism Act 2000. Under the provisions of Act, the UK Government also proscribed 21 foreign terrorist organisations with effect from 28 March 2001 (see p. 218).

Terrorist Attack on the United States

On 11 September 2001 terrorists launched suicide attacks on US landmarks using hijacked civil airliners. Two aircraft were flown into the twin towers of New York's World Trade Centre, which subsequently collapsed, and another plane hit the Pentagon (Defence Department) in Washington. A fourth jet crashed in Pennsylvania before reaching any specific target. Around 6,000 people are thought to have died in the attacks and ensuing devastation, including British citizens. The US Government condemned the attacks as an act of war and pledged military retaliation against known terrorist networks and their state sponsors. In the UK, Parliament was recalled on 14 September to debate the atrocity. The Prime Minister emphasised Britain's solidarity with the United States and its support for an international alliance against terrorism. NATO invoked the article in its treaty which states that an attack on any of its members is an attack on all. On 21 September EU Heads of Government declared that Member States were ready to engage in targeted action against states supporting terrorism.

DEVELOPMENT COOPERATION

The UK's development aid policy is focused on its continuing commitment to the international development targets, agreed by the world's governments at UN conferences in the 1990s, to halve the proportion of people living in abject poverty by 2015. The UK Government believes that, if properly managed, the wealth now being created by globalisation—involving, for example, increased flows of goods, services, capital, trade, people and information—can provide new opportunities for the elimination of world poverty and for equitable and environmentally sustainable growth in the poorest countries. However, these countries need to be brought into the global economy so that they can gain greater access to knowledge and technology, new trade and investment.

UK official development assistance will rise from 0.26% of GNP in 1997 to 0.33% in 2003–04, with the longer-term objective of attaining the UN target of 0.7%. In line with this, the budget for the Department for International Development (DFID) will reach almost £3.6 billion in 2003–04, a 45% increase in real terms on 1997–98.

In December 2000 the Government published a White Paper, *Eliminating World Poverty: Making Globalisation Work for the Poor.* This set out an agenda to help bring sustainable benefits to the one in five of the world's population (1.2 billion people) who live in extreme poverty. It announced:

- the ending, from 1 April 2001, of the practice of providing aid on condition that a proportion of the goods and services were from UK companies;
- financial support for the eradication of polio from the world within five years;
- help for African countries to trade more effectively;
- new opportunities for investing in developing countries;
- strong action against corruption;
- the establishment of a commission on intellectual property rights to protect the interests of developing countries; and
- an increase in support for world environmental initiatives.

Poverty Reduction

DFID supports poorer countries in developing and implementing national strategies for poverty reduction (based on growth, equity and security) which have broad political support and meet local needs. DFID considers that growth requires market-based policies, with a commitment to economic reform and liberalisation together with support for effective governance and institutions. Poor people's participation in growth, using their own assets and capabilities, requires tackling inequalities of opportunity, especially access to education, information, and health, transport and financial services. It may also necessitate measures to redistribute income and assets. Physical and economic vulnerability must also be addressed.

Debt Relief

The heavy burden of servicing debt reduces the ability of the poorest countries to tackle poverty effectively. The UK is focusing on accelerating the implementation of the revised 1999 Heavily Indebted Poor Countries (HIPC) debt initiative designed to deliver wider and faster relief to countries committed to poverty reduction. At least 23 HIPC countries will receive debt relief by 2002 (reducing their debts by two-thirds on average). All aid debts owed to the UK by the poorest countries—some £1.2 billion—have been cancelled. In 1999 the Government announced that it would provide full debt relief on the remaining ECGD debt—about £2 billion—for countries when they qualify for the HIPC initiative.

Good Governance and Human Rights

The quality of governance has a major impact on economic growth and the effectiveness of services. DFID is focusing on issues such as democratic accountability (bringing poor people into the democratic process); fundamental freedoms (including rights to education, health and an adequate livelihood); combating child labour; tackling corruption and money laundering; better revenue and public finance management; access to basic services; and personal safety and security in the community with access to justice.

Women's Empowerment

An estimated 70% of the world's poor are female. Removing gender discrimination and supporting measures to improve women's equality are fundamental to reducing poverty and upholding human rights. A priority in DFID assistance is the promotion of equal access to education for all girls and boys.

Health

Since 1997 DFID has committed around £1 billion to improving basic health systems in developing countries. The improvement of poor people's access to healthcare and to new and existing drugs and vaccines needs substantial investment (including from the private sector) in health service infrastructure, and financial and human resources. The impact of major communicable diseases, such as HIV, tuberculosis and malaria, on the poor is a major obstacle to social and economic development. The UK is working with the G8 countries, developing countries and the UN to establish a Global Health Fund to increase access to effective treatments against these diseases. It is planned that this fund will have become operational by the end of 2001.

Education

About 113 million children around the world do not go to school and a further 150 million drop out before attaining useful levels of basic education. Almost 900 million adults are illiterate, two-thirds of them women. DFID resources are being focused on basic and primary education. Nearly 80% of UK current commitments—£800 million—are now in this area, with two-thirds going to 11 of the poorest countries in sub-Saharan Africa and South Asia.

The UK is working with governments to develop well-integrated and sustainable education systems, helping them to provide high-quality primary education for all their children, especially girls. To increase the supply of teachers, the UK is initiating programmes and working with the Commonwealth of Learning (an intergovernmental organisation created by the Commonwealth) to encourage the use of distance learning and information technology programmes for teacher training and the sharing of skills.

The Environment

DFID's main priority is to promote better environmental management that can contribute to poverty reduction—by trying to reverse trends in environmental degradation,

Figure 7.1: DFID Programme 1999–2000: Bilateral Aid by Form of Aid

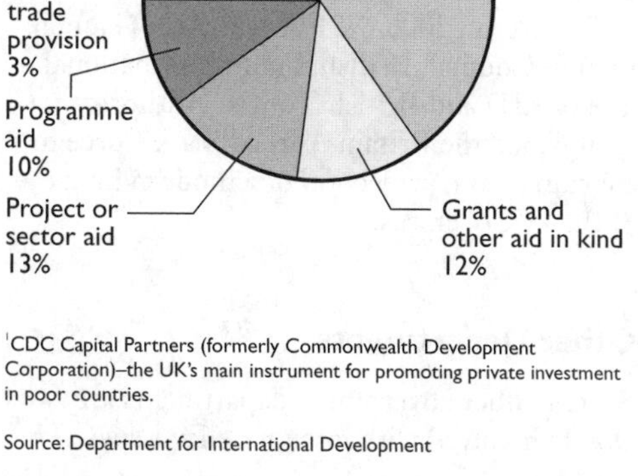

[1]CDC Capital Partners (formerly Commonwealth Development Corporation)–the UK's main instrument for promoting private investment in poor countries.

Source: Department for International Development

Figure 7.2: DFID Programme 1999–2000: Bilateral Aid by Region

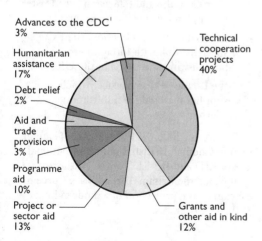

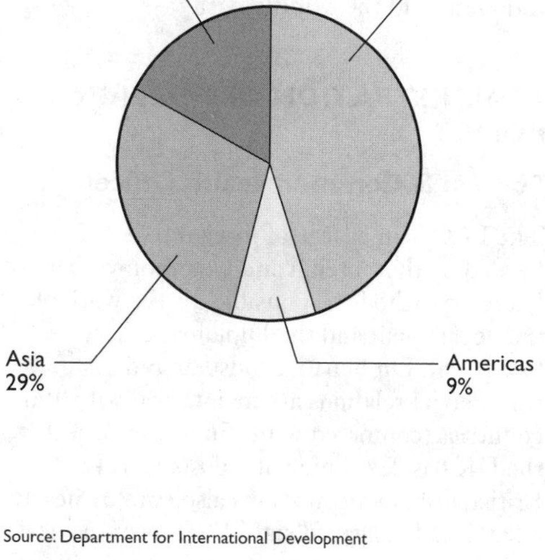

Source: Department for International Development

and reducing poor people's vulnerability to the effects of global environmental trends (particularly climate change).

Conflict and Natural Disasters

Conflict and natural disasters are major barriers to development in many of the world's poorest countries. More than half of the 40 poorest countries are either in the midst of armed conflict or have only recently emerged from it. DFID's objectives are to reduce the tensions that lead to conflict, limit the means of waging warfare, and provide the assistance and support needed to help societies cope and eventually rebuild.

DFID's humanitarian assistance is targeted at improving the quality and speed of response to a disaster; promoting effective recovery and early transition from emergency assistance to rehabilitation and reconstruction; and helping countries to reduce their vulnerability to natural, environmental and industrial disasters. DFID provides humanitarian assistance through governments, UN agencies and non-governmental organisations. Between 1997–98 and 1999–2000, UK expenditure on humanitarian assistance rose from £186 million to £323 million.

During 2000–01 the UK responded to a number of natural disasters, including flooding in Mozambique and earthquakes in India and El Salvador. It also funded winter relief for Serbia, as well as assistance for refugees in West Africa, Sudan, Afghanistan, Indonesia and the Middle East.

ADMINISTRATION OF FOREIGN POLICY

Foreign & Commonwealth Office

The FCO is in charge of foreign policy. It is headed by the Foreign and Commonwealth Secretary, who is responsible for the work of the department and the Diplomatic Service (see p. 66). Diplomatic, consular and commercial relations are maintained with 190 countries (compared with 136 in 1968), and the UK has 224 diplomatic posts worldwide. British diplomatic missions also employ nearly 8,000 locally engaged staff. Staff overseas deal with political, commercial and economic work; entry clearance to the UK and consular work; aid administration; and information and other activities, such as culture, science and technology.

The FCO's executive agency, Wilton Park International Conference Centre in West Sussex, contributes to the solution of international problems by organising conferences in the UK, attended by politicians, business people, academics and other professionals from all over the world.

An important function of the FCO is to promote understanding of British foreign policies and to project an up-to-date image of the UK worldwide, beyond the sphere of government-to-government diplomacy. Key elements of FCO-funded public diplomacy work include:

- publications, television and radio programmes, and the FCO and Planet Britain websites (*www.fco.gov.uk* and *www.planet-britain.org*);
- scholarship schemes for overseas students (see p. 145) and programmes for influential foreign visitors;
- the BBC World Service (see p. 272);
- the British Council (see p. 97);
- the London Radio Service and British Satellite News, used extensively by overseas radio and television broadcasters to supplement their news coverage;
- International Press Section, the FCO's specialist link with foreign journalists, both visiting and based in the UK; and
- the London Press Service, which supplies material for publication overseas.

In autumn 2000 the FCO, British Council, Design Council, British Trade International (see p. 421) and British Tourist Authority established the Britain Abroad Task Force to coordinate the projection of a modern image of the UK overseas.

Other Departments

Several other government departments are closely involved with foreign policy issues. The

DFID administers the UK's development aid programmes. It is also responsible for the UK's relations with the World Bank and international organisations concerned with development. The Ministry of Defence maintains military liaison with the UK's NATO and other allies. The Department of Trade and Industry (DTI) has an important influence on international trade policy and commercial relations with other countries, including EU Member States. The joint work of the FCO and DTI in support of British trade and investment overseas is coordinated through British Trade International. HM Treasury is involved in British international economic policy and is responsible for the UK's relations with the International Monetary Fund.

BRITISH COUNCIL

The British Council is the UK's principal agency for cultural relations overseas. Its purpose is to promote a wider knowledge of the UK and the English language and to encourage cultural, scientific, technological and educational cooperation between the UK and other countries. Its work also supports the FCO's objective of increasing respect and goodwill for the UK. The Council:

- helps people to study, train or make professional contacts in the UK;
- enables British specialists to teach, advise or establish joint projects abroad;
- teaches English and promotes its use;
- provides library and information services;
- supports legal reform overseas and works to enhance the protection of human rights;
- promotes scientific and technical training, research collaboration and exchanges; and
- encourages appreciation of British arts and literature.

In 2000–01 the Council worked in 229 towns and cities in 111 countries. It issued nearly 8 million books and videos to 350,000 British Council library members, and dealt with almost 2 million enquiries in its libraries and information centres. It also organised more than 1,500 science events in over 60 countries; managed or supported 3,000 arts events worldwide; administered 700,000 professional and academic examinations; helped 13,000 young people take part in exchange projects; and supported over 4,000 trainers and trainees for vocational projects across Europe.

It is financed partly by a grant from the FCO and partly by income from revenue-earning activities, such as English language teaching, the administration of examinations, and bilateral and international aid contract work. Some of the training and education programmes organised by the Council as part of the British aid programme receive funding from the DFID.

In November 2000 the Council announced a new five-year strategy to realign its global operations—increasing its activities in 'transitional' countries such as China and Russia, and investing in information technology to provide a better service to a wider audience.

Educational Exchanges

The British Council recruits teachers for work overseas, organises short overseas visits by British experts, encourages cultural exchange visits, and organises academic interchange between British universities and colleges and those in other countries.

The British aid programme has helped fund certain Council programmes, such as:

- recruitment of staff for overseas universities;
- secondment of staff from British higher education establishments; and
- organisation of short-term teaching and advisory visits.

The British Council's Central Bureau for International Education and Training aims to raise standards in UK education and training through international partnership and exchange. This is achieved by the promotion of international mobility, vocational training and development, linking and exchange programmes, lifelong learning and multilateral partnerships. The government-funded Bureau is the UK national agency for many EU education and training programmes. It also hosts the Secretariat of the new UK National Commission for UNESCO (UN Educational, Scientific and Cultural Organisation), inaugurated at the start of 2001.

Further Reading

Foreign & Commonwealth Office Departmental Report 2001: The Government's Expenditure Plans 2001–02 to 2003–04. Cm 5110. The Stationery Office, 2001.

Department for International Development Departmental Report 2001. The Government's Expenditure Plans 2001–02 to 2003–04. Cm 5111. The Stationery Office, 2001.

Eliminating World Poverty: Making Globalisation Work for the Poor. Department for International Development. Cm 5006. The Stationery Office, 2000.

Websites

Foreign & Commonwealth Office: www.fco.gov.uk

Department for International Development: www.dfid.gov.uk

Ministry of Defence: www.mod.uk

British Council: www.britcoun.org

United Nations: www.un.org

Commonwealth: www.thecommonwealth.org

Organisation for Security and Co-operation in Europe: www.osce.org

Council of Europe: www.coe.fr

8 Defence

UK Security	99	Force Structures and Capabilities	103
North Atlantic Treaty Organisation	100	Defence Equipment	104
Defence Tasks	101	The Armed Forces	105
Nuclear Forces	103	Administration	106

The defence of the United Kingdom, as well as its economic and other wider interests, is linked with the stability of Europe. The primary means of ensuring British and European security is NATO (the North Atlantic Treaty Organisation), of which the UK is a founder member and to which its armed forces are assigned. The Government is involved in the development of a European military capability as a complementary role to NATO in crisis operations in which NATO as a whole is not engaged. The armed forces also contribute to the peacetime security of the UK and its Overseas Territories, and assist in humanitarian and peacetime operations throughout the world.

UK SECURITY

Defence Policy

The 1998 Strategic Defence Review (SDR), which set out the changes required for the UK's armed forces to meet the needs of new strategic issues in the 21st century, remains the foundation of the country's defence policy and plans for reshaping and modernising the services and their support. The SDR concluded that there was no direct military threat to the UK or its Overseas Territories, but that the end of the Cold War had introduced instability and uncertainty. There remained the potential threat of the proliferation of nuclear, chemical and biological weapons, organised crime and the break-up of existing states with attendant ethnic and religious conflict. The SDR laid out a force structure in which the armed services would be able to respond to a major international crisis. This might involve operations of a similar scale and duration to the Gulf War, or of more extended overseas deployment on a lesser scale (such as in Bosnia and Kosovo), while retaining the ability to mount a second, substantial deployment (up to a combat brigade and supporting naval and air forces).

This assessment was confirmed and restated in the 1999 Defence White Paper and in later analyses—*Defence Policy 2001* and *The Future Strategic Context for Defence*—in 2001. The growth and type of planned and coordinated missions undertaken by UK forces since 1997 have indicated the increasing likelihood of the armed services conducting smaller, but frequent assignments—often simultaneous and sometimes prolonged, and some at short notice—rather than preparing for one large-scale warfighting operation.

The changes outlined in the SDR are designed to reinforce the UK's contribution to international peace and security through NATO and the European Union (EU—see p.75), and through other international organisations such as the United Nations (UN—see p. 75) and the Organisation for Security and Co-operation in Europe (OSCE—see p. 76).

Defence Missions

Defence missions which underpin the UK's defence planning are:

- peacetime security;
- security of the Overseas Territories;
- defence diplomacy (see p. 103);
- support to wider British interests;
- peace support and humanitarian assistance operations;
- contributing forces for a regional conflict outside the NATO area;
- providing forces to respond to regional aggression against NATO; and
- responding to strategic attack on NATO.

NORTH ATLANTIC TREATY ORGANISATION

The UK is a founding member of NATO, membership of which is the cornerstone of British defence policy, and most of the UK's forces are assigned to it. The Alliance embodies the transatlantic relationship that links North America and Europe in a unique defence and security partnership. The number of members was increased to 19 with the accession of the Czech Republic, Hungary and Poland in 1999. The Alliance remains open to new members willing and able to assume the obligations and responsibilities of membership. Nine countries (Albania, Bulgaria, Estonia, Latvia, Lithuania, Macedonia, Romania, Slovakia and Slovenia) have expressed an interest in joining NATO. The Alliance is committed to reviewing enlargement by the autumn 2002 summit to be held in Prague.

Adaptation of NATO

NATO is adapting to the changed security environment in Europe. The Partnership for Peace programme, aimed at enhancing both political consultation and practical military cooperation between NATO and Partner states, and the Euro-Atlantic Partnership Council, which provides the framework for cooperation between NATO and its Partner countries, are key to the development of the security relationship between NATO and other countries in Europe. Following the 1999 NATO summit, measures were put in place to increase the ability of Partner countries to operate effectively in NATO-led crisis management operations. These include

European Defence

While NATO is the primary means of ensuring UK and European security and defence, operations such as in Bosnia and Kosovo (see p. 89) have led the EU to decide that it needs to make a stronger and more coherent contribution to the Alliance, and to improve the collective capability to undertake EU-led crisis management operations where NATO as a whole is not engaged. At the Helsinki European Council in December 1999, on the basis of proposals developed by the UK, Italy and France, EU member states committed themselves to the goal of modernising their armed forces so that by 2003 they would have a pool of deployed units from which a force up to corps level (50,000 to 60,000 personnel, together with appropriate air and naval elements) could be swiftly assembled for a crisis management operation, as well as for humanitarian, rescue, and peacekeeping tasks (see also p. 84). This force would be sustainable for at least a year. The UK contribution to an individual operation could be up to 12,500 ground troops, 18 warships and 72 combat aircraft. A crucial priority in achieving this objective is the setting up of permanent arrangements for consultation and cooperation with NATO and for drawing on NATO planning and other capabilities. Collective defence remains the responsibility of NATO, which will also continue to have a major role in crisis management.

greater involvement of the 27 non-NATO Partner states in the political consultation and decision-making process and in the operational planning and command arrangements. NATO is also committed to the sustained development of its relationship with Russia and Ukraine, following consultation and cooperation agreements signed in 1997.

NATO has also undertaken a period of internal adaptation, including a major review of the military command structure and the implementation of the Combined Joint Task Force concept. At the 1999 summit the allies approved an updated strategic concept for NATO to reflect the changed political environment and the launch of an initiative to improve its defence capability and effectiveness in all multinational Alliance missions.

DEFENCE TASKS

The UK and its Overseas Territories

The armed forces are responsible for safeguarding Britain's territory, airspace and territorial waters. They also provide for the security and reinforcement of the Overseas Territories and for support to the civil authorities in both the UK and the Overseas Territories.

Maritime Defence

The Royal Navy aims to ensure the integrity of the UK's territorial waters and the protection of its rights and interests in the surrounding seas, and of British interests around the world. The maintenance of a 24-hour, year-round presence in waters around the British Isles provides reassurance to merchant ships and other mariners, as well as security of the seas. The Royal Air Force (RAF) also contributes to maritime requirements, for instance through the Nimrod force, which provides air surveillance of surface vessels and submarines.

Land Defence

The British Army aims to provide, through either the deployment of the whole or appropriate elements of its available forces, the capability to defend the UK and its Overseas Territories. In addition, the Army is committed to such tasks as giving military aid to peace support and humanitarian operations, responding to regional conflict outside the NATO area and contributing forces to counter a strategic attack on NATO.

Air Defence

Air defence of the UK and the surrounding seas is maintained by a system of layered defences. Continuous radar cover is provided by the Air Surveillance and Control System (ASACS) supplemented by the NATO Airborne Early Warning Force, to which the RAF contributes six aircraft. The RAF also provides five squadrons of Tornado F3 air defence aircraft, supported by tanker aircraft and, in wartime, an additional F3 squadron. Royal Navy air defence destroyers can also be linked to the ASACS, providing radar and electronic warfare coverage and surface-to-air missiles. Ground-launched Rapier missiles defend the main RAF bases. Naval aircraft also contribute to British air defence.

Overseas Garrisons

The UK maintains garrisons in Gibraltar, the Sovereign Base Areas of Cyprus, the Falkland Islands and Brunei. Gibraltar provides headquarters and communications facilities for NATO in the western Mediterranean, while Cyprus provides strategic communications facilities as well as a base for operations in the eastern Mediterranean and beyond. The garrison on the Falkland Islands is a tangible demonstration of the Government's commitment to uphold the right of the islanders to determine their own future (see p. 81). The garrison in Brunei is maintained at the request of the Brunei Government. In addition, a jungle warfare-training unit is maintained in Belize.

Northern Ireland

The armed forces provide support to the police in Northern Ireland (see p. 19) in maintaining law and order and countering terrorism. The number of units deployed at any one time is dependent on the prevailing security situation. The Royal Navy patrols territorial waters around Northern Ireland and its inland waterways in order to deter and intercept the movement of terrorist weapons. The Royal Marines provide troops to meet Navy and Army commitments, while the RAF provides elements of the RAF Regiment and Chinook, Wessex and Puma helicopters.

Other Tasks

Other tasks include the provision of:

- military assistance to civil ministries, for example in maintaining the essentials of life in the community, carrying out fishery protection duties and helping in the fight against drugs;
- military aid to the civil community, including during emergencies; and
- military search and rescue.

Britain in NATO

Maritime Forces

Most Royal Navy ships are committed to NATO. Permanent contributions are made to NATO's Immediate Reaction and Rapid Reaction Forces in the Atlantic, the English Channel and the Mediterranean. The UK also contributes to NATO's Maritime Augmentation Forces, which are held at the lowest state of readiness and in peacetime comprise ships mainly in routine refit or maintenance.

The main components of the Fleet available to NATO are:

- three aircraft carriers operating Joint Force Harrier aircraft and Sea King anti-submarine helicopters;
- 32 destroyers and frigates, and 22 mine counter-measure vessels;
- 12 nuclear-powered attack submarines; and
- amphibious forces, including a commando brigade of the Royal Marines, two assault ships and a helicopter carrier.

Land Forces

The multinational Allied Command Europe Rapid Reaction Corps (ARRC) is the key land component of NATO's Rapid Reaction Forces. Capable of immediately deploying up to four NATO divisions, the ARRC is commanded by a British general, and some 55,000 British regular troops are assigned to it. The UK provides two of the ten divisions available to the Corps—a division of three armoured brigades stationed in Germany, and a division of three mechanised brigades based in Britain. An air-mobile brigade, assigned to one of the Corps' multinational divisions, is also sited in the UK.

Air Forces

The RAF contributes to NATO's Immediate and Rapid Reaction Forces. Around 100 aircraft and 40 helicopters are allocated to them. Tornado F3, Harrier and Jaguar aircraft, and Rapier surface-to-air missiles form part of the Supreme Allied Commander Europe's Immediate Reaction Force, while Harrier, Jaguar and Tornado GR1/4 aircraft provide offensive support and tactical reconnaissance for the Rapid Reaction Force. Chinook and Puma helicopters supply troop airlift facilities for the ARRC or other deployed land forces. The RAF provides Nimrod maritime patrol aircraft and search and rescue helicopters.

Wider Security Interests

Military tasks to promote the UK's wider security interests may be undertaken by British forces whether working within NATO, assisting the United Nations, in coalition with allies, or acting alone. Contingents are deployed on UN operations in Cyprus, Georgia, East Timor, Bosnia, Sierra Leone, the Democratic Republic of Congo and on the Iraq/Kuwait border. Over Iraq (see p. 86), Tornado GR1/4s and Jaguars, supported by VC-10s, are policing the no-fly zones to ensure that Iraq does not resume repression of minorities and that it does not threaten its neighbours. The Royal Navy is deployed to the Gulf to enforce UN sanctions against Iraq.

A substantial British contingent is deployed in Kosovo to help implement a peace agreement following the conclusion of air operations over the Federal Republic of Yugoslavia in 1999 (see p. 89).

The number of operations against trafficking in illicit drugs has increased in recent years, for example in the Caribbean, where a Royal Navy destroyer or frigate works closely with the authorities of the United States, the Overseas Territories and the Regional Security System to combat drug trafficking. Although primary responsibility for this task rests with the local law enforcement agencies or other government departments, the armed forces assist where they can do so without detriment to the performance of their other military tasks.

In recent years, British forces have taken part in international evacuation or humanitarian relief operations in Rwanda, Somalia, Angola, Eritrea, the Democratic Republic of Congo, Sierra Leone, Mozambique, East Timor, the Caribbean and Central America.

Defence diplomacy—the use of defence assets to build and promote stability and assist in the development of democratically accountable armed forces—is an established defence mission. British service personnel and civilians working in defence are involved in a range of non-operational activities including:

- help in verifying arms control agreements (see p. 90);
- outreach programmes of bilateral assistance and cooperation with other countries in areas such as English language training, advice on the management of defence training and provision of short-term military training teams to assist in modernising and reforming armed forces; and
- training of some 4,000 military and civilian students from over 100 countries each year at UK defence establishments.

NUCLEAR FORCES

Although the four Trident submarines are retained as the ultimate guarantee of national security, the UK and other members of NATO have radically reduced their reliance on nuclear weapons. The UK is committed to pressing for progress in the negotiations towards mutual, balanced and verifiable reductions in nuclear weapons (see p. 90). When satisfied that verified progress has been made towards the goal of global elimination of nuclear weapons, the Government has said it will ensure that the British nuclear weapons are included in the talks.

The Government undertook a fundamental re-examination of all aspects of Britain's nuclear position in the SDR and concluded that fewer than 200 operationally available nuclear warheads were needed—a reduction of one-third. Therefore, the UK now has only one Trident submarine on patrol at a time. It carries a reduced load of up to 48 warheads compared with the previously announced ceiling of 96. The submarine's missiles are not targeted and it is normally at several days' 'notice to fire'.

FORCE STRUCTURES AND CAPABILITIES

To achieve its policy objectives, the UK needs forces with a high degree of mobility, at sufficient readiness and with a clear sense of purpose, for combat operations, conflict prevention, crisis management and humanitarian activities. These forces must therefore be flexible and able to undertake the full range of military tasks.

Measures to increase a joint-service approach to defence, outlined in the SDR, have led to the establishment of:

- Joint Rapid Reaction Forces, a pool of deployable forces (including 50 warships and support vessels, four army brigades and 100 combat aircraft), able to carry out a range of short-notice missions from warfighting to peacekeeping operations, and to provide a first stage of a larger deployment;
- Joint Force Harrier, a joint command of Royal Navy and RAF Harrier aircraft able to operate from aircraft carriers or land bases;
- a new helicopter command of some 350 battlefield helicopters—Navy commando

helicopters, Army helicopters (including Apache attack helicopters entering service) and RAF support helicopters;
- a joint nuclear, biological and chemical defence regiment; and
- a joint doctrine and concepts centre for the development of defence doctrine.

These initiatives should enhance the services' ability to work together efficiently and effectively and to project power to potential trouble spots and crises. As well as addressing the equipment requirements for the services, the SDR sought to improve the way they are supported by:

- creating a Defence Logistics Organisation, under a new post of Chief of Defence Logistics, covering all three services;
- establishing two logistic lines of communication, each with a Joint Force Logistic Component Headquarters, which will each be able to provide support to an operation of the type conducted in Bosnia and in Kosovo; and
- restructuring of management and organisation of the Defence Medical Services (including closer integration with the National Health Service) and a commitment to spend an additional £140 million on medical support to deployed forces in the period to March 2002.

All of these joint organisations have been established, and most are up to their full operational capability.

Royal Navy

The focus for the Navy will continue to move from large-scale, open-ocean warfare to force projection and offshore operations in conjunction with the other services, based on:

- two new large aircraft carriers, capable of operating up to 50 aircraft and helicopters, which will enter service from 2012;
- a force of 32 destroyers and frigates, with the Type 42 destroyer being replaced by the Type 45 from 2008, and 22 mine counter-measure ships; and
- ten attack submarines, able to fire Tomahawk land-attack missiles by 2008.

Army

Among measures aimed at improving mobility, firepower and the projection of forces are:

- an increase in the number of the armoured or mechanised brigades from five to six through the conversion of the airborne brigade to a mechanised brigade;
- the creation of a new, powerful air assault brigade (combining two battalions of the Parachute Regiment) equipped with the new Apache attack helicopter;
- the creation of an additional armoured reconnaissance regiment from an existing armoured regiment, which will be brought back from Germany;
- the conversion of the tank regiments from eight units to six larger ones, with significantly more personnel and tanks; and
- increasing the operational utility of the Territorial Army (TA—see p. 106).

RAF

The emphasis of the new plans is on the ability to deploy appropriate types of aircraft rapidly to crises. Measures include:

- the procurement of new air-to-air, anti-armour and air-to-surface missiles for Tornado, Harrier and Eurofighter aircraft;
- improving the capability of the Nimrod reconnaissance aircraft to support both peacekeeping and warfighting operations; and
- modernising the strategic airlift capability of the air transport fleet, in the short term by the leasing of four Boeing C-17 aircraft and, later in the decade, by the acquisition of 25 Airbus A400M aircraft.

DEFENCE EQUIPMENT

Modern equipment is essential if one of the key aims of Britain's force restructuring programme is to be achieved, namely that of increasing the flexibility and mobility of its armed forces.

Improvements for the Royal Navy equipment programme include:

- the fourth Trident submarine (now in service) and the building of the Astute-class attack submarines;
- new aircraft, replacing the current Sea Harriers, for the two new aircraft carriers;
- a modernised destroyer and frigate fleet, including the introduction of the Type 45 destroyer, which will deploy an anti-air missile system developed with France and Italy;
- new amphibious shipping to strengthen the amphibious force; and
- the Merlin anti-submarine helicopter.

The Army front line is being strengthened by:

- the introduction of the Challenger 2 tank;
- Apache attack helicopters equipped with new anti-tank missiles;
- improved Rapier and new Starstreak air defence missiles;
- new bridging equipment to increase mobility and flexibility; and
- a range of advanced surveillance, target acquisition and reconnaissance equipment.

Improvements for the RAF include:

- upgrading the Tornado GR1 fleet;
- upgrading the Jaguar aircraft until it is replaced, together with the Tornado F3 aircraft, by the Eurofighter;
- new Nimrod maritime patrol aircraft;
- orders for new air-launched missiles and guided bombs; and
- the introduction of EH101 and additional Chinook support helicopters and of improved Hercules aircraft.

Defence Procurement

Some £10 billion is spent each year on military equipment, including the procurement of spares and associated costs. When assessing options, consideration is given to the initial costs of a project and to those necessary to support it throughout its service life. Competition for contracts takes place wherever possible. Measures to improve the procuring of defence equipment, identified by the SDR's 'smart procurement' initiative, are the introduction of integrated teams, including representatives from industry, to closely control a project throughout its life. Equipment is to be acquired incrementally, with the basic equipment entering into service quickly and then being upgraded as technology improves. All defence acquisition projects are run on 'smart procurement' lines. The involvement of the private sector through Public-Private Partnerships is a major element of procurement strategy: under this policy, capital investment with a value of some £1 billion is being undertaken.

International Procurement Collaboration

The UK is a member of NATO's Conference of National Armaments Directors, which promotes equipment collaboration between NATO nations. It is also a founder member of OCCAR, an armament cooperation organisation formed with France, Germany and Italy for managing joint procurement activities. Current collaborative programmes in which the UK participates include:

- development of the Eurofighter (with Germany, Italy and Spain);
- a maritime anti-air missile system (France and Italy);
- a battlefield radar system (France and Germany);
- the EH101 helicopter (Italy);
- a multi-role armoured vehicle (France and Germany); and
- the large transport Airbus A400M aircraft (Belgium, France, Germany, Italy, Spain and Turkey).

THE ARMED FORCES

Commissioned Ranks

Commissions, either by promotion from the ranks or by direct entry based on educational and other qualifications, are granted for short, medium and long terms. All three services have schemes for school, university and college sponsorships.

Commissioned ranks receive initial training at the Britannia Royal Naval College, Dartmouth; the Commando Training Centre, Lympstone (Devon); the Royal Military Academy, Sandhurst; or the Royal Air Force College, Cranwell. This is followed by specialist training, which may include degree courses at service establishments or universities. Courses of higher training for officers, designed to emphasise the joint approach to the tactical and operational levels of conflict, are provided at the Joint Services Command and Staff College at Shrivenham (Wiltshire).

Non-commissioned Ranks

Engagements for non-commissioned ranks vary widely in length and terms of service. Subject to a minimum period, entrants may leave at any time, giving 18 months' notice (12 months for certain engagements). Discharge may also be granted on compassionate or medical grounds.

In addition to their basic training, non-commissioned personnel receive supplementary specialist training throughout their careers. Study for educational qualifications is encouraged, and service trade and technical training leads to nationally recognised qualifications. New vocational training and educational initiatives to improve recruitment and retention were announced in the SDR. The Army Foundation College offers a 42-week course combining military training and the opportunity to acquire national qualifications. The course is intended to attract high-quality recruits who will go on to fill senior posts in front-line roles.

Table 8.1: Strength of Service and Civilian Personnel, April 2001

Royal Navy	42,900
Army	114,000
RAF	54,000
Regular reserves	234,700
Volunteer reserves	47,300
Civilians	111,700
UK-based	*98,400*
Locally based	*13,300*

Source: Defence Analytical Services Agency

Reserve Forces

The Reserve Forces serve alongside the regular forces and are integral to the ability to expand the services in times of crises. For example, under the current commitment, around 10% of UK forces in Bosnia are reservists at any one time. In particular, reserves can provide skills and units not available or required in peacetime. The reserves include former members of the regular armed forces liable for service in an emergency (regular reserve) and volunteer reserves, recruited directly from the civilian community—the Royal Naval Reserve, the Royal Marines Reserve, the TA and the Reserve Air Forces (which comprise the Royal Auxiliary Air Force and the Royal Air Force Reserve).

The main contribution of reserves—both individuals and formed units—is to support regular forces in clearly identifiable and worthwhile roles. This requires their full integration into regular formations and ready availability for service, where necessary through selective compulsory call-out during situations short of a direct threat to the UK. Reserves should also be able to serve in peace support operations. A Reserve Training Mobilisation Centre at Chilwell near Nottingham has been set up for this purpose. Under the SDR, Royal Naval and RAF volunteer reserve numbers will increase, and, while the strength of the TA has been reduced from 56,000 to 41,200, it is more closely integrated with the Regular Army, with greater emphasis on combat support.

ADMINISTRATION

The Defence Budget

The defence budget for 2001–02 is £23.8 billion, rising to £24.2 billion in 2002–03 and £25.4 billion in 2003–04. The Ministry of Defence believes these increases will allow it to build on the measures outlined in the SDR, while also taking into account the lessons learned from recent operations and other

o: Wig

Festivals, Boards and Blades

Texting Socialising Piercing

Apex Photo Agency Ltd

Apex Photo Agency Ltd

britainonview.com

PA Photos

Fast Forward is a National Voluntary Organisation based in Edinburgh. Since 1987 it has been working with young people in schools, youth work and residential settings, and with parents and professionals, focusing on the prevention of drug, alcohol and tobacco misuse.

Thirty young volunteers aged between 16 and 25 are involved at every level of the organisation. They are trained in relevant interpersonal skills, as well as gaining knowledge of legal and illegal drugs and their side effects. Many volunteers attend national conferences on relevant topics.

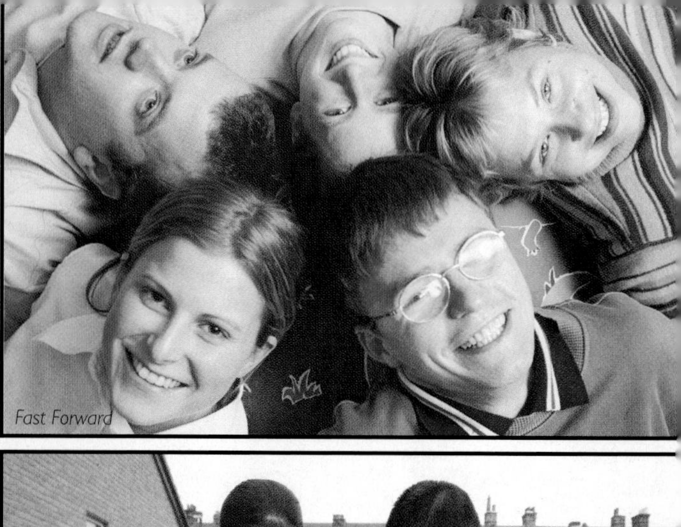

Fast Forward

Volunteers in The Community

Jane Alexander/BTCV (both)

In 1970 **BTCV** (founded as the British Trust for Conservation Voluntee was established as an independent organisation to involve volunteers practical conservation work. It is now active throughout the UK an abroad. The Trust offers a wide variety of activities in both urban and rural environments and works with communities to help impro their surroundings. It also arranges conservation holidays and employment programmes for people wishing to develop a career in environmental work.

Above: Volunteers working in a garden at Newham Sixth Form Colle in London, built for (and by) people with special needs.
Left: Volunteers clearing some of the reeds around Sanderstead Pon near Croydon, in Surrey.

At the Cefn Golau Family Centre in Tredegar, South Wales, young people aged 15 to 19 are taught to recondition unroadworthy motorbikes. This is part of the NCH (founded as National Childrens Homes) **'Youthbike Scheme'**, which is funded by a Millennium Volunteers grant of £3,000. Through this scheme, up to a dozen young people will be helped to obtain a qualification in motorcycle mechanic skills.

The Millennium Volunteer Grant Scheme was set up in 1999 by the Government to encourage young people to develop personally through projects which make an impact on their community. Grants of up to £5,000 are available to help support Millennium volunteer programmes and are awarded every three months.

Photo: Gareth Morgan

priorities such as accommodation and the retention of personnel.

Defence Management

The Ministry of Defence is both a Department of State and the highest-level military headquarters. The Secretary of State for Defence is responsible for the formulation and conduct of defence policy and for providing the means by which it is conducted. Three junior ministers support the Secretary of State and have responsibilities for operational and policy issues for all armed services; defence equipment procurement, equipment collaboration and research; and defence estate, environmental and public services respectively.

Ministers are in turn supported by two key officials: the Chief of the Defence Staff (CDS) and the Permanent Secretary. The CDS is the professional head of the armed forces and the principal military adviser to the Secretary of State and the Government. The Permanent Secretary is the Government's principal civilian adviser on defence and has primary responsibility for policy, finance and administration of the department. The Permanent Secretary is also personally accountable to Parliament for the expenditure of all public money voted for defence purposes.

A number of senior-level committees underpin the management of defence:

- the Defence Council, the highest departmental committee with a range of statutory and prerogative powers vested in it. Chaired by the Secretary of State, it provides the formal legal basis for the conduct of defence;
- the Defence Management Board, which provides senior-level leadership and strategic management of defence and is chaired mainly by the Permanent Secretary; and
- the Chiefs of Staff Committee, chaired by the CDS and the forum in which collective military advice is given to the Secretary of State and the Government.

An integrated civilian and military staff support ministers, senior officials and top-level committees in the day-to-day management of defence. The department is divided into a number of budget areas responsible for the major functions of the Ministry. These include the operational and personnel arms of each service; the Defence Logistics Organisation; and the Defence Procurement Agency, which is responsible for the acquisition and support of defence equipment. A large proportion of the Ministry of Defence's support activities is undertaken by defence agencies (see p. 540).

Further Reading

The Strategic Defence Review: Modern Forces for the Modern World. Cm 3999. Ministry of Defence. The Stationery Office, 1998.

Defence Policy 2001. Ministry of Defence. The Stationery Office, 2001.

The Future Strategic Context for Defence. Ministry of Defence. The Stationery Office, 2001.

The Government's Expenditure Plans 2001/2002 to 2002/2003 and Main Estimates 2001/2002. Cm 5109. Ministry of Defence. The Stationery Office, 2001.

Performance Report 1999/2000. Cm 5000. Ministry of Defence. The Stationery Office, 2000.

Websites

Ministry of Defence: www.mod.uk

NATO: www.nato.int

9 The Social Framework

Population Profile	108	National Identity and Ethnic Groups	114
Households and Families	109	Economic Changes	117
Migration	111	Social Trends	119

The structure of the UK population is changing, with increases in life expectancy and lower fertility rates leading to an ageing population. Family life is more diverse—although the majority of men and women still get married, marriage has declined and cohabitation has increased while the proportion of people living alone has also risen. Women have contributed heavily to the growth of the labour force. Technological change has been rapid and telephone, radio, television and the Internet have all transformed communications.

POPULATION PROFILE

The population of the UK in mid-2000 was estimated to be 59.8 million, the second largest in the European Union (EU) and the 20th largest in the world. Projections, based on an analysis of recent demographic trends, suggest that population growth in the UK will continue until it peaks at nearly 65 million people in 2036, before gradually declining.

In mid-2000, 50.0 million people lived in England (about 84% of the UK population). Northern Ireland had the smallest population of the four countries, at 1.7 million (3%). The population density in England was the highest, with about 383 inhabitants per square kilometre.

The ten-year Census of Population was held on 29 April 2001 (see pp. 34–6).

Age and Gender

The UK has an ageing population. The proportion of the population aged 65 and over increased from one person in 20 in 1901 to just over one in six in 2000. Projections suggest that this trend will continue so that by 2016 it is expected that the number of people aged 65 and over will exceed those under the age of 16.

Although more boys are born each year than girls, in 2000 there were about 838,000 more women in the UK than men. Men outnumbered women in the younger age groups, until around the age of 50 when the numbers of men and women were about equal. Above this age women increasingly outnumbered men. This reflects the longer life expectancy of women. In 1999 the expectation of life at birth was 75 years for males and just under 80 years for females. However, life expectancy has been increasing faster for males than females—about two years every decade for males and one-and-a-half years for females.

Births and Deaths

The annual number of births in the UK peaked following both of the World Wars. The highest number of births in any year of the 20th century was 1.1 million in 1920, shortly after the end of the First World War. A lower peak of 1.0 million was reached after the Second World War and the most recent peak was in 1964. The number of births has been relatively stable since 1984 and in 2000 there were 679,000 live births in the UK, representing 11.4 live births per 1,000 population.

Although the number of deaths in the UK remained relatively constant throughout the 20th century, this masks large declines in mortality rates. There were nearly 611,000 deaths registered in 2000, a death rate of 10.3 per 1,000 population. Infant and childhood mortality declined considerably during the 20th century, while in recent years the death rates among older people have also fallen. Rising standards of living and developments in medical technology help to explain the decline in mortality rates. The infant mortality rate (deaths of infants under one year old per 1,000 live births) was 6.1 for boys and 5.1 for girls in 2000. In general, in all age groups, death rates are higher for males than females, and this helps to explain the gender imbalance among the older population.

Changes in the causes of death have accompanied this improvement in mortality. Sharp peaks in mortality occurred around the First World War, when deaths were mainly due to respiratory and infectious diseases. Such diseases now account for a relatively small proportion of all deaths. They have been overtaken by causes such as cancer and circulatory diseases which are much less responsive to modern preventive and curative medicine and whose incidence is concentrated at older ages.

HOUSEHOLDS AND FAMILIES

The number of households in Great Britain rose by almost half between 1961 and 1999, from 16.3 million to 24.1 million. Over the same period the population increased by 13% and the average household size fell from 3.1 to 2.4 people per household. If recent trends continue, official projections in England suggest that household size will continue to decline to 2.2 in 2021.

Household composition has been transformed in recent decades. Although most people still live in a couple household, an increasing proportion of people are living on

Table 9.1: Households by Type of Household and Family, Great Britain *Per cent*

	1961	1981	1991	2000
One person				
Under pensionable age	4	8	11	14
Over pensionable age	7	14	16	15
Two or more unrelated adults	5	5	3	3
One-family households[1]				
Couple				
No children	26	26	28	29
1–2 dependent children[2]	30	25	20	19
3 or more dependent children[2]	8	6	5	4
Non-dependent children only	10	8	8	6
Lone parent				
Dependent children[2]	2	5	6	6
Non-dependent children only	4	4	4	3
Multi-family households	3	1	2	1
All households (millions)	**16.3**	**20.2**	**22.4**	**n.a.**

[1] Other individuals who were not family members may also be included.

[2] May also include non-dependent children.

Sources: Office for National Statistics, Department for Transport, Local Government and the Regions, National Assembly for Wales and Scottish Executive

their own. In spring 2000 almost three in ten households in Great Britain comprised one person living alone, which was two-and-a-half times the proportion in 1961. During the 1970s and 1980s there was emphasis on the provision of first public, and then private, housing which enabled households to occupy separate accommodation. There is also evidence that lone parents, who historically were more likely than other families to live in multi-family households, increasingly became one-family households during the period. Households containing a lone parent family living on their own formed one in 17 of all households in 1961, but one in 11 in 2000.

Cohabitation, Marriage and Divorce

The pattern of partnership formation has changed since the mid-1970s. Although the majority of men and women still get married, the proportion who marry has been declining and the proportions who cohabit or live outside a relationship have increased. It was estimated that there were just over 1.5 million cohabiting couples in England and Wales in 1996—representing about one in six of the adult non-married population; the number of cohabiting couples is projected to double by 2021.

Some people never marry and this proportion has also increased over the last few decades. Among people born in the 1940s, 4% of men and 8% of women had neither married nor been in a cohabiting relationship by the time they were 50. If current trends continue, official projections suggest that this will be the case for over 10% of women and 16% of men born in the 1960s.

In 1999 there were 301,000 marriages in the UK, one of the lowest numbers in the 20th century. Of the marriages that took place in 1999, 179,000 were first marriages for both partners, less than half the number in the peak year of 1970. First marriages accounted for 83% of all marriages in 1970 but only 59% in 1999. In 1970 the average age at first marriage

Figure 9.2: Marriages and Divorces, UK

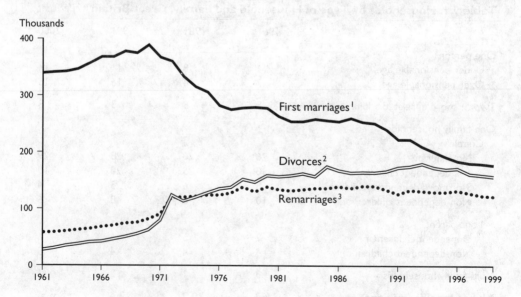

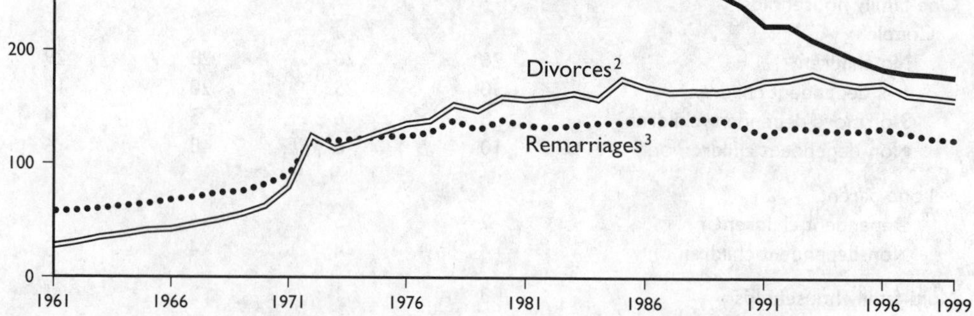

[1] For both partners.
[2] Includes annulments.
[3] For one or both partners.

Source: Office for National Statistics; General Register Office for Scotland; Northern Ireland Statistics and Research Agency

for both partners in England and Wales was 24 for men and 22 for women; by 1999 this had risen to 29 and 27 respectively.

Although there was a long-term rise in the number of divorces in the UK each year, the number has recently been declining. Around 155,000 divorces were granted in 2000—14% below the peak in 1993. The divorce rate in England and Wales similarly peaked in 1993, at 14.2 per 1,000 married people, and has since fallen slightly. Provisional figures suggest that the rate in 2000 was 12.7 per 1,000 married people, the lowest since 1984.

Family Formation

In general, fertility rates for older women have increased since the early 1980s while those for younger women have declined. Women in their late twenties still have the highest fertility rates, although the rate continued to fall in 2000 when there were 96 births per 1,000 women aged 25 to 29 in England and Wales. The fertility rate for those aged 35 to 39 continued its slow but steady increase, nearly doubling between 1981 and 2000 to 41 births per 1,000 women in this age group, although it still remains lower than in 1961. Mothers giving birth are now on average nearly three years older than in the early 1970s—in 2000 the mean age of mothers at birth was 29.1 years, compared with 26.2 in 1972.

The average completed family size has fallen from a recent peak of 2.4 children per woman born in the mid-1930s and is projected to fall below two children per woman for women born around 1960. Throughout the 1980s and 1990s fertility fell below the level needed for long-term natural replacement of the population. Average completed family size is expected to continue declining and eventually level off for women born after 1970 at 1.8 children per woman.

Not all couples have children and the proportion of women remaining childless has risen. About 16% of women born in 1924 were childless by the age of 45. It is projected that over 20% of women born in or after 1965 will remain childless.

Most children are born to married couples but an increasing proportion of births occur outside marriage. Almost two-fifths of all births in the United Kingdom in 2000 occurred outside marriage, around five times greater than in 1971. Much of this growth is accounted for by the increase in births to cohabiting couples. In 2000, 81% of all births outside marriage were jointly registered by both parents. For just over three-quarters of these—62% of all births outside marriage—the parents were living at the same address. The proportion of births outside marriage has always been higher for teenagers; in 2000, almost 90% of births to women under 20 occurred outside marriage. In the same year, 28% of births to teenagers were sole registrations compared with only 4% of births to women in their late thirties or early forties.

MIGRATION

Population movements occur both within the UK and internationally. The most mobile age-group within the UK is young adults in their twenties, when many young people leave their parental home to study, work or set up their own home. During the second half of the 20th century there was a movement of population from the coal, shipbuilding and steel industry areas in the north of England and Wales to the light industries and services of the south of England and the Midlands.

International Migration

During most of the 20th century the net natural change in the UK population (the difference between births and deaths) exceeded the effects of net migration and other changes. However, in recent years net inward migration has become an increasingly important determinator of population growth. Between 1991 and 1999 net natural change was almost matched by net migration and other changes. In 1999 an estimated 182,000 more people migrated to the UK than emigrated from the UK. This was the highest on record and nearly double the figures for 1997 (92,000) and for 1996 (93,000). The net gain of EU citizens in 1999 was 7,000; this was just a quarter of the number in the previous year.

Immigration into the UK is largely governed by the Immigration Act 1971 and the Immigration Rules made under it. The Rules set out the requirements to be met by those who are subject to immigration control and seek entry to, or leave to remain in, the UK. The 1971 Act has been amended by subsequent legislation, including the Immigration and Asylum Act 1999. Most of the key provisions of the 1999 Act have already been implemented and the implementation of the remainder is continuing. The major provisions of the Act include:

- modernising immigration control with the aim of helping it to deal with increasing passenger traffic and make enforcement of the control more effective;
- introducing measures to tackle clandestine entry, including a new civil penalty for drivers of lorries and other vehicles found to contain clandestine entrants, and strengthening the carriers' liability regime;
- replacing the existing multiple rights of appeal with a single, comprehensive right of appeal;
- creating new arrangements to support asylum seekers who are considered to be in genuine need, involving a new national system, separate from the main benefits system. Accommodation is being provided on a 'no choice' basis, with other support generally being provided in kind;
- strengthening enforcement of the immigration control by extending powers of immigration officers, extending and strengthening the existing immigration offences of deception and facilitation, and extending fingerprint powers; and
- providing greater safeguards for those who are detained, including putting the management and operation of detention centres on a statutory footing.

In implementing the Act, priority has been given to the provisions relating to the new asylum support arrangements, and to the civil penalty for carrying clandestine entrants. The single, comprehensive right of appeal was introduced on 2 October 2000 to coincide with the implementation of the Human Rights Act 1998 (see p. 214). The 1999 Act also introduced changes to the Marriage Act 1949 which applies in England and Wales. These changes came into effect on 1 January 2001 and consist of:

- a common 15-day notice procedure (which may only be waived in exceptional circumstances on application to the Registrar-General);
- a requirement for both parties to a marriage to personally give notice of their intention to marry, including a declaration of their nationality; and
- powers for registration officers to request evidence of name, age, marital status and nationality from couples, underpinned by a power to refuse to give authority for the marriage when a registration officer is not satisfied that a person is free, legally, to contract the marriage.

The 1999 Act also places a duty on registration officers to report to the Home Office those marriages suspected of having been arranged for the purpose of evading immigration controls.

In 2000 some 125,000 people were accepted for settlement, 28,000 more than in 1999. When analysed by nationality there were substantial increases in acceptances from Africa (see Table 9.3). Africa, which accounted for 36% of total acceptances in 2000, was the leading region, followed by the rest of Asia, the Indian subcontinent and then Europe.

Under the Immigration Rules, nationals of certain specified countries or territorial entities must obtain a visa before they can enter the UK. Other nationals subject to immigration control require entry clearance when coming to work or settle in the UK. Visas and other entry clearances are normally obtained from the nearest or other specified British diplomatic post in a person's home country.

Nationals of the European Economic Area (EEA)—EU Member States plus Norway, Iceland and Liechtenstein—are not subject to substantive immigration control. They may work in the UK without restriction. Provided

Table 9.3: Acceptances for Settlement by Nationality

	1997	1998	1999	2000
Europe	7,740	7,570	15,990	15,110
Americas	7,790	10,780	8,520	11,520
Africa	13,200	16,090	27,020	44,460
Asia	25,610	30,120	40,090	47,540
of which:				
Indian subcontinent	*13,080*	*16,420*	*21,440*	*22,730*
Rest of Asia	*12,530*	*13,700*	*18,650*	*24,810*
Oceania	3,100	3,690	4,120	4,900
Other nationalities[1]	1,280	1,540	1,380	1,560
All nationalities	**58,720**	**69,790**	**97,120**	**125,090**

[1] Includes refugees from South-East Asia.
Source: Home Office

they are working or able to support themselves financially, EEA nationals have a right to reside in the UK.

Asylum

The UK has a tradition of granting protection to those in need, and is a signatory to the 1951 United Nations Convention, and its 1967 Protocol, relating to the Status of Refugees. These provide that refugees lawfully resident should enjoy treatment at least as favourable as that accorded to the indigenous population. In the late 1980s applications for asylum (based on the principal applicant) started to rise dramatically from around 4,000 a year during 1985 to 1988 to 44,800 in 1991, and reached a record 80,300 in 2000 (provisional data). The main nationalities applying for asylum in the UK in 2000 were people from Iraq (9%), Sri Lanka (8%), the Federal Republic of Yugoslavia (8%), Afghanistan (7%) and Iran (7%). In the first six months of 2001, applications for asylum averaged 5,550 a month. This was 15% lower than in the same period a year earlier. Between January and June 2001 an average of 720 applications a month were received from people from Afghanistan; an average of 495 applications a month were from Iraq and 460 from Somalia.

An estimated 109,205 asylum decisions were made in 2000, more than three times the number in 1999, reflecting a drop in the backlog of cases. In 2000, 11% of these decisions were grants of asylum, less than a third of the proportion in 1999. A further 12% were grants of exceptional leave to remain. Many failed asylum seekers appeal against their refusal decision. Nearly 19,400 appeals were determined by independent adjudicators in 2000, of which 3,340 (17%) were successful.

In January 2001 the Home Office published research on the social and economic impacts of migration. Its key findings included:

- migrants experience mixed success in the labour market, but on average earn more than the existing population, contributing to economic growth;
- there is little evidence that migration damages the employment prospects of existing resident workers;
- migrants make significant cultural and social contributions to UK society, including the contributions of many notable figures in the arts, academia, medicine, science and sport; and
- reduced transport and transaction costs and increased economic integration, as a result of globalisation, have led to increased flows of people around the world in recent years, both to and from the UK.

On 3 April 2000 the National Asylum Support Service took over responsibility for the provision of support for those asylum seekers who are destitute. The new arrangements apply to those seeking asylum on or after this date. Support will be provided until the asylum claim is finally decided. Those granted refugee status or who are allowed to remain exceptionally on humanitarian grounds are entitled to claim public funds.

Support under the new system is provided principally in kind, with vouchers issued to enable asylum seekers to obtain essential living needs. Where accommodation is provided, this is on a 'no choice' basis and dispersal is throughout the UK. Legal advice for asylum seekers is available from immigration law advisers and firms of solicitors contracted to provide immigration services under the Community Legal Services Fund (formerly the Legal Aid scheme). They will provide advice on the initial claim and any appeal.

NATIONAL IDENTITY AND ETHNIC GROUPS

Citizenship

Under the British Nationality Act 1981 there are three main forms of citizenship:

- British citizenship for people closely connected with the UK;
- British Dependent Territories citizenship for people connected with the dependent territories (now commonly referred to as 'Overseas Territories'—see p. 79); and
- British Overseas citizenship for those citizens of the UK and Colonies who did not acquire either of the other citizenships when the 1981 Act came into force.

British citizenship is acquired automatically at birth by a child born in the UK if his or her mother or, if legitimate, father is a British citizen or is settled in the UK. A child adopted in the UK by a British citizen is also a British citizen. A child born abroad to a British citizen born, adopted, naturalised or registered in the UK is generally a British citizen by descent. The Act safeguards the citizenship of a child born abroad to a British citizen in Crown service, certain related services, or in service under an EU institution.

British citizenship may also be acquired:

- by registration for certain children, including those born in the UK who do not automatically acquire such citizenship at birth, or who have been born abroad to a parent who is a citizen by descent;
- by registration for British Dependent Territories citizens, British Overseas citizens, British subjects under the Act, British Nationals (Overseas) and British protected persons after five years' residence in the UK, except for people from Gibraltar who may be registered without residence;
- by registration for stateless people and those who have previously renounced British nationality;
- by registration for British Dependent Territories citizens connected with the Falkland Islands;
- by registration for certain women who are, or have previously been, married to men who served in the defence of Hong Kong during the Second World War;
- by registration for certain British nationals who are ordinarily resident in Hong Kong; and
- by naturalisation for all other adults aged 18 or over.

Naturalisation is at the Home Secretary's discretion. Requirements include five years' residence, or three years if the applicant's spouse is a British citizen. Those who are not married to a British citizen are also required to have a sufficient knowledge of English, Welsh or Scottish Gaelic; they must in addition intend to have their main home in the UK or be employed by the Crown, or by an international organisation of which the UK is a member, or by a company or association established in the UK.

In 2000 around 82,000 people were granted British citizenship in the UK, compared with 55,000 in 1999. Some 6,800 were refused in 2000, 2,900 more than in 1999. A little over one in four of all successful applications were from citizens of Indian subcontinent countries, with Africa accounting for a similar proportion and Europe about one in seven. The largest nationalities were Pakistan and India (10% each), and Bangladesh and Nigeria (7% each). Residence in the UK continued to be the most frequent basis on which persons were granted British citizenship in 2000, amounting to 45% of the total, while marriage to a British citizen accounted for 35%.

Ethnic Groups

For centuries people from overseas have settled in the UK, either to escape political or religious persecution or in search of better economic opportunities. The Irish have long formed a large section of the population. Jewish refugees who came to the UK towards the end of the 19th century and in the 1930s were followed by other European refugees after 1945. Substantial immigration from the Caribbean and Indian subcontinent dates principally from the 1950s and 1960s, when the Government encouraged immigration as a means of addressing labour shortages, while many people of South Asian descent entered the UK as refugees from Kenya, Malawi or Uganda in the 1960s and 1970s.

An analysis of the Labour Force Survey by the Office for National Statistics found that, on average between the spring 2000 and winter 2000–01 quarters, over 4 million people in Great Britain described themselves as belonging to an ethnic group other than 'White', about one person in 14. In general, minority ethnic groups tend to have a younger age profile than the White population, reflecting past immigration and fertility patterns.

In spring 2000 members of minority ethnic groups were heavily concentrated in the most populous areas of England, with relatively small numbers in Scotland, Wales and Northern Ireland. Over half lived in the South East of England. The highest concentration was in the London borough of Newham, where over 60% of the local population were not from the White group. There were also variations in the regional concentrations of particular ethnic groups. Nearly two-thirds of people from Black ethnic groups lived in

Figure 9.4: Grants of British Citizenship in the United Kingdom in 2000, by Previous Nationality

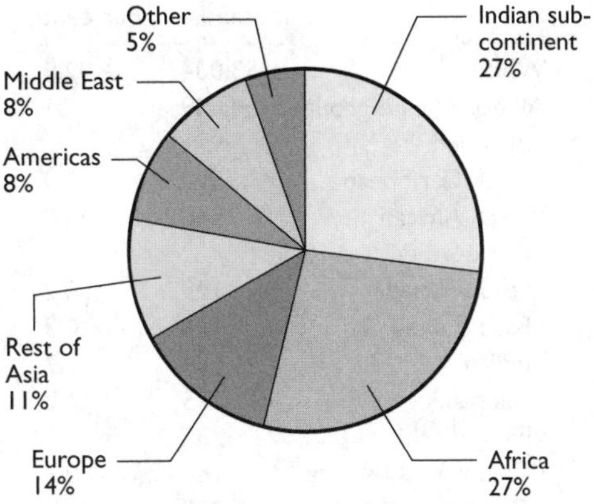

Source: Home Office

London, compared with over a third of Indians and about a sixth of Pakistanis. Outside London there were relatively high concentrations of Indians in Leicester, Wolverhampton and Birmingham, and relatively high concentrations of Pakistanis in Birmingham, Greater Manchester and West Yorkshire.

Alleviating Racial Disadvantage

Many members of the Black and Asian communities are concentrated in the inner cities, where there are problems of deprivation and social stress. Unemployment rates for some of these groups are well above the national average. For example, on average between spring 2000 and winter 2000–01, the unemployment rate was around 17% for both Black and Pakistani/Bangladeshi men, compared with 13% for White men and 8% for Indian men.

However, some progress has been made in tackling racial disadvantage over the last 20 years. For example, young people from some minority ethnic groups are leading the way for participation in education. In 2000–01, 86% of Indian, and 95% of Black, 16 year olds were in

Table 9.5: Resident Population by Ethnic Group, 2000–01,[1] Great Britain

	Number of people (thousands)	Per cent
White	53,004	92.9
All non-White groups	4,039	7.1
of which:		
Black Caribbean	529	0.9
Black African	440	0.8
Black Other (non-mixed)	129	0.2
Black Mixed	176	0.3
Indian	984	1.7
Pakistani	675	1.2
Bangladeshi	257	0.5
Chinese	149	0.3
Other groups	700	1.2
All groups[2]	**57,057**	**100.0**

[1] Four-quarter average of spring (March to May) 2000 to winter (December to February) 2000–01 quarters. Population in private households only.
[2] Includes those who did not state their ethnic group.
Source: Office for National Statistics (Labour Force Survey)

full-time education, compared with 79% of their White counterparts.

Many individuals have achieved distinction in their careers and in public life, and the proportion of people from minority ethnic groups occupying professional and managerial positions is increasing. In July 2001 there were 12 Members of the House of Commons from minority ethnic groups.

The Home Office has overall responsibility within the Government for race equality policy and the legislation that is in place to help achieve that. Central and local government have economic, environmental, educational and health programmes that are intended to combat disadvantage. There are also special allocations that channel extra resources into specific projects including, for example, the provision of specialist teachers for children needing English language tuition. The Government promotes equal opportunities through training programmes, including provision for unemployed people who need training in English as a second language. The Northern Ireland Executive has established a unit to promote equality of opportunity and good relations between people of different ethnic backgrounds.

Race Relations Legislation

In Great Britain the Race Relations Act 1976, as amended by the Race Relations (Amendment) Act 2000, makes it unlawful for anybody to discriminate on grounds of race, colour, nationality (including citizenship), or ethnic or national origin (referred to as 'racial grounds'). The legislation applies to employment, training, education and the provision of goods and services. Legislation along similar lines to the 1976 Act was introduced in Northern Ireland in 1977.

The Race Relations (Amendment) Act imposed a statutory general duty on listed public authorities to have due regard in carrying out their functions to the need to eliminate unlawful discrimination and to promote equality of opportunity and good relations between people of different racial groups. Secondary legislation will detail specific actions which key public bodies need to take in order to comply with this duty. The Commission for Racial Equality (see below) will be issuing codes of practice for public bodies. The Northern Ireland Act 1998 similarly requires public authorities to have due regard to the desirability of promoting good relations between people of different ethnic backgrounds.

The Crime and Disorder Act 1998 created racially aggravated versions of a number of existing offences in England and Wales, including assault, criminal damage and harassment. These racially aggravated offences carry a higher maximum penalty. Other provisions in criminal law prohibit incitement to racial hatred and the publication or dissemination of materials that are likely to incite racial hatred.

Commission for Racial Equality

The Commission for Racial Equality (CRE), established by the 1976 Race Relations Act, is a publicly funded independent organisation working in Great Britain to tackle racial discrimination and promote racial equality. It also helps individuals with complaints about racial discrimination; in 2000 about 11,000 people approached the CRE for advice on such matters, and 1,553 applications for assistance were received. It has the power to investigate unlawful discriminatory practices and to issue non-discrimination notices requiring such practices to cease. It also has an important promotional and educational role and can undertake or fund research. In Northern Ireland equivalent responsibilities for tackling racial discrimination and promoting racial equality rest with the Equality Commission for Northern Ireland, which also covers other types of unlawful discrimination.

The CRE supports the work of nearly 100 racial equality councils. These are autonomous voluntary bodies set up across the UK to promote equality of opportunity and good race relations at local level. The Commission helps to pay the salaries of officers employed by the racial equality councils, most of which also receive funds from their relevant local authority.

ECONOMIC CHANGES

The trend in the UK's standard of living, using Gross Domestic Product (GDP) per head at constant market prices as an indicator, has generally been one of steady growth since 1971. However, within this long-term trend the UK is subject to cycles of weaker and stronger growth. The year-on-year growth rates for GDP in volume terms at constant prices suggest that the UK's economy contracted during the mid-1970s, at the time of the oil crisis, and again in the early 1980s and early 1990s. However, growth has exceeded 4% a year 11 times in the post-war period, most recently in 1994. The long-term average annual growth rate was 2.5% between 1948 and 2000.

GDP per head shows marked variations between the regions of the UK. In 1999, it was highest in London, at £16,900 per head (30% higher than the UK average). The South East and East were the only other regions above the UK average. The North East had the lowest regional GDP per head in 1999—£10,000—followed by Northern Ireland, at £10,100, and Wales at £10,400.

Income and Wealth

Real household disposable income per head doubled between 1971 and 2000. During the 1970s and early 1980s growth fluctuated, and there were some year-on-year falls. Since then, there has been growth each year with the exception of 1998 when there was a slight fall. The gap between those on high and low disposable incomes grew rapidly during the second half of the 1980s, and then fell slightly in the first half of the 1990s, although this only reversed a small part of the rise seen in the previous decade. The latest figures show that the gap rose again in the late 1990s.

The spread of income distribution is uneven. Individuals living in lone parent families are more than twice as likely as the average individual to be in the bottom fifth of the income distribution. Pensioners are also over-represented in the bottom two-fifths. In 1999–2000, over 40% of individuals living in lone parent families were in the bottom fifth of the income distribution and around half of pensioners were in the bottom two-fifths. Children are also disproportionately present in low-income households. In 1999–2000, 23% of children—around 3 million—were living in households below 60% of median income (before housing costs) in Great Britain.

Wages and salaries remain the main source of household income for most households, although the proportion they contribute has declined, from 59% in 1987 to 56% in 1999. The main sources of household income differ considerably in their importance between different types of household. The largest source of income for pensioners is social security benefits. In 1999–2000 benefits accounted for 56% of the income of a single pensioner under the age of 75 and 68% of the income of a single pensioner over that age. Students, on the other hand, received 24% of their income from student loans in 1998–99, 16% from parental contributions, 14% from grants, 12% from earnings and the rest from a variety of sources such as gifts, overdrafts and withdrawal of savings.

The tax and benefit system redistributes income from households on high incomes to those on lower incomes. Households make payments through direct and indirect taxes, and social security contributions, while benefits are received through both cash payments and provision of benefits in-kind, such as the National Health Service. Households with high incomes tend to pay more in taxes than they receive in benefits, while those on low incomes benefit more than they are taxed. The average original income of the top fifth of households in 1999–2000—£54,400—was 19 times the average of the bottom fifth—£2,800. Benefits and, to a lesser extent, taxes reduce this inequality so that the ratio for final income is four to one. The types of household that tend to be net beneficiaries from the redistribution of taxes and benefits include lone parent families, families with three or more children, and retired households. Wealth continues to be much more unequally distributed than income, with the most wealthy 10% of the adult population owning 56% of the total marketable wealth of the household sector in 1998.

Social Exclusion

Social exclusion is the term given to what can happen when individuals or areas suffer from a combination of linked problems, such as unemployment, poor skills, low incomes, poor housing, high crime environments, bad health and family breakdown. A Social Exclusion Unit (SEU) was set up in the Cabinet Office in 1997 to coordinate and improve government action to reduce social exclusion in England. It looks at issues that involve a range of government departments. There is close liaison with the Scottish, Welsh and Northern Ireland devolved administrations which have their own strategies for tackling social exclusion. The Social Exclusion Unit has produced reports on five main areas which have led to new policies on truancy and school exclusion, rough sleeping, a national strategy for neighbourhood renewal, teenage pregnancy and 16 to 18 year olds not in employment, education or training. The Government's approach is intended to prevent people from becoming socially excluded, to help people to get back on their feet if they have become excluded, and to ensure that there is a necessary framework of minimum standards in areas including health, education, employment, in-work income and in tackling crime.

The SEU's current projects are:

- Young runaways—a report published by the SEU in March 2001 suggests that by the age of 16 one in nine school-age children in England will run away for at least one night; a quarter of those who run away sleep on the streets and one in 14 survive through begging, stealing, drug dealing and prostitution; 80% of young people run away because of family problems.
- Children in care and education—in England, those who have been children in care are over-represented among rough sleepers, prisoners and runaways. In 1997, 75% of children in care left school with no formal qualifications. Children in care are ten times more likely to be excluded from school; a quarter of all prisoners and up to a third of rough sleepers have been in care; and children in care are two-and-a-half times more likely to become teenage parents.
- Transport and social exclusion—two-thirds of the poorest fifth of the population in the UK have no car and depend on public transport. If public transport is unavailable or does not meet their needs this can be a barrier to inclusion. The SEU is working with other government departments to analyse the nature of the transport barriers that make it difficult for people to get to work, or to access critical services, including healthcare, learning and shops.
- Reducing reoffending by ex-prisoners—the SEU is working with other government departments to cut rates of re-offending by ex-prisoners, in particular by boosting levels of employment and reducing homelessness. Poor literacy and numeracy skills mean that 90% of those leaving prison do so without any immediate prospect of employment, while two-fifths will be homeless.

Neighbourhood Renewal

The Neighbourhood Renewal National Strategy Action Plan sets out how the

Government is responding to problems such as unemployment, educational failure and crime in England's most deprived communities.

The aim is to narrow the gap between deprived areas and the rest of the country, so that within 10 to 20 years no one should be seriously disadvantaged by where they live. The specific objectives are to ensure:

- economic prosperity;
- safe communities;
- high-quality schools;
- decent housing; and
- better health.

The emphasis is on attacking the core problems of deprived areas, such as weak economies and poor schools; harnessing the power of all sectors to work in partnership; and focusing existing programmes more explicitly on these areas.

By 2004, annual expenditure will be increased by: £10 billion on education; £1.6 billion on the police; and £1.6 billion on housing. This additional funding is underpinned by minimum targets which mean that, for the first time, government departments will be judged on the areas where they are doing worst, and not on the national average. In 2001 a new Neighbourhood Renewal Unit in the Department for Transport, Local Government and the Regions took over the leadership of the Neighbourhood Renewal National Strategy from the Social Exclusion Unit.

> One of the priorities of the National Strategy is to get better information about neighbourhoods in order to provide evidence of the problems they face, to assess need, and to monitor progress. The Office for National Statistics is leading the development of a new Internet-based service—the Neighbourhood Statistics Service (*www.statistics.gov.uk/neighbourhood*)—which has the aim of meeting these information needs. It will be developed over several years in partnership with the many organisations that collect the kind of data that can inform the National Strategy for Neighbourhood Renewal. The information will come from making better use of existing administrative data and from developing methodologies and estimates to meet other requirements.

SOCIAL TRENDS

Women and Men

Employment and Income

The economic and domestic lives of women have changed considerably in the last 30 years and women have taken an increasingly important role in the labour market. According to the 1971 Census, 91% of men of working age, compared with 56% of women, were economically active in the UK. By spring 2001 the rate for women had increased to 72% of women of working age, while the rate for men had declined to 84%. The number of women in the UK labour force increased from 10 million in 1971 to nearly 13 million in spring 2001; projections indicate that the number will rise by 1.1 million between 1999 and 2011. The increase in the female labour force came mainly from a strong rise in the participation of married women. By spring 2001, 75% of married or cohabiting women were economically active. The likelihood of being economically active varies considerably according to whether or not they have dependent children; activity rates are lowest for those with a child under the age of five, at 57%.

Despite the growth in female employment in recent years, women and men still tend to work in different occupations and pay rates are considerably lower in sectors dominated by women. In spring 2001 women employees outnumbered men in clerical and secretarial occupations by four to one, while there were more than twice as many men as women managers and senior officials. Around 41% of male employees and 29% of female employees had some form of managerial or supervisory responsibility in spring 2001.

The average individual income of men was higher than that of women in all age bands in 1999–2000, largely because of their higher levels of earnings, self-employment income and their longer hours of working. Gross income varied across age bands and was

Figure 9.6: Median Individual Income by Age Band, for All Women and All Men, 1999–2000, Great Britain

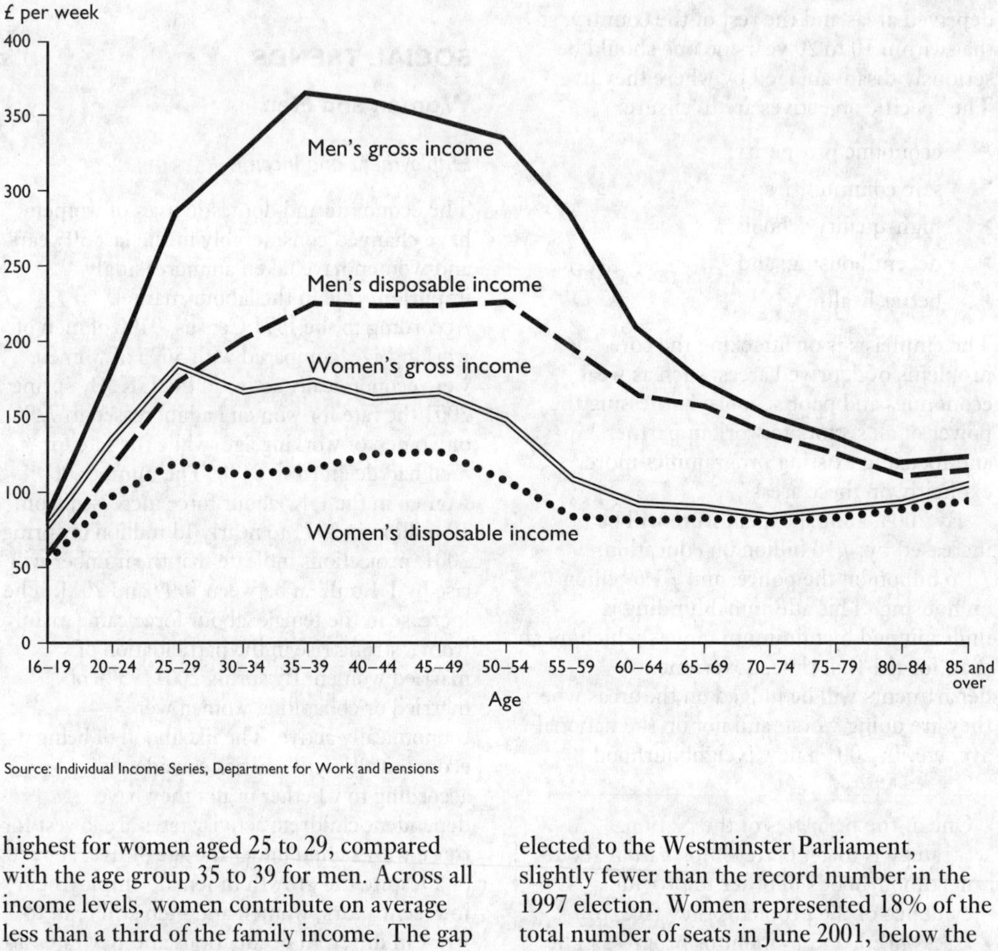

Source: Individual Income Series, Department for Work and Pensions

highest for women aged 25 to 29, compared with the age group 35 to 39 for men. Across all income levels, women contribute on average less than a third of the family income. The gap between male and female earnings has been closing but the differential remains, with female full-time employees earning around 82% of the corresponding male hourly rate in April 2000. However, the difference in weekly earnings was even greater—women only earned 75% of men's weekly earnings—because men tend to work longer hours than women, and are more likely than women to receive overtime payments.

Public Policy

In the June 2001 General Election, 118 women Members of Parliament (MPs) were elected to the Westminster Parliament, slightly fewer than the record number in the 1997 election. Women represented 18% of the total number of seats in June 2001, below the EU average of 25% for lower houses. Women account for 37% of the Members of the Scottish Parliament, 42% of the Welsh Assembly and 14% of the members of the Legislative Assembly in Northern Ireland. In July 2001 seven women sat in the UK Cabinet.

Ministerial responsibility for women's issues changed following the 2001 General Election. There is a separate Minister for Women, who reports to a Cabinet minister with responsibility for this subject among her other duties, but the Minister for Women now has responsibility for coordinating a wider range of gender equality issues, including sexual orientation. She chairs the Cabinet Committee on Equality and has day-to-day responsibility for the Women and Equality Unit (formerly the Women's Unit) in the Cabinet Office, which remains the sponsor department for the Women's National Commission—an advisory committee ensuring that women's views are heard and considered by government.

In Scotland, four out of 11 Cabinet ministers are women and the Scottish Executive has established an Equality Unit to take forward its work in this area. The Northern Ireland Executive has established a Gender Policy Unit whose remit covers the promotion of equality between men and women, people of different sexual orientation, people with and without dependants and people of different marital status.

The Government is working to ensure that the perspective of women is automatically taken into account in the development of government policies. It is also encouraging the development of 'family-friendly' employment policies and practices (see chapter 11).

Equal Opportunities

The Sex Discrimination Act 1975 makes discrimination between men and women unlawful, with certain limited exceptions, in employment, education, training and the provision of housing, goods, facilities and services, and protects complainants and their supporters from victimisation. Discrimination against married people and discriminatory job recruitment advertisements are also unlawful. Under the Equal Pay Act 1970, women in Great Britain are entitled to equal pay with men when doing work that is the same or broadly similar, work which is rated as equivalent, or work which is of equal value. Parallel legislation on sex discrimination and equal pay applies in Northern Ireland.

The Equal Opportunities Commission (EOC), an independent statutory body, has the duties of working towards the elimination of sex discrimination; promoting equality of opportunity between women and men; promoting equality of opportunity in the fields of employment and vocational training for people who intend to undergo, are undergoing or who have undergone gender reassignment; and keeping under review the working of, and proposing amendments to, the Sex Discrimination Act and the Equal Pay Act. It provides advice to individuals and in some cases provides legal representation for individuals to bring sex discrimination and equal pay claims. The EOC runs an 'Equality Exchange', with around 800 members, which enables employers to exchange information on good practice. In Northern Ireland equivalent responsibilities for tackling discrimination and promoting gender equality rest with the Equality Commission for Northern Ireland. The remit of this Commission also includes race, religious and political beliefs, age, marital status, sexual orientation, disability and people with dependants.

Further details of the Government's equal opportunities policies may be found in chapter 6, p. 66.

The Voluntary and Community Sector

Across the UK there are many thousands of voluntary and community organisations, ranging from national bodies to small local groups. Serving the community through volunteering and more informal involvement is a long-established tradition. One in five adults interviewed in the 1998 British Social Attitudes Survey said that they had taken part in unpaid charitable work in the previous year. Many volunteers are involved in activities which improve the quality of life in their local communities, or give their time to help organise events or groups in areas as diverse as social welfare, education, sport, heritage, the environment and the arts.

The Government is keen to encourage productive partnerships between the statutory and voluntary and community sectors and also wants to see a greater public involvement in community life. It funds a number of initiatives to support this aim. It is particularly keen to encourage more involvement by younger people, older people and employees, and to work with voluntary organisations to improve the delivery of public services. In January 2001 the Government announced an additional £300 million in funding to support voluntary and community activity over the

Table 9.7: Income and Expenditure of the Top[1] Fund-raising Charities, UK, 1998–99 *£ million*

	Voluntary income	Total income	Total expenditure
Oxfam	106	170	155
National Trust[2]	100	221	190
Imperial Cancer Research Fund	96	118	102
Cancer Research Campaign[3]	80	89	88
Royal National Lifeboat Institution	79	94	60
British Heart Foundation	78	88	93
Salvation Army[2]	69	86	79
Help the Aged	60	67	63
Diana Princess of Wales Memorial Fund[4]	59	97	20
Barnardo's	59	110	125

[1] Ranked by voluntary income.
[2] Figure not confirmed by charity.
[3] Now merged with North of England Cancer Research Campaign.
[4] Accounts are for the period of 15 months.
Source: Charities Aid Foundation

next three years. In July 2001 it also announced that the Cabinet Office Performance and Innovation Unit would carry out a review of voluntary sector law and regulation, with the intention of bringing forward proposals for reform.

Charities

The Charity Commission for England and Wales, a non-ministerial government department, is responsible for the registration, monitoring and support of organisations that are charitable in law. The Commission does not make grants. There are over 185,000 charities in England and Wales sharing a combined annual income of over £24 billion. The financial wealth of registered charities, measured by annual income, is concentrated in a few very large charities. The Commission gives advice to trustees of charities on their administration, and has a statutory responsibility to ensure that charities make effective use of their resources. Recent legislation has strengthened the Commissioners' powers to investigate and supervise charities. These include measures to protect charities and donors from bogus fund-raisers and a new framework for charity accounts and reports. In the reporting period from January 1999 to March 2000, 8,300 applications were received for registration from organisations, of which 5,400 were accepted and placed on the Public Register of Charities. As part of the duty to investigate allegations of abuse or maladministration and evaluate them for cause for concern, 1,300 evaluations were carried out in the 12 months to March 2000. Where these show a cause for concern, a formal inquiry is opened—255 formal inquiries were completed in the year.

Funding

Voluntary organisations may receive income from several sources, including:

- central and local government grants;
- contributions from individuals, businesses and trusts;
- earnings from commercial activities and investments; and
- fees from central and local government for services provided on a contractual basis.

The introduction of the National Lottery (see p. 123) has given charities and voluntary organisations the opportunity to secure substantial new funding for projects across a range of activities.

CAF (Charities Aid Foundation) is a registered charity that works to increase resources for the voluntary sector in the UK and overseas. As well as providing services that are both charitable and financial, CAF undertakes a comprehensive programme of research, and is established as a leading source of information on all aspects of the sector.

Another valuable source of revenue for charities is through tax relief and tax exemptions. The Gift Aid scheme provides tax relief on one-off and regular cash donations of any amount, while under the Payroll Giving scheme, employees and those drawing a company pension can make tax-free donations from their earnings. In addition, gifts of quoted stocks and shares are free of capital gains tax and can be offset against income.

National Lottery

National lotteries have existed in Britain intermittently since 1569. The National Lottery, launched in 1994, currently comprises a twice weekly draw, a weekly draw and scratchcard games.

Tickets or scratchcards are available from around 36,000 retail outlets. Camelot Group plc, the current private sector consortium operating the Lottery, has been awarded a new seven-year licence, which will start on 27 January 2002. In the 1999–2000 Family Expenditure Survey, 53% of households reported participating in the Saturday or Wednesday night Lottery draws during the two-week diary-keeping period following interview. Those households that played spent an average of £4.00 a week on the Lottery. In 1999 the British Gambling Prevalence Survey was carried out by the National Centre for Social Research. Overall, 68% of men and 62% of women said that they had participated in the National Lottery Draw in the previous year and 22% of both men and women said that they had bought scratchcards.

Of every pound spent on the National Lottery, an average of around 28 pence goes to good causes. By the end of June 2001 some £11.0 billion, including interest, had been raised for good causes and over 92,000 awards totalling £9.4 billion had been made. By October 2001 the amount raised for good causes is expected to have reached at least £11.6 billion, around £2.6 billion more than originally forecast. Almost three-quarters of the awards have been for less than £50,000. The average size of a lottery grant is now £49,000, down from a peak of more than £250,000 in 1995–96. Lottery money is shared among several areas—health, education, environment, arts, sport, heritage and charities.

The National Lottery Commission regulates the Lottery. It is headed by five commissioners and its duties are to protect players' interests, to ensure the Lottery is run with propriety, and—subject to satisfying those two criteria—to maximise the amount raised for good causes. Its functions include selecting the Lottery operator, setting the terms of its licence and ensuring that it complies with those terms; vetting individuals and companies associated with the National Lottery to ensure they are 'fit and proper'; licensing individual games that form part of the National Lottery; and ensuring that the operator pays the right amount of money to the good causes.

Leisure Trends

The most common leisure activities are home-based, or social, such as visiting relatives or friends. Television viewing is by far the most popular leisure pastime, with average viewing time for all people aged four and over being around 24 hours a week for males and around 27 hours for females. In a poll in September 2000 by the British Film Institute the all-time favourite British television programme was *Fawlty Towers* which ran for two series made in 1975 and 1979. It has been shown again on several occasions and also sold to over 70 countries. Nearly all households have one television set or more, and almost nine in ten have a video recorder. In 1999–2000, 32% of households had satellite television.

Despite the increasing number of television channels in recent years, the proportion of people listening to the radio has remained fairly stable, with about nine in ten adults reporting listening in the four weeks prior to interview. The average amount of time spent listening to the radio in 1999 for people aged four and over was around 20 hours for males and 18 hours for females. Purchases of compact discs (CDs) have risen rapidly, and 72% of households had a CD player in 1999–2000.

Other popular pursuits include reading, do-it-yourself home improvements, gardening and going out for a meal, for a drink or to the cinema. Taking part in sporting activities remains a popular way of spending leisure time. Around two-fifths of adults said that they had been walking or rambling for 2 miles or more in the four weeks prior to interview in the General Household Survey and the Continuous Household Survey. Football is the most common team sport among men—10% had played in the previous four weeks.

Results from the 1998–2000 National Travel Survey show that men in Great Britain travelled, on average, 9,200 miles a year, making an average of 1,087 trips a year. Women made a similar number of trips (1,048) but travelled far less distance (6,213 miles a year). Part of this difference is related to the different types of trips that men and women make. Travel to work trips account for a high proportion of men's trips, while shorter trips, such as shopping and escorting children to school, account for a higher proportion of women's trips. Men also make more trips than women as a car driver—59% compared with 39%. More men than women have driving licences—82% compared with 60% respectively—and men are more often than women the main car driver in households with only one car. Car ownership increased steadily from three out of ten households in Great Britain in the early 1960s to seven out of ten households in 2000. Whereas the proportion of households with one car has changed little since the end of the 1960s, the proportion with two or more cars has grown from 2% in the early 1960s to 27% in 2000.

Technological Change

The rapid expansion of communication and technology has dramatically changed the way in which people in Britain live and work. The number of communication tools have increased as mobile telephones, e-mail and the Internet have become more affordable. Very few households are now without a home telephone, and mobile telephones have become increasingly popular. In 1999–2000, 95% of households in the UK had a home telephone and 44% had at least one mobile telephone. Some mobile telephones are now more than just a means of talking to someone as technological advances have allowed people to send and receive e-mail and access the Internet through them. The number of households owning home computers in the UK has almost tripled since 1985 to 38% in 1999–2000. In the first quarter of 2001, 9.2 million households could access the Internet from home. This amounts to 37% of all UK households and is just over three times the number two years earlier (see p. 286). Half of adults in Great Britain have accessed the Internet at some time, the equivalent of 23.0 million adults. Two-fifths of adults had accessed the Internet in the preceding month. Men were more likely to have ever used the Internet than women. The proportion steadily decreased with age—from 82% of all 16 to 24 year olds to 16% of those aged 65 and over. Although there is a range of technology available, virtually all those—98%—who used the Internet for personal use had done so mostly or exclusively using a computer. Among those who had accessed the Internet for personal use, three-quarters of adults had done so from their own home.

Holidays

Although the proportion of British residents who did not take a holiday of four days or more has remained relatively unchanged over the past three decades (41% in 1998), the proportion taking two or more holidays increased from 15% in 1971 to 25% in 1998. The number of holidays taken in Great Britain has been broadly stable over the last decade while the number taken abroad has grown. France overtook Spain as the most popular holiday destination abroad in 2000. The United States and Irish Republic were the next most popular destinations. Among adult residents of Great Britain who spent their holiday (of four nights or more) in Great

Britain in 1999, the West Country was by far the most popular destination, accounting for about a quarter of such holidays. The East of England and Scotland were the next most popular destinations.

Further Reading

Population Trends. Office for National Statistics. The Stationery Office.

Social Focus on Families. Office for National Statistics. The Stationery Office, 1997.

Social Focus on Men. Office for National Statistics. The Stationery Office, 2001.

Social Focus on Older People. Office for National Statistics. The Stationery Office, 1999.

Social Focus on Women and Men. Office for National Statistics and Equal Opportunities Commission. The Stationery Office, 1998.

Social Focus on Young People. Office for National Statistics. The Stationery Office, 2000.

Social Inequalities. Office for National Statistics. The Stationery Office, 2000.

Annual Reports

Annual Abstract of Statistics. Office for National Statistics. The Stationery Office.

British Social Attitudes. Ashgate Publishing.

Family Spending. Office for National Statistics. The Stationery Office.

Home Office Annual Report. Home Office. The Stationery Office.

International Migration. Office for National Statistics. The Stationery Office.

Living in Britain: Results from the General Household Survey. Office for National Statistics. The Stationery Office.

National Travel Survey Update. Department for Transport, Local Government and the Regions.

Social Trends. Office for National Statistics. The Stationery Office.

Travel Trends. Office for National Statistics. The Stationery Office.

Websites

Charity Commission: www.charity-commission.gov.uk

Commission for Racial Equality: www.cre.gov.uk

Equality Commission for Northern Ireland: www.equalityni.org

Equal Opportunities Commission: www.eoc.org.uk

Home Office: www.homeoffice.gov.uk

Office for National Statistics: www.statistics.gov.uk

Women and Equality Unit: www.womens-unit.gov.uk

10 Education and Training

Administrative Arrangements	126	Links with Other Countries	144
Schools	127	The Youth Service	145
Education and Training after 16	137		

Parents in the United Kingdom are required by law to see that their children receive full-time education until the age of 16. About 70% of young people choose to stay in full-time education after this age, either at school or further education colleges. Around 10% of 16 year old school leavers go into work and the remainder are guaranteed a place on government training programmes. About a third of all young people enter universities or other institutions of higher education.

Increasing emphasis is being placed on lifelong learning as a way of creating skills and improving employment prospects in a changing labour market. People who move more frequently between jobs and careers will need to be able to change and update their qualifications.

At the beginning of the 20th century school attendance was compulsory but the average class size was 50 and most pupils left by the age of 14. Many teachers were not professionally trained and much learning was done by rote. In England and Wales, local authorities became responsible for state schooling in 1902 and the 1944 Education Act subsequently led to an expansion of secondary education. Eleven year olds took a test (the '11-plus') which determined the type of secondary school that they attended. Those who passed (about 20%) went to grammar schools and the rest to secondary modern or technical schools. In the 1960s a new system of comprehensive education was adopted by most education authorities. The emphasis switched to mixed ability teaching and the 11-plus was largely abandoned, although it continued in Northern Ireland. Since the 1980s approved national curricula have been introduced and pupils are assessed against the level of attainment expected at certain ages. Measures have also been taken to increase parental choice and involvement.

ADMINISTRATIVE ARRANGEMENTS

State schools in England and Wales are maintained by local government education authorities (LEAs). With a few exceptions, this is also the position in Scotland. In Northern Ireland five education and library boards fund all controlled and maintained schools and the Department of Education funds voluntary grammar and grant-maintained integrated schools (see p. 128). Further education colleges in the UK are controlled by autonomous governing bodies, with representation from businesses and the local community. Universities and higher education colleges are legally independent corporate institutions with individual governing bodies.

A number of central government departments are responsible for education policy:

- the Department for Education and Skills (DfES) in England;
- the National Assembly for Wales Training and Education Department (NATED);
- the Scottish Executive Education Department (primary and secondary education) and the Scottish Executive Enterprise and Lifelong Learning Department; and
- the Department of Education and the Department for Employment and Learning in the Northern Ireland Executive.

> The Government published a White Paper in September 2001: *Schools: Achieving Success*. This proposes a number of reforms to improve standards, encourage innovation, reduce and simplify regulations, enhance the diversity of secondary education and improve the ability of that sector to respond to the talents and aspirations of individual students. The policy objectives in the White Paper are for England, but the legislation that is planned to achieve these goals will cover England and Wales. Many of the provisions will be enabling in character and, in accordance with the principles of the devolution settlement, the National Assembly for Wales will decide whether they should apply in Wales.

The education service in Great Britain is financed in the same way as other local government services (see chapter 6, p. 68), with education authorities funding schools largely on the basis of pupil numbers. Specific central government grants are made to education authorities in Great Britain in order to improve school performance in literacy, numeracy and information and communications technology (ICT). The Government also allocates some resources direct to schools for them to use as they wish. The costs of education and library boards are met directly by the Northern Ireland Executive.

In England, public funding is given to further education colleges by the Learning and Skills Council and in Wales by the National Council for Education and Training for Wales. Colleges in Northern Ireland are financed through the Northern Ireland Executive. Government finance is distributed to higher education institutions by higher education funding councils in England, Scotland and Wales and by the Department for Employment and Learning in Northern Ireland.

Planned spending on education in the UK as a proportion of Gross National Product in 2001–02 is 5% and will rise to a projected 5.3% in 2003–04.

SCHOOLS

Parents are required by law to see that their children receive full-time education between the ages of 5 and 16 in England, Scotland and Wales and between 4 and 16 in Northern Ireland. About 94% of pupils receive free education from public funds, while the others attend independent fee-paying schools or are educated at home.

In England and Wales, schools supported by public funds are now classified into three broad categories. Community schools consist in the main of schools that were traditionally owned and funded by LEAs. Foundation schools include many of the former grant-maintained schools. Many schools in the voluntary category are connected to a particular religious faith. The White Paper proposes that new faith schools should be encouraged where there is local support and where they would add to the inclusiveness and diversity of the school system. More generally, schools would be encouraged to work with external partners—for example from the voluntary, private or faith-based sectors—and LEAs would advertise when a new school is

Figure 10.1: Children under Five[1] in Schools as a Percentage of Children aged Three and Four, UK

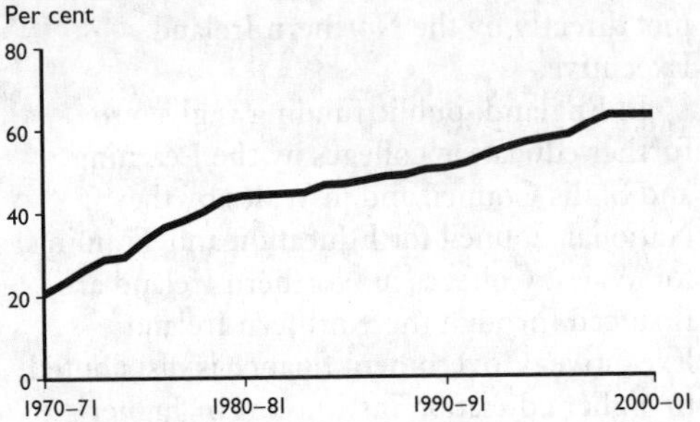

[1] Pupils aged three and four at 31 December each year. The figure for 2000–01 includes 1999–2000 data for Wales and Scotland and is provisional.

Sources: Department for Education and Skills, National Assembly for Wales, Scottish Executive and Northern Ireland Department of Education

required so that any interested party can put forward proposals and have them considered on their merits.

In Scotland, state schools managed by local authorities form the majority, but there are also seven grant-aided schools, one self-governing school and a number of independent schools.

Table 10.2: Number of Schools by Type in the UK, 2000–01[1]

Type of school	Number
State nursery	2,813
State primary	22,919
State secondary	4,337
Independent schools	2,462
Special schools[2]	1,499
Pupil referral units	338
All schools	**34,368**

[1] Provisional figures.
[2] Catering for children with special educational needs (see p. 135). The great majority of special schools are publicly maintained.
Sources: Department for Education and Skills, National Assembly for Wales, Scottish Executive and Northern Ireland Department of Education

In Northern Ireland all schools must be open to all religions. In practice, however, most Protestant children attend one of the 643 controlled schools, managed by education and library boards, while most Roman Catholic children attend one of 542 voluntary maintained schools. There are, in addition 54 voluntary grammar schools (which tend to be Catholic or non-denominational in character). The 44 integrated schools aim to educate Roman Catholic and Protestant children together. These schools are controlled or grant-maintained. The Government has a statutory duty to encourage integrated education as a way of breaking down sectarian barriers. Publicly financed schools can apply to become integrated, following a majority vote by parents.

Table 10.3: Number of Pupils by School Type in the UK, 2000–01[1]

Type of school	Thousands
State nursery[2,3]	143
State primary[2,3]	5,298
State secondary[2]	3,915
Non-maintained schools	626
Special schools[4]	114
Pupil referral units	10
All schools	**10,105**

[1] Provisional figures based on head counts.
[2] Excludes special schools.
[3] Nursery classes within primary schools are included in primary schools.
[4] Includes maintained and non-maintained sectors.
Sources: Department for Education and Skills, National Assembly for Wales, Scottish Executive and Northern Ireland Department of Education

Pre-school Education

Pre-school education is expanding considerably in order to ensure that all children begin school with a basic foundation in literacy and numeracy. The proportion of three and four year olds enrolled in UK schools rose from 21% in 1970–71 to 63% in 2000–01. Private and voluntary providers have also increased their provision.

National Child Care Strategy

The National Child Care Strategy was launched in 1998 to address the need for good quality affordable childcare for working parents. The aim is to provide childcare places for 1.6 million children in England by 2004. Some 45,000 new daycare places will be created in neighbourhood nursery centres. Similar strategies apply in Wales and Scotland.

Sure Start

The Sure Start Programme supports local projects for families with children under four years of age. The aim is to establish 500 local programmes in England by 2004: this will cover 400,000 children. By September 2001, 437 programmes had been announced, 192 of which had started delivering services. Core services include visits to new parents within two months of a birth, support for improved childcare, play, early learning and access to health care. Parents also receive advice on ante-natal support, healthy eating and help to find work. Similar Sure Start programmes cover the rest of the UK.

England

In January 2000, 97% of four year old children in England whose parents wanted one had a free part-time early education place. Half of three year olds are also in early education and it is intended to make a place available to every three year old by 2004.

Scotland

Every four year old child whose parents want one has a part-time pre-school place, as do 80% of three year olds. The Scottish Executive has set a number of targets, which include making a nursery place available to every three year old by April 2002, training more childcare workers and expanding provision outside of schools.

Northern Ireland

In Northern Ireland the aim is to provide a year of pre-school education for every child whose parents wish them to have one. A phased expansion programme is increasing free provision from 45% in 1997–98 to 85% in 2001–02.

Primary Schools

Age Ranges

In England and Wales, infant schooling begins at age five, primary schooling at age seven and secondary education at age 11. However, some schools cater for different age ranges. Primary education in Scotland starts at the age of five and continues until the age of 12. School classes are organised by age group, from primary 1 to primary 7. In Northern Ireland, children attend primary school for seven years from the beginning of the school year following their fourth birthday.

Class Sizes

In recent years steps have been taken to reduce the size of infant school classes. In England, for example, only 2% of infants were in classes of 31 or more in January 2001, compared with 29% in January 1998. The overall average class size in primary schools is 26.8 in England (January 2001) and 24.4 in Scotland.

Secondary Schools

England and Wales

Over 87% of the 3,180,000 state secondary pupils in England and all pupils in Wales attend comprehensive schools. These largely take pupils without reference to ability or aptitude, providing a wide range of secondary education for all or most of the children in a district. Some are middle schools with a pupil age range of 8 to 14. Some 600,000 pupils attend non-maintained schools, including independent fee-paying schools.

Scotland

Scottish state secondary education is non-selective, without reference to ability or aptitude. Nearly all the schools cover ages 12 to 18. In 2000–01 there were 317,704 pupils in state secondary schools and a further 17,537 attended private schools.

Northern Ireland

Secondary education is organised largely on selective lines, with grammar schools admitting pupils on the basis of tests in English, mathematics and science. In 2000–01, 62,574 pupils attended grammar schools (40% of secondary pupils) and 92,979 attended non-grammar secondary schools, of whom 8,688 were educated in integrated schools (see p. 128).

City Technology Colleges and City Academies

There are 15 City Technology Colleges situated in English cities. They are state-funded independent schools run by private sponsors, operating outside the normal local government framework. They provide free education for 11 to 16 year olds in inner city areas with a curriculum focusing on science, mathematics and technology.

City Academies are publicly funded independent schools involving sponsors from the private and voluntary sectors. Their aim is to offer new responses to the persistent school failure that sometimes occurs in city areas. The initiative was launched in March 2000 and 13 partnerships had been announced by September 2001. The White Paper proposes at least 20 City Academies by 2005 and an extension of the model to rural as well as urban areas.

State Specialist Schools

An increasing number of state secondary schools in England have been designated as specialist schools. This status can be achieved by raising private sector sponsorship, preparing development plans for the teaching of specialist subjects and sharing resources and good practice with other schools and the local community. The schools specialise in technology, mathematics and science; modern foreign languages; sport; or the arts—in addition to providing the National Curriculum (see p. 132). New specialisms will be introduced in September 2002.

By September 2001 there were 685 specialist schools in England: 367 technology colleges, 126 language colleges, 101 sports colleges and 91 arts colleges. Some are located in Excellence in Cities areas and Education Action Zones while some are Beacon Schools (see p. 131). From September 2002, high performing schools can become Advanced Specialist Colleges with an additional focus, for example, on teacher and leadership training.

The White Paper proposes a new target of at least 1,500 specialist schools by 2005. Schools will be able to apply for 'working towards' status and be offered support to develop a distinct specialism.

Excellence in Cities

Excellence in Cities was launched in England by the Government in 1999 to address educational problems in the big cities. By September 2001 it included 1,000 schools and one-third of all secondary age pupils. The programme has six elements:

- Learning Mentors—paid staff who help pupils overcome learning obstacles;
- over 1,000 Learning Support Units where pupils with problems can be taught until they are ready to return to the classroom;
- a network of new school-based City Learning Centres which share their latest ICT facilities with other schools;
- more Beacon and specialist schools;
- small Education Action Zones; and
- extended opportunities for gifted and talented pupils.

Education Action Zones

Education Action Zones have been formed in deprived areas in order to help raise educational standards. A zone is typically made up of two or three secondary schools, with their associated primary and special school provision, working in partnership with parents, schools, businesses, the LEA, the local Learning and Skills Council (see p. 138) and others. Each zone is run by an action forum comprising these partners.

Latest figures indicate that 1,650 schools with 583,000 pupils are participating in 113 zones. In September 2001 about one in ten schools was in a zone.

Beacon Schools

The Beacon Schools initiative is intended to raise standards by sharing and spreading good practice. As part of Excellence in Cities, the initiative is supporting schools in the most under-achieving areas. Beacon Schools are given extra funding to build partnerships with other schools in order to foster the exchange of knowledge between professionals. By September 2001, there were 1,000 Beacon Schools in England, including 250 secondary schools. The White Paper proposes an expansion of secondary Beacon Schools to 400 by 2005.

Independent Schools

Independent schools providing full-time education for five or more pupils of compulsory school age must register by law with the appropriate government department and are subject to inspection. There are about 2,400 independent schools in the UK educating over 600,000 pupils. Independent schools are not funded by the state and obtain most of their finances from fees paid by parents and income from investments. Some of the larger independent boarding schools are known as public schools.

Under the Music and Ballet Schools Scheme, the Government gives income-related help with fees to 800 pupils at five music schools, three ballet schools and for 80 choristers attending cathedral choir schools. Some 1,900 children attend the music and ballet schools.

School Management

England and Wales

All state schools work in partnership with, and receive recurrent funding from, LEAs, while managing 85% of their budgets and staffing. They are run by governing bodies, comprising parents, school staff, LEA and local community representation. The White Paper proposes giving schools more flexibility by replacing some of the current legislative requirements in respect of school governance with statutory guidance, and by removing barriers to cooperation between schools.

LEAs and school governing bodies responsible for pupil admissions are expected to work with head teachers, the churches and others in local forums to coordinate admission arrangements, taking account of statutory codes of practice. Any disagreements on school organisation or admissions in England are referred to an independent Adjudicator; those regarding religious or denominational admission criteria are referred to the Secretary of State for Education and Skills. In Wales the National Assembly decides all cases of disagreement.

Admission authorities are not allowed to introduce selection by ability, unless it is for sixth form admission or is designed to ensure that pupils of all abilities are admitted and that no one level of ability is over- or under-represented. Where existing partial selection by ability is challenged, the Adjudicator (in Wales the National Assembly) decides whether it should continue.

In England local parents are allowed to petition for a ballot and (if sufficient numbers locally wish it) to vote on whether to keep selective admission arrangements in the case of the 164 designated grammar schools which select pupils by high ability.

Scotland

Nearly all Scottish schools are education authority schools financed by the authorities and central government. The head teacher is responsible for decision-making on at least 80% of school-level expenditure. A review of devolved school management is nearing completion.

In May 2000, 83% of eligible education authority schools had a school board consisting of elected parents and teachers and members coopted from the local community. In addition to promoting contact between parents, the school and the community, they are involved in procedures to appoint senior staff and for the community use of school premises. They may also take on further executive functions by delegation from their education authority.

Seven grant-aided schools, for children with special educational needs, are run by boards of managers who receive government grants.

Northern Ireland

Boards of governors are responsible for the management of individual schools and include elected parents and teachers among their members. Virtually all schools have delegated budgets under which school governors determine spending priorities.

Rights of Parents

England and Wales

Parents have a statutory right to information about schools and to express a preference for a school for their child. There is an appeal system (see p. 131) if their choice is not met. The information to which they are entitled includes:

- annual national performance tables on a school-by-school basis;
- an annual prospectus, including summaries of the school's results in National Curriculum assessment tests, public examinations, vocational qualifications (if applicable) and rates of pupil absence.

Parents must be given a written annual report on their child's achievements in all subjects, including results of tests and examinations. Arrangements must also be made for the discussion of reports with teachers.

Parents are also entitled to see or be provided with a copy of their child's pupil record within 15 school days of making a written request. Unless there is a court order preventing it, all parents have a right to participate in decisions about their child's education.

Home/school agreements set out the responsibilities of schools, pupils and parents and are a statutory requirement for all maintained schools.

Scotland

Parents have a statutory right to express their choice of school and the education authority must meet this request except in certain circumstances set out in law. Information is published on school costs, examination results, pupil attendance/absence, 5–14 attainment targets and results, and the destinations of school leavers. Schools are required to provide parents with information about their children's attainment in each subject, pupil attainment targets and teachers' comments on their progress.

Northern Ireland

The system of reporting to parents is broadly similar to that in England and Wales, except that no annual performance tables on a school-by-school basis are published.

School Curriculum

England and Wales

Subjects taught to children between the age of 5 and 16 are largely determined by the National Curriculum which has four Key Stages (see Table 10.4). At each Key Stage the core subjects of English (and in Wales, Welsh), mathematics and science must be taught. History, geography, art/design and music are also compulsory in the earlier stages but become optional at Key Stage 4. A modern foreign language is compulsory at Key Stages 3 and 4, although this is optional at Key Stage 4 in Wales. Physical education, design/technology and information and communications technology are also compulsory at all four Key Stages. In 2002 the subject of 'citizenship' will become compulsory at Key Stages 3 and 4.

Other subjects, such as drama, dance and classical languages, are optional. It is intended that over time every primary school child should have the opportunity to learn to play a musical instrument and explore one of a range of sports.

Table 10.4: Key Stages of the National Curriculum

	Pupil ages	Year groups
Key Stage 1	5–7	1–2
Key Stage 2	7–11	3–6
Key Stage 3	11–14	7–9
Key Stage 4	14–16	10–11

The National Curriculum contains programmes of study for each Key Stage outlining what pupils should be taught as well as targets setting out expected standards of pupil performance.

Religious education—all state schools must provide religious education. Locally agreed syllabuses must reflect Christianity while taking account of the other main religions practised in the UK. Parents have the right to withdraw their children from religious education classes.

Sex education—state secondary schools are required to provide sex education for all pupils, including education about HIV/AIDS and other sexually transmitted diseases. Parents are entitled to withdraw their children from sex education classes other than those required by the National Curriculum. All state schools must provide information to parents about the content of their sex education courses.

Assessment and testing—at the ages of 7, 11 and 14, school pupils are assessed by their teachers on their progress in the core subjects of English, mathematics and science (and Welsh in Welsh medium schools in Wales). They also take tests in English and mathematics at these ages, and in science at 11 and 14. The results are shown as a level on the National Curriculum scale. A typical seven year old is expected to achieve level two, a typical 11 year old level four, and a typical 14 year old between levels five and six. At 14, pupils are also assessed in other subjects.

Literacy and numeracy—the Government has set national targets to improve literacy and numeracy for 11 year olds in England. These are for 80% of them to reach the standards for their age (level four in Key Stage 2) in English and 75% in mathematics by 2002. The Government has proposed higher targets for 2004 and will be consulting about these in late 2001.

Summer schools are available to help those 11 year olds who have failed to meet national standards in mathematics and literacy. In 2001 funding was provided for 2,200 such schools, assisting 66,000 pupils. New tests have been introduced to monitor the progress of these pupils in the first year of their secondary education.

Following a pilot covering 205 schools, a Key Stage 3 National Strategy is being introduced in order to raise standards in the early years of secondary education. The strategy is beginning with English and mathematics but will be extended to science and ICT. Targets have been set for the proportion of pupils achieving level five or above at the end of Key Stage 3 in both 2004 and 2007. The White Paper proposes that national results for 14 year olds and new measures of progress between the ages of 11 and 14 should be published.

In Wales the National Assembly has adopted targets for attainments in English, Welsh (first language), mathematics and science.

Qualifications—the General Certificate of Secondary Education (GCSE) is the main examination taken by pupils at the age of 16. GCSE short courses are also available in a limited range of subjects, occupying half the time of full GCSEs. In addition, the Part One General National Vocational Qualification (GNVQ) is available for 14 to 16 year olds. It covers arts and design, business, engineering, health and social care, ICT, leisure and tourism, and manufacturing. In a bid to expand vocational opportunities, GNVQs will be replaced in 2002 by vocational GCSEs.

All GCSE and other qualifications offered to pupils in state schools must be approved by the Government. Syllabuses and assessment procedures must comply with national guidelines and be approved by the Qualifications and Curriculum Authority (QCA) in England and by its Welsh counterpart, ACCAC. Both are independent government agencies responsible for ensuring that the curriculum and qualifications are of high quality, coherent and flexible.

The proportion of final-year pupils achieving five or more GCSE grades A* to C or equivalent in the United Kingdom was over 50% in 2000, compared with just over 46% in 1997. Extra assistance will be given to every school with under 25% achieving these results.

Scotland

There is no statutory national curriculum in Scotland. National guidelines for pupils aged 5–14 set out the ground to be covered and the way pupils' learning should be assessed and reported. Progression is measured by attainment of five levels, based on the expectation of the performance of the majority of pupils at certain ages between 5 and 14. It is recognised that pupils learn at different rates and that some will reach the various levels before others. There are curriculum guidelines for languages, mathematics, ICT, environmental studies, expressive arts, religious and moral education, health education, and personal and social development.

Pupils can study a modern European language during the last two years of primary education. There are 57 units in primary schools where education takes place through the Gaelic language. There are some other schools where Gaelic can be learned as a second language.

Education authorities must ensure that pupils are given religious instruction, though parents can withdraw their children if they wish. Government guidance on sex education is given to education authorities and head teachers.

Pupils are assessed by their teachers in all aspects of the curriculum through primary years and the first two years of secondary education. In addition, teachers select and administer tests in reading, writing and mathematics from a national catalogue. Tests can take place at any time during the school year and at any age.

Pupils take National Qualifications (NQ) at Standard Grade after four years of secondary education at the age of 16. These examinations are conducted by the Scottish Qualifications Authority (SQA). In 2000 some 34% of these pupils gained five or more Standard Grades at levels 1–2; the proportions of those achieving these grades at levels 1–4 and 1–6 were 76% and 89% respectively.

Northern Ireland

The Northern Ireland curriculum, compulsory in all publicly financed schools, consists of six broad areas of study: English, mathematics, science and technology, the environment and society, creative and expressive studies and, in secondary schools and some primary schools, language studies. The main churches have approved a core syllabus for religious education which must be taught in all grant-aided schools.

There are also a number of cross-curricular themes, including cultural heritage, education for mutual understanding, health education and information and communications technology. Secondary schools have two additional themes, namely, economic awareness and careers education.

Sex education is taught through the compulsory science study programme and the health education cross-curricular theme.

Statutory pupil assessment is broadly in line with practice in England and Wales, taking place at 8, 11, 14 and 16. The GCSE examination is used to assess 16 year old pupils.

The Northern Ireland curriculum is currently under review.

Educational Standards

England and Wales

The Office for Standards in Education (OFSTED) in England and the Office of Her Majesty's Chief Inspector in Wales (Estyn) aim to improve the quality and standards of education through independent inspections and advice. Schools are inspected at least once in six years, but more often where weaknesses have been identified in an earlier inspection. Schools must produce an action plan to address the key issues raised in the inspection report.

In cases where inspectors find that a school is failing to provide an acceptable education and is in need of special measures to turn it round, OFSTED inspectors make regular visits to the school to monitor implementation of the action plan. The average time for a school to come off these special measures is just under two years. If the school does not improve during this period, the Secretary of State for Education and Skills can require the LEA to close the school and replace it with a Fresh Start school which receives further targeted finance and professional support. Since OFSTED inspections began in 1993, nearly 800 schools have improved and been taken off special measures.

The Government has announced plans to allow weak or failing schools to be managed by private or voluntary sponsors, including other successful schools. The White Paper (see p. 127) proposes new powers to replace governing bodies with an interim executive board if the former are part of the problem. LEAs would be expected to invite external partners to help turn round failing schools.

OFSTED data indicate that teaching has improved in all types of school over the past five years. Unsatisfactory teaching has been reduced from one lesson in five to one in 20 and good teaching increased from 40% of lessons to 60%.

Scotland

HM Inspectorate of Education began operating as an executive agency of the Scottish Executive in April 2001. It inspects, reviews and reports on state and independent schools, further education colleges and the education functions of local authorities. Reports are published and are usually followed up within two years.

Northern Ireland

The purpose of inspection is to help promote the highest possible standards of education and professional practice, and to provide information and policy advice to the Department of Education, the Department of Culture, Arts and Leisure, and the Department for Employment and Learning.

Children with Special Educational Needs

A child is said to have special educational needs (SEN) if he or she has significantly greater difficulty in learning than other children of the same age or a disability which makes it difficult to use normal educational facilities. Each SEN child has the right to receive a broad and balanced education. State schools must publish information for parents about their SEN policy.

England and Wales

In January 2001 approximately 1.8 million pupils were identified as having special educational needs. If an LEA believes that it should determine the education for an SEN child, it must draw up a formal statement of the child's special needs and the action it intends to meet them. About 260,000 children with SEN have these statements. The LEA is required to comply with the parents' choice of school unless this is inappropriate for the child or incompatible with the efficient education of other children or with the efficient use of resources. Parents have a right of appeal to the Special Educational Needs Tribunal if they disagree with certain LEA decisions about their child. The Tribunal's verdict is final and binding on all parties. Over 60% of SEN pupils with statements are educated in mainstream schools while most of the others are educated in special schools.

In March 2001 the Government announced a £25 million package to improve the prospects of children with SEN. Much of the money will be used to train specialist child care and educational needs officers, including 850 area specialists. Regional networks of SEN experts are to be set up to work with local authorities.

Legislation was passed in 2001 covering England, Scotland and Wales. It states that LEAs and schools must not treat disabled pupils less favourably, without justification, than non-disabled pupils. Reasonable steps will have to be taken in cases where education arrangements have placed a disabled pupil at a substantial disadvantage compared with non-disabled pupils. The legislation will also strengthen the right of SEN children to be educated in mainstream schools where parents wish it and where the interests of other children can be protected.

LEAs are required to provide parents of SEN children with advice and information and a means of resolving disputes with schools and LEAs. They must also comply, within a prescribed period, with any order made by the SEN Tribunal.

Information and Communications Technology in Schools

England and Wales

The National Grid for Learning programme was launched in 1998 in order to increase the use made by pupils and teachers of computer (and especially Internet) resources. By 2001, 96% of primary and 99% of secondary schools were connected to the Internet and schools had achieved computer to pupil ratios of 1:12.6 in primary and 1:7.9 in secondary schools. By 2001 nearly one in eight teachers had received a subsidised computer through various government schemes.

The National Grid for Learning has commissioned courses in mathematics, Latin and Japanese at Key Stage 3 to be delivered using ICT and has also launched a Grid Club for 7–11 year olds.

Scotland

Learning & Teaching Scotland provides independent advice to Scottish ministers on the use of ICT in schools and supports research work on ICT and the school curriculum. All schools will be connected to the Internet in 2001. In September 2000 there was one computer for every 18 primary school pupils and one for every seven secondary pupils. A National Grid for Learning is also being developed in Scotland.

Northern Ireland

All schools are connected to the Internet through the Northern Ireland Network for Education, the local arm of the National Grid for Learning. Computer to pupil ratios range from 1:14 at Key Stage 1 to 1:6.5 at Key Stage 5 and 1:5 in special schools. About 12,000 laptop computers have been provided to facilitate teacher training and to improve their competence in ICT.

Teachers

England and Wales

New teachers in state primary and secondary schools are required to be graduates and must hold Qualified Teacher Status (QTS). There are two main ways to become a teacher:

- by taking a Bachelor of Education degree at a university or college of higher education. The course includes subject and professional studies, combined with practical teaching experience in schools where students teach a limited timetable under the supervision of an experienced teacher; or
- by enabling graduates to take a one-year Postgraduate Certificate in Education course leading to QTS. All postgraduate courses focus on professional preparation for teaching in a chosen subject and include the National Curriculum.

A third route into the profession will allow undergraduates on traditional academic degrees to take education modules and so gain part of a teacher education qualification.

Other programmes offer the opportunity for people aged 24 and over to earn a salary while following a teacher training programme in a school. These programmes are particularly suitable for overseas-trained teachers who do not hold QTS, mature career changers, school support staff and people who have had previous teaching experience.

Revised arrangements for the development of the teaching profession in England were implemented from September 2000. Key aspects include the creation of the National College for School Leadership (responsible for training head teachers); the introduction of a new pay system; and measures to attract high-quality graduates to teaching and to move outstanding teachers quickly through the profession.

All teachers working in state schools must be registered with the General Teaching Council for England, a teachers' professional body which, among other things, has power to strike a teacher from the register on grounds of professional misconduct or incompetence.

Similar reforms are taking place in Wales, including the establishment of a General Teaching Council for Wales in 2000.

The White Paper (see p. 127) states that the Government will be examining the potential for providing more time during the working week for planning, preparation and management.

Scotland

All teachers in education authority schools must be registered with the General Teaching Council for Scotland. The Council gives advice to the Scottish Executive on teacher supply and the professional suitability of teacher training courses. It is also responsible for disciplinary procedures under which a teacher guilty of professional misconduct may be removed temporarily or permanently from the register.

Teacher qualification procedures are similar to those in England and Wales, including the Bachelor of Education degree and the Postgraduate Certificate in Education. There is also a combined degree, sometimes known as a concurrent degree. All pre-service courses are validated by a higher education institution accredited by the Council and approved by the Scottish Executive. The Education Inspectorate has powers to inspect teacher education and training.

Northern Ireland

All entrants to teaching in grant-aided schools are graduates and hold an approved teaching qualification. Initial teacher training is integrated with induction and early in-service training, the latter covering a period of three years. A Professional Qualification for Headship is being developed, equivalent to the arrangements in England and Wales. A General Teaching Council is also being established. The main teacher training courses are Bachelor of Education Honours (four years) and the one-year Postgraduate Certificate of Education.

The education and library boards have a statutory duty to provide curricular support services and in-service training.

Careers

All young people in full-time education are entitled to career information, advice and guidance.

In England the current work of school careers services with 13 to 19 year olds will be subsumed within the new Connexions Service which is being implemented across the country by 2002–03. It coordinates careers, youth and other statutory and voluntary services for young people and is delivered by a network of personal advisers based in a variety of settings, including schools and colleges.

The National Assembly for Wales launched Careers Wales—an information, advice and guidance service for all age groups—in April 2001. Additional help will be aimed at those most at risk of failing to realise their potential. In Northern Ireland careers education forms part of the secondary school curriculum (see p. 134).

All secondary schools in England and Wales, and primary and secondary schools in Northern Ireland, provide leavers with a Record of Achievement setting out their attainments, including public examination and National Curriculum assessment results. The Record is not compulsory in Scotland.

Education Business Links

The Learning and Skills Council (LSC—see p. 138) is responsible for developing education business links in England. Local and national organisations have formed local consortia in each of the 47 LSC areas to help the Council to carry out this responsibility. The aim is to ensure that all young people have high-quality work experience during their time at school in order to raise standards, develop key skills and prepare effectively for adult and working life.

Careers Wales works with schools and colleges to ensure that all young people undertake work experience placements and have the opportunity to learn about business and enterprise. Business support for the delivery of the curriculum is organised by the National Council for Education and Training.

In Northern Ireland, links are fostered through the Northern Ireland Business Education Partnership, which supports a network of local partnerships and five area partnerships aligned to the five education and library boards.

EDUCATION AND TRAINING AFTER 16

After compulsory education is finished, young people can choose to stay on at school, attend college or take part in work-based learning. About 70% of 16 year olds continue in full-time education in school sixth forms, sixth form colleges or further education colleges.

The Government is keen to promote lifelong learning and the Learning and Skills

Table 10.5: Students[1] in Further and Higher Education: by Type of Course and Gender, UK

Thousands

	Males	Females
1998–99		
Further education[2]		
Full-time	532	533
Part-time	1,257	1,721
All further education	**1,789**	**2,254**
1999–2000		
Higher education[3]		
Undergraduate		
Full-time	513	594
Part-time	220	301
Postgraduate		
Full-time	78	75
Part-time	121	122
All higher education	**932**	**1,092**

[1] Home and overseas students.
[2] Further education figures (except Northern Ireland) are whole year counts. Excludes adult education centres.
[3] Higher education figures are based on an annual snapshot—students starting courses after that date will not be counted. Includes Open University.
Sources: Department for Education and Skills, National Assembly for Wales, Scottish Executive and Northern Ireland Department of Education

Council was established in April 2001 in order to play a lead role in planning and funding all post-16 learning outside higher education.

Under the Welfare-to-Work programme (see p. 154), all young unemployed people are guaranteed education and training, while those with poor basic skills can take part in full-time study on an approved course.

As part of a pilot programme in one-third of England, there is a weekly Education Maintenance Allowance (EMA) for 16 and 19 year olds who continue their education. Students can qualify for allowances of up to £30 a week with bonuses for achievement.

England and Wales

Students may continue to study for examinations leading to higher education, professional training or vocational qualifications. They can also take non-examination courses.

The academic General Certificate of Education Advanced (GCE A) level is usually taken at the age of 18 after two years' full-time study; it is graded on a scale from A to E. The Advanced Subsidiary (AS) qualification is worth 50% of the marks of an A level; it is designed to encourage the take up of more subjects, particularly in the first year of post-16 study, and to help the transition from GCSE into advanced level study.

New GCE A level specifications were introduced in 2000, made up of six units and offering candidates the choice of end-of-course or staged assessment. Figure 10.6 shows increases in A level or equivalent achievements.

National Vocational Qualifications

England, Wales and Northern Ireland have a wide range of National Vocational Qualifications (NVQs), awards which recognise work-related skills and knowledge in areas such as business, engineering and health and social care. Prepared by industry and business, including representatives from trade unions and professional bodies, NVQs are based on national standards of competence and can be achieved at levels 1 to 5. Vocational A levels replaced Advanced GNVQs in September 2000. The remaining two classes of GNVQ are to be replaced by Vocational GCSEs.

The Qualifications and Curriculum Authority is responsible for supervising academic and vocational qualifications in England. Corresponding bodies in Wales (ACCAC) and Northern Ireland perform similar functions.

Learning and Skills Council

In England, the Learning and Skills Council (LSC) is responsible for planning, funding, monitoring and improving the quality of post-16 education and training up to higher education level. Its remit covers basic skills, higher level skills in further education, work-based training for young people and adult and community education. From 2002–03 it will also take on responsibility for school sixth form funding. The Council has a statutory

Figure 10.6: Achievement at GCE A Level or Equivalent:[1,2] by Gender, UK

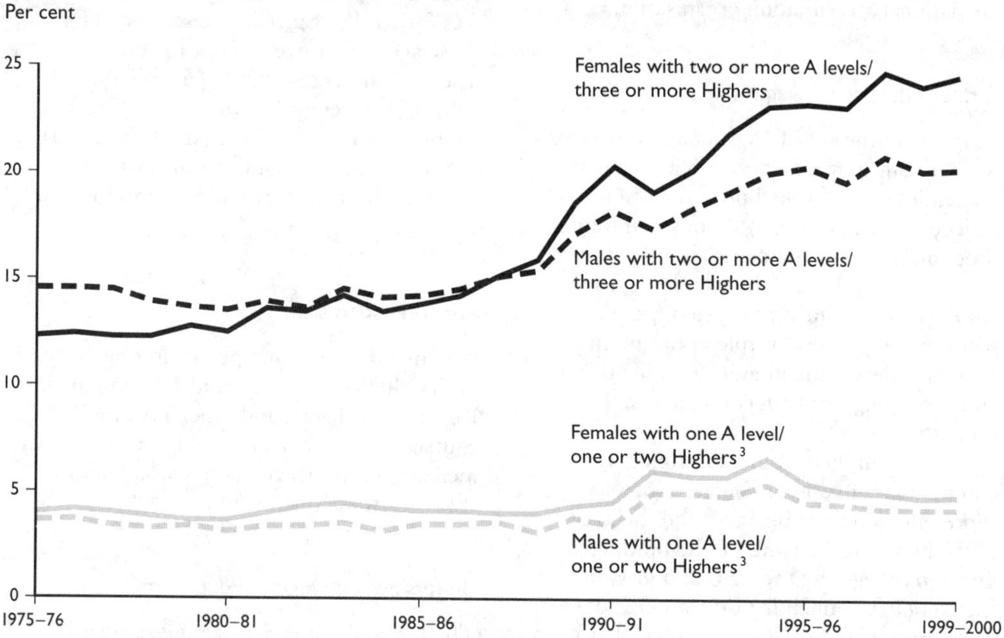

[1] Based on population aged 17 at the start of the academic year. Data to 1990–91 (1991–92 in Northern Ireland) relate to school leavers. From 1991–92 data relate to pupils of any age for Great Britain, while school performance data are used for Northern Ireland from 1992–93. Figures exclude sixth form colleges in England and Wales which were reclassified as further education colleges from 1 April 1993. Excludes GNVQ Advanced Qualifications.

[2] Data for 1999–2000 are provisional.

[3] From 1996–97 figures only include two Highers.

Sources: Department for Education and Skills, National Assembly for Wales, Scottish Executive and Northern Ireland Department of Education

duty to encourage participation in learning and works with employers and others to promote workforce development and economic regeneration. There is a network of 47 local LSC offices.

National Council for Education and Training for Wales

The National Council has a very similar remit to the LSC. It is responsible for post-16 education and training, with the exception of higher education. There are 21 local voluntary partnerships (Community Consortia for Education and Training) linking LEAs, schools, colleges, voluntary organisations, private training providers, employers and trade unions. The National Council and the Higher Education Funding Council for Wales operate together under the name Education and Learning Wales.

Scotland

In Scotland education for those aged 16 to 18 has been reformed. Traditional, fairly academic Highers (Higher Grade Scottish Certificate of Education) have been replaced by National Qualifications (NQ) courses and units offering students greater flexibility and, through a revised assessment system, more opportunities to demonstrate academic and vocational achievement. It is intended that the new system should be fully in place by 2003.

The Scottish Qualifications Authority is the national accreditation organisation.

Further Education Colleges

People over the age of 16 can take courses in further education colleges with a choice of academic and vocational provision. Many colleges offer government-sponsored training programmes. Most students attend part-time, either by day release or block release from employment or during the evenings. The sector has an important role in promoting economic development and social inclusion, and has strong ties with commerce and industry.

Colleges in the UK are controlled by autonomous governing bodies, with representation from business and the local community. In England, public funding is given to colleges by the LSC and in Wales by the National Council for Education and Training for Wales. Colleges in Northern Ireland are financed through the Northern Ireland Executive.

The LSC is providing £100 million over the next three years to help colleges meet the economy's rising skill needs by developing centres of vocational excellence in subjects such as construction, engineering, electronics and ICT. By 2003–04, 50% of general further education colleges will have a specialism.

An online National Learning Network links all further education colleges to super JANET, the UK's education and research network.

Independent inspectors assess the quality of education provided by colleges, which are required to explain how they will put things right if there are major criticisms. In England OFSTED (see p. 134) inspects provision for 16 to 19 year olds in schools and colleges and the Adult Learning Inspectorate performs the same function for post-19 provision in colleges and for work-based learning for all post-16s.

In Scotland colleges are inspected by Her Majesty's Inspectorate of Education (see p. 135); in Northern Ireland by the Education and Training Inspectorate and in Wales by Estyn.

Student Support

Support for further education students in England includes a subsidy towards course fees for 16–18 year olds, fee remission for those aged 19 or over on low incomes and a discretionary access fund (£62 million in 2001–02) to help meet the costs of books, equipment, travel and fees. The Child Care Support Fund (£30 million in 2001–02) provides discretionary child care support for students.

Higher Education

Around 30% of young people in England and Wales, 40% in Scotland and 45% in Northern Ireland take degree and other advanced courses in universities and other colleges. An increasing number of mature students also study for these qualifications.

Universities and Higher Education Colleges

The UK's 87 universities enjoy academic freedom, appoint their own staff, admit students and award their own degrees. The universities of Oxford and Cambridge date from the 13th century and the Scottish universities of St Andrews, Glasgow and Aberdeen from the 15th century. The University of Edinburgh was established in the 16th century. All the other universities were founded in the 19th and 20th centuries.

In addition, there are 64 higher education colleges which have different backgrounds and missions. Some are very specialised, such as art and design, teacher education and agriculture colleges, while others are multi-disciplinary. Some award their own degrees and qualifications, while in others these are validated by a university or national body.

Applications for first degrees are usually made through the Universities and Colleges Admission Service (UCAS).

Students at university in England, Wales and Northern Ireland usually spend three years of study, leading to a Bachelor's degree, for example Bachelor of Arts (BA) or Bachelor of Science (BSc). There are some four-year courses and medical and veterinary courses normally require five or six years. A full-time first degree in Scotland generally takes four years for Honours and three years for the broad-based Ordinary degree.

In 2000, some 265,300 students gained a first degree in the UK compared with 232,200 in 1995. Of these, 31,900 graduated with a first degree in business and administration, by far the highest category. From 2001 new foundation degrees will be introduced allowing students to combine work with study.

Some students go on to do postgraduate studies. These usually lead to a Masters degree, for example Master of Arts (MA) or Master of Science (MSc) or a doctorate (PhD).

The Open University

The Open University (OU) is a non-residential university offering 186 degree and other courses for adult students who wish to study in their own time. Teaching is through a combination of printed texts, correspondence tuition, television broadcasts, audio/video cassettes and, for some courses, short residential schools. Some 110,000 of its students are online from home and many OU learning resources are delivered on interactive CD-ROM or computer software. There is a network of local tutorial centres for contact with part-time tutors and fellow students. Students do not need formal academic qualifications to register for most courses.

Its first degrees are the BA (Open) and the BSc (Open) which are awarded on a system of points for each course completed. Either degree can be awarded with honours. The OU offers honours degrees in named subject areas and an MEng degree to enable students to achieve the highest professional status of Chartered Engineer. There are a number of certificates and diplomas. Higher degrees are also available.

Finance

Government finance is distributed to higher education institutions by higher education funding councils in England, Wales and Scotland, and in Northern Ireland by the Department for Employment and Learning. The private University of Buckingham does not receive public funds.

Institutions also charge tuition fees, which are partly funded by students. In addition, they provide paid training, research or consultancy for commercial firms. Many establishments have endowments or receive grants from foundations and benefactors.

Student Support

Support for higher education students in England and Wales includes:

- help to pay tuition fees—a maximum fee contribution of £1,050 is charged per student, but the amount paid depends on student and family income; more than half of students do not pay any fees;
- student loans—these are the main form of help for students in meeting living costs. The maximum loan in 2001–02 for full-time students is £4,590. Loans are repaid on the basis of income after the student has completed his/her course;
- a number of additional grants, allowances or bursaries—available to students from disadvantaged backgrounds, disabled students, young people leaving local authority care and students with children or other dependants; and
- hardship funds—made at the discretion of the institution, the amount depending on the student's individual circumstances.

The Department for Education and Skills has announced a review of student support arrangements.

The Scottish Executive has introduced a new support scheme for full-time higher education. The main feature is that tuition fees are no longer payable by eligible full-time Scottish-domiciled students or EU students studying in Scotland. Student loan entitlement may be reduced, however, because any assessed parental or spouse contribution is set against the means-tested student loan entitlement rather than tuition fees.

In Northern Ireland support for higher education students generally operates on a parity basis with England and Wales.

Training

Several programmes are available to help increase work-related skills. These are offered as alternatives to academic education for 16 to 19 year olds or as part of an existing employee's training.

Modern Apprenticeships

Modern Apprenticeships (MAs) provide structured learning programmes for young people in which workplace training is integrated with off-the-job learning. They are available at Foundation and Advanced levels. Foundation MAs (National Traineeships in Wales) lead to NVQ at level 2. Advanced MAs lead primarily to NVQ level 3 and above and are designed to increase the number of young people trained to technician, supervisory and equivalent levels. Over 400,000 people have started an MA at this level since 1995. The quality of MAs is being improved through technical certificates that develop knowledge and understanding, and through an Apprenticeship diploma. Every young person with the necessary aptitude and ability will be entitled to a Modern Apprenticeship and there will be better access from an MA to higher education.

Other Training Schemes

Other workplace training includes:

- The right for 16 and 17 year old employees with few, if any, qualifications to reasonable paid time off work to study or train for an approved qualification at NVQ level 2 or equivalent.
- Career development loans to help people pay for vocational education or training in Great Britain. Loans of between £300 and £8,000 are provided through major banks; interest payments on the loan during training and one month after training are funded by the Government. They help to pay for courses lasting up to two years. Since the scheme began in 1988, over 154,000 loans have been made with an average value of £3,391.
- Small Firms Training Loans which help firms with 50 or fewer employees to meet a range of vocational training-related expenses, including training consultancy. Loans of between £500 and £125,000 are available through major banks and repayments can be deferred for between six and 12 months. Since the scheme began in 1994, nearly £3.8 million has been lent to 574 small firms.
- Work-based learning for adults is open to those aged 25 and over who have been unemployed for six months or longer.

In Wales, Skill Build, targeted at those young people who are most at risk in the labour market, aims to develop social skills, literacy, numeracy, ICT and other skills. A new programme—the Modern Skills Diploma for Adults—has been introduced to provide skills training for people aged over 25 who are in employment.

In Scotland all young people aged between 16 and 17 are entitled to training under the government-funded Skillseekers scheme. Its key elements are:

- training leading to a recognised qualification, up to Scottish Vocational Qualification (SVQ) level 3;
- an individual training plan; and
- employer involvement.

A network of Local Enterprise Companies are responsible for the delivery of the Scottish Executive's national training programmes. They run under contract to two non-departmental public bodies: Scottish Enterprise and Highlands and Islands Enterprise. This system is currently under review.

In Northern Ireland the Jobskills Programme is available to all 16–17 year olds. It provides training to NVQ level 2 with progress routes to NVQ level 3 through Modern Apprenticeship arrangements.

National Training Organisations

National Training Organisations (NTOs) are employer-led bodies responsible for the development of skills to meet the business needs of employers throughout the UK. In particular, they encourage employer involvement in the development and uptake of competence-based standards, education, training and qualifications in order to help businesses improve their competitiveness in UK and overseas markets. There are 72 NTOs covering 90% of the workforce.

New Technology Institutes

The Government is planning to develop New Technology Institutes in each English region to boost the supply of ICT and other high technology skills and to help transfer this know-how to small and medium-sized businesses.

Information and Advice

There are 75 Information, Advice and Guidance partnerships in England. Working closely with the Learning and Skills Council, their role is to coordinate information about opportunities in learning or work and to provide a free service to all members of the community. Particular attention is given to the needs of disadvantaged clients.

Learndirect

This is a new national online and distributed network making learning available to people at home, in the workplace and at over 1,200 centres throughout England, Wales and Northern Ireland. Its primary objective is to stimulate demand for lifelong learning among adults and small and medium-sized enterprises and to increase the availability of high-quality learning through the use of ICT. There is a learndirect telephone helpline and a learndirect website (*www.learndirect.co.uk*). The Scottish University for Industry is developing a similar network called learndirect Scotland. Careers Wales provides free information and advice on learning options to all adults, plus more in-depth guidance for some people not covered by the New Deal (see chapter 11). These services are delivered face to face or by the learndirect freephone service.

UK Online Centres

A network of 6,000 UK online centres is being established by the end of 2002 in order to reduce the gap between those who have access to ICT and those who do not. Internet and e-mail access is provided and there is support from staff, who help clients develop ICT skills and explore opportunities for learning. The network is underpinned by the learndirect helpline and website.

Individual Learning Accounts

The Government helps people plan and pay towards the cost of their learning through Individual Learning Accounts.

This national network was launched in September 2000. Some £150 million is being used to contribute £150 each to the first million account holders to book eligible learning, provided that the individual pays at least £25. People also receive 20% and 80% discounts on the costs of learning; the 20% discount can be used on a wide range of learning while the 80% discount is mainly restricted to ICT, literacy, basic mathematics and (in Wales) learning Welsh. By May 2001 over 1 million people in the UK had opened an Individual Learning Account.

Union Learning Fund

In 1998 the Government introduced the Union Learning Fund. This assists some 3,250 trade union learning representatives to promote learning in the workplace, especially among people with basic skills needs. The Government is consulting on a proposal that these representatives be given formal recognition in the workplace.

The Wales Union Learning Fund, launched in 1999, has funded over 40 projects.

Adult Education

Education for adults is provided by further education colleges, adult education centres and colleges run by LEAs, community organisations and voluntary bodies such as the Workers' Educational Association. The duty to secure such education rests with the Learning and Skills Council in England and the National Council for Education and Training for Wales. Adult education in Scotland is a statutory duty of education authorities and is generally known as community learning or community education. In Northern Ireland it is provided by the further education sector, supplemented by the work of a range of non-statutory providers.

General adult education courses include languages, physical education/sport/fitness and practical craft skills such as embroidery or woodwork.

The National Institute of Adult Continuing Education (NIACE) and the Basic Skills Agency (BSA) jointly manage the Adult and Community Learning Fund on behalf of the Department for Education and Skills; the Fund supports innovative learning opportunities and aims to encourage people who have been reluctant to participate in learning in the past and who may be disadvantaged as a result.

Skills for Life

The Government has launched Skills for Life, a programme designed to help the 7 million adults who have problems with literacy or numeracy. This funds community and workplace provision, teacher training in literacy and numeracy, and support for adults with learning difficulties. A new curriculum and standardised tests are being introduced in nine pathfinder areas. A new university-based national research centre will help develop best practice in teaching methods. In addition, a network of up to 2,000 fully equipped learning centres will be established to provide courses at colleges, workplaces and schools.

National Targets for Education and Training in England

In 1998 the Government launched its National Learning Targets for England for the year 2002. They cover key stages of people's lives and progress is measured every autumn. The targets state that 85% of 19 year olds should be qualified to NVQ level 2 (equivalent to five GCSEs at grades A* to C) and 60% of 21 year olds to NVQ level 3 (equivalent to 2 GCE A levels). Some 75% of 19 year olds and 54% of 21 year olds met these standards in 2000.

A set of targets also exists for adults of working age. The first states that by the year 2002, 50% of the workforce should be qualified to NVQ level 3. The second states that 28% of the workforce should have a professional, vocational, management or academic qualification at NVQ level 4 or above (which is equivalent to a first degree). By 2000, 47% and 26% of adults had achieved levels 3 and 4 respectively.

LINKS WITH OTHER COUNTRIES

Large numbers of people from other countries come to the UK to study, and many British people work and train overseas. The British aid programme (see chapter 7) encourages links between educational institutions in the UK and developing countries.

European Union Schemes

Exchange of students is promoted by the EU's SOCRATES-ERASMUS programme which provides grants enabling university students from the EU, Norway, Iceland, Liechtenstein, Central and Eastern European and EU pre-accession countries (see pp. 82–3) to study in other states. All academic subjects are covered, the study period normally lasting between three and 12 months. Between 1995 and 2000, some 512,000 students participated, of whom 65,000 were from the UK.

The SOCRATES programme also supports partnerships between schools, language learning, mobility opportunities for educational staff and a range of multinational projects, including open and distance learning and adult education. Competence in another European language is supported in all activities.

The LEONARDO DA VINCI programme supports vocational training policies and practices through multinational pilot projects, placements and exchanges and research projects. Between 1995 and 2000, 1,188 projects were supported in the UK. Of these, 578 were placement-type projects through which 12,212 young people undertook part of their vocational training in another Member State.

The YOUTH Programme supports youth exchanges and volunteering activities throughout the EU, the European Economic Area and pre-EU accession countries. Between 1995 and 2000 some 513,000 young people took part, including 56,000 from the UK.

EU member states have created ten European schools, including one at Culham, Oxfordshire, for pupils aged between 4 and 19 in order to provide a multilingual education for the children of staff employed in EU institutions. Around 16,000 pupils attend these schools.

Overseas Students in the UK

About 341,900 overseas students follow courses in the UK at higher and further education institutions. Most of them pay fees covering the full costs of their courses. Nationals of other EU states generally pay the lower level of fees applicable to British home students.

Government Scholarship Schemes

The Government makes provision for foreign students and trainees through its overseas aid programme and other award and scholarship schemes. Around 2,450 receive awards from schemes, funded in part by the Foreign & Commonwealth Office (FCO) and the Department for International Development (DFID). These are:

- British Chevening Awards, a worldwide programme offering outstanding graduate students and young professionals the opportunity to spend time studying at British universities and other academic institutions; and
- the Commonwealth Scholarship and Fellowship Plan, offering scholarships for study in other Commonwealth countries. In the UK these scholarships are for postgraduate study or research for one to three years at a higher education institution.

The FCO is also increasing the number of scholarships jointly funded with British or foreign commercial firms, and with academic and other institutions.

Other Schemes

The Overseas Research Students Award Scheme, funded by the higher education funding councils, provides help for overseas full-time postgraduate students with outstanding research potential. In addition, most British universities and colleges offer bursaries and scholarships for which graduates of any nationality are eligible. Other public and private scholarships are available to students from overseas and to British students who want to study in other countries.

THE YOUTH SERVICE

The youth service is a partnership between local government and voluntary organisations concerned with the informal personal and social education of young people aged 11 to 25 (5 to 25 in Northern Ireland).

Local authorities manage their own youth centres and clubs and provide most of the public support for local and regional organisations. In England, the service is estimated to reach around 3 million young people, with the voluntary organisations contributing a significant proportion of overall provision.

The DfES in England gives grants to the National Youth Agency, the National Council for Voluntary Youth Services and to the headquarters of some 80 national voluntary youth organisations. Funded primarily by local government, the National Youth Agency supports those working with young people and provides information and publishing services. In 2001 the DfES published a consultation document about the future of the Youth Service (*Transforming Youth Work*).

The National Assembly for Wales sponsors the Welsh Youth Agency which pays grant aid to national youth service bodies with headquarters in Wales, and accredits training and staff development for youth workers. The Assembly also supports the work of CWVYS (the Council for Wales of Voluntary Youth Services). In autumn 2000 the Assembly launched a consultation document *Extending Entitlement: supporting young people in Wales*, which proposed a new framework for young people aged 11–25. These proposals are now being taken forward.

In Scotland the youth service is part of community education provision made by local authorities. It is also promoted by Community Learning Scotland.

In Northern Ireland the education and library boards provide and fund youth clubs and outdoor activity centres. They assist with the running costs of registered voluntary youth organisations and provide advice and support for youth groups. In addition, they help young people visit the rest of the UK, the Irish Republic and overseas. The Youth Council for Northern Ireland advises the education system and other bodies on the development of the youth service. It encourages cross-community activity and pays grants to the headquarters of voluntary bodies.

Voluntary Youth Organisations

National voluntary organisations work mainly through local groups which raise most of their day-to-day expenses by their own efforts. Many receive financial and other help from local authorities. They vary greatly in character and include uniformed organisations such as the Scouts and Girl Guides, church-based and other religious organisations and particular interest groups. In Wales, Urdd Gobaith Cymru (the Welsh League of Youth) provides cultural, sporting and language-based activities for young Welsh speakers and learners.

Many voluntary organisations and local authorities provide services for young unemployed people, young people from ethnic minorities, young people in inner city or rural areas and those in trouble or especially vulnerable. Many authorities have youth committees on which official and voluntary bodies are represented. They employ youth officers to coordinate youth work and to arrange in-service training.

Youth Workers

In England and Wales a two-year training course at certain universities and higher education colleges produces qualified youth and community workers; several undergraduate part-time and postgraduate courses are also available. In Scotland courses lasting between one and three years are provided at teacher education institutions. Students from Northern Ireland attend courses at universities and colleges in the UK and the Irish Republic.

Other Organisations

Many grant-giving foundations and trusts provide finance for activities involving young people. The Prince's Trust and the Royal Jubilee Trust provide grants and practical help to individuals and organisations; areas of concern include urban deprivation, unemployment, homelessness and young offenders. Efforts are also made to assist ethnic minorities.

The Duke of Edinburgh's Award Scheme challenges young people from the UK and other Commonwealth countries to meet certain standards in activities such as community service, expeditions, social and practical skills and physical recreation.

Further Reading

Education and Training Statistics for the United Kingdom. Department for Education and Employment, 2000.

The Government's Expenditure Plans 2001–02 to 2003–04. Department for Education and Employment and Office for Standards in Education. Cm 5102. The Stationery Office, 2001.

Learning to Succeed: a new framework for post-16 learning. Department for Education and Employment. Cm 4392. The Stationery Office, 1999.

Schools: Achieving Success. Department for Education and Skills. Cm 5230. The Stationery Office, 2001.

Transforming Youth Work. Department for Education and Skills, 2001.

An Education and Training Action Plan for Wales. National Assembly for Wales, 1999.

Extending Entitlement: supporting young people in Wales. National Assembly for Wales, 2000.

The Learning Country—A Comprehensive Education and Lifelong Learning Programme to 2010 in Wales. National Assembly for Wales, 2001.

Websites

Department for Education and Skills: www.dfes.gov.uk

Scottish Executive: www.scotland.gov.uk

National Assembly for Wales: www.wales.gov.uk

Northern Ireland Assembly: www.ni-assembly.gov.uk

Department of Education (NI): www.deni.gov.uk

Connexions: www.connexions.gov.uk

11 The Labour Market

Patterns of Employment	148	Pay and Conditions	157
Labour Market Policy	152	Industrial Relations	158
Recruitment and Job-finding	153	Health and Safety at Work	162

In recent years the United Kingdom labour market has seen a growth in employment, which now exceeds 28 million. Both full-time and part-time employment have risen. The increase in employment has been predominantly in the service sector, in which over three-quarters of employees now work. Unemployment, on the other hand, has fallen considerably since the last peak at the end of 1992 and is at its lowest level since the introduction of the International Labour Organisation measure of unemployment in 1984.

PATTERNS OF EMPLOYMENT

The Office for National Statistics (ONS) carries out the Labour Force Survey (LFS) on a continuous basis. The LFS shows that, on a seasonally adjusted basis, 29.6 million people aged 16 and over were economically active[1] in the UK in spring (March to May) 2001. The economic activity rate was 63.3% for all persons aged 16 and over and 78.8% for those of working age (men aged 16 to 64 and women aged 16 to 59). Among the working-age group, some 7.7 million people were economically inactive, of whom 5.5 million people did not want a job and 2.2 million people wanted a job but were either not seeking work or not available to start work.

The number of people aged 16 and over in employment[2] rose by 267,000 in the year to spring 2001 to 28.2 million (see Table 11.1): some 15.5 million men and 12.7 million women. Employment was up by 1% during the year: 1.2% for women and 0.8% for men. The employment rate (among those of working age) was 74.9%, close to the high achieved in 1990.

Unemployment

The UK unemployment rate is similar to that for the major G7 group of nations and substantially below the EU average. In spring 2001, 1.5 million people were unemployed, a fall of 12.5% since spring 2000. This represents 4.9% of the labour force, compared with 5.6% in the same period of 2000, according to the International Labour Organisation (ILO) definition of unemployment. The rate in spring 2001 is the lowest since the adoption of the ILO definition of unemployment in 1984. Unemployment has been falling in all regions—areas with the lowest levels of unemployment include the South East and East of England.

[1] Defined as those who are either in employment (employee, self-employed, unpaid family worker or on a government-supported training programme) or unemployed and actively seeking work.

[2] There are two main measures of employment: the number of people in employment and the number of jobs; they represent different concepts, as one person can have more than one job.

Table 11.1: Employment in the UK, Spring 2001 *Thousands, seasonally adjusted*

	Males	Females	Total
All aged 16 and over	22,917	23,915	46,832
Total economically active	16,406	13,228	29,634
of whom:			
In employment	15,530	12,650	28,180
ILO unemployed[1]	876	578	1,453
Economic activity rate (%)[2]	84.2	72.9	78.8
Employment rate (%)	67.8	52.9	60.2
ILO unemployment rate (%)	5.3	4.4	4.9

[1] International Labour Organisation definition of unemployment.
[2] For men aged 16 to 64 and women aged 16 to 59.
Source: Labour Force Survey, Office for National Statistics

There have been substantial falls in long-term unemployment. In spring 2001 some 379,000 people had been unemployed for a year or more, of whom 218,000 had been out of work for two years or more. These figures represent falls of 15.6% and 13.5% respectively since spring 2000.

The picture for youth unemployment is similar, with some 380,000 people aged 18 to 24 unemployed in spring 2001, 7.3% lower than in spring 2000. Much larger percentage falls were recorded for those who had been out of work for one year or more (17.9%) and two years or more (35.7%).

In June 2001 the claimant count (the count of claimants of unemployment-related benefit, such as Jobseeker's Allowance—see chapter 12) was 963,100, a rate of 3.2% of the total of workforce jobs and the number of claimants. It is below 1 million for the first time since 1975.

The number of workless households (among working-age households) was 3.1 million in spring 2001, 6,000 fewer than in spring 2000 and 384,000 fewer than five years earlier. This represented a rate of worklessness of 16.3% in spring 2001, compared with 18.9% in spring 1996.

Women in Employment

One of the main long-term trends in the labour market has been the growth in the number of women in employment. Among the key figures illustrating this trend are:

- the number of women in work in spring 2001 was 12.6 million—an increase of nearly 1.1 million, or 9.5%, over ten years;
- nearly 70% of women of working age are working;
- 65% of women with dependent children are in work; and
- the number of women in permanent jobs has risen by around 347,000 (6.0%) in the three years to spring 2001.

Among several reasons for the greater involvement of women in the workplace is that more women are putting off having children until their thirties. When they do have children, they are far more likely to return to work, making use of a range of childcare options (see chapter 12).

Part-time Working

Another major long-term trend in employment has been a move towards people working part time, and women are more likely to do so than men. In spring 2001, 7.0 million people aged 16 and over, 25% of those in employment, worked part time. About 44% of women in employment work part time, compared with 9% of men.

Occupations

In terms of occupations, long-term trends have included growth in managerial and

Table 11.2: Employment Status of the UK Workforce *Thousands, seasonally adjusted*

	Spring				
	1997	1998	1999	2000	2001
Employees	23,218	23,657	24,084	24,497	24,760
Self-employed	3,358	3,290	3,214	3,160	3,171
Unpaid family workers	118	102	101	108	97
Government-supported training and employment programmes	222	178	162	148	153
Employment	**26,916**	**27,227**	**27,560**	**27,913**	**28,180**
of whom:					
Full-time workers	*20,219*	*20,473*	*20,718*	*20,967*	*21,161*
Part-time workers	*6,697*	*6,755*	*6,843*	*6,946*	*7,020*
Workers with a second job	*1,258*	*1,190*	*1,283*	*1,190*	*1,182*
Temporary workers	*1,791*	*1,745*	*1,715*	*1,729*	*1,726*

Source: Labour Force Survey, Office for National Statistics

Figure 11.3:
Working Age[1] Employment Rates,[2,3,4] UK

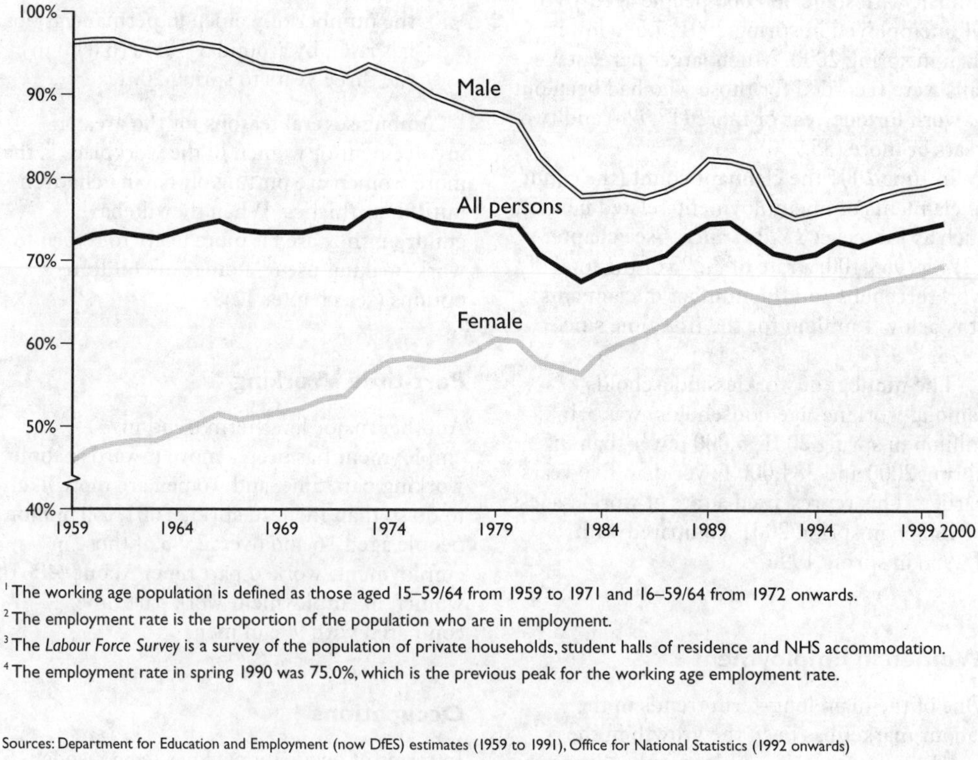

[1] The working age population is defined as those aged 15–59/64 from 1959 to 1971 and 16–59/64 from 1972 onwards.

[2] The employment rate is the proportion of the population who are in employment.

[3] The *Labour Force Survey* is a survey of the population of private households, student halls of residence and NHS accommodation.

[4] The employment rate in spring 1990 was 75.0%, which is the previous peak for the working age employment rate.

Sources: Department for Education and Employment (now DfES) estimates (1959 to 1991), Office for National Statistics (1992 onwards)

professional occupations, whereas skilled trades occupations, elementary occupations and process, plant and machine operatives have generally experienced declines. Two sectors experiencing change include occupations related to information and communications technology (ICT) and customer service occupations. Between winter 1996–97 and summer 2000 in England and Wales employment in ICT-related occupations grew substantially. In particular, employment of IT operations technicians increased by 138%, and IT user support technicians by 70% in this period. The number of people working in 'traditional' customer service occupations, such as counter clerks and telephonists, has been declining, but 'newer' customer service occupations have been rising: between winter 1996–97 and summer 2000 employment of call centre operatives in England and Wales rose by 220%, customer care occupations by 60% and telephone sales persons by 50%.

Second Jobs and Temporary Employment

Around 1.2 million people had a second job in spring 2001. The most common industries in which people have second jobs are education, health and social work, and hotels and restaurants.

About 1.7 million (7% of employees) were engaged in temporary jobs (see Table 11.2). Temporary employment is lower in the UK than in most other EU countries. The recent rise in employment as a whole has been concentrated in permanent jobs, and the number of temporary employees was virtually the same in spring 2001 as a year earlier. Of temporary employees in spring 2001, 480,000 (28%) worked in temporary jobs because they could not find a permanent one, and 522,000 (30%) worked in temporary jobs because they preferred to do so.

Teleworking

'Teleworking'—people working from home using ICT—is continuing to grow, although from a relatively low level. In spring 2001 some 347,000 people were classed as teleworkers whose main job was primarily in their own home; extending the definition to cover those working in different places using home as a base and those who spent at least one day a week working from home raised the number to 1.8 million. In a survey in Great Britain in 2000 around 22% of workplaces reported that they had staff who worked from home, usually professional and managerial staff and mostly on an occasional basis.

Self-employment

In spring 2001 nearly 3.2 million people were self-employed in the UK: 15% of men and 7% of women in employment were self-employed. Agriculture and fishing, and construction had the highest proportions of self-employed people, while relatively few of those engaged in manufacturing and public administration were self-employed.

The private sector share of employment rose from 71% in 1981 to 76% (21.5 million) in spring 2001. A separate analysis by ONS of public and private sector jobs showed that in June 2000, 82% of the 29 million jobs in the UK were in the private sector. Jobs in the private sector rose by 5% to 23.9 million in the ten years to June 2000. In the same period jobs in the public sector fell by 16% (959,000) to 5.1 million, of which 873,000 were in central government and 2.7 million in local government (including education and the police). The main falls occurred in public corporations, excluding National Health Service (NHS) Trusts, mainly as a result of the privatisation of former nationalised industries, and in education. Employment in public corporations (excluding NHS Trusts) fell by 400,000 to 385,000 and in education by 131,000 to 1.3 million. However, in the 12 months to June 2000 jobs in education rose by about 60,000 and there was also a rise in employment in NHS Trusts in this period, of 14,000 to 1.145 million.

Table 11.4: Workforce Jobs by Industry, UK, March 2001 *Seasonally adjusted*

	Workforce jobs (thousands)	Per cent of workforce jobs	Per cent change 1981–2001
Agriculture and fishing	494	1.7	–23.2
Energy and water	197	0.7	–71.2
Manufacturing	4,116	14.1	–34.1
Construction	1,884	6.5	1.4
Services:	22,482	77.1	34.2
Distribution, hotels and restaurants	*6,805*	*23.3*	*24.1*
Transport and communication	*1,822*	*6.2*	*9.8*
Finance and business services	*5,453*	*18.7*	*86.3*
Public administration, education and health	*6,694*	*22.9*	*20.5*
Other services	*1,708*	*5.9*	*52.2*
All jobs	**29,172**	**100.0**	**11.4**

Source: Office for National Statistics

Employment by Sector

The major long-term trend in employment by sector in the UK has been a big increase in employment in service industries (see Table 11.4). Between March 1981 and March 2001 the number of workforce jobs in service industries increased from 16.8 million to 22.5 million, a rise of 34%, compared with a rise in the total number of jobs of 11%. Growth in finance and business services was particularly strong, up by 86% in this period, although recently growth has been slower.

Transport and communications is one service sector where growth in the number of jobs has been below the average for the economy as a whole. However, in the year to March 2001 jobs in this sector grew by 4.1%, compared with a rise of 1.5% in finance and business services and of 1.1% in services as a whole.

In recent years most other sectors have experienced falling levels of employment. Traditional manufacturing industries, such as steel, shipbuilding and textiles, have recorded particularly large falls in employment. By March 2001 manufacturing accounted for 14% of workforce jobs, compared with 24% in 1981. Agriculture and fishing has also seen a fall in the number of jobs, and in the year to March 2001 jobs in the sector fell by 5%. The biggest long-term decline though has been in energy and water (see Table 11.4), reflecting, among other things, a big fall in jobs in the coal industry.

LABOUR MARKET POLICY

In March 2001 the Government published a Green Paper, *Towards Full Employment in a Modern Society*, setting out its strategy on labour market policy. This aims to ensure employment opportunity for all who can work, encourage flexible labour markets and raise skills. The Government's strategy for ensuring employment opportunity for all is based on:

- helping people to move from welfare to work, through extending the series of 'New Deals' (see pp. 154–5);
- easing the transition into work by removing barriers to working and ensuring that people are financially secure when moving from welfare to work;
- making paid work more attractive, through promoting incentives to work and reforming the tax and benefit system (see chapters 23 and 12); and
- securing progression in work, through lifelong learning (see chapter 10), to ensure that people are well trained and able to adapt to changing economic circumstances.

In June 2001 the Government established a new Department for Work and Pensions (see also chapter 12). The Department combines the employment and disability responsibilities of the former Department for Education and

Employment (now the Department for Education and Skills) with the welfare and pensions responsibilities of the former Department of Social Security. It will be responsible for Jobcentre Plus (see box).

> *Jobcentre Plus*
>
> From October 2001, the Government plans to launch a new Agency, Jobcentre Plus. This will bring together the Employment Service, which runs Jobcentres, and those parts of the Benefits Agency providing services to people of working age. It will start with around 50 'pathfinder' offices across England, Scotland and Wales. It will deal with all people's work and benefits needs, providing a single point of contact for all working-age people to access Jobseeker's Allowance and other social security benefits (see chapter 12) and will:
>
> - offer practical job-finding assistance through a personal adviser service;
> - ensure those people unable to work receive the correct benefits on time; and
> - help employers to fill their vacancies, including assistance in recruiting new groups of potential employees.

RECRUITMENT AND JOB-FINDING

Government Employment Services

The Employment Service (*www.employmentservice.gov.uk*) provides a range of services to jobseekers including:

- a network of over 1,000 local offices, at which people can find details of job vacancies;
- advice and guidance so that people can find the best route back into employment, for example, by training; and
- a range of special programmes, including those for people with disabilities.

The Employment Service has a budget in Great Britain of over £2 billion for 2001–02. In 2000–01 it placed 1.23 million unemployed people into jobs. It has a key role in the delivery of the Government's Welfare-to-Work measures (see p. 154).

Advisory Services

Through the main Jobcentre services, unemployed people have access to vacancies, employment advice and training opportunities. Employment Service advisers see all jobseekers when a claim is made for Jobseeker's Allowance (see p. 176) to assess their eligibility and to provide advice about jobs, training and self-employment opportunities. To receive the allowance, each unemployed person has to complete a Jobseeker's Agreement, which sets out his or her availability for work, the types of job for which he or she is looking, and the steps which, if taken, offer the best chance of securing work. Jobseekers are required to attend a job search review each fortnight and periodic intensive advisory interviews to assess their situation and see what additional help, if any, is needed and, if appropriate, to revise the Jobseeker's Agreement.

Programme Centres have been introduced nationally and are gradually replacing traditional fixed-length job search courses with a modular approach that addresses the needs of individual jobseekers, and allows providers to take a flexible approach so that job search help can be adapted for local delivery. Other programmes include Jobclubs (offering guidance on jobseeking, interview skills and other practical assistance), Jobplan workshops (a mandatory five-day programme of individual assessment) and work trial, where jobseekers spend up to a maximum of 15 days in an actual vacancy.

The Employment Service is implementing a modernisation programme using information and communications technology with the intention of improving its services to jobseekers and employers. All of the Service's vacancies are now available over the Internet, on one of the largest job banks in the world. Vacancies are also available through electronic touch-screen kiosks, known as 'Jobpoints', which are replacing traditional vacancy display boards in Jobcentres. In March 2001 the Employment Service began the phased introduction, which is expected to be completed by early 2002, of a new service, Employer Direct, to provide a single national telephone number for employers to have their vacancies advertised on the Internet and on all Jobpoint terminals.

In Northern Ireland arrangements for the joint delivery of services between the Department for Employment and Learning and the Social Security Agency are under consideration.

Welfare-to-Work

The Government's Welfare-to-Work programme is a series of measures, including a number of New Deals, designed with the aim of promoting an efficient labour market and tackling structural unemployment, economic inactivity and social exclusion. Common features of the measures for those seeking employment include the assistance of personal advisers, providing a single point of contact and help; and an emphasis on trying to obtain sustainable employment.

The Welfare-to-Work programme was originally funded by a windfall tax on the excess profits of the privatised utilities. Since April 2001 it has been funded from the new Employment Opportunities Fund, bringing together the remaining windfall tax receipts and additional resources allocated in the Spending Review 2000. Planned expenditure on Welfare-to-Work from the Fund is £1.05 billion in 2001–02, rising to £1.4 billion in 2002–03. In 2001–02 the provision for expenditure on New Deals includes £350 million on the New Deal for Young People, £190 million for the 25 plus programme, £100 million for lone parents and £50 million for disabled people.

Young People

The New Deal for Young People is available to those aged 18 to 24 who have been unemployed for more than six months. It begins with an intensive period of up to four months, of counselling, advice and guidance—the 'gateway'. If a young person has not left the gateway after that time, he or she must choose one of five options:

- a job attracting a wage subsidy of £60 a week, payable to employers for up to six months;
- self-employment;
- a work placement with a voluntary organisation;
- a six-month work placement with an Environment Task Force; and
- for those without basic qualifications, a place on a full-time education and training course, which might last for up to one year.

All these options include an element of education and training. By the end of June 2001 there had been 669,300 starts on this New Deal since its launch in April 1998: 577,700 people had left, of whom 39% had entered sustained unsubsidised jobs.

Long-term Unemployed

Under the New Deal for the long-term unemployed, which started in 1998, employers receive a subsidy of up to £75 a week for 26 weeks if they employ anyone who has been unemployed for two years or longer. From April 2001 the programme was extended and renamed the New Deal 25 plus programme, with eligibility reduced to 18 months for those aged 25 and over. The programme includes:

- a gateway period, lasting up to four months, aimed at getting people into work through an intensive period of weekly interviews and job search support from a personal adviser;
- a period of full-time activity where individuals are able to choose a mix, based on their needs, of subsidised employment, work-focused training, work experience, help with job search or help with moving into self-employment;
- a period for those who do not find work through the full-time activity period involving intensive help to take advantage of their experience and move into work; and
- benefit penalties, if individuals do not take advantage of this assistance.

By the end of June 2001 there had been 358,600 starts on this New Deal since its launch in April 1998: 322,800 people had left, with 73,600 people in jobs, of which 60,800 were sustained jobs.[3]

Lone Parents

The New Deal for Lone Parents provides for all lone parents on Income Support to meet a personal adviser and receive guidance to help improve their employment prospects.

From autumn 2001 eligibility will gradually be extended to all lone parents who are not in work, or work less than 16 hours a week but are not on Income Support. The Government is also phasing in, from 2001–02, compulsory meetings with a personal adviser for lone parents claiming Income Support who have a youngest child of five or over. This was piloted in three areas (Shropshire, South Tyneside and Fife) from October 2000. The 2001 Budget announced that the meetings would be extended to all lone parents on Income Support from April 2002, with an additional interview at the six-month stage of the claim. Intended further enhancements to this provision will include a new outreach service to attract more lone parents to the New Deal, help with starting up in self-employment, and extra childcare support.

Disabled People

Under the New Deal for Disabled People (NDDP), a wide range of innovative approaches in helping people on incapacity benefits were tested. From September 1998 to June 2001, 24 innovative schemes and 12 Personal Adviser Pilots, covering a range of disabilities and areas of the country, tested ways of helping disabled people and carers who want to work. In July 2001 the NDDP was extended throughout Great Britain, and a new network of job brokers is providing services and support to sick and disabled people who want to work, so as to help them find and keep paid work. The extended service will continue to be tested and evaluated.

[3] Figures relate to pre-April 2001 entrants to the New Deal.

Partners

The New Deal for Partners is a voluntary programme available to partners of those claiming Jobseeker's Allowance. Since 23 April 2001 it has also been available to partners of those receiving Income Support, Invalid Care Allowance, Severe Disablement Allowance and Incapacity Benefit. The New Deal aims to ensure that they have the opportunity to receive help to return to work; those involved are able to improve their skills and employability through employment programmes and training.

50 Plus

New Deal 50 plus was introduced nationally from April 2000. This programme helps people of 50 or over after they or their partners have been on benefits for six months or more and provides an Employment Credit payment of £60 a week for full-time work (30 hours or more a week) or £40 a week for part-time work (29 hours or less a week). This is paid for up to 52 weeks.

Northern Ireland

In Northern Ireland there is a broadly similar system to Welfare-to-Work, although programmes such as ONE (see p. 156) may be at a different stage of development. Responsibility for administration of programmes and services rests with the Northern Ireland Department for Employment and Learning and the Department for Social Development and their executive agencies.

Employment Zones

Pilot Employment Zones began running in April 2000 in 15 areas of Great Britain with unemployment rates above the national average. New approaches to tackle unemployment—including financial help for individual jobseekers through personal job accounts and the use of personal advisers—are being adopted and are being provided by public, private and voluntary sector organisations selected to run the zones by open competition. Originally £112 million was made available to support this initiative, providing help to around 48,000 long-term unemployed jobseekers aged 25 and over, between April 2000 and March 2002. In February 2001 the Government announced a one-year extension to the Employment Zones until March 2003; this is expected to benefit up to an additional 29,000 jobseekers at a cost of £81 million.

ONE

ONE is a pilot initiative for people of working age who work for less than 16 hours each week on average, to help them find jobs, training, benefits and a range of other advice and support to become independent. It is managed in partnership by the Benefits Agency (BA), Employment Service and local authorities in the 12 pilot areas.

Four of these pilots started in June 1999, testing delivery through existing Employment Service and BA outlets and local authority premises, and eight other pilots began in November 1999, with four testing the use of call centre technology and four innovative private/voluntary sector methods of delivery. The pilots, which are being evaluated, are expected to run until March 2002.

Individuals who wish to claim one or more of the ONE benefits must attend a work-focused meeting with a personal adviser at the outset of the claim, and thereafter at intervals as long as they remain on benefits. The purpose of the meeting is to identify the state of readiness for work, and any help or support the individual might need to help him or her move towards independence. Apart from those who claim Jobseeker's Allowance, there is no obligation on individuals to actively seek work, although they are encouraged to draw up an action plan and follow up their commitments. However, failure to attend, and participate in, the work-focused meeting without good cause can result in reduction or withdrawal of benefit until the condition is met.

Action Teams

In October 2000 Action Teams were set up, initially for one year, in 40 communities in the UK with the lowest employment and highest unemployment, including the 15 Employment Zones. From October 2001 there will be 38 Teams led by the Employment Service and from January 2002, 25 Teams led by private sector contractors. Funding of £135 million from October 2001 to March 2004 will enable the Teams to work with jobless people in the most deprived wards in the most deprived local authority areas of England, Wales and Scotland. The aim of the Teams is to remove the barriers to employment faced by jobless people and, by working with employers, to move them into suitable vacancies. The Teams will look at innovative ways of achieving their aim.

Job Transition Service

The Job Transition Service became operational from April 2001 and a number of initiatives are being piloted. It is led by the Employment Service working with local partners. The Service aims to provide additional help and support to those being made redundant, particularly where a significant redundancy has been recognised. This is done by working with employers in the local and national labour markets to identify skill shortages and to put in place arrangements to equip the redundant workforce for these opportunities. Where appropriate, the Service can also provide support to families and the wider community, to cope with the impact.

Employment Agencies

There are many private employment agencies, including several large firms with significant branch networks. The law governing the conduct of employment agencies is less restrictive than in many other EU countries, but agencies must comply with legislation which establishes a framework of minimum standards designed to protect agency users, both workers and hirers. Following a review of the regulatory framework by the Department of Trade and Industry (DTI) in 1999, a revised series of regulations should be in force by the end of 2001, providing, among other things, greater protection for temporary workers from exploitation. Another objective is to make it easier for temporary workers to move to permanent work status by removing current barriers within the market.

PAY AND CONDITIONS

Earnings

Average gross weekly earnings of full-time employees on adult rates in Great Britain whose pay was unaffected by absence were £411 in April 2001, according to the ONS New Earnings Survey. Average earnings for men were £453 and for women £338. Earnings were higher for non-manual employees (£452) than for manual employees (£324), with managerial and professional groups the highest paid.

Minimum Wage

The National Minimum Wage Act 1998 set out the regulatory framework for the national minimum wage which was introduced on 1 April 1999. Minimum wage rates, from 1 October 2001, are:

- £4.10 an hour for those aged 22 or above; and
- £3.50 an hour for workers aged 18 to 21, and for those aged 22 or over in the first six months of a new job with a new employer, and receiving accredited training.

The Government has agreed in principle that the rates will increase to £4.20 and £3.60 respectively on 1 October 2002, subject to favourable economic conditions.

Almost all workers who are 18 or over are covered by the minimum wage—there are no exemptions for casual workers, agency workers, part-time workers, overseas workers or workers in small businesses. The only workers to whom the national minimum wage does not apply are the self-employed, people under 18 years of age, prisoners, voluntary workers, members of the armed forces, family members of the employer living in the employer's home, and unrelated people living in their employer's home who are treated as part of the family (for example, au pairs). Apprentices and trainees are exempted for the first year of their training.

Around 1.5 million low-paid workers are estimated to have become entitled to higher pay following the introduction of the national minimum wage, some two-thirds of whom are women. This includes around 140,000 young people. Sectors most affected have been hospitality (hotels and catering), retailing, cleaning, hairdressing, social care, footwear and clothing manufacture, and private security.

Fringe Benefits

Fringe benefits are used by many employers to provide additional rewards to their employees. They include schemes to encourage financial participation by employees in their companies, pension schemes, medical insurance, subsidised meals, company cars and childcare schemes.

By the end of March 2000, 3,790 profit-related pay schemes, which link part of pay to changes in a business's profits, were registered with the Inland Revenue, covering around 1.6 million people. Many companies have adopted employee share schemes, where employees receive free shares or options to buy shares at a discount from their employer without paying income tax. A new all-employee share ownership plan was introduced in 2000, allowing employees to buy shares from their pre-tax salary and to receive free shares, with tax incentives for longer-term shareholding.

Hours of Work

Most full-time employees have a basic working week of between 34 and 40 hours, and work a five-day week. When overtime is taken into account, average weekly hours worked by full-time workers in their main job in the UK in spring 2001 were 38 hours: 40 hours for men and 34 hours for women. For part-time workers the average was 16 hours.

Both male and female full-time employees tend to work more hours than people in other EU countries. Hours worked tend to be longest in agriculture, construction, and transport and communications, and shortest in public administration, education and health. Self-employed people work, on average, longer hours than full-time employees.

Holiday entitlements have generally been determined by negotiation. In spring 2001 the average paid holiday entitlement for full-time workers was just under five weeks. However, some employees, such as part-time and temporary employees, may have much less holiday entitlement.

Regulations implementing two EC Directives, on working time and on young workers (in relation to hours of work of adolescents), came into force in the UK in 1998. They apply to full-time, part-time and temporary workers, although workers in certain sectors—including transport, sea fishing, other work at sea, and doctors in training—are currently exempt. They provide for:

- a maximum working week of 48 hours (on average), although individual workers can choose to work longer;
- a minimum of four weeks' annual paid leave;
- minimum daily and weekly rest periods;
- a limit for night workers of an average eight hours' work in a 24-hour period; and
- a right for night workers to receive free health assessments.

There are specific provisions for adolescent workers in respect of these rights and entitlements.

INDUSTRIAL RELATIONS

Around 36% of employees in Great Britain in 2000 were in workplaces covered by collective bargaining, which is generally more prevalent in large establishments and in the public sector. Collective bargaining mainly concerns pay and working conditions. In general, negotiations are now conducted more at a local level, although many large firms retain a degree of central control over the bargaining process. There are relatively few industry-wide agreements; where they do exist, they are often supplemented by local agreements in companies or factories (plant bargaining). The EC's European Works Councils Directive requires firms with 1,000 or more employees and which operate in two or more member states to establish European-level information and consultation procedures. Regulations implementing the Directive in the UK took effect in January 2000. About 100 UK-based companies have a European Works Council.

The Government is encouraging partnership at work by supporting the spread of best practice and promoting changes to workplace relations designed to benefit employees, business and the competitiveness of the UK economy. The Partnership Fund was launched in 1999 and is providing £5 million over four years to support partnership at work projects. Among 76 projects approved by July 2001 are schemes designed to reduce harassment and bullying at work, improve work-life balance, and implement modern manufacturing techniques through partnership.

Investors in People

Investors in People is the National Standard which sets a level of good practice for improving an organisation's performance through its people. It is designed to improve business performance by linking the training and development of employees to an organisation's business objectives. Reported benefits include increased productivity, higher profits, lower rates of absenteeism, and improved morale. Investors in People UK, which is responsible for the promotion, quality assurance and development of the Standard, has carried out an extensive review to simplify the Standard and make it more accessible, especially for small firms. At the end of March 2001, 24,259 organisations in the UK had been recognised as Investors in People. Over 5 million employees work in recognised organisations, covering around 24% of the UK workforce.

Individual Employment Rights

Employment protection legislation provides a number of safeguards for employees. For example, most employees have a right to a written statement setting out details of the main conditions, including pay, hours of work and holidays. Employees with at least two years of continuous employment with their employer are entitled to lump-sum redundancy payments if their jobs cease to exist and their employers cannot offer suitable alternative work.[4]

Minimum periods of notice are laid down for both employers and employees. Most employees who believe they have been unfairly dismissed have the right to complain to an employment tribunal (see p. 160), subject to the general qualifying period of one year's continuous service. If the complaint is upheld, the tribunal may make an order for re-employment or award compensation.

Legislation prohibits discrimination on grounds of sex or marital status (see p. 121) or disability or on grounds of race, nationality (including citizenship) or ethnic or national origin (see p. 116), in employment, training and related matters. In Northern Ireland discrimination in employment on grounds of religious belief or political opinion is unlawful. Under the Equal Pay Act 1970, women in Great Britain are entitled to equal pay with men when doing work that is the same or broadly similar, work which is rated as equivalent, or work which is of equal value. Despite this, there is a continuing pay gender gap. Among men and women working full-time the gap between their hourly earnings has narrowed since the mid-1970s. In March 2001 the Government announced a review of women's employment and pay.

Under the Disability Discrimination Act 1995, disabled people have the right not to be discriminated against in employment. Employers with 15 or more employees have a duty not to discriminate against disabled employees or applicants. The Disability Rights Commission (see p. 167) has powers to investigate cases of discrimination at work against people with disabilities, and to ensure employers comply with the appropriate legal regulations.

All pregnant employees have the right to statutory maternity leave with their non-wage contractual benefits maintained, and protection against detriment and dismissal because of pregnancy. Statutory maternity pay is payable by an employer for up to 18 weeks to women with at least six months' service with that employer.

New Rights

The Employment Relations Act 1999, and in Northern Ireland the Employment Relations (NI) Order 1999, introduced a package of family-oriented employment rights. With later modifications, the key elements are:

- a minimum of 18 weeks' maternity leave for all pregnant employees (in line with statutory maternity pay), with additional maternity leave for women after one year's service (reduced from the previous two years);
- 13 weeks' unpaid parental leave after one year's service for mothers and fathers—

Following a government review of the issues surrounding maternity rights and paternity leave, several new measures have been announced, including:

- an increase in the flat rate of Statutory Maternity Pay (SMP) and Maternity Allowance (see chapter 12)—from 2003 women will receive 90% of their previous earnings if that is less than the flat rate;
- an extension of the period of maternity pay from 18 weeks to 26 weeks from 2003;
- an extension of additional maternity leave to 26 weeks, enabling mothers to take up to a year's maternity leave;
- the right to two weeks of paid paternity leave for working fathers from 2003;
- an increase in the Sure Start Maternity Grant in April 2002, for 215,000 low-income families a year; and
- an increase in the amount of parental leave for parents of disabled children from 13 weeks to 18 weeks.

[4] The statutory redundancy payment is calculated according to a formula based on a person's age, the number of years of continuous service and his or her weekly pay. However, many employers pay more than the statutory amount.

the leave can be taken in the first five years following the child's birth or adoption;

- being able to return to the same job, or its equivalent, at the end of maternity and parental leave;
- clarification of the status of an employee's employment contract during periods of paternal or maternity leave;
- a reasonable amount of unpaid time off to deal with an emergency or unexpected problem involving a dependant; and
- protection against dismissal or detriment for exercising any of these rights.

Trade Union and Industrial Relations Law

Among the legal requirements governing industrial relations are:

- All individuals have the right not to be dismissed or refused employment (or the services of an employment agency) because of membership or non-membership of a trade union.
- Where a union is recognised by an employer for collective bargaining purposes, union officials are entitled to paid time off for undertaking certain trade union duties and training. The employer is also obliged to disclose information to the union for collective bargaining purposes.
- A trade union must elect every member of its governing body, its general secretary and its president. Elections must be held at least every five years and be carried out by a secret postal ballot under independent scrutiny.
- If a trade union wishes to set up a political fund, its members must first agree in a secret ballot a resolution adopting those political objectives as an aim of the union. The union must also ballot its members every ten years to maintain the fund. Union members have a statutory right to opt out of contributing to the fund.
- For a union to have the benefit of statutory immunity when organising industrial action, the action must be wholly or mainly in contemplation or furtherance of a trade dispute between workers and their own employer. Industrial action must not involve workers who have no dispute with their own employer (so-called 'secondary' action) or involve unlawful forms of picketing. Before calling for industrial action, a trade union must obtain the support of its members in a secret postal ballot.

Recent Changes

Various changes to industrial relations legislation are being implemented through the Employment Relations Act 1999 and in Northern Ireland the Employment Relations (NI) Order 1999. For example, there are new statutory procedures, which came into force in June 2000, for trade unions to seek recognition in organisations with more than 20 employees where the majority of the workforce is in favour. Parties are encouraged to reach a voluntary agreement where possible, but if this proves impossible the Central Arbitration Committee (CAC) will decide the issues concerned. In the first year, 80 applications were made to the CAC. Other provisions include:

- extended protection against unfair dismissal for employees taking part in lawfully organised official industrial action which started on or after 24 April 2000;
- a legal right for employees to be accompanied by a fellow employee or trade union representative in serious disciplinary and grievance hearings;
- powers to prohibit the blacklisting of trade unionists; and
- a new Partnership Fund (see p. 158) to contribute to the training of managers and employee representatives in order to assist and develop partnerships at work.

Employment Tribunals

Employment tribunals in Great Britain have jurisdiction over complaints covering a range of employment rights, including unfair dismissal, redundancy pay, equal pay, and sex and race discrimination. New tribunal regulations, including provisions designed to deter cases with weak claims and defences, took effect in July 2001. Tribunals received 130,000 applications in 2000–01. Northern Ireland has a separate tribunal system.

Labour Disputes

In the past 20 years there has been a substantial decline in working days lost through labour disputes. In 2000 there were 212 stoppages of work arising from labour disputes, and 499,000 working days were lost as a result. Although this was the highest annual total since 1996, it was below the average of 660,000 days lost in the period 1990 to 1999. Stoppages over pay accounted for 77% of days lost in 2000. Some 49% of stoppages lasted for no more than one working day. The UK has a good record in employment relations: in 1999 only 10 days were lost per 1,000 employees to labour disputes, compared with the EU average of 37.

Trade Unions

Trade unions have members in nearly all occupations. As well as negotiating pay and other terms and conditions of employment with employers, they provide benefits and services, such as educational facilities, financial services, legal advice and aid in work-related cases.

In autumn 2000 there were 7.3 million trade union members in Great Britain, according to the Labour Force Survey, 17% fewer than in 1990, although there were small increases in membership in 1999 and 2000.[5] The proportion of those in employment who are union members was 27.0% in autumn 2000 (compared with 33.9% in 1990), and the proportion among employees was 29.4% in 2000 (38.1% in 1990). Trade union membership is more prevalent among older employees, those with long service and those in the public sector. By occupation, union membership is most prevalent among professionals, half of whom were trade union members in 2000. The long-term decline in membership has been particularly noticeable where membership has traditionally been high—among male employees, manual workers and those in production industries. Public administration has the highest density of union members, around 60% of all employees. Sectors with relatively few union members include agriculture, forestry and fishing, hotels and restaurants, and wholesale and retail trade.

The largest union in the United Kingdom is Unison with around 1.3 million members. Other unions with membership over 500,000 are:

- the Transport and General Workers Union;
- the Amalgamated Engineering and Electrical Union; and
- the GMB—a general union with members in a wide range of industries.

At the end of March 2001 there were 206 trade unions on the list maintained by the Certification Officer, who, among other duties, is responsible for certifying the independence of trade unions. To be eligible for entry on the list a trade union must show that it consists wholly or mainly of workers and that its principal purposes include the regulation of relations between workers and employers or between workers and employers' associations. A further 22 unions were known to the Certification Officer.

The national body of the trade union movement is the Trades Union Congress (TUC), founded in 1868. At the beginning of 2001 its affiliated membership comprised 74 trade unions, which together represented some 6.7 million people.

There are six TUC regional councils for England and a Wales Trades Union Council. The annual Congress meets in September to discuss matters of concern to trade unionists. A General Council represents the TUC between annual meetings.

In Scotland there is a separate national central body, the Scottish Trades Union Congress, to which UK unions usually affiliate their Scottish branches. Nearly all

[5] There are two main sources of information on trade union membership: the ONS Labour Force Survey and data provided by trade unions to the Certification Office. Differences in coverage can result in different estimates. For example, the Certification Officer's figure for trade union membership in 1999–2000 was 7.9 million, compared with the Labour Force Survey figure in autumn 2000 of 7.3 million members among those in employment.

trade unions in Northern Ireland are represented by the Northern Ireland Committee of the Irish Congress of Trade Unions (ICTU). Most trade unionists in Northern Ireland are members of unions affiliated to the ICTU, while the majority also belong to unions based in Great Britain, which are affiliated to the TUC.

The TUC participates in international trade union activity, through its affiliation to the International Confederation of Free Trade Unions and the European Trade Union Confederation. It also nominates the British workers' delegation to the annual International Labour Conference.

The TUC initiated the TUC Partnership Institute in spring 2001 to provide an advisory and training service to help unions and employers establish partnerships at work.

Employers' Organisations

Many employers in the UK are members of employers' organisations, some of which are wholly concerned with labour matters, although others are also trade associations concerned with commercial matters in general. Employers' organisations are usually established on an industry basis rather than a product basis, for example, the Engineering Employers' Federation. A few are purely local in character or deal with a section of an industry or, for example, with small businesses; most are national and are concerned with the whole of an industry. At the end of March 2001, there were 98 employers' associations on the list maintained by the Certification Officer and a further 94 were known to the Certification Officer.

Most national organisations belong to the CBI (see p. 397), which represents around 200,000 businesses.

ACAS

The Advisory, Conciliation and Arbitration Service (ACAS) is an independent statutory body with a general duty of promoting the improvement of industrial relations. ACAS aims to operate through the voluntary co-operation of employers, employees and, where appropriate, their representatives. Its main functions are collective conciliation; provision of arbitration and mediation; advisory mediation services for preventing disputes and improving industrial relations through the joint involvement of employers and employees; and the provision of a public enquiry service. ACAS also conciliates in disputes on individual employment rights, and in April 2001 introduced a new voluntary arbitration system for resolving unfair dismissal claims.

In Northern Ireland the Labour Relations Agency, an independent statutory body, provides services similar to those provided by ACAS in Great Britain.

HEALTH AND SAFETY AT WORK

There has been a long-term decline in injuries to employees in the UK, partly reflecting a change in industrial structure away from the traditional heavy industries, which tend to have higher risks. In 1999–2000 the number of deaths of employees and the self-employed from injuries at work was 220, which represented a fatal injury rate of 0.8 per 100,000 workers. About 6.5 million working days were lost in 1997–98 as a result of work-related injuries.

The principal legislation is the Health and Safety at Work etc. Act 1974. It imposes general duties on everyone concerned with work activities, including employers, the self-employed, employees, and manufacturers and suppliers of materials for use at work. Associated Acts and regulations deal with particular hazards and types of work. Employers with five or more staff must prepare a written statement of their health and safety policy and bring it to the attention of their staff.

In June 2000 the Government announced targets to cut workplace deaths, injuries and illness. It aims to:

- cut deaths and major injury accidents by 10% by 2010;
- reduce the rate of work-related ill-health by 20% by 2010;
- cut working days lost per 100,000 workers due to work-related injury and ill-health by 30% by 2010; and
- achieve half of the above improvements by 2004.

A new Safety Bill is planned, which will include proposals to meet these targets as well as proposals aimed at making travel by air, rail, sea and road safer (see chapter 21).

Health and Safety Commission

The Health and Safety Commission (HSC) has responsibility for developing policy on health and safety at work in Great Britain, including proposals for new or revised regulations and approved codes of practice. Recent work has concentrated on a simpler and more effective system of regulation.

The HSC has advisory committees covering subjects such as toxic substances, genetic modification and the safety of nuclear installations. There are also several industry advisory committees, each covering a specific sector of industry.

Health and Safety Executive

The Health and Safety Executive (HSE) is the primary instrument for carrying out the HSC's policies and has day-to-day responsibility for enforcing health and safety law, except where other bodies, such as local authorities, are responsible. Its field services and inspections are carried out by the Field Operations Directorate, which includes the Railway Inspectorate, the Safety Policy Directorate, the Health Directorate and the Hazardous Installations and Nuclear Safety Inspectorates.

The HSE's Technology Division provides technical advice on industrial health and safety matters. The Health and Safety Laboratory (HSL), an agency of the HSE, aims to ensure that risks to health and safety from work activities are properly controlled. This involves HSL in two main areas: operational support through incident investigations and studies of workplace situations; and longer-term work on analysis and resolution of occupational health and safety problems.

In premises such as offices, shops, warehouses, restaurants and hotels, legislation is enforced by inspectors appointed by local authorities, working under guidance from the HSE. Some other official bodies work under agency agreement with the HSE.

Northern Ireland

The general requirements of health and safety legislation in Northern Ireland are broadly similar to those for Great Britain and are enforced by the Health and Safety Executive for Northern Ireland (HSENI) and the district councils, with the latter having an enforcement role similar to that of local authorities in Great Britain.

Further Reading

Labour Market Trends. Office for National Statistics. Monthly.

Labour Market Bulletin. Northern Ireland Department for Employment and Learning. Annual.

Towards Full Employment in a Modern Society. Department for Education and Employment, Her Majesty's Treasury and the Department of Social Security. Cm 5084. The Stationery Office, 2001.

Work and Parents: Competitiveness and Choice. Department of Trade and Industry. Cm 5005. The Stationery Office, 2001.

Annual Reports

Advisory, Conciliation and Arbitration Service. ACAS.

Certification Officer. Certification Office for Trade Unions and Employers' Associations.

Health and Safety Commission. HSC.

Websites

Department for Work and Pensions: www.dwp.gov.uk

Department of Trade and Industry: www.dti.gov.uk

Health and Safety Executive: www.hse.gov.uk

Office for National Statistics: www.statistics.gov.uk

Trades Union Congress: www.tuc.org.uk

12 Social Protection

Personal Social Services	164	Contributions	173
Social Security	171	Benefits	174
Modernising the System	172	Arrangements and Comparisons	
Administration	173	with Other Countries	183

The responsibility for delivering social care support to children, older people, those who are physically disabled and sensorily impaired, people with learning disabilities or mental health problems, and to the carers of such individuals, falls to local authorities and voluntary organisations, working within a policy framework set out by central government. The Department for Work and Pensions was established in June 2001 to continue the reform of the welfare state.

Provisions in the Care Standards Act 2000 aim to improve standards in care services, set new checks on private healthcare and reform regulation of early years childcare and education. The National Service Framework for Older People sets standards for preventing illness and improving care of older people. The Adoption and Children Bill seeks to improve the performance of the adoption service and promote greater use of adoption, putting the needs of children first. Through the Criminal Justice and Services Act 2000, the Government has changed the law to protect children from paedophiles when using the Internet.

Personal Social Services

Personal social services help older people, people with disabilities, children and young people, those with mental health problems or learning disabilities, their families and carers. Major services include residential, day care, short-break and domiciliary services (provided for people needing support to live in their own homes). In certain circumstances direct cash payments may be made to enable individuals to obtain relevant services for themselves. Services are administered by local authorities, but central government is responsible for establishing national policies, issuing guidance and overseeing standards.

Much of the care given to older people and disabled people comes from families and self-help groups. One in eight adults gives informal care and one in six homes has a carer. Many of these carers are elderly themselves. There are around 6 million informal carers in the UK, about 58% of whom are women. The Carers and Disabled Children Act 2000 ensures for the first time that support is specifically directed at carers, bringing their needs in line with those of the person they are looking after.

Caring for Vulnerable People

The number of places in residential care homes provided by the public sector has been

Table 12.1: Places available in Residential Care Homes in the UK, by Sector

Thousands

	1994	1995	1996	1997	1998	1999
Public sector						
Older people	81.2	75.7	67.4	66.2	64.3	60.5
People with physical or sensory or learning disabilities	13.6	13.0	11.9	11.1	11.3	10.2
People with mental health problems	5.6	5.2	5.0	5.3	4.9	3.8
Other people	0.5	0.4	0.4	0.5	0.6	0.6
All places in the public sector	**100.9**	**94.3**	**84.7**	**83.2**	**81.1**	**75.1**
Independent sector						
Older people	202.7	204.1	196.8	212.0	219.1	219.5
People with physical or sensory or learning disabilities	40.0	43.9	45.7	53.1	55.9	57.6
People with mental health problems	20.9	21.0	22.7	34.1	36.5	37.1
Other people	4.2	4.3	3.9	4.4	5.5	4.5
All places in the independent sector	**267.9**	**273.2**	**269.1**	**303.6**	**316.9**	**318.7**

Sources: Department of Health; National Assembly for Wales; Scottish Executive; Department of Health, Social Services and Public Safety, Northern Ireland

declining since 1994, while the number of places provided by the independent sector (the private sector and the voluntary sector) has been increasing over the same period (see Table 12.1).

The Care Standards Act 2000 aims to raise the standards in care services in England and Wales, to monitor private healthcare provision and reform the regulation of care for young people. Under the Act, the National Care Standards Commission (NCSC) was established in April 2001. The NCSC takes over its regulatory functions in April 2002 and will be responsible for regulating social care services as well as private and voluntary healthcare. Its remit includes all care homes, children's homes as well as private hospitals and clinics. The independent Commission has strong powers of enforcement to make sure that services meet required standards.

The Act also establishes a General Social Care Council (GSCC) which will operate from October 2001. This will raise professional and training standards for the social care workforce and offer an increased level of protection to users of social care services in England. It will regulate the social care workforce by publishing Codes of Practice for workers and their employers and by registering the workforce, beginning with social workers. Equivalent bodies are being established in Scotland, Northern Ireland and Wales.

Alongside the GSCC, the Government is also to establish the Social Care Institute for Excellence (SCIE), which will help to raise the standard of social care provision in England and Wales. SCIE will establish a database of knowledge about what works in social care, drawing on existing practice, user and carer experience and the results of Social Services Inspectorate and Joint Review inspections. The information that SCIE gathers will be rigorously reviewed and SCIE will produce Best Practice guidelines based on this review process. These guidelines will be disseminated across the social care sector in order to eliminate variations in quality and standards. The improvement of training standards will be taken forward by the Training Organisation for the Personal Social Services (TOPSS), which is responsible for developing and promoting the National Occupational Standards for care work.

Older People

Older people represent the fastest growing section of the community. Services are designed to help them live at home whenever possible. These services may include advice and help given by social workers, domestic help, the provision of meals in the home, sitters-in, night attendants and laundry services, as well as direct payments, day centres, lunch clubs and recreational facilities. The Warm Homes Act 2000 addressed the issue of fuel poverty. As a result, schemes have been set up in the different countries of the UK to provide free central heating and free insulation.

Adaptations to the home can overcome a person's difficulties in moving about. A range of equipment is available for people with poor hearing or eyesight and for those with physical disabilities. Alarm systems help older people obtain assistance in an emergency. In some areas 'good neighbour' and visiting services are arranged by the local authority or a voluntary organisation.

Over the past few years, there has been a fall in the number of residential places provided for older people by the public sector (see Table 12.1). In 1994, the public sector provided 29% of places for older people. This had fallen to 22% in 1999. Older people who live in residential care homes or nursing homes are subject to means-test charging. Local authorities contribute to care costs for those who cannot pay the full charge.

Better Care for all our futures, published by the Scottish Executive in April 2001, sets out pre-legislative consultation on a range of proposals to develop long-term care in Scotland. The proposals include:

- measures to extend joint working on health and social care between local authorities and health bodies;
- expansion of direct payments made by local authorities allowing people to purchase non-residential care services;
- optional deferred payment agreement with local authorities to give people the choice of whether to sell their home in order to pay for their residential care;
- enabling certain people in care homes funded by local authorities to top up the fees if they choose a more expensive home; and
- improving consistency of charging for non-residential care by local authorities.

The National Service Framework (NSF) for Older People

This NSF, published in 2001, sets standards for preventing illness and improving care among older people in England. (NSFs for mental health and coronary heart disease were published in September 1999 and March 2000 respectively—see chapter 13.) The NSF for older people contains eight standards on: rooting out age discrimination; person-centred care; intermediate care; general hospital care; stroke; falls; mental health in older people; and promoting an active healthy life.

The standards will be delivered locally and monitored by independent bodies, including the National Care Standards Commission.

Implementation of free personal and nursing care for older people in Scotland will begin in April 2002.

Following publication of *Improving Health in Wales—A Plan for the NHS with its Partners* and the introduction of the Health and Social Care Act 2001, the National Assembly for Wales is also implementing a policy to ensure that the services of a Registered Nurse are free of charge in all care settings.

The development of a strategy for older people is being taken forward by the National Assembly for Wales. The main purpose of the strategy is to provide a structured basis for the Assembly and other public bodies to develop future policies and plans which reflect the needs of older people and recognise changing demographic and social circumstances. The strategy will be completed for consultation by spring 2002 and will include a review of the consequences of introducing free personal care in Wales.

People with Disabilities

Over the past decade there has been increasing emphasis on rehabilitation and the provision of day, domiciliary and respite support services to enable disabled people to live independently in the community whenever possible.

Local authority social services departments help with social rehabilitation and adjustment to disability. They are required to identify the number of disabled people in their area and to provide and publicise services. These may include advice on personal and social problems arising from disability, as well as occupational, educational, social and recreational facilities, either at day centres or elsewhere. Other services provided may include adaptations to homes (such as ramps for wheelchairs, stairlifts and ground-floor toilets), the delivery of cooked meals, support with personal care at home and direct payments with which disabled people can purchase support to meet their assessed need. Local authorities and voluntary organisations may provide severely disabled people with residential accommodation, either on a permanent basis or temporarily in order to relieve their existing carers. Special housing may be available for those able to look after themselves. Some authorities provide free or subsidised travel for disabled people on public transport, and they are encouraged to provide special means of access to public buildings.

The Department for Work and Pensions is responsible for disability issues. The department manages WORKSTEP (previously called the Supported Employment Programme). This exists to recognise the right of disabled people to the same work opportunities as others and, where possible, to allow them to move from supported employment to open employment. Quality standards will be developed to ensure consistency throughout the programme for those employers who take part.

A Disability Rights Commission (DRC), established in Great Britain in April 2000, aims to eliminate discrimination against disabled people, promote equal opportunities, encourage good practice and advise the Government on the operation of the Disability Discrimination Act 1995 and the Disability Rights Commission Act 1999. The Equality Commission (see p. 117) has a similar role in Northern Ireland.

People with Learning Disabilities

The Government encourages the development of local services for people with learning disabilities and their families through cooperation between health authorities, local authorities, education and training services and voluntary and other organisations.

Local authority social services departments are the leading statutory agencies for planning and arranging such services. They provide or arrange short-term care, support for families in their own homes, residential accommodation and support for various types of activity outside the home. People with learning disabilities may also be able to receive direct payments. The main aim is to ensure that, as far as possible, they can lead full lives in the community. They form the largest group for local authority-funded day centre places and the second largest group in residential care. The National Health Service (NHS) provides specialist services when the ordinary primary care services cannot meet healthcare needs. Residential care is provided for those with severe or profound disabilities whose needs can effectively be met only by the NHS. The White Paper *A new strategy for Learning Disability for the 21st Century* was published in March 2001. The proposals are intended to result in improvements to education, social services, health, employment, housing, and support for people with learning disabilities, their families and carers in England.

In May 2000, the Scottish Executive published *The Same As You?*, its review of services for people with a learning disability. By focusing on inclusion, it aims to improve the lives of people with learning disabilities and their families.

People with a Mental Health Problem

Government policy aims to ensure that people with mental health problems should have access to all the services they need as locally as possible. Under the Care Programme Approach, each patient should receive an assessment leading to the formulation of an agreed care plan. A care coordinator is appointed to keep in touch with him or her, and the care plan is regularly reviewed in the light of the individual's changing needs. The separate Welsh Mental Health Strategy employs many of the same principles in delivering services in Wales. In Scotland, each health board works with its local authority care partners, with users of mental health services and with their carers in order to develop joint strategies and provide local and comprehensive mental health services.

While the total number of places for people with mental health problems in the large hospitals has continued to fall, the provision of alternative places has increased. More people are now cared for in smaller NHS hospitals, local authority accommodation and private and voluntary sector homes. In 1999 there were 37,100 places available in independent sector (private sector and voluntary sector) residential care homes for people with mental health problems in the UK, compared with 20,900 places in 1994 (see Table 12.1).

Arrangements made by social services authorities for providing care in the community include direct payments, day centres, social centres and residential care. Social workers are increasingly being integrated with NHS staff in community mental health teams under single management. This includes the newer functional teams specified in the NHS Plan—assertive outreach, crisis resolution, home treatment and early intervention. Social workers help patients and their families with problems caused by mental illness. In some cases they can apply for a mentally disordered person to be compulsorily admitted to and detained in hospital. Special bodies provide safeguards for patients to ensure that the law is used appropriately.

Currently supervision registers for discharged patients most at risk are maintained by the providers of services for mentally ill people. However, mental health provider trusts will be allowed to discontinue their supervision registers once Regional Offices are satisfied that they have suitable arrangements for delivering the Care Programme Approach.

In December 2000 the Government set out detailed plans covering the reform of the Mental Health Act (1983), in the White Paper *Reforming the Mental Health Act*. This set out new arrangements for managing dangerous people with severe personality disorders, including significant programmes of research and service development. Modern mental health legislation will make it possible to treat people with severe mental disorder either in their own best interest or to protect the wider public. The legislation will also introduce new safeguards for patients subject to compulsory care and treatment and enable people to be treated in the community, where appropriate, rather than being detained in hospital.

Help to Families

Local authorities and Health and Social Services—HSS—Trusts in Northern Ireland are required to safeguard the welfare of any child in need and promote the upbringing of such children by their families. The services provided to achieve these aims include advice, guidance, counselling, help in the home and family centres. Help is available to the immediate family of the child in need or to any other member of the family, if this will safeguard the child's welfare. Local authorities can provide these services directly or arrange them through another agency such as a voluntary organisation. They are also required to publicise the help available to families in need. Many local authorities and specialist voluntary organisations run refuges for women whose home conditions have become intolerable because of, for example, domestic violence. The refuges provide short-term accommodation and support for women and children while attempts are made to relieve the longer-term problems.

Day Care for Children

Day care facilities are provided for young children by childminders, voluntary agencies, private nurseries and local authorities. In 2000 in England and Wales, there were 334,000 childminder places for children under eight; 275,000 day nursery places; 149,000 out-of-school clubs; and 377,000 playgroup places.

In allocating local authority places, priority is given to children with special social, learning or health needs. In September 2001 the newly formed Early Years Directorate of OFSTED (see p. 134) took over responsibility from local authorities for the regulation of day care providers for children aged under eight.

In Scotland, local authority responsibility transferred to the new Scottish Commission for the Regulation of Care in April 2001. Regulation has been extended to cover provision for children up to the age of 16.

Child Protection

Child protection is the joint concern of a number of different agencies and professions. Local authority area child protection committees determine how the different agencies should cooperate to help protect children from abuse and neglect in their area. In Scotland, a review of child protection was announced in March 2001. The report of the review will be published by June 2002.

New guidance for schools in England has been issued by the Department for Education and Skills on protection against paedophiles using the Internet. It covers e-mails for pupils, filtering systems, school websites and chat rooms, and stipulates that no child be identified by name or other personal details.

The Government announced in March 2001 that a new taskforce would be established to help improve the protection of those using the Internet in the UK, particularly children. The taskforce will include representatives from the Internet industry, child welfare organisations, the police and government.

In January 2001, the Government changed the law to tackle Internet crime in England and Wales. Through the Criminal Justice and Court Services Act 2000, the age below which children are protected under the Indecency with Children Act 1960 was raised from 14 to 16. The same Act also significantly increased the maximum sentences for child pornography offences. Through the Regulation of Investigatory Powers Act 2000, the police will undertake computer network investigations and forensic examinations of suspects' and victims' computers in order to secure evidence to bring before a court.

Children in Care

Local authorities and HSS Trusts must provide accommodation for children who have no parent or guardian, who have been abandoned, or whose parents are unable to provide for them. They can also be accommodated by a local authority through a voluntary agreement with their parents.

In England and Wales a child may be brought before a family proceedings court if he or she is neglected or ill-treated, exposed to moral danger, beyond the control of parents, or not attending school. The court can commit children to the care of a local authority under a care order. Certain pre-conditions have to be satisfied to justify such an order. These are that the children are suffering or are likely to suffer significant harm because of a lack of reasonable parental care or because they are beyond parental control. However, an order is made only if the court is also satisfied that this will positively contribute to the children's well-being and be in their best interests. In court proceedings children are entitled to separate legal representation. All courts have to treat the welfare of children as the paramount consideration when reaching any decision about their upbringing. There is a general principle that, wherever possible, children should remain at home with their families.

In Scotland children who have committed offences or are in need of care and protection may be brought before a Children's Hearing, which can impose a supervision requirement on a child. Under these requirements, most children are allowed to remain at home under the supervision of a social worker, but some may live with foster parents or in a residential establishment while under supervision. Supervision requirements are reviewed at least once a year until ended by a Children's Hearing.

The Government has set up the Quality Protects programme in England to improve the management and delivery of children's social services and hence improve the life chances of children in need, including children in care. This is a key part of the wider strategy for tackling social exclusion (see p. 118). A special grant of £885 million over five years from April 1999 is supporting this programme. Payment of each local authority's share of the grant is subject to the preparation and achievement of satisfactory action plans. In Wales the National Assembly's Children First programme has similar objectives.

Fostering and Children's Homes

Local authorities and HSS Trusts have a duty to ensure that the welfare of children being looked after away from home is properly safeguarded. This includes their health, education and contact with their families and way of life. When appropriate, children in care are placed with foster parents, who receive payments to cover the child's living costs. Alternatively, the child may be placed in residential care. Children's homes may be provided by local authorities, voluntary organisations or private companies or individuals. Voluntary children's homes, which are registered by the Department of Health, are inspected by the Social Services Inspectorate. Local authority social services departments inspect the children's homes that they are responsible for registering.

Under the Care Standards Act (see p. 165), all children's homes are required to register with the NCSC. The Commission will also inspect all children's homes, including small private children's homes accommodating three or fewer children, which are not currently subject to any inspection process.

Local authorities are as far as possible expected to work in partnership with the parents of children who are in their care. They are required to produce a plan for the future of each child in their care and to prepare a child for leaving care. Local authorities are also expected to have a complaints procedure for considering representations about children's services. The Children Act 1989 requires the involvement of an independent person at each stage of consideration of a representation or complaint. The Children (Leaving Care) Act 2000 (see below) introduced a 14-day resolution stage for complaints brought under this Act; if the complaint is not resolved by that deadline the same procedure applies as for the Children Act complaints process.

The number of children looked after by local authorities in England, Wales and Northern Ireland increased from 55,000 in 1994 to 61,000 in 1999. The number of children placed in foster homes increased by around 13% over the same period and the number placed in children's homes declined by 19%. Scotland has a different definition of children in care which means data are not comparable with the rest of the UK. Social services also help children who are considered to be at risk of abuse and hold a central register of such children. At 31 March 2000, 34,200 children in England, Wales and Northern Ireland were on child protection registers.

Young People Leaving Local Authority Care

Improving the life chances of young people living in and leaving local authority care is the principal aim of the Children (Leaving Care) Act 2000, which will be implemented from October 2001. The Act:

- imposes a new duty on local authorities to assess and meet the needs of eligible people aged 16 or 17 who are in care or care leavers. Wherever the young person lives in England or Wales the local authority must keep in touch with them until they are at least 21;
- ensures that, on or shortly after becoming 16, every eligible young person in or leaving care has a plan mapping out a clear route to independence;
- ensures that local authorities provide all eligible 16 to 17 year olds who are in care or care leavers with personal and practical support to meet the objectives identified in their pathway plans;
- ensures each young person has a young person's adviser to coordinate provision of support and assistance. Emphasis will be placed on helping the young person into education, training or employment;
- ensures a new financial regime for care leavers; and
- ensures continuing assistance for care leavers aged 18 to 21, especially with education and employment. Assistance with education or training continues to the end of the agreed programme, even if it takes someone past the age of 21.

The Act applies to England and Wales, although regulations are made separately for the two countries. Scotland intends to bring in similar legislation as soon as parliamentary time allows. In Northern Ireland a consultation document on proposals for a Children Leaving Care Bill was published by the Department of Health, Social Services and Public Safety in March 2001.

Adoption

Local authority social services departments and HSS Trusts are required by law to provide an adoption service, either directly or by arrangement with approved voluntary adoption societies. Adoption is one way children in care are able to leave care—around a third of all children adopted are looked after by a local authority prior to their adoption. Around 5,000 children were entered on the Adopted Children Register in 2000 in England and Wales.

In August 2001, the final National Adoption Standards for England were published. The Standards have been developed to ensure that children, prospective adopters and birth families receive a consistent and high-quality adoption service no matter where they live. Adoption Standards for Wales, Scotland and Northern Ireland will be issued at a later date.

At the same time, the Adoption Register for England and Wales was launched in England (the launch in Wales will follow later). It will hold information on children waiting to be adopted and approved adoptive families from across England and Wales. The Register will tackle delays in finding suitable adoptive families for children from across the country where a local family cannot be found, or the child needs to move away from the area.

The Adoption and Permanence Taskforce is a new source of practical help for authorities. Its function is to help councils to improve their performance and to spread best practice. A Partnership Council has also been established to support this work and act as a sounding board for the Government on adoption issues.

In April 2001 provisions in the Adoption (Intercountry Aspects) Act 1999 came into force in England and Wales. These placed a duty on local government to provide an inter-country adoption service and made it an offence to bring a child into the UK for the purposes of adoption without complying with prescribed procedures including the usual assessment and approval arrangements. Scotland brought the same provisions into force in July 2001.

Adoption and Children Bill

An Adoption and Children Bill will be introduced during the current session of Parliament. It will implement the proposals in the White Paper *Adoption—a new approach,* published in December 2000, and underpin the Government's drive to improve the adoption service and promote greater use of adoption. It will include provisions to:

- introduce a new duty on local authorities to provide an adoption support service and a right for adoptive families to request and receive an assessment of their needs for adoption support services;
- establish an independent review mechanism for applicants who consider they are being turned down unfairly;
- legally underpin the new Adoption Register for England and Wales; and
- improve the legal controls on inter-country adoption and advertising children for adoption, and make clear the steps in relation to adoption which may only be taken by an adoption agency.

In Scotland, the Adoption Policy Review was announced in April 2001. This will look at adoption law and practice.

Finance

In 1998–99, gross expenditure on personal social services was £12.4 billion in Great Britain. In England local authorities' expenditure on services for older people and children accounted for nearly three-quarters of all expenditure on personal social services in 1998–99 (see Figure 12.2).

Social Security

The social security system is designed to secure a basic standard of living for people in

Figure 12.2:
Local Authority Personal Social Services Gross Expenditure by Client Group, England, 1998–99

Total: £11 billion

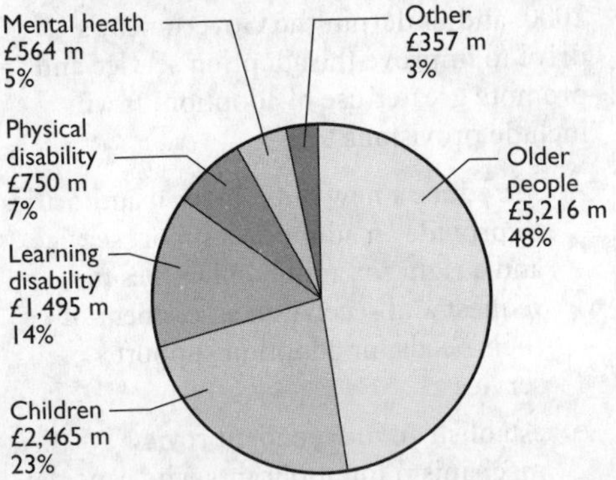

Source: Department of Health

financial need. It provides income during periods of inability to earn (including periods of unemployment), help for families and assistance with costs arising from disablement.

Social security is the largest single area of government spending. In each year from 1995–96 to 2000–01 spending on social security benefits in Great Britain represented about 29% of total government expenditure. At 2000–01 prices, spending grew from £100.8 billion to £105.5 billion over this five-year period, representing a growth rate of about 0.9% a year on average.

MODERNISING THE SYSTEM

Welfare Reform

The Government's central aim for welfare reform is to promote an ethic of work and savings. The Welfare Reform and Pensions Act 1999 came into force in November 1999. Its main measures are: the introduction of new stakeholder pension schemes (see below); pension sharing for divorced couples; revisions to benefits for widows and widowers; a single gateway to the benefit system for those of working age; and a new benefits structure for people with disabilities or long-term illness.

The Government aims to support and strengthen the framework for occupational pensions. The new stakeholder pensions were introduced in April 2001. They will provide a new pension option for those earners who do not have access to a good occupational pension. All employers, if they do not have an occupational pension scheme or contribute at least 3% to their employees' personal pension, must provide their employees with access to a stakeholder pension scheme. Employers are exempt if they have fewer than five employees.

Stakeholder pensions, which are provided by private sector companies, must satisfy a number of minimum government standards to ensure that they offer value for money and flexibility. These standards include:

- not charging more than 1% a year on the value of each member's funds;
- enabling members to transfer into or out of a stakeholder pension, or stop payment for a time, without facing any charge;
- accepting contributions of £20 or more, weekly, monthly or at less regular intervals; and
- being run in the interest of their members by trustees or scheme managers.

The Government also plans to reform the state earnings-related pension scheme (SERPS) (see p. 175) in 2002 to provide a more generous additional state pension for low and moderate earners, and certain carers and people with a long-term illness or disability. This will be called the State Second Pension.

The statutory framework necessary to establish State Second Pensions is contained in the Child Support, Pensions and Social Security Act 2000. For the first time, carers, others with domestic responsibilities who were unable to contribute to a second pension in their own right, and people suffering a long-term illness or disability with broken work records would benefit from additional pension provision. It is expected that about 11 million people nationwide will be better off when they retire as a result of these changes.

Other measures in the Act will strengthen arrangements for child maintenance (see p. 178). These include:

- giving the Child Support Agency (CSA) far-reaching powers to enforce maintenance payments;
- introducing fines of up to £1,000 for absent parents who deliberately try to evade the CSA; and
- requiring absent parents to pay 15% of their wages for a single child, rising to 20% for two children and 25% for three children or more.

Fighting Fraud

Around £2 billion is lost each year in Great Britain where social security benefit fraud is known to have taken place. To combat this, the Benefits Fraud Inspectorate was set up in 1997 to strengthen the administration and security of benefits through inspection, reporting and monitoring and support of delivery organisations. The Inspectorate covers the Department for Work and Pensions' agencies and the benefits administered by local authorities. It also carries out work for the Social Security Agency in Northern Ireland.

Among the provisions included in the Social Security Fraud Act 2001 are those to obtain and share information; withdraw or reduce benefits for repeat offenders; and use penalties as an alternative to prosecution.

ADMINISTRATION

In June 2001 the Department for Work and Pensions (DWP) was formed (see p. 62). The Department will:

- provide a single point of delivery for jobs, benefits advice and support through Jobcentre Plus—a new service which will begin to operate in October 2001 (see p. 153);
- help employers to fill job vacancies;
- set up The Pension Service—to be phased in between April 2002 and 2003—to provide information and support to current and future pensioners;
- deliver a simplified and efficient Child Support system and;
- ensure equality of opportunity and social inclusion.

Other responsibilities of the new department include:

- the Benefits Agency (BA), administering and paying the majority of benefits;
- the Child Support Agency, assessing and collecting maintenance payments for children (see p. 178) and;
- The Appeals Service (TAS), providing an impartial re-examination of decisions under appeal.

Advice about Benefits

The DWP produces a range of information material in English and other languages as well as in different formats (audio and videotapes, braille and large print). There are telephone helplines, and a website provides general information on entitlement and liability.

CONTRIBUTIONS

Entitlement to National Insurance benefits such as Retirement Pension, Incapacity Benefit and contributory Jobseeker's Allowance is dependent upon the payment of contributions. The amount an employee can earn before employer NI contributions (NICs) are charged is aligned with the personal allowance for income tax (see p. 406). There are six classes of contributions. *The rates given below are effective from April 2001 to April 2002*:

- Class 1—paid by employees and their employers. No NICs are payable for employees earning less than £72 a week. Employees earning between £72 and £87 a week are liable to make contributions, but at present they do not make any payments. Contributions on earnings at or above £87 a week in non-contracted-out employment are at the rate of 10% up to the upper earnings limit of £575 a week. Employers' contributions are at the rate of 11.9% and are charged on everything earned at or above £87 per week. There is no upper earnings limit for employers' contributions.

- Class 1A—paid by employers who provide their employees with a variety of benefits in kind.
- Class 1B—paid by employers who enter into a PAYE Settlement Agreement with the Inland Revenue for tax.
- Class 2—paid by self-employed people. Contributions are at a flat rate of £2 a week. The self-employed may claim exemption from Class 2 contributions if their net earnings are expected to be below £3,955 for the 2001–02 tax year. Self-employed people are not eligible for unemployment and industrial injuries benefits.
- Class 3—paid voluntarily to safeguard rights to some benefits. Contributions are at a flat rate of £6.75 a week.
- Class 4—paid by the self-employed on their taxable profits over a set lower limit (£4,535 a year), and up to a set upper limit (£29,900 a year) in addition to their Class 2 contribution. Class 4 contributions are payable at the rate of 7%.

Employees who work after pensionable age (currently 60 for women and 65 for men) do not pay contributions but the employer continues to be liable. Self-employed people over pensionable age do not pay contributions.

BENEFITS

Social security benefits can be grouped into three types:

- **means-tested**, available to people whose income and savings are below certain levels;
- **contributory**, paid to people who have made the required contributions to the National Insurance Fund,[1] from which benefits are paid; and

Figure 12.3: Social Security Benefit Expenditure, Great Britain, 2001–02: by Broad Groups of Beneficiaries

Total: £106.7 billion

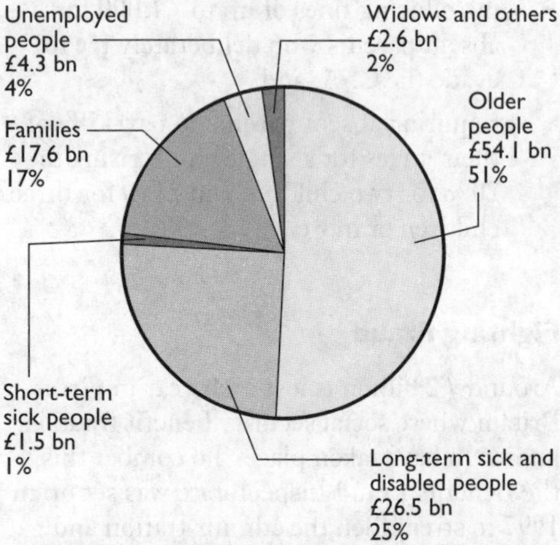

Source: Department for Work and Pensions

- benefits which are neither means-tested nor contributory (mainly paid to cover extra costs, for example of disability, or paid universally, for example Child Benefit).

General taxation provides over half the income for the social security programme, employers' NI contributions around a quarter and employees' NI contributions about a fifth.

For most contributory benefits there are two conditions. First, before benefit can be paid at all, a certain number of contributions must have been made. Second, the full rate of benefit cannot be paid unless contributions have been made or credited to a specific level over a set period. A reduced rate of benefit may be payable, dependent on the level of contributions made or credited. For example, a great many of those receiving retirement pensions and widows' benefits receive a percentage-based rate of benefit. Benefits are increased annually in line with percentage increases in retail prices. The main benefits (payable weekly) are summarised on pp. 175–182. *Rates given are those effective from April 2001 until April 2002.*

[1] The National Insurance Fund is a statutory fund into which all NI contributions payable by employers, employees and self-employed people are deposited, and from which contributory benefits and their administration costs are paid.

Table 12.4: Estimated Numbers Receiving Benefits in Great Britain 2000–01 (forecast)[1]

Benefit	*Contributory (C) or non-contributory (NC)*	*Thousands*
Retirement Pension	C	10,947
Widow's Benefit	C	257
Jobseeker's Allowance		
contribution-based	C	196
income-based	NC	899
Incapacity Benefit	C	
Short-term (lower rate)		96
Short-term (higher rate) and long-term		1,490
Maternity Allowance	C	17
Non-contributory Retirement Pension	NC	24
War Pension	NC	286
Attendance Allowance	NC	1,284
Disability Living Allowance	NC	2,171
Invalid Care Allowance	NC	382
Severe Disablement Allowance	NC	400
Industrial Injuries Disablement Benefit[2]	NC	322
Reduced Earnings Allowance[2]	NC	165
Industrial Death Benefit	NC	15
Income Support	NC	3,892
Child Benefit	NC	
number of children		12,763
number of families		7,072
One parent benefit/ Child Benefit (Lone Parent)	NC	842
Housing Benefit	NC	
rent rebate		2,356
rent allowance		1,836
Council Tax Benefit	NC	5,090

[1] Figures are for beneficiaries at any one time.

[2] Figures refer to the number of pensions being paid, and not to the number of recipients.

Source: *The Government's Expenditure Plans 2000/01–2001/02* : Social Security Departmental Report

Retirement

A state **Retirement Pension** is a taxable weekly benefit payable, if the contribution conditions have been met, to women from the age of 60 and men from the age of 65. Legislation was introduced in 1995 to equalise the state pension age for men and women at 65. The change will be phased in over ten years, starting from April 2010. Women born before 6 April 1950 will not be affected; their pension age will remain at 60. The new pension age of 65 will apply to women born on or after 6 April 1955. Pension age for women born between these dates will move up gradually from 60 to 65.

The state pension scheme consists of a basic weekly pension of £72.50 for a single person and £115.90 for a married couple on a standard rate pension, together with an additional earnings-related pension (SERPS). Pensioners may have unlimited earnings without affecting their pensions. Those who have put off their retirement during the five years after state pension age may earn extra pension, but they will not get any pension for the weeks they gave up.

A *non-contributory retirement pension* of £43.55 a week is payable to people who are over 80, satisfy certain residence conditions and are either not entitled to a retirement pension or are entitled to one of less than £43.30 a week. People whose pensions do not give them enough to live on may be entitled to the Minimum Income Guarantee (see p. 177).

Rights to basic pensions are safeguarded for people whose opportunities to work are limited while they are looking after a child or a sick or disabled person. Men and women may receive the same basic pension, provided they have paid full-rate NI contributions when working. The earnings-related pension scheme will eventually be calculated as 20% rather than 25% of earnings, and is being phased in over ten years from 1999. However, the pensions of people who retired in the 20th century will be unaffected.

Occupational and Personal Pensions

Employers may 'contract out' their employees from SERPS and provide a pension via their own occupational pension instead. Contracted-out salary-related schemes must meet a statutory test of overall quality and offer benefits that are broadly the same as, or better than, SERPS. They receive a flat-rate refund of National Insurance contributions and an age-related top-up based on a percentage of earnings between the lower and upper earnings limit on which National Insurance contributions are based. Membership of an employer's contracted-out scheme is voluntary; the State remains responsible for the basic pension.

Occupational pension schemes currently have over 10.3 million members accruing pension rights. The occupational pension rights of those who change jobs before pensionable age and are unable or do not want to transfer their contracted-out salary-related pension rights are now offered some protection against inflation. Most workers leaving a scheme at least a year before its pension age and with two years' pensionable service have the right to a fair transfer value. The trustees or managers of pensions have to provide full information about their schemes. Occupational schemes must provide equal treatment between male and female members.

As an alternative to their employer's scheme or SERPS, people are entitled to choose a personal pension available from a bank, building society, insurance company or other financial institution.

Employees can also contract out of SERPS using a personal pension plan rather than an occupational scheme. A personal pension used this way is called an appropriate personal pension and it also receives National Insurance rebates which are age-related.

The Pensions Ombudsman deals with complaints of maladministration against occupational and personal pension schemes and adjudicates on disputes. A pensions registry helps people trace lost benefits.

Unemployment

Jobseeker's Allowance

Jobseeker's Allowance (JSA) is a benefit for unemployed people seeking work. Claimants must be capable of, available for, and actively seeking work. They must normally be aged at least 18 years and under pension age. JSA can be either contribution-based or income-based:

- *Contribution-based JSA*: those who have paid enough NI contributions are entitled to a personal JSA for up to six months (£53.05 a week for a person aged 25 or over), regardless of any savings or partner's income.
- *Income-based JSA*: those on a low income are entitled to an income-based JSA, payable for as long as the jobseeker requires support and continues to satisfy the qualifying conditions. The amount a claimant receives comprises an age-related personal allowance (£53.05 a week for a person aged 25 or over), allowances for dependent children and premium payments for those with extra expenses, for example, disabled children.

Income-based JSA's benefit rates are determined by circumstances on a basis similar to Income Support (see p. 177).

Back to Work Bonus

Recipients of JSA and people aged under 60 who receive Income Support can benefit from a Back to Work Bonus. The aim of the scheme is to encourage people to keep in touch with the labour market by undertaking small amounts of work while claiming benefit.

The Back to Work Bonus scheme allows people to accrue a tax-free lump sum of between £5 and £1,000 if working part-time while in receipt of Income Support or Jobseeker's Allowance.

To begin accruing the Bonus, the person must have been entitled to Income Support or Jobseeker's Allowance for at least 91 days. Back to Work Bonus can be accrued by either member of a couple and is payable if their benefit ceases due to starting remunerative work or increasing their earnings. Remunerative work is defined as 16 hours or more of employment for the claimant or 24 hours or more for the partner.

An amount equal to half of any earnings above the appropriate weekly earnings disregard (normally £5 for a single person, £10 for couples, and £20 for single parents, disabled people and some people in special occupations) will count towards the bonus.

Income Support

Income Support is payable to certain people aged 16 or over who are not required to be available for work, and whose income and savings are below certain set levels. They include lone parents, pensioners, carers and long-term sick and disabled people. Income Support is made up of: a personal allowance based on age and on whether the claimant is single, a lone parent or has a partner; age-related allowances for dependent children and additional sums known as premiums; and housing costs. From this total amount other income, including some other social security benefits, is deducted. Income Support for people aged 60 and over is now known as the Minimum Income Guarantee.

Income Support is not payable if savings exceed £8,000. Savings between £3,000 and £8,000 will reduce the amount received. For people living permanently in residential care or a nursing home, the allowance is not payable if savings exceed £16,000; and savings between £10,000 and £16,000 will affect the amount received. For people aged over 60, Income Support is not payable if savings exceed £12,000, while savings between £6,000 and £12,000 will reduce the amount received.

Families

Most pregnant working women receive **Statutory Maternity Pay** directly from their employer. It is paid for a maximum of 18 weeks to any woman who has been working for the same employer for 26 weeks and who earns on average at least £72 a week. She will receive 90% of her average weekly earnings for the first six weeks and a rate of £62.20 a week for the remaining 12 weeks.

Women who are not eligible for Statutory Maternity Pay because, for example, they are self-employed, or have recently changed jobs or left their job, may qualify for a weekly **Maternity Allowance**, which is payable for up to 18 weeks and is based on average earnings. If average weekly earnings are equal to or more than the lower earnings limit, this amounts to £62.20 a week. If average weekly earnings are at least £30 a week but less than the lower earnings limit, the sum paid is 90% of average earnings. All pregnant employees have the right to take a minimum of 18 weeks maternity leave.

A **Sure Start Maternity Grant** of up to £200 may be made if the mother or her partner receive Income Support, income-based Jobseeker's Allowance, Working Families' Tax Credit or Disabled Person's Tax Credit and have savings under £500 (£1,000 for people aged 60 and over). It is also available if a baby is adopted.

The main social security benefit for children is **Child Benefit**. This is a tax-free, non-contributory payment of £15.50 a week for the eldest qualifying child of a couple, and £10.35 for each other child. Child Benefit is payable for children up to the age of 16, and for those up to 19 who continue in full-time non-advanced education. It is generally not payable to people whose entry into the UK is subject to immigration control.

People claiming Child Benefit for an orphaned child they have taken into their family may be entitled to **Guardian's Allowance**. This is a tax-free non-contributory benefit of £9.70 a week for the eldest child and £11.35 for each other child

Table 12.5: Recipients of Benefits for Families, Great Britain *Thousands*

	1994–95	1999–2000
Child Benefit		
Children	12,640	12,867
Families	6,950	7,108
Lone parent families		
One parent benefit only	548	n.a.
One parent benefit and Income Support[1]	373	311
Income Support only[1]	676	614
Other benefits		
Maternity Allowance	11	11
Statutory Maternity Pay[2]	95	100

[1] Income Support data includes some income–based Jobseeker's Allowance claimants. Income–based JSA replaced Income Support for the unemployed from October 1996.

[2] Estimated average weekly number of recipients, rounded to the nearest 5,000.

Source: Department for Work and Pensions

who qualifies. In certain circumstances Guardian's Allowance can be paid even if one parent is still alive.

Child Support Agency (CSA)

An estimated 1 million lone parents in the UK bring up 1.7 million children in households where no one is working. If any person is living with and caring for a child, and one, or both, of the child's parents are living elsewhere in the UK, he or she may apply to have child support maintenance assessed and collected by the CSA (or its Northern Ireland counterpart). If that person or their present partner claims Income Support or income-based Jobseeker's Allowance, they may be required to apply for child support maintenance if asked to do so by the CSA (or its Northern Ireland counterpart).

Assessments for child support maintenance are made using a formula which takes into account each parent's income and makes allowance for essential outgoings. (A system of departures from the formula allows the amount of maintenance payable to be varied in a small number of cases.) A child maintenance bonus worth up to £1,000 may be payable to parents living with and caring for a child who have been in receipt of Income Support or income-based Jobseeker's Allowance and in receipt of child maintenance when they leave benefit for work.

Working Families' Tax Credit

Working Families' Tax Credit (WFTC) gives working families with children additional financial help. It is administered by the Inland Revenue and paid through workers' pay packets. Families (couples or lone parents) are eligible if they:

- have one or more children;
- work at least 16 hours a week;
- are resident and entitled to work in the UK; and
- have savings of £8,000 or less.

WFTC is made up of:

- basic credit—£59.00;
- credit for working over 30 hours per week—£11.45;
- tax credit for each child —£26.00 (aged up to 15 years) —£26.75 (aged 16 to 18);
- a childcare tax credit—up to 70% of eligible costs up to a maximum of £135 for one child and £200 for two or more children;
- a disabled child tax credit of £30.00 for each child who gets Disability Living Allowance, or who is registered blind or who has left the register in the last 28 weeks; or a child enhanced disability tax

credit of £41.05 for each child who gets the higher care component of Disability Living Allowance; and

- an adult enhanced disability tax credit of £16.00 where applicants or their partner get the higher rate care component of Disability Living Allowance.

The WFTC award, which normally lasts for 26 weeks, is calculated by adding the credits together. If the family income (after tax and National Insurance contributions) is above £92.90 per week, this is reduced by 55 pence for each £1 above £92.90.

Social Fund

Payments, in the form of loans or grants, may be available to people on low incomes to help with expenses which are difficult to meet out of regular income. There are two kinds of payment. *Discretionary* payments are:

- budgeting loans for important intermittent expenses;
- community care grants to help, for example, people resettle into the community from care, or to remain in the community, to ease exceptional pressure on families, to set up home as part of a planned resettlement programme and to meet certain travel expenses; and
- crisis loans to help people in an emergency or as a result of a disaster where there is serious risk to health or safety. People do not have to be receiving any form of benefit to qualify for this.

The Social Fund also provides *regulated* payments (payments that are not cash-limited) to help people awarded certain income-related benefits with the costs of maternity or funerals, or with heating during very cold weather and winter fuel payments.

Widows and Widowers

Bereavement Payment. Widows under the age of 60, and widowers under the age of 65—or those over 60/65 whose spouses were not entitled to a category A state Retirement Pension when they died—receive a tax-free single payment of £2,000 following the death of their spouses, provided that their spouses have paid a minimum number of National Insurance contributions. Those whose spouses have died of an industrial injury or prescribed disease may also qualify, regardless of whether their spouses have paid NI contributions.

Widowed Parent's Allowance is a taxable benefit of £72.50 a week, and is payable to widowed parents with at least one child for whom they are getting Child Benefit. Additional tax-free amounts of £9.70 for a child for whom the higher rate of Child Benefit is payable, and £11.35 for each subsequent child, are available. Entitlement to this benefit is dependent on the NI contributions of the spouse, and it ceases if the parent moves in with a partner or re-marries, or once entitlement to Child Benefit ends.

Widowed Mother's Allowance is a benefit for mothers who were widowed before April 2001, and it is paid on terms similar to those for Widowed Parent's Allowance.

Bereavement Allowance is a taxable benefit of £72.50 a week payable to widows and widowers without dependent children, who are 55 or over when their spouse dies. It is payable for 52 weeks following the date of widowhood. A percentage of the full rate is payable to widows and widowers who are aged between 45 and 54. Entitlement to this benefit is dependent on the NI contributions of the spouse, and it ceases after 52 weeks of the date of widowhood or if the widow or widower moves in with a partner, or re-marries before the 52-week date has been reached.

Widow's Pension is a taxable weekly benefit of £72.50 payable to a woman who was widowed before April 2001, and was 55 or over when her husband died or when her entitlement to Widowed Mother's Allowance ends due to her entitlement to Child Benefit ceasing. A percentage of the full rate is payable to a widow aged between 45 and 54 when her husband dies, or when her entitlement to Widowed Mother's Allowance ends due to her entitlement to Child Benefit ceasing. Special rules apply for widows whose husbands died before April 1988. Entitlement continues unless the widow moves in with a partner or re-marries or until she begins to draw Retirement Pension.

Sickness and Disablement

A variety of benefits are available for people unable to work because of sickness or disablement. Employers are responsible for paying **Statutory Sick Pay** to employees from the fourth day of sickness for up to a maximum of 28 weeks. There is a single rate of Statutory Sick Pay for all qualifying employees provided their average gross weekly earnings are at least £72 a week. The weekly rate is £62.20.

Incapacity Benefit is also for people who become incapable of work. Entitlement to Incapacity Benefit begins when entitlement to Statutory Sick Pay ends or, for those who do not qualify for Statutory Sick Pay, from the fourth day of sickness. There are three types:

- short-term benefit for people under pension age—a lower rate of £52.60 a week for the first 28 weeks; and a higher rate of £62.20 a week between the 29th and 52nd week;
- short-term benefit for people over pension age—lower rate of £66.90; and a higher rate of £69.75; and
- long-term benefit rate of £69.75 a week (after 52 weeks of incapacity).

Extra benefits may be paid for dependent adults and children. Incapacity Benefit is taxable from the 29th week of incapacity.

The medical test of incapacity for work usually applies after 28 weeks' sickness. It assesses ability to perform a range of work-related activities rather than the ability to perform a specific job.

Severe Disablement Allowance is a tax-free benefit for people who have not been able to work for at least 28 weeks because of illness or disability but who cannot get Incapacity Benefit because they have not paid enough NI contributions. The benefit is £42.15 a week, plus additions of up to £14.65 depending on the person's age when they became incapable of work. Additions for adult dependants and for children may also be paid. Claims may be made by people aged between 16 and 65. Once a person has qualified for the allowance, there is no upper age limit for receipt. New claimants must satisfy the same incapacity test as that used in Incapacity Benefit.

People who become incapable of work after their 20th birthday must also be medically assessed as at least 80% disabled for a minimum of 28 weeks. People already in receipt of certain benefits, such as the higher rate of the Disability Living Allowance care component (see below), will automatically be accepted as 80% disabled.

In April 2001, Severe Disablement Allowance was abolished for new claims. People under 20, or 25 if they were in education or training before reaching 20, may now be able to receive Incapacity Benefit without having to satisfy the contributions conditions.

Other Benefits

Disability Living Allowance is a non-contributory tax-free benefit to help severely disabled people aged under 65 with extra costs incurred as a result of disability. Entitlement is measured in terms of personal care and/or mobility needs. There are two components: a care component which has three weekly rates—£55.30, £37.00 and £14.65; and a mobility component which has two weekly rates—£38.65 and £14.65. The higher rate is payable from age three and above; the lower rate is payable from age five and above.

Attendance Allowance is a non-contributory tax-free benefit to provide financial help to severely disabled people aged 65 or older with extra costs incurred as a result of disability. It is measured in terms of personal care needs by day and/or night. The two rates are £55.30 and £37.00.

A non-contributory **Invalid Care Allowance** (ICA) of £41.75 weekly may be payable to people between 16 and 65 at the time of claim who have given up the opportunity of a full-time paid job because they are providing regular and substantial care of at least 35 hours a week, to a severely disabled person in receipt of either Attendance Allowance or the higher or middle care component of Disability Living Allowance. ICA is taken fully into account when calculating entitlement to Income Support, income-based JSA, Housing Benefit and Council Tax Benefit, as it is an earnings replacement benefit. Carers do, however, receive the carer premium, which is intended to focus help on those who have lost the opportunity to gain income from work because of caring, and who do not gain from receipt of ICA.

Disabled Person's Tax Credit (DPTC) provides support to people with disabilities who work. DPTC structure is similar to that of the WFTC (see p. 178). Some of the individual tax credit amounts are set at different levels and applicants do not have to have dependent children to qualify.

Industrial Injuries Disablement Benefit

Various benefits are payable for disablement caused by an accident at work or a prescribed disease caused by a particular type of employment. The main benefit is the tax-free **Industrial Injuries Disablement Benefit**: up to £112.90 a week is usually paid after a qualifying period of 15 weeks if a person is at least 14% or more physically or mentally disabled as a result of an industrial accident or a prescribed disease.

Basic Disablement Benefit can be paid in addition to other NI benefits, such as Incapacity Benefit. It can be paid whether or not the person returns to work and does not depend on earnings. The degree of disablement is assessed by an independent medical authority and the amount paid depends on the extent of the disablement and on how long it is expected to last. Except for certain progressive respiratory diseases, disablement of less than 14% does not attract Disablement Benefit. In certain circumstances additional allowances may be payable.

Housing and Council Tax Benefits

Housing Benefit is an income-related, tax-free benefit which helps people on low incomes meet the cost of rented accommodation. The amount paid depends on personal circumstances, income, savings, rent and other people sharing the home. It also normally depends on the general level of rents for properties with the same number of rooms in the locality.

Most single people under 25 years old who are not lone parents and who are renting privately have their Housing Benefit limited to the average cost of a single non-self-contained room (that is, with shared use of kitchen and toilet facilities) in the locality.

Council Tax Benefit helps people to meet their council tax payments (the tax set by local councils to help pay for services—see p. 70). The scheme offers help to those claiming Income Support and income-based Jobseeker's Allowance and others with low incomes. It is subject to rules broadly similar to those governing the provision of Housing Benefit (see above). A person who is solely liable for the council tax may also claim benefit for a second adult who is not liable to pay the council tax and who is living in the home on a non-commercial basis. In Northern Ireland, where council tax does not apply, people on low incomes may get help to pay for their domestic rates from a means-tested housing benefits scheme.

War Pensions and Related Services

Pensions are payable for disablement as a result of service in the armed forces or for certain injuries received in the merchant navy or civil defence during wartime, or to civilians injured by enemy action. The amount paid depends on the degree of disablement: the pension for 100% disablement for an officer is £6,251 a year; for other ranks it is £119.80 a week.

There are a number of extra allowances. The main ones are for unemployability, restricted mobility, the need for care and attendance, the provision of extra comforts, and as maintenance for a lowered standard of occupation. An age allowance of between £8.00 and £24.70 is payable weekly to war pensioners aged 65 or over whose disablement is assessed at 40% or more.

Pensions are also paid to war widows and other dependants. (The standard rate of pension for a private soldier's widow is £90.45 a week.) War Widow's Pension is also payable to a former war widow who has remarried and then become widowed again, divorced or legally separated.

The War Pensioners' Welfare Service helps and advises war pensioners, war widows and other dependants. It works with ex-Service organisations and other voluntary bodies which give financial and personal support to those disabled or bereaved as a result of war.

Concessions

Other benefits for which unemployed people and those on low incomes may be eligible include exemption from health service charges (see p. 192), vouchers towards the cost of spectacles (see p. 193), publicly funded legal help (see p. 235) and free school meals for their children. People on low incomes, pensioners, widows and long-term sick people on Incapacity Benefit, receive extra help to meet the cost of VAT (value added tax) on their fuel bills.

Reduced charges are often made to unemployed people, for example, for adult education and entry into exhibitions, and pensioners are usually entitled to reduced transport fares. Since November 2000, pensioners aged 75 and over have no longer been required to pay for their television licence.

Taxation

The general rule is that benefits which replace lost earnings are subject to tax, while those intended to meet a specific need are not (see Table 12.6). Various income tax reliefs and exemptions are allowed on account of age or a need to support dependants.

Benefit Controls on People from Abroad

Residence Test

All claimants must be habitually resident in the Common Travel Area (that is, the UK, the Irish Republic, the Channel Islands or the Isle of Man) before a claim for Income Support, income-based Jobseeker's Allowance, Housing Benefit or Council Tax Benefit can be paid. This in line with most other European countries, which also limit access to their benefit systems to those who have lived in the country for some time.

Asylum Seekers

Generally only people who claim refugee status as soon as they arrive in the UK can claim income-based Jobseeker's Allowance, Income Support, Housing Benefit and Council Tax Benefit. Their eligibility to receive these will stop if their asylum claim is refused by the Home Office. The Immigration and Asylum Act 1999 (see p. 112), among other things, replaced cash benefits for asylum seekers with a voucher system.

Table 12.6: Tax Liability of Social Security Benefits

Not taxable	*Taxable*
Attendance Allowance	Bereavement Allowance
Bereavement Payment	Incapacity Benefit (long-term or short-term higher rate)
Child Benefit	Industrial Death Benefit Pensions
Child's Special Allowance	Invalid Care Allowance
Council Tax Benefit	Jobseeker's Allowance[1]
Disability Living Allowance	Retirement Pension
Guardian's Allowance	Statutory Maternity Pay
Housing Benefit	Statutory Sick Pay
Incapacity Benefit (short-term lower rate)	Widowed Mother's Allowance
Income Support	Widowed Parent's Allowance
Industrial Injuries Disablement Benefit/Reduced Earnings Allowance	Widow's Pension
Maternity Allowance	
Severe Disablement Allowance	
War Disablement Pension	
War Widow's Pension	

[1] That part of the Jobseeker's Allowance equivalent to the individual or couple rate of personal allowance, as appropriate.
Source: Inland Revenue

ARRANGEMENTS AND COMPARISONS WITH OTHER COUNTRIES

As part of the European Union's efforts to promote the free movement of labour, regulations provide for equality of treatment and the protection of benefit rights for people who move between member states. The regulations also cover retirement pensioners and other beneficiaries who have been employed, or self-employed, as well as dependants. Benefits covered include Child Benefit and those for sickness and maternity, unemployment, retirement, invalidity, accidents at work and occupational diseases.

The UK has reciprocal social security agreements with a number of other countries which also provide cover for some NI benefits and family benefits.

A comparison of the expenditure on social protection benefits per head for the 15 EU countries indicates that, in general, spending is much higher in the more northerly countries than in the south. Luxembourg spent the most per head in 1998; at just over £6,500 this was over three times the amount spent by Portugal, the country which spent the least. The UK spent around £4,000 per head of population, just below the average for the EU.

Further Reading

With Respect to Old Age: Long-term Care—Rights and Responsibilities. Cm 4192; vols I–II. Royal Commission on Long-term Care. The Stationery Office, 1999.

The Government's Expenditure Plans 2001–02 to 2003–04 and Main Estimates 2001–02. Social Security Departmental Report. Cm 5115. The Stationery Office, 2001.

The Government's Expenditure Plans 2001–2002 to 2003–2004 and Main Estimates 2001–2002. Department of Health Departmental Report. Cm 5103. The Stationery Office, 2001.

Websites

Department of Health: www.doh.gov.uk

Department for Work and Pensions: www.dwp.gov.uk

13 Health

The State of Public Health	184	Family Health Services	198
The National Health Service	187	Hospital and Specialist Services	199
England	188	Health Arrangements with Other Countries	211
Wales	189	Health Provision Outside the NHS	211
Scotland	190		
Northern Ireland	191		
Administration	192		
New Initiatives	196		

Strategies for dealing with health problems and improving healthcare services have been published for England, Wales, Scotland and Northern Ireland. They contain many common elements, such as commitments to reduce avoidable ill-health, with particular emphasis on cancer, heart disease and mental health, improving clinical performance through a more integrated and inclusive network of local health provision, and tackling the various health inequalities which exist across the United Kingdom.

The State of Public Health

Overall mortality declined in the 20th century; this is generally regarded as a result of a number of major social and economic trends, including an increase in real incomes, improvements in nutrition and housing, higher levels of education, improved health services, and developments in medicines and their wider availability to the population.

Life Expectancy

Life expectancy provides a useful summary measure of mortality. Since the middle of the 19th century the expectation of life at birth for both females and males has almost doubled. Neither women nor men born in England and Wales in 1841 had an average life expectancy from birth much beyond 40, mainly because of high infant and child mortality; by 1998 the life expectancy at birth for females in Great Britain had reached almost 80, and for males nearly 75 years. However, life expectancy takes no account of quality of life. Healthy life expectancy, on the other hand, combines mortality and morbidity data into a single index. Healthy life expectancy at birth, defined as life expectancy in good or fairly good self-perceived general health, increased from 64.4 years to 66.9 years between 1981 and 1997 for males, and for females from 66.7 to 68.7 years.

Cancer

About a third of the population develop cancer at some time in their lives. Over the 20th century cancer has become more prominent as a cause of death when compared with other major causes. While death rates from some other major types of illness have fallen considerably, those from cancer have not done so to the same extent. By 1999 cancer was responsible for around a quarter of deaths among males in Great Britain and about a fifth of female deaths, compared with a tenth and a sixth respectively in 1911. However, despite the greater prominence of cancer deaths in the latter half of the 20th century, the death rates have declined since the 1980s. The particular cancers which people are diagnosed with have changed over the last 20 years. The incidence of breast and prostate cancer has risen considerably since 1981, partly because increased awareness and screening have led to earlier diagnosis, while lung cancer among males has fallen dramatically, mainly because fewer men now smoke. In 1981 there were 112 new cases of lung cancer per 100,000 males, but the rate had fallen to around 80 by the mid-1990s.

Coronary Heart Disease

The United Kingdom has one of the highest premature death rates from circulatory disease (which includes heart disease and strokes) in Europe. Coronary heart disease (CHD) killed around 132,000 people in the UK in 1999. However, death rates from coronary heart disease for both males and females under 65 fell steadily between 1979 and 1999, from 139 to 56 per 100,000 males and from 39 to 16 per 100,000 females. Among patients of all ages in 1998 in England and Wales, 37 per 1,000 males and 22 per 1,000 females were treated for coronary heart disease. These figures represent a rise over the past few years.

Mental Health

Mental ill-health is also a major cause of disability and mortality. In 1999–2000, there were 2.1 million attendances at National Health Service (NHS) outpatient facilities for psychiatric specialties in England, 282,000 of which were new attendances.

Communicable Diseases

Although communicable (or infectious) diseases were the cause of less than 1% of deaths in England and Wales in 1999, they are still a public health concern, especially as the occurrence of some diseases is rising. In the 40 years up to 1987, the number of notifications of tuberculosis (TB) in England and Wales fell considerably. However, over the next 13 years they increased by 34%, so that in 2000 there were around 6,800 notifications. The rise has been particularly noticeable in London and among young men.

Another communicable disease which has risen in prominence comparatively recently is the Human Immuno-deficiency Virus (HIV). The UK has a relatively low prevalence of HIV as a result of public education and health campaigns. The use of combination drug therapy to delay disease progression has helped HIV-related deaths fall during the second half of the 1990s. However, the number of people diagnosed with HIV each year is rising: in 1999 there were more new diagnoses of HIV than in any year previously, at around 2,900. There are now 20,800 people living with HIV in England and Wales, and this is expected to rise to 29,000 by the end of 2003.

Substance Misuse

Alcohol

The consumption of alcohol in excessive amounts can lead to ill health, and an increased likelihood of problems such as high blood pressure, cancer and cirrhosis of the liver. The current Department of Health (DH) advice on alcohol is that consumption of between three and four units[1] a day for men and two to three units a day for women will not lead to significant health risks, but consistently drinking four or more units a day for men, and three units or more for women, is not advised because of the progressive health risks. In 1998–99, around two-fifths of

[1] A unit of alcohol is 8 grams by weight or 10 millilitres (ml) by volume of pure alcohol. This is the amount contained in half a pint of ordinary strength beer or lager, a single measure of pub spirits (1/6 gill or 25 ml), one glass of ordinary wine and a small pub measure of sherry or other fortified wine.

Table 13.1: Percentage of Adults consuming over Specified Levels of Alcohol:[1] by Gender and Age, United Kingdom, 1998–99

Percentages

	16–24	25–44	45–64	65 and over	All aged 16 and over
Males					
More than 4 units and up to 8 units	13	18	20	12	17
More than 8 units	37	28	17	4	21
Females					
More than 3 units and up to 6 units	18	17	12	3	13
More than 6 units	23	11	4	1	8

[1] On the heaviest drinking day last week.

Sources: General Household Survey, Office for National Statistics and Continuous Household Survey, Northern Ireland Statistics and Research Agency

men aged 16 and over and a fifth of women aged 16 and over in the United Kingdom had exceeded the recommended amount of alcohol on their heaviest drinking day in the week prior to being interviewed (see Table 13.1). However, the proportions for 16 to 24 year olds were much higher, with half of young men having consumed more than four units and two-fifths of young women having consumed more than three units.

Smoking

More cancer deaths in the United Kingdom can be attributed to smoking tobacco than to any other single risk factor. The then Health Education Authority estimated that smoking was the direct cause of 120,000 deaths in 1995. The proportion of people who smoked fell steadily through the 1970s and 1980s. The gap between males and females has narrowed: in 1974, 51% of males aged 16 and over and 41% of females of the same age smoked in Great Britain, compared with 28% and 26% respectively in 1998–99.

The prevalence of smoking also varies by social class. For both men and women, the proportion of smokers is higher among those in the manual socio-economic groups than among those in the non-manual groups. Just over a quarter of people aged 16 and over in the United Kingdom were smokers in 1998–99, but while only 13% of male professionals and 14% of female professionals smoked, almost half of unskilled males and a third of unskilled females did so. Smoking during pregnancy can have harmful effects on the health of the child. Between 1985 and 1995 the proportion of women who smoked during pregnancy in the United Kingdom fell from 30% to 24%.

Drugs

Findings from the 1998 British Crime Survey indicate that about 500,000 of 16 to 24 year olds in England and Wales had used Class A drugs[2] in the previous 12 months, and about 200,000 in that age group had done so during the last month. These figures represent 8% and 3% of 16 to 24 year olds respectively. Young people are more likely than older people to misuse drugs. The most commonly used illegal drug in 1998 among both young men and young women was cannabis, which had been used by more than a quarter of young people aged 16 to 24 in England and Wales in the previous year. Along with age, lifestyles are a good indicator of likely drug use. In particular, young people who go out more than three times a week, those who visit pubs and bars and those who go to nightclubs are all much more likely to use drugs than other young people. The use of more harmful drugs, such as heroin and crack, appears to be associated more with those living in relatively deprived areas.

[2] Heroin, cocaine (both cocaine powder and 'crack'), ecstasy, magic mushrooms, LSD and unprescribed use of methadone.

Health Inequalities

In July 2000, the Government gave a commitment in the *NHS Plan* (see p. 188) that, for the first time ever in England, local targets for reducing health inequalities would be reinforced by the creation of national health inequalities targets:

- starting with children under one year, by 2010 to reduce by at least 10% the gap in mortality between manual groups and the population as a whole; and
- by 2010 to reduce by at least 10% the gap between the fifth of areas with the lowest life expectancy at birth and the population as a whole.

These two targets address health inequalities for the more disadvantaged groups in the community, since they die sooner and suffer more illness in their lives. The national health inequalities targets will be delivered by a combination of specific health and broader government policies. Action on the priority areas, such as cancer, CHD and stroke and mental health, will help to reduce inequalities, as all of these have high prevalence in lower socio-economic groups.

Smoking reduction will be a significant factor in the achievement of both the national inequalities targets. They are therefore supported by the government target to reduce smoking rates among manual groups from 32% in 1998 to 26% by 2010.

Reducing inequalities in health is a priority for the National Assembly for Wales. It has launched an Inequalities in Health Fund to stimulate and support new action to address health inequalities and the factors that cause them, including inequities in access to health services. Fifty-four projects lasting for up to three years were announced in July 2000 and will result in new local action in deprived communities across Wales.

The Scottish Executive has appointed a Health and Homelessness Coordinator, responsible for working with Primary Care Trusts (see p. 189) and NHS Boards (see p. 190) to develop strategies to tackle the health needs of Scotland's homeless people.

The National Health Service

The body responsible for public health in the UK is the National Health Service (NHS).

Table 13.2 Satisfaction with Local Hospital and Community Health Services,[1] Great Britain

Percentages

	1991	1999
Hospital services		
Quality of medical treatment	65	66
Time spent waiting for an ambulance after a 999 call	n.a.	60
General condition of hospital buildings	40	53
Time spent waiting in outpatient departments	17	28
Time spent waiting in accident and emergency departments before being seen by a doctor	24	20
Waiting lists for non-emergency operations	13	20
Waiting time before getting appointments with hospital consultants	14	17
GP services		
Quality of medical treatment by GPs	73	76
Being able to choose which GP to see	72	71
Amount of time GP gives to each patient	65	69
GP appointment systems	54	54

[1] Percentage of respondents who said that each service was 'very good' or 'satisfactory' when asked 'From what you know or have heard, say whether you think the NHS in your area is, on the whole, satisfactory or in need of improvement'.
Source: British Social Attitudes Survey, National Centre for Social Research

The NHS is founded on the principle of providing a universal service to all its resident population, based upon need rather than ability to pay. The services are intended to provide treatment and care where necessary while making the best use of the resources available. All taxpayers, employers and employees contribute to the cost so that members of the community who do not require healthcare help to pay for those who do. Most forms of treatment are provided free, but others incur a charge, such as prescription drugs and eye tests.

The Department of Health (DH) is responsible for national strategic planning in England and for developing and implementing policies for the provision of health services. The National Assembly for Wales, the Scottish Executive Health Department and the Department of Health, Social Services and Public Safety in Northern Ireland have similar responsibilities for health provision in their respective countries.

ENGLAND

The Government's strategy for healthcare in England was set out in the NHS Plan, published in July 2000. The plan sets out a programme of reform and investment that is intended to tackle the systemic problems that have affected the NHS.

Key to the principles laid down in the NHS Plan are modernisation and improvement. In April 2001 the Modernisation Agency was launched, with a brief to take a lead role in modernising the NHS by helping local clinicians and managers redesign services around the needs of patients. The Commission for Health Improvement (CHI) now provides independent advice and expertise to the NHS on developing and improving the quality of NHS services. The CHI also has an inspection role: every NHS organisation is to be inspected every four years. Those that perform well are given more freedom to run their own affairs, and obtain access to extra funds. Those which fail receive intensive support from the Modernisation Agency and NHS regional offices, and could have their responsibilities removed.

The NHS Plan includes a number of targets for the NHS to achieve by 2004. Among these are:

- patients to be able to see a GP within 48 hours;
- hospital consultants, currently working only in hospitals, to deliver approximately 4 million outpatient consultations a year in primary care and community settings;
- GPs to be able to refer patients to around 1,000 GPs with a special interest, for example in ophthalmology, orthopaedics, dermatology and ear, nose and throat surgery, instead of referring them to hospital; and
- waiting time in accident and emergency departments in hospitals to fall to 1 hour 15 minutes on average.

Targets to be met by the NHS by the end of 2005 include:

- the replacement of waiting lists for appointments and admission by booking systems (see p. 200);
- a reduction in the maximum waiting time for a routine outpatient appointment from six to three months; and
- a reduction in the maximum waiting time for inpatient treatment from 18 to six months.

The National Institute for Clinical Excellence (NICE) was established in 1999 to develop national standards for best practice in clinical care within the NHS in England and Wales. This includes drawing up new guidelines based on clinical and cost effectiveness and ensuring that they apply to all parts of the NHS. The Institute's membership is drawn from the health professions, the NHS, academics, health economists and patients. It appraises new drugs and technologies and produces clinical guidelines. In 2000, its first full year of operation, NICE issued 16 appraisals of new technologies. (Details of some of these appraisals can be found elsewhere in the chapter.)

The Government sees the local management of healthcare as important in reducing health inequalities. There are 99 health authorities in England responsible for identifying the healthcare needs of the people living in their areas. They secure hospital and community health services and arrange for the provision of services by family doctors, dentists, pharmacists and opticians, as well as administering their contracts. Health authorities now have a duty to prepare health improvement programmes, and to work with Primary Care Groups (PCGs), Primary Care Trusts (PCTs) and NHS Trusts to achieve the targets set out in them.

In 2000 the first Primary Care Trusts were established, and by April 2001 there were 164 in total. They bring together medical and social care professionals with other organisations and agencies, to shape local health and social care services. PCTs have taken over many functions formerly performed by health authorities; they can also provide some community health services directly.

Primary Care Groups, which are smaller than Primary Care Trusts, were established in 1999. They control about two-thirds of local NHS budgets and are responsible for commissioning services for their local communities. PCGs are accountable to local health authorities. They are the bodies which enable control of the nature of services to be held by GPs, community nurses, other health professionals, managers, social services, health authorities and NHS Trusts.

The actual provision of healthcare at a local level is carried out by NHS Trusts. These existed prior to the Primary Care Groups and Trusts, but they now carry out healthcare according to local long-term service agreements with the Primary Care Groups and Trusts. Each NHS Trust has autonomy over recruitment, pay, research and training, and publishes details of its performance, including the cost of treatments and services.

Patient opinion and involvement have been given greater emphasis by the Health and Social Care Act 2001. Under the Act, NHS bodies have a duty to make arrangements with a view to ensuring that the public are consulted and involved in planning and decisions about local health services. The Act also provides for local authority overview and scrutiny committees (established under the Local Government Act 2000) to examine the health service in their area.

Responsibility for health education lies with separate NHS authorities working alongside the national health departments. In England the former Health Education Authority was succeeded in April 2000 by two new bodies: the Health Development Agency (HDA) and Health Promotion England.

The HDA is a special health authority, working to improve the health of people and communities in England, and in particular to reduce health inequalities. In partnership with others, it gathers evidence of what works, advises on standards and develops the skills of all those working to improve health.

Health Promotion England runs national campaigns on a number of subjects, including childhood immunisation, drugs, alcohol and sexual health. In addition, almost all NHS health authorities have their own health education service, which works closely with health professionals, health visitors, community groups, local employers and others to determine the most suitable local programmes.

WALES

In Wales, the operation of the NHS is the responsibility of the National Assembly for Wales (NAW). In January 2001 it published *Improving Health in Wales—A Plan for the NHS with its Partners*. The document describes the Assembly's programme over the next ten years.

The Assembly has the power to make changes to the structure of the NHS in Wales. By April 2003, the Assembly will abolish the five health authorities in Wales and put in place a new structure, with changes at two levels:

- at a local level, Local Health Groups will be developed into Local Health Boards and their role strengthened—they will take on new responsibilities for commissioning, securing and delivering healthcare in their localities; and
- at a national level, the National Assembly will hold both Local Health Boards and NHS Trusts fully accountable for the services they provide and commission.

Effective partnership working is an important theme of the Welsh Plan. At a national level, a Health and Well-being Partnership Council will be established, chaired by the Health and Social Services Minister. The Council will bring together key personnel from the NHS, local government, the voluntary and independent sectors, staff and professional groups, and patients' representatives to ensure the direction and leadership of the new agenda for health and well-being. The council will be supported by a network of similar partnerships at a local level.

Since devolution, the NAW also has some control over the finances of the NHS in Wales, and in February 2001 it announced additional investment, so that by 2003–04 health expenditure will be £3.6 billion, an increase of £1 billion on 1999–2000. Much of this new investment is to be directed towards tackling the priorities outlined in *Improving Health in Wales*: coronary heart disease, cancer services, mental health services, intensive care, primary and community care, children's services and local priorities in Health Improvement Programmes. Other areas targeted are integrated working methods to address waiting lists and waiting times, pressures on admissions, human resource development for the NHS workforce, and the establishment of a new Inequalities in Health Fund.

SCOTLAND

The Scottish Executive Health Department is an integrated body, responsible both for the executive leadership of NHSScotland and for the development and implementation of health and community care policy. The Health Department works with NHSScotland bodies:

- to improve, protect and monitor the health of the people of Scotland;
- to develop and deliver modern primary care and community care services; and
- to provide modern, high-quality, responsive hospital and specialist services.

Prior to devolution in 1999, healthcare in Scotland was already distinct from healthcare in England and Wales in many ways, and in December 2000 the Scottish Executive Health Department published the Scottish Health Plan—*Our National Health: A plan for action, a plan for change*—which described its priorities. These are to:

- improve Scotland's health, and narrow the health gap between rich and poor;
- set national standards of care to be delivered locally across Scotland;
- improve patients' practical access to health services;
- give patients and communities a voice in the way the NHS is run;
- provide better care for the young, and for older people;
- tackle coronary heart disease, cancer and poor mental health; and
- change the ways in which the NHS works with its staff so as to improve care and standards.

To underpin these aims, the Scottish Executive's core spending on health will rise from £4.9 billion in 2001–02 to £6.7 billion in 2003–04—this represents approximately one-third of the devolved Scottish budget. In addition, a new way of sharing NHS funds across Scotland—the 'Arbuthnott formula'—is now in place to address relative healthcare needs, including those caused by deprivation.

In September 2001, the decision-making powers of the 15 Health Boards and 28 NHS Trusts are being brought together in 15 new unified NHS Boards, each of which will be responsible for all NHS services in its area. The introduction of the new NHS Boards will ensure that national clinical and service standards are delivered in all parts of Scotland by unified local systems of care.

The 15 NHS Boards and 32 local authorities will be expected to work together to strengthen the localised focus of health provision, and every local authority will have a seat on its principal NHS Board. Acute services and primary care will continue to be delivered through NHS Trusts, although the Island Boards will remain as integrated structures with no separate Trusts. Other NHS bodies, such as the Scottish Ambulance Service, the Health Education Board for

Scotland and the Clinical Standards Board for Scotland, provide services on a national basis. One of the priorities for the new NHS Boards is involving people and communities. The Scottish Executive is investing £14 million in improving NHSScotland's ability to communicate with, listen to and work with patients. One such initiative is the Patients' Project, a systematic assessment of patient information which intends to capture and disseminate best practice and to act as a national source of patient information and advice. NHS Boards will be required to show how they are involving the public, and how this has affected the provision of services. Local Health Councils also provide a voice for the local public in each area.

The Scottish Health Plan includes the same clinical priorities as the NHS Plan for England: CHD, cancer and poor mental health. In July 2001, the Scottish Executive published *Cancer in Scotland: Action for Change*, a comprehensive cancer plan for Scotland. The Scottish CHD Task Force is due to report in autumn 2001 and the Framework for Mental Health, published in 1997, is in its implementation phase. Specific targets have also been set, including:

- by 2002, the maximum wait for angiography (radiographic examination of arteries and veins) will be 12 weeks from the time of seeing a specialist;
- by 2002, the maximum wait for surgery or angioplasty (a treatment for CHD) will be 24 weeks from the time of angiography;
- by October 2001, women who have breast cancer and are referred for urgent treatment will begin that treatment within one month of diagnosis, where clinically appropriate; and
- by 2005, the maximum wait from urgent referral to treatment for all cancers will be two months.

The Health Technology Board for Scotland was established in April 2000 and acts as a single source of national advice on the most clinically and cost-effective health technologies, playing a similar role to NICE in England and Wales (see p. 188).

A new service, NHS24, is also planned. Similar to NHS Direct in England (see p. 196), it is due to be introduced in Scotland from April 2002 onwards.

NORTHERN IRELAND

Northern Ireland also has a new public health strategy. *Investing for Health* was released for consultation in November 2000 and was finalised by the Northern Ireland Executive in 2001. It is focusing on avoidable chronic sickness and disability, and inequalities in the health of different groups in the population.

Northern Ireland's equivalent bodies to health authorities are the four health and social services boards. They are responsible for identifying the healthcare needs of the people in their area, securing hospital and community health services, providing primary care services, and administering contracts. The boards will play a major role in the implementation of *Investing for Health*. They are each responsible for establishing an 'Investing for Health Partnership' between the main public, voluntary and community interests which have a contribution to make in their area, and producing 'Health and Well-being Investment Plans'.

The Health Promotion Agency is responsible for providing a statutory regional focus for health promotion in Northern Ireland, and it plays a key role in identifying needs and in developing and implementing programmes designed to promote health and prevent ill-health. It coordinates regional health promotion activities throughout Northern Ireland, undertakes public education campaigns, evaluates and disseminates research findings, provides training and works with the wider health and personal social services and other bodies in helping to implement the Government's public health policies.

One of the wider impacts of the Belfast (Good Friday) Agreement in 1999 (see p. 16) was the setting up of bodies for cross-border cooperation between Northern Ireland and the Irish Republic. Cooperation on health matters was identified as an area suitable for consideration by the North/South Ministerial Council, and Joint Working Groups have been set up in five areas: accident and emergency services, emergency planning, high technology equipment, cancer research and health promotion. These groups are looking in detail at where cooperation can yield the greatest benefit for people in both Northern Ireland and the Irish Republic. Joint ventures have included the production of an all-Ireland cancer incidence report, a folic acid advertising campaign, promotion of physical fitness, training and research initiatives, and preliminary work to establish plans and protocols for dealing with major incidents.

ADMINISTRATION

Finance

The NHS is financed mainly through general taxation, along with an element of National Insurance contributions (see chapter 12) paid by employed people, their employers and self-employed people. In 2000–01 an estimated 80.4% of the NHS was financed through general taxation, with 12.1% from National Insurance contributions and 7.4% from charges and other receipts.

The Government's Expenditure Plans, published in May 2001, detailed the funding strategy for the NHS in England. Planned expenditure (net of receipts) by the DH has been set at around £49.8 billion in 2001–02, £54.7 billion in 2002–03, and £59.2 billion in 2003–04. Capital investment is also set to rise, to £3.1 billion in 2001–02, £3.4 billion in 2002–03, and £3.6 billion in 2003–04. Core spending on health by the Scottish Executive will rise from £5.9 billion in 2001–02 to £6.7 billion in 2003–04. Capital spending on NHSScotland buildings and equipment will rise to £312 million by 2003–04, more than double the amount spent in 1997.

Health authorities may raise funds from other, non-government, sources. For example, some hospitals increase revenue by taking private patients, who pay the full cost of their accommodation and treatment. They can also use private finance for NHS capital projects, under the Private Finance Initiative. This is a scheme which aims to promote commercial partnership between the public and private sectors (see p. 403). In the context of the NHS, it involves new facilities being designed, built, maintained and owned by the private sector, which then leases them back to the NHS. The NHS retains control of key planning and clinical decisions. In addition, the National Lottery's New Opportunities Fund provides funding for health, education and the environment.

Figure 13.3: NHS Gross Expenditure, England, 2000–01

Total: £47.9 billion

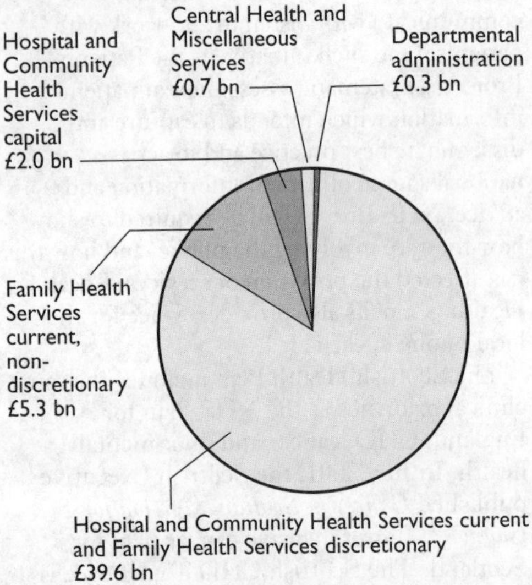

Source: *Department of Health. The Government's Expenditure Plans 2001–2002 to 2003–2004 and Main Estimates 2001–2002*

Charges

Around 552 million prescription items, worth around £5.6 billion, were dispensed in England in 2000, an increase of 6.0% in real terms since 1995. The proportion of items provided free of charge was 85% in 2000, a rise of 1% since 1995. The following groups are exempt from prescription charges: people aged 60 and over; children under 16 and people aged under 19 who are in full-time education; women who are pregnant or have given birth in the previous 12 months; and people with certain medical conditions. In addition, people who receive (or whose partners receive) certain social security benefits (see chapter 12), or who otherwise qualify on low income grounds, do not pay prescription charges. In 2000, 54% of all prescription items dispensed by community pharmacies and appliance contractors in England were for elderly people, compared with 45% five years earlier. War pensioners (if not otherwise entitled to free prescriptions) get free prescriptions for treatment of their pensionable disability, and they may receive refunds of the costs of sight tests, glasses or contact lenses and dental treatment. Prescription charges and exemptions in Wales are now different from those in England.

There are charges for most types of NHS dental treatment, including examinations. However, the following people are entitled to free treatment: women who begin a course of treatment while pregnant or within 12 months of having a baby; children under 18; full-time students under 19; and adults on low incomes or receiving the same benefits or tax credits as for free prescriptions.

Free NHS sight tests are available for people aged 60 and over, children, full-time students under the age of 19, adults on low incomes or receiving the same benefits or tax credits as for free prescriptions, and people who have, or are at particular risk of, eye disease. Over 10 million sight tests were paid for by health authorities in England and Wales in the year to 31 March 2001.

NHS Workforce

The NHS is one of the largest employers in the world, with a workforce of nearly 1 million people. In 1999 there were the equivalent of 943,000 whole-time direct care employees in NHS hospital and community health services in Great Britain.

For the most part, family practitioners (GPs, dentists, optometrists and community pharmacists) are either self-employed or (in the case of pharmacists and optometrists) are employed by independent businesses. They, or their companies, agree to provide services on the NHS's behalf, and are paid by health authorities for doing so.

By 2005, the Government intends the number of places in medical schools in England to have risen to 5,894, compared with 3,749 in October 1997. It has set NHS Plan targets to increase the number of GPs by at least 2,000, the number of consultants by 7,500 and the number of nurses by 20,000 between 1999 and 2004. In the first year of the NHS Plan period (September 1999 to September 2000) there were 6,300 more nurses, 1,100 more consultants and 126 more GPs. By 2003, the Scottish Executive intends to have invested an additional £11.5 million to recruit 375 extra junior doctors.

Doctors and Dentists

Only people on the medical or dentists' registers may practise as doctors or dentists in the NHS. University medical and dental schools are responsible for undergraduate teaching, and the NHS provides hospital and community facilities for training.

Full registration as a doctor requires five or six years' training in a medical school, in a hospital and in the community, with a further year's hospital experience. Most GPs are paid by a system of fees and allowances designed to reflect responsibilities, workload and practice expenses. The regulating body for the medical profession in the UK is the General Medical

In the 2001 Budget, new initiatives costing £835 million over three years were announced, aimed at recruiting more NHS staff in England, particularly GPs and nurses. These included:

- a £5,000 'golden hello' to every new GP who joins the NHS;
- a scheme to encourage GPs to return to the NHS;
- a £10,000 payment to GPs who wait until the age of 65 before retiring from the NHS;
- extra payment to GPs who work in deprived areas;
- a 10.4% rise in bursaries for student nurses, midwives and therapists; and
- funding for 50 new NHS workplace nurseries.

Council (GMC), and the main professional association is the British Medical Association. As a result of high-profile cases, such as that of Harold Shipman,[2] clinical governance has become an increasing concern. From 2001 all doctors are being appraised annually, and the GMC plans to revalidate doctors regularly to ensure that they keep their professional practice up to date. A National Clinical Assessment Authority was established in April 2001, to provide a rapid objective assessment of a doctor's performance where necessary.

For a dentist, five years' training at a dental school and satisfactory completion of one year's mandatory vocational training are required before permission is granted to work as a principal in the General Dental Services of the NHS. All general dental practitioners are paid by a combination of capitation fees for children registered with the practice, continuing care payments for adults registered, and a prescribed scale of fees for individual treatments. The regulating body for the dental profession in the UK is the General Dental Council, and the main professional association is the British Dental Association.

Nurses, Midwives and Health Visitors

The majority of nursing students undertake the pre-registration Diploma in Higher Education programme, which emphasises health promotion as well as care of the sick and enables students to work either in hospitals or in the community. The programme lasts three years and consists of periods of university study combined with practical experience in hospital and in the community. In addition, there are now over 60 cadet schemes in England, encompassing over 800 people. They offer a non-academic route into professional training by combining work experience with theoretical learning, leading to achievement of qualifications sufficient to meet entry requirements to a pre-registration programme, usually a National Vocational Qualification (NVQ). The Government intends to expand the scheme to cover at least 2,000 people over the next three years.

[2] In January 2000, a Manchester GP, Harold Shipman, was convicted of murdering 15 elderly patients.

Between 1997 and 1999, the number of qualified nurses in the NHS increased by more than 10,000.

Midwifery education programmes for registered general/adult nurses take 18 months, but the direct entry programme lasts three years. Health visitors are registered adult nurses who have a further specialist qualification in health visiting. District nurses are registered adult nurses who have a further specialist qualification in district nursing and care for clients in the community. By 2005, the Government aims to raise the number of midwives by 2,000.

The United Kingdom Central Council for Nursing, Midwifery and Health Visiting is responsible for regulating and registering these professions. Four National Boards—for England, Wales, Scotland and Northern Ireland—are responsible for ensuring that training courses meet Central Council requirements as to their type, content and standard. The Government intends to replace all of these bodies with a single regulatory body, the Nursing and Midwifery Council, which will be more responsive to patients' needs. This body was set up in shadow form in May 2001, and is expected to be established formally from April 2002.

Pharmacists

Only people on the register of pharmaceutical chemists may practise as pharmacists. Registration requires four years' training in a school of pharmacy, followed by one year's practical experience in a community or hospital pharmacy approved for training by regulatory bodies for the profession—the Royal Pharmaceutical Society of Great Britain or the Pharmaceutical Society of Northern Ireland. Community pharmacists are paid professional fees for dispensing NHS prescriptions, as well as being reimbursed for the cost of the drugs and appliances concerned.

Optometrists (Ophthalmic Opticians)

The General Optical Council regulates the professions of ophthalmic optician (or ophthalmic medical practitioner) and

Table 13.4: Health and Personal Social Services Staff, Great Britain *Thousands*

	1981	1991	1999
NHS hospital and community health service			
Direct care staff			
Medical and dental	48	56	72
Nursing, midwifery and health visitors[1]	457	470	414
Other non-medical staff	473	429	457
All direct care staff	978	955	943
General medical practitioners[2]	27	31	36
General dental practitioners[3]	15	18	21
Personal social services[4]	240	289	274

[1] Excludes nurse teachers, nurses in training and certain students.
[2] Excludes GP retainers.
[3] Principals on a health authority or family health list, assistants and vocational dental practitioners.
[4] Staff employed only at local authority social work departments (whole time equivalent).
Sources: Department of Health, National Assembly for Wales and NHSScotland

dispensing optician. Only registered ophthalmic opticians may test sight. Their training takes four years, including a year of practical experience under supervision. Dispensing opticians take a two-year full-time course with a year's practical experience, or follow a part-time day-release course while employed with an optician. Ophthalmic medical practitioners and optometrists providing general ophthalmic services for the NHS receive approved fees for each sight test.

Other Health Professions

The Council for Professions Supplementary to Medicine (CPSM) and its 12 professional boards regulate the initial training and subsequent practice of arts therapists, chiropodists, clinical scientists, dieticians, medical laboratory scientific officers (commonly known as medical laboratory technicians or biomedical scientists), occupational therapists, orthoptists, paramedics, physiotherapists, prosthetists and orthotists, radiographers, and speech and language therapists. The boards are responsible for promoting high standards of professional education and conduct among members, approving training institutions, qualifications and courses, and maintaining registers of those who have qualified for state registration, which is mandatory for employment in most of these professions in health authorities, trusts and local authority social services. However, by April 2002, the Government plans to replace the CPSM and all of the boards with the Health Professions Council (HPC), a single statutory regulatory body which is intended to be more responsive to patients' needs, and which will have scope to regulate new professions.

Standards and Openness in the NHS

The 1997 White Paper *The New NHS* and the 1998 consultation document *A First Class Service* introduced a range of measures to raise quality and decrease variations in service, including National Service Frameworks (NSFs). The NHS Plan re-emphasised the role of NSFs in modernising the service. NSFs set national standards and define service models for a defined service or care group, put in place strategies to support implementation, and establish performance milestones against which progress within an agreed timescale can be measured.

The rolling programme of NSFs, launched in April 1998, takes forward established frameworks on cancer and paediatric intensive care, and published NSFs include those for mental health (1999), coronary heart disease (2000) and older people (2001). Other NSFs will be for diabetes, renal services, children's services, and long-term conditions focusing on neurological conditions.

NHS Complaints System

Under the current NHS complaints system, complaints should be resolved speedily at local level, but if the complainant remains dissatisfied with the local response he or she can request an independent review. Where such an investigation takes place, a report setting out suggestions and recommendations will be produced. Complainants who remain dissatisfied, or whose request for a panel investigation is turned down, can refer their complaint to the Health Service Commissioner.

In 1999–2000, 86,536 written complaints were made about hospital and community health services in England, and 39,725 complaints (covering general medical and dental services and health authority/family health services administration) were made about family health services. In Scotland in 1999–2000, there were 7,027 written complaints about hospital and community health services and 2,581 about family health services.

Health Service Commissioners

England, Wales and Scotland each have Health Service Commissioners. They are responsible for investigating complaints directly from members of the public about health service bodies. The three posts are at present held by one person (with a staff of about 250), who is also Parliamentary Commissioner for Administration (the Ombudsman—see p. 57). As Health Service Commissioner, he reports annually to Parliament, the Welsh Assembly and the Scottish Parliament. In Northern Ireland complaints about health and social services bodies are investigated by the Commissioner for Complaints.

The Health Service Commissioner can investigate complaints that a person has suffered hardship or injustice as a result of a failure in a service provided by a health service body; a failure to provide a service which the patient was entitled to receive or maladministration by an NHS authority; or action by health professionals arising from the exercise of clinical judgment.

NHS Charters

In 2001 a new NHS Charter for England—*Your Guide to the NHS*—replaced the Patient's Charter. It provides information on how patients can access appropriate services to meet their healthcare needs, sets out a series of standards for each stage in the patient's care, and includes improvements patients can expect in the future. In Wales, a Health and Social Care Charter was launched in 2001, backed up with local charters at local health group level. A revised Charter for NHSScotland is planned.

NEW INITIATIVES

NHS Direct

In 1998 NHS Direct, a nurse-led telephone helpline, was launched in England. NHS Direct aims to provide people at home with fast and convenient access to health information and advice. The service helps people to be better able to care for themselves and their families, when it is appropriate to do so, and to direct them to the most appropriate level of care when they need professional help.

During 2000–01 NHS Direct handled 3.42 million calls. At present, the service handles between 100,000 and 110,000 calls each week.

NHS Direct Online, an Internet extension of the telephone-based services, was launched in December 1999, and receives around 5 million 'hits' a month, or around 150,000 site visits. The website (*www.nhsdirect.nhs.uk*) features an electronic version of the NHS Direct Healthcare Guide, and a conditions and treatment database with information and links to support groups for hundreds of different conditions. Work is in progress to develop an interactive e-mail enquiry service for health information. A pilot scheme making NHS Direct Online services available via digital television is also in progress.

The NHS Plan set out a programme of developments for NHS Direct. These focus around the closer integration of NHS Direct with other parts of the NHS and should ensure the development of the service in the next two to three years into one of the most important 'gateways' into the NHS, with an estimated call volume of 20 million calls a year by 2004.

Wales has a similar service, NHS Direct Wales, which offers advice in both English and Welsh.

In Scotland, a new service—NHS24—is due to be rolled out from April 2002 onwards. Similar to NHS Direct in England, NHS24 will be available 24 hours a day throughout the year. A single telephone call will allow members of the public to obtain confidential and reliable health advice from qualified nurses, gain access to care services when appropriate, and get information on healthcare services in their area.

NHS Walk-in Centres

By the end of 2001 a total of 43 NHS Walk-in Centres will exist across England. NHS Walk-in Centres are a network of centres—where no appointment is necessary—offering quick access to a range of services, including healthcare advice and information, and treatment for minor ailments and injuries such as coughs, colds, cuts and bruises, and sprains. They are intended to complement GP surgeries and help reduce pressure on GPs.

Health Action Zones

There are 26 Health Action Zones (HAZs) in deprived areas of England, including inner city, rural and ex-coalfield communities. The zones are local partnerships between the health service, local councils, voluntary groups and local businesses, and receive government funding. Their aim is to make measurable improvements in the health of local people and in the quality of treatment and care. Working closely with DH, the participants cooperate to tackle inequalities and deliver better services and healthcare. They focus on areas such as programmes to stop smoking, children's and young people's health, mental health, CHD and cancer, older people's health, and the health of ethnic minorities. HAZs play an important role in the development of Local Strategic Partnerships and the NHS modernisation agenda.

Four Health Action Zones have been established in Northern Ireland and an initiative to encourage local healthcare partnerships has been launched in Scotland. The Scottish Executive is supporting Social Inclusion Partnerships to tackle exclusion at a local level. The 48 Partnerships deliver local solutions in deprived areas and for particular groups facing disadvantage, including health inequalities. Thirty-four are area-based and include the majority of the areas within the 10% most deprived postcode sectors in Scotland. The others are thematic and target groups of people with specific needs, such as young people leaving care and ethnic minority groups.

Electronic Initiatives

The NHS is making increasing use of new technology in patient care. In March 2001 the DH and the Scottish Executive both agreed to pilot electronic prescription schemes, whereby prescriptions could be sent electronically from GPs to community pharmacies. Consortia are concentrating on preparatory work in readiness to begin piloting once amended regulations have been approved. In addition, by 2004 the Government has said that every patient in England will be able to access his or her own electronic health record—a summary of key personal and health data about the patient. There are other health information websites: the Medicines Control Agency (MCA) website, which was relaunched in 2001, contains information on medicines; and the British Library's telemedicine website, which was launched in 2001 and aims to give medical professionals, patients and carers access to information on the latest projects and developments. Scotland's first pilot scheme for the electronic transmission of prescriptions from local surgeries to community pharmacies was launched in March 2001. NHSnet is a range of voice and data services used by the NHS, covering radio, telephone and computer-based communications. Health authorities and most Trusts are connected to NHSnet, as are a number of major NHS suppliers and all GPs in Scotland. By 2002 every GP practice in England will be connected to NHSnet and will be able to receive hospital pathology test results. NHSnet will also support the longer-term goal of introducing electronic health records to replace the paper-based records. This will make possible secure access by doctors to patients' records in an emergency when they are away from home. An equivalent scheme, HPSSnet, has been set up in Northern Ireland by Northern Ireland Health and Personal Social Services (HPSS).

FAMILY HEALTH SERVICES

The Family Health Services are those provided to patients by doctors (GPs), dentists, opticians and pharmacists. According to estimates based on the ONS's General Household Survey, there were 255.3 million consultations with GPs in Great Britain in 1998–99.

GPs provide the first diagnosis in the case of illness, give advice and may prescribe a suitable course of treatment. They may refer a patient to the more specialised services and hospital consultants. Primary healthcare teams also include health visitors, district nurses, midwives, social workers and other professional staff employed by the health authorities. A long-term investment programme to improve GP premises is under way and since 1998 over 1,000 premises have been improved.

Between 1981 and 1999, the number of GPs in Great Britain rose by a third, from 27,000 to 36,000, and the number of general dental practitioners increased by more than a third, from 15,000 to 21,000 (see Table 13.4).

Initiatives in Primary Care

The NHS Plan envisages that by 2004 patients in England will be able to see a primary care professional routinely within 24 hours and a GP within 48 hours. Additional funding has been made available to PCTs over the four years to 2003–04 to help GP practices achieve this target. An interim target has been set, that by March 2002 six in ten patients will be able to see a GP within 48 hours. More services will also be available in primary care centres, and there are targets (see p. 188) of some 4 million consultant outpatient appointments a year in primary care and community settings and up to 1,000 GPs with a special interest being able to take referrals from other GPs.

A major target of the NHS Plan is reducing inequality in access to services. To improve the fair distribution of GPs across the NHS, from 2002–03 the formula for allocating resources to the NHS will be improved to take greater account of expenditure on GPs, and responsibility for deciding if more GPs are needed in particular areas will be transferred to health authorities from the national Medical Practices Committee, which is to be abolished.

In September 2000 the DH published *Modernising NHS Dentistry: Implementing the NHS Plan*, its dental strategy for England. It states that, by the end of 2001, everyone who wants to will be able to be treated by an NHS dentist. A Dental Care Development Fund has been set up, aimed at making it easier for up to 250,000 people to find an NHS dentist. Pilot dental services are being set up to encourage innovation to meet differences in local dental needs, and Dental Access Centres are being set up in a number of locations to relieve the most acute access problems. The first were launched in October 1998, and by April 2002 there will be around 60 Dental Access Centres, providing both routine and emergency dental care. The Scottish Executive published *An Action Plan for Dental Services in Scotland* in August 2001 and is currently implementing its plans, including free toothbrushes and toothpaste for 100,000 children in Scotland.

Pharmacy in the Future—Implementing the National Plan was published by the DH in September 2000. By 2004 all Primary Care Groups and Trusts should have schemes which enable people to get more advice from pharmacists in using their medicines. In Scotland, work is under way to develop a national strategy for pharmaceutical care.

Midwives, Health Visitors and District Nurses

Nurses, midwives and health visitors working in primary and community care provide care, treatment, rehabilitation and preventive services to individuals, families and communities. They deliver this care in the home, health centres, schools, and other community settings.

District nurses give skilled nursing care to people at home or elsewhere outside hospital; they also play an important role in health promotion and education. Practice nurses are based in GP surgeries. They carry out treatments and give advice on health promotion, working closely with GPs and with other community nurses. Midwives provide care and support to women throughout pregnancy (see p. 206), birth and the postnatal period (up to 28 days after the baby is born). They work in both hospital and community settings. The Government has emphasised the importance of both nurses and midwives in their planned reforms of the NHS (*Making a Difference—Strengthening nursing, midwifery and health visiting in England*, issued in July 1999, and *Caring for Scotland—the Strategy for Nursing and Midwifery in Scotland*, issued in March 2000). It intends nurses and midwives to play a stronger role in the health service, and has committed itself to investment in developing nurses' and midwives' skills and in expanding their training. In both Scotland and England there are plans to expand the prescribing powers of some nurses, after appropriate training, so that patients can obtain quicker access to medicines. Following the publication of the review of public health nursing in Scotland, *Nursing for Health*, in March 2001, the Scottish Executive is creating 84 new 'public health practitioner' posts, who will be drawn from the nursing profession and whose job will be to help families and communities make improvements in their own health.

HOSPITAL AND SPECIALIST SERVICES

District general hospitals offer a broad spectrum of clinical specialities, supported by a range of other services, such as anaesthetics, pathology and radiology. Almost all have facilities for the admission of emergency patients, either through accident and emergency departments or as direct referrals from GPs. Treatments are provided for inpatients, day cases, outpatients and patients who attend wards for treatment such as dialysis. Some hospitals also provide specialist services covering more than one region or district, for example for heart and liver transplants and rare eye and bone cancers. There are also specialist hospitals such as the

Table 13.5: Use of Health Services: by Gender and Age, Great Britain, 1998–99

Percentages

	16–24	25–34	35–44	45–54	55–64	65–74	75 and over	All aged 16 and over
Males								
Consultation with GP[1]	7	9	10	12	16	17	21	12
Inpatient	4	4	5	7	10	15	21	8
Outpatient visit[2]	12	14	13	15	20	25	29	17
Casualty visit[2,3]	7	7	5	4	3	3	3	5
Females								
Consultation with GP[1]	15	18	16	19	17	19	20	18
Inpatient	11	15	8	8	10	10	15	11
Outpatient visit[2]	13	13	12	17	19	21	26	17
Casualty visit[2,3]	6	4	3	3	3	3	3	4

[1] Consultations with an NHS GP in the last two weeks.
[2] In the last three months; includes visits to a hospital casualty department.
[3] The question was only asked of those who had an outpatient visit.
Source: General Household Survey, Office for National Statistics

world-famous Hospital for Sick Children at Great Ormond Street, Moorfields Eye Hospital, and the National Hospital for Neurology and Neurosurgery, all in London. These hospitals combine specialist treatment facilities with the training of medical and other students, and international research.

Less than a third of hospitals now pre-date the formation of the NHS in 1948. While much has been done to improve existing hospital buildings, the largest building programme in the history of the NHS is currently in progress, including several major Private Finance Initiative schemes. Altogether over 100 new hospital schemes are planned between 2000 and 2010.

The main contribution of NHS Trusts (see p. 189) remains the provision of hospital and community services to patients. The services provided are subject to quality standards set by NICE (see p. 188) and, in England, to the new 'earned autonomy' system to be established under the NHS Plan (see p. 188).

Waiting Lists

Half of all admissions to hospital are immediate. The other half are placed on a waiting list before the admission takes place. Of patients admitted from waiting lists, half are admitted within six weeks, and around two-thirds within three months. Under the NHS Plan, the maximum waiting time for admission to hospital is intended to be reduced from 18 months to 6 months by the end of 2005. By the same date patients needing a hospital outpatient appointment will face a maximum wait of 3 months. At the end of March 2001 just over 1 million patients were waiting to be admitted to NHS hospitals in England. The Government has developed a new National Booked Admissions Programme, under which, by the end of 2005, all patients will be able to pre-book their hospital appointments and operations for a convenient date and time. This will be facilitated by the introduction of electronic booking systems throughout the NHS by the end of 2005. An extra £40 million was made available by the National Assembly for Wales to reduce waiting lists by 15,000 during 2000–01.

Cancer Care

Cancer was one of the three clinical priorities outlined by the UK Government in its NHS Plan. Cancer services are organised at three levels:

- *primary care* for initial care;
- *cancer units* in many local hospitals of sufficient size to support a team with the expertise and facilities to treat more common cancers; and
- *cancer centres* situated in larger hospitals to treat less common cancers and to support smaller cancer units.

Cancer networks are also being developed as an additional element in this structure. These bring together NHS providers (cancer units and centres), health authorities, Primary Care Groups and the voluntary sector.

In September 2000, the NHS published its *Cancer Plan, A plan for investment. A plan for reform*. This sets out targets for investment, waiting times, staffing levels, screening and reducing the risk of cancer. For 1999–2000, £280 million was made available for the achievement of the Government's cancer targets, and by 2003–04 funding will rise to £570 million a year.

In July 2001, the Scottish Executive published a comprehensive cancer plan for Scotland: *Cancer in Scotland: Action for Change*, which builds on the work of the Scottish Cancer Group, established in 1998. The plan sets out objectives for improving the prevention of cancer and its diagnosis and treatment. The Scottish Health Plan pledged new maximum waiting times for cancer treatment.

Targets

The NHS Cancer Plan set out a range of targets, including:

- reducing smoking rates among manual groups of workers from 32% in 1998 to 26% by 2010;
- employing 1,000 more cancer specialists by 2006;
- pre-planned and pre-booked care for every patient diagnosed with cancer by 2004;

- a maximum one-month wait from urgent GP referral to treatment for children's and testicular cancer and acute leukaemia by the end of 2001;
- a maximum one-month wait from diagnosis to treatment for breast cancer by 2001, and for all cancers by 2005; and
- a maximum two-month wait from urgent GP referral to treatment for breast cancer by 2002, and for all cancers by 2005.

The Cancer Services Collaborative programme was launched in 1999 to find the best ways of cutting delays in treatment. In January 2001, the DH published national standards for cancer care, allowing the quality of care provided to be assessed across the country on a consistent basis.

Research

Research is an important way to reduce the number of deaths from cancer in the long term. The National Cancer Research Institute was formed in April 2001 to coordinate all cancer research in the United Kingdom. At the same time the National Cancer Research Network was also established. It aims to double the number of patients involved in clinical trials as well as recruiting more specialist nurses and other staff. By 2003–04, the Government will be investing an additional £20 million a year on this initiative.

> The National Institute for Clinical Excellence (NICE) has recommended several cancer drugs since its formation in 1999. These have included the ovarian cancer drug Taxol, the breast cancer drug Taxotere, the brain cancer drug Temodal and the pancreatic cancer drug Gemzar.

Screening

Cancer screening programmes are in operation for breast cancer and cervical cancer. At present, under the United Kingdom's breast cancer screening programme, every woman aged between 50 and 64 is invited for mammography (breast X-ray) every three years by computerised call-up and recall systems. This facility is to be extended to women aged 65 to 70 by 2004 in England. In Scotland, the extension of the routine age of invitation to women aged 65–70 will begin in 2003–04 and be implemented over a three-year round of screening. Also at present, all women over the age of 64 can refer themselves for screening. In England, 1.3 million women of all ages were screened, and 8,215 cases of cancer were diagnosed. In Scotland 106,816 women aged 50–64 years were routinely screened in 1999–2000, and 712 cases of cancer were diagnosed.

National policy for cervical screening is that women should be screened every three to five years (three-and-a-half to five-and-a-half years in Scotland) so as to detect indications of the long developmental stage which may proceed to invasive cancer. The programme invites women aged 20 to 64 (20 to 60 in Scotland) for screening. However, since many women are not invited immediately when they reach their 20th birthday, the age group 25 to 64 is used to give a more accurate estimate of coverage of the target population in England. By the end of March 2000, more than four-fifths of women in the target population had been screened in England, Scotland and Wales. This is a considerable increase on the figures for 1989, when less than half of the target population in England had undergone a smear test in the previous five years.

The NHS Cancer Plan set out the Government's intention to introduce prostate cancer screening if and when screening and treatment techniques have developed sufficiently. The evidence for this is kept under review. In the meantime, a prostate cancer risk management programme has been launched. One element of this is the Informed Choice Project for prostate specific antigen (PSA) testing. Pilot studies are under way for colorectal screening, and other possibilities for future screening programmes are lung and ovarian cancers.

Coronary Heart Disease

As well as being a major clinical health concern, coronary heart disease is also linked to the Government's aim of reducing health inequality. Death rates for CHD are three times higher among manual workers than among managers. By 2003–04, an extra £230 million should have been invested in heart disease services, and capital funding from the Capital Modernisation Fund (see p. 400) is also being made available. To help streamline the delivery of coronary heart care, in 2000 the Coronary Heart Disease Partnership Programme was set up, bringing together doctors, nurses, paramedics and other staff involved in heart care. The Government has set the following targets and priorities for CHD in England:

- an increase of 10% each year to 2003–04 in the number of consultant cardiologists, and no Trust to have a 'single-handed' consultant cardiologist by 2004;
- all practices to have disease management registers in place by 2003;
- rapid access chest pain clinics to be established by 2003 (by April 2001, 139 had been opened);
- 'clot-busting' drugs to be administered within 60 minutes of a call for professional help;
- a reduction in waiting times for cardiac surgery to three months by 2008; and
- 6,000 more heart operations by 2003.

Improving Health in Wales recognised that clinical networks for cardiac care are essential for the development and improvement of clinical services, and the Welsh Assembly is to spend an extra £208,000 on heart disease and critical care managed clinical networks. It is also spending £2 million on attempts to reduce waiting lists for cardiac surgery.

The Scottish Health Plan, *Our National Health*, includes a range of measures to tackle heart disease and stroke in Scotland, focusing on primary and secondary prevention, improving access to diagnostic services, and reducing waiting times for treatment. In autumn 2001, the national CHD Task Force is due to report on its comprehensive review of CHD services in Scotland.

Mental Health

The Mental Health Services NSF sets out a ten-year programme designed to raise standards of mental healthcare. The NHS Plan involves extra annual investment of over £300 million by 2003–04 and includes provision for:

- 1,000 new mental healthcare workers helping GPs, and 500 additional community mental health staff;
- 50 teams to be established over the next three years to help reduce the period of untreated psychosis in young people;
- over 300 'crisis resolution' teams to help deal quickly with people with acute mental illness experiencing a crisis and who would otherwise need to be admitted to hospital;
- 230 teams to deal with the small number of high users of services, many of whom also have a problem with substance misuse;
- women-only day centres in every health authority by 2004; and
- more staff to increase respite care.

In addition, the NHS Plan established a Mental Health Taskforce, which has a specific remit to look at minority ethnic mental health and the development of culturally appropriate mental health services. In 2000 the DH carried out a survey of attitudes to mental illness in Great Britain, which revealed that three-quarters of adults felt that 'mental illness was an illness like any other'. However, 80% of young people believe that mental illness will lead to discrimination, and in 2001 the DH launched a campaign designed to reduce discrimination against people with mental health problems and users of mental health services. In Scotland, the *Framework for Mental Health*, published in 1997, is in its implementation phase.

Communicable Disease Prevention and Immunisation

Health authorities/health boards are responsible for the prevention and control of infectious disease, liaising closely with colleagues in environmental health departments of local authorities. They are assisted by the Public Health Laboratory

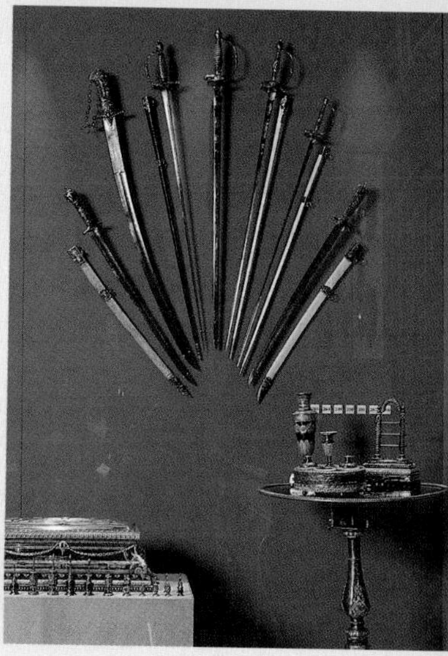

photos: Copyright, The Hermitage Development Trust

In November 2000 permanent exhibition space was opened at Somerset House, London, devoted to rotating exhibitions for the State Hermitage Museum of St Petersburg. During 2001 the inaugural exhibition entitled 'Treasures of Catherine the Great' transformed this suite of rooms into a miniature Winter Palace.

Catherine was born in 1729 and is now considered one of the greatest collectors of all time. The exhibition was designed not only to reflect her passion for collecting art and antiquities from around the world, but also her patronage of contemporary craftsmen.

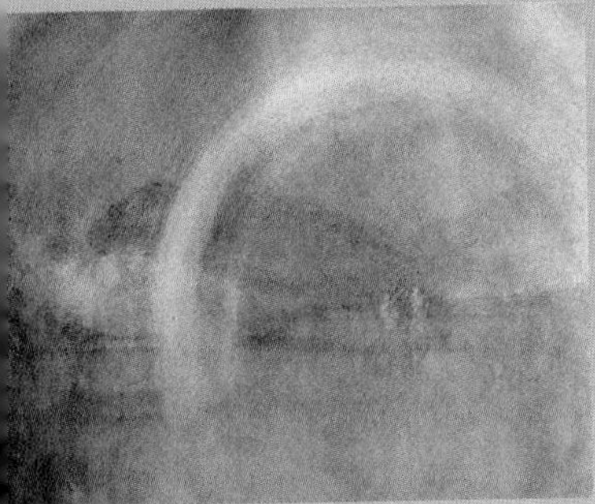

Both: The Hickman Bacon Collection

Guild of St George Collection, Sheffield Galleries and Museums Trust

2001 marked the 150th anniversary of J. M. W. Turner's death. He is regarded as one of the founders of English watercolour landscape painting, having demonstrated his prodigious artistic talent at the age of 15, when one of his paintings was exhibited at the Royal Academy.

'Malmesbury Abbey' (right), 'A Low Sun' and 'Lake and Rainbow' (both top left) are all part of the Sir Hickman Bacon private collection of British landscape drawings and watercolours, on display at the Dulwich Picture Gallery during 2001–02. 'A Low Sun' and 'Lake and Rainbow' are typical of his late, ethereal style of painting. The portrait of 'Turner on Varnishing Day' (top right) by S. W. Parrott may have been painted from a surreptitious sketch, as Turner disliked being watched as he worked.

The Hickman Bacon Collection

© Sue Crossfield: www.suecrossfield.co.uk Photo: Chris Johnson

© Sally MacDonell: www.macdonell-ceramics.co.uk Photo: Fotek

© Christine Cox: www.potfest.co.uk

CUMBRIA CERAMICA

'Cumbria Ceramica', a new ten-day ceramic festival held in and around Cumbria, was launched in the summer of 2001, with internationally known potters exhibiting alongside recent graduates. As well as promoting the sales of ceramics being produced in small workshops throughout the UK, the festival gave the public an opportunity to participate in the ceramic production process through workshops, demonstrations in open studios, illustrated talks and kiln firings.

The page shows the work of five contributors to the festival: Sue Crossfield (top left), Sally MacDonell (centre left), Christine Cox (bottom left), Ralph Jandrell (below) and Syl Macro (bottom).

© Ralph Jandrell Pottery: www.ralphjandrell.co.uk

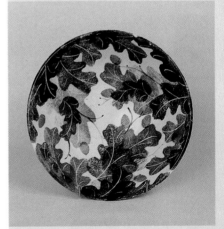

© Syl Macro: sylmacro@hotmail.com

Reliquary of Holy Cross of Khotakerats, 1300.

Holy See of Ēĵmiadsin

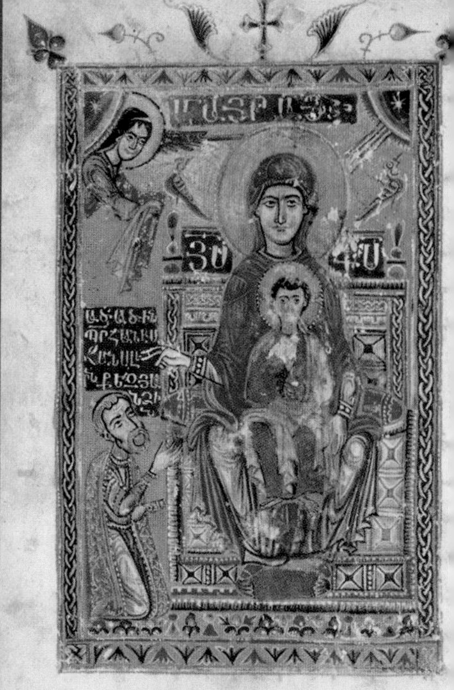

The Psalter of King Levon III, 1283.

The British Library

The year 2001 marked the 1,700th anniversary of the adoption of Christianity as the state religion of Armenia. A celebratory exhibition held at The British Library, called **'Treasures from the Ark'**, brought together Armenian Christian art and artefacts, many of which have not been seen outside the country before. Armenian culture is also being promoted through a series of events linked to the exhibition such as film shows and free gallery talks.

Gonfalon of St Gregory the Illuminator, 1448.

Holy See of Ēĵmiadsin

Deacon holding a cross, fragmentary tile, 18th–19th century.

British Museum

Service (PHLS), which aims to protect the population from infection through the detection, diagnosis, surveillance, prevention and control of communicable diseases in England and Wales. Similar facilities are provided in Scotland by the Scottish Centre for Infection and Environmental Health and, in Northern Ireland, by the Communicable Disease Surveillance Centre, the Department of Health, Social Services and Public Safety, and other hospital microbiology laboratories.

Immunisation

Health authorities/health boards carry out programmes of immunisation against diphtheria, measles, mumps, rubella, poliomyelitis, tetanus, tuberculosis, whooping cough (pertussis) and haemophilus influenzae type B infection ('Hib'). The UK was the first country in the world to use a new vaccine to protect against meningitis C. This vaccine was introduced into the immunisation programme in 1999, and by the end of 2000 all people aged under 18 had been offered the vaccine. The programme has led to dramatic reductions in the incidence of meningitis C among 15 to 17 year olds and babies under the age of one.

Immunisation is not compulsory. Parents are provided with information about the safety and effectiveness of vaccines and are encouraged to have their children immunised. Immunisations are mainly given by GPs and their practice nurses. Virtually every child under the age of two is now immunised against diphtheria, tetanus, whooping cough and polio. Since the introduction of the Hib vaccine in 1992, Hib meningitis has been almost completely eliminated in young children.

Vaccination against influenza is recommended for people with certain other illnesses, and for everybody aged 65 and over. In 1988, the measles/mumps/rubella (MMR) vaccine was introduced and a higher coverage of immunisation was achieved as it became widely available. Adverse publicity about the MMR combined vaccine led to a fall in the number of children immunised against MMR by their second birthday in England, from 92% in 1995–96 to 88% in 1999–2000.

Tuberculosis

A schools immunisation programme against tuberculosis (TB), which had been suspended in 1999, was restarted in March 2001. The Government intends routine immunisation for pupils aged between 13 and 15 to be back in place by 2002–03.

Much of the recent rise in TB in the UK (see p. 185) is thought to be the result of the disease being 'imported' from other countries. The Government has a dual approach to prevention and control of TB in new immigrants to the UK: first to screen those at highest risk at ports of entry, and then to offer more detailed screening, including skin testing, when they arrive at their destination.

HIV/AIDS

Government strategies to reduce HIV transmission include:

- HIV/AIDS health promotion aimed at both the general population and groups at risk;
- information on antenatal HIV testing to help pregnant women to reach informed decisions, for example about ways of reducing the risk of transmission to babies; and
- the National AIDS Helpline, which provides confidential information and advice on all aspects of HIV and AIDS.

The Government has also introduced a range of initiatives to encourage pregnant women to have an HIV test as an integral part of their antenatal care. Most HIV-infected pregnant women accept measures to decrease the risk of passing the infection to their babies.

Substance Misuse

Alcohol

Part of the funds allocated to Health Promotion England (see p. 189) is for promoting sensible drinking in England, and equivalent bodies are similarly funded in other parts of Britain. 'Drinkline' provides confidential telephone advice about alcohol problems and services in England and Wales. Treatment and rehabilitation within the NHS includes inpatient and outpatient services in general and psychiatric hospitals and some specialised alcohol treatment units. Primary care teams and voluntary organisations also play an important role in providing treatment and rehabilitation in hostels and day centres.

There is also close cooperation between statutory and voluntary organisations. In England, Alcohol Concern plays a prominent role in improving services for problem drinkers and their families, increasing public awareness of alcohol misuse, and improving training for professional and voluntary workers. The Scottish Council on Alcohol has a similar function in Scotland.

The Scottish Executive will publish a *Plan for Action on Alcohol Misuse* in autumn 2001, following an extensive public consultation exercise. In Northern Ireland, a Regional Drug Strategy Coordinator was appointed in February 2001 to take forward the Drug Strategy and the Strategy for Reducing Alcohol Related Harm.

Tobacco

The NHS Plan envisages an expansion in specialist services for those smokers who need extra help to give up. Smokers can now get nicotine replacement therapy (NRT) on prescription from GPs. NRT provides the body with nicotine in decreasing doses until the craving can be coped with. This complements the newly available treatment, buproprion. Reduction in the proportion of people smoking since 1965 has almost halved the number of lung cancer deaths that would otherwise have been expected in the UK.

In September 1999, the licensed hospitality industry, supported by the Government, produced a voluntary Public Places Charter which committed signatories to improve the facilities for customers who do not smoke in public houses, bars and restaurants.

In Northern Ireland a working group has been established to oversee the implementation of an action plan to tackle the use of tobacco.

Drugs

The misuse of drugs, such as heroin, cocaine and amphetamines, is a serious social and health problem (see p. 186). In response to this, the Government launched its ten-year anti-drugs strategy *Tackling Drugs to Build a Better Britain* in April 1998. The strategy acknowledged the link between drug misuse and social conditions and problems; signalled a change in spending priorities in order to stop the problem happening, rather than reacting to it when it does; and developed targets for reducing drug misuse based on evidence and experience.

Over the past four years, the Government's strategy has been:

- encouraging young people to resist taking drugs in the first place;
- helping communities to protect themselves from drug-related anti-social and criminal behaviour;
- providing treatment to help people overcome their drug addiction; and
- tackling the availability of drugs.

By 2008 the Government aims to:

- halve the number of young people using the most dangerous illegal drugs, such as heroin and cocaine;
- double the number of drug misusers in treatment;
- halve the level of re-offending by drug misusing offenders; and
- halve the availability of the most dangerous drugs, such as heroin and cocaine, on the streets.

The Welsh Assembly's anti-drugs strategy was published in May 2000 in *Tackling Substance Misuse in Wales: a Partnership Approach*. Scotland's drugs strategy is set out in *Tackling Drugs in Scotland—Action in Partnership*, published in 1999, and in the Scottish Executive's Drug Action Plan, published in May 2000. A £100 million package of expenditure on drugs misuse over three years was announced in September 2000, covering NHS Boards, local authorities and other agencies. This is the biggest programme of anti-drugs initiatives in Scotland and will fund a series of interlinked activities, to ensure that every school pupil, both primary and secondary, has effective drugs education. The strategy for Northern Ireland is set out in *Drug Strategy for Northern Ireland*, published in 1999.

The National Drugs Helpline gives advice and information to anyone in the UK concerned about drugs. The telephone number is 0800 77 66 00.

Solvents

Government policy aims to prevent solvent misuse through educating young people, parents and health professionals about the dangers and signs of misuse, and, where practicable, restricting the sales of solvent-based liquefied gas and aerosol products to young people.

In England, Wales and Northern Ireland it is an offence to supply such substances to children under 18 if the supplier knows or has reason to believe they are to be used to induce intoxication. In Scotland proceedings can be taken under the common law. Since October 1999 it has been an offence in the UK to sell butane lighter refills to people under 18—these refills are implicated in more than half of all deaths from solvent abuse.

The DH funds a hospital-based unit in London to collect and publish annual mortality statistics associated with volatile substance abuse. There were 73 deaths in the UK in 1999.

Organ Transplants

United Kingdom Transplant (a special health authority of the NHS) provides a 24-hour support service to all transplant units in the UK and the Irish Republic for the matching and allocation of organs for transplant. In many cases transplants are multi-organ.

During 2000, 1,695 kidney transplants were performed, and at the end of 2000 there were 6,126 patients waiting for kidney transplants. At the end of 2000 there were seven designated thoracic transplant centres in England, and one in Scotland. In 2000, 204 heart, 98 lung, and 33 heart/lung transplants were performed. There are six designated liver transplant units in England and one in Scotland. In 2000, 671 liver transplants were performed. A similar service exists for corneas and, in 1999, 2,271 were transplanted in the UK. The Government has set targets for increasing the kidney transplant rate by almost 100% and the heart and lung and liver transplant rates by 10% by 2005. A voluntary organ donor card system enables people to indicate their willingness to become organ donors in the event of their death. The NHS Organ Donor Register is a computer database of those willing to be organ donors. At December 2000 it contained around 8 million names. The Government aims to double this figure by 2010. Commercial dealing in organs for transplant is illegal in the UK.

Blood Services

Blood services are run by the National Blood Services in England and North Wales, the Welsh Blood Service, the Scottish National Blood Transfusion Service and the Northern Ireland Blood Transfusion Agency. The UK is self-sufficient in blood components.

In the UK over 3 million donations are made each year by voluntary unpaid donors. These are turned into many different life-saving products for patients. Red cells, platelets and other components with a limited 'life' are prepared at blood centres, while the production of plasma products is undertaken at the Bio Products Laboratory in Elstree (Hertfordshire) and the Protein Fractionation Centre in Edinburgh.

Each of the four national blood services coordinates programmes for donor recruitment, retention and education, and donor sessions are organised regionally, in towns and workplaces. Donors are normally aged between 17 and 70. Blood centres are responsible for blood collection, screening, processing and supplying hospital blood banks. They also provide laboratory, clinical, research, teaching and specialist advisory services and facilities. These blood centres are subject to nationally coordinated quality audit programmes, through the MCA.

Ambulance and Patient Transport Services

NHS emergency ambulances are available free to the public through the 999 telephone system for medical emergencies and accidents, as well as for doctors' urgent calls. Rapid response services, in which paramedics use cars and motorcycles to reach emergency cases, have been introduced in a number of areas, particularly major cities with areas of high traffic density. Helicopter ambulances, provided through local charities, serve many parts of the country and an integrated NHS-funded air ambulance service is available throughout Scotland. In England between 1999–2000 and 2000–01 the number of emergency calls to the NHS rose by 6% to 4.4 million and the number of emergency patient journeys grew by 2% to 2.9 million.

Non-emergency patient transport services are free to NHS patients considered by their doctor, dentist or midwife to be medically unfit to travel by other means. In many areas the ambulance service organises volunteer drivers to provide a hospital car service for non-urgent patients. Patients on low incomes may be eligible for reimbursement of costs of travelling to hospital.

Rehabilitation

The NHS and social services undertake rehabilitation work for large numbers of people of all ages, to restore and maintain their independence and social participation. Rehabilitation plays an important role in improving quality of life, enabling people to return to, or remain in, employment or education and preventing future admissions to hospital or long-term care. Health and social services are encouraged to develop a range of rehabilitative options and to be flexible in meeting people's needs.

Hospices

Hospice (or palliative) care is a special type of care for people whose illness may no longer be curable; it enables them to achieve the best possible quality of life during the final stages. It was first developed in the UK in 1967 by the voluntary hospices and continues to be provided by them, but is also increasingly provided within NHS palliative care units, and in hospitals and community services. The care may be provided in a variety of settings: at home (with support from specially trained staff), in a hospice or palliative care unit, in hospital or at a hospice day centre.

Hospice care focuses on controlling pain and other distressing symptoms and providing psychological support to patients, their families and friends, both during the patient's illness and into bereavement. Hospice care services mostly help people with cancer, although patients with other life-threatening illnesses, such as AIDS, motor neurone disease and heart failure are also cared for. Currently 22 specialist hospice inpatient units provide respite care for children from birth to 16 years of age.

The National Council for Hospices and Specialist Palliative Care Services brings together voluntary and health service providers in England, Wales and Northern Ireland, in order to provide a coordinated view of the service. Its Scottish counterpart is the Scottish Partnership Agency for Palliative and Cancer Care.

Parents and Children

Special preventive services are provided under the NHS to safeguard the health of pregnant women and mothers with young children. Services include free dental treatment; health education; and vaccination and immunisation of children against certain infectious diseases (see p. 203). Under the NHS Plan, further screening programmes are planned by 2004.

Nearly all births take place in hospital, although there was a slight increase during the 1990s in the popularity of home births: these accounted for around 2% of births in England and Wales in 2000, compared with around 1% during the 1980s. Home births in Scotland remain relatively constant at under 1%. A woman is entitled to care throughout her pregnancy, the birth and the postnatal period. Care may be provided by a midwife, a community-based GP, a hospital-based obstetrician, or a combination of these. The birth may take place in a hospital maternity unit, a midwife/GP-led unit, or at home. After the birth, a midwife will visit until the baby is at least ten days old and after that a health visitor's services are available. Throughout her pregnancy and for the first year of her baby's life, a woman is entitled to free prescriptions and dental care.

There is a welfare food scheme for mothers on low income, providing formula feed and vitamins free of charge. The NHS Plan envisages that the scheme will be reformed by 2004 to improve access to a healthy diet for children in poverty. As part of the drive to tackle health inequalities, breastfeeding is being encouraged by the Infant Feeding Initiative in England and the Scottish Breastfeeding Group and the National Breastfeeding Adviser in Scotland.

A comprehensive programme of health surveillance, provided for pre-school children (under five years of age), is run by community health trusts and GPs who receive an annual payment for every child registered on the programme. (In Scotland this is carried out by the Community Paediatric Service which may be based in the primary care or acute services trust.) This enables doctors, dentists and health visitors to oversee the health and development of pre-school children so that any health problems are picked up and appropriate intervention arranged as early and as quickly as possible. Health Promotion England (see p. 189) produces *The Pregnancy Book*, a complete guide to a healthy pregnancy, labour and giving birth as well as life with a new baby, and *Birth to Five*, a guide to the early stages of development, nutrition, weaning and common childhood ailments; both are made available to all first-time mothers free of charge. The Scottish equivalent is *Ready, Steady, Baby!*, produced by the Health Education Board for Scotland. New mothers also receive a Personal Child Health Record for their child. This helps parents to keep a record of immunisation (see p. 203), tests, birth details and health checks.

In February 2001 the Scottish Executive published the national *Framework for Maternity Services in Scotland*, designed to ensure choices for women and their families while recognising the need for clinical safety. It sets out a basis against which each NHS Trust and NHS Board should judge its own service provision, and covers key aspects of maternity care, the organisation of maternity services, and women's and parents' information needs. In England, the DH is developing a NSF for maternity care, and is investing an extra £100 million to fund capital improvements to modernise the facilities in maternity units, as well as separate additional investment to provide 2,000 extra midwives by 2005.

Children of school age attending a state school have access to the school health service, as well as usually being registered with a GP and a dentist. In addition to providing health advice to children and young people, the school health service assists teachers with pupils who have medical needs.

Child guidance and child psychiatric services provide help and advice to families and children with psychological or emotional problems. In recent years efforts have been made to improve cooperation between community-based child health services and local authority education and social services for children. This is particularly important in the prevention of child abuse and for the health and welfare of children in care (see p. 169).

Fertility and Sexual Health

The Government's public health strategy aims to ensure the provision of effective sexual health services. Free contraceptive advice and treatment are available from GPs, family planning clinics and tailored services for young people. Clinics are able to provide condoms and other contraceptives free of charge. The DH has developed a national sexual health and HIV strategy to bring together current initiatives in sexual health and HIV, including work on chlamydia. The Scottish Executive is also developing plans for a sexual health strategy for Scotland. The National Assembly for Wales' *Strategic framework for promoting sexual health*, launched in October 2000, is now being implemented. Local sexual health strategies are in place, and a two-year HIV prevention campaign targeted at homosexual men has been commissioned.

Teenage Pregnancies

The Social Exclusion Unit's report on teenage pregnancy, launched in 1999, set out a national strategy for England to halve the rate of conception among women aged under 18 and to increase the participation of teenage parents in education and work. The strategy sets out an action plan to help prevent teenage pregnancy and provide support for teenage parents. Every top-tier local authority area has agreed a ten-year local teenage pregnancy strategy, beginning in 2001, outlining how local authorities will work with health bodies and other local agencies to take forward the aims of the national strategy. The conception rate for women aged under 18 declined by 4% between 1998 and 1999.

Abortion

Under the Abortion Act 1967, as amended, a time limit of 24 weeks applies to the largest category of abortion—risk to the physical or mental health of the pregnant woman—and also to abortion because of a similar risk to any existing children of her family. There are three categories in which no time limit applies: to prevent grave permanent injury to the physical or mental health of the woman; where there is a substantial risk of serious foetal handicap; or where continuing the pregnancy would involve a risk to the life of the pregnant woman greater than if the pregnancy were terminated. The Act does not apply in Northern Ireland.

Between 1999 and 2000 the rate of legal abortions on women resident in England rose by 1% to 175,542, and the overall age-standardised rate rose slightly, from 16.8 to 16.9 abortions per 1,000 women aged between 15 and 49.

Human Fertilisation and Embryology

The world's first 'test-tube baby' was born in the UK in 1978, as a result of the technique of *in vitro* fertilisation. This provided new possibilities for dealing with the problems of infertility and for the science of embryology. The social, ethical and legal implications were examined by a committee of inquiry and led eventually to the passage of the Human Fertilisation and Embryology Act 1990. The Human Fertilisation and Embryology Authority (HFEA) licenses and controls centres providing certain infertility treatments, undertaking human embryo research or storing gametes or embryos. The HFEA maintains a code of practice giving guidance to licensed centres and reports annually to Parliament.

Eating Habits, Nutrition and Exercise

Since the early 1970s there have been marked changes in the British diet. One feature has been the long-term rise in consumption of poultry, while that of red meat (such as beef and veal) has fallen (see Figure 13.6). Consumption of fresh fruit has increased since 1970, while consumption of fresh green vegetables was lower in 2000 than in 1970. In addition, the use of convenience food—both frozen and ready meals—has increased. Despite these changes, the British diet is still noticeably different from that in other countries such as those in the Mediterranean, being relatively low in fruit, vegetables and fish. Health considerations appear to have been influencing some aspects of diet in recent years, such as the fall in sales of red meat and the rise in consumption of low-fat spread. However, the proportion of adults who are obese or overweight has increased—in 1999, 19% of women and 21% of men aged 16 and over in England were classified as obese, compared with 8% and 6% respectively in 1980 in Great Britain. The likelihood of being obese increases up to the age of 65 and then declines at older ages.

In 1997, three-quarters of children aged 4 to 18 had not eaten any citrus fruits (excluding fruit juice) during the seven-day dietary record, and three-fifths had not eaten any leafy green vegetables. The Department of Health is piloting 'five a day' projects testing the feasibility and practicalities of new approaches to improving access to and increasing awareness of fruit and vegetables. Lessons learned from these pilot projects will be used to provide guidance on the national roll-out

Figure 13.6:
Changing Patterns in Consumption of Foods at Home, Great Britain

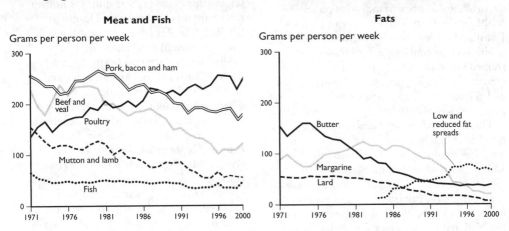

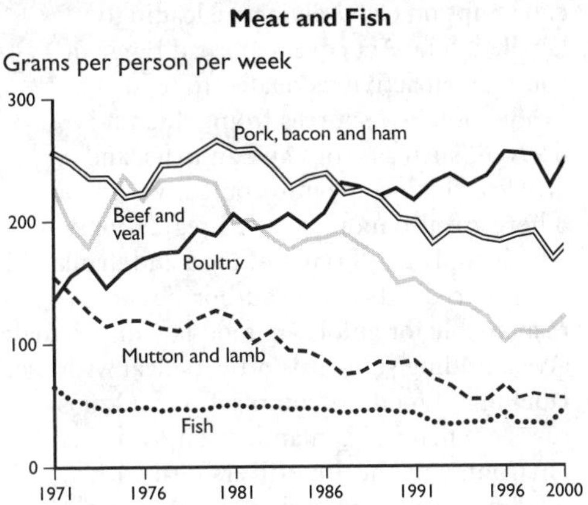

Source: National Food Survey, Department for Environment, Food and Rural Affairs

beginning in 2002. Under the National School Fruit Scheme, launched in 2000 and expanded in spring 2001, over 80,000 children in 27 areas and 548 schools are receiving free fruit each school day. By 2004 every child in nursery and children aged four to six in infant schools will be entitled to a free piece of fruit on each school day. The Scottish Diet Action Plan—*Eating for Health*—provides the framework for wide-ranging action to tackle Scotland's poor health, with a particular focus on children and young people. The most recent initiatives in this area include fruit for infants, breakfast clubs, and school fruit and salad bars.

The Committee on the Medical Aspects of Food and Nutrition Policy published its report *Nutritional Aspects of the Development of Cancer* in 1998. It noted that research suggests that diet might contribute to about a third of all cancers. Its main recommendations are consistent with the Government's healthy eating advice to the effect that a healthy and balanced diet is one which is varied and rich in fruit and vegetables and dietary fibre. The report also underlined the importance of maintaining a healthy body weight throughout adult life.

The major supermarket groups and most food manufacturers have introduced voluntary labelling schemes indicating the energy, fat, protein and carbohydrate content of food. Nutrition labelling is compulsory on products for which a nutritional claim is made.

Physical activity helps give protection against coronary heart disease and stroke. It also has beneficial effects on weight control, blood pressure and diabetes, all of which are cardiovascular disease risk factors in their own right. Regular exercise also protects against osteoporosis (brittle bones), maintains muscle power and increases people's general sense of well being. Among males in England aged 16 to 24, almost a fifth said they took part in seven or more hours of sport or exercise per week in 1998. However, almost two-fifths engaged in less than an hour's sport or exercise. Three-fifths of women aged 16 to 24 took part in less than an hour's sport or exercise per week. Only one in 20 young women took part in more than seven hours per week.

ENVIRONMENT AND HEALTH

According to the DH, the public's health also needs protection through control of the physical environment. Atmospheric pollution, noise, radiation, contaminated land and water, waste management and housing are all important aspects of environmental health. In the United Kingdom no single government department is responsible for environmental health as a whole, but the DH advises other departments and health ministers on the health implications of Government policies. Local authorities provide environmental health services and employ professionally trained environmental health officers, concerned with inspection, health promotion and regulation. The Environment Agency also regulates pollution from large-scale industry.

The Government sponsors or funds a number of bodies to support its work in this area. For example: the DH Toxicology Unit and the Small Area Health Statistics Unit (SAHSU), both at Imperial College London; the Institute for Environment and Health, established by the Medical Research Council; the National Focus, which coordinates work on responses to chemical incidents and surveillance of health effects of chemicals; and the National Poisons Information Service, which provides a 24-hour advice service to health professionals in the NHS on suspected poisoning cases. The Government has also established a number of independent expert committees to provide scientific advice.

Accidents

In 2000 there were 234,000 road accidents involving personal injury in Great Britain, and there were over 3,400 deaths and nearly 317,000 injuries (see p. 364). The Department of Trade and Industry records home and leisure accidents needing hospital treatment. Data for 1999 show that every 6 hours one elderly person dies from an accidental fall in the home. Altogether 1.2 million people in the UK go to a hospital casualty department each year as a result of a fall in the home. Over 35,000 people experience falls from ladders each year, and burns from barbecues are thought to affect around 600 people. Results from the DH's Health Survey for England show that 19 in every 100 men and 15 in every 100 women had a major accident—one which necessitated treatment by a doctor or in a hospital—in 1999. In 1999–2000 there were 218 worker fatalities, compared with 253 the previous year.

Food Safety

Under the Food Safety Act 1990, it is illegal to sell or supply food that is unfit for human consumption or falsely or misleadingly labelled. The Act covers a broad range of commercial activities related to food production, the sources from which it is derived, such as crops and animals, and articles which come into contact with food. There are also more detailed regulations, which apply to all types of food and drink and their ingredients. Local authorities are responsible for enforcing food law in two main areas: trading standards officers deal with the labelling of food, its composition and most cases of chemical contamination; and environmental health officers deal with hygiene, cases of microbiological contamination of foods, and food which is found to be unfit for human consumption.

The Food Standards Agency (FSA), which began operating in April 2000, is responsible for all aspects of food safety and standards in the UK. The Agency has set a target to reduce foodborne disease by 20% by 2006, and will be seeking new ways to help disadvantaged consumers improve their diets. It also sets and audits standards for the enforcement of food law by local authorities. In 1999, 47% of the food premises inspected by local environmental health officers were found to be infringing food safety rules in some way, compared with 44% in the previous year.

CJD and Public Health

Creutzfeldt-Jakob disease (CJD) is a rare transmissible spongiform encephalopathy in humans. Since the discovery in 1996 of variant CJD, or vCJD, which is linked to exposure to BSE (see p. 460), there have been 102 cases of definite and probable vCJD in the UK (up to the end of June 2001). To safeguard public health the Government is providing additional funding for research into CJD and BSE, including the work carried out at the National CJD Surveillance Unit, which monitors the incidence of the disease. In 2001, the Government announced interim payments of £25,000 to each of the families of people who had been diagnosed with vCJD. A compensation scheme is currently being developed. The Government also announced that arrangements would be made for the funding of health and social care for patients with CJD.

An independent public inquiry set up to establish and review the history of the emergence and identification of BSE and vCJD in the UK reported in October 2000 (see p. 460).

Safety of Medicines

Only medicines that have been granted a marketing authorisation issued by the European Agency for the Evaluation of Medicinal Products or the MCA may be supplied to the public. Marketing authorisations are issued following scientific assessment on the basis of safety, quality and effectiveness.

HEALTH ARRANGEMENTS WITH OTHER COUNTRIES

The member states of the European Economic Area (EEA—see p. 83) have special health arrangements under which EEA nationals resident in a member state are entitled to receive emergency treatment, either free or at a reduced cost, during visits to other EEA countries. Treatment is provided, in most cases, on production of a valid Form E111 which, in the United Kingdom, people normally obtain from a post office before travelling. There are also arrangements for people who go to another EEA country specifically for medical care, or who require continuing treatment for a pre-existing condition. Unless falling into an exempted category (for instance foreign students), visitors to the United Kingdom are generally expected to pay for routine, non-emergency treatment, or if the purpose of their visit is to seek specific medical treatment. The United Kingdom also has a number of separate bilateral agreements with some other countries, such as Australia and New Zealand.

HEALTH PROVISION OUTSIDE THE NHS

Private Healthcare and Regulation

As an alternative to the NHS, people are entitled to pay for their own health and social care, by joining a private healthcare organisation. In addition, there is the option of private medical insurance, which, depending on the premium paid, will cover people's healthcare in times of need. In 2000, 11.5% of the population of the United Kingdom were covered by private medical insurance.

The Government does, however, still play some role in this type of care, through regulation. At present, local councils and health authorities are responsible for monitoring care provision by the private and voluntary sectors. However, during 2001–02 the National Care Standards Commission (NCSC) is to be set up. It will cover public, private and voluntary care services in institutions such as care homes, children's homes, private hospitals and private clinics. It will carry out regular inspections of services and will have the power to ensure that standards meet national minima. In Wales, these functions will be performed by the Care Standards Inspectorate for Wales, a new division within the Welsh Assembly.

Partnerships

The Government is beginning to work formally in partnership with the private sector. In October 2000, the DH signed an agreement with the independent healthcare sector (the private and voluntary sectors), under which health authorities will be able to bring private sector providers into the planning of local healthcare on a systematic and long-term basis. The agreement covers care, workforce planning and service planning, and will involve the NHS using the private sector's spare capacity, transfer of patients between the two sectors, exchange of information, and joint working on preventive and rehabilitation services.

Complementary and Alternative Medicine

There is a growing interest in complementary and alternative medicine (CAM). In November 2000 the House of Lords Select Committee reported its findings on CAM, and in March 2001 the Government published its response. The Government agreed that acupuncture and herbal medicine were early candidates for regulation on a statutory basis, and that others, such as chiropractic, homeopathy and osteopathy, might also be regulated in due course. The Government also said that, for voluntary regulation to be effective, each type of therapy should have its own single regulatory body, and that funding for research into CAM was a possibility, if it supported the Government's clinical priorities—cancer, heart disease and mental health. Information on CAM is now available through NHS Direct Online.

Further Reading

The NHS Plan: A plan for investment, a plan for reform. Cm 4818. The Stationery Office, 2000.

Department of Health Departmental Report. The Government's Expenditure Plans 2001–2002 to 2003–2004 and Main Estimates 2001–2002. Cm 5103. The Stationery Office, 2001.

Improving Health in Wales—A Plan for the NHS with its Partners. National Assembly for Wales, 2001.

Our National Health: A plan for action, a plan for change. Scottish Executive Health Department, 2000.

Investing for Health. Department of Health, Social Services and Public Safety, Northern Ireland, 2000.

Annual publications

Health and Personal Social Services Statistics for England. The Stationery Office.
Scottish Health Statistics. Information and Statistics Division, NHSScotland.
Health Statistics Wales. National Assembly for Wales.
On the State of the Public Health. The Annual Report of the Chief Medical Officer of the Department of Health. The Stationery Office.
Health in Scotland. The Annual Report of the Chief Medical Officer on the State of Scotland's Health. Scottish Executive.
Welsh Health: Annual Report of the Chief Medical Officer. National Assembly for Wales.

Websites

Department of Health: www.doh.gov.uk
National Assembly for Wales: www.wales.gov.uk
Scottish Executive Health Department: www.scotland.gov.uk
NHSScotland, Information and Statistics Division: www.show.scot.nhs.uk/isd
Department of Health, Social Services and Public Safety, Northern Ireland: www.dhsspsni.gov.uk
Public Health Laboratory Service: www.phls.co.uk

14 Criminal and Civil Justice

Introduction	213
Crime in the UK	215
Police Service	219
Legal System in England and Wales	222
Legal System in Scotland	229
Legal System in Northern Ireland	232
Prison Service	233
Probation	234
Publicly Funded Legal Help	235

The United Kingdom does not have a single legal system. Instead, England and Wales, Scotland and Northern Ireland have their own, with considerable differences in law, judicial procedure and court structure. There is, however, substantial similarity on many points and a large volume of modern legislation, including EC legislation, applies throughout the UK. In all three systems there is a common distinction between criminal law and civil law.

Introduction

Criminal and Civil Law

Criminal law deals with wrongs affecting the community for which a prosecution may be brought in the criminal courts. Civil law is about deciding disputes between two or more parties—individuals, companies or other organisations—and for providing a means of legal scrutiny of the actions of public bodies. The purpose of civil proceedings is not to punish, but to obtain compensation or some other appropriate remedy, although in England and Wales the payment of damages may sometimes have a punitive element.

The distinction between civil and criminal matters is not precise. All courts in England and Wales, and Northern Ireland have both a civil and a criminal jurisdiction (apart from county courts, whose jurisdiction is exclusively civil). However, the court of trial and the rules of procedure and evidence will usually differ in civil and criminal cases.

Sources of Law

Statutes passed by Parliament are the ultimate source of law. There are no legal limits on what may be done by Act of Parliament, although a legal duty exists to comply with European Community (EC) law. In addition, statutes passed by the Scottish Parliament are a source of law in Scotland. A statute may also confer power on a minister, local authority or other executive body to make delegated legislation (see p. 54).

Modern statutes are usually brought into effect by an Order made by a minister of the Crown. The Order allows provisions to become effective when practical. Pilot schemes can be set up to test the operation of statutory provisions. Changing policies or circumstances may sometimes mean that provisions are not brought into effect, and may be repealed.

Common law in England and Wales covers many key areas which have, over the centuries, developed through the decisions of the courts. The concept of binding precedent means that decisions of higher courts bind those courts lower down in the court hierarchy, ensuring consistency of judicial approach. Judges give reasons for their decisions, and principles of law are stated, developed and modified. When government action is being tested, the court is considering the legality of that action and will try to ensure that government is not overstepping its proper role; the court does not seek to substitute its discretion for that of the public authority being challenged. Sources of law in Scotland include decisions of the courts as well as Acts of the previous Scottish parliament which ended in 1707.

European Sources

EC law, which applies in the UK as a member of the European Union (see p. 72), is derived from the EC treaties, from the Community legislation adopted under them, and from the decisions of the European Court of Justice. That court has the highest authority, under the Treaty of Rome, to decide points of EC law. Where a point arises before a British court, it may refer the point of law to the Court of Justice for it to decide. Sometimes a court is obliged to make a reference to the European Court.

The decisions of the Court of Justice do not directly bind British courts, but the UK is under treaty obligation to uphold EC law. Consequently, British courts are obliged to apply EC law, even at the expense of not applying the provision of an Act of Parliament. If a rule of statute or common law is incompatible with Community law, it is Community law that will be applied by a British court. Under the Scotland Act 1998, the Parliament and the Executive are bound, as a matter of domestic law, to act in accordance with EC obligations.

European Convention on Human Rights

The European Convention on Human Rights is an international treaty covering, among other rights, an individual's right to life, prohibition of torture, right to a fair trial, right to respect for family and private life, freedom of expression and freedom of assembly. Most Convention rights can be limited by public authorities under certain circumstances. Individual rights sometimes have to be balanced against one another or the wider public interest.

The Convention was incorporated into UK law under the Human Rights Act 1998 on 2 October 2000. It requires all public authorities, including the courts, to act compatibly with the Convention rights (unless an Act of Parliament leaves no choice). It enables individuals to rely on those rights in any legal proceedings and to bring a claim against a public authority which has acted incompatibly with those rights. The Act requires a court to give effect to legislation, as far as possible, in a way that is compatible with Convention rights. A court cannot declare invalid an Act of Parliament which is incompatible with the Convention, but the higher courts may make a declaration of incompatibility. It will be up to Parliament to decide what action to take, if any, following such a declaration. In this way the Human Rights Act lays down a set of basic human rights against which laws and administration can be tested. In Scotland, as with EC law, the Scottish Executive and Scottish Parliament have to act in a way which is compatible with the Convention.

Personnel of the Law

The law is enforced by judicial officers, both professional judges and lay justices who, together with juries in certain cases, are responsible for deciding disputed cases. The law also depends on officers of the court who have general or specialised functions of an administrative, and sometimes of a judicial, nature in the courts to which they are attached.

Judges are legally qualified, being appointed from the ranks of practising barristers and advocates or solicitors. They have independence of office, and can be removed only in rare and limited circumstances involving misconduct or incapacity. They are not subject to ministerial control or direction. Full-time judges are generally expected to have previously sat in a part-time capacity (for about 15 days a year) in the same or a similar jurisdiction. There are approximately 3,500 full and part-time judges, including District Judges (Magistrates' Courts), sitting in the civil and criminal courts in England and Wales plus approximately 10,000 full and part-time judiciary and members sitting in tribunals handling a range of disputes and appeals.

Magistrates in England and Wales, and justices of the peace in Scotland, are trained in order to give them sufficient knowledge of the law, including the rules of evidence, and of the nature and purpose of sentencing. There are nearly 30,000 lay magistrates working on a part-time, voluntary basis in England and Wales and around 260 full and part-time professional District Judges and Deputy District Judges (Magistrates' Courts).There are 4,000 justices of the peace in Scotland. In Northern Ireland there are 19 resident magistrates, who are drawn from practising solicitors or barristers, with powers similar to those of District Judges (Magistrates' Courts) and 18 deputy (part-time) magistrates.

Although people are free to conduct their own cases if they so wish, barristers (in Scotland, advocates) and solicitors, or other authorised litigators, generally represent the interests of parties to a dispute. There are over 10,000 practising barristers in England and Wales and around 85,000 practising solicitors. Scotland has over 400 practising advocates and some 8,600 solicitors; in Northern Ireland there are about 450 barristers. Barristers practise as individuals, but join a group of other barristers, in Chambers. Advocates in Scotland practise as individuals; they do not operate from Chambers and work independently of each other. Solicitors usually operate in partnership with other solicitors, unless they are self-employed. Large firms of solicitors employ not only qualified staff, but also legal executives and support staff. Certain legal functions may be performed by non-lawyers—licensed conveyancers (qualified conveyancers in Scotland) can act in conveyancing matters (the transfer of interests in land).

Only barristers and advocates, who are regarded as specialist court pleaders, have traditionally had rights of audience in the higher courts—the Judicial Committee of the Privy Council, House of Lords, Court of Appeal, High Court and Crown Court, High Court of Justiciary (Scotland) and Court of Session (Scotland). Legislation in 1990 opened the door for other professional bodies to apply to become authorised to grant their members rights of audience in the higher courts, making it possible for solicitors in private practice to obtain the same rights of audience as barristers and advocates. In 1999 the Institute of Legal Executives and the Chartered Institute of Patent Agents were authorised to grant rights of audience to their members. The Access to Justice Act 1999 (not applicable in Scotland) established the principle that all barristers and solicitors should acquire full rights of audience on call to the Bar or admission to the Roll. It also allowed suitably qualified employed barristers and solicitors to acquire rights of audience in the higher courts, from which they had previously been excluded. (See civil justice reforms, p. 229.)

The Bar Council is the professional body representing barristers (in Scotland, the Faculty of Advocates); and the Law Society of England and Wales, Law Society of Scotland and Law Society of Northern Ireland represent solicitors. The profession is self-regulating, with the professional bodies exercising disciplinary control over their members.

The Legal Services Ombudsman for England and Wales oversees the way in which relevant professional bodies handle complaints about barristers, solicitors, legal executives, licensed conveyancers and patent agents. The Scottish Legal Services Ombudsman performs a similar task.

Crime in the UK

Crime Statistics

There are two main measures of the scale of crime in the UK: the recording of crimes by the police; and surveys which ask representative samples of the population about their experiences of crime.

Recorded Crime

Notifiable crimes recorded by the police broadly cover the more serious offences.

Table 14.1: Notifiable Crimes Recorded by the Police in England and Wales for the Year ended March 2001 *Thousands*

Offence group	
Violence against the person	600.9
Sexual offences	37.3
Burglary	836.0
Robbery	95.2
Theft and handling stolen goods	2,145.4
Fraud and forgery	319.3
Criminal damage	960.1
Drug offences	113.5
Other	63.2
Total	**5,170.8**

Source: Home Office

In the year ended March 2001 in England and Wales:

- overall recorded crime totalled 5.2 million offences, representing an increase of 2.5% over the previous 12 months (see Table 14.1);
- the overall clear-up rate was 24%;
- about 82% of offences recorded by the police were against property, while 14% involved violence; and
- theft of, or from, vehicles accounted for about 19% of all recorded crimes.

In Scotland there were 423,000 crimes recorded by the police in 2000, a decrease of 3% compared with 1999. The overall crime clear-up rate was 44%.

Recorded crime in Northern Ireland in 2000–01 totalled 120,000 offences. The overall clear-up rate was 27%.

Principal Crime Surveys

The British Crime Survey (BCS) is a large household survey first conducted in 1982, which has a sample representative of people aged 16 and over in private households in England and Wales. The BCS asks respondents whether they have experienced certain personal and household crimes in the preceding year, regardless of whether or not they reported the incident to the police. The survey therefore provides a measure of those crimes not reported to, or recorded by, the police. The latest BCS, published in October 2000, estimated that there were 14.7 million crimes in 1999, 10% fewer than in 1997. Burglary was down 21% from 1997 (to its lowest level since 1991) and theft of vehicles decreased by 11% from its 1997 level. The number of violent crimes fell by 4%. The proportion of people who were victims of some type of crime once or more during 1999 fell from 34% to 30%.

The 2000 Scottish Crime Survey estimated that around 845,0000 crimes were committed against individuals and private households in Scotland during 1999. This was 13% fewer than the number estimated in the 1996 survey.

Official estimates put the total impact of crime in 1999–2000 at around £60 billion; roughly 30% of this cost represents an estimate of the value to the victim of the pain and trauma suffered, while the remainder reflects actual transactions such as insurance claims and making good damage to property. Violent crime represented almost 40% of the total cost of crime, compared with 3% of the volume of crimes committed.

Crime Reduction

An aim of the Home Office is to reduce crime and the fear of crime. It has developed a Crime Reduction Strategy to tackle crime and the causes of crime. Crime and Disorder Reduction Partnerships, set up under the Crime and Disorder Act 1998, bring together the police, local authorities and other relevant agencies to develop strategies in local districts.

A Crime Reduction Programme (CRP) started in England and Wales in 1999 to run for three years. This is taking an evidence-based approach to reducing crime. The CRP is funding a range of programmes to deliver crime reduction and to obtain evidence on what works in tackling crime and its causes. A website (*www.crimereduction.gov.uk*) has been developed with the aim of helping practitioners around the country and abroad to

> Crime reduction 'toolkits' provide web-based information and advice to Crime and Disorder Reduction Partnerships. They cover the main areas of crime and criminality, and are designed to provide the Partnerships and their constituent agencies—including police, local authorities, probation, health, and the private and voluntary sectors—with a practical approach to identifying and understanding local problems, and implementing effective strategies to reduce crime and disorder in their area. The toolkits contain evaluated good practice and local solutions and provide information on central initiatives, policies and funding opportunities.

reduce crime. A number of toolkits (see box) can be found on the website.

Key elements of the Crime Reduction Programme include:

- around £170 million of investment in closed-circuit television (CCTV) surveillance systems in public areas such as housing estates, shopping centres, railway stations and car parks;
- crime reduction action teams, set up to examine problems which affect particular types of crime (vehicles, retailers and property crime in general) in their area;
- youth inclusion projects to provide assistance and support for young people at risk of offending;
- work to help schools develop effective behaviour management techniques to deal with disruptive pupils;
- burglary and targeted policing projects; and
- initiatives to prevent and identify best practice in preventing domestic violence and sexual assault.

Other recent crime reduction initiatives, building on previous work, include:

- a commitment to reduce domestic burglary by 25% by 2005;
- a commitment to reduce robbery by 14% in principal cities by 2005; and
- the setting up of new neighbourhood wardens schemes to act as a channel of communication between the community and the police.

Since April 2000 every police authority and Crime and Disorder Reduction Partnership has been asked to set five-year targets for the reduction of two key offences—vehicle crime and domestic burglary—and five metropolitan forces have been set the additional target of reducing street robberies.

Within the Scottish Executive Justice Department, the Crime Prevention Unit has responsibility for developing crime prevention, community safety and domestic abuse policy on behalf of Scottish Executive ministers. All 32 local councils in Scotland have formed community safety partnerships. The Scottish Executive has formed a Scottish Forum on Community Safety. In Northern Ireland, there is a Crime Prevention Panel.

Drug and Alcohol Misuse

The UK-wide drugs strategy, launched in 1998 to coordinate the fight against illegal drugs, has four main elements:

- helping young people resist drug misuse in order to achieve their full potential in society;
- protecting communities from drug-related anti-social and criminal behaviour;
- enabling people to overcome drug problems through treatment; and
- stifling the availability of illegal drugs on the streets.

Scotland has its own drugs strategy within this framework and has also introduced national standards for drugs services.

The Crime and Disorder Act 1998 introduced drug treatment and testing orders, targeted at persistent offenders (aged 16 and over) with drug problems who show a willingness to cooperate with treatment. The orders were introduced in England and Wales in October 2000 and are currently being piloted in Scotland. A pilot 'drug court' has been set up in Glasgow to deal specifically with drugs-related offending (see p. 27).

The Drugs Prevention Advisory Service (DPAS) was launched in England and Wales in April 1999 to promote community-based drugs prevention at local, regional and national level in line with the objectives of the Government's national strategy. In particular, the DPAS provides information, advice and support to local Drug Action Teams to encourage good drugs prevention practice and promotes prevention policy across Government. DPAS teams have been established in each of the nine Government Regions in England. In an effort to reduce the availability of drugs in Scotland and to target organised drug crime, the Scottish Drug Enforcement Agency was launched in June 2000.

Under provisions in the Criminal Justice and Court Services Act 2000, the drug-testing of offenders will be extended across the criminal justice process. Drug testing will be introduced at the police station after charge; under probation supervision through a new drug abstinence order and as a condition of other forms of community sentence (see p. 226); and for offenders released from prison on licence. Drug test results will also be used to inform decisions on bail.

In 2001, the Government announced a new programme to tackle drugs and drug-related crime in communities—'Communities Against Drugs'—and channelled over £200 million to Crime and Disorder Reduction Partnerships with the aim of tackling local drugs markets, and cutting drug-related crime.

Other recent initiatives have focused on curbing alcohol misuse, recognised to be a contributory factor in 40% of all incidents of violent crime committed in England and Wales. The programme in England and Wales has three main objectives:

- reducing the problems arising from under-age drinking;
- reducing public drunkenness; and
- prevention of alcohol-related violence.

In order to achieve these objectives, there are tougher regulations on licensing laws relating to off-licences and pubs giving them, among other things, more discretionary powers and responsibilities to restrict the sale of alcohol to young persons or persons already intoxicated. Additionally, regulations and proposals to curb the use of glass bottles as weapons in incidents of street violence are also being considered. A plan for action on alcohol misuse in Scotland will be produced by the Scottish Executive by the end of 2001.

Countering Terrorism

In order for the UK to be better able to deal with the threats which terrorism imposes, legislation was introduced in Parliament in December 1999. The Terrorism Act 2000 came into force in February 2001. The Act provides for:

- permanent UK-wide anti-terrorist legislation (to replace the existing separate pieces of temporary legislation for Northern Ireland and Great Britain);
- the adoption of a new definition of terrorism (including ideological and religious motivation for terrorist acts) which would extend to domestic and international terrorism (see below);
- a new offence of inciting terrorist acts abroad from within the UK;
- new powers to seize suspected terrorist cash at borders;
- a new judicial authority to consider applications for extensions of detention of terrorist suspects; and
- specific offences relating to training for terrorist activities.

The Terrorism Act 2000 (Proscribed Organisations) (Amendment) Order 2001 added international organisations to Schedule 2 of the Act (which lists proscribed Terrorist Organisations) and came into force on 29 March 2001 following approval by both Houses of Parliament. A total of 21 organisations have been added to Schedule 2, which also includes 14 organisations connected to terrorism in Northern Ireland.

In the light of the terrorist attacks in the United States in September 2001 (see p. 93), the Government has announced its intention to strengthen current counter-terrorist legislation.

Police Service

Government ministers, together with police authorities and chief constables, are responsible for providing an effective and efficient police service in the UK.

Organisation

There are 52 police forces organised on a local basis—43 in England and Wales, eight in Scotland and one in Northern Ireland. The Metropolitan Police Service and the City of London force are responsible for policing London. The Police (Northern Ireland) Act 2000 created a new framework for the police service in Northern Ireland (see p. 19). Each force in Great Britain has volunteer special constables who perform police duties in their spare time, without pay, acting in support of regular officers. They number about 20,000 in all (around 12,700 in England and Wales). Civilian staff in England and Wales number about 54,600.

Police strength in England and Wales is about 125,500 (of which the Metropolitan Police numbers around 25,000). There are just over 15,100 officers in Scotland and 8,500 (plus 5,000 reserves) in the Northern Ireland Police Service (formerly called the Royal Ulster Constabulary—RUC).

Police forces are maintained in England and Wales by local police authorities. In the 41 police areas outside London, they normally have 17 members—nine locally elected councillors, three magistrates and five independent members. In July 2000 the Home Secretary's duties as the police authority for the Metropolitan Police District were assumed by a new Metropolitan Police Authority (MPA), the majority of whose 23 members are elected representatives from the Greater London Assembly (see p. 9). For the City of London Police Area, the authority is the Common Council of the Corporation of London. Police authorities, in consultation with the chief constables and local community, set local policing objectives, while the Government sets ministerial priorities for the police as a whole. The police authorities in Scotland are composed of elected councillors. In Northern Ireland the Secretary of State appoints the newly formed Police Board.

Police forces are headed by chief constables (in London the Commissioner of the City of London Police, and the Commissioner of the Metropolitan Police), appointed by their police authorities with government approval. They are responsible for the direction and control of their forces and for the appointment, promotion and discipline of all ranks below assistant chief constable. On matters of efficiency they are generally answerable to their police authorities.

Independent inspectors of constabulary report on the efficiency and effectiveness of police forces.

National Crime Bodies

The National Criminal Intelligence Service (NCIS), which was put on an independent statutory footing in 1998, has the leading role in collecting and analysing criminal intelligence for use by police forces and other law enforcement agencies in the UK. It has a headquarters and South East regional office in London, five other regional offices in England and offices in Scotland and Northern Ireland. NCIS coordinates the activities of the Security Services in support of the law enforcement agencies against organised crime, and liaises with the International Criminal Police Organisation (INTERPOL), which promotes international cooperation between police forces. It also provides the channel for communication between the UK and EUROPOL (see p. 93).

In 1998 a National Crime Squad, with 1,400 officers, replaced six regional crime squads in England and Wales. Its role is to prevent and detect organised and serious crime across police force and national boundaries and to support provincial forces in their investigation of serious crime. The Scottish Crime Squad performs the same function in Scotland. The two organisations are each headed by a Director General, who is accountable to a body known as the Service Authorities.

Forensic Science Service (FSS)

The FSS, a Home Office executive agency, provides scientific support in the investigation of crime to police forces in England and Wales through six regional laboratories. It also operates the national DNA database, which provides intelligence information to police forces by matching DNA profiles taken from suspects to profiles from samples left at the scenes of crime. In Scotland forensic science services are provided by four regional laboratories. The largest of these is based in Dundee. Northern Ireland has its own laboratory.

Powers and Procedures

England and Wales

Police powers and procedures are defined by legislation and accompanying codes of practice. Evidence obtained in breach of the codes may be ruled inadmissible in court. The codes must be available in all police stations.

- *Stop and search*—Police officers can stop and search people and vehicles if they reasonably suspect that they will find stolen goods, offensive weapons or implements that could be used for burglary and other offences. An officer must record the grounds for the search, and anything found, and the person stopped is entitled to a copy of the officer's report. Some 857,200 stop and searches were carried out by the police in England and Wales in 1999–2000.
- *Arrest*—The police may arrest a suspect on a warrant issued by a court, but can arrest without a warrant for *arrestable* offences (for which the sentence is fixed by law or for which the term of imprisonment is five years or more).
- *Detention and questioning*—Suspects must be cautioned before the police can ask any questions about an offence. For *arrestable* offences, a suspect can be detained in police custody without charge for up to 24 hours. Someone suspected of a *serious arrestable* offence can be held for up to 96 hours, but not beyond 36 hours unless a warrant is obtained from a magistrates' court. If someone thinks that his or her detention is unlawful, he or she may apply to the High Court for a writ of *habeas corpus* against the person responsible, requiring them to appear before the court to justify the detention. *Habeas corpus* proceedings take precedence over others.
- *Charging*—Once there is sufficient evidence, the police have to decide whether a detained person should be charged with an offence. If the police institute criminal proceedings against a suspect, the Crown Prosecution Service (see p. 223) then takes control of the case.

Scotland and Northern Ireland

The police in Scotland can arrest someone without a warrant, under wide common law powers, if suspects are seen or reported as committing a crime or are a danger to themselves or others. They also have specific statutory powers of arrest for some offences. In other cases they may apply to a justice of the peace for a warrant. As in England and Wales, Scottish police have powers to enter a building without a warrant if they are pursuing someone who has committed, or attempted to commit, a serious crime. A court can grant the police a warrant to search premises for stated items in connection with a crime, again as in England and Wales. The police may search anyone suspected of carrying an offensive weapon. Someone suspected of an imprisonable offence may be held for police questioning without being arrested, but for no more than six hours without being charged. If arrested, suspects must be charged and cautioned. The case is then referred to the procurator fiscal (see p. 230).

The law in Northern Ireland relating to police powers in the investigation of crime and to evidence in criminal proceedings is similar to that in force in England and Wales.

Firearms

The policy in Great Britain is that the police should not generally be armed but that there should be specialist firearms officers, deployed on the authority of a senior officer where an operational need arises. In 1999–2000 there were over 11,000 operations in Great Britain where firearms were issued to the police. Most forces operate armed response vehicles to contain firearms incidents. In Northern Ireland police officers are issued with firearms for their personal protection.

Police Discipline

An officer may be prosecuted if suspected of a criminal offence. Officers are also subject to a code of conduct. If found guilty of breaching the code, an officer can be dismissed. There is a civil standard of proof at police disciplinary hearings; a fast-track procedure to deal with officers caught committing serious criminal offences; and separate formal procedures for dealing with unsatisfactory performance.

Complaints

Members of the public can make complaints against the police if they feel that they have been treated unfairly or improperly. In England and Wales the investigation of the more serious cases is supervised by the Police Complaints Authority. In 1999–2000, over 800 of the 30,000 complaints received by police forces were supervised by the Authority. Less than 3% of all complaints were substantiated. The Government intends to introduce legislation in the current session which will establish a new complaints system and a new Independent Police Complaints Commission (IPCC) by April 2003. Unlike the Police Complaints Authority, the IPCC will have its own investigating teams, independent from the police. In Scotland complaints of misconduct against police officers are overseen by chief constables. Police authorities have statutory responsibility for dealing with complaints against chief officers. Allegations of criminal misconduct are referred to the procurator fiscal for investigation. HM Inspectorate of Constabulary for Scotland also considers representations from complainants dissatisfied with the way the police have handled their complaints. A consultation paper with proposals for strengthening the independence of the police complaints system in Scotland was published in July 2001. In Northern Ireland the Independent Commission for Police Complaints has been superseded by a Police Ombudsman.

Community Relations

Within every police authority there are police/community liaison consultative arrangements, involving representatives from the police, local government and community groups. Home Office and police service initiatives have sought to ensure that racist crime is treated as a police priority.

The Government is committed to a policy of ensuring that the police service is representative of society. In 1999, the Government set employment targets for the recruitment, retention and progression of minority ethnic officers in England and Wales. The targets are intended to ensure that by 2009 forces will reflect their local minority ethnic population. On 31 March 2001 there were 2,955 officers from minority ethnic backgrounds (representing 2.4% of the police service in England and Wales). The corresponding figure for Scotland is about 70 (less than 1% of police numbers).

Measures introduced to promote better relations between the police and the communities they serve include:

- an extension of the race relations legislation—through the Race Relations (Amendment) Act 2000. This makes direct and indirect discrimination in all public authorities unlawful, and places a duty on public authorities to promote race equality;
- citizenship classes in schools, to be introduced into the National Curriculum (see p. 132) in England and Wales in 2002, to ensure that pupils are taught about the cultural diversity of Britain;
- enforcing specific criminal offences of racially aggravated violence, harassment and criminal damage; and
- a programme to reform the use by the police of their powers to stop and search people (with the aim of ensuring these powers are used fairly).

Statistics on race and the criminal justice system can be found on the Home Office website *www.homeoffice.gov.uk/rds/index*.

Legal System in England and Wales

Various government departments, agencies and individuals share the responsibility of administering the system which dispenses justice in England and Wales. Most Acts of Parliament and the common law apply equally in both countries, although since devolution some legislation has applied differently in Wales.

The *Lord Chancellor* heads the judiciary and sits as a member of the judicial committee of the House of Lords. He also presides over the upper House in its law-making role, and, as a senior Cabinet minister, is in charge of the Lord Chancellor's Department. This Department has overall responsibility (through the Court Service) for the court system in England and Wales, which includes the Supreme Court—comprising the Court of Appeal, High Court and Crown Court—the county courts and some tribunals. The Lord Chancellor advises the Crown on the appointment of all senior judges in England and Wales, and appoints most other judges and magistrates, consulting national executives and Senior Judiciary in Scotland and Wales where appropriate for tribunal appointments. In addition, he has policy responsibility for locally managed magistrates' courts and responsibility for the civil justice process; promoting general reforms of the civil law; and arrangements for publicly financed legal services. He is also responsible for open government, including freedom of information and data protection; royal, Church and hereditary issues and Lords Lieutenants; Crown Dependencies and human rights issues.

The *Home Secretary* has overall responsibility for criminal law, the police service, the prison system, the probation service, and for advising the Crown on the exercise of the royal prerogative of mercy.

The *Attorney-General* and the *Solicitor-General* are the Government's main legal advisers, providing advice on a range of legal matters, including proposed legislation. They may also represent the Crown in difficult or publicly important domestic and international cases. In addition to his various civil law functions, the Attorney-General has final responsibility for enforcing the criminal law. The Solicitor-General is the Attorney-General's deputy.

The Crown Prosecution Service (CPS—see p. 223) is headed by the *Director of Public Prosecutions (DPP)*, who reports to the Attorney-General. Other prosecuting authorities include the Serious Fraud Office (see p. 224), which also answers to the Attorney-General, and bodies such as the Inland Revenue, Customs and Excise Commissioners, local authorities and trading standards departments which prosecute cases in their own discrete areas of work. Individual citizens may bring private prosecutions for most crimes, but some need the consent of the Attorney-General and these may be taken over by the DPP.

The four Heads of Division and other senior members of the judiciary may perform specific administrative functions. The Lord Chief Justice of England and Wales,[1] for example, has some responsibilities for the organisation and work of the criminal courts, including issuing practice directions to the courts and members of the legal professions on criminal law and court procedures. Individual judges may be asked to carry out specific duties such as chairing a national inquiry, while other functions are performed by statutory committees comprising legal professionals and lay representatives. The Civil Procedure Rule Committee is responsible for making rules that govern the civil justice process.

Executive bodies or agencies such as the Prison Service and the Forensic Science Service manage their own functions. Since 1998 the Youth Justice Board for England and Wales has monitored the youth justice system, promoted good practice and advised the Home Secretary on its operation and the setting of national standards.

In addition, a wide range of other statutory and non-statutory advisory bodies gives advice to the Government. These include

[1] The Lord Chief Justice presides over the Criminal Division of the Court of Appeal and the Queen's Bench Division of the High Court, and ranks second only to the Lord Chancellor in the judicial hierarchy.

Figure 14.2: The Prosecution Process

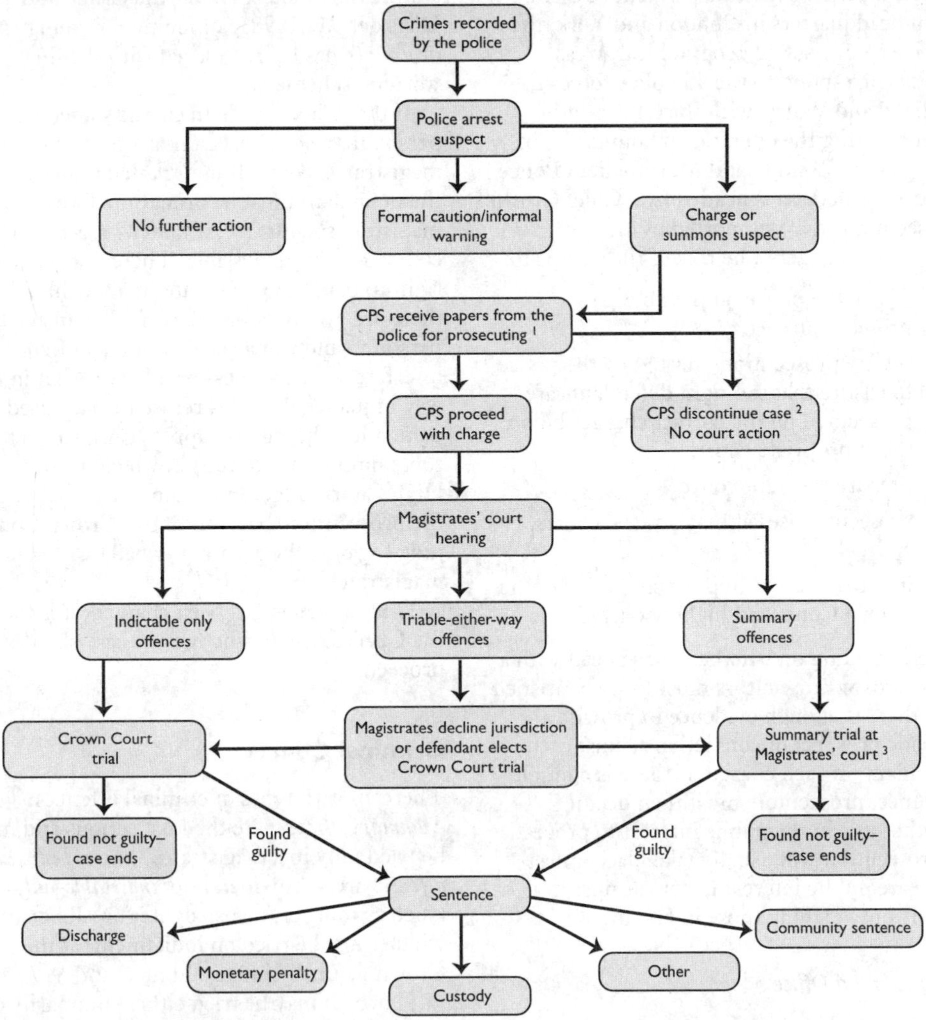

[1] Although the majority of prosecutions are handled by the Crown Prosecution Service, other organisations can also bring prosecutions.

[2] A case will be under continued review, and may be discontinued at any stage before the hearing at the magistrates' court or the prosecution may offer no evidence. In addition, the charge may be altered up to the final decision of the court.

[3] Magistrates may commit to the Crown Court for sentence.

Derived from Figure 1.2 in *A Guide to the Criminal Justice System in England and Wales*, Home Office, 2000

the police inspectorates, the magistrates' courts service, the probation service, the Audit Commission, the Criminal Justice Consultative Committee, law reform bodies such as the Law Commission and *ad hoc* Royal Commissions and departmental committees.

PROSECUTION AND THE CRIMINAL COURTS

Prosecution Arrangements

Crown Prosecution Service

The CPS is responsible for prosecuting people in England and Wales who have been charged by the police with a criminal offence. Although it works closely with the police, it is a governmental body independent of them. With headquarters in London and York, the service comprises 42 geographical Areas. These correspond to the 43 police forces in England and Wales, with the CPS London Area covering the operational boundaries of both City of London and Metropolitan Police Forces. Each Area is headed by a Chief Crown Prosecutor (CCP) supported by an Area Business Manager. The role of the CPS is to:

- advise the police on possible prosecutions;
- review prosecutions started by the police to ensure that the right defendants are prosecuted on the correct charges before the appropriate court;
- prepare cases for court;
- prosecute cases at magistrates' courts; and
- instruct counsel to prosecute cases in the Crown Court and higher courts.[2]

When deciding on whether to go ahead with a case, Crown Prosecutors must first be satisfied that there is enough evidence to provide a realistic prospect of conviction against each defendant on each charge. If there is enough evidence, prosecutors must then decide whether it is in the public interest to proceed. A prosecution will usually take place unless there are public interest factors against it clearly outweighing those in favour.

Serious Fraud Office

The Serious Fraud Office prosecutes cases of serious or complex fraud, with teams of lawyers, accountants, police officers and other specialists conducting investigations. The Office has wide powers that go beyond those normally available to the police and prosecuting authorities.

Initial Stages

For minor offences, the police may decide to caution an offender rather than prosecute. A caution is not the same as a conviction, and will not be given unless the person admits the offence. Under the Crime and Disorder Act 1998, cautioning for young offenders has been replaced with the final warning scheme.

If the police decide to charge someone, that person may be released on bail to attend a magistrates' court. If not granted police bail, the defendant must be brought before a magistrates' court (or, if under 18, a youth court) as soon as possible. There is a general right to bail, but magistrates may withhold it if there are grounds for believing that an accused person would run away, commit an offence, interfere with a witness or otherwise get in the way of justice. If bail is refused, an accused person has the right to apply again, subject to some limitations, to the Crown Court or to a High Court judge. In certain circumstances, the prosecution may appeal to a Crown Court judge against the granting of bail by magistrates.

Once a person has been charged, it is for the CPS to decide whether the case should proceed.

Criminal Courts

There are two types of criminal offences. *Summary offences* are the least serious and may be tried only in a magistrates' court. *Indictable offences* are subdivided into *'indictable-only'* (such as murder, manslaughter or robbery) which must be tried on indictment[3] at the Crown Court by judge and jury, and *'either-way'*, which may be tried either summarily or on indictment. Under a new procedure introduced in January 2001, indictable-only cases are sent straight to the Crown Court from an initial appearance before the magistrates. The defence may, if it wishes, challenge the prosecution case as soon as it has been served by making an application to the judge for the case to be dismissed.

Either-way offences, such as theft and burglary, can vary greatly in seriousness and a magistrates' court must decide whether the

[2] Under a change in legal rules, a number of CPS lawyers are now qualified to appear in some cases in the Crown Court and other higher courts.

[3] An indictment is a written accusation against a person, charging him or her with serious crime triable by jury.

case is serious enough to be sent to the Crown Court. If the magistrates decide in favour of summary trial, however, the accused person has the right to a trial by jury in the Crown Court if he or she chooses.

Where an either-way case is to be tried on indictment, the magistrates' court commits it to the Crown Court for trial if it is satisfied that there is a case to answer. In most cases this is accepted by the defence and the magistrates do not need to consider the evidence, but if the defence challenges the case, the magistrates consider the documentary evidence—without witnesses being called. In 1999, 1.9 million defendants were dealt with by magistrates' courts, while 77,000 were dealt with in the Crown Court.

A magistrates' court usually comprises three representatives of the local community who do not have professional legal qualifications, known as lay magistrates or justices of the peace (JPs). They sit with a court clerk who advises them on law and procedure. In some areas a paid professional District Judge (Magistrates' Courts) sits alone instead of the JPs. District Judges (Magistrates' Courts) are becoming more common, although most cases are still dealt with by lay magistrates.

Magistrates' courts committees (MCCs), made up of magistrates selected by their colleagues, are responsible for running the magistrates' courts service locally. During 2000–01 the MCCs were reorganised and their number reduced, improving efficiency and bringing their boundaries into closer alignment with those of other criminal justice agencies, such as the police and the CPS.

Youth courts are specialist magistrates' courts, which sit separately from those dealing with adults. They handle all but the most serious charges against people aged at least ten (the age of criminal responsibility) and under 18. Young offenders may also be tried in an adult magistrates' court or in a Crown Court, depending on the type of offence they have committed. Only JPs who have been specially trained for the job sit in youth courts. Proceedings are held in private.

The Crown Court sits at about 90 venues, in six regional areas called circuits, and is presided over by High Court judges, circuit judges and part-time recorders. The type of judge dealing with a case and instructing the jury of 12 members of the general public will depend on which Crown Court the case is being heard in. Not all Crown Courts handle cases of the same level of seriousness.

An independent review of the practices and procedures of, and the rules of evidence applied by, the criminal courts in England and Wales was announced by the Lord Chancellor in December 1999. A report on its findings is expected to be published in autumn 2001.

Trial

The prosecution and the defence form the two opposing sides in criminal trials. The law presumes an accused person is innocent until proved guilty beyond reasonable doubt by the prosecution. Accused people have a right at all stages to stay silent; however, when questioned, failure to mention facts which they later rely upon in their defence may not be helpful to their case. There are rules governing the pre-trial disclosure of material by both the prosecution and the defence. A judge may, in a case to be tried on indictment, hold a preliminary hearing, where pleas of guilty or not guilty are taken. If the defendant pleads guilty, the judge will simply decide upon the appropriate sentence. If a not guilty plea is entered, the prosecution and defence are expected to help the judge identify the key issues and provide any additional information required for the proper and efficient trial of the case.

Criminal trials normally take place in open court (that is, members of the public and press are allowed to hear the proceedings, unless there are specific reasons why this would not be appropriate) and it is the prosecution's job to prove their case. Strict rules of evidence govern how this may be done. Certain types of evidence may be excluded because they could be prejudicial or unreliable. Written statements by witnesses are allowed with the consent of the other party or in limited circumstances at the discretion of the court. Otherwise evidence is taken from witnesses testifying orally on oath. Child witnesses may testify without taking the oath and their evidence must be received by the court unless the child is incapable of giving intelligible testimony. A child in some circumstances can testify via a live TV link or the court may consider a video-recorded interview, subject to the defence having the right to question the child in cross-examination.

Helping Victims and Witnesses

In England and Wales a government-funded organisation, Victim Support, provides practical help and emotional support to victims of crime with the help of around 16,000 volunteers. It also runs the Witness Service, which advises victims and other witnesses attending Crown Court centres (and is developing similar services in magistrates' courts). Victim Support Scotland provides a volunteer-based service similar to that provided by Victim Support in England and Wales. A separate scheme operates in Northern Ireland.

In 1998 the Government published a report—*Speaking up for Justice*—on improving the treatment of witnesses (including children) who become involved in the criminal justice system in England and Wales. Twenty-six of the report's recommendations required statutory force and were included in the Youth Justice and Criminal Evidence Act 1999. The implementation plan includes the provision of pagers for intimidated witnesses, new rules on cross-examination and evidence, and practical help and protection for vulnerable witnesses (including children).

Blameless victims of violent crime in England, Wales and Scotland may be eligible for compensation from public funds under the Criminal Injuries Compensation Scheme. In Northern Ireland there are separate statutory arrangements for compensation for criminal injuries, and for malicious damage to property.

The Jury

In jury trials the judge decides questions of law, sums up the case to the jury, and discharges or sentences the accused. The jury is responsible for deciding questions of fact. The jury's verdict may be 'guilty' or 'not guilty' and the latter would result in an acquittal. Juries may, subject to certain conditions, reach a verdict by a majority of at least 10–2.

If an accused person is acquitted, there is no right of appeal from the prosecution, and the accused cannot be tried again for that same offence. However, an acquittal may be set aside and a retrial ordered if there is proof that a juror has been interfered with or intimidated.

A jury is independent of the judiciary and any attempt to interfere with its members is a criminal offence. People aged between 18 and 70 whose names appear on the electoral register are liable to be chosen at random for jury service. Various occupations, such as police officers, lawyers and doctors, are exempted from serving.

Sentencing

The court will sentence the offender after considering all the relevant information it has on the case, which may include a pre-sentence or any other specialist report, and a mitigating plea by the defence. Magistrates may impose a fine of up to £5,000 and/or a maximum sentence of six months' imprisonment, but can send the offender to the Crown Court if they feel their sentencing powers are not sufficient.

Taking away someone's freedom is only done where the offence is so serious that this action alone is justified. In 1999, 8% of males and 3% of females found guilty of all offences were given a custodial sentence. A term of up to two years' imprisonment may be suspended. Courts are required to impose minimum three-year sentences on offenders convicted of a third offence of domestic burglary. A second serious violent or sexual offence requires a court to order a life sentence unless there are exceptional circumstances. Life imprisonment is the mandatory sentence for murder, and is also available for certain other serious offences. The death penalty is no longer available for any offence; it has not been used in the United Kingdom since 1965.

Community sentences may include community rehabilitation orders (involving supervision in the community—see p. 235); community punishment orders (unpaid work within the community); community punishment and rehabilitation orders (elements of both probation supervision and community service work); curfew orders (requiring the offender to remain at a specified place for specified periods, usually monitored by electronic tagging); and drug treatment and testing orders (see p. 217). The Criminal Justice and Court Services Act 2000 contained two new measures: drug abstinence orders, which require an offender to abstain from misusing Class A drugs and to undertake drugs tests on instruction; and exclusion orders (likely to be monitored by electronic tagging) requiring offenders to stay away from a certain place for specified periods. Both types of order are to be piloted during 2001 before being introduced nationally.

A fine is the most common punishment, and most offenders are fined for summary offences. A court may also make compensation orders, which require the offender to pay compensation for personal injury, loss or damage resulting from an offence; or impose a conditional discharge, where the offender, if he or she offends again, may be sentenced for both the original offence and for the new one.

In May 2000 the Government announced a review of the legal framework for sentencing and its impact on reducing re-offending. The review—the Halliday Report—was published in May 2001. It made wide-ranging proposals, including increased severity of sentencing of persistent offenders, and restructuring of sentences under 12 months.

Sentencing Young Offenders

The main custodial sentence for 12 to 17 year olds is the *detention and training order* which was introduced in April 2000 and replaced detention in a young offender institution and the secure training order. It is a two-part sentence which combines a period of custody with a period under supervision in the community. It may last for a minimum of four months to a maximum of two years and there is provision for the custodial element to be shortened or lengthened depending on the young offender's progress.

Offenders under 18 convicted of certain serious offences may be detained for a period not exceeding the maximum term of imprisonment which would be available for that offence in the case of an adult. Those convicted of murder are detained 'during Her Majesty's pleasure'—the equivalent of a life sentence in the case of an adult.

Non-custodial penalties include: *conditional discharge*; *fines* and *compensation orders* (with the offender's parents having to pay); *supervision orders* (where the offender must comply with specific requirements, such as staying in local authority accommodation); and *attendance centre orders*. Those aged 16 or 17 may also be given the same community rehabilitation, community punishment, community punishment and rehabilitation, drug treatment and testing, curfew and exclusion orders as older offenders. From February 2001 the courts have been able to sentence offenders aged 10–15 to a curfew order with electronic tagging. This was previously only available for offenders aged 16 or over.

Other new orders are also available, including a *reparation order*, which requires young offenders to compensate the victim(s) of their offence or the community which they have harmed in some non-financial way; and an *action plan order*, making them comply with an individually tailored programme intended to alter their offending behaviour.

Complementing these are *parenting orders*, which require a parent or guardian to attend counselling and guidance sessions, and may direct them to comply with other requirements; and *child safety orders*, which place a child under ten who is at risk of becoming involved in crime or is behaving in an anti-social manner under the supervision of a specified, responsible officer.

Prohibitive anti-social behaviour orders (ASBOs) may be applied to individuals or groups whose threatening and disruptive conduct harasses the local community. Anyone in breach of such an order is guilty of a criminal offence. ASBOs and sex offender orders are applicable throughout the UK. By the end of March 2001, around 215 ASBOs had been issued.

A young offender convicted in court for the first time and pleading guilty may be sentenced to a *referral order* where an absolute discharge or custodial sentence is not appropriate. These orders are being piloted in seven areas in England and Wales. The offender is referred to a panel of two community volunteers and a member of the Youth Offending Team who agree a programme of activity aimed primarily at preventing re-offending. The target date for national implementation of referral orders is April 2002.

Appeals

A person convicted by a magistrates' court may appeal to the High Court, on points of law, and to the Crown Court, for their trial to be re-heard. Appeals from the Crown Court go to the Court of Appeal (Criminal Division). A further appeal can be made to the House of Lords on points of law of public importance, if permission is given. A prosecutor cannot appeal against an acquittal, but there is a system for reviewing rulings of law and sentences which are too lenient. The Criminal Cases Review Commission, which is independent of both government and the courts, reviews alleged miscarriages of justice in England, Wales and Northern Ireland. Referral of a case to this body depends on some new argument or evidence coming to light, not previously raised at the trial or on appeal.

Coroners' Courts

The coroner (usually a senior lawyer or doctor) must hold an inquest if a person died a violent or unnatural death, or died suddenly while in prison or in other specified circumstances. He or she may also need to hold an inquest if the cause of death remains unknown following a post-mortem examination. The coroner's court establishes how, when and where the death occurred. A coroner may sit alone or, in certain circumstances, with a jury.

CIVIL JUSTICE SYSTEM

Jurisdiction in civil matters is split between the High Court and the county courts and, to a limited extent, magistrates' courts. Some 90% of all cases are dealt with by the county courts, but most civil disputes do not go to court at all, and most of those which do, do not reach a trial. Many are dealt with through statutory or voluntary complaints mechanisms, or through mediation and negotiation. Arbitration is common in commercial and building disputes. Ombudsmen have the power to determine complaints in the public sector, and, on a voluntary basis, in some private sector activities (for example, banking, insurance and pensions).

A large number of tribunals exist to determine disputes. Most deal with cases that involve the rights of private citizens against decisions of the State in areas such as social security, income tax and mental health. Some tribunals deal with other disputes, such as employment. In all, there are some 70 tribunals which together deal with over 1 million cases a year.

Courts

The High Court is divided into three Divisions:

- The Queen's Bench Division deals with disputes relating to contracts, general commercial matters (in a specialist Commercial Court), and breaches of duty—known as 'liability in tort'—(covering general civil wrongs, such as accidents caused by negligence, or defamation of character). The Administrative Court has special responsibility for dealing with applications for judicial review of the actions of public bodies, and has the power to declare the action of a public individual, department or body unlawful.
- The Chancery Division deals with disputes relating to land, wills, companies and insolvency.
- The Family Division deals with matrimonial matters, including divorce, and the welfare of children.

About 220 county courts handle claims in contract and in tort (of these, 179 deal with family issues including divorce and the welfare of children) and a wide range of statutory matters. The majority of claims dealt with concern the recovery and collection of debt. The next most common types of claims relate to recovery of land and personal injury. Magistrates' courts have limited civil jurisdiction: in family matters (when they sit as a Family Proceedings Court) and in miscellaneous civil orders.

Appeals in most civil cases were reformed by the Access to Justice Act 1999 (see below). Appeals from magistrates' courts in civil matters go to the High Court, on matters of law, or to the Crown Court, if the case is to be re-heard. A further appeal on points of law of public importance goes to the House of Lords.

Reform of the Civil Justice System

Changes to the civil justice system were implemented in 1999, introducing:

- a unified code of procedural rules, replacing separate sets for the High Court and county court and enabling both to deal with cases more appropriately. Courts now take a more active case management role than before, handling them in a way which is proportionate to their value, complexity and importance;
- pre-action protocols (for clinical negligence, personal injury, construction and other professional negligence disputes), which set standards and timetables for the conduct of cases before court proceedings are started; and
- a system of three tracks to which disputed claims are assigned by a judge according to the value and complexity of the case. These are the:

  —small claims track, for cases worth less than £5,000, at an informal hearing by a district judge;

  —fast track, for cases from £5,000 to £15,000, setting a fixed timetable from allocation to trial; and

  —multi-track, for cases worth over £15,000 or of unusual complexity, which are supervised by a judge and given timetables tailored to each case.

Judges have a key role in reducing cost, delay and complexity, by managing cases to ensure that people going to law and their representatives keep to the timetable, and undertake only necessary work.

The Access to Justice Act 1999 reformed the workings of the appeals system according to the principles of proportionality and efficiency, by:

- diverting from the Court of Appeal those cases which, by their nature, do not require the attention of the most senior judges in the country; and
- making various changes to the working methods and constitution of the Court, which will enable it to allocate its resources more effectively.

The Civil Justice Council oversees the working of the civil justice system, and makes proposals for its improvement.

Legal System in Scotland

Scots law has legal principles, rules and concepts modelled on a combination of medieval church laws and those borrowed from other European systems. The main sources are judge-made law, certain legal treatises having 'institutional' authority, legislation, and EC law. The first two sources are sometimes referred to as the common law of Scotland. Legislation, as in the rest of the UK, consists of statutes (Acts of Parliament) or subordinate legislation authorised by Parliament.

PROSECUTION AND THE CRIMINAL COURTS

Awaiting Trial

When arrested, an accused person may be released by the police to await summons, on an undertaking to appear in court at a specified time, or be held in custody to appear in court on the next working day. Following that appearance, the accused may be remanded in custody until trial or released by the court on bail. If released on bail, he or she must agree to appear at trial when required, not to commit an offence while on bail, and not to interfere with witnesses or obstruct justice. There is a right of appeal to the High Court against the refusal of bail, or by the prosecutor against the granting of bail, or against the conditions imposed.

Prosecution Arrangements

The Crown Office and Procurator Fiscal Service provides Scotland's independent public prosecution and deaths investigation service. The Department is headed by the Lord Advocate, assisted by the Solicitor-General for Scotland (who are the Scottish Law Officers and members of the Scottish Executive). The Crown Agent, a senior civil servant, is responsible for the running of the Department.

Procurators fiscal and Crown Office officials prepare prosecutions in the High Court which are conducted by the Lord Advocate and the Solicitor-General for Scotland; they in turn delegate the bulk of their work to advocates depute, collectively known as Crown Counsel, of whom there are 13. In all other criminal courts the decision to prosecute is made, and prosecution carried out, by procurators fiscal, who are the Lord Advocate's local representatives (one for each sheriff court). They are lawyers and full-time civil servants subject to the direction of the Department.

The police report gives details of alleged crimes to the local procurator fiscal who has discretion whether or not to prosecute. He or she may receive instructions from the Crown Counsel on behalf of the Lord Advocate.

The office of coroner does not exist in Scotland. Instead the local procurator fiscal inquires into sudden or suspicious deaths. When appropriate, a fatal accident inquiry may be held before the sheriff; this is mandatory in cases of death resulting from industrial accidents and deaths in custody.

Criminal Courts

There are three criminal courts in Scotland: the High Court of Justiciary, the sheriff court and the district court. Cases are heard under one of two types of criminal procedure:

- In *solemn procedure* in both the High Court of Justiciary and the sheriff court, an accused person's trial takes place before a judge sitting with a jury of 15 people selected at random from the general public. As in England and Wales, the alleged offence is set out in a document called an indictment. The judge decides questions of law and the jury decides questions of fact and may reach a decision by a simple majority. They may decide to find the accused 'guilty', 'not guilty' or 'not proven'; the last two are acquittals and have the effect that the accused cannot be tried again for the same offence.
- In *summary procedure* in sheriff and district courts, the judge sits without a jury and decides questions of both fact and law. The offence charged is set out in a document called a summary complaint.

Pre-trial hearings (called 'diets') in summary and solemn cases are intended to establish the state of readiness of both the defence and the prosecution.

The *High Court of Justiciary* is the supreme criminal court in Scotland, sitting in Edinburgh, Glasgow and on circuit in other towns. It tries the most serious crimes and has exclusive jurisdiction in cases involving murder, treason and rape.

The 49 *sheriff courts* deal mainly with less serious offences committed within their area of jurisdiction. These courts are organised in six sheriffdoms; at the head of each is a sheriff principal. There are over 100 permanent sheriffs, most of whom are appointed to particular courts. The sheriff has jurisdiction in both summary and solemn criminal cases. Under summary procedure, the sheriff may impose prison sentences of up to three months (although more in some cases) or a fine of £5,000. Under solemn procedure, the sheriff may impose imprisonment for up to three years and unlimited financial penalties, and has an additional power of remit to the High Court of Justiciary if he or she thinks a heavier sentence should be imposed. The sheriff also has available a range of non-custodial sentences, principally community service and probation.

District courts, which deal with minor offences, are the administrative responsibility of the local authority. The longest prison sentence which can be imposed is generally 60 days and the maximum fine is £2,500. The bench of a district court will usually be made up of one or more Justices of the Peace. A local authority may also appoint a stipendiary magistrate, who must be a professional lawyer of at least five years' standing, and who has the same summary criminal jurisdiction and powers as a sheriff. At present, only Glasgow has stipendiary magistrates sitting in the district court. A government review of the operation of the district courts was announced in May 2000.

Sentencing

In Scotland a court must obtain a social enquiry report before imposing a custodial sentence if the accused is aged under 21 or has not previously served a custodial sentence. A report is also required before making a probation or community service order, or in cases involving people already subject to supervision.

Non-custodial sentences available to the courts include fines, probation orders, community service orders, restriction of liberty orders (monitored by electronic tagging) and supervised attendance orders (which provide an alternative to imprisonment for non-payment of fines, and incorporate aspects of work and training).

Children

Criminal proceedings may be brought against any child aged eight or over, but the instructions of the Lord Advocate are necessary before anyone under 16 years of age is prosecuted. Most children under 16 who have committed an offence or are considered to be in need of care and protection may be brought before a Children's Hearing. The hearing, consisting of three people who are not lawyers, determines whether compulsory measures of care are required and, if so, the form they should take.

Young people aged between 16 and 21 serve custodial sentences in young offender institutions. Remission of part of the sentence for good behaviour, release on parole and supervision on release are available.

Appeals

The High Court of Justiciary sits as the Scottish Court of Criminal Appeal. In both solemn and summary procedure, a convicted person may appeal against conviction, or sentence, or both. The Court may authorise a retrial if it sets aside a conviction. There is no appeal from this court in criminal cases. The Scottish Criminal Cases Review Commission is responsible for considering alleged miscarriages of justice and referring cases meeting the relevant criteria to the Court of Appeal for review.

CIVIL COURTS

The main civil courts are the Court of Session (the supreme court, subject to appeal only to the House of Lords in London) and sheriff court (the principal local court).

The *Court of Session* sits in Edinburgh, and may hear cases from the outset or on transfer from sheriff courts and tribunals on appeal. A leading principle of the court is that cases starting there are both prepared for decision, and decided, by judges sitting alone whose decisions are subject to review by several judges. The total number of judges is 32, of whom 24, called Lords Ordinary, mainly decide cases in the first instance. This branch of the court is called the Outer House. The other eight judges are divided into two divisions of four judges each, forming the Inner House. The First Division is presided over by the Lord President of the Court of Session and the Second Division by the Lord Justice-Clerk. The main business of each division is to review, on appeal, the decisions of the Lords Ordinary or inferior courts.

In addition to its criminal jurisdiction, the *sheriff court* deals with most civil law cases in Scotland. There is, with very few exceptions, no upper limit to the financial level with which the court can deal, and a broad range of remedies can be granted. Cases may include debts, contracts, reparation, rent restrictions, actions affecting the use of property, leases and tenancies, child protection issues and family actions. There is a right of appeal in some cases from the sheriff to the sheriff principal and then, in some cases, to the Court of Session.

The House of Lords hears relatively few appeals in civil matters from Scotland but, since devolution, the Judicial Committee of the Privy Council (JCPC) has had jurisdiction to consider disputes involving devolution issues. When dealing with Scottish cases, the JCPC usually includes at least two Scottish judges and can sit in London or elsewhere as appropriate.

Civil Proceedings

The formal proceedings in the Court of Session are started by serving the defender with a summons or, in sheriff court cases in ordinary actions, an initial writ. A defender who intends to contest the action must inform the court; if he or she fails to do so, the court normally grants a decree in absence in favour of the pursuer. Where a case is contested, both parties must prepare written pleadings, after which a hearing will normally be arranged.

In summary cause actions involving sums between £750 and £1,500 in the sheriff court, a summons incorporates a statement of claim. The procedure is designed to let most actions be settled without the parties having to appear in court. Normally, they, or their representatives, need appear only when an action is defended.

In cases below £750 a special small claim procedure allows those who do not have legal advice to raise claims themselves. The procedures are similar to, but less formal than, the summary cause procedure. In addition to the courts, there is a wide range of tribunals which administer justice in special types of case. Many of these are the same as in the rest of Great Britain; others, such as the Land Court, the Lands Tribunal and the Children's Hearings, only apply to Scotland.

ADMINISTRATION OF THE SCOTTISH LEGAL SYSTEM

The Scottish Executive Justice Department, under the Minister for Justice, is responsible for civil law and criminal justice, including criminal justice social work services, police, prisons, courts administration, legal aid, and liaison with the legal profession in Scotland. The Scottish Court Service, an executive agency of the Scottish Executive Justice Department, deals with the work of the Supreme Courts and the sheriff courts.

The Lord Advocate and the Solicitor-General for Scotland provide the Scottish Executive with advice on legal matters and represent its interests in the courts. Since devolution, the Advocate-General for Scotland has provided advice on Scots law to the UK Government.

The role of the Scottish Parliament is to make laws on matters devolved to it (see chapter 4). In these areas, it is able to amend or repeal existing Acts of the UK Parliament and to pass new legislation for Scotland of its own. It can also consider and pass private legislation, promoted by individuals or bodies (for example, local authorities).

The Court of Session and the High Court of Justiciary enact the rules regulating their own procedure and the procedures of the sheriff courts and the lay summary courts. The Court of Session and Criminal Courts Rules Councils, and the Sheriff Court Rules Council, consisting of judges and legal practitioners, advise the courts about amending the rules.

Legal System in Northern Ireland

Northern Ireland's legal system is similar to that of England and Wales. Jury trials have the same place in the system, except in the case of offences involving acts of terrorism (see p. 218). In addition, cases go through the same stages in the courts and the legal profession has the same two branches.

Superior Courts

The Supreme Court of Judicature comprises the Court of Appeal, the High Court and the Crown Court. All matters relating to these courts are under the jurisdiction of the UK Parliament. Judges are appointed by the Crown.

The *Court of Appeal* consists of the Lord Chief Justice (as President) and two Lords Justices of Appeal. The High Court is made up of the Lord Chief Justice and five other judges. The practice and procedure of the Court of Appeal and the High Court are virtually the same as in the corresponding courts in England and Wales. Both courts sit in the Royal Courts of Justice in Belfast.

The Court of Appeal has power to review the civil law decisions of the High Court and the criminal law decisions of the Crown Court, and may in certain cases review the decisions of county courts and magistrates' courts. Subject to certain restrictions, an appeal from a judgment of the Court of Appeal can go to the House of Lords.

The *High Court* is divided into a Queen's Bench Division, dealing with most civil law matters; a Chancery Division, dealing with, for instance, trusts and estates, title to land, mortgages and charges, wills and company matters; and a Family Division, dealing principally with such matters as matrimonial cases, adoption, children in care and undisputed wills.

The *Crown Court* deals with all serious criminal cases.

Inferior Courts

The inferior courts are the county courts and the magistrates' courts, both of which differ in a number of ways from their counterparts in England and Wales.

County courts are primarily civil law courts. They are presided over by one of 14 county court judges, two of whom—in Belfast and Londonderry—have the title of recorder. Appeals go from the county courts to the High Court. The county courts also handle appeals from the magistrates' courts in both criminal and civil matters. In civil matters, the county courts decide most actions in which the amount or the value of specific articles claimed is below a certain level. The courts also deal with actions involving title to, or the recovery of, land; equity matters such as trusts and estates; mortgages; and the sale of land and partnerships.

The day-to-day work of dealing summarily with minor local criminal cases is carried out in *magistrates' courts* presided over by a full-time, legally qualified resident magistrate (RM). The magistrates' courts also exercise jurisdiction in certain family law cases and have a very limited jurisdiction in other civil cases.

Terrorist Offences

People accused of offences specified under emergency legislation (see p. 218) are tried in the Crown Court without a jury. The prosecution must prove guilt beyond reasonable doubt and the defendant has the right to be represented by a lawyer of his or her choice. The judge has to set out in a written statement the reasons for conviction and there is an automatic right of appeal to the Court of Appeal against conviction and/or sentence on points of fact as well as of law.

Administration of the Law

The Lord Chancellor is responsible for court administration, while the Northern Ireland Office, under the Secretary of State, deals with policy and legislation concerning criminal law, the police and the penal system. The Lord Chancellor has general responsibility for legal aid, advice and assistance.

The Director of Public Prosecutions for Northern Ireland, who is responsible to the Attorney-General, prosecutes all offences tried on indictment, and may do so in other (summary) cases. Most summary offences are prosecuted by the police.

Prison Service

The Prison Service in England and Wales, the Scottish Prison Service and the Northern Ireland Prison Service are all executive agencies. There are currently 138 prison establishments in England and Wales (nine of which are run by private contractors), 17 Scottish establishments and three establishments in Northern Ireland.

Prison accommodation ranges from open prisons to high-security establishments. Sentenced prisoners are classified into different risk-level groups for security purposes. Women prisoners are held in separate prisons or in separate accommodation in mixed prisons. There are no open prisons in Northern Ireland.

Many of the prisons currently used were built in Victorian times. Few new prisons were built at the start of the 20th century. In the late 1980s a number of new prisons were built, including those at Doncaster, Lancaster Farms and Milton Keynes. New prisons continued to open in the 1990s including Altcourse (Liverpool) and Parc (Bridgend) which were designed, constructed, managed and financed by the private sector under the PFI (Private Finance Initiative).

Independent Oversight of the Prison System

Every prison establishment in England, Wales and Northern Ireland has a board of visitors, comprising volunteers drawn from the local community appointed by the Home Secretary or Secretary of State for Northern Ireland. Boards, which are independent, monitor complaints by prisoners and concerns of staff, and report as necessary to ministers. In Scotland, visiting committees to prisons are appointed by local authorities.

Independent Prisons Inspectorates report on the treatment of prisoners and prison conditions, and submit annual reports to Parliament. Each prison establishment is visited about once every three years.

In England and Wales prisoners who fail to get satisfaction from the Prison Service's internal request and complaints system may complain to the independent Prisons Ombudsman. In Scotland, prisoners who exhaust the internal grievance procedure may apply to the independent Scottish Prisons Complaints Commissioner.

Privileges and Discipline

Prisoners in the UK may write and receive letters, be visited by relatives and friends, and make telephone calls. Privileges include a personal radio; books, magazines and newspapers; and watching television. Earnable privileges, dependent on good behaviour, include extra and improved visits, higher rates of pay, community visits, and longer periods out of cell.

Offences against prison discipline are dealt with by prison governors, who act as adjudicators. In England, Wales and Scotland measures to counter drug misuse in prisons include mandatory drug testing. Voluntary testing has been piloted in Northern Ireland, but there is no mandatory programme. People awaiting trial in custody have certain rights and privileges not granted to convicted prisoners.

Early Release of Prisoners

There are statutory arrangements governing the early release of prisoners. Offenders serving shorter terms (less than four years) may be automatically released at specific points in their sentences, while those detained for longer require Parole Board approval or the consent of a government minister.

Probation

The Probation Service in England and Wales supervises offenders in the community under direct court orders and after release from custody. It also advises offenders in custody. All young offenders and all prisoners in

Table 14.3: Average Daily Prison Population

	1993	1995	1998	2000
England and Wales	44,566	51,047	65,298	64,800
Scotland	5,637	5,626	6,017	6,176
Northern Ireland	1,933	1,762	1,402	947

Sources: Home Office, Scottish Executive and Northern Ireland Office

England and Wales sentenced to 12 months' imprisonment and over are supervised on release by the Probation Service, or, in the case of certain young offenders, by local authority social services departments or youth justice teams.

A court probation order requires offenders to maintain regular contact with their probation officer, who is expected to supervise them. The purpose of supervision under a probation order is to secure the rehabilitation of the offender, to protect the public and to prevent the offender from committing further offences. A probation order can last from six months to three years; an offender who fails to comply without good reason with any of the requirements can be brought before the court again. The Probation Service also supervises those subject to community service orders, combination orders (see p. 226) and those released from prison on parole. The Probation Service in England and Wales dealt with around 130,000 new offenders in 2000. Just under half this total were starting probation orders; a similar number were beginning community service orders.

HM Inspectorate of Probation has both an inspection and an advisory role, and also monitors any work that the Probation Service carries out in conjunction with the voluntary and private sectors.

In Scotland local authority social work departments supervise offenders on probation, community service and other community disposals, and ex-prisoners subject to statutory supervision on release from custody. With effect from September 2002, arrangements for delivery of community disposals—equivalent to community sentences—will pass to 11 mainland groupings of local authorities.

In Northern Ireland the probation service is administered by the government-funded Probation Board, whose membership is representative of the community.

Publicly Funded Legal Help

Someone who needs legal assistance or representation may be able to get help with costs from publicly funded schemes. Those who qualify may have all their legal costs paid for, or they may be asked to make a contribution, depending on their personal financial circumstances and, in civil cases, the outcome of the case.

England and Wales

Provisions in the Access to Justice Act 1999 set up the Legal Services Commission (LSC) which administers two separate schemes for funding services:

- the Community Legal Service (CLS) operates the CLS Fund, through which funding in civil cases is targeted on quality-assured services in priority areas of need; and
- the Criminal Defence Service, which aims to achieve quality assurance and improve value for money in publicly funded criminal defence services.

The CLS Fund provides legal help and representation if applicants qualify for it, which depends on their personal financial circumstances and the nature of their case. It supports eligible people in cases of divorce, mediation and other family issues, welfare benefits, credit and debt problems, housing and property disputes, immigration and nationality issues, clinical negligence cases, challenges to decisions by government departments and other public bodies, and actions against the police and others. The CLS Fund is not available for most personal injury cases (except clinical negligence cases), as the Government believes that these are best conducted by way of conditional fee ('no win, no fee') arrangements between solicitors and clients.

In criminal proceedings the LSC, through the Criminal Defence Service, makes arrangements for solicitors to assist unrepresented defendants in the magistrates' courts and advocacy assistance is also available in some other specified circumstances. Solicitors are also available, on a 24-hour basis, to give advice and assistance to people being questioned by the police and others. These services are not means-tested and are free.

Publicly funded representation in criminal cases may be granted by the court if it appears to be in the interests of justice. A contribution towards the costs may be payable in cases which reach the Crown Court or the higher criminal courts on appeal. During 2000 over 3 million acts of assistance, including offering advice and payment of legal bills, were granted at a total cost of around £1.7 billion.

Scotland

The Scottish Legal Aid Board manages legal aid in Scotland. Its main tasks are to grant or refuse applications for legal aid; to pay solicitors or advocates for the legal work that they do; and to advise Scottish ministers on legal aid matters. Where legal aid is granted to the accused in criminal proceedings, he or she is not required to pay any contribution towards expenses.

Northern Ireland

Civil legal aid is administered by the Law Society for Northern Ireland. Where legal aid is granted for criminal cases it is free.

Other Legal Advice

The CLS brings together organisations offering legal and advice services into local networks throughout England and Wales. These include solicitors' firms, Citizens Advice Bureaux, law centres, local authority services and other independent advice centres.

Further Reading

The Lord Chancellor's Departments: Departmental Report. The Government's Expenditure Plans 2001–02 to 2003–04 and Main Estimates 2001–02. Cm 5107. The Stationery Office, 2001.
Home Office Annual Report 2000–2001. The Government's Expenditure Plans 2001–02 to 2003–2004 and Main Estimates 2001–02. Cm 5106. The Stationery Office, 2001.

Websites

Community Legal Service: www.justask.org.uk
Home Office: www.homeoffice.gov.uk
Legal Services Commission: www.legalservices.gov.uk
Lord Chancellor's Department: www.lcd.gov.uk
Northern Ireland Executive: www.northernireland.gov.uk
Scottish Executive: www.scotland.gov.uk

15 Religion

Church and State	237	Places of Worship	243
Background and Membership	237	Ceremonies marking Life Events	244
Organisation	241	Religion and Society	244
Guidance and Leadership	242	Cooperation between Religions	246

The United Kingdom in the 21st century is a multifaith society. Everyone has the right to religious freedom. Religious organisations and groups may conduct their rites and ceremonies, promote their beliefs within the limits of the law, own property and run schools and a range of other charitable activities. The 2001 Census included, for the first time in the UK since 1851, a question on religion.[1] When the answers to this question have been analysed, they will provide extensive official information on patterns of religious identity in the United Kingdom.

CHURCH AND STATE

Christianity has been the most influential religion in the UK, and it remains the declared faith of the majority of the population. Two churches have a special status with regard to the State. In England, following the rejection by Henry VIII of the supremacy of the Pope in 1534, the Anglican *Church of England* has been legally recognised as the official, or established, Church. The Monarch is the 'Supreme Governor' of the Church of England and must always be a member of the Church, and promise to uphold it. A similar situation applied in Scotland until the early 20th century regarding the Presbyterian *Church of Scotland.* Since then the Church has continued to be recognised as the national Church. The Monarch holds no constitutional role in the government of the Church of Scotland but is represented at the General Assembly (see p. 241) in the office of the Lord High Commissioner. There are no 'established' churches in Wales or Northern Ireland. In Wales, the Anglican Church is known as the Church in Wales.

BACKGROUND AND MEMBERSHIP

A distinction is often drawn between 'community size' figures and 'active membership' figures, with the former representing identification with a religion, or a religious ethic, in the broadest sense, and the latter a much closer association. Current community size estimates suggest 40 million people in the UK identify themselves as Christians. On the same basis it is estimated that there are over 1.5 million Muslims; around half a million Hindus, half a million Sikhs, and nearly a third of a million Jews.

[1] Questions about religious beliefs have, however, been asked previously for official purposes in Northern Ireland. For more information on the 2001 Census, see pp. 34–6.

Table 15.1: Estimated Active Faith Membership[1] in the United Kingdom

Thousands

Group	1970	1980	1990	2000
Christian: Trinitarian[2]	9,272	7,529	6,624	5,917
of whom:				
Anglican	*2,987*	*2,180*	*1,728*	*1,654*
Catholic[3]	*2,746*	*2,455*	*2,198*	*1,768*
Free Churches	*1,629*	*1,285*	*1,299*	*1,278*
Presbyterian	*1,751*	*1,437*	*1,214*	*989*
Orthodox	*159*	*172*	*185*	*235*
Christian: Non-Trinitarian	276	349	455	533
Buddhist	10	15	30	50
Hindu	80	120	140	165
Jewish	120	110	100	95[4]
Muslim	130	305	495	665
Sikh	100	150	250	400
Others	20	40	55	85
Total membership	**10,010**	**8,620**	**8,150**	**7,910**

[1] Active *adult* members.

[2] Trinitarian means acceptance of the historic formulary of the Godhead as three eternal persons. Owing to the existence of many smaller churches whose membership figures are not included in the table, membership of the five Christian Trinitarian Churches mentioned here will not add up to the total.

[3] Based on attendance at Mass.

[4] Synagogue-affiliated households. In some parts of the country membership is through a household which may contain more than one adult. Figures relate to 1996.

Note: Many religious gatherings are small and of an informal nature. Consequently, reliable data on the level of religious observance and activity in the UK can sometimes be difficult to obtain.

Sources: Christian Research and Board of Deputies of British Jews

In addition to the 7.9 million active faith members of religions (see Table 15.1), many other people involve themselves in formal religious ceremonies at times of crisis or for significant events such as birth, marriage and death.

Organisations such as the British Humanist Association and the National Secular Society offer the opportunity for members to debate and explore moral and philosophical issues in a non-religious setting.

The Christian Community

The Church of England is part of a worldwide Communion of Anglican churches, 38 in all, with a UK membership of 1.7 million. The Presbyterian Church of Scotland has an adult communicant membership in the UK of over 600,000.

The Catholic Church has the largest active adult membership of any single Christian denomination in the UK, with average weekly Mass attendance of over 1 million in England and Wales and 225,000 in Scotland.

The rise of the Puritan movement in the 16th and 17th centuries led to a proliferation of nonconformist churches. The term 'Free Churches' is often used to describe those Protestant churches in the UK which, unlike the Church of England and the Church of Scotland, are not 'established' churches. The major Free Churches include Methodist, Baptist, United Reformed, Salvation Army and Pentecostal churches.

The British Methodist Church, the largest of the Free Churches, originated in the 18th century following the evangelical revival under John Wesley (1703–91). It has 332,000 adult full members. The present Church is based on the 1932 union of most of the separate Methodist Churches.

The Baptists first achieved an organised form in the UK in the 17th century. Today they are mainly organised in groups of churches, most of which belong to the Baptist

Union of Great Britain (re-formed in 1812) with about 145,000 members. There are also separate Baptist Unions for Scotland, Wales and Ireland, and other independent Baptist Churches.

The third largest of the Free Churches is the United Reformed Church, with some 93,000 members. It was formed in 1972 from the union of the Congregational Church in England and Wales with the Presbyterian Church in England. In 1982 and 2000 there were further unions with the Reformed Churches of Christ and the Congregational Union of Scotland.

Among the other Free Churches are: the Presbyterian Church in Ireland, the largest Protestant church in Northern Ireland, where it has around 300,000 members; the Presbyterian (or Calvinistic Methodist) Church of Wales, with 49,750 members and the largest of the Free Churches in Wales; the Union of Welsh Independents, with 40,750 members; and a number of independent Scottish Presbyterian churches which are particularly active in the Highlands and Islands.

The Salvation Army was founded in the East End of London in 1865 by William Booth (1829–1912). It runs over 800 local church and community centres, and has a strong musical tradition.

The Religious Society of Friends (Quakers), with about 17,000 adult members, was founded in the middle of the 17th century under the leadership of George Fox (1624–91). Other Protestant churches include the Christian Brethren, a Protestant body organised by J. N. Darby (1800–82). There are two branches: the Open Brethren and the Closed or Exclusive Brethren. Unitarians and Free Christians, whose origins go back to the Reformation, belong to a similar tradition.

The rich tradition of people of different cultures coming to settle in the United Kingdom since the Middle Ages has also contributed to the diversity of Christian denominations found here. Christian communities founded by migrants include those of the Orthodox, Lutheran and Reformed Churches of various European countries, the Coptic Orthodox Church and the Armenian Church. These tend to be concentrated in the larger cities, particularly London, and operate in a variety of languages. The largest is probably the Greek Orthodox Church, many of whose members are of Cypriot origin.

More recent developments within the Christian tradition have included the rise of Pentecostalism and the charismatic movement. A number of Pentecostal bodies were formed in the UK at the turn of the 20th century. The two main Pentecostal organisations in the UK today are the Assemblies of God, with approximately 54,000 members, and the Elim Pentecostal Church, with around 62,000 members. Since the Second World War immigration from the Caribbean has led to a significant number of Black Majority Pentecostal churches, and these are a growing presence in British (and especially English) church life.

The Christian 'house church' movement (or 'new churches') began in the 1970s when some of the charismatics began to establish their own congregations. The movement, whose growth within the UK has been most marked in England, is characterised by lay leadership and is organised into a number of loose fellowships.

Inter-church Cooperation

Churches Together in Britain and Ireland is the main coordinating body for the Christian churches in the UK. It coordinates the work of its 33 member churches and associations of churches, in the areas of social responsibility, international affairs, church life, world mission, racial justice, care of international students and inter-faith relations. Its international aid agencies—Christian Aid, CAFOD and SCIAF[2]—are major charities. Member churches are also grouped in separate ecumenical bodies, according to country: Churches Together in England, Action of Churches Together in Scotland, Churches Together in Wales (Cytûn), and the Irish Council of Churches.

The Free Churches Group, with 18 member denominations, was in 2001 incorporated into Churches Together in England. It promotes cooperation among the

[2] Catholic Agency for Overseas Development and Scottish Catholic International Aid Fund.

Free Churches, especially in hospital chaplaincy and in education matters. The Evangelical Alliance, with a membership of individuals, churches or societies drawn from 20 denominations, represents over 1 million evangelical Christians.

Inter-church discussions about the search for Christian unity take place internationally, as well as within the UK, and the main participants are the Anglican, Baptist, Lutheran, Methodist, Orthodox, Reformed and Catholic Churches. In 1999 the Church of England and the Methodist Church began formal discussions on a move towards unity. An initial report is expected to be published in December 2001. The Baptist Union, the Moravian Church, the Catholic Church and the United Reformed Church had participating observers at the discussions. Informal talks were held between the Church of England, the Methodist Church and the United Reformed Church from 1999 to 2001. A report from these conversations will be published alongside the report of the formal discussions between the Church of England and the Methodist Church. In Scotland, several churches, including the Church of Scotland, have been pursuing unity through the Scottish Churches' Initiative for Union. Among them was the United Reformed Church, itself the outcome of a 1999 union between the United Reformed Church in the UK and the Scottish Congregational Church. In Wales there are moves towards a United Free Church, and towards establishing in one small area an ecumenical bishop.

Other Faith Communities

In addition to Christianity, the United Kingdom is also home to adherents of many other world religions.

The Buddhist community in the UK has around 50,000 followers, both of British or Western origin, and of South Asian and Asian background.

The Hindu community in the UK originates largely from India, although others have come from countries to which earlier generations had previously migrated, such as Kenya, Tanzania, Uganda, Zambia and Malawi. The number of members is around 400,000 to 550,000, although some community representatives suggest a considerably higher figure (of close to 1 million). They are predominantly Gujaratis (between 65% and 70%) and Punjabis (between 15% and 20%). Most of the remainder have their ancestral roots in other parts of India, such as Uttar Pradesh, West Bengal, and the Southern states, as well as other countries such as Sri Lanka.

Jews first settled in England at the time of the Norman Conquest. They were banished by royal decree in 1290, but readmitted following the English Civil War (1642–51). Sephardic Jews, who originally came from Spain and Portugal, have been present in the UK since the mid-17th century. The majority of the 300,000 Jews in the UK today, while British born, are Ashkenazi Jews, of Central and East European origin, who fled persecution in the Russian Empire between 1881 and 1914, and Nazi persecution in Germany and other European countries from 1933 onwards.

A significant Muslim community has existed in the UK since Muslim seamen and traders settled around the major ports in the early 19th century. Most came from the Middle East and the areas that are now Pakistan and Bangladesh. There was further settlement after the First World War, and again in the 1950s and 1960s as people arrived to meet the shortage of labour following the Second World War. The 1970s saw the arrival of significant numbers of Muslims of Asian origin from Kenya and Uganda. There are also well-established Turkish Cypriot and Iranian Muslim communities, while more recently Muslims from Somalia, Iraq, Bosnia and Kosovo have sought refuge in the UK. There are smaller numbers of English and West Indian Muslims. In total, there are around 1.5 million people who identify themselves as Muslims in the UK, the majority of whom are now British-born. Sunni and Shi'a are the two principal traditions within Islam and both are represented among the Muslim community in the UK. Sufism, the mystical aspect of Islam, can be found in both traditions, and members of some of the major Sufi traditions have also developed branches in British cities.

Most of the Sikh community in the UK are of Punjabi ethnic origin. A minority came from East Africa and other former British colonies to which members of their family had migrated, but the majority have come to the UK directly from the Punjab. There are between 400,000 and 500,000 members, making it the largest Sikh community outside the Indian subcontinent.

Jainism is an ancient religion brought to the UK by immigrants mainly from the Gujarat and Rajasthan areas of India. It is estimated that there are between 25,000 and 30,000 members in the UK. The Zoroastrian religion is mainly represented in the UK by the Parsi community. Founders of the UK community originally settled in the 19th century and it is estimated that there are between 5,000 and 10,000 members. The Bahá'í movement originated in Persia in the 19th century. The UK community has around 6,000 members.

Rastafarianism, with its roots in the return-to-Africa movement, emerged in the West Indies early in the 20th century. It arrived in the UK with immigration from Jamaica in the 1950s.

Other religious groups in the UK were originally founded in the United States in the 19th century. These include the Church of Jesus Christ of Latter-Day Saints (the Mormon Church, with about 180,000 members in Britain), the Jehovah's Witnesses (146,000 members), the Christadelphians, the Christian Scientists, and the Seventh-day Adventists. The Spiritualists have about 35,000 members.

A number of newer religious movements, established since the Second World War and often with overseas origins, are now active in the UK. Examples include the Church of Scientology, the Transcendental Meditation movement, the Unification Church and various New Age groups. INFORM (Information Network Focus on Religious Movements) carries out research and seeks to provide information about new religious movements.

ORGANISATION

The *Church of England* is divided into two geographical provinces, each headed by an archbishop: Canterbury, comprising 30 dioceses, including the Diocese in Europe; and York, with 14 dioceses. The dioceses are divided into archdeaconries and deaneries, which are in turn divided into about 13,000 parishes, although in practice many of these are grouped together.

Church of England archbishops, bishops and the deans of some cathedrals are appointed by the Monarch on the advice of the Prime Minister. The Crown Appointments Commission, which includes lay and clergy representatives, plays a key role in the selection of archbishops and diocesan bishops. The Archbishops' Council is the centre of an administrative system dealing with inter-church relations, inter-faith relations, social questions, recruitment and training for the ministry, and missionary work.

The Church Commissioners are responsible for the management of a large part of the Church of England's invested assets. The Crown appoints a Member of Parliament from the backbenches of the governing party to the unpaid post of Second Church Estates Commissioner, to represent the Commissioners in Parliament. The Church Commissioners provide a fifth of the Church of England's total annual income, with most of the remainder provided by local voluntary donations.

The *Church of Scotland* became the national church following the Scottish Reformation in the late 16th century and legislation enacted by the Scottish Parliament. It has a Presbyterian form of government—that is, government by church courts or councils, composed of ministers, elders, and deacons. The 1,600 congregations are governed locally by courts known as Kirk Sessions. The courts above these are the 'Presbyteries', responsible for a geographical area made up of a number of parishes. The General Assembly, or Supreme Court, meets annually under the chairmanship of an elected moderator, who serves for one year.

There are eight provinces of the Catholic Church in Great Britain and Northern Ireland—four in England, two in Scotland, one in Wales and one which includes Northern Ireland. There is a Bishops' Conference of England and Wales, and a Bishops' Conference of Scotland. The Irish

Episcopal Conference includes the whole of Ireland. The Bishops' Conference is a permanent institution of the Catholic Church whereby the bishops of a country exercise together pastoral, legislative and teaching offices as defined by the law of the Catholic Church.

In Great Britain there are 30 territorial Catholic dioceses: 22 in England and Wales and eight in Scotland. Each diocesan bishop is appointed by the Pope and governs a diocese according to Canon Law and through reference to a Council of Priests, College of Consultors and a Pastoral Council.

There are 2,843 Catholic parishes in England and Wales and 483 in Scotland. Northern Ireland is covered by seven dioceses, some of which have territory in the Irish Republic. There are 1,329 parishes in the whole of Ireland.

The Network of Buddhist Organisations links many of the various Buddhist educational, cultural, charitable and teaching organisations. The Buddhist Society of Great Britain and Ireland, formed in 1907, eventually evolved into a new and independent organisation—the Buddhist Society—in 1943. The Society promotes the principles, but does not adhere to any particular school, of Buddhism.

The main administrative body for Hindus is the National Council of Hindu temples. Other national bodies serving the Hindu community include the Hindu Council (UK) and Vishwa Hindu Parishad.

Jewish congregations in the UK number about 365. The Board of Deputies of British Jews is the officially recognised representative body for these groups. Founded in 1760, it is elected mainly by synagogues, but a growing number of community organisations are also represented. The Board serves as the voice of the community to both government and the wider non-Jewish community. Of the total number of synagogue-affiliated households, most Ashkenazi Jews (60%) acknowledge the authority of the Chief Rabbi. The Reform Synagogues of Great Britain (founded in 1840) cover almost 20% of synagogue-affiliated community membership. The Union of Liberal and Progressive Synagogues (founded in 1901) and the recently established Assembly of Masorti synagogues together account for most of the remaining synagogue-affiliated community membership. The more strictly observant have their own spiritual leaders, as do the Sephardim.

The Muslim Council of Britain, founded in 1997, represents established national and regional Muslim bodies as well as local mosques, professional associations and other organisations. The Council aims to promote cooperation, consensus and unity on Muslim affairs in the UK. A number of other representative bodies, such as the Union of Muslim Organisations, have been set up to coordinate the social, cultural and economic aspects of Muslim life in the UK.

The Network of Sikh Organisations (NSO) was formed in 1995 to facilitate cooperation between British Sikhs. It provides a forum for organising the celebration of major events in the Sikh calendar, and works with government departments and a number of national organisations to represent Sikh interests at a national level.

GUIDANCE AND LEADERSHIP

Most religions depend, to a greater or lesser degree, on ministers of religion to interpret doctrine, advise on moral issues and lead their respective communities.[3] Church of England ministers, Catholic priests, and other ordained ministers often receive a guaranteed annual stipend and rely to a lesser extent on gifts and donations from members of their communities. Some ministers (particularly lay ministers) combine their religious ministries with other paid employment.

The two archbishops of the Church of England (of Canterbury and York), together with its bishops of London, Durham and Winchester and 21 other senior bishops, sit in the House of Lords as Lords Spiritual. There are currently proposals to appoint a third archbishop. Prior to the House of Commons (Removal of Clergy Disqualification) Act 2001, all clergy who had been ordained by a bishop, and Ministers of the Church of Scotland, were disqualified from sitting as

[3] Although not all—the Quakers, for example, have no ordained ministers and no formal liturgy or sacraments.

MPs in the House of Commons. The new Act removed these restrictions, except for those bishops who sit as Lords Spiritual in the House of Lords.

The Church of England, which has about 13,000 ordained ministers and 10,300 licensed Readers, reported an increase in the ordination of new clergy between 1999 and 2000 (from 481 to 569). There are at present just over 1,400 people in training. The first women priests were ordained in 1994 and by 2000 they numbered 2,100. Women priests cannot yet be appointed bishop or archbishop. The Church of Scotland has around 1,200 ministers in parishes. The Methodists have 3,727 ministers (including student ministers), the Baptists 1,780 and the United Reformed Church 1,090. All these admit women to the ministry.

The Catholic Church in Great Britain has approximately 3,800 active diocesan priests and 1,800 priests who are members of religious congregations. In the Catholic tradition, men are ordained to the priesthood and diaconate.

Rabbis provide leadership for the Jewish community. Sadhus provide leadership and guidance for the Hindu community. There is no priesthood in Islam. However, the British Muslim community has a number of associations of religious scholars—ulema—and shariah councils that provide religious legal rulings on matters such as matrimonial disputes.

PLACES OF WORSHIP

The State does not contribute to the general expenses of church maintenance, although some state aid does help repair historic churches. In 1999–2000 English Heritage and the Heritage Lottery Fund jointly offered grants to churches totalling £26 million. Assistance is also given to meet some of the costs of repairing cathedrals, and £3 million was available from English Heritage in 2000–01.

The Churches Conservation Trust (formerly the Redundant Churches Fund), funded jointly by the Government and the Church of England, preserves Anglican churches of particular cultural and historical importance that are no longer used as regular places of worship. At present over 300 churches are maintained in this way.

The Historic Chapels Trust was established to take into ownership redundant chapels and other places of worship in England of outstanding architectural and historic interest (other than those which are eligible for vesting in the Churches Conservation Trust). Buildings of all denominations and faiths can be and have been taken into care, including nonconformist chapels, Catholic churches, private Anglican chapels and synagogues. In April 2001 the Government announced a new grant for repairs to listed buildings used as places of worship. While not a tax rebate, it will have the same effect as if the level of VAT (value added tax) for repairs had been reduced from 17.5% to 5%.

Although religious buildings are not as central to Buddhist life as to that of some other religious traditions, there are some 50 Buddhist monasteries and temples in the UK.

The first Hindu temple, or mandir, was opened in London in the 1950s and there are now over 140 mandirs in the UK; many are affiliated to the National Council of Hindu Temples (UK). The Swaminarayan Hindu Temple, in north London, is the first purpose-built Hindu temple in Europe, having a large cultural complex with provision for conferences, exhibitions, marriages, sports and health clinics.

Jewish synagogues in the UK number slightly fewer than 300, a lower figure than the number of congregations.

There are over 1,000 mosques and numerous community Muslim centres throughout the UK. Mosques are not only places of worship; they also offer instruction in the Muslim way of life and facilities for education and welfare. Mosques range from converted buildings in many towns to the Central Mosque in Regent's Park, London, and its associated Islamic Cultural Centre. The main conurbations in the Midlands, North West and North East of England, and in Scotland also have their own central mosques with a range of community facilities.

The largest gurdwara, or Sikh temple, in the UK is situated in Southall, Middlesex.

Gurdwaras cater for the religious, educational, welfare and cultural needs of their community. A granthi is usually employed to take care of the building and to conduct prayers. There are over 200 gurdwaras in the UK, the vast majority being in England and Wales.

A new use has been found for Anglican church steeples. Mobile telephone companies have, by agreement with individual parishes, recently placed telephone aerials on a number of church steeples, generating income in the form of annual rent for the churches concerned. The Archbishop's Council is considering proposals for a national scheme which would increase the number of aerials on churches, while ensuring that installations are made to the highest aesthetic and environmental standards.

CEREMONIES MARKING LIFE EVENTS

Historically, one of the major roles of religion has been to commemorate as a community the birth, marriage and death of members of that community. The state and organisations such as the British Humanist Society have long offered a secular alternative for marriage. Some local authorities offer a secular alternative for celebrating births. Secular funerals and memorial meetings can also be held.

In 1999, 179,000 people were baptised in the Church of England's two provinces, excluding the Diocese in Europe; of these, 126,000 were under one year old. In the same year there were 37,000 confirmations. In 1999 there were over 67,000 baptisms in the Catholic Church in Great Britain and almost 6,000 adults became Catholics. Over 67,000 marriages were solemnised in 1999 in the Church of England and Church in Wales. There were over 12,000 Catholic weddings and 14,000 nonconformist weddings in England and Wales during the same year. Religious ceremonies in 1999 in England and Wales accounted for fewer than two-fifths of marriages, compared with just over half in 1991.

Traditionally, deaths have been followed by a burial ceremony. However, as UK cemeteries have grown increasingly overcrowded, cremation ceremonies, whether religious or secular, have become more common. In 2000 an estimated 72% of all deaths resulted in cremation. Concerns about future land-use have also led to an increasing number of burials in 'green' cemeteries, with minimal disruption to the countryside and a greater use of biodegradable coffins.

Hindus, Sikhs and Muslims likewise commemorate the birth, marriage and death of their community members, together with other rites of passage. The Jewish bar mitzvah for boys and bat mitzvah for girls are coming of age ceremonies for children approaching adulthood.

RELIGION AND SOCIETY

The influence of Christianity and other religions in the UK has always extended far beyond the comparatively narrow spheres of organised and private worship. Churches and cathedrals make a significant contribution to the architectural landscape of the nation. Religious organisations are actively involved in voluntary work and the provision of social services—many schools and hospitals, for example, were founded by men and women who were strongly influenced by Christian motives. Easter and Christmas, the two most important events in the Christian calendar, are the year's major public holidays. Festivals and other events observed by other religions—such as Diwali (Hindu), Ramadan (Muslim), Vaisakhi (Sikh) and Passover (Jewish)—are adding to the visible diversity of life in the UK today

The moral codes of behaviour associated with many religions have helped to determine how young people are educated. The way individuals dress, eat, express themselves artistically and view themselves as belonging to an immediate community can often be derived from, and inspired by, a particular religious tradition.

Art

All major world religions have been a rich source of inspiration for art and artists, and public interest in religious art shows no sign of diminishing. 'Seeing Salvation', a major exhibition held in the National Gallery in London, was the most visited show in 2000 of all the major galleries and museums of Great Britain, and the fourth most visited in the world. There was an exhibition 'Arts of the Sikh Kingdoms' at the Victoria and Albert Museum in 1999 and one on Jainism in 1998. Regular annual events such as the Islam Awareness Week help to promote the social, cultural and artistic contribution of British Muslims.

Religious Education

In England and Wales all state schools must provide religious education, each local education authority being responsible for producing a locally agreed syllabus. Syllabuses must reflect Christianity, while taking account of the teaching and practices of the other principal religions represented in the UK. State schools must provide a daily act of collective worship. Parents may withdraw their children from religious education.

The vast majority of the maintained schools that have a religious character are either Anglican (nearly 4,700 schools) or Catholic (around 2,100 schools). In addition, there is a well-established tradition of Methodist and Jewish schools, with about 30 schools provided by each. Recently the Government has helped set up, and given support to, a number of schools reflecting other religious traditions—Greek Orthodox, Muslim, Seventh-day Adventist and Sikh. All the churches and faith groups involved with the provision of these schools have organisations at national or regional level to provide support and help when opportunities arise to promote new schools.

In Scotland, education authorities must ensure that schools provide religious education and regular opportunities for religious observance. The law does not specify the form of religious education, but it is recommended that pupils should be provided with a broad-based curriculum, through which they can develop a knowledge and understanding of Christianity and other world religions, and develop their own beliefs, attitudes and moral values and practices.

In Northern Ireland a core syllabus for religious education has been approved by the main churches and this must be taught in all state schools. Integrated education is encouraged and all schools must be open to pupils of all religions, although in practice most Catholic pupils attend Catholic maintained or Catholic voluntary grammar schools, and most Protestant children are enrolled at controlled schools or non-denominational voluntary grammar schools. However, the number of inter-denominational schools is increasing. In 2000–01, over 13,800 primary and secondary school pupils received their education at 'integrated' schools not attached to any particular religion.

Welfare

Charitable concern is a feature of many religions. There are currently over 3,000 charities (see p. 122) with religious connections helping to translate charitable concern into charitable action, usually involving some sort of practical or financial help given by the charity to those in need. Around two-thirds of such charities have a Christian connection, such as Oxfam or CAFOD, but there are also many Jewish and Islamic charities operating within this sector. Muslim Aid and Islamic Relief are two British Muslim charities that organise appeals and deliver relief aid globally.

Within the UK the Salvation Army is the largest, most diverse provider of social services after the Government. It is one of the biggest providers of hostel accommodation, offering over 3,000 beds every night. Other services include work with alcoholics, prison chaplaincy and a family-tracing service which receives 5,000 enquiries each year. The Quakers have a long tradition of social concern and peacemaking.

The Church of England's Church Urban Fund is an independent charity which raises money to enable those living in the most disadvantaged urban areas to set up local projects to help alleviate the effects of poverty. These projects help support a wide range of community-based programmes concerned with issues such as education, employment, young people and poverty. Although rooted in the Christian faith, the Fund does not restrict its grants on the basis of religious belief. By 2001 it had made grants totalling £37 million to nearly 2,900 different projects.

The General Assembly of the Church of Scotland debates annual reports from its Committee on Church and Nation, on social, economic and political matters; and, through its Board of Social Responsibility, it is the largest voluntary social work agency in Scotland. The Board currently runs more than 80 projects offering care and support to over 4,000 people every day. Churches in Wales and Northern Ireland, and other faith communities also have a concern for social issues.

In England, the Inner Cities Religious Council, based in the Department for Transport, Local Government and the Regions, provides a forum in which the Government and the faith communities work together on issues relating to urban policy. Chaired by a government minister, the Council comprises senior leaders of the Christian, Hindu, Jewish, Muslim and Sikh faiths. The Churches Regional Network coordinates church involvement in Regional Development Agencies and Regional Assemblies. Churches in Scotland have created a Scottish Churches Parliamentary Office for formal representation of their interests in the new Scottish Parliament. In Wales, the churches have worked together to appoint a Churches National Assembly Liaison Officer to relate to the National Assembly for Wales.

> December 2000 saw the end of the Jubilee 2000 coalition in the UK, a group of over 100 national and regional organisations, including many churches and other religious groups. It campaigned for 100% cancellation of the debts of the world's poorest countries and was influential in persuading the G7 countries (see p. 76) to promise to do so. Jubilee 2000 was succeeded by the Jubilee Debt Campaign, a similar coalition that aims to build upon the work of its predecessor.

COOPERATION BETWEEN RELIGIONS

The Inter Faith Network for the United Kingdom links a wide range of organisations with an interest in inter-faith relations, including the representative bodies of the Bahá'í , Buddhist, Christian, Hindu, Jain, Jewish, Muslim, Sikh and Zoroastrian communities. The Network promotes good relations between faiths in the UK, and runs a public advice and information service on inter-faith issues. The Council of Christians and Jews works for better understanding among members of these two religions and deals with educational and social issues. The Three Faiths Forum and the Calamus Foundation have as their focus relationships between the Christian, Jewish and Muslim traditions. There are many other organisations in the UK dealing wholly, or in part, with inter-faith issues.

Churches Together in Britain and Ireland (see pp. 239–40) has a Commission on Inter Faith Relations. The Interfaith Unit of the Islamic Foundation was set up with the specific aim of developing better relations between the Muslim and Christian traditions.

Further Reading

UK Christian Handbook 2000/2001, ed. Peter Brierley and Heather Wraight. Harper Collins.

UK Christian Handbook—Religious Trends 2000/2001, No. 2, ed. Peter Brierley. Paternoster Publishing.

Religions in the UK Directory, 2001–03, ed. Paul Weller, Religious Resource and Research Centre at the University of Derby and The Inter Faith Network for the United Kingdom, 2001.

16 Culture

Introduction	247	Visual Arts	259
Administration	248	The Written Word	262
Finance	251	Libraries and Archives	262
Cultural Events	254	Education and Training	264
Live Performance	255	Awards	266
Broadcast Performance and Film	258	Audiences and Expenditure	266

Culture makes an important contribution to the wider economy in the United Kingdom. Arts and culture are a major influence on business location and tourism. The arts are seen by the Government as having a role in helping to lift personal and community self-esteem, and in developing skills and confidence that open up wider economic and social opportunities.

INTRODUCTION

The United Kingdom has a diverse cultural heritage. It is the birthplace of Shakespeare, Jane Austen, Burns, Elgar, Constable and numerous other men and women who have contributed over the centuries to the growth of a rich, complex and eclectic cultural tradition. Culture in the UK is forward-looking too, with many artists and performers currently working in the sector seeking out innovative ways of expressing themselves. As a nation, the appetite for culture remains undimmed, with more people spending more on cultural leisure and entertainment services than ever before. Many people come from abroad to visit the UK for cultural reasons. Collections in the UK's museums and galleries are among the best in the world. British popular music has enjoyed considerable success at home and overseas.

Increasingly, however, 'culture' extends far beyond the traditional participation of an individual at a formal cultural event. The communication and enjoyment of personal and imaginative experiences can take place at school, at home, in a street or community festival, or even in the workplace.

The Indian Mahila Cultural Committee in Glasgow and the Scottish African and Caribbean Resource Centre celebrate the richness and diversity of contemporary culture in the United Kingdom. CADMAD[1] runs a cultural diversity training programme for artists and arts organisations. Measures to foster cultural diversity in Northern Ireland include funding for arts in both the Irish language and Ulster Scots language. A feature of the richness of cultural life in the United Kingdom has been the growth of Caribbean carnival, of which the most famous is the annual Notting Hill Carnival, the largest street festival in Europe. The Regional Black Theatre Initiative, Kuumba, an arts centre in Bristol, takes part in youth projects with the Bristol Old Vic.

The personal and imaginative experiences of other voices in society are also encouraged.

[1] Cardiff and District Multicultural Arts Development.

National Disability Arts Forum and other similar national agencies are funded by the Arts Council of England (ACE), as are creative organisations, such as Candoco Dance Company, composed of disabled and non-disabled dancers, and Graeae, a theatre company promoting performers with disabilities. Dance Division is another group looking to push back the boundaries of what is commonly understood as performing art, offering trainee footballers new approaches to movement and fitness.

Innovations

The Government's 24-hour Museum website (*www.24hourmuseum.org.uk*), which provides a gazetteer of all UK museums and galleries, a magazine, search facilities and educational resources, receives about 300,000 'hits' a month. SCRAN (*www.scran.ac.uk*), the Scottish Cultural Resources Access Network, is a history and culture site providing access to images, movies, sounds and virtual reality records from museums, galleries, archives and media.

Cultureonline (*www.cultureonline.gov.uk*), another government Internet initiative, which was launched in September 2000, will eventually act as one of the main sources of information about cultural events across the United Kingdom, as well as being an educational tool. After a consultation period, a full business case for Cultureonline will be produced, which will form the basis of a bid to the Capital Modernisation Fund (see p. 400). It is proposed that the new service will be set up and run by a new autonomous body, to be established as a company limited by guarantee. Its position will be regularised as a statutory body at the first legislative opportunity.

A growing number of operas, concerts, ballets and plays can now be viewed via the Online Classics webpage (*www.onlineclassics.net*). The British Library has put on its Internet catalogue details of more than 10 million documents from the past 500 years, including books, journals and reports. The National Library of Wales has established a substantial digitisation programme in order to make available online copies of large numbers of items from its collections. The expansion of cultural experiences communicated via the Internet remains a potentially enormous growth area, although there are copyright difficulties associated with posting such information on the Internet which have yet to be fully addressed.

ADMINISTRATION

The expression of creativity is first and foremost a personal or group activity, but there is an official and commercial side to culture too. Many artists and performers engaged in cultural activity rely on subsidies and funding from government and other patrons of the arts. The Government has a role in protecting the rights of authors through copyright legislation (see p. 251); providing a regulatory framework for cultural activities in areas such as film classification (see p. 251); and encouraging greater public participation in the arts. Public sector involvement in the arts is expressed in a number of different ways: through the work of the four Administrations directly responsible for culture in England, Wales, Scotland and Northern Ireland; through local government support for local initiatives (see p. 250); or through intermediate groups such as the Arts Councils (see pp. 249–50), which act independently from the Government but are nonetheless publicly funded and take on the role of patrons of the arts.

UK and England

The Department for Culture, Media and Sport (DCMS) has policy responsibilities within government for the arts, broadcasting, the built heritage, creative industries, film, museums, galleries and libraries, the National Lottery (see p. 123), press freedom and regulation, sport and tourism, along with new areas of responsibility that include film and video classification.

The DCMS's stated aim is to improve the quality of life for all through cultural activities and to strengthen the creative industries. The Department, in partnership with others, works to:

- create an efficient and competitive market by removing obstacles to growth and unnecessary regulation so as to promote Britain's success in the fields of culture, media, sport and tourism, both in the UK and abroad;

- broaden access to cultural events and to the built environment;
- raise the standards of cultural education and training;
- ensure that everyone has the opportunity to achieve excellence in areas of culture and to develop talent, innovation and good design; and
- maintain public support for the National Lottery and ensure that the objective of the Lottery Fund supports DCMS and other national priorities.

Future plans under consideration by the DCMS include:

- the creation of new regional centres of excellence, involving greater partnership between national and regional museums and galleries; and
- the piloting of plans for local authorities to draw up cultural strategies appropriate for their area.

> As part of its commitment to encourage greater participation in the arts, the Government will enable museums to recover VAT (value added tax) on their purchases under a scheme which makes it possible (subject to the agreement of the trustees of the museums and galleries concerned) for a scrapping of all entry charges on the major collections (see p. 259) to take effect from December 2001. In Scotland admission to the National Galleries of Scotland is free of charge, and the Scottish Executive made provision for the National Museums of Scotland to abolish admission charges from 1 April 2001.

Other national organisations acting in an advisory capacity are:

- the Creative Industries Task Force, which was set up in 1998 to identify issues vital to the economic health of the creative industries. It has organised a work programme covering skills development, access to capital, intellectual property, export promotion, regional activity, and the UK's image overseas;
- the Quality, Efficiency and Standards Team (QUEST), which monitors financial management across DCMS sectors; and
- the Music Industry Forum, a DCMS initiative which works closely with interested parties and trade associations to identify what can be done to improve the economic performance of the music industry.

Wales

The National Assembly for Wales has responsibility for the arts in Wales, including museums, galleries and libraries. Responsibility for funding and developing the arts in Wales falls to the Arts Council of Wales (ACW). ACW launched its Cultural Diversity Strategy in the summer of 2001. The Council's work includes support for events such as the Hay Festival of Literature and organisations such as Welsh National Opera. The promotion of the Welsh language and support for the National Eisteddfod is the responsibility of the Welsh Language Board.

Scotland

The Scottish Executive published a National Cultural Strategy in August 2000, providing additional funding for the arts in Scotland, promoting Scotland's languages and cultural heritage, and developing further the work started by the three-year Scotland Onstage initiative towards the goal of a fully fledged national theatre. Other plans to promote culture in Scotland include the building of a 'creative media campus' on Tayside, a hub for Scotland's flourishing computer games industry, which will provide employment for designers and other creative talent.

Northern Ireland

'To the Millennium: A Strategy for the Arts in Northern Ireland', a five-year plan for the arts, produced jointly by the Northern Ireland

Arts Council and its parent organisation at the time, the Department of Education, has provided the basis for planning in the arts, outlining goals for achieving wider community participation and encouraging greater access in all aspects of cultural activity. Since devolution, responsibility for the arts has been taken over by the Department of Culture, Arts and Leisure. An independent report 'Opening up the Arts' was published in May 2000, providing the basis for directions in arts policy up to 2006. Practical plans for boosting culture in Northern Ireland include the construction of major theatres and arts centres in Cookstown, Ballymena and Omagh.

Local Authorities

Although policy is worked out by the four UK administrations, many new initiatives are carried out at a local level. Local authorities maintain about 1,000 museums and art galleries, and a network of public libraries. They also provide grant aid for professional and amateur orchestras, theatres, and opera and dance companies. Fourteen authorities are piloting Local Cultural Strategies, a DCMS scheme to bring cultural issues into the heart of local government planning. The Greater London Authority (see p. 9) will prepare a cultural strategy and proposes to introduce a Capital Culture Card, allowing students, pensioners and the unemployed to attend theatres, cinemas and concerts at reduced rates.

The Arts Councils

The independent Arts Councils of England, Scotland, Wales and Northern Ireland are the main channels for the distribution of government grants and Lottery funding to the visual, performing and community arts and to literature. They act as national 'champions' of the arts and give financial assistance and advice not only to the major performing arts organisations, but also to small touring theatre companies, experimental performance groups and literary organisations. They provide funds for training arts administrators and help to develop sponsorship and local authority support. In addition to promoting education and public access to, and participation in, performing and visual arts and literature, the Arts Councils commission research into the impact of the arts on society and develop forward strategies.

ACE funds the major national arts-producing organisations in England—including the Royal Opera, the Royal Ballet, the Birmingham Royal Ballet, English National Opera (ENO), the Royal Shakespeare Company (RSC), the Royal National Theatre (RNT) and the South Bank Centre—and the main touring companies, such as Opera North and English National Ballet.

The year 2000 was designated Year of the Artist by ACE, with 1,000 artists given residencies in 1,000 places across England. Residencies ranged from sound artist Kate Tierney working on the Radio 4 programme *Today*, to the Cornelius Cardew ensemble creating a pub opera at the Miller's Arms in Canterbury (Kent). The Scottish Arts Council operated a similar scheme with 100 artists in residence, including Barnaby Brown recording Gaelic choirs from Skye in a series of sea-caves.

Resource: the Council of Museums, Archives and Libraries

Resource is the strategic agency working with, and on behalf of, museums, archives and libraries across the UK; it replaced the Museums and Galleries Commission in April 2000. It also provides funds to the seven English Area Museum Councils, which supply services and their own small grants to individual museums, the Museum Documentation Association and to the Cultural Heritage National Training Organisation. Resource advises ministers on the Acceptance in Lieu (AIL) scheme, whereby pre-eminent works of art may be accepted by the Government in settlement of tax and allocated to public galleries. A review of the scheme in 2001 found there was scope for promoting greater public awareness of AIL, and recommended the establishment of a new fast-track claims procedure to reduce processing delays.

Film Council and *bfi*

The Film Council, which came into being in April 2000, channels the majority of public funding for film production in the UK. It has a wide remit, with both cultural and industry objectives: to develop film culture in the UK, and to create a coherent structure for the UK film industry. The Council also helps to fund the British Film Office in Los Angeles, which acts as an information service to promote both British exports and the advantages of British studios to US film-makers. Recently, the responsibilities of the British Film Office were broadened to include television programmes and commercials.

The moving image as an art form is promoted by the British Film Institute (*bfi*), Scottish Screen, the Northern Ireland Film Commission and Sgrîn, the Media Agency for Wales. The *bfi* has an extensive library and runs a number of film festivals, including the London Film Festival. It also supports a new UK cinema exhibition strategy to bring non-mainstream films into high street multiplexes, and gives financial assistance to a network of independent cinemas across the UK. Its educational activities include courses, conferences and other events, and helping to formulate national film education policy.

Cinema Licensing and Film Classification

Public cinemas must be licensed by local authorities, which have a legal duty to prohibit the admission of children to unsuitable films, and may prevent the showing of any picture. In assessing films the authorities normally rely on the judgment of an independent non-statutory body, the British Board of Film Classification (BBFC), to which all items must be submitted. Films passed by the BBFC are put into one of the following categories:

- U (universal), suitable for all;
- PG (parental guidance), in which some scenes may be unsuitable for young children;
- 12, 15 and 18, for people of not less than those ages; and
- Restricted 18, for restricted showing only at premises to which no one under 18 is admitted, for example, licensed cinema clubs.

The BBFC is also legally responsible for classifying videos under a system similar to that for films. It is an offence to supply commercially a video which has not been classified or to supply it in contravention of its designation.

Authors' Copyright and Performers' Protection

Original literary, dramatic, musical or artistic works (including computer programs and databases), films, sound recordings, cable programmes, broadcasts and the typographical arrangement of published editions are automatically protected by copyright in the UK if they meet the legal requirements for protection. The copyright owner has rights against unauthorised reproduction, distribution, public performance, rental, broadcasting and adaptation of his or her work (including putting material on the Internet without permission). In most cases the author is the first owner of the copyright, and the term of copyright in literary, dramatic, musical and artistic works is generally the life of the author and a period of 70 years. There are similar rules governing copyright on films. Sound recordings and broadcasts are protected for a period of 50 years.

British Council

The British Council (see p. 97) is the UK's international organisation for educational and cultural relations. It works in 243 cities in 111 countries to promote international understanding of British creativity in the arts, literature and design, as well as education, good governance and science. It aims to present a modern and culturally diverse picture of the UK. In 2000 it supported some 3,000 cultural events overseas. The Visiting Arts Office of Great Britain and Northern Ireland is a joint venture of the British Council with the Foreign & Commonwealth Office and the Arts Councils. It encourages the inward flow to the UK of arts from other countries.

FINANCE

In England planned central government expenditure through the DCMS in 2001–02 amounts to £246 million for museums and galleries; £253 million distributed through the Arts Council for England for the visual and performing arts; and £115 million for libraries and archives.

Planned 2001–02 expenditure by the Arts Councils for Scotland, Wales and Northern Ireland is respectively £34.8 million, £16.6 million and £7.4 million. The Scottish Executive is also providing £41 million for Scotland's National Galleries and Museums, and National Library, while the National Assembly for Wales is giving £23.2 million for Wales's National Museum, National Library and other arts. Total planned spending by the Department of Culture, Arts and Leisure in Northern Ireland on the National Museums (see p. 261), arts and libraries amounts to just over £43.3 million in 2001–02.

Figure 16.1: Arts Council of England Funding, 1999–2000

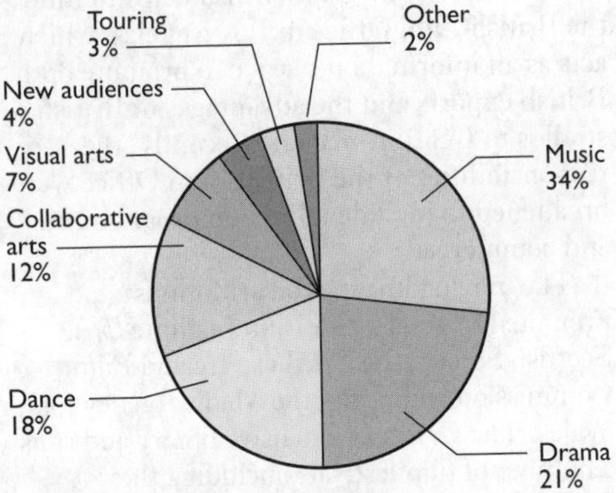

Source: Arts Council of England

National Lottery

By December 2000, Lottery awards of over £1.47 billion had been announced by the Arts Council of England for arts projects. Between June 1995 and April 2000, grants for the acquisition of works of art from the Heritage Lottery Fund (HLF—see p. 322) to museums, galleries and other organisations amounted to £1.57 billion.

By August 2001 UK museums and galleries were estimated to have benefited from £656 million of Heritage Lottery Fund money, as well as £117 million from the Millennium Commission. Recent Arts Lottery grants have included nearly £16 million to the New Art Gallery, Walsall, and £20 million to the new Milton Keynes Theatre and Art Gallery. Heritage Lottery grants included £15 million to the development of Manchester's City Art Gallery and £11.9 million to the new wing of the National Portrait Gallery. Scottish Arts Council lottery grants included £7 million for the Centre for Contemporary Arts in Glasgow.

Nesta

The National Endowment for Science, Technology and the Arts has initial finance of £200 million from the National Lottery. It aims to help talented individuals or groups to develop their full potential; to turn creativity into exploitable or commercial products and services with protected rights, and to contribute to public knowledge and appreciation of science, technology and the arts. It grants fellowships worth up to £75,000 spread over a fellowship of three to five years, with around 40 awards made each year.

Business and Other Sponsorship

Total UK business investment in the arts in 1999–2000 was over £150 million. London attracted most of the investment—£80 million—followed by Scotland and the West Midlands. Museums and galleries received £12 million each, drama and theatre received £7 million, music £8 million, festivals £6.6 million and opera £2.4 million. As one example, HSBC, one of the UK's largest banks, is giving £1.5 million over three years to the National Youth Theatre, the National Youth Orchestra, the National Youth Ballet and the National Opera Studio.

Arts & Business promotes and encourages partnerships between business and the arts. It has over 350 business members and manages the Arts & Business New Partners Programme on behalf of ACE and the DCMS. Under the programme, investments can be made in arts/business partnerships, which bring benefits to both parties. Arts & Business New Partners was launched in April 2000, replacing the former Pairing Scheme, which raised £10 million from business and contributed over £160 million (including £52 million from the Government) to the arts over 16 years. Arts & Business also runs the Arthur Andersen Skills Bank and the NatWest Board Bank, which enable 3,000 volunteers from companies to loan their skills, in computing, accountancy, marketing or personnel, to local arts groups on a part-time basis.

The Corporation of London, the local authority for the City of London, is one of the largest sponsors of the arts in the UK, with a budget of £56 million in 2001–02. The Corporation owns, funds and manages the Barbican Centre (Europe's largest multi-arts and conference centre), which has the London Symphony Orchestra as resident and presents an international theatre programme; owns, funds and manages the Guildhall School of Music and Drama; jointly funds and manages the Museum of London with the DCMS; and funds various other cultural activities.

Among sponsorship from charitable trusts, the Jerwood Foundation gave over £5.5 million a year in capital and revenue grants in 2000, with emphasis on encouraging young performers. In January 2000 the Foundation pledged £500,000 over five years to the Young Singers Programme at English National Opera. In addition to its £3 million towards the renewal of the Royal Court Theatre in London, it plans to continue with revenue funding for the theatre of up to £100,000 a year, providing it produces new plays by young writers. The Arvon Foundation, a charitable trust which also attracts sponsorship from the private sector, runs residential courses for new writers, attracting over 1,000 students a year.

Approximately £3 million from the Foundation for Sport and the Arts, run by the Pools Promoters Association, was used to help the arts in 2000 in the form of awards. Many arts organisations also benefit from the fund-raising activities of friends, groups and from private individuals' financial support. For example, theatre companies have traditionally relied on the support of 'angels', individual sponsors putting up often quite small amounts of money to meet the costs of putting on a show, and subsequently recouping their investment from box office proceeds.

Sector Finance

Museums and galleries maintained by local authorities, universities and independent or privately funded bodies may receive help in building up their collections through grants through Area Museum Councils—throughout the UK—which are funded by Resource: the Council of Museums, Archives and Libraries. Support to national and regional public and independent museums and galleries is also given by the Arts Councils and by trusts, voluntary bodies, the Heritage Lottery Fund and the National Art Collections Fund.

Government help for the film industry allows a 100% tax write-off on the production and acquisition costs for British movies with budgets of up to £15 million.

The Film Council will be responsible for distributing £150 million of Lottery and government grant to the UK film industry during 2000–03.The Council's New Cinema Fund will make £1.5 million available to radical and innovative film-makers looking to use the latest digital technology. Its £10 million Premiere Production Fund is geared towards the making of popular mainstream films and the £5 million Film Development Fund will be targeted at the pre-production stage of film-making. The Film Council has absorbed the British Film Commission, whose aim has been to attract foreign film-making and production investment into the UK, and British Screen Finance, a private sector company which previously provided funding to British productions and co-productions. The Council has earmarked 20% of its production funds for encouraging European co-productions. It also funds the British Film Institute (*bfi*; see p. 251) to deliver its cultural and educational objectives and has fully absorbed *bfi* Production.

In 2000–01 ACE spent more than £50 million on support for drama, including regional theatre—21% of ACE's total grant. New funding announced in early 2001 made

London Underground is becoming an increasingly popular location for film-makers, a popularity that has been boosted by the commercial success of recent films such as *Sliding Doors*. In 1999 London Underground received over 200 filming requests, and provided some scenes for the hit film *Billy Elliott*. Canary Wharf station was the most popular for film-makers because of its futuristic appeal. A record 28 feature films produced by foreign production teams were made in Britain in 2000 with budgets totalling £366 million.

an extra £25 million available for theatre companies, spread over two financial years. Nearly 200 individual venues are to benefit from substantial increases in their grants, and 85 touring companies will share over £4 million. The Arts Council of Wales has established Clwyd Theatr Cymru as a Wales National Performing Arts Company, supported major building work at the Grand Theatre in Swansea, and funded new equipment at the Sherman Theatre in Cardiff.

CULTURAL EVENTS

Since the end of the 19th century the means of cultural expression have rapidly expanded from their traditional roots, as practitioners of the arts have exploited the opportunities presented by new media—cinema, radio, television, electronics and the Internet. Continuing technological development and innovative work from artists have helped blur distinctions between traditional art forms and created richer and more diverse outlets for the communication of cultural experiences. The most recent Turner Prize winner, a competition traditionally reserved for artists, was a photographer; even theatre, one of the most traditional of art forms, can now be directly experienced online.

Arts Centres

Over 200 arts centres in the UK give people the chance of seeing a range of art forms and taking part in activities, especially educational projects. Nearly all the centres are professionally managed, while using the services of volunteers. They are assisted mainly by the Arts Councils, and local authorities, while ACE currently funds two centres in London—the South Bank Centre and the Institute of Contemporary Arts—the latter being popular for its art films and avant-garde exhibitions. The Pier Arts Centre at Stromness (Orkney) and Dundee Contemporary Arts (which has two galleries, two cinemas, a print studio and activity rooms) are two of the centres supported by the Scottish Arts Council. Among other centres, the Arts Council of Wales funds Chapter Arts Centre in Cardiff and the Aberystwyth Arts Centre, which helps to promote international artists and collaborations.

Festivals

Some 500 professional arts festivals take place in the UK each year. Their appeal has broadened; for example, whereas classical music once dominated music festivals, there are now those that offer jazz, folk, pop, rock, world and early music as well. Sixty or so festivals concentrate on poetry, and other festivals are devoted to the visual arts, such as the Liverpool Biennial.

The 2001 Edinburgh International Festival featured some 180 performances of music, theatre, opera and dance, as well as lectures and discussions. Performances included Sir Charles Mackerras conducting the Scottish Chamber Orchestra and Chorus with the BT Scottish Ensemble in a programme of Handel concerti and Wagner's *Die Walküre*, performed by Scottish Opera. The Edinburgh Festival Fringe, with programmes (including street events) to suit all tastes, takes place alongside the main events. In recent years it has proved a fertile training ground for comedians and actors who have progressed to successful careers elsewhere. In 2001 the Fringe hosted over 1,462 performances by 666 different companies. Other annual Edinburgh events include the International Film Festival, the International Book Festival and the international Jazz and Blues Festival.

The 53rd Aldeburgh Festival in 2001 included Janáček piano recitals by Thomas

Adès, and performances of Beethoven and Shostakovich by the Borodin String Quartet. The Hay festival, held in Hay-on-Wye, originally focusing on literature—the town is renowned for its second-hand bookshops—has broadened its range in recent years and its programme in 2001 included appearances by best-selling author Louis de Bernières, rock band Pulp and former US President Bill Clinton. Film festivals include the annual London Film Festival, the 45th in 2001, and newer festivals such as the Leeds Children's Film Festival and the Brief Encounters short film festival in Bristol.

LIVE PERFORMANCE

Drama

Some of the UK's 300 professional theatres are privately owned, but most belong to local authorities or to not-for-profit organisations.

In England, the Royal National Theatre (RNT) on the South Bank in London relies in part on public subsidy for support, allowing it to take greater artistic risks and offer cheaper tickets than unsubsidised theatres in London's West End. Under the directorship of Trevor Nunn, recent plays produced at the RNT have included the revival of musicals such as *Oklahoma!* and the staging of work such as Michael Frayn's *Copenhagen*.

Elsewhere in London, revivals of classic musicals such as *The King and I* and *My Fair Lady* (with Martine McCutcheon in the starring role) have proved a success. Other, more literary, lower-budget plays such as the comedy *Stones in their Pockets*, by Marie Jones, have proved popular with audiences too. The Almeida Theatre, one of London's leading independent venues, closed briefly for refurbishment in 2001, and reopened in temporary accommodation with a staging of Wedekind's masterpiece *Lulu* at a refashioned disused coach depot in King's Cross. Productions from the Donmar Warehouse, another leading West End theatre, included a revival of Christopher Hampton's *Tales from*

Selection of Arts Events, 2002

Aldeburgh Festival, Suffolk—music, visual arts, film
Belfast Festival at Queen's University
Brecon Jazz Festival
Brighton Festival—the largest in England, including theatre, music, opera and street arts
Chelsea Crafts Fair
Cheltenham International Music Festival
Edinburgh International Festival—opera, dance, theatre, music, and the Fringe; also Edinburgh International Book and Film Festivals
Glyndebourne Festival—opera
Henry Wood Promenade Concerts ('the Proms') at the Royal Albert Hall, London
Knebworth, Hertfordshire—rock festival
London Book Fair
London Film Festival, hosted by the *bfi*, which shows some 250 new international films
Notting Hill Carnival
Royal National Eisteddfod, alternating each year in south and north Wales
RSC Summer Festival, at Stratford-upon-Avon
Salisbury Festival—various events, including sculpture and street arts
Singer of the World Competition in Cardiff
Spitalfields Festival, London—music
T in the Park, Perthshire—rock festival
Urdd National Eisteddfod—Europe's largest youth arts festival, held at a different location around Wales each year
WOMAD at Reading—festival of world music and dance.

Hollywood and *Boston Marriage*, by David Mamet. The 2001 season of the Globe Theatre—a reconstruction of Shakespeare's playhouse—featured *King Lear*, *Cymbeline* and *Umabatha*, the Zulu Macbeth. The Royal Shakespeare Company, based at Stratford-upon-Avon, presents spring and autumn seasons of Shakespeare's plays in a repertory programme.

Northern Ireland has six major theatre spaces, including the Opera House and the recently opened Waterfront Hall; and several young theatre companies—among them Tinderbox Theatre, specialising in small-scale productions of new work. In Scotland, the Royal Lyceum Theatre and King's and Festival Theatres in Edinburgh, and the Citizen's Theatre Glasgow, all have full programmes covering a wide range of productions—the spring season at Citizen's featured a Borderline Theatre Company production of Marie Jones' comedy *Women on the Verge of HRT*. The Traverse Theatre in Edinburgh is Scotland's leading centre for new writing. The Sherman Theatre in Wales has a specific mission of attracting younger audiences, and recently staged *Everything Must Go* by Patrick Jones, featuring musical contributions from the successful Welsh pop group Manic Street Preachers.

Music

Orchestral and Choral Music

London leads the world in its wide range of music available throughout the year. In classical music alone, there are four symphony orchestras with public subsidy, two more at the BBC, one at English National Opera and one at Covent Garden. The largest of these, the London Symphony Orchestra, performs at the Barbican. Recent concerts by English orchestras at the Royal Festival Hall were given by the Philharmonia, the London Philharmonic (under its new principal director Kurt Masur), the BBC Symphony (under Andrew Davis), and the City of Birmingham Symphony. The smaller Queen Elizabeth Hall featured the Orchestra of the Age of Enlightenment and chamber groups: the London Mozart Players, the Academy of St Martin-in-the-Fields and the English Chamber Orchestra. The Bournemouth Symphony, Manchester's Hallé Orchestra and the Royal Liverpool Philharmonic are other well-known and highly rated English orchestras.

The Royal Scottish National Orchestra and the Scottish Chamber Orchestra each give over 100 performances a year. The Ulster Orchestra, Northern Ireland's only fully professional orchestra, has established a world-class reputation under the artistic direction of conductors such as Vernon Handley and Dmitri Sitkovetsky. In Wales the BBC National Orchestra of Wales offers a year-round programme of orchestral and choral music featuring the BBC National Chorus of Wales.

English and Welsh choral societies have done much to foster the oratorio tradition at the leading music festivals. English ecclesiastical choral singing is a speciality of the choirs of cathedrals and Oxford and Cambridge colleges.

Two celebrated events in the musical calendar are the Leeds International Piano Competition for young pianists and the biennial Cardiff Singer of the World Competition, which attracts outstanding young singers, and distinguished adjudicators, from all countries. The 18-year-old cellist Guy Johnston won the biennial BBC Young Musicians contest in 2000.

Attendance at the 2000 Promenade Concerts (the 'Proms'), the world's largest music festival, was 89% of capacity, with attendance figures reaching 259,700. 'Pastoral' and 'Exile' were two themes linking performances in the 2001 season, which included new work commissioned from Sally Beamish, Alexander Goehr and Sir Harrison Birtwistle, and premières of material by Bernstein, Boulez and Tavener.

A number of classical musicians have in recent years achieved 'celebrity' status. The violinist Vanessa Mae has been making solo recordings and appearing at top international venues for the past decade. The tenor Russell Watson was, until recently, a relatively unknown singer. However, after an intensive television promotion campaign for his debut album 'The Voice', he became the top-selling classical performer of 2000. Charlotte Church, still only 15, has in recent years given many international concerts and achieved great popularity as a soprano, making her one of Britain's highest-paid entertainers. The repertoire, marketing, and celebrity appearances of classical artists have helped break down traditional barriers between hitherto distinct genres of classical and pop music.

Pop and Rock Music

The pop and rock music industry continues to thrive in the United Kingdom and has seen the continuing chart success of bands such as SClub7 and Steps—whose work is often characterised by the emphasis placed on dance routines in their live and video performances. One of the latest groups to emerge is the all-girl group Atomic Kitten, which has had two chart-topping singles in 2001. Craig David has won critical acclaim and achieved commercial success through his development of 'garage' music, an innovative soul sound.

> Hear'say, the winners of a musical talent competition on television, is one of the most notable new groups to emerge in 2001. In the course of the year, Hear'say became the first British band to top both album and single charts simultaneously with their debut releases. The band achieved instant success largely because it was selected in a series of ratings-topping, 'fly on the wall' television documentaries broadcast in autumn 2000.

In 2000–01 Welsh artists and bands made significant contributions to British pop, with the Stereophonics, Manic Street Preachers and Super Furry Animals achieving commercial success. Another success for the industry was the release of the greatest hits compilation album '*1*' of perennial favourites the Beatles, which sold over 20 million copies and reached the number one slot in the pop charts in over 30 countries.

Folk

Folk music has always been strong in all parts of the UK. In Northern Ireland, for example, bands perform in pubs and clubs, playing fiddles and other traditional Celtic instruments. Scottish and Welsh festivals honour Gaelic and Celtic music and song. The Scottish Arts Council highlights the diversity of Scottish traditional music: a CD, *Seriously Scottish*, places traditional music alongside contemporary forms. English morris dancing, in which traditional musical instruments and centuries-old dance forms are practised by groups or 'sides', remains popular since its revival in the 1970s and 1980s. Currently there are about 800 morris dancing sides in the United Kingdom.

Jazz and Blues

The Brecon, Cheltenham and London Jazz festivals, Edinburgh International Jazz and Blues Festival, and venues such as Ronnie Scott's in London's Soho have helped win new audiences for jazz in the UK and have shown how it can evolve when exposed to other musical influences, such as pop and Latin American, and how its rhythms can change. The 2001 Bishopstock Blues Festival, held in Devon in June, attracted artists from all over the world, including Booker T and the MGs, Johnny Winter and Nina Simone.

Opera

London's Royal Opera House (ROH) at Covent Garden reopened in December 1999 after a £214 million restoration and redevelopment. Recent performances include *Boulevard Solitude*, staged as a 75th birthday tribute to the German composer Hans Werner Henze. The English National Opera, Welsh National Opera and Scottish Opera companies all have international reputations.

Glyndebourne Opera (East Sussex), which relies on private patrons for its summer season, is another prestigious venue. One of its main season offerings in 2001 included traditional favourites in the operatic repertoire, *Fidelio* and *A Midsummer Night's Dream*. Other country house opera ventures include Garsington (Oxfordshire), where the stage is a garden terrace, Longborough (Gloucestershire) and Castleward Opera in County Down (Northern Ireland).

Dance

The Royal Ballet is to have an enhanced status and more performances at the ROH. In 2001 English National Ballet was at the Coliseum. Other important ballet companies include Birmingham Royal Ballet and Northern Ballet Theatre. Alongside traditional repertoires of classic ballet favourites such as Tchaikovsky, contemporary dance has grown in stature in recent years. Scottish Ballet has embarked on a new era of classical and contemporary dance, and Dance Base, Scotland's new national centre for dance, opened in Edinburgh in 2001. The Rambert Dance Company, Britain's oldest ballet troupe, has become known for its forward-looking creativity. It remains the UK's only large-scale contemporary dance repertory company, touring nationally and internationally. In 2001 it presented a programme of work in the intimate setting of Linbury Studio, London, featuring work from new choreographers—'Beach Birds' by Merce Cunningham and 'Hurricane' by Christopher Bruce. It also focuses on education and community work. Other dance companies with growing reputations are Spring Loaded and the Richard Alston Dance Company.

BROADCAST PERFORMANCE AND FILM

Television

Now that 99% of households own a television set, and the average person watches well over 20 hours of programmes a week (see p. 123), television has become an enormously popular medium for the communication of cultural experiences. Plays, films, 'soaps' (long running serials often focusing on family relationships) and specialist arts and music programmes—which might together be referred to as 'cultural' programmes in the traditional sense—form a significant part of the broadcasting output of many terrestrial, cable and satellite channels. However, the format of television programmes is constantly changing and in this medium the concept of culture has expanded beyond, or fused, traditional art forms. Many quiz shows and 'fly on the wall' documentaries, for example, have a strong cultural element, and the broadcast media are adept at combining popular and supposedly highbrow culture in a seamless and acceptable form for huge and varied audiences. For information on individual programmes broadcast on television, see p. 274.

Arts programmes broadcast by BBC radio and television and the independent companies have won many international awards, for example at the Prix Italia and Montreux International Television Festivals. Independent television companies give grants for arts promotion in their regions. The BBC plans to introduce a new digital television channel, BBC FOUR (see p. 272), with the specific aim of giving more primetime space to cultural debate.

Radio

The BBC broadcasts each week about 150 hours of classical and other music (both live and recorded) on Radio 3 (see p. 272). BBC Radio 1 broadcasts rock and pop music, and much of the output of BBC Radio 2 is popular and light music. Classic FM offers mainly classical and Virgin Radio plays rock. Much of the output of the UK's local radio stations is popular and light music, news and information. Radio 4's output is mainly talk-based and includes a wealth of drama, documentary discussions and full-length plays. Latest estimates indicate that radio programmes reach 92% of the adult population aged 15 and over, with BBC local and national stations taking just over half of the audience share. *The Archers*, Radio 4's serial chronicling the lives of a fictional rural community in the village of Ambridge, recently celebrated its 50th anniversary.

Film

At the end of 2000 there were 754 cinema sites in Great Britain and 3,017 screens. The average number of screens per site increased from just over three in 1993 to just over four in 2000, reflecting the growth in 'multiplex' (multi-screen cinema sites sometimes built in out-of town locations) which currently account for over half of all screens and over two-thirds of all admissions. More than £539 million was invested in the British production sector for films such as *Harry Potter and the Sorcerer's Stone*, *The Mummy Returns*, *Proof of Life*, and *Pearl Harbor*. Shepperton and Pinewood, two leading British film studios, merged at the start of 2001 in a move designed to strengthen the UK's production base, and attract more US investment.

Billy Elliott, a feature film about a working-class boy in the North East of England wishing to train as a professional ballet dancer, was one of the notable success stories of 2000 and the seventh most popular film in the United Kingdom, bringing in revenue of over £16 million at the box office. The top three films in 2000 in terms of box office revenue were *Toy Story 2* (US), *Gladiator* (US) and *Chicken Run* (a jointly funded, UK-US production).

VISUAL ARTS

Museums and Galleries

Over 80 million visits a year are made to the UK's 2,500 or so museums and galleries open to the public (in contrast to the 800 museums in 1980), which include the major national collections (permanent displays of art and artefacts), about 1,000 independent museums, and 800 receiving support from local authorities. The £15 million Designated Challenge Fund made its second round of awards in 2000. Nearly £7 million has so far been awarded to 62 institutions in England, to encourage them to raise their standards of collection care and access. Exhibitions in the form of smaller shows (often housed in the same building as the national collections) or less permanent displays of works of art also attract thousands of visitors.

Current exhibitions include *Paper Assets*, a wide-ranging collection of prints and drawings (including cigarette cards) at the British Museum; *Zero to Infinity*, *Arte Povera 1962–1972* at Tate Modern; new installations by Daphne Wright and retrospectives of established names such as Barbara Hepworth at the New Art Centre Sculpture Park and Gallery, Salisbury; *Rembrandt's Women* and *Lee Miller: the Photographer* at the National Galleries of Scotland; and an exhibition of Japanese woodblock prints at the National Museums and Galleries of Wales.

The English national museums and galleries are:

- British Museum, housing one of the most comprehensive collections of European and world culture. It also houses many documents relating to Britain's rich literary heritage.
- Natural History Museum.
- Victoria and Albert Museum (concentrating on fine and decorative arts).
- National Museum of Science & Industry, including the Science Museums in London and Wroughton, the National Railway Museum (York) and the National Museum of Photography, Film and Television (Bradford). Their exhibits commemorate the role played by the UK in the industrial and technological revolutions of the 19th and 20th centuries.
- National Gallery (Western painting from about 1260 to 1900)—a collection of worldwide importance, including the Leonardo da Vinci Cartoons and *The Haywain* by Constable.
- Tate Britain, devoted to British art since the 15th century, with additional collections in Liverpool and St Ives, Cornwall (St Ives School and modern art).
- Tate Modern (20th-century international art). Visitors at the recently opened former power station in London reached over 4 million in 2000, reflecting renewed public interest in modern art.
- National Portrait Gallery, containing pictures, sculptures and photographs of people who have shaped Britain's past.

The ten most popular art exhibitions (usually but not exclusively in galleries rather than museums) which took place in the United Kingdom in 2000 were as follows:

Exhibition	Location
Seeing Salvation: Images of Christ	National Gallery, London
Kingdom Come: Botticelli's Mystic Nativity	National Gallery, London
1900: Art at the Crossroads	Royal Academy of Arts, London
10 Religious Masterpieces	Laing Art Gallery, Newcastle upon Tyne
Art Nouveau 1890–1914	Victoria and Albert Museum, London
Cornelius Gijsbrecht	National Gallery, London
Chardin 1699–1779	Royal Academy of Arts, London
Apocalypse	Royal Academy of Arts, London
The Show: Design, Communications	Royal College of Art, London
Polly Borland: Australians	National Portrait Gallery, London

- Imperial War Museum, which has three sites in London and one at Duxford (which includes the American Air Museum) in Cambridgeshire.
- Royal Armouries, the UK's oldest museum, which has exhibits in the Tower of London (relating to the Tower's history), Leeds (arms and armour) and Fort Nelson, near Portsmouth (artillery).
- National Army Museum.
- Royal Air Force Museum.
- National Maritime Museum.
- Wallace Collection (paintings, furniture, arms and armour, and *objets d'art*).
- National Museums & Galleries on Merseyside.

The Royal Academy of Arts in London holds an annual Summer Exhibition (the 233rd in 2001) which is the world's largest open display of present-day art, and other important shows during the year. Anyone claiming the status of an artist of 'distinguished merit' and seeking 'reputation and encouragement' may submit works to the Summer Exhibition. In 2000, 1,516 were chosen, representing 628 artists, from an entry of over 13,000. The Royal Academy also puts on children's shows, including the National Exhibition of Children's Art.

Other important displays housed in galleries and museums include: the New Art Gallery, Walsall, containing a collection of European art bequeathed by Kathleen Garman (widow of the sculptor Jacob Epstein) and Sally Ryan. The Lowry at Salford Quays, Manchester, costing £96 million (£64 million of which came from ACE Lottery funds), houses galleries dedicated to the works of L. S. Lowry. The Hermitage Rooms, a new permanent display in Somerset House, London, which opened in November 2000, contains exhibitions originating from the collection of the Hermitage Museum in St Petersburg (see colour section between pp. 202 and 203). Other important collections in London include the Museum of London; the Courtauld Institute Galleries (containing masterpieces of 14th–20th-century European painting); and the London Transport Museum. Museums outside London include those associated with universities.

Scotland

In Scotland the national collections are held by the National Museums of Scotland and the National Galleries of Scotland. The former include the Royal Museum, the Museum of Scotland, the Scottish National War Museum and the Scottish Agricultural Museum, in Edinburgh; the Museum of Flight, near North Berwick; and the Museum of Costume at Shambellie House near Dumfries. The new Museum of Scotland, built at a cost of £52 million and devoted to the history of Scotland, has imaginative displays and distinctive architecture.

The National Galleries of Scotland comprise the National Gallery of Scotland, the Scottish National Portrait Gallery, the Scottish National Gallery of Modern Art, and the Dean Gallery, housing the Paolozzi gift of sculpture and graphic art, and renowned Dada and Surrealist collections. The National Galleries also have deposits at Paxton House near Berwick upon Tweed and Duff House in Banff. In 2000 the National Museums of Scotland attracted nearly 1.1 million visitors, while in 2000–01 the National Galleries of Scotland attracted over 1.1 million.

Wales

The National Museum of Wales in Cardiff has a number of branches, including the Museum of Welsh Life at St Fagans, the Slate Museum at Llanberis and the National Waterfront Museum Swansea, which is currently under development and will be housed in Swansea's Maritime Quarter.

> Contemporary museums are distancing themselves from their traditional image of dusty exhibits in glass cases. Many have interactive displays and programmes of lectures and demonstrations catering specifically for school trips. One of the most popular single exhibits in 2001, in the Natural History Museum, was a three-quarters size replica of a dinosaur, which moved and reproduced swamp smells from the Jurassic era. The dinosaur attracted over 180,000 visitors in its opening week.

Northern Ireland

The Museums and Galleries of Northern Ireland comprise the Ulster Museum in Belfast, the Ulster Folk and Transport Museum in County Down, and the Ulster-American Folk Park in County Tyrone.

'Living Museums'

Open-air museums depicting the life of an area or preserving early industrial remains, such as the Weald and Downland Museum in West Sussex, the Ironbridge Gorge Museum in Shropshire and the North of England Open Air Museum at Beamish in County Durham, are becoming increasingly popular tourist attractions. Skills of the past are revived interactively in a number of 'living' museums such as the Gladstone Pottery Museum near Stoke-on-Trent and the Quarry Bank Mill at Styal in Cheshire. Here, actors play the parts of people living in a particular 'bygone age', allowing visitors to ask questions about their working life and conditions.

Art Sales

The UK art market is second only to that of the United States. The UK's art and antiques trade handles about 70% of European art sales, employs about 40,000 people, had exports valued at £629 million in 1999 and in the same year had a turnover of £3.5 billion. Auctions of works of art take place in the main auction houses (two of the longest established being Sotheby's and Christie's), and through private dealers. *Art 2001*, the UK's leading contemporary art fair, was held in London in January, and has been influential in promoting the careers of innovative artists such as Tomoko Takahashi.

Crafts

'Crafts' in the United Kingdom is an umbrella term covering a huge range of activities, from the making of pots to rugs to handmade toys and other personal and household products. The crafts industry gives people another opportunity to express their creativity, adds richness and diversity to cultural life, and provides significant employment.

The crafts in the UK have an annual turnover estimated at £400 million. Government aid amounted to £2.5 million in 1999–2000. Policy and funding for the crafts in England are the responsibility of ACE, which is required to allocate at least £3.4 million, £3.6 million and £3.8 million to crafts for the years 1999–2000, 2000–01 and 2001–02 respectively, with a further £750,000 for development.

The Crafts Council is the official organisation for crafts in England. Its objectives include raising the profile of crafts in England and abroad and strengthening and developing, through its publications and exhibition work, the crafts economy in support of craftspeople. Activities and responsibilities of the Crafts Council include organising the annual Chelsea Crafts Fair and other programmes from its London venue; and coordinating British groups at international fairs. Craft Forum Wales has a membership of 640 craft business groups in Wales; they had a turnover of £27.5 million in 1999. Craftworks, an independent company, is the craft development agency for Northern Ireland. The Arts Council of Northern Ireland funds crafts promotion. In Scotland, the Scottish Arts Council has a Crafts Department, which promotes crafts and helps craftworkers.

THE WRITTEN WORD

Books have been central to the preservation and dissemination of UK culture for centuries. Despite the growth of television and the Internet, demand for books remains as strong as ever. In 2000 British publishers issued over 116,000 separate titles (including new editions). The UK book industry exported books worth £1,172 million in 2000.

J. K. Rowling's Harry Potter books have continued their success, both in the domestic and overseas markets. Sales of the four Harry Potter books totalled 3.2 million in 2000, and they occupied the top four places in the bestsellers list. The latest in the series, *Harry Potter and the Goblet of Fire*, was the best-selling book of 2000, with sales of just over 1 million. Fictional works of literature are just part of the range of books on offer. Non-fiction, in particular gardening, lifestyle, and travel books, as well as books tied to particular television series, are consistently among the lists of best-selling titles. Excluding the Harry Potter series, the top ten best-selling titles of 2000 in Great Britain were as follows:

1. *Angela's Ashes* Frank McCourt
2. *The Return of the Naked Chef* Jamie Oliver
3. *Hannibal* Thomas Harris
4. *The Testament* John Grisham
5. *Bridget Jones: The Edge of Reason* Helen Fielding
6. *Delia's How to Cook Book Two* Delia Smith
7. *Man and Boy* Tony Parsons
8. *Guinness World Records 2001*
9. *Black Notice* Patricia Cornwell
10. *'Tis* Frank McCourt

Among the leading trade organisations are the Publishers Association (PA), which has 200 members; and the Booksellers Association, with about 3,300 members. The PA, through its international division, promotes the export of British books. The Welsh Books Council promotes the book trade in Wales in both Welsh and English and the Gaelic Books Council supports the publication of books in Gaelic. The Book Trust encourages reading and the promotion of books through an information service and a children's library.

Literary and Philological Societies

Societies to promote literature include the English Association, the Royal Society of Literature and the Welsh Academy (Yr Academi Gymreig). The leading society for studies in the humanities is the British Academy for the Promotion of Historical, Philosophical and Philological Studies (the British Academy).

Other specialist societies are the Early English Text Society, the Bibliographical Society and several devoted to particular authors, such as Jane Austen and Charles Dickens. The Poetry Society sponsors poetry readings and recitals, as does the Scottish Poetry Library. London's South Bank Centre and the British Library run programmes of literary events.

The National Poetry Competition, sponsored by the Poetry Society, has established itself as a major cultural event. Ian Duhig won the 2000 competition, beating around 8,000 other entries (the winners were announced in April 2001).

LIBRARIES AND ARCHIVES

Local authorities in Great Britain and education and library boards in Northern

Ireland have a duty to provide a free lending and reference library service. There are almost 5,000 public libraries in the UK. In Great Britain more than 34 million people (58% of the population) are members of their local library and about half of these borrow at least once a month. About 430 million books and 37 million audio-visual items were borrowed from UK public libraries in 1999–2000. Adult fiction accounted for 43%, adult non-fiction for 29% and children's books for 28%. The Government is advised on library and archives policy by Resource (see p. 250).

Many libraries have collections of CDs, records, audio- and video-cassettes, DVDs and musical scores for loan to the public, while a number also lend from collections of works of art, which may be originals or reproductions. Most libraries hold documents on local history, and all provide services for children, while reference and information sections, and art, music, commercial and technical departments meet a growing demand.

The information role is important for all libraries: nearly all have personal computers for public use and, in early 2000, 62% had Internet connections. A government initiative under the New Opportunities Fund is providing £20 million for information and communications technology training of library staff and £50 million for enabling library material to be stored and accessed in digitised form. The Government is committed to networking all public libraries and connecting them to the National Grid for Learning by 2002. The DCMS/Wolfson Public Libraries Challenge Fund has mounted a £3 million campaign to persuade people, especially the young, of the joys of reading as a leisure pursuit.

Films are also archived. The *bfi* maintains the J. Paul Getty Conservation Centre, which contains over 275,000 films and 200,000 television programmes, together with extensive collections of stills, posters and designs. The *bfi* National Library forms the world's largest collection of film-related books, periodicals, scripts and other written materials.

The Library Association is the principal professional organisation for those engaged in library and information management. Founded in 1877, the Association has some 24,000 members. It maintains a Register of Chartered Members and is the designated authority for the recognition of qualifications gained in other EU Member States.

Public Lending Right Scheme

The Public Lending Right Scheme gives registered authors royalties from a central fund (totalling just over £5 million in 1999–2000) for the loans made of their books from public libraries in the UK. Payment is made according to the number of times an author's books are lent out. The maximum yearly payment an author can receive is £6,000.

> The top 12 most borrowed authors in 2000 from public libraries in the UK were:
>
> Catherine Cookson, R. L. Stine, Danielle Steel, Josephine Cox, Dick Francis, Janet and Allan Ahlberg, Jack Higgins, Ruth Rendell, Agatha Christie, Roald Dahl, Lucy Daniels and Enid Blyton.

The British Library and National Libraries

The British Library (BL), the national library of the UK, is custodian of the most important research collection in the world (150 million items spanning 3,000 years). It is housed in the largest wholly publicly funded building constructed in the UK in the 20th century. The total floor space is approximately 100,000 square metres. The basements, the deepest in London, have 340 km of shelving for 15 million books. There are 11 reading areas, three exhibition galleries and a conference centre with a 255-seat auditorium. British publishers are legally obliged to deposit a copy of their publications at the BL. The National Libraries of Scotland and of Wales, the Bodleian at Oxford and the Cambridge University Library (and the Library of Trinity College, Dublin) can also claim copies of all new British publications under legal deposit.

Some 456,000 reader visits are made to the BL each year. The reading rooms are open to those who need to see material (for example, manuscripts, newspapers, journals, stamps, maps and CD–ROMs as well as books) not readily available elsewhere or whose work or studies require the facilities of the national library.

The BL's Document Supply Centre at Boston Spa (West Yorkshire) is the national centre for inter-library lending within the UK and between the UK and other countries. It dispatches over 3.5 million documents a year.

University Libraries

As well as public and national libraries there are nearly 700 in higher and further education institutions, about 5,600 in schools and 2,220 specialised libraries within other public and private sector organisations (such as government bodies and commercial companies).

The university book collections of Oxford and Cambridge number over 7 million and more than 6 million items respectively. The combined stores of the colleges and institutions of the University of London total 9 million volumes. The John Rylands University Library of Manchester contains 3.5 million volumes, Edinburgh 2.5 million, Leeds 2.3 million, and Durham, Glasgow, Liverpool and Aberdeen each have over 1 million volumes. Many universities have vital research collections in special subjects, the Barnes Medical Library at Birmingham and the British Library of Political and Economic Science at the London School of Economics, for example.

Manuscripts and Other Records

The Historical Manuscripts Commission locates, reports on, and gives information and advice about historical papers outside the public records. It also advises private owners, grant-awarding bodies, record offices, local authorities and the Government on the acquisition and maintenance of manuscripts. The Commission maintains the National Register of Archives (the central collecting point for information about British historical manuscripts) and the Manorial Documents Register, which are available to researchers.

The Public Record Office (PRO) in Kew (Surrey) houses the records of the superior courts of law of England and Wales and of most government departments, as well as millions of historical documents, such as *Domesday Book* (1086) and autograph letters and documents of the sovereigns of England. Public records, with a few exceptions, are available for inspection by everyone 30 years after the end of the year in which they were created. The National Archives of Scotland (formerly the Scottish Record Office) in Edinburgh and the PRO of Northern Ireland in Belfast serve the same purpose.

EDUCATION AND TRAINING

The National Curriculum specifies that all children at school should receive training in the arts, music and literature. For many, involvement in art classes, the school play, or orchestra is the first time their interest in culture is awakened. The Government is keen to encourage artistic talent at school. In England, Artsmark, a new initiative from the Department for Education and Skills (DfES) and the Department for Culture, Media and Sport in conjunction with ACE, gives formal recognition to schools which achieve a certain standard in the cultural education they offer. Additional initiatives to encourage cultural excellence in schools include:

- the Music Standards Fund, receiving £270 million from the DfES over five years. Some £60 million a year from the DfES Standards Fund will be used over the next three years to protect and expand a range of music services, such as buying musical instruments for schools, providing instrumental tuition and providing extra training for teachers;
- the National Foundation for Youth Music, funded by a £30 million Lottery grant and donations from other sources, including the British Phonographic Industry; and
- the Space for Sport and Arts initiative, creating around 300 multi-purpose facilities for primary schools in the most deprived areas.

In Scotland, education is the responsibility of the Scottish Executive Education Department (SEED). Expressive arts are a key component of the pre-school and 5–14 curricular guidelines, and are available as examination subjects at Standard Grade, Higher and Advanced Higher levels.

For those wishing to pursue the route of a career in the arts, training available at post-16 tends to concentrate on particular specialisms within the arts. The DCMS and DfES disburse £19 million a year in grants for drama and dance students for tuition and maintenance. Over 800 students a year cover their tuition fees in this way, on the same basis as other higher and further education pupils. All training must be at accredited institutions and towards recognised qualifications, with annual evaluation by the DCMS and DfES to ensure that standards are maintained. Among drama schools which train actors, directors, technicians and stage managers are the Royal Academy of Dramatic Art (RADA), the Central School of Speech and Drama, the London Academy of Music and Dramatic Art (LAMDA), and the Drama Centre (all in London); the Bristol Old Vic School; the Royal Scottish Academy of Music and Drama (Glasgow); Queen Margaret University College (Edinburgh); and the Welsh College of Music and Drama (Cardiff). Competition to enter all the Schools of Performing Arts is keen.

The Royal National Theatre's Education Programme encourages access to drama on a national level through youth theatre projects, touring productions, workshops, rehearsed readings, work in schools and a nationwide membership scheme. The National Youth Theatre in London, the touring National Youth Theatre of Wales, the Scottish Youth Theatre in Glasgow and the Ulster Youth Drama Theatre offer early acting opportunities to the young. ACE supports several national touring companies that produce plays for children, including Pop-Up, Quicksilver and Theatre Centre. The Scottish Arts Council supports many youth theatre initiatives and several theatre companies touring Scotland with work for children, including TAG, Visible Fictions, Wee Stories and Catherine Wheels.

Professional training in music is given at universities and conservatoires. The leading London conservatoires are the Royal Academy of Music, the Royal College of Music, the Guildhall School of Music and Drama, and Trinity College of Music. Outside London are the Royal Scottish Academy of Music and Drama (RSAMD), including the Alexander Gibson School in Glasgow, the Royal Northern College of Music in Manchester, the Welsh College of Music and Drama in Cardiff, and the Birmingham Conservatoire.

Nearly a third of the players in the European Community Youth Orchestra come from the UK. There is also a National Youth Jazz Orchestra, a Scottish Youth Jazz Orchestra and a network of other youth jazz orchestras and wind bands.

Professional training for dancers and choreographers is provided mainly by specialist schools, which include the Royal Ballet School, the Central School of Ballet, the Northern School of Contemporary Dance (Leeds) and the London Contemporary Dance School.

All government-funded dance companies provide dance workshops and education activities. Phoenix Dance Company and English National Ballet, for example, have won awards for their projects, and Scottish Ballet has a long history of education work. Ludus Dance Company, in Lancaster, works mainly with young people. The National Youth Dance Company gives a chance for young people to work with professionals, as does Scottish Youth Dance.

The National Film and Television School is financed jointly by the Government and the film, video and television industries (£5.5 million in 1999–2000). It offers postgraduate and short course training for directors, editors, camera operators, animators and other specialists. The School enrols 50–60 full-time students a year and about 850 on short course programmes. The London International Film School, the Royal College of Art and some universities and other institutions of higher education also offer courses in production. The Skills Investment Fund, worth £1.5 million and run by Skillset, the National Training Organisation for the industry, aims to boost UK film production training. The Film Council makes £5 million available for the Film Training Fund, for screenwriters to gain expertise in producing commercially attractive screenplays; and a further

£1 million to First Movies, to enable children to make a first film using low-cost digital technology.

Most practical education in art and design is provided in the art colleges and fine and applied art departments of universities (these include the Slade School of Art and Goldsmiths College of Art, London), which have absorbed the former independent art schools, and in further education colleges and private art schools. Some of these institutions award degrees at postgraduate level. The Royal College of Art in London is the only postgraduate school of art and design in the world. Art is also taught to degree level at the four Scottish art schools.

University courses concentrate largely on academic disciplines, such as the history of art. The Courtauld and Warburg Institutes of the University of London and the Department of Classical Art and Archaeology at University College London are leading institutions. Art is a foundation subject in the National Curriculum in England (see p. 132). The Society for Education through Art, among other activities, encourages schools to buy original works by organising an annual 'Pictures for Schools' exhibition.

AWARDS

The granting of awards remains a popular means of recognising and rewarding outstanding cultural achievement. Awards ceremonies generate large amounts of publicity for the industry concerned; and the careers of individual performers are often boosted enormously by the awards they receive. The number of awards ceremonies grows by the year; a selection of some of the most important awards—given in 2001 unless otherwise stated—is given in Table 16.2.

British actors and filmmakers have enjoyed success at Hollywood's Oscars in recent years. A Lifetime Achievement award was given in 2001 to cinematographer Jack Cardiff.

AUDIENCES AND EXPENDITURE

Recent official estimates included in a creative industries mapping report produced by the DCMS creative industries initiative suggest that, taken as a whole, these industries generate around £112.5 billion a year in revenue, contribute some £10.2 billion in export earnings, employ 1.3 million people and account for over 5% of Gross Domestic Product.

By sector, the music industry as a whole in 2000 was worth over £4 billion (with exports worth £1.3 billion). It employed about 120,000 people. Over 200 million pop albums and 66 million pop singles were sold in the UK domestic market, generating a turnover of £1,170 million, a 3.3% increase on the previous year. Year-on-year sales of classical albums increased by 13% in 2000 to £66.5 million.

In 2000, cinemas took £507 million at the box office, from 349 films on release, compared with £583 million in 1999, from 360 films. An estimated 45,000 people were employed in the film and video industry in 2000. Exports in 1999 were worth around £653 million.

In 2000 the London West End theatres were credited with bringing around £1 billion into the UK economy, when additional expenditure on travel, accommodation and meals has been added to the cost of a ticket.

Figures from the ONS Family Expenditure Survey provide further evidence that the culture and leisure industries are strong growth areas for the economy: in 1999–2000 the average household spent more on leisure goods and services (including holidays) than food (see chapter 22). Increasing amounts are also being spent on satellite subscriptions to channels and cable TV subscriptions and connections. Investment in new museums and galleries (particularly those in Salford, Walsall and Bankside, London) has also helped to regenerate local communities.

Attendance figures at cultural events are also either steady or increasing (see Table 16.3). In the UK more people attend live music performances than football matches. Admissions to cinemas rose from 139 million in 1999 to 143 million in 2000, reaching their highest level since 1974. Museum and gallery attendance in England rose from 25 million in 1999–2000 to over 27 million in 2000–01 (see Table 16.4).

Callanish Standing Stones, Eilean Siar, c.2,900–2,600 BC

alton Cross, Islay, c.800AD

Pictish Slab, Aberlemno, Angus, c.750AD

The earliest continuous human settlements in what is now the United Kingdom appeared after the last Ice Age, between approximately 13,000 and 10,000 BC. Ever since, the landscape has been successively, and at times dramatically, transformed by the cultures, beliefs, conflicts and technologies of its generations of inhabitants. Many subtleties of this archaeological record can be seen clearly in aerial photographs. The following pages display archaeological sites and features from around the UK

Balnvaran of Clara, Inverness-shire, late 3rd millennium BC

Navan Fort, County Armagh, 1st century BC–4th century AD

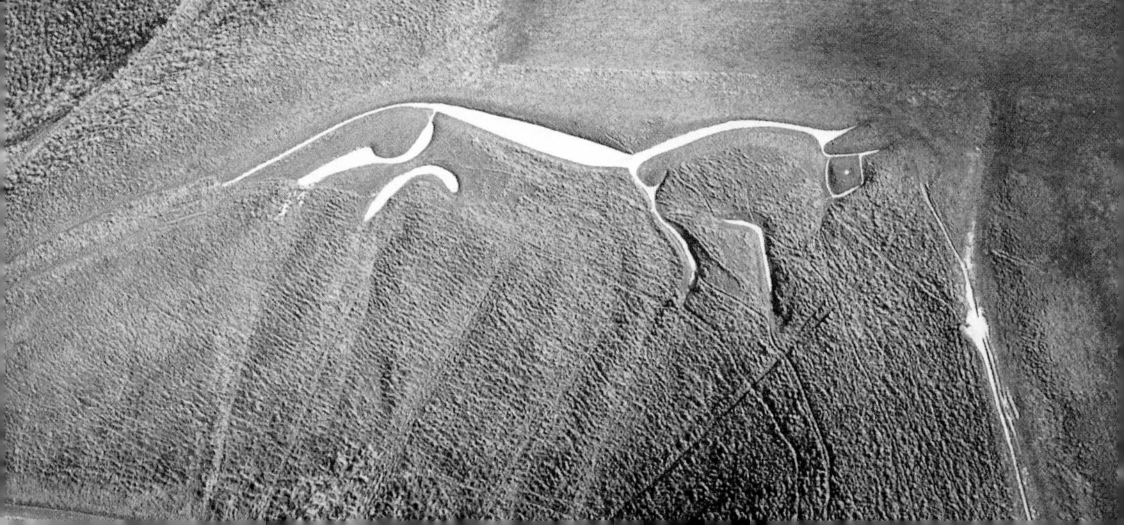

The Uffington White Hors
Oxfordshire, c.1,600–560

h of Gurness, Aikerness, Orkney.
upied c.1st century BC–10th century AD

Repeat detail of Prehistoric Rock Carving at Dod Law, Northumberland

Photo manipulation: Collection of Ian Hewitt, Bournemouth University

Beaumaris Castle, Anglesey, constructed *c.*1295–1330

Mosaic of Medusa, Bignor Roman Villa, West Sussex *c.* 350 AD

Reproduced by kind permission of the Tupper family, Bignor Roman Villa, West Sussex

Roman Baths *c.* 1st–4th centuries AD and Bath Abbey, Somerset. The present Abbey church was founded in 1499.

Reproduced by courtesy of Bath & North East Somerset C
Photo: Simon McBride

xterior and interior of the early 14th century Tithe Barn, Bradford on Avon, Wiltshire.

Ironbridge Gorge, Shropshire

Main picture and inset: Courtesy of the Ironbridge Gorge Museum Trust

The Ironbridge Gorge is celebrated for its role in the Industrial Revolution. The mass production of iron began here in the 18th century, helping to create the British engineering industry and laying the foundations for the railway age in the next century. The revolution changed the landscape of the United Kingdom forever.

In 1986 a two-mile stretch of the Ironbridge Gorge was added to the World Heritage List by UNESCO.

Detail of Bridge, Ironbridge Gorge

Table 16.2 Selected Major Award Winners, United Kingdom, 2001

Award	Category	Title of Work	Winner
Turner Prize (2000) *(Art)*	Overall	—	Wolfgang Tilmans[1]
Whitbread Prizes *(Literature)*	Overall	*English Passengers*	Matthew Kneale
	Biography	*Bad Blood*	Lorna Sage
	Poetry	*Asylum Dance*	John Burnside
	First Novel	*White Teeth*	Zadie Smith
Booker Prize (2000) *(Literature)*	Overall	*Blind Assassin*	Margaret Atwood[1]
Brit Awards *(Popular Music)*	Best Male Artist	—	Robbie Williams
	Best Female Artist		Sonique
	Best Pop Act		Westlife[1]
	Best Newcomer		A1
	Best International Group		U2[1]
BAFTA Awards *(Film)*	Best Film	*Gladiator*	
	Best Director	*Crouching Tiger, Hidden Dragon*	Ang Lee[1]
	Best Actor	*Billy Elliott*	Jamie Bell
	Best Actress	*Erin Brokovitch*	Julia Roberts[1]
BAFTA Awards *(TV and Video)*	Best Drama Series	*Clocking Off*	
	Best Soap	*Emmerdale*	
	Best Comedy	*Da Ali G Show*	
	Best Feature	*The Naked Chef*	Jamie Oliver
	Innovation	*Big Brother*	
	Best Actor	*Longitude*	Michael Gambon
	Best Actress	*Last of the Blonde Bombshells*	Judi Dench
Stirling Prize (1999) *(Architecture)*	Overall	*NatWest Media Centre*	Future Systems
Queen's Award for Poetry	Overall	—	Michael Longley
Olivier Awards *(Theatre)*	Best Director	*All My Sons*	Howard Davies
	Best Actor	*Stones in His Pockets*	Conleth Hill[1]
	Best Actress	*All My Sons*	Julie Walters
	Best New Opera	*Greek Passion*	Bohuslav Martinu[1]
	Best New Musical	*Merrily We Roll Along*	Steven Sondheim[1]
	Outstanding Achievement in Dance	*MIX*	Deborah Colker

[1] Winners from outside UK.

Table 16.3: Attendance[1] at Cultural Events, Great Britain *Per cent*

	1987–88	1991–92	1996–97	1997–98	1999–2000
Cinema	34	44	54	54	56
Theatre	24	23	24	23	23
Art galleries/exhibitions	21	21	22	22	22
Classical music	12	12	12	12	12
Ballet	6	6	7	6	6
Opera	5	6	7	6	6
Contemporary dance	4	3	4	4	4

[1] Per cent of resident population aged 15 and over attending.
Source: Target Group Index, BMRB International

Table 16.4: Visits to National Museums and Galleries in England, 2000–01

	Number of visits *Million*	% increase/decrease over 1999–2000
British Museum	5.7	4
Imperial War Museum	1.5	6
National Gallery	4.6	2
National Maritime Museum	0.8	–7
National Museum of Science & Industry	2.8	0
National Museums & Galleries on Merseyside	0.7	–2
National Portrait Gallery	1.2	18
Natural History Museum	1.7	0
Royal Armouries	0.2	5
Tate Gallery	6.7	172
Tate Britain	*1.1*	*–34*
Tate Liverpool	*0.6*	2
Tate Modern[1]	*4.8*	
Tate St Ives	*0.2*	35
Victoria and Albert Museum (V&A)	1.3	4
Wallace Collection	0.2	16

[1] Tate Modern (part of the Tate Gallery) opened its doors to the public in May 2000.
Source: DCMS

Further Reading

Department for Culture, Media and Sport: Annual report 2001. Cm 5114. The Stationery Office, 2001.

Websites

Department for Culture, Media and Sport: www.culture.gov.uk

Artsonline: www.artsonline.com

Arts Council of England: www.artscouncil.org.uk

Arts Council of Wales: www.ccc-acw.org.uk

Scottish Arts Council: www.sac.org.uk

Arts Council of Northern Ireland: www.artscouncil-ni.org

17 Media and Communications

Television and Radio	**269**	The Periodical Press	281
Digital Broadcasting	270	Press Institutions	282
The BBC	271	Press Conduct and Law	282
Independent Broadcasting	273	**Media Ownership**	**283**
Teletext, Cable and Satellite Services	275	**Communications**	**284**
Other Aspects	277	Telecommunications	284
The Press	**279**	Internet Services	286
National and Regional Titles	279	Postal Services	287

A Government White Paper proposing a new framework for communications regulation in the UK was published jointly by the Department of Trade and Industry and the Department for Culture, Media and Sport in December 2000. It set out the Government's response to the new communications environment, encompassing digital media, multi-channel television, telecommunications and Internet services. The aim is to promote the global competitiveness of the UK's media and communications industries as well as to protect the interests of the consumer.

Television and Radio

The Department for Culture, Media and Sport is responsible for government policy on broadcasting. Three public authorities oversee television and radio services. They are accountable to Parliament, but are otherwise independent in their day-to-day operations. The authorities are:

- the BBC (British Broadcasting Corporation), which broadcasts television and radio programmes and online services;
- the ITC (Independent Television Commission), which licenses and regulates commercial television services, including cable, satellite and independent teletext services; and
- the Radio Authority, which licenses and regulates commercial radio services, including cable and satellite.

There are five terrestrial analogue television channels, offering a mixture of drama, light entertainment, films, sport, educational, children's and religious programmes, news and current affairs, and documentaries. These comprise two national BBC networks, financed almost wholly by a licence fee, and the commercial ITV (Channel 3), Channel 4 and Channel 5 services, which are funded by advertising and sponsorship. In Wales, S4C—Sianel Pedwar Cymru—broadcasts programmes on the fourth channel.

Satellite television and cable services are funded mainly by subscription income. The largest satellite programmer is BSkyB (British

Figure 17.1: Television Audience Share Figures (in the 12 months to December 2000)

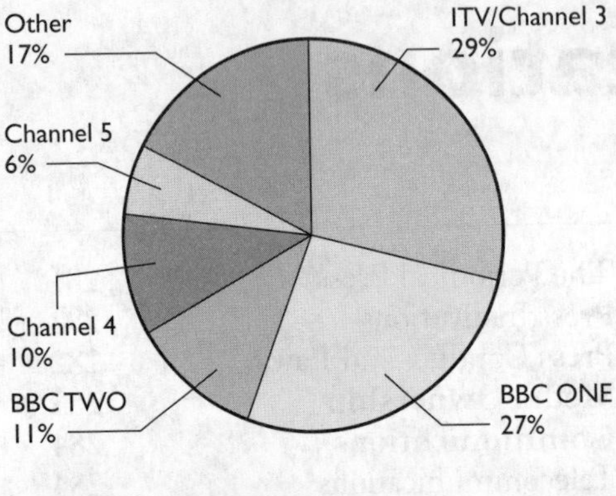

Source: Independent Television Commission

Sky Broadcasting), which dominates subscription-based television in the United Kingdom.

The UK's first digital satellite and terrestrial television services (see pp. 274 and 277) started in 1998, providing the existing analogue programmes in a digital format, together with free-to-air and subscription and pay-per-view[1] services. Digital cable services began in 1999.

The BBC has five national radio networks (see p. 272), which together transmit all types of music, news, current affairs, drama, education, sport and a range of features programmes. There are also 39 BBC local radio services covering England and the Channel Islands, and national radio services in Scotland, Wales and Northern Ireland, including Welsh and Gaelic language stations. BBC radio takes a 52% share of the total UK radio audience.

There are three national commercial radio stations (see p. 275). About 240 independent local radio (ILR) services also supply local news and information, sport, music and other entertainment, education and consumer advice. The first commercial digital radio services started in 1999.

[1] A free-to-air service can be received without charge to the viewer. Pay-per-view allows subscribers to pay for a specific programme, such as a film, sporting event or concert.

DIGITAL BROADCASTING

The transition from analogue to digital transmission technology has the potential to expand broadcasting capacity enormously. Digital broadcasting, which uses computer technology instead of standard signals, allows much more information than before to be transmitted, and can offer many more channels, extra services, interactivity, and higher quality picture and sound to viewers and listeners with new receiving equipment.

Digital television services can be received through an existing television aerial, a cable connection or a satellite dish. Viewers need either a special set-top box decoder, enabling reception of digital broadcasts through an analogue television set, or an integrated digital television set. Radio listeners need to invest in new sets to hear digital radio.

Legislation was passed in 1996 setting out a regulatory framework for the introduction of digital terrestrial broadcasting (and paving the way for more broadly based competitive media groups—see p. 283). The Broadcasting Act 1996 provided for:

- the licensing of six digital terrestrial television (DTT) 'multiplexes',[2] and of the providers of the programmes or other services on them; and
- the licensing of digital radio services on two national multiplexes, with multiplexes for local services in most parts of the UK.

The existing public service broadcasters have guaranteed capacity on the multiplexes. Licences to operate commercial DTT multiplexes were awarded by the ITC in 1997, and all DTT multiplexes started broadcasting in 1998. The Radio Authority awarded the national *commercial* radio multiplex licence in 1998, and is inviting applications for local commercial multiplex licences in most of the main population centres across the UK.

Many of the new services on digital television are available on a subscription or

[2] Through the process known as multiplexing, the signals of several broadcasters are combined into a single stream on a single-frequency channel. There is therefore no longer a direct one-to-one relationship between a television service and a frequency.

pay-per-view basis. Any broadcaster wishing to offer pay-television needs to use a 'conditional access' system (covering encryption, scrambling and subscription management services) to ensure that only those who have paid for a particular service receive it.

Existing analogue transmissions will continue for some time, but the Government wants to announce a switch-off date for analogue services as soon as is practicable. It has said that the switch-over to digital broadcasting could start to happen as early as 2006 and be completed by 2010, provided that all viewers who can receive the current free-to-air analogue services can receive them digitally. By the end of 2000 about 30% of households in the UK had access to digital television (the great majority via satellite). In April 2001, to encourage the digital switch-over, the Government announced a scheme to provide a series of targeted neighbourhoods with free conversion to digital TV (including access to interactive Internet services and e-mail). This programme is intended to provide practical experience to plan the switch-over from analogue services.

THE BBC

The BBC is the UK's main public service broadcaster.[3] A Royal Charter and Agreement govern its constitution, finances and obligations. Its Board of Governors appoints the Director-General, who heads the bodies in charge of the daily running of the Corporation. It has a regional structure throughout the UK.

The domestic services of the BBC are financed almost wholly by a licence fee. All households or premises with a television set must buy an annual licence. This costs £109 for colour and £36.50 for black and white in 2001–02, although people aged 75 and over have been entitled to free licences since 1 November 2000. Licence income is supplemented by profits from the commercial activities of BBC Worldwide (see p. 273). BBC World Service's radio broadcasting operations (see p. 272) are financed by a grant from the Foreign & Commonwealth Office.

In 2000 the Government announced new funding plans for the BBC over the period to 2006–07, aimed at ensuring that the Corporation can continue to meet its public service obligations and operate effectively in a competitive market.

BBC Television

The BBC broadcasts 17,000 hours of television each year on its two analogue domestic channels to national and regional audiences. BBC ONE is the channel of broad appeal (including documentaries and current affairs, features, drama and light entertainment, sport, religion and children's programmes), while BBC TWO aims for more innovation and originality in its programming.

Network programmes are made at, or acquired through, Television Centre in London and six bases throughout the UK (Glasgow in Scotland, Cardiff in Wales, Belfast in Northern Ireland, and Birmingham, Bristol and Manchester in England); or they are commissioned from independent producers—the BBC must ensure that at least 25% of its original programming comes from the independent sector.

The Corporation provides a range of digital channels available free-to-air, including:

- an extended BBC ONE and BBC TWO in widescreen;
- BBC News 24 (a 24-hour news channel);
- BBC Choice, a supplementary service to complement and enhance the network schedules;
- BBC Parliament (coverage of proceedings in the House of Commons, House of Lords, the Parliament in Scotland and the assemblies in Wales and Northern Ireland—see p. 278); and
- BBC Knowledge (the UK's first fully integrated public service multimedia learning service).

It also offers BBC Text, a new digital teletext service for its digital viewers.

---

[3] Public service broadcasting remains at the heart of UK broadcasting. Its goals are education, information and entertainment for all.

In February 2001 the BBC announced plans to introduce four new digital services. Subject to government approval, its existing BBC Choice and BBC Knowledge channels would be replaced by BBC THREE (an entertainment channel for young adults) and BBC FOUR (devoted to culture). There would also be two daytime children's channels. In September 2001 the Government approved conditionally three of the proposed services, but not BBC THREE. However, the BBC was offered the opportunity to put forward fresh proposals for a replacement for BBC Choice.

The BBC's Online channel on the Internet provides constantly updated news, sport, finance, travel and other information, attracting 4.9 million users in 2000–01.

Education is a central component of the Corporation's public service commitment across all platforms. A range of educational programmes is broadcast for primary and secondary schools (over 90% of which use BBC schools television), further education colleges and the Open University (see p. 141), while programmes for adults cover numeracy, literacy, language learning, health, work and vocational training. Books, pamphlets, computer software, and audio and video cassettes supplement the programmes.

BBC Network Radio

BBC Network Radio, broadcasting to the whole of the UK, transmits almost 43,000 hours of programmes each year on its five networks (broadcasting 24 hours a day):

- Radio 1 is a contemporary music station, serving a young target audience (with nearly 10% of the overall radio audience share during January–March 2001);
- Radio 2 offers a broad range of music, light entertainment, documentaries, public service broadcasting and popular culture (over 14% of audience share);
- Radio 3 covers classical and jazz music, drama, documentaries and discussion (over 1% share);
- Radio 4 offers news and current affairs coverage, complemented by drama, science, the arts, religion, natural history, medicine, finance and gardening features; it also carries parliamentary coverage and cricket in season on Long Wave, and BBC World Service overnight (over 11% share);
- Radio 5 Live broadcasts news, current affairs and extensive sports coverage (over 4% share).

BBC plans to provide five new digital radio services (for launch in 2001 and 2002) were approved by the Government in September 2001. They will be available via digital satellite and cable, the Internet and digital radio sets. Three services will focus on: black music, news and speech aimed at a young audience; popular music from the 1970s to the 1990s (drawing on the BBC's archive of musical performances, concerts and interviews); and a speech-based service, offering comedy, drama, stories and features (mixing original and archive programming). Two other services—5 Live Sports Plus and a national BBC Asian Network—will be enhancements of existing services. The BBC World Service (see below) will also be available as part of BBC Radio's digital portfolio.

BBC World Service

BBC World Service broadcasts by radio in 43 languages (including English) worldwide. It has an estimated global weekly audience of 153 million listeners. This excludes any estimate for listeners in countries where it is difficult to survey audiences. The core programming of news, current affairs, business and sports reports is complemented by cultural programmes, including drama, literature and music.

While maintaining short wave broadcasts for mass audiences, BBC World Service is making programmes more widely available on FM frequencies and delivering services in major languages through digital broadcasting and on the Internet.

BBC World Service programmes in English and many other languages are made available by satellite for rebroadcasting by agreement with local or national radio stations, networks and cable operators.

BBC Monitoring, the international media monitoring arm of BBC World Service, provides transcripts of radio and television broadcasts from 150 countries. As well as providing a vital source of information to the BBC, this service is used by other media organisations, government departments, the commercial sector and academic institutions.

BBC Worldwide

BBC Worldwide Limited is the main commercial arm, and a wholly owned subsidiary, of the BBC. It was formed in 1994 to coordinate the Corporation's commercial activities (television, publishing, product licensing, the Internet and interactive services), which are not funded by the licence fee. Its role is to generate money that can be reinvested in public service programming for the benefit of UK licence payers.

BBC Worldwide is Europe's largest exporter of television programmes, the world's biggest television channel operator based outside the United States, and the UK's third largest publisher of consumer magazines. These activities accounted for turnover of £587 million in 2000–01, which in turn delivered £96 million back to the BBC for reinvestment in programming and other services.

It operates 12 commercial channels in the UK and overseas. These include the wholly owned BBC World (news and information), BBC Prime (entertainment) and BBC America channels, and nine other channels in joint ventures with other companies (Discovery Communications, Flextech, and FOXTEL and Pearson). Together, they reach about 365 million households across the world.

BBC Worldwide is the market leader in audio publishing. It also operates online services (beeb.com and beeb.net).

INDEPENDENT BROADCASTING

Independent Television Commission

The ITC is responsible for licensing and regulating commercial television services (including BBC commercial services) operating in, or from, the UK. It does not make, broadcast or transmit programmes.

The ITC must ensure that a wide range of commercial television services is available throughout the UK and that they are of a high quality and appeal to a variety of tastes and interests. It must also ensure fair competition in the provision of these services, and compliance with the rules on media ownership.

The Commission regulates the various television services through licence conditions, codes and guidelines. The codes cover programme content, advertising, sponsorship and technical standards. If a licensee does not comply with the conditions of its licence or the codes, the ITC can impose penalties. These range from a formal warning or a requirement to broadcast an apology or correction, to a fine. In extreme circumstances, a company's licence may be shortened or revoked.

ITV (Channel 3)

ITV is made up of 15 regionally based television companies, which are licensed to supply programmes in the 14 independent television geographical regions. There are two licences for London, one for weekdays and the other for the weekend. An additional ITC licensee provides a national breakfast-time service, transmitted on the ITV network.

The ITV licences for Channel 3 are awarded for a ten-year period by competitive tender to the highest bidder (who has to have passed a quality threshold). Licensees must provide a diverse programme service designed to appeal to a wide range of tastes and interests. Each company plans the content of the programmes to be broadcast in its area. These are produced by the company itself, by other programme companies, or are bought from elsewhere. As with the BBC, at least 25% of original programming must come from the independent sector. About one-third of the output is made up of informative programmes—news, documentaries, and coverage of current affairs, education and religion—while the remainder covers drama, entertainment, sport, the arts and children's programmes. Programmes are broadcast 24 hours a day throughout the country. A common national and international news service is provided by Independent Television News (ITN).

ITV (Channel 3) companies are obliged to operate a national programme network. The ITV Network Centre, which is owned by the companies, independently commissions and schedules programmes.

Operating on a commercial basis, licensees derive most of their income from selling advertising time. Their financial resources and programme production vary considerably, depending largely on the population of the areas in which they operate. Newspaper groups can acquire a controlling interest in ITV companies, although measures are in force to deter any undue concentrations of media ownership (see p. 284).

Granada and Carlton, the two dominant regional ITV (Channel 3) television companies, jointly own ITV Digital (known as ONdigital until July 2001), which occupies three of the six multiplexes licensed for digital terrestrial television. It offers over 30 channels, including subscription and non-subscription TV channels and some interactive services. ITV Digital services were launched in 1998 and had attracted 1 million subscribers by the end of 2000.

Channel 4 and S4C

Channel 4 provides a national 24-hour television service, although Wales has its own corresponding service—S4C (Sianel Pedwar Cymru). Channel 4 is a statutory corporation, licensed and regulated by the ITC, and funded by selling its own advertising time. Its remit is to provide programmes with a distinctive character and to appeal to tastes and interests not generally catered for by ITV (Channel 3). It must present a suitable proportion of educational programmes, and encourage innovation and experiment. Channel 4 commissions programmes from the ITV companies and independent producers, and buys programmes from overseas. In February 2001 Channel 4 announced a restructure, and launched a new incorporated company, 4Ventures, to manage all its film and other new business activities.

The fourth analogue channel in Wales is allocated to S4C, which is regulated by the Welsh Fourth Channel Authority. Members of the Welsh Authority are appointed by the Government. S4C must ensure that a significant proportion of programming—and the majority between 18.30 and 22.00 hours—is in the Welsh language. At other times it transmits Channel 4 programmes. In 1998 S4C launched a digital service incorporating current analogue Welsh programmes and additional material. Roughly 5% of S4C's income comes from advertising, programme sales, merchandising and publicity; the rest comes from a government grant, which is fixed by statute.

Channel 5

The UK's most recent national terrestrial channel went on air in 1997, its ten-year licence having been awarded by competitive tender to Channel 5 Broadcasting Limited. Channel 5 serves about 70% of the population and is supported by advertising revenue.

Like ITV (Channel 3), the new service is subject to positive programming requirements. It must show programmes of

Popular Television Programmes

The most consistently popular television programmes in the UK are soap operas (everyday-life drama serials), notably ITV's *Coronation Street* and the BBC's *EastEnders* (which are broadcast several times a week and attract average audiences of 16–17 million viewers for each episode). Other current peak-time favourites are quiz shows, such as *Who Wants To Be a Millionaire?* (ITV) and *The Weakest Link* (BBC), and leisure and lifestyle programmes. Channel 4 has meanwhile pioneered competitive 'people-watching' shows in the UK, particularly the successful *Big Brother* series.

British programmes also sell well abroad. In addition to historical drama and quiz shows, particular recent successes have included the computer graphic BBC documentary *Walking with Dinosaurs*, and the children's programmes *Tweenies* and *Bob the Builder*.

quality and diversity, with a range of original productions and commissions from independent producers.

Gaelic Broadcasting

The Gaelic Broadcasting Committee is an independent statutory body committed to ensuring that a good selection of quality television and radio programmes is broadcast in Gaelic for reception in Scotland. Its members are appointed by the ITC, in consultation with the Radio Authority. The Committee is responsible for the distribution of government money to programme makers through the Gaelic Broadcasting Fund.

The Radio Authority

The Radio Authority's licensing and regulatory remit covers all independent radio services, including national, local, cable and satellite services. Its three main tasks are to plan frequencies, appoint licensees with a view to broadening listener choice, and regulate programming and advertising.

The Radio Authority has to make sure that licensed services are of a high quality, and offer programmes which will appeal to many different tastes and interests. It has published codes covering engineering, programmes, news and current affairs, and advertising and sponsorship, to which licensees must adhere.

Independent National Radio

There are currently three independent national radio services, whose licences were awarded by the Radio Authority through competitive tender, and which broadcast 24 hours a day:

- Classic FM, which broadcasts mainly classical music, together with news and information;
- Virgin 1215, which plays broad-based rock music (and is supplemented by a separate Virgin station which operates under a local London licence); and
- Talk Sport, a speech-based service.

Independent Local Radio

Independent local radio (ILR) stations broadcast a wide range of programmes and news of local interest, as well as music and entertainment, traffic reports and advertising. There are also stations serving ethnic minority communities. The Radio Authority awards independent local licences, although not by competitive tender; the success of licence applications is in part determined by the extent to which applicants widen choice and meet the needs and interests of the people living in the area, and in part by whether they have the necessary financial resources for the eight-year licence period. Local radio stations do not have guaranteed slots on digital local radio multiplexes.

The Radio Authority also issues restricted service licences (RSLs). Short-term RSLs, generally for periods of up to 28 days, are for special events or trial services, and long-term RSLs, primarily for student and hospital stations, broadcast to specific establishments.

TELETEXT, CABLE AND SATELLITE SERVICES

Teletext Services

Teletext is written copy broadcast on television sets. There are several teletext services, operated by the BBC (including a new digital service—see p. 271) and by independent television. They offer constantly updated information on a variety of subjects, including news, sport, travel, weather and entertainment. The teletext system allows the television signal to carry additional information which can be selected and displayed as 'pages' of text and graphics on receivers equipped with the necessary decoders. Around 16 million homes have sets with teletext decoders. The BBC and Channels 3, 4 and 5 provide subtitling for people with hearing difficulties. The ITC awards teletext licences for Channels 3, 4 and 5 by competitive tender for a period of ten years.

Cable Services

Cable services are delivered to consumers through underground cables and are paid for

Communications White Paper

Following a review of the future regulation of broadcasting and telecommunications, taking account of the implications of the increasing convergence of the two sectors, the Government published a White Paper, *A New Future for Communications*, in December 2000. The main proposals in the White Paper are:

- the establishment of a new unified, independent regulator—the Office of Communications (OFCOM)—combining the functions of the Broadcasting Standards Commission, Independent Television Commission, Office of Telecommunications (OFTEL; see p. 285), Radio Authority and the Radiocommunications Agency;
- while the BBC would be subject to OFCOM's regulation with regard to standards, its Board of Governors would retain the role of overseeing the Corporation's public service remit and upholding its political and editorial independence;
- the BBC's and S4C's present roles would remain, but Channel 4's remit would be reviewed, as would Channel 5's public service obligations;
- ITV companies would continue as the main commercial providers of public service broadcasting, but with less prescriptive regulation; and
- OFCOM would have powers to promote effective competition in the communications services sector for the benefit of consumers.

The White Paper also invited comments for reform of cross-media ownership rules, including television ownership rules (see p. 283), where the present disqualification on holding two or more independent television licences where the licensee has 15% or more of the total television audience share would be reviewed and a simplification of the present regulations governing radio ownership considered.

In July 2001 the Government published legislative proposals providing for the formal establishment of OFCOM. A broader draft communications bill should follow later in the parliamentary session.

by subscription. The franchising of cable systems and the regulation of cable television services are carried out by the ITC, while the Radio Authority issues cable radio licences. ITC licences are required for systems capable of serving more than 1,000 homes. Systems extending beyond a single building and up to 1,000 homes require only an individual licence regulated by OFTEL (see p. 285).

'Broadband cable' systems can carry between 30 and 65 television channels using analogue technology (including terrestrial broadcasts, satellite television and channels delivered to cable operators by landline or videotape), as well as a full range of telecommunications services. Digital technology is being introduced which will support up to 500 television channels. The two major cable companies (NTL and Telewest) started converting their networks to digital transmission during 1999.

There are no specific quality controls on cable services. However, if cable operators also provide their own programme content as opposed to just conveying services, they require a programme services licence from the ITC, which includes consumer protection requirements.

There are currently around 140 operating cable franchises in the UK. By the end of 2000 over 12.6 million homes were able to receive broadband cable services; of these 3.6 million subscribed to television services.

Cable also has the capacity for computer-based interactive services, such as video-on-demand,[4] home shopping, home banking, security and alarm services, e-mail and high-speed Internet access. It can additionally supply television services tailored for, and

[4] Video-on-demand enables viewers to dial into a video library, via a cable or telephone network, and call up a programme or film of their choice, which is then transmitted to that household alone.

directed at, local communities. Local television services operate under location-specific restricted service licences (making use of spare frequencies as and when they are available). These services began in 1998.

Satellite Services

Direct broadcasting by satellite, by which television is transmitted directly by satellite into people's homes, has been available throughout the UK since 1989. The signals from satellite broadcasting are received through specially designed aerials or 'dishes'. Most services are paid for by subscription. All satellite television services provided by broadcasters established in the UK are licensed and regulated by the ITC.

Some services offer general entertainment, while others concentrate on specific areas of interest, such as sport, music, religion, health, children's programmes and feature films. They also include foreign language services, some of them designed for ethnic minorities within the UK and others aimed primarily at audiences in other countries. Viewers in the UK can likewise receive a variety of television services from other European countries. Satellite services must comply with the ITC's programmes, advertising and sponsorship codes, but they are not subject to any positive programming obligations.

BSkyB is the UK's largest satellite programmer, with 5.1 million 'direct to home' subscribers. BSkyB's digital satellite service, SkyDigital, which offers over 200 channels including TV and radio services (subscription and non-subscription), was launched in 1998. New interactive services started in 1999.

Satellite radio services must be licensed by the Radio Authority if they are transmitted from the UK for general reception within the country, or if they are transmitted from outside the UK but are managed editorially from within it.

OTHER ASPECTS

Advertising and Sponsorship

The BBC may not raise revenue from broadcasting advertisements or from commercial sponsorship of programmes on its public service channels. It must not give publicity to any firm or organised interest except when this is necessary in providing effective and informative programmes. It does, however, cover sponsored sporting and artistic events. Advertising and sponsorship are allowed on all commercial television and radio services, subject to controls. The ITC and the Radio Authority operate codes governing advertising standards and programme sponsorship, and can impose penalties on broadcasters who do not comply.

Advertisements on independent television and radio are broadcast in breaks during programmes as well as between programmes, and must be distinct and separate from them. Advertisers are not allowed to influence programme content. Advertising is prohibited in broadcasts of religious services and in broadcasts to schools. Political advertising and advertisements for betting (other than the National Lottery, the football pools and bingo) are prohibited. All tobacco advertising is banned on television and cigarette advertisements are banned on radio. Religious advertisements may be broadcast on commercial radio and television, provided they comply with the guidelines issued by the ITC and the Radio Authority.

Sponsorship in Independent Broadcasting

In return for their financial contribution, sponsors receive a credit associating them with a particular programme. The ITC's Code of Programme Sponsorship and the Radio Authority's Advertising and Sponsorship Code aim to ensure that sponsors do not exert influence on the editorial content of programmes and that sponsorships are made clear to viewers and listeners. News and current affairs programmes on television may not be sponsored. References to sponsors or their products must be confined to the beginning and end of a programme and around commercial breaks; on television they must not appear in the programme itself. All commercial radio programmes other than news bulletins may be sponsored.

The ITC permits masthead programming (programmes with the same title as a magazine and made or funded by its publishers) on all UK commercial television services.

Broadcasting Standards

The independence of the broadcasting authorities carries certain obligations concerning programme content. Broadcasters must try to achieve a wide and balanced range of subject matter, impartiality in controversial issues and accuracy in news coverage, and must not offend against good taste. Broadcasters must also obey the law relating to obscenity and incitement to racial hatred.

The BBC, the ITC and the Radio Authority apply rules on impartiality, the portrayal of violence, and standards of taste and decency in programmes, particularly during hours when children are likely to be viewing or listening. Television programmes broadcast before 21.00 hours (or 20.00 hours on certain cable and satellite services) must be suitable for a general audience, including children.

Broadcasting Standards Commission (BSC)

The BSC, a statutory body, monitors standards and fairness on television and radio (both terrestrial and satellite). It considers complaints received from the public, and adjudicates on claims of unfair treatment in broadcasts and of unwarranted infringement of privacy in programmes or in their preparation. In 2000–01 the Commission received 360 fairness complaints, of which 111 were within its remit; of these, 80 complaints were considered further, and 21% were upheld in part or in full. The BSC also received 4,920 complaints about standards, of which 3,944 were within its remit; 3,123 complaints were pursued, of which 25% were upheld in part or in full.

Parliamentary Broadcasting

The proceedings of both Houses of Parliament may be broadcast on television and radio, either live or, more usually, in recorded and edited form on news and current affairs programmes. The BBC has a specific obligation to transmit on radio an impartial account day by day of the proceedings in both Houses of Parliament. The BBC Parliament digital channel (see p. 271) transmits continuous coverage of daily proceedings. The proceedings of the Scottish Parliament and the Assemblies for Wales and Northern Ireland are also broadcast live on occasions and in recorded and edited form on a regular basis by the BBC.

Party Political Broadcasts

In the absence of paid political advertising in the UK, broadcasters make time available for party political and election broadcasts on television and radio. Changes have been introduced by broadcasters to reflect the increased number of elections in the UK following devolution and to refocus broadcasts between elections at key times in the political calendar (for example, the Budget, the Queen's Speech and party conferences). The content of these broadcasts is the responsibility of the parties, although they have to comply with broadcasters' rules. The Government may make ministerial broadcasts on radio and television, with opposition parties also being allotted broadcast time.

Audience Research

The BBC and the commercial sector are required to monitor the state of public opinion about the programmes and advertising that they broadcast. This is done through the continuous measurement of the size and composition of audiences and their opinions of programmes. For television, this work is undertaken through BARB (the Broadcasters' Audience Research Board). Joint research is undertaken for BBC radio and for commercial radio by RAJAR (Radio Joint Audience Research).

The BBC, the commercial sector and the BSC conduct regular surveys of audience opinion on television and radio services.

European Agreements

The UK has implemented two European agreements on cross-border broadcasting—the European Community Broadcasting Directive and the Council of Europe Convention on Transfrontier Television. These oversee the free flow of television programmes and services throughout participating countries, setting minimum standards on advertising, sponsorship, taste and decency, and the portrayal of sex and violence. If a broadcast meets these standards, no participating country may prevent reception in its territory.

The Press

On an average weekday it is estimated that 54% of people aged 15 and over in the UK read a national morning newspaper (59% of men and 50% of women in 2000–01). About 84% of adults read a regional or local newspaper every week. National papers have an average (but declining) total circulation of some 13 million on weekdays and about 14 million on Sundays. There are more than 1,300 regional and local newspaper titles.

While newspapers are almost always financially independent of any political party, they often express obvious political leanings in their editorial coverage, which may derive from proprietorial and other non-party influences. Ownership of the national press lies in the hands of a number of large corporations (see Table 17.2), most of which are involved in the whole field of publishing and communications. There are around 100 regional press publishers—ranging from those owning just one title (about half of them) to a few controlling more than 100 each.

In addition to sales revenue, newspapers and periodicals earn considerable amounts from advertising. Indeed, the press is the largest advertising medium in the UK. The British press receives no subsidies from the state.

NATIONAL AND REGIONAL TITLES

The National Press

The national press consists of ten morning daily papers and nine Sunday papers (see Table 17.2). At one time London's Fleet Street area was the centre of the industry, but now all the national papers have moved their editorial and printing facilities to other parts of London or away from the capital altogether. Editions of several papers, such as the *Financial Times*, *Guardian* and *Daily Mirror*, are also printed in other countries.

National newspapers are often described as 'quality', 'mid-market' or 'popular' papers on the basis of differences in style and content. Five dailies and four Sundays are usually described as 'quality' newspapers, which are directed at readers who want full information on a wide range of public matters. Popular newspapers tend to appeal to those who want to read shorter, entertaining stories with more human interest. 'Mid-market' publications cater for the intermediate readership. Quality papers are normally in the larger broadsheet format, while mid-market and popular papers are smaller-size 'tabloid' format.

Many newspapers are printed in colour and most produce extensive supplements as part of the Saturday or Sunday edition, with articles on personal finance, travel, gardening, home improvement, food and wine, fashion and other leisure topics.

Increasing competition from other media in the delivery of news, information and entertainment has had an effect on the national press, with a gradual decline in circulation discernible for many titles. Most national newspaper groups have set up Internet websites in recent years, initially experimenting with the new medium and offering editorial, directory and advertising services, and later developing networks of additional special interest sites to cater for a growing alternative readership.

Regional Newspapers

Most towns and cities throughout the UK have their own regional or local newspaper. These range from morning and evening dailies to Sunday papers and others which are published just once a week. They mainly include stories of regional or local attraction, but the dailies also cover national and international news, often looked at from a local viewpoint. In addition, they provide a valuable medium for local advertising. Circulation figures for the period July–December 2000 indicate that the regional press sells 42 million paid-for newspapers and distributes 30 million

Table 17.2: National Newspapers (UK)

Title and foundation date	Controlled by	Circulation average (January–June 2001)
Dailies		
Populars		
Daily Mirror (1903)	Trinity Mirror	2,150,711
Daily Star (1978)	Northern & Shell[1]	676,671
Sun (1964)	News International	3,497,302
Mid-market		
Daily Mail (1896)	Daily Mail & General Trust	2,381,154
Express (1900)	Northern & Shell	906,539
Qualities		
Financial Times (1888)	Pearson	461,095
Daily Telegraph (1855)	Telegraph Group	968,926
Guardian (1821)	Guardian Media Group	390,278
Independent (1986)	Independent Newspapers	196,089
Times (1785)	News International	666,576
Sundays		
Populars		
News of the World (1843)	News International	3,971,478
Sunday Mirror (1963)	Trinity Mirror	1,809,691
People (1881)	Trinity Mirror	1,385,859
Mid-market		
Mail on Sunday (1982)	Daily Mail & General Trust	2,309,008
Express on Sunday (1918)	Northern & Shell	876,755
Qualities		
Sunday Telegraph (1961)	Telegraph Group	769,370
Independent on Sunday (1990)	Independent Newspapers	216,055
Observer (1791)	Guardian Media Group	419,724
Sunday Times (1822)	News International	1,353,900

[1] In November 2000 Northern & Shell bought the *Daily Star*, *Express* and *Express on Sunday* from United News and Media.
Source: Audit Bureau of Circulations

issues of free titles each week, reflecting an expanding market. About 90% of local and regional titles are now available online.

London has one paid-for evening paper, the *Evening Standard*. Its publisher (Associated Newspapers) also produces a free daily newspaper, *London Metro*, launched in 1999. There are also local weekly papers for every district in Greater London; these are often different local editions of one centrally published paper.

Of the Scottish papers, the *Daily Record* has the highest circulation. The press in Wales includes Welsh-language and bilingual papers (Welsh community newspapers receive an annual grant as part of the Government's wider financial support for the Welsh language). Newspapers from the Irish Republic, as well as the British national press, are widely read in Northern Ireland.

Around 640 free distribution newspapers, mostly weekly and financed by advertising, are published in the UK. Top free weekly titles include the *Manchester Metro News* and *The Glaswegian*.

Table 17.3 lists the average net circulations of the leading paid-for regional daily, Sunday and weekly newspapers across the UK.

Table 17.3: Top Regional Newspaper Circulations (July–December 2000 average)

	Circulation
Regional daily newspapers	
Daily Record (Scotland)	613,927
Evening Standard (London)	433,696
Express & Star (West Midlands)	179,029
Manchester Evening News	170,436
Liverpool Echo	151,229
Birmingham Evening Mail	130,405
Belfast Telegraph	111,115
Glasgow Evening Times	104,060
Evening Chronicle (Newcastle upon Tyne)	101,835
Leicester Mercury	101,032
Regional Sunday newspapers	
Sunday Mail (Glasgow)	725,234
Sunday Post (Dundee)	634,585
Sunday Mercury (Birmingham)	103,653
Scotland on Sunday (Edinburgh)	103,035
Sunday Sun (Newcastle upon Tyne)	100,556
Sunday Life (Belfast)	94,644
Sunday World (Northern Ireland edition)	79,921
Wales on Sunday (Cardiff)	60,564
Sunday Herald (Glasgow)	55,409
Regional weekly newspapers	
West Briton (Cornwall)	50,785
Essex Chronicle	49,749
Kent Messenger	48,162
Surrey Advertiser	43,445
Western Gazette (Somerset)	42,367
Hereford Times	42,216
Derbyshire Times	41,943
Kent & Sussex Courier	40,495
Barnsley Chronicle	40,352

Source: Audit Bureau of Circulations/Newspaper Society

Ethnic Minority Publications

Many newspapers and magazines in the UK are produced by ethnic minority communities. Most are published weekly, fortnightly or monthly. A Chinese newspaper, *Sing Tao*, the Urdu *Daily Jang* and the Arabic *Al-Arab*, however, are dailies. Afro-Caribbean newspapers include *The Gleaner*, *The Voice* and *Caribbean Times*, which are all weeklies. The *Asian Times* is an English language weekly for people of Asian descent. Publications also appear in other languages, particularly Bengali, Gujarati, Hindi and Punjabi. The fortnightly *Asian Trader* is a successful business publication, while *Cineblitz International* targets those interested in the Asian film industry.

THE PERIODICAL PRESS

There are around 9,000 separate periodical publications that carry advertising. They are generally defined as either 'consumer' titles, offering readers leisure-time information and entertainment, or 'business and professional' titles, which provide people with material of relevance to their working lives. Within the former category, there are general consumer titles, which have a wide appeal, and consumer specialist titles, aimed specifically at groups of people with particular interests, such as motoring, sport or music. A range of literary and political journals, appearing monthly or quarterly, caters for a more academic readership. There are also many in-house and customer magazines produced by businesses or public services for their employees and/or clients.

The two top-selling weekly consumer titles, *What's on TV* (published by IPC Magazines) and *Radio Times* (BBC-owned), carry full details of the forthcoming week's television and radio programmes and have sales of around 1.7 million and 1.3 million respectively. *Reader's Digest*, which covers a broad range of topics, has the highest sales (over 1 million) among monthly magazines.

Women's magazines traditionally enjoy large circulations, while several men's general interest titles similarly reached high levels of circulation (see Table 17.4) during the 1990s.

Children have an array of comics and papers, while magazines like *Sugar*, *Smash Hits* and *It's Bliss*, with their coverage of pop music and features of interest to young people, are very popular with teenagers.

Leading journals of opinion include the *Economist*, an independent commentator on national and international affairs, finance and business, and science and technology; *New Statesman*, which reviews social issues, politics, literature and the arts from a

Table 17.4: Top Women's and Men's Titles

	Average net circulation (July–December 2000)
Women's titles	
Take a Break	1,137,952
Woman	636,528
OK!	586,176
That's Life	569,804
Woman's Own	553,701
Men's general interest titles	
FHM	716,679
Loaded	351,353
Maxim	328,463
Men's Health	235,851

Source: Audit Bureau of Circulations/Periodical Publishers Association

left-wing point of view; and the *Spectator*, which covers similar subjects from a conservative point of view. A rather more irreverent approach to public affairs is taken by *Private Eye*, a satirical fortnightly. *New Scientist* comments on the latest developments in science and technology.

Weekly listings magazines such as *Time Out* provide details of cultural and other events in London and other large cities.

PRESS INSTITUTIONS

Trade associations include the Newspaper Publishers Association (NPA), whose members publish national newspapers, and the Newspaper Society (NS), which represents British regional and local newspapers (and is believed to be the oldest publishers' association in the world). The Scottish Daily Newspaper Society represents the interests of daily and Sunday newspapers in Scotland; the Scottish Newspaper Publishers Association acts on behalf of the owners of weekly newspapers in Scotland; and Associated Northern Ireland Newspapers is made up of proprietors of weekly newspapers in Northern Ireland. The membership of the Periodical Publishers Association (PPA) includes most publishers of business, professional and consumer magazines. UK Publishing Media, an alliance of the NPA, NS, PPA and the Publishers Association, was formed in January 2001.

The Society of Editors is the officially recognised professional body for newspaper editors and their equivalents in radio and television. It exists to defend press freedom and to promote high editorial standards. There is also a British Society of Magazine Editors. Organisations representing journalists are the National Union of Journalists, Chartered Institute of Journalists and British Association of Journalists. The main printing union is the Graphical, Paper and Media Union. The Foreign Press Association helps the correspondents of overseas newspapers in their professional work.

The Press Association is the national news agency of the UK and Irish Republic, delivering comprehensive news and sports coverage, photographs, weather reports and listings to the national and regional print, broadcast and electronic media. A number of other British and foreign agencies and news services have offices in London, and there are smaller agencies based in other British cities. Most regional agencies are members of the National Association of Press Agencies.

PRESS CONDUCT AND LAW

Press Complaints Commission

In a free society, there is a delicate and sometimes difficult balance in the relationship between the responsibilities of the press and the rights of the public. A policy of press self-regulation, rather than statutory control or a law of privacy, operates in the UK. The Press Complaints Commission, a non-statutory body whose 16 members are drawn from both the public and the industry, deals with complaints about the content and conduct of newspapers and magazines, and operates a Code of Practice agreed by editors covering inaccuracy, invasion of privacy, harassment and misrepresentation by the press. The Commission's jurisdiction also extends to online versions of newspaper and magazine titles by publishers who already subscribe to the Code. In 2000 it received 2,225 complaints, 44% of which related to national newspapers, 34% to regional papers,

10% to newspapers specific to Scotland, 7% to magazines and 5% to other publications. Most complaints breaching the Code are resolved by editors following the intervention of the Commission. It had to adjudicate on just 57 complaints—upholding 24 and rejecting 33.

The Press and the Law

There is no state control or censorship of the newspaper and periodical press, and newspaper proprietors, editors and journalists are subject to the law in the same way as any other citizen. However, certain statutes include sections which apply to the press. There are laws governing the extent of newspaper ownership in television and radio companies (see p. 284), the transfer of newspaper assets, and the right of press representatives to be supplied with agendas and reports of meetings of local authorities.

There is a legal requirement to reproduce the printer's imprint (the printer's name and address) on all publications, including newspapers. Publishers are legally obliged to deposit copies of newspapers and other publications at the British Library (see p. 263).

Publication of advertisements is governed by wide-ranging legislation, including public health, copyright, financial services and fraud legislation. Legal restrictions are imposed on certain types of prize competition.

Laws on contempt of court, official secrets and defamation are also relevant to the press. A newspaper may not publish comments on the conduct of judicial proceedings which are likely to prejudice the reputation of the courts for fairness before or during the actual proceedings; nor may it publish before or during a trial anything which might influence the result. The unauthorised acquisition and publication of official information in such areas as defence and international relations, where such unauthorised disclosure would be harmful, are offences under the Official Secrets Acts. These are restrictions on publication generally, not just through the printed press.

Most legal proceedings against the press are libel actions brought by private individuals.

Advertising Practice

Advertising in all non-broadcast media, such as newspapers, magazines, posters, sales promotions, cinema, direct mail, and electronic media (such as CD-ROM and the Internet) is regulated by the Advertising Standards Authority (ASA). The ASA is an independent body whose role is to ensure that advertisers conform to the British Codes of Advertising and Sales Promotion. These require that advertisements and promotions are legal, decent, honest and truthful; are prepared with a sense of responsibility to the consumer and society; and respect the principles of fair competition generally accepted in business.

The ASA monitors compliance with the Codes and investigates complaints received. Pre-publication advice is available to publishers, agencies and advertisers from the Committee of Advertising Practice. If an advertisement is found to be misleading or offensive, the ASA can ask the advertiser to change or remove it. Failure to do so can result in damaging adverse publicity in the ASA's monthly report of its judgments, the refusal of advertising space by publishers, and the loss of trading privileges. Advertisers found guilty of placing irresponsible or offensive posters can face a two-year period of mandatory pre-vetting. The ASA can also refer misleading advertisements to the Director General of Fair Trading (see p. 394), who has the power to seek an injunction to prevent their publication.

Media Ownership

Legislation in 1990 laid down rules enabling the ITC and Radio Authority to keep ownership of the broadcasting media widely spread and to prevent undue concentrations of single and cross-media ownership, in the broader public interest. The Broadcasting Act 1996 relaxed those rules, both within and across different media sectors, to reflect the needs and aspirations of the industry against the background of accelerating technological change:

- allowing for greater cross-ownership between newspaper groups, television companies and radio stations, at both national and regional levels; and

- introducing 'public interest' criteria by which the regulatory authorities can assess and approve (or disallow) mergers or acquisitions between newspapers and television and radio companies.

The 1996 Act overturned the rule that no one company could own more than two of the ITV (Channel 3) licences; instead, a new limit was set whereby no company could control franchises covering more than 15% of the total television audience. Local newspapers with more than a 50% share of their market may own a local radio station, providing at least one other independent local radio station is operating in that area. An additional regulation is the Office of Fair Trading's limit of 25% on any company's share of television advertising revenue. Newspaper transfers and mergers are subject to the consent of the Secretary of State for Trade and Industry, usually after reference to the Competition Commission (where the total paid-for daily circulation of newspapers owned by the proprietors involved is 500,000 or more). Government plans to revise or reconsider ownership regulations were proposed in December 2000 in the White Paper, *A New Future for Communications* (see p. 276).

Communications

TELECOMMUNICATIONS

Turnover of the UK telecommunications services sector grew by 9% in 2000 to £38.4 billion. Growth has been particularly strong in new services, notably mobile telephones and services provided over the Internet. In the UK over 300 licences have been issued to service providers and more than 100 to telecommunications operators to build and run their own networks. According to a report on telecommunications regulation issued by the European Commission in December 2000, the UK has one of the most competitive telecommunications markets in Europe.

Telephone Services

Telephone traffic is growing quickly. Calls from fixed links were 21% higher in 2000, at 241.9 billion call minutes, than in 1999 (see Table 17.5). There are 35 million fixed lines. A telephone is one of the most popular consumer durable goods in the home. According to the 1998 ONS General Household Survey, an estimated 96% of households had a telephone. A survey for OFTEL, conducted in May 2001, found that a significant and growing number of people preferred to use a mobile telephone rather than a fixed-line telephone as they favoured the former's flexibility and the ability to be contactable at all times. Around 6% of homes now have a mobile telephone instead of a fixed line. By the beginning of March 2001 there were some 43.5 million mobile telephone users, 60% more than a year earlier.

BT, which became a private sector company in 1984, remains the biggest fixed-line UK operator, although competitors have increased their share of the market, especially the business market. BT runs one of the world's largest public telecommunications networks, including about 20 million residential lines and 8.8 million business lines. Turnover in 2000–01 totalled £20.4 billion. In May 2001 BT announced a major restructuring, including a proposed demerger (creating a separate company) for its BT Wireless operations (including the mobile telephone operator BT Cellnet—see p. 285), which would become one of the UK's biggest companies on its establishment, scheduled for later in 2001. BT currently operates five main businesses: BT Retail and BT Wholesale, concentrating on customers and the network in the UK; and BTopenworld, BT Ignite and BT Wireless, which operate internationally, although concentrating on Western Europe.

The two main cable operators are NTL and Telewest. By the end of March 2001 cable operators had installed around 5.2 million telephone lines in the UK.

In November 2000 the Government held an auction for licences to run broadband fixed wireless services, which would allow companies to provide high-speed Internet and multimedia services over the airwaves in the 28 gigahertz band. Six companies were awarded licences. Some licences were left unsold, and in February 2001 the Government announced proposals for

Table 17.5: Telecommunications Statistics

	Call minutes 2000 (million)	Per cent increase in call minutes 2000 over 1999	Per cent increase in revenue 2000 over 1999
Fixed link			
Local calls	83,135	*–6.0*	*–8.0*
National calls	51,083	*5.2*	*–7.6*
International calls	7,477	*5.7*	*–2.2*
Calls to mobile telephones	11,390	*38.5*	*27.7*
Other calls[1]	88,795	*88.4*	*14.9*
All calls[2]	241,880	*21.3*	*4.3*
Cellular services			
UK calls	34,835	*53.0*	*n.a.*
Outgoing international calls	420	*31.1*	*n.a.*
Calls while abroad	846	*26.6*	*n.a.*
All calls	36,101	*52.1*	*n.a.*

[1] Other calls include number translation services, premium rate calls, directory enquiries, operator calls, the speaking clock, public payphones and calls to Internet Service Providers (ISPs).
[2] Figures may include a small amount of double counting, as in some instances calls supplied by an operator to a reseller may be counted by both operator and reseller.
Source: *OFTEL Market Information*

allocating these licences. In addition, licences will be offered in three other bands later in 2001.

Mobile Communications

The number of mobile telephone subscribers, and the volume of calls, are continuing to rise rapidly. There has been particularly strong growth in the volume of text messages handled by cellular network operators, which increased by over 240% between 1999–2000 and 2000–01. About 90% of new subscribers in 2000–01 bought pre-paid packages—pre-paid subscribers tend to have lower usage than subscribers on annual contracts with a supplier.

Vodafone, one of the UK's biggest companies by market capitalisation (see p. 384), is the world's largest mobile telephone operator in terms of the number of subscribers. It has over 93 million customers worldwide through its operations in 29 countries, including 12.5 million in the UK in May 2001. There are three other network suppliers in the UK:

- BT Cellnet (with 11.4 million subscribers in May 2001);
- Orange (11.3 million), part of France Telecom; and
- One 2 One (9.2 million), a subsidiary of Deutsche Telekom.

In addition, there are around 50 independent service providers.

In 2000 the Government held an auction for licences to run systems to provide the next generation of mobile telephone services, known as 'third generation'. These will provide users with high-speed access to the Internet, e-mail facilities, video conferencing and access to a large number of information services. Bids for the five licences available totalled £22.5 billion. Licences were won by Vodafone, BT Cellnet, Orange and One 2 One, with the licence reserved for a new entrant going to a subsidiary of TIW of Canada (now Hutchison 3G).

Regulation

OFTEL (the Office of Telecommunications), a non-ministerial government department headed by the Director General of Telecommunications, is the independent regulatory body for the telecommunications industry. Among its current initiatives are promoting greater broadband and narrowband Internet access (see below), and market reviews to ensure the appropriate level of regulation. It is involved in regulating 'local loop unbundling', a process giving BT's competitors access to its telephone exchanges in order to deliver their own high-speed services via BT's local telephone wires/lines; the first unbundled loops became available in early 2001. OFTEL has begun public consultation on the creation of a Telecoms Ombudsman with powers to resolve disputes between consumers and telecommunications companies; the new post is expected to begin operating in April 2002. OFTEL is one of the nine regulatory bodies whose functions would be absorbed within those of the proposed new Office of Communications (see p. 276).

A new legal framework for liberalising telecommunications markets in the European Union (EU) took effect in 1998. The UK Government is in the process of negotiating a regulatory framework for electronic communications networks and services with its EU partners. The European Commission has proposed new legislation for the converging electronic communications sector that would remove existing barriers to the single market and promote competition.

INTERNET SERVICES

The Internet plays an increasingly important role in the provision and distribution of information and entertainment. Broadly, it is a loose collection of computer networks around the world—it links thousands of academic, government and public computer systems, giving hundreds of millions of people access to a wealth of stored information and other resources. The World Wide Web (WWW or the web) has given the Internet its user appeal and accessibility—it consists of many thousands of 'sites' on the Internet. No one owns the Internet and there is no centralised controlling or regulating body.

The use of the Internet in the UK is growing rapidly (see Figure 17.6). According to the ONS Family Expenditure Survey, in the first quarter of 2001 an average of 9.2 million households (37% of households) in the UK could access the Internet from home, almost three times the number in the same period in 1999. Nearly all access the Internet through a home computer, although a small proportion access the Internet in another way, such as through digital television or a mobile telephone. Many people use the Internet at work, in education establishments and in libraries; over 99% of secondary schools and 96% of primary schools in England are connected to the Internet, according to the Department for Education and Skills. For information on e-commerce (electronic commerce) see the essay on p. 536.

Figure 17.6: Households with Home Access[1] to the Internet, UK

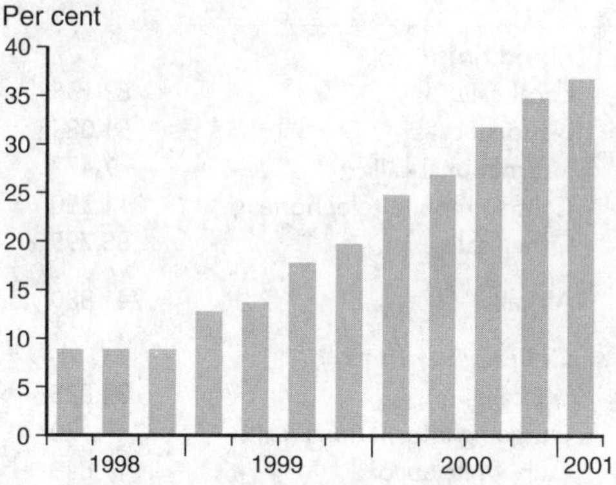

[1]Since April–June 2000 the data cover the percentage of households with home access using all forms of access, while prior to April–June 2000 the data cover the percentage of households with access from home computers.

Source: Office for National Statistics

Research conducted by OFTEL in May 2001 found that over one-third of homes used some form of unmetered access to the Internet, while in November 2000, 25% of households with Internet access were considering installing high-speed ADSL (asymmetric digital subscriber line) broadband access, which is now becoming available.

According to the National Statistics Omnibus Survey, conducted in July 2001, 51% of adults in Great Britain have accessed the Internet, equivalent to 23 million adults. Activities undertaken included:

- finding information about goods or services (74% of users);
- using e-mail (71%);
- general browsing or surfing (57%);
- finding information related to education (35%);
- buying or ordering tickets, goods or services (35%);
- personal banking, financial or investment activities (27%); and
- downloading software, including games (23%).

There are over 400 Internet Service Providers (ISPs). Freeserve is the biggest ISP and has some 2 million registered users; it was acquired by Wanadoo of France in 2001.

POSTAL SERVICES

The Post Office, founded in 1635, pioneered postal services and was the first to issue adhesive postage stamps as proof of advance payment for mail. In March 2001 it experienced one of the most significant changes in its history. Under the Postal Services Act 2000, which implemented the Government's programme of postal services reforms, the Post Office ceased to be a statutory authority and its business was transferred to a successor company, Consignia Holdings plc, wholly owned by the Government. Consignia serves its UK customers through three main operations: Royal Mail, Parcelforce Worldwide and the Post Office retail network.

Regulation

The Government's reforms are intended to modernise the Post Office and give it greater commercial freedom so that it can compete more effectively in the changing global communications market. The Act requires any postal operator conveying letters costing less than £1 per item and weighing less than 350 grams to be licensed. Licensing is the responsibility of a new independent regulator, the Postal Services Commission (known as 'Postcomm'). By mid-2001 it had licensed Consignia and was considering licence applications from other potential operators.

The Act also enables the UK to meet objectives under the EC Postal Services Directive, of which the most important concerns the provision of a universal service. Consignia is required to provide a universal postal service throughout the UK, involving the daily delivery and collection of mail at a uniform, affordable price. Its Royal Mail service cannot raise prices for most of its products without the prior approval of Postcomm. The Act also established a consumer protection body, the Consumer Council for Postal Services (known as 'Postwatch'), which is monitoring service standards and acting as a focus for consumer issues and complaints.

Consignia's Operations

Consignia's Royal Mail service delivers to 27 million addresses in the UK, handling around 80 million items each working day. In 2000–01 it processed more than 19.1 billion inland letters and 792 million outgoing international letters. Mail is collected from about 113,000 posting boxes, and from post offices and large postal users. Its International Services uses 1,400 flights a week to send mail direct to 280 postal 'gateways' worldwide. Consignia employs some 200,000 people.

High-speed mail-handling machinery—the Integrated Mail Processor—has cut the sorting time for processing letters. Automatic sorting utilises the information contained in the postcode; the UK postcode system allows mechanised sorting down to part of a street on a delivery round and, in some cases, to an individual address.

Parcelforce Worldwide provides a door-to-door overnight delivery service throughout the UK and an international service to 239 countries and territories. It handles 150 million packages a year. Parcelforce Worldwide is modernising its facilities for handling parcels. Two new sorting centres in Coventry—one for international parcels and the other for domestic traffic—have been opened, forming one of the largest and most modern distribution centres in Europe, handling some 50,000 items an hour.

Consignia owns nearly 20 international companies, based on the continent of Europe and in North America. It is also involved in a cross-border business mail joint venture with TNT Post Group of the Netherlands and Singapore Post.

Post Offices

The nationwide network of Post Office branches handles a wide range of transactions, with a total value of £140 billion in 2000–01. It acts as an agent for Royal Mail and Parcelforce Worldwide, government departments, local authorities, and Alliance & Leicester Giro and other banks' banking services. There are some 18,000 Post Office branches in the UK, and nearly all branches have recently been automated under a £1 billion programme, 'Horizon', which was completed by summer 2001. As part of the 'Modernising Government' programme (see p. 63), the concept of Post Offices as 'government general practitioners', helping their customers to access public information electronically and 'face to face', is being investigated; a pilot scheme in Leicestershire and Rutland will run for six months from September 2001. In May 2001 the Government reached agreement with the main UK banks on the introduction of new Universal Banking services (see p. 514), which would be available through Post Offices and aimed particularly at people who do not currently have a bank account.

Private Courier and Express Services

Private sector couriers and express operators can operate, subject to charging a minimum fee, currently £1. Postcomm is considering the scope for changing that part of the postal market requiring a licence.

Further Reading

Department for Culture, Media and Sport Annual Report 2001: The Government's Expenditure Plans 2001–02 to 2003–04 and Main Estimates 2001–02. Cm 5114. The Stationery Office, 2001.

A New Future for Communications. Department of Trade and Industry and Department for Culture, Media and Sport. Cm 5010. The Stationery Office, 2000.

Post Office Reform: A world class service for the 21st century. Department of Trade and Industry. Cm 4340. The Stationery Office, 1999.

Websites

Department for Culture, Media and Sport: www.culture.gov.uk

Department of Trade and Industry: www.dti.gov.uk

British Broadcasting Corporation (BBC): www.bbc.co.uk

Broadcasting Standards Commission: www.bsc.org.uk

Channel 4: www.channel4.com

Consignia: www.consignia.com

Independent Television Commission (ITC): www.itc.org.uk

ITV (Channel 3): www.itv.co.uk

Newspaper Society: www.newspapersoc.org.uk

Office of Telecommunications (OFTEL): www.oftel.gov.uk

Periodical Publishers Association: www.ppa.co.uk

Postal Services Commission: www.psc.gov.uk

Radio Authority: www.radioauthority.org.uk

18 Sport and Active Recreation

Sports Policy	291	Drug Misuse	298
Organisation and Administration	293	Funding	298
Sports Facilities	295	Popular Sports	299
Support Services	297		

Sport is one of the UK's most popular leisure activities, with two-thirds of all adults taking part in one or more sporting activities. According to UK Sport (see p. 293), the UK can claim to be among the top five most successful nations in world sport. UK sportsmen and sportswomen hold over 50 world titles in a variety of sports, such as professional boxing, modern pentathlon, rowing, snooker, squash and motorcycle sports. In the 2000 Olympics in Sydney the Great Britain team won 28 medals (including 11 gold medals) and in the subsequent Paralympics the team was second in the medals table, winning 131 medals.

In 1996–97 (the latest period for which information is available), 71% of men and 57% of women took part in at least one sporting activity in the four-week period before they were interviewed for the General Household Survey in Great Britain and the Continuous Household Survey in Northern Ireland. Walking (including rambling and hiking) was by far the most popular form of active recreation in the UK (see Table 18.1).

Many important sporting events are held each year in the UK, including the Wimbledon Lawn Tennis Championships, the FA Cup Final, the Open Golf Championship and the Grand National steeplechase. In 1999 the UK hosted both the cricket and rugby union world cups, while in 2000 most of the matches in the Rugby League World Cup were staged in the UK, and the World Track Cycling Championships were held in

Table 18.1: Participation in the Most Popular Sports, Games and Physical Activities 1996–97

% participation by those aged 16 and over

Males		**Females**	
Walking	49	Walking	41
Snooker/pool/billiards	19	Keep fit/yoga	17
Cycling	15	Swimming	16
Swimming	13	Cycling	8
Soccer	10	Snooker/pool/billiards	4

Sources: *General Household Survey* and *Continuous Household Survey* (Northern Ireland)

Table 18.2: British Medals won at the Olympics since 1972

	Gold	Silver	Bronze	Total
1972 Munich	4	5	9	18
1976 Montreal	3	5	5	13
1980 Moscow[1]	5	7	9	21
1984 Los Angeles[1]	5	11	21	37
1988 Seoul	5	10	9	24
1992 Barcelona	5	3	12	20
1996 Atlanta	1	8	6	15
2000 Sydney[2]	11	10	7	28

[1] A number of countries did not attend the 1980 and 1984 Olympic Games, mainly as a result of the Western bloc boycott following the Soviet Union invasion of Afghanistan and the Soviet bloc's subsequent boycott of the Los Angeles Games.
[2] British medallists are given in the appropriate reference in the section on Popular Sports (see pp. 299–310), with the exception of six medallists in sports that do not have an individual reference: canoeing, where Paul Ratcliffe won a silver medal in the K1 slalom and Tim Brabants a bronze in the K1 1,000 metre sprint; modern pentathlon, where Stephanie Cook and Kate Allenby won gold and bronze respectively; and shooting, in which Richard Faulds won a gold medal in the men's double trap and Ian Peel a silver in the Olympic trap.

Table 18.3: Selected Domestic Sporting Champions 2000–01

Basketball
BBL Championship—Leicester

Cricket
Cricinfo Championship—Yorkshire
Cheltenham & Gloucester Trophy—Somerset
Benson & Hedges Cup—Surrey
Norwich Union National Cricket League—Kent

Football
FA Carling Premiership—Manchester United
AXA-sponsored FA Cup—Liverpool
Worthington Cup—Liverpool
Bank of Scotland Premier League—Celtic
Tennents Scottish Cup—Celtic

Hockey
English Premiership Final (Men)—Surbiton
English Premiership Final (Women)—Slough

Ice Hockey
Sekonda Superleague—Sheffield Steelers
Sekonda Superleague play-off final—Sheffield Steelers
Benson & Hedges Cup (2000)—Sheffield Steelers

Rugby League
Super League Grand Final (2000)—St Helens
Silk Cut Challenge Cup—St Helens

Rugby Union
Zurich Premiership—Leicester
Tetley's Bitter Cup—Newcastle
Welsh/Scottish League—Swansea
WRU Cup—Newport

Tennis (2000)
National Champion (men)—Lee Childs
National Champion (women)—Lorna Woodroffe

Note: This table gives a list of champions from selected sports. For details of major international sporting achievements, see the section on Popular Sports, pp. 299–310.

Manchester. Major events in the UK in 2001 included the world modern pentathlon championships in Millfield (Somerset)[1] and the world amateur senior boxing championships in Belfast. The world athletics half marathon championships will take place in Bristol in October. The Commonwealth Games will take place in Manchester in 2002. The European Champions League Final will take place at Hampden, Scotland's national football stadium, in May 2002. The 2003

[1] In the women's event Stephanie Cook won the gold medal to become the first woman to hold the Olympic, European and world titles, and she was a member of the British gold medal winning squad in both the team and relay events.

world indoor athletics championships will be staged in the UK.

SPORTS POLICY

A 'Sports Cabinet', headed by the Secretary of State for Culture, Media and Sport and including the ministers responsible for sport in England, Wales, Scotland and Northern Ireland, is involved in identifying strategic priorities for sport, which is a devolved function.[2] In April 2000 the Government published *A Sporting Future for All*, its strategy designed to increase participation in sport in England and encourage greater success for the top sportsmen and sportswomen. It also seeks to ensure that sporting opportunities are widely available to the entire community, irrespective of age, gender, social background, location or ability. In March 2001 the Government published its Plan for Sport, containing a series of measures to support sport at every level: in schools, in the community and in elite competition.

For young people the Government's plan includes measures to ensure that all children have more opportunities to take part in physical education (PE) and sport in schools, including:

- the allocation of over £750 million for improving sports facilities in schools from the next round of funding from the National Lottery's New Opportunities Fund, with priority for schools in areas of urban and rural deprivation;
- investment of £130 million under a new fund, Space for Sport and Arts, in primary schools in the 65 most deprived areas of England;
- the creation by 2004 of 200 Specialist Sports Colleges, of which 101 had been designated by September 2001—they are providing high-quality facilities and training to support the most talented and promising pupils;
- a commitment to offer a new entitlement for children of two hours a week of good-quality school sport and PE; and
- investment of £120 million to provide school sports coordinators.

Community Participation

The Government's strategy also includes measures to raise participation more widely in the community, with investment of between £1.5 billion and £2 billion from the Lottery envisaged in community sports facilities in England in the next ten years. Local authorities are being encouraged to conduct audits of sports facilities in England to determine where the need for new or improved facilities is greatest, and with a view to the establishment of a comprehensive national database of sports facilities, which will form the basis of strategic planning for sports development.

The Government's view is that sport is an important component of regeneration, and can have a beneficial effect in helping the development of run-down areas. Sport England has established 12 Sport Action Zones in areas of high economic and social deprivation where basic sports provision falls below an acceptable standard. Eventually up to 30 zones will be established. Sport England will target these areas for improving sporting provision.

Sport England, the Youth Justice Board for England and Wales and the UK Anti-Drugs Co-ordination Unit have established 'Positive Futures', an initiative set up in 24 locations in England to reduce anti-social behaviour, crime and drug use among young people aged 10 to 16 within local neighbourhoods. The programme is to be expanded during 2001.

In Scotland about £87 million will be available through the New Opportunities Fund over the four-year period to 2004 to stimulate schemes that will encourage the improvement of school facilities and their

[2] Most of the strategies and funding programmes in this section relate to England. The devolved administrations have separate, but similar, strategies, policies and funding programmes.

wider use in the community, and for schemes in which sport can be part of a wider strategy in action being taken against youth crime.

Sporting Excellence

As well as the Specialist Sports Colleges, two main schemes are designed to promote sporting excellence:

- *The World Class Performance Programme* provides support to the UK's most talented athletes to enable them to improve their performance and win medals in major international competitions.
- *The World Class Events Programme* aims to ensure that major international events can be attracted to, and staged successfully in, the UK. About £1.6 million a year is available to support funding of up to 35% of the cost of bidding for and staging events.

Following the UK successes in the Olympics and the Paralympics (see pp. 294–5), the Sports Cabinet has agreed to maintain funding for the UK's world-class performers.

Sport on Television and Radio

Major sporting events (such as the Olympic Games) receive extensive television and radio coverage in the UK and are watched or listened to by millions of people. Football matches attract very high ratings, especially when the UK's national teams are involved in the final stages of international tournaments. A number of other sports, including rugby, horse racing, cricket and athletics, also achieve high ratings figures. Several of the UK's leading sports events, such as the Grand National and FA Premier League football matches (see pp. 305 and 304 respectively), are now watched on television by viewers in many other countries.

There are a number of satellite and cable channels concentrating on sport, and they have won the rights for live coverage of several major events and competitions. In the Government's view, however, there are some leading sporting occasions to which everyone should have access. These events are included on a protected list ('Group A') and cannot be shown on subscription channels unless they have first been offered to the UK's universally available free-to-air broadcasters (the BBC, the ITV network and Channel 4). Live coverage of events on the 'Group B' list may be shown by satellite and cable channels on the condition that an acceptable level of secondary coverage—a combination of delayed coverage and edited highlights—is made available to the universally available free-to-air channels. The current list is:

Group A Events (with full live coverage protected)
Olympic Games
FIFA World Cup football finals tournament
European Football Championship finals tournament
FA Cup Final
Scottish FA Cup Final (in Scotland)
The Grand National
The Derby
Wimbledon Tennis Championships finals
Rugby League Challenge Cup Final
Rugby World Cup Final

Group B Events (with secondary coverage protected)
Cricket Test matches played in England
Wimbledon Tennis Championships (other than the finals)
Rugby World Cup Finals tournament (other than the Final)
Six Nations Rugby Union matches involving home countries
Commonwealth Games
World Athletics Championship
Cricket World Cup—Final, semi-finals and matches involving home nations' teams
Ryder Cup
Open Golf Championship

Crowd Safety and Control

The Football Licensing Authority (FLA) has a wide-ranging role in advising football and other sports on outdoor ground safety. In England and Wales, licences issued by the Authority require all clubs in the Premier League and those in the First Division of the

Football League to have all-seater grounds. Clubs in the second and third divisions of the Football League have to ensure that any terracing with standing complies with the highest safety standards, as outlined in guidance from the FLA.

The Government works closely with the police, football authorities and the governments of other European countries to implement crowd control measures. The Football (Disorder) Act 2000 has introduced new measures to deal with English football hooliganism overseas. Domestic and international banning orders, which ban individuals from attending football matches, have been merged and can be imposed for between two and ten years. Courts have greater powers for imposing banning orders. For example, they can now impose a banning order on people who have not been convicted of a football-related offence if they believe that such an order would help prevent violence or disorder at football matches. The police can also request the courts to impose bans on particular individuals. Anyone subject to a domestic or international ban has to surrender his or her passport when major international 'away' games involving England are imminent.

ORGANISATION AND ADMINISTRATION

Sports Councils

Government responsibilities and funding for sport and recreation are largely channelled through five Sports Councils:

- the United Kingdom Sports Council, operating as UK Sport;
- the English Sports Council, operating as Sport England;
- the Sports Council for Wales;
- the Scottish Sports Council, operating as **sport**scotland; and
- the Sports Council for Northern Ireland.

UK Sport takes the lead on those aspects of sport and physical recreation that require strategic planning, administration, coordination or representation for the UK as a whole. Its main functions include:

- coordinating support to sports in which the UK competes internationally (as opposed to the four home countries separately);
- tackling drug misuse in sport;
- coordinating policy for bringing major international sports events to the UK; and
- representing British sporting interests overseas at international level.

All the Sports Councils distribute Exchequer and Lottery funds. UK Sport focuses on elite sportsmen and sportswomen, while the home country Sports Councils are more concerned with the development of sport at the community level by promoting participation, giving support and guidance to facility providers, and supporting the development of talented sportsmen and women, including people with disabilities. They also manage the National Sports Centres (see pp. 295–7).

Sports Governing Bodies

Individual sports are run by over 400 independent governing bodies. Some have a UK or Great Britain structure, while others are constituted on an individual home country basis. Their functions include drawing up rules, holding events, regulating membership, selecting and training national teams, and producing plans for their sports. There are also organisations representing people who take part in more informal physical recreation, such as walking. Most sports clubs in the UK belong to, or are affiliated to, an appropriate governing body.

Governing bodies that receive funding from the Sports Councils are required to produce development plans, from the grass roots to the highest competitive levels. In order to have access to Lottery funds for their top athletes, they need to prepare 'world-class performance' plans with specific performance targets. The Government is encouraging governing bodies to develop strategic plans for widening participation and developing sporting talent and to include high-quality youth sport programmes and coaching education systems, a talent development framework and targets for the development of their sport. A number of governing bodies that adopt such strategic plans will be given greater control of the distribution of funding from the Sports Councils and the National Lottery. Under the new arrangements, all major sports bodies receiving significant revenues from broadcasting will be required to set aside at least 5% of these revenues for investment in grass-roots facilities in their sports.

There are 12 international federations that have their headquarters in the UK: the Commonwealth Games Federation and federations for badminton, billiards and snooker, bowls, cricket, curling, golf, netball, sailing, squash, tennis and wheelchair sports.

Other Sports Organisations

The main sports associations in the UK include:

- The Central Council of Physical Recreation (CCPR), the largest sport and recreation federation in the world, comprises 202 UK bodies and 66 English associations, most of which are governing bodies of sport. The British Sports Trust is the charity arm of the CCPR that runs a volunteer sports leadership programme, in which some 50,000 people participated in 2000. The Scottish Sports Association, the Welsh Sports Association and the Northern Ireland Sports Forum are equivalent associations to the CCPR. Their primary aim is to represent the interests of their members to the appropriate national and local authorities, including the Sports Councils, from which they may receive some funding.
- The British Olympic Association (BOA), comprising representatives of the 35 national governing bodies of Olympic sports, which organises the participation of British teams in the Olympic Games, sets standards for selection and raises funds. Its team of over 300 competitors in the 2000 Olympics won more medals than in recent Olympics (see Table 18.2), gaining 11 gold, 10 silver and 7 bronze medals. The number of gold medals was the best performance by the team since the Olympics of 1920. The BOA is supported by sponsorship and by donations from the private sector and the general public, and works closely with UK Sport. It makes important contributions to the preparation of competitors in the period between Games, such as arranging training camps, and for the Sydney Olympics had a camp on the Gold Coast in Queensland for all team members. The BOA also has programmes to support national governing bodies and their athletes in areas such as acclimatisation, psychology and physiology. Its British Olympic Medical Centre at Northwick Park Hospital in Harrow provides medical services for competitors before and during the Olympics. The BOA's educational arm aims to educate youngsters on the Olympic Games and the Olympic movement.
- The Women's Sports Foundation, which promotes the interests of women and girls in sport and active recreation. It encourages the establishment of women's sports groups throughout the UK and organises events and activities. It runs both the Sportswomen of the Year Awards and an annual nationwide awards scheme for girls and young women between the ages of 11 and 19.

Sport for Disabled People

Sport for people with disabilities is organised by a wide range of agencies in the UK. Single-disability, multi-sport organisations coordinate disability-specific recreation and development opportunities and events. These agencies are the British Amputee and Les Autres Sports Association, British Blind Sport, British Wheelchair Sports Foundation, Cerebral Palsy Sport and the United Kingdom Sports Association for People with Learning Disability. The British Deaf Sports Council organises sporting opportunities for hearing-impaired people and coordinates British interests at the World Deaf Games.

At the Paralympics in Sydney in October 2000 the Great Britain team was second to Australia in the medals table, winning a total of 131 medals: 41 gold, 43 silver and 47 bronze. Gold medals were won in archery, athletics, boccia,[3] equestrian sports, powerlifting, shooting and swimming, while silver or bronze medals were also won in cycling, judo and table tennis.

Winners of more than one gold medal were:

- in athletics, Tanni Grey-Thompson (who won four gold medals, in the 100 metre, 200 metre, 400 metre and 800 metre T53 wheelchair events), Caroline Innes and Lloyd Upsdell;
- in swimming, James Crisp, Jody Cundy, Sascha Kindred, Giles Long and David Roberts; and
- in equestrian dressage, where three of the winners of the team dressage also won individual gold medals—Kay Gebbie, Lee Pearson and Nicola Tustain.

Multi-disability, multi-sport organisations are responsible for the coordination and development of sport on a pan-disability basis within each home country and, where possible, endorse integration into mainstream sport activities. These agencies are the English Federation of Disability Sport, Disability Sport Cymru, Scottish Disability Sport and Disability Sport Northern Ireland.

The remit of the British Paralympic Association (BPA) is to ratify selection, and fund and manage the Great Britain Paralympic Team in the winter and summer Paralympic Games. The BPA is the British member of the International Paralympic Committee.

UK Sport is reviewing disability sport, with a key objective being the organisational inclusion/integration of able-bodied and disabled sport across a range of sports, particularly at the high-performance level.

Nine sports already have a degree of integration: athletics, swimming, cycling, sailing, judo, equestrianism, powerlifting/weightlifting, wheelchair tennis/tennis and archery. The Commonwealth Games in Manchester in 2002 will be the first to include an integrated programme of events for people with disabilities. All distributing bodies of Lottery funding are required to ensure that applicants incorporate access and availability for people with disabilities.

SPORTS FACILITIES

The UK has a range of world-class sporting facilities including 13 National Sports Centres, operated by the home country Sports Councils. A number of major facilities have been improved in recent years, including many football grounds and the Wimbledon tennis complex. The Millennium Stadium in Cardiff was completed in 1999, with a capacity of 72,500; it hosted the final of the Rugby World Cup in 1999, and in May 2001 for the first time staged the FA Cup Final. In Manchester modern facilities are being provided for the Commonwealth Games in 2002, including a new 50,000-seat sports stadium costing £90 million, and an Olympic-sized swimming complex costing £32 million. The Games are expected to attract over 5,000 athletes from the Commonwealth nations.

United Kingdom Sports Institute

The United Kingdom Sports Institute (UKSI) is being set up under the strategic direction of UK Sport and in partnership with the home country Sports Councils, and will be fully operational by summer 2002. It will provide facilities and integrated support services to potential and elite athletes and teams. Its Athlete Career and Education (ACE UK) programme is designed to enhance athletes' personal development and sporting performance, and more than 700 athletes have already undergone an initial assessment and over 230 have attended personal development courses. All sports have access to the UKSI's services, although it concentrates on Olympic sports and those minority sports that lack a commercial element. The UKSI central

[3] One of two disability-specific sports in the Paralympics, boccia is played by those with cerebral palsy and is similar to bowls.

services team is part of UK Sport and based in London. It coordinates a network of regional centres in England and national institutes in Scotland, Wales and Northern Ireland. The UKSI's funds come mainly from the National Lottery, although the costs of the central services team are being provided from government funds.

UKSI Regional and National Network

England

In England the UKSI network is managed by the English Institute of Sport (part of Sport England). It is based around a number of key centres, of which four are based around National Sports Centres: Crystal Palace (London), Bisham Abbey (Berkshire), Lilleshall (Shropshire) and the National Water Sports Centre at Holme Pierrepont in Nottinghamshire. The other network centres are based around the Don Valley Stadium in Sheffield, Gateshead International Stadium, Manchester Sports City, the University of Bath and Norwich Sports Park.

Investment in new facilities planned by the English Institute includes:

- £21 million to fund a regional high-performance centre at Crystal Palace, with improved facilities for athletics, boxing, swimming and tennis;
- £21 million at Loughborough University, including facilities for athletics, badminton, gymnastics, hockey, netball and swimming;
- £20 million in sports science, sports medicine and conditioning facilities (such as gym facilities, including loose weights and fitness machines);
- £10 million in water sports facilities for sailing, canoeing and rowing;
- £6 million in water-based hockey pitches; and
- £3 million in judo facilities.

Wales

The centre of the UKSI network in Wales is the Welsh Institute of Sport in Cardiff, which is the premier venue in Wales for top-level training and for competition in many sports. The Institute, which is run by the Sports Council for Wales, has close links with other specialist facilities, including the National Watersports Centre at Plas Menai in north Wales, a centre of excellence for sailing and canoeing; the national indoor athletics centre at the University of Wales Institute, Cardiff; and the cricketing school of excellence at Sophia Gardens, Cardiff.

Plas y Brenin National Mountain Centre, in Snowdonia National Park in north Wales, is run by Sport England. It offers courses in rock climbing, mountaineering, canoeing, orienteering, skiing and most other mountain-based activities, and is the UK's leading training institution for mountain instructors.

Scotland

Sportscotland has set aside funding of £20 million over five years to develop the network comprising the Scottish Institute of Sport and six area institutes. The institutes have focused initially on supporting the development of top talent in seven sports: athletics, badminton, curling, football, hockey, rugby and swimming. Golf and judo were added to these 'core' sports in 2001. The network also includes three National Sports Centres, run by **sport**scotland, which provide training and coaching facilities for a range of sports:

- Glenmore Lodge near Aviemore, which caters for outdoor sports, including canoeing, mountaineering, mountain biking, orienteering and skiing;
- Inverclyde in Largs, which caters for 23 sports and has many indoor and outdoor facilities, including a gymnastics hall, golf training, and sports medicine and sports science facilities of an international standard; and
- the Scottish National Water Sports Centre—Cumbrae—on the island of Great Cumbrae in the Firth of Clyde.

Northern Ireland

The Sports Council for Northern Ireland has announced a partnership with the University of Ulster for the development of a Northern Ireland network centre of the UKSI. This will involve creating high-quality training facilities and support services, primarily at the University's Jordanstown campus, with the establishment of links with nearby facilities.

The Tollymore Mountain Centre in County Down, run by the Sports Council for Northern Ireland, offers courses in mountaineering, rock climbing, canoeing and outdoor adventure. Leadership and instructor courses leading to nationally recognised qualifications are also available.

The Council's Youth Sport programme has pioneered innovative ways of involving young people in sport.

Local Facilities

Local authorities are the main providers of basic sport and recreation facilities for the local community, including indoor sports centres, parks, lakes, playing fields, playgrounds, tennis courts, natural and artificial pitches, golf courses and swimming/leisure pools. The English sports strategy (see p. 291) provides for a major investment in the improvement of school sports facilities which will also be available for community use. The Lottery Sports Fund is also providing investment of £1.56 billion over ten years in community sports facilities in England.

Over 150,000 voluntary sports clubs are affiliated to the national governing bodies of sport in the UK. Some local clubs cater for indoor recreation, but more common are those which provide sports grounds, particularly for bowls, cricket, football, rugby, hockey, tennis and golf. In the March 2001 Budget the Government announced its intention to consult on the best way for tax relief to help community amateur sports clubs that make a positive contribution to their local communities. Many clubs linked to businesses and other employers cater for sporting activities. Commercial facilities include health and fitness centres (which are increasingly popular, as indicated by a growing number of clubs and rising membership), tenpin bowling centres, ice and roller-skating rinks, squash courts, golf courses and driving ranges, riding stables and marinas.

SUPPORT SERVICES

Coaching

Sports coach UK (formerly the National Coaching Foundation) works closely with sports governing bodies, local authorities, and higher and further education institutions. Supported by the Sports Councils, it provides a comprehensive range of services for coaches in all sports. In 2000, over 50,000 coaches and schoolteachers participated in its programmes.

The Government wishes to see improvements in coaching, and in March 2001 announced a review of coaching in England with the intention of establishing a framework for developing more world-class coaches.

Volunteering

In 1996 there were an estimated 1.5 million volunteers involved in the running of sport in the UK, according to a survey commissioned by Sport England and conducted by Sheffield University. The Government's Plan for Sport recognises the contribution of volunteers and calls on Sport England and the national governing bodies of sport to develop a cross-sport strategy for volunteering. In addition, some £7 million is being allocated to the training and support of up to 60,000 volunteers who will become mentors, coaches, officials and administrators.

Sports Medicine

The National Sports Medicine Institute of the United Kingdom (NSMI) was established in 1992 to serve as the national focus for all those concerned with sport and exercise medicine. It aims to provide optimum levels of safety and care in order to enhance the ability of those engaged in exercise and sport from grass-roots to international levels throughout the UK. The NSMI is funded through contracts with the Sports Councils and it also generates income from its services, many of which are developed or delivered through collaboration with other organisations.

Sports Science

The development of sports science support services for the national governing bodies of sport is being promoted by the Sports Councils, in collaboration with the BOA and sports coach UK, in an effort to raise the standards of performance of national squads. The type of support provided may be biomechanical (human movement), physiological or psychological.

DRUG MISUSE

UK Sport aims to prevent doping and achieve a commitment to drug-free sport and ethical sporting practices. Its Anti-Doping Directorate coordinates an independent drugs-testing programme and conducts an information programme aimed at changing attitudes to drug misuse. Samples are analysed at a laboratory accredited by the International Olympic Committee, at King's College, University of London; UK Sport is responsible for reporting the results to the appropriate governing body. The drugs-testing programme involves 50 national governing bodies and 20 international sporting federations from 44 sports. UK Sport provides a Drug Information Line to allow athletes to check whether a licensed medication is permitted or banned under their governing body's regulations, and issues a comprehensive guide on drugs and sport for competitors and officials; information is also available on its website (*www.uksport.gov.uk*). The UK is working closely with international colleagues in the World Anti-Doping Agency.

FUNDING

Sport is a major industry in the UK: a joint Department of Trade and Industry/Sports Industries Federation competitiveness analysis, published in 1999, found that it is worth almost £5 billion a year.

Sport is one of the main recipients of funds raised by the National Lottery, and 62 sports have received Lottery funding. By mid-2001 awards totalling £1.58 billion had been made to over 15,500 sport projects in the UK from Lottery funds.

Sponsorship may take the form of financing specific events or championships, such as horse races or cricket leagues, or support for sports organisations or individual performers. Motor sport and football receive the largest amounts of private sponsorship. Two recent examples of major sport sponsorship are in cricket—Vodafone has recently extended its sponsorship of the England cricket team until the end of 2005, and in January 2001 Npower agreed to sponsor Test matches in England for the next three years.

Sponsorship is encouraged by a number of bodies, including the Institute of Sports Sponsorship (ISS), which comprises some 100 UK companies involved in sponsoring sport.

Sportsmatch

Sportsmatch aims to increase the amount of business sponsorship going into grass-roots sport and physical recreation. It offers matching funding for new sponsorships and for the extension of existing ones. Priority is given to projects involving disabled people, the young and ethnic minorities and to projects in deprived areas.

In England the ISS runs the scheme on behalf of Sport England, while in Wales the scheme is managed by the Sports Council for Wales and in Scotland by **sport**scotland. In England since 1992 Sportsmatch has approved 3,120 awards, totalling £25 million and covering 70 different sports, while in Scotland over £6.2 million has been invested, in partnership with business, through 1,050 awards.

SportsAid

SportsAid raises funds to help encourage and support young and disabled people with sporting talent. Financial grants are provided on an individual basis, with each application being conducted on the criteria of talent and need. Those receiving funds must normally be aged between 12 and 18, but there is no age limit for disabled people. SportsAid relies on commercial sponsorship and donations from the public, and the corporate and public sectors. The Scottish Sports Aid Foundation, SportsAid Cymru/Wales and the Ulster

ra London Marathon

ra London Marathon (both)

© Newcastle Document Services

The BUPA Great North Run in Newcastle upon Tyne–a half-marathon–and the Flora 26.2 mile London Marathon are popular annual sporting events. Thousands of people take part every year. Both races have a strong competitive element, attracting top athletes from around the world. Many people take part to raise money for charity. In 2001 the official charities for the Great North Run and the Flora London Marathon were Leukaemia Research and the Multiple Sclerosis Society respectively. Both races also raised funds for many other organisations.

© Newcastle Document Services

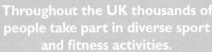

Throughout the UK thousands of people take part in diverse sport and fitness activities. Many individuals belong to local sports clubs or associations, playing competitively as well as purely for recreation. Working out in a gym is a popular way to keep fit. As well as traditional sports, such as football, a wide range of other sports is played in schools.

Swimming is recommended as a comfortable way to exercise throughout pregnancy. Many people keep fit through jogging, rambling, or even exercising with a dog. Football remains one of the most popular national sports and is increasingly played by both sexes.

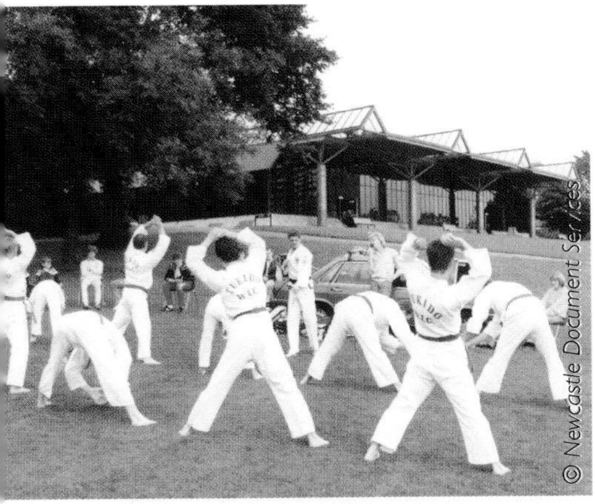

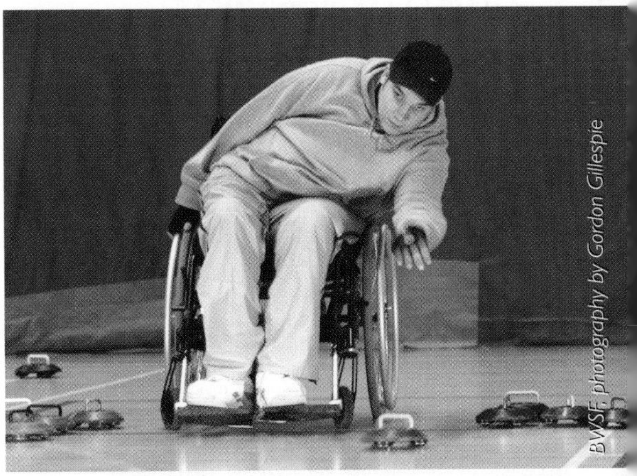

BWSF, photography by Gordon Gillespie

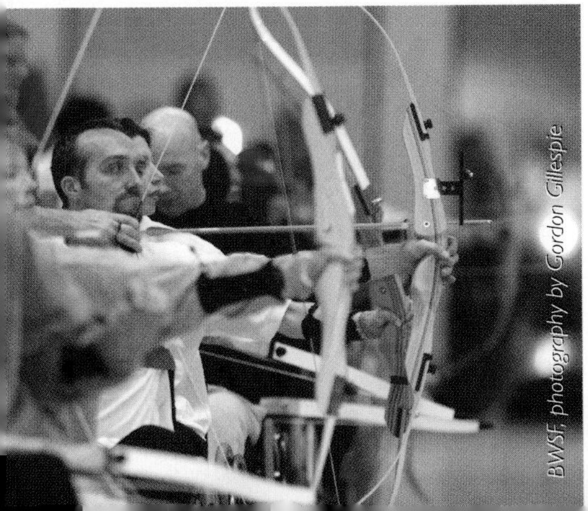

BWSF, photography by Gordon Gillespie

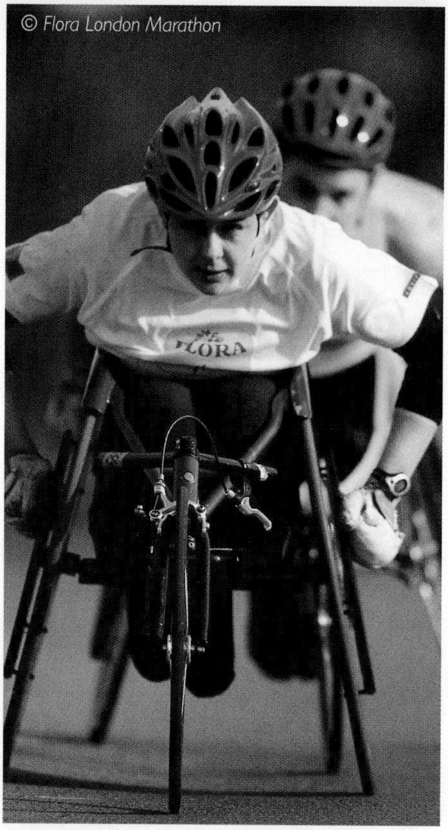

© Flora London Marathon

SPORTS PERSONALITIES

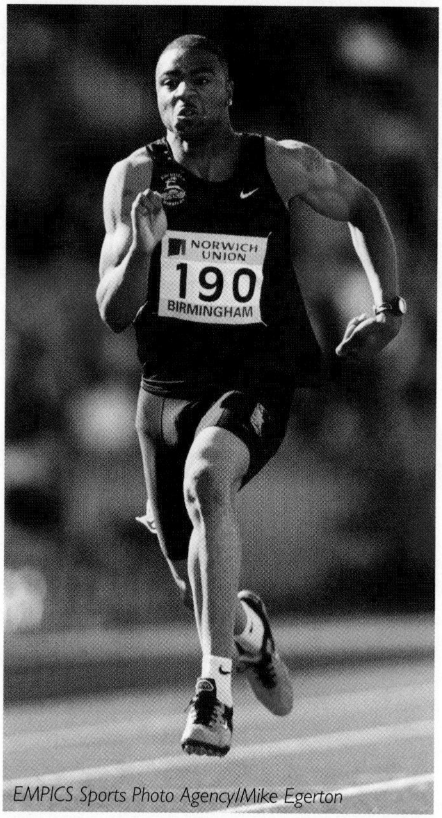

EMPICS Sports Photo Agency/Mike Egerton

Tanni Grey-Thompson, OBE, is the world's most successful disabled athlete. She comes from Cardiff. Tanni has competed at world-class level for the past 13 years, is a multiple paralympic gold medal winner and has achieved a comprehensive set of British and World Records. Tanni has also won the women's wheelchair division of the London Marathon five times.

Tanni has won awards reflecting achievement, inspiration and personality, including the BBC Wales Sports Personality of the Year in 2000. She spends a great deal of her time contributing to sports administration.

© Erik Lindkvist

Ellen MacArthur is from Whatstandwell in Derbyshire. In November 2000, Ellen set out to race in the Vendée Globe Yacht Race, spending over 94 days alone at sea as she sailed round the world, becoming the youngest person ever to achieve this. She finished this intensely demanding race in second place. Ellen was nominated 'Yachtsman of the Year' in 1999.

Mark Lewis-Francis is one of the UK's brightest sprinting prospects. He comes from Darlaston in the West Midlands. At 18 he was one of the youngest participants in the World Athletics Championships at Edmonton (Canada) in August 2001, where he competed in the 100 metres. He won this event in the World Junior Championships in Santiago (Chile) in October 2000.

Sports and Recreation Trust have similar functions.

Foundation for Sport and the Arts

The Foundation for Sport and the Arts, set up by the football pools promoters in 1991, funds small-scale projects in sport and the arts. This initiative followed the 1991 Budget, in which pools betting duty was reduced by 2.5%, provided that the money forgone by the Government was paid into the new Foundation. Funding will continue until at least 2002. The Foundation has made awards to schemes benefiting over 100 sports.

Betting and Gaming

A survey, published in June 2000, found that 72% of adults in Great Britain gamble at least once a year. The survey was carried out by the National Centre for Social Research for a consortium representing the gambling industry, the Home Office and other regulatory authorities, and GamCare (the national centre addressing the social impact of gambling). It found that the National Lottery was by far the most popular gambling activity in the UK. Some 65% of the adult population had bought Lottery tickets in the year leading up to the survey, and the results indicate that up to half the adult population take part each week. According to the survey, other forms of gambling in which people had participated over the previous year included scratchcards (22% of adults), fruit machines (14%), horse racing (13%), private bets with friends or workmates (11%), football pools (9%) and bingo (7%). The survey found that less than 1% of adults would be classed as problem gamblers.

Gross expenditure on all forms of gambling, including the National Lottery, is estimated at approximately £42 billion a year. In July 2001 the Government published an independent review of the controls on gambling, with recommendations designed to simplify regulation and extend choice for adult gamblers. The review proposes that all gambling activities, including betting other than spread betting, should be regulated by a single regulator, a new Gambling Commission. Casinos would be permitted to provide a wider range of gambling activities, including betting and bingo. The proposals are designed to ensure that permitted forms of gambling remain crime-free and that there is protection for children and vulnerable groups. The Government has asked for comments on the report by 31 October 2001, and intends to publish early in 2002 its plans on how the reform of gambling will be taken forward.

> The Government has announced that general betting duty of 6.75% on total stakes will be replaced in October 2001 with a 15% tax on bookmakers' gross profits. Off-course punters will no longer be liable for tax on their stakes. The change is designed to help bookmakers develop their domestic and international business from an onshore base, while protecting the future revenue received by the Government from betting. Several UK bookmaking firms had set up separate offshore operations to cater for the growing global market for telephone and Internet betting and in order to avoid what they considered to be onerous UK taxes, but under the new arrangements almost all have said they would relocate their offshore operations to the United Kingdom.

POPULAR SPORTS[4]

Some of the major sports in the UK, many of which were invented by the British, are described below. During 2001 several sports, such as horse racing and field sports, have been affected by the outbreak of foot-and-mouth disease (see p. 460). The Government's key priority has been to try to eradicate the foot-and-mouth virus. As a result, some sporting fixtures and events were postponed or cancelled.

---

[4] Statistics for participation in particular sports in this section are usually provided by the relevant governing body. Website addresses are included for selected sporting governing bodies.

Angling

Angling is one of the most popular sports, with an estimated 3 million anglers in the UK. In England and Wales the most widely practised form of angling is for coarse fish (freshwater fish other than salmon or trout). The rivers and lochs of Scotland, Wales and Northern Ireland are the main areas for salmon and trout fishing. Separate organisations represent game, coarse and sea fishing clubs in England, Wales, Scotland and Northern Ireland, and there are separate competitions in each of the three disciplines.

The UK has several world champion coarse anglers. Alan Scotthorne is the only person to have won three consecutive world titles, and in 1999 Bob Nudd became the first angler to be world champion for the fourth time. England won the team gold in the 2000 European freshwater fishing championships held in Nottingham and the team silver in the championships in Hungary in 2001. Paul Starbuck is the current junior world champion.

Athletics

In the UK athletics incorporates many activities, including track and field events, cross-country and road running, race walking, and fell and hill running. Mass participation events, notably marathons and half marathons, are popular. Many runners are sponsored, raising considerable amounts for charities and other good causes.

The largest UK marathon is the London Marathon each April, with over 30,000 runners competing in the 2001 event. The Great North Run, a half marathon, takes place between Newcastle upon Tyne and South Shields each September/October.

The governing body for the sport is UK Athletics (*www.ukathletics.org*). It has made successful bids to host major championships, including the World Half Marathon in Bristol in 2001; the World Indoor Championships, which will be held at Birmingham in 2003; and the European Cross Country Championships, to be held in Edinburgh in 2003.

At the Sydney Olympics in September 2000 Jonathan Edwards and Denise Lewis won gold medals in the triple jump and the heptathlon respectively. Four other athletes won medals: two silver, for Steve Backley in the javelin and Darren Campbell in the 200 metres, and two bronze, for Kelly Holmes in the 800 metres and Katharine Merry in the 400 metres. At the world championships in Edmonton (Canada) in August 2001 Jonathan Edwards won the triple jump and Dean Macey won the bronze medal in the decathlon. Paula Radcliffe followed her gold medal in the world half marathon championships in Veracruz (Mexico) in November 2000 by winning the 8 km world cross-country championships and finishing second in the 4 km event in Ostend (Belgium) in March 2001. British athletes held world records in two events in mid-2001: Jonathan Edwards in the triple jump and Colin Jackson in the 110 metre hurdles.

Badminton

Badminton takes its name from the Duke of Beaufort's country home, Badminton House, where the sport was first played in the 19th century. The game is organised by the Badminton Association of England and the Scottish, Welsh and Irish (Ulster branch) Badminton Unions. Around 2 million people play badminton regularly. The Badminton Association of England (*www.baofe.co.uk*) has a coach education system to develop coaches for players of all levels and a development department with a network of part-time county development officers.

The All England Badminton Championships, staged at the National Indoor Arena in Birmingham, is one of the world's leading tournaments. At the Olympic Games in 2000, Simon Archer and Joanne Goode won the bronze medal in the mixed doubles.

Basketball

Over 3 million people participate in basketball in the UK. The English Basketball Association is the governing body in England, with similar associations in Wales, Scotland and Ireland (Ulster Branch). All the associations are represented in the British and Irish Basketball Federation, which acts as the coordinating body for the UK and the Irish Republic.

The leading clubs play in the British Basketball League and the National Basketball League, which cover four divisions for men and two for women, while there are also leagues for younger players in the RAF Junior/Cadet League and the Passerelle competition. Mini-basketball has been developed for players under the age of 12. Wheelchair basketball is played under the same rules, with a few basic adaptations, and on the same court as the running game.

The English Basketball Association (*www.basketballengland.org.uk*) runs various development schemes for young people which aim to increase participation and improve the quality of basketball. With support from National Lottery funds, some 10,000 outdoor basketball goals have been installed in parks and play areas in England.

Bowls

The two main forms of bowls are lawn flat green (outdoor and indoor) and crown green. About 6,000 flat green outdoor lawn bowling clubs are affiliated to the English, Scottish, Welsh and Irish Bowling Associations, which, together with the Women's Bowling Associations for the four countries, play to the laws of the World Bowls Board. Crown green, indoor, English bowls federation and short mat bowls have their own separate associations. The World Bowls Tour now organises bowls at the professional level. A new single world governing body, World Bowls Ltd, has been set up, with headquarters in Edinburgh.

UK bowlers have achieved considerable success in international championships. At the world outdoor championships in April 2000 in Johannesburg, gold medals were won by Scotland (represented by Alex Marshall and George Sneddon) in the pairs event and by the four representing Wales: Mark Williams, Stephen Rees, Robert Weale and Will Thomas. At the women's outdoor championships held in Australia in March 2000, the Scottish pairing of Margaret Letham and Joyce Lindores won the women's world pairs title and England won the overall team title. At the 2001 world indoor championships, held in Hopton-on-Sea (Norfolk), Paul Foster won the singles event, while Les Gillett and Mark McMahon won the pairs title.

Boxing

Boxing in its modern form is based on the rules established by the Marquess of Queensberry in 1865. In the UK boxing is both amateur and professional, and in both strict medical regulations are applied.

All amateur boxing in England is controlled by the Amateur Boxing Association of England. There are separate associations in Scotland and Wales, and boxing in Northern Ireland is controlled by the Irish Amateur Boxing Association. The associations organise amateur boxing championships as well as training courses for referees and coaches. Headguards must be used in all UK amateur competitions.

Professional boxing in the UK is controlled by the British Boxing Board of Control (*www.bbbofc.com*). The Board appoints referees, timekeepers, inspectors, medical officers and representatives to ensure that regulations are observed, and that contests take place under carefully regulated conditions. Medical controls and safety measures must be in place at all licensed tournaments, to minimise the risk to boxers. The Board nominates challengers for British championships and represents the interests of British licensed boxers in the international championship bodies of which it is a member.

In mid-2001 the UK had two world champions (as recognised by organisations of which the British Boxing Board of Control is a member): Joe Calzaghe, who holds the World Boxing Organisation (WBO) super-middleweight title; and Johnny Nelson (WBO cruiserweight).

Audley Harrison, who won the gold medal in the super-heavyweight division at the Sydney Olympics, has recently turned professional and won his first professional contest in May 2001. At the world amateur boxing championships in Belfast in June 2001 UK boxers won two medals: David Haye, a silver in the heavyweight division; and Carl Froch, a bronze in the middleweight.

Chess

There are local chess clubs and leagues throughout the UK, and chess is also played widely in schools and other educational establishments. Domestic competitions include the British Championships, the National Club Championships and the County Championships. The Hastings Chess Congress, which started in 1895, is the world's longest running annual international chess tournament. A number of UK chess players feature among the world's best, including Michael Adams and Nigel Short.

The governing bodies are the British Chess Federation (*www.bcf.ndirect.co.uk*) (responsible for chess in England and for coordinating activity among the home nations), the Scottish Chess Association and the Welsh and Ulster Chess Unions.

Cricket

The rules of cricket became the responsibility, in the 18th century, of the Marylebone Cricket Club (MCC), based at Lord's cricket ground in north London, and it still frames the laws today. The England and Wales Cricket Board (ECB) (*www.ecb.co.uk*) administers men's and women's cricket in England and Wales. The Scottish Cricket Union administers cricket in Scotland.

Cricket is played in schools, colleges and universities, and amateur teams play weekly games in cities, towns and villages. There is a network of First Class cricket, minor county cricket and club games with a variety of leagues. Recent changes to two of the main professional cricket competitions have involved the creation of a two-division structure for the Cricinfo Championship, which is played by 18 county teams in four-day matches, and for the one-day Norwich Union League. Two other main one-day competitions are held: the Cheltenham & Gloucester Trophy and the Benson & Hedges Cup.

Each summer two visiting teams play Test cricket against England in a number of five-day Test Matches; a ten-match one-day triangular competition, the NatWest Series, is also contested. In 2001 the visiting teams were Pakistan and Australia. The other Test-playing countries are Bangladesh, India, New Zealand, South Africa, Sri Lanka, the West Indies and Zimbabwe. A team representing England usually tours one or more of these countries in the UK winter. The International Cricket Council (ICC) is introducing a ranking system for Test nations, the ICC Test Championship, in which the Test-playing nations will play each other on a regular basis over a rolling five-year period.

Cycling

Cycling includes road and track racing, time-trialling, mountain biking (downhill, cross-country and dual slalom), cyclo-cross (cross-country racing), touring and BMX (bicycle moto-cross). Mountain bikes are increasingly popular and make up the majority of the sales of bicycles.

The British Cycling Federation (BCF) (*www.bcf.uk.com*) has 14,000 members and 1,200 affiliated clubs. It is the internationally recognised governing body for British cycle sport. The Road Time Trials Council controls road time trials and has around 1,030 member clubs. In 2000 some 85,100 rides were completed in open time trials in England and Wales. CTC (Cyclists' Touring Club) (*www.ctc.org.uk*), with 71,000 members and affiliates, is the governing body for recreational (including off-road) and urban cycling, and hosts the CTC rally each year in York. CTC Scotland and the Scottish Cyclists' Union represent cyclists in Scotland. CTC Cymru represents CTC in Wales. Wales and Northern Ireland have separate federations affiliated to the BCF.

The British cycling team achieved success in 2000 at both the Sydney Olympics and the World Track Championships held at the Manchester Velodrome. At the Olympic Games Jason Queally won a gold medal in the 1 km time trial and, together with Craig MacLean and Chris Hoy, won a silver medal in the men's sprint. Bronze medals were won by Yvonne McGregor in the 3,000 m pursuit and by the men's pursuit team. At the World Track Championships the team won five medals—Yvonne McGregor won her first world 3,000 m pursuit title, while there were silver medals for the men's sprint and the men's pursuit teams, and bronze medals for Jason Queally in the 1 km time trial and Rob Hayles in the men's individual pursuit.

Equestrianism

Leading equestrian events are held at a number of locations throughout the year. The Badminton Horse Trials, sponsored by Mitsubishi Motors, is normally one of the UK's largest sporting events, attracting around 250,000 spectators. However, in 2001 it did not take place as a result of foot-and-mouth disease. The major show jumping events include the Horse of the Year Show at Wembley in London and the Hickstead Derby in West Sussex.

The British Equestrian Federation (BEF) (*www.bef.co.uk*) acts as the international secretariat on behalf of its members. They include the British Show Jumping Association, British Eventing, British Dressage, British Horse Driving Trials Association, British Endurance Riding Association and British Equestrian Vaulting. These associations act as the governing bodies of the different sporting disciplines in the UK and oversee the organisation of the major national and international events. The British Horse Society, which includes Riding Clubs, is responsible for promoting training, road safety, rights of way and the welfare of horses, while the Pony Club provides training for children.

At the 2000 Olympic Games, the British team of Jeanette Brakewell, Pippa Funnell, Leslie Law and Ian Stark won the silver medal in the three-day event.

Exercise and Fitness

Exercise and fitness is a term covering a variety of activities—such as exercise to music, aqua exercise, weight training and circuit training—which aim to improve health and fitness. The Keep Fit Association (KFA) (*www.keepfit.org.uk*), which has 900 teachers and a membership of 8,500, promotes fitness through movement, exercise and dance for people of all ages and abilities. Its national certificated training scheme for KFA teachers is recognised by local education authorities throughout the UK. Autonomous associations serve Scotland, Wales and Northern Ireland.

Field Sports

Field sports in the UK include hunting, shooting, stalking, ferreting, falconry and hare coursing. There are over 300 recognised packs of quarry hounds in the UK, of which more than 180 are foxhound packs recognised by the Masters of Fox Hounds Association. Most hunts organise 'point-to-point' race meetings (see p. 305). The Countryside Alliance promotes, among several other issues, the interests of field sports.

In June 2000, following the report of the Committee of Inquiry into Hunting with Dogs in England and Wales, the Government announced its intention to introduce a Bill containing a series of legislative options. In a free vote on the Hunting Bill in January 2001, Members of Parliament voted by 387 to 174 to ban hunting and hare coursing with dogs in England and Wales, although subsequently the House of Lords supported self-regulation of hunting by a vote of 249 to 108. However, the Bill did not complete its passage through Parliament. Following the General Election, the Government has indicated that the House of Commons will be given an early opportunity to make its views known in the new parliamentary session and that it will enable Parliament to reach a conclusion on the issue.

Football

Association football is controlled by separate football associations in England, Wales, Scotland and Northern Ireland. In England 314 clubs are affiliated to the Football Association (FA) (*www.the-fa.org*) and about 42,000 clubs to regional or district associations. The FA, founded in 1863, and the Football League (*www.football-league.co.uk*), founded in 1888, were both the first of their kind in the world. In Scotland there are 78 full and associate clubs and nearly 6,000 registered clubs under the jurisdiction of the Scottish Football Association (*www.scottishfa.co.uk*).

In England the FA Premier League comprises 20 clubs. A further 72 full-time professional clubs play in three main divisions run by the Football League. Over 2,000 English League matches are played during the season, from August to May.

Three Welsh clubs play in the Football League, while the National League of Wales contains 20 semi-professional clubs. In Scotland 12 clubs play in the Scottish Premier League, while a further 30 clubs play in the Scottish Football League, which has three divisions. In Northern Ireland, 20 semi-professional clubs play in the Irish Football League.

The major knock-out competitions are the FA Cup (sponsored by AXA) and the Worthington Cup in England, the Tennents Scottish Cup and the CIS Insurance Cup in Scotland, the Irish Cup and the Welsh FA Cup.

Football is popular among spectators, and some 42.2 million spectators attended the main English and Scottish League matches in 1999–2000. Turnover of the FA Premier League's clubs reached £772 million in 1999–2000. The FA is investing substantially in developing grass-roots football facilities. In 2001 it announced plans for a new National Football Centre in Burton-on-Trent, to be opened in 2003. Meanwhile, **sport**scotland has invested over £18 million of Lottery funds in developing Scottish football, at both grass-roots and elite level, and in March 2001 announced two football academies, at Kilmarnock and Rangers football clubs, to help develop talented young footballers into top-class international players.

In 2001 Liverpool won the UEFA Cup, defeating Alaves of Spain in the final in Dortmund (Germany), the team's third Cup victory during the year following victories in the AXA-sponsored FA Cup and in the Worthington Cup. Leeds reached the semi-finals of the Champions League.

Gaelic Games

Gaelic Games, popular in Northern Ireland, cover the sports of Gaelic football, ladies' Gaelic football, handball, hurling, camogie (women's hurling) and rounders. There are over 700 clubs (incorporating more than 2,550 teams) in Northern Ireland affiliated to the Gaelic Athletic Association, the Ladies Gaelic Football Association and the Camogie Association, the official governing bodies responsible for Gaelic Games.

Golf

Since 1897 the rules of golf have been administered worldwide (excluding the United States and Mexico) by The Royal and Ancient Golf Club (R & A) (*www.randa.org*), which is situated at St Andrews. Club professional golf is governed by the Professional Golfers' Association (PGA) (*www.pga.org.uk*) and tournament golf by the European PGA Tour and the European Ladies Professional Golfers' Association. The home country governing bodies for men's amateur golf are affiliated to the R & A and are represented on the Council of National Golf Unions, which is the UK coordinating body responsible for handicapping and organising home international matches. Women's amateur golf in Great Britain is governed by the Ladies' Golf Union.

The main tournament of the British golfing year is the Open Championship, one of the world's four 'major' events. Other important competitions include the World Matchplay Championship at Wentworth; the Walker Cup and Curtis Cup matches for amateurs, played every two years between Great Britain and Ireland and the United States; and the Ryder Cup and Solheim Cup matches for men and women professionals respectively, played every two years between Europe and the United States.

There are over 2,000 golf courses in the UK. Some of the most famous include St Andrews, Royal Lytham and St Anne's (which staged the 2001 Open Championship), Royal Birkdale, and Carnoustie.

In October 2000 Lee Westwood won the World Matchplay Championship. He also headed the European list of money winners in 2000, succeeding Colin Montgomerie, who had been top for the previous seven years.

Greyhound Racing

Greyhound racing is one of the UK's most popular spectator sports, with about 4 million spectators a year. The rules for the sport are drawn up by the National Greyhound Racing Club (NGRC), the sport's judicial and administrative body. The representative body is the British Greyhound Racing Board.

Meetings are usually held three times a week at each track, with at least ten races a meeting. The main event of the year is the Greyhound Derby, run in June at Wimbledon Stadium, London. Tracks are licensed by local authorities. There are 32 major tracks that operate under the rules of the NGRC and around 30 smaller independent tracks.

Gymnastics

Gymnastics is divided into seven main disciplines: artistic (or Olympic) gymnastics, rhythmic gymnastics, sports acrobatics, general gymnastics, sports aerobics, trampolining, and gymnastics and movement for people with disabilities.

The governing body for the sport is British Gymnastics, to which 925 clubs are affiliated. It is estimated that between 3 million and 4 million schoolchildren take part in some form of gymnastics every day.

Highland Games

Scottish Highland Games cover a wide range of athletic competitions, including running, cycling and dancing. The heavyweight events are the most popular and include throwing the hammer, tossing the caber and putting the shot. Over 70 events of various kinds take place throughout Scotland, the most famous being the annual Braemar Gathering.

The Scottish Games Association is the official governing body responsible for athletic sports and games at Highland and Border events in Scotland.

Hockey

The modern game of hockey was founded in England in 1886. A single association—English Hockey (*www.hockeyonline.co.uk*)—now governs men's and women's hockey in England, with similar single associations in Scotland and Wales. Cup competitions and leagues exist at national, divisional or district, club and school levels, both indoors (six-a-side) and outdoors, and there are regular international matches and tournaments. The National Hockey Stadium in Milton Keynes is the venue for all major hockey matches played in England.

Horse Racing

Horse racing takes two main forms—flat racing and National Hunt (steeplechasing and hurdle) racing. The turf flat race season lasts from late March to early November, but all-weather flat racing and National Hunt racing take place throughout the year. Great Britain has 59 racecourses and about 14,000 horses currently in training. Point-to-point racing, restricted to amateur riders on horses which are qualified by having gone hunting, takes place between January and June.

The Derby, run at Epsom, is the outstanding event in the flat racing calendar. Other classic races are: the 2,000 Guineas and the 1,000 Guineas, both held at Newmarket; the Oaks (Epsom); and the St Leger (Doncaster). The meeting at Royal Ascot in June is another significant flat racing event. The most important National Hunt meeting is the National Hunt Festival held at Cheltenham in March, which features the Gold Cup and the Champion Hurdle. The Grand National, run at Aintree, near Liverpool, since the 1830s, is the world's most famous steeplechase. The race is televised around the world, with an estimated total audience of approximately 500 million in 150 countries in 2001.

As the governing authority for racing, the British Horseracing Board (BHB) (*www.bhb.co.uk*) is responsible for strategic and financial planning, the fixture list, race programmes, relations with the Government and the betting industry, and central marketing. The Jockey Club, as the regulatory authority, is responsible for licensing, disciplinary matters and security.

The Government has announced that the Horserace Totalisator Board (the Tote), which provides pool betting facilities on racecourses and a range of other betting facilities, will be sold to the racing industry. It also intends to abolish the Horserace Betting Levy Board and the annual levy under which a proportion of horserace betting turnover of bookmakers and the Tote is returned to the racing industry. Discussions are in progress between the racing and betting industries on a successor commercial arrangement.

Ice Hockey

Ice hockey is a significant indoor sport, with over 2 million spectators each season. There are two professional leagues, with seven teams in the Ice Hockey Superleague and a further 12 teams in the Findus British National Ice Hockey League. The English Premier League is a development league, with ten teams in its Premier Division while there are also two lower divisions (North and South). There are around 11,500 players in the UK.

Ice Skating

Ice skating has four main disciplines: ice figure (single and pairs), ice dance, speed skating and synchronised skating. Participation in ice skating is concentrated among the under-25s, and it is one of the few sports that attracts more female than male participants. The governing body is the National Ice Skating Association of UK Ltd. The Association has 75 affiliated clubs and over 4,500 individual members. There are over 70 rinks in the United Kingdom.

> In a major £40 million development, a new National Ice Centre has been opened at Nottingham. The first Olympic-sized ice rink was opened in April 2000 and a second rink in April 2001. The Centre houses many ice sports, including free skating, ice dance, precision skating, ice hockey and short track speed skating. It is also the base of the National Ice Skating Association, part of the English Institute of Sport network and home to the Short Track Speed Team national squad.

Judo

Judo is popular not only as a competitive sport and self-defence technique, but also as a means of general fitness training. There is an internationally recognised grading system, which is in operation through the sport's governing body, the British Judo Association (*www.britishjudo.org.uk*).

At the world championships in Munich in July 2001 Kate Howey won a silver medal in the under 70 kg category and Karina Bryant won a silver in the open category, and John Buchanan won a bronze medal in the under 60 kg division. At the Olympic Games in 2000 Kate Howey won the silver medal in the middleweight event.

Martial Arts

Various martial arts, mainly derived from the Far East, are practised in the UK. There are recognised governing bodies for karate, ju-jitsu, aikido, Chinese martial arts, kendo, taekwondo and tang soo do. The most popular martial art is karate, with over 100,000 participants.

Motor-car Sports

Four-wheeled motor sport includes motor racing, autocross, rallycross, rallying and karting. In motor racing the Formula 1 Grand Prix World Championship is the pinnacle of the sport. The British Grand Prix takes place at Silverstone (Northamptonshire), and the 2001 race reverted to its traditional time of July.

The governing body for four-wheeled motor sport in the UK is The Royal Automobile Club Motor Sports Association, which issues licences for competitors and events. It also organises the British Grand Prix and the Rally of Great Britain, an event in the World Rally Championship.

The UK has had more Formula 1 world champions than any other country, the most recent being the 1996 champion Damon Hill. David Coulthard finished in third place in the 2000 World Championship and in September 2001 was in second place in the 2001 Championship. In November 2000 Richard

Burns won the Rally of Great Britain for the third year running and finished runner-up in the World Rally Championship, while Colin McRae (the 1995 world champion) was fourth. In the 2001 Championship Colin McRae took his number of career victories to 23, and in September 2001 he was sharing the lead in the Championship.

UK car constructors, including McLaren and Williams, have enjoyed outstanding success in Grand Prix and many other forms of racing. Seven of the 11 Formula 1 racing teams are based in the United Kingdom, as are half the World Rally teams. The UK produces around 75% of the world's single-seat racing cars, including a large proportion of the cars used in the US Indy and Champ Car series. The British motor sport industry is estimated to generate an annual turnover of over £4.8 billion (of which exports account for 50%) and to directly employ over 40,000 people.

> A major new motor racing circuit, at Rockingham (Northamptonshire), on the site of the former Corby steelworks, was opened in May 2001. Its first event was a historic racing festival. In September 2001 it staged a round of the US Champ Car series.

Motorcycle Sports

Motorcycle sports include road racing, moto-cross, grass track, speedway, trials, drag racing, enduro (endurance off-road racing) and sprint. There are between 40,000 and 50,000 competitive motorcyclists in the UK.

The governing bodies of the sport are the Auto-Cycle Union (ACU) (*www.acu.org.uk*), for Great Britain, and the Motor Cycle Union of Ireland (in Northern Ireland). The major events of the year include the Isle of Man TT Races, the British Road Race Grand Prix, two rounds of the World Superbike series, and the British Superbike series. The ACU also provides road race training through the ACU Road Race Academy and off-road training by approved instructors for riders of all ages.

In September 2000 Mark Loram won the world speedway title, the first British winner of the event since 1992. In June 2001 the British Speedway Grand Prix was held in the Millennium Stadium in Cardiff for the first time, having previously been staged at Coventry. In 2001 Dougie Lampkin won his fifth successive outdoor title in the world motorcycle trials championship.

Mountaineering

The representative body is the British Mountaineering Council (BMC) (*www.thebmc.co.uk*), which works closely with the Mountaineering Councils of Scotland and Ireland. Their main areas of work include access and conservation, training and the provision of information. The BMC estimates that the number of active climbers is around 150,000, while there are also a large number of hill walkers. There are over 300 mountaineering and climbing clubs in the UK, and three National Centres for mountaineering activities run by the Sports Councils (see pp. 296–7). UK mountaineers have been prominent among the explorers of the world's great mountain ranges.

Netball

More than 60,000 adults play netball regularly in England alone and a further 1 million young people play in schools. The sport is played almost exclusively by women and girls, although male participation has increased in recent years.

The All England Netball Association (*www.england-netball.co.uk*) is the governing body in England, with Scotland, Wales and Northern Ireland having their own separate organisations. National competitions are staged annually for all age-groups, and England plays a series of international matches against other countries, both in England and overseas.

Rowing

Rowing takes place, both on inland waterways and on the coast, in many schools, universities and rowing clubs throughout the UK. The boats used range from singles and pairs to fours and eights. The governing bodies are the

Amateur Rowing Association (ARA) (*www.ara-rowing.org*) in England, with similar bodies in Scotland, Wales and Northern Ireland. The ARA is also the governing body for representative international teams for Great Britain, in World and Olympic competition.

The Head of the River Race is the largest assembly of racing craft in the world, with more than 420 eights racing in procession on the Thames. Similar events are run throughout the winter months for fours, pairs and singles. Racing over the same course, the University Boat Race, between two eights from Oxford and Cambridge, has been rowed almost every spring since 1836. Cambridge won the event in March 2001, to take its total number of victories to 77; Oxford has won 69 races and there has been one dead heat. The National Championships are held at the National Water Sports Centre at Holme Pierrepont, with a series of races over 2,000 metres. At the Henley Regatta in Oxfordshire crews from all over the world compete each July in various kinds of race over a straight course of 1 mile 550 yards (about 2.1 km).

In the 2000 Sydney Olympics the British rowing team won two gold medals and a silver medal , its best result since 1948. Sir Steve Redgrave (who has since retired) became the first competitor in Olympic history to win five gold medals in an endurance sport in consecutive Olympics when he won the coxless four, together with Matthew Pinsent (with whom he had won the coxless pairs in the 1992 and 1996 Olympics), James Cracknell and Tim Foster. The men's eight also won gold, while the women's quadruple scull won a silver medal, Britain's first women's Olympic medal in rowing.

Rugby League

Rugby league (a 13-a-side game) originated in 1895 following the breakaway from rugby union (see below) of 22 clubs in the north of England, where the sport is still concentrated. In the UK there are 30 professional clubs, with about 2,000 professional players, and some 400 amateur clubs with a total of around 40,000 players.

The governing body of the professional game is the Rugby Football League (*www.rfl.uk.com*), while the amateur game is governed by the British Amateur Rugby League Association. The major domestic club match of the season is the Challenge Cup Final.

Matches in the two main leagues are played in the summer. The Tetley's Super League consists of 12 clubs—11 from the north of England and one from London—while 19 clubs play in the Northern Ford Premiership.

Sixteen nations contested the Lincoln Financial Group World Cup in 2000. In the final at Old Trafford (Manchester) Australia defeated New Zealand. Wales and England were the other two teams to reach the semi-finals.

Rugby Union

Rugby union football (a 15-a-side game) originated at Rugby School in the first half of the 19th century. The sport is played under the auspices of the Rugby Football Union (RFU) (*www.rfu.com*) in England (the International Rugby Board internationally) and parallel bodies in Wales, Scotland and Ireland. In July 2001 an agreement was reached under which the RFU and the Premiership Clubs in England formed a joint venture, England Rugby Ltd, to manage their international and professional game together. Each of the four home unions has separate national league and knock-out competitions for its domestic clubs; however, the two premier sides in Scotland play in a league with Welsh clubs. Leicester became the new European champions in May 2001 when winning the Heineken Cup, beating Stade Français in the final in Paris.

The Lloyds TSB Six Nations Championship is contested by England, Scotland, Wales, Ireland (a team from the Irish Republic and Northern Ireland), France and Italy. Overseas tours are undertaken by the national sides and by the British and Irish Lions, a team representing Great Britain and Ireland. Tours to the UK are made by teams representing the major rugby-playing nations.

Sailing

Sailing is a broad term used to cover yacht and dinghy racing and cruising, powerboat racing,

In finishing second in the yacht *Kingfisher* in the Vendée Globe race in February 2001, Ellen MacArthur (see picture opposite p. 299) became the fastest woman to circumnavigate the world in a single-handed race. At the age of 24, she was also the youngest person to achieve this feat.

motor cruising, jet skiing and windsurfing on inland and offshore waters. The Royal Yachting Association (RYA) (*www.rya.org.uk*) is the national governing body for boating in the UK and aims to make boating in all its forms as accessible as possible. The Association also includes RYA Sailability, the charity for disabled sailors. It also administers the Yachtmaster yachting qualification. According to the British Marine Industries Federation, about 7.8 million people participate in the sport. Among well-known yachting events in the UK are Cowes Week and the Fastnet Race.

In the 2000 Olympic Games the British team was the most successful nation in sailing, winning five medals. Gold medals were won by Ben Ainslie (in the Laser class), Iain Percy (Finn class) and Shirley Robertson (Europe class), while silver medals were won by Ian Barker and Simon Hiscocks in the 49er event and by Ian Walker and Mark Covell in the Star class.

Skiing and Other Winter Sports

Skiing takes place in Scotland from December to May and also at several English locations when there is sufficient snow. The five established winter sports areas in Scotland are Cairngorm, Glencoe, Glenshee, the Lecht and Nevis Range. All have a full range of ski-lifts, prepared ski-runs and professional instructors.

There are over 115 artificial or dry ski-slopes throughout the UK. The British Ski and Snowboard Federation is the representative body for international competitive skiing and snowboarding. The four home country ski councils are responsible for the development of the sport at grass-roots level.

Snooker and Billiards

Snooker was invented by the British in India in 1875 and is played by approximately 7 million people in the UK. British players have dominated the major professional championships. The main tournament is the annual Embassy World Professional Championship, held at the Crucible Theatre in Sheffield. In May 2001 Ronnie O'Sullivan won the title, defeating John Higgins in the final by 18 frames to 14.

World Snooker (*www.worldsnooker.com*) organises professional events and holds the copyright for the rules. The representative body for women is the World Ladies' Billiards and Snooker Association.

Squash

Squash derives from the game of rackets, which was invented at Harrow School in the 1850s. The governing body for squash in England is the Squash Rackets Association (*www.squash.co.uk*); there are separate governing bodies in Wales, Scotland and Northern Ireland. The British Open Championships is one of the major world events in the sport.

The number of players in the UK is estimated at over 1.5 million, of whom more than 500,000 compete regularly in inter-club league competitions. There are nearly 9,000 squash courts in England, provided mainly by squash clubs, commercial organisations and local authorities.

Peter Nicol is the current men's world squash champion. The England team of Tania Bailey, Stephanie Brind and Linda Charman won the women's team title in Sheffield in November 2000, defeating Australia in the final.

Swimming

Swimming is a popular sport and form of exercise for people from all age-groups (see Table 18.1). Competitive swimming is governed by the Amateur Swimming Association (ASA) (*www.britishswimming.org*) in England and by similar associations in Scotland and Wales. Together these three associations form the Amateur Swimming Federation of Great Britain Ltd, which coordinates the selection of Great Britain teams and organises international competitions. Instruction and coaching are provided by qualified teachers and coaches who hold certificates awarded mainly by the ASA. Northern Ireland forms part of Swim Ireland. The British team won seven medals in the World Championships in Fukuoka (Japan) in July 2001, including a gold medal for the 4 x 200 m women's freestyle relay team of Nicola Jackson, Janine Belton, Karen Legg and Karen Pickering.

Table Tennis

Table tennis originated in England in the 1880s. Today it is played by all age-groups, and in a variety of venues, ranging from small halls to specialist, multi-table centres. It is also a major recreational and competitive activity for people with disabilities. The governing body in England is the English Table Tennis Association (*www.etta.co.uk*) and there is also an English Schools Association. Separate associations exist in Scotland, Wales and Ireland (where the association covers both Northern Ireland and the Irish Republic).

Tennis

The modern game of tennis originated in England in 1873 and the first championships were played at Wimbledon in 1877. The governing body for tennis in Great Britain is the Lawn Tennis Association (LTA) (*www.lta.org.uk*), to which Tennis Wales and the Scottish LTA are affiliated. Tennis in Northern Ireland is governed by Tennis Ireland (Ulster Branch).

The Wimbledon Championships, held within the grounds of the All England Club, are one of the four tennis 'Grand Slam' tournaments. They attracted a record 490,000 spectators in 2001. Prize money totalled £8.5 million. In 2000 the Championships generated a surplus of £31.1 million, which was invested in British tennis. The UK's two leading players, Tim Henman (a Wimbledon semi-finalist in 1998, 1999 and 2001) and Greg Rusedski, have both won titles on the main tennis tour in 2001. Lee Childs and James Nelson won the boys' doubles at the US Open in September 2000, and at the end of 2000 they became the first British players to be declared world junior champions by the International Tennis Federation.

About 5 million people play tennis in the UK. There are national and county championships, while national competitions are organised for schools. The LTA has a five-year plan for developing tennis in Great Britain, with the aim of expanding participation, encouraging regular competition and producing more world-class tennis players. Tennis facilities are being improved, with more indoor tennis centres, clay courts and floodlit courts.

Further Reading

The Government's Plan for Sport. Department for Culture, Media and Sport, 2001.

A Sporting Future for All. Department for Culture, Media and Sport, 2000.

Sport 21: A Strategy for Sport in Scotland. **sport**scotland, 1998.

Websites

Department for Culture, Media and Sport: www.culture.gov.uk

Department of Culture, Arts and Leisure (Northern Ireland): www.dcalni.gov.uk

UK Sport: www.uksport.gov.uk

Sport England: www.sportengland.org

Sportscotland: www.sportscotland.org.uk

Sports Council for Northern Ireland: www.sportni.org

Sports Council for Wales: www.sports-council-wales.co.uk

Design

Design—sometimes unnoticed, often highly creative—is a pervasive influence in UK society today. It covers a huge range of activities: the packaging of a tin of beans, the latest fashion styles, the layout and appearance of websites and the special effects produced in a film are all the responsibility of designers. Design boosts the economy and exports, introduces new and updated products into everyday life, and helps to change the way we communicate and think about ourselves.

British business spends an estimated £27 billion on design either as an in-house resource or as a bought-in service, and around 1 million people are employed in design in the UK in either full- or part-time positions.[1] A relatively small number of these (around 7,000) work for the top 100 specialist firms, selling design services to other companies. British design consultancies earn around £1 billion a year in export revenue. In 1998–99 some 18,000 students were studying design courses at colleges of further and higher education, including graphic design, theatre and interior design, photography, craft and animation courses.[2] The UK's expertise in areas such as airport and transport design is acknowledged worldwide, with British designers having a strong presence in all the international large automotive design studios.

Designer fashion is another growth area. Individual designers such as Alexander McQueen, Julien Macdonald and Stella McCartney have gained international reputations, and London Fashion Week is now firmly established as a leading event in the fashion house circuit. The UK designer fashion industry is currently ranked fourth largest in the world, behind those of the United States, France and Italy.

[1] Design Council research, 2001.

[2] As a comparison, there were about 8,000 creative arts graduates from Great Britain institutions in 1991–92.

Better design is supported and encouraged in the UK by the Design Council, an independent organisation working with partners in business, education and government to inspire and enable the effective use of design. Its work includes web-based knowledge sharing, events, publications and educational materials highlighting design best practice, as well as the development of tools to enable the integration of design into management. The Design Council also runs two annual awareness-raising initiatives: Design in Business Week and Design in Education Week.

Changing patterns in the UK economy have resulted in the increasing dominance of service sector and technology-intensive businesses. The expansion of e-commerce, the shorthand name given to many of these changes,[3] has opened up fresh opportunities for design. In 2000, seven of the top ten UK design consultancies specialised in digital media.[4] As more and more business is conducted over the Internet, the design of websites will become increasingly important in attracting new customers.

The ability to generate new ideas or develop innovative products or processes is a much prized but often elusive skill. The traditional workplace is not always the best environment for such creativity. In a recent survey of company directors, 39% of those questioned said that their best ideas came to them while travelling; thinking in bed worked best for 18% of directors; and 12% favoured bathtime as a source of creative ideas. Only 11% replied that their best ideas came to them while they were at work.[5]

[3] See the essay on e-commerce on p. 536 and chapter 29: Finance and Other Service Industries.

[4] See chapter 17: Media and Communications.

[5] Mori/3M sponsored research. Survey of 102 FTSE 500 company and finance directors. Taken from *Design in Britain 2000*.

19 Environmental Protection

Conservation	312	Land, Waste, Recycling and Litter	324
Administration	312	Water	328
Countryside and Wildlife	312	Air and the Atmosphere	330
Buildings and Monuments	321	Noise	334
World Heritage Sites	323	Radioactivity	336
Pollution Control	323	**Businesses and the Consumer**	337
Administration	323	**Environmental Research**	338
Industrial Pollution Control	324		

Recent initiatives to support the countryside and environmental protection include the Countryside and Rights of Way Act 2000 for England and Wales and the rural White Papers in England and Scotland.

Government funding for countryside and wildlife programmes in 2002–03 will be £207 million in England and Wales, £52.6 million in Scotland and £1.6 million in Northern Ireland.

Conservation

Administration

The Department for Environment, Food and Rural Affairs (DEFRA) is responsible for countryside policy and environmental protection in England. It was formed from the Ministry of Agriculture, Fisheries and Food (MAFF) and parts of the Department of the Environment, Transport and the Regions (DETR) in June 2001 to ensure that objectives for the countryside are integrated with agricultural policies. The Environment Group of the Scottish Executive Environment and Rural Affairs Department, the National Assembly for Wales (NAW) and the Northern Ireland Executive have broadly equivalent responsibilities for other parts of the UK. The four bodies are responsible for implementing the Biodiversity Action Plan, the overarching framework for conservation work in the UK (see p. 320). Many of the conservation functions are delegated to agencies, which are described below. In addition, local authorities and many voluntary organisations are actively involved in environmental conservation and protection.

Countryside and Wildlife

Countryside and Wildlife Agencies, and Voluntary Organisations

The Wildlife and Countryside Directorate within DEFRA is responsible for policy on wildlife and countryside in England. It sponsors three non-departmental public bodies: the Countryside Agency, English Nature and the National Forest Company. DEFRA also sponsors the Joint Nature Conservation Committee (JNCC), a committee of three statutory nature conservation agencies (see p. 314).

The Countryside Agency (*www.countryside.gov.uk*) is the statutory body in England whose aims are to conserve and enhance the countryside; promote social equality and economic opportunity for the people who live there; and help everyone, wherever they live, to enjoy this natural asset. It has a budget of around £73 million for 2001–02 which includes £10 million set aside for initiatives announced in the rural White Paper; £2.2 million for its Rural Transport Partnerships Scheme; and £3.5 million for Areas of Outstanding Natural Beauty (AONBs—see p. 315) and for the preparations for the introduction of greater access to open country (see below).

In 2001 the Agency set out its strategy to address the key issues facing the countryside. The strategy comprises eight major work programmes to:

- increase awareness of the impact of policies on rural people and places;
- develop markets for local products and influence subsidy reform;
- establish more areas where visitors can enjoy the countryside;
- revitalise rural service centres;
- create attractive, accessible green spaces around towns;
- secure the quality of the best landscapes;
- equip rural communities to shape their future; and
- help people to care for their landscapes, landmarks and traditions.

The Agency has already started a number of these programmes. In January 2001 it commissioned work on mapping the areas that are open country and common land. The *Countryside Character* database will bring together map-based and trend information on a Geographical Information System (GIS) map of England in order to develop a landscape typography that provides a deeper insight into the components of the English countryside. Once the typography is finalised in 2002, it will be used to assess the impact on the landscape of changes in agricultural practices, new housing, industrial development and transport infrastructure, and mineral extraction.

In April 2001 the Countryside Agency published its third annual comprehensive analysis: *The State of the Countryside 2001*. For the first time the report presents information about 20 thematic indicators illustrating rural economic, social and environmental conditions. The indicators can track changes and the cumulative impact of organisational and individual decisions and policies. The 2001 report details how:

- tourism contributes more than £12 billion a year to the rural economy;
- the rapid decline in farmland birds slowed between 1986 and 1999;
- hedgerow decline appears to have halted;
- one-third of all England's businesses are in rural areas; and
- the growth of rural populations continues to outstrip that of urban populations, as more people move into the countryside.

The Agency has established more than 250 new Millennium Greens in and on the edge of cities, towns, villages and hamlets across England, with the aid of a £10 million Lottery grant from the Millennium Commission.

English Nature (*www. english-nature.org.uk*) promotes the conservation of England's wildlife and natural features and provides advice to the Government on nature conservation. Its budget for 2001–02 is £62.6 million. This includes £8 million to enable it to implement the new provisions on Sites of Special Scientific Interest (SSSIs) (see p. 319) in the Countryside and Rights of Way Act 2000 (see p. 314). In Scotland, the Countryside and Natural Heritage Unit of the Environment Group sponsors *Scottish Natural Heritage* (SNH) (*www.snh.org.uk*), a body with both the nature conservation duties and powers of English Nature, and the countryside and landscape powers of the Countryside Agency. The *Countryside Council for Wales* (CCW) (*www.ccw.gov.uk*) has responsibilities in Wales for landscape and nature conservation and countryside recreation. The budgets for these two organisations for 2001–02 are £48.5 million and £40.2 million respectively. In Northern Ireland, the

Environment and Heritage Service (EHS) (*www.ehsni.gov.uk*), an agency within the Department of the Environment (DOE), protects and manages the natural and built environment and also has an environmental protection role. Its budget for 2001–02 is £35 million.

English Nature, CCW and SNH are also responsible for providing advice and information to the Government and the public on nature conservation, for notifying land as being of special interest due to its wildlife, geological and natural features, and for establishing National Nature Reserves (NNRs).

The JNCC (*www.jncc.gov.uk*) is the statutory committee through which English Nature, CCW and SNH exercise their joint functions. These include: providing advice on amendments to the Wildlife and Countryside Act 1981 and on the development and implementation of policies that affect nature conservation in Great Britain and internationally; and establishing common standards for monitoring of, and research into, nature conservation and the analysis of resultant information. At the international level, the JNCC is working on implementing the Convention on Biological Diversity (see p. 320).

Voluntary organisations are well represented in conservation work. Although they are funded largely by subscription, private donations and entrance fees, many receive government support and grants, sometimes in recognition of statutory responsibilities that they perform.

The *National Trust*, a charity with nearly 2.7 million members, owns and protects places of historic interest and natural beauty for the benefit of the nation. It looks after around 270,000 hectares (667,000 acres) of land in England, Wales and Northern Ireland, including: 200 historic houses; 160 gardens; 40,000 ancient monuments and archaeological remains; forests, woods, fens, farmland, downs, moorland and islands; nature reserves; coastline; and 46 villages. Some 2.6 million people visit National Trust 'pay for entry' properties each year and an estimated 50 million visits are made annually to its coasts and countryside properties.

The separate *National Trust for Scotland* owns 125 properties and 75,000 hectares (185,000 acres) of countryside. Established in 1931, it is supported by a membership of 240,000 and over 2 million people visit its properties each year.

Countryside and Wildlife Legislation

The primary conservation legislation in Great Britain is the Wildlife and Countryside Act 1981, which provides for a range of measures to protect plants and animals from damage and destruction. The Countryside and Rights of Way Act 2000 strengthened this legislation. The Act—the first major piece of countryside legislation to be introduced in England and Wales for nearly 20 years—creates a new statutory right of access, giving people greater freedom to explore the open countryside, while also providing safeguards for landowners. Other provisions within the Act, which came into force in February 2001, include:

- greater protection for SSSIs (see p. 319) and AONBs (see p. 315);
- establishing statutory local access forums to advise local authorities on the improvement of access and rights of way in their area;
- new provisions to tackle wildlife crime (see p. 318);
- enabling courts to order the removal of obstructions from highways;
- requiring vegetation overhanging bridleways to be cut back to a height suitable for horseriders;
- power to regulate traffic for conservation purposes;
- promoting the conservation of important habitats and species; and
- revising and clarifying the definition of town and village greens.

National Parks, Areas of Outstanding Natural Beauty and National Scenic Areas

National Park status recognises the national importance of the area concerned, in terms of landscape, biodiversity and as a recreational resource. However, the name National Park

Table 19.1: National Parks and Other Designated Areas, 2000

	National Parks area (sq km)[1]	% of total area	Areas of Outstanding Natural Beauty (sq km)[2]	% of total area
England	9,934[3]	8[3]	20,439	15
Wales[4]	4,129	20	727	4
Scotland	—	—	10,018	13
Northern Ireland	—	—	2,849	20

[1] 1 square kilometre = just over a third of a square mile.
[2] National Scenic Areas in Scotland.
[3] Including the Broads.
[4] AONBs include 326 sq km of a cross-border area covering England and Wales.
Sources: Countryside Agency, Countryside Council for Wales, Scottish Natural Heritage, Environment and Heritage Service (NI)

does not signify national ownership and most of the land in National Parks is owned by farmers and other private landowners. In England and Wales, each Park is administered by an independent National Park Authority. There are eight National Parks in England (including the Broads) and three in Wales. The oldest is the Peak District National Park, established in 1951. Although there are currently no National Parks in Northern Ireland or Scotland, the Scottish Parliament passed the National Parks (Scotland) Act in July 2000, paving the way to establish Scotland's first National Park—Loch Lomond and the Trossachs—by summer 2002.

The primary objective of AONBs is the conservation and enhancement of the natural beauty of the landscape, although many of them also fulfil a greater recreational purpose. There are 37 in England and five in Wales. Designation started in 1956 with the Gower Peninsula in Wales, and the most recent addition was the Tamar Valley in Cornwall in 1995. The Countryside and Rights of Way Act 2000 gives authorities and communities greater powers to improve the conservation of AONBs.

The Countryside Agency and the CCW designate National Parks and AONBs, subject to confirmation by the Secretary of State for Environment, Food and Rural Affairs or NAW respectively. The Agency is currently considering National Park designations for the New Forest and the South Downs.

In Northern Ireland the Council for Nature Conservation and the Countryside (CNCC) advises the Government on natural landscapes and the designation of AONBs. Nine such areas have been designated and two more areas—Erne Lakeland and Fermanagh Caveland—have been proposed for designation. While Scotland does not have any AONBs it does have four regional parks and 40 National Scenic Areas (NSAs), together covering around 11,000 sq km (4,250 sq miles). In NSAs certain developments are subject to consultation with SNH and, in the event of a disagreement, with the Scottish Executive.

Forest and Country Parks

There are 17 forest parks in Great Britain, covering nearly 3,000 sq km (1,150 sq miles), which are administered by the Forestry Commission (see pp. 465–7). The Countryside Agency recognises over 200 country parks and more than 250 picnic sites in England. A further 36 country parks in Wales are recognised by the CCW, and there are 36 country parks in Scotland. Northern Ireland has eight forest parks, three forest drives and over 40 minor forest sites. All are administered by the Forest Service, an agency of the Department of Agriculture and Rural Development for Northern Ireland (DARD).

Tree Preservation and Planting

Tree Preservation Orders enable local authorities to protect trees and woodlands. Once a tree is protected, it is, in general, an offence to cut down or carry out most types of work to it without permission. Courts can impose substantial fines for breaches of such

Orders. Where protected trees are felled in contravention of an Order or are removed because they are dying, dead or dangerous, replacement trees must be planted and local authorities have powers to enforce this.

Tree planting is encouraged through various grant schemes, including the Forestry Commission's Woodland Grant Scheme (see p. 466). Consequently, the planting of broadleaved trees has greatly increased since the 1980s.

Major afforestation projects involving the Forestry Commission, the Countryside Agency and 58 local authorities include the creation of 12 Community Forests in and around major cities, with a total designated area of 450,000 hectares (1.1 million acres). The aims of these forests are: to increase woodland cover near the cities from 6.5% to about 30%; to restore areas scarred by industrial dereliction; to create sites for recreation, sport and environmental education; and to form new habitats for wildlife. In 1999–2000, about 1,200 hectares of new woodlands were created in Community Forest areas, bringing the total since 1991 to just over 7,400 hectares. This compares with total new woodland creation in Britain of over 15,000 hectares a year.

In July 2001 NAW published its woodland strategy, which will be managed by the Forestry Commission. The strategy will focus on community woodlands, the environmental management of existing woodland, and the contribution that woodlands make to rural, social and economic development.

Other organisations involved in protecting existing woods and planting new areas of woodland include voluntary bodies such as the Woodland Trust, which owns over 1,100 woods across the UK covering 18,300 hectares (45,300 acres) and, since 1976, has planted over 4 million trees.

> The outbreak of foot-and-mouth disease in 2001 (see p. 460) had a severe impact on the rural economy as a whole, with rural enterprises, farming support services and countryside tourism being badly affected. In response to this, in March 2001, the Government set up the Rural Task Force to work on a package of measures to help ease hardship in rural areas. Key issues for the Task Force included: improving information about access to the countryside; restoring confidence, both at home and abroad, in the tourist industry; and implementing a package of measures to help to sustain rural communities.
>
> The Countryside Agency has given almost £1.5 million to three charities: the ARC-Addington Fund, the Rural Stress Information Network and the Cumbrian Community Foundation to help them as they deal with the problems that rural people are facing as a result of foot-and-mouth disease.

Public Rights of Way and Open Country

England has about 188,700 km (122,800 miles) of rights of way: 146,600 km of footpaths, 32,400 km of bridleways, 3,700 km of byways open to all traffic and 6,000 km of roads used as public paths. There are 13 long-distance routes in England and Wales and three in Scotland, designated as National Trails. Ten of the National Trails have been fully developed and three are in the process of being completed.

About a quarter of the rights of way in England may be lawfully used by horseriders and cyclists, although the Pennine Bridleway—currently under construction—will be the first long-distance trail designed specifically for horseriders and cyclists.

In 1996 SNH launched *Paths for All*, an initiative established to facilitate the creation of 40 path networks across Scotland by 2000 for walkers, riders and cyclists.

County, metropolitan and unitary councils in England and Wales (see pp. 67–8) are responsible for keeping public rights of way signposted and free from obstruction. Public paths are usually maintained by these 'highway authorities', which also supervise landowners' duties to repair stiles and gates. In Scotland planning authorities are responsible for asserting and protecting rights of way. Subject to public consultation, and, if necessary, a public inquiry, local authorities in

Great Britain can create paths, close paths no longer needed for public use, and divert paths to meet the needs of either the public or landowners. Farmers in England and Wales are required by law to restore any cross-field public paths damaged or erased by agricultural operations.

Common land in England and Wales totals more than 550,000 hectares (1.36 million acres). The open character of commons has made them popular for informal recreation although significant areas are still important for agriculture. Four-fifths of common land is privately owned and although only 20% has a right of public access, there is also *de facto* access. The Countryside and Rights of Way Act 2000 will provide a right of access to all registered common land, subject to management restrictions. DEFRA estimates that 65% of common land is no longer subject to rights of common. Commons are largely unimproved and therefore have high amenity and wildlife value; many are protected by law and by nature conservation designations. For example, around half of the common land in England is found within National Parks (see p. 314) and a similar amount is designated as SSSIs (see p. 319). Ministerial consent is usually required to undertake work on commons or to enclose areas by fencing. In 2000 the Government launched a public consultation exercise aimed at finding ways to improve the protection and management of common land in England and Wales.

The Coast

Local planning authorities are responsible for planning land use at the coast; they also aim to safeguard and enhance the coast's natural attractions and preserve areas of scientific interest. The policy for the protection of the coastline against erosion and flooding is administered by DEFRA, NAW, the Scottish Executive and DARD. Operational responsibility lies with local authorities and, in England and Wales, the Environment Agency.

DEFRA and the NAW are jointly funding a project which aims to predict how the coastline in England and Wales will change. This will help local operating authorities update their shoreline management plans and coastal defence systems. It will also allow coastal management decisions to be placed within a longer-term and wider-scale framework, by looking at current coastal processes such as erosion, beach slipping and sand movement, cliff stability problems and landslip. The results of the research are expected to be available in February 2002.

Certain stretches of undeveloped coast of particular beauty in England and Wales are defined as Heritage Coast. There are 45 Heritage Coasts, protecting 1,540 km (960 miles), about 35% of the total length of coastline.

The National Trust (see p. 314), through its Neptune Coastline Campaign, raises funds to acquire and protect stretches of coastline of great natural beauty and recreational value. Around £36 million has been raised since 1965 and the Trust now protects around 960 km (600 miles) of coastline in England, Wales and Northern Ireland. The National Trust for Scotland cares for more than 400 km (250 miles) of the Scottish coastline and protects others through conservation agreements.

English Nature has supported 13 groups in developing and managing a variety of marine conservation initiatives. So far, 36 estuary management plans have been completed or are in preparation, covering 39 estuaries or 85% of England's total estuaries by area (the Dee and Severn estuary plans were jointly funded with the CCW). There are also 29 informal marine consultation areas in Scotland. In addition, SNH has established the Focus on Firths initiative to coordinate management of the main Scottish estuaries. In Wales the CCW provides grants to the Arfordir (or Coastal) Group, which is concerned with the sustainable management of the whole coast of Wales. Altogether there are 163 estuaries in the UK, representing about 30% of the North Sea and Atlantic seaboard of Western Europe. The UK also has about 75% of the European chalk coast.

Wildlife Protection

The protection of wildlife is an essential element of the UK Government's sustainable development agenda (see p. 378). DEFRA intends to bring 95% of all nationally

Table 19.2: Areas in the UK Protected for their Wildlife, March 2001

Type of site[1]	Number of sites	Area (sq km)[2]
National Nature Reserves	392	2,261
Local Nature Reserves	759	449
Sites of Special Scientific Interest (SSSIs) (Great Britain only)	6,573	22,802
Areas of Special Scientific Interest (ASSIs) (Northern Ireland)	182	896
Statutory Marine Nature Reserves	3	213
Areas protected by international agreements		
Candidate Special Areas of Conservation (cSACs)	546	22,320
Special Protection Areas (SPAs)	219	12,486
Ramsar sites	138	7,347

[1] Some sites may be included in more than one category.
[2] One square kilometre = 100 hectares (247 acres), or just over a third of a square mile.
Source: Joint Nature Conservation Committee

important wildlife sites into a favourable condition by 2010, compared with the 60% of sites currently estimated to be in that state.

The UK has over 100,000 separate species, out of a global total estimated by the JNCC as being between 5 million and 15 million. The list of protected species is reviewed by the three statutory nature conservation agencies, acting jointly through the JNCC, every five years, when recommended changes can be submitted to the Government. As elsewhere in the world, urban development, changes in farming methods and other factors have put pressure on a number of species and plants.

Bird populations are good indicators of the state of wildlife in the countryside, since they have a wide habitat distribution and are near the top of the food chain. There are concerns about the decline in certain bird species, as modern farming and forestry methods have removed the food supply they need for breeding and surviving the winter. In 2001 the British Trust for Ornithology (BTO) published findings from a survey, *Breeding Birds in the Wilder Countryside*, which found that populations of 20 of Britain's most common birds have dropped by more than 50% in 25 years. It is for this reason that wild bird populations are one of the headline indicators in the UK's sustainable development strategy. DEFRA will increase funding up to 2007 for agri-environment schemes to restore farmland habitats, and is funding a study led by the BTO to investigate the long-term declines of the house sparrow and starling, as both species have declined by more than 50% since 1973.

The UK Biodiversity Action Plan (see p. 320) also includes targets to reverse bird population decline; 26 species have been identified, including the skylark, grey partridge, corn bunting, song thrush and bullfinch.

Wildlife Crime

Wildlife crime takes many forms and has been increasing in recent years: for example, theft of eggs from birds of prey, illegal shooting, trapping, poisoning, digging up of wild plants, and the illicit trade in endangered species. DNA testing is playing an increasing role in combating crime of this kind, and there are now specialist wildlife officers in almost every police force in the UK.

An important role in combating wildlife crime is played by the Partnership for Action Against Wildlife Crime, which is chaired by the police and DEFRA. It provides a forum for communication and cooperation between the statutory enforcement authorities and non-governmental organisations which have an active interest in wildlife law enforcement in the UK. The Partnership provides a strategic overview of wildlife law enforcement issues and promotes increased awareness of

Figure 19.3: Populations of Wild Birds, UK

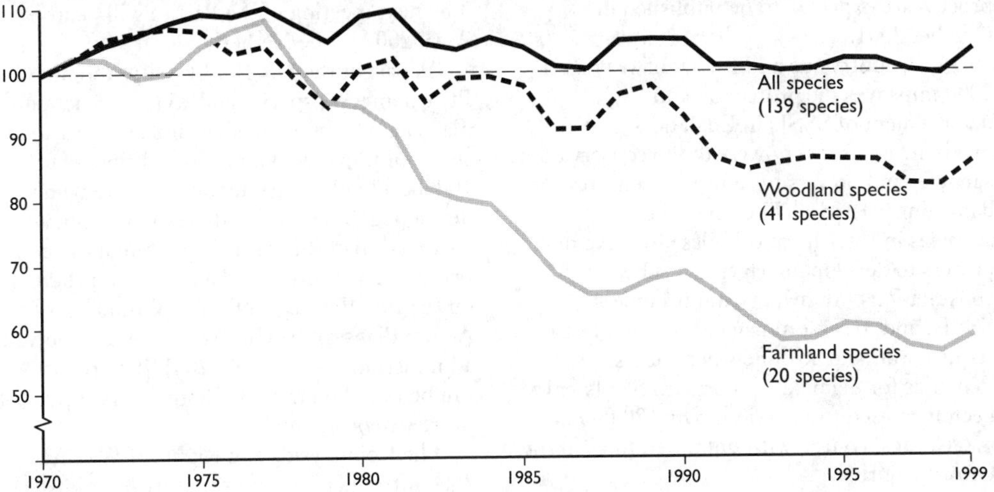

Note: Index (1970 = 100)

Sources: Royal Society for the Protection of Birds; British Trust for Ornithology; Department for Environment, Food and Rural Affairs

wildlife crime and the damage it causes to certain threatened species. DEFRA manages a team of around 100 wildlife inspectors whose main role is to carry out visits to premises to verify information submitted to them for permits, certificates and other documents to keep or trade in wildlife species and to check that people are complying with the administrative controls contained in certain wildlife legislation.

The Countryside and Rights of Way Act 2000 has introduced stronger measures to combat wildlife crime, including greater powers for police officers and DEFRA wildlife inspectors, and new penalties, including jail sentences of up to six months and fines of up to £5,000. In Scotland, a process of pre-legislative consultation on reform of wildlife law has been completed and is being considered by Scottish ministers.

Habitat Protection

Habitat protection is mainly achieved through the networks of Sites of Special Scientific Interest (SSSIs) in Great Britain, and Areas of Special Scientific Interest (ASSIs) in Northern Ireland. By the end of March 2001, 4,115 SSSIs had been notified in England, 1,009 in Wales, 1,449 in Scotland and 182 ASSIs in Northern Ireland, for their plants, animals or geological or physiographical features. Some SSSIs and ASSIs are of international importance and have been designated for protection under the EC Wild Birds and Habitats Directives or the Ramsar Convention (see p. 321). In England, the Government's target is to bring 95% of SSSIs into favourable condition by 2010. Most SSSIs and ASSIs are privately owned, but about 40% are owned or managed by public bodies such as the Forestry Commission, Ministry of Defence and the Crown Estate.

English Nature, the CCW and SNH have powers to enter into land management agreements with owners and occupiers of SSSI land, where this is necessary to support the management of their natural features. The CNCC advises on the establishment and management of land and marine nature reserves and the declaration of ASSIs in

Northern Ireland. In March 2001 the DOE published a consultation document, *Partners in Protection*, which seeks further protection for the ASSIs. Proposals from this consultation process are expected to be published in October 2001.

The Countryside and Rights of Way Act 2000 improves the protection and management of SSSIs in England and Wales, by giving enhanced powers to the conservation agencies and powers to refuse consent for damaging activities. The conservation agencies in England and Wales also have new powers to develop management schemes, in consultation with owners and occupiers of SSSIs, and to serve a management notice to require works to be done where necessary. Penalties for deliberate damage to SSSIs have been increased to a maximum of £20,000 in magistrates' courts, with unlimited fines in the Crown Court.

Wildlife Trusts (based on conurbations, counties or regions), the Royal Society for the Protection of Birds (RSPB) and the Scottish Wildlife Trust play an important part in protecting wildlife throughout the UK. The RSPB manages 168 reserves in the UK covering 114,657 hectares (283,300 acres) of land. During 2000–01 it acquired 2,910 hectares of land, including six new reserves. It is the largest voluntary wildlife conservation body in Europe, with over 1 million members. The Scottish Wildlife Trust, with a membership of around 19,000, manages 126 wildlife reserves covering approximately 22,500 hectares (55,600 acres). The Trust has recently secured funding from the Heritage Lottery Fund for a £5 million, five-year reserves enhancement project.

Biodiversity, and Species Recovery and Reintroduction

The UK is one of 180 Parties to the Convention on Biological Diversity Treaty, agreed at the Earth Summit in Rio de Janeiro in 1992 (see p. 378). The Parties have agreed to develop national strategies and programmes for the conservation and sustainable use of biological diversity and ensure the fair and equitable sharing of benefits from the use of genetic resources. While the prime focus for implementation is at national level, much activity is under way internationally to elaborate the Convention's obligations, share experience and help identify good practice. The next meeting of the Parties will be in April 2002 in the Netherlands.

As part of the UK Biodiversity Action Plan, some 391 species and 45 habitat action plans have been established and are at various stages of implementation. In addition, over 100 local biodiversity action plans are being developed. The UK Biodiversity Group, a partnership of the statutory, voluntary and private sectors presented a report on progress on the first five years of the UK Biodiversity Action Plans to the Government and devolved administrations in March 2001. The report can be found on the UK Biodiversity website (*www.ukbap.org.uk*).

The Countryside and Rights of Way Act 2000 introduced a statutory duty on ministers and government departments in England and Wales to have regard to the conservation of biological diversity in carrying out their functions. The National Biodiversity Network Trust is a charity representing 11 voluntary and public organisations. It was established in 2000 with the aim of bringing together biodiversity information to meet a wide range of conservation, research, educational and public participation needs. The National Biodiversity Network provides an Internet service (*www.searchnbn.net*) to deliver access to dispersed information sources. The service provides geographical, species, habitat and thematic ways of accessing and integrating information.

The Royal Botanic Gardens at Kew (see p. 444) has been successful for many years in the reintroduction of species. Its Millennium Seed Bank in the Wellcome Trust Millennium Building, at Wakehurst Place, West Sussex, holds seeds of 1,312 native UK wild flowers, plants and trees—90% of British plant species. It aims to hold 10% of flowering plants from the arid regions of the world by 2010 and 25% by 2025. The Royal Botanic Garden Edinburgh (RBGE) (see p. 444) promotes conservation programmes for rare plants in Scotland and for coniferous trees worldwide, maintaining genetically diverse populations in cultivation at many sites, as pools for eventual reintroduction to the wild. Currently RBGE's Living Collections consists of 6% of the world's flowering plant species in cultivation and also includes 1,400 threatened plants.

International Action

The UK's international obligations to conserve wildlife include membership of the World Conservation Union and of several international Conventions and Directives, some of which are described below.

The IUCN—the *World Conservation Union*—is the largest nature conservation body in the world, having a membership of nearly 1,000 governmental and non-governmental organisations. The purpose of the Union is to influence, encourage and help societies throughout the world to conserve the integrity and diversity of nature and to ensure that any use of natural resources is equitable and ecologically sustainable.

The *Convention on Wetlands of International Importance* (the *Ramsar Convention*) is an intergovernmental treaty which covers all aspects of wetland conservation and use, recognising wetlands as ecosystems that are extremely important for biodiversity conservation and for the well-being of human communities. By March 2001, 138 Ramsar sites covering 7,347 sq km (2,837 sq miles) had been established within the UK. There are a further 11 sites in the British Overseas Territories: seven in Bermuda and one each in the British Indian Ocean Territory, the British Virgin Islands, the Cayman Islands, and the Turks and Caicos Islands, collectively covering over 55,000 hectares.

The *Convention on the Conservation of European Wildlife and Natural Habitats* (the *Bern Convention*) aims to ensure conservation and protection of all wild plants and animal species, to increase cooperation between states in these areas, and to afford special protection to the most vulnerable or threatened species. It was the inspiration for the EC Habitats and Wild Birds Directives and had a direct influence on the Wildlife and Countryside Act. Under the EC Wild Birds Directive, 219 UK sites have been designated as Special Protection Areas (SPAs). The Forest of Clunie is the most recent area to be designated in August 2001. Under the EC Habitats Directive, 546 sites in the UK have been put forward to the European Commission as candidate Special Areas of Conservation (cSACs). Collectively, SPAs and cSACs form the EU network of nature conservation sites known as Natura 2000.

The *Convention on International Trade in Endangered Species of Wild Fauna and Flora* (*CITES*) strictly regulates trade in endangered species by means of a permit system. The parties meet every two years, with the next round of talks taking place in Chile in 2002. At these talks, the UK Government will be pressing for restrictions to the international trade in basking sharks, and has already pledged funds of £215,000 for research. The UK's bid follows a similar unsuccessful proposal at the previous talks held in Nairobi in April 2000.

The *Convention on the Conservation of Migratory Species of Wild Animals* (the *Bonn Convention*), which is held every two or three years, coordinates international action on a range of endangered migratory species. The UK has signed a number of species-related agreements under the Convention covering the conservation of bats, cetaceans, waterbirds and seabirds. The next meeting of the parties will be held in Bonn in September 2002.

The *Darwin Initiative*, launched at the Earth Summit (see p. 378), is designed to bring British expertise to bear on the biodiversity needs of developing countries to help them implement the Convention on Biological Diversity (see p. 320). Nine rounds of funding have so far been approved for over 230 projects at a total cost of £27 million.

Buildings and Monuments

In England, lists of buildings of special architectural or historic interest are compiled by the Department for Culture, Media and Sport (DCMS) with advice from English Heritage. In Scotland and Wales, buildings are listed by Historic Scotland and Cadw: Welsh Historic Monuments, an executive agency within NAW. It is against the law to demolish, extend or alter the character of any 'listed' building without prior consent from the local planning authority or—on appeal or following call-in—the appropriate government minister. A local planning authority can issue a 'building preservation notice' to protect for six months an unlisted building which it considers to be of special architectural or historic interest and is at risk while a decision is taken on whether it should be listed. In Northern Ireland, the EHS has responsibility for historic buildings, following consultation with the advisory Historic Buildings Council (HBC) and the relevant local district council.

Ancient monuments are protected through a system of scheduling. English Heritage assesses all known archaeological sites in England in order to identify those nationally important sites—out of a total of some 600,000—that should be afforded statutory protection. It then makes its recommendations to the DCMS, which maintains the schedule of ancient monuments. Similar arrangements exist to identify buildings and ancient and historic monuments eligible for statutory protection in Scotland and Wales. In Northern Ireland the EHS assesses all known archaeological sites in order to identify those sites which should be afforded statutory protection. It then makes recommendations to the Historic Monuments Council (HMC) and maintains the schedule.

In England details of all listed buildings are contained in about 2,000 volumes which can be inspected at the English Heritage offices in Swindon (National Monuments Record Centre) and London. The lists for particular areas are also held by the relevant local planning authorities, where they are available for inspection, and at some public libraries. In Wales records are kept at Cadw in Cardiff, and in Scotland at Historic Scotland's head office in Edinburgh or the relevant local planning authority. The EHS's Monuments and Buildings Record in Belfast holds information on all historic monuments and buildings in Northern Ireland.

English Heritage is responsible for the maintenance, repair and presentation of 409 historic properties in public ownership or guardianship, and gives grants for the repair of ancient monuments and historic buildings in England. In 2000–01 English Heritage offered £6.2 million to conservation areas throughout

Table 19.4: Listed Buildings and Scheduled Monuments, May 2001

	Listed buildings	Scheduled monuments
England	496,456	19,006[1]
Wales	25,597	3,440
Scotland	45,534	7,432[2]
Northern Ireland	8,274	1,485

[1] As at 30 June 2001.
[2] As at 31 March 2001.
Sources: Department for Culture, Media and Sport, Cadw: Welsh Historic Monuments, Scottish Executive and Environment and Heritage Service (NI)

England under its Heritage Economic Regeneration Schemes. Most of its properties are open to the public, and there were nearly 5.7 million visitors to its staffed properties alone in 2000–01. Government funding for English Heritage is £112.3 million in 2001–02.

In Scotland and Wales, Historic Scotland, which cares for over 330 monuments, and Cadw, with 130 monuments, perform similar functions. There were nearly 3 million visitors to Historic Scotland's properties in 2000–01 and 1.1 million to Cadw properties in 2000. An Ancient Monuments Board and an HBC advise Scottish ministers and similar arrangements exist in Wales. The DOE in Northern Ireland has 189 historic monuments in its care, managed by the EHS (another 1,485 are scheduled).

Local planning authorities have designated more than 9,000 conservation areas of special architectural or historic interest in England; there are 504 in Wales, 602 in Scotland and 58 in Northern Ireland. These areas receive additional protection through the planning system, particularly over the proposed demolition of unlisted buildings.

The National Heritage Memorial Fund (NHMF) helps towards the cost of acquiring, maintaining or preserving land, buildings, objects and collections that are of outstanding interest and of importance to the national heritage. In addition, trustees are responsible for distributing the heritage share of the proceeds from the National Lottery (see p. 123). By August 2001 over £1.72 billion had been awarded from the Heritage Lottery Fund for more than 7,000 projects.

Many of the royal palaces and all the royal parks are open to the public; their maintenance is the responsibility of the DCMS and Historic Scotland. Historic Royal Palaces, the Royal Household and the Royal Parks Agency carry out this function on behalf of the Secretary of State in England.

Industrial, Transport and Maritime Heritage

As the first country in the world to industrialise on a large scale, the UK has a rich industrial heritage, including such sites as the Ironbridge Gorge, where Abraham Darby (1677–1717) first smelted iron using coke instead of charcoal (now a World Heritage Site—see below).

Several industrial monuments in Scotland are in the care of the First Minister, including Bonawe Iron Furnace, the most complete charcoal-fuelled ironworks surviving in Britain; the working New Abbey Corn Mill; and Dallas Dhu Malt Whisky Distillery.

The UK pioneered railways, and has a fine heritage of railway buildings and structures. A large number of disused railway lines have been bought by railway preservation societies, and there are several railway museums.

Reminders of the UK's maritime past are also preserved. Portsmouth is home to HMS *Victory* (Admiral Nelson's flagship), HMS *Warrior* (the world's first iron battleship, launched in 1860), and the remains of King Henry VIII's *Mary Rose*, the world's only surviving 16th-century warship.

A voluntary body, the Maritime Trust, preserves vessels and other maritime items of historic or technical interest. The Trust's vessels include the steam coaster *Robin* (1890) and Sir Francis Chichester's *Gipsy Moth IV* (1966). In all, about 400 historic ships are preserved in the UK, mostly in private hands.

World Heritage Sites

The World Heritage List was established under the United Nations Educational, Scientific and Cultural Organisation's (UNESCO's) 1972 World Heritage Convention to identify and secure lasting protection for sites of outstanding value. The UK has 20 World Heritage sites (see map at the front of the book), including three in Overseas Territories: the town of St George in Bermuda, Henderson Island and Gough Island Wildlife Reserve. The UK has drawn up a list of 25 potential World Heritage sites, and nomination for World Heritage Status will be drawn from the sites included in this list over the next five to ten years. Four sites nominated in June 2000 were Derwent Valley Mills in Derbyshire; Saltaire in West Yorkshire; New Lanark in Central Scotland; and the Dorset and East Devon Coast.

Pollution Control

Administration

Executive responsibility for pollution control is divided between local authorities and central government agencies. The central government departments make policy, promote legislation and advise pollution control authorities on policy implementation. The Secretary of State for Environment, Food and Rural Affairs has general responsibility for coordinating the work of the Government on pollution control in England and for some regulations in Wales. Similar responsibilities are exercised in Scotland by the Minister for Environment and Rural Affairs, in Wales by the National Assembly Environment Secretary, and in Northern Ireland by the DOE. Local authorities are responsible for:

- collection and disposal of domestic waste;
- keeping the streets clear of litter;
- controlling air pollution from domestic premises and, in England and Wales, from many industrial premises;
- reviewing, assessing and managing local air quality; and
- noise and general nuisance abatement.

The Environment Agency for England and Wales and the Scottish Environment Protection Agency (SEPA) (*www.sepa.org.uk*) regulate the major pollution risks to air, water and land, and waste. In Northern Ireland, the EHS exercises similar functions.

The Royal Commission on Environmental Pollution (*www.rcep.org.uk*) is an independent standing body that advises the Government on dangers to the environment, and suggests ways of integrating environmental objectives with other economic and social objectives in order to achieve sustainable development. It has produced 22 reports so far, on a variety of topics, such as climate change and environmental standards. It intends to publish its 23rd report on environmental planning early in 2002.

Industrial Pollution Control

The Environmental Protection Act 1990 established two pollution control regimes for the UK: Local Air Pollution Control (LAPC), which regulates emissions to air; and Integrated Pollution Control (IPC), which regulates emissions to land and water, as well as air.

In England and Wales, LAPC is operated by local authorities and IPC by the Environment Agency. In Scotland SEPA operates both IPC and LAPC. In Northern Ireland IPC is operated by the Chief Industrial Pollution Inspector. The Chief Inspector also regulates some processes subject to an Air Pollution Control (APC) regime. District councils regulate the remaining APC processes.

A new Pollution Prevention and Control (PPC) regime, which implements an EC Directive on Integrated Pollution Prevention and Control (IPPC), came into force in England and Wales in August 2000, and in Scotland in September 2000. PPC succeeds IPC and part of LAPC and will be fully established by 2007.

Under both the old and new regimes, regulators are required to ensure that pollution from industry is prevented or reduced through the use of best available techniques, subject to assessment of costs and benefits. Both regimes require regulators to take account of the special characteristics of each installation and its local environment.

Under PPC, the issuing of integrated permits will apply to a larger number of industrial activities. These include, for example, animal rendering, the food and drink industry, and intensive livestock installations, which have not previously been controlled under this type of regime. Regulators are also required to take into account a wider range of environmental impacts (including noise, energy efficiency and site restoration) when issuing integrated permits.

Existing installations are being phased into the new PPC regime on a sectoral basis until 2007. Regulators, with some exceptions, continue to be responsible for those installations they currently regulate under IPC and LAPC. In Scotland, SEPA will continue to regulate all installations falling within the regime.

A Pollution Inventory for England and Wales, administered by the Environment Agency, provides details of emissions to air, water and land from processes regulated under IPC and their contributions to national emission levels. The data are updated annually and can be found on the Agency's website (*www.environment-agency.gov.uk*). The implementation of the IPPC Directive will increase the number of sites reporting from 2,000 to around 7,000 in 2003. A similar inventory will be developed to include information on emissions to air and water from PPC installations.

Land, Waste, Recycling and Litter

Land Quality

Land quality in the UK is relatively good, but faces pressure from a range of factors, including urbanisation, localised erosion, declining organic content and contamination.

Contaminated land is the legacy of an industrial age that generated wealth but also caused much pollution. The Environment Agency estimates that some 300,000 hectares of land in Great Britain are contaminated to some degree. Government policy emphasises the importance of voluntary action to clean up contaminated land, and most attempts to clean up sites occur when they are redeveloped. A strengthened regulatory regime for dealing with contaminated land came into force in England in April 2000, in Scotland in July 2000 and in Wales in July 2001.

In 2001 the former DETR and MAFF jointly published a draft soil strategy for England promoting the sustainable use of soil and raising public awareness of the importance of soil as part of the environment. The strategy sets out five actions:

- to ensure that all policies and programmes which affect soil take into account the strategy's aims and objectives;
- to develop a national set of key soil indicators to help provide assessments of, for example, the extent of soil lost to development;
- to review current soil monitoring and develop a national framework for it;
- to examine existing soil research, and recommend ways to improve its coordination; and
- to set a five-year goal for evaluating the success of the soil strategy.

One key objective includes managing and protecting the diversity of soil, to ensure that the right balance of soil types is available to support England's ecosystems, landscape and agriculture. Many of the 400 species identified in the UK Biodiversity Action Plan depend on the right type and quality of soil for their survival. By managing soil correctly, wildlife can be given greater protection.

Also in 2001, SEPA published its first report on soil quality. It highlighted the range of pressures on soil from air pollution, agriculture and forestry practices, and industrial contamination.

Waste Management and Disposal

In England and Wales, waste regulation is the responsibility of the Environment Agency, while local authorities in England and Wales are responsible for the collection and disposal of all household waste and some commercial waste. In 'two-tier' areas, district councils are responsible for waste collection and county councils for waste disposal, while in unitary areas the council has both roles. In Scotland, local authorities carry out both roles while waste regulation rests with SEPA. In Northern Ireland, responsibility for waste regulation is being transferred from district councils to the DOE.

The Environmental Protection Act 1990 (as amended) and the Waste Management Licensing Regulations 1994 regulate waste management. A waste management licence is required by anyone wanting to deposit, recover, or dispose of waste. Licences are issued by the Environment Agency in England and Wales and SEPA in Scotland. A duty of care requires waste producers, and anyone else with responsibility for waste, to take all reasonable steps to keep their waste safe. If they give their waste to someone else they must be sure that those people are authorised to take it and can transport, recycle or dispose of it safely. Failure to comply with either the licensing requirements or a duty of care is an offence.

The management of waste arisings is one of the headline indicators of sustainable development (see p. 378). In 1999–2000 it is estimated that 29.3 million tonnes of municipal waste was produced—90% of which came from households. Although 11% of municipal waste was recycled, the majority (81%) was disposed of in landfill—a method which makes little practical use of waste.[1] In the 1999 Budget, a staged increase in landfill tax to encourage less disposal of waste to landfill and more recycling was announced, bringing the standard rate of tax to £15 per tonne by 2004, with a review thereafter. The landfill tax credit scheme enables landfill site operators to channel up to 20% of their landfill tax liability into environmental bodies for approved projects, which include reclamation of polluted land, research and education activities to promote re-use and recycling, provision of public parks and amenities, and restoration of historic buildings.

In May 2000 the Government published *Waste Strategy 2000 for England and Wales*, setting out its views on waste and resource management, and the changes needed to deliver more sustainable waste management during the next 20 years. It requires action by many different organisations—including local authorities, the waste industry and the business sector—and by individuals. By 2005 the Government aims to reduce the amount of industrial and commercial waste disposed of in landfill sites to 85% of 1998 levels and to recycle or compost at least 25% of household waste, increasing to 33% by 2015. Between

[1] Some landfill sites produce gas that is used for energy.

1998–99 and 1999–2000, the household recycling rate increased from 8.8% to 10.3%.

Scotland has its own waste strategy, launched in 1999. The strategy's objectives include: ensuring that waste is disposed of without endangering human health and without harming the environment; establishing an integrated and adequate network of waste disposal installations; encouraging the prevention or reduction of waste production; and encouraging the recovery of waste. Current planning policy advice on waste management in Scotland is contained in National Planning Policy Guidance 10: Planning and Waste Management. The Scottish Executive will be publishing further advice on this issue in a Planning Advice Note on waste management by the end of 2001.

A similar waste management strategy in Northern Ireland was launched in March 2000. This strategy was designed as a framework within which planning and developments will be shaped to achieve sustainable waste management and to meet the targets for diversion away from landfill. The main goals for the term of the strategy are: by 2010 a reduction of 25% for biodegradable municipal waste going to landfill, increasing to 50% by 2013 and 75% by 2020 (all set against 1995 levels).

In May 2001 the DOE published a draft Planning Policy Statement (PPS11) on Planning and Waste Management for public consultation. PPS11 will facilitate changes in waste management proposed in the waste management strategy. It contains the DOE's planning polices for the development of waste management facilities and explains the relationship between the planning system and the authorities responsible for the regulation and management of waste.

NAW currently has a budget of £40 million over the three years 2001–02 to 2003–04 for waste management programmes. In July 2001 it published a draft waste strategy—*Managing Waste Sustainably*—for consultation, and intends publishing a final version early in 2002.

Under the EC Directive on Packaging and Packaging Waste, at least 50% of the UK's packaging waste must be recovered and at least 25% recycled. Regulations that came into force in 1998 in Great Britain and in 1999 in Northern Ireland stipulate, among other things, that all packaging must be 'recoverable' through at least recycling, incineration with energy recovery, and composting or biodegradation.

Across the UK, banks are available for the public to deposit various waste material for recycling, including bottles, cans, clothes, paper and plastics. In addition, some local authorities provide kerbside collection of recyclable material. In early 2001 the Northern Ireland DOE launched a new reference manual for businesses entitled *Recycling Directory of Ireland*, aimed at helping businesses throughout Ireland to recycle materials discarded as waste.

The Spending Review 2000 (see chapter 23) provided substantial extra resources for waste and recycling—£140 million specifically for local authority waste and recycling in England. It also provided significant resources for the Waste and Resources Action Programme (WRAP) to overcome market barriers to the recovery and recycling of waste—total funding of around £30 million is planned during 2000–01 to 2002–03. In Scotland a Strategic Waste Fund has been established to assist local authorities in their implementation of Area Waste Plans. The fund has been allocated £50.4 million over three years (2001–04). Scotland has also allocated £2.1 million to WRAP over the same time period.

Hazardous Waste

There is an extensive framework of national and EC legislation on the manufacture, distribution, use and disposal of hazardous chemicals. New and existing chemicals are subject to notification and assessment procedures under EC legislation. Pesticides, biocides and veterinary medicines are subject to mandatory approval procedures. International movements of hazardous waste are controlled by the Basel Convention on the Control of Transboundary Movements of Hazardous Wastes and their Disposal. In December 2000 the UK became one of the first countries to sign the Basel Convention Protocol on Liability and Compensation. Once fully ratified the Protocol requires any exporter of hazardous waste to be insured against any damage caused on the journey to the recycler or disposer of that waste.

Table 19.5: Management of Municipal Waste, England and Wales, 1999–2000

	Thousand tonnes	%
Landfill	23,714	81
Incineration without energy from waste	9	—
Incineration with energy from waste	2,276	8
Refuse-derived fuel manufacture	111	—
Recycled/composted	3,218	11
Other	4	—
Total	**29,332**	

Source: Department for Environment, Food and Rural Affairs

In Great Britain, the Special Waste Regulations 1996 are the centrepiece of hazardous waste controls. However, since 1996, the Hazardous Waste List that defines the scope of the EC Hazardous Waste Directive has been refined and increased in length, and these changes need to be implemented in national law by 1 January 2002. Furthermore, a number of new Directives have been or will be made, which will have an impact on the sector, notably the Hazardous Waste Incineration Directive, the Landfill Directive and the IPC Directive (see p. 324).

The Government is conducting a review of the Special Waste Regulations and is consulting on a number of changes. These include: resolving inconsistencies between the EC Hazardous Waste Directive/List and the Special Waste Regulations; encouraging reductions in the amount of hazardous waste produced; providing a better audit trail for hazardous waste and improving its management by waste producers and the waste management industry; reducing the administrative burden on the waste industry and the Environment Agency; and shifting the burden of responsibility onto the producer rather than the recycler or disposer of the waste.

Litter and Dog Fouling

It is a criminal offence to leave litter in any public place in the open air or to dump rubbish except in designated places. The maximum fine upon successful prosecution is £2,500 for littering or up to £20,000 for fly-tipping offences. The optional litter fixed penalty fine, which discharges a person's liability to prosecution, is £25.

Local authorities have a duty to keep their public land free of litter and refuse, including dog faeces, as far as is practicable. Members of the public have powers to take action against authorities which fail to comply with their responsibilities. In England and Wales local authorities also have powers to make it an offence not to clear up after one's dog in a public place, and may issue a fixed penalty fine of £25 under the Dogs (Fouling of Land) Act 1996. In Scotland it is an offence to allow a dog to foul in specified places under the Civic Government (Scotland) Act 1982.

The Tidy Britain Group, Keep Wales Tidy, Keep Scotland Beautiful and Tidy Northern Ireland are the national agencies for tackling litter, in collaboration with local authorities and the private sector. In 2001 the Tidy Britain Group launched the National Local Environmental Quality Survey, whose purpose is to produce reliable national and regional estimates of cleanliness and other environmental standards for England. The survey will be continuous and will be used to identify factors affecting standards of cleansing and environmental maintenance. Conditions to be monitored include cleanliness, graffiti, physical obstructions and observed cleansing operations.

The environment agencies, local authorities, police and the Tidy Britain Group have been monitoring the incidence of 'fly tipping' (illegal dumping of waste) since the introduction of the landfill tax, and have found that it has increased since 1994–95. If indicted to the Crown Court, the maximum penalty for fly tipping (and other offences relating to waste) is up to five years' imprisonment and/or an unlimited fine.

In 2001 the Government proposed a new code of conduct to reduce litter from 'takeaway' outlets. Existing litter legislation would be overhauled, including doubling the fixed penalty for littering from £25 to £50.

Water

Water Quality

Water quality in England and Wales has continued to show steady improvement in recent years as a result of strict regulation by the Environment Agency and substantial investment by the water industry.

In the UK, 94% of the population live in properties connected to a sewer, and the waste water from the majority of these properties is given secondary treatment or better. Within the current round of planning, further investment will be made in effluent treatment up to 2005. This is expected to deliver:

- improved compliance with EC Directives such as those on EC bathing waters and freshwater fish;
- improved compliance with river quality objectives; and
- improvements to over 3,800 Combined Sewer Overflows (CSOs) that are currently regarded as unsatisfactory due to their environmental impact.

Scottish ministers published a consultation paper in June 2001, entitled *Rivers, Lochs, Coasts: the Future for Scotland's Waters*, which contains proposals for a new approach to the sustainable management of the natural water environment in Scotland and for implementing the EC Water Framework Directive. Scottish ministers plan to introduce primary legislation in the Scottish Parliament to implement the Directive in 2002.

In November 2000 the Government published a draft Water Bill which includes measures to improve customer protection, by setting up an independent consumer council; improvements to water conservation and drought planning; and improvements to the water abstraction licensing system in England and Wales. For details on the water supply industry and the Drinking Water Inspectorate, see pp. 504–8.

Discharges to Inland Waters, Coastal Waters and Groundwaters

In the UK, all discharges to water are regulated by the appropriate authority. For England and Wales this is the Environment Agency, which controls water pollution by issuing legally binding documents, known as consents, for all effluent discharges into controlled waters (groundwaters, inland and coastal waters). The effluent quality is monitored against the conditions set within the consents. The Agency maintains public registers containing information about water quality, performance and compliance, consents, authorisations and monitoring. Trade effluent discharges to the public sewers are controlled by the water companies.

In Scotland, controlling water pollution is the responsibility of SEPA; appeals are dealt with by the Scottish Executive and trade effluent discharges to the public sewer are controlled by the Water Authorities. In December 1999 SEPA produced the National Waste Strategy: Scotland, providing a framework within which Scotland can reduce the amount of waste it produces and deal with the waste which has been produced in more sustainable ways. In Northern Ireland, the EHS is responsible for controlling water pollution. From autumn 2001, the EHS proposes to introduce a cost recovery scheme of application fees in respect of all discharges to waterways and underground strata. In addition, from 2002–03 annual charges will be payable by those industries that discharge effluent to waterways and underground strata that are subject to compliance sampling by the EHS.

In 1999, the Environment Agency responded to 36,623 reports of environmental pollution in England and Wales; 14,374 were substantiated as having an impact on the water environment. In 1999–2000, SEPA reported 2,588 routine water pollution incidents in Scotland; the DOE reported 1,510 in Northern Ireland.

Under the 1999 Groundwater Regulations certain dangerous substances may not be disposed of to land in case they also pollute groundwater, and others may only be disposed of following prior authorisation. The regulations also give the Environment Agency (in England and Wales) and SEPA (in

Scotland) powers to stop activities which might cause groundwater pollution.

There are 68 Nitrate Vulnerable Zones (NVZs) in England and Wales, designated under the EC Nitrates Directive, covering 8% of the total agricultural land area. There are a further two zones in Scotland and three in Northern Ireland. Farmers in NVZs are required to follow rules known as 'Action Programme Measures', which control the timing and rate of application of fertilisers and organic manures. The aim of these measures is to reduce or prevent the pollution of water caused by the application and storage of inorganic fertiliser and manure on farmland. This will have the effect primarily of safeguarding drinking water supplies, and secondarily curtailing wider ecological damage in the form of eutrophication (excess nitrogen deposition) of freshwater and saline waters.

Bathing Waters and Coastal Sewage Discharges

Bathing water quality is influenced by natural factors such as temperature, salinity and sunlight, discharges from coastal sewerage treatment works, the operation of CSOs in wet weather, and run-off from agricultural land. Over the past 12 years the overall quality of UK bathing waters has improved considerably. In 2000, 94% of UK waters complied with the mandatory coliform standards of the EC Bathing Waters Directive, compared with 91% in 1999 and 66% in 1988. The Thames and Anglian regions, and Northern Ireland achieved 100% compliance, while the North West had the lowest compliance rate—with 82% of bathing waters meeting the required standard. Consistent compliance with the mandatory standards of the EC Bathing Waters Directive is expected to increase from 95% in England and Wales in 2000 to 97% by 2005 as a result of the investment programme to improve water quality (see p. 507).

In 2001 the Tidy Britain Group (*www.tidybritain.org.uk*) gave Seaside Awards (*www.seasideawards.org.uk*) to 308 beaches in the UK for meeting appropriate standards of water quality and beach management. The Seaside Award was introduced in 1992 to provide information about a wide range of beaches in the UK and is given to beaches that comply with the EC Bathing Waters Directive standards, are clean, safe and well managed, and provide appropriate information about water quality.

Figure 19.6: Percentage of Bathing Waters complying[1] with the EC Bathing Waters Directive, UK

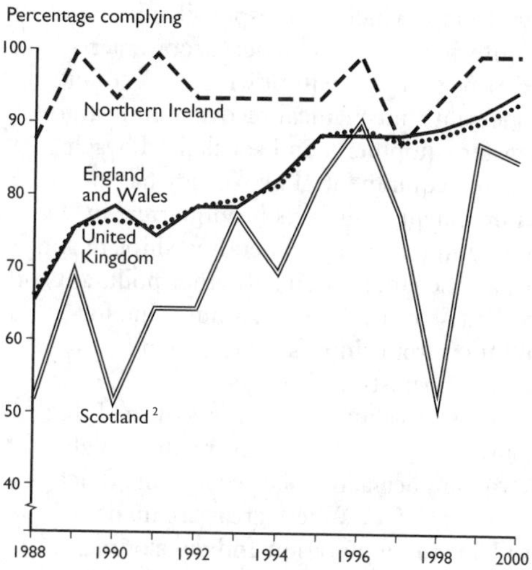

[1] The small number of designated bathing waters in Scotland (60 in 2000, 23 in 1988 to 1999) and Northern Ireland (16) causes greater fluctuations in percentage compliance than in England and Wales (over 471 sites).

[2] A direct comparison cannot be drawn between the results for 2000 and the results since 1988 because of the additional 37 waters that were identified before the start of the 1999 season.

Sources: Environment Agency; Scottish Environment Protection Agency; and Environment and Heritage Service, Northern Ireland

The European Blue Flag Campaign (*www.blueflag.org*) is an initiative of the Foundation of Environmental Education in Europe and is administered in the UK by the Tidy Britain Group. To be considered, a beach must have attained the guideline standard of the EC Bathing Waters Directive before being assessed for 24 other criteria including bathing water quality, beach cleanliness, dog control, wheelchair access, the provision of life-saving equipment and other facilities. In 2001, 55 beaches in the UK were awarded a 'Blue Flag' compared with 57 in 2000. In 1999 a 'Blue Flag' for marinas category was introduced in the UK and in 2001 there were 26 flags flying in harbours.

Marine Environment

The Maritime and Coastguard Agency (see p. 373) is responsible for dealing with spillages of oil or other hazardous substances from ships at sea. The various counter-pollution facilities for which it is responsible include: remote-sensing surveillance aircraft; aerial and seaborne spraying equipment; stocks of oil dispersants; mechanical recovery and cargo transfer equipment; and specialised beach cleaning equipment. The Agency has an Enforcement Unit at its headquarters in Southampton for apprehending ships making illegal discharges of oil and other pollutants off the British coast. The maximum fine for pollution from ships is £250,000 in cases heard in magistrates' courts.

Decisions about which areas of the UK Continental Shelf should be made available for petroleum licensing take account of advice from the JNCC. Where areas are made available for exploration and development, special conditions may be imposed on the licence holders to minimise or avoid any impact on the marine environment. These conditions are agreed with the JNCC.

Government policy is not to permit any deposit of waste in the sea when there is a safe land-based alternative, unless it can be demonstrated that disposal at sea is the best practicable option. Disposal of sewage sludge at sea ceased at the end of 1998. The only types of waste that are now routinely considered for deposit in the sea are dredged material from ports and harbours, and small quantities of fish waste.

Air and the Atmosphere

Air Quality

Air quality has improved considerably since the smogs of the 1950s. The first step towards these improvements was the introduction of the Clean Air Act in 1956, which controlled smoke from industrial and domestic coal burning, a major source of pollution at the time. Since then, the large-scale replacement of coal by natural gas for domestic heating, tighter regulation and structural changes in industry, and the introduction of progressively more stringent standards for vehicle exhaust emissions, have all led to considerable improvements in air quality. For example, in 1970, 8.5 million tonnes of carbon monoxide (CO) and 6.5 million tonnes of sulphur dioxide (SO_2) were emitted into the air in the UK. By 1999 these emissions had fallen to 4.8 million and 1.2 million tonnes respectively.

Industrial processes with the greatest potential for producing harmful emissions are subject to regulation under IPC and IPPC (see p. 324). Processes with a significant but lesser potential for air pollution require approval, in England and Wales from local authorities, in Scotland from SEPA and in Northern Ireland from the Chief Pollution Inspector or district council, depending on the process. Local authorities also control emissions of black smoke from commercial and industrial premises, and implement smoke control areas to deal with emissions from domestic properties.

The Air Quality Strategy for the UK was launched in 1997, with a revised version published in January 2000. The Strategy contains air quality standards and objectives for eight pollutants of particular concern to human health: nitrogen dioxide, PM_{10} (particulate matter that is less than 10 microns), SO_2, CO, ozone, lead, benzene and 1,3-butadiene. It sets out a programme of action to reduce air pollution and so reduce any remaining risks to people's health and the natural and built environment.

The UK has an automatic air quality monitoring network with sites covering much of the country, in both urban and rural areas. In recent years this network has undergone a rapid expansion, with the number of sites increasing from 74 at the end of 1996 to 119 by April 2001. The increase was mainly in urban sites to provide more comprehensive coverage of air quality in UK cities.

In 2000, in urban areas, air pollution was recorded as moderate or higher for 16 days on average per site, compared with 30 days in 1999 and 23 days in 1998. The main causes of moderate or higher air pollution at urban sites are ground level ozone arising from chemical reactions of other pollutants such as nitrogen oxides (NO_X) and volatile organic compounds (VOCs), PM_{10} and SO_2. Pollution caused by PM_{10} and SO_2 has fallen steeply since 1993, so

The NERC Centre for Ecology and Hydrology/Paul Rosier

NERC–the Natural Environment Research Council–was established in 1965 by Royal Charter. It undertakes research in a wide variety of environmental sciences, in the UK and overseas, as well as training scientists. NERC funds research in universities and operates from a series of research centres located throughout the UK.

Scientists from NERC's Centre for Ecology and Hydrology have been assisting the South Atlantic island of St Helena with the control of unmanaged flax plantations in its Diana Peak National Park. Removal of the overgrown plants, which use up almost all the water in the soil, and replacement with endemic plants, has so far shown that this is likely to result in an increased water supply in the local streams. A longer-term monitoring programme has also been established, as the demand for water for agriculture, tourism and the islanders themselves is likely to increase over the next few years.

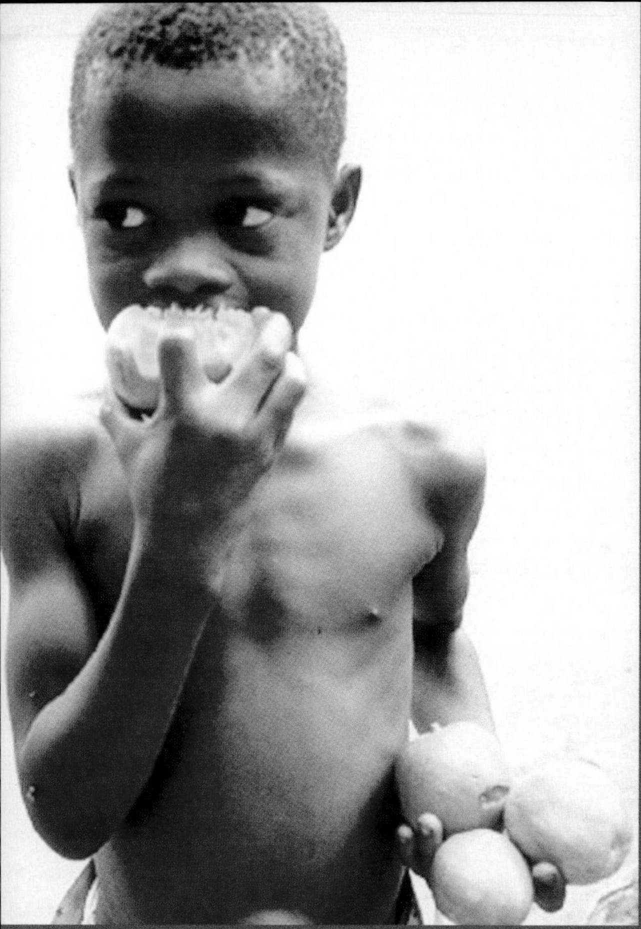

The NERC Centre for Ecology and Hydrology/Dr David Ladipo

The NERC Centre for Ecology and Hydrology/Roger Leakey

Farmers in Cameroon and Nigeria have been improving their domestication of wild fruit trees, with the help of a partnership of scientists from the UK and West Africa and the Department for International Development's Forestry Research Programme. The scientists helped them identify the best individual Bush Mango and African Plum trees in each village. They analysed different characteristics of the fruit, including size and taste. Having found the best trees, the scientists showed the farmers how to take cuttings and set up a village nursery in which to produce cultivars of the trees. The farmers now plant the trees among their cocoa and coffee crops. The trees supply staple foods, enrich the biodiversity of the village and provide extra income from selling surplus fruit.

UK partner organisations in the project:
Overseas Development Institute, Centre for Ecology and Hydrology, Institute for Ecology and Resource Management, Campden and Chorleywood Food Research Association.

West African Partners:
International Centre for Research in Agroforestry, L'Institut des Recherches Agricoles pour le Développement, Limbe Botanic Garden, Cameroon Extension Service and non-governmental organisations.

The above information is taken from a research project partly funded by the United Kingdom Department for International Development (DFID) for the benefit of developing countries. The views expressed in the research to which the above refers are not necessarily those of DFID. (DFID project code (R7190) Forestry Research Programme).

Jonathan Rainsford/Oxfam

Following the devastating earthquake in January 2001 in the state of Gujarat, India, Oxfam worked with Gujarati Water Supply and Sanitation Board to provide emergency water and sanitation to more than 20,000 people. In these situations Oxfam offers expertise and provides specialist equipment developed over many years.

Oxfam–originally known as 'The Oxford Committee for Famine Relief'–was founded in 1942. After the war the Committee saw a need for its work to continue and enlarged its objectives. During the 1960s it employed a growing network of overseas Field Directors, supporting self-help schemes whereby communities improved their own water supplies, health provision and farming practices. The name 'Oxfam' was formally adopted in 1965.

During the 1970s Oxfam decided to employ local people to run and work on projects. In 1992 Oxfam celebrated its 50th anniversary and was nominated for the Nobel Peace Prize. Today Oxfam GB is part of Oxfam International and continues to work with communities and other agencies to bring an end to poverty and suffering around the world.

Howard Davies/Oxfam

Oxfam's work has included the design of an award-winning special bucket, to be used in emergency situations. These buckets, plus hygiene packs, were handed out by Oxfam staff at Stankovic refugee camp in Macedonia, set up for Kosovar refugees in 1999. Refugees were recruited to help Oxfam staff–several of whom were refugees themselves–having previously worked with Oxfam in Kosovo.

Shafiqul Alam/Oxfa

Members of a community group meeting with Oxfam Project Officer Kafil Ahmed in central Bangladesh in 1996, to discuss the progress of their work together.

By raising the level of their homesteads–and that of a piece of land to keep their cattle on–the families were able to reduce significantly the damage caused by the year's floods. A good harvest of wheat and groundnuts, the latter sold for income, offset the effects of weeks with no work when their farmland was covered by water. This meant that the families did not need to ask for emergency relief. Similar work continues today.

Jenny Matthews/Ox

Sierra Leone, 1999. Oxfam provides water and sanitation for thousands of families displaced from their homes by the long-running civil war. This Oxfam trainer is explaining how to make oral rehydration solution to an audience of volunteer health promoters in Nyawama camp for displaced people. Oxfam continues to promote good hygiene in the area.

that ozone is now the principal cause of these criteria being exceeded in urban areas. In rural areas, air pollution was recorded as moderate or higher on 25 days on average per site in 2000 compared with 48 days in 1999. This variability reflects ozone levels—again, the main cause of the threshold of the 'moderate air pollution' criterion being exceeded.

Daily Air Quality Bulletins make air pollution data from the monitoring network available to the public. These give the concentrations of the main pollutants, together with an air pollution forecast. The information features in television and radio weather reports, and appears in many national and local newspapers. Information on the Internet may be accessed through the UK's National Air Quality Archive website (*www.aeat.co.uk/netcen/airqual*).

Between 1998 and 2001, DEFRA and the former DETR contributed around £1.4 million to research on the health impact of outdoor pollution.

Vehicle Emissions

Measures to reduce pollution from road transport are seen as being key to achieving the objectives set out in the UK air quality strategy. Progressively tighter standards for fuels and vehicle emissions mean that urban road transport emissions of CO, NO_X and particulates are projected to fall by around 70% between 1995 and 2015.

Vehicle emissions standards are governed by a series of EC Directives enforced in the UK under the Motor Vehicles Construction and Use and Type Approval Regulations.

All new petrol-engined passenger cars in the UK are fitted with catalytic converters, which typically reduce emissions by over 75%. These measures to reduce vehicle emissions from new vehicles have been accompanied by improvements in fuel quality with, for instance, reductions in components such as benzene and sulphur, which have an environmental impact, and the phasing out of leaded petrol. In the UK from 1 March 2001, people buying a new car must pay vehicle excise duty according to the amount of carbon dioxide (CO_2) their car produces and the type of fuel it uses (see also chapter 23).

> In 2003 three fuel-celled buses running on hydrogen will be put into operation in London, as part of a trial involving nine cities in Europe and 27 buses. A fuel cell combines hydrogen with oxygen to produce electricity, heat and water. As water vapour is the only emission from fuel-celled vehicles, they are significantly cleaner than existing petrol and diesel vehicles. Following the end of the trials in 2005, Transport for London will give consideration to using more fuel-celled buses.

Compulsory testing of emissions from vehicles is a key element in the UK's strategy for improving air quality. Metered emission tests and smoke checks feature in the annual 'MoT' roadworthiness test. Enforcement checks carried out at the roadside or at operators' premises also include a check for excessive smoke. The Vehicle Inspectorate (see p. 364) carried out 85,300 roadside emissions checks in 2000–01 (on cars, coaches, goods vehicles, buses and taxis), and 3,482 vehicles failed. Under a trial scheme introduced in 1997, seven local authorities in Great Britain (five in England, one in Scotland and one in Wales) were given powers to enforce vehicle exhaust emissions standards by random testing at the roadside, with a £60 fixed penalty fine for offenders exceeding prescribed standards. The Government has completed consultation on proposals to extend these powers to local authorities in England and Wales which have designated air quality management areas. The Scottish Executive is consulting on extending the powers to other Scottish local authorities.

Climate Change

Several gases naturally present in the atmosphere keep the Earth at a temperature suitable for life by trapping energy from the sun—the 'greenhouse' effect. However, emissions from human activities are increasing the atmospheric concentrations of several important gases, causing global warming and climate change. Globally the temperature rose by about 0.6°C during the 20th century. In

England, four of the five warmest years since records began in 1659 occurred in the 1990s, with 1990 and 1999 being the joint warmest years ever. Research at the Hadley Centre, part of the Met Office, is focused on improving climate predictions and investigating the causes of recent climate change. Results from its latest climate model suggest that, with the current levels of increase in greenhouse gases, the global mean sea level will rise by between 9 and 88 cm by 2100 and there will be a rise in average global temperature of up to 6°C over the next 100 years. Emissions of greenhouse gases are one of the UK Government's sustainable development headline indicators (see p. 378).

The most significant greenhouse gas emitted by the UK is CO_2, followed by methane and nitrous oxide (N_2O). Although still comparatively low, there has been an upward trend in emissions of hydrofluorocarbons (HFCs), which have high global warming potential. This has been due to an increase in consumption in response to the phasing out of ozone-depleting substances under the Montreal Protocol (see p. 333). HFCs were virtually unused before 1990, but their emissions accounted for nearly 3% of total UK greenhouse gas emissions in 1998 and then fell to about 1% in 1999 in response to pollution control regulations.

In 1997, the Government established the UK Climate Impacts Programme to help those likely to be affected by climate change to assess their vulnerability, so that they can plan to adapt accordingly. Several regional and sectoral impact assessments have been implemented and many others are under way. Possible impacts of climate change in the UK include more droughts in the south and east of England, more flooding in the north and west of England, more damage as a result of severe storms, threats to the coast and low-lying agricultural land from rising sea levels, and changes in wildlife and habitats. The extensive flooding to parts of the country during autumn 2000 illustrated the UK's vulnerability to extreme events.

Control of global and regional air pollution requires international cooperation and action. The first international action dealing with climate change dates from the Earth Summit (see p. 378), at which the UN Framework Convention on Climate Change was adopted, calling for the stabilisation of greenhouse gas concentrations in the atmosphere at a level that would prevent dangerous man-made interference with the climate system. At the third Conference of the Parties to the Framework Convention, held in Kyoto in 1997, developed countries established a Protocol agreeing legally binding targets to reduce emissions of the basket of six main greenhouse gases: CO_2, methane, N_2O, HFCs, perfluorocarbons (PFCs) and sulphur hexafluoride. The Protocol committed developed nations to a 5.2% reduction in greenhouse gas emissions below 1990 levels by 2008–12 (in 1990 the UK emitted 164 million tonnes of CO_2, 21 million tonnes of carbon equivalent of methane and 18 million tonnes of carbon equivalent of N_2O). The European Union agreed to a collective reduction target of 8%. At a subsequent meeting in June 1998, the Member States agreed to share out the EU's target to reflect national circumstances. Individual countries' targets range from a reduction of 28% for Luxembourg to a permitted increase of 27% for Portugal. The UK is on course to meet its legally binding target, a reduction of 12.5%. Between 1990 and 1999 emissions, weighted by global warming potential, fell by 14.5%.

In November 2000 *Climate Change: The UK Programme* was published. The programme sets out how the Government and the devolved administrations intend to:

- deliver the UK's Kyoto target;
- meet the legally binding target and move towards a domestic goal of a 20% cut in CO_2 emissions by the year 2010;
- move the UK towards a more sustainable, lower carbon economy; and
- ensure that all sectors of the economy and all parts of the UK play their part.

In July 2001 the UK attended the second part of the sixth Conference of the Parties to the Framework Convention on Climate Change in Bonn to discuss the details of the Kyoto Protocol, following the break-up of talks in The Hague in November 2000. The following issues were agreed:

- commitment of additional funding to developing countries for climate change-related activities;
- rules on how to make the Kyoto provisions workable;
- rules on the extent to which 'carbon sinks' (the temporary storage of carbon in forests and soils) can be used to meet Kyoto commitments; and
- tighter targets, for subsequent periods, for countries that fail to achieve their emission reductions, along with compliance action plans to show what measures they will take to get back on track.

The integrated package of policies and measures contained in the programme includes the climate change levy package (see below) which includes negotiated agreements with energy-intensive sectors; extra money for improving business use of energy; emissions trading (where companies can buy and trade reductions in emissions) where emission caps have been taken; reform of the building regulations; EU-level voluntary agreements with manufacturers to increase fuel efficiency in vehicles; a target to deliver 10% of the UK's electricity from renewable sources of energy by 2010; and the promotion of energy efficiency in the domestic sector. The programme also looks at what the UK may need to do to adapt to the effects of climate change.

In May 2001 the Climate Change Projects Office was launched. This interdepartmental initiative—between DEFRA and the Department of Trade and Industry—provides advice to companies interested in carrying out climate change projects that reduce greenhouse gases.

As part of its contribution to ocean climate monitoring, the UK has commissioned research to assess the rapid collapse of the western Antarctic ice sheet. This is due to be published in 2001–02. The Government has also funded an instrument to provide highly accurate temperature readings for the sea surface, and delivered it to the European Space Agency for inclusion on its ENVISAT satellite, due to be launched in 2001.

Stratospheric Ozone Layer

Stratospheric ozone forms a layer of gas about 10 km to 50 km (6 to 30 miles) above the Earth's surface, protecting it from the more harmful effects of solar radiation. British scientists first discovered ozone losses over much of the globe, including a 'hole' in the ozone layer over Antarctica, in 1985. This 'hole' has been growing steadily and its edges now reach beyond the Antarctic continent to the tip of South America. Similar but less dramatic thinning of the ozone layer occurs over the North Pole each year as well. Ozone depletion is caused by man-made chemicals containing chlorine or bromine, such as chlorofluorocarbons (CFCs), hydrochlorofluorocarbons (HCFCs) and halons, which have been used in aerosol sprays, refrigerators and fire extinguishers.

In an effort to repair this damage, over 170 countries have ratified the Montreal Protocol, an international treaty for the protection of the stratospheric ozone layer. This is enforced in the UK by an EC Regulation. In October 2000 a new EC Regulation was introduced with tougher restrictions, including controls on the use of most ozone-depleting substances, production controls on HCFCs, a ban on a new list of substances, trade controls and an export licensing system.

Acid Rain

The pollutant gases SO_2 (mainly from power stations), NO_X (from road transport and power stations), and ammonia (NH_3) (mainly from livestock) can be carried over long distances before being deposited directly on to vegetation and soil or being washed out as acid rain. Acidification results when sensitive ecosystems are not capable of neutralising the deposited acidity. In the UK, the ecosystems that are most sensitive to acidification are located in the northern and western uplands. The damaging effects of high levels of acid deposition on soils, freshwaters and trees, and on buildings, have been demonstrated by scientific research.

In 1998 the National Expert Group on Transboundary Air Pollution was set up to advise the Government on biological and

The climate change levy came into force on 1 April 2001. The levy applies to sales of electricity, coal, natural gas and liquefied petroleum gas (LPG) to the non-domestic sector (business, commerce, agriculture and the public sector) within the UK. It aims to encourage business energy efficiency and is expected to save at least 5 million tonnes of carbon emissions a year by 2010. It is forecast to raise around £1 billion in 2001–02, which will be returned, in full, to the non-domestic sector through a cut in employers' National Insurance contributions and provision of £120 million of additional support for energy efficiency measures in its first year of operation. By July 2001, 43 energy-intensive industry sectors—such as chemicals, cement and steel—had signed up to formal targets for cutting carbon emissions in the period to 2010.

chemical trends in the UK environment and the prospects for ecosystem recovery as a result of current and projected transboundary air pollution. In 2001 it published its draft report for comment, *Transboundary Air Pollution: Acidification, Eutrophication and Ground Level Ozone in the UK*.

The UK is a party to the UNECE (United Nations Economic Commission for Europe) Convention on Long Range Transboundary Air Pollution, which was set up in 1979 in response to evidence that acidification of lakes in Scandinavia was linked to European emissions of SO_2. Under the Convention, there have been a number of Protocols to reduce emissions of acidifying pollutants. The latest 'Gothenburg' Protocol, signed in December 1999, tackles the three environmental problems of acidification, eutrophication and ground-level ozone (summer smog). Under the Protocol, the UK agreed annual emission ceilings of 625 kilotonnes for SO_2, 1,181 kilotonnes for NO_X and 297 kilotonnes for NH_3, to be achieved by 2010. By comparison, UK emissions in 1999 were 1,187 kilotonnes for SO_2, 1,605 kilotonnes for NO_X, and 348 kilotonnes for NH_3. The Protocol also sets a ceiling of 1,200 kilotonnes for VOCs (for example, solvents used in industry, domestic products, dry cleaning, fumes at petrol pumps and paints). VOCs contribute to the formation of ground-level ozone. In 1999 the UK emitted 1,744 kilotonnes of VOCs.

Running in parallel to the UNECE Gothenburg Protocol is the EC National Emission Ceilings Directive (NECD), provisionally agreed in June 2001, which is intended to tackle the harmful effects to human health and the environment from transboundary air pollution. The NECD sets ceilings for 2010 for the same four pollutants. The figures negotiated commit the UK to further cuts in SO_2 and NO_X emissions, reducing the ceilings to 585 kilotonnes and 1,167 kilotonnes respectively.

Noise

The Air and Environmental Quality Division (EAQD) in DEFRA is responsible for the coordination and development of policies and the promotion of initiatives to address the problem of noise in England, with the aim of improving quality of life. The Air Quality Team, part of the Environment Group in the Scottish Executive, has equivalent responsibility in Scotland. The EAQD also acts as the UK lead organisation in negotiations on environmental noise in Europe.

Local authorities have a duty to inspect their areas for 'statutory nuisances', including noise nuisance from premises and vehicles, machinery or equipment in the street. They must take reasonable steps to investigate complaints, and serve a noise abatement notice where it is judged to be a statutory nuisance. There are specific provisions in law to control noise from construction and demolition sites, to control the use of loudspeakers in the streets and to enable individuals to take independent action through the courts against noise nuisance.

The Noise Act 1996 strengthened the law in England, Wales and Northern Ireland on action that can be taken against noisy neighbours, and a review of this Act is currently being undertaken. The Housing Act

Figure 19.7: Emissions of Sulphur Dioxide, Nitrogen Oxide, VOCs and Ammonia and UNECE Obligation Targets, UK

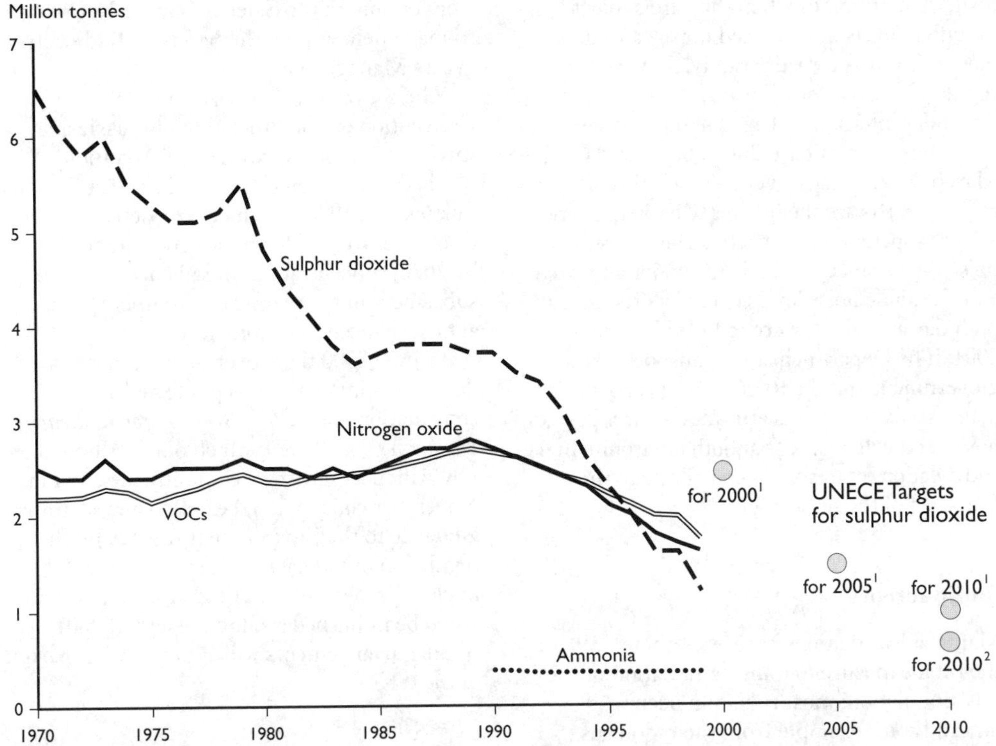

[1] Targets set by the UNECE Second Sulphur Protocol, 1994.
[2] Targets set by the UNECE Gothenburg Protocol, 1999.

Source: Department for Environment, Food and Rural Affairs

1996 gave local authorities new powers to deal with anti-social behaviour by tenants, including noise. However, these two Acts do not apply in Scotland, where action against noisy neighbours is taken under earlier legislation. The Crime and Disorder Act 1998 introduced Anti-Social Behaviour Orders in England, Scotland and Wales, which can be used against any person who is causing harassment, alarm or distress to others.

The Government announced in the rural White Paper (see p. 356) its intention to consult on a proposed national ambient noise strategy. The strategy will include mapping the main sources and areas of noise to enable policy to take better account of the implications of noise sources for rural areas. The first stage is expected to be completed by 2004, and £13 million has been allocated for this.

The National Noise Incidence Survey and the National Noise Attitude Study are undertaken by DEFRA to establish a baseline for, and monitor changes in, the noise climate in Britain. Both surveys (which have recently been expanded to cover the whole of the UK) have now taken place and results are expected to be published in late 2001.

Compensation may be payable for loss in property values caused by physical factors, including noise from new or improved public works such as roads, railways and airports. Highway authorities (in Scotland, local road authorities and the Trunk Roads Authority) are required to make grants available for the insulation of homes when they are subject to specified levels of increased noise caused by new or improved roads. Equivalent regulations exist for railways.

Under international agreements, noisier subsonic jet aircraft are due to be phased out by March 2002: already over 95% of UK-registered jets are the quieter 'Chapter 3' types. Various operational restrictions aim to reduce noise disturbances at the UK's major airports, and allowable noise levels over airports, during both day and night, were reduced in spring 2001. The Department for Transport, Local Government and the Regions is to carry out a major study to reassess attitudes to aircraft noise, and will ensure that both environmental and aviation interests can contribute to the oversight of the project.

Radioactivity

Man-made radiation represents about 15% of the total exposure to ionising radiation of the UK population; most radiation occurs naturally (for example from the radon gas given off by some rock formations). A large proportion of the exposure to man-made radiation comes from medical sources, such as X-rays. This and other man-made radiation is subject to stringent control. Users of radioactive materials must be registered by the Environment Agency in England and Wales, SEPA in Scotland and the Chief Radiological Inspector in Northern Ireland. The Health and Safety Executive (HSE—see p. 163) is responsible for regulating safety at civil nuclear installations. The National Radiological Protection Board (NRPB) advises on health risks posed by radiation and how to guard against them.

International Commitments

An EC Directive lays down basic standards for the protection of the health of workers and the general public against the dangers arising from ionising radiation. The provisions of the Directive are implemented in the UK through a number of Acts including the Radioactive Substances Act 1993. The UK is also a Contracting Party to the International Joint Convention on the Safety of Spent Fuel Management and on the Safety of Radioactive Waste Management.

The contracting parties to the Oslo and Paris Convention on the Protection of the Marine Environment of the North East Atlantic (OSPAR), including the UK, agreed at Sintra, Portugal, in 1998 to reduce radioactive discharges to the North East Atlantic so that, by 2020, concentrations of radioactive substances in the marine environment, are almost reduced to historic levels.

In June 2000 the Government and the devolved administrations published a consultation paper, *UK Strategy for Radioactive Discharges 2001–2020*, which outlines how the UK will meet its Sintra commitments, and in November consultation began on new statutory guidance to the Environment Agency on the regulation of radioactive discharges from nuclear licensed sites in England. Final versions are to be published around the end of 2001. Similar arrangements will apply in other parts of the UK.

Radioactive Waste Management

All solid radioactive waste in the UK is either disposed of in suitable facilities on land or safely stored pending the adoption of a final management strategy. The disposal of such waste is regulated by law under the Radioactive Substances Act 1993. This Act makes the Environment Agency in England and Wales and SEPA in Scotland responsible for regulating the safe use and storage of radioactive materials and the management of waste.

Radioactive wastes vary widely in nature and level of activity, and the methods of management reflect this. Most solid waste—of low radioactivity—is disposed of at the shallow disposal facility at Drigg in Cumbria. Some small quantities of very low-level waste are disposed of at authorised landfill sites. Some intermediate-level waste is stored at nuclear licensed sites, usually those sites where it is generated, but most of the UK's inventory is at Sellafield in Cumbria. High-level or heat-generating waste is stored in either raw (liquid) or vitrified (glass-like) form. Once vitrified it will be stored for at least 50 years to allow it to cool to a safe temperature for final management.

Businesses and the Consumer

A number of initiatives have been introduced to encourage businesses and consumers to develop environmentally sound practices.

Envirowise—formally known as the *Environmental Technology Best Practice Programme*—launched in 1994, is a programme that promotes the use of better environmental practices that reduce business costs for industry and commerce. It provides information and advice on environmental technologies and techniques by means of publications, events and a freephone UK helpline. By the end of 2000, it was helping business to save £120 million a year. It works in partnership with the Energy Efficiency Best Practice Programme (EEBPP) (see p. 493), which supports energy efficiency measures.

In April 1999 the Government launched the *Sustainable Technologies Initiative* (STI), to build on Envirowise and the EEBPP. The STI provides financial support for developing new technologies that will help businesses to be more efficient in their use of resources, and produce less waste and pollution.

The Advisory Committee on Business and the Environment (ACBE) (*www.defra.gov.uk/environment/acbe/index.htm*) consists of business leaders appointed by the Government and serving in a personal capacity. It enables government and business to discuss environmental issues and aims to help the business community to demonstrate good environmental practice and management. The ACBE was instrumental in the establishment of the *Carbon Trust* in April 2001 (see p. 492).

Environmental Management Systems

In 1996 the International Organisation for Standardisation (ISO) published ISO 14001 which specifies the requirements for an environmental management system against which an organisation may be certified. ISO 14001 is an international standard which provides organisations with a tool to help them control and minimise the impact of their products, services and activities on the environment. Certification is achieved only after an audit of the organisation's environmental management system by an independent 'certification body' which has been accredited by the United Kingdom Accreditation Service.

The EU Eco-Management and Audit Scheme (EMAS) is a voluntary registration scheme which registers organisations from the public and private sector that have established an environmental management system consistent with ISO 14001. The scheme was launched in April 1995 and revised in 2001. There are currently 124 organisations registered for EMAS.

Many leading companies now address environmentally issues in their annual reports and over 90 publish separate environmental performance reports. To encourage the top 350 UK businesses to report publicly on their major environmental impacts, the Government has produced guidance to help companies measure and report on greenhouse gas emissions, water consumption and waste.

Environmental Labelling

Consumers can need assistance in making environmentally sound decisions about the goods they buy, and often rely on the information given on product labels. To help them, the Government encourages accurate and relevant environmental labelling, as part of an integrated approach to reduce the environmental impact of consumer products. It also administers the voluntary EU ecolabelling scheme in the UK. The voluntary Green Claims Code sets out guidance for businesses that make environmental claims about their products. In June 2000 the code was revised in line with ISO 14021—the international standard on environmental labelling.

The Government's Market Transformation Programme encourages the take-up of more

The Queen's Awards for Enterprise: Sustainable Development are presented in recognition of products, technology or processes developed by British industry which offer major environmental benefits. Awards are granted only for products, technology or processes which have achieved commercial success. In 2001 there were 15 awards. Examples include B&Q plc in Eastleigh (Hampshire), for its QUEST (QUality, Ethics, SafeTy) programme and Cooks' Delight Ltd in Berkhamsted (Hertfordshire) for its organic food.

The biennial *European Environmental Awards*, sponsored by the European Commission and the United Nations Environmental Programme, recognise and reward companies that are making significant contributions to economic and social development without detriment to the environment. In 2000, a UK company, Entec UK Ltd, was one of four winners chosen from 80 nominations across Europe. It won the award for international partnership in sustainable development, for a project created to develop environmental programmes in Egypt.

energy-efficient domestic appliances. The mandatory EU energy labelling scheme provides graded information on product performance, and EU measures have also resulted in the removal of inefficient appliances from the market.

Environmental Research

Several government departments have substantial environmental research programmes. For example, DEFRA's planned expenditure on research and development for 2001–02 is £186 million.

The European Wildlife Division within DEFRA manages a significant research effort, of which the biggest element in 2000 was the *Countryside Survey 2000*, carried out by the Natural Environment Research Council Centre for Ecology and Hydrology. This was the fourth survey of its kind—carried out every six to eight years—of habitats and landscape features in Great Britain. However, it was the first survey to combine both the latest satellite image analysis techniques with traditional field survey methods to obtain full national coverage and detailed information on vegetation, soils and freshwater. The survey found, among other things, that in the past ten years, in Great Britain, there has been a 22% expansion of fen, marsh and swamp, a halt in hedgerow destruction, and an increase of 38% in plant diversity around the edges of fields. It also found there were declines in the quality of grassland, downland and heaths and a loss of some plant species. A similar survey was also carried out in Northern Ireland by the University of Ulster on behalf of the EHS. This survey found that: land use intensification has resulted in a reduction in habitat biodiversity; the most widespread wildlife habitats in Northern Ireland are species-rich grasslands, wetlands, bogs and hedges; and improved grassland now covers 42% of the Northern Ireland land area.

Early in 2001, thousands of people across Britain took part in the fifth in a series of public attitude surveys commissioned by the former DETR to investigate people's environmental concerns, awareness and behaviour. This latest study was extended to cover sustainable development and quality of life issues such as housing development, health, jobs, air quality, educational achievement, wildlife and economic prosperity.

Most of the government-funded Research Councils (see pp. 431–6) have a role in environmental science research, but the Natural Environment Research Council (NERC) (*www.nerc.ac.uk*) takes the lead. NERC, whose R&D budget for 2001–02 is about £220 million, funds and carries out scientific research in the sciences of the environment. It carries out research into five environmental and natural resource issues of priority to the UK: biodiversity; environmental risks and hazards; global climate change; natural resource management; and pollution and waste. In 2000–01, NERC opened four important research centres, the Tyndall Centre for Climate Change, based at the University of East Anglia, the NERC Centres for Atmospheric Science and Data

Assimilation, mainly based at the University of Reading, and the Centre for Polar Observation and Modelling, based at University College London. Other organisations that carry out environmental research include the Met Office (including the Hadley Centre); the Environment Agency, whose R&D budget for 2001–02 is around £11 million; the Natural Resources Institute of the University of Greenwich at Chatham (Kent); and the Climatic Research Unit at the University of East Anglia. Around 100 British universities and colleges run courses on environmental studies or natural resource management; many also carry out research. In addition to research funded directly by SEPA and the EHS, the Scotland and Northern Ireland Forum for Environmental Research also commissions research.

A computer program has been developed by the Natural History Museum which should enable experts to find combinations of areas to represent as many species as possible and which are therefore most worth preserving. *Worldmap* divides up the area of interest (anything up to and including the whole planet) into cells, and then displays a colour-coded map showing the relative biodiversity of the cells. *Worldmap* can also be used to plot maps and prioritise areas by their genetic diversity (*www.nhm.ac.uk/science/projects/worldmap*).

Further Reading

Accounting for Nature: Assessing Habitats in the UK Countryside (Countryside Survey 2000). DETR, 2000.
A Fair Deal for Rural England. DETR, 2000.
Climate Change: The UK Programme. DETR, 2000.
Digest of Environmental Statistics. DEFRA. Available only on the Internet: www.defra.gov.uk/environment/statistics/des/index.htm
Energy—the changing climate. Royal Commission on Environmental Pollution. The Stationery Office, 2000.
An environmental vision: the Environment Agency's contribution to sustainable development. Environment Agency, 2001.
Municipal Waste Management Survey 1999/2000. DEFRA, 2001.
National Waste Strategy: Scotland. SEPA, 1999.
The Air Quality Strategy for England, Scotland, Wales and Northern Ireland. DETR, 2000.
The Environment in your Pocket 2000. DEFRA, 2001.
The State of the Countryside 2001. The Countryside Agency, 2000.
Waste Management Strategy for Northern Ireland. The Stationery Office, 2000.
Waste Strategy 2000: England and Wales. DETR, The Stationery Office, 2000.
The Way Forward: The Final Report of the Cleaner Vehicles Task Force. The Stationery Office, 2000.
State of the Environment: Soil Quality. SEPA, 2001.

Websites

Department for Environment, Food and Rural Affairs: www.defra.gov.uk
Scottish Executive: www.scotland.gov.uk
National Assembly for Wales: www.wales.gov.uk
The Countryside Information System: www.cis-web.org.uk

20 Planning, Housing and Regeneration

Land Use Planning	**340**	Rented Housing	349
Planning Policy Guidance	341	Homelessness	353
Development Plans	343	**Regeneration**	**354**
Development Control	344	England	354
Housing	**345**	Wales	356
Housing Stock and Housebuilding	346	Scotland	357
Home Ownership	346	Northern Ireland	357

As a result of an increase in the population, changes in household composition and the demands of a growing economy, there are increasing pressures on land use in the United Kingdom. Planning policy guidance issued by the Government aims to create a fair and efficient land use planning system, to promote sustainable, high-quality development and to respect regional differences. The Government seeks to encourage the use of 'brownfield' sites, particularly in inner cities, to promote urban regeneration—thereby minimising the use of 'greenfield' land for housing and other development and preserving the countryside as far as possible.

LAND USE PLANNING

Planning systems regulate development and land use and contribute to the Government's strategy for promoting a sustainable pattern of physical development in cities, towns and the countryside.

Land use planning is the direct responsibility of local authorities in Great Britain. The Secretary of State for Transport, Local Government and the Regions has responsibility for the operation of the system in England. In Wales and Scotland control rests with the National Assembly for Wales and the Scottish Executive respectively. In Northern Ireland, the Department of the Environment functions as the single planning authority. The Planning Service, an executive agency within the Department, administers most planning functions.

The Department for Transport, Local Government and the Regions (DTLR) issues national planning policy guidance in England and provides guidance on the operation of the planning system at regional and local levels. Working with the Government Offices (for the Regions), it ensures that regional planning guidance, local authorities' development plans and decisions on planning applications are consistent with national policies.

In both Wales and Scotland, operation of the planning system—including the determination of most planning applications, and the preparation of development plans—is the responsibility of planning authorities. The National Assembly for Wales and the Scottish

Executive regulate and provide guidance on the operation of planning systems. The Scottish ministers approve structure plans and take decisions on planning applications that raise issues of national importance.

In Northern Ireland, the Planning Service is responsible for issuing operational planning, policy and guidance, determining planning applications and preparing development plans.

The National Land Use Database is a partnership project between the DTLR, English Partnerships (see p. 354), the Improvement and Development Agency (representing the interests of local government) and Ordnance Survey. It aims to establish a complete geographical record of land use in England, and to assist in a variety of policy issues, such as identifying previously developed land which may be available for redevelopment. Urban and rural pilot projects are seeking to develop methodologies for providing a land use map based on Ordnance Survey's new Digital National Framework.

Planning Policy Guidance

The Government's policy on the planning system is contained in *Planning Policy Guidance (PPG) Note 1 General Policy and Principles*, and taken further in other PPG Notes on housing, economic development, transport, retail and town centres, the countryside, green belts, sports and recreation, minerals and waste, and other topics—25 in all. PPG notes are subject to a period of consultation before issue and revision as necessary.

Housing

The revised *Planning Policy Guidance Note 3 on Housing*, providing national planning guidance on the future of housebuilding and development in England, was issued in March 2000. The guidance set out proposals for planning authorities to recycle brownfield (previously developed) sites and empty properties in preference to greenfield sites; for using land more efficiently; for assisting with the provision of affordable housing in both rural and urban areas; and for promoting mixed-use developments which integrate housing with shops, local services and transport. The Government's national target is that, by 2008, 60% of additional housing in England should be provided on previously developed land or by re-using existing buildings. This is one of the Government's 'headline' indicators of sustainable development (see p. 378).

The DTLR has published three good practice guides[1] in support of PPG3, covering design, monitoring and urban capacity studies (all available on its website). The Department has also consulted on a fourth guide on managing the release of sites and will publish this as soon as possible.

Research undertaken on behalf of the DTLR and published in March 2001 suggested that between 18,000 and 26,500 additional homes in England could be provided each year through the conversion of buildings and redevelopment of existing housing. It found that most of the sites for redeveloping and converting dwellings were available in town centres, throughout the south, particularly in Greater London. Possibilities for re-use were greatest in areas with a buoyant housing market and a large supply of older housing.

In 1998, 57% of all new dwellings in England were provided on previously developed land. In the same year, 47% of land changing to residential use was previously developed, compared with 38% in 1985. In 1996 the percentage of dwellings built on previously developed land varied from 82% in London to 35% in the South West.

Draft planning guidance for the provision of sports and recreational facilities, including further protection for open spaces, was published in March 2001.

Transport

New planning policy guidance, in line with the Government's policy on transport (see chapter 21), was issued in March 2001. It is aimed at integrating planning and transport at the national, regional and local level so as to promote more sustainable transport choices

---

[1] *By Design: Urban Design in the Planning System; Monitoring Provision of Housing through the Planning System* and *Tapping the Potential: Assessing Urban Housing Capacity.*

(both for people and for moving freight), and accessibility to jobs, shopping, leisure facilities and services by public transport, walking and cycling—thereby reducing the need to travel, especially by car.

Flooding

Following the extensive floods in parts of England and Wales in autumn 2000 (see chapter 1), new planning guidance for development and flood risk was issued in July 2001. Nearly 2 million homes and businesses are located in areas at risk of flooding. In higher-risk areas, including the functional flood plains used to hold excess water in times of flood, only a very limited amount of development of essential infrastructure should be permitted. In lower-risk areas, further development may be permitted if it can be properly defended from flooding and does not add to flood risk. Local planning authorities should make flood risk information available to prospective developers and property owners.

Regional Planning Guidance (England)

Regional Planning Guidance (RPG) provides the regional framework for local authorities' preparation of development plans (see p. 343) and local transport plans (see p. 360–1) in England. It is produced by the regional planning bodies in consultation with Government Offices (for the Regions) and other regional stakeholders. The Guidance is tested at a non-statutory public examination before being issued by the Secretary of State. It sets out a broad development framework for each region over a period of 15–20 years, and identifies the scale and distribution of provision for new housing and priorities for the environment, transport, infrastructure, economic development, agriculture, minerals, and waste treatment and disposal. New planning policy guidance (*PPG11: Regional Planning*), issued in October 2000, places greater responsibility on regional planning bodies working together with local authorities, Regional Development Agencies (see p. 392), the Government Offices and the public to resolve planning issues at the regional level through the production of draft RPG. By mid-2001, two RPGs (RPG 9 for the South East and RPG 6 for East Anglia) had been issued and most of the remainder are expected to be issued by the end of the year.

The Greater London Authority Act 1999 introduced new arrangements for planning in London. The Mayor has responsibility for the production of a 'spatial development strategy' covering development, regeneration and transport issues in London.

Wales and Scotland

Planning guidance in Wales is supplemented by a series of Technical Advice Notes. The National Assembly's draft *Planning Policy Wales* document, published in February 2001, contains proposed guidance on land use planning across Wales. It includes policies aimed at keeping development away from flood risk areas; the possible establishment of Wales' first Green Belt areas; and measures to ensure that the development of land and buildings creates a more accessible environment for everyone, including those with limited mobility. The document includes guidance on the extension of sustainable use of previously developed land in urban areas beyond housing needs alone, and encourages both rural and farm diversification. It proposes a change to the current strict control of all developments in the open countryside so that development on farm complexes can be permitted, subject to controls to prevent adverse environmental and transport effects.

National Planning Policy Guidelines (NPPGs) provide statements of Scottish Executive policy on nationally important land use and other planning matters. Circulars provide guidance on policy implementation and Planning Advice Notes provide advice on good practice. The revised NPPG1, which sets out policy on the planning system, was issued in November 2000. NPPG6, published at the same time, sets out the role of the planning system in promoting renewable energy. NPPGs on housing and on business and industry are being reviewed, with revised versions expected to be issued in 2002.

Green Belts

Green Belts are areas of land that are intended to be left open and protected from inappropriate development. They aim to control the unrestricted sprawl of large built-up areas, prevent towns from merging with one another, preserve the heritage of historic towns and encourage the recycling of derelict and other urban land, thereby encouraging urban regeneration. Not all Green Belt land is countryside. It can cover small villages comprising a mixture of residential, retail, industrial and recreational land as well as fields and forests. Development on Green Belts is only permitted under exceptional circumstances.

The first major Green Belt was established around the fringes of Greater London, under the London and Home Counties Green Belt Act 1938. Green Belts have also been established around Glasgow, Edinburgh, Aberdeen, Greater Manchester, Merseyside and the West Midlands, as well as several smaller towns. In 1997, there were 14 separate designated Green Belt areas in England, amounting to 1.65 million hectares, about 13% of the land area.

In Scotland there were six Green Belt areas totalling 156,000 hectares. Proposals for Green Belts around St Andrews and Dunfermline are included in the Fife Council Structure Plan which is currently under consideration by Scottish ministers. There are 245,000 hectares of Green Belt in Northern Ireland; this represents about 18% of the total land area. There are no Green Belts at present in Wales, but their creation is under consideration (see p. 342).

Development Plans

Development plans play an integral role in shaping land use development in an area, and provide a framework for consistent decision-making. Planning applications are determined in accordance with relevant development plan policies unless 'material considerations' indicate otherwise. In England, local planning authorities are required to prepare development plans in line with the Town and Country Planning Act 1990. Regulations, which took effect in 2000, provide a statutory framework for new procedures designed to improve the delivery of development plans. Unless justified by specific local considerations, plans should not conflict with either national or regional policies.

In England, outside metropolitan areas and certain non-metropolitan unitary authority areas, the development plan comprises:

- *structure plans*, which are produced by county councils, some unitary authorities and National Park authorities (in many cases on a joint basis). They set out the key strategic policies and provide a framework for local plans;
- *local plans*, which are produced by district councils, some unitary authorities and National Park authorities, and contain more detailed policies to guide development in a particular local authority area. The plans may include proposals for specific sites; and
- *minerals and waste local plans*, which are produced by county councils, some unitary authorities and National Park authorities (which are usually the development control authorities for these issues).

Within metropolitan areas and in some non-metropolitan unitary authorities, the development plan comprises a single *unitary development plan (UDP)*. There are two parts to the UDP: Part I consists of the local authority's strategic policies for the development and use of land in its area, and forms the framework for the detailed proposals for the use and development of land set out in Part II.

All unitary authorities and National Park authorities in Wales are required to prepare a UDP for their area. The UDP is the development plan for each county or borough council and each National Park, replacing the structure plan, local plan and any other existing plan. Three-quarters of the land area and almost 80% of the population of Wales are currently covered by area-wide plans. It is expected that UDPs will be reviewed in full at least once every five years.

The planning system in Scotland is governed by the Town and Country Planning

(Scotland) Act 1997. Development plans are prepared by councils and consist of structure and local plans. Councils are also responsible for making decisions on most applications for planning permission and for taking action against development that has not been approved.

In November 2000 the Scottish Executive announced that current arrangements for strategic planning were to be reviewed. A consultation paper was issued in June 2001 inviting views on a range of issues, including a proposal for strategic development plans based on city regions as well as local plans for each planning authority, and single-tier plans for other areas. An objective of these changes would be to guide investment in new development and infrastructure by identifying priority areas for physical renewal and regeneration. The Scottish Executive's Planning Audit Unit was set up to work with planning authorities to establish the underlying reasons for contrasting development control performance and to identify best practice in handling planning applications. The work of the Unit has recently been broadened to consider development planning as well as development control.

In Northern Ireland, the Planning Service put in place its Development Plan Programme in 1998. The programme is reviewed annually, and is designed to meet the development planning needs of all districts. During 2000–01, a new development plan for Londonderry was adopted, together with the Armagh Countryside Proposals, an alteration to the Armagh Area Plan.

Development Control

Development control is the process for regulating the development of land. Most forms of development, such as the construction of new buildings, alterations of existing buildings or changes of land use, require permission from the planning authority. Applications are dealt with on the basis of the development plans and other material considerations, including national and regional guidance. In 2000–01 district planning authorities in England received 545,000 applications for permission, 4% more than in the previous year, and made 504,000 planning decisions, an increase of 5%. Applications granted averaged 87% overall, varying between 91% in the North East and 81% in London. Householder developments accounted for 46% of all decisions in 2000–01, compared with 11% for new dwellings and 19% for other commercial and industrial developments. Other decisions involved listed buildings or conservation areas, advertisements, or change of use. In 2000–01, 63% of all planning decisions in England were made within the statutory eight-week period. The Government's target is for 80% of applications to be dealt with within this time frame. Similar targets apply in Wales and Scotland, with comparable targets in Northern Ireland.

In England and Wales, a small number of planning applications are called in to be decided by the Secretary of State or National Assembly for Wales rather than being decided by the local planning authority. Generally this only happens where the planning issue is of national or regional importance. A small number of cases end up as public inquiries.

If a local authority refuses to grant planning permission, grants it with conditions attached or fails to decide an application within eight weeks, or two months in Scotland, the applicant has a right of appeal to the Secretary of State in England, the National Assembly in Wales and Scottish ministers in Scotland. In August 2000 a package of revised rules and guidance was introduced aimed at speeding up decisions on planning appeals in England. New arrangements are expected to come into effect in Wales in 2002. In Northern Ireland, the applicant has the right of appeal to the Planning Appeals Commission.

The Planning Inspectorate serves both the Secretary of State for Transport, Local Government and the Regions in England and the National Assembly for Wales on appeals and other casework on planning, housing, the environment, highways and related legislation. It also provides information and guidance to appellants and other interested parties about the appeal process. In 2000–01, almost 13,000 planning appeal cases were determined.

In Scotland, the Scottish Executive Inquiry Reporters Unit is responsible for the determination of the majority of planning appeals and organises public local inquiries into planning proposals and related matters. In Northern Ireland, major planning applications can be referred to a public inquiry in certain circumstances.

The Royal Institute of British Architects and the Architects Registration Board exercise control over standards in architectural training and encourage high standards in the profession. The Royal Town Planning Institute carries out similar functions for the planning profession.

HOUSING

In England, the Secretary of State for Transport, Local Government and the Regions has responsibility for determining housing policy and supervising the housing programme. Responsibility for housing policy in Wales, Scotland and Northern Ireland rests with the National Assembly for Wales, the Scottish Executive and the Northern Ireland Executive respectively.

In Great Britain, the Government works with local authorities (which are responsible for preparing local housing strategies) and with the private and voluntary sectors. In England, the DTLR also works with the Housing Corporation, which regulates registered social landlords (RSLs—see p. 350) and provides financial support to help them supply affordable housing. In Wales, the National Assembly has responsibility for the funding and regulation of RSLs. The main purpose of Scottish Homes is to help provide good housing and contribute to the regeneration of local communities. From November 2001 it will become Communities Scotland, an executive agency of the Scottish Executive. In Northern Ireland, the Housing Division of the Department for Social Development is responsible for the development of housing policy issues throughout Northern Ireland and for the legislative framework to support the policy. The Division funds the Northern Ireland Housing Executive (NIHE) and the housing association movement and has regulatory powers over both, together with oversight of the section of the private rented sector which is controlled by the Rent (Northern Ireland) Order 1978.

The Government issued a housing policy statement in December 2000, *The Way Forward for Housing*, which set out its strategy for ensuring that everyone in England has the opportunity to live in a decent home. The aim is to deliver greater quality and choice across the housing market, through improving the quality of stock in all tenures; improving the quality of housing services; delivering affordable housing where it is needed; and giving people greater choice over where they live. Specific measures include:

- ➢ legislation to strengthen the safety net provided by local authorities for the homeless;
- ➢ introduction of a new 'commonhold' scheme for the ownership of flats;
- ➢ provision of new affordable housing where it is needed and in forms which are more sustainable; and
- ➢ a starter homes initiative for key workers in areas where both housing costs and demand are high.

By 2003–04, annual capital investment in housing will be more than £4 billion, compared with just over £1.5 billion planned spending in 1997–98. The Government intends that all housing provided by local authorities and RSLs should be of a decent standard by 2010, with a third of improvements taking place by 2004.

Better Homes for People in Wales, which sets out the National Assembly's proposals for a national housing strategy for Wales, was issued for consultation in January 2001. The proposals included increased emphasis on tackling problems of homelessness, including the establishment of a homelessness commission, continued support for sustainable home ownership, and an extension of the Care and Repair service to the whole of Wales, providing help and advice for elderly and disabled persons, and assisting with repairs and improvements.

In Scotland, the *Housing (Scotland) Act 2001* lays the basis for a radical re-shaping of social housing in Scotland, through strengthened and extended rights for homeless people; the establishment of a single tenancy (the Scottish secure tenancy) for tenants of both local authorities and RSLs; improved rights for tenants to be consulted and to participate; an enhanced strategic housing role for local authorities; a single regulator of providers of social housing; and a revised institutional framework, including the transformation of Scottish Homes into Communities Scotland (see p. 345).

The Executive announced the formation of a Housing Improvement Task Force in December 2000. This will consider current arrangements to promote housing improvement and maintenance in the private sector and will make recommendations for change. It will report during 2002.

In Northern Ireland a new housing Bill is currently being drafted. It is hoped that this will be placed before the Assembly in 2002.

Housing Stock and Housebuilding

The number of dwellings in Great Britain increased from almost 2 million at the start of the 19th century to nearly 25 million at the start of the 21st century. During the 20th century the number of households tripled, partly as a result of decreasing household and family sizes, and, in the latter part of the century, partly as a result of the increase in the numbers of people living on their own. The number of households in England is projected to increase from 20.2 million in 1996 to 24.0 million in 2021, with the largest increase being projected in one-person households from 5.8 million in 1996 to 8.5 million by 2021—71% of the total increase in the number of households.

In Scotland, the number of households is projected to increase by 12% from 2.17 million in 1998 to 2.43 million in 2012. One-person households accounted for an estimated 32% of households in 1998 and are projected to increase to 38% by 2012 (234,000 extra households).

A fifth of dwellings in England were built before the end of the First World War. In the early post-Second World War years, councils undertook most of the housebuilding construction. In 1999–2000, however, private sector enterprises in the United Kingdom were responsible for almost 90% of all housebuilding completions. RSLs now dominate building in the social sector. An estimated 17,300 new RSL homes were built in England during 2000–01.

To minimise new greenfield development and encourage urban regeneration, the Government wishes to see empty homes brought back into use. The number of vacant dwellings in England was 763,900 at the start of 2000–01. Four-fifths of all vacant dwellings are private housing, although two-thirds of these have been vacant for 12 months or less. Some dwellings may be vacant for short periods between purchase and sale or re-let, while others may be vacant for a longer period as they are awaiting demolition or renovation.

Home Ownership

A notable feature of the 20th century was the increase in owner-occupation. At the beginning of the century, around 10% of dwellings in England were owner-occupied, but by the beginning of the 21st century, this had increased to over two-thirds (16.7 million) in Great Britain (see Table 20.1).

The increase in the proportion of dwellings that are owner-occupied is in part due to a number of schemes that aim to increase low-cost home ownership. In England, these include the Right to Buy, Right to Acquire and Voluntary Purchase Grants, which offer tenants in social housing a discount against the market value of the homes they rent if they are eligible and choose to buy them. In addition, funding to support low-cost ownership is provided through the Housing Corporation and local authorities, including:

- *Conventional Shared Ownership*, which allows people to part buy and part rent homes developed by RSLs. The scheme allows people to increase their share of ownership in their home over time;
- *Do-It-Yourself Shared Ownership*, which is funded by local authorities in partnership with RSLs and enables people to select a house in the private market and then part own and part rent it, with the RSL taking on ownership of the rented share of the property;

Table 20.1: Tenure of Dwellings in the UK, 2000[1] *Per cent*

	Owner-occupied	Rented from local authority[2]	Rented from private owners or with job or business	Rented from registered social landlord
England	69	14	10	6
Wales	72	15	9	4
Scotland	62	25	7	6
Great Britain	**69**	**15**	**10**	**6**
Northern Ireland[3]	73	19	5	3

[1] As at 31 March (England), 1 April (Wales) and 31 December 1999 (Scotland and Northern Ireland).
[2] Including Scottish Homes and Northern Ireland Housing Executive.
[3] Figures for Northern Ireland are not directly comparable with those for the rest of the UK.
Sources: Department for Transport, Local Government and the Regions, National Assembly for Wales, Scottish Executive and Department for Social Development, Northern Ireland

Figure 20.2: Housebuilding Completions

United Kingdom

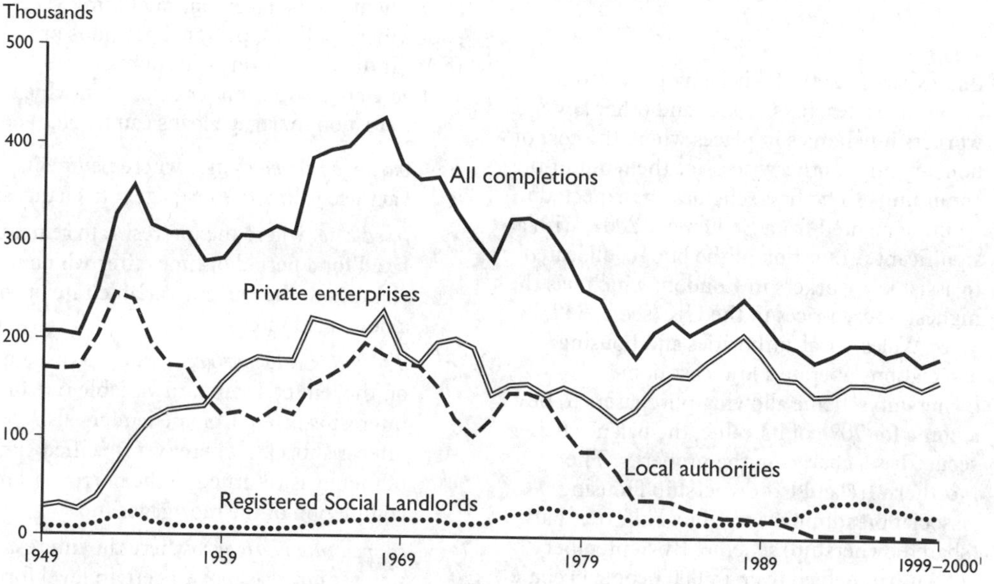

[1] From 1990–91 data are financial year.

Sources: Department for Transport, Local Government and the Regions; National Assembly for Wales; Scottish Executive; Department for Social Development, Northern Ireland

- *Homebuy*, which allows people to buy a home in the private market with an interest-free equity loan from an RSL for 25% of the value of the property. The loan is repayable, at 25% of the current market value, when the home is sold; and
- the *Cash Incentive Scheme*, in which local authorities offer cash grants for the purchase of a home in the private market.

Under the Starter Home Initiative, government funding of £250 million over the

Figure 20.3: Households: by Type of Dwelling, UK 1999–2000[1]

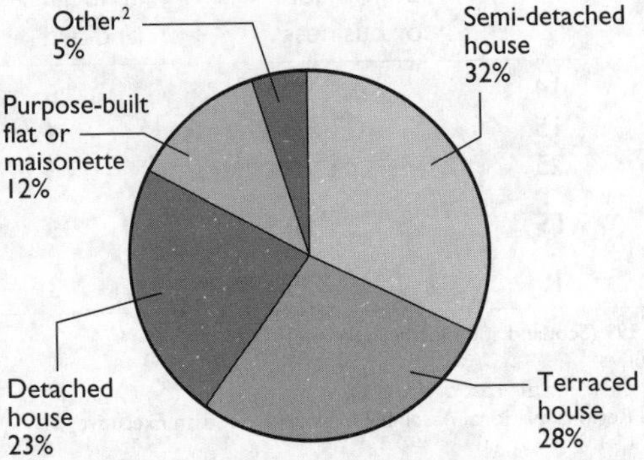

[1] Data for Wales and Scotland are for 1998–99.

[2] Includes converted flats which are particularly common in London.

Sources: Department for Transport, Local Government and the Regions, Office for National Statistics and Northern Ireland Statistics and Research Agency

three years to 2003–04 is being provided to help nurses, teachers, police and other key workers buy homes in places where the cost of housing might otherwise price them out of the community. The first schemes are expected to be implemented from September 2001, with a significant proportion of the budget allocated to assist key workers in London, which has the highest house prices in the UK (see p. 349).

In Wales, local authorities and housing associations operate a low-cost home ownership scheme allowing purchasers to buy a home for 70% of its value, the balance being secured as a charge on the property. The Northern Ireland Co-ownership Housing Association administers a 'buy half, rent half' (shared ownership) scheme. By September 2000 it had helped over 15,000 people become homeowners, while 91,000 NIHE tenants have bought their homes.

Mortgage Loans

A feature of home ownership in the UK is the relatively high proportion of homes purchased with a mortgage; approximately three-quarters of all homes are purchased with a mortgage loan facility. In 2000 loans for home purchase were obtained mainly through banks (70%) and building societies (21%), with 9% of loans being obtained from other lenders. Some companies offer low-interest loans to their employees.

Lenders differ in the amount they will lend relative to annual income. In 2000 the ratio of the average advance to income for all borrowers was 2.26: 2.30 for first-time buyers and 2.23 for owner-occupiers moving to another home. There are several different types of mortgage. A repayment mortgage provides for regular monthly repayments so that, over the life of the mortgage (usually 25 years), the debt, together with interest, is entirely repaid. With an investment-linked mortgage, only the interest on the loan is paid from the beginning, so that the capital sum borrowed does not decrease. Usually the borrower makes a long-term investment at the same time as taking out the mortgage, with the aim of achieving a capital sum sufficient to repay the mortgage loan. Different types of investment can be taken out, including endowment policies, personal pensions or ISAs (Individual Savings Accounts).

There are also a number of ways in which the interest on mortgage loans can be charged:

- *variable rate mortgage*, where payments vary according to mortgage rate changes;
- *fixed rate*, where the interest rate remains fixed for a period of time, after which it changes to the current variable rate or to a new fixed rate;
- *discounted rate mortgage*, where a discount on the lender's standard variable rate of interest is offered. Some lenders also offer cashbacks, whereby a specified sum of money is returned to the borrower on completion of the mortgage; and
- *capped rate mortgage*, where the interest rate cannot rise above a certain level for a given term, but it can fall.

Other types of mortgages exist for those who want to be able to vary their mortgage payments without having to pay extra charges. There are various types of flexible mortgage, including current account mortgages and flexible payment mortgages.

Since the late 1980s there has been a decrease in the popularity of endowment policies because of the possibility that investments may not grow fast enough to repay the capital borrowed. In 1988, 83% of new mortgages for house purchase in the United Kingdom were of this type, but by 2000 this had fallen to 17%. Around 60% of new mortgages were standard repayment mortgages in 2000. There has also been an increase in the take-up of variable-rate loans (which accounted for 66% of new mortgage loans in 2000) and a greater willingness to remortgage in order to take advantage of price differentials between lenders.

Statutory regulation of mortgages is expected to begin in summer 2002, when mortgage lenders will have to be authorised by the Financial Services Authority (FSA). The Authority will help consumers make informed decisions and its proposed regulatory approach will aim to protect those who subsequently fall into arrears or face repossession.

In Scotland, the *Mortgage Rights (Scotland) Act 2001* provides for people in mortgage debt to seek suspension of the creditor's right of enforcement if, in the view of the court, taking the whole circumstances into consideration, it is reasonable to do so.

The Executive is also considering a mortgage to rent scheme.

In 2000 the sample average dwelling price in the United Kingdom was £101,550, although there were marked regional variations (see Table 20.4), with buyers in London paying the most for their property. Dwelling prices also vary according to type, with detached homes being the most expensive.

In 1999–2000 average weekly mortgage payments for owner-occupiers ranged from £35 in Northern Ireland to £82 in London. Average weekly housing costs for all owner-occupiers were lowest in Wales and highest in London.

The number of properties that were taken into possession by mortgage lenders in the United Kingdom in 2000 was the lowest since 1989, at 22,960. This was a 24% decrease on the previous year; the number of mortgage accounts with mortgage arrears also fell significantly, by 29% for mortgages with long-term arrears (over 12 months).

Rented Housing

As owner-occupation has increased, the number of dwellings that are rented has

Table 20.4: Average Dwelling Prices by Region, 2000 £

Region	Type of dwelling: Bungalow	Detached house	Semi-detached house	Terraced house	Flat/ maison-ette	All dwellings	% increase on 1999
North East	70,236	107,868	55,920	45,232	51,812	63,921	*3.7*
North West	82,532	130,236	66,637	52,641	66,961	77,932	*8.2*
Yorkshire and the Humber	78,071	115,479	60,414	50,221	58,646	72,176	*7.1*
East Midlands	83,472	121,726	60,965	51,276	51,509	79,323	*9.5*
West Midlands	108,597	144,073	73,700	58,330	62,605	88,431	*10.9*
East	109,803	179,089	104,930	84,017	64,688	111,813	*15.5*
London	171,146	295,534	191,788	172,223	137,506	163,577	*14.9*
South East	160,467	232,212	132,347	101,882	86,351	142,790	*17.4.*
South West	117,355	163,259	93,603	78,809	67,590	104,233	*16.8*
England	111,297	162,110	91,748	82,295	98,277	106,998	*11.3*
Wales	74,720	115,505	60,621	47,771	55,880	72,285	*7.1*
Scotland	87,572	116,615	62,304	54,831	52,576	69,961	*0.9*
Northern Ireland	77,833	111,971	66,894	50,252	48,148	72,514	*9.4*
United Kingdom	**103,390**	**155,167**	**88,098**	**78,264**	**88,831**	**101,550**	**9.8**

Sources: Survey of Mortgage Lenders and Department for Transport, Local Government and the Regions

decreased. Between 1981 and 2000, the number of rented dwellings in Great Britain fell by 14% to 7.9 million. The Law Commission is to undertake a major review of the law on housing tenure in the social and private rented housing sectors. It will aim to produce a less complex framework for housing law which is better understood by everyone, particularly landlords and tenants.

Private Rented Sector

In England, households renting privately fell from 1.9 million in 1981 to 1.6 million in 1989 but rose to 2.1 million in 2000. The recovery may be linked to the deregulation of rents and to earlier repossession. In its policy statement, *The Way Forward for Housing*, the Government seeks to encourage good practice through voluntary accreditation schemes for landlords, through development of the National Approved Lettings Scheme and through a pilot tenancy deposit scheme. Legislation is proposed in order to raise the standards of houses in multiple occupation and to target bad landlords in areas of low demand. For a diminishing number of regulated tenancies and a few assured tenancies, five Rent Assessment Panels in England (and one each in Scotland and Wales) determine 'fair rents'. This occurs when either the landlord or the tenant objects to the rent fixed by a rent officer.

Social Housing

Much of the Government's expenditure on social housing (rented housing at below market rent) is provided as subsidies to local authorities to help pay for the costs of nearly 3.8 million rented council homes in the UK. More than 2,000 housing associations (most of them RSLs) provide other social housing. The RSLs manage and build new homes for rent and sale with the aid of government grants.

Most social housing in England is provided by local housing authorities which are responsible for preparing local housing strategies. In its housing policy statement, the Government confirmed its commitment to bring all social housing up to a decent standard by 2010, and proposes to improve the supply of social housing by doubling capital investment.

Most capital expenditure on housing goes towards renovating and improving existing council homes. Finance for the authorities' housing capital programmes comes partly from their own resources (mainly from receipts from sales of assets not used to repay debt and from contributions from the authorities' Housing Revenue Account and their general fund) and partly from central government. From 2001–02 some of the capital resources for local authorities provided in the 2000 Spending Review are being channelled through the Housing Revenue Account subsidy, in the form of a new major repairs allowance (MRA), which was introduced in April 2001 to ensure that authorities have the resources necessary to maintain their stock. The MRA in England will be around £1.6 billion in 2001–02, declining to £1.5 billion in 2002–03 and £1.4 billion in 2003–04, reflecting an estimated fall in the number of council homes. Total housing allocations for 2003–04 are approximately £2.6 billion (including MRA).

The Government's housing policy statement proposes to promote diversity and a wider range of landlords through stock transfer and through new investment and ownership options for council housing. By March 2001 there had been 146 approved large-scale voluntary transfers from local authorities to RSLs, involving 582,500 homes and raising more than £9.2 billion in private finance.

Supporting People, a new programme to be launched in 2003, will help vulnerable people live independently in the community by providing them with a wide range of housing support.

Local authorities in Wales own around 200,000, or approximately 15%, of all Welsh homes. By law they have to manage their own stock efficiently and in consultation with their tenants, address current housing needs in their area and plan to meet future needs and demands. Planned provision for local housing capital expenditure in 2001–02 is £149 million for local authorities and £56 million for RSLs.

The Scottish Executive has provided local authorities with nearly £175 million in capital allocations for 2001–02. Scottish Homes (Communities Scotland from November 2001) plans to invest almost £215 million in Scotland's housing to help build 5,360 new and improved homes, and is seeking to attract a further £120 million in private sector investment. The majority of homes—5,100—will be for rent from RSLs. The remaining homes will be offered to first-time buyers.

The *Housing (Scotland) Act 2001* introduced a new legislative framework for the provision and management of homes in the social rented sector. It introduced a common tenancy for local authority and RSL housing, with an enhanced package of rights including a new tenant participatory framework. This is being supported by £4.5 million to improve tenant involvement and a further £10 million to help landlords and tenants implement the new provisions. Communities Scotland will regulate local authority landlords and RSLs and be charged with improving housing management standards. Four local authorities (Glasgow, Dumfries and Galloway, Scottish Borders and Shetland) will be transferring their stock to new RSLs in 2002. A number of others are considering such transfers or will be transferring part of their stock via regeneration and development partnerships.

In Northern Ireland, the Government's contribution to housing of £209 million in 2000–01, supplemented by rental income and capital receipts, meant that gross resources available were £602 million. The Northern Ireland Housing Executive (NIHE) is the landlord of nearly one-third of rented homes in Northern Ireland—125,000 properties. It is responsible for assessing the need for, and arranging for the supply of, social housing. The NIHE's gross resources in 2001–02 are £540 million, with some £61 million for housing associations. An additional £35 million from private finance will supplement the social housing new build programme carried out by the Northern Ireland Co-ownership Housing Association and 41 other housing associations.

Improving Existing Housing

Whereas slum clearance and large-scale redevelopment used to be major features of housing policy in urban areas in the UK, the modernisation and conversion of sub-standard homes is now undertaken wherever practicable.

Action against unfit homes is based on a fitness standard covering disrepair; structural stability; dampness; provision for lighting, heating and ventilation; water supply; drainage; WC, wash hand basin and bath/shower; and facilities for food preparation. The standard is also used to guide decisions on the declaration of renewal areas and in surveying the condition of housing stock. It is generally recognised that the standard does not reflect a modern approach to health and safety hazards in the home and the Government has been developing a Housing Health and Safety Rating System. The system was made available to local authorities in July 2000 and consultation on enforcement arrangements (which would require primary legislation) began in March 2001.

Almost £50 million has been allocated to local authorities in Wales via the Supplementary Credit Approval to improve standards of housing quality and safety in 2001–02. The money will fund crime reduction and security and safety work, as well as stock condition and housing needs surveys.

The Scottish Executive is consulting on the introduction of an Index of Housing Quality to focus action on improvement to ensure that homes have an acceptable level of comfort, are sustainable and safe, and are fit for the households that live in them. The Index would not be statutory but implemented through local housing strategies.

Run-down estates are being improved through various initiatives, including Housing Action Trusts, Estate Action and the Single Regeneration Budget Challenge Fund (see p. 355). Five Housing Action Trusts are working to regenerate some of the worst housing estates in England. The Estate Action programme helps local authorities transform unpopular housing estates, but it now only funds schemes approved before 1995. Outside London it is expected that approved work will come to an end by March 2002, and within London by March 2005. Over the past year,

DTLR has continued to work with eight pathfinder authorities and the first contracts will be signed in 2002. A further 12 schemes are being developed and a third round of schemes is in prospect. In all, £760 million of funding under the Private Finance Initiative (PFI) (see p. 403) is available for housing projects in the current spending review period—up to 2004.

Local authorities in England have powers to help home owners and tenants to improve the worst quality housing and to assist with the regeneration of communities. They were expected to invest about £280 million in private housing renewal in 2000–01, providing repairs for some 75,000 homes. Local authorities also pay disabled facilities grants so that disabled people can adapt their homes and live more independently. A subsidy of £72 million was provided in 2000–01, generating £120 million of local authority investment. This was expected to pay for adaptations to 25,000 dwellings. The allocation for 2001–02 is £87 million. Independent advice and assistance with repairs, improvements and adaptations is available to elderly, vulnerable or disabled people via 284 Home Improvement Agencies (HIAs) operating in 227 local authority areas in England and via a Care and Repair service in Scotland.

In Wales, Estate Partnership was set up to assist local authorities in tackling the worst problems on local authority housing estates by coordinating efforts to raise the quality of the housing stock, along with social and environmental improvements. Options include transferring ownership to the private sector.

In Scotland, local authorities and Scottish Homes have powers to provide grants for the improvement and repair of private sector housing. Funding of £6.8 million has been made available by the Scottish Executive to councils to assist with housing improvement and repair programmes. In Northern Ireland, funding is allocated through the house renovation grants scheme, administered by the NIHE, on a similar basis to that in England and Wales. In rural areas, financial assistance to replace isolated dwellings that cannot be restored is also on offer.

Registered Social Landlords

Registered social landlords (RSLs) are the major providers of new subsidised homes for those in housing need. They own and manage 1.4 million self-contained units in England and are diverse bodies, ranging from small almshouses to very large housing associations managing many thousands of homes. They also include large-scale voluntary transfer and local housing companies, set up to own and manage council houses transferred out of local authorities.

The Housing Corporation, which regulates RSLs in England, gives capital grants to provide homes for rent and for sale under shared ownership terms. The rental programme includes building new homes and the purchase or rehabilitation of existing dwellings. The home ownership initiatives help tenants (and other first-time buyers) to buy homes of their own. The capital comes from the Approved Development Programme (ADP). Over the next three years, it is expected that the ADP will provide around 56,000 affordable homes for rent and 7,700 homes for low-cost ownership. In 2000–01 it anticipated providing around 22,000 homes for rent and sale to those in housing need. Local authorities can also fund RSL schemes. In 2000–01, RSLs were expected to provide about 10,000 affordable homes through the local authority social housing grant scheme.

Similar arrangements apply in Wales through the National Assembly's Housing Department and currently in Scotland through Scottish Homes. However, the situation in Scotland is set to change under Communities Scotland, the new executive agency. Scottish local authorities will eventually be expected to take on responsibility for development funding. Although stock transfer remains the only guaranteed method for securing funding, development funding could also transfer if the appropriate checks and balances are in place and there is local support. The Northern Ireland Housing Executive has continued to transfer its new build programme to registered housing associations. The 2002–03 transfer programme will involve 102 schemes, representing 1,395 dwellings.

Rural Housing

The Housing Corporation finances a special rural programme to build houses in villages with a population of 3,000 or less. Following the publication of the Rural White Paper *A Fair Deal for England* in November 2000 (see p. 356), the Government announced plans for the Housing Corporation programme for small settlements to increase from 800 to 1,100 units in 2002, rising to 1,600 by 2003–04. The National Assembly for Wales supports the development of housing in rural areas if it is regarded as a strategic priority by the local authority. Under the Homebuy scheme (see p. 347), RSLs in rural communities will now be able to take an increased equity share in the property. In Scotland, the Rural Partnership for Change Initiative is a pilot scheme, bringing together Highland Council, Scottish Homes and local housing providers. It is designed to tackle rural housing problems and target resources more effectively. In Northern Ireland, a revised rural housing policy was introduced in April 2000. It includes a programme of around 120 new rural dwellings a year, improvement or replacement of some 600 rural cottages over the next three to five years and provision of central heating in some 7,000 rural dwellings within the next three years.

Homelessness

Local housing authorities in England and Wales have a statutory obligation to ensure that suitable accommodation is available for applicants who are eligible for assistance, have become homeless through no fault of their own and who fall within a priority need group. The priority need groups cover households which include a dependent child or a pregnant woman; people who are vulnerable as a result of old age, mental or physical illness or disability or other special reason; and people who are homeless as a result of an emergency. Where these criteria are met, the authority must ensure that suitable accommodation is available for at least two years. Subject to a review of the household's circumstances, these arrangements can be extended beyond the initial two-year period. The local authority duty is likely to continue until settled accommodation can be found—in most cases through the allocation of a secure council tenancy or an assured tenancy with an RSL.

It is proposed to extend the priority needs categories, through secondary legislation, to include certain young people and other applicants who are vulnerable as a result of having an institutionalised background or as a result of fleeing violence. The Homelessness Bill, introduced in the House of Commons in June 2001, would strengthen the obligations of housing authorities towards homeless people and provide new powers for them to secure accommodation for non-priority need applicants where resources permit. Authorities would be required to adopt a homelessness strategy, based on a review of homelessness in their district, at least every five years. The Bill would also encourage authorities to give applicants more choice when allocating long-term social housing.

In the year ended March 2001, local housing authorities in England made over 252,000 decisions on applications for housing from households eligible under the existing legislation, and accepted around 113,600 households as meeting the conditions. Of these households, 57% contained dependent children, and a further 10% included a pregnant woman. Over three in ten acceptances arose because parents, relatives or friends (mostly parents) were no longer able, or willing, to accommodate the applicants. Almost a quarter (23%) of acceptances were because of the breakdown of a relationship with a partner, of which over two-thirds involved violence.

The types of accommodation used for households accepted under the legislation include hostels, women's refuges, bed and breakfast accommodation, properties owned by private landlords, and dwellings owned by the local authority and let on a non-secure tenancy. A new unit has been set up within the DTLR to help local authorities in England reduce the number of homeless families living in bed and breakfast accommodation. Some 10,800 households (14% of those accommodated under the legislation) were in bed and breakfast accommodation at the end of March 2001.

In Scotland there were 46,000 applications under the homeless persons legislation during

1999–2000. At the end of December 2000, 3,900 households were in temporary accommodation. The Housing (Scotland) Act 2001 includes a duty to ensure that unintentionally homeless people in priority need are entitled to permanent accommodation. There is also a basic package of rights for non-priority applicants, including enhanced advice and assistance and access to temporary accommodation. The new measures are supported by funding of £27 million over the next three years. A further £6 million has been made available to reduce the use of bed and breakfast as temporary accommodation for the homeless and £1.1 million has been awarded to voluntary groups for homelessness projects.

The Government aims to reduce the number of people sleeping rough in England to as close to zero as possible, and by at least two-thirds between 1998 and 2002. The Rough Sleepers Unit has a budget of almost £200 million in order to achieve this target. Almost £80 million of the budget has been administered by the Housing Corporation for permanent accommodation. Between June 1998 and June 2001, there was a reduction in the number of rough sleepers of 62%, to around 700. In coordination with other government departments, the Unit has set up projects to help some of the people who may be most at risk of rough sleeping—namely those leaving care, prison, or the armed forces.

Responsibility for rough sleeping initiatives in Wales and Scotland rests with the National Assembly for Wales and the Scottish Executive respectively. Over the next three years £3.5 million is being made available to support projects whose aim is to reduce the number of people sleeping rough in Wales. In Scotland, the Executive has set a target to remove the need for anyone to have to sleep rough by 2003. Funding of £42 million is provided though the Rough Sleepers Initiative to March 2002, after which time local authorities will assume more responsibility under Local Outcome Agreements with the Executive.

REGENERATION

Regeneration policies aim to enhance economic development and social cohesion through effective regional action and integrated local regeneration programmes. These programmes work through partnership between the public and private sectors and involve a substantial contribution from the latter. They support and complement other programmes tackling social and economic decline, and initiatives such as Sure Start (see p. 129), Health Action Zones (see p. 197), the Crime Reduction Programme (see p. 216) and the work of the Cabinet Office Social Exclusion Unit (see p. 118). Rundown areas in the UK benefit from European Union Structural Funds, which assist a variety of projects in the least prosperous industrial, urban and rural areas of the European Union. Over £10 billion of Structural Funds, including £3 billion covering Objective 1 areas (see p. 393), have been allocated to the UK for the period 2000–06.

England

In England, government departments and public agencies work together to develop national regeneration policies. The Government and the nine Regional Development Agencies (RDAs) set out the priorities for regeneration and ensure that programmes aim to enhance and complement those already in place. RDA regional strategies provide, after consultation, a regional framework for economic development and regeneration. The DTI is the lead sponsor of the RDAs, with the Government Offices (for the Regions) responsible for day-to-day RDA sponsorship issues. In London, the development agency reports to the Greater London Authority (see p. 9). The DTI, DTLR, the Department for Environment, Food and Rural Affairs and the Department for Education and Skills are jointly responsible for financing RDAs and for advising and assisting them on the implementation of regional strategies. English Partnerships, sponsored by the DTLR, works together with central and local government, the RDAs, local authorities and other public and private sector partners, and seeks to create new jobs and investment through sustainable economic regeneration and development in the English regions.

The Single Regeneration Budget (SRB), operated by the RDAs, provides funding for regeneration schemes and supports a range of economic, physical and social regeneration activities. Some 80% of new SRB funding goes to schemes in the most deprived areas, and 20% to smaller areas elsewhere, including rural, coastal and former coalfield areas. Regeneration partnerships, consisting of key local organisations including the voluntary sector, bid for resources from the SRB. There have been six SRB rounds. Under round six, announced in summer 2000, 189 schemes were approved, involving planned expenditure of around £1.2 billion over the following seven years. The successful bids from the first six rounds of the SRB are expected to involve expenditure of more than £23.2 billion over their lifetime: more than £5.6 billion from the SRB, £9.0 billion from other public service support and European funds and an estimated £8.6 billion of private sector investment. From 2001–02 it is for individual RDAs to decide on the appropriate level of new SRB activity in their region and from April 2002 the SRB will become part of their single budget (see below).

In April 2001, the Government announced that the European Commission had approved the five new schemes proposed as partial replacements for the Partnership Investment Programme which was managed by English Partnerships and the RDAs and closed to new projects in December 1999. The new schemes are designed to regenerate derelict, disused and vacant land, including projects which can be taken forward in partnership with the private sector. From 2002 the RDAs will be supporting these schemes from a single budget worth £1.55 billion in 2002–03 and £1.7 billion in 2003–04, giving them greater budgetary flexibility and freedom. Under this new framework, they will be required to deliver outcome and output targets set collectively by government departments, moving away from separate funding streams.

Urban Living

Following recommendations from the Urban Task Force for improving towns and cities, the Government published a White Paper on urban policy, *Our Towns and Cities: The Future—Delivering an Urban Renaissance*, in November 2000. It set out the Government's plans for towns, cities and suburbs, with the aim of encouraging people to return to live in town and city centres, thereby easing the pressure on the countryside and helping to protect it from development. Among the measures in the White Paper are plans for:

- a £1 billion series of taxation measures to increase investment in urban areas, including plans to exempt from stamp duty all property transactions in disadvantaged communities, higher tax credits for cleaning up contaminated land, 100% capital allowances for creating flats (suitable for letting) above shops, and a package of reforms to value added tax to encourage additional conversions of properties for residential use;
- new planning policy guidance putting urban renaissance at the centre of the planning system, and a drive to implement planning policy on housing;
- more Urban Regeneration Companies (see below) and more Millennium Communities—such as the ones in Greenwich (London), Allerton Bywater (Leeds), the Cardroom Estate in Manchester and at Nar Ouse in King's Lynn;
- the promotion of a culture of innovation and enterprise through services such as the Small Business Service and programmes such as the Phoenix Fund (see chapter 22);
- a Neighbourhood Renewal Fund of £900 million over the three years to 2004 in the 88 most deprived local authority areas; and
- a comprehensive programme to improve the quality of parks, play areas and open spaces.

Urban regeneration companies (URCs) have been set up in Liverpool, Manchester, Sheffield and Corby. They are new independent companies established by the relevant local authority, RDA, English Partnerships (if appropriate), the private sector and other key partners. They coordinate approaches to problems and opportunities in their target areas, with the aim of engaging the private sector in an agreed physical and economic regeneration strategy. The Urban White Paper announced a rolling programme to create around 12 new companies over the next three years, with a limited number in each region.

In April 2001 the Government announced funding of £30 million over the next three years for Home Zones, which aim to improve the quality of life in residential streets. The zones are intended to enable local authorities to design streets as places for people and not just for traffic.

In November 2000 the former DETR published an action plan to revitalise England's rural areas. The plan, set out in a White Paper entitled *A Fair Deal for Rural England*, includes measures to:

- deliver high-quality health, education, transport and housing services, backed up with new standards;
- tackle the causes of social exclusion by boosting the provision of jobs and affordable housing;
- support the rural economy with new measures to encourage diversification, attract new businesses and support existing shops and pubs;
- provide better protection for the countryside; and
- give more local choice with new powers for parish and town councils.

The implementation plan and timetable for the measures and initiatives in the White Paper were published in March 2001. Some of the key elements of the implementation package include:

- £37 million of government funding over three years to help create a £100 million regeneration programme, with partnership funds, for around 100 market towns;
- legislation to extend 50% mandatory rate relief to all village food shops, new small-scale, non-agricultural enterprises on farms and sole village pubs and petrol stations;
- new Countryside Agency grant schemes worth £35 million to support village shops and services; and
- £62 million to improve rural bus services and encourage greater bus use.

Rural Regeneration

Although most problems arising from dereliction and unemployment occur in urban areas, some rural areas have also been affected as employment in traditional sectors, such as mining and rurally based defence establishments, has declined. Low wages and a decline in local public transport and other services have caused problems for some rural residents.

The RDAs outside London are responsible for rural regeneration. The Countryside Agency (see p. 313) promotes and advises on conserving and enhancing the countryside, people's access to the countryside for recreation, and the economic and social development of England's rural areas. It also administers a number of grants designed to help meet village needs for transport, shops or other services.

Wales

Parts of Wales have been adversely affected by the decline in traditional industries, especially coal and steel.

Wales will receive up to £1.4 billion from the European Union to fund a variety of programmes until 2006. These include Objective 1 Funds (see p. 393) for West Wales and the Valleys. The programmes will be aimed at developing a stronger, more sustainable economy (especially with an expanded small and medium-sized company sector), better infrastructure, a more highly skilled workforce, and the regeneration of urban and rural communities.

The new Local Regeneration Fund (LRF) was established in 2000–01 by merging budgets available under the Welsh Capital Challenge and Local Authority Rural Scheme, which will be phased out. The National Assembly for Wales has allocated £36.5 million to LRF in 2001–02. The purpose of the Fund is to support sustainable regeneration or development within, or benefiting, the most deprived areas, including the Objective 1 area in West Wales and the Valleys. Some of the money is used to match funding provided by European structural funds.

The Welsh Development Agency contributes to economic regeneration across Wales. Its programmes include physical and environmental regeneration activities, such as land reclamation and urban, rural and environmental improvements; activities to provide site development works to assist with business infrastructure; and financial support for community initiatives such as the Market Towns Initiative and the Small Towns and Villages programmes.

The National Assembly's most recent annual report on social inclusion (published in March 2001) highlights the steps being taken to combat poverty and social disadvantage. Communities First is an area-based regeneration strategy that will benefit 88 deprived communities in 119 electoral wards. Sixteen communities have been awarded funding under the People in Communities programme. Both emphasise the involvement of local people in decision-making.

Scotland

During 2000 the Scottish Executive set out its strategy for tackling poverty and injustice in the publication *Social justice . . . a Scotland where everyone matters*. Supporting communities is central to the strategy. The Social Inclusion Partnership (SIP) programme, established in 1999, involves 48 local partnerships tackling the problems that disadvantaged groups and communities face across rural and urban Scotland. The SIPs are multi-agency partnerships, consisting of all relevant local public agencies, the voluntary and private sectors, and representatives from the community. The SIPs are supported over three years from 2001–02 by £169 million from the Social Inclusion Partnership Fund.

Funding is also provided through the Working for Communities and Empowering Communities programmes. These programmes are testing and developing new models for delivering integrated local services in deprived areas, and for developing the capacity of excluded communities to influence decisions about their lives. Future directions for regeneration and community empowerment work in Scotland will be set out in a Neighbourhood Renewal Statement due to be produced before the end of 2001.

The Better Neighbourhood Services Fund (BNSF) is a new programme designed to advance the Executive's social justice objectives and narrow the gap between the poor and better off. Over the next three years £90 million has been allocated to 12 local authorities for pilot programmes to improve the delivery of services in deprived neighbourhoods and encourage greater community involvement. Local Outcome Agreements will be used to link national and local policy priorities.

Local Enterprise Companies working as part of the Highlands and Islands Enterprise Network (in the north of Scotland) and the Scottish Enterprise Network (in the south), have a range of functions and powers to engage in regeneration, and to encourage business and employment in their areas. Among recent regeneration projects in Scotland is *Pacific Quay* in Glasgow—a development comprising three elements: a business park, the Glasgow Science Centre and the Digital Media Campus, which will house a new headquarters and production facility for BBC Scotland.

Communities Scotland (see p. 345) will also have a responsibility for regeneration. It will work closely with relevant partners, and particularly local authorities, which have a lead role in community planning in Scotland.

Northern Ireland

The Department for Social Development's (DSD's) Urban Generation and Community Development Group is responsible for the establishment of policy and strategy; implementation of programmes targeting resources to areas of social need; addressing the social, economic and physical regeneration of cities, towns and villages in Northern Ireland; and promoting partnership between the Government and the voluntary and community sector. It also has responsibility for the Laganside Corporation, a non-departmental public body managing the regeneration of Belfast's riverside and waterfront areas. The DSD administers the Urban Development Grant (UDG) scheme, a discretionary grant used to promote job creation, inward investment and environmental improvement in priority areas in both Belfast and Londonderry by stimulating the development of vacant, derelict or underused land or buildings. In Belfast, priority is currently given to schemes within the Making Belfast Work areas, while UDG in Londonderry is targeted at the City Centre and Waterside Business District. Underused or derelict land and buildings in selected areas of towns and cities are identified for planning and regeneration by the DSD via *Comprehensive Development Schemes*.

The Londonderry Regeneration Initiative has an annual budget of £2.7 million and from its launch in 1988 to the end of 2000–01 provided almost £33.5 million for a variety of projects in the most deprived and disadvantaged areas. The Making Belfast Work Initiative has an annual budget of around £13.7 million and has provided £248 million for a variety of projects over the same period.

The International Fund for Ireland's Urban Development Programme is designed to assist in the regeneration of towns and villages by providing financial assistance for the renovation of derelict and run-down commercial properties. Priority will be given to projects situated in the most disadvantaged areas and to those which are judged to have the potential to make the greatest impact. Grants of up to £100,000 are available. Assistance is also available, through the Community Property Development Scheme, to cross-community groups for the regeneration of key properties in the most run-down non-disadvantaged areas. Some £5 million has been committed by the International Fund for Ireland to nearly 20 projects.

The Community Regeneration and Improvement Special Programme (CRISP) is aimed at assisting communities in the regeneration of the most disadvantaged towns and villages with a population of less than 10,000. The programme was introduced in 1990 and 70 community-led projects have been supported, involving financial assistance of £55 million.

Further Reading

DETR Annual Report 2001: The Government's Expenditure Plans 2001–02 to 2003–04. The Stationery Office, 2001.

English Partnerships: Annual Report and Financial Statements 2000/2001.

Housing Statistics. The Stationery Office, 2000.

The Housing Corporation: Annual Review. The Housing Corporation.

Our Countryside: The Future—A Fair Deal for Rural England. DETR, 2000.

Our Towns and Cities: The Future—Delivering the Urban Renaissance. DETR, 2000.

Quality and Choice: A Decent Home for All. DETR, 2000.

Social Trends (Annual). Office for National Statistics, The Stationery Office.

Websites

Department for Transport, Local Government and the Regions: www.dtlr.gov.uk

Scottish Executive: www.scotland.gov.uk

National Assembly for Wales: www.wales.gov.uk

Northern Ireland Executive: www.nics.gov.uk

English Partnerships: www.englishpartnerships.co.uk

Housing Corporation: www.housingcorp.gov.uk

21 Transport

Travel Trends	359	Inland Waterways	372
Transport Policy	360	Shipping	372
Roads	362	Ports	373
Railways	368	Civil Aviation	374

Responsibility for transport policy in the UK is divided between Government in Whitehall and the devolved administrations of Scotland, Wales and Northern Ireland. The Transport Act 2000, implemented in England and Wales in 2001, established the Strategic Rail Authority, required local authorities to offer concessionary fares to pensioners and certain groups of disabled people using public transport, and provided for the establishment of a Public-Private Partnership for air traffic services. In 2001 detailed funding plans were announced for the first five years of the Government's ten-year plan, which aims to modernise the UK transport system.

TRAVEL TRENDS

Passenger travel was 721 billion passenger-kilometres in Great Britain in 2000 (see Table 21.1). Travel by car, van and taxi has more than doubled in the past 30 years, but recently the rate of growth has slowed, and car traffic in 2000 was virtually the same as in 1999. Travel by bus has shown a steady decline since the 1950s, but usage is now increasing, with the number of bus passenger journeys up 0.5% in the year to 31 March 2001. Rail travel rose by around 2.0% in 2000–01, and travel on the various light rail/supertram systems is also growing. Air traffic, particularly international travel, has grown substantially.

Travel by car accounted for 85% of passenger mileage in Great Britain in 2000. Over the last ten years, the proportion of households with regular use of one car has remained relatively constant, at 45%, but there has been an increase in households with two cars (from 19% in 1990 to 22% in 2000), while in 2000, 5% of households had regular use of three or more cars. Most freight is carried by road, which accounts for 81% of goods by tonnage and 65% in terms of tonne-kilometres.[1]

At the end of 2000 there were 28.9 million vehicles licensed for use on the roads of Great Britain, according to the Driver and Vehicle Licensing Agency, which maintains official records of drivers and vehicles in Great Britain. There were 23.9 million cars (2.4 million company-owned); 2.5 million vans and light goods vehicles; 418,000 goods vehicles over 3.5 tonnes; 825,000 motorcycles, scooters and mopeds; and 86,000 public transport vehicles with nine or more seats.

[1] A tonne-kilometre is equivalent to 1 tonne transported for 1 kilometre.

Table 21.1: Passenger Transport in Great Britain by Mode[1]

Billion passenger-kilometres

	1990	1995	1998	1999	2000
Buses and coaches	46	44	45	45	45[2]
Cars, vans and taxis	588	596	617	614	613
Motorcycles, mopeds and scooters	6	4	4	5	5
Pedal cycles	5	4	4	4	4
All road	**645**	**648**	**671**	**668**	**666**
Rail[3]	40	37	44	46	47
Air[4]	5	6	7	7	8
All modes[5]	**690**	**691**	**722**	**722**	**721**

[1] Figures for 1999 and 2000 have been produced on a new basis and are not directly comparable with those for earlier years.
[2] Provisional.
[3] Financial years. Former British Rail companies and urban rail systems.
[4] Scheduled and non-scheduled services. Excludes air taxi services, private flying and passengers paying less than 25% of the full fare. Includes Northern Ireland and the Channel Islands.
[5] Excluding travel by water within the UK (including the Channel Islands), estimated at 0.7 billion passenger-kilometres in 2000.
Source: *Transport Statistics Great Britain, 2001 Edition*

TRANSPORT POLICY

In July 2000 the Government issued its ten-year transport spending plan, which envisages public spending and private investment in transport of some £180 billion: £60 billion for railways in Great Britain, £59 billion for local transport in England, £25 billion for transport in London, £21 billion for strategic roads in England and £15 billion on future projects and other transport areas. The total includes capital investment of £121 billion, which the Government intends to be implemented through partnerships between the private and public sectors.

Many of the provisions in the Transport Act 2000 are closely linked to the targets of the ten-year plan. The Act provides for the establishment of the Strategic Rail Authority (see p. 368) and a Public-Private Partnership (PPP) to deliver air traffic services provided by National Air Traffic Services Ltd (NATS); requires local authorities to prepare five-year plans to improve their local transport facilities; enables local authorities outside London to introduce road charges and workplace parking levies to help tackle congestion; and gives local authorities new powers to improve local bus services and requires them to offer concessionary fares for all pensioners and certain groups of disabled people.

The powers allocated to local authorities under the Act cover England and Wales only. Local Transport Plans (LTPs) have been drawn up by local transport authorities in England (outside London), and by Welsh authorities; in Scotland all local authorities and Strathclyde Passenger Transport have produced local transport strategies. Capital allocations to English authorities were made in the LTP capital settlement for 2001–02 (see box). The London Mayor and Assembly are responsible for delivering integrated transport for the city, and a draft transport strategy was released by the Mayor in January 2001 for consultation. London authorities produce Local Implementation Plans in line with the Mayor's transport strategy. Key priorities include reducing congestion, increasing investment in the Underground system, improving bus and national rail systems in London and expanding the overall capacity of the rail and bus networks. Transport for London, which took up its powers in July 2000, will be responsible for delivering the strategy.

The Government has announced its intention to draft a Safety Bill aimed at making travel by rail, air, sea and on the roads safer, and the Bill will include proposals relating to health and safety at work (see p. 162). Elements of the Safety Bill would:

Local Transport Capital Settlement
The settlement, covering the first five years of the ten-year transport plan, provided £8.4 billion for authorities to implement their LTPs: up to £4.4 billion on integrated and public transport, and up to £4 billion on new and existing roads. Major schemes given full or provisional approval include 31 major public transport schemes, such as two new light rail lines, guided bus schemes, new public transport interchanges and 39 road improvement schemes, including urban relief roads and 14 by-passes.

Authorities have discretion over the exact package of smaller schemes (which have a gross cost of less than £5 million) that they deliver using LTP funding. However, over the five-year period, LTPs are expected to deliver up to 4,500 km of faster, more reliable bus routes and up to 8,200 local safety measures, including 20 mph (32 km/h) zones and traffic calming.

- allow the Government to implement the recommendations which came from Lord Cullen's wide-ranging review of rail safety;
- tackle alcohol and drug use by 'safety critical' personnel in civil aviation and shipping;
- raise port and maritime safety standards; and
- set a framework for delivery of government commitments on road safety strategy and on meeting new road safety targets.

The *Traveline* national public transport information system is to be developed into the more comprehensive *Transport Direct* service by 2003. This system will allow people to compare prices and routes, and will cover all types of transport within the UK.

Wales

The National Assembly for Wales continues to develop an integrated approach to transport planning, and a £300 million package was announced in January 2001 to support local authority transport delivery over the next five years. Measures included:

- indicative dates for the implementation of a number of road improvement schemes;
- rail infrastructure improvements, including reopening the Vale of Glamorgan line to passenger services;
- £23.2 million for support for integrated transport schemes; and
- extra support for Safe Route to Schools initiatives, which aim to improve children's safety and reduce reliance on the car for school trips.

In addition, all Welsh local authorities published local transport plans during summer 2000, and the Bus Subsidy Grant and the Welsh Rural Transport Grant were combined under the control of local authorities to promote integration.

The Assembly plans to publish its Transport Framework for Wales in autumn 2001. This will provide the basis for a coordinated approach to transport for local authorities, transport operators and the Assembly when drawing up investment programmes. The trunk road programme is to be published by the end of 2001, and is expected to include schemes intended to improve accessibility between north and south Wales.

Scotland

The Transport (Scotland) Act 2001 provides local authorities with additional powers to enable them to develop an integrated transport system at the local level. The Act contains many provisions similar to those in the Transport Act for England and Wales, including the establishment of statutory bus 'quality partnerships' and 'quality contracts' between local authorities and bus operators.

Expenditure on transport of £986 million is planned in 2001–02, rising to £1,029 million in 2002–03. Priorities include: creating an integrated transport system; encouraging the use of public transport; tackling congestion; moving freight off the roads onto both the railways and waterways, with a target of 21 million lorry miles taken off Scottish roads by March 2002; and maintaining affordable lifeline services to islands and other remote areas. In April 2001 the Scottish Executive acquired responsibility from the former Department of the Environment, Transport and the Regions (DETR) for funding rail services in Scotland.

The Executive is preparing a plan which will set out its transport policy and investment priorities.

Northern Ireland

The Department for Regional Development is preparing a Regional Development Strategy. One aim of the strategy is to develop a modern, sustainable and safe transport system based on an integrated approach. An important element is the development of five key transport corridors: strategic long-distance routes connecting a number of towns to the major regional 'gateways', including links to transport corridors within the Belfast metropolitan area.

Within this context, the Department for Regional Development is preparing a Regional Transport Strategy (RTS), taking into account the ten-year plan and Strategy 2010 (which sets out a range of recommendations and targets for the Northern Ireland economy). The draft RTS, which aims to develop a modern, sustainable, safe transport system, identifies current problems in three key areas:

- the key transport corridors, where Northern Ireland has a low proportion of motorway carriageway compared with the rest of the UK;
- urban areas, for example the lack of a rail link to Belfast international airport; and
- rural areas, for example the age of the rural bus fleet and underfunding of bus services compared with the rest of the UK.

ROADS

The total road network in Great Britain in 2000 was 391,700 kilometres (243,400 miles).

Figure 21.2: Road Traffic in Great Britain by Vehicle Type, 2000

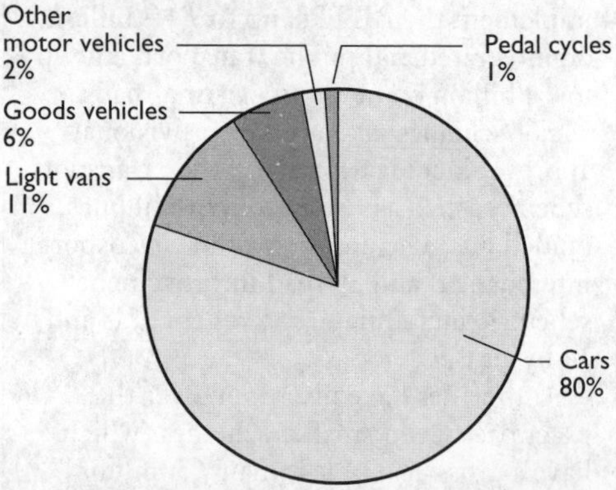

Note: Light vans = goods vehicles under 3.5 tonnes gross weight. Goods vehicles = goods vehicles over 3.5 tonnes gross weight. Other motor vehicles include two-wheel motor vehicles and large buses and coaches.

Source: Department for Transport, Local Government and the Regions

Trunk motorways[2] accounted for 3,422 kilometres (2,126 miles) of this, less than 1%, and other trunk roads for over 11,740 kilometres (7,300 miles), or 3.0%. However, motorways carry 20% of all traffic, and trunk roads another 16%. Combined, they carry over half of all goods vehicle traffic in Great Britain. In Northern Ireland the road network is over 24,960 kilometres (15,510 miles), of which 226 kilometres (165 miles) are motorways.

Motor traffic in Great Britain increased only very slightly in 2000, to an estimated 467.7 billion vehicle-kilometres (see Table 21.3). Traffic on motorways was up by 1%, to 94.1 billion vehicle-kilometres.

Road Programme

The Highways Agency—an executive agency of the Department for Transport, Local Government and the Regions (DTLR)—is responsible for maintaining, operating and improving the national road network in England, except for London, where

[2] That is, those motorways that are the direct responsibility of the central administration rather than the local authority.

Table 21.3: Motor Vehicle Traffic in Great Britain[1] *Billion vehicle-kilometres*

	1990	1995	1998	1999	2000
Motorways	61.6	70.9	81.3	93.4	94.1
Trunk roads	69.1	70.4	75.0	76.5	76.1
Principal roads	124.1	131.2	136.4	128.1	128.4
Minor roads	156.1	158.4	166.6	168.0	169.1
All roads	**410.8**	**430.9**	**459.2**	**466.0**	**467.7**

[1] Figures for 1999 and 2000 have been produced on a new basis and are not directly comparable with those for previous years.

responsibility has been transferred to the Greater London Authority. In Wales, Scotland and Northern Ireland responsibility for the motorway and trunk road network rests with the devolved administrations. The Roads Service, an agency within the NI Department for Regional Development, maintains and improves the road network on behalf of the Assembly.

The Highways Agency is responsible for 6,065 miles (9,760 km) of motorway and trunk roads in England. The Agency and the relevant local authorities are in consultation over the transfer of some 310 miles (500 km) of this network to local authorities. Its budget is £1.77 billion in 2002–03, when it expects to spend £759 million on major network improvements, £668 million on motorway and trunk road maintenance and £252 million on making better use of the network. In addition, local authorities have a budget of nearly £2.1 billion for maintaining roads. In Scotland, the motorway and trunk road programme for 2001–04 will cost £680 million.

The Government's ten-year plan envisages public investment of £21.3 billion in the Highways Agency's strategic road network, together with £2.5 billion of private capital investment. Investment will tackle the main congestion pressures. Extra capacity will be provided through 30 trunk road by-passes, 80 major schemes to ease bottlenecks at junctions, and the widening of some 5% of the strategic road network and associated junction improvements. For example, one major scheme is to widen to 12 lanes sections of the M25 near Heathrow Airport, the most heavily used sections of the UK motorway network.

The Local Transport Plans settlement also contained new money to fund capital maintenance on local highways, in addition to funding for major new maintenance schemes, such as for the Central Motorway East in Newcastle upon Tyne.

Private sector finance is playing a role through 'Design, Build, Finance and Operate' (DBFO) contracts, under which the private sector provides the funding for construction and maintenance, and receives government payments linked to usage and performance.

Standards

Minimum ages for driving are:

- 16 for riders of mopeds, drivers of small tractors, and disabled people receiving a mobility allowance;
- 17 for drivers of cars and other passenger vehicles with nine or fewer seats (including that of the driver), small motorcycles, and goods vehicles not over 3.5 tonnes maximum authorised mass (MAM);
- 18 for goods vehicles weighing over 3.5, but not over 7.5, tonnes MAM; and
- 21 for passenger-carrying vehicles with more than nine seats, goods vehicles over 7.5 tonnes MAM and large motorcycles.

New drivers of motor vehicles must pass both the computer-based touch screen theory test and the practical driving test in order to acquire a full driving licence. In 2000, just over 1.1 million driving tests were conducted in Great Britain by the Driving Standards Agency (DSA), the national driver testing authority. The average pass rate was nearly 46%. About 32 million people hold a full driving licence for a car. The DSA also supervises professional driving instructors, the compulsory basic training scheme for learner motorcyclists and a voluntary register for instructors of drivers of large goods vehicles.

Before most new cars and goods vehicles are allowed on the roads, they must meet safety and environmental requirements, based primarily on standards drawn up by the European Union (EU). The Vehicle Certification Agency is responsible for ensuring these requirements are met through a process known as 'type approval'.

The Vehicle Inspectorate is responsible for ensuring the roadworthiness of vehicles, through their annual testing. It also uses roadside and other enforcement checks to ensure that drivers and vehicle operators comply with legislation. In Northern Ireland the Driver and Vehicle Testing Agency is responsible for testing drivers and vehicles.

Motorcycling

There has been a resurgence of interest in motorcycling in the UK over the last few years, after a long period of decline. The number of licensed motorcycles has risen from a low of 594,000 in 1995 to around 825,000 in 2000, the highest figure since 1990. Motorcycles have a role to play in an integrated transport policy, and mopeds and small-engined motorcycles can offer environmental benefits. An Advisory Group on Motorcycling has been set up, bringing together all interested parties to discuss issues of concern to motorcycle users. In its first interim report, the Group requested that local authorities consider specific measures to assist motorcyclists, such as better parking and interchange facilities, and appropriate road maintenance.

Road Safety

Since 1981–85 there has been a significant decline in road deaths and serious casualties in Great Britain, by 39% and 49% respectively, while road traffic has risen by 59%. In 2000 there were 233,000 road accidents involving personal injury in Great Britain, 1% fewer than in 1999, of which 35,600 involved death or serious injury. There were 3,409 deaths in road accidents, 38,200 serious injuries and 278,700 slight injuries.

The Government has set a target of reducing the number of people killed or seriously injured on the roads of Great Britain by 40% by 2010, compared with the average levels for 1994–98. A higher target reduction, of 50%, has been set for deaths and serious injuries to children. Measures to be taken include:

- creating more 20 mph (32 km/h) zones around schools and in residential areas;
- enforcing road traffic law more effectively, with greater use of speed cameras;
- improving driver training;
- the mandatory fitting of seat belts in new coaches and minibuses from October 2001;
- setting appropriate speed limits for local conditions;
- supporting the development of safer car design; and
- improving road safety education.

The Safety Bill (see p. 360) contains measures that set a framework for the delivery of these targets. In addition, local authorities in England and Wales are now required to include specific road safety measures as part of their Local Transport Plans, while local authorities in Scotland are expected to set out in their local transport strategies their plans for reducing road casualties.

Congestion

About 7% of the Highways Agency's network experiences regular heavy peak and occasional non-peak congestion, and a further 13% sees heavy congestion on at least half the days in the year. Traffic congestion also occurs in many towns and cities in the main morning and evening peak periods and for much of the day in central London. Traffic management schemes aim to reduce congestion through measures such as traffic-free shopping precincts, bus lanes and other bus priority measures, and parking controls. In London a 512-km (318-mile) network of priority 'red routes', with special stopping controls, is designed to improve traffic flow.

The DTLR has a target to reduce congestion on the inter-urban road network and in large urban areas to below 2000 levels by 2010, as part of its commitment to the Government's Sustainable Development Programme (see essay on p. 378).

Under the Greater London Authority Act 1999 and the Transport Act 2000, local authorities in London and the rest of England and Wales are able to introduce congestion charging schemes for road users and a levy on workplace parking, as part of their Local Transport Plans, and to retain the net revenue generated from charges for at least ten years, provided that it is used to fund local transport improvements. Congestion charging schemes in Scotland are provided for by the Transport (Scotland) Act 2001. Local authorities will need to consult local people and businesses and to make improvements to public transport before starting such schemes. Schemes—in the Peak District National Park in Derbyshire and in Durham—are planned to start early in 2002, and future schemes are expected to be brought forward by local authorities over the duration of the ten-year plan.

The Government is encouraging major employers to adopt travel plans to reduce car use for travel to work and on business, for example by promoting alternatives such as car sharing, cycling and use of public transport.

Traffic Information

Traffic information is provided throughout Great Britain by a variety of means, such as the media, roadside signs and in-vehicle systems. Information originates from a range of sources, such as roadside sensors, the traffic police and highway authorities. It is collated by motoring organisations, such as the Automobile Association (AA) and the Royal Automobile Club (RAC), and by information service providers like Integrated Traffic Information Services (ITIS), Metro Networks and Trafficmaster. Local traffic control centres across Great Britain help to manage traffic and provide information about traffic conditions. Centres covering wider areas exist in Scotland and Wales. The Highways Agency has entered into a Public-Private Partnership with Traffic Information Services (TiS) to set up and run the Traffic Control Centre (TCC). Costing £160 million, the object of the TCC is to provide a coordinated national information service to travellers in England by early 2003. Up-to-the-minute details will be available via variable message signs, the Highways Agency information line, the Internet, the media and commercial driver information services.

Cycling

The National Cycling Strategy aims to increase the number of cycling journeys fourfold by 2012 (based on 1996 figures). The National Cycling Forum is coordinating the implementation of the strategy, which has been endorsed by the Government. The Scottish Cycle Forum coordinates implementation of the strategy in Scotland. The DTLR announced its own target of trebling the number of cycling journeys by 2010, as part of the Government's ten-year plan. Cycling strategies form part of Local Transport Plans, and include measures to make cycling safer and more convenient.

The first 5,000 miles (8,000 kilometres) of the National Cycle Network were officially opened in June 2000. Developed by the transport charity Sustrans, the network will cover 10,000 miles (16,000 kilometres) when it is completed in 2005. Over a third of the network will be entirely free from motor traffic by utilising old railway lines, canal towpaths, river paths and derelict land. The remainder of the network will follow existing roads, with traffic calming and cycle lanes being implemented where necessary. Some 60 million journeys were made on the network in 2000; 48% of users were cyclists and 51% pedestrians.

Walking

People in the UK are walking significantly less than in the past, with fewer journeys on foot and many more by car. The Government wishes to reverse this trend, and is expecting local authorities to give more priority to walking by providing, for example, wider pavements, pedestrianisation schemes and more pedestrian crossings.

Almost all local authorities included walking strategies in their Local Transport Plans, many identifying targets to encourage walking through a variety of initiatives. LTP funding is likely to be used to make walking safer and more accessible, for example by improving pavement and footway maintenance, removing obstructions and improving pedestrian crossings.

The DTLR is monitoring nine pilot Home Zones in England and Wales, with further schemes operating in Scotland and Northern Ireland. Home Zones are residential streets in which the road space is shared between the drivers of motor vehicles and other road users, with the wider needs of residents (including people who walk or cycle, and children) in mind. The aim is to change the way that streets are used, improving the quality of life of local residents. The Government has announced a £30 million Home Zone challenge fund for England, which is expected to fund about 100 schemes.

Road Haulage

An operator's licence is required for operating goods vehicles over 3.5 tonnes gross weight in the UK. About 87% of the 105,700 licences in issue are for fleets of five or fewer vehicles, and there are around 423,000 heavy goods vehicles (HGVs). Road haulage traffic by HGVs amounted to 150 billion tonne-kilometres in Great Britain in 2000, 15% more than in 1990. Road hauliers are tending to use larger vehicles carrying heavier loads—85% of the traffic, in terms of tonne-kilometres, is now carried by vehicles of over 25 tonnes gross weight.

International road haulage has grown rapidly. In 2000 about 2.3 million road goods vehicles travelled by ferry or the Channel Tunnel to mainland Europe, of which 544,800 were powered vehicles registered in the UK. UK vehicles carried 14.7 million tonnes internationally—97% of this traffic was with the EU.

The Government has a long-term strategy for freight in the UK, which aims to promote a competitive and efficient distribution sector to support future economic growth while minimising the effects on society and the environment. The strategy seeks to reduce the extent to which economic growth generates additional lorry movements, by improving efficiency, making the most of rail, shipping and inland waterways, and improving interchange links between the different types of transport. Measures introduced include an increase in the maximum weight of lorries on domestic journeys to 44 tonnes, and the provision of grants towards the costs of fitting HGVs with emission-reducing equipment or converting them to run on alternative fuels.

Bus Services

In 1999–2000 some 4,279 million passenger journeys were made on local bus services in Great Britain, nearly 16% less than in 1989–90, but a small increase on 1998–99. In London (which accounts for nearly a third of bus journeys in Great Britain) passenger journeys in 1999–2000 were some 10% higher than ten years earlier. The ten-year plan target for bus use in England is growth of 10% by 2010 from 2000 levels.

There are around 85,000 buses and coaches in Great Britain, of which 22% are minibuses, while 21% are double-deckers. Most local bus services are provided commercially, with 83% of bus mileage outside London operating on this basis. Local authorities may subsidise services not commercially viable which are considered socially necessary.

Operators

Almost all bus services in Great Britain are provided by private sector concerns, apart from 17 bus companies owned by local authorities. Transport for London is responsible for providing or procuring public transport in the capital. It oversees about 750 bus routes run by about 30 companies under contract.

Five main groups operate bus services: Arriva, FirstGroup, Go-Ahead Group, National Express and Stagecoach. All also run rail services and some have expanded into transport services in other countries, notably the United States.

In Northern Ireland almost all road passenger services are operated by subsidiaries of the publicly owned Northern Ireland Transport Holding Company (NITHC), collectively known as 'Translink'. Citybus Ltd operates services in Belfast, and Ulsterbus Ltd runs most of the services in the rest of Northern Ireland, carrying 21 million and 48 million passengers a year respectively.

Services

The Transport Act 2000 introduced a new statutory framework that aims to improve bus services outside London. Local authorities in England and Wales are required to develop bus strategies as part of their Local Transport Plans. Although there is no statutory requirement in Scotland, local authorities are expected to set out their views on bus services in their local transport strategies. Statutory backing also exists for 'bus quality partnerships' and 'quality contracts' between local authorities and bus operators. Similar partnerships have already been developed voluntarily in around 130 towns and cities, and have led to better services with higher-quality buses, and typically 10% to 20% greater passenger use. The Transport Acts also give authorities powers to promote joint ticketing, including through tickets and to work with train operating companies on bus/rail ticketing.

Bus priority measures, such as bus lanes, are becoming more extensive, while in some areas innovative measures, such as guided busways (with buses travelling on segregated track), are being adopted. Around 70 park and ride schemes, in which car users park on the outskirts of towns and travel by public transport to the central area, are in operation in England and are being increasingly used to relieve traffic congestion in busy urban centres; over 100 new schemes are envisaged over the next ten years.

FirstGroup is to pilot US-style yellow school buses to provide a door-to-door service for children, using the same driver each day and giving each child an allocated seat.

The Government is seeking to improve rural and local bus services. A number of schemes are in place which have led to 1,800 extra bus services in rural communities, carrying 16 million passengers a year. In England, the Rural Bus Subsidy Grant (RBSG) is providing £41.5 million to local authorities in 2001, with another £21.2 million coming from the Rural Bus Challenge (RBC) competition. The RBC is an annual competition in which local authorities bid for funding for schemes aimed at stimulating innovation in rural transport. Among the award-winning schemes in 2001 was an initiative in Cornwall to create a demand-responsive service in the Bodmin Moor area, which will provide information and infrastructure improvements. An Urban Bus Challenge, broadly following the lines of the RBC, is now being developed to support improved public transport links to deprived urban estates.

The Countryside Agency, on behalf of the DTLR, administers the Rural Transport Partnership, which encourages partnerships between the public, private and voluntary sectors to develop local solutions to local needs, often at the parish level. The Scottish Executive's £6 million Rural Transport Fund is funding over 350 new and improved rural bus services.

Coaches

Coaches account for much of the non-local mileage operated by public service vehicles, and amounted to 1,417 million vehicle-kilometres in 1999–2000. Organised coach tours and holiday journeys account for about 60% of coach travel in Great Britain. High-frequency scheduled services, run by private sector operators, link many towns and cities, and commuter services run into London and some other major centres each weekday. The biggest coach operator, National Express, has a national network of scheduled coach services and carries more than 15 million passengers each year.

Taxis

There are about 61,000 licensed taxis in England and Wales (mainly in urban areas), around 9,000 in Scotland, and about 11,000 in Northern Ireland. In London (which has over 20,000 taxis) and several other major cities, taxis must be purpose-built to conform to strict requirements. In many districts, taxi drivers have to pass a test of their knowledge of the area.

Private hire vehicles ('minicabs') may only be booked through the operator and not hired on the street. Outside London, private hire vehicles are licensed; there are about 76,000 in England and Wales, outside the capital, and 8,000 in Scotland. The Private Hire Vehicles (London) Act 1998 is currently being implemented by Transport for London. Operators must be licensed by October 2001: driver and vehicle licensing will follow when the necessary regulations have been made.

RAILWAYS

Railways were pioneered in Britain: the Stockton and Darlington Railway, which opened in 1825, was the first public passenger railway in the world to be worked by steam power. Most railway services in the UK are now operated by the private sector.

Railtrack is responsible for operating all track and infrastructure in Great Britain. Its assets include 32,000 kilometres (20,000 miles) of track; 40,000 bridges, tunnels and viaducts; 2,500 stations; and connections to over 1,000 freight terminals. Apart from 14 major stations operated directly by Railtrack, nearly all stations and passenger depots are leased to the passenger Train Operating Companies (TOCs) that run passenger services under franchise. There are currently ten TOCs operating 25 franchises. In April 2001 Railtrack agreed to new licence conditions under which it operates the rail network, in return for a £1.5 billion advance payment from the Government. In addition to increasing public accountability, the company will now concentrate on maintenance, and improving safety and the service to passengers, with private sector participants, such as TOCs or construction firms, helping to expand the network.

The TOCs, such as Great Western Trains, Virgin and GNER, lease their rolling stock from the four main rolling stock companies: Angel Trains, HSBC Rail, Porterbrook Leasing and GLRailease. Freight services are run by four companies, and there are a number of infrastructure maintenance companies.

There are also over 100 other passenger-carrying railways, often connected with the preservation of steam locomotives. Services are operated mostly on a voluntary basis and cater mainly for tourists and railway enthusiasts.

Rail Regulation

The Transport Act 2000 established the Strategic Rail Authority (SRA) to promote rail use, plan the strategic development of the rail network, work closely with transport providers and promote integration between different types of transport. The SRA also acquired the consumer protection functions of the Office of the Rail Regulator, including responsibility for sponsoring the rail users' consultative committees that represent the interests of passengers.

The SRA is responsible for negotiating, awarding and monitoring the franchises for operating rail services. The public subsidy for passenger rail services amounted to approximately £700 million in 2000–01. Most franchises are for around seven years, but some are for 10, 12 or 15 years. The SRA published its strategic agenda in March 2001. This sets out the progress and next steps of the replacement of the rail operating franchises, where the objective is establishing stronger TOCs with longer franchises and the ability to invest to provide extra capacity to meet growing demand. It also includes objectives for developing rail freight and enhancing the infrastructure, and covers ancillary areas such as better training and staff development. Renegotiation of the shorter-term franchises is currently in progress.

The Rail Regulator provides independent economic regulation of the monopoly and dominant elements of the rail industry, particularly Railtrack's stewardship of the national rail network. In addition, the

Regulator licenses the railway operators, approves or directs agreements governing access to track, stations and depots, and enforces competition law in connection with the provision of rail services.

Rail Safety

There have been a number of fatal rail accidents in recent years, including incidents at Southall (London) in 1997, Ladbroke Grove, near Paddington (London), in 1999, Hatfield (Hertfordshire) in 2000 and Selby (Yorkshire), primarily caused by a road vehicle, in February 2001. Nevertheless, there is evidence that some trends in railway safety are improving. For example, Health and Safety Executive (HSE) figures show that in 1999–2000, there were 94 train collisions and 89 derailments, the lowest numbers recorded. Measures taken to improve the safety of the railway network include:

- the fitting of the train protection and warning system (TPWS) to the Railtrack network by the end of 2003. The TPWS is designed to reduce the risk associated with signals passed at danger (SPADS—where a train passes a signal without authority);
- the introduction of automatic train protection (ATP) as lines that are included in the European high-speed network are upgraded;
- the removal by the end of 2002 of all rolling stock which does not meet modern crash resistance standards, with some modified stock allowed to remain in service until the end of 2004;
- more consistent and better standards for driver training; and
- the development of a new national safety plan to improve safety management and ensure best practice across the rail network.

Passenger Services

The passenger network (see map facing inside back cover) comprises a fast inter-city network, linking the main centres of Great Britain; local and regional services; and commuter services in and around the large conurbations, especially London and the South East. Passenger traffic is growing (see Table 21.4) and on the national railways rose by 2% in 2000–01 to 39,100 million passenger kilometres, representing some 973 million passenger journeys.

Investment

The Government's ten-year plan includes substantially increased rail investment to provide a large expansion of rail services to meet the growing demand and improve the quality of service to passengers. Over £34 billion of capital investment is envisaged from the private sector and nearly £15 billion from the public sector, of which £7 billion will be provided through the Rail Modernisation Fund. The Fund will allow the SRA and the

The Hatfield Crash

The fatal rail crash just north of London, which occurred in October 2000, killed four people and injured 34 when a high-speed train came off the rails. The HSE interim report said that the reason for the derailment was the fracture and subsequent fragmentation of a rail.

Following the derailment, Railtrack imposed temporary speed restrictions (TSRs) on around 1,000 sites throughout the network where earlier monitoring had identified problems similar to that believed to have caused the accident. The TSRs meant that revised timetables had to be issued for many services, and the disruption was compounded by severe flooding in some areas. However, normal timetables were restored on most routes by the end of May 2001. Following the accident, Railtrack spent £180 million on re-railing 450 miles (720 km) of track and renewing points, in addition to paying £400 million in compensation to the TOCs.

Despite disruption caused by the emergency timetables, use of the railways still increased in 2000–01 (see Table 21.4).

Table 21.4: Passenger Traffic on Rail,[1] Underground and Selected Light Rail Services in Great Britain

Million passenger-kilometres

	1990–91	1995–96	1998–99	1999–2000	2000–01
National railways	33,200	30,000	36,300	38,400	39,200
London Underground	6,164	6,337	6,716	7,171	7,456
Glasgow Underground	40	41	47	49	46
Docklands Light Railway	33	70	144	172	200
Greater Manchester Metro	—	81	117	126	152
Tyne and Wear Metro	290	261	238	230	229
Croydon Tramlink	—	—	—	—	96
Centro West Midlands Metro	—	—	—	50	56
Stagecoach Supertram	—	20	35	37	38

[1]Excludes Heathrow Express.
Source: *Transport Statistics Great Britain, 2001 Edition*

railway industry to formulate a long-term investment programme and is designed to encourage a much greater level of private sector capital investment. Funds will go towards new rolling stock, modern signalling, safety improvements and the provision of greater capacity by removing bottlenecks. The first tranche of this investment was announced in April 2001 and is aimed at major projects, including expansion of the capacity of the East Coast main line and construction of the second and final phase of the Channel Tunnel Rail Link from north Kent to London St Pancras.

Freight

Rail freight traffic totalled an estimated 18.4 billion tonne-kilometres, representing the carriage of 102.9 million tonnes, in 1999–2000. Over 80% of traffic by volume is in bulk commodities, mainly coal, coke, iron and steel, building materials and petroleum. The two largest operators are English, Welsh & Scottish Railway (EWS), which also runs trains through the Channel Tunnel to the continent of Europe; and Freightliner, which operates container services between major ports and inland terminals.

The Government and the devolved administrations are keen to encourage more freight to be moved by rail, to relieve pressure on the road network and to bring environmental benefits. The SRA published a strategy in May 2001 which aims to increase rail freight carriage by 80% by 2010, by upgrading freight tracks and introducing longer trains. Grants are available to encourage companies to move goods by rail or water rather than by road. In 2001 the SRA gave grants totalling £6 million to three companies for the development of innovative rail schemes.

Northern Ireland

In Northern Ireland, Northern Ireland Railways, a wholly owned subsidiary of the NITHC (see p. 367), operates the railway service on about 336 kilometres (211 miles) of track and handled 6 million passenger journeys in 2000–01. A task force was set up in 2000 to advise on how to improve the network. Following its interim report, the Department for Regional Development intends to improve the present network over the next three years, and has increased expenditure in 2001–02 by 150% over 2000–01.

Channel Tunnel

The Channel Tunnel was opened to traffic in 1994. It cost about £9 billion and was constructed by TML (Transmanche Link) on behalf of Eurotunnel, an Anglo-French group, under an operating concession from the British and French Governments.

Eurotunnel Services

As well as managing the infrastructure of the Channel Tunnel—tunnels, terminals and track—Eurotunnel operates a drive-on, drive-off shuttle train service, with separate shuttles for passenger and freight vehicles, between terminals near Folkestone and Calais. In 2000 the service carried nearly 2.8 million cars (54% of car traffic on the Dover/Folkestone –Calais route), 1.1 million goods vehicles (48% of accompanied freight traffic) and 79,500 coaches (35% of coach traffic).

Eurostar Passenger Services

Eurostar high-speed train services are operated jointly by Eurostar (UK) Ltd, French Railways and Belgian Railways under the commercial direction of Eurostar Group. Frequent services connect London (Waterloo) and Paris or Brussels, taking less than 3 hours and 2 hours 40 minutes respectively. Trains also serve Ashford (Kent), Calais, Lille, Disneyland Paris and, during the winter, Bourg St Maurice in the French Alps. Eurostar carried over 7 million passengers in 2000.

Channel Tunnel Rail Link

The first section of the Channel Tunnel Rail Link (CTRL) is under construction between the Channel Tunnel terminal and Ebbsfleet, near Gravesend (Kent), and is planned to be completed in 2003. Construction work on the second section, from Ebbsfleet to St Pancras (London), began in 2001, and the section is due to open in 2006. The whole project is forecast to cost some £5.2 billion. Eurostar trains will be able to travel at speeds of 300 km/h (185 mph), reducing journey times by 40 minutes. A new international station for the CTRL will also be built at Stratford in east London, enabling services from regional centres to by-pass central London.

Underground Railways

In 1863 the world's first Underground railway opened in London. Today London Underground is a major business, serving 275 stations on 408 kilometres (253 miles) of railway. In 2000–01, 972 million passenger journeys were made on the network.

Under a proposed Public-Private Partnership (PPP), responsibility for maintaining and upgrading London Underground's infrastructure would transfer to the private sector, while London Underground would continue to have responsibility for safety and all aspects of operating passenger services across the network. The private sector would work under contract to London Underground for a 30-year period, after which all the assets would return to the public sector. The PPP is expected to deliver about £8 billion of investment in the network and up to £5 billion of maintenance over 15 years. London Underground Ltd will become part of Transport for London once the PPP is in place.

The Glasgow Underground, a heavy rapid transit system, operates on a 11-km (7-mile) circle in central Glasgow.

Light Railways and Tramways

There has been a revival in interest in tram/light rail services, and the Government's ten-year plan indicates a growing role for tramways, with the provision of up to 25 new lines in major cities and conurbations.

Two systems are in operation in London. The Croydon Tramlink is a 28-km (18-mile) light rail network, built and run as a joint operation between Tramtrack Croydon Ltd (a private sector consortium) and Transport for London. The Docklands Light Railway (DLR) connects Docklands with surrounding areas and the City, and is operated under franchise by Docklands Railway Management Ltd. A link to London City Airport is planned and could be opened by 2004.

Four other light rail systems are in operation: the Tyne and Wear Metro, Manchester Metrolink, Stagecoach Supertram (in South Yorkshire) and the Midland Metro. DTLR approval has been given for the £100 million extension of the Tyne and Wear Metro to Sunderland; for the £180 million Nottingham Express Transit system, which will run for 13 kilometres (8 miles) and link Hucknall to the centre of Nottingham from 2003; and for a £190 million light rail system in South Hampshire. Approval has also been given for three further extensions, costing over £500 million, of the Manchester Metrolink to Manchester Airport, to Oldham and Rochdale, and to Ashton-under-Lyne. Four other lines were approved by the Government in April 2001—three in Leeds and one in Bristol/South Gloucestershire.

INLAND WATERWAYS

Inland waterways are now used mainly for leisure and general recreation, but they have a number of other important roles: as a heritage and environmental resource, as a catalyst for regeneration, and in land drainage and water supply. Some inland waterways still carry freight.

The UK's waterways are managed by about 30 different navigation authorities. British Waterways, a public corporation sponsored by DEFRA and the Scottish Executive, is the largest, responsible for some 2,600 kilometres (1,600 miles) of fully navigable waterways, about half the UK total (see map at the front of the book).

In June 2000 the then DETR issued *Waterways for Tomorrow*, a policy document which envisages greater recreational use of, and access to, the waterways; their wider use as a catalyst for regeneration; encouragement for the transfer of freight from road to waterway; and closer links between British Waterways and other navigation authorities. The Government is encouraging partnerships between navigation authorities and the private and voluntary sectors and British Waterways is developing a number of PPPs.

The Millennium Link project in Scotland reopened the Forth & Clyde Canal and the Union Canal to navigation in 2001, and the reconnection of Glasgow and Edinburgh by canal will be completed in 2002. The Huddersfield Narrow Canal was also reopened to navigation for the first time since 1945, following a major restoration project.

The cross-border body Waterways Ireland is responsible for the management, maintenance, development and restoration of the inland navigable waterways system throughout the island of Ireland, principally for recreational purposes.

SHIPPING

It is estimated that about 95% by weight (75% by value) of the UK's foreign trade is carried by sea. The UK fleet has declined considerably in tonnage terms in the last 25 years, reflecting changing trade patterns, removal of grants, and greater competition. International revenue (including freight revenue) earned by the UK shipping industry in 1999 was £3.4 billion and represented over 5% of the total export of services from the UK.

At the end of 2000 there were 624 UK-owned merchant trading ships of 100 gross tonnes or more, with a total tonnage of 10.5 million deadweight tonnes. There were 160 vessels totalling 5.2 million deadweight tonnes used as oil, chemical or gas carriers, and 425 vessels totalling 5.2 million deadweight tonnes employed as dry-bulk carriers, container ships or other types of cargo ship, together with 39 passenger ships. In all, 72% of UK-owned vessels are registered in the UK, the Channel Islands, the Isle of Man or British Overseas Territories such as Bermuda.

The Government is implementing a series of measures aimed at reviving the shipping industry and reversing the downward trend in the UK fleet. The Finance Act 2000 provided for a new fiscal regime, under which shipping can be taxed on the basis of tonnage, as occurs in a number of other countries. Other measures include more training and career opportunities for seafarers.

Cargo Services

International revenue earned by the UK shipping industry in 2000 was £3.8 billion: £2.9 billion from freight (£2.3 billion on dry cargo and passenger vessels and £0.6 billion on tankers and liquefied gas carriers); £0.2 billion from charter receipts; and £0.6 billion from passenger revenue.

Nearly all scheduled cargo-liner services from the UK are containerised. British tonnage serving these trades is dominated by a relatively small number of companies. Besides the carriage of freight by liner and bulk services between the UK and the rest of Europe, many roll-on, roll-off services carry cars, passengers and commercial vehicles.

Passenger Services

Over 30 million passenger journeys a year take place on international and domestic ferry services linking the UK with Ireland and with mainland Europe. A further 18 million passengers are carried on ferry services to many of Britain's offshore islands, such as the Isle of Wight, Isle of Man, Orkney and Shetland, and the islands off the west coast of Scotland. Traffic from southern and south-eastern ports accounts for a large proportion of traffic to the continent.

P&O Ferries is the UK's largest ferry operator, with a fleet of about 50 ships operating on 18 routes around the UK coast. Cross-Channel services are operated by roll-on, roll-off ferries, high-speed catamarans and high-speed monohulls.

Maritime Safety

The DTLR's policies for improving marine safety and pollution control are implemented by the Maritime and Coastguard Agency (MCA), which inspects UK ships and foreign ships using UK ports to ensure that they comply with international safety, pollution prevention and operational standards. In 2000–01, 116 foreign-flagged ships were detained in UK ports.

In 2000 the MCA was alerted to 12,016 incidents, of which 6,825 were accidents requiring search and rescue assistance. In an emergency HM Coastguard coordinates facilities, such as its own helicopters; cliff rescue teams; lifeboats of the Royal National Lifeboat Institution (a voluntary body); aircraft, helicopters and ships from the armed forces; and merchant shipping and commercial aircraft.

Some locations around the UK are potentially hazardous for shipping. There are over 1,000 marine aids to navigation around the UK coast and responsibility for these rests with three regional lighthouse authorities. Measures to reduce the risk of collision include the separation of ships into internationally agreed shipping lanes, as applies in the Dover Strait, one of the world's busiest seaways, which is monitored by radar from the Channel Navigation Information Service near Dover.

In 2000 the Government launched the Port Marine Safety Code, designed to ensure the highest standards of marine safety in UK ports. All harbour authorities are being asked to implement the code by the end of 2001.

PORTS

There are about 70 ports of commercial significance in Great Britain, while several hundred small harbours cater for local cargo, fishing vessels, island ferries or recreation. There are three broad types of port: ports owned and run by boards constituted as trusts; those owned by local authorities; and company-owned facilities.

Associated British Ports (ABP) is the UK's largest port owner and operates 22 ports, including Cardiff, Grimsby and Immingham, Hull, Ipswich, Newport, Port Talbot, Southampton and Swansea. Other major facilities owned by private sector companies include Felixstowe, Harwich and Thamesport (all owned by the Hong Kong group Hutchison Whampoa).

The Government launched *Modern Ports: a UK Policy* in November 2000. It intends to assist ports in maintaining competitiveness, develop nationally agreed safety standards, promote environmental best practice, and build on the approach detailed in the ten-year plan, which recognised the importance of port hubs within integrated transport systems.

Port Traffic

In 2000 traffic through the 52 major UK ports (generally those handling over 1 million tonnes a year) amounted to 561 million

Table 21.5: Traffic through the Principal Ports of Great Britain *Million tonnes*

	1996	1997	1998	1999	2000[1]
Grimsby and Immingham	46.8	48.0	48.4	49.7	52.2
Tees and Hartlepool	44.6	51.2	51.4	49.3	51.5
London	52.9	55.7	57.3	52.2	47.9
Forth	45.6	43.1	44.4	45.4	41.2
Sullom Voe	38.2	32.1	31.1	37.7	38.2
Southampton	34.2	33.1	34.3	33.3	36.8
Milford Haven	36.6	34.5	28.8	32.2	33.8
Liverpool	34.1	30.8	30.4	28.9	30.4
Felixstowe	25.8	28.9	30.0	31.5	29.7
Orkneys	11.5	10.5	16.2	17.0	22.8

[1] Provisional.
Source: Department for Transport, Local Government and the Regions

tonnes: 308 million tonnes of inward traffic and 252 million tonnes of outward traffic. Minor ports handled an additional 16 million tonnes.

The main ports, in terms of total tonnage handled, are shown in Table 21.5. Forth, Milford Haven and Sullom Voe mostly handle oil, while the principal destinations for non-fuel traffic are London, Felixstowe, Grimsby and Immingham, Tees and Hartlepool, and Liverpool. Crude oil now accounts for one-third of all port traffic.

By far the most important port for container traffic is Felixstowe (which handles about two-fifths of this type of traffic), while Dover is the leading port for roll-on, roll-off traffic. Dover is also the major arrival and departure point for sea passengers, handling well over half of all international movements to and from the UK. The top four UK ports are among the ten largest ports in northern Europe.

Northern Ireland has four main ports, at Belfast, Larne, Londonderry and Warrenpoint. Belfast handles around three-fifths of Northern Ireland's seaborne trade.

CIVIL AVIATION

In 2000 UK airlines flew a record 1,471 million aircraft kilometres, 74% higher than in 1990: 1,016 million kilometres on scheduled services and 455 million kilometres on non-scheduled flights. They carried 70 million passengers on scheduled services and 33 million on charter flights. Passenger seat occupancy was 77%, being much higher on charter flights (89%) than on scheduled services (72%). It was also higher for international flights (78%) than internal services (65%).

UK airlines are entirely in the private sector, as are many of the major airports. Day-to-day responsibility for the regulation of civil aviation rests with the Civil Aviation Authority (CAA).

Airlines

British Airways

British Airways is the world's largest international airline. During 2000–01 its turnover from airline operations was £9.3 billion, and the British Airways group carried over 44 million passengers, achieving an occupancy of 72% on its main scheduled services. The airline's worldwide network covers 268 destinations in 97 countries, and its main operating bases are London's Heathrow and Gatwick airports.

British Airways was one of the founders, together with American Airlines, Canadian International Airlines, Cathay Pacific and Qantas, of the 'Oneworld' alliance. The alliance now has 31 member airlines and serves 565 scheduled destinations in 133 countries.

The British Airways group has a fleet of 340 aircraft, including seven Concordes, 54 Boeing

737s, 72 Boeing 747s, 51 Boeing 757s, 35 Boeing 777s and 27 Boeing 767s. Ten Airbus A320s and 15 A319s are in service, with a further 20 and 33 respectively on order.

Other UK Airlines

BMI, formerly British Midland, is the second largest scheduled carrier and operates an extensive network of scheduled services with 40 aircraft, carrying 7.1 million passengers in 2000. The company commenced transatlantic services for the first time in 2001. Britannia Airways is the world's biggest charter airline and carried 8.2 million passengers in 2000 on its 44 aircraft. Virgin Atlantic operates scheduled services to 18 overseas destinations with 27 aircraft. Low fare 'no-frills' airlines operating in the UK include easyJet and Go.

Airports

Of the 150 or so licensed civil aerodromes in the UK, nearly a quarter handle more than 100,000 passengers a year each. In 2000 the UK's civil airports handled a total of 181.2 million passengers (180 million terminal passengers and 1.2 million in transit), and 2.3 million tonnes of freight.

Passenger traffic has been growing at the UK's main airports (see Table 21.6). Heathrow is the world's busiest airport for international travellers and is the UK's most important for passengers and air freight, handling 64.6 million passengers (excluding those in transit) and 1.3 million tonnes of freight in 2000. Gatwick is the world's sixth busiest international airport and has the world's busiest single runway. Stansted is the fastest growing airport in Europe, with terminal passengers increasing by 24% in 2000–01.

Ownership and Control

BAA plc is the world's largest commercial operator of airports. Its airports handle almost 200 million passengers a year worldwide. In 2000 its seven UK airports—Heathrow, Gatwick, Stansted and Southampton in southern England, and Glasgow, Edinburgh and Aberdeen in Scotland—handled 124.1 million passengers. Overseas, BAA manages all or part of 12 airports: four in the United States, six in Australia, including Melbourne and Perth airports, Naples Airport in Italy and Mauritius. The UK's second largest operator is TBI, which has an interest in 37 airports worldwide, including Belfast International and Cardiff.

All UK airports used for public transport must be licensed by the CAA for reasons of safety. Stringent requirements, such as adequate firefighting, medical and rescue

Table 21.6: Passenger Traffic at the UK's Main Airports[1] *Million passengers*

	1990	1995	1998	1999	2000
London Heathrow	42.6	54.1	60.4	62.0	64.6
London Gatwick	21.0	22.4	29.0	30.4	32.0
Manchester	10.1	14.5	17.2	17.4	18.5
London Stansted	1.2	3.9	6.8	9.4	11.8
Birmingham	3.5	5.2	6.6	6.9	7.5
Glasgow	4.3	5.4	6.5	6.8	6.9
Luton	2.7	1.8	4.1	5.3	6.1
Edinburgh	2.5	3.3	4.5	5.1	5.5
Newcastle	1.6	2.5	2.9	2.9	3.2
Belfast International	2.3	2.3	2.6	3.0	3.1
Aberdeen	1.9	2.2	2.7	2.5	2.4
East Midlands	1.3	1.9	2.1	2.2	2.2

[1] Terminal passengers, excluding those in transit.
Source: Civil Aviation Authority

services, have to be satisfied before a licence is granted.

Airport Development

Investment to expand passenger facilities is in progress at many UK airports. At Heathrow, BAA has invested over £960 million in the last five years. A £100 million redevelopment of departure facilities at Terminal 3 is scheduled for completion in 2002. BAA's plans for a fifth terminal, which could eventually cater for 30 million passengers a year, have been considered by a public inquiry. If approval is granted, the new terminal could be operational by 2007. Expansion at Gatwick's two terminals over the next ten years is designed to raise annual capacity to around 40 million passengers. Manchester Airport's second runway became fully operational during summer 2001, increasing the airport's capacity to over 40 million a year.

Among other large-scale projects at UK airports are:

- a major £360 million expansion plan at Birmingham Airport, which will increase capacity to around 10 million passengers a year;
- a £200 million investment programme at Stansted over the next five years to increase capacity to around 15 million passengers a year; and
- a £30 million expansion scheme at Belfast City Airport over the next five years.

As there is a shortage of capacity at some of the UK's major airports, the Government is seeking ways to increase provision, and make more efficient use of the existing infrastructure, while also reducing the environmental impact of aviation. A series of studies on regional airports has been undertaken, and a study of airport issues in south-east and east England is in progress. These will contribute to the development of a White Paper which will provide a long-term framework for the future of civil aviation and airports in the UK.

The DTLR, along with BAA and local councils, is looking at ways of reducing the environmental impact of air travel. Both daytime and night-time noise levels were reduced in 2001, and plans for the expansion of Gatwick Airport include legally binding agreements with the local authorities to reduce emissions from the airport and protect air quality. Aircraft noise is discussed further in chapter 19.

Air Traffic Control

Civil and military air traffic control over the UK and the surrounding seas, including much of the North Atlantic, is undertaken by National Air Traffic Services Ltd (NATS), working in collaboration with military controllers. Previously a subsidiary of the CAA, NATS became a separate organisation under the Transport Act 2000, and the company is being restructured, bringing in private sector investment through a PPP. The Government's strategic partner in this venture is the Airline Group, a consortium of seven UK airlines—British Airways, BMI, Virgin, Britannia, Monarch, easyJet and Airtours. Under the deal, the Airline Group has a 46% share (with rights giving it voting control), the Government 49%, and NATS employees 5%. The CAA retains responsibility for air safety regulation, and will also regulate the NATS PPP.

The PPP is intended to attract large-scale investment, from the private sector, to undertake the improvements needed in air traffic control operations. To cope with the rapid growth in air traffic, NATS is planning to replace the three existing UK centres for civil and military *en route* air traffic control operations at Prestwick, Manchester and West Drayton (near Heathrow) with two major centres. Swanwick (Hampshire) is due to open in 2002, while a new Scottish centre at Prestwick will replace the existing centre in 2006–07.

Air Safety

The CAA is responsible for safety standards on UK airlines. It certifies aircraft and crews, licenses air operators and air travel organisers, and approves certain air fares and airport charges. To qualify for a first professional licence, a pilot must undertake a full-time course of instruction approved by the CAA—or have acceptable military or civilian flying experience—and pass ground examinations and flight tests. Every company operating aircraft used for commercial air transport purposes must possess an Air Operator's Certificate, which the CAA grants when it is satisfied that the company is competent to operate its aircraft safely. All aircraft registered in the UK must be granted a certificate of airworthiness by the CAA before being flown. The CAA works closely with the Joint Aviation Authorities (JAA), a European grouping of aviation safety regulation authorities.

The DTLR's Air Accidents Investigation Branch investigates accidents and serious incidents in UK airspace and those that occur overseas to aircraft registered or manufactured in the UK.

Further Reading

Transport Statistics Great Britain, annual report. The Stationery Office.

Transport 2010: The 10 Year Plan. DETR, 2000.

Waterways for Tomorrow. DETR, 2000.

Websites

Department for Transport, Local Government and the Regions: www.dtlr.gov.uk
National Assembly for Wales: www.wales.gov.uk
Northern Ireland Department for Regional Development: www.drdni.gov.uk
Scottish Executive: www.scotland.gov.uk
British Waterways: www.britishwaterways.co.uk
Civil Aviation Authority: www.caa.gov.uk
Highways Agency: www.highways.gov.uk
Railtrack: www.railtrack.co.uk
Strategic Rail Authority: www.sra.gov.uk
Sustrans: www.sustrans.co.uk
Transport for London: www.transportforlondon.gov.uk

Sustainable Development

The year 2002 marks the tenth anniversary of the UN Conference on Environment and Development, held in Rio de Janeiro. At the conference, known as the 'Earth Summit', for the first time global attention was focused on the links between environmental problems, economic conditions and social justice. From it emerged a commitment to the concept widely known as 'sustainable development'.

The Earth Summit brought together policy-makers, diplomats, scientists, and media and non-governmental representatives from 179 countries to discuss how environmental protection and management of natural resources could be integrated with socio-economic issues of poverty and under-development. It set in motion integrated approaches to social, economic and environmental management in many countries, including the UK.

The first UK sustainable development strategy was published in 1994. In 1996 a programme was established to monitor a set of 120 indicators. In 1999 the programme was expanded to 150 indicators in a revised strategy which emphasised a simultaneous pursuit of social progress that recognises the needs of everyone, effective protection of the environment, prudent use of natural resources, and maintenance of high and stable levels of economic growth and employment. It included 15 headline indicators intended to focus attention on what sustainable development means:

Economic: economic output (Gross Domestic Product—GDP); investment (as % of GDP); and employment.
Social: poverty and social exclusion; education (qualifications at age 19); health (expected years of healthy life); housing; and crime.
Environmental: climate change (greenhouse gases); air quality (days of air pollution); road traffic; river water quality; wildlife (farmland birds); land use (percentage of new homes on previously developed land); and waste (arisings and management).

In January 2001 the Government's first annual report reviewing progress made against the 15 indicators was published, showing improvement in eight of them in 2000. At the same time the first breakdown of the headline indicators for each of the English regions and for Wales was published. A website on sustainable development (*www.sustainable-development.gov.uk*) was also launched to provide both a means for continuous reporting of progress and a forum for debate and exchange of information.

In November 2000 the National Assembly for *Wales* adopted its own sustainable development scheme, providing the overarching framework for all the Assembly's work. The first annual report on implementation of the scheme will be produced in late 2001.

In *Scotland*, sustainable development is being built into programmes and policies across the board. The Scottish Executive is considering its own set of indicators.

Planned consultation in *Northern Ireland* will outline a framework for implementing a sustainable development strategy aiming for better coordination of action within and between central government and other key sectors.

The principal body responsible for encouraging and promoting sustainable development within the UK is the Sustainable Development Commission (*www.sd-commission.gov.uk*). It acts to advocate sustainable development in the UK, review progress and build consensus on the actions needed for further progress.

In September 2002 many UN members, including the UK, and other concerned parties will attend the World Summit on Sustainable Development (known as Rio + 10) in Johannesburg, South Africa (*www.johannesburgsummit.org*). The Summit will identify areas for further action and examine the obstacles to the implementation of Agenda 21 (the plan of action adopted at Rio).

22 The Economy

Structure and Performance	379	Industrial and Commercial Policy	388
Economic Strategy	385	Corporate Affairs	396

The Government's central economic objective is to raise the UK economy's sustainable rate of growth and achieve rising prosperity. It has set five key long-term economic goals: raising productivity; increasing employment opportunity for all; providing educational opportunity for all; abolishing child poverty; and delivering strong and dependable public services.

In 2000 growth in the UK economy continued for the ninth consecutive year. Gross Domestic Product (GDP) at constant market prices rose by 3.1% over the year, with quarterly growth reaching 0.9% in the second quarter and 0.8% in the third quarter, although there was a weakening to 0.4% in the fourth quarter. Employment grew by a further 225,000 during the course of the year, contributing to a total rise of more than 1 million since spring 1997. The economy is seeing the longest period of sustained low inflation since the 1960s. Underlying inflation was modestly below the Government's 2½% inflation target throughout 2000, averaging 2.1% for the year as a whole.

STRUCTURE AND PERFORMANCE

The value of all goods and services produced in the UK economy for final consumption is measured by Gross Domestic Product. In 2000 GDP at current market prices—'money GDP'—totalled £935 billion. Average annual growth in GDP at 1995 market prices over the past five years has been 2.8% (see also Table 22.3). Values for two of the main economic indicators, inflation and GDP, are shown in Figures 22.1 and 22.2 overleaf.

Output

Real GDP grew by 3.1% in 2000, above its post-war average of around 2½% a year. Strong growth in domestic demand more than accounted for the expansion, driven by a 3.7% rise in household consumption, well above average rates. Business investment growth slowed significantly in 2000 following rapid expansion over previous years, although it gathered pace in the second half of the year. Whole economy fixed capital formation was supported by a 15.4% increase in general government investment. In the 2001 Budget, HM Treasury expected GDP growth to ease back to its assumed trend rate of between 2¼% and 2¾% a year in the period 2001 to 2003.

Recent decades have generally seen growth dominated by the service sector (see chapter 29) and this pattern continued during the 1990s. In 2000, at constant basic prices—that is, adjusted for inflation, and excluding taxes and subsidies on products—output of the service industries increased by 3.4%, with particularly strong growth in transport,

Figure 22.1:
RPI Inflation, UK (All Items)

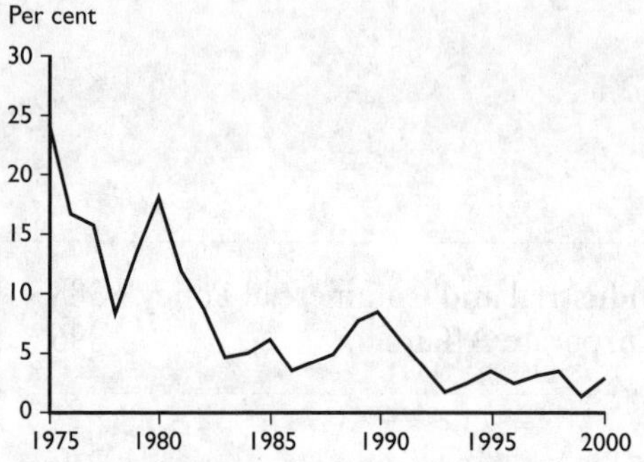

Source: Office for National Statistics

Figure 22.2:
Percentage Change in GDP at 1995 Market Prices, UK

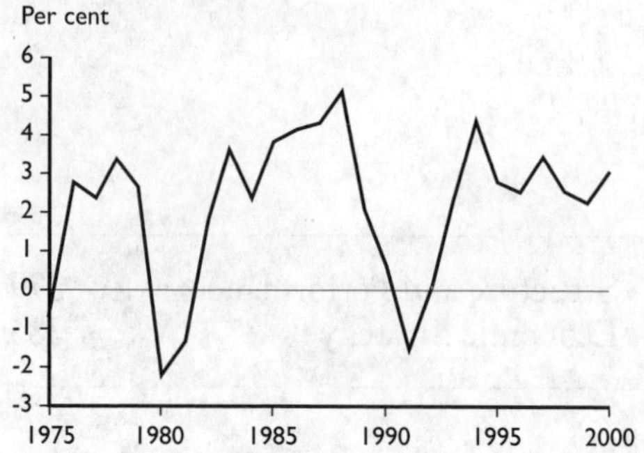

Source: Office for National Statistics

Table 22.3: Gross Domestic Product and Gross National Income *£ million*

	1990	1995	1998	1999	2000
Final consumption expenditure					
Households	336,492	438,453	530,851	562,915	589,235
Non-profit institutions	11,401	16,481	20,972	22,537	22,454
General government	110,620	141,075	154,767	164,999	174,184
Gross capital formation					
Gross fixed capital formation	114,314	116,360	148,071	157,610	166,114
Changes in inventories	–1,800	4,512	4,461	–1,946	1,206
Acquisitions less disposals of valuables	–113	–92	487	245	–3
Total exports	133,501	202,412	225,474	231,023	254,348
Gross final expenditure	704,415	919,201	1,085,083	1,137,383	1,207,538
less Total imports	–148,198	–205,221	–233,429	–245,924	–272,206
Statistical discrepancy	—	—	—	–459	–408
GDP at current market prices	**556,217**	**713,980**	**851,654**	**891,000**	**934,924**
Gross national income at current market prices	**550,521**	**715,028**	**862,462**	**896,988**	**936,586**
GDP at 1995 market prices	**659,486**	**713,980**	**777,937**	**795,747**	**820,195**
GDP index at 1995 market prices (1995 = 100)	**92.4**	**100.0**	**109.0**	**111.5**	**114.9**

Source: ONS Quarterly National Accounts

storage and communication (6.6%) and in business services and finance (4.4%). Within the production industries, output of electricity, gas and water rose by 3.4%, and manufacturing growth—at 1.6%—showed the biggest increase since 1994. Manufacturing (see chapter 27) now contributes around 18% of GDP, compared with over a third in 1950.

The UK experienced lower economic growth than its major competitors in both the 1970s and the 1980s, according to the Organisation for Economic Co-operation and

Table 22.4: Output by Industry

	Gross value added at current basic prices 2000 (£ million)	% of gross value added 2000	% change in gross value added 1990–2000 at 1995 basic prices
Agriculture, hunting, forestry and fishing	8,912	1.1	1.1
Mining and quarrying	24,244	2.9	46.0
Manufacturing	155,531	18.7	6.2
Electricity, gas and water supply	15,677	1.9	30.8
Construction	43,287	5.2	–2.4
Wholesale and retail trade	104,854	12.6	30.7
Hotels and restaurants	25,928	3.1	–3.3
Transport, storage and communication	68,195	8.2	65.0
Financial intermediation	42,602	5.1	18.8
Adjustment for financial services	–37,091	–4.5	31.2
Real estate, renting and business activities	191,777	23.1	47.3
Public administration and defence	42,091	5.1	–6.4
Education	46,176	5.6	16.5
Health and social work	56,313	6.8	45.5
Other services	42,560	5.1	44.4
Total gross value added	**831,053**	**100.0**	**24.8**
Intermediate consumption at purchasers' prices	987,792		
Total output at basic prices	1,818,849		

Sources: ONS Quarterly National Accounts and *United Kingdom National Accounts 2001—the Blue Book*

Development. Average annual GDP growth in the 1970s was 1.9% compared with 3.0% in the EU and 3.4% in the G7 countries. In the 1980s, annual growth of 2.7% was slightly above the EU average of 2.4% but a little below the G7 average of 3.0%. By the 1990s, however, UK growth was the same as for the EU and G7 countries, at 2.0% a year.

Household Income and Expenditure

Total resources of the households sector—including non-profit institutions serving households—rose by 4.6% in 2000 to £915 billion. Gross disposable income—after deductions, including taxes and social contributions—totalled £622 billion. In 1995 prices, real households' disposable income—the amount of money the household sector has available for spending after taxes and other deductions—was 3.0% higher in 2000 than in 1999. Wages and salaries accounted for 60% of household primary income in 2000, rising by 5.3% during the year to £449 billion. Household net financial wealth fell by 10% in 2000 to £2,149 billion.

Household final expenditure—spending by the household sector on products or services to satisfy immediate needs or wants—rose in 2000 by 4.7% at *current market prices* to £589 billion, representing 74.9% of total final consumption expenditure (£786 billion). Expenditure on services remained relatively strong, rising by 5.6%, with expenditure on durable goods up by 3.6% and on non-durable goods by 3.8%. In *constant price* terms total expenditure grew by 3.7%.

Households' saving ratio—saving as a percentage of total available households' resources—fell slightly between 1999 and 2000, from 5.2% to 4.5%, partly due to increases in tax payments and consumption growth continuing to outstrip income.

Table 22.5: Household Final Consumption Expenditure

	Expenditure in 1990 (£ million)[1]	Expenditure in 2000 (£ million)[1]	% of expenditure in 2000[1]	% change in expenditure at constant 1995 prices 1990–2000
Durable goods				
Cars, motorcycles and other vehicles	19,034	27,930	4.7	14.7
Other durable goods	15,483	28,932	4.9	110.0
Total	**34,517**	**56,862**	**9.7**	**55.5**
Non-durable goods				
Food	41,817	55,850	9.5	13.9
Alcohol and tobacco	30,009	46,063	7.8	−11.4
Clothing and footwear	21,212	34,458	5.8	67.9
Energy products	22,422	30,673	5.2	−1.5
Other goods	39,659	76,405	13.0	50.9
Total	**155,119**	**243,449**	**41.3**	**22.7**
Services				
Rent, water and sewerage charges	36,543	79,454	13.5	13.1
Catering	30,076	50,954	8.6	10.6
Transport and communication	30,969	57,247	9.7	44.3
Financial services	13,856	28,506	4.8	38.7
Other services	35,412	72,763	12.3	40.1
Total	**146,856**	**288,924**	**49.0**	**27.0**
TOTAL	**336,492**	**589,235**	**100.0**	**28.1**

[1] At current market prices.
Source: ONS Quarterly National Accounts

The 2000 figure is the lowest level since 1988, when it was 3.9%.

Table 22.5 shows the changing pattern of households' final consumption expenditure. Over the longer term, with rising incomes, people tend to spend increasing proportions of their disposable income on durable goods, clothing and certain services. Spending on leisure pursuits and tourism, communications, health and financial services have all shown significant growth in recent years. Declining proportions are being spent on alcohol and tobacco, and energy products.

Investment

Gross fixed capital formation represents investment in assets which are used repeatedly or continuously over a number of years to produce goods, such as machinery used to create a product. Total investment at constant 1995 prices grew by 2.8% in 2000 (see Table 22.6), slower growth than the 5.4% increase in 1999. Business investment rose by 1.9%, and at 14.1% of GDP, remained very close to 1999's record high share.

UK whole economy investment has accounted for a smaller share of GDP than for other industrialised countries—in 1999 around 19.1% of GDP (at 1995 prices), compared with the average for the G7 excluding the UK of 22.3%—but strong growth of business investment in recent years has helped to narrow the gap.

General government investment rose by 15.4% in 2000 following a 3.0% decline in

Table 22.6: Gross Fixed Capital Formation at Constant 1995 Prices *£ million*

	1995	1998	1999	2000
Transport equipment	11,055	14,913	16,122	15,700
Other machinery and equipment	44,464	63,833	68,708	70,741
Dwellings	21,588	23,231	23,123	23,752
Other buildings and structures[1]	35,314	38,304	40,246	42,084
Intangible fixed assets	3,939	4,156	4,004	4,115
Gross fixed capital formation	**116,360**	**144,437**	**152,203**	**156,392**
of which:				
Business investment[2]	76,437	105,866	113,807	115,972
General government	14,005	9,993	9,692	11,188
Public corporations	1,912	1,679	1,655	1,864
Private sector	24,006	26,899	27,049	27,368

[1] Including costs associated with the transfer of ownership of non-produced assets.
[2] Excluding dwellings and costs associated with the transfer of non-produced assets; these are included under the private sector.
Source: ONS Quarterly National Accounts

1999, and is forecast by HM Treasury to increase at an average of around 20% a year between 2001 and 2003, reflecting the Government's commitment to the renewal and modernisation of the public sector capital stock (see also p. 400).

International Trade

International trade plays a key role in the UK economy (see chapter 24). The UK is the world's fifth largest exporter of goods and services, with exports accounting for 27% of GDP in 2000. Other EU countries took 57.3% of UK exports of goods in 2000 and supplied 50.5% of imported goods.

The UK's current account deficit (see p. 411) deteriorated sharply from £9.9 billion in 1999 to £16.2 billion in 2000 as domestic production continued to be outstripped by domestic demand. This increased deficit was partly caused by a record trade in goods deficit of £28.8 billion, and a decreased surplus on investment income to £5.5 billion. There was a continued surplus on trade in services of £11.0 billion and a £3.8 billion deficit on current transfers.

Business Structure

The UK has around 3.7 million businesses including many large companies. According to a *Financial Times* survey of the world's 500 largest companies in January 2001, 40 were UK-based, with a market capitalisation of US$1,637 billion (£1,115 billion). In Europe, 143 of the top 500 companies were UK-based, with market capitalisation of almost US$2,148 million (£1,462 billion). There are around 3,485 UK businesses employing over 500 people, representing 39.8% of total employment by UK businesses and 41.7% of turnover. A small number of large companies and their subsidiaries are responsible for a substantial proportion of total production in some sectors. This is particularly true for chemicals, pharmaceuticals, motor vehicle assembly and aerospace. Of the top 20 UK companies by market capitalisation, five are in the retail banking sector, three in telecommunications and two each in pharmaceuticals, life assurance and oil and gas (see Table 22.7).

Expenditure on acquisitions abroad by UK companies reached a record level of £181.3 billion in 2000, 63% higher than in 1999, which had itself been a record. The two largest reported transactions were the acquisition of Mannesmann AG of Germany by Vodafone AirTouch (now Vodafone) for a reported £101.2 billion and of Atlantic Richfield Company of the United States by BP Amoco (now BP) for £18.0 billion. Expenditure on acquisitions in the UK by

Table 22.7: Top UK Companies by Market Capitalisation, 2001[1]

Company/ business sector	Market capitalisation (£ million)[2]
Vodafone/telecommunications	154,684
BP/oil and gas	121,205
GlaxoSmithKline/pharmaceuticals	109,221
HSBC/retail banking	95,798
AstraZeneca/pharmaceuticals	56,335
Shell Transport & Trading/ oil and gas	54,540
Royal Bank of Scotland/ retail banking	42,805
Lloyds TSB/retail banking	41,306
British Telecommunications/ telecommunications	40,185
Barclays/retail banking	36,517
Cable & Wireless/ telecommunications	26,553
CGNU/life assurance	24,707
Diageo/alcoholic beverages	22,851
Prudential/life assurance	21,681
British Sky Broadcasting/ cable and satellite	21,123
Marconi/IT hardware	19,680
Tesco/food & drug retailers	17,771
Abbey National/retail banking	17,653
Reuters/publishing & printing	16,269
Anglo-American/mining finance	16,118

[1] As at 4 January. During 2001 there have been some changes in this ranking and in August the top three companies were BP, GlaxoSmithKline and Vodafone.
[2] Market capitalisation represents the number of shares issued multiplied by their market value.
Source: *FT 500 Survey*

foreign companies also reached a record level—£64.6 billion—slightly higher than the previous record in 1999. The largest reported acquisition was of Orange by France Telecom for £23.4 billion.

Small firms play an important part in the UK economy: around 43.6% of the private sector workforce work for companies employing fewer than 50 people. Around 2.6 million businesses are sole traders or partners without employees, while a further 738,685 businesses employ one to four people. Together these 3.3 million enterprises account for 89.5% of the number of businesses, over 23.5% of business employment and 16.4% of turnover.

Private sector firms predominate in the economy. The public sector has become much less significant following the privatisation since 1979 of many public sector businesses, including gas, electricity supply, coal and telecommunications. The remaining major nationalised industries are Consignia (formerly the Post Office), BNFL (British Nuclear Fuels) and the Civil Aviation Authority.

Inflation

Three main measures of retail prices are used in the UK:

- the all items Retail Prices Index (RPI), the main domestic measure of prices in the UK. RPI inflation measures the average change from month to month in the prices of goods and services purchased by most households in the UK and is commonly called 'headline' inflation;
- the RPI excluding mortgage interest payments (RPIX), which is used to calculate 'underlying' inflation, the target measure set by the Government (see p. 386); and
- the harmonised index of consumer prices (HICP), calculated for each Member State of the European Union for the purposes of European comparisons; it is also used to derive inflation rates for the eurozone and the EU as a whole.

Annual underlying inflation (RPIX) in the last 20 years or so has fluctuated considerably, peaking at 20.8% in the year to May 1980. However, it was much lower in the 1990s, and since 1993 has been in a relatively narrow range, from around 2% to 3.5%. In 2000 it averaged 2.1% and has been modestly below the Government's current target of 2½%—set in May 1997—since April 1999.

In 2000 the all items RPI averaged 3.0%: goods inflation averaged 0.3% and services inflation 3.5%. There were above average increases of 8.9% for housing costs, 8.6% for tobacco and 4.9% for leisure services; conversely, clothing and footwear costs fell by 3.8% and leisure goods by 3.5%.

In 2000 UK inflation on the HICP measure was 0.8%, the lowest in the EU and well below the average of 2.1%. During the early months of 2001 the UK's HICP continued at this low level. This situation is partly a consequence of sterling relative to the euro.

Producer input prices for materials and fuels purchased by manufacturing industry rose by 11.5% in 2000 as a whole, but dropped back slightly in the first half of 2001. This compares with a 1.6% increase in 1999 and a 9.1% fall in the previous year. Producer output price inflation was 1.2% in 1999 as a whole, and 2.6% in 2000, but output prices were broadly stable in the first half of 2001.

Labour Market

Employment in the UK has continued to grow, and there were falls both in the International Labour Organisation (ILO) unemployment rate and in the number of people claiming unemployment-related benefits. Latest figures show that employment—at 28.2 million in the three months to May 2001—was at a record level, 267,000 higher than in the same period a year earlier (see chapter 11). Those people economically inactive (of men aged 16 to 64 and women aged 16 to 59) rose by 166,000 over the same period to 7.74 million, but 5.55 million people did not want jobs. Unemployment continued to fall, and at 1,453,000 in the three months to May 2001 was 208,000 lower than a year earlier, according to ILO measures. This represented 4.9% of the workforce, well below the figure (7.6%) for all EU countries and the lowest UK rate since the series began in 1984. Long-term (over two years) and youth unemployment have both declined substantially.

ECONOMIC STRATEGY

The main elements of the Government's economic strategy, which is designed to deliver high and stable levels of economic growth and employment, are as set out in the 2001 Budget:

- delivering macroeconomic stability;
- meeting the productivity challenge;
- increasing employment opportunity for all (see chapter 11);
- ensuring fairness for families and communities; and
- protecting the environment.

HM Treasury is the department with prime responsibility for the Government's monetary and fiscal frameworks. It is also responsible for wider economic policy, which it carries out in conjunction with other government departments, such as Trade and Industry; Education and Skills; Work and Pensions; and Transport, Local Government and the Regions.

The Government's policy on UK membership of the European single currency (see p. 82) is that the determining factor underpinning any decision on membership is the national economic interest and whether the economic case for joining is clear and unambiguous. As the Chancellor of the Exchequer said in his October 1997 statement, the five economic tests will define whether a clear and unambiguous case can be made. These tests are:

- sustainable convergence between Britain and the economies of the single currency;
- whether there is sufficient flexibility to cope with economic change;
- the effect on investment;
- the impact on the UK financial services industry; and
- whether it is good for employment.

The Government has said that it will complete an assessment of the five economic tests within two years of the start of the current Parliament.

Economic Stability

The Government's central economic objective is to raise the economy's sustainable rate of growth, and achieve rising prosperity, through creating economic and employment opportunities for all. It has introduced new frameworks for the operation of both monetary and fiscal policy in order to achieve low and stable inflation and sound public finances. The Government ensures the coordination of monetary and fiscal policy by setting mutually consistent objectives for both.

The Bank of England's Monetary Policy Committee (see p. 512) is responsible for setting interest rates to meet the Government's inflation target of 2½%, as defined by the 12-month change in RPIX. Official interest rates peaked at 7½% in 1998, compared with a peak of 14⅞% in 1989 in the previous economic cycle, and had fallen to 5% by August 2001.

International Stability

The crises in emerging markets in the 1990s brought to light what the Government saw as fundamental weaknesses in the architecture of the international financial system and highlighted the need for new measures to promote stability at the international level in parallel with the reforms to the UK's macroeconomic framework. The Government supported the need for all governments to pursue transparent, consistent and credible macroeconomic policies with enhanced international surveillance, greater international cooperation in financial regulation and a new framework for managing crises. In 1998 the G7 Finance Ministers pledged to create a new international financial architecture for an integrated global economy. The UK Government has played a leading role in taking forward this agenda, building on the structural changes introduced domestically. In the past three years there have been developments in a number of important areas, including:

- a new framework of codes and standards against which countries can assess their performance and improve their economic accounts and financial policy frameworks;
- a new model of cooperation in global financial regulation—the Financial Stability Forum—which was established in 1999 to bring together the International Monetary Fund, World Bank and key finance ministries, central banks and regulatory authorities with the objective of tackling areas of vulnerability in the international financial system;
- a new framework of partnership for crisis prevention and resolution between the private and public sectors which will help ensure that all parties benefiting from the international financial system play their part in maintaining its stability; and
- a new mechanism for informal dialogue between major developed and emerging market economies—the G20. This Group was also established in 1999 to provide a forum for broader discussion and cooperation on key economic and financial issues.

Fiscal Policy

The *Code for Fiscal Stability*, set up under the Finance Act 1998, requires fiscal and debt management policy to be carried out in accordance with five key principles:

- *transparency* in setting fiscal policy objectives, the implementation of fiscal policy and the presentation of the public accounts;
- *stability* in the fiscal policy-making process and in the way that fiscal policy affects the economy;
- *responsibility* in the management of the public finances;
- *fairness*, including between present and future generations; and
- *efficiency* in the design and implementation of fiscal policy, and in managing both sides of the public sector balance sheet.

Consistent with these principles, the Government established key objectives for fiscal policy as:

- over the medium term, to ensure sound public finances and that spending and taxation impact fairly, both within and between generations; and
- over the short term, to support monetary policy and, in particular, to allow the 'automatic stabilisers' to play their role in

smoothing the path of the economy over the economic cycle.

These objectives are implemented through the Government's two fiscal rules, set out in HM Treasury's Economic and Fiscal Strategy Report (see below), against which the performance of fiscal policy can be judged:

- *the golden rule*—over the economic cycle, the Government will borrow only to invest and not to fund current spending; and
- *the sustainable investment rule*—public sector net debt as a proportion of GDP will be held over the economic cycle at a stable and prudent level: other things being equal, net debt will be maintained below 40% of GDP.

These rules promote economic stability by ensuring sound public sector finances, while allowing flexibility in two key respects. First, the rules are set over the economic cycle, allowing fiscal balances to vary between years in keeping with the cyclical positions of the economy. This allows the automatic stabilisers to operate freely to dampen the effects of the economic cycle, boosting aggregate demand when the economy is below trend, and reducing aggregate demand when it is above trend. Second, the interaction of the two rules promotes capital investment while ensuring the sustainability of the public finances in the longer term.

Across the public sector, planning for the long term and increasing capital investment have been supported by the new public spending framework. The key elements are:

- three-year spending allocations for departments (Departmental Expenditure Limits—DELs), providing departments with greater certainty and flexibility over their budgets and thereby enabling improved planning and management of resources over the medium term;
- Annually Managed Expenditure (AME), which covers those elements of spending that cannot reasonably be subject to firm multi-year limits and are instead subject to tough annual scrutiny as part of the Budget process. DEL and AME sum to Total Managed Expenditure (see p. 402);
- separate resource (current) and capital budgets for each department, consistent with the distinction in the fiscal rules. Departments are required to manage their resource and capital budgets separately, removing the bias against investment which was present in the previous planning regime;
- new Public Service Agreements (PSAs) through which each department is committed to deliver challenging outcome-focused targets; and
- Resource Accounting and Budgeting, which measures the full economic costs of government activity and provides better information and incentives for public sector managers.

The Budget

The Budget is the Government's main economic statement of the year and is usually issued in March. In a major speech to Parliament, the Chancellor of the Exchequer reviews the nation's economic performance and describes the Government's economic objectives and the economic policies it intends to follow in order to achieve them. The 2001 Budget report comprised two documents:

- the *Economic and Fiscal Strategy Report*, describing the comprehensive strategy which the Government is pursuing to meet its economic objectives, the progress that has been made so far, and how the 2001 Budget took further steps to meet the Government's objectives; and
- the *Financial Statement and Budget Report*, providing a summary of each of the main Budget measures and updated forecasts for the economy and the public finances.

In advance of the spring Budget, the Government publishes a Pre-Budget Report, usually in the previous November. As well as setting out economic and fiscal developments and prospects, it describes the direction of government policy and sets out for consultation measures under consideration for the forthcoming Budget.

INDUSTRIAL AND COMMERCIAL POLICY

The Department of Trade and Industry (DTI) aims to increase UK competitiveness and scientific excellence in order to generate higher levels of sustainable growth and productivity. It has four specific objectives:

- to promote enterprise, innovation and higher productivity;
- to make the most of the UK's scientific, engineering and technological capabilities;
- to create strong and competitive markets within a fair and effective regulatory framework; and
- to assist the competitiveness of UK companies through export promotion and inward investment.

Competitiveness

In February 2001 the DTI published the second in its series of UK competitiveness indicators, which showed that the UK was well placed to meet the challenges of the global economy, although its productivity was still lagging significantly behind that of its main competitors in the G7 group of countries. Among the UK's strengths highlighted were:

- economic stability based on low inflation and strong public finances;
- an open and competitive economy, relatively free from regulation;
- an economy open to international trade and investment, with foreign direct investment reaching record levels in 2000;
- higher levels of business investment;
- an increase in the level of employment, with unemployment rates at their lowest since the 1970s;
- a strong science base, with UK research highly regarded around the world; and
- strengths in some key knowledge-intensive sectors (such as software, pharmaceuticals and biotechnology), with exports of these goods and services having grown strongly and now representing a higher proportion of UK exports than in any other G7 country.

The indicators found that the UK's economic performance was held back by low levels of basic skills (such as literacy and numeracy) and vocational skills, low spending levels on research and development (R&D) and low levels of investment. However, in recent years there has been a rapid rise in business investment in the UK, progress towards the national learning targets (see p. 144) and the new R&D tax credit (see p. 406), which is designed to help increase UK spending on innovation.

> In February 2001 the Government issued a White Paper, *Opportunity for All in a World of Change*, setting out its policy for improving competitiveness and closing the productivity gap with its competitors. It includes measures designed to:
>
> - improve the level of skills, including literacy, numeracy and vocational skills (see chapter 10) and those in information and communications technology (ICT);
> - increase the rate of growth in all regions of the UK, through a new regional policy (see p. 391);
> - promote the exploitation of scientific advances by business (see chapter 25); and
> - create a regulatory and financial environment that helps to foster enterprise and growth.

Enterprise, Innovation and Business Support

The DTI promotes enterprise and innovation by encouraging successful business start-ups and offering businesses a number of support services. Most support is designed to assist business, especially small and medium-sized enterprises (SMEs), to expand and invest, and to adopt best practice.

The Small Business Service (SBS) was set up in April 2000 as a separate DTI agency to act as a strong voice within government for small businesses and to improve government programmes promoting small businesses. It also aims to reduce the burden of regulation on small businesses, and to ensure that the interests of SMEs are considered in future regulations. The SBS is advised by the Small Business Council, a non-departmental public body with 20 members, most of whom are entrepreneurs with experience of running an SME.

The Business Link network, which reports to the SBS, was restructured in March 2001. The network now comprises 45 operators throughout England formed by partnerships between local enterprise agencies, local authorities, chambers of commerce and some commercial organisations with wider interests. In addition, the network can be accessed nationally via a contact centre and associated website (*www.businesslink.org*). Business Link, which offers information and advice on a wide range of subjects, is the 'gateway' to a network of business support organisations, as well as to information from the public, private and voluntary sectors. The main advice services are delivered by personal business advisers, who either give advice or arrange appointments with the relevant experts.

Elsewhere in the UK similar business support arrangements apply:

- in lowland Scotland, the Small Business Gateway, launched in July 2000, offers a package of measures designed to improve the quality and consistency of public sector support for new and small businesses in the Scottish Enterprise area, while the Business Information Source of Highlands and Islands Enterprise operates equivalent services;
- in Wales, Business Connect covers all the main business support agencies and has a network of business support and front-line advice centres; and
- in Northern Ireland, small firms are helped by the Local Enterprise Development Unit (LEDU), with its headquarters in Belfast and its network of five regional offices. LEDU will form part of the new single agency planned for the beginning of 2002 (see p. 393).

Business Finance

Small businesses can face particular difficulties accessing finance and, in the Government's view, it has a role to play in addressing this market weakness. The SBS is developing new early-growth funding in order to encourage risk funding of start-ups and growth firms that are currently too risky for the banks or too small for traditional venture capital. Funding will be stimulated to facilitate the availability of small amounts of risk capital for innovative and knowledge-intensive businesses as well as for smaller manufacturers needing fresh investment to pursue new opportunities. The SBS will target businesses seeking to raise up to £50,000 and aims to help 1,000 businesses over the next three years, committing up to £50 million.

The Phoenix Fund has been set up to encourage entrepreneurship in disadvantaged areas and within disadvantaged groups. Funding is awarded to individuals and companies investing in Community Development Financial Institutions to encourage private investment in under-invested communities. Funding is on the basis of a competitive bidding process. Of the 57 bids received in the first round of bidding, 16 were assessed as suitable for support, involving funds of some £6 million over three years from 2001–02. A further round of bidding will be held in autumn 2001.

The Government has created the £180 million Enterprise Fund to stimulate more finance for small businesses and to address market weaknesses in the provision of that finance. The main elements of the Fund are:

- the Small Firms Loan Guarantee Scheme, which offers guarantees on loans to small firms with viable business proposals that are unable to obtain conventional finance as they lack security to offer against a loan. For established businesses that have been trading for two years or more, the SBS provides a guarantee of 85% on loans of up to £250,000 and for other businesses, including start-ups, the guarantee is 70% on loans of up to £100,000. Since the scheme started in 1981 over 71,000 loans, valued at over £2.5 billion, have been guaranteed;

- the UK High Technology Fund, which has raised £126 million and has been established as a 'fund of funds'—it is making commitments to invest in existing venture capital funds that specialise in investing in early-growth, high-technology companies; and
- new Regional Venture Capital Funds specialising in the provision of small-scale equity (up to £500,000) to small businesses with growth potential—they are being established on the basis of at least one in each of the English regions.

The £75 million Small Business Service Business Incubation Fund will provide loans to those in the English regions setting up or running business incubation projects (helping SMEs to survive and grow when they are at their most vulnerable in their start-up and early growth stages) whose development plans are hindered by a shortfall in funding from other sources. Loans averaging £1 million will be available for new incubators, and of up to £500,000 for refurbishment of workspace premises into incubators and the installation of infrastructure, such as broadband communications and relevant support services. The Fund will be open from autumn 2001 until 2004–05.

The SBS will be inviting proposals from a variety of organisations, including Business Links, for initiatives aimed at helping small businesses to better understand external finance and to become more investment-ready. The Small Business Investment Taskforce was set up in October 2000 and includes representatives of banks and other finance providers, accountancy bodies, academics and representatives of small firms. It advises the SBS on how best to stimulate the operation of markets providing finance for small business. It is also working with the Regional Development Agencies (see p. 392) and other bodies towards the creation of a new fund, with a target of £1 billion, comprising investment from the UK Government, the EU and private sector sources to develop the market in venture capital.

The Queen's Awards for Enterprise

The Queen's Awards for Enterprise scheme recognises outstanding performance by UK firms. The Awards, which are made annually and are valid for five years, are granted by the Queen on the advice of the Prime Minister, who is assisted by an advisory committee consisting of senior representatives from business, trade unions and government departments. Any self-contained 'industrial unit' in the UK with at least two full-time employees is eligible to apply so long as it meets the scheme's criteria. Winners are entitled to display the Award Emblem on their goods, packaging, advertising and letter headings. In 2001, 133 companies received Awards: 76 for International Trade, 42 for Innovation and 15 for Sustainable Development.

Information and Communications Technology

The Government is keen to ensure that the UK benefits fully from the rapid developments in ICT, including the growth of the Internet (see p. 286) and of 'e-commerce'. Its e-commerce strategy aims to ensure that the UK is the best environment in the world to do business electronically, and that, by 2005, there will be universal access to the Internet within the UK, with everyone who wants it having access. The Office of the 'e-Envoy' has been set up to take forward this strategy. For further information on ICT and e-commerce, see the essay on p. 536.

Quality, Standards and Design[1]

Quality is important throughout the business cycle—design, production, marketing and delivery to customers. Conformity assessment is a key part of the quality infrastructure encompassing certification of products,

---

[1] For more information on Design see the essay on p. 311.

processes, services and personnel to indicate that they meet certain criteria, such as standards and technical regulations. Conformity assessment conducted by third-party organisations can provide an impartial assessment, which is given greater emphasis when these bodies are themselves accredited by an authoritative body. In the UK the United Kingdom Accreditation Service is recognised by the Government as the sole national accreditation body. Companies that use accredited conformity assessment bodies in certain sectors are entitled to use the national accreditation mark—the 'tick and crown'.

British Standards Institution

The British Standards Institution (BSI) is the national standards body and is independent of the Government. It works with business, consumers and the Government to produce standards relevant to the needs of the market and suitable for public purchasing and regulatory purposes. The Kitemark is BSI's registered product certification trade mark. Government support for BSI is directed particularly towards European and international standards, which account for over 90% of its work.

National Measurement System

The National Measurement System (NMS) is the UK's national infrastructure of laboratories (see p. 437), which provides standards of measurement for use in trade, industry, academia and government. The NMS supports innovation in industry generally, by enabling the benefits of new products and processes to be measured, and specifically, by stimulating new product development in the instrument sector. It also raises productivity through improved process and quality control. The DTI is responsible for government programmes for the NMS and for policy on measurement standards.

Regional Development

The White Paper *Opportunity for All in a World of Change* set out the Government's new regional policy, which aims to raise GDP in the regions, improve skills, and help industry through restructuring and encouraging new industries as they develop. Measures planned include:

- establishing University Innovation Centres (long-term research partnerships between major business interests and the universities) and New Technology Institutes (based on partnerships between universities, colleges and local business), with the aim of boosting the levels of R&D, innovation and technology transfer, and of increasing skills in ICT and high technology;
- creating a Business Incubation Fund (see p. 390) and Regional Venture Capital Funds (see p. 390);
- introducing a Manufacturing Advisory Service, which will be set up in partnership with the Regional Development Agencies and the SBS to provide practical help with new manufacturing technology;
- setting up the Job Transition Service (see p. 156), to enable individuals affected by large-scale redundancies to find new jobs more quickly, and to help growing companies tackle skill shortages; and
- supporting the development of business 'clusters', local concentrations of businesses in a particular sector—the UK has a number of successful clusters, such as high technology industries in Cambridge and Oxford, and several developing clusters, such as biomedical industries in the North West and leisure software in Yorkshire.

Financial help is focused on the Assisted Areas, covering some 16.5 million people in Great Britain and all 1.7 million people in Northern Ireland. Regional Selective Assistance (RSA) is the main instrument of government support to industry in the Assisted Areas in Great Britain, and is now focusing more on high-quality, knowledge-based projects that provide skilled jobs. In 2000–01, 304 offers of RSA grants totalling £205 million were accepted in England in support of projects with total investment of £2.2 billion, which is expected to create or safeguard 32,000 jobs. The Enterprise Grant scheme is providing grants towards capital projects to growing SMEs in England in the Assisted Areas and other specified areas with particular needs.

England

Nine Regional Development Agencies (RDAs) have been set up in England (see also chapter 2). They aim to stimulate economic development and regeneration; promote business efficiency, investment, competitiveness and employment; raise the level of skills; and contribute to the achievement of sustainable development. The RDAs have developed regional economic strategies, which have identified the importance of developing their skills base, encouraging enterprise, and building a stronger capacity for innovation and technology transfer. They work closely with other bodies, such as Government Offices for the Regions, chambers of commerce, the SBS and Business Links.

Funding for RDAs totalled £1.5 billion in 2001–02, which will rise to £1.7 billion by 2003–04. RDA programmes include the Single Regeneration Budget (focused on community-based regeneration) and the Rural Development Programme (see chapter 26), and the Skills Development Fund. Financial support available to stimulate regional innovation includes DTI's Regional Innovation Fund, which will provide funding of £50 million a year for RDAs to invest in projects which will promote regional competitiveness, innovation and enterprise, and to support cluster development and networks of businesses in their regions. From April 2002 the different funding streams used to provide RDA funding will be pooled together into a single budget, allowing RDAs the flexibility to concentrate their resources according to regional priorities.

Scotland

In Scotland the Scottish Executive Enterprise and Lifelong Learning Department, which has overall responsibility for development of the Scottish economy, operates a range of schemes to support business. Scottish Enterprise and Highlands and Islands Enterprise are the lead economic development agencies in lowland and highland Scotland respectively, operating mainly through the network of Local Enterprise Companies (LECs—see p. 142).

Following a major review of the structure, functions and activities of the enterprise networks in 2000–01, a number of significant changes have been implemented with the aim of delivering a more streamlined and effective development network in Scotland. The strategy for enterprise, 'A Smart Successful Scotland' is aimed at clarifying the relationships with the Scottish Executive and at laying the foundation for a sustained improvement in economic performance by focusing the enterprise networks on three main aspects of raising productivity: encouraging entrepreneurship, raising skill levels and improving international links.

Changes include the launch of the Small Business Gateway scheme (see p. 389); a change in the status of LECs, so that they will become wholly owned by either Scottish Enterprise or Highlands and Islands Enterprise; and the creation of Local Economic Forums, which will consider local needs within the national framework and aim to achieve a simpler, more cohesive structure in local economic development.

Wales

The National Assembly for Wales is preparing a new national economic development strategy, which will be launched in December 2001. The Assembly's priorities are improving productivity, through focusing on particular sectors and clusters, and improving skills and entrepreneurship; tackling unemployment and supporting community regeneration; ensuring balanced and sustainable development; and delivering better government. Following a review of business support and development services by the Economic Development Committee of the National Assembly, published in January 2001, the Welsh Development Agency (WDA) is to become responsible for the 'gateway' for all public sector business support services; the new arrangements are expected to take effect in April 2002.

The Welsh Development Agency is the lead body for economic development. Its main role is to support and sustain business success, enabling businesses to prosper in both the local economy and the global marketplace. The WDA is focusing its activities on encouraging businesses to increase the level of value added, on supporting innovation and encouraging entrepreneurship and e-commerce.

Northern Ireland

A new agency, to be known as Investment Northern Ireland (INI), is to be set up by the beginning of 2002 to promote and support innovation and entrepreneurship in the Northern Ireland economy. As well as the business support aspects of the Northern Ireland Tourist Board, INI will be responsible for the functions currently undertaken by three bodies:

- the Industrial Development Board, which deals with overseas companies considering Northern Ireland as an investment location, as well as the development of local companies with more than 50 employees;
- the Local Enterprise Development Unit, which promotes enterprise and the development of small business; and
- the Industrial Research and Technology Unit, which provides advice and assistance on R&D, innovation and technology transfer.

European Union Regional Funding

The EU seeks to promote economic and social cohesion, reducing disparities between the regions and countries of the Union. The principal responsibility for helping poorer areas remains with national authorities, but the EU provides additional funding and targets the worst affected areas through its Structural Funds. The major fund is the European Regional Development Fund (ERDF), which supports regional competitiveness, training, economic development and innovation.

The UK is due to receive nearly £10.7 billion from the Funds in 2000–06. Funding is supporting a range of projects, designed to encourage businesses to grow, create suitable conditions for inward investment and new jobs, assist the most disadvantaged areas and the socially excluded, and help people to learn new skills.

The highest level of assistance is available to areas with 'Objective 1' status, where GDP is less than 75% of the EU average. In the UK about £3 billion is allocated to four Objective 1 areas: Cornwall and the Isles of Scilly, Merseyside, South Yorkshire, and West Wales and the Valleys. In recognition of the special position of Northern Ireland and the structural problems faced by the Highlands and Islands of Scotland, both of which used to have Objective 1 status, these two areas are eligible for special transition packages, with funding levels broadly equivalent to Objective 1 status.

Aid is also available to areas qualifying for 'Objective 2' status, which covers industrial and urban areas in need of regeneration, declining rural areas, and depressed areas dependent on fisheries. About 13.8 million people in the UK are in Objective 2 areas and a further 6 million benefit from transitional programmes.

Competitive Markets

In the Government's view, competitive markets provide the best means of ensuring that the UK economy's resources are put to their most effective use by encouraging enterprise and efficiency, and widening choice. The Government is committed to modernising and strengthening the UK's competition laws, with the aim of ensuring that effective and dynamic competition is delivered across the economy, as part of its wider agenda for promoting competitiveness and growth.

In July 2001 the Government published a White Paper *Productivity and Enterprise—A World Class Competition Regime*, setting out a consultation process scheduled for completion in October 2001. The White Paper proposals include:

- reforms to the merger and monopoly regimes, with decisions being taken by independent competition authorities;
- new duties for the *Office of Fair Trading* (OFT) (*www.oft.gov.uk*) to promote competition;
- consultation on criminal penalties for those involved in cartels; and
- a proposal to give the OFT and other competition regulators a new role to assess when laws and regulations might create barriers to entry and competition, or channel markets in a particular direction.

Competition Act 1998

The Competition Act 1998 came into force in March 2000 and is enforced by the Director General of Fair Trading and the utility regulators who have concurrent powers in their sectors. The Act introduced two prohibitions:

- of agreements which prevent, restrict or distort competition and which may affect trade within the UK (the Chapter I prohibition); and
- of conduct by undertakings that amounts to an abuse of a dominant position in a market and may affect trade in the UK (the Chapter II prohibition).

The Chapter I and II prohibitions are based on articles 81 and 82 of the Treaty of Rome, and the 1998 Act sets out principles which provide for the UK authorities to handle cases in such a way as to ensure consistency with EC law.

An agreement will infringe the Chapter I prohibition only if it has as its object or effect an appreciable prevention, restriction or distortion on competition in the UK. The Director General takes the view that an agreement will generally have no appreciable effect on competition if the parties' combined share of the market does not exceed 25%, although there will be circumstances when this is not the case.

For the purposes of the Chapter II prohibition, an undertaking will be considered dominant if it can behave 'to an appreciable extent independently of its competitors and customers and ultimately of consumers' when making commercial decisions. This has to be judged against the background of a properly defined relevant market through the assessment of the goods and services that form part of the market (the product market) and the geographical extent of the market.

The Act gives the Director General the power to impose financial penalties of up to 10% of turnover in the UK on an undertaking that has infringed either prohibition.

Between March 2000 and the end of May 2001 the OFT received over 5,000 complaints alleging breach of the Competition Act 1998 or concerning the complex monopoly provisions of the Fair Trading Act 1973. These complaints resulted in 2,065 preliminary inquiries being opened to consider the allegations; 68 resulted in investigations.

The OFT's review of competition in the legal, accountancy and architecture professions in England and Wales, published in March 2001, found that there were numerous possible restrictions on competition in the professions. It recommended that the professions should be fully subject to competition law and that unjustified restrictions on competition should be removed, although it recognised that there might be countervailing benefits to some of the potential restrictions it identified. The Secretary of State for Trade and Industry agreed that the professions should be fully subject to competition law and announced that the entitlement to exclusion from the provisions of the Competition Act 1998 should be removed. Consultation on those aspects of the report that fall to the Government is planned for autumn 2001.

The *Competition Commission* (*www.competition.commission.org.uk*) has two main arms:

- a reporting arm, which investigates various aspects of monopolies and mergers referred by the Director General of Fair Trading or a utility regulator; and
- an Appeal Tribunals arm, which hears appeals against decisions of the Director General of Fair Trading and the regulators on the prohibitions of anti-competitive agreements and abuse of a dominant position.

Monopolies

The framework under the Fair Trading Act 1973 for dealing with scale and complex monopolies[2] has been retained alongside the Competition Act. The Director General of Fair Trading, and those utility regulators which have parallel powers to apply the monopoly provisions of the 1973 Act, may examine such monopolies and make a reference to the Competition Commission to establish whether a monopoly operates, or may be expected to operate, against the public interest.

Mergers

A merger qualifies for investigation if it involves the acquisition of assets of more than £70 million or the creation or enhancement of a 25% share of the supply of a particular good or service in the UK or a substantial part of it. There is a voluntary procedure for pre-notification of proposed mergers. Qualifying mergers are considered by the Director General of Fair Trading, who then advises the Secretary of State for Trade and Industry on whether the merger should be referred to the Competition Commission. The Secretary of State's policy is to follow the advice of the Director General on reference, unless there are exceptional circumstances. In general, a reference to the Competition Commission will be made where the merger raises competition concerns. In rare cases a merger reference may be based on other public interest issues. Alternatively, the Secretary of State may ask the Director General to obtain suitable undertakings from the companies involved to remedy the adverse effects identified. Most mergers are cleared without being referred to the Competition Commission.

If the Competition Commission finds that a merger could be expected to operate against the public interest, the Secretary of State can prohibit it, allow it, or allow it subject to certain conditions being met. Where the merger has already taken place, action can be taken to reverse it. There are special provisions for newspaper and water company mergers.

The European Commission has exclusive jurisdiction in mergers which meet certain domestic, EC and global turnover thresholds. The Commission can ban mergers if it concludes that they would create or strengthen a dominant position which would significantly impede effective competition within the EU or a substantial part of it; alternatively, it may negotiate undertakings to correct the adverse effect.

Utility Regulation

There are a number of organisations regulating the privatised utilities, and their aim is to promote the interests of consumers, for example through ensuring effective competition. The Utilities Act 2000 replaced the two separate regulators for gas and electricity with a single regulatory body, Ofgem (see p. 500).

EU Single Market

The Government is working with the European Commission and other Member States to ensure effective competition within the single market (see p. 417). It is looking to improve the way the market operates through

[2] A scale monopoly exists where a single company (or a group of interconnected companies) supplies or acquires at least 25% of the goods or services of a particular type in all or part of the UK. A complex monopoly exists where a group of companies which are not connected and together account for at least 25% of the supply of, or acquisition of, any particular description of goods or services in all or part of the UK engage in conduct which has, or is likely to have, the effect of restricting, distorting or preventing competition.

wide-ranging economic reforms which target 'weak areas' (those areas where the single market does not work as well as it could) identified by the Commission. By the end of May 2001, 96.7% of single market measures had been incorporated into UK law.

CORPORATE AFFAIRS

Corporate Structure

There are about 1,406,000 'live' companies registered in Great Britain with the Registrar of Companies. Companies incorporated overseas with a place of business or branch in Great Britain must also register. Most corporate businesses are 'limited liability' companies, in which the liability of members is restricted to contributing an amount related to their shareholding (or to their guarantee where companies are limited by guarantee). The Limited Liability Partnerships Act 2000 created a new type of body, the limited liability partnership (LLP). Since April 2001 a firm has been able to be incorporated as an LLP, with the organisational flexibility and tax status of a partnership but with limited liability for its members.

Companies may be either public or private; about 12,800 are public limited companies (plcs). A company must satisfy certain conditions before it can become a plc. It must be limited by shares and meet specified minimum capital requirements. Private companies are generally prohibited from offering their shares to the public.

Company Law and Corporate Governance

Company law is designed to meet the need for proper regulation of business, to maintain open markets and to create safeguards for those wishing to invest in companies or do business with them. It takes account of EC Directives on company law, and on company and group accounts and their auditing.

In 1998 the DTI initiated a fundamental review of company law to produce a modern framework which encourages both competitiveness and accountability. The review was overseen by an independent steering group of experts, and the group's final report and recommendations to the Government were published in July 2001. Key recommendations, which, if accepted by the Government, would need to be implemented through a new Companies Act, include:

- simplification of the law for small companies, with simpler decision-making and administrative requirements and less burdensome accounting and audit obligations;
- a statutory statement of directors' duties to encourage responsible and informed decision-making;
- an operating and financial review, to improve the quality of reporting by larger companies;
- tighter annual reporting cycles, with more effective use of new technology to open up financial and other information for shareholders and others; and
- streamlined procedures to remove unnecessary constraints and costs, and to improve the operation of the law.

The Government believes that greater business involvement in corporate social responsibility (CSR) can make an important contribution to addressing social problems, help to tackle deprivation and promote a fairer, more inclusive society, while at the same time improving business competitiveness. In March 2001 it produced its first report on CSR, business and society, and identified four key priorities for government:

- promoting good practice, in particular in the provision of advice to SMEs;
- supporting work to demonstrate the business case, in particular in two areas where the Government is keen to see greater business involvement—investment in deprived communities and work to improve adult literacy and numeracy skills;
- promoting international action on CSR; and
- coordinating action across government departments.

Insolvency and Bankruptcy

The Government has announced its intention to make major changes to the law on insolvency and bankruptcy. In the White Paper *Opportunity for All in a World of Change*, it announced that insolvency law and practice would be brought up to date to help enhance entrepreneurial culture. Further details were given in the White Paper *Productivity and Enterprise: Insolvency—A Second Chance*, published in July 2001. This modernisation would build on the provisions of the Insolvency Act 2000, which gives more time to small firms in short-term financial difficulties to agree a rescue plan with their creditors, and has speeded up the process of disqualifying unfit company directors. Following a review of the law on personal bankruptcy, the Government is developing proposals to distinguish between those who fail to save their business for reasons beyond their control (such as insufficient funds) despite their best efforts and those who are irresponsible, reckless or negligent. For the large majority of bankrupts whose failure is genuine, the Government is proposing a much earlier discharge from bankruptcy. Those who are irresponsible, reckless or negligent may be subject to restrictions for up to 15 years.

Regulation of Business

The Regulatory Reform Act 2001 provides a new mechanism for reforming regulatory regimes affecting business and other sectors. The Government has identified over 50 potential reforms using the Act, to deal with outdated and over-complex legislation. Consultation documents have been issued containing proposals in a number of areas, including grants and loans for modernising private sector housing, licensing hours for public houses, business leases, gaming machines (allowing people to use banknotes and 'smartcards') and partnerships (where the restriction on professional and other groups from forming partnerships of over 20 people would be ended).

The Cabinet Office's Regulatory Impact Unit works to ensure that all proposals for regulations are fully assessed before their introduction and that the benefits justify the costs, while the Small Business Service assesses proposals from the point of view of small firms to ensure that they are not disproportionately affected. Each government department has a minister responsible for its regulatory reform programme, and these ministers are called to account by the Panel for Regulatory Accountability, which is chaired by the Minister for the Cabinet Office.

Industrial Associations

The Confederation of British Industry (CBI) (*www.cbi.org.uk*) is the largest business organisation in the UK. With a membership comprising companies and trade associations, it represents some 200,000 firms which employ about 7.5 million people. The CBI's objective is to help create and sustain the conditions in which British business can compete and prosper, both in the UK and overseas. Examples of its work include lobbying to minimise the burden of regulation and campaigning to spread best practice. The CBI also offers a wide range of advisory services, including a series of regular economic surveys. It is the British member of the Union of Industrial and Employers' Confederations (UNICE). The CBI has 13 regional offices and an office in Brussels, and opened an office in Washington in the United States in 2001.

The British Chambers of Commerce (BCC) comprise nationally a network of chambers of commerce, which are local, independent, non-profit-making organisations funded by membership subscriptions. With over 2,500 staff covering more than 100 locations, the network provides a wide range of services for its membership of over 135,000 businesses. Services provided include business training, commercial services, export-related services, financial services and access to information resources. The BCC represents business views to the Government at national and local levels and is also part of the global network of chambers of commerce.

The Institute of Directors (IOD) has around 53,000 members in the UK. It provides business advisory services on matters affecting company directors, such as corporate management, insolvency and career counselling, and represents the interests of members to authorities in the UK and EU. In autumn 2000 it opened the first of 20 new business centres for SMEs in UK cities.

Enterprise Insight (*www.enterpriseinsight.co.uk*), a government-supported initiative launched in 2000 and led by a company owned jointly by the BCC, CBI and IOD, is aiming to encourage more positive attitudes to enterprise among young people aged 5 to 30 and to develop their entrepreneurial skills. Up to 1,000 'ambassadors' from business are helping to develop closer links between schools and the business community.

The Federation of Small Businesses is the largest pressure group promoting the interests of the self-employed and small firms. The Federation has 160,000 members, and provides them with expert information and guidance on subjects such as taxation, employment, health and safety, and insurance.

Trade associations represent companies that produce or sell a particular product or group of products. They exist to supply common services, regulate trading practices and represent their members in dealings with government departments. For information on trade associations and trade unions see chapter 11.

Further Reading

Budget 2001. Investing for the Long Term: Building Opportunity and Prosperity for All. Economic and Fiscal Strategy Report and Financial Statement and Budget Report March 2001. HM Treasury. The Stationery Office, 2001.

Modern Company Law for a Competitive Economy. Final Report of the Company Law Review Steering Group. 2 vols. Department of Trade and Industry, 2001.

Opportunity for All in a World of Change. Cm 5052. Department of Trade and Industry and Department for Education and Employment. The Stationery Office, 2001.

Productivity and Enterprise: Insolvency—A Second Chance. Cm 5234. Department of Trade and Industry. The Stationery Office, 2001.

Productivity and Enterprise: A World Class Competition Regime. Cm 5233. Department of Trade and Industry. The Stationery Office, 2001.

Trade and Industry: The Government's Expenditure Plans 2001–02 to 2003–04 and Main Estimates 2001–02. Cm 5112. The Stationery Office, 2001.

UK Competitiveness Indicators: Second Edition. Department of Trade and Industry, 2001.

United Kingdom National Accounts—the Blue Book (annual). Office for National Statistics. The Stationery Office.

Websites

Department of Trade and Industry: www.dti.gov.uk
HM Treasury: www.hm-treasury.gov.uk
National Statistics: www.statistics.gov.uk

23 Public Finance

Main Programmes	399	Main Sources of Revenue	404
Debt Management	403		

The UK Government's spending and revenue are forecast to approach £400 billion in 2001–02. Total public expenditure is forecast to grow by 3¾% a year in real terms in the three years to 2003–04. Public finances have been improving, reflecting higher revenues and the relatively low growth in social security spending and the lower cost of interest payments on government debt. As a result, more resources are available and are being allocated to key public services, such as education and health.

Total Managed Expenditure—the main concept in the management of public expenditure (see p. 401)—rose, in terms of 1999–2000 prices, from £262.4 billion in 1979–80 to £343.5 billion in 1999–2000. During this period it peaked as a proportion of Gross Domestic Product (GDP) at 48.6% in 1982–83, but by 1999–2000 had fallen to 37.9%. In the same period net taxes and social security contributions as a proportion of GDP ranged between 33% and 39%, and in 1999–2000 were 36.9%.

MAIN PROGRAMMES

The 2000 Spending Review rolled forward the three-year planning cycle, established in the Comprehensive Spending Review in 1998, and set new *departmental* spending plans for 2001–02 to 2003–04. Current spending is planned to grow by 2½% a year in real terms, in line with the UK's economic growth rate, while net public sector investment is expected to rise to 1.7% of GDP by 2003–04.

Spending Priorities

The main categories of expenditure are shown in Figure 23.2 on p. 401. Social security is the biggest single element, involving expenditure of £109 billion (nearly 28% of spending) in 2001–02, followed by spending on the National Health Service (NHS) of £59 billion and on education of £50 billion.

Areas in which the Government is planning higher expenditure include education, health, transport, law and order, deprived neighbourhoods, and science. For example, spending on the NHS is planned to rise at an annual rate of growth in real terms of 6.3% between 1999–2000 and 2003–04, and is being accompanied by reforms to the NHS under the NHS Plan (see p. 188). In the March 2001 Budget the Government announced an additional £2.3 billion of spending over the next three years in three areas:

- £1 billion on education, including £600 million which will be made available to head teachers to modernise school buildings and equipment and to improve

Table 23.1: Current and Capital Budgets *£ billion*

	Outturn 1999–2000	Estimate 2000–01	Projections 2001–02	2002–03	2003–04
Current budget					
Current receipts	358.7	383.2	398	416	432
Current expenditure	325.3	346.0	367	386	407
Depreciation	14.6	14.9	15	16	17
Surplus on current budget[1]	**19.2**	**23.1**	**17**	**15**	**8**
Capital budget					
Gross investment	23.0	26.3	30	35	39
less asset sales	–4.8	–4.1	–4	–4	–4
less depreciation	–14.6	–14.9	–15	–16	–17
Net investment	3.5	7.4	11	15	19
Net borrowing[1]	**–16.0**	**–16.4**	**–6**	**1**	**10**
Public sector net debt at end of year	340.1	307.5	307	314	330

[1] Excluding windfall tax receipts and associated spending.
Source: *Budget 2001. Investing for the Long Term: Building Opportunity and Prosperity for All. Economic and Fiscal Strategy Report and Financial Statement and Budget Report March 2001*

pupil attainment, and £200 million to help schools implement recruitment and retention incentives for teachers;

- £1 billion on health, including £450 million for hospital investment to help pay for new equipment, such as scanners; and
- £300 million to help tackle misuse of drugs, with extra resources, for example, to Crime and Disorder Reduction Partnerships (see p. 216).

Local authorities are estimated to have spent about £91 billion in 2000–01, around a quarter of public expenditure. The main categories of expenditure are education, law and order, personal social services, housing and other environmental services, and roads and transport.

Net public investment is planned to rise to £19 billion by 2003–04 (see Table 23.1). The Capital Modernisation Fund is supporting innovative capital projects aimed at improving delivery of public services, and funds have been allocated to departments on a competitive basis. Allocations in the first three rounds of funding totalled £3.3 billion, including £470 million to provide 1,000 UK Online and City learning centres across the UK (see p. 143) and £68 million to match job seekers to employers online. Under the Invest to Save Budget, some £380 million will have been allocated up to the period 2003–04 to projects designed to improve public service operations through partnership between public sector bodies.

Control of Spending

In the 1998 Comprehensive Spending Review, the Government introduced a new framework for public spending. The main elements of the reforms include:

- replacing the annual Public Expenditure Survey with firm plans set for three years, through Departmental Expenditure Limits (DELs). Where expenditure such as social security benefit payments cannot be planned on a multi-year basis, it is subject to annual scrutiny as part of the Budget process—such expenditure is denoted Annually Managed Expenditure;
- separating spending into capital and resource (formerly current) budgets with tight controls on transfers from capital to resource spending to ensure that short-term pressures do not squeeze out essential investment;
- allowing underspending within DELs in a given year to be carried over to the

Figure 23.2:
Forecast UK Government Expenditure and Revenue 2001–02

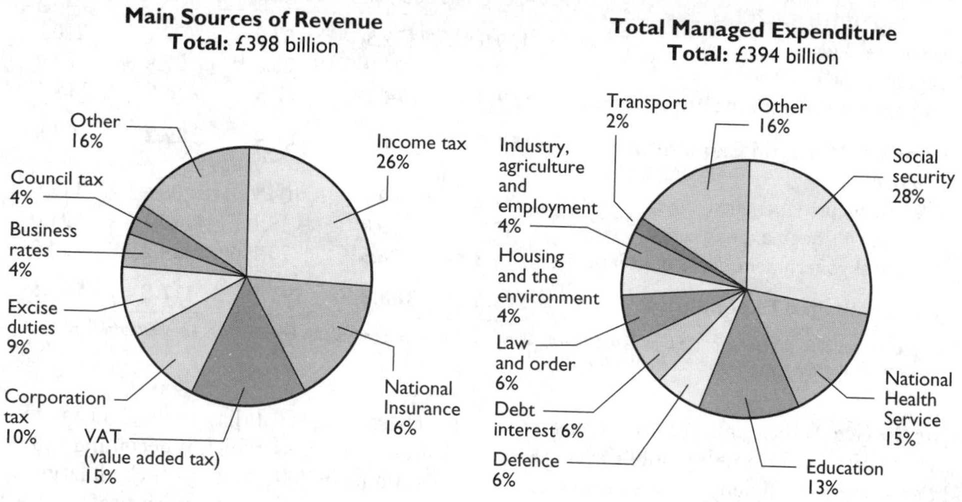

Source: HM Treasury

> In the third round of the Invest to Save Budget, announced in March 2001, 123 projects were selected for funding totalling £60 million. Among the projects are:
>
> - 'Police Direct', a project involving the police and criminal justice organisations that will develop a police 'portal' to provide services electronically to the citizen in the most efficient and cost-effective manner;
> - 'Skill Force', in which retired military instructors in a number of pilot schemes will train disaffected youngsters aged 15 or 16, with the aim of reducing truancy and exclusion from school, cutting juvenile crime and raising educational attainment; and
> - '21st Century Citizen', a project that will support the inclusion of citizenship as a subject in the National Curriculum (see p. 132) by pooling the resources of the Office for National Statistics, the Public Record Office and the British Library to create an online resource for schools.

following year, so assisting departments in managing their budgets and avoiding wasteful end-of-year spending surges;

- establishing the National Asset Register to improve the utilisation of existing public sector assets (valued at over £500 billion, around one-eighth of the UK's total assets), while encouraging departments to dispose of surplus assets;
- establishing Departmental Investment Strategies to demonstrate that capital investment is being used efficiently and effectively—these strategies are taken into account in the allocation of resources from the Capital Modernisation Fund; and
- introducing cross-departmental reviews to tackle problems such as crime, drugs and social exclusion—15 were conducted in the 2000 Spending Review.

The main concept in the measurement of public expenditure is Total Managed Expenditure (see Table 23.3), over half of which is managed through DELs and the remainder is Annually Managed Expenditure.

In connection with the 2000 Spending Review, departments have prepared new

Table 23.3: Total Managed Expenditure *£ billion*

	Outturn 1999–2000	Estimate 2000–01	Projections 2001–02	2002–03	2003–04
Resource Budget	159.9	172.3	187.0	199.1	210.7
Capital Budget	19.4	21.9	25.3	29.4	34.4
Departmental Expenditure Limits	**179.3**	**194.2**	**212.3**	**228.5**	**245.1**
Annually Managed Expenditure	**164.1**	**174.0**	**181.4**	**189.2**	**197.5**
of which:					
Social security benefits	97.2	99.1	104.9	108.6	113.5
Locally financed expenditure	17.2	18.0	19.1	20.1	21.0
Central government gross debt interest	25.3	26.6	23.1	24.2	24.0
Total Managed Expenditure	**343.5**	**368.3**	**393.7**	**417.8**	**442.6**

Source: *Budget 2001. Investing for the Long Term: Building Opportunity and Prosperity for All. Economic and Fiscal Strategy Report and Financial Statement and Budget Report March 2001*

Public Service Agreements (PSAs), listing specific targets for improving public services and departmental efficiency. For example, there are PSA targets on reducing preventable deaths from cancer and heart disease (see chapter 13) and on increasing pupil attainment. Departmental performance against the targets is scrutinised by a Cabinet Committee, which is chaired by the Chancellor of the Exchequer, and supported by a Public Services Productivity Panel of experts from outside government. In November 2000 a White Paper was issued, containing new Service Delivery Agreements for every government department, setting out how the PSAs will be achieved.

The Office of Government Commerce (OGC) was established as an office of HM Treasury in 2000 to improve the efficiency and effectiveness of the Government's civil procurement budget, of around £13 billion a year. It aims to work with civil departments, agencies and non-departmental public bodies as a catalyst to achieve value for money in their commercial activities. The OGC's activities include development of best practice, the management of strategic suppliers, wider use of 'e-procurement', improving the management of major projects, and raising the professionalism and skills of staff involved in procurement and project management. The OGC is leading a wide-ranging programme to modernise procurement in government and to deliver substantial value for money gains by developing the Government's collective purchasing power. It has established a new 'Gateway' process, which is becoming fully operational in 2001, under which all large, complex or novel projects must use independent review teams to inform each stage of procurement decision-making.

Under the Government Resources and Accounts Act 2000, new Resource Accounting and Budgeting (RAB) procedures (see p. 387) became fully operational in April 2001. They apply the financial reporting practices of the private sector and much of the rest of the public sector to government departments' accounts, Estimates and Budgets. The changes are designed to improve efficiency and focus more on departmental objectives and outputs in terms of resources used rather than the money available for spending. According to HM Treasury, this represented the biggest overhaul of financial management in central government since the 1860s.

Examination of Public Expenditure

Examination of public expenditure is carried out by select committees of the House of Commons. These study in detail the activities of particular government departments and question ministers and officials. The Public Accounts Committee considers the accounts of government departments, executive agencies and other public sector bodies, and examines reports by the Comptroller and Auditor General on departments and their use of resources.

Audit of the Government's spending is exercised through the functions of the Comptroller and Auditor General, the head of the National Audit Office (NAO). The NAO's responsibilities include certifying the accounts of all government departments and executive agencies, and those of a wide range of other public sector bodies; scrutinising the efficiency and effectiveness of their operations; examining revenue accounts and inventories; and reporting the results of these examinations to Parliament. The Government is considering a review of central government audit arrangements and accountability, published in February 2001.

Public-Private Partnerships

The Government sees Public-Private Partnerships (PPPs) as a key factor in the delivery of high-quality public services, by bringing in private sector management, finance and ownership with the intention of improving the value for money, efficiency and quality of these services. The PPPs cover a variety of arrangements, including joint ventures; outsourcing; the sale of equity stakes in government-owned businesses; and the Private Finance Initiative (PFI), in which the public sector specifies the service needed, in terms of the outputs required, and private sector companies compete to meet the requirements. Major PPP projects include the Channel Tunnel Rail Link (see p. 371), a scheme for investment in the National Air Traffic Services (see p. 376) and several projects for investment in health and education.

Partnerships UK was set up in 2000 to help the public sector develop more effective partnerships with the private sector by building on the work previously carried out by a task force within HM Treasury. In April 2001 Partnerships UK became a PPP, following the sale of 51% of the company to private sector investors, with 49% shareholding retained by HM Treasury and the Scottish Executive.

DEBT MANAGEMENT

The Government finances its borrowing requirement by selling debt to the private sector. Public sector net debt has generally been falling since 1996–97. At the end of March 2001 it was £306 billion, 31.6% of GDP, compared with 36.8% at the end of March 2000. Public sector net borrowing has declined substantially, and was in surplus in 2000–01 by around £16 billion (see Table 23.1) as a consequence of the strict fiscal frameworks employed by the Government.

The objective of the Government's debt management policy is to minimise, over the long term, the cost of meeting the Government's financing needs, taking into account risk, while ensuring that debt management policy is consistent with the objectives of monetary policy. Responsibility for managing government debt rests with a Treasury agency, the United Kingdom Debt Management Office.

Gilt-edged Stock

The major debt instrument, government bonds, is known as gilt-edged stock ('gilts'), as government securities are judged by the market as having the lowest risk of default. Gilts include 'conventionals', which generally pay fixed rates of interest and redemption sums; and index-linked stocks, on which principal and interest are linked to movements in the Retail Prices Index. Gilt issues are primarily by auction. The annual Debt and Reserves Management Report sets out the framework for issuing gilts in the coming year. The financing requirement has been reduced to a relatively low level. In 2000–01, £5.5 billion of debt was bought back: six reverse auctions were held, which enabled the Government to buy back £4.1 billion (cash) debt from the market and £1.4 billion of gilts were bought back as a result of net purchases in the secondary market.

At the end of December 2000 holdings of marketable gilts were estimated at £287 billion. This comprised £215 billion of conventional gilts, £70 billion of index-linked gilts and £2 billion of Treasury Bills. Insurance companies and pension funds hold just over 65% of gilts, UK households just over 7% and participants in the rest of the world 18%.

MAIN SOURCES OF REVENUE

Government revenue is forecast to be £398 billion in 2001–02. The main sources (see Figure 23.2) are:

- taxes on income (together with profits), which include personal income tax, corporation tax and petroleum revenue tax (see p. 493);
- taxes on capital, which include inheritance tax, capital gains tax, council tax and non-domestic rates;
- taxes on expenditure, which include VAT (value added tax) and customs and excise duties; and
- National Insurance contributions (see chapter 12).

The March 2001 Budget included:

- support for families and children, including increases in the new children's tax credit, with a higher rate in the first year of a child's birth (see p. 405) and a series of measures on maternity pay and parental leave (see p. 159);
- a widening of the 10p tax band (see p. 405) by more than the rate of increase in inflation;
- a series of measures aimed at encouraging cleaner road transport, and improving the efficiency of the road haulage industry (see p. 408);
- measures to assist regeneration; and
- additional public expenditure in three of the Government's priority areas (see p. 399).

Taxation Policy

The primary aim of tax policy is to raise sufficient revenue for the Government to pay for the services that its policies require, and to service its debt, while keeping the overall burden of tax as low as possible. The Government has based its tax policy on the principles of encouraging work, raising investment, and promoting fairness and opportunity. It has taken measures designed to improve productivity, increase employment opportunities, tackle child poverty and protect the environment.

Collection of Taxes and Duties

The Inland Revenue assesses and collects taxes on income, profits and capital, and stamp duty (see p. 409), and its Contributions Office is responsible for collecting National Insurance contributions. HM Customs and Excise collects the most important taxes on expenditure (VAT and most duties). Local authorities collect the main local taxes, such as council tax.

Most wage and salary earners pay their income tax under a Pay-As-You-Earn (PAYE) system whereby tax is deducted and accounted for to the Inland Revenue by the employer, in a way which enables most employees to pay the correct amount of tax during the year.

Under the self-assessment system for collecting personal taxation, some 8 million people—primarily higher-rate taxpayers, the self-employed and those receiving investment income (particularly where this is paid without tax being deducted at source)—are required to complete an annual tax return for the Inland Revenue. Such taxpayers may calculate their own tax liability, although they can choose to have the calculations done by the Inland Revenue if they return the form by the end of September.

Electronic transmission is already used to a limited extent in the collection of taxes and duties. To encourage greater use, tax discounts have been introduced for electronic filing of tax returns and payment of tax.

The UK has agreements governing double taxation with over 100 countries, the largest network of tax treaties in the world. They are intended to avoid double taxation arising, to deal with cross-border economic activity, and to prevent fiscal discrimination against UK business interests overseas. They also include provisions to counter tax avoidance and evasion.

Following a review of the informal economy, published in March 2000, which found that substantial sums were being lost to the Exchequer, the Government set up a confidential helpline and provided advice on tax and National Insurance for people starting their own business. To combat persistent tax offences and benefit fraud, it has introduced a number of measures, including making fraudulent evasion of income tax a statutory offence and requiring newly self-employed people to notify the Inland Revenue within three months of starting up a business.

Taxes on Income

Income Tax

Income tax is the biggest single contributor to government receipts, accounting for around 11% of GDP in 2000–01, when it brought in net receipts of £106.7 billion. In general, it is charged on all income originating in the UK—although some forms of income, such as child benefit, are exempt—and on all income arising abroad of people resident in the UK. Income tax is imposed for the year of assessment beginning on 6 April. The tax rates and bands for 2000–01 and 2001–02 are shown in Table 23.4. The basic rate of 22% is the lowest basic rate for nearly 70 years. As part of the Government's reforms designed to make it financially worthwhile for people to work at all levels of the labour market, especially those with low incomes, a 10% starting rate of income tax took effect in April 1999. In the March 2001 Budget the starting rate band was widened by £300 above indexation (to take account of inflation) from April 2001. Of around 27.6 million income taxpayers, 2.9 million are expected to pay tax only at the starting rate of 10% in 2001–02, 21 million at 22% and 2.8 million at 40%, while 0.8 million 'savers' will have a marginal rate of 10% or 20%.

Allowances and reliefs reduce an individual's income tax liability. All taxpayers are entitled to a personal allowance against income from all sources, with a higher allowance for the elderly (see Table 23.4). One of the most significant reliefs, which is designed to encourage people to save towards their retirement, covers contributions to pension schemes, including the new stakeholder pension introduced in April 2001 (see p. 172). Personal tax-free saving is also encouraged through the Individual Savings Account (ISA) (see p. 521).

In line with its policies of improving work incentives, promoting a fair and efficient tax system, and supporting families, the Government has changed the system of allowances and is introducing a series of tax credits. The married couple's allowance was abolished in April 2000, except for married couples where at least one of the two was aged 65 or over on 5 April 2000. Its successor, introduced in April 2001, is the Children's Tax Credit (CTC), worth up to £520 a year for families with one or more children under 16 living with them; the credit is reduced where the main earner in the family is a higher rate taxpayer. From April 2002 a higher rate of CTC, worth up to £1,040 a year, will be introduced for families in the year of a child's birth, to recognise the extra costs associated with having a baby. The Working Families' Tax Credit (WFTC—see chapter 12) is designed to provide a guaranteed minimum income for working families. From 2003 an integrated child credit will bring together the support for children in the WFTC, the CTC and other forms of support, while a new employment tax credit will extend the principles of the WFTC to people without children. A new Pension Credit is also planned for 2003, with the aim of rewarding pensioners for having built up savings during their working lives or for continuing to work beyond the state pension age (see p. 175).

Corporation Tax

The UK rate of corporation tax, payable by companies on their income and capital gains, is the lowest among major industrial countries. The main rate of tax is 30%. Two lower rates are also levied: a starting rate of 10% for the smallest firms (those with annual profits of up to £10,000) and a small companies' rate of 20% levied on firms with annual profits between £50,000 and £300,000. A sliding scale of relief is allowed for companies with annual profits between £10,000 and £50,000 and between £300,000 and £1.5 million, so that the overall average rate paid by these firms is between 10% and 20% and between 20% and 30% respectively.

Some capital expenditure—on machinery and plant, industrial buildings, agricultural

Table 23.4: Tax Allowances and Bands £

	2000–01	2001–02
Income tax allowances:		
Personal allowance:		
age under 65	4,385	4,535
age 65–74	5,790	5,990
age 75 and over	6,050	6,260
Married couple's allowance:[1]		
for those born before 6 April 1935	5,185	5,365
age 75 and over	5,255	5,435
minimum amount[2]	2,000	2,070
Income limit for age-related allowances	17,000	17,600
Children's tax credit[1]	—	5,200
Blind person's allowance	1,400	1,450
Bands of taxable income:[3]		
Starting rate of 10%	0–1,520	0–1,880
Basic rate of 22%	1,521–28,400	1,881–29,400
Higher rate of 40%	over 28,400	over 29,400

1 The rate of relief for these allowances is restricted to 10%.
2 The minimum amount of married couple's allowance is the level at which the tapered withdrawal of the allowance ceases for taxpayers who have income over the income limit.
3 The rate of tax applicable to savings income in the basic rate band is 20%. For dividends the rates applicable are 10% for income below the basic rate upper limit and 32.5% above that.
Source: Inland Revenue

buildings and scientific research, for example—may qualify for relief in the form of capital allowances. To boost investment in manufacturing and services, the 40% first-year allowance for expenditure on machinery or plant by small or medium-sized businesses has been made permanent. To encourage more companies to invest in information and communications technology (ICT) and adopt electronic commerce, small businesses are able to claim 100% first-year allowances on investments in ICT between 1 April 2000 and 31 March 2003, so enabling them to write off immediately the entire cost against their taxable income. A new research and development (R&D) tax credit for small firms took effect in April 2000. In March 2001 the Government published a consultation document containing its proposals for a new tax credit to encourage R&D and innovation among larger firms.

Taxes on Capital

Capital Gains Tax

Capital gains tax (CGT) is payable by individuals and trusts on gains realised from the disposal of assets. It is payable on the amount by which total chargeable gains for a year exceed the exempt amount (£7,500 for individuals and £3,750 for most trusts in 2001–02). Gains on some types of asset are exempt from CGT, including the principal private residence, government securities, certain corporate bonds, and gains on holdings of Personal Equity Plans and ISAs. For individuals, CGT in 2001–02 will be payable at 10%, 20% or 40%, depending on a person's marginal income tax rate.

CGT taper relief was introduced in 1998 to succeed the previous system of indexation relief to take account of inflation. The relief reduces the amount of the chargeable gain depending on how long an asset has been held. Changes to the taper relief were introduced in 2000 with the intention of boosting productivity, stimulating employee share ownership, and encouraging 'business angel' investors to provide risk capital for growing companies. The current CGT taper reliefs reduce the percentage of the gain that is chargeable for a business asset from 100% for assets held for less than one year to 25% for assets held for four years or more. For non-business assets the chargeable gain falls from

100% for assets held for less than three years to 60% for assets held for ten years or longer.

Inheritance Tax

Inheritance tax is charged on estates at the time of death and on gifts made within seven years of death; most other lifetime transfers are not taxed. There are several important exemptions, including transfers between spouses, and gifts and bequests to UK charities, major political parties and heritage bodies. In general, business assets and farmland are exempt from inheritance tax, so that most family businesses can be passed on without a tax charge.

Tax is charged at a single rate of 40% above a threshold: £242,000 in 2001–02. Only about 4% of estates a year become liable for an inheritance tax bill.

Taxes on Expenditure

Value Added Tax (VAT)

VAT is a broadly based expenditure tax, which is collected at each stage in the production and distribution of goods and services. The final tax is payable by the consumer. The standard rate is 17.5%, with a reduced rate of 5% on a number of goods and services, including domestic fuel and power, and the installation of energy-saving materials in homes. Under the Finance Act 2001, the 5% rate is being extended to cover the cost of converting residential properties into a different number of dwellings (such as a house into flats or into a residential care home), the renovation of homes empty for three years or longer, and the purchase of children's car seats.

Certain goods and services are relieved from VAT, either by being charged at a zero rate or by being exempt:

- Under zero rating, a taxable person does not charge tax to a customer but reclaims any VAT paid to suppliers. Among the main categories where zero rating applies are goods exported to other countries; most food; water and sewerage for non-business use; domestic and international passenger transport; books, newspapers and periodicals; construction of new residential buildings; young children's clothing and footwear; drugs and medicines supplied on prescription; specified aids for handicapped people; and certain supplies by or to charities.
- For exempt goods or services, a taxable person does not charge any VAT but is not entitled to reclaim the VAT on goods and services bought for his or her business. The main categories where exemption applies are many supplies of land and buildings; financial services; postal services; betting; gaming; lotteries; much education and training; and health and welfare.

The March 2001 Budget contained a package of measures designed to help small businesses. A series of measures is being introduced with the intention of helping small companies as they grow, allowing them to manage their entry into the VAT system and improve their cash flow. This has included raising the annual level of turnover above which traders must register for VAT to £54,000 from April 2001. More businesses are expected to benefit from lower compliance costs as a result of the decision to raise the upper limit for filing VAT returns on an annual rather than a quarterly basis from £300,000 to £600,000 in April 2001.

Customs Duties

Customs duties are chargeable on goods from outside the European Union in accordance with its Common Customs Tariff. Goods can move freely across internal EU frontiers without making customs entries at importation or stopping for routine fiscal checks. For commercial consignments, excise duty and VAT are charged in the Member State of destination, at the rate in force in that state.

Excise Duties

Mineral oils used as road fuel are subject to higher rates of duty than those used for other purposes. As part of government measures to encourage the use of more environmentally friendly fuels, there are lower rates on fuels such as ultra low sulphur petrol, ultra low sulphur diesel, and on road fuel gases, such as liquefied petroleum gas and compressed natural gas. The March 2001 Budget further reduced the duty on these fuels. Kerosene not used as road or motor fuel, most lubricating oils and oils used for certain industrial, horticultural and marine uses are free of duty or attract very low rates. Fuel substitutes are taxed at the same rate as the corresponding mineral oil.

Cigarette duty is charged partly as a cash amount per cigarette and partly as a percentage of retail price. Duty on other tobacco products is based on weight. To support the Government's health objectives (see chapter 13), tobacco duty has been increased in real terms in recent years and was increased in line with inflation in the March 2001 Budget. A new strategy was introduced in March 2000 to tackle the rise in smuggling, including extra Customs officers, additional specialist investigators and new equipment, such as X-ray scanners. In the first nine months of operation Customs confiscated 2.1 billion cigarettes destined for the UK market.

Duties are levied on spirits, beer, wine, cider and other alcoholic drinks according to alcoholic strength and volume. Spirits used for scientific, medical, research and industrial processes are generally free of duty.

Duties are charged on off-course betting, pool betting, gaming in casinos, bingo and amusement machines. Rates vary with the particular form of gambling. In October 2001 a new 15% tax on bookmakers' gross profits will replace general betting duty of 6.75% on total stakes (see p. 299). On the National Lottery (see p. 123) there is a 12% duty on gross stakes, but no tax on winnings.

Insurance premium tax is levied on most general insurance at a rate of 5%, with a higher rate of 17.5% on travel insurance and on insurance sold by suppliers of cars and domestic appliances.

A new structure for air passenger duty took effect in April 2001, introducing a differential when there are different classes of travel on a flight. The rate of duty for flights to UK and to European Economic Area (EEA) destinations is £5 for the lowest class and £10 for any other class; the equivalent rates to non-EEA destinations are £20 and £40 respectively. All flights from airports in the Scottish Highlands and Islands are now exempt from duty in recognition of their remoteness and dependence on air travel.

The system of **vehicle excise duty (VED)** changed on 1 March 2001 with the introduction of graduated annual rates on new cars. There are four VED bands, depending on the rate of carbon dioxide emissions and the type of fuel used: £100 to £155 for cars using petrol, and £110 to £160 for those using diesel. In addition, cars using cleaner fuels are subject to a VED discount, with the overall duty varying from £90 to £150. For cars first registered before 1 March 2001 the standard rate of VED is £160, with a lower rate of £105 for cars up to 1,549 cc.

A new system of VED for goods vehicles will come into operation in December 2001, with seven broad rate bands replacing the current system of around 100 different rates. These new rates better reflect the environmental and road damage caused by goods vehicles, and are set according to the gross vehicle weight and the number of axles. The new annual standard rate will range from £165 to £1,850, with the rate for lorries with reduced pollution certificates ranging from £160 to £1,350. The UK rates will be among the lowest in Europe for the cleanest lorries. Duty on buses varies according to seating capacity, and duty on motorcycles according to engine capacity.

Landfill tax is levied at £12 a tonne, and this will rise by £1 a tonne each year until 2004, when it will be reviewed; a lower rate of £2 a tonne applies for inert waste. To reduce the environmental impact of quarrying, a new aggregates levy of £1.60 a tonne on the extraction of sand, gravel and crushed rock will be introduced in April 2002. Some of the revenue from the levy will be used through a new Sustainability Fund to address the environmental costs associated with aggregates extraction, including noise, dust, visual intrusion, loss of amenity and damage to biodiversity.

The climate change levy was introduced on 1 April 2001 on the non-domestic use of energy at the rate of 0.43p per kilowatt-hour (kWh) for electricity, 0.15p per kWh for gas,

0.96p per kilogramme (kg) for liquefied petroleum gas and 1.17p per kg for solid fuels. All revenues are recycled back to business through a reduction in employers' National Insurance contributions and additional support for energy efficiency measures (see p. 492). An 80% discount on the levy is available to energy-intensive business sectors that have agreed targets with the Government for increasing energy efficiency and reducing greenhouse gas emissions.

Stamp Duty

Some transfers are subject to stamp duty. Transfers of shares generally attract duty at 0.5% of the cost, while certain types of document, such as declarations of trust, generally attract a small fixed duty of £5. Transfers by gift and transfers to charities are exempt. Duty on land and property is payable at 1% of the total price when above £60,000, 3% above £250,000 and 4% over £500,000.

Local Authority Revenue

Local authorities in Great Britain have four main sources of revenue income: grants from central government; council tax; non-domestic rates (sometimes known as business rates); and sales, fees and charges. About 75% of expenditure (excluding sales, fees and charges) is financed by government grants and redistributed non-domestic rates.

Non-domestic rates are a tax on the occupiers of non-domestic property. The rateable value is assessed by reference to annual rents and reviewed every five years. Separate non-domestic rates are set for England, Wales and Scotland, and collected by local authorities. They are paid into separate national pools and redistributed to local authorities in proportion to their population.

Domestic property in Great Britain is generally subject to the council tax. Each dwelling is allocated to one of eight valuation bands, based on its capital value (the amount it might have sold for on the open market) in April 1991. Discounts are available for dwellings with fewer than two resident adults, and those on low incomes may receive council tax benefit of up to 100% of the tax bill (see p. 181). In 2001–02, in England the average council tax payable per dwelling will be £741: £764 in London, £684 in other metropolitan areas and £755 in shire areas.

In Northern Ireland, rates—local taxes on domestic and non-domestic properties—are based on the rental value of the property. For 2001–02 the average domestic rates bill in Northern Ireland will be £420.

Further Reading

Budget 2001. Investing for the Long Term: Building Opportunity and Prosperity for All. Economic and Fiscal Strategy Report and Financial Statement and Budget Report March 2001. HM Treasury. The Stationery Office, 2001.

Prudent for a Purpose: Building Opportunity and Security for All. 2000 Spending Review: New Public Spending Plans 2001–2004. Cm 4807. HM Treasury. The Stationery Office, 2000.

Annual Reports

Debt and Reserves Management Report. HM Treasury.

Public Expenditure Statistical Analyses. HM Treasury. The Stationery Office.

Websites

HM Treasury: www.hm-treasury.gov.uk

Inland Revenue: www.inlandrevenue.gov.uk

HM Customs and Excise: www.hmce.gov.uk

24 International Trade and Investment

Balance of Payments	410	Government Services	421
International Trade Policy	415		

Trade has been of vital importance to the British economy for hundreds of years. Although it has under 1% of the population, the UK is the world's fifth largest trading nation, accounting for over 5% of world trade in goods and services in 1999. About one in four British jobs is linked to business overseas. As one of 15 Member States of the European Union (EU), the world's largest established trading group, 52% of the UK's trade in goods and services in 2000 was with fellow EU members. The UK has a higher degree of inward and outward investment than any of the other G7 economies, relative to Gross Domestic Product (GDP), and was second only to the United States as a destination for international direct investment in 1999. Within the World Trade Organisation (WTO), the UK as part of the EU is calling for a new round of negotiations aimed at lowering tariffs, eliminating non-tariff barriers and liberalising world markets.

The UK exports more per head than the United States and Japan. Its sales abroad of goods and services were 21% of gross final expenditure in 2000. Receipts from trade in services (such as financial services, business services, travel, transport and communications) and investment income account for about half of total UK current account credits, and the UK consistently runs large surpluses on these accounts. The UK was the world's biggest foreign investor in 1999 and UK direct investment abroad since 1992 has significantly exceeded direct investment into the UK.

BALANCE OF PAYMENTS

The UK balance of payments measures the economic transactions between UK residents and the rest of the world. It also draws a series of balances between inward and outward transactions, provides an overall net flow of transactions between UK residents and the rest of the world, and reports how that flow is funded. Economic transactions include:

- exports and imports of goods, such as oil, agricultural products, other raw materials, machinery and transport equipment, computers, white goods (such as refrigerators and washing machines) and clothing;
- exports and imports of services, such as international transport, travel, financial and business services;
- income flows, such as dividends and interest earned by non-residents on investments in the UK and by the UK investing abroad;

- financial flows, such as investment in shares, debt securities, loans and deposits; and
- transfers, such as payments to, and receipts from, EU institutions, foreign aid and funds brought by migrants to the UK.

The balance of payments classification comprises the following groups of accounts:

- the *current account*, which comprises trade in goods and services, income (compensation of employees and investment income) and current transfers;
- the *capital account*, which comprises capital transfers and the acquisition and disposal of non-produced, non-financial assets (such as copyrights);
- the *financial account*, which covers direct, portfolio and other investment and reserve assets; and
- the *international investment position*, which measures the UK's stock of external financial assets and liabilities.

Table 24.1 summarises the UK's balance of payments position over recent years. In 2000 the current account was in deficit, at £16.2 billion, the largest since 1990. This compares with a recorded deficit of £9.9 billion in 1999. There were sharp deteriorations in both the deficit on goods and services and in the surplus on income in 2000. The capital account surplus rose from £0.8 billion in 1999 to a record £1.9 billion in 2000.

Trade in Goods and Services

Table 24.2 summarises the UK's trade in goods and services over recent years. More detailed analyses for 2000 can be found in subsequent tables. In 2000, UK exports of goods amounted to £187.1 billion and imports to £215.9 billion, giving a deficit on trade in goods of £28.8 billion, slightly higher than in 1999 and the largest deficit on record. The trade in services surplus in 2000 of £11.0 billion was marginally lower than the £11.3 billion surplus recorded in the previous year.

Commodity Composition of Goods

UK exports of goods are dominated by manufactures—finished manufactures and semi-manufactured goods. In 1971 they accounted for 84% of total goods exports. Although the advent of North Sea oil meant their share declined into the early 1980s, they have subsequently recovered and in 2000 again stood at 84% of exports of goods (see Table 24.4).

Historically the UK was predominantly an importer of foods and basic materials. However, over the last 30 years, imports of manufactures have grown rapidly. Between 1970 and 2000 the share of finished manufactures in total imports rose from 24% to 61%, while the share of basic materials fell from 14½% to just under 3%. The percentage of food, beverages and tobacco has been dropping since the 1950s, down to 7½% of imports in 2000. The UK has not had a surplus on manufactured goods since 1982.

Table 24.1: UK Balance of Payments Summary[1] *£ million*

	1990	1995	1998	1999	2000
Current account					
Trade in goods and services	–14,697	–2,809	–7,955	–14,901	–17,858
Income	–558	5,976	14,245	9,169	5,515
Current transfers	–4,258	–6,912	–6,370	–4,150	–3,828
Current balance	**–19,513**	**–3,745**	**–80**	**–9,882**	**–16,171**
Capital account	497	534	473	808	1,949
Financial account	17,529	937	–4,677	11,410	17,213
Net errors and omissions[2]	1,487	2,274	4,284	–2,336	–2,991

[1] Balance of payments basis.
[2] Amount necessary to bring the sum of all balance of payments entries to zero.
Source: ONS Quarterly Balance of Payments

Table 24.2: External Trade in Goods and Services[1] *£ million*

	1990	1995	1998	1999	2000
Exports of goods	102,313	153,725	164,092	166,198	187,131
Exports of services	31,188	48,687	61,382	64,825	67,217
Exports of goods and services	**133,501**	**202,412**	**225,474**	**231,023**	**254,348**
Imports of goods	121,020	165,449	184,629	192,365	215,940
Imports of services	27,178	39,772	48,800	53,559	56,266
Imports of goods and services	**148,198**	**205,221**	**233,429**	**245,924**	**272,206**
Balance of trade in goods	–18,707	–11,724	–20,537	–26,167	–28,809
Balance of trade in services	4,010	8,915	12,582	11,266	10,951
Balance of trade in goods and services	**–14,697**	**–2,809**	**–7,955**	**–14,901**	**–17,858**

[1] Balance of payments basis.
Source: ONS Quarterly Balance of Payments

Figure 24.3:
UK Balance of Payments in Goods and Services

Source: Office for National Statistics

Machinery and transport equipment accounted for 47% of exports and 46% of imports in 2000. Aerospace, chemicals and electronics have become increasingly significant export sectors, while textiles have declined in relative importance. Sectors with a positive balance of trade in 2000 included fuels, chemicals, beverages and tobacco.

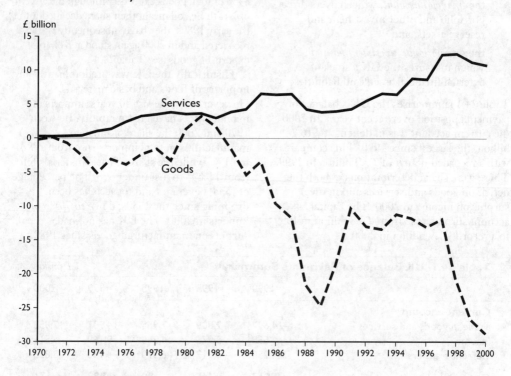

Table 24.4: Commodity Composition of Trade in Goods, 2000[1] *£ million*

		Exports	Imports	Balance
Food, beverages and tobacco		**9,900**	**16,215**	**–6,315**
Food and live animals		5,830	13,249	–7,419
of which:	Meat and meat preparations	631	2,342	–1,711
	Dairy products and eggs	657	1,177	–520
	Cereals and animal feeding stuffs	1,594	1,750	–156
	Vegetables and fruit	401	3,886	–3,485
Beverages		3,055	2,646	409
Tobacco		1,015	320	695
Basic materials		**2,600**	**6,330**	**–3,730**
Crude materials		2,442	5,834	–3,392
of which:	Wood, lumber and cork	70	1,199	–1,129
	Pulp and waste paper	79	771	–692
	Textile fibres	496	416	80
	Metal ores	752	1,816	–1,064
Animal and vegetable oils and fats		158	496	–338
Oil		**15,211**	**9,050**	**6,161**
Other fuels		**1,472**	**959**	**513**
Semi-manufactured goods		**47,580**	**49,827**	**–2,247**
Chemicals		24,895	20,588	4,307
of which:	Organic chemicals	5,682	5,335	347
	Inorganic chemicals	1,491	1,051	440
	Colouring materials	1,563	1,006	557
	Medicinal products	7,220	4,720	2,500
	Toilet preparations	2,564	1,993	571
	Plastics	3,349	4,134	–785
Manufactures classified chiefly by material		22,685	29,239	–6,554
of which:	Wood and cork manufactures	253	1,246	–993
	Paper and paperboard manufactures	2,107	4,410	–2,303
	Textile manufactures	3,059	4,364	–1,305
	Iron and steel	2,853	2,738	115
	Non-ferrous metals	3,168	3,712	–544
	Metal manufactures	3,582	4,064	–482
Finished manufactured goods		**108,682**	**131,708**	**–23,026**
Machinery and transport equipment		87,547	99,129	–11,582
	Mechanical machinery	22,142	17,837	4,305
	Electrical machinery	42,303	50,564	–8,261
	Road vehicles	15,608	23,328	–7,720
	Other transport equipment	7,494	7,400	94
Miscellaneous manufactures		21,135	32,579	–11,444
of which:	Clothing	2,701	8,510	–5,809
	Footwear	513	1,998	–1,485
	Scientific and photographic	7,334	7,244	90
Unspecified goods		**1,686**	**1,851**	**–165**
Total		**187,131**	**215,940**	**–28,809**

[1] Balance of payments basis.
Sources: ONS Quarterly Balance of Payments and *Monthly Digest of Statistics*

Table 24.5: Distribution of Trade in Goods, 2000[1]

	Value (£ million)			%	
	Exports	Imports	Balance	Exports	Imports
European Union	107,142	108,976	−1,834	57.3	50.5
Other Western Europe	7,475	13,172	−5,697	4.0	6.1
North America	33,823	33,637	186	18.1	15.6
Other OECD countries	10,926	18,093	−7,167	5.8	8.4
Oil-exporting countries	6,048	4,289	1,759	3.2	2.0
Rest of the world	21,717	37,775	−16,058	11.6	17.5
Total	**187,131**	**215,942**	**−28,811**	**100.0**	**100.0**

[1] Balance of payments basis.
Source: Office for National Statistics

Geographical Distribution of Goods

Most of the UK's trade in goods is with other developed countries (see Table 24.5). In 2000, 85% of UK exports were to other member countries of the Organisation for Economic Co-operation and Development (OECD), and 81% of imports came from the same countries. The proportion of export trade with the European Union was 57%, while imports from the EU accounted for over 50% of the total. Western Europe as a whole took 61% of UK exports in 2000.

EU countries accounted for eight of the UK's top ten export markets in 2000—the United States and Japan took the other two places—and seven of the top ten leading suppliers of goods to the UK (see Table 24.6); the other three places were taken by the United States, Japan and Hong Kong. The United States maintained its position as the UK's largest external market for the fourth year running and regained its position as the UK's largest single supplier, with Germany in second position. Both total exports and imports grew strongly in 2000—by 13% and 12% respectively. In particular, exports to the United States rose by 21% and imports from the same country by 17%.

Table 24.6: Trade in Goods—Main Markets and Suppliers, 2000[1]

	Value (£ million)	Share of UK trade in goods (%)
Main markets		
United States	29,371	15.7
Germany	22,570	12.1
France	18,510	9.9
Netherlands	14,947	8.0
Irish Republic	12,227	6.5
Belgium and Luxembourg	10,267	5.5
Italy	8,381	4.5
Spain	8,274	4.4
Sweden	4,189	2.2
Japan	3,679	2.0
Main suppliers		
United States	28,566	13.2
Germany	27,687	12.8
France	17,817	8.3
Netherlands	14,901	6.9
Japan	10,201	4.7
Belgium and Luxembourg	10,169	4.7
Irish Republic	9,510	4.4
Italy	9,365	4.3
Spain	5,972	2.8
Hong Kong	5,933	2.7

[1] Balance of payments basis.
Source: ONS *Monthly Digest of Statistics*

Services

There has been a surplus recorded for trade in services every year since 1966. Exports of services grew by 3.7% to £67.2 billion in 2000 (see Table 24.7), with the largest contributions to growth from financial and other business services. Imports of services were 5.1% higher at £56.3 billion, with the travel sector contributing almost 45% of the total.

Table 24.7: Trade in Services, 2000 *£ million*

	Exports	Imports	Balance
Transport	12,059	14,554	–2,495
Travel	14,364	25,192	–10,828
Communications	1,501	1,493	8
Construction	89	39	50
Insurance	2,793	635	2,158
Financial services[1]	8,391	227	8,164
Computer and information services	2,261	1,008	1,253
Royalties and licence fees	4,773	3,957	816
Other business services	18,520	6,590	11,930
Personal, cultural and recreational services	1,289	648	641
Government	1,177	1,923	–746
Total	**67,217**	**56,266**	**10,951**

[1] Service earnings of financial institutions are recorded net of their foreign expenses. Imports of financial services only cover imports by non-financial institutions.
Source: ONS Quarterly Balance of Payments

Income and Transfers

Earnings on UK investment abroad rose sharply from £110.4 billion in 1999 to £145.2 billion in 2000, while debits (earnings of foreign-owned assets in the UK) also increased significantly, by 38%, to £139.9 billion, giving a modest surplus of £5.3 billion (see Table 24.8), down appreciably on the record surplus of £9.0 billion in 1999. The surplus on direct investment income of £11.0 billion, down a little from the £12.4 billion surplus in 1999, was partly offset by an increased deficit of £6.1 billion on other investment income (including earnings on reserve assets). The deficit on current transfers fell slightly from £4.2 billion in 1999 to £3.8 billion in 2000.

Financial Account and International Investment Position

The financial account (see Table 24.9) shows that in 2000 UK direct investment abroad was £165.1 billion, compared with £128.1 billion in 1999. Foreign direct investment in the UK was £86.2 billion, compared with £52.1 billion in 1999. The increased investment reflects the high level of acquisition and merger activity taking place throughout the year (see p. 383). Portfolio investment abroad in 2000 amounted to £85.5 billion compared with £5.3 billion in 1999. Portfolio investment in the UK rose from £109.7 billion in 1999 to £174.6 billion in 2000—a large increase in investment in UK equity securities reflecting the counterpart to the large outward direct investment paid for by the issue of new shares. Other investment abroad rose from £56.8 billion in 1999 to £270.8 billion in 2000, mainly due to increased deposits by banks. Other investment in the UK was £281.8 billion compared with £39.1 billion in 1999. This large increase was mainly due to deposits of sterling and foreign currency with UK banks. Reserve assets increased by £3.9 billion in 2000.

At the end of 2000, direct investment in the UK was £323 billion (see Table 24.10), while direct investment abroad was £604 billion—a net balance of £281 billion. Inward portfolio investment stood at £1,032 billion, while the stock of UK portfolio investment abroad was £858 billion. In total, UK external liabilities exceeded assets by £123 billion.

INTERNATIONAL TRADE POLICY

The Department of Trade and Industry (DTI) pursues the UK's interest in international trade policy in cooperation with other government departments. This covers goods, services and investment, and involves

Table 24.8: Income and Transfers, 2000 *£ million*

	Credits	Debits	Balance
Income			
Compensation of employees	1,025	842	183
Investment income	145,209	139,877	5,332
of which:			
Earnings on direct investment	47,584	36,557	11,027
Earnings on portfolio investment	33,780	33,397	383
Earnings on other investment[1]	63,845	69,923	–6,078
Total	**146,234**	**140,719**	**5,515**
Current transfers			
Central government	12,117	7,799	4,318
Other sectors	8,621	16,767	–8,146
Total	**20,738**	**24,566**	**–3,828**

[1] Including earnings on reserve assets.
Source: ONS Quarterly Balance of Payments

Table 24.9: Financial Account Summary[1] *£ billion*

	1990	1995	1998	1999	2000
UK investment abroad (net debits)					
Direct investment abroad	10.6	28.2	71.9	128.1	165.1
Portfolio investment abroad	15.9	39.3	36.7	5.3	85.5
Other investment abroad	52.5	48.1	15.9	56.8	270.8
Reserve assets	0.1	–0.2	–0.2	–0.6	3.9
Total	**79.0**	**115.3**	**124.4**	**189.5**	**525.4**
Investment in the UK (net credits)					
Direct investment in the UK	18.6	12.9	38.4	52.1	86.2
Portfolio investment in the UK	13.4	37.2	17.9	109.7	174.6
Other investment in the UK	64.6	66.1	63.4	39.1	281.8
Total	**96.6**	**116.2**	**119.7**	**200.9**	**542.6**
Net transactions (net credits less net debits)					
Direct investment	8.0	–15.2	–33.5	–76.0	–78.9
Portfolio investment	–2.5	–2.1	–18.8	104.5	89.1
Other investment	12.1	18.1	47.5	–17.7	10.9
Reserve assets	–0.1	0.2	0.2	0.6	–3.9
Total	**17.5**	**0.9**	**–4.7**	**11.4**	**17.2**

[1] Balance of payments basis.
Source: ONS Quarterly Balance of Payments

working through the EU and drawing on the UK's bilateral relations and membership of international organisations and groupings such as the WTO, OECD and the Commonwealth. The EU's common commercial policy coordinates the external trade of all the EU's Member States. In consultation with a wide range of businesses, consumer and non-governmental interests, the DTI seeks to safeguard and promote open markets in the interest of economic growth, employment and international development, and to ensure coherence between commercial, financial, environmental and social policies.

Table 24.10: International Investment Position[1] *£ billion*

	1990	1995	1998	1999	2000
UK assets					
Direct investment abroad	120.7	200.9	301.1	429.3	604.2
Portfolio investment abroad	197.3	487.2	685.5	752.4	858.0
Other investment abroad	555.9	819.5	1,102.6	1,135.1	1,426.6
Reserve assets	22.5	31.8	23.3	22.2	28.8
Total	**896.4**	**1,539.4**	**2,112.5**	**2,338.9**	**2,917.6**
UK liabilities					
Direct investment in the UK	113.5	137.9	192.8	239.3	323.5
Portfolio investment in the UK	189.2	386.4	686.7	852.1	1,032.1
Other investment in the UK	602.0	1,007.5	1,351.2	1,386.4	1,685.3
Total	**904.6**	**1,531.8**	**2,230.7**	**2,477.8**	**3,040.8**
Net international investment position					
Direct investment	7.2	63.0	108.3	190.0	280.7
Portfolio investment	8.1	100.8	–1.2	–99.8	–174.0
Other investment	–46.0	–188.0	–248.5	–251.3	–258.7
Reserve assets	22.5	31.8	23.3	22.2	28.8
Total	**–8.2**	**7.6**	**–118.1**	**–138.9**	**–123.2**

[1] Balance of payments basis.
Source: ONS Quarterly Balance of Payments

European Union

The establishment of the Single Market is one of the key achievements of the EU, although in the Government's view further reform is needed in key areas such as services, public procurement, liberalisation of utilities, simplifying the regulatory environment, and tightening up on state aids. UK priorities are to push forward this reform and improve the level of transposition and enforcement of Single Market legislation across the EU.

In the Government's view, the benefits of the Single Market include:

- a wider market for UK goods, comprising 380 million consumers, with intra-EU trade accounting for around 25% of world trade;
- greater competition and liberalisation, which have helped to bring about lower prices;
- better consumer protection;
- British manufacturers can sell their products throughout the EU without expensive re-testing in every country as a result of the Single Market principle of mutual recognition of standards;
- there has been a significant reduction in export bureaucracy for UK business—the Single Market is in effect a domestic market for European business; and
- the right of UK citizens to work, study or retire in all other Member States—around 750,000 Britons live in other EU countries.

The European Commission sets out in its Internal Market Strategy a long-term strategic vision and framework for measures aimed at achieving better functioning of the Single Market. First produced in 1999, it is reviewed annually. The 2001 review, endorsed by the Internal Market, Consumer and Tourism Council, largely reflects UK views on priorities for action to further improve the operation of the Single Market, including completion of work by the end of 2001 on patents and public procurement. In the longer term, the UK looks to take forward work on other key elements in the Strategy, such as on services and plans to simplify the regulatory environment.

More than 88% of Directives have now been implemented in all Member States. At the Stockholm European Council in March 2001, EU Heads of Government agreed a target of no more than 1.5% of Single Market directives to be overdue in any Member State by the time of the Barcelona Summit in 2002.

In addition, a framework for ensuring the even and effective enforcement of Single Market rules has been established. This involves encouraging cooperation between national administrations, setting up contact points for businesses and citizens, and improving the efficiency of the Commission's complaints procedure. In the UK, the DTI's Action Single Market acts not only as a contact point for UK business and citizens but also as a first port of call for similar units in other Member States when Single Market problems arise. Initiatives for simplifying national and Community rules include SLIM (Simpler Legislation for the Internal Market) and the European Business Test Panel, which allows for consultation of business during the drafting stage of new legislation.

World Trade Organisation (WTO)

The UK Government works to promote an open and stable economic environment in which trade flows freely and which stimulates prosperity. It believes that this can best be achieved through a multilateral framework of rules that are designed to promote an open and liberal trading system, where barriers to a free flow of trade—such as high import duties or subsidies—are minimised. These rules are held and enforced primarily by the WTO.

The WTO (*www.wto.org*) was established in 1995 and currently has a membership of 141 countries. It and its predecessor, the General Agreement on Tariffs and Trade, have helped to establish a multilateral trading system through successive rounds of trade negotiations. However, the WTO Ministerial Conference in Seattle in November 1999 failed to agree on the launch of a new round of trade negotiations. With the next Ministerial Conference in Doha, Qatar, scheduled for November 2001, the UK and its EU partners are pressing for the launch of a new round, which they see as having the potential to deliver a substantial liberalising package for the benefit of all countries, so promoting economic growth and new job creation. The Government, in partnership with UK businesses, has identified a number of priority areas which they would like to see included in such a round, including a further substantial reduction of tariffs, removal of other barriers to trade, simplification of trade procedures and further opening of government procurement markets. The UK would also like a round to consider investment, competition and environmental issues.

The DTI monitors actions by third countries which represent obstacles to UK exports. It seeks to resolve problems bilaterally in conjunction with EU partners where such efforts fail through the initiation of WTO dispute settlement action. In particular, the UK is seeking to ensure that the current major trade disputes between the EU and the United States are carefully handled and, if possible, resolved at minimum cost to the UK and world economy. The Department is keen to ensure that bilateral agreements between the EU and third countries (for example the Transatlantic Economic Partnership and the Asia-Europe Meeting) are established and implemented in a way which secures open markets. A similar approach is adopted in the negotiations with countries seeking to join the WTO, including the People's Republic of China, Russia, Saudi Arabia and the Ukraine.

Developing Countries

The DTI works closely with the Department for International Development (DFID) to ensure that developing countries benefit from, and participate in, the world trade system. An inter-departmental Working Group on Trade and Development, chaired by the DTI, meets regularly to ensure consistency of approach.

In June 2000 the EU and the 71 African, Caribbean and Pacific (ACP) countries signed in Cotonou, Benin, a new agreement, which sets out a framework for economic and political cooperation, development aid and trade. After a transitional period of eight years, during which the ACP countries will continue to enjoy their current preferential access to the EU, new WTO-compatible arrangements will be put in place.

Other developments in 2000–01 have included:

- a commitment in the White Paper *Eliminating World Poverty: Making Globalisation Work for the Poor* (see p. 94) to make the next round of negotiations a Development Round that brings real benefits to developing countries across a range of issues;
- a proposal by the European Commission, agreed by the General Affairs Council in February 2001, to open up immediately duty- and quota-free access for all exports from Least Developed Countries, except arms. Only three products—sugar, rice and bananas—are treated differently, with full duty-free access being phased in gradually in the period up to 2009; and
- encouraging a Commonwealth consensus in favour of development of the multilateral trading system, in particular by working to remove barriers which prevent developing countries playing their part in the global economy.

Special Trading Arrangements

The multilateral trading system provides the foundation for the EU's common commercial policy. However, the EU has preferential trading arrangements with a number of countries, falling into three main categories:

- those that prepare countries in Central and Eastern Europe for possible EU membership. Europe (Association) Agreements (see p. 86) are designed to facilitate closer political and economic ties and the eventual full liberalisation of trade with a view to helping these countries prepare for becoming full EU members. Similar agreements—Stabilisation and Association Agreements—are being negotiated with the Western Balkan countries;
- the EU has association and cooperation agreements with virtually all non-member countries with Mediterranean coastlines, plus Jordan. These provide for the setting up by 2010 of a free trade area between the EU and these countries; and
- those that provide an economic dimension to its assistance to former dependent territories. Trade relations with these ACP countries, formerly beneficiaries of the Lomé Convention, are now governed by the EU/ACP Cotonou Partnership Agreement, which gives them tariff-free access, subject to certain safeguards, to the EU for industrial and agricultural products. The EU also operates a Generalised System of Preferences (GSP), available to nearly all developing countries and applying to industrial products, including textiles and certain (mainly processed) agricultural products. The EU will negotiate a new GSP Regulation to take effect once the current scheme expires in December 2001.

New trade relationships with countries and regions of Latin America and the Gulf Cooperation Council are being pursued. A free trade agreement with Mexico came into force in July 2000, and negotiations for new agreements with the Mercosur regional economic area (Argentina, Brazil, Paraguay and Uruguay) and Chile are under way.

Partnership and cooperation (non-preferential) agreements have been concluded with ten states of the former Soviet Union. Non-preferential cooperation agreements have also been made with countries in South Asia and Latin America, as well as the People's Republic of China, the Association of South East Asian Nations, the Andean Pact, and the Central American States.

Controls on Trade

Import Controls

Following the completion of the Single European Market, all national quantitative restrictions were abolished. However, the EU does restrict imports of textiles and clothing, steel, footwear and ceramics from certain countries under EU import regimes using licensing controls; these are also used to monitor imports and deter quota fraud.

Imports into the UK may also be subject to prohibition or restriction, either as a result of UN resolutions (for example imports of rough diamonds from Angola, Liberia and Sierra Leone) or for reasons of national security. These include firearms and ammunition, nuclear materials, landmines and chemical weapons.

The DTI's Import Licensing Branch has responsibility for issuing import licences in accordance with UK and EC law. Its principal customers are UK importers dealing in goods controlled by the DTI. In 2001 it expected to issue 280,000 licences.

Other products may be prohibited or restricted to protect human, animal or plant life or health. Examples include certain drugs, explosives, endangered wildlife and derived products (under the CITES Convention), pornographic material, and certain agricultural, horticultural and food products. These are controlled and enforced by other government departments such as the Department for Environment, Food and Rural Affairs, and HM Customs and Excise.

Strategic Export Controls

Governments control the export of goods and technology for a variety of reasons. In particular, irresponsible transfers of arms, ammunition and related material can contribute to internal repression or regional instability, while goods intended for civil purposes can also contribute to the development of weapons of mass destruction and the missiles to deliver them. Controls are also imposed to meet various international commitments.

Licences to export arms and other goods controlled for strategic reasons are issued by the DTI acting through its Export Control Organisation (ECO). All relevant individual licence applications are circulated by the DTI to other departments with an interest, including the Foreign & Commonwealth Office (FCO), the Ministry of Defence and DFID. The ECO also issues licences for exports and some other activities that are only controlled because of trade sanctions.

Strategic export controls apply to a range of goods, components and spare parts and technology and include the following:

- military equipment, such as arms, ammunition, bombs, tanks, imaging devices, military aircraft and warships;
- nuclear-related items, including nuclear materials, reactors and processing plant;
- dual-use goods—goods designed for civil use but which can be used for military purposes—such as certain materials, machine tools, electronic equipment, computers, telecommunications equipment, cryptographic goods, sensors and radar, navigation and avionics equipment, marine equipment and space and propulsion equipment;
- chemical weapons precursors, and related equipment and technology;
- certain micro-organisms, biological equipment and technology; and
- goods used in programmes involved in weapons of mass destruction and missiles used for their delivery.

The Export Control Bill was introduced in the House of Commons in June 2001. Among the powers in the Bill are those to impose controls on:

- trafficking and brokering;
- the transfer of technology from the UK and by UK persons anywhere by any means (other than by export); and
- the provision of technical assistance overseas.

Inward and Outward Investment

The UK has an open economy, with no restrictions on the outward flow of capital. Outward investment helps develop markets for UK exports while providing earnings in the form of investment income (see p. 415). Inward investment is promoted by Invest UK (see p. 421). This inward investment is seen as a means of introducing new technology, products and management styles to the UK.

Inward Investment

The UK was ranked second in the world at attracting inward investment according to the latest (2000) United Nations *World Investment*

Report. North America continues to be the largest source in terms of stock levels. Britain is the premier inward investment location in Europe and inward investment is a significant contributor to the economy. It attracted 24% of all inward investment into the EU in 1999. There are nearly 18,000 foreign investors in the UK, including 5,600 from the United States.

Recent inward investment announcements have included:

- the Japanese car maker Nissan will invest around £214 million to build its new Micra model at its Sunderland plant;
- the Matsushita Communication Industrial Co. of Japan plans a new telecommunications R&D centre creating 400 highly skilled jobs and developing Panasonic's third generation (3G) mobile telephone systems;
- the Bertelsmann Group of Germany has set up its new European customer service centre in Liverpool, and expects to create 350 jobs over the next three years;
- the IT group Insight from Arizona in the United States will build its new European headquarters in Sheffield, creating around 1,750 jobs—700 of which will be in software development and programming; and
- Ford will invest £250 million at its Bridgend plant in south Wales where around 600 new jobs will be created, building engines for Ford's premium models, including Jaguar.

Outward Investment

According to the latest United Nations Conference on Trade and Development (UNCTAD) report, the UK was the world's largest outward investor in 1999 (US$199 billion), surpassing the United States for the first time since 1988.

GOVERNMENT SERVICES

The Government provides a wide range of advice and practical support to meet the needs of exporters. This is designed to help businesses, especially small and medium-sized enterprises (SMEs), through all stages of the exporting process.

British Trade International

British Trade International (BTI), established in 1999, brings together the work of the DTI and FCO in support of international trade and investment. It aims to enhance the competitiveness of companies in the UK through overseas sales and investments, and to maintain a high level of inward direct investment. Its two operating units, Trade Partners UK and Invest UK (formerly the Invest in Britain Bureau), are responsible for these activities respectively.

The Group Chief Executive reports to the Secretary of State for Trade and Industry and the Secretary of State for Foreign & Commonwealth Affairs, and to the Board of BTI. A single Minister for International Trade and Investment was appointed for the first time in June 2001.

Trade Partners UK

Trade Partners UK (*www.tradepartners.gov.uk*) provides a single point of access to the full range of support in Britain and in over 200 diplomatic posts overseas, delivering a range of services to its customers including:

- providing basic trade information—delivered via its website and by market-based staff;
- offering access to information sources and data through the Trade Partners UK Information Centre—increasingly focused on providing access to electronic sources which SMEs would not otherwise be able to access; and
- facilitating participation in overseas trade fairs and enabling visits and meetings for exporters travelling abroad, and supporting inward missions from overseas countries to the UK.

Invest UK

Invest UK (*www.invest.uk.com*) is a business service organisation, which communicates the benefits of the UK to potential investors, identifies and approaches potential investors, and assists them with all aspects of locating and expanding in the UK. It works with Regional Development Agencies in England, as well as national agencies in Scotland, Wales and Northern Ireland. Invest UK is represented in Embassies and Consulates in over 41 cities around the world.

In 2000–01, 869 inward investment decisions were notified to Invest UK and these are expected to create 71,488 new jobs (see also Table 24.11). Around a third of these investment projects were from companies with an existing presence in the UK. The largest single investor country was the United States, with 48.4% of projects, followed by Germany (8.2%), Canada (6.4%) and Japan (5.9%). The UK is particularly successful at attracting investment in industries linked to the knowledge-driven economy—computer software, Internet, telecommunications, electronics and e-business sectors—together forming the largest category of foreign direct investment, with some 455 projects (52.4%). Other main sectors for UK inward investment are the automotive sector, pharmaceuticals and financial services.

Table 24.11: UK Inward Investment Cases and Effect on Jobs

	1999–2000	2000–01
Invest UK		
Active cases	604	655
Inward investment decisions in which it was significantly involved	145	219
New jobs created	15,519	16,909
UK figures		
Inward investment decisions	757	869
New jobs created	52,783	71,488

Source: Invest UK

Export Insurance

The Export Credits Guarantee Department (ECGD) (*www.ecgd.gov.uk*), Britain's official export credit agency, is a separate department reporting to the Secretary of State for Trade and Industry. It aims to benefit the economy by helping UK exporters win business, and UK firms to invest overseas, by providing guarantees, insurance and reinsurance against loss, taking into account the Government's international policies. ECGD charges premiums for its guarantees to reflect the risk and seeks to break even in the longer term. It plays a key role in the Government's export strategy, working closely with Trade Partners UK and other government departments involved in export promotion. Its facilities are intended to complement those available in the private sector.

In 1999–2000, ECGD provided £4.7 billion of new guarantees for UK capital goods exporters, a 43% increase on the previous year's figure—£1.3 billion of this supported exports in the aerospace sector. Its overseas investment insurance portfolio reached a record £797 million; two of the largest investments covered were the San Lorenzo power station in the Philippines and the Mozal aluminium smelter in Mozambique.

Further Reading

Trade and Industry. The Government's Expenditure Plans 2001–02 to 2003–04 and Main Estimates 2001–02. Cm 5112. The Stationery Office, 2001.

United Kingdom Balance of Payments—the Pink Book 2001. Office for National Statistics. The Stationery Office.

Export Credits Guarantee Department Annual Report and Resource Accounts 1999–2000. The Stationery Office, 2000.

Websites

Department of Trade and Industry: www.dti.gov.uk

National Statistics: www.statistics.gov.uk

25 Science, Engineering and Technology

Background	423	Government Departments	436
Research and Development Expenditure	425	International Collaboration	440
Government Role	425	Research in Higher Education Institutions	442
Research Councils	431	Other Organisations	443

More Nobel Prizes for science (over 70) have been won by scientists from Britain than any country except the United States. The UK is responsible for about 4.5% of global expenditure on science, produces about 8% of scientific publications and receives 9% of citations. UK scientists claimed about 10% of internationally recognised prizes in the 20th century. Government policy aims to reinforce the UK's international scientific standing, and maximise the contribution of science, engineering and technology (SET) to economic competitiveness and the quality of life by promoting innovation.

BACKGROUND

The public sector is the prime funder of basic science in Britain. As well as playing a crucial part in advancing scientific knowledge and producing well-trained people, such research can often lead to exploitable results. Business has the prime responsibility for researching and developing new and improved products and services. The Government's aim is to create a knowledge-driven economy by building on the UK's science base and promoting the right climate to encourage innovation and the exploitation of new ideas.

The Government's policies for science, engineering and technology were set out in the July 2000 White Paper *Excellence and Opportunity—a science and innovation policy for the 21st century*. The White Paper set out the actions being taken by the Government to ensure that UK science remains world class, to open up opportunities for innovation throughout the economy and to increase public confidence in science. Details are set out in the *Science Budget 2001–02 to 2003–04*. Specific priority research areas for the Spending Review 2000 period are genomics, e-science and basic technology.

The Fifth Framework Programme of the European Union (EU)—a further round of its collaborative research and development (R&D) programme (see p. 440)—was launched in March 1999 with a budget of 14.96 billion euro. UK companies, higher education institutions and research organisations are playing an active role in this transnational collaborative research programme. EU proposals to create a European Research Area are expected to offer new opportunities for the UK to compete as part of the EU in global markets.

The Sanger Centre at Hinxton in Cambridgeshire (funded mainly by the

Wellcome Trust) has contributed a third of the sequence data to the international Human Genome Project, while the Medical Research Council (MRC) Human Genome Mapping Project Resource Centre on the same site also played a major role in supporting work on the human genome. The near complete set of human genes was announced in February 2001 and has involved scientists working at 16 research institutes in six countries. In addition, the Centre for Genome Research, supported by the Biotechnology and Biological Sciences Research Council (BBSRC) at the University of Edinburgh, is now a world leader in stem cell biology.

The UK has been at the forefront of many other world-class advances in science. For example, in the latter part of the 20th century there was the discovery by Natural Environment Research Council (NERC) British Antarctic Survey scientists of the hole in the ozone layer over the Antarctic. Earlier, researchers at the MRC Laboratory of Molecular Biology, Cambridge, had produced the first monoclonal antibodies—proteins with enormous potential in the diagnosis and treatment of disease. Among British breakthroughs in genetics research are the identification of the gene in the Y chromosome responsible for determining sex, and of other genes linked to diseases such as cystic fibrosis and a form of breast cancer. Another internationally recognised breakthrough came with the birth of the first cloned mammal, Dolly the sheep, at the BBSRC-funded Roslin Institute near Edinburgh. Pioneering studies into the transfer of the nucleus between cells at Roslin have made the research institute a world leader in this field. Professor Sir Harold Kroto of Sussex University shared the 1996 Nobel Prize for chemistry with two US scientists for discovering in 1985 the fullerene molecule—60 carbon atoms arranged in a symmetrical cage.

Notable areas of UK achievement in R&D include biotechnology, biomedicine, materials, chemicals, electronics and aerospace. Among the British research achievements reported in the first half of 2001 are:

- Professor A. Fabian of the Cambridge Institute of Astronomy shared the 2001 Bruno Rossi Prize (in high-energy astrophysics). This was awarded for observations revealing the very large black holes at the centre of distant galaxies. He is the first to have observed X-ray spectra of active galactic nuclei being broadened by the strong pull of gravity, thus indicating that black holes lurk at their core. This is an important confirmation of Einstein's theory of gravity—the General Theory of Relativity.
- Researchers at the University of Plymouth and the Institute of Arable Crops Research investigating environmentally friendly pest control have undertaken field-trials of a novel method for controlling aphid populations—using predatory ground beetles.
- It used to be thought that plants could take up nitrogen from the soil only if it is in an inorganic form. Researchers at the University of Lancaster have found that most grasses can take up and use organic nitrogen in the form of amino acids—a form of nitrogen less 'mobile' than inorganic forms such as nitrate, which can leach into and pollute watercourses.
- The MRC Programme on AIDS in Uganda has established that survival times and disease progression rates in HIV-1 infection in rural Uganda are similar to those in industrialised countries before anti-HIV drugs were used. This research has disproved the idea that AIDS in Africa is a distinct disease from AIDS in developed countries and shows that there is an opportunity to mitigate the effects of the African AIDS epidemic.
- Research from the MRC Laboratory of Molecular Cell Biology has provided the first evidence that specialised precursor cells, destined to become a particular cell type, can be re-programmed into stem cells, which are able to self-renew and generate a diverse range of other cells. The work could have implications for developing stem cell therapies, because precursor cells are easier to purify and expand than stem cells.

RESEARCH AND DEVELOPMENT EXPENDITURE

Gross domestic expenditure in the UK on R&D in 1999 was £16.7 billion, 1.8% of Gross Domestic Product (GDP) and a 5% increase over 1998. Of this, £14.4 billion was on civil R&D, with the rest going to defence projects.

Business enterprise provided 49% of total funding of R&D and government 28% in 1999; a further 18% came from abroad. Other contributions were made by private endowments, trusts and charities. As well as financing R&D carried out within business enterprise itself, business enterprise supports university research and finances contract research at government establishments. Some charities have their own laboratories and offer grants for outside research. Contract research organisations (see p. 443) carry out R&D for companies and are playing an increasingly important role in the transfer of technology to British industry.

Total spending on R&D in business enterprise amounted to £11.3 billion in 1999. Of this total, business enterprise's own contribution was 67%, with 10% coming from government and the rest (23%) from overseas. The two biggest investors in R&D—AstraZeneca and GlaxoSmithKline (formed by a merger of Glaxo Wellcome and SmithKline Beecham)—both operate in the pharmaceuticals sector, and pharmaceuticals account for 22% of UK R&D expenditure. The motor vehicles and parts and aerospace sectors are also big investors in R&D.

GOVERNMENT ROLE

Science, engineering and technology (SET) base issues are the responsibility of the Secretary of State for Trade and Industry assisted by a Minister for Science; they are supported by the Office of Science and Technology (OST). A Cabinet Office Science Policy Committee has been created for the collective consideration of, and decisions on, major science policy issues. The OST, headed by the Government's Chief Scientific Adviser, is responsible for policy on SET, both nationally and internationally, and coordinates science and technology policy across government departments. The Chief Scientific Adviser also reports directly to the Prime Minister. An independent Council for Science and Technology advises the Prime Minister on the strategic policies and framework for science and technology in the UK. Its members are drawn from academia,

Figure 25.1:
Expenditure on R&D in 1999, UK

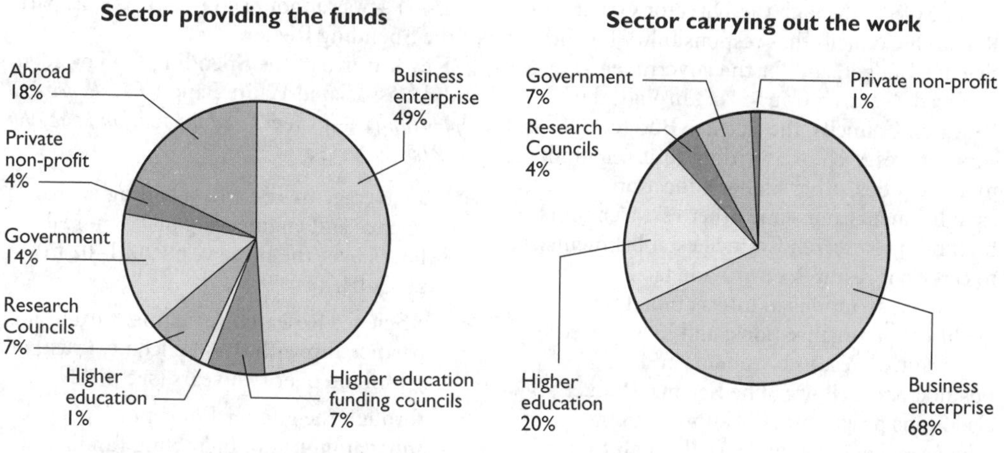

Source: Office for National Statistics

business and charitable foundations/institutions. The policy and management of some aspects of science and technology are reserved to the UK Government, while in other instances this has been devolved to the new administrations in Scotland, Wales and Northern Ireland.

In 1999 the Government announced a new framework for overseeing developments in biotechnology. The Human Genetics Commission, which advises on genetic technologies and their impact on humans, and the Agricultural and Environment Biotechnology Commission, which advises on all other aspects of biotechnology except food, work alongside the Food Standards Agency (see p. 210) as part of the strategic framework.

The term 'science and engineering base' is used to describe the research and postgraduate training capacity based in the universities and colleges of higher education and in establishments operated by the Research Councils (see pp. 431–6), together with the national and international central facilities (such as CERN—see p. 441) supported by the Research Councils and available for use by British scientists and engineers. There are also important contributions from private institutions, chiefly those funded by charities. The science and engineering base is the main provider of basic research and much of the strategic research (research likely to have practical applications) carried out in the UK. It also collaborates with the private sector in the conduct of specific applied research.

The OST, through the Director General of Research Councils, has responsibility for the Science Budget, and for the government-financed Research Councils. Through the Research Councils, the Science Budget supports research by awarding research grants to universities, other higher education establishments and some other research units; by funding Research Council establishments to carry out research or provide facilities; by paying subscriptions to international scientific facilities and organisations; and by supporting postgraduate research students and postdoctoral Fellows. The Science Budget also funds programmes of support to the science and engineering base through the Royal Society and the Royal Academy of Engineering. The other main sources of funds for universities are the higher education funding councils (see p. 442).

Strategy and Finance

Planned total government expenditure on SET (both civil and defence) in 2001–02 is £7.8 billion. This represents an increase of about 9% in real terms over the estimated outturn of expenditure in 2000–01. Of the 2001–02 total, £4.9 billion is devoted to civil science, including £1.8 billion for the Science Budget.

In 1998 the Government announced that it would provide an additional £1 billion for the science and engineering base between 1999 and 2002—£700 million through the Science Budget and £300 million through the Department for Education and Employment (now the Department for Education and Skills). A further £400 million is being provided by the Wellcome Trust. About £700 million of the extra funding, including £300 million of the Wellcome contribution, is devoted to upgrading university laboratories and other essential equipment (see p. 428). Another £400 million is being used by the Research Councils to support research in priority areas, such as life sciences (including genetic research, medical science and biotechnology). In July 2000 a further £1 billion investment partnership with the Wellcome Trust—for the years 2002–03 and 2003–04—was announced (see p. 429) as part of the Spending Review.

Key features of the Spending Review 2000 and the associated White Paper, *Excellence and Opportunity—a science and innovation policy for the 21st century*, are:

- an average increase in spending on science and engineering of 7% in real terms over the three years 2001–02 to 2003–04;
- a Science Research Investment Fund, in partnership with the Wellcome Trust, of £1 billion over two years (see p. 429);
- through the Higher Education Innovation Fund, increasing funding to £140 million over three years, to help

© FCO/John Martin

Many shows and exhibitions take place every year throughout the UK, relating to all aspects of industry and commerce, including leisure and food.

The Daily Mail **Ideal Home Show** has showcased domestic trends and tastes annually since 1908. Over the years the exhibition has grown in size and has a strong international flavour. The displays include purpose-built showhomes. In 2001 many exhibits had a futuristic feel, such as the robotic lawnmowers shown above. The exhibition has been held at Earl's Court in London since 1979.

Offshore Europe Partnership

Offshore Europe is a bie
show which has been helc
the Aberdeen Exhibition a
Conference Centre since 1
It is the largest oil and gas s
in Europe and presents a
opportunity for internatio
exhibitors to showcase th
products and services to
visitors from around the wo
There are International
Pavilions within the exhibit
and in 2001 the show attra
several countries who exhib
for the first time.

National Boat Shows (both)

The annual **Southampton Boat Show**
provides a showcase for manufacturers o
boats and marine equipment. Water displa
and demonstrations are staged for the
entertainment of families and sailing
professionals in the largest purpose-built
marina in Europe. The show also features
number of indoor exhibitions.

Every year at the Cardiff International Arena a number of different exhibitions are held, including the annual **Welsh and Southwest Manufacturing Show.** A conference is held at the event, which includes demonstrations of machinery, manufacturing innovations and IT solutions.

The King's Hall Conference and Exhibition Centre/photo: Phil Smyth

The **Northern Ireland Manufacturing and Product Technology Exhibition** takes place biennially in the King's Hall, Belfast. Many aspects of engineering were reflected in the 2001 exhibition, which featured shipbuilding, production equipment and aerospace technology.

British Educational Suppliers Association

BETT, The Education and Technology Show, has taken place for the last 18 years. The last five shows have been held in Olympia, London. The event attracts both national and international educationalists who come to see the latest products and services provided by educational information, communication and technology (ICT) suppliers.

© EmapMaclaren, organisers of the Recycling and Waste Management Exhibition

The Outdoor Recycling and Waste Management Exhibition is an annual event which takes place at the National Exhibition Centre (NEC), in Birmingham. The event attracts a wide range of suppliers and buyers of products and services from the two industries. Visitors can also attend seminars and demonstrations.

The **Asian Wedding Exhibition** was established in 1994 and is held at the Wembley Conference and Exhibition Centre, London. The event takes place over two days and attracts a large number of exhibitors who show a wide range of products and services to the public.

The **Organic Food and Wine Festival** took place for the first time in 1999. It presents an opportunity for the public to buy organic products as well as offering the chance to attend lectures by leading authors, growers and producers. Cooking demonstrations also take place. In 2001 the Festival was held at Alexandra Palace, London.

Figure 25.2: Government Expenditure on R&D, UK

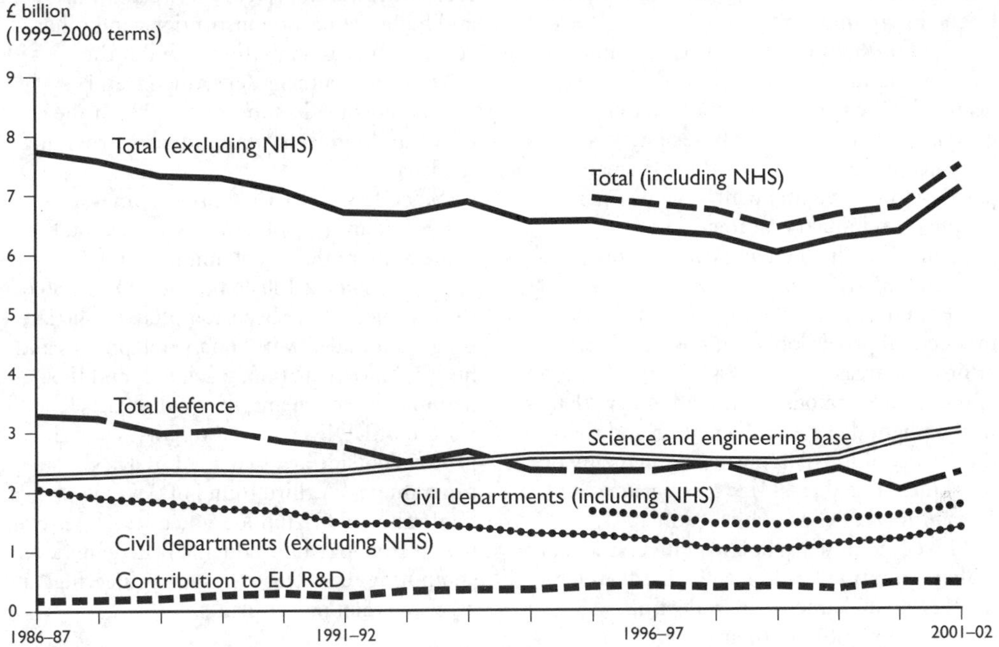

Source: Office for National Statistics

universities to work with business to create jobs and wealth from the science base;

- an extra £250 million to boost key research areas—genomics, e-science, nanotechnology, quantum computing and bioengineering;
- in partnership with the Wolfson Foundation and the Royal Society, a fund, initially of £4 million a year, to help in the recruitment of up to 50 top researchers (see p. 430);
- an annual £50 million Regional Innovation Fund to enable Regional Development Agencies (see p. 10) to support business incubators and clusters and new clubs of scientists, entrepreneurs, managers and financiers to collaborate more closely in the regions; and
- a new Small Business Research Initiative to encourage more high-technology small firms to start up or develop their research expertise by bidding for government research contracts.

The *Opportunity for All* White Paper (see p. 388) announced an additional £90 million to promote the commercial exploitation of research in the priority areas of basic technologies, genomics and e-science.

The Foresight Programme

The funding and organisation of British SET aim to create a close partnership between government, industry and the scientific community in developing strengths in areas of importance to the future economic well-being of Britain. In particular, the Government's Foresight Programme encourages the public and private sectors to work together to identify opportunities in markets and technologies likely to emerge over the next 10 to 20 years that would support sustainable growth, and the actions needed to exploit them. Government priorities in SET programmes, and in overall policy, regulation, and education and training, are being guided by the Programme.

The Foresight Programme is coordinated by a joint industry/academic steering group headed by the Chief Scientific Adviser. The current (second) round of Foresight was launched in 1999. This has three thematic panels and ten sectoral panels, made up of people from industry, academia and government. The thematic panels addressed the issues of ageing population, crime prevention and manufacturing in 2020, while the sectoral panels looked at business sectors or broader areas. The panels produced visions of the future—published in December 2000—which might drive wealth creation and shape the quality of life. A report bringing many of these ideas together—*Messages from the Current Round*—was published in 2001.

Government departments, universities and higher education funding councils, as well as the Research Councils, are reflecting Foresight priorities in their research spending allocations. The private sector is being encouraged to take account of the priorities both in its participation in collaborative research programmes and in its own strategic planning.

A new Foresight fund, initially of up to £15 million, was announced to implement the best ideas from the current round quickly. This has resulted in a third round of Foresight LINK Awards, recipients of which were announced in July 2001.The Foresight website (*www.foresight.gov.uk*) is an integral part of this round—it has an electronic library of strategic visions, information and views about the future.

The Secretary of State for Trade and Industry announced a review of Foresight in December 2000. Proposals for the future of the programme are due to be announced in late 2001.

LINK

The LINK scheme provides a government-wide framework for collaborative research in support of sustainable growth and improvements in the quality of life, in line with Foresight priorities. LINK aims to promote partnerships in commercially relevant research projects between industry and higher education institutions and other research base organisations. Under the scheme, government departments and Research Councils fund up to 50% of the cost of research projects, with industry providing the balance.

Since 1988, 71 LINK programmes have supported over 1,300 projects with a total value of more than £650 million and involving some 2,100 companies. Over 950 of these projects have been completed. The latest programmes deal with mobile telephones and health; bioremediation; e-science; and the manufacture of chemicals. Within LINK, Foresight LINK Awards support research projects outside areas covered by LINK programmes. A third round of Awards, with a total value of £12 million, includes: the use of nanotechnology in producing next-generation computing technology; tissue engineering; and zero-emission power plants.

Joint Research Equipment Initiative

The Joint Research Equipment Initiative brings together the higher education funding councils, the Department for Employment and Learning in Northern Ireland and the Research Councils. It directs funds for research equipment in strategic priority areas. Since 1996 over £275 million of public and private money has been committed for 'leading edge' equipment for UK universities and colleges.

Joint Infrastructure Fund

The Joint Infrastructure Fund (JIF) was a three-year programme to address the infrastructure problems of universities and was created by the Wellcome Trust and the Department of Trade and Industry (DTI), each contributing £300 million. The Higher Education Funding Council for England also contributed £150 million, raising the total fund to £750 million. A competition was run over five rounds from May 1999 to March

2001. More than 150 projects from over 40 universities shared the £750 million. Successful bids included a new research laboratory for research into tissue engineering; infrastructure for research on global climate change; equipment for developing optical fibre technology—photonic crystal fibre; astronomy facilities to help with the identification of black holes, stellar collapses and pulsars; a fire safety engineering research facility; and a post-genomic research centre to make advances in healthcare using data amassed by the Human Genome Project.

Science Research Investment Fund

A £1 billion initiative, announced in July 2000, builds on the Joint Infrastructure Fund. The Science Research Investment Fund (SRIF)—a two-year partnership between the Government and the Wellcome Trust—will finance new infrastructure schemes across the spectrum of science and engineering during 2002–04. The Government will provide £775 million and the Wellcome Trust £225 million. Funds will be allocated to universities for them to decide priorities. Universities will be required to find 25% of the total investment in projects from their own resources, business or other third parties. Contributions from SRIF already announced by the Wellcome Trust include grants of more than £10 million each towards: a new biomedical sciences research building at Leicester University; a research institute for medical cell biology at the new Royal Infirmary of Edinburgh; and a research institute for molecular medicine at Leeds University.

University Challenge Fund

The University Challenge Fund is a competitive scheme that offers financing to universities to help them in the early stages of turning research into commercial products. The first round involved over £65 million of investment funds: the Government contributed £25 million, the Wellcome Trust £18 million and the Gatsby Charitable Foundation £2 million, with the remainder raised by universities. Fifteen seed funds were established, allowing 37 institutions (28 universities and nine institutes) to access investment capital. A second round of the University Challenge Fund competition was launched in April 2001 and awards will be announced later in 2001.

Science Enterprise Challenge

In 1999 UK universities were invited to bid for a share of a £25 million fund to establish centres that would teach enterprise and business skill to scientists, and promote commercialisation of technological innovation. Since then a total of £28.9 million has been invested in 12 Science Enterprise Centres located throughout the UK. Each centre is hosted by a leading research university, and seven centres are run by university consortia, drawing in an additional 22 institutions. A further round of bidding was announced in the 2000 Spending Review and White Paper, with an additional £15 million available to fund either new centres or expand existing ones: awards will be announced later in 2001.

Cambridge-MIT Institute

A strategic collaboration has been established between Cambridge University and the Massachusetts Institute of Technology to carry out joint educational and research initiatives to improve the competitiveness of UK industry, focusing on the role of technology and enterpreneurship. The Institute is funded by a £65.1 million award over five years from its launch in 2000.

Faraday Partnerships

The Faraday Partnership scheme (*www.faradaypartnerships.org.uk*) is intended to improve the exploitation of SET in the UK. The partnerships bring together universities, independent research organisations, industry associations and manufacturers, with support from DTI, DEFRA and some of the Research Councils. It is intended to have a national network of 24 Faraday Partnerships by 2002–03.

The first awards under the Wolfson Foundation and Royal Society scheme to attract and retain the best scientific talent in the UK were announced in mid-2001. Research specialisms represented by these initial winners range across health, the environment, the economy and computing. The awards range from £45,000 to £75,000. Of the first seven winners of awards, four are at, or associated with, University College London. A further 30 awards are expected to be made in 2001 and about 35 in the second year of the scheme. The awards are jointly funded by the Wolfson Foundation and the OST.

National Science Week 2001, held in March, was marked by science events and activities throughout the UK. From 'I wonder for Tots' in Halifax to 'Granny on the Net' in Kidderminster, all age groups were catered for in a wide-ranging array of events that also included a 'how balls really bounce' look at the science of ball impacts at Loughborough and a 'magical mystery tour' through the sounds of 'Scouse' at the Liverpool Museum. In total, about 6,200 activities received some 1.4 million visitors. The week is coordinated by the BAAS and aims to popularise science and provide debates on key scientific issues. See the picture section between pp. 426 and 427.

Public Engagement in Science

The Government seeks to raise the status of SET among the general public, by increasing awareness of the contribution of SET to the UK's economic wealth and quality of life. To this end, the Government supports activities such as the annual science festival of the British Association for the Advancement of Science (BAAS), National Science Week and the Committee on the Public Understanding of Science (COPUS). COPUS—set up by the Royal Society, BAAS and the Royal Institution (see p. 444)—provides a strategic focus for science communication in the UK and promotes best practice in the field.

Science festivals are also a growing feature of local cooperative efforts to further understanding of the contribution made by science to everyday life. Schools, museums, laboratories, higher education institutions and industry contribute to a variety of special events. The longest established single-location annual science festival is the Edinburgh International Science Festival.

Activities such as these are important in assuring continued interest in SET among young people making educational and career choices. They also help to enhance the public's ability to relate to scientific issues in general and to make informed judgments about scientific developments.

An increase in the number of science centres in the UK is intended to change the way that the public interacts with science. Investment in these new centres will total more than £500 million—half of which will come from UK National Lottery funding with matching funding from other public and private sources. The centres aim to bring science and technology to the public in an informative and enjoyable way (see p. 445).

Science Year is a government-funded initiative which was launched in September 2001. The Year aims to increase pupil engagement in science subjects; increase parents' engagement in science, both for themselves and to help them support their children; raise the profile of science; and celebrate achievements in science and identify role models through a Science and Engineering Ambassadors initiative. Other planned activities include a Science Discovery Day at the Royal Albert Hall in South Kensington, London; a 'Future of Science in Society' conference at the BAAS Festival of Science in Leicester; mass participation experiments around the UK; and events and conferences enabling people to take part in debates on important issues.

Women

The Promoting SET for Women Unit within OST was established in 1994 in response to a report which found that women were under-represented in the SET sectors, especially at senior levels. The Unit has highlighted the benefits to business of providing a working environment sensitive to the needs of women scientists and engineers who combine a career and family responsibilities. It seeks to ensure that careers information for girls and women is widely available and to promote good employment practices, such as the provision of childcare facilities and job sharing. The Unit's website (*www.set4women.gov.uk*) promotes SET for girls and women and gives details of the Unit's activities.

Industrial and Intellectual Property

The Government supports innovation through the promotion of a national and international system for the establishment of intellectual property rights. These matters are the responsibility of the Patent Office, an executive agency of the DTI. The Office is responsible for the granting of patents, and registration of designs and trade marks. In 2000 it received over 31,400 applications for patents and almost 76,000 applications for trade marks. The Patent Office encourages worldwide harmonisation of rules and procedures, and the modernisation and simplification of intellectual property law. International patenting arrangements include the European Patent Convention and the Patent Co-operation Treaty. For trade marks the European Community Trade Mark System and the Madrid Protocol provide means of extending rights beyond the borders of the United Kingdom. The Patent Office Central Enquiry Unit and the website (*www.patent.gov.uk*) offer detailed information about intellectual property rights.

R&D's important role in a knowledge-driven economy is further recognised in an intellectual property rights action plan, which focuses on making these rights more affordable and accessible. In August 1999 the Baker report on the exploitation of public sector research, *Creating Knowledge: Creating Wealth—Realising the Economic Potential of Public Sector Research Establishments*, was published. The key recommendations were: reducing the risk avoidance culture in central government that inhibits entrepreneurial behaviour; giving government laboratories greater financial and management freedom; and reforming Civil Service conduct rules so as to reward scientists for exploiting their work. The Government has welcomed the report and has announced:

- guidelines on intellectual property in government research contracts;
- changes and guidelines to provide government scientists with greater incentives and rewards for participating fully, subject to safeguards, in exploitation; and
- a £10 million fund to support commercialisation of the intellectual property from research carried out in the public sector, including public sector research establishments, Research Council institutes and the National Health Service (NHS).

RESEARCH COUNCILS

Each Research Council is an autonomous body established under Royal Charter, with members of its governing council drawn from the universities, professions, industry and government. The Councils support research, study and training in universities and other higher education institutions, and carry out or support research, through their own institutes and at international research centres, often jointly with other public sector bodies and international organisations. They provide awards to about 15,000 postgraduate students in science, social sciences, engineering and technology. In addition to funding from the OST, the Councils receive income from research commissioned by government departments and the private sector.

The Quinquennial Review of the seven Research Councils was launched in 2001. The review has two stages: the first stage, now complete, considered the role and organisation of the Councils; and the second stage will examine the efficiency and effectiveness of the Councils' operations.

Engineering and Physical Sciences Research Council (EPSRC)

The EPSRC (*www.epsrc.ac.uk*), the Research Council with the largest budget (£461 million in 2001–02), promotes and supports high-quality basic, strategic and applied research and related postgraduate training in engineering and the physical sciences. It also provides advice, disseminates knowledge and promotes public understanding in these areas. Its remit is delivered through ten programme areas: physics, chemistry, mathematics, the generic technologies of information technology and materials, three engineering programmes (engineering, innovative manufacturing and infrastructure, and environment), the life sciences and basic technology. The life sciences programme covers research and training at the interface between the life sciences and all areas of engineering and the physical sciences. The basic technology programme is a joint council programme managed by the EPSRC on behalf of all the Research Councils.

EPSRC 'Partnerships for Public Awareness' awards were launched in 1998 to improve public awareness of leading research and its possible impact on society. The awards encourage researchers to communicate the value of their work to the public. In the first three years, 68 projects received awards totalling over £1.7 million. The *Maths on the Underground* project from Cambridge University has reached a large audience through its use in schools and on a Channel 4 TV programme as well as on Circle Line trains of the London Underground and a series of events. It received the 'Heist' Merit Award for marketing, and a book of the posters is planned. A Reading University 'Robot League' project for schools had coverage on two Channel 4 programmes, including a broadcast

The Research Councils were awarded additional funding under the Government's 2000 Spending Review for three priority areas—genomics, basic technology and e-science:

- *Genomics*—the Research Councils have established a Genomics Co-ordinating Group to integrate post-genome strategies, including interfacing with the industrial sector, engagement of the public, and analysis of the UK's strengths and weaknesses in genomics research within the international context.
- *Basic Technology*—this programme will contribute to the development of fundamental new technology that will be available to scientific, engineering and technology endeavour in the next 10 to 20 years. The £41 million programme is being taken forward by the EPSRC, on behalf of and in discussion with the other Councils. It will support a different type of project, that aims to encourage consortia and develop a new 'technology community' unconstrained by Research Council remit or academic discipline.
- *E-science*—Science is increasingly undertaken through global collaboration, enabled by the Internet, and involves very large volumes of data and using the most powerful computer resources. The e-science programme has two strands: tackling generic grid infrastructure problems common to all Research Council disciplines and developing e-science test beds specific to each Council. It will help scientists to develop the computing technology and infrastructure that will be necessary to process, store and analyse increasing amounts of data. This £120 million programme will be overseen by the EPSRC. The Research Councils are working closely together to capitalise on potential joint funding opportunities. In addition, links have been established with other international programmes; for example, there is collaboration with the EU DataGrid Project, and Computer Science Fellowships are being funded at CERN in grid technologies.

Developments in quantum cryptography could lead to completely secure 'unhackable' Internet, data and voice communications. Researchers based at Imperial College, London and the University of Oxford are carrying out research based on exploiting quantum principles—the Heisenberg uncertainty principle and quantum entanglement—instead of the current mathematical methods. They are working towards new encryption systems. As industry and commerce become increasingly reliant on secure communications, the potential for code-breaking techniques of the future being able to breach current security methods makes improving data encryption a priority.

of one of the Christmas Lectures from the Royal Institution (see p. 444).

Medical Research Council (MRC)

The MRC (*www.mrc.ac.uk*), with an overall budget of £393 million for 2001–02, is the main source of public funds for biomedical and related sciences research. It supports research and training aimed at maintaining and improving human health. The MRC advances knowledge and technology to meet the needs of user communities, including the providers of healthcare and the biotechnology, food, healthcare, medical instrumentation, pharmaceutical and other biomedical-related industries. About half the MRC's research expenditure is allocated to its own institutes and units, the rest going mainly on grant support and research training awards to teams and individuals in higher education institutions. The Council has three major institutes, including the National Institute for Medical Research at Mill Hill in London, the Laboratory of Molecular Biology in Cambridge and the Clinical Sciences Centre at Imperial College, London. It has some 30 smaller research units and scientific teams in the UK, most of which are attached to higher education institutions and hospitals. The MRC works closely with a number of government bodies, in particular the UK Health Departments; this includes cooperation in developing research priorities, and joint initiatives in areas such as primary care research and in research training.

The Government has identified cancer as one of the three most important service priorities for the NHS (see p. 200). The MRC is contributing in a number of ways to research that will underpin improvements in cancer health care. The Council has established a Cancer Cell Unit at Addenbrooke's Hospital, Cambridge, that will work with the university's Department of Clinical Oncology to translate basic research into new tests, treatments and preventive measures. Research at the nearby MRC Laboratory of Molecular Biology has led to the design of cytotoxic molecules that specifically target cancer cells, rather than attacking normal cells as well. This may lead to clinical treatment for common cancers. MRC funds many cancer clinical trials and is hosting the new National Cancer Research Institute, launched in April 2001, that will provide a strategic focus for all aspects of cancer research.

Natural Environment Research Council (NERC)

The NERC (*www.nerc.ac.uk*) carries out Earth system science. In 2001–02 it will spend its budget of £220 million addressing issues related to biodiversity, environmental risks and hazards, global change, natural resource management, and pollution and waste.

The Council invests in research in its own and other research centres as well as research and training in universities. It also provides a range of facilities for use by the wider environmental science community, including a marine research fleet. NERC research centres include the British Geological Survey, the British Antarctic Survey, the Centre for Ecology and Hydrology, the Southampton Oceanography Centre (a partnership with Southampton University), the Plymouth Marine Laboratory and the Proudman Oceanographic Laboratory. The NERC also supports a number of university-based units. One of these is the Tyndall Centre for Climate Change, jointly funded by NERC, EPSRC and ESRC (see p. 435), with headquarters at the University of East Anglia. The Tyndall Centre brings together scientists, economists, engineers and social scientists, who together are working to develop sustainable responses to climate change. Their research involves dialogue with the research community, with business leaders, policy advisers, the media and the general public.

> Scientists at the Plymouth Marine Laboratory (PML) have been researching how the microscopic floating algae of the sea—the phytoplankton—produce ultraviolet sunscreen compounds of low molecular weight to protect themselves from the potentially damaging effects of the sun. There is commercial interest in these compounds—for algal sunscreens—as the chemical properties match requirements for a marketable product and because they derive from a natural, renewable source.

Biotechnology and Biological Sciences Research Council (BBSRC)

The BBSRC (*www.bbsrc.ac.uk*) has a budget of £226 million for 2001–02. It supports basic and strategic research and research training related to the understanding and exploitation of biological systems, which underpin the agriculture, bioprocessing, chemical, food, healthcare, pharmaceutical and other biotechnology-related industries. The scientific themes are biomolecular sciences; genes and developmental biology; biochemistry and cell biology; plant and microbial sciences; animal sciences; agri-food; and engineering and biological systems. As well as funding research in universities and other research centres, the BBSRC sponsors eight research institutes.

The BBSRC funds research that provides the UK with world-class genetics resources, databases and genomics technologies for a variety of model laboratory species and for important microbes, crops and livestock. The BBSRC has launched a £25 million initiative, Exploiting Genomics, on research that brings together genetics, engineering and information science to address industrial and policy needs in areas such as improving food safety, overcoming bacterial resistance to antibiotics, and developing new cell- and gene-based therapies.

The BBSRC has established six specialist Centres for Structural Biology, the science that underpins understanding of, and ability to predict how, the function of individual biological molecules and large molecular assemblies, such as virus particles, is determined by their structure.

The Bioscience Business Plan competition has been developed and piloted by the BBSRC with support from the MRC and private sector funding. It encourages the formation of new bioscience ventures by enabling participants to develop and submit ideas for new start-up businesses.

> *Campylobacter jejuni* is a major cause of debilitating food poisoning in the UK and around the world. A collaborative study by scientists at the London School of Hygiene and Tropical Medicine, and the Universities of Leicester and Birmingham has used comparative genomics, microarrays and protein analysis (proteomics) to look at patterns of gene activity in this organism. The organism has been shown to possess a capsular coat, which has implications for its survival inside its host and outside. Some of its proteins have carbohydrate attachments—something that was thought not to occur in bacteria, and which is probably important in *Campylobacter's* ability to alter its surface characteristics and camouflage itself against a host's immune system. These findings will help suggest new strategies for controlling *C. jejuni* and for designing vaccines.

Particle Physics and Astronomy Research Council (PPARC)

The main task of the PPARC (*www.pparc.ac.uk*), which has a budget of £212 million for 2001–02, is to encourage and support a balanced and cost-effective research programme into fundamental physical processes. Its four main areas of research are:

- particle physics—theoretical and experimental research into elementary particles and the fundamental forces of nature;
- particle astrophysics—theoretical and computational studies of the structure of the early Universe following the Big Bang;
- astronomy (including cosmology and astrophysics)—the origin, structure and evolution of the Universe, stars and galaxies; and
- planetary science (including solar and terrestrial physics)—the origin and evolution of the solar system and the influence of the Sun on planetary bodies, particularly Earth.

> Researchers at Imperial College, London and the University of Durham have been investigating the possibilities of adaptive optics techniques—methods of reducing the distorting effects of the Earth's atmosphere on images produced by large telescopes—in studies of the eye (ophthalmology). Imaging the eye's retina is an important diagnostic tool but is difficult because of the internal aberrations of the eye. Adaptive optics can correct for the aberrations and enable doctors to see the retina in detail. It could also help to simplify and improve the accuracy of optometry and allow the production of specialised contact lenses for correcting the vision of people whose eyes have complicated aberrations.

The PPARC's support involves the provision of funds to universities to undertake research and the provision of facilities to enable that research to take place. Facilities are provided on a national and international basis, the latter including membership of ESA and CERN, and, from July 2002, ESO (see pp. 439–42).

> The 2001 Census of Population in the UK (see pp. 34–6) is using a new measure of social class—the National Statistics Socio-economic Classification (NS–SEC). This was developed through a collaborative arrangement between the ESRC and the Office for National Statistics. Information about the eight NS–SEC categories—which replace earlier Social Class categories—can be found on the National Statistics website (*www.statistics.gov.uk*).

Economic and Social Research Council (ESRC)

The ESRC (*www.esrc.ac.uk*), with an R&D provision of £78 million for 2001–02, supports research and training in the social sciences to address economic and social concerns of importance to business, the public sector and government—including economic competitiveness, the quality of life, and the effectiveness of public services and policy. Research funded by the ESRC is conducted in higher education institutions or independent research establishments. The Council has seven priority themes: economic performance and development; environment and human behaviour; governance and citizenship knowledge, communication and learning; lifecourse, lifestyles and health; social stability and exclusion; and work and organisations.

A major research programme on devolution and constitutional change in the UK has been launched. It will explore the political, economic, social and geographical effects of constitutional changes connected with the creation of the Scottish Parliament, the National Assembly for Wales, the Northern Ireland Assembly, Regional Development Agencies (see p. 10) and the London Assembly and Mayor (see pp. 9–10). The programme's aim is to increase understanding of these processes of change and the consequent effects on people's lives.

Council for the Central Laboratory of the Research Councils (CCLRC)

The CCLRC (*www.cclrc.ac.uk*) promotes scientific and engineering research by providing facilities and technical expertise primarily to meet the needs of the research communities supported by the other Research Councils. Its R&D budget for 2001–02 is £114 million, of which £83 million comes through agreements with other Research Councils and another £23 million from contracts and agreements with the EU, overseas countries, and other industries and organisations. It covers a broad range of science and technology, including materials, structural and biomolecular science using accelerators, synchrotrons and lasers, satellite instrumentation and data processing, remote sensing, electronics, sensor technology, computing, mobile communications, micro-engineering, microsystems and particle physics.

The CCLRC is responsible for three research establishments: the Rutherford Appleton Laboratory in Oxfordshire; the Daresbury Laboratory in Cheshire; and the Chilbolton Observatory in Hampshire. These centres provide facilities too large or complex to be housed by individual academic institutions. Among the facilities are ISIS (the world's leading source of pulsed neutrons and muons), some of the world's brightest lasers and the pioneering Daresbury synchrotron source.

GOVERNMENT DEPARTMENTS

Department of Trade and Industry

In 2001–02 DTI's planned expenditure on SET is £418 million: £274 million on R&D and £144 million on technology transfer. Expenditure covers innovation and technology for a number of industrial sectors, including aeronautics, biotechnology, chemicals, communications, engineering, environmental technology, IT, space (see pp. 439–40), and nuclear and non-nuclear energy. DTI is committed to helping UK businesses successfully exploit their ideas, and to promoting a business environment to encourage this. DTI's innovation expenditure in 2001–02 will be some £334 million, of which £58 million will be for industrial exploitation of science, £87 million on support for competitiveness and £76 million on technical and design infrastructure.

Innovation embraces the development, design and financing of new products, services and processes, exploitation of new markets, creation of new businesses and associated changes in management of people and organisational practices. Through its Innovation Unit, a mixed team of business secondees and government officials, DTI seeks to promote a culture of innovation in all sectors of the economy. In Northern Ireland the Industrial Research and Technology Unit has a similar role to that of DTI, supporting industrial R&D, technology transfer and innovation.

Technology and Knowledge Transfer

DTI aims to increase collaboration and the flow of knowledge between the SET base and businesses; improve access to sources of technology and technological expertise; improve the capacity of business to use technology effectively; and increase the uptake of the latest technology and best practice techniques.

One example of a technology and knowledge transfer mechanism is TCS (previously known as the Teaching Company Scheme). Now a Business Link service in England, TCS is managed by the Small Business Service (see p. 389) and funded by DTI, two other government departments, five of the Research Councils and the devolved administrations, and by the participating companies. As well as facilitating technology and knowledge transfer between the knowledge base and businesses, TCS also provides business-based training and experience for high-calibre graduates. They work in companies on two-year projects that are central to the needs of the businesses and are jointly supervised by personnel from the knowledge base and the companies. There are around 900 individual TCS Programmes, each involving one or more graduates, with around 90% of the Programmes involving small and medium-sized enterprises (SMEs).

To help UK companies remain competitive in an increasingly global market, DTI's International Technology Service (ITS) enables UK companies to become aware of, and gain access to, new technological developments and management practices not present in the UK. The ITS highlights developments and opportunities overseas; and assists companies to access technology, set up licensing agreements and collaborative ventures, and gain experience of new technology and leading management practices.

Smart

The 'Smart' scheme helps individuals and SMEs review their use of technology, access technology, and research and develop technologically innovative products and processes. Traditionally, help has been available for feasibility studies into innovative technology and for projects to develop new products and processes up to prototype stage. Since 1999, Smart has also provided help for:

- technology reviews, which provide grants towards the consultancy costs of an expert review of a company's use of technology compared to best practice in its industry sector;
- technology studies, which provide grants for a more in-depth consultancy to help a business identify technological opportunities leading to innovative products and processes; and
- micro projects, which provide grants of up to £10,000 to help individuals and small firms with fewer than ten employees to develop low-cost prototypes of products and processes involving technical advances and/or novelty.

Business Links (see p. 389) have an important role in providing advice on all aspects of Smart, generating suitable feasibility studies and development projects, and in helping firms to submit applications. Smart is managed in England by the Small Business Service. Separate Smart schemes are operated in Scotland, Wales and Northern Ireland.

Aeronautics

DTI's Civil Aircraft Research and Technology Demonstration Programme (CARAD) supports research and technology demonstration in aeronautics as part of the industrial exploitation of science programme. In 2001–02 the CARAD budget is £20 million. CARAD is part of the national aeronautics research effort, with most of the supported research work being conducted in industry, and with significant involvement of QinetiQ, formerly the Defence Evaluation and Research Agency (see p. 438). Universities and other research organisations receive about 7% of funding. CARAD and earlier programmes have supported a range of projects, including aluminium and composite airframe materials, more efficient and environmentally friendly engines, and advanced aircraft systems.

Measurement Standards

DTI is responsible for the National Measurement System (NMS—see p. 391) which funds science and technology programmes in measurement science, including materials metrology. DTI invests £50 million on the NMS and a further £8 million a year on materials metrology. The NMS provides world-class measurement standards and calibration facilities. These enable businesses and public authorities to make accurate measurements which are nationally and internationally accepted. Although most of the work is carried out at the National Physical Laboratory, the Laboratory of the Government Chemist, the National Engineering Laboratory and the National Weights and Measures Laboratory, DTI is taking steps to increase competition in these programmes and to work more closely with business in order to identify its future needs.

Ministry of Defence

The Government invests about £450 million a year in technological research to ensure that the UK's armed forces stay ahead of threats from potential adversaries. The MoD has a research budget and also a much larger equipment procurement budget. Some £2 billion a year is spent on equipment procurement, including the development—the design and testing (normally by industry for the MoD as customer)—of specific equipment.

All MoD research was previously carried out by the Defence Evaluation and Research Agency (DERA), which used to be the largest single scientific employer in the UK. In July 2001 DERA was disbanded and replaced by two new organisations—Defence Science and Technology Laboratory (Dstl) and QinetiQ plc. About 25% of the staff (some 3,000) have been retained in MoD to form Dstl which is a trading fund agency. It will carry out research in key areas, provide a high-level overview of defence science and technology, act as an in-house source of impartial advice and manage international research collaboration.

About 75% of DERA's staff were transferred to QinetiQ plc. This is a wholly government-owned company which will be floated during 2002, with the Government probably retaining a financial stake initially.

Department for Transport, Local Government and the Regions (DTLR)

The DTLR funds research to provide the evidence base for all its major policy and operational responsibilities: local and regional government; housing, urban policy and planning; roads and local transport; and railways, aviation and shipping. Total expenditure for 2001–02 is £87 million, including spending by executive agencies.

Department for Environment, Food and Rural Affairs (DEFRA)

DEFRA coordinates its research programme with the devolved administrations and the Research Councils. The programme supports the Department's wide-ranging responsibilities for protecting the public in relation to farm produce and animal diseases transmissible to humans; protecting and enhancing the rural and marine environment; reducing risks from flooding and coastal erosion; improving animal health and welfare; and encouraging modern, efficient and competitive agriculture, fishing and food industries. The budget for research expenditure in 2001–02 is £186 million, including support for the Royal Botanic Gardens, Kew (see p. 444). Through the Darwin Initiative (see p. 321), British expertise is being made available to assist countries that are rich in biodiversity but have insufficient financial or technical resources to implement the Biodiversity Convention.

The Report of the BSE (Bovine Spongiform Encephalitis) Inquiry headed by Lord Phillips was published in late 2000 (see p. 460) and the Government's response to the report was published in September 2001. A Review of the origin of BSE, presenting results of a committee headed by Professor Horn, was published in July 2001.

Department of Health (DH)

The DH supports R&D to provide the evidence needed to inform policy and practice in public health, healthcare and social care. It delivers this objective through:

- National Health Service (NHS) R&D funding, which supports projects funded by other non-commercial R&D sources (including charities) carried out in the NHS, and also specific health and social care projects meeting identified research needs of the DH and the NHS;
- a Policy Research Programme (PRP), directly commissioned by the DH; and
- *ad hoc* project funding from other DH R&D budgets and support for non-departmental public bodies (NDPBs).

The DH expects to spend some £538 million on research in 2001–02: £476 million on NHS R&D, £33 million on the PRP and about £29 million involving the NDPBs and *ad hoc* budgets.

Department for International Development (DFID)

DFID commissions and sponsors knowledge generation and sharing in natural resources, health and population, engineering, education and social sciences. Financial provision in 2001–02 is about £90 million, covering research projects and programmes that respond to identified development needs and that help build research capacity in developing countries. DFID also contributes to international centres and programmes generating knowledge on development issues. These contributions include support for the EU Framework Programmes, which sponsor research and technological development in renewable natural resources, agriculture, health and information technologies, for the Consultative Group on International Agricultural Research (CGIAR) and for the World Health Organisation which administer programmes that include international research and research capacity strengthening.

Scottish Executive

In many areas—electrical and electronic engineering, medicine, agriculture and biological sciences, fisheries and marine science—Scotland's science base has an international reputation for research excellence. The majority of the Scottish Executive's support for the science base is disbursed by the Scottish Higher Education Funding Council. In total this amounts to some £616 million for 2001–02, including £133 million for research and £23 million to support the strategic development of the sector. A further £52 million encourages and funds agricultural and fisheries research, and related biological, food, environmental, economic and social science—most of this goes to the Scottish Agricultural and Biological Research Institutes, the Fisheries Research Service and the Scottish Agricultural College. In addition, about £145 million goes to Scottish research institutions from the UK Research Councils.

The Scottish Executive Enterprise and Lifelong Learning Department encourages the development of science-based industry, for example, by promoting and administering government and EU industrial R&D schemes. The enterprise network in Scotland, including Scottish Enterprise and Highlands and Islands Enterprise, addresses the need for innovation and technology transfer, both through grant support for innovation and through a wide range of initiatives.

Space Activities

The UK's civil space programme is brought together through the British National Space Centre (BNSC), a partnership of government departments and the Research Councils. BNSC's key aims are to develop practical and economic uses of space, to promote the competitiveness of British space companies in world markets, to maintain the UK's position in space science, to foster the development of innovative technology and to improve understanding of the Earth's environment and resources. These are realised primarily by collaboration with other European nations through the European Space Agency (ESA).

Through BNSC, the Government spends around £180 million a year on space activities. About three-quarters of this is channelled through ESA for collaborative programmes on Earth observation, telecommunications and space science, much of which returns to the UK through contracts awarded to British industry. The remaining quarter of the space budget is spent on international meteorological programmes carried out through the European Meteorological Satellite Organisation (EUMETSAT), developing experiments (such as the Beagle 2 Mars Lander) for ESA satellites, and on the national programme, which is aimed at complementing R&D supported through ESA. Around half of the British space programme is concerned with satellite-based Earth observation (remote sensing) for commercial and environmental applications.

The UK is also a major contributor to ESA's latest Earth observation satellite, ENVISAT, due to be launched in 2001. This will carry a new generation of radar and radiometer systems as well as other scientific environmental instruments, some of which have been either designed or constructed in Britain. British companies are also active in the development of microsatellites.

A quarter of the UK's space budget is devoted to space science led by the Particle

Physics and Astronomy Research Council, in support of astronomy, planetary science and geophysics. The UK is contributing substantially to the SOHO mission to study the Sun; to the Cluster mission launched in 2000 to study solar-terrestrial relationships; to the Infrared Space Observatory, which is investigating the birth and death of stars; and to the Cassini Huygens mission, a seven-year programme to send a probe to Saturn and its moon Titan, launched in 1997. It is also participating in XMM, ESA's X-ray spectroscopy mission launched in December 1999 to investigate X-ray emissions from black holes.

The UK is taking an active role in the largest current international project in ground-based astronomy. The Gemini project involves building two 8 m telescopes at Mauna Kea (Hawaii) and Cerro Pachón (Chile): the former became operational in 1999 and the latter in 2001. The other partners are the United States, Canada, Argentina, Brazil and Chile. The UK has a 25% stake in the work, with major responsibility for the primary mirror support system and much of the control software.

ESA's £400 million Living Planet environmental research programme, to help scientists understand and predict the Earth's environment and humankind's effects upon it, was launched in 1999. BNSC will contribute £67 million to this programme. The first project to benefit from the programme will be the British CRYOSAT mission, to be launched in 2002, which will study the effects of global warming on the polar ice caps and floating Arctic sea ice. UK environmental scientists also have a significant interest in a second mission, which will measure soil moisture and ocean salinity.

Two new centres of excellence in Earth observation will use satellites and models to help forecast environmental change and play a role in exploiting data from ENVISAT and the Living Planet programme. The Data Assimilation Research Centre will forecast changes in the Earth's systems, while the Centre for Polar Observation Modelling will measure changes in polar ice which could cause rising sea levels and changes in ocean circulation.

The UK is also developing the Geostationary Earth Radiation Budget instrument, which is intended to provide accurate measurements of the energy source for the Earth's climate and, together with the National Aeronautics and Space Administration (NASA), the High Resolution Dynamics Limb Sounder, which will provide measurements of upper atmosphere trace chemicals and temperature.

The UK has many bilateral agreements for scientific research with other countries, such as Russia, Japan and the United States. For example, British scientists contributed to the high-resolution camera for Chandra (the NASA X-ray satellite).

Another major area of British space expertise is satellite communications and navigation. In Europe, the UK is both a leading producer and user of satellite communications technology (see p. 487). It is taking a leading role in preparations for future ESA satellite communications missions, including ARTEMIS, which will provide important communications links for the ENVISAT programme. Britain is also contributing to the Galileo global navigation satellite system.

INTERNATIONAL COLLABORATION

European Union

Since 1984 the EU has operated a series of R&D framework programmes, across a range of disciplines and sectors, to strengthen the scientific and technological basis of European industry and support the development of EU policies. The Fifth Framework Programme, which runs for four years (1999–2002), supports strategic and applied multi-disciplinary research targeted at tackling pressing European problems, such as aeronautics, land transport and marine technologies, the ageing population, e-commerce and climate change. The six grant-giving Research Councils maintain a joint office in Brussels to promote UK participation in European research programmes. The UK is actively engaged in the development of a common European Space Strategy involving ESA, EU and others.

Other International Activities

Over 800 UK organisations have taken part in EUREKA (*www.eureka.be*), an industry-led scheme to encourage European cooperation in developing advanced products and processes with worldwide sales potential. There are 32 members of EUREKA, including the 15 EU countries and the European Commission. Some 650 projects are in progress, involving firms, universities and research organisations. About 1,100 projects have finished. Examples of projects include the development of biological tracers for use during oil spills to identify the source of the spill; new designs for lamp posts which will be less dangerous if hit by oncoming vehicles; and a 'biopackaging' project to develop food trays made from potato starch, coated in a waterproof film, which will biodegrade harmlessly when they come into contact with soil.

The COST programme (European co-operation in the field of scientific and technical research) is a multilateral agreement involving 32 countries (including all the EU member states, many Mediterranean, Central European and Eastern European countries and Israel). Its purpose is to encourage co-operation in national research activities across Europe, with participants from industry, academia and research laboratories. Transport, telecommunications and materials have traditionally been the largest areas supported. New areas include physics, chemistry, neuroscience and the application of biotechnology to agriculture, including forestry. The UK participates in the majority of COST actions and in the management of the COST programme.

Another example of international collaboration is CERN, the European Laboratory for Particle Physics, based in Geneva, where the Large Hadron Collider is due to be completed by 2006. Scientific programmes at CERN aim to test, verify and develop the 'standard model' of the origin and structure of the Universe. There are 20 member states. The Particle Physics and Astronomy Research Council (see p. 435) leads UK participation in CERN. The Engineering and Physical Sciences Research Council provides the UK contribution to the costs of access by UK researchers to the high-flux neutron source at the Institut Laue-Langevin and to the European Synchrotron Radiation Facility, both in Grenoble.

The PPARC is a partner in the European Incoherent Scatter Radar Facility within the Arctic Circle, which conducts research on the ionosphere. The Natural Environment Research Council has a major involvement in international programmes of research into global climate change organised through the World Climate Research Programme and the International Geosphere-Biosphere Programme. It also supports the UK's subscription to the Ocean Drilling Program.

The Medical Research Council pays the UK subscription to the European Molecular Biology Laboratory (EMBL), which has its home research base at Heidelberg. The European Bioinformatics Institute, an outstation of the EMBL, at Hinxton, near Cambridge, provides access to important molecular biology, sequencing and structural databases. The MRC is also responsible for the UK's subscriptions to the International Agency for Cancer Research and the Human Frontier Science Programme, which supports international collaborative research into brain function and biological function through molecular-level approaches .

The Research Councils have a number of bilateral arrangements to promote international collaboration. For example, the BBSRC has agreements with its equivalent organisations in France, the Netherlands, the United States, China, Japan, the Republic of Korea and India, and provides travel funding and fellowships to encourage international linkages.

The UK is a member of the science and technology committees of such international organisations as the OECD and NATO, and of various specialised agencies of the United Nations, including the United Nations Educational, Scientific and Cultural Organisation (UNESCO). The Research Councils, the Royal Society and the British Academy are members of the European Science Foundation—an association of 67 international funding agencies in 24 European countries, representing all scientific

From July 2002, the UK will become a member of the European Southern Observatory (ESO). ESO owns a number of world-class telescope facilities in Chile, in particular the recently completed four 8-metre ground-based telescopes. Membership of ESO will allow UK astronomers access to these world-leading telescopes, and also to participate in the next world ground-based astronomy project, the Atacama Large Millimetre Array (ALMA), which will involve European, US and Japanese collaboration to build an array of telescopes in the Atacama Desert in Chile.

disciplines—and a number of British scientists are involved in its initiatives.

The British Government also enters into bilateral agreements with other governments to encourage closer collaboration in science, engineering and technology. Staff in British Embassies, High Commissions and British Council offices conduct government business on, and promote contacts in, SET between the UK and overseas countries; and help to inform a large number of organisations in the UK about developments and initiatives overseas. There are science and technology (S&T) attachés in British Missions in Washington, Tokyo, Moscow, Ottawa, Paris, Bonn, Munich, Rome, Beijing, Taipei and Seoul. The S&T network is being expanded by the creation of some 30 new posts across the world—likely to be in North and South America, Europe and Asia—and a London-based S&T unit. A number of British Council offices have designated Science Officer posts.

The British Council promotes the creativity and innovation of cutting-edge UK science through events, partnership programmes, seminars, exhibitions and information provision. It balances one-to-one scientific links with projects aimed at raising awareness of scientific issues among overseas public audiences through popular communication.

RESEARCH IN HIGHER EDUCATION INSTITUTIONS

Universities carry out most of the UK's long-term strategic and basic research in science and technology. The higher education funding councils provide the main general funds to support research in universities and other higher education institutions in Great Britain. These funds pay for the salaries of permanent academic staff, who usually teach as well as undertake research, and contribute to the infrastructure for research. The quality of research performance is a key element in the allocation of funding. In Northern Ireland institutions are funded by the Department for Employment and Learning.

Basic and strategic research in higher education institutions is also financed by the Research Councils. Institutions undertaking research with the support of Research Council grants have the rights over the commercial exploitation of their research, subject to the prior agreement of the sponsoring Research Council. They may make use of technology transfer experts and other specialists to help exploit and license the results of their research. The other main channels of support are industry, charities, government departments and the EU. The high quality of research in higher education institutions, and their marketing skills, have enabled them to attract more funding from a larger range of external sources, especially in contract income from industry and charities.

Science Parks

A Science Park is a business support and technology transfer initiative—it has formal or operational links to a higher education institution or other major research centre, encouraging and supporting the start-up, incubation and growth of innovation-led, high-growth, knowledge-based businesses. The UK Science Park Association (*www.ukspa.org.uk*) numbers 63 such initiatives, which between them host over 1,600 firms employing over 28,000 people in total. Many of these firms are spin-offs from the associated institution or are start-up enterprises in fields of high technology such as software, biotechnology, analytical services or consultancy.

OTHER ORGANISATIONS

Research and Technology Organisations (RTOs)

RTOs are independent organisations carrying out commercially relevant research and other services on behalf of industry, often relating to a specific industrial sector. Others are contract research organisations undertaking specific projects for any client. The Association of Independent Research and Technology Organisations has 44 members that together employ about 10,000 people.

Charitable Organisations

Medical research charities are a major source of funds for medical research in the UK. Their combined contribution to research activities in the UK in 2000–01 was £632 million (excluding capital and infrastructure costs). The three largest contributors are the Wellcome Trust, the Imperial Cancer Research Fund and the Cancer Research Campaign.

Professional and Learned Institutions

There are numerous technical institutions, professional associations and learned societies in the UK, many of which promote their own disciplines or the education and professional well-being of their members. The Council of Science and Technology Institutes has ten member institutes representing biology, biochemistry, chemistry, the environment, food science and technology, geology, hospital physics and physics.

The Engineering Council (*www.engc.org.uk*) promotes and regulates the engineering profession. It is supported by over 125 industry affiliates, which include large private sector companies and government departments, and 35 professional engineering institutions. In partnership with the institutions, the Council accredits higher and further education courses and advises the Government on academic, industrial and professional issues. It also runs a number of promotional activities. Some 257,000 individuals have satisfied the Council's regulations for registration through their institution as either Chartered Engineers, Incorporated Engineers or as Engineering Technicians.

Royal Society

The Royal Society (*www.royalsoc.ac.uk*), founded in 1660, is the UK's academy of science and has 1,130 Fellows and 113 Foreign Members. Many of its Fellows serve on governmental advisory councils and committees concerned with research. The Society has three roles: as the national academy of science, as a learned society and as a funding agency for the scientific community. It offers independent advice to government on science matters, acts as an international forum for discussion of ground-breaking scientific research, supports many of the brightest young scientists and engineers in the UK, facilitates dialogue between scientists and the public and promotes science education. Its government grant for 2001–02 is £26 million.

> One of the 42 new Fellows of the Royal Society (FRS) in 2001, Professor Timothy Berners-Lee was elected in recognition of his work that has 'revolutionised communication via the Internet, enabling universal access to information placed on the web, and has had a profound economic impact'. Professor Berners-Lee, now at the Massachusetts Institute of Technology, in the United States, invented the web's address system and layout while working at CERN in Switzerland in 1990, thus revolutionising the way information is presented and accessed.

Royal Academy of Engineering

The national academy of engineering in Britain is the Royal Academy of Engineering (*www.raeng.org.uk*), which has 1,175 Fellows and 82 Foreign Members. It promotes excellence in engineering for the benefit of society, and advises government, Parliament and other official organisations. The Academy's programmes are aimed at attracting first-class students into engineering, raising awareness of the importance of engineering design among undergraduates, developing links between industry and higher education, and increasing industrial investment in engineering research in higher education institutions. It has a government grant of £4.3 million in 2001–02.

Other Societies

In Scotland the Royal Society of Edinburgh, established in 1783, promotes science by offering postdoctoral research fellowships and studentships, awarding prizes and grants, organising meetings and symposia, and publishing journals. It also acts as a source of independent scientific advice to the Government and others.

Three other major institutions publicise scientific developments by means of lectures and publications for specialists and schoolchildren. Of these, the British Association for the Advancement of Science, founded in 1831, is mainly concerned with science, while the Royal Society of Arts (*www.rsa.org.uk*), dating from 1754, deals with the arts and commerce as well as science. The Royal Institution (*www.ri.ac.uk*), founded in 1799, also performs these functions and runs its own research laboratories. It also arranges a large and varied public programme of events to bring science to a wider audience, including the *Christmas Lectures* and the *Friday Evening Discourses*. These are all presented in the Royal Institution's historic Albemarle Street lecture theatre—some 35,000 schoolchildren and 25,000 members of the public attend events here each year. The *Christmas Lectures* now reach a worldwide audience, being broadcast in Britain, other parts of Europe, Japan and the Republic of Korea.

Zoological Gardens

The Zoological Society of London (ZSL) (*www.zsl.org*), an independent conservation, science and education charity founded in 1826, runs London Zoo, which occupies about 15 hectares (36 acres) of Regent's Park (London). It also owns and runs Whipsnade Wild Animal Park (243 hectares/600 acres) in Bedfordshire. ZSL is responsible for the Institute of Zoology, which carries out research in support of conservation. The Institute's work covers topics such as ecology, reproductive biology and conservation genetics. ZSL also operates in overseas conservation projects, and is concerned with practical field conservation, primarily in East and Southern Africa, the Middle East and parts of Asia. Other well-known zoos in the UK include those in Edinburgh, Bristol, Chester, Dudley and Marwell (near Winchester).

Botanic Gardens

The Royal Botanic Gardens, Kew (*www.rbgkew.org.uk*), founded in 1759, covers 121 hectares (300 acres) at Kew in south-west London and a 187-hectare (462-acre) estate at Wakehurst Place (Ardingly, in West Sussex). They contain one of the largest collections of living and dried plants in the world. Research is conducted into all aspects of plant life, including physiology, biochemistry, genetics, economic botany and the conservation of habitats and species. The Millennium Seed Bank, containing the world's most comprehensive collection of seeds of flowering plants, at Wakehurst Place in Sussex, opened in August 2000. By August 2001 it held 266,425,433 seeds. These are stored in large underground vaults at –20°C in the Wellcome Trust Millennium Building. Staff are also active in programmes to reintroduce endangered plant species to the wild. Kew participates in joint research programmes in some 50 countries.

The Royal Botanic Garden in Edinburgh was established in 1670 and is the national botanic garden of Scotland. Together with its three associated specialist gardens, which were acquired to provide a range of different climatic and soil conditions, it has become an internationally recognised centre for taxonomy (classification of species); for the conservation and study of living and preserved plants and fungi; and as a provider of horticultural education.

A National Botanic Garden and research centre for Wales has been developed on a 230-hectare (570-acre) site on the Middleton Hall estate at Llanarthne, near Carmarthen and was opened in May 2000—the first botanic garden to be built in Britain for two centuries.

'Sleepovers' at the Science Museum, as they are popularly known, are Science Nights, catering for 380 children aged between 8 and 11 years. The all-night programme of demonstrations, talks, 'hands-on' workshops and team activities starts at around 7 p.m. and finishes at 10 a.m. the next morning. Each season of Science Nights has a theme—Light Fantastic, Space and Stars, Forces and Motion, and Material World. The programme provides a mixture of education and fun, and is designed to introduce science to children and interest them in science at an early age.

Scientific Museums

The Natural History Museum (*www.nhm.ac.uk*) is one of Britain's most popular visitor attractions (with 1.7 million visitors in 2000–01), with exhibitions devoted to the Earth and the life sciences. It is founded on collections of 68 million specimens from the natural world, has 350 scientists working in 60 countries, and has 500,000 historically important original works of art. It also offers an advisory service to institutions all over the world. The Science Museum (*www.nmsi.ac.uk*), which had 1.4 million visitors in 2000–01, promotes the public understanding of the history of science, technology, industry and medicine.

Around 80 science and discovery centres in the UK have formed a new network which will be the UK wing of ECSITE—the European Collaborative for Science Industry and Technology Exhibitions. It will be known formally as ECSITE-UK, the Science and Discovery Centre Network. It brings together more than 40 regional science centres and a similar number of discovery centres in a wide range of museums, botanic gardens, aquariums and zoos. In recent years the number of science centres has increased rapidly through Millennium Commission funding, matched by capital investment from other public and private sources. The largest private supporter is the Wellcome Trust, which has invested £45 million in science centres in Birmingham, Bristol, Dundee, Glasgow, London, Manchester and Newcastle upon Tyne.

A new wing added 10,000 sq m of display space to the Museum in June 2000. This contains galleries on biomedical science and information technology and a 450-seat 3D IMAX (large-format screen) theatre. These two museums are in South Kensington, London. Other important collections include those at the Museum of Science & Industry in Manchester, the Museum of the History of Science in Oxford, and the Royal Scottish Museum, Edinburgh.

Further Reading

Excellence and Opportunity—a science and innovation policy for the 21st century. Cm 4814. The Stationery Office, 2000.
The Science Budget 2001–02 to 2003–04. DTI/OST, 2001.
The Forward Look 1999. DTI/OST. Cm 4363. The Stationery Office, 1999.
Creating Knowledge: Creating Wealth—Realising the Economic Potential of Public Sector Research Establishments. DTI, 1999.
Guidelines 2000: Scientific Advice and Policy Making. OST, 2000.
The Government's Response to the Baker Report: 'Creating Knowledge, Creating Wealth': Realising the Economic Potential of Public Sector Research Establishments. OST, 2000.

Websites

Office of Science and Technology: www.dti.gov.uk/ost
Council of Science and Technology: www.cst.gov.uk
The Wellcome Trust: www.wellcome.ac.uk

26 Agriculture, Fishing & Forestry

Agriculture	446	Animal Health and Welfare	459
Production	448	**The Fishing Industry**	461
Exports, Marketing and Promotion	453	**Research**	464
Government Role	454	**Forestry**	464

Although agriculture, forestry and fishing together accounted for only 1.1% of the total economy in terms of gross value added in 2000, their impact across the United Kingdom was far greater. The UK is about 66% self-sufficient for all food and about 80% for indigenous food.

Agriculture

The major issue facing the farming community in the UK in 2001 was the outbreak of foot-and-mouth disease (see p. 460). This dealt the industry another blow, coming as it did after the BSE epidemic and then the severe flooding which affected many parts of the UK, especially parts of south-east England, and areas close to the River Severn and the Yorkshire Ouse, during autumn 2000. Farm incomes remained low in 2000, another key factor being the further decline in the value of the euro against sterling during the year.

In 2000 UK agriculture contributed £6.6 billion to the total economy, employed some 557,000 people and used nearly three-quarters of the country's land area.

A new Department for Environment, Food and Rural Affairs (DEFRA) was created after the 2001 General Election. It has a crucial role in promoting sustainable development, rural renewal, and sustainable and competitive food chains, both in the UK and internationally. It brings together all the functions of the former Ministry of Agriculture, Fisheries and Food (MAFF), the Environment Protection Group and Wildlife and Countryside Directorate from the former Department of the Environment, Transport and the Regions (DETR) and responsibility for certain animal welfare issues and hunting with hounds from the Home Office. DEFRA administers support policies agreed in Brussels which provide around £3 billion a year to UK agriculture from the European Union (EU) budget.

Farming

In 2000 there were some 233,200 farm holdings in the UK (excluding minor holdings in Great Britain but including all active farms in Northern Ireland). These holdings had an average area of 70.9 hectares (175.2 acres). About 27% of them are smaller than eight European size units (ESUs).[1] About two-thirds of all agricultural land is owner-occupied; the rest is tenanted or rented. Agricultural land represents about 75% of

[1] ESUs measure the financial potential of the holding in terms of the margins which might be expected from stock and crops: 8 ESU is judged the minimum for full-time holdings.

Figure 26.1: Agricultural Land Use, UK, 2000

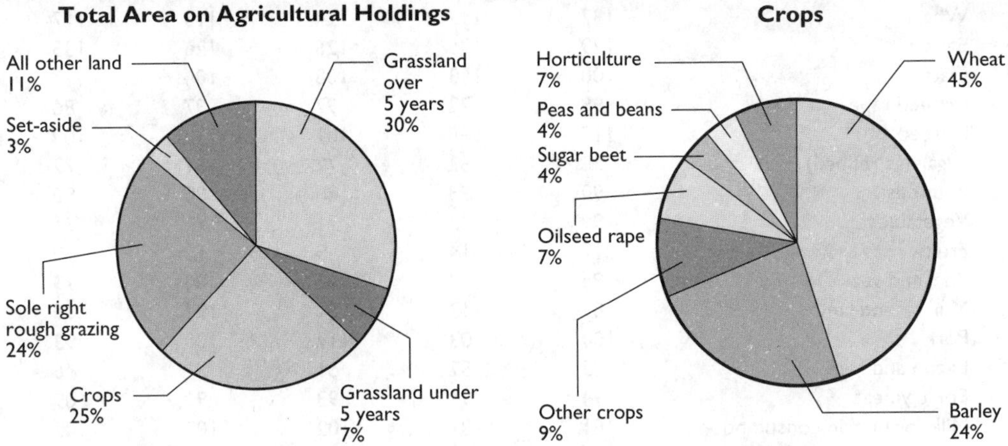

Source: Department for Environment, Food and Rural Affairs

total land area in the UK, compared with 42% for the EU as a whole.

Total income from farming in the UK is estimated to have fallen by 27% in real terms, from £2,578 million in 1999 to £1,882 million in 2000. The *value of output* (including subsidies directly related to products) was 4.5% (£729 million) lower in current prices than in 1999. This fall is largely due to pressure on prices for agricultural outputs caused by a further rise in sterling against the euro, compared with 1999. Prices have fallen particularly for milk and cereals and also, because of domestic market conditions, for potatoes. The wet autumn caused problems for many farmers. *Industry productivity* rose by 2.5% in 2000; the volume of inputs fell by 3.8%, largely due to an 11% fall in the volume of paid labour, whereas a lesser fall of 1.4% in the volume of final output reflected significant drops in the production of oilseed rape, linseed, potatoes, pigs and breeding livestock.

The first of over 300 *farmers' markets* now operating in the UK—selling produce directly to consumers—started in 1997, and a National Association (*www.farmersmarkets.net*) was launched in May 2000.

Agricultural Landlords and Tenants

About 34% of agricultural land in England and 21% in Wales is rented. Since 1995 a simplified legal framework for new tenancies, known as farm business tenancies, has allowed landowners to benefit from full income tax relief.

There is a similar proportion of rented land in Scotland, much of it under crofting tenure (see below), including common grazings. The Scottish Executive is committed to changing the law relating to agricultural tenure.

Most farms in Northern Ireland are owner-occupied, but the conacre system allows owners not wishing to farm all their land to let it annually to others. Conacre land, about 30% of agricultural land, is used mainly for grazing.

Smallholdings and Crofts

In England and Wales county councils let smallholdings to experienced people who want to farm on their own account. Councils may lend working capital to them. In January 2001 there were approximately 31,000 smallholdings in England and 7,000 in Wales.

Table 26.2: Production as a Percentage of Total New Supply for Use in the UK

Food product	1990	1995	1998	1999	2000
Wheat	137	117	124	113	117
Barley	129	135	126	126	135
Oats	100	153	108	104	117
Oilseed rape	99	72	97	97	86
Linseed	117	68	101	152	109
Sugar (as refined)	56	62	72	71	72
Potatoes	90	88	88	90	90
Vegetables	99	73	71	72	71
Fruit	17	14	9	12	10
Beef and veal	95	114	83	80	79
Mutton and lamb	89	113	101	104	99
Pork	100	103	112	100	93
Bacon and ham	43	52	51	51	46
Poultrymeat	94	94	93	91	89
Milk for human consumption (as liquid)	101	101	102	102	102
Butter	67	69	78	71	67
Cheese	66	70	64	63	62
Eggs	93	95	97	93	92

Source: DEFRA: *Agriculture in the United Kingdom 2000*

Land settlement in Scotland has been carried out by the Scottish Executive, which still owns and maintains about 104,500 hectares (668,800 acres) of land settlement estates, comprising 1,390 crofts and holdings.

Crofting is a system of land tenure regulated through the Crofting Acts and found only in the Highlands and Islands of Scotland. A croft is a unit of land subject to these Acts, *not* a house. It rarely provides a full-time income and most crofters have other off-croft employment. An estimated 30,000 family members live on 17,500 crofts, the main crofting areas being in the Western Isles (about 6,000 crofts), Shetland (2,700), Skye and the Inner Hebrides (1,800) and the north-west Highlands (2,300). Croft land covers some 800,000 hectares (2 million acres) and accounts for more than 25% of the agricultural land area of the Highlands and Islands. The Crofters Commission develops and regulates the crofting system and promotes the interests of crofters. The Scottish Executive plans to issue a White Paper in 2002 containing proposals for an amended crofting Act.

PRODUCTION

Home production of the principal foods is shown in Table 26.2 as a percentage by weight of total supplies. Total new supply is home production plus imports less exports.

Livestock

About half of full-time farms are devoted mainly to dairy farming or to beef cattle and sheep. Most of the beef animals and sheep are reared in the hill and moorland areas of Scotland, Wales, Northern Ireland and northern and south-western England. Among world-famous British livestock are the Hereford, Welsh Black and Aberdeen Angus beef breeds, the Jersey, Guernsey and Ayrshire dairy breeds, the Large White pig breed and a number of sheep breeds. Livestock totals are given in Table 26.3.

Cattle and Sheep

Cattle and sheep constitute about 35% of the value of the UK's gross agricultural output.

Table 26.3: Livestock and Livestock Products

	1990	1995	1998	1999	2000
Cattle and calves ('000 head)	12,192	11,857	11,519	11,423	11,133
Sheep and lambs ('000 head)	44,469	43,304	44,471	44,656	42,261
Pigs ('000 head)	7,548	7,627	8,146	7,284	6,482
Poultry ('000 head)[1]	112,718	119,474	152,886	153,581	157,252
Milk (million litres)[2]	14,554	14,015	13,937	14,303	13,775
Hen eggs (million dozen)[3]	804	774	792	743	745
Beef and veal ('000 tonnes)	1,002	1,002	699	679	706
Mutton and lamb ('000 tonnes)	397	403	385	403	390
Pork ('000 tonnes)	762	791	931	832	738
Bacon and ham ('000 tonnes)	191	245	236	233	213
Poultrymeat ('000 tonnes)	1,140	1,415	1,546	1,523	1,514
Butter ('000 tonnes)	151	133	137	141	134
Cheese ('000 tonnes)	320	362	366	368	344
Cream—fresh, frozen, sterilised ('000 tonnes)	230	281	266	275	258
Condensed milk ('000 tonnes)	204	181	192	177	160
Milk powder—full cream ('000 tonnes)	70	90	97	102	107
Skimmed milk powder ('000 tonnes)	166	117	107	102	83

[1] Includes ducks, geese and turkeys. In England and Wales a new approach to collecting poultry information has been used. The figures from 1998 onwards are not therefore directly comparable with previous years.
[2] For human consumption. Including the production of dairy products.
[3] For human consumption only; does not include eggs for hatching.
Source: DEFRA: *Agriculture in the United Kingdom 2000*

Dairy production is the largest part of the sector, followed by cattle and calves, and then sheep and lambs. In 2000 the average size of dairy herds in England was 79. The average yield of milk for each dairy cow in the UK was 5,915 litres (1,300 gallons). The total value of milk and milk products for human consumption fell by 10%.

More than half of home-fed beef production originates from the national dairy herd, in which the Holstein Friesian breed predominates. The remainder derives from suckler herds producing high-quality beef calves, both in the hills and uplands and in lowland areas. The traditional British beef breeds (see p. 448) and, increasingly, imported breeds, such as Charolais, Limousin, Simmental and Belgian Blue, are used for beef production.

The size of both the beef-breeding and dairy herds decreased by 4.3% in 2000. The value of beef and veal production fell by 2.3% to £2,011 million. Despite increased production—output rose by 4.0% to 706,000 tonnes—there were falls in finished cattle prices and in subsidy payments.

The UK has more than 60 native sheep breeds and many cross-bred varieties. The size of the British breeding flock declined by 4.7% in 2000 to 20.4 million and the value of sheepmeat production by 1.9% to £982 million. Prices were generally higher than in 1999. Exports fell in 2000, hampered by the continued strength of the pound.

Pigs

The output value of pigs increased by 5.0% in 2000 to £826 million due to a 20% increase in prices which offset a 12% fall in the home-fed production of pigmeat. Marketing of clean pigs[2] fell by 14%, reflecting the continuing contraction of the breeding herd and also an outbreak of Classical Swine Fever (see

[2] Pigs which have not been used for breeding.

pp. 460–1) in the autumn, which removed over 220,000 pigs from the food chain.

Poultry

The total UK poultry population in 2000 comprised 105.7 million chickens and other table fowls; 28.7 million birds in the laying flock; 9.9 million fowls for breeding; and 12.9 million turkeys, ducks and geese.

Poultrymeat production in 2000 was 1.5 million tonnes, a 0.6% decrease on 1999. The overall value of production in 2000 rose by 2.0% to £1,299 million. Poultry prices overall rose by 1.3%, with the price for turkeys increasing by 11% to the highest level since 1996. The value of hen eggs for human consumption increased by 6.7%.

Crops

Farms devoted primarily to arable crops are found mainly in eastern and central-southern England and eastern Scotland. The main crops are shown in Table 26.4. In the UK in 2000, the area planted to *cereals*—predominantly wheat, barley and oats—totalled 3.35 million hectares, an increase of 6.6% on 1999, largely as a result of good planting conditions and a switch away from oilseed rape and linseed. Total cereal production increased by 8.4% to 24.0 million tonnes and total value by 1.0% to £2,350 million.

The output value of *oilseed rape* fell by 32% to £249 million in 2000 and that of *linseed* by 74% to £34 million, due to lower plantings and a reduction in subsidy rates. The output value of *sugar beet* fell by 9% to £253 million.

Large-scale *potato and vegetable cultivation* takes place on the fertile soils throughout the UK, often with irrigation. Principal areas are the peat and silt fens of Cambridgeshire, Lincolnshire and Norfolk; the sandy loams of Norfolk, Suffolk, West Midlands, Nottinghamshire, South Yorkshire and Lincolnshire; the peat soils of south Lancashire; and the alluvial silts by the River Humber. Early potatoes are produced in Shropshire, Pembrokeshire, Cornwall, Devon, Essex, Suffolk, Kent, Cheshire and south-west Scotland. Production of high-grade seed potatoes is confined mainly to east Scotland, Northern Ireland, the northern uplands of England and the Welsh borders. Total area for all potatoes fell by 7.3% in 2000, with an overall reduction in production of 7.6%. Waterlogged ground caused by continuous rain from mid-October onwards meant that over 20,000 hectares of the Great Britain crop remained unlifted by the end of the year. The output value of potatoes fell by 33% to £501 million.

Arable Area Payments Scheme

Under this scheme within the Common Agricultural Policy (CAP—see p. 457), farmers may claim area payments on cereals, oilseeds, proteins and linseed, and on fibre flax and hemp for fibre. A condition for claiming area payments is that large-scale farmers must 'set aside' a certain percentage of their land, thereby avoiding overproduction, and must comply with the strict rules for managing set-aside. The minimum rate for set-aside for 2001 is 10% of the total area claimed.

In 2000 there were approximately 59,200 claims for area payments in the UK in respect of nearly 4.5 million hectares of land. Payments of approximately £990 million were made.

Pesticides

The Pesticides Safety Directorate (PSD), an executive agency of DEFRA, administers the regulation of agricultural, horticultural, forestry, food storage and home garden pesticides. Its principal functions are to evaluate and process applications for approval of pesticide products for use in Great Britain and provide advice to government on pesticides policy. The PSD aims:

- to protect the health of human beings, creatures and plants;
- to safeguard the environment; and
- to ensure that methods of pest control are safe, efficient and humane by providing effective controls on the sale, supply and use of pesticides.

Horticulture

Table 26.5 gives details of the main horticultural products. As at June 2000 the

Table 26.4 Cereals and Other Crops

	1990	1995	1998	1999	2000
CEREALS					
Wheat					
Area ('000 hectares)	2,014	1,859	2,045	1,847	2,086
Production ('000 tonnes)	14,033	14,310	15,470	14,870	16,700
Yield (tonnes per hectare)	7.0	7.7	7.6	8.0	8.0
Value of production (£ million)	1,426	2,079	1,652	1,525	1,585
Barley					
Area	1,518	1,193	1,255	1,179	1,127
Production	7,910	6,840	6,630	6,580	6,490
Yield	5.2	5.7	5.3	5.6	5.8
Value	776	1,110	781	735	693
Oats					
Area	107	112	98	92	109
Production	530	615	585	540	640
Yield	5.0	5.5	6.0	5.9	5.9
Value	53	89	61	58	65
Total[1]					
Area	3,660	3,182	3,420	3,141	3,347
Production	22,582	21,870	22,790	22,120	23,980
Yield	6.2	6.9	6.7	7.0	7.2
Value	2,259	3,287	2,502	2,326	2,350
OTHER CROPS					
Oilseed rape					
Area	390	439	534	537	402
Production	1,207	1,234	1,566	1,737	1,129
Yield	3.1	2.8	2.9	3.2	2.8
Value	240	380	411	365	250
Linseed					
Area	34	62	101	213	74
Production	62	81	143	302	43
Yield	1.9	1.3	1.4	1.4	0.6
Value	15	40	67	132	34
Sugar beet					
Area	194	196	189	183	173
Production	7,902	8,431	10,002	10,584	9,335
Yield	40.7	43.0	53.0	58.0	53.8
Value	276	355	298	277	253
Potatoes					
Area	178	173	165	178	165
Production	6,579	6,435	6,439	7,156	6,611
Yield	36.9	37.3	39.1	40.1	40.0
Value	574	1,095	630	750	501

[1] Also includes rye, mixed corn and triticale.

Source: DEFRA: *Agriculture in the United Kingdom 2000*

Table 26.5: Horticulture

	1990	1995	1998	1999	2000
Vegetables[1]					
Area ('000 hectares)	189.1	163.8	155.9	149.1	144.5
Value of production (£ million)	655	726	665	644	650
Fruit					
Area ('000 hectares)	47.0	38.6	34.4	34.2	34.2
Value (£ million)	260	259	259	260	251
of which:					
Orchard fruit					
Area ('000 hectares)	32.4	26.6	25.2	25.3	25.3
Value (£ million)	144	118	126	108	101
Soft fruit					
Area ('000 hectares)	14.5	12.1	9.1	8.9	8.9
Value (£ million)	116	137	125	140	139
Ornamentals					
Area ('000 hectares)	18.9	20.2	19.2	19.7	20.0
Value (£ million)	506	630	649	719	714

[1] Includes peas harvested dry for human consumption.
Source: DEFRA: *Agriculture in the United Kingdom 2000*

total area devoted to horticulture (excluding mushrooms, potatoes, and peas for harvesting dry) amounted to 172,310 hectares, a decrease of 3.7% on the 1999 figure. This area relates to field area and does not take into account the number of crops in the year. Vegetables and salad grown in the open for human consumption accounted for 118,500 hectares; total orchards, small fruit and grapes 37,500 hectares; other horticultural crops grown in the open 14,100 hectares; and area under glass or plastic covered sheets 2,200 hectares.

The output value of all horticultural products (including seeds and peas harvested dry) in 2000 was £1.9 billion, virtually unchanged from 1999. A slight rise of 1.9% in the value of production for vegetables was offset by decreases of 0.6% for ornamentals and 3.2% for fruit.

Agri-industrial Materials

The Agri-Industrial Materials (AIMS) section in DEFRA is responsible for the coordination and development of plant-based renewable raw materials. It aims:

- to encourage the development of crops for energy and industry, to the benefit of UK agriculture, manufacturing businesses, and the environment;
- to stimulate market-led opportunities for renewable raw materials from environmentally acceptable crops with prospects of commercial viability;
- to ensure cohesion between agriculture and other areas of government policy, and between policies on different agricultural crops and other aspects of agriculture so that worthwhile and potential developments are not hindered; and
- to provide the strategic research on which future developments can be based.

AIMS is also providing the secretariat for a new government-industry forum on non-food uses of crops.

Genetically Modified Crops

Now that the location and function of individual crop genes are being discovered, scientists have the chance to alter the genetic make-up of plants by adding or removing specific genes. Some 44 million hectares of genetically modified crops were estimated to have been grown in 14 countries across the world in 2000.

A three-year UK programme of farm-scale evaluations (FSEs), begun in 1999, will allow independent researchers to study the effect, if any, that the management practices associated with genetically modified (GM) herbicide tolerant crops might have on farmland wildlife, when compared with those used with non-GM crops. Three crops are involved: oilseed rape (both spring and autumn sown); beet (fodder and sugar varieties); and maize. The project will involve between 60 and 75 fields of each crop in total. Sites for autumn 2001 were announced in July 2001. At the end of the programme in 2002–03, the results will be reported, made publicly available and considered by the Government. The FSE programme includes a project to monitor gene-flow, including cross-pollination. There will be no commercial growing of GM crops until the FSEs are completed and unless they are assessed as posing no unacceptable effects on the environment.

Food Safety

The Food Standards Agency (FSA—see chapter 13) (*www.foodstandards.gov.uk*), launched in 2000, aims to ensure that the food consumers eat is safe, and to offer independent, balanced advice to government throughout the UK. The Meat Hygiene Service, an executive agency of the FSA, is responsible for enforcing legislation on meat hygiene, inspection, animal welfare at slaughter and specified risk materials controls in all licensed abattoirs and cutting premises in Great Britain.

EXPORTS, MARKETING AND PROMOTION

Exports of food, feed and drink were around £8.8 billion in 2000, compared with £17.0 billion for imports. EU countries accounted for 61% of all UK food and drink exports. In 2000 the main markets were the Irish Republic (£1.2 billion) and France (£1.0 billion). Sales to the United States increased by 4% to £832 million and to Asia by 12%, to £961 million.

Drinks and cereals were key contributors to exports. Drinks were up overall by 5% for the year, with whisky and fruit juices recording the highest gains, at 7% and 19% respectively. Rising world prices for wheat and barley resulted in a 5% increase in exports of cereals.

Food from Britain (FFB) (*www.foodfrombritain.com*), an organisation funded by DEFRA on behalf of the four agricultural Departments (£5.4 million in 2000–01) and by industry (£7.0 million), provides specialist marketing and international business development services to the food and drink industry. It has a network of 11 international offices, each with local food industry expertise and trade contacts. It also fosters the development of the speciality food and drink industry in the UK through a range of tailored business development and marketing services, delivered nationally by FFB and locally by regional and county food groups. Speciality companies have an annual turnover of about £3.6 billion and a workforce of 52,000.

The British Farm Standard red tractor logo, launched in June 2000, has been designed by the National Farmers' Union as an authoritative mark to identify food that meets high—and independently verified—production standards covering food safety, animal welfare and environmental issues.

Several major shows are held annually[3] across the UK including:

- the Royal Show, Stoneleigh, Warwickshire (early July), enabling visitors to see the latest techniques and improvements in British agriculture. Some 160,400 visitors attended in 2000, of whom 9% were from overseas;
- the Royal Highland Show, Edinburgh, the largest trade exhibition of agricultural machinery in Great Britain (June)—145,000 visitors in 2000;
- the Royal Welsh Show, Llanelwedd, Builth Wells (late July);

[3] Many of the shows had to be cancelled in 2001 because of the foot-and-mouth outbreak.

- the Royal Welsh Agricultural Winter Fair, Llanelwedd, Builth Wells, for livestock and carcases (December);
- the Royal Ulster Agricultural Society Show, Belfast (May); and
- the Royal Smithfield Show, London (every other year), for agricultural machinery, livestock and carcases.

GOVERNMENT ROLE

DEFRA, the Scottish Executive Environment and Rural Affairs Department (SEERAD), the National Assembly for Wales Agriculture Department (NAWAD), and the Department of Agriculture and Rural Development in Northern Ireland (DARD) have varying degrees of responsibility for agriculture and fisheries affairs. Matters not devolved or transferred to the devolved administrations, such as relations with the EU and other international organisations, remain with the Government in London. The work of DEFRA's nine Regional Service Centres in England and SEERAD's eight areas in Scotland relates to payments under domestic and EU schemes, licensing and other services for farmers and growers.

UK Agriculture Strategy

The Government launched a long-term strategy for the agriculture industry—*A New Direction*—in December 1999. It is designed to help the farming industry become more competitive, diverse, flexible, responsive to consumer wishes and environmentally responsible. The strategy aims to deliver short-term support to those sectors hit hardest by the farming crisis and longer-term action to encourage industry restructuring and adaptation.

New Rural Development Programmes (see pp. 455–6), implementing the EU Rural Development Regulation, will help implement the strategy. These programmes have been approved by the European Commission. In total, these will invest nearly £3 billion in the UK rural economy over seven years. A new partnership between government across the EU and the farming community will mean that some of the existing production-linked payments to farmers will be recycled into rural development measures and matched with equivalent UK government funding.

These programmes have been supplemented by other measures, in particular the *Action Plan for Farming*, which was launched in March 2000 in response to the crisis in farm incomes in the UK. The plan provides short-term financial relief and longer-term support for business restructuring and development, improved marketing and food chain cooperation, training and innovation. Although a number of measures in the Plan are UK-wide, others are focused on England. The devolved administrations are developing strategies to meet priorities in their own areas. For example, in *Scotland* the Scottish Executive published a policy document, *A Forward Strategy for Scottish Agriculture*, in June 2001.

The Government announced in August 2001 the establishment of an independent Policy Commission on the future of farming and food in England. The Commission will advise the Government how a sustainable, competitive and diverse farming and food sector can be created which contributes to a thriving and sustainable rural economy, and advances environmental, economic, health and animal welfare goals. Its work will be consistent with the Government's aims for CAP reform, enlargement of the EU and increased trade liberalisation.

In *Wales*, an advisory group has been established to assist in the preparation of a long-term direction for farming. The National Assembly's Agriculture and Rural Development Committee has been invited to discuss and comment on the draft strategy prior to its publication, planned for autumn 2001.

In *Northern Ireland*, a separate strategic review, aimed at developing a vision for the future development of the local agri-food sector, is expected to produce a final report in autumn 2001.

The Government published a Rural White Paper, *Our Countryside: the future—a fair deal for rural England*, in November 2000. The main areas of focus were:

- sustainable growth and regeneration in rural areas;
- a new direction for agriculture;
- access to services in rural areas and countering social exclusion; and
- conservation and recreation.

The Scottish Executive published *Rural Scotland: a New Approach* in May 2000. This set out the Executive's priorities on rural issues and how it is working to deliver its rural commitments. The Executive commissioned a report into innovative service provision, and is currently considering how to take the report forward. It also set up the Rural Poverty and Inclusion Working Group to advise on rural poverty and social exclusion matters.

Rural Development Programmes

The ***England Rural Development Programme*** (ERDP), launched in October 2000, will invest £1.6 billion in rural development and agri-environment measures over seven years. The programme identifies two priority areas for funding: the conservation and improvement of the environment and creation of a productive and sustainable rural economy. It sets out how these priorities will be met through a substantial expansion in funds for four schemes described below:

- the Countryside Stewardship Scheme;
- the Organic Farming Scheme;
- the Woodland Grant Scheme; and
- the Farm Woodland Premium Scheme.

The Environmentally Sensitive Areas Scheme will continue, with support for hill farming refocused through the new Hill Farm Allowance Scheme. Four new schemes opened to applications in October 2000:

- the Rural Enterprise Scheme;
- Processing and Marketing Grants;
- the Energy Crops Scheme; and
- the Vocational Training Scheme.

These schemes aim to assist the creation of more diverse and competitive agriculture and forestry sectors, more jobs in the countryside, the development of new products and markets and greater collaboration, and to provide training to support these new activities.

The ***Scottish Rural Development Programme*** incorporates the new Rural Stewardship Scheme and the Organic Aid Scheme, the new area-based scheme to support Less Favoured Areas, and the continuation of the Farm Woodland Premium Scheme and the Woodland Grant Scheme. The new Less Favoured Areas Support Scheme will be worth £61 million in 2000–01. Payments are based on area, and land capability and remoteness are taken into account. Around £685 million will be spent over the lifetime (seven years) of the Rural Development Programme on these schemes. Under the Highlands and Islands Special Transitional Programme, which operates under the Rural Development Regulation, SEERAD introduced the Agricultural Business Development Scheme across the programme area. The scheme will provide assistance to farmers and crofters for investments in agricultural holdings and diversification projects, while immediate family members may apply for assistance with diversification projects. Assistance is also available for marketing and training.

The ***Wales Rural Development Plan***, published in December 2000, will involve the investment of around £450 million in rural development and agri-environment measures over seven years. The National Assembly is supporting a number of the measures permitted under the Plan, aimed at conserving and improving the environment and enabling farming, forestry and other rural businesses and communities to adapt to changing circumstances and to develop. The programme will make funds available for Tir Gofal (Land in Care); the Organic Farming Scheme; support for hill farming through Tir Mynydd; a range of forestry and farm woodland initiatives; training for farmers and their families; investment in agricultural holdings; and the processing and marketing of agricultural products through the Processing and Marketing Grant Scheme.

The Rural Development Regulation Plan for ***Northern Ireland***, worth £266 million between 2000 and 2006, comprises a new Less Favoured

Area support scheme to replace the existing Hill Livestock Compensatory Allowances; an enhanced agri-environment programme, with additional funding for the Countryside Management Scheme and the Organic Farming Scheme; continuation of the Environmentally Sensitive Areas Schemes; and a continuation of the private forestry programme.

DARD also manages a Rural Development Programme targeted at the broader rural community. It is expected to be worth about £80 million between 2001 and 2007, and combines several programmes, such as the Northern Ireland Programme for Building Sustainable Prosperity (see p. 457).

Agri-environment Schemes

Environmentally Sensitive Areas (ESAs)

The Environmentally Sensitive Areas scheme, introduced in 1987, offers incentives to farmers to adopt agricultural practices which will safeguard and enhance parts of the country of particularly high landscape, wildlife or historic value. There are now 22 ESAs in England, covering some 10% of agricultural land, and six in Wales (operating under Tir Gofal), ten in Scotland and five in Northern Ireland. In 2000–01 a forecast £68.4 million was spent in the UK under ESAs.

Hill Farm Allowance Scheme (HFA)

The new HFA scheme is designed to compensate hill farmers for the difficulties of farming in Less Favoured Areas. It replaces the Hill Livestock Compensatory Allowance scheme, under which farm incomes continued to decline. Some £12.6 million is forecast to have been spent on the new scheme in 2000–01.

Countryside Stewardship

The Countryside Stewardship scheme is the main scheme for the wider countryside which aims, through the payment of grants, to improve the natural beauty and diversity of the English countryside; to enhance, restore and recreate targeted landscapes, their wildlife habitats and historical features; and to improve opportunities for public access. It operates outside ESAs. Farmers and land managers enter ten-year agreements to manage land in an environmentally beneficial way in return for annual payments. Grants are also available towards capital works, such as hedge laying and planting, or repairing dry stone walls. Some £34.7 million is forecast to have been spent on the scheme in 2000–01. In Scotland, the Rural Stewardship Scheme has replaced both ESA and the Countryside Premium scheme as the main scheme for encouraging environmentally friendly farming practice.

Organic Farming Schemes

Organic Farming Schemes offer payments to farmers—in the form of financial help during the conversion process—to aid them in converting to organic farming and to manage their land in some additional environmentally beneficial ways. Total expenditure on these schemes is budgeted at £18 million in the UK in 2001–02.

There are over 425,000 hectares (about 1 million acres) of land converted or in the process of conversion to organic farming, representing 2.5% of the agricultural area of the UK. It is estimated that the UK market for organic food is currently worth around £500 million a year.

The Organic Conversion Information Service, funded by DEFRA in England, provides free advice to farmers considering conversion to organic farming. In Scotland SEERAD funds the Scottish Agricultural College to operate a telephone helpline for farmers considering conversion. Standards of organic food production in the UK are set by the UK Register of Organic Food Standards.

Farm Woodland Premium Scheme

The Farm Woodland Premium Scheme (partly funded by the EU) aims to encourage farmers to convert productive agricultural land to woodlands by providing annual payments for ten years (for predominantly conifer woodland) or 15 years (for predominantly broadleaved woodland) to help offset agricultural income foregone. It is intended to enhance the environment through the planting of trees, improve the landscape, provide new habitats and increase biodiversity. In the eight years to 1999–2000, in England, 5,829 applications covering 23,277 hectares had been approved for planting (of which 662 applications covering 3,412 hectares were for 1999–2000). A total of £77 million over seven years has been provided for under the ERDP. In Wales, from 1992–93 to 1999–2000, 580 applications were approved covering 2,769 hectares and in Scotland some 2,707 applications covering 43,933 hectares had been approved for planting to the end of 2000.

Structural Funds Programmes in Northern Ireland

In parallel with the Rural Development Regulation Plan, Northern Ireland will benefit from two further EU-funded programmes. The Northern Ireland Programme for Building Sustainable Prosperity is worth some £80 million between 2000 and 2006 and comprises training and development, processing and marketing of agricultural products, afforestation of non-agricultural land and investment in forests and rural development. The programme provides an additional £23 million towards assisting the fishing sector. The Programme for Peace and Reconciliation in Northern Ireland and the Border Counties of Ireland provides some £38 million between 2000 and 2004 towards assisting the agri-food and wider rural economy to address the legacy of the conflict and take opportunities arising from peace. Assistance is available for training, investment in agricultural holdings, diversification, rural tourism and rural development.

Common Agricultural Policy (CAP)

In 2000–01 total UK public expenditure on agriculture—under the CAP and on national grants and subsidies—is forecast to have increased to £3,182 million. Spending in the UK under the CAP is forecast to have increased from £2,816 million in 1999–2000 to £2,869 million in 2000–01. The increase is

Figure 26.6: Public Expenditure[1] under the CAP by the Intervention Board and Agriculture and Other Departments, UK, 2000–01

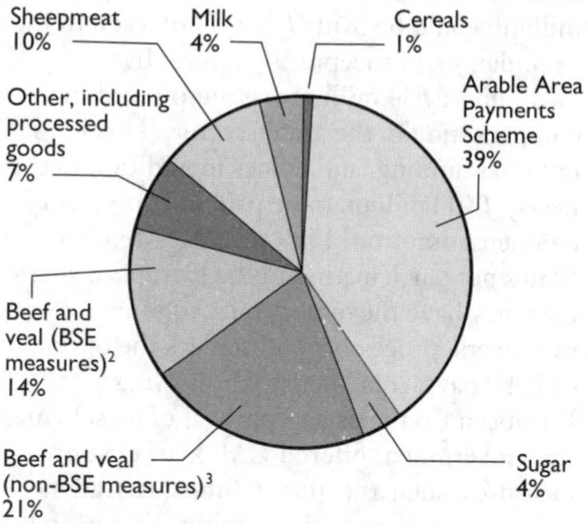

[1] Forecast.

[2] Payments to farmers under schemes to compensate for losses caused by BSE.

[3] Payments to farmers under schemes unrelated to BSE measures.

Source: Department for Environment, Food and Rural Affairs

mainly attributable to additional BSE compensation and disposal costs. There was a sharp increase in beef intervention sales activity during the last quarter of 1998–99, which was sustained throughout 1999–2000 resulting in significantly higher receipts. For 2000–01 beef intervention sales are forecast to be significantly reduced. The increased forecast for expenditure on pigs arose from the outbreak of Classical Swine Fever, which resulted in the creation of the Pig Welfare (Disposal) Scheme (see p. 461). Decreases in non-BSE-related expenditure are mainly attributable to higher receipts following the sale of intervention cereals and skimmed milk powder, a reduction in animal numbers and rates on the sheep annual premium, and a reduction in the level of sugar export refund rates. The continuing depreciation of the euro on the foreign exchanges was also a contributory factor to the reduction in support prices in sterling terms.

Agrimoney Compensation

In 2000 the Government announced a series of packages of agrimonetary compensation to offset falls in CAP direct payments to the UK resulting from the euro/sterling exchange rate. In March, it was announced that £66 million would be paid: £22 million each to the beef, dairy and sheepmeat sectors. In November, £34 million was announced in compensation to the arable sector. This is all optional funding, and comes in addition to the nearly £400 million to be paid in compulsory compensation from 1999 to 2001. Member States not participating in the European single currency have the opportunity to offer producers, processors and traders the option of CAP payments in euros. Following European Commission approval of its scheme, the Government offered CAP market support measures, such as export refunds, to traders and processors from the autumn. By the end of the year 14 businesses had taken up the offer, receiving £100 million in euro payments in a full year (around 3.5% of total CAP market support payments in the UK). Further consideration is being given to extending this option to direct aid recipients.

Other EU Developments

Developments in the past year have included:

- Agreement in December 2000 on a comprehensive EU proposal for submission to the *World Trade Organisation agriculture negotiations* (see p. 418). The proposal meets a key UK objective in committing the EU to constructive negotiations on continuing trade liberalisation and reform of agricultural policy.
- Agreement of EU-wide rules on compulsory *beef labelling*: these require fresh, chilled and frozen beef, offered for sale throughout the supply chain, to be labelled from 1 September 2000 with information on place of slaughter and cutting/mincing, and from 1 January 2002 with full country of origin information (place of birth, raising and slaughter).
- *New EU-wide feed controls*: against a background of rising incidence of BSE (see p. 460) in other EU Member States (notably France) and of the first reports of BSE in homebred animals in Spain and Germany, new controls were agreed requiring Member States to prohibit, until the end of 2001, the feeding of processed animal protein to any animals kept, fattened or bred for the production of food. This decision was made to avoid the risk of cross-contamination of cattle feed with feed intended for other animals containing animal proteins possibly contaminated by the BSE agent.
- *Beef Market Support Measures*: among other proposals it was agreed that meat and other materials derived from cattle over 30 months of age not tested for BSE should be removed from the food chain. A purchase and destruction scheme for such animals was introduced; and
- *Specified Risk Materials*: intestines of bovine animals of all ages were added to the list of materials which must be removed and destroyed in all Member States with effect from 1 January 2001.

Integrated Administration and Control System (IACS)

The purpose of IACS is to protect expenditure under the CAP arable and livestock schemes. Controls to prevent and detect fraud and irregularity are major features of the System. These include verification checks of claimed land and animals, including on-the-spot inspections and remote sensing by observation satellites.

Professional, Scientific and Technical Services

In the UK, professional, scientific and technical services are provided by a number of organisations:

- in England the Rural Development Service of DEFRA provides scheme implementation services for the ERDP, involving professional and technical work in relation to the enhancement and protection of the environment, including biodiversity and rural development;

- in Scotland the Scottish Agricultural College (SAC) provides professional, business, scientific and technical services in the agriculture, rural business, food and drink, and environmental markets;
- the Department of Agriculture and Rural Development (DARD) has a similar remit in Northern Ireland; and
- Lantra, the UK National Training Organisation for the sector, which receives government support under contracts from DEFRA and the Scottish Executive.

ANIMAL HEALTH AND WELFARE

Professional advice and action on the statutory control of animal health and the welfare of farm livestock are the responsibility of the State Veterinary Service. It is supported by the Veterinary Laboratories Agency (VLA), which also offers its services to the private sector on a commercial basis. Similar support is provided in Scotland by the SAC. In Northern Ireland, DARD's Veterinary Service carries out a similar role to the State Veterinary Service in Great Britain, supported by its Veterinary Sciences Division.

Farm Animal Welfare

DEFRA works to ensure priority is given to maintaining the standards for welfare of animals on the farm, during transport, at markets and at slaughter. Work currently being undertaken on the farm includes improved welfare conditions for laying hens; broiler chicken welfare standards; a new sheep code and negotiations on pig welfare. Since June 2001 DEFRA has also been responsible for welfare work concerning farm animals, previously the responsibility of the Home Office.

Farm Animals

Britain enforces controls on imports of live animals and genetic material, including checks on all individual consignments originating from outside the EU and frequent checks on those from other EU Member States at destination points. Measures can be taken to prevent the import of diseased animals and genetic material from regions or countries affected by disease. Veterinary checks also include unannounced periods of surveillance at ports.

Cattle Tracing System (CTS)

The British Cattle Movement Service (BCMS) for Great Britain, at Workington, Cumbria, was launched in 1998 to record all cattle in the national herd on a CTS database. A recommendation that herd cover should be extended to all cattle has now been implemented. Cover has been extended to over 98% of the 10 million cattle in the herd. Work is in hand to collect the remaining data and apply checks to help ensure that information held on the database is accurate and complete. Since the end of January 2001 it has been a legal requirement to notify the BCMS of all movements. In Northern Ireland, all cattle and cattle movements are recorded on the Animal and Public Health Information System (APHIS), which has been approved by the EU since 1999 as a fully operational database for cattle traceability.

Tuberculosis (TB) in Cattle

The Government's strategy is to find a science-based policy to control TB in cattle. An annual £5 million research programme has been put in place to find out how the disease is spread among cattle and wildlife, including research into improved diagnostic tests and the development of a TB vaccine. An on-farm epidemiological survey, known as TB99, to identify the factors causing TB in cattle herds, is starting to provide data to help understand the disease and focus future research. A sample survey of badger carcases found dead on the roads started in November 2000 to collect data on the prevalence of TB in badgers, but was suspended in February 2001 due to foot-and-mouth disease. The former Ministry of Agriculture, Fisheries and Food also commissioned and published an independent report on the role husbandry might play in reducing TB risk and this work is being taken forward in 2001 by DEFRA.

Foot-and-mouth

A significant outbreak of foot-and-mouth disease occurred in the UK during 2001. By the time that foot-and-mouth disease was confirmed in pigs at an abattoir, and in cattle on a neighbouring farm in Brentwood (Essex) on 20 February 2001, the disease had already been present in the country, undetected, for two to three weeks—the original outbreak was subsequently found to have been a farm at Heddon-on-the-Wall, Northumberland. During this time it had already been spread widely throughout the country by large-scale commercial movements of sheep. As a result, cases occurred in many areas of the country, with particular clusters in Cumbria, Dumfries and Galloway, Devon and North Yorkshire, together accounting for over two-thirds of all confirmed cases. Up to 16 September a total of 2,020 cases had been confirmed and 3,117,000 sheep, 597,000 cattle, 139,000 pigs, 2,000 goats and 500 deer slaughtered. There were 9,395 premises on which animals had been or were due to be slaughtered. The number of cases peaked at between 40 and 50 a day at the end of March 2001, but subsequently declined and by early September averaged between one and two a day.

Foot-and-mouth disease is highly virulent in pigs, cattle, sheep and other ungulates, spreading rapidly by contact between animals, transmission via people or transport, or through the air. Strict controls on the movement of animals in affected areas were introduced as was an export ban. Estimated compensation costs are £1,142 million, of which £986 million had been paid to farmers up to 13 September. In addition, a Livestock Welfare Disposal Scheme was opened as an outlet of last resort for livestock farmers whose animals face welfare difficulties as a result of foot-and-mouth related movement restrictions. The scheme provides for the removal and disposal of animals, for which the Government will bear the costs. Up to 13 September, claims totalling £174 million had been paid.

A major consequence of the outbreak was the postponement of local council elections in England and Wales, from 3 May to 7 June, the same date as the General Election. Several prestigious agricultural shows (see p. 453) and sporting events were also cancelled.

An important element of the Government's strategy is the badger culling trial, designed to establish the contribution that badgers, as opposed to other factors, make in spreading TB to cattle. By the end of 2000, ten areas had been enrolled in the trial and initial culling had been carried out in seven of these. The trial is expected to produce conclusions by 2004 and possibly earlier.

BSE Inquiry

In October 2000 the Government published the report of the public inquiry into the history of BSE (bovine spongiform encephalopathy) and variant CJD (Creutzfeldt-Jakob disease) and how the diseases were handled by the Government and others in the period up to 20 March 1996. The report found that most of those responsible for responding to the challenge posed by BSE emerged with credit. However, it identified a number of aspects of the response that were inadequate, and set out some fundamental lessons for public policy and administration in the future. An interim government response to the report in February 2001 formed the basis of further consultations and discussions, which enabled those interested to contribute to the final response the Government made to the report's recommendations in September 2001.

Classical Swine Fever

The first outbreak of Classical Swine Fever in Great Britain since 1986 was confirmed in August 2000. Disease was confirmed on 16 premises in East Anglia, the last being in November. By the end of December, all area movement restrictions around those premises had been lifted. In order to deal with the animal welfare problems resulting from movement restrictions, the UK introduced a Pig Welfare (Disposal) Scheme in August 2000. The scheme came to an end when all movement controls were lifted. Payments to producers under the scheme were linked strictly to dealing with animal welfare problems and were in addition to the free transport, slaughter and disposal of pigs made available by the scheme.

The Pet Travel Scheme

The Pet Travel Scheme, launched in February 2000, allows pet cats and dogs from 24 Western European countries and 26 'long-haul' countries—including Australia, New Zealand, Singapore and Japan—to enter or re-enter the UK without quarantine, provided they meet certain conditions, including vaccination against rabies. The scheme operates on certain approved sea, air and rail routes into the UK. UK residents can, having taken their pets to these countries, bring them back without the need for quarantine, providing the scheme's requirements are met. By the end of July 2001, 26,271 pets had been brought into the UK under the scheme.

Veterinary Medicinal Products

The *Veterinary Medicines Directorate* (*www.vmd.gov.uk*), an executive agency of DEFRA, aims to protect public health, animal health and the environment and to promote animal welfare, by ensuring the safety, quality and efficacy of all aspects of veterinary medicines in the UK. The Government is advised by the independent scientific *Veterinary Products Committee* on standards to be adopted in the authorisation procedures for veterinary medicines.

The Fishing Industry

Overview

The UK has a major interest in sea fisheries, reflecting its geographical position in the North East Atlantic, and is one of the EU's largest fishing countries, taking about a fifth of the total catch in major species. It has an interest in more than 100 'allowable catches' set by the European Commission (see p. 463). In 2000 the British fishing industry provided around 50% by quantity of total UK fish supplies, and household consumption of fish in the UK was provisionally estimated at 442,000 tonnes.

Fisheries Departments, in partnership with the European Commission, are responsible for the administration of legislation concerning the fishing industry, including fish and shellfish farming. The *Sea Fish Industry Authority* (*www.seafish.co.uk*), a largely industry-financed body, undertakes R&D, provides training and promotes the marketing and consumption of sea fish.

British vessels have exclusive rights to fish within 6 miles of the British coast. Certain other EU Member States have historic rights in British waters between 6 and 12 miles. British vessels have similar rights in other Member States' 6 to 12 mile belts. Between 12 and 200 miles, EU vessels may fish wherever they have access rights. Non-EU countries' vessels may fish in these waters if they negotiate reciprocal fisheries agreements with the EU. British fishery limits extend to 200 miles or the median line (broadly halfway between the UK coast and the opposing coastline of another coastal state), measured from baselines on or near the coast of Britain.

Fish Caught and the Fishing Fleet

UK fishing industry statistics are shown in Table 26.7. Altogether, some 526,000 tonnes of sea fish, with a total value of £483 million, were landed into the UK by both the UK fleet and foreign fishing vessels in 2000. Another major source of supply is the import into the UK in bulk of fish caught by other countries.

In 2000 demersal fish (caught on or near the bottom of the sea) accounted for 34% by weight of total landings by British fishing vessels, pelagic fish (caught near the surface) for 48% and shellfish for 18%. Landings of all types of fish (excluding salmon and trout) by British fishing vessels into the UK totalled 748,000 tonnes. Cod and haddock represented 15% and 14% of the total value of demersal and pelagic fish landed respectively. The

Table 26.7: UK Fishing Industry: Summary Table

	1990	1995	1998	1999	2000
Fleet size at end of year					
Number of vessels	11,189	8,458	8,271	8,039	7,818
Employment					
Number of fishermen	n.a.	19,921	17,889	15,961	15,121
Total landings by UK vessels[1]					
Quantity ('000 tonnes)	763.2	911.8	923.8	836.2	748.1
Value (£ million)	472.2	590.1	661.5	587.6	550.3
Household consumption					
Quantity ('000 tonnes)	431.0	438.8	447.8	446.0	442.0

[1] Figures relate to landings both into the UK and abroad.
Source: *UK Sea Fisheries Statistics*

quayside value of landings of all sea fish, including shellfish, by British vessels in 2000 was £550 million.

Catches of crabs, lobsters, scampi and other shellfish have increased to supply a rising demand. In 1985 British fishermen landed 75,000 tonnes of shellfish worth about £65 million. By 2000, landings were 135,400 tonnes worth £170 million.

Britain aims to achieve the EU target for reducing its fleet by both cutting its numbers and limiting the time some vessels spend at sea. At the end of 2000 the UK fleet consisted of 7,818 registered vessels, including 115 vessels greater than 24.39 m (80 ft). There are an estimated 15,121 professional fishermen in Britain. A national licensing scheme now limits the shellfish fleet to 3,000, mainly small boats. New minimum landing sizes for shellfish to be introduced across the EU in 2002, and which make it illegal to land a lobster smaller than 87 mm (3.4 inches), now apply in the UK.

There is a substantial fish processing industry of around 700 businesses which employ some 19,000 people. At the retail level, there are approximately 3,000 fishmongers employing 7,000 people. An increasing proportion of all fish (67.7% by volume and 66.4% by value, excluding canned produce) is sold through supermarkets. Fish is also consumed in restaurants and in takeaway form from fish and chip shops. A small proportion of the catch is used to make fish oils and animal feeds. Some of the species caught by UK fishing vessels find a better market overseas and these species are usually exported or landed directly abroad. In 2000 UK vessels landed directly into non-UK ports 283,500 tonnes of sea fish with a value of £128 million.

Aquaculture

Fish farming is a significant industry in remote rural areas on the west coast of Scotland, as well as in Orkney, Shetland and the Western Isles, producing primarily salmon. In addition, species such as cod, halibut and turbot are entering commercial production. Trout is also farmed as a freshwater species in Scotland, England and Northern Ireland, and various shellfish species are produced all round the coast of the United Kingdom. Total value at first sale in 1999 is estimated at over £300 million, and the industry employs over 3,000 people. Production in 1999 was 127,000 tonnes of salmon, 16,000 tonnes of trout, 125 tonnes of other fish, and some 10,500 tonnes of shellfish.

Aquaculture is subject to a comprehensive regulatory regime covering such issues as fish health and disease control, control of discharges into the marine environment, site leasing and planning, and the use of medicines and other chemicals.

Common Fisheries Policy (CFP)

The primary aim of the CFP is to ensure rational and sustainable exploitation of fish stocks through conservation and management policies designed to protect resources and reflect the needs of the fishing industry. The

CFP aims to improve the balance between catching capacity and available resources by regulating the amount of fishing and the quantities of fish caught, through a system of Total Allowable Catches (TACs) based on scientific advice. These TACs are then distributed to Member States according to the system of relative stability. This means that national quota allocations are based each year on a fixed proportion reflecting, among other things, historical fishing patterns. Catch limits are complemented by a series of technical conservation measures intended to achieve more selective fishing, for example by setting rules on minimum landing sizes, minimum mesh sizes and gear design, as well as defining areas of seasonal closures, methods of fishing and target species. Opportunities to fish in third country waters are also secured through the CFP.

Fish Quotas

EU fisheries ministers set TACs for a wide range of stocks each year in December. The TACs are then divided into Member States' quotas. The UK's separate quotas are then apportioned between various groups within the UK fishing fleet. The size and structure of the fishing fleet is governed by a licensing system (see below), and vessels work to an agreed quota of allowable catches, based on scientific assessment of fish stocks. Some allocations are managed by fishermen's organisations, known as Producer Organisations. However, overall responsibility for managing the UK's quotas rests with DEFRA and the other Fisheries Departments in the UK administrations. Quotas, technical conservation and other management measures allow balanced fish populations to renew themselves.

In December 2000 at the EU Fisheries Council in Brussels, the UK secured a deal on fishing quotas which sought to strike a balance between the advice given by international scientists on rescuing threatened fish stocks and the needs of UK fishermen. The European Commission had in some cases suggested cuts in TACs for some species which were even more severe than the serious reductions suggested by scientists from the International Council for the Exploration of the Sea. However, the UK succeeded in halving the TAC cuts initially put forward by the Commission for some species, reflecting the need to leave open fishing opportunities where there are no risks to the state of the stocks.

North Sea Cod Recovery Plan

Agreement in principle was reached with Norway in January 2001 on emergency closures of large areas of the North Sea to protect cod at spawning time. Trawling for all white fish species was prohibited, between 14 February and 30 April, in an area of more than 40,000 square miles, with closures concentrated in the north, east and south of the North Sea. Local inshore fishermen were allowed to continue fishing within 12-mile limits. All EU Member States with North Sea fishing interests will continue to share the burden of reduced fishing effort and increased protection for spawning cod in 2002 through a series of additional technical conservation measures.

Restrictive Licensing System for Fishing Vessels

This system, also operated by the Government, controls the activities of the UK fishing fleet in accordance with the EU and UK aims on fleet and catch management. All engine-powered UK-registered or British-owned vessels which fish for profit for sea fish (other than salmon, migratory trout and eels) are required to hold a licence issued by UK Fisheries Departments. In order to keep the fleet the same size, additional licences are not granted. Licences must therefore be transferred and aggregated according to detailed rules.

Sea Fisheries Committees

There are 12 Sea Fisheries Committees (SFCs) which regulate local sea fisheries around virtually the entire coast of England and Wales out to 6 miles. SFCs were established in the 19th century and are empowered to make bye-laws for the management and conservation of their districts' fisheries. In Scotland, inshore fisheries legislation has allowed the establishment of local management bodies.

Salmon and Freshwater Fisheries

A Salmon and Freshwater Fisheries Review Group has reviewed all aspects of existing policies and legislation on salmon and freshwater fisheries in England and Wales. The Group's report was published in 2000 and the Government accepted most of its proposals in February 2001. Its main recommendations were:

- an increase of £3 million a year in fisheries grant-in-aid to the Environment Agency from April 2002. The Agency will be able to increase its work on conserving and restoring salmon stocks, and improving controls over unauthorised transfers of coarse and non-native fish;
- up to £750,000, subject to matching funds from interested parties, to launch compensation arrangements to accelerate the phase-out of mixed stock fisheries on a voluntary basis; and
- a commitment to introduce proposals for new legislation when parliamentary time permits.

Research

Departmental funding of R&D in agriculture, fisheries and food in 2000–01 included about £105 million commissioned by MAFF—now DEFRA—which acts in this context on behalf of the National Assembly for Wales, and £6 million conducted by DARD in Northern Ireland. In Scotland about £50 million is invested annually in the agricultural and biological sciences-related research programme and £15.3 million in fishery research. Priority areas in the DEFRA programme are public health (covering food safety, transmissible spongiform encephalopathies and zoonoses) and protection of the environment (improved sustainability in production methods, with benefits for the environment and agricultural efficiency). The total expenditure of DEFRA on research and development in 2001–02 is planned to be some £186 million.

Research Bodies

The Biotechnology and Biological Sciences Research Council (BBSRC, see p. 434) supports research related to food and agriculture. The Natural Environment Research Council includes some agricultural aspects in its remit. Research institutes sponsored by these Councils receive income from work commissioned by DEFRA, industry and other bodies.

ADAS carries out R&D, at a network of research centres across England and Wales and on clients' premises, for DEFRA and other organisations and companies. DEFRA receives scientific expertise and technical support from two of its other agencies: the Veterinary Laboratories Agency and the Central Science Laboratory. Horticulture Research International, a non-departmental public body, receives funding for its research from DEFRA, BBSRC and industry, transfers the results of its R&D to the British horticulture industry and the wider public.

SEERAD supports agricultural, biological and related sciences primarily through sponsorship of the five Scottish Agricultural and Biological Research Institutes, the Scottish Agricultural College (SAC) and the Royal Botanic Garden in Edinburgh. It contracts additional research through these bodies and provides funding for Education and Advisory Services at the SAC. In Northern Ireland DARD maintains an integrated Science and Technology programme to improve the economic performance of the agri-food, fishing and forestry sectors, to conserve the rural environment and to strengthen the economy and social infrastructure of disadvantaged rural areas. Fisheries research is undertaken by the Fisheries Research Service (FRS) in Scotland and by the Centre for Environment, Fisheries and Aquaculture Science (CEFAS) in England and Wales.

Forestry

Land area under forestry in 2000 amounted to 16.9% in Scotland, 14.1% in Wales, 8.7% in England and 6.1% in Northern Ireland, giving

Table 26.8: Area of Woodland, Great Britain, 31 March 2000 *Thousand hectares*

	High forest					
	Conifers	Broad-leaves	Coppice	Total productive woodland	Other woodland	Total woodland
Forestry Commission						
England	164	35	1	199	17	216
Wales	105	6	0	111	4	116
Scotland	458	6	0	463	30	493
Great Britain	**727**	**46**	**1**	**774**	**51**	**825**
Private woodlands						
England	206	596	22	825	94	919
Wales	79	84	1	164	12	176
Scotland	572	144	1	717	108	825
Great Britain	**858**	**824**	**24**	**1,706**	**214**	**1,920**
Total						
England	370	631	24	1,024	111	1,136
Wales	185	90	1	275	16	292
Scotland	1,030	150	1	1,180	138	1,318
Great Britain	**1,584**	**870**	**26**	**2,480**	**266**	**2,745**

Source: Forestry Commission

a total of 11.6% for the UK, or 2.828 million hectares (7 million acres), almost double the cover in 1947. This compares with 36% for the EU as a whole. The area of total productive woodland in Great Britain at 31 March 2000 was nearly 2.5 million hectares (6.1 million acres) (see Table 26.8), 31.2% of which was managed by the Forestry Commission.

The area of new planting (including natural regeneration) in 1999–2000 was 300 hectares (740 acres) by the Forestry Commission and Northern Ireland Forest Service and 17,600 hectares (43,500 acres) by other woodland owners. In 1999–2000, 14,600 hectares (36,000 acres) of broadleaved trees were planted, both new planting and restocking. Table 26.9 gives more details.

In 1999–2000, 306 hectares (756 acres) of land were acquired by the Forestry Commission/Forest Service, which disposed of 5,305 hectares (13,109 acres).

Forestry and primary wood processing in Great Britain employed around 30,000 people in 1998–99, around 43% of whom were engaged in forest activity. Its woodlands produced 9.56 million cubic metres (338 million cubic feet) of timber in 1999, 92% of which was softwood.

The UK uses a large amount of timber, paper, board and other wood products each year, equivalent to about 50 million cubic metres (over 1,750 million cubic feet). Around 85% of this has to be imported at a cost of about £8 billion—the fourth largest single import commodity. The development of the British timber industry, using wood from Britain's sustainable forests, has been a major success story. Over £1.6 billion has been invested in sawmills and paper and board mills over the last 15 years, and a further £2 billion is expected to be invested over the next 15 years, creating many new jobs. The volume of wood supplied from Britain's forests each year has more than doubled from 4 million cubic metres in the 1970s to more than 9 million. This is forecast to increase to over 15 million cubic metres by 2020, offering scope for further substantial investment in the processing industry.

Table 26.9: New Planting and Restocking, UK, Year ended 31 March

Thousand hectares

	1990	1995	1998	1999	2000
New planting					
Broadleaf	5.8	10.8	9.9	10.4	11.4
Conifer	15.5	9.4	7.0	6.6	6.5
Total	**21.3**	**20.2**	**16.9**	**17.0**	**17.9**
of which: Forestry Commission/Forest Service	*4.6*	*1.2*	*0.2*	*0.2*	*0.3*
Restocking					
Broadleaf	4.5	3.6	3.0	2.8	3.3
Conifer	10.1	11.0	11.2	11.3	11.9
Total	**14.6**	**14.7**	**14.2**	**14.1**	**15.2**
of which: Forestry Commission/Forest Service	*8.3*	*8.4*	*8.5*	*8.5*	*8.8*

Sources: Forestry Commission and Northern Ireland Forest Service

Very few, if any, woodlands in Britain are planted without some form of grant. The Forestry Commission offers grants through the *Woodland Grant Scheme* (WGS), and operates the *Farm Woodland Premium Scheme* (FWPS) on behalf of DEFRA and SEERAD. In Wales, there is a joint application form for farmers who enter land into the WGS and FWPS, which is administered by the National Assembly. The WGS aims to encourage the creation of new woodlands and the management of existing woodlands by providing money towards the cost of the work involved. The FWPS is designed to encourage the creation of new woodlands on farms but can only be given where the WGS is also payable. Expenditure of £139 million over seven years on the WGS is provided for under the England Rural Development Programme.

The Forestry Commission and Forestry Policy

The *Forestry Commission* (*www.forestry.gov.uk*) is the government department responsible for forestry throughout Great Britain and is the UK's largest land manager and biggest single provider of countryside recreation. It has a Board of Commissioners with duties and powers prescribed by statute which, following devolution, they exercise separately in England, Scotland and Wales. DEFRA directs the Commissioners' activities in England and, after consultation with Scottish ministers, the National Assembly for Wales and the Northern Ireland Assembly, represents the UK's forestry interests within the EU and in the wider world. Scottish ministers and the National Assembly for Wales direct the Commissioners' activities in Scotland and Wales respectively. The Commission is responsible for advising ministers and for implementing each country's separate and distinct forestry policy. It is funded separately in each country.

Its objectives are to:

- protect Britain's forests and woodlands;
- expand Britain's forest area;
- enhance the economic value of forest resources;
- conserve and improve the biodiversity, landscape and cultural heritage of forests and woodlands;
- develop opportunities for woodland recreation; and
- increase public understanding and community participation in forestry.

The Forestry Commission has two executive agencies. *Forest Enterprise* is responsible for managing the forests and woodlands owned by the nation. It aims to maintain and increase the productive potential of the forest estate and to increase opportunities for public recreation, the conservation value of its forests and the net value of commercial activities. Forest Enterprise has a total forest estate of

826,000 hectares of mainly productive forest with complementary land for grazing, conservation and recreation, and employs around 2,300 staff. A further 3,000 people work in the forests as contractors or are employed by the timber purchasers.

Forest Research aims to deliver high-quality scientific research and surveys, to inform the development of forestry policies and practices, and to promote high standards of sustainable forest management. It is the principal organisation in the UK engaged in forestry and tree-related research.

Forestry Initiatives

The new National Forest covers 520 sq km (200 sq miles) of the English Midlands spanning parts of Derbyshire, Leicestershire and Staffordshire and incorporates the towns of Ashby-de-la-Zouch, Burton upon Trent, Coalville, and Swadlincote. The aim is for woodland to increase from 6% to about one-third of the area, a third to remain in agriculture with the remainder comprising the towns and villages. Thirty million trees (60% broadleaf and 40% conifer) will eventually be planted. For Community Forests, see p. 316.

Forestry in Northern Ireland

Woodland and forest cover about 83,000 hectares (201,000 acres) of Northern Ireland. State-owned forest constitutes 61,000 hectares (151,000 acres).

The *Forest Service* (*www.dardni.gov.uk/forestry*) is an executive agency within DARD and promotes the interests of forestry through sustainable management and expansion of state-owned forests. It encourages private forestry through grant aid for planting. The Forest Service offered 350,981 cubic metres (12.4 million cubic feet) of timber for sale during 2000–01, with receipts of £4.4 million. Forestry and timber processing employ about 1,050 people. It is estimated that some 2.0 million people visited forests during the year.

Further Reading

Agriculture in the United Kingdom 2000. DEFRA and the Agriculture Departments. The Stationery Office, 2001.
Economic Report on Scottish Agriculture 2000. The Stationery Office, 2000.
Forestry Statistics. The Forestry Commission, 2001.
The Report of the BSE Inquiry. The Stationery Office, 2000.
Scottish Agriculture Facts and Figures 2000. Scottish Executive, 2000.
United Kingdom Sea Fisheries Statistics. DEFRA. The Stationery Office.
Statistical Review of Northern Ireland Agriculture 2000. Department of Agriculture and Rural Development, 2001.
MAFF, the Intervention Board and the Forestry Commission. The Government's Expenditure Plans 2001–02 to 2003–04 and Main Estimates 2001–02. Cm 5113. The Stationery Office, 2001.

Websites

DEFRA: www.defra.gov.uk
Department of Agriculture and Rural Development (Northern Ireland): www.dardni.gov.uk
National Assembly for Wales: www.wales.gov.uk
Scottish Executive Environment and Rural Affairs Department: www.scotland.gov.uk/agri

27 Manufacturing and Construction

Introduction 468
Sectors of Manufacturing 468
Construction 488

Manufacturing continues to play an important role in the UK economy, even though service industries generated 3.8 times as much Gross Domestic Product (GDP) and over five times as much employment in 2000. Important industries include chemicals, plastics, pharmaceuticals, electronics, motor vehicles and components, aerospace, offshore equipment, and paper and printing, where British companies are among the world's largest.

Introduction

Manufacturing accounted for 18.7% of gross value added (at current basic prices) in 2000 and for 15.2% of employment (3.9 million people) in the UK at the end of December 2000. The highest proportions of employees in manufacturing are to be found in the East Midlands (23%) and West Midlands (22%), with London the lowest (7%). Overseas companies have a strong presence.

The recession in the early 1990s led to a decline in manufacturing output, but it began to rise again in 1993. By 1999, the volume of output was 10% above the level in 1992, rising by a further 1.6% in 2000. Some industries, notably electrical and optical equipment—where output was up by 76% between 1992 and 2000—but also chemicals and rubber and plastic products, have achieved substantial growth following the recession. However, output of other sectors, such as textiles and leather, remains well below their 1990 levels.

The construction industry contributed 5.2% of gross value added in 2000. Following a period of marked decline as recession affected the industry in the early 1990s, output picked up and was 11.8% higher in 2000 than in 1993, although still a little below pre-recession levels.

Sectors of Manufacturing

Relative sizes of enterprises are shown in Tables 27.1 and 27.2, with output and investment, industrial production and employment by sector in Tables 27.3 to 27.5. An outline of the main manufacturing sectors follows. In some cases statistics in the text and in tables have come from alternative sources to National Statistics, such as trade associations. Any variations usually reflect differences in coverage of the industry concerned.

Food, Drink and Tobacco

In December 2000 the food, drink and tobacco industry employed over 466,000 people.

Food and Drink

The UK's food and drink manufacturing and processing industry has accounted for a growing proportion of total domestic food supply since the 1940s. The largest

Table 27.1: Manufacturing—Size of UK Businesses by Turnover, 2001

Annual turnover (£'000)	Number of businesses
1–49	23,760
50–99	25,615
100–249	32,415
250–499	20,920
500–999	16,705
1,000–1,999	11,605
2,000–4,999	9,185
5,000–9,999	3,925
10,000–49,999	3,835
50,000+	1,130
Total	**149,095**

Source: Office for National Statistics

Table 27.2: Manufacturing—Size of UK Businesses by Employment, 2001

Employment size	Number of businesses
1–9	108,440
10–19	17,330
20–49	11,955
50–99	4,955
100–199	2,845
200–499	1,910
500–999	635
1,000+	440
Total	**148,510**

Not all businesses have been allocated by employment size—hence the difference in totals between this table and Table 27.1.
Source: Office for National Statistics

concentration of enterprises is in the production of bread, cakes and fresh pastry goods, followed by those engaged in processing and preserving meat and meat products. The greatest number of food and drink manufacturing jobs are in the South East and London (15.8% of the total for Great Britain), Yorkshire (13.8%) and the North West (12.5%). Spirits production gives Scotland the highest concentration of employment in the alcoholic and soft drinks manufacturing industry, with a significant proportion of jobs in its economically deprived rural areas. The biggest food and drinks export category in 2000 was alcoholic drinks, accounting for 35% of the total (£8.8 billion) value of food and drink sales overseas. The largest food-exporting sector was biscuits and confectionery, worth £395 million.

Among the best-known companies involved in food and drink manufacturing and processing are Unilever, Cadbury Schweppes, Nestlé, Associated British Foods, Tate and Lyle, Ranks Hovis McDougall and Allied Domecq. Specialist small and medium-sized firms in the food and drink manufacturing industry thrive alongside these large concerns, supplying high-quality 'niche' products, often to small retail outlets, such as delicatessens.

Frozen foods and chilled convenience foods, such as frozen potato products and ready-prepared meals, fish and shellfish dishes, salads and pasta, together with yogurts, desserts and instant snacks, have formed some of the fastest-growing sectors of the food market in recent years. The trend towards snacking—eating less, more often—and higher consumption outside the home means that snacks are filling the gap left by the decline of the traditional family meal. Many new low-fat and fat-free items are being introduced, ranging from dairy products to complete prepared meals. Organic foods are also becoming more widely available. There has been a substantial rise in sales of vegetarian foods (both natural vegetable dishes and vegetable-based substitutes of meat products, where soya plays a big role). For genetically modified foods, see chapter 26.

The UK *bread and morning goods* market is worth over £3 billion each year and is one of the largest sectors in the food industry—total volume is about 2.9 million tonnes. Large plant bakers accounted for 81% of bread production by volume in 2000, with 13% by in-store bakeries (ISBs) and 6% by high street retail bakers. Some ISBs use the bake-off method, where dough is part-baked and frozen and then baked off later at the retail outlet—this is particularly popular at smaller supermarkets. The two largest bread producers are Allied Bakeries and British Bakeries, with 33 manufacturing sites between

Table 27.3: Output and Investment in UK Manufacturing, 2000 *£ million*

1992 Standard Industrial Classification (SIC) category	Gross value added at current basic prices	Business investment at current prices
Food, drink and tobacco	20,014	2,356
Textiles and textile products	6,202	255
Leather and leather products	841	54
Wood and wood products	2,150	170
Pulp, paper and paper products, publishing and printing	20,710	2,191
Coke, petroleum products and nuclear fuel	2,568	306
Chemicals, chemical products and man-made fibres	15,062	2,733
Rubber and plastic products	7,958	887
Other non-metal mineral products	4,729	552
Basic metals and fabricated metal products	17,814	1,369
Machinery and equipment not elsewhere classified	12,620	1,186
Electrical and optical equipment	23,272	1,716
Transport equipment	15,214	2,658
Other manufacturing	6,378	414
Total	**155,531**	**16,847**

Sources: ONS *United Kingdom National Accounts 2001—the Blue Book* and ONS Quarterly Business Investment Inquiry

Table 27.4: Index of Production, UK 1995 = 100

1992 SIC category	1990	1998	1999	2000
Food, drink and tobacco	97.2	101.9	101.5	100.1
Textiles, leather and clothing	111.9	89.2	83.0	78.5
Textiles and textile products	111.8	89.2	82.5	78.5
Leather and leather products	112.1	89.5	86.6	79.0
Wood and wood products	111.6	94.7	89.7	91.5
Pulp, paper, printing and publishing	96.4	98.8	98.9	98.7
Coke, refined petroleum products and nuclear fuel	77.4	88.3	79.3	82.6
Chemicals and man-made fibres	83.5	103.8	107.6	112.5
Rubber and plastic products	88.2	101.6	101.1	100.3
Non-metallic mineral products	109.4	96.4	95.3	95.5
Basic metal and metal products	111.2	99.0	95.1	95.0
Engineering and allied industries	97.3	108.6	111.1	115.9
Machinery and equipment	110.6	95.8	89.9	89.3
Electrical and optical equipment	80.8	112.4	121.2	137.4
Transport equipment	108.8	115.8	117.6	112.5
Other manufacturing	112.5	102.2	101.6	101.0
Total manufacturing	**97.7**	**102.2**	**102.2**	**103.8**

Source: Office for National Statistics

Table 27.5: Employee Jobs in Manufacturing Industries, UK *Thousands, June*

1992 SIC category	1990	1995	2000
Food, drink and tobacco	525	474	497
Textiles, leather and clothing	525	398	290
Wood and wood products	98	83	84
Pulp, paper, printing and publishing	473	466	468
Chemicals and man-made fibres	306	254	239
Rubber and plastic products	230	234	235
Non-metallic mineral, metal and metal products	878	709	671
Machinery and equipment	481	386	357
Electrical and optical equipment	544	473	493
Transport equipment	489	372	373
Coke, nuclear fuel, other manufacturing	245	227	241
Total manufacturing	**4,794**	**4,076**	**3,950**

Source: Office for National Statistics

them. In terms of volume, 66% of bread sold in the UK in 2000 was white, and 23% brown/wholemeal. Morning goods, or bakery snacks (including rolls and baps, scones, teacakes and croissants), account for 11% by volume of the bread market. Sandwiches are the UK's most frequently consumed snack food and have a wider range of distribution outlets than other bread sales. Some 2.6 billion sandwiches are consumed each year in a market valued at £3.0 billion in 2000 which is growing at around 7% to 8% a year.

Around 30% of household *liquid milk* supplies in Great Britain are distributed through a doorstep delivery system employing about 15,000 people. However, the proportion is declining (employees have declined by 58% since 1991) as supermarkets have increased their share of the market. Household consumption of liquid milk per head—2.2 litres (3.9 pints) a week—is among the highest in the world. Consumption of skimmed and semi-skimmed milk accounted for 65% of total milk sales in 2000. The British dairy industry accounts for 67% of butter and 62% of cheese supplies to the domestic market, and achieves significant sales in overseas markets. Over 400 different types of cheese are produced in the UK.

Beer (including lager) production in 2000, at 55.3 million hectolitres, was 4.5% lower than in 1999; beer released for home consumption amounted to 57.0 million hectolitres. Exports were valued at £244 million in 2000, amounting to some 2.5 million barrels. The brewing industry currently has three major national brewery groups—Scottish & Newcastle (incorporating Scottish Courage, Britain's leading beer company), Bass (whose brewery operations were acquired by Interbrew of Belgium in 2000, although in September 2001 the DTI ordered Interbrew to dispose of three Bass brands) and Carlsberg-Tetley—and over 470 regional and local breweries. Brewers throughout the world use British malt, which is made almost entirely from home-grown barley. Beer consumption per head in the UK in 2000 was 168 pints, equivalent to 27.4 million pints sold every day or 34.8 million barrels a year. Lager accounted for 63.7% of all sales, up from 62.2% in 1999, but there is still a strong demand for the vast range of traditional cask-conditioned and brewery-conditioned ales and stouts. Recently there has been a shift towards stronger bottled beers, many of which are imported. Another recent trend has been a sizeable import of beer bought on the continent, mainly in Calais, by British travellers. The main brewers are modernising their brewing and distribution facilities to meet the changing pattern of demand.

Home-produced *whisky* production in 2000 was 3.62 million hectolitres, 13% down on 1999. The Scotch whisky industry is one of the UK's top export earners, with overseas sales worth £2.2 billion in 2000, 3% higher

Table 27.6: Alcoholic Drink Production, UK *Thousand hectolitres*

	1990	1995	2000
Beer	61,783	56,800	55,279
Potable spirits			
Home-produced whisky	4,370	4,026	3,620
Other	373	481	590
Released for home consumption			
Beer	65,184	59,129	57,016
Wine of fresh grapes			
Still	6,271	6,907	8,653
Sparkling	365	315	543
Made wine	706	1,419	3,286
Cider and perry	3,666	5,575	6,006
Spirits			
Home-produced whisky	413	310	314
Other[1]	567	481	615

[1] Includes imported spirits.
Source: HM Customs and Excise

than in 1999. By volume, about 90% of production was exported to over 200 markets worldwide, the European Union (EU) taking 40%, the United States 14% and Japan 6%. Some 11,000 people work in the Scotch whisky industry and a further 30,000 are employed in associated sectors, for instance supplying ingredients and materials. There were 97 malt whisky distilleries and eight grain distilleries in Scotland in 2000, the majority in the Highlands and in Speyside, producing either malt whisky or grain whisky—most Scotch consumed is a blend of the two. Well-known blended brands include Ballantine's, Bell's, Famous Grouse, J & B, Johnnie Walker and Teacher's. Glenfiddich, Glen Grant, Glenmorangie and Macallan are some of the best-known single malt Scotch whiskies. *Gin and vodka* production is another important part of the spirits industry, with over 70% of UK-produced gin and 32% of vodka exported, worth nearly £192 million in 2000.

In a highly competitive market, *English and Welsh wines* have a distinctive local identity. There are nearly 400 vineyards, covering approximately 800 hectares (2,000 acres) of land, nearly all in the southern half of the two countries. Over 90% of wine produced each year is white, mainly from Germanic vines. Quality continues to improve with a combination of more experienced winemakers, modern technologies and better winemaking equipment. *Cider and perry* are made predominantly in the west and south-west of England.

The *soft drinks* industry produces still and carbonated drinks, dilutable drinks, fruit juices and juice drinks, and bottled waters. The UK market was worth £8.0 billion by retail value in 2000, with Coca-Cola Enterprises (formerly Coca-Cola and Schweppes Beverages) the largest supplier. Soft drinks are one of the fastest-growing sectors of the grocery trade, responsible for introducing many innovative products each year. Bottled waters—natural mineral waters, spring and table waters—have experienced the fastest growth within the sector during the period 1994–2000, averaging increases in volume of 12% a year, and with sales of £600 million in the UK in 2000. In 2000 UK consumption of soft drinks was 11.96 billion litres, compared with 8.33 billion litres in 1989—an increase of 44%. There was a 5% decline in 2000 in the volume of the still fruit drinks market. Sales of energy and sports drinks have risen by 366% since 1996, with sales of £700 million in the UK in 2000.

Tobacco

Around 7,500 people in the UK are directly employed in tobacco manufacturing with a further 53,000 jobs indirectly supported in supplier industries, and through forward linkages into distribution and retailing. Three major manufacturers—Imperial Tobacco Ltd, Gallaher Ltd and Rothmans (UK) Ltd (now part of British American Tobacco)—supply the market. British American Tobacco, which mainly manufactures cigarettes in the UK for export only, is the second largest tobacco company in the world. UK consumers spent almost £12.5 billion on tobacco products in 2000, of which £9.6 billion was accounted for by taxes. Although the figures in Table 27.7 show a substantial decline in sales, in recent years there has been a rapid growth in 'bootlegging' and smuggling. The official

Table 27.7: Tobacco—UK Sales to Trade[1]

	1990	1995	2000
Cigarettes (million)	98,325	79,560	56,012
Handrolling tobacco ('000 kg)	4,170	2,570	2,135
Pipe tobacco ('000 kg)	1,975	1,090	640
Cigars (million)	1,480	1,070	895

[1] Based on UK manufacturers' sales to the wholesale and retail trade and estimates of imported goods.
Source: Tobacco Manufacturers Association

estimate of revenue lost through tobacco smuggling in 2000 was £3.8 billion, making a total of almost £9 billion since 1996. The industry achieves significant export sales—in excess of £1 billion in 2000—with Europe, the Middle East and Africa important overseas markets. The UK tobacco industry remains one of the top ten balance-of-payments earners in the UK economy.

Textiles, Clothing and Footwear

Around 276,000 people were employed in the UK textiles, clothing and footwear industry in December 2000. Annual turnover in 1999 was £18.0 billion. The sector has been adversely affected by imports from low labour-cost suppliers, changing sourcing patterns in the UK high street and the weakness of the euro and related European currencies—in 2000 output was over 21% below the level in 1995. UK manufacturers have modernised their domestic operations to meet these challenges, in some cases investing in production facilities abroad. In addition, to compete in areas other than price, firms have shifted into higher-value products to benefit from the UK's strengths in fashion, design, product and process innovation, and information technology. New technologies, largely designed to improve response times and give greater flexibility in production, are used throughout the industry.

Textiles and Clothing

The textiles industry has a high degree of regional concentration, reflecting the traditional centres for this sector: cotton textiles in the North West, fine knitwear in Scotland, linen in Northern Ireland, woollens and worsteds in Yorkshire and Scotland, and knitted fabrics in the East Midlands. The clothing industry is more dispersed throughout the UK, but also has significant concentrations in the Midlands, north and east London and the North East.

The UK textile and clothing industry comprises a few multi-process companies, but in the main companies operate vertically. However, small and medium-sized firms dominate, some of which subcontract work to other companies or to homeworkers. Two of the mainstays of the industry, Coats Viyella and Courtaulds Textiles, have undergone radical changes over the past year or so. Courtaulds has been taken over by the US conglomerate Sara Lee, and Coats Viyella has withdrawn from a number of markets, including home furnishing and contract clothing.

The principal textile and clothing products are yarns, woven and knitted fabrics, interior (including printed) textiles, technical textiles, carpets and a full range of clothing (including knitwear). Tables 27.8 and 27.9 show manufacturers' sales for a range of products. Worsted yarns are finely spun for use mainly in suit fabric and fine knitwear. As well as spinners, weavers and knitters, the sector supports a number of other processes, such as scouring of raw wool and dyeing and finishing of wool, yarn or fabric. British mills also process rare fibres such as cashmere and angora. In addition, the UK produces synthetic fibres, cotton/synthetic mixed yarns and fabrics, and has a large dyeing and finishing sector (which includes fabric printing).

Axminster and Wilton are the main types of woven carpets in the UK, which is recognised for its high-quality products, variety of design and use of new technology. UK companies are also continually improving their capability in the manufacture of higher-volume, lower-value tufted carpets.

Technical textiles are usually defined as such for their performance characteristics. They include non-wovens for filtration and absorbency, textiles used in construction,

Table 27.8: Textiles—UK Manufacturers' Sales by Industry *£ million*

	1998	1999	2000
Soft furnishings	493.5	443.7	465.7
Canvas goods, sacks, etc	127.4	161.2	138.7
Household textiles	914.5	941.6	982.4
Carpets and rugs	1,083.1	1,028.9	992.3
Cordage, rope, twine and netting	82.7	80.1	76.1
Non-wovens excluding apparel	144.6	158.0	n.a.
Preparation and spinning of textile fibres	999.0	891.4	811.5
Textile weaving	1,082.8	972.0	904.6
Finishing of textiles	716.6	628.9	578.2
Lace	61.7	39.3	33.9
Narrow fabrics	235.6	223.4	209.7
Other textiles not elsewhere classified	523.8	497.9	503.8
Knitted and crocheted fabrics	n.a.	n.a.	376.6
Knitted and crocheted hosiery	451.3	363.0	n.a.
Knitted and crocheted pullovers, cardigans and similar articles	771.0	663.5	579.8

n.a. = not available—data suppressed as it could identify individual enterprises concerned.
Source: Office for National Statistics

Table 27.9: Clothing—UK Manufacturers' Sales by Industry *£ million*

	1998	1999	2000
Leather clothes	19.8	13.9	15.9
Workwear	290.2	278.7	264.7
Men's outerwear	759.4	612.5	390.8
Women's outerwear	1,302.1	1,001.2	904.2
Men's underwear	572.2	436.8	305.1
Women's underwear	938.0	779.0	742.7
Hats	71.0	62.7	51.0
Other wearing apparel and accessories	661.4	603.5	593.6
Dressing and dyeing of fur and fur articles	6.5	5.8	6.3

Source: Office for National Statistics

automotive textiles, sewing thread, rope and medical/healthcare textiles and a very wide range of fabrics used in the automotive, aviation, aerospace and defence sectors.

The clothing industry is more labour-intensive than textiles. Although a broad range of clothing is imported, British industry still supplies about two-fifths of domestic demand. As a result of the rising prominence of the British fashion designer industry in the 1980s, and continued strength of traditional branded clothing companies such as Burberry and Jaeger, exports rose consistently until 1996. UK firms have also had success in the growing market for branded street and club-wear. However, exports fell by 20% between 1996 and 2000 to £2.7 billion.

Footwear

Britain is home to some of the world's leading footwear brands. UK shoemakers are renowned for high-quality formal footwear, youth street fashion footwear, safety and protective footwear, high-quality children's shoes and 'made to order' shoes. With around

Table 27.10: British Footwear Market

	1998	1999	2000
Volume (million pairs)			
Manufacturers' sales	82.8	62.9	35.5
Exports[1]	37.0	38.4	37.1
Imports	260.0	290.2	279.6
Domestic supplies	305.8	314.7	278.0
Value (£ million)			
Manufacturers' sales	1,067.5	1,015.4	920.7
Exports[1]	517.1	506.8	486.3
Imports	1,754.8	1,923.4	1,889.5
Domestic supplies	2,305.3	2,432.2	2,323.9

[1] Including re-exports.
Source: British Footwear Association

12,000 employees, manufacturers are predominantly found in Northamptonshire, Leicestershire, Somerset and Lancashire. Manufacturers' sales were over 35 million pairs in 2000, worth around £920 million (see also Table 27.10). The domestic market is, however, dominated by increasingly competitive imports and has been particularly affected by the strength of sterling.

Paper, Printing and Publishing

In total, the UK paper, printing and publishing industry employed some 466,000 people in December 2000. Output has been fairly constant in recent years and was only 6% higher in 2000 than in 1992.

Paper

The paper and board sector is dominated by a small number of medium and large firms—97 pulp, paper and board mills, employing 18,800 people in 2000, concentrated in the north of Kent, Lancashire, the West Country and central Scotland. UK production in 2000 was 6.6 million tonnes, over 40% higher than in 1989, with 1.4 million tonnes exported, 73% to the EU. Imports amounted to 7.7 million tonnes, 85% of which came from the EU and Norway. Hundreds of different grades of paper and board are converted into a wide range of products for use in industry, commerce, education, communications and distribution, and in the home—such as tissues for household and personal use—together with a host of speciality papers for industrial use, for example filters and papers which are subsequently coated, sensitised or laminated. There has been a significant trend towards waste-based packaging grades. Recycled paper made up 60.4% of the raw material for UK newspapers in the first half of 2000 (including imports).

Printing and Publishing

Unlike the paper and board sector, the printing industry in particular has many small businesses—only about 500 firms employ more than 50 people and approximately 90% of firms employ fewer than 20 employees. Much publishing and printing employment and output is carried out in firms based in south-east England. Mergers have led to the formation of large groups in newspaper, magazine and book publishing. The British book-publishing industry is a major exporter, with exports of £1.17 billion in 2000, 4.5% higher than in 1999 (see also Table 27.11). Over 116,000 new titles (including new editions) were issued in 2000, a 6.8% increase on 1999.

The UK printing industry has an annual turnover of around £12 billion and employed

Table 27.11: Top Ten UK Export Destinations for Books *£ million*

	1998	1999	2000
United States	206.9	201.9	212.6
Netherlands	71.5	64.8	72.9
Irish Republic	65.7	66.0	72.8
Germany	76.3	68.5	70.8
Australia	76.0	75.9	69.5
Spain	42.5	45.0	49.3
Italy	37.5	38.3	44.7
Japan	36.3	38.0	42.2
France	46.8	42.1	41.2
South Africa	35.4	33.1	33.3

Source: Department of Trade and Industry

around 198,000 people in Great Britain in December 2000. It has undergone significant technological change recently, with digital technology enabling much greater automation and standardisation. With exports of £2,023 million and imports of £1,568 million, the printing industry had a £455 million trade balance in 2000. Exports are dominated by books and periodicals (see Table 27.12).

Table 27.12: UK Printing Industry: Top Ten Export Categories, 2000

	£ million
Books, booklets and brochures	1,019.1
Newspapers and periodicals	402.4
Trade advertising	119.0
Single sheets	84.9
Postcards and greetings cards	69.7
Cartons, boxes, etc	60.8
Printed labels	57.5
Security printing	48.6
Transfers	22.6
Dictionaries and encyclopaedias	20.7

Source: HM Customs and Excise

Chemicals and Chemical Products

The chemicals industry is one of the primary manufacturing sectors in the UK. It employed almost 238,000 people directly in December 2000 in over 3,400 companies, and had total product sales of £32 billion in 2000, of which 77% was exported (see also Table 27.13). The sector underpins much of the rest of UK manufacturing industry, with chemicals being essential feedstocks for most other industrial processes. Growth in output was strong in 2000—up 4.6%—and was over 27% higher than in 1992.

It is a diverse industry, with important representation in all principal chemical sectors—ranging from bulk petrochemicals to low-volume, high-value specialised organics. It includes key industrial materials such as plastics and synthetic rubber, and other products such as man-made fibres, soap and detergents, cosmetics, adhesives, dyes and inks, and intermediates for the pharmaceutical industry.

Bulk Chemicals

The UK's North Sea oil and gas provide accessible feedstocks for its large organics sector, including such products as ethylene, propylene, benzene and paraxylene. These provide the basic building blocks for the manufacture of many chemical products, including plastics whose strength, durability and light weight have led to their increasing use in transport and packaging applications; and synthetic fibres such as nylon, and polyester used in textiles, clothing and home furnishings.

There is substantial inorganics production, including sulphuric acid (1 million tonnes in 2000), chlorine and caustic soda, based on minerals such as salt, sulphur, and phosphate ores, or reaction between gases. These also serve many other chemical processes.

Formulated Products

The UK is strong in the 'formulation' of chemical products, in areas such as coatings, inks, soaps and detergents, and cosmetics and toiletries. This group includes familiar household items such as decorative paint, home laundry and cleaning products and personal care items like toothpaste, shampoos and skincare products.

Speciality Chemicals

Speciality chemicals meet specific needs through the development and application of sophisticated 'chemistry'. The pharmaceutical and agrochemical sectors are at the forefront of this kind of innovation. In recent years, the application of chirality[1] in synthesis has allowed firms to make drugs more closely tailored to specific targets. Leading-edge research by international pharmaceutical companies in the UK is supported both by a strong academic research capability and a network of specialist manufacturers of 'fine'

[1] Chiral compounds are mirror images of each other, analogous to left- and right-handed forms. One form may be more effective, or safer, than the other.

Table 27.13: Chemicals—UK Manufacturers' Sales by Industry *£ million*

	1998	1999	2000
Basic chemicals, etc			
Industrial gases	600.3	530.1	556.8
Dyes and pigments	1,031.0	1,048.6	1,055.8
Inorganic basic chemicals	1,365.9	1,251.0	1,172.7
Organic basic chemicals	4,045.2	4,152.2	5,340.6
Fertilisers and nitrogen compounds	631.1	736.7	729.3
Plastics	3,341.6	3,500.2	3,720.3
Synthetic rubber in primary forms	349.5	n.a.	349.0
Pesticides and other agrochemical products	n.a.	725.2	739.1
Pharmaceutical products			
Basic products	515.4	520.6	639.0
Preparations	6,029.2	7,298.3	7,380.5
Soaps and detergents, etc	1,839.7	1,922.3	1,849.1
Perfumes and essential oils			
Perfumes and toilet preparations	2,470.5	2,528.8	2,606.5
Essential oils	466.5	526.0	n.a.
Other chemical products			
Paints, varnishes, printing ink, etc	2,482.5	2,627.5	2,558.1
Explosives	111.6	106.8	112.8
Glues and gelatines	449.1	353.3	323.4
Photographic chemical material	1,209.5	n.a.	597.5
Prepared unrecorded media	137.0	141.0	123.3
Other chemical products not elsewhere classified	2,230.3	2,315.1	2,351.9
Man-made fibres	755.6	673.4	727.7

n.a. = not available—data suppressed as it could identify individual enterprises concerned.
Source: Office for National Statistics

chemicals. The latter specialise in the highly skilled processes needed to produce commercial quantities of the complex molecules identified by the pharmaceutical companies' research.

Pharmaceuticals

The UK pharmaceuticals industry, largely based in the South East, North West and North East of England, is the world's third largest exporter of medicines, accounting for 12% of the developed world's export market. It researches and manufactures the complete range of medicinal products—human and veterinary medicines, medical dressings and dental materials. Latterly, the largest growth has been in medicines that act on the respiratory system, followed by cardiovascular, muscular and skeletal, anti-infective and alimentary tract remedies. Exports in 2000 were worth £7.1 billion. The main overseas markets are Western Europe, North America and Japan.

Over 300 pharmaceutical companies operate in the UK, with indigenous and US parent multinationals dominating production. GlaxoSmithKline (employing 21,000 people in the UK) and AstraZeneca (UK-Swedish: 10,000) are the two largest UK-based companies (see p. 384).

Some 62,000 people are directly employed in the UK pharmaceutical industry, with another 250,000 in related sectors. About a third are engaged in R&D, expenditure on which grew by 162% between 1990 and 2000; the industry invested £2.9 billion in UK-based R&D in 2000, around 23% of all UK manufacturing industry R&D. AstraZeneca and GlaxoSmithKline are the UK's top two companies in terms of R&D expenditure, with Pfizer (US), Merck (US) and Novartis (Swiss) also significant investors.

Major developments pioneered in the UK are semi-synthetic penicillins and cephalosporins, both powerful antibiotics, and new treatments for ulcers, asthma, arthritis, Meningitis C, cancer, migraine, HIV/AIDS, coronary heart disease, hypertension, fungal infections, erectile dysfunction and schizophrenia. The UK pharmaceuticals industry is second only to the United States in the discovery and development of leading medicines, including five of the world's current top 25 best-selling drugs. UK laboratories place about 20 new pharmaceutical products on the market each year. Among the best-selling drugs produced by the two largest UK-owned companies are:

- GlaxoSmithKline—Seroxat/Paxil (central nervous system), Augmentin (infections), Avandia (diabetes), Flixotide/Flovent (asthma) and Imigran (migraine); and
- AstraZeneca—Losec (anti-ulcer), Nexium (successor to Losec), Zestril (heart disease), Seroquel (schizophrenia/ Parkinson's disease/Alzheimer's disease) and Zoladex (cancer).

Biotechnology

The UK has the leading biotechnology sector in Europe, with 281 biotechnology companies, employing an estimated 18,400 people. As well as AstraZeneca, GlaxoSmithKline, Celltech, Cambridge Antibody Technology Group and Oxford Glycoscience, there are numerous smaller specialist biotechnology firms—about 18% of the number in Europe—with particular strengths in biopharmaceuticals. Of the potential new drugs under development in Europe, 46% are from publicly quoted UK companies. Companies are clustered particularly around Cambridge, Oxford and southern Scotland. The industry benefits strongly from the UK's science base. Bioscience research in UK universities is of world renown, and the major research laboratories of leading pharmaceutical multinationals are based here. The UK has a number of world-class research institutes, such as the Sanger Centre in Cambridge, which played an important part in the Human Genome project (see p. 424).

Rubber and Plastics Products

In December 2000 around 229,000 people were employed by 6,565 enterprises in the rubber and plastics industries. Output fell slightly by 0.8% in 2000 although it was 18% higher than in 1992.

Rubber products include tyres and tubes, pipes, hoses, belting and floor coverings, many of which have applications in the automotive industry. The industry employs around 40,000 people in 1,000 enterprises. The largest firms in this sector are major tyre manufacturers such as Goodyear, making tyres in the UK since 1927, and Michelin.

Cellulose nitrate, or celluloid, was the first *plastic* to achieve real success, and was displayed at the Great International Exhibition in London in 1862. Since then plastics have made great advances and have a multitude of applications today. The packaging industry is the largest user, accounting for 36% of the market, followed by the construction (23%), electrical and electronic goods (11%) and transport industries (8%). The highest concentrations of plastics employment are in the Midlands (25% of the total), the South East, North West and the South West of England. The UK's plastics industry continues to be a world leader in material specification and design, with new processes allowing stronger plastics to replace traditional materials and develop new applications. Among the larger firms in a sector characterised by many small and medium-sized businesses is British Polythene Industries, manufacturing products such as carrier bags, sacks and shrink film. In the moulded plastics sector, Linpac's output includes trays, fast food packaging, egg cartons and disposable tableware.

Glass, Ceramics and Building Materials

Around 142,000 people were employed in this sector in December 2000; output was little changed from 1999 and just 1% higher than in 1992.

Glass

The UK is a world leader in the manufacture of glass. Flat glass is made through the float process, invented by Pilkington in 1952, which manufactures clear, tinted and coated glass for buildings, and clear and tinted glass for vehicles. It is licensed to more than 40 glass manufacturers in 30 countries. About 48% of Pilkington's total sales are in building products and another 47% in automotive products—the company is one of the world's largest suppliers of glass for cars, trucks and buses—with around one in four of the world's cars containing its glass. The company employs 5,500 people in the UK. The manufacture and supply of building components containing glass, windows, doors, partitioning and cladding is carried out by many other companies operating from within the timber, metal (aluminium and steel) and plastic (UPVC) sectors. The UK also has several leading lead crystal suppliers, such as Waterford-Wedgwood, Dartington and Edinburgh Crystal.

Ceramics

'Ceramics' covers tableware, giftware, ornamentalware and catering ware; floor and wall tiles and sanitaryware; bricks, clay roofing tiles, clay pipes and land drains; industrial ceramics and refractories; and ceramic materials and machinery. The industry has sales of more than £2 billion a year, employs over 46,000 people and is heavily concentrated in the West Midlands. Domestic tableware production includes fine china, bone china, earthenware and stoneware and is produced predominantly in the Potteries (Stoke-on-Trent) area of Staffordshire. Wedgwood, Spode and Royal Doulton are among the most famous names in fine bone china, and the UK is one of the world's leading manufacturers and exporters. Research is being conducted into the use of ceramics in housebuilding and diesel and jet engines. Important industrial ceramics invented in the UK include some forms of silicon carbide and sialons, which can withstand ultra-high temperatures.

Building Materials

Most crushed rock, sand and gravel quarried by the aggregates industry (some 221 million tonnes in Great Britain in 1999) is used in construction. In 2000, 2.86 billion bricks were produced by, and 2.89 billion bricks were delivered from, sites in Great Britain. Portland cement, a 19th-century British innovation, is the most widely used chemical compound in the world. Blue Circle Industries (now part of the French group Lafarge) is the UK's largest producer of cement—6.3 million tonnes in 2000, of which 400,000 tonnes were exported—and has 1,620 employees.[2]

Metals and Fabricated Metal Products

The Industrial Revolution in the UK was based to a considerable extent on the manufacture of iron and steel and heavy machinery. These sectors remain important parts of the industrial economy; around 519,000 people were employed in December 2000. Output in 2000 was little changed from 1999 and at the same level as in 1993.

The major areas of *steel* production are concentrated in south Wales and northern England, with substantial processing in the Midlands and Yorkshire. Major restructuring in the steel industry took place during the 1980s and 1990s. Metals can be recycled many times; every year the British metals recycling industry processes about 8 million tonnes of scrap metal.

From total crude steel output of 15.1 million tonnes, British producers delivered 14.4 million tonnes of finished steel in 2000; 50% was exported. Over three-quarters of UK steel exports go to other EU Member States. Germany is the UK's biggest market. Annual steel industry exports have risen from 4.7 million tonnes in 1985 to 7.8 million tonnes in 2000. Exports of UK steel products were valued at £2.7 billion in 2000. The main UK markets for steel are in the construction (22%), engineering (24%), automotive (17%) and metal goods industries (14%). Corus, Europe's third largest steelmaker and the

[2] For china clay see chapter 28.

Table 27.14: Production of Building Materials and Components, Great Britain

	1998	1999	2000
Bricks (millions)	3,000	2,939	2,864
Concrete building blocks ('000 sq m)	84,662	87,767	90,219
Cement ('000 tonnes)[1]	12,409	12,697	12,522
Sand and gravel ('000 tonnes)[2]	85,968	88,209	86,960
Ready mixed concrete ('000 cu m)[1, 3]	22,983	23,550	23,043
Slate (tonnes)[4]	104,899	98,870	85,858
Concrete roofing tiles ('000 sq m)	24,981	25,972	26,316

1 United Kingdom.
2 Sales.
3 Deliveries.
4 Excluding slate residue used for fill.
Source: Department of Trade and Industry—*Construction Statistics Annual 2001*

seventh largest in the world, employed 33,200 people in the UK at the end of June 2000 and produced 85% of the UK's total crude steel. Its output is based on strip mill products, plate, sections, specialist engineering steels, bars, wire rods and tubes. The company owns 23% of Avesta Polarit, formed in 2001 from the merger of Avesta Sheffield (the Anglo-Swedish stainless steel group) and the stainless steel division of Outokumpu of Finland. Corus's worldwide aluminium output is around 500,000 tonnes.

Products manufactured by other UK steel companies include reinforcing bars for the construction industry, wire rod, hot rolled bars, bright bars, tubes, and wire and wire products. The production of special steels is centred on the Sheffield area and includes stainless and alloy special steels for the aerospace and offshore oil and gas industries.

Steel has had a notable success in UK construction, with its market share in buildings of two or more storeys more than doubling from 30% in the early 1980s to 70% today. It has 90% of the single storey market. Total iron and steel sales in this sector are £2.3 billion a year and consumption of constructional steelwork 1.1 million tonnes.

Several multinational companies have plants in Britain producing *non-ferrous metals* from both primary and recycled raw materials. The *aluminium* industry supplies customers in the aerospace, transport, automotive and construction industries. Other important non-ferrous metal sectors are *copper and copper alloys*, used for electrical wire and cables, power generation and electrical and electronic connectors, automotive components, plumbing and building products, and components for industrial plant and machinery; *lead* for lead acid batteries and roofing; *zinc* for galvanising to protect steel; *nickel*, used principally as an alloying element to make stainless steel and high temperature turbine alloys; and *titanium* for high-strength, low-weight aerospace applications. Despite an overall decline in the *castings* industry, some foundries have invested in new melting, moulding and quality control equipment.

Fabricated metal products include those made by forging, pressing, stamping and roll forming of metal. They are used for builders' carpentry and joinery equipment; tanks, reservoirs and metal containers; central heating radiators and boilers; steam generators; treatment and coating of metals; cutlery, tools and general hardware.

Machinery and Equipment

Around 353,000 people were employed in this sector in December 2000, with highest concentrations found in the West Midlands, followed by the South East and the East region. Output declined marginally in 2000 and was 6% lower than in 1992–93. Mechanical machine-building is an area in which British firms excel, especially internal combustion engines, power transmission

Table 27.15: Machinery and Equipment—Turnover and Orders, UK

£ billion

	1998	1999	2000
Home			
Orders on hand	6.9	7.4	7.7
New orders[1]	20.1	21.4	20.7
Turnover	21.5	20.9	20.3
Export			
Orders on hand	3.5	3.3	3.6
New orders[1]	12.3	11.1	11.9
Turnover	12.7	11.3	11.5
Total			
Orders on hand	10.4	10.6	11.3
New orders[1]	32.4	32.4	32.5
Turnover	34.2	32.2	31.8

[1] Net of cancellations.
Source: Office for National Statistics

Table 27.16: Metalworking Machine Tools—Turnover and Orders, UK

£ million

	1998	1999	2000
Home			
Orders on hand	139.2	94.2	92.8
New orders[1]	549.9	440.2	503.8
Turnover	586.9	485.1	505.3
Export			
Orders on hand	108.3	114.2	197.3
New orders[1]	403.9	387.7	514.7
Turnover	415.1	381.8	431.6
Total			
Orders on hand	247.5	208.4	290.1
New orders[1]	953.8	827.9	1,018.5
Turnover	1,001.9	867.0	936.8

[1] Net of cancellations.
Source: Office for National Statistics

equipment, pumps and compressors, wheeled tractors, lawnmowers, construction and earth-moving equipment, and textile machinery. The UK is a major producer of industrial engines, pumps, valves and compressors, and of pneumatic and hydraulic equipment. Companies manufacture steam generators and other heavy equipment for power plants.

Alstom, a global specialist in transport and energy infrastructure, is one of the world's leading suppliers of major components for complete power station projects along with the transformers and switchgear needed in transmission and distribution of electricity. In the UK the company's strengths are steam turbine manufacture, switchgear manufacture, industrial gas turbines, and project design and management.

The mechanical lifting and handling equipment industry makes cranes and transporters, lifting devices, escalators, conveyors, powered industrial trucks and air bridges, as well as electronically controlled and automatic handling systems. The commercial heating, ventilation, air-conditioning and refrigeration sector is served to a great extent by small and medium-sized firms, although several large multinational companies have sites in Britain.

Tractors and equipment used in agriculture, horticulture, forestry, sportsturf and gardens achieved export sales of £1.2 billion in 2000. Most tractor exports were supplied by three major multinationals with plants in the UK which, together with JCB Landpower, export to nearly every country in the world. A wide range of specialist golf, parks and sports field machinery, lawn and garden products, and agricultural equipment complement the tractor business.

Machine tools, most of which are computer-controlled, are used in all sectors of manufacturing, including the engineering, aerospace and automotive industries. In 2000 total turnover of companies classified to the metalworking machine tools industry was £937 million, of which exports accounted for £432 million, or 46%.

The mining and tunnelling equipment industry leads the world in the production of coal-cutting and road-heading (shearing) equipment, hydraulic roof supports, conveying equipment, flameproof transformers, switchgear, and subsurface transport equipment and control systems. In construction equipment, the UK has the largest production volume in Europe, approximately one-third of the total. It also has the highest export ratio of any major producing country. JCB and a number of major multinational companies contribute to construction equipment exports of over £2 billion a year.

The UK has one of the largest engineering construction sectors in the world, serving the whole spectrum of process industries, with particular strengths in oil, gas and related industries. Most sales of textile machinery are to export markets. British innovations include computerised colour matching and weave simulation, friction spinning, high-speed computer-controlled knitting machines and electronic jacquard attachments for weaving looms. British companies also make advanced printing machinery and ceramic processing equipment, and other types of production machinery.

The *domestic appliances* sector includes the manufacture of refrigerators and freezers, dishwashers, washing machines, tumble dryers, vacuum cleaners, floor polishers, microwave ovens and cookers, as well as water heaters and showers, ventilation products and small appliances for the kitchen and bathroom. Energy efficiency and water conservation are progressively improving in home laundry products, and new technology is being applied to many products. Visual design of what were traditionally 'white goods' is changing, giving a new look to kitchens, and modern design is also being applied to vacuum cleaners and small appliances such as kettles and toasters. The UK is Europe's largest manufacturer of tumble dryers, with an annual trade surplus in this product of around £23 million.

Electrical and Optical Equipment

In total 490,000 people were employed in this sector in December 2000. There were 52,000 working in the office machinery and computers sector, 178,000 in electrical machinery, 132,000 in radio, TV and communications equipment and 129,000 in medical, precision optical equipment and watches. Overall, output has been rising sharply—by over 13% in 2000, when it was almost 76% higher than in the early 1990s. Production of office machinery and computers rose by 274% between 1990 and 2000, while radio, television and communications equipment output was up by 132%. However, output of medical and optical instruments fell by 2%, while that of electrical machinery and apparatus fell by 5%.

Table 27.17: Electrical and Optical Equipment—Turnover and Orders, UK *£ billion*

	1998	1999	2000
Home			
Orders on hand	7.6	9.5	11.2
New orders[1]	31.1	35.0	37.8
Turnover	31.2	33.0	36.1
Export			
Orders on hand	6.1	6.6	7.3
New orders[1]	28.6	29.0	31.5
Turnover	27.9	28.5	30.9
Total			
Orders on hand	13.7	16.2	18.5
New orders[1]	59.7	64.0	69.3
Turnover	59.1	61.6	67.0

[1] Net of cancellations.
Source: Office for National Statistics

Southern England provides a substantial proportion of employment (especially sales and administrative jobs) in these sectors, with Scotland and Wales having become important areas for inward investors. Scotland's electronics industry ('Silicon Glen'—in effect all of central Scotland) directly employed about 40,600 people in 1998. In 2000 electrical and instrument engineering accounted for exports worth £10 billion, 56% of Scotland's manufactured exports.

Many of the world's leading overseas-based multinational electronics firms have substantial manufacturing investment in the UK. The main electronic consumer goods produced are television sets, with UK production concentrated in the high-value market and with an increasing proportion of widescreen and digital sets. High-fidelity audio and video equipment is also produced.

The computer industry in the UK is the largest in Europe, producing an extensive range of systems for all uses—for information on software, see p. 533. There are several multinational computer manufacturers in the UK. Others, such as Psion (a British pioneer of the 'palmtop' computer), have concentrated on developing new lines for specialised markets.

A broad range of other electrical machinery and apparatus is produced in the UK by both British and foreign companies, covering power plant, electric motors, generators, transformers, switchgear, insulated wire and cable (including optical fibre cables for telecommunications), and lighting equipment.

The past few years have seen the development of electronic service providers (contract electronic manufacturers) which manufacture and assemble products to the specification of other companies. This global trend has encouraged some multinational producers to move away from manufacture to become designers, developers, marketers or sellers of their products; the UK is one of the leading locations in Europe for this type of business.

Communications Equipment

The domestic telecommunications equipment market is worth £15 billion a year. Manufacturers have invested heavily in facilities to meet rapidly increasing demand for telecommunications services (see chapter 17). The main products are switching and transmission equipment, telephones and terminals. Transmission equipment and cables for telecommunications and information networks include submarine and high-specification data-carrying cables.

There was remarkable growth in the mobile communications sector in 2000 (see p. 285), with the UK among Europe's leading markets and manufacturing bases. Many producers have UK production or design centres. Fibre optics (a UK invention) and other optoelectronic components have also experienced rapid growth, due to the demand for ultra high-speed transmission rates for Internet use. However, in 2001, there has been a general downturn in the telecommunications sector due mainly to the downturn in the US economy. This has led to rationalisation and job losses across the sector in recent months.

Another sector of the industry manufactures radio communications equipment, radar, radio and sonar navigational aids for ships and aircraft, thermal imaging systems, alarms and signalling apparatus, public broadcasting equipment and other capital goods. Radar was invented in the UK and British firms are still in the forefront of technological advances. Solid-state secondary surveillance radar is being supplied to numerous overseas civil aviation operators.

Medical Electronics

The high demand for advanced medical equipment in the UK stems from its comprehensive healthcare system and extensive clinical research and testing facilities in the chemical, biological, physical and molecular sciences. Important contributions have been made by British scientists and engineers to basic R&D in endoscopy, computerised tomography scanning, magnetic resonance imaging (pioneered in the UK), ultrasonic imaging, CADiagnosis and renal analysis. Firms in the UK medical electronics sector continue their tradition of developing and manufacturing a range of medical equipment for domestic and overseas health sectors.

Instrumentation and Control

The instrumentation and control sector covers the design, development and manufacture of scientific and industrial equipment and systems for analysis, measurement, testing and control. The instrumentation sector is generally broken down into six specific categories: navigation and surveying; electronic and electrical testing; laboratory/analytical; process monitoring and control; automotive; and drafting and dimensional measurement. The UK instrumentation and control sector has an estimated annual output of £9 billion, with a trade balance of £884 million. The sector is diverse and exceeds 3,000 firms, employing 79,000 people. It is the fourth most important manufacturer of instrumentation and process control equipment in the world behind the United States, Japan and Germany.

Motor Vehicles

New UK car *registrations* rose by 1.1% in 2000 to 2.22 million, the fourth highest figure on record. UK-based manufacturers' share of the UK market in 2000 was 28.3%, marginally down on 1999. By customer type, the private sector took 44.7% of the total, the fleet sector 45.8% and the business sector 9.5%. Commercial vehicle registrations, at 298,000, were 3.5% higher than in 1999. Car *production*, at 1.63 million, was 8.8% lower than in 1999, but has risen almost 26% since 1990. Vehicle manufacturers are increasingly pursuing a global market, with production no longer dominated by their traditional home markets. This is reflected in the rise in both UK exports and imports of motor vehicles. Over 1 million passenger cars were produced for export in 2000, more than two-and-a-half times as many as in 1990 and the highest figure ever. Commercial vehicle production in 2000 was 184,000, 1% lower than in 1999 and significantly down on previous years; 87,000 units were for export. The sector is dominated by light commercial vehicles.

Around 720,000 jobs are dependent on the UK automotive industry, including 220,000 engaged in vehicle and component production and manufacturing activities. There are around 40 motor vehicle manufacturers in the UK. Seven groups now dominate car output, accounting for 99% of the total: Ford (including Jaguar, Land Rover and Aston Martin), Vauxhall/IBC, Peugeot, Honda, Nissan, Toyota and the newly independent MG Rover. There are still many companies making cars and commercial vehicles in Britain: Table 27.18 shows the main producers, plus some specialist manufacturers.

Since 1997 motor vehicle manufacturers have announced over £4 billion in new capital investment in the UK, which is expected to create over 10,000 new jobs. This includes £440 million by Nissan at its Sunderland plant to introduce the new Micra and Primera models; £150 million by Toyota at its engine plant in Deeside, raising capacity to 400,000 engines a year; £330 million invested by GM in its Vauxhall and IBC plants for the new Vectra and van projects; £400 million by BMW at Hams Hall (West Midlands) to create the world's most advanced engine plant; and £130 million by Ford to modernise Land Rover's Solihull plant. Ford will also invest £360 million in the Dagenham diesel engine plant to enhance its status as Ford's European centre of excellence. Investment by component manufacturers includes four Unipart joint ventures totalling over £80 million, and investment by Visteon on four facilities in the UK.

The main truck manufacturers are Paccar (which manufactures Leyland Trucks) and ERF, now owned by MAN of Germany. Medium-sized vans are manufactured by LDV at Birmingham, Ford at Southampton and by the new GM/Renault joint venture at the IBC plant in Luton. The merger of the UK bus manufacturing interests of Mayflower and Henlys to form Transbus has resulted in a powerful new group able to compete successfully in European and other world markets. London Taxis International, owned by Manganese Bronze Holdings, the engineering and automotive components group, now produces 3,000 taxis a year at its Coventry factory.

The *automotive components manufacturing* sector, with an annual turnover of £8 billion and employing 95,000 in Great Britain, is a major contributor to the UK motor industry. There are around 1,400 companies involved (some 23% of them small and medium enterprises, in terms of employment), many of which also supply other sectors. The sector has enjoyed strong growth and rising productivity in recent years.

Shipbuilding and Marine Engineering

The UK *merchant shipbuilding* industry, located mainly in Scotland and northern England, consists of some 19 yards employing in the region of 3,500 to 4,000 people, producing ships ranging from tugs and fishing vessels to fast ferries and large specialist craft for offshore exploration and exploitation work. The industry's current order book is in the region of 20 ships. The merchant ship repair and conversion industry, which has a strong presence in the UK, comprises over 60 companies employing 4,000 to 7,000 people depending on workload. Naval construction accounts for a further 15,000 people. Vosper Thornycroft and BAE SYSTEMS dominate warship production. During 2000 the Ministry of Defence announced orders for the

Table 27.18: UK Vehicle Production in 2000

Manufacturer	Cars	Manufacturer	Commercial vehicles[1]
Aston Martin	1,029	Dennis Eagle	489
Caterham	468	Dennis SV	1,874
Ford	155,085	ERF	2,698
General Motors	290,679	Foden	1,121
Honda	74,751	Ford	110,291
Jaguar-Daimler	88,844	Land Rover	15,611
Land Rover	159,997	LDV	13,081
Lotus	2,861	Leyland Trucks	9,743
LTI	3,327	Optare	296
Metrocab	472	Peugeot	1,723
MG Rover	174,885	Seddon Atkinson	646
Morgan	550	Vauxhall	14,869
Nissan	327,701	**Total**	**172,442**
Peugeot	186,074		
Rolls-Royce/Bentley	1,938		
Toyota	171,339		
TVR	1,317		
Total	**1,641,317**		

[1] Includes buses and coaches.

Source: Society of Motor Manufacturers and Traders

construction of troop landing ships and troop carriers which will safeguard and create thousands of jobs at UK shipyards. Overall, shipyards employ about 26,000 people and tend to concentrate around Southampton, Liverpool, Newcastle upon Tyne, Glasgow and Belfast. In addition, the UK has a range of world-class companies in the boat-building sector. A few internationally known builders dominate the sector.

The UK marine equipment industry has an annual turnover of £1.7 billion and employs an estimated 16,600 people in about 700 companies. About 60% of its output is exported. Production ranges from traditional marine equipment to sophisticated navigational and propulsion systems, as well as equipment and supplies for the cruise industry.

Oil and gas exploitation in the North Sea has generated a major offshore industry (see pp. 495–6). Shipbuilders and fabricators design and build semi-submersible units for drilling, production andemergency/ maintenance support; drill ships; jack-up rigs; modules; and offshore loading systems as well as undertaking 'floating production storage and offload' vessel (FPSO) conversions. Harland and Wolff of Belfast is a world leader in the offshore sector, specialising in drill ships, while Swan Hunter and Aker McHulty have had recent successes in the FPSO field. Many other firms supply equipment and services to the industry, notably diving expertise, consultancy, design, project management and R&D. A number have used their experience of North Sea projects to establish themselves in oil and gas markets throughout the world.

Railway Equipment

There are several hundred UK companies engaged in the manufacture of railway equipment for both domestic and overseas markets, mainly producing specialist components and systems for use in rolling stock, signalling, track and infrastructure applications. Two large multinational train builders, the UK/French-owned Alstom and the Canadian-owned Bombardier—which acquired German-owned Adtranz in 2000—have UK bases. After a period in the early

1990s with few orders, privatised train operating companies have placed orders for more than 3,000 passenger carriages. One notable order is for 53 electric tilting trains, due to begin operating on Virgin West Coast routes out of London Euston in 2002.

Aerospace and Defence

The UK's aerospace industry is one of the few in the world with a complete capability across the whole spectrum of aerospace products and technology. For the aerospace industry as a whole, turnover in 2000 was £18.3 billion, of which £11.95 billion (60%) was exported. It contributed £3.8 billion to the UK's balance of payments in 2000. Around 151,000 people are directly employed in the industry in Great Britain, with the North West, South West and East Midlands providing the highest number of jobs. Farnborough International, held in July every other year, and organised by the Society of British Aerospace Companies, is the world's premier aerospace business event. At the 2000 show there were 1,287 exhibitors from 30 countries, with trade attendance of 170,000 and public attendance of 133,000. Orders worth £35 billion were announced during the event.

Industry activities cover designing and constructing airframes, aero-engines, guided weapons, simulators and space satellites, materials, flight controls including 'fly-by-wire' and 'fly-by-light' equipment (see p. 487), avionics and complex components, with their associated services. The UK also has the Western world's second largest defence manufacturing industry after that of the United States.

Among the leading companies are BAE SYSTEMS and Rolls-Royce, both of which are among the UK's top five exporters. BAE SYSTEMS is a global systems, defence and aerospace company. It employs more than 100,000 people around the world and has annual sales of some £12 billion; its order book in 2000 was £41 billion. It designs and manufactures civil and military aircraft, surface ships, submarines, space systems, radar, avionics, guided weapons systems, communications, electronics and a range of other defence equipment.

Civil Aircraft

BAE SYSTEMS has a 20% share of Airbus—EADS (European Aeronautic Defence and Space Company) controls the other 80%. BAE SYSTEMS has responsibility for designing and manufacturing the wings for the whole family of Airbus airliners, from the short- to medium-haul A320 series (the first civil airliner to use fly-by-wire controls) to the large long-range four-engined A340. The company will also design and manufacture the wings for the new A380 'superjumbo'—a twin-deck, twin-aisle jetliner with 555 or more seats—expected to directly create 8,000 jobs in the UK. Airbus and its related businesses support 62,000 UK jobs. In 2000 Airbus received firm orders for 520 new aircraft worth a total of US$41.3 billion from 42 customers around the world, and in the first half of 2001 it had 52% of the world market for large civil aircraft.

Short Brothers, owned by Bombardier of Canada, the third largest civil aircraft manufacturer in the world, employs about 6,000 people, the vast majority of whom are based in Northern Ireland. The company is mainly engaged in design and production of major civil aircraft sub-assemblies, advanced engine nacelles and components for aerospace manufacturers as well as the provision of aviation support services.

Military Aircraft and Missiles

The Eurofighter Typhoon is being built by BAE SYSTEMS, EADS and Alenia of Italy. BAE SYSTEMS also has the Harrier, a vertical/short take-off and landing (V/STOL) military combat aircraft, the Tornado combat aircraft (built jointly with EADS) and the Hawk fast-jet trainer, being supplied to 17 customers worldwide. The company is involved in the Joint Strike Fighter programme teams of both Boeing and Lockheed Martin of the US.

BAE SYSTEMS is a major supplier of tactical guided weapon systems for use on land, at sea and in the air, having merged its missile business with that of France's Matra Corporation and subsequently Alenia to form Europe's largest guided weapons concern, MBDA (Matra BAe Dynamics Alenia). Shorts

Missile Systems Ltd (SMS), which has been acquired by Thomson-CSF of France, now THALES, operates in the area of very short-range air defence systems.

Helicopters

Agusta Westland manufactures the multi-role EH101 medium-lift helicopter for civilian and military markets—two British variants are the Royal Navy's Merlin HM.1 advanced anti-submarine warfare helicopter and the RAF's Merlin HC.3 combat transport helicopter. It also manufactures the Super Lynx light battlefield and naval helicopter, and is currently building the Apache attack helicopter for the UK Army, under licence from Boeing. Agusta Westland is now, after Boeing, the world's second largest helicopter manufacturer, when including its product line inherited from Agusta and the manufacturing facilities in Italy.

Land Systems

The UK's main armoured fighting vehicle capability is concentrated in two companies: Rolls-Royce, which acquired Vickers (Defence Systems) in 1999, and Alvis. RO Defence, a division of BAE SYSTEMS, is the UK's only indigenous ordnance company.

Engines and Other Aviation Equipment

Rolls-Royce is one of the world's three leading manufacturers of aero-engines, with a turnover in 2000 of £3.2 billion for its aerospace business. More than 17,000 Rolls-Royce civil engines are in service, in over 130 countries. Customers include over 500 airlines, 2,400 corporate and utility operators and 100 armed forces. Rolls-Royce is a partner in the low-emission V2500 aero-engine, now in service on the Airbus A320 family. It produces military engines for both fixed-wing aircraft and helicopters, and is a partner in the EJ200 engine project for the Eurofighter and with GE on the alternative US Joint Strike Fighter programme.

A number of UK companies produce aerostructures (doors, windows and aircraft body parts), equipment and systems for engines, aircraft propellers, navigation and landing systems, engine and flight controls, environmental controls and oxygen breathing and regulation systems, electrical generation, mechanical and hydraulic power systems, cabin furnishings, flight-deck controls and information displays. BAE SYSTEMS is the world's largest manufacturer of head-up displays (HUDs). British firms have made important technological advances, for example, in developing fly-by-wire and fly-by-light technology, in which control surfaces on the wings and elsewhere are moved by means of automatic electronic signalling and fibre optics respectively. UK companies provide radar and air traffic control equipment and ground power supplies to airports and airlines worldwide (see also p. 483).

Space Equipment and Services

Between 300 and 400 organisations employing more than 5,000 people are engaged in industrial space activities (see pp. 439–40), with turnover of £365 million in 1999. UK participation in the European Space Agency, and the British National Space Centre's role in coordinating UK space policy (see p. 439), has enabled UK-based companies to participate in many leading space projects covering telecommunications, satellite navigation, Earth observation, space science and astronomy. The industry is strong in the development and manufacture of civil and military communications satellites and associated Earth stations and ground infrastructure equipment. In the field of Earth observation, it plays a major role in manufacturing platforms, space radar and meteorological satellite hardware, and in the exploitation of space data imaging products.

The largest British space company is Astrium Limited. Jointly owned by BAE SYSTEMS and EADS, it is one of the world's major space companies. It has become the leading provider of direct broadcast television satellites, and is involved in all of Europe's space science and Earth observation projects and its launcher and navigation programmes.

Construction

The total value of work done in the construction industry in Great Britain during 2000 was £69.5 billion at current prices, of which £37.5 billion was new work and £32.0 billion repair and maintenance (see also Table 27.19). The volume of output at constant 1995 prices grew by 1.5% compared with 1999. The main areas of construction work within the GB industry covered by these statistics are:

- building and civil engineering—ranging from major private sector companies with diverse international interests to one-person enterprises carrying out domestic repairs; and
- specialist work—companies or individuals undertaking construction work ranging from structural steelwork and precast concrete structures to mechanical and electrical services (including the design and installation of environmentally friendly building control systems).

Other areas of construction work not covered in the above statistics include:

- the supply of building materials and components—ranging from large quarrying companies, and those engaged in mass production of manufactured items, to small, highly specialised manufacturers; and
- consultancy work—companies or individuals engaged in the planning, design and supervision of construction projects.

In December 2000, there were 1,845,000 workforce jobs in Great Britain in the construction industry, just over 6% of the total workforce. Of these, 721,000 (39%) were self-employed and 15.0% of employees were female.

Table 27.19: Value of Construction Output by Type of Work, Great Britain *£ million*

	1998	1999	2000
New work	32,491	35,587	37,510
New housing	8,430	8,418	9,946
Other new work	24,060	27,168	27,565
Repair and maintenance	29,569	30,117	32,016
Housing	16,202	16,370	16,906
Other work	13,367	13,747	15,110
All work	**62,060**	**65,704**	**69,527**

Source: Department of Trade and Industry

Housing

In 2000 the total value of new housing orders in Great Britain was £7 billion, 1.9% higher than in 1999—the private sector accounted for 87% of the total compared with 75% in 1993. In 2000 construction of over 176,000 dwellings was *started* in Great Britain. Starts by private enterprise concerns were 158,300, by registered social landlords 18,000, and by the public sector 300. New dwellings *completed* by sector are shown in Table 27.20 below.

Table 27.20: Permanent Dwellings completed by Sector in Great Britain

	1990	1995	2000
Private enterprise	161,300	150,900	144,000
Registered social landlords	17,600	38,300	21,000
All public sector	16,600	2,100	600
Total	**195,500**	**191,300**	**165,600**

Sources: Department of Trade and Industry, National Assembly for Wales and Scottish Executive

Project Procurement, Management and Financing

Private and public sector projects are managed in a variety of ways. Most clients invite construction firms to bid for work by competitive tender, having used the design services of a consultant. The successful contractor will then undertake on-site work with a number of specialist subcontractors. Alternative methods of project procurement have become more common in recent years—for example, contracts might include subsequent provision of building maintenance, or a comprehensive 'design-and-build' service where a single company oversees every stage of a project from conception to completion.

Financing of major projects has also been changing. Traditionally, clients raised the finance to pay for schemes themselves. Today, they often demand a complete service package that includes finance; as a result, larger construction companies are developing closer links with banks and other financial institutions. In public sector construction the Government's Private Finance Initiative/ Public-Private Partnerships (see p. 403) have also heralded a move away from traditional financing.

Overseas Contracting and Consultancy

UK companies operate internationally and in any one year British consultants work in almost every country in the world.

UK contractors have pioneered management contracting and design and build, and also the financing mechanisms that have been developed in the domestic market through innovations such as the Private Finance Initiative. During 2000 they won new international business valued at £4.0 billion, 8% more than in 1999 (see Table 27.21). Contractors have been particularly successful in North America, their most valuable market, which accounted for 47% of all new contracts. Recent major contracts have included:

- liquid natural gas terminal, India;
- station for East Rail Extension, Hong Kong;
- station depot, Hong Kong;
- 29-storey office development, Hong Kong;
- high-rise commercial development, Munich;
- High Falls Redevelopment Project, Newfoundland; and
- water treatment works, Malaysia.

Table 27.21: Overseas Construction Activity by British Companies *£ million*

	1998	1999	2000
Europe	444	385	824
of which EU	*294*	*306*	*618*
Middle East	446	522	368
Far East	892	914	466
of which Hong Kong	*527*	*703*	*278*
Africa	174	261	128
Americas	2,017	1,216	1,868
of which North America	*1,904*	*1,145*	*1,748*
Oceania	259	384	321
Total	**4,232**	**3,682**	**3,975**

Source: Department of Trade and Industry

The main categories of work in which *British consultants* are involved include structural commercial (roads, bridges, tunnels and railways); electrical and mechanical services; chemical, oil and gas plants; and water supply. Award-winning recent major contracts have included:

- Institut Supérieur des Finances Publiques, Kigali, Rwanda;
- Water and Sewerage Concession Project, Sofia, Bulgaria;
- Hanging Glass Façade, Samsung Jong-Ro Building, Seoul, Korea;
- the Oresund Tunnel and Bridge, Sweden;
- Jumeirah Beach Resort, Dubai; and
- Road Management Capacity Building Project, Uganda.

Websites

Department of Trade and Industry: www.dti.gov.uk
National Statistics: www.statistics.gov.uk

28 Energy and Natural Resources

Energy Resources	**490**	Gas Supply Industry	497
Energy Policy	490	Coal	498
Energy Consumption	492	Electricity	499
Energy Efficiency	492	New and Renewable Sources of Energy	503
Oil and Gas Exploration and Production	493	**Non-energy Minerals**	**504**
Downstream Oil	496	**Water Supply**	**504**
Trade	496		

UK energy production fell by 3% in 2000 and primary energy consumption was 0.4% higher. Oil production was 7.9% down, while production and consumption of gas rose by 9.2% and 3.8% respectively, although the growth rate of its use in power stations was lower than in recent years. The Government has allocated £267 million over three years to promote new and renewable energy technologies.

Energy Resources

Production of coal continued to fall in 2000, by 16% on 1999, to just over 31 million tonnes. Nuclear electricity output went down by 10.6% to 85.1 terawatt hours. Production of natural gas rose to 108.5 billion cubic metres—a record level for the eleventh consecutive year. Coal still supplied a significant proportion of the country's primary energy needs: 32% of the electricity supplied in 2000 was from coal, while gas supplied 39% and nuclear 21%.

For 2000, in value terms, total imports of fuels were 85% higher than in 1999, largely owing to a 75% increase in the value of petroleum product imports. Exports were 69% higher, mainly because of a 66% increase in the value of exports of crude oil. These increases reflect high world oil prices during 2000 (see p. 495).

Overall the UK remains a net exporter of all fuels, with a surplus on a balance of payments basis of £6.7 billion in 2000, nearly £2.4 billion higher than in 1999. The trade surplus in crude oil and petroleum products was £6.2 billion. In volume terms, imports of fuel in 2000 were 18% higher than in 1999, while exports were 6% higher. The UK had a trade surplus in fuels of 43.5 million tonnes of oil equivalent—the eighth year in succession that it has had a trade surplus in volume terms.

ENERGY POLICY

The Government's energy policy is based on diversity of sources and on sustained and secure energy production at competitive prices, within a framework where competition can flourish, markets can operate efficiently for the benefit of suppliers and consumers, and the UK can make best use of its indigenous resources. The electricity and gas markets in Great Britain are open to full competition, with the aim of giving consumers a choice from a growing number of suppliers.

In June 2001 the Government announced a review of the strategic issues surrounding energy policy in Great Britain. This is being carried out by the Cabinet Office's Performance and Innovation Unit and is due to be completed by the end of 2001. The main aim of the review is to set out the objectives of energy policy and to develop a strategy that ensures current policy commitments are consistent with longer-term goals. In particular, the review is considering the impact of current and projected energy demand and supply on: the potential conflict with environmental objectives; continued security and diversity of energy supplies over the long term; and managing potentially conflicting policy goals for energy prices. The review covers the roles of coal, gas, oil and renewables in the country's future energy balance, as well as Combined Heat and Power and energy efficiency. It is also considering what part the nuclear industry should play. The results of the review will be a key input to the Government's future policy on security and diversity of energy supply and on climate change.

In April 2001 the Government introduced the climate change levy, a tax on business use of energy, designed to encourage energy efficiency across business, and thus help to bring about lower emissions of greenhouse gases. It is a key component in the Government's Climate Change Programme, published in November 2000. It will contribute towards climate change commitments, including the UK's binding target under the Kyoto Protocol to reduce greenhouse gas emissions by 12.5% from 1990 levels by 2008–12 (see p. 332).

The levy is designed to balance environmental gains and the protection of business competitiveness. It is expected to cut carbon emissions by about 5 million tonnes a year by 2010 and to raise £1 billion in 2001–02. All revenues, however, are being recycled, mainly through an offsetting cut in employer National Insurance contributions, but also through support for energy efficiency programmes and renewables (see pp. 492–3 and 503). To protect the international competitiveness of energy-intensive industries, an 80% levy discount is available to users who can demonstrate high emissions-saving targets in negotiated agreements with the Government.

International Developments

Since 1999 the European Union's (EU) Fifth Framework Programme of Research and Technological Development (see p. 440) has been the focus of research, development and demonstration of energy technologies in the EU. It has a non-nuclear energy budget of 1,042 million euro over 1999–2002. In addition, the EU Energy Framework Programme has six separate components: ETAP (shared studies and analyses); SYNERGY (international cooperation); ALTENER (renewable energy); SAVE (strategic action for vigorous energy efficiency); SURE (safe transport of nuclear materials and safeguards); and CARNOT (clean and efficient use of solid fuels). The programme has a total budget of 170 million ecu (£119 million) over five years (1998–2002). Since 1999 eight agencies, which conduct research into, and promote, energy conservation, have been established in the UK under the SAVE II programme, which provides up to 50% of start-up funding.

The European Commission (EC) collaborates with specialist international organisations, such as the International Energy Agency (IEA), which monitors world energy markets on behalf of industrialised countries and whose membership consists of all members of the Organisation for Economic Co-operation and Development except Iceland and Mexico.

Over 60% of the EU internal electricity market has been legally opened to competition. Great Britain, Finland, Germany and Sweden have introduced the right of consumer choice for all domestic, industrial and commercial customers. The UK gas

Table 28.1: Inland Consumption for Energy Use (in terms of primary sources), UK

Million tonnes oil equivalent

	1990	1996	1997	1998	1999	2000
Natural gas	51.2	80.9	82.7	86.2	91.4	94.9
Oil	77.2	77.8	75.4	76.0	75.9	75.2
Coal	66.9	45.7	40.8	41.0	36.7	38.1
Nuclear energy	16.3	22.1	23.0	23.4	22.2	19.6
Hydro-electric power[1]	0.4	0.3	0.4	0.5	0.5	0.5
Renewables and waste	0.7	1.8	1.9	2.1	2.2	2.5
Net imports of electricity	1.0	1.4	1.4	1.1	1.2	1.2
Total[2]	**213.6**	**230.3**	**226.1**	**230.7**	**230.7**	**232.5**

[1] Excludes pumped storage. Includes generation at wind stations.
[2] Total includes losses of electricity during transmission and distribution.
Source: Department of Trade and Industry

market has been fully open to competition since 1998.

An EC Green Paper, launching a debate on the future of EU energy policy, calls for stronger demand management (using taxes and efficiency measures), and greater promotion of renewable energy sources. Otherwise the EU would increase its dependency on imported energy from 50% to 70% by 2030, raising the share of fossil fuels in meeting total energy demand from 79% to 86%. The EC has also proposed a directive that aims to achieve full liberalisation of the electricity and gas markets by 2005.

ENERGY CONSUMPTION

In 2000 consumption of primary fuels (oil, gas, coal, nuclear) in the UK was only 9% higher than in 1970, while Gross Domestic Product (at constant market prices) rose by 96%. Energy consumption by final users in 2000, allowing for losses in conversion and distribution, and excluding non-energy use, amounted to 16.1 million tonnes of oil equivalent,[1] of which transport took 34.5%, residential users 29.3%, industrial users 22.6%, commerce, agriculture and public services 12.1%, and other users 1.6%.

Primary energy demand in 2000 was 0.4% higher than in 1999. Primary demand for coal and other solid fuels was 3.8% higher than in 1999, reflecting a late surge in coal use for electricity generation. Primary demand for oil fell by 1.7%, but gas rose by 3.8%, again fuelled by the demand for gas for electricity generation. On a temperature-corrected basis, which shows what the annual intake might have been if the average temperature during the year had been the same as the average for 1961–90, energy consumption grew by 1.2% in 2000, compared with an increase of 0.2% between 1998 and 1999.

[1] 1 tonne of oil equivalent = 41.868 gigajoules.

ENERGY EFFICIENCY

The Government funds a number of energy efficiency programmes in the UK. Over £200 million of the revenue from the climate change levy in its first two years will go to support energy efficiency measures and renewables, including 100% first-year capital allowances for energy-saving investments. These initiatives are an essential part of the UK strategy for reducing greenhouse gas emissions (see p. 332) and achieving the Government's domestic goal of a 20% reduction in carbon by 2010.

The Carbon Trust was set up in April 2001 as an independent, non-profit-making company with the aim of accelerating take-up by business of low carbon technologies. The Trust's first-year funding is about £50 million—from recycled receipts from the climate change levy and the Energy Efficiency Best Practice Programme (EEBPP), which the Trust will manage. It will also administer a new Enhanced Capital Allowance scheme for energy-saving technologies. This will be worth about £70 million in 2001–02 and £130 million in 2002–03, depending on take-up.

The EEBPP is the prime national source of independent authoritative information and advice on energy efficiency. It is estimated to have stimulated energy savings worth about £800 million a year (at 1990 prices). These energy savings are equivalent to saving more than 4 million tonnes of carbon a year by 2000. The 2000–01 EEBPP budget was £16.7 million.

The Energy Saving Trust (EST) was set up by the Government and the major energy companies. Its purpose is to work through partnerships towards the sustainable and efficient use of energy. In 2000–01 it received an estimated £24.2 million in direct government funding for work with the domestic and small business sectors and £16.4 million on transport-related programmes; its UK-wide programmes brought in an extra £75 million of investment. Under the government-funded programme of work, advice was given to some 430,000 individuals and organisations during 2000–01. Since 1994 the public electricity suppliers (see p. 499) have invested nearly £26 million a year in energy efficiency under the regulator's successive Energy Efficiency Standards of Performance (EESOP) schemes. The energy companies are increasing their investment in schemes under EESOP3 to about £55 million a year over 2000–02, including scheme delivery costs. Since 1994 EESOP programmes have resulted in more than 500,000 insulation improvements and the sale of 13.5 million energy-efficient light bulbs. The Utilities Act 2000 has transferred the power to set future EESOPs to the Government. The Department for Environment, Food and Rural Affairs (DEFRA) has published proposals for its Energy Efficiency Commitment (EEC) to cover 2002–05.

The Home Energy Efficiency Scheme (HEES) is to be relaunched in England as the Warm Front Team in autumn 2001. It has a budget of over £600 million during 2000–04, and is aimed at those households for whom the health risks are the greatest: the elderly, those with children, and the disabled and chronically sick. A fuel-poor household is one that needs to spend more than 10% of its income on maintaining a satisfactory heating regime—about 4.5 million households in the UK in 1999. HEES offers grants of up to £1,000 for insulation and heating improvements (not central heating) for low-income families with children and for the disabled, and up to £2,000, including insulation and central heating packages, for those aged 60 or more on low incomes. In accordance with the Warm Homes and Energy Conservation Act 2000, the Government published in February 2001 a draft Fuel Poverty Strategy setting out its goal to assist all vulnerable 'fuel poor' by 2010.

OIL AND GAS EXPLORATION AND PRODUCTION

The UK Continental Shelf (UKCS) comprises those areas of the seabed and subsoil up to and beyond the territorial sea over which the UK exercises sovereign rights of exploration and exploitation of natural resources. In 2000, either through direct use or as a source of energy for electricity generation, oil and gas accounted for 73% of total UK energy consumption, with UK production supplying 98% of gas consumed. About 10% of UK production was exported to Ireland or through the UK–Belgium interconnector (see p. 495), although on some winter days imports were required to meet demand. In 2000 output of crude oil and natural gas liquids (NGLs) in the UK averaged 2.7 million barrels (about 359,500 tonnes) a day, making it the world's tenth largest producer.

Taxation

The North Sea fiscal regime is a major mechanism for gaining economic benefit for the UK from its oil and gas resources. The Government grants licences to private sector companies to explore for and exploit oil and gas resources (see p. 494). Its main sources of revenue from oil and gas activities are petroleum revenue tax, levied on profits from fields approved before 16 March 1993; corporation tax, charged on the profits of oil

Table 28.2: Oil Statistics *Million tonnes*

	1990	1996	1997	1998	1999	2000
Oil production						
Land	1.8	5.3	5.0	5.2	4.3	3.2
Offshore	89.9	116.7	115.3	118.9	124.0	114.6
Refinery output	82.3	89.9	90.4	87.1	82.0	82.7
Deliveries	73.9	75.4	72.5	72.0	72.0	71.2
Exports						
Crude, NGL, feedstock	54.3	81.6	79.4	84.6	91.8	92.9
Refined petroleum	20.7	23.7	26.8	24.3	21.7	20.7
Imports						
Crude, NGL, feedstock	43.5	50.1	50.0	48.0	44.9	54.4
Refined petroleum	24.5	9.3	8.7	11.4	13.9	14.2

Source: Department of Trade and Industry

and gas companies—the only tax on profits from fields approved after 15 March 1993; and royalty, which applies only to fields approved before April 1982 and is paid at 12.5% of the value of petroleum 'won and saved'.

Licensing

The 19th seaward licensing round, inviting applications for blocks in the White Zone—the most recently designated part of the UKCS between the Faroes and Shetland Islands—was concluded in May 2001, with the award of nine licences covering 12 blocks. In addition, a tenth round of landward licensing was announced in July 2001. By the end of 2000, some 7,675 wells had been, or were being, drilled in the UKCS: 2,126 exploration wells, 1,333 appraisal wells and 4,216 development wells. Some 26 exploration wells and 33 new appraisal wells were started in 1999. The Government must approve all proposed wells and development plans.

Production and Reserves

Some 223 offshore fields were in production in March 2001: 113 oil, 93 gas and 17 condensate (a lighter form of oil). During 2000, 12 new development projects were approved. Offshore, these comprised six oilfields and five gasfields; onshore, one gasfield. In addition, approval for 12 incremental offshore developments (elaborations to existing fields) was granted.

Cumulative UKCS crude oil production to the end of 2000 was 2,448 million tonnes, with Forties (327 million tonnes) and Brent (250 million tonnes) the largest producing fields. Britain's largest onshore oilfield, at Wytch Farm (Dorset), produces 85% of the total crude oils and NGLs originating onshore. Possible maximum remaining UKCS reserves of oil are estimated at 1,490 million tonnes.

Offshore Gas

Natural gas now accounts for over 40% of total inland primary fuel consumption in the UK. In 2000 indigenous production amounted to a record 115 billion cubic metres, 9.5% up on 1999.

Production from the three most prolific offshore gasfields—Leman, Indefatigable and the Hewett area—has accounted for 34% of the total gas produced so far in the UKCS. The Southern Basin fields, the Morecambe fields and the Liverpool Bay fields in the Irish Sea produce more gas in winter to satisfy increased demand, with the North Sean and South Sean fields also augmenting supplies to meet peak demand on very cold days in winter. The partially depleted Rough field is used as a gas store for rapid recovery during peak winter periods (see map at the end of the book).

Cumulative gas production to the end of 2000 is 1,604 billion cubic metres. Maximum possible remaining gas reserves in present discoveries now stand at just under 1,630 billion cubic metres.

Pipelines

Some 10,640 km (6,650 miles) of major submarine pipelines transport oil, gas and condensate from one field to another and to shore. Nine landing places on the North Sea coast bring gas ashore to supply a national and regional high- and low-pressure pipeline system some 273,000 km (170,625 miles) long, which transports natural gas around Great Britain. A pipeline (40 km; 25 miles) takes natural gas from Scotland to Northern Ireland; exports to the Irish Republic are conveyed by the Britain–Ireland interconnector. The pipeline from Bacton to Zeebrugge in Belgium (232 km; 145 miles), which opened in 1998 and cost £420 million, has an export capacity of 20,000 million cubic metres a year and an import capacity of 8,500 million cubic metres a year.

Economic and Industrial Aspects

Throughout 2000 world oil prices continued to rise; the average price received by producers from sales of UKCS oil was £137 a tonne, compared with £108 a tonne at the end of 1999. UKCS oil and gas production rose from 1.9% of the UK's gross value added in 1999 to an estimated 2.7% in 2000. Total revenues from the sale of oil (including NGLs) produced from the UKCS in 2000 rose to some £17.2 billion, while those from the sale of gas rose to £6.6 billion. Taxes and royalty receipts attributable to UKCS oil and gas rose to some £4.8 billion in 2000–01.

PILOT, the successor to the Oil and Gas Industry Task Force, is pursuing specific initiatives, with industry support, to maintain exploration and development momentum on the UKCS in the face of increasing maturity of its oil reserves, and to prolong UK self-sufficiency. Among its targets are a production level of 3 million barrels of oil equivalent a day in 2010, a sustained investment level of £3 billion a year, a 50% increase in the value of industry-related exports by 2005, an additional revenue of £1 billion from new businesses, and 100,000 more jobs in 2010 than there would otherwise have been.

Production investment in the oil and gas extraction industry fell back to some £2.8 billion in 2000. Including exploration and appraisal investment of a further £0.4 billion, it formed about 12% of total British industrial investment and some 2% of gross fixed capital investment. Some 26,400 people were engaged in extraction offshore and onshore by the industry (which also supports about 360,000 jobs in related sectors) in 2000. Various initiatives, such as LOGIC (Leading Oil and Gas Industry Competitiveness), are currently aimed at making the UKCS more attractive to investors and sustaining activity through 2010 and beyond.

> Since 1965 the oil and gas production industry has generated operating surpluses of some £272 billion, of which about £108 billion (including £24 billion of exploration and appraisal expenditure) has been reinvested in the industry, £95.7 billion paid in taxation, and about £68.3 billion retained by the companies. Total annual income of the oil and gas sector rose to over £25 billion in 2000.

The Offshore Environment

Environmental impact assessments (under the EC Environmental Impact Directive) are mandatory for all field developments. The Offshore Chemicals (Pollution Prevention and Control) Regulations 2001 require the use and discharge of offshore chemicals to be subject to a permit issued by the Secretary of State for Trade and Industry.

The EC Habitats and Wild Birds Directives were applied to offshore oil and gas activities on the UKCS through the Offshore Petroleum Activities (Conservation of Habitats) Regulations 2001, which came into force in May 2001.

During 2000, 300 hours of unannounced aerial surveillance of oil and gas rigs detected minimal amounts of oil on the surface of the sea. Offshore environmental inspections were also carried out. The 2000 figure for accidental oil spills (78 tonnes) was lower than that for 1999 (120 tonnes).

Decommissioning

The Petroleum Act 1998 places a decommissioning obligation on the co-venturers of every offshore installation and the owners of every offshore pipeline on the UKCS. Companies have to submit a decommissioning programme for ministerial approval and ensure that its provisions are carried out. In 1998 the OSPAR Commission (see p. 336) agreed rules for the disposal of defunct offshore installations at sea. This decision prohibits the dumping of offshore installations and leaving them wholly or partly in place. Derogations, however, are possible for concrete platforms and for the footings of steel installations with a jacket weight above 10,000 tonnes. All installations put in place after 9 February 1999 must be completely removed. The Government encourages the re-use of facilities and expects operators to show that they have investigated such a course. It also encourages free trade in mature offshore oil and gas assets, as a means of extending field life and maximising economic recovery.

Offshore Safety

Offshore health and safety are the responsibility of the Health and Safety Executive (HSE—see p. 163). In 1999 Aberdeen University's Petroleum and Economic Consultants Ltd published an evaluation of the offshore health and safety regime, which resulted from the Cullen inquiry into the explosion that destroyed the Piper Alpha oil platform in 1988. The evaluation, which considered the regime among the safest in the world, covers offshore installations, pipeline works, prevention of fire and explosion and emergency response, and design and construction.

Suppliers of Goods and Services

The number employed in UK fabrication yards declined to about 2,000 by early 2001. Many companies have needed to seek work in other sectors and overseas, and the Oil and Gas Directorate of the Department of Trade and Industry (DTI) works with the PILOT initiatives and by other direct action to help the industry realign to the changed market circumstances. Britain's largest ever overseas offshore contract, worth £300 million and placed by Shell with Amec to build an oil-processing module for Nigeria, announced in March 2001, will create over 4,000 jobs in north-east England and in London, and will inject work worth £100 million into the UK supply chain.

DOWNSTREAM OIL

Oil Consumption

Deliveries of petroleum products for inland consumption (excluding refinery consumption) in 2000 included 21.4 million tonnes of petrol for motor vehicles, 15.6 million tonnes of DERV (diesel-engined road vehicles) fuel, 10.7 million tonnes of aviation turbine fuel, 6.5 million tonnes of gas oil (distilled from petroleum) and 1.8 million tonnes of fuel oils (blends of heavy petroleum).

Oil Refineries

In 2000 the UK's 13 refineries processed 88 million tonnes of crude and process oils, a slightly lower level than in 1999, but higher than might have been expected after the closure of Shell's Shell Haven refinery in December 1999. About 80% of UK output by weight is in the form of lighter, higher-value products, such as gasoline, DERV and jet kerosene. The UK is much more geared towards petrol production than its European counterparts; this accounts for about a third of each barrel of crude oil, compared with a European average of just over a fifth.

TRADE

In 2000 UK exports of refined petroleum products rose by 60% to £1.4 billion. Virtually all exports went to its partners in the EU and in the IEA, especially France and Germany, and the United States.

Exports of UKCS gas rose by 73% over 1999. Some 13.5 billion cubic metres went to the Netherlands, from the British share of the Markham transboundary field and the neighbouring Windermere field, to the Irish Republic and to Belgium through the UK–Belgium interconnector. About 2.3 billion cubic metres were imported from

Norway, and from Belgium via the interconnector, representing 2.5% of total supplies in 2000, compared with 1.3% in 1999.

GAS SUPPLY INDUSTRY

Structure of the Industry

The holder of a public gas transporter's licence in Great Britain may not also hold licences for supply or shipping in a fully competitive market.[2] Of the two entirely separate companies formed from the demerged British Gas plc, the supply business is now part of the holding company Centrica plc (which still trades under the British Gas brand name in Great Britain), while the pipeline and storage businesses, most exploration and production, and research and technology (R&T) became part of the holding company BG Group plc. In October 2000 BG Group plc demerged its transport, telecommunications, R&T and other businesses into a separately listed company, Lattice Group plc, while the rest of the group continues as BG Group plc.

The national and regional gas pipeline network is owned by Transco, now part of Lattice Group, which retains responsibility for dealing with leaks and emergencies, and also has had a monopoly in gas metering, which the energy regulator, Ofgem (see p. 500), plans to open to competition. Shippers participate in balancing supply and demand in the pipeline network, within a regime partly driven by commercial concerns, and utilising gas trading arrangements, which include a screen-based on-the-day commodity market for trading in wholesale supplies of gas. In addition, there are auctions for the allocation of entry capacity into the high-pressure national transmission system; and commercial incentives for Transco to operate and balance the system efficiently. Because of the increasing use of gas for electricity generation, the energy regulator is considering changes to the gas balancing regime—the way gas supply is matched to demand, at present on a daily basis.

[2] Suppliers sell piped gas to consumers; public gas transporters (PGTs) operate the pipeline system through which gas will normally be delivered; shippers arrange with PGTs for appropriate amounts of gas to go through the pipeline system.

In Northern Ireland supplies of natural gas have been available since 1996, when the Scotland to Northern Ireland gas pipeline was put into operation. Phoenix Natural Gas Ltd has been awarded a combined licence for the conveyance and supply of gas in Greater Belfast. There are proposals both to extend the gas system to other parts of Northern Ireland and for a South–North pipeline from outside Dublin to the Belfast area.

Competition

Since 1994 suppliers other than British Gas have captured 83% of the industrial and commercial gas market. Some 60 companies are licensed to sell gas to the commercial sector.

By December 2000 about 6 million (out of 20 million) domestic customers had switched from British Gas to one of 25 other companies now in the domestic market, and also between these other companies; but about 1 million have since returned to British Gas. In 2000 the changes that competition has brought about were estimated to have brought each standard credit customer average savings of about £60 a year on a gas bill (the average annual bill now being £300, including VAT).

Only companies that have been granted a supplier's licence are allowed to sell gas. Licence conditions include providing gas to anyone who requests it and is connected to the mains gas supply. Special services must be made available for elderly, disabled and chronically sick people. Suppliers must offer customers a range of payment options; they are able to set their own charges, but have to publish their prices and other terms so that customers can make an informed choice.

Ofgem (Office of Gas and Electricity Markets) has removed price controls from British Gas Trading, as it considers the market to be competitive. However, it continually monitors the market to ensure that anti-competitive practices do not take place.

Consumption and the Market

Natural gas consumption, at an estimated 1,030.7 terawatt hours (TWh)[3] in 2000, was up

[3] 1 TW = 1,000 gigawatts (GW). 1 GW = 1,000 megawatts (MW). 1 MW = 1,000 kilowatts (kW).

3.3% on 1999, with gas supplied for electricity generation (amounting to 312.5 TWh) up 1.5%. Sales to industry (214.4 TWh) were 4.1% up and to the commercial sector (126.8 TWh) 5.8% up, while domestic sales (369.9 TWh) were nearly 3.3% higher.

Sharp rises in the wholesale prices of gas have occurred since spring 2000, affecting in particular industrial and commercial customers (for whom prices have risen on average by about 50% in the year to March 2001). The major causes have been arbitrage (trading on the price differences) across the UK–Belgium gas pipeline, at a time when continental gas prices are linked to oil prices, which have themselves been at high levels, and the associated tightening of the UK supply/demand balance. Liberalisation and competition in the continental European markets are not yet as developed as in Great Britain.

COAL

The UK coal industry is entirely in the private sector. The main deep-mine operators in the UK are UK Coal plc (formerly known as RJB Mining plc, in England); Mining Scotland Ltd; Tower Colliery (in south Wales); Hatfield Colliery in South Yorkshire; and Blenkinsopp Collieries Ltd in north-east England. UK Coal plc, Mining Scotland Ltd, H. J. Banks and Company Ltd, and Celtic Energy, which operates in Wales, are the main opencast operators. In May 2001 there were 33 underground mines in production, including 17 major deep mines, employing 8,600 workers; and 45 opencast sites, employing 2,600. Opencast production accounts for most of the relatively low sulphur coal mined in Scotland and south Wales, and contributes towards improving the average quality of coal supplies. Opencast mining is subject to approval by local authorities and can take place only where it can comply with strict environmental guidelines, which stress the highest standards of operation, restoration and aftercare.

Market for Coal

In 2000 inland consumption of coal, at 59 million tonnes, was up 5.8% on 1999, partly because high gas prices at the end of the year led to an increase in generation by coal-fired power stations. About 78% was used by the electricity generators, 15% by coke ovens and blast furnaces, 1% by other fuel producers, 2.5% by industry, 3% by domestic consumers and 0.5% by other final consumers. Exports were 661,000 tonnes, while imports amounted to 23.4 million tonnes—mainly of steam coal for electricity generation and coking coal. Total production from British deep mines fell by 18%, from 20.9 million tonnes in 1999 to 17.2 million tonnes in 2000. Opencast output went down from 15.3 million tonnes to 13.4 million tonnes in the same period.

The Government's lifting of the stricter consents policy on the building of gas-fired power stations has helped win EC approval for the UK Coal Operating Aid Scheme, which provides for up to £170 million to help the coal industry through short-term energy market problems while its production costs are higher than world market prices for coal.

Clean Coal

Cleaner coal technologies reduce the environmental impact of coal used for power and industrial applications by increasing the efficiency of its conversion to energy and reducing harmful emissions which are the cause of acid rain. Improvements in the efficiency of coal-fired power stations lead directly to reductions of carbon dioxide (CO_2), a major contributor to climate change. The DTI allotment of £12 million during 1999–2000 to 2001–02 to the cleaner coal research and development (R&D) programme aims to encourage collaboration between UK industry and universities in the development of the technologies and expertise. The DTI is also developing a sub-commercial underground coal gasification project to meet government criteria on cleaner coal.

The Coal Authority

The Coal Authority is a public body sponsored by the DTI. It has five main responsibilities: licensing coal-mining operations; repairing coal subsidence damage; managing coalfield property; managing minewater pollution and other environmental problems associated with coal-mining; and providing information to house buyers, other purchasers of property and local authorities about mining activity near property.

ELECTRICITY

England and Wales

In December 2000, over 60 companies held generation licences in England and Wales. The largest generators are Innogy (formerly National Power), PowerGen, AES, British Energy, TXU Europe (which has taken over Energy Group, including Eastern Electricity), Edison Mission Energy, and British Nuclear Fuels' (BNFL's) Magnox Generation Group. The National Grid Company (NGC) owns and operates the transmission system, and is responsible for balancing electricity supply and demand.

Distribution—transfer of electricity from the national grid to consumers via local networks—is carried out by the 12 regional electricity companies (RECs) in England and Wales. Supply—the purchase of electricity from generators and its sale to consumers—has been fully open to competition since 1999. All consumers in Great Britain, including 24 million homes and 2 million small businesses, are free to choose their electricity supplier.

Cross-border acquisitions and takeovers have become a feature of the European power market. RECs are now restructuring as separate distribution and supply companies, most of them overseas-owned. All the main UK generators are vertically integrating through ownership of supply businesses. British electricity companies continue to invest overseas.

In 2000–01, 2 GW of coal-fired plant was sold by major generators to other concerns. Coal-fired plant is now owned by eight unrelated companies and the total market shares in generation of Innogy and PowerGen, now demerged, have fallen to 10.5% and 14% respectively.

Reform of Electricity Trading

In March 2001 new wholesale electricity trading arrangements (NETA) came into operation. NETA introduces greater competition into electricity trading, which should ensure downward pressure on prices. In a wholesale market worth about £7.5 billion a year in 1998, such pressure could result in a saving of up to £2 billion, or about 30% in real terms. Generators, suppliers, traders and customers are encouraged to enter into bilateral contracts in forwards and futures markets and short-term power exchanges. Participants are free to trade electricity until 3½ hours ahead of real time for any half-hour period. From that point until real time, the market operates through a balancing mechanism run by the NGC—because of the need to balance the system on a second-by-second basis. NETA has taken effect through new conditions inserted into generation, supply and transmission licences. These have been designated by the Secretary of State for Trade and Industry under the Utilities Act 2000.

Scotland

ScottishPower plc and Scottish and Southern Energy plc generate, transmit, distribute and supply electricity within their respective franchise areas. They are also contracted to buy all the output from British Energy's two Scottish nuclear power stations (Hunterston B and Torness) until 2005. The over-100-kW market in Scotland comprises about 6,750 customers and accounts for around 45% of all electricity consumed. ScottishPower and Scottish and Southern Energy have second-tier licences that allow them to compete in each other's area. In 2000–01, 29.5% of customers in the over-100-kW market obtained their power from holders of second-tier supply licences. In 1999 Ofgem proposed the establishment of BETTA (British Electricity Transmission and Trading Arrangements), an extension of NETA to Scotland, aimed at bringing greater competition to the Scottish market. Included in the BETTA proposals is the creation of a single system operator, which would monitor the balancing of supply and demand and trading; establish new interconnector and transmission access arrangements; and develop new connections policies.

Northern Ireland

Three private companies, AES (NI) Ltd, Premier Power Ltd and Coolkeeragh Power Ltd, generate electricity from four power stations. Most of the electricity generated is sold to Northern Ireland Electricity plc (NIE), which has a monopoly of transmission and distribution, and a right to supply. As required by the EC Electricity Liberalisation Directive, the market has been gradually opened up to competition since 1999. From 2001 the right to choose a supplier has been extended to 35% of the total market (mainly large industrial and public sector consumers). In addition, a number of second-tier suppliers are now operating.

Northern Ireland has a power surplus, with a peak demand of 1,500 MWh. However, two of the four power stations are due to close within four years. Plans have been announced to replace the Coolkeeragh station by a 400 MW CCGT (see p. 501). Additional capacity will also be available when the Northern Ireland–Scotland ('Moyle') interconnector (500 MW capacity) is commissioned early in 2002, and when work finishes later in 2001 on strengthening the links between the networks in Northern Ireland and the Irish Republic, with an interconnector capacity of 660 MW.

Northern Ireland's Energy Action Plan (Vision 2010) envisages—within a European context—an all-Ireland energy market with the aim of increasing competition and consumer choice, tackling the consequences that arise from two small markets operating on the periphery of Europe, and reducing costs, particularly in Northern Ireland, where standard domestic consumers paid some 25% more for electricity than their counterparts in Great Britain in 2000. Consultants have been appointed to advise on the steps needed to create a more cohesive energy market.

Regulation and Other Functions

The gas and electricity markets in Great Britain are regulated by Ofgem, which is governed by an authority whose powers are provided under the Gas Act 1986, the Electricity Act 1989 and the Utilities Act 2000. Ofgem's principal objective is to protect the interests of gas and electricity customers, wherever appropriate, by promoting effective competition. Other duties and objectives include ensuring that reasonable demands for electricity are met and that electricity and gas licensees are able to finance their statutory obligations. Ofgem is responsible for setting performance standards for gas and electricity companies, and for price regulation of companies where competition has not yet fully emerged or where there is a natural monopoly.

In Northern Ireland the energy regulator holds two separate statutory appointments: Director General of Electricity Northern Ireland and Director General of Gas Northern Ireland.

Figure 28.3:
Electricity Demand by Sector, UK, 2000[1]

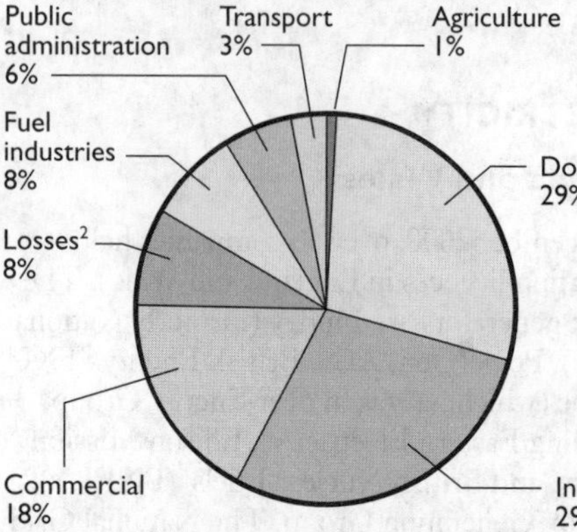

[1] Percentages sum to more than 100 because of rounding.
[2] Mainly losses in transmission and distribution.

Source: Department of Trade and Industry

Consumption

In 2000 sales of electricity through the public distribution system in the UK amounted to 314.6 TWh. Domestic users took 36% of the total, industry 32%, and commercial and other users the remainder. The average price for electricity in the UK has fallen by 22% in real terms between 1990 and 2000 for domestic customers and by 32% for industrial customers. In 2000 an average annual domestic electricity bill for a customer paying by standard credit is estimated at £257.40.

Generation

The shares of generating capacity during 1999–2001 are shown in Table 28.4.

Non-nuclear power stations owned by the UK's major power producers consumed 53.5 million tonnes of oil equivalent in 2000, of which coal accounted for 51.9% and natural gas for 45.6%. Other power companies (for which gas is the most widely used fuel), and over 2,000 small autogenerators (which produce power for their own use), have equal access with the major generators to the grid transmission and local distribution systems. A ten-year programme to control emissions of oxides of nitrogen (NO_X) through the installation of low-NO_X burners at 12 major power stations in England and Wales is in progress. Scottish and Southern Energy has completed a £220 million refitting of Peterhead power station, which has reduced the emissions by 50%. ScottishPower has fitted low-NO_X burners at Longannet power station.

Combined Cycle Gas Turbines (CCGT)

In 2000 CCGT stations accounted for 35% of the electricity generated by major power producers, compared with 16% in 1995. This increase has been balanced by a fall in coal- and oil-fired generation. CCGT stations, favoured by the smaller, independent producers and using natural gas, offer cheap generation, and give out almost no sulphur dioxide and some 55% less CO_2 than coal-fired plant per unit of electricity. At the end of March 2001, 29 such stations in the UK (with a total registered capacity of 20.6 GW) were generating power. With the introduction of NETA (see p. 499), the Government has lifted restrictions on the building of new CCGTs.

Table 28.4: Shares of Generating Capacity in England and Wales

Per cent

	Winter 1999–2000	Winter 2000–01
Innogy	18.7	12.3
PowerGen	16.1	14.9
British Energy	11.3	13.8
Eastern Group	10.3	8.8
Edison Mission Energy	9.2	5.9
AES	7.3	6.9
BNFL/Magnox	5.2	5.2
Interconnectors	4.9	4.7
Others	17.1	27.5
Total	**100.0**	**100.0**
Total (MW)	65,330	67,695

Source: *The Energy Report 2000* (DTI)

Table 28.5: Generation by and Capacity of Power Stations Owned by the Major Power Producers in the UK

	Electricity generated (GWh) 1990	1995	2000	% 2000	Output capacity (MW)[1]
Nuclear plant	61,308	88,964	85,063	*25*	12,486
Other conventional steam plant	230,376	169,866	130,771	*38*	35,221
Gas turbines and oil engines	432	190	261	—	1,243
Pumped storage plant	1,982	1,552	2,694	*1*	2,788
Natural flow hydro-electric plant	4,393	4,096	4,331	*1*	1,327
CCGTs	—	48,720	117,965	*35*	19,349
Renewables other than hydro	4	570	700	—	117
Total	**298,495**	**313,958**	**341,785**	***100***	**72,531**
Electricity supplied (net)[2]	276,003	295,166	323,333	—	—

[1] At end December 2000.

[2] Electricity generated less electricity used at power stations (both electricity used on works and that used for pumping at pumped storage stations).

Source: Department of Trade and Industry

Combined Heat and Power (CHP)

CHP plants are designed to produce both electricity and usable heat. They convert about 80% of fuel input into useful energy, compared with conventional generation, which wastes at least half the energy content of the fuel and emits considerably more CO_2. CHP thus benefits the environment by reducing emissions of greenhouse gases. It is also used for cooling and chilling.

CHP can be fuelled by a variety of energy sources. It offers particular benefits where there is a regular need for heat as well as electricity—in hospitals, leisure centres and housing developments for example—and can be provided on a local scale. About 83% of CHP plants are less than 1 MW capacity; large-scale plant (above 10 MW) represents just under 80% of total CHP capacity. In 2000 over 1,500 CHP schemes supplied more than 4,600 MW of generating capacity (with some 2,700 MW under development) and produced a total of 23.3 TWh. This represents 6% of the UK's total electricity generated (and 16.5% of electricity consumption). The Government aims to have at least 10,000 MW by 2010. EU strategy is to double CHP's share of the electricity market from 9% to 18% by the same year.

The Government promotes CHP by administering a quality assurance programme under the EEBPP (see p. 493)—to assess CHP schemes for exemption from the climate change levy and for other benefits.

Trade

The NGC and Electricité de France run a 2,000 MW cross-Channel cable link, allowing transmission of electricity between the two countries. The link has generally been used to supply 'baseload' power—which needs to be generated and available round the clock—from France to England. Imports met just over 4% of the UK's electricity needs in 2000.

Scotland has a peak winter demand of under 6 GWh and generating capacity of over 9 GW. The additional available capacity is used to supply England and Wales through transmission lines linking the Scottish and English grid systems. This interconnector's capacity is now 1,600 MW, with plans to increase it to 2,200 MW. The 60-km (37-mile) 500 MW undersea interconnector between Scotland and Northern Ireland (see p. 500) will allow further exports of power from Scotland.

The capacity of the interconnector between Northern Ireland and the Irish Republic is being doubled to 660 MW along with the upgrading of the two present standby connectors to full system interconnectors, each with a capacity of 125 MW.

Nuclear Power

Nuclear power generates about one-sixth of the world's energy and over a third of Europe's. It substantially reduces the use of fossil fuels that would otherwise be needed for generation. In the UK nuclear stations generated 85.1 TWh in 2000 and contributed 23% of total electricity generation.

The private sector company British Energy owns and operates seven advanced gas-cooled reactor (AGR; five in England and Wales) stations and the pressurised water reactor (PWR) at Sizewell B. British Energy's reactors have a rated output of 7,281 MW in England and 2,440 MW in Scotland. British Nuclear Fuels (see below) and Magnox Electric, which merged in 1998, operate seven magnox power stations, and four more that are being decommissioned.

There are currently no proposals for new nuclear power stations in the UK, principally because the cost, compared with new generation from other sources, is not competitive. While projecting a 17% reduction in nuclear output by 2010, the Government sees nuclear as having an important role well into the future. This role will depend on nuclear competitiveness and on securing public confidence in nuclear safety and its environmental impact.

British Nuclear Fuels (BNFL)

BNFL is Britain's primary provider of nuclear products and services, including spent fuel management, recycling, reprocessing oxide fuel, decommissioning and cleaning up redundant nuclear facilities, and treating historic wastes, to both UK and international customers. The company's turnover in 2000–01 was £2.1 billion. In February 2000 the Nuclear Installations Inspectorate (NII) issued three critical reports after quality checks on mixed oxide fuel (MO_X) manufactured at Sellafield were found to have been falsified. In early 2000 both Japan and Germany, two of BNFL's biggest customers, put contracts to buy large quantities of MO_X on hold. The Government has ordered BNFL to make improvements and has delayed consideration of a proposal to introduce a Public-Private Partnership into the company until at least 2002. Following a fifth public consultation, the Government has given permission for the Sellafield Mox plant (to mix oxide fuel with depleted, natural or recycled plutonium) to begin operations.

UK Atomic Energy Authority (UKAEA)

UKAEA's main function is to maintain and decommission safely and cost-effectively its redundant nuclear facilities used for the UK's nuclear R&D programme. UKAEA owns the sites at Dounreay (Caithness), Culham and Harwell (Oxfordshire), and Winfrith (Dorset); and operates the Windscale (Cumbria) site. In 2000 it published a comprehensive plan for decommissioning the Dounreay site and its environmental restoration. UKAEA is also responsible for Britain's fusion programme (see below).

Fusion Research

Nuclear fusion in the UK is funded by the DTI and Euratom. The UK Government spends £15 million a year on fusion research, of which the main focus is magnetic confinement, based at Culham science centre, where Britain's own nuclear fusion research is carried out. The UK also operates the experimental JET (Joint European Torus) project at Culham. Through the EU, the Euratom/UKAEA Fusion Association contributes to the international effort to demonstrate the principle of power production from fusion, currently embodied in the International Thermonuclear Experimental Reactor.

Nuclear Safety

Responsibility for ensuring the safety of nuclear installations falls to nuclear operators within a system of regulatory control enforced by the HSE.

The International Convention on Nuclear Safety has been ratified by 46 countries, including the UK, and each has reported on how it has progressed towards meeting its nuclear safety obligations. The UK's main contribution to the international effort to improve safety in Central and Eastern Europe and in the former Soviet republics is channelled through the EU PHARE and TACIS nuclear safety programmes.

NEW AND RENEWABLE SOURCES OF ENERGY

The Government is committed to meeting ambitious targets to reduce UK emissions of greenhouse gases. It is putting in place measures designed to ensure that the UK exceeds its commitment to reduce emissions of these gases by 12.5% below 1990 levels by 2010. A growth in the proportion of electricity generated from renewable sources will play a vital role in these efforts. The Government aims to increase the percentage of electricity generated from renewable sources from the current level of just under 3% to 10% by 2010, subject to the cost being acceptable to consumers. The proposed Renewables Obligation for England and Wales, and the associated Scottish Renewables Obligation, will oblige all licensed electricity suppliers to ensure that a specified proportion of their supplies is derived from renewable sources.

The Government is allocating over £260 million during 2001–04 to promote renewables technologies. This includes £89 million for capital grants for offshore wind power, energy crops and small-scale biomass from the DTI and the New Opportunities Fund; £55.5 million for an expanded DTI R&D programme; and a further £100 million that will be allocated after a report on renewable energy by the Cabinet Office's Performance and Innovation Unit. Solar voltaics will also benefit through a

Britain's coastal waters offer the potential of an abundant supply of wind power, if it can be harnessed effectively and efficiently. The UK's first offshore wind farm (two 2 MW turbines off the Northumberland coast) began generating enough power to supply 3,000 homes in October 2000. It was developed by the Border Wind consortium, with financial help from the Non Fossil Fuel Obligation (which preceded the Renewables Obligation) and an EU THERMIE grant. The Government is seeking to streamline the planning consent process for wind power. A major step has been the announcement of 18 potential sites as having pre-qualified for leases from the Crown Estates, which could result in a maximum of 540 turbines if all were to go ahead.

TXU Europe has introduced 'net metering' at its Eastern subsidiary in the UK. This involves utilities buying excess electricity from solar-powered households at the same price as it is sold.

Elean power station at Sutton (Cambridgeshire) is the UK's first straw-fired power plant. With a potential output of 36 MW, it will burn 200,000 tonnes of straw a year and generate enough power for 80,000 homes. The world's first commercial wave power station has been commissioned on the coast of Islay in Scotland: the Land Installed Marine Powered Energy Transformer (LIMPET), developed by Wavegen and the Queen's University Belfast with EU support, harnesses oscillating water column technology to provide 500 kW for the national grid.

major installation programme, the first phase of which has been allocated £10 million. DEFRA will distribute £12.5 million in the form of establishment grants to aid the further development of energy crops.

A large number of British companies are involved in an expanding global market for renewables technologies, directly employing several thousand people, and with a multi-million-pound export business.

Non-energy Minerals

Output of non-energy minerals in 1999 came to 309 million tonnes, valued at nearly £2.4 million. The total number of employees in the extractive industry was about 24,300.

The UK is virtually self-sufficient in construction minerals, and produces and exports several industrial minerals, notably china clay, ball clay, potash and salt. The Boulby potash mine in north-east England is the UK's most important non-energy mineral operation. Production in 1999 was down to 825,000 tonnes, of which 51% was exported. Sales of china clay (or kaolin), the largest export, were 2.3 million tonnes, of which 88% was exported. A UK company, Baseresult, bought the South Crofty tin mine (closed in 1998) in Cornwall in September 2000 and has announced plans to restart mining in 2001.

The largest non-energy mineral imports are metals (ores, concentrates and scrap—valued at £1.5 billion in 1999), refined non-ferrous metals (£3.1 billion), iron and steel (£2 billion) and non-metallic mineral products (£5.9 billion, of which rough diamonds account for £3.8 billion).

Water Supply

About 75% of the UK's water supplies is obtained from mountain lakes, reservoirs and river intakes; and about 25% from underground sources (stored in layers of porous rock). South-east England and East Anglia are more dependent on groundwater than any other parts of the UK. Scotland and Wales have a relative abundance of unpolluted water from upland sources. Northern Ireland also has plentiful supplies for domestic use and for industry.

Water put into the public supply system (including industrial and other uses) in England and Wales averaged 15,331 megalitres a day (Ml/d)[4] in 1999–2000, of which average daily consumption per head was about 151 litres. An average of 2,443 Ml/d was supplied in Scotland in 1999–2000. In Northern Ireland the figure was 704 Ml/d.

[4] 1 megalitre = 1 million litres.

Some Minerals Produced in Britain

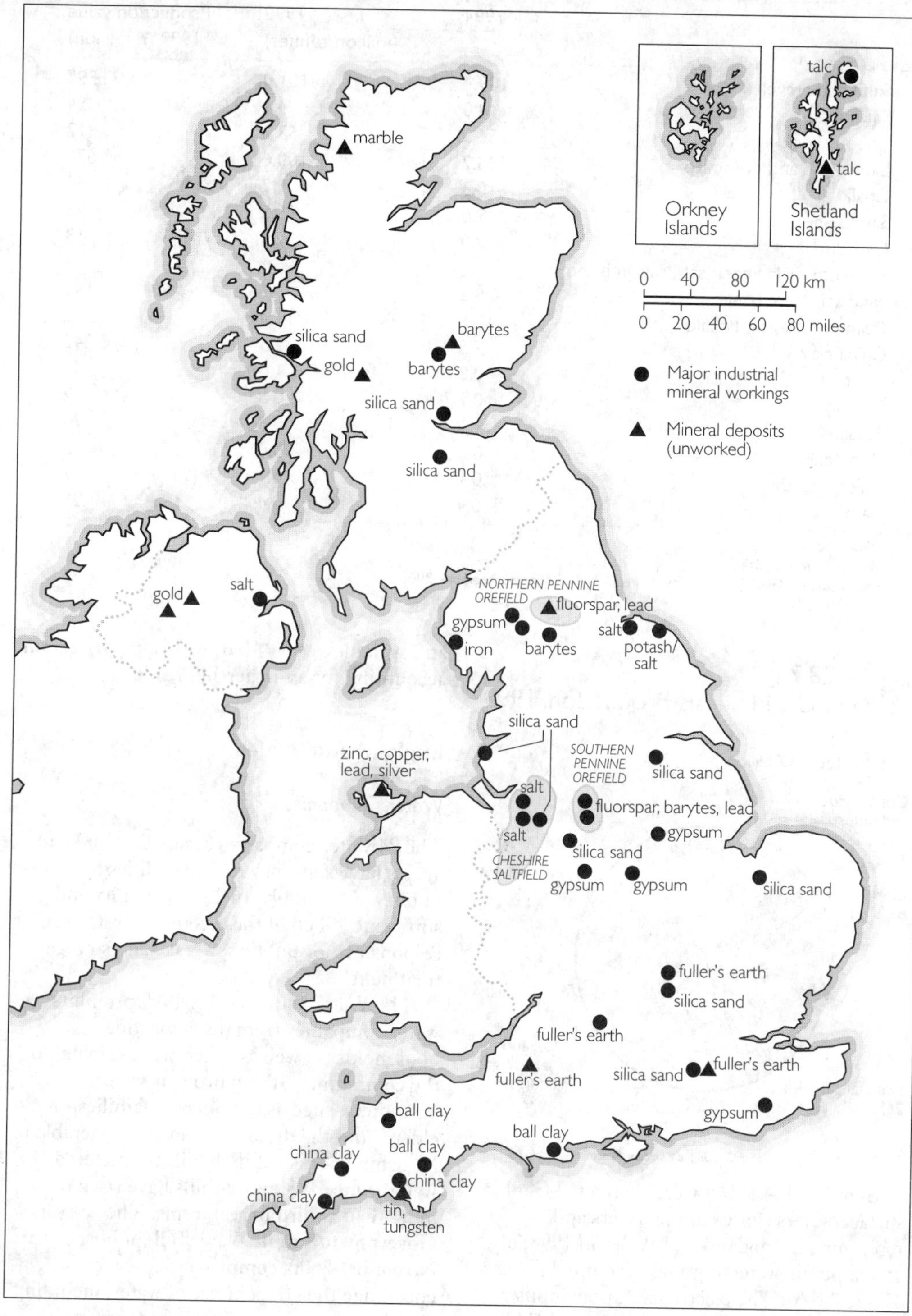

Table 28.6: Production of Some of the Main Non-energy Minerals in the UK

	1994	1999	Production value 1999 (£ million)
	(million tonnes)		
Sand and gravel	109.4	101.0	597
Silica sand	4.0	4.1	54
Igneous rock	56.5	53.2	312
Limestone and dolomite	124.2	100.6	670
Chalk[1]	10.3	9.7	56
Sandstone	19.0	15.5	95
Gypsum	2.0	1.8	13
Salt, comprising rock salt, salt in brine and salt from brine	5.3	5.7	146
Common clay and shale[1]	12.5	11.4	22
China clay[2]	2.5	2.3	242
Ball clay	0.8	1.0	45
Fireclay[1]	0.7	0.5	2
Potash	1.0	0.8	74
Fluorspar	0.1	0.0	5
Fuller's earth	0.1	0.1	7
Slate	0.4	0.4	29

[1] Great Britain only.
[2] Moisture-free basis.
Source: British Geological Survey, *United Kingdom Minerals Yearbook 2000*

Figure 28.7: Value of UK Minerals Production, 1999

Total value: £17 billion

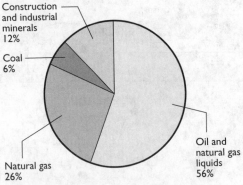

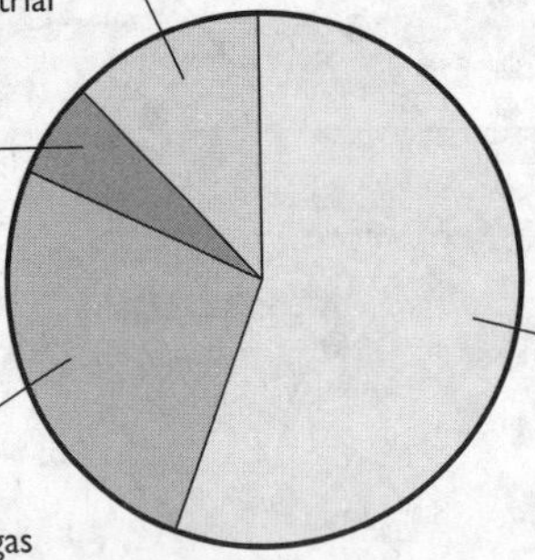

Source: British Geological Survey, *United Kingdom Minerals Yearbook 2000*

Some 35,144 Ml/d were abstracted from surface waters (for example, rivers and reservoirs) in England and Wales in 1998, of which public water supplies accounted for 11,723 Ml/d. The electricity supply industry took 15,955 Ml/d; fish farming 5,182 Ml/d; and agriculture 11 Ml/d, with spray irrigation accounting for a further 144 Ml/d.

England and Wales

Water Companies

The 24 water companies across England and Wales have statutory responsibilities for public water supply, including quality and sufficiency. Ten of these companies are also responsible for public sewerage and sewage treatment.

The Water Industry Act 1999 prohibits water companies from disconnecting households, as well as other premises vital to the community. It also protects water customers, such as low-income families, the elderly and the disabled, who are vulnerable to hardship because of high bills for metered water. Since 1989 water bills have risen by more than a third in real terms. The Government's draft Water Bill, published in November 2000, comprises clauses to encourage the efficient use of water, including changes to the licensing system for water abstraction (with increased penalties for abstraction and impounding offences), and provisions to improve the regulation of the water industry and promote the interests of consumers.

Watermark, a government-backed initiative, aims to develop a database that will give the public sector, which has a water bill of £600 million a year, reliable benchmarks against which to measure its consumption. Such data, it is estimated, could save £60 million of this amount.

During 2000–05 the Government requires the water companies to pay for a capital investment programme costing an estimated £15.6 billion,[5] including £7.4 billion on improving water quality and on meeting new UK and EU environmental standards. It also wants to ensure that customers do not have to face unreasonably high bills.

The Director General of Water Services, who heads Ofwat (Office of Water Services), the industry's regulatory body, has determined that the companies' efficiency improvements will mostly fund the investments specified. Household customers are expected to see an average increase of 2.3% in their bills for water and sewerage services for 2001–02, coming after an average 11.3% reduction in their bills for 1999–2000.

By the end of 2001–02 about 22% of households and 90% of commercial and industrial customers will be charged for water on the basis of consumption measured by meter. Most homes are still charged according to the rateable value of their property. The Government has given customers increased choice over whether or not to have their bills based on a water meter. As a result, all water companies now supply free meters to households on request. Average water and sewerage bills for households without a meter, at £227 in 1999–2000, are expected to be £18 lower in real terms by 2005.

Of some 2.8 million tests on drinking water in England and Wales in 1999, 99.82% met standards that are in some cases stricter than those in the 1980 EC Drinking Water Directive. A new EC Directive, adopted in 1998, requires Member States to meet a number of even more stringent standards, for example an obligation to ensure maximum concentrations of lead in water of 25 microgrammes per litre within five years and 10 μg/l within 15 years.

The Drinking Water Inspectorate (DWI) checks that water companies meet the drinking water quality regulations. Enforcement action is taken when there are infringements of standards. The DWI also investigates incidents and consumer complaints about quality, and initiates prosecution if water unfit for human consumption has been supplied.

Competition

The Government has proposed to extend the opportunities for competition in the water industry in England and Wales, but will take steps to safeguard water quality, public health and wider social policies. These proposals will license new entrants in the market for production and retail activities, while the incumbent water companies will remain vertically integrated statutory undertakers. A consultation paper setting out the regulatory and legislative framework will be published in autumn 2001. By September 2000 eight 'inset appointments' had been made, under which a water company can seek to be appointed to supply customers in the area of another appointed water company. Five of these appointments involve Anglian Water, and one a new entrant. Since April 2000 every water company has been subject to the Competition Act 1998, which could result in others using its pipe network to supply customers. In August 2000 the Government lowered the 'inset' threshold, allowing customers who use between 100 million and 250 million litres a year—such as hospitals and universities—to seek alternative suppliers.

Water Leakage

In response to mandatory targets set by the Director General of Water Services the companies reduced water leakage by some 30% between 1996–97 and 1999–2000, from

[5] The programme includes dismantling what remains of Victorian sewerage systems; providing new sewers, and tanks to prevent sewage overflows; removal of lead from supply pipes; and replacement of iron water mains, which cause discoloration.

4,528 Ml a day to 3,306 Ml a day. The industry spent £816 million on leakage repair and £1.7 billion on mains rehabilitation and replacement over 1998–2000.

Scotland

Responsibility for the provision of water and sewerage services rests with the North, West and East of Scotland Water Authorities. The Scottish Executive intends to replace these authorities with an all-Scotland water and sewerage authority, called Scottish Water. As with the existing authorities, Scottish Water will be a public sector body accountable to Scottish ministers and the Parliament for the provision of water and sewerage services. The Water Industry Commissioner for Scotland promotes customer interests and advises the Executive about the level of water charges.

Modernisation of the water industry is in progress, with the authorities investing some £1.8 billion over 1999–2002, including projects worth about £700 million in partnership with the private sector. New water treatment plants are being built and all major towns are benefiting from new wastewater treatment works. Prices for water services depend on the type of consumer: domestic consumers pay amounts based on their council tax band (see p. 409) or, in very few cases, metered charges; and non-domestic consumers pay non-domestic water rates, or metered charges and trade effluent charges.

The Executive also intends to introduce legislation to regulate the provision of water and sewerage services on the public networks, with a licensing regime to ensure that only fit and proper operators gain access to the networks.

Northern Ireland

The Northern Ireland Executive envisages expenditure of up to £2.5 billion over 15–20 years to bring water and sewerage services up to standard and to meet increasing demand. (Some of the main sewers of Belfast date from Victorian times and may be at risk of collapse.) An extra 10% in water bills would be necessary to pay for these improvements.

Further Reading

Annual Publications

Digest of Environmental Statistics. Department for Environment, Food and Rural Affairs. Available only on the Internet. www.defra.gov.uk/environment/statistics/des/index.htm

Digest of United Kingdom Energy Statistics. Department of Trade and Industry. The Stationery Office.

Energy Report (the Blue Book). Department of Trade and Industry. The Stationery Office.

Oil and Gas Resources of the United Kingdom (the Brown Book). Department of Trade and Industry. The Stationery Office.

United Kingdom Minerals Yearbook. British Geological Survey.

Websites

Department of Trade and Industry: www.dti.gov.uk

Department for Environment, Food and Rural Affairs: www.defra.gov.uk

Northern Ireland Executive: www.nio.gov.uk

Scottish Executive: www.scotland.gov.uk

Ofgem: www.ofgem.gov.uk

Ofwat: www.ofwat.gov.uk

British Geological Survey Minerals UK: www.mineralsUK.com

Energy Efficiency Best Practice Programme: www.energy-efficiency.gov.uk

29 Finance and Other Service Industries

Financial Services	509	Retailing	524
Regulation	510	Consumer Protection	527
Bank of England	512	Hotels, Restaurants and Catering	529
Banking Services	513	Travel Agents	529
Insurance	518	Tourism and Leisure	530
Investment	520	Exhibition and Conference Centres	532
Financial Markets	521	Rental Services	533
Other Services	523	Computing Services	533
Wholesaling	523	Other Business Activities	534

The service sector in the United Kingdom is continuing to grow and contributed 70.2% of gross value added at current basic prices and 77% of employment in 2000. Nearly 22.5 million people had jobs in the service sector at the end of 2000, a rise of over 800,000 in two years.

Financial services make a major contribution to the UK economy, and London is by far the largest international financial centre in Europe. The UK's financial services sector accounts for around 5% of Gross Domestic Product (GDP) and employs more than 1 million people. Net overseas earnings have risen substantially, reaching a record £31.2 billion in 1999.

As a result of rising real incomes, consumer spending on financial, personal and leisure services has increased considerably. Travel, hotel and restaurant services in the UK are among those to have benefited from the long-term growth in tourism, and the UK is one of the world's leading tourist destinations. Computer activities and research and development are among the non-financial sectors which experienced strong growth in turnover in 2000 (see Table 29.1).

Financial Services

Historically, the heart of the financial services industry has been in the 'Square Mile' in the City of London, and this remains broadly the case. Among the major financial institutions and markets in the City are the Bank of England, the London Stock Exchange and Lloyd's insurance market. The City is one of the world's three leading financial centres, along with Tokyo and New York. An important feature is the size of its international activities. It is noted for having:

- more overseas banks than any other financial centre;
- the biggest market in the world for trading foreign equities, accounting for 48% of global turnover in 2000;
- by far the world's biggest foreign exchange market, actively trading the largest range of currencies;

Table 29.1: Turnover in Selected Non-financial Services, 2000

	£ million	% increase on 1999
Motor trades	122,031	–0.9
Wholesale trades	358,004	9.0
Hotels and restaurants	52,596	2.8
Renting	16,832	6.2
Computer and related activities	40,976	12.5
Research and development	5,715	15.9
Business services	145,829	5.0
Education[1]	23,326	7.8
Sewage and refuse disposal, etc	7,463	–3.9
Recreation[2]	25,392	13.7
Other services	3,780	7.5

[1] Excludes public sector activities.
[2] Excludes sporting, betting and gaming activities.
Source: Office for National Statistics—annual data derived from short-term turnover inquiries

London has a full range of ancillary and support services, including legal, accountancy and management services. For example, of the world's 50 largest legal firms, ten are based in London, more than in any other centre. A report by IFSL in May 2001 confirmed London's position as a leading international centre for the provision of accounting and management consulting services. The UK management consultancy market (see p. 534) is the second largest in Europe, accounting for about 10% of the international market. Between 1996 and 1999 the UK's net overseas earnings of management consultancy firms more than doubled, from £358 million to £811 million, while those of accounting firms rose from £50 million to £477 million.

- the largest fund management centre;
- the leading international insurance centre; and
- the major international centre for primary and secondary dealing in the Euromarket.

Scotland (Edinburgh and Glasgow) is a major fund management centre, with over £350 billion of funds under management. Manchester, Cardiff, Liverpool and Leeds are also important financial centres.

International Financial Services London (IFSL) (*www.ifsl.org.uk*), formerly BI (British Invisibles), promotes the international activities of UK-based financial institutions and related professional and business services. It also seeks to raise awareness of the UK's leading role in international financial markets and highlight the major contribution of financial services to the UK economy.

REGULATION

Major reforms have been made to the regulation of financial services, including the creation of the Financial Services Authority (FSA) (*www.fsa.gov.uk*). The Financial Services and Markets Act 2000 provides for the formal establishment of the FSA, bringing together the regulation of investment business, banks, building societies and insurance companies previously handled by nine regulatory bodies. New compensation arrangements and a single Financial Ombudsman are being set up. The new regulatory regime will be fully operational by the end of November 2001.

FSA Objectives and Functions

The FSA's statutory objectives are maintaining confidence in the UK financial system and promoting public understanding of it, providing an appropriate degree of consumer protection and reducing the potential for financial crime. In delivering these objectives, the FSA has to be efficient and economic, facilitate innovation in financial services, take account of the international nature of financial services business and minimise any adverse effects of regulation on competition.

Until the end of November 2001 the FSA will continue to supply regulatory and other services under contract to several of the regulatory bodies which it will replace when the Act is fully implemented. It is also supplying services to HM Treasury in its prudential regulation of insurance business, including regulatory oversight of the Lloyd's market (see p. 519). The FSA's new risk-based strategy for the regulation of financial services is designed to help the Authority achieve its statutory objectives. It aims to identify and address the most important risks to firms, markets and consumers, with less routine monitoring for well-run firms. Each year the FSA will identify key regulatory themes for priority attention by managers and regulators.

The FSA has acquired responsibility from the London Stock Exchange for acting as the competent authority for listing companies in the UK, determining the rules for companies that wish to be listed. The FSA has been making preparations for the new regime under the Act, focusing on how the Act will interact with the listing rules; under the Act, the FSA, as listing authority, will also acquire the power to impose financial penalties. The FSA has issued guidance for recognised investment exchanges (RIEs)—there are eight UK RIEs and 11 overseas investment exchanges currently recognised in the UK—and the two recognised clearing houses, and published its sourcebook on regulating the Lloyd's market.

The FSA will become responsible in September 2002 for statutory regulation of key aspects of mortgage lending (but not mortgage advice), as part of the Government's plans to reform the selling of mortgages (see p. 349). It will also implement a new statutory system for regulating credit unions (see p. 517), which is due to come into operation in summer 2002.

The FSA is to publish comparative information on the Internet for retail consumers on long-term investment products, including personal pensions, investment bonds, unit trust Individual Savings Accounts, savings endowments and mortgage endowments. This information is intended to make a contribution to the transparency of retail products, so encouraging consumers to shop around.

Banking Supervision

Banks are required to meet minimum standards on the integrity and competence of directors and management, the adequacy of capital and cash flow, and the systems and controls to deal with the risks they experience. If a bank fails to meet the criteria, its activities may be restricted, or it may be closed. These arrangements are intended to strengthen, but not guarantee, the protection of bank depositors, thereby increasing confidence in the banking system as a whole.

Changes are planned to the international agreement governing the adequacy of capital (the Basel Accord), which are designed to link the level of capital required by banks more closely to the degree of risk taken. The new Accord, which is planned to be implemented by the end of 2005, would be consistent with current UK practice. In addition, the European Commission issued proposals in February 2001 for updating the EU capital adequacy regime and these would apply to EU banks, building societies and investment firms.

Compensation

The Financial Services and Markets Act 2000 provides for a single Financial Services Compensation Scheme (FSCS). When the Act is fully in force the FSCS will provide compensation if a firm collapses owing money to investors, depositors or policyholders. It will replace a number of schemes, including the Investors Compensation Scheme (ICS), for private investors; the Deposit Protection Scheme (DPS), for bank customers; and the Building Societies Investor Protection Scheme. Since February 2001 the FSCS has had operational responsibility for managing the ICS and DPS; since their creation they have made compensation payments to investors and depositors of £238 million and £118 million respectively.

Financial Ombudsman Service

A new Financial Ombudsman Service is being set up as a one-stop service for dealing with complaints about financial services, and will have an annual budget of around £20 million. It will replace eight schemes, including those covering banks, building societies, insurers and firms conducting investment business. All firms authorised by the FSA will be subject to the Ombudsman's procedures, but consumers will have to seek a resolution to a complaint from the firm in the first instance. If the matter is not resolved satisfactorily, consumers can ask the Ombudsman to intervene. Firms not authorised by the FSA will be able to join the scheme on a voluntary basis.

International Agreements

The UK plays a major role in international efforts to maintain global prosperity and prevent financial crises. The Group of Seven (G7) leading industrialised countries agreed in 1998 on measures to reform the international financial architecture, including enhanced global supervision and strengthened cooperation between regulatory authorities. The Financial Stability Forum was set up in 1999, bringing together senior representatives of G7 national governments, central banks and statutory regulators, together with international financial institutions and the key global financial regulatory standard-setting agencies.

HM Treasury represents the UK in negotiating EC Directives on the financial services sector, coordinating as necessary with the FSA and other bodies.

BANK OF ENGLAND

The Bank of England (*www.bankofengland.co.uk*) was established in 1694 by Act of Parliament and Royal Charter as a corporate body. Its capital stock was acquired by the Government in 1946. Fundamental changes to the Bank's role took effect under the Bank of England Act 1998, including the acquisition of operational responsibility for setting interest rates.

As the UK's central bank, the Bank's overriding objective is to maintain a stable and efficient monetary and financial framework for the effective operation of the economy. In pursuing this goal, it has three main purposes:

- maintaining the integrity and value of the currency;
- maintaining the stability of the financial system; and
- seeking to ensure the effectiveness of the financial services sector.

Monetary Policy Framework

The Bank's monetary policy objective is to maintain price stability and, subject to that, to support the Government's economic policy, including growth and employment objectives. Price stability is defined in terms of the Government's inflation target (see p. 386). The responsibility for meeting this target rests with the Bank's Monetary Policy Committee, which comprises the Governor, the two Deputy Governors and six other members. The Committee meets every month and interest rate decisions are announced as soon as is practicable after the meeting. The Committee is accountable to the Bank's Court of Directors as regards its procedures, to government and to Parliament.

Financial Stability

Under the Memorandum of Understanding between the Bank, HM Treasury and the FSA, the Bank is responsible for the overall stability of the financial system, and its Financial Stability Committee oversees the Bank's work in this area. In exceptional circumstances, the Bank may provide financial support as a last resort to prevent problems affecting one financial institution from spreading to other parts of the financial system. It also oversees the effectiveness of the financial sector in meeting the needs of customers and in maintaining the sector's international competitiveness.

Other Main Functions

The Bank, through its daily operations in the money market, supplies the funds which the banking system as a whole needs to achieve balance at the end of each day. By setting the interest rate for these operations, the Bank influences the general level of interest rates as the interest rate at which the Bank deals is quickly passed on through the financial system, which in turn affects the whole pattern of interest rates across the UK economy.

The Bank provides banking services to its customers, principally the Government, the banking system and other central banks. It plays a key role in payment and settlement systems, and has sole right in England and Wales to issue banknotes, which are backed by government and other securities. The profit from the note issue is paid directly to the Government. Three Scottish and four Northern Ireland banks may also issue notes, but these have to be fully backed by Bank of England notes.

Court of Directors

The Court of Directors is responsible for managing the affairs of the Bank other than the formulation of monetary policy. It comprises the Governor, the two Deputy Governors and 16 Directors. The Directors form a subcommittee; functions include reviewing the Bank's performance in relation to its objectives and strategy, and the internal procedures of the Monetary Policy Committee. The Court is required to report annually to the Chancellor of the Exchequer.

Table 29.2: Households[1] with Different Types of Account or Savings in Great Britain 1999–2000

	Per cent of households
Accounts	
Current account	86
Post Office account	8
Individual Savings Account (ISA)	11
Tax Exempt Special Savings Account (TESSA)	14
Other bank or building society accounts excluding current accounts, ISAs and TESSAs	61
Other savings	
Stocks and shares	26
Unit trusts or investment trusts	6
Personal Equity Plans	14
Gilt-edged stock	1
Premium Bonds	26
National Savings Bonds	5
Save as you earn	2
Any type of account	**92**

1 Households in which at least one member has an account. Covers accounts held by adults only.
Source: Family Resources Survey, Department for Work and Pensions

BANKING SERVICES

At the end of March 2001, there were 309 banks authorised to accept deposits in the UK under the Banking Act 1987. In addition, 355 branches of European-authorised institutions were entitled to accept deposits in the UK. With around 20% of cross-border bank lending, the UK is the world's largest single market for international banking. Banks from around 80 countries have subsidiaries, branches or representative offices in London.

'Retail' banking primarily caters for personal customers and small businesses, offering services including current accounts, savings accounts, loan arrangements, credit and debit cards, mortgages, insurance, investment products, share-dealing services and 'wealth management' services. Nearly all banks engage in some 'wholesale' activities, which involve taking larger deposits, deploying funds in money-market instruments, and making corporate loans and investments, while some concentrate on wholesale business. Many dealings are conducted on the inter-bank market, among banks themselves.

Around 92% cent of households have at least one member with a bank or building society current account (see Table 29.2).

Retail Banks and Banking Groups

The 'big four' bank groups are HSBC, Lloyds TSB, Royal Bank of Scotland and Barclays. Two other large banks, Halifax and Bank of Scotland, merged in September 2001 to form HBOS, while the Competition Commission has rejected a proposed bid by Lloyds TSB for

Abbey National. Other large-scale banks include Alliance & Leicester, Bradford & Bingley and Northern Rock, all of which used to be building societies. Standard Chartered, which mainly operates overseas, has a network of around 615 offices in 56 countries, notably in Asia, Africa and the Middle East. As well as the move by several building societies into the banking sector, other businesses, notably insurance companies and supermarkets (see p. 525), have also entered the sector, although relatively few offer current accounts. Several US banks have entered the market for issuing credit cards.

Traditionally, the major banks have operated through their branches, but the number of branches is falling, as banks have taken steps to cut costs, such as through centralising 'back office' processing operations. This is partly because more customers are using telephone and Internet banking. According to APACS (see p. 515), over 12 million people used telephone and/or personal computer (PC)/Internet banking services in 2000, of whom around 3.3 million used PC/Internet banking. Most customers use these services to view balances and transactions or to transfer funds between accounts, with only a small proportion using them for making payments. Banking services using the Internet are becoming much more widely available. Most major banks have introduced Internet banking, either as an additional option for customers or as a separate stand-alone facility. Several are planning to introduce Internet banking with access through mobile telephones and/or digital television.

Review of UK Banking Services

A major independent review of banking services, *Competition in UK Banking: A Report to the Chancellor of the Exchequer*, published in March 2000, found that, although the UK had a stable financial system and one of the most open regulatory regimes in the world, a more competitive policy framework was needed. In its response to the report, published in August 2000, the Government announced a number of measures designed to improve competition in UK banking markets and to deliver benefits to consumers, including:

- reviewing self-regulatory redress mechanisms, with the aim of ensuring that they deliver sufficient consumer benefits—an independent report was published in July 2001, and the Government has asked the industry to respond by the end of September 2001;
- encouraging the provision of comparative information on banking products;
- agreeing to a review of the effect of the Financial Services and Markets Act 2000 on competition two years after the Act's commencement; and
- reforming the Treasury's objectives on promoting competition in financial services.

Following the review's recommendation, the Competition Commission is conducting a review of the supply of banking services to small businesses.

In December 2000 the Government issued a consultative document containing proposals for a new regulatory framework governing UK payment systems. Under these proposals, banks and other organisations offering payment services would, among other things, have to set out clearly their charges, let new competitors into the market on fair and

Universal Banking Services

In May 2001 the Government reached agreement with the main UK banks on the introduction of 'universal banking services', which will be available through post offices from 2003. The services are intended to tackle financial exclusion and bring those people without bank accounts into the financial mainstream. They will also ensure that benefit recipients and pensioners can continue to receive their money in cash at their local post office when such payments are automated in January 2003. Facilities available through post offices will include a new Post Office card account, while the banks will make their basic bank accounts accessible through the Post Office and contribute £180 million to the costs of running the Post Office card account.

reasonable terms, and work together to develop new and innovative payment systems. Responsibility for enforcing the rules would rest with the Office of Fair Trading.

Investment Banks

London is a major international centre for investment banking and many overseas investment banks have a substantial presence. Many investment banks in London, including those from the United States and continental Europe, have been developing their international operations. Investment banks offer a range of professional financial services, including corporate finance and asset management. A major activity is the provision of advice and financial services to companies, especially in respect of mergers, takeovers and other forms of corporate reorganisation. Investment banks have considerable expertise in advising governments on privatisation.

Building Societies

Building societies are mutual institutions, owned by their savers and borrowers. As well as their retail deposit-taking services, they specialise in housing finance, making long-term mortgage loans against the security of property—usually private dwellings purchased for owner-occupation. Some of the larger societies provide a full range of personal banking services. Building societies have about 2,100 branches. According to the Building Societies Association (BSA) (*www.bsa.org.uk*), about 15 million savers have building society savings accounts (around 18.5 million accounts), and building societies hold some £120 billion in savings accounts. Over 2.5 million borrowers are buying their homes through mortgage loans from a building society. The chief requirements for societies are that:

- their principal purpose is making loans which are secured on residential property and are funded substantially by their members;
- at least 75% per cent of lending has to be on the security of housing; and
- a minimum of 50% of funds must be in the form of deposits made by individual members.

There are 67 authorised building societies, all of which are members of the BSA, with total assets of over £165 billion. The largest is the Nationwide, with assets of £71 billion.

The number of societies has fallen substantially as a result of mergers and the decision by several large societies to give up their mutual status and become banks. Many of the remaining societies have taken steps to defend their mutual status, for example, by requiring new members to assign to charity any 'windfall' payments arising from a conversion.

Payment Systems

Apart from credit and debit card arrangements, the main payment systems are run by three separate companies operating under an umbrella organisation, the Association for Payment Clearing Services (APACS) (*www.apacs.org.uk*). One system, Cheque and Credit Clearing, covers bulk paper clearings—cheques and credit transfers. A second, CHAPS (Clearing House Automated Payment System), is a nationwide electronic transfer service dealing with high-value clearings for real-time gross settlement. A third, Bankers' Automated Clearing Services (BACS), covers bulk electronic clearing for direct credits, standing orders and direct debits. A total of 26 banks and building societies are members of one or more clearing companies, while several hundred others obtain access to APACS clearing through agency arrangements with one of the members.

Trends in Financial Transactions

Major changes in the nature of financial transactions have included the rapid

Table 29.3: Transaction Trends in the UK *Million*

	1990	1995	1999	2000
Plastic card purchases	930	2,023	3,537	3,909
of which:				
Debit card	*192*	*1,004*	*2,062*	*2,332*
Credit and charge card	*690*	*908*	*1,344*	*1,452*
Store card[1]	*48*	*109*	*131*	*125*
Plastic card withdrawals at ATMs and counters	1,045	1,512	2,025	2,102
Direct debits, standing orders, direct credits and CHAPS	1,741	2,402	3,255	3,470
Cheques	3,975	3,283	2,854	2,700
of which:				
For payment	*3,537*	*2,938*	*2,641*	*2,515*
For cash acquisition	*438*	*345*	*213*	*185*
Total non-cash transactions	**7,691**	**9,220**	**11,672**	**12,180**
Cash payments[1]	28,023	26,270	25,596	27,910
Post Office Order Book payments and passbook withdrawals	1,061	1,163	962	880
Total transactions	**36,775**	**36,654**	**38,230**	**40,970**

[1] Estimated figures.
Source: APACS

growth in the use of plastic cards (which first appeared in 1966) and of automated teller machines (ATMs). According to APACS, there were around 3.8 billion plastic transactions in the UK in 2000 when 127 million bank and building society plastic cards were in circulation, with 90% of adults holding one or more cards. Most non-regular payments are still made by cash, but the trend is away from cash and cheques towards greater use of plastic cards (see Table 29.3).

Consumers now acquire more than half their cash through withdrawals from ATMs. The number of ATMs has risen by three-quarters in the last ten years, to 34,300 at the end of 2000. There were 2,027 million cash withdrawals from ATMs in 2000. About three-fifths of adults use ATMs regularly, making on average 68 withdrawals a year.

Direct debit and standing order payments account for over half of all regular bill payments, and 73% of adults have set up at least one direct debit or standing order. Direct debit payments rose by 8% to reach 2.0 billion in 2000.

Plastic Cards

The main types of plastic card are debit cards, credit/charge cards, cash cards and cheque guarantee cards, although individual cards frequently cover more than one use. Charge cards are similar to credit cards, but are designed to be paid off in full each month and are usually available only to those with relatively high income or substantial assets. Several major retailers issue store cards for use within their own outlets. Electronic purse cards are being tested: cards are 'charged' with money from the card holder's bank account, and can be used to purchase goods or services at retailers through electronic tills.

There are about 51 million credit cards (including charge cards) in use in the UK, and 53% of adults have at least one credit card. According to the Credit Card Research Group, credit card expenditure in the UK is a higher proportion of GDP than in the rest of the European Union, reflecting the competitive nature of the UK credit card market, where consumers can choose between over 1,300 different brands of card. Most credit cards are affiliated to one of the two major international organisations, Visa and MasterCard. Many new providers have entered the market and there has been particularly rapid growth in the number of 'affinity' cards, where the card is linked to an organisation such as a charity or trade union.

Debit cards, where payments are deducted directly from the purchaser's bank or building society account, were first issued in 1987. Purchases using debit cards are rising rapidly, with the volume of debit card payments up by 13% in 2000. About 50 million cards have been issued, and around four-fifths of adults in the UK hold a debit card, often combined with cheque guarantee and ATM facilities in a single card.

To tackle the problem of fraud on plastic cards, which rose by 55% to £293 million in 2000, banks are investing in 'smart' cards, in which information is contained on a microchip embedded in the card. These are very difficult to counterfeit and can also store securely much more information than was previously possible.

National Savings

National Savings (*www.nationalsavings.co.uk*), an executive agency of the Chancellor of the Exchequer, is a source of finance for government borrowing and offers personal savers a range of investments. Its operational services—including its three main sites in Blackpool, Durham and Glasgow—are now run under a Public-Private Partnership agreement with Siemens Business Services. National Savings retains responsibility for policy and marketing. Sales of National Savings products totalled £10.2 billion in 2000–01 and around £62 billion is invested in National Savings. Premium Bonds are held by 23 million people and are entered in a monthly draw, with tax-free prizes ranging from £50 to a single top prize of £1 million. Other savings products include Savings Certificates (both Fixed Interest and Index-linked), Pensioners' Bonds, Children's Bonus Bonds, a cash mini ISA (Individual Savings Account—see p. 521) and Ordinary and Investment Accounts (where deposits and withdrawals can be made at post offices).

Friendly Societies

Friendly societies have traditionally been unincorporated societies of individuals, offering their members a limited range of financial and insurance services, such as small-scale savings products, life insurance and provision against loss of income through sickness or unemployment. The Friendly Societies Act 1992 enabled societies to incorporate, take on new powers and provide a wider range of financial services through subsidiaries. Under the Financial Services and Markets Act 2000, the Government will remove the remaining restrictions on the activities of friendly society subsidiaries.

There are around 245 friendly societies, with total funds of £15 billion and an estimated membership of over 5 million. The largest society is the Liverpool Victoria, which has over 1 million members and manages some £5 billion of funds.

Credit Unions

Credit unions are mutually owned financial co-operatives. They are less widespread in the UK than in some other countries, but grew rapidly during the 1990s. There are 688 credit unions registered in Great Britain, with a membership of 296,000 and assets of £181 million.

As part of its policy for dealing with financial exclusion, the Government is introducing a number of measures designed to help credit unions by improving the services that they can offer savers and borrowers. For example, in April 2001 new regulations took effect to allow credit unions to make loans for longer periods. Further measures to relax restrictions on credit unions are planned. Under the Financial Services and Markets Act 2000, the FSA will become responsible for regulation. From mid-2002 a new and more comprehensive regulatory regime for credit unions will come into effect. Credit union members will also have some protection under the new Financial Services Compensation Scheme (see p. 511) from around the same time.

Venture Capital

Venture capital companies offer medium- and long-term equity financing for new and developing businesses, management buy-outs and buy-ins, and company rescues. The UK sector is the largest and most developed in Europe. The British Venture Capital Association (BVCA) (*www.bvca.co.uk*) has 151 full members, which represent a large majority of private equity and venture capital sources in the UK. During 2000, according to a report for the BVCA based on data provided by 96% of its members, UK venture capital companies invested a record £8.3 billion worldwide in 1,523 businesses, 5% more than in 1999. Investment in the UK rose by 3% to £6.4 billion. The Government is encouraging the further development of venture capital, particularly for smaller firms, including new Regional Venture Capital Funds (see chapter 22).

Other Credit and Financial Services

Finance houses and leasing companies provide consumer credit, business finance and leasing, and motor finance. The 100 full members of the Finance and Leasing Association carried out new business worth £69 billion in 2000.

Factoring and invoice discounting comprises a range of financial services, including credit management and finance in exchange for outstanding invoices. The industry provides working capital to more than 27,000 businesses a year. Member companies of the Factors & Discounters Association (*www.factors.org.uk*) handled business worth £77 billion in 2000, 18% higher than in 1999.

INSURANCE

The UK insurance industry is the third largest in the world and the largest global centre for international insurance and reinsurance. In 1999 it employed some 359,000 people in insurance companies, Lloyd's, insurance brokers and other related activities, representing in total over a third of all employment in financial services. About 50,000 of these jobs are supported by the London Market, a unique international wholesale insurance market (see p. 519).

Main Types of Insurance

There are two broad categories of insurance: long-term (such as life insurance), where contracts may be for periods of many years; and general, where contracts are for a year or less. Most insurance companies reinsure their risks; this performs an important function in spreading losses and in helping insurance companies to manage their businesses.

Long-term Insurance

At the end of 2000, 225 companies were authorised to handle long-term insurance, which includes life insurance and pensions, permanent health insurance, endowment policies and annuities. As well as providing life cover, life insurance is a vehicle for saving and investment as premiums are invested in securities and other assets. About 58% of households have life insurance cover. Several companies are now offering the new stakeholder pensions which became available from April 2001 (see p. 172). Total long-term insurance assets under management by companies in 1999 were £1,043 billion on behalf of their worldwide operations. Total long-term premium income by companies in 1999 was £106 billion.

General Insurance

General insurance business is undertaken by insurance companies and by underwriters at Lloyd's. It includes fire, accident, general liability, motor, marine, aviation and other transport risks. Competition has intensified in areas like motor and household insurance, particularly with the growth of insurers offering telephone-based services. Total worldwide premium income of members of the Association of British Insurers (ABI) (*www.abi.org.uk*) in 1999 was £33 billion, of which £23 billion was earned in the UK.

Structure of the Industry

At the end of 2000, 822 companies were authorised to carry on one or more classes of insurance business in the UK. About 400 companies belong to the ABI.

The industry, which includes both public limited companies and mutual institutions (companies owned by their policyholders), has seen considerable restructuring in recent years. The largest insurance group in the UK is CGNU, formed in 2000 from a merger of CGU and Norwich Union. It controls over £200 billion in funds under management and has more than 25 million customers worldwide. Standard Life is the largest mutual insurer in Europe. However, the mutually owned sector is gradually contracting—Scottish Widows was acquired by the banking group Lloyds TSB in 2000, Scottish Provident was bought by Abbey National in 2001, Scottish Life is being acquired by another mutual insurer Royal London, and Friends Provident became a public limited company in July 2001.

The London Market

The London Market is an international wholesale insurance market-place accepting risk from around the world. It is the main centre for world reinsurance business and for marine, aviation, satellite and other forms of transport insurance. It consists of insurance and reinsurance companies, Lloyd's, protection and indemnity clubs (originally created to serve the marine industry) and brokers. Gross premiums of the London Market from reported returns were estimated at £14.2 billion in 1999. Virtually all companies participating in the company sector of the London Market are members of the International Underwriting Association of London (IUA) (*www.iua.co.uk*), which in mid-2001 had 112 members. Over three-quarters of the companies operating in the London Market are overseas-owned. Lloyd's and the IUA have set up a joint forum to help update business procedures, with the aim of ensuring that London retains its position as the leading international centre. Working with the broking community, the forum is taking steps to streamline processes and increase the use of e-commerce.

Lloyd's

Lloyd's (*www.lloydsoflondon.com*) is an incorporated society of private insurers in London. It is not a company but a market for insurance administered by the Council of Lloyd's and Lloyd's Regulatory and Market Boards.

The net premium income of the market in 1998 was £6.03 billion. For 2001 the market has a total projected allocated capacity of £11.04 billion, of which some £9.09 billion will be capacity provided by 894 limited liability members, representing both companies and individuals who have converted to limited liability. The number of individual 'Names'—wealthy individuals who accept insurance risks for their own profit or loss, with unlimited liability—was 2,852 in 2001. Members underwrite through 108 syndicates. Each syndicate is managed by an underwriting agent responsible for appointing a professional underwriter to accept insurance risks and manage claims on behalf of the members.

In January 2001 the market was opened up so that more UK and overseas brokers could gain direct access, subject to meeting certain technical and customer service standards. Around one-sixth of Lloyd's current work is in its traditional marine market, and it has a significant share of the UK motor insurance market. Lloyd's is a major insurer of aviation and satellite risks, and underwrites in other areas of insurance except long-term life insurance. Reinsurance constitutes a large part of Lloyd's business.

Under the Financial Services and Markets Act 2000, the FSA will have regulatory oversight of Lloyd's. The FSA's primary concern will be protecting the interests of Lloyd's policyholders.

Insurance Brokers and Intermediaries

Medium to large insurance brokers almost exclusively handle commercial matters, with the biggest dealing in worldwide risks. Smaller brokers deal mainly with personal lines, such as motor, household and holiday insurance, or specialise in a particular type of commercial insurance. Some brokers specialise in reinsurance business. There are also auxiliary services, such as loss adjusters and actuaries, and other support services. Under the Financial Services and Markets Act 2000, the statutory regime of professional standards governing insurance brokers was abolished in April 2001. The sector is now regulated by the General Insurance Standards Council. For intermediaries arranging life insurance constituting an investment (such as a personal pension), regulation is by the FSA.

INVESTMENT

The UK has considerable expertise in fund management, which involves managing funds on behalf of investors, or advising them how best to invest their funds. The main types of investment fund include pension schemes, life insurance, unit trusts, open-ended investment companies and investment trusts.

> The final report of the Myners review of institutional investment, published in March 2001, found that there were a number of distortions affecting institutional investment decision-making. Its central proposal is for a set of clear principles of investment decision-making, which would apply to pension funds and, in due course, other institutional investors. For example, the principles envisage that trustees should set out an overall investment objective for the fund, while decision-makers should consider a full range of investment opportunities across all major asset classes, including private equity. Other recommendations in the review include the replacement of the minimum funding requirement (MFR) for pension funds, and a legislative change to raise the duty of care for fund trustees. The Government is consulting on a number of the recommendations, and intends to legislate to replace the MFR with a long-term scheme-specific funding standard, with additional protective measures to protect scheme members.

Pension Funds

Total net assets of UK pension funds were estimated at about £755 billion at the end of 2000, according to the National Association of Pension Funds. Pension funds are major investors in securities markets, holding around 20% of securities listed on the London Stock Exchange. Funds are managed mainly by the investment management houses.

Unit Trusts/Open-ended Investment Companies

Over 1,900 authorised unit trusts and open-ended investment companies (oeics) pool investors' money in funds divided into units or shares of equal size, enabling people with relatively small amounts of money to benefit from diversified and managed portfolios. In April 2001 total funds under management were £260 billion, of which £54 billion represented funds in Personal Equity Plans and £21 billion in Individual Savings Accounts (ISAs). Most unit trusts are general funds, investing in a wide variety of UK or international securities, but there are also many specialist funds.

There are over 150 unit trust and oeic management groups, of which 62 had total fund values exceeding £1 billion in April 2001. Investment fund management groups are represented by the Association of Unit Trusts and Investment Funds (AUTIF) (*www.investmentfunds.org.uk*).

Oeics are similar to unit trusts, but investors buy shares in the fund rather than units. They were set up in 1997 to enable UK companies to compete on an equal footing with similar schemes operating elsewhere in the EU. By April 2001, 549 oeics had been set up by 51 management groups.

Investment Trusts

Investment trust companies are listed on the London Stock Exchange and their shares can be bought and sold in the same way as other companies. Like unit trusts, they offer the opportunity to diversify risk on a relatively small lump-sum investment or through regular savings. Investment trusts are exempt from tax on gains realised within the funds and invest principally in the shares and securities of other companies. Assets are purchased mainly out of shareholders' funds, although investment trusts are also allowed to borrow money for investment.

There are about 380 investment trusts, which form the largest listed sector of the

London Stock Exchange. Around 35% of their shares by value are held by private investors. Over 310 listed trust companies are members of the Association of Investment Trust Companies (*www.aitc.co.uk*). At the end of May 2001 the industry had £77 billion of assets under management and a stock market capitalisation of £62 billion.

Share Ownership

Financial institutions hold the bulk of equities. At the end of 2000 UK financial institutions held ordinary shares valued at £855 billion (47% of the total market value of £1,811 billion), with insurance companies holding £381 billion and pension funds £321 billion. Holders from outside the UK had £587 billion (32%). The value of holdings of UK individual shareholders was £290 billion (16%). About 26% of households have at least one adult owning shares (see Table 29.2).

According to ProShare (an independent organisation encouraging share ownership), the number of investment clubs—groups of individuals, usually about 15 to 20 people, who regularly invest in shares—has risen to around 10,000. The conversion of a number of building societies to banks, privatisation, employee share schemes and measures to increase tax-free savings have led to increased share ownership by individuals.

Tax-free Savings

The main method of tax-free saving is now the Individual Savings Account (ISA). The Government introduced ISAs in 1999 to help encourage people to save more and to distribute the tax relief on savings more fairly. ISAs succeeded Personal Equity Plans (PEPs), which allowed tax-free investment in shares, unit trusts and certain corporate bonds, and TESSAs (Tax Exempt Special Savings Accounts).

ISAs are guaranteed to run until at least April 2009. Until April 2006 each individual can contribute up to £7,000 a year in total. There are three main elements of an ISA:

- cash—up to £3,000 each year—such as in a bank or building society ISA account;
- stocks and shares—up to £7,000 a year; and
- life insurance—up to £1,000 a year.

In addition, savers can roll over capital from a matured TESSA into a cash ISA or a special TESSA-only ISA.

There are two main types of ISA: a maxi ISA, which can include all three elements in a single ISA with one manager; and mini ISAs, which allow savers to have different managers, for cash, stocks and shares, and life insurance. Savers can choose to put money into mini ISAs or a maxi ISA, but not both, in each tax year.

In 2000–01 subscriptions were made to about 11.3 million ISAs—7.9 million mini ISAs and 3.4 million maxi ISAs—attracting £29.8 billion (see Table 29.4 overleaf).

FINANCIAL MARKETS

London Stock Exchange

The London Stock Exchange (*www.londonstockexchange.com*) is one of the world's leading exchanges. In 2000 turnover in international equities was £3,520 billion and in UK equities £1,900 billion, 40% and 35% higher respectively than in 1999. In mid-2001, 1,882 UK and 482 international companies were listed on the main market, with a market capitalisation of £1,700 billion and £3,300 billion respectively. A further 567 companies, with a total capitalisation of £13.8 billion, were listed on AIM, the Alternative Investment Market, primarily for small, young and growing companies. The 'techMARK' market brings together 248 of the listed companies engaged in technology or related sectors. In July 2001 shares in the Exchange became more widely available when it listed on its own Exchange.

Several other products for raising capital are handled, including Eurobonds (see p. 522), warrants, depositary receipts and gilt-edged stock (see p. 403). The London Stock Exchange provides a secondary or trading market where investors can buy or sell gilts.

Each day the CREST computerised settlement system for shares and other company securities settles around 230,000 transactions with a value of over £200 billion.

Table 29.4: Subscriptions to ISAs in the UK

	Subscriptions in 1999–2000 (£ million)	Subscriptions in 2000–01 (£ million)	% of subscriptions in 2000–01
Mini ISAs			
Stocks and shares	1,587	1,839	*6.2*
Cash	11,575	13,864	*46.6*
Life insurance	56	108	*0.4*
Total invested in mini ISAs	**13,218**	**15,811**	***53.1***
Maxi ISAs			
Stocks and shares	14,467	13,337	*44.8*
Cash	731	606	*2.0*
Life insurance	15	18	*0.1*
Total invested in maxi ISAs	**15,213**	**13,961**	***46.9***
Total invested in ISAs	**28,431**	**29,772**	***100.0***

Source: Inland Revenue

Other Equity Exchanges

Three other markets in the City of London for trading equities are virt-x, OM London, and Ofex (a trading facility run by J. P. Jenkins). Virt-x is a new pan-electronic trading exchange formed from a merger of the Tradepoint exchange and the Swiss stock exchange; it became fully operational in June 2001.

Euromarket

The Euromarket began with Eurodollars—US dollars lent outside the United States—and has developed into a major market in a variety of currencies lent outside their domestic markets. London is at the centre of the Euromarket and houses most of the leading international banks and securities firms. Its share of trading in the two main types of international bond—Eurobonds and foreign bonds—is around 70%. Coredeal, which started operations in 2000, acts as an exchange for transactions involving such bonds.

Foreign Exchange Market

A survey by the Bank for International Settlements in 1998 showed that daily foreign exchange turnover in the UK was US$637 billion and that London was the world's biggest trading centre, with over 30% of global net daily turnover. Dealing is conducted through telephone and electronic links between the banks, other financial institutions and a number of firms of foreign exchange brokers which act as intermediaries. The institutions keep close contact with financial centres abroad and quote buying and selling rates throughout the day for both immediate ('spot') and forward transactions in many currencies. Following the introduction of the euro in 1999 (see p. 82) and associated with a number of other factors, including a move to greater use of multilateral electronic trading platforms for foreign exchange, global turnover in a number of currencies fell, but there are indications that turnover in London, at least in some of the major firms, has grown.

LIFFE

The London International Financial Futures and Options Exchange (LIFFE) (*www.liffe.com*) handles financial derivatives (including 'futures' and 'options'), which offer a means of protection against changes in prices, exchange rates and interest rates. It also handles trade in commodities, such as coffee, cocoa and sugar. LIFFE transacts

The Centre for Alternative Technology (CAT)

Machynlleth, Powys. CAT is a working demonstration of alternative technology. The centre generates its own electricity and uses alternative sewage systems. Buildings on the site have the latest developments in energy conservation, such as roof-mounted solar energy collectors. In 2001 the Centre won the National Eisteddfod of Wales' Gold Medal for Architecture for its new visitor information centre.

CAT is situated on a 40-acre site. Seven acres are open to the public, who are encouraged to explore ways in which natural resources can be used more sustainably. Volunteer work placements, a consultancy service and various courses, such as the Alternative Building Methods Course, help students to learn more about environmentally conscious technology. The earthball oven (left), shows part of the coursework of students on CAT's MSc in Architecture.

Entering the Centre through a water-powered cliff railway.

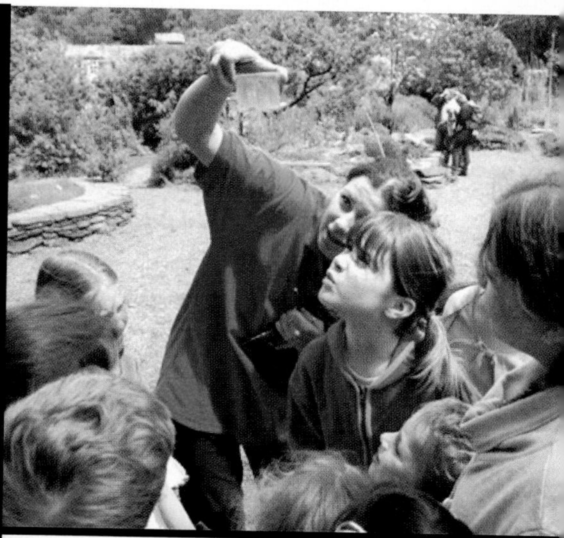

Learning about the science of ecology on a slug and bug hunt.

Visitors in front of a photovoltaic panel, which generates electricity from sunlight.

A hydro-power display circuit shows how renewable energy works.

SCUBA AND THE JAMES CLERK MAXWELL TELESCOPE

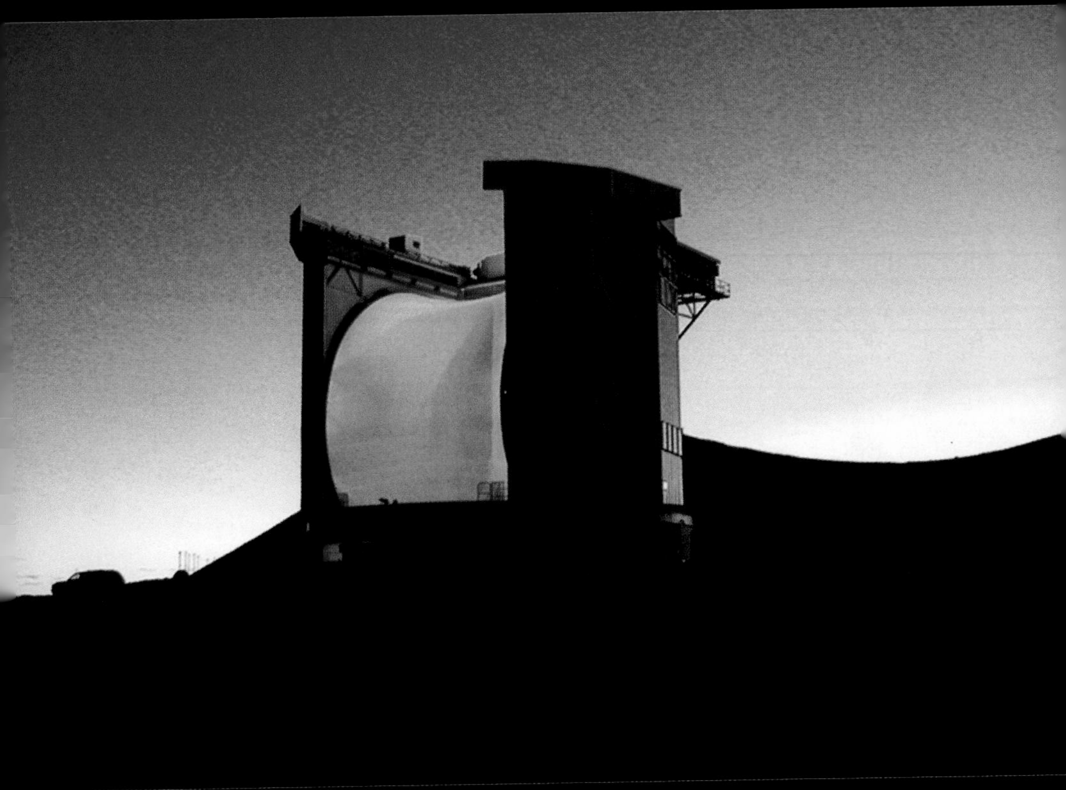

(Top): Panoramic view of Mauna Kea, Hawaii, the site of the James Clerk Maxwell Telescope.
(Above): The JCMT against the dusk sky, illuminated from within by high-intensity sodium lamps.

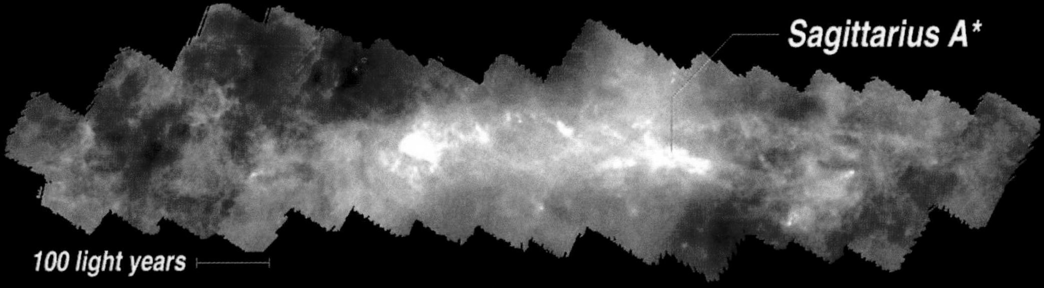

With a diameter of 15 m, the James Clerk Maxwell Telescope (JCMT) is the largest astronomical telescope in the world capable of operating throughout the millimetre and sub-millimetre wavebands. The telescope is owned and operated by the UK, Canada and the Netherlands, on behalf of astronomers worldwide, through the Particle Physics and Astronomy Research Council's Joint Astronomy Centre in Hilo, Hawaii. It is situated close to the summit of Mauna Kea, at an altitude of 4,092 m and is named after the 19th century Scottish physicist.

The JCMT is used to study the Solar System, interstellar dust and gas, and distant galaxies. In 1996, the **Sub-millimetre Common-Use Bolometer Array (SCUBA)** constructed by the Royal Observatory, Edinburgh, in collaboration with Queen Mary and Westfield College, London, was installed on the JCMT. The SCUBA is an extremely powerful sub-millimetre wave camera (right). Since 1997 it has been taking observations of the Milky Way and other galaxy and star formations for the astronomical community. In 2000 the camera obtained the most advanced map of the Milky Way to date (above). It is the first detailed map to show all the interstellar gas in the Galactic Centre. The SCUBA does this by using sub-millimetre wavelengths, which are tuned to detect the clouds of interstellar gas and dust where new stars are born.

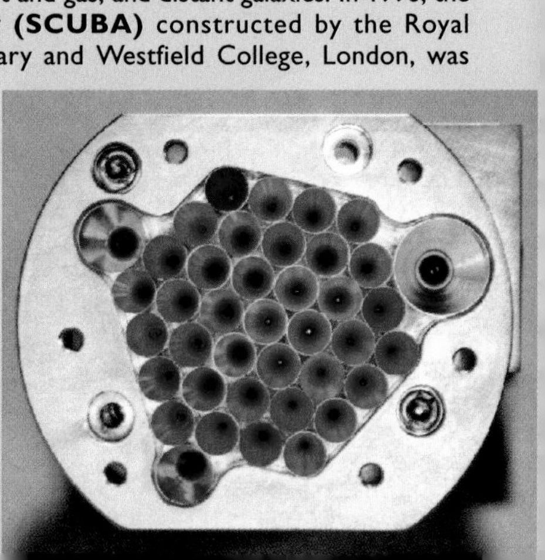

A more powerful version, SCUBA 2, is currently being developed in the UK. It is due to be delivered to JCMT in Hawaii in 2005–06, and will enable increasingly magnified images to be studied by astronomers.

SET Week) has taken place annually to promote the public's understanding of science, engineering and technology. A variety of events are coordinated by the British Association for the Advancement of Science and held at locations throughout the UK. During the week scientists have the opportunity to explain their work to the public. School children attend many of the workshops and demonstrations and are encouraged to consider a career in science and technology.

Courtes

Courtesy CLRC

As part of the 2001 National Science Week children examine a model of the earth's magnetic fields (left) and experiment with wind power at the two centres of the Central Laboratory of the Research Councils.

The

A visitor to the 2001 National Science Week 'Bodyworks' display at Newcastle-under-Lyme College studies a plasma ball. The gas inside the ball glows as negative charges of electricity repel each other.

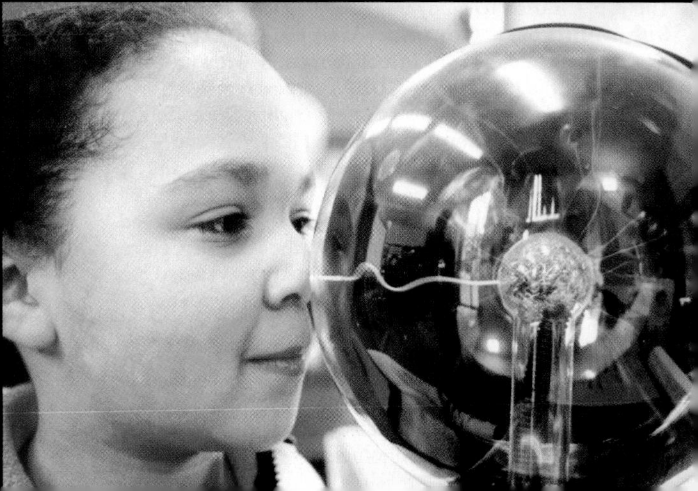

business worth US$523 billion every day through its electronic trading platform, LIFFE CONNECT. The LIFFE market and its broad range of products can now be accessed from 440 locations in 23 countries. LIFFE employs 700 people in offices in London, New York, Chicago, Paris and Tokyo.

LIFFE's strategy includes extending its core exchange business, with new products such as universal stock futures, which were launched in 2001. It is also developing its technology assets and investing in infrastructure to meet the needs of third-party customers and to deliver on three major contracts secured in the first half of 2001. One of the contracts is with the Nasdaq exchange, where the joint venture, Nasdaq LIFFE Markets, is intended to expand LIFFE's US business by creating a market to trade single stock futures as soon as US regulations are in place to permit this.

Other Exchanges

Other important City exchanges include:

- the *London bullion market*—around 60 banks and other financial trading companies participate in the London gold and silver markets;
- the *London Metal Exchange (LME)*—the primary base metals market in the world, trading contracts in aluminium, aluminium alloy, copper, lead, nickel, tin and zinc;
- the *International Petroleum Exchange (IPE)*; and
- the *Baltic Exchange*—the world's leading international shipping market.

The London Clearing House (LCH) clears and settles business at LIFFE, LME, IPE and virt-x.

Other Services

The distribution of goods, including food and drink, to their point of sale is a major economic activity. The large wholesalers and retailers of food and drink operate extensive distribution networks, either directly or through contractors.

WHOLESALING

In 2001 there were over 110,000 enterprises (see Table 29.5) engaged in wholesaling in the UK; 25% were sole proprietors and 15% partnerships. There were over 1.1 million employee jobs in the UK in this sector in December 2000 and turnover in 2000 amounted to £358 billion, 9.0% higher than in 1999.

In the food and drink trade almost all large retailers have their own buying and central distribution operations. Many small wholesalers and independent grocery retailers belong to voluntary 'symbol' groups, which provide access to central purchasing facilities and coordinated promotions. This has helped smaller retailers to remain relatively competitive; many local and convenience stores and village shops would not otherwise be able to stay in business. London's wholesale markets play a significant part in the distribution of fresh foodstuffs. New Covent Garden at Nine Elms is the main market for fruit and vegetables, London Central Markets at Smithfield for meat and Billingsgate at Canary Wharf for fish.

In April 2000 Co-operative Wholesale Society (CWS) and Co-operative Retail Services (CRS) merged; the merged society was renamed the Co-operative Group (CWS) in January 2001. As well as food retailing, the Group's operations cover funeral businesses, travel retailing, motor trading, non-food department stores and a chain of opticians. The merger created the UK's largest mutual retail group, with sales of £3.1 billion in 2000, over 1,000 stores and 47,000 employees.

The Co-operative Group has been the principal supplier of goods and services to the Co-operative Movement—comprising 44 independent retail societies and around 2,340 stores—and was a founder member of the Co-operative Retail Trading Group (CRTG). Formed in 1993, the CRTG acts as a central marketing, buying and distribution partnership for retail co-operative societies, and now accounts for around 90% of Co-op food trade. The Co-op is also one of the largest co-operative retailers in Europe, with stores located in most parts of the United Kingdom. Retail co-operative societies are voluntary organisations controlled by their

Table 29.5: Wholesale and Retail Enterprises in the UK, 2001

	Number of enterprises					
Annual turnover (£'000)	Wholesale Total	*of which:* Sole proprietors	Partner-ships	Retail Total	*of which:* Sole proprietors	Partner-ships
1–49	17,895	8,580	2,605	20,210	11,725	4,520
50–99	16,160	7,230	2,810	47,690	27,935	13,390
100–249	22,615	7,215	4,295	69,370	30,360	27,020
250–499	14,905	2,790	2,895	33,510	10,100	14,225
500–999	13,045	1,360	1,970	16,535	3,390	5,760
1,000+	25,830	780	1,760	11,030	965	2,175
of which:						
1,000–1,999	*10,130*	*n.a.*	*n.a.*	*6,670*	*n.a.*	*n.a.*
2,000–4,999	*8,535*	*n.a.*	*n.a.*	*2,800*	*n.a.*	*n.a.*
5,000–9,999	*3,490*	*n.a.*	*n.a.*	*705*	*n.a.*	*n.a.*
10,000–49,999	*2,950*	*n.a.*	*n.a.*	*605*	*n.a.*	*n.a.*
50,000+	*725*	*n.a.*	*n.a.*	*250*	*n.a.*	*n.a.*
Total	**110,445**	**27,955**	**16,330**	**198,345**	**84,475**	**67,090**

n.a. = not available.
Note: Turnover relates mainly to a 12-month period ended in spring 2000.
Source: Office for National Statistics. *Size Analysis of UK Businesses 2001*. Business Monitor PA1003

members, membership being open to anyone paying a small deposit on a minimum share.

RETAILING

The retail sector accounts for 43% of all consumer expenditure and employs one in ten of the workforce. In 2001 there were over 198,000 retail enterprises in the UK (see Table 29.5); 43% were sole proprietors and 34% partnerships. In December 2000 there were 2.6 million employee jobs in the UK in this sector. Total turnover in the retail trade sector (including repair of personal and household goods) in 1999 amounted to £208 billion, 4.2% higher than in 1998. Businesses range from national supermarket and other retail chains to independent corner grocery shops, hardware stores, chemists, newsagents and a host of other types of retailer. The large multiple retailers have grown considerably, tending to increase outlet size until relatively recently and to diversify product ranges. Some also operate overseas, through either subsidiaries or franchise agreements. Small independent retail businesses and co-operative societies have been in decline for some time.

Sunday trading laws have been relaxed to allow retailers to open for specified periods on Sundays. To help their competitive position, smaller retailers can open for longer hours than the larger supermarkets and department stores, which are restricted to six hours, except in Scotland. Some major supermarket branches now open for 24 hours, six days a week.

The volume of retail sales rose by almost 21% between 1995 and 2000 (see Table 29.6). Growth in non-food stores (28%) has been higher than predominantly food stores (14%), with the most significant increase in household goods stores, 49% higher than in 1995.

The four biggest supermarket chains (as at July 2001) by sales value were Tesco (840 stores), J. Sainsbury (440), Asda (246) and Safeway (nearly 500). They accounted for 65% of total grocery sales, worth £47.3 billion in 2000. Asda was taken over by US discount giant Wal-Mart in 1999. Other significant food retailers are Somerfield, Co-ops, Marks & Spencer and Morrisons, which, together with independent food retailers, account for 35% of grocery sales. Alcoholic

Table 29.6: Volume of Retail Sales in the UK 1995 = 100

	1990	1995	1998	1999	2000
Predominantly food stores	89.4	100.0	108.8	110.8	113.6
Predominantly non-food stores					
Non-specialised stores	94.3	100.0	111.5	114.7	122.2
Textile, clothing and footwear stores	89.9	100.0	112.0	117.1	124.7
Household goods stores	89.7	100.0	125.2	135.2	148.6
Other stores	102.5	100.0	109.2	113.2	117.0
Total	93.9	100.0	114.3	119.9	127.9
Non-store retailing and repair	109.4	100.0	111.6	115.2	115.6
All retailing	**93.0**	**100.0**	**111.7**	**115.6**	**120.8**

Source: Office for National Statistics

drinks are sold mainly in supermarkets and in specialist 'off licences'.

The leading mixed retail chains are found in high streets nationwide. Competition with lower-priced outlets and discount chains is squeezing some of the more traditional suppliers selling a range of items. Several chains of DIY (Do-It-Yourself) stores and superstores cater for people carrying out repairs and improvements to their own homes and gardens; they stock tools, decorating and building materials, kitchen and bathroom fittings, and garden products. Specialist shops, such as those selling mobile telephones, have shown substantial growth.

The large multiple groups have broadened their range of goods and services. Large food retailers are also placing greater emphasis on selling own-label groceries (which in Sainsbury's case accounts for 40% of sales) and environmentally friendly products (including organic produce), together with household wares and clothing. In-store pharmacies, post offices, customer cafeterias and dry-cleaners are now a feature of large supermarkets, which also sell newspapers, magazines, books, audio cassettes, pre-recorded videos, compact discs and electrical goods. 'Stores within stores' are common; for example, sportswear and sports goods retailers are found in several of the big mixed department stores. Major supermarket chains have their own petrol stations at some of their bigger outlets (see p. 526). Several large retailers offer personal finance facilities in an attempt to encourage sales, particularly of high-value goods, while others have diversified into financial services. Some supermarkets now offer banking facilities. 'Loyalty' cards were introduced in the mid-1990s by supermarket and other retail groups, giving regular customers cash discounts related to the size of their purchases and providing the stores with detailed information on shoppers' buying habits.

The British Franchise Association (BFA) Annual Survey 2001 estimated that there were 665 fully fledged business-format franchises, with around 35,600 outlets, accounting for 316,000 direct jobs in the UK and with annual turnover of £9.3 billion. Franchising is the granting of a licence by one company (the franchisor) to another (the franchisee), usually by means of an initial payment with continuing royalties. Franchised activities operate in many areas, including cleaning services, film processing, print shops, fitness centres, courier delivery, car rental, engine tuning and servicing, and fast-food retailing. About 170 franchisors are members of the BFA.

Vehicle, Vehicle Parts and Petrol Retailing

In December 2000 there were 548,000 employee jobs in the UK in retailing motor vehicles and parts, and in petrol stations. Turnover in the motor trades industry in 2000 amounted to £122.0 billion, 0.9% lower than in 1999 (see Table 29.7).

Most businesses selling new vehicles are franchised by the motor manufacturers.

Table 29.7: Turnover in the Motor Trades Industry *£ million*

	1999	2000	Percentage change
Sale of motor vehicles	86,503	80,912	–6.5
Maintenance and repair of motor vehicles	8,750	9,782	11.8
Sale of motor vehicle parts and accessories	11,481	11,677	1.7
Sale, maintenance and repair of motorcycles and related parts and accessories	1,629	1,959	20.3
Retail sale of automotive fuel	14,821	17,701	19.4
Total	**123,183**	**122,031**	**–0.9**

Source: Office for National Statistics—annual data derived from short-term turnover inquiries

Vehicle components are available for sale at garages which undertake servicing and repair work and also at retail chains and at independent retailers. Drive-in fitting centres sell tyres, exhaust systems, batteries, clutches and other vehicle parts. There were over 13,000 retail outlets for petrol at the end of 2000, with the top three companies accounting for about 34% of the total. The number of petrol stations has declined by about a third between 1989 and 2000, reflecting intense competition in the sector, relatively low profit margins and consolidation among operators. This is particularly so in rural areas. Petrol stations have increasingly offered other retail services, such as shops, car washes and fast-food outlets, with the aim of increasing business. Over one-quarter of petrol sold in the UK comes from supermarket forecourts, of which there were around 1,040 operating at the end of 2000.

Shopping Facilities

Government policy is to focus new retail development in existing centres. This is to ensure that everyone has easy access to a range of shops and services, whether or not they have a car; and to enable businesses of all types and sizes to prosper. Many smaller and middle-range retailers traditionally concentrated in high streets have experienced high costs, with a result that many have closed down. The Government aims to revitalise town centres by focusing new shopping, leisure and other facilities in these centres. One of the most significant trends in retailing has been the spread of superstores, many of which were built away from urban centres until recently. Since 1996, social, economic and environmental considerations have led the Government and local planning authorities to limit new retail developments outside town centres, as these had undermined the vitality and viability of existing town and district centres, were not always readily accessible by those without a car and encouraged greater car use.

All new retail development requires planning permission from the local planning authority, which must consult central government before granting permission for most retail developments of 2,500 sq m (27,000 sq ft) or more. Retailers' attentions are now being turned back to town centres, redeveloping existing stores and building smaller outlets. Almost 50 new small (1,000 sq m) stores have been opened by two of the major supermarket chains so far and up to 50 smaller (300 sq m) stores are planned.

There are eight regional out-of-town shopping centres, located at sites offering good road access and ample parking facilities. The latest, and likely to be the last such out-of-town centre, is Bluewater near Dartford, Kent, which opened in 1999. It is the largest out-of-town retail development in Europe, covering 160,000 sq m (1.7 million sq ft). With 320 shops and parking for 13,000 cars, it attracted 25.3 million shoppers in 2000. The other out-of-town regional shopping centres are: the MetroCentre at Gateshead in Tyne and Wear; Meadowhall near Sheffield; Trafford Centre in Manchester; Merry Hill at

Dudley in the West Midlands; Cribbs Causeway at Bristol; Lakeside at Thurrock in Essex; and Braehead, near Glasgow. About half of total food sales are accounted for by superstores away from town centres, compared with a fifth at the beginning of the 1980s.

Retailers of non-food goods, such as DIY products, toys, furniture and electrical appliances, sportswear, and office and computer products, have also built outlets away from urban centres. There was a trend in the 1990s towards grouping retail warehouses into retail warehouse parks, often with food and other facilities, although planning controls now limit approvals for such developments.

Computers monitor stock levels and record sales figures through electronic point-of-sale (EPOS) systems by means of product bar codes. Techniques such as 'just-in-time' ordering, in which products arrive at the store at the last possible moment before sale, have become widespread as a result. Electronic data interchange (EDI) systems enable retailers' and suppliers' computers to communicate and transmit orders and invoices electronically, so reducing errors and saving time. 'Superscan' technology—where customers use an electronic scanning device to calculate their own bills—is operational in a number of supermarkets.

Home Shopping

Traditionally, all kinds of goods and services have been, and can still be, purchased through mail-order catalogues. In 1999 sales by direct and agency mail order totalled £8.15 billion. The largest-selling items are clothing, footwear, furniture, household textiles and domestic electrical appliances. More recently introduced have been electronic home shopping, using a television and telephone, and 'online' shopping, where personal computers are linked to databases—this 'e-commerce' is growing rapidly (see e-commerce essay on p. 536). Supermarkets are looking closely at different forms of home shopping (by telephone, fax and Internet) and delivery.

CONSUMER PROTECTION

The Government aims to maintain and develop a clear and fair regulatory framework that gives confidence to consumers and contributes to business competitiveness. It works closely with outside bodies that have expert knowledge of consumer issues to develop policies and legislation. In 1999 a White Paper, *Modern Markets: Confident Consumers*, set out a range of initiatives to improve consumer protection. The main proposals included: a hallmark for consumers identifying companies signed up to a code of practice and a digital hallmark for Internet traders abiding by codes guaranteeing security of payment and privacy of information; increased powers to deal with dishonest traders; new advice networks, including a consumer 'gateway' on the Internet; new measures to ensure information is accurate, comprehensive and easy to understand; a review of consumer protection legislation; and a review by the Director General of Fair Trading of his consumer protection functions.

Consumer Legislation

- The *Trade Descriptions Act 1968* prohibits misdescriptions of goods and services, and enables regulations to be made requiring information or instructions relating to goods to be marked on, or to accompany, the goods or to be included in advertisements.
- Under the *Fair Trading Act 1973*, the Director General of Fair Trading can recommend legislative or other changes to stop practices adversely affecting consumers' economic interests; to encourage trade associations to develop codes of practice promoting consumers' interests; and to disseminate consumer information and guidance. The Director General can also demand assurances as to future conduct from traders who persistently breach the law to the detriment of consumers.
- The *Consumer Credit Act 1974* is intended to protect consumers in their dealings with credit businesses. Most businesses

connected with the consumer credit or hire industry or which supply ancillary credit services—for example, credit brokers, debt collectors, debt counsellors and credit reference agencies—require a consumer credit licence. The Director General is responsible for administering the licensing system, including refusing or revoking licences of those unfit to hold them. The Director General also has powers to prohibit unfit people from carrying out estate agency work; to take court action to prevent the publication of misleading advertisements; and to stop traders using unfair terms in standard contracts with consumers.

- The *Sale of Goods Act 1979* (as amended in 1994) ensures that consumers are entitled to receive goods which fit their description and are of satisfactory quality.
- The *Consumer Protection Act 1987* covers misleading indications about prices of goods. The Act also makes it a criminal offence to supply unsafe products, and provides product liability rights for consumers. The regulatory framework to control product safety is a mixture of European and UK legislation, voluntary safety standards and industry codes of practice. The Department of Trade and Industry (DTI) runs a programme of safety awareness initiatives. This aims to reduce accidents by increasing consumer awareness of potential hazards in the home and by encouraging consumers to change their behaviour.[1]

The marking and accuracy of quantities are regulated by weights and measures legislation. Other law provides for the control of medical products, and certain other substances and articles, through a system of licences and certificates. New regulations have been introduced to strengthen the protection of consumers from unscrupulous doorstep sellers.

The EU's consumer programme covers activities such as health and safety, protection of the consumer's economic interests, promotion of consumer education and strengthening the representation of consumers. The interests of UK consumers on EU matters are represented by a number of organisations, including the Consumers' Association and the National Consumer Council (see below).

Consumer Advice and Information

Citizens Advice Bureaux in England, Wales and Northern Ireland handled almost 5.9 million enquiries during 2000–01 (see Table 29.8). Their work is coordinated by a national association (*www.nacab.org.uk*) linked to the bureaux by local and regional committees. In addition, over 500,000 problems are handled by Citizens Advice Scotland each year. Similar assistance is provided by trading standards and consumer protection departments of local authorities in Great Britain and, in some areas, by specialist consumer advice centres.

The *National Consumer Council* (*www.ncc.org.uk*), a non-departmental public body which receives much of its funding from the DTI, gives its view to government, industry and others on consumer issues. Associate Councils in Scotland, Wales and Northern Ireland deal with the particular concerns of consumers in those countries.

Table 29.8: Citizens Advice Bureaux Enquiries by Category in England, Wales and Northern Ireland *Thousand*

	1999–2000	2000–01	% change
Benefits	1,757	1,723	–1.9
Consumer and utilities	1,217	1,175	–3.5
Employment	687	632	–8.0
Housing	620	600	–3.2
Legal	503	479	–4.8
Relationships	415	388	–6.6
Tax	160	154	–3.8
Other	747	705	–5.3
Total	**6,107**	**5,858**	**–4.1**

Source: National Association of Citizens Advice Bureaux

[1] According to the DTI, there were 3,974 home accident deaths and 2.8 million injuries in the UK in 1999.

Consumer bodies for privatised utilities investigate questions of concern to the consumer. Some trade associations have set up codes of practice. In addition, several organisations work to further consumer interests by representing the consumer's view to government, industry and other bodies. The largest is the *Consumers' Association*, with 676,000 members in June 2001, funded largely by subscriptions to *Which?* and related magazines.

HOTELS, RESTAURANTS AND CATERING

The hotel and restaurant trades, which include public houses (pubs), wine bars and other licensed bars in addition to all kinds of businesses offering accommodation and prepared food, had 1.4 million employee jobs in the UK in December 2000. Total turnover in 2000 amounted to £52.6 billion, 2.8% higher than in 1999. There are estimated to be some 60,000 hotels and guest houses in the UK, ranging from major hotel groups to small guest houses, individually owned. Over 20,400 hotels in the UK were registered with a tourist board in 2000—offering 884,000 bedspaces—although this is a fall of 7.5% since 1998. Holiday centres, including traditional holiday camps with full board, such as Butlins and Pontins, self-catering centres and caravan parks, are run by several companies.

In 2000 there were 45,875 enterprises in the UK in the licensed restaurant industry (including fast-food and takeaway outlets), an increase of 1.7% on 1999, with a total turnover of £16.1 billion, 6.1% higher than in 1999. Burger restaurants accounted for 11.2% of the total restaurant market in 2000, public house restaurants 9.0%, pizza and pasta restaurants 5.0%, roadside restaurants 4.0%, and chicken restaurants 2.9%. Turnover at these types of outlet amounted to £4.8 billion.

Restaurants offer cuisine from virtually every country in the world, and several of the highest-quality ones have international reputations. Chinese, Indian, Thai, Italian, French and Greek restaurants are among the most popular. 'Fast-food' restaurants are widespread, many of which are franchised. They specialise in selling hamburgers, chicken, pizza and a variety of other foods, to be eaten on the premises or taken away. Traditional fish and chip shops are another main provider of cooked takeaway food. Sandwich bars are common in towns and cities, typically in areas with high concentrations of office workers.

There were an estimated 49,500 pubs in the UK in 2001, a decline of over 8% since 1990. They account for 57% of all fully licensed premises, compared with 65% in 1990. Turnover was estimated at £14.7 billion in 2000, approaching an annual average of £300,000 per pub. Pubs sell alcoholic drinks (beer, wines and spirits) to adults for consumption on the premises, with non-alcoholic (soft) drinks and hot and cold food a growing part of their trade. Although brewers still own many of the tightly controlled, and often branded, pub chains, their share has declined to less than 25% of UK pubs. Such pubs either provide managers to run them or offer tenancy agreements and tend to sell only their own brands of beer, although some also offer 'guest' beers. Multiple pub-owning 'pub companies' and venture capital companies account for over 40% of the ownership. The remaining 36% of pubs, called 'free houses', are independently owned and managed—these frequently serve a variety of different branded beers. Wine bars are normally smaller than pubs and tend to specialise in wine and food. 'Themed' pubs, for example Irish bars, are becoming increasingly popular.

TRAVEL AGENTS

Many British holidaymakers travelling overseas buy 'package holidays' from travel agencies, where the cost covers both transport and accommodation. According to a MORI survey in September 2000, the top destination for British package holidaymakers in the previous 12 months was Spain and the Balearics/Canaries with 43% of the total market, followed by Greece and the Greek Islands. Long-haul holidays to places like North America, the Caribbean, Australia and New Zealand have gained in popularity in recent years. Some people prefer more independence, and many travel agents will make just the travel arrangements.

Table 29.9: Spending on Tourism in the UK *£ billion*

	1997	1998	1999
Spending by:			
Overseas residents			
Visits to the UK	12.24	12.67	12.50
Overseas fares to UK carriers	3.05	3.20	3.17
Domestic tourists			
Trips of one night or more	15.07	14.03	16.25
Day trips	22.00	31.30	32.01
Total	**52.36**	**61.20**	**63.93**

Source: British Tourist Authority

In 2000 turnover in the travel agency and tour operator businesses amounted to £16.8 billion, 5.3% higher than in 1999. Around 80% of high street travel agencies are members of the Association of British Travel Agents (ABTA) (*www.abta.com*). Although most are small businesses, a few large firms have hundreds of branches. The Association's over 600 tour operators and 2,300 travel agency companies have over 7,000 offices and are responsible for the sale of more than 90% of UK-sold package holidays. ABTA operates financial protection schemes to safeguard its members' customers and maintains codes of conduct drawn up with the Office of Fair Trading. It also offers a free consumer affairs service to help resolve complaints against members, and a low-cost independent arbitration scheme for members' customers. The British Incoming Tour Operators Association (*www.bitoa.co.uk*) represents the commercial and political interests of incoming tour operators and suppliers to the British inbound tourism industry.

TOURISM AND LEISURE

Tourism is one of the UK's key long-term growth sectors, with total spending in 1999 estimated at £64 billion (see Table 29.9). In Great Britain there were an estimated 2.1 million jobs in tourism and related activities in March 2001. Some 553,000 were in bars, public houses and nightclubs; 539,000 in restaurants and cafés; 383,000 in sport and other recreational activities; 376,000 in hotels and other tourist accommodation; 146,000 in travel agencies and tour operators; and 88,000 in libraries, museums and other cultural activities. Of the total, around 166,000 were self-employment jobs. The bulk of tourism services are provided by some 127,800 mainly independent small businesses such as hotels and guest houses, restaurants, holiday homes, caravan and camping parks. In all about 7% of small businesses are engaged in tourism.

The outbreak of foot-and-mouth disease in February 2001 (see chapter 26) had a severe impact on the tourism industry in many parts of the UK. With large areas of the countryside in effect out of bounds to visitors, many holiday bookings and leisure trips were cancelled. Overseas visitor numbers have been affected too—they were down an estimated 5.5% in the second quarter of 2001 compared with a year earlier. It is too early to say what the overall impact of the outbreak has been on the economy, but the Government has estimated that tourist revenue worth over £5 billion has been lost as a result.

There were an estimated 25.2 million overseas visits to the UK in 2000, generating nearly £12.8 billion. The UK's share of world tourism earnings reached 4.6% in 2000 and ranked fifth behind the United States, Italy, France and Spain. The number of overseas visitors to the UK fell slightly by 1% (see Table 29.10) although spending was 2% higher than in 1999. The number of visitors from North America rose by 6% but those from Western Europe fell by 4%. From all other areas, visitor numbers increased by 5%. Table 29.11 shows that the United States topped the league of overseas visitors to the UK. Business travel accounts for about

Table 29.10: Overseas Visitors to the UK and Overseas Earnings

	1998	1999	2000
All visits (thousands)	25,745	25,394	25,209
of which from:			
North America	4,553	4,599	4,869
Western Europe	16,642	16,081	15,378
Other areas	4,551	4,714	4,961
Total earnings (£ million)	12,671	12,498	12,805

Source: ONS, International Passenger Survey

£4.0 billion, 32% of all overseas tourism revenue. London's Heathrow and Gatwick airports, the seaport of Dover and the Channel Tunnel are the main points of entry.

Some 54% of overseas tourists spend at least half of their visit in London, while others venture further afield to see the many attractions in the English regions as well as in Scotland, Wales and Northern Ireland.

Domestic tourism generated £48 billion in 1999. For British residents opting to take their main holiday in the UK, 23% choose a traditional seaside destination, such as Blackpool, Bournemouth, Eastbourne, Llandudno and resorts in Devon and Cornwall. Short holiday breaks (up to three nights), valued at £3.5 billion in 1999, make up a significant part of the market.

The UK's historic towns and cities and its scenic rural and coastal areas continue to have great appeal for domestic and overseas tourists alike. Their popularity reflects a growing interest in British heritage, arts and culture. There are an estimated 6,100 visitor attractions in the UK. These include museums, art galleries and historic buildings and monuments (together making up just over half the total), cathedrals, gardens, wildlife sites, country parks, farms, steam railways, visitor centres and workplaces, as well as leisure parks and other recreational facilities. Domestic and foreign tourists play an increasingly important role in supporting the UK's national heritage and creative arts, in addition to the large financial contribution they make to hotels, restaurants, cafés and bars, and public transport.

Table 29.11: Top Countries of Origin for Overseas Visitors to the UK, 2000

	Visits ('000)	Spending (£ million)
United States	4,097	2,752
France	3,087	684
Germany	2,758	887
Irish Republic	2,087	570
Netherlands	1,440	374

Source: ONS, International Passenger Survey

Business travel includes attendance at conferences, exhibitions, trade fairs and other business sites. *Activity holidays* are often based on walking, canoeing, mountain climbing, or artistic activities. *Youth Hostel Associations* operate a comprehensive network of hostels—227 in England and Wales, 77 in Scotland and eight in Northern Ireland—offering young people and families a range of facilities, including self-catering.

Theme parks attract over 35 million visitors a year. Alton Towers (Staffordshire) was the biggest in terms of visitor numbers in 1999, and was the top UK attraction charging admission (see Table 29.12). Attractions in these parks include spectacular 'white knuckle' rides and overhead cable cars and railways, while some also feature domesticated and wild animals. The largest tourist attraction in 1999 with free admission was Blackpool Pleasure Beach in Lancashire (see Table 29.13). The Millennium Dome in Greenwich, London, attracted just over 6.5 million visitors in the 12 months it was open in 2000.

Tourism Promotion

Tourism in England is the responsibility of the Department for Culture, Media and Sport, and the Scottish Parliament, Welsh Assembly and Northern Ireland Assembly

Table 29.12: Top UK Tourist Attractions Charging Admission

Visitors, *million*

	1998	1999
Alton Towers, Staffordshire	2.78	2.65
Madame Tussaud's, London	2.77	2.64
Tower of London	2.55	2.42
Natural History Museum, London	1.90	1.74
Legoland, Windsor	1.51	1.62
Chessington World of Adventures, Surrey	1.65	1.55
Science Museum, London	1.60	1.48
Royal Academy, London	0.91	1.39
Canterbury Cathedral	1.50	1.35
Windsor Castle, Berkshire	1.50	1.28
Westminster Abbey, London	n.a.	1.27
Edinburgh Castle	1.22	1.22
Flamingo Land Theme Park, North Yorkshire	1.11	1.20
Drayton Manor Park, Staffordshire	1.00	1.17
Windermere Lake Cruises, Cumbria	1.06	1.14

n.a. = not applicable.
Source: British Tourist Authority

Table 29.13: Top UK Free Tourist Attractions, 1999

Visitors, *million*

Blackpool Pleasure Beach	7.2[1]
British Museum, London	5.5
National Gallery, London	5.0
Palace Pier, Brighton	3.7[1]
Segaworld, The Trocadero, London	3.5
Eastbourne Pier	2.8[1]
Pleasureland, Southport	2.5[1]
Peter Pan's Adventure Island, Southend	2.0[1]
Tate Gallery, London	1.8
York Minster	1.8[1]
Pleasure Beach, Great Yarmouth	1.5[1]
Hampton Court Gardens, London	1.2[1]
Kelvingrove Art Gallery and Museum, Glasgow	1.1
Chester Cathedral	1.0[1]
National Portrait Galley, London	1.0

[1] Estimated visitor numbers.
Source: British Tourist Authority

have responsibility for tourism in their respective countries. The government-supported British Tourist Authority (BTA) (*www.britishtouristauthority.org*), which is receiving £35.5 million grant-in-aid in 2001–02, promotes Britain through its network of 27 overseas offices, located in markets offering the best potential return and covering 88% of all visitors to Britain. There are separate national tourist boards—in England the English Tourism Council (ETC)—which support domestic tourism and work with the BTA to promote Britain overseas. The ETC is to receive a planned £9.6 million grant-in-aid in 2001–02.

The Government is working with the tourism industry to raise standards of accommodation and service, and to address certain key issues facing the industry. These include: improving visitor attractions; boosting business tourism; encouraging best practice for the development of workforce skills; and government-industry communication. The Government is also considering how best to support tourism growth which is economically, socially and environmentally sustainable. The BTA and the national tourist boards inform and advise the Government on issues of concern to the industry. They also help businesses and other organisations to plan by researching and publicising trends affecting the industry. The national tourist boards work closely with regional tourist boards, on which local government and business interests are represented. There are 561 local Tourist Information Centres in England, 78 in Wales, 141 in Scotland and 26 in Northern Ireland. The national tourist boards, in conjunction with motoring organisations, operate accommodation classification and quality grading schemes.

EXHIBITION AND CONFERENCE CENTRES

The UK is one of the world's three leading countries for international conferences—along with the United States and France. London and Paris are the two most popular conference cities. Many British towns and cities—including several traditional seaside holiday

Table 29.14: UK Exhibitions and Attendance[1]

	1998	1999	2000
Number of events	843	817	868
Number of visitors (thousand)	10,994	10,096	11,082
Visitors per exhibition	13,042	12,357	12,767

[1] Excludes one-day public events; covers only venues of 2,000 sq m and over.
Source: Association of Exhibition Organisers

resorts diversifying to take advantage of the growing business tourism market—have conference and exhibition facilities.

Among the most modern purpose-built centres are the National Exhibition and International Conference Centres in Birmingham, celebrating 25 years' opening in 2001; the Queen Elizabeth II and Olympia Conference Centres, both in London; Cardiff International Arena; and the Belfast Waterfront Hall. In Scotland, Edinburgh, Glasgow and Aberdeen have major exhibition and conference centres. Brighton (East Sussex), Harrogate (North Yorkshire), Bournemouth (Dorset), Manchester, Nottingham and Torquay (Devon) all have exhibition and conference centres. Other important exhibition facilities in London are at the Barbican, Earls Court, Alexandra Palace and Wembley Arena. A new exhibition and conference centre, ExCel, costing £240 million, opened in London Docklands in November 2000, with an initial area of 90,000 sq m.

The Association of Exhibition Organisers (*www.aeo.org.uk*) estimates that between 1995 and 1999 exhibitor spending grew by 5% a year to £1.75 billion.

RENTAL SERVICES

A varied range of rental services, many franchised, are available throughout the UK. These include hire of cars and other vehicles; televisions, video recorders and camcorders; household appliances such as washing machines; tools and heavy decorating equipment (such as ladders and floor sanders); and video films and computer games. Retailing of many types of service is dominated by chains, although independent operators are still to be found in most fields. In December 2000 there were 162,000 employee jobs in the UK in the rental sector, with turnover in 2000 amounting to £16.8 billion, 6.2% higher than in 1999.

COMPUTING SERVICES

The computing software and services industry comprises businesses engaged in software development; systems integration; IT consultancy; IT 'outsourcing'; processing services; and the provision of complete computer systems. It also includes companies that provide IT education and training; independent maintenance; support, contingency planning and recruitment; and contract staff. In December 2000 there were 451,000 employee jobs in the UK in computer and related activities. Turnover of companies in this sector amounted to £41.0 billion in 2000, 12.5% higher than in 1999. British firms and universities have established strong reputations in software R&D. A number of international IT conglomerates, such as Microsoft, have set up R&D operations in the UK. Academic expertise is especially evident in such areas as artificial intelligence, neural networks, formal programming for safety-critical systems, and parallel programming systems.

Software firms have developed strengths in sector-specific applications, including systems for retailing, banking, finance and accounting, the medical and dental industries, and the travel and entertainment industries. Specialist 'niche' markets in which UK software producers are active include artificial intelligence, scientific and engineering software (especially computer-aided design), mathematical software, geographical information systems, and data visualisation packages. Some firms specialise in devising multimedia software. Distance learning, 'virtual reality' and computer animation all benefit from a large pool of creative talent.

One of the biggest users of software is the telecommunications industry (see p. 284).

The provision of almost all new telecommunications services, including switching and transmission, is dependent on software.

A special survey by ONS in July 2001 estimated the size of the computer services market in Great Britain in 2000 as £32.0 billion (including exports). Table 29.15 below shows a breakdown of the activities. There was a further £5.4 billion of sales activity in non-computer (but related) services, the largest of which were wholesaling or retailing of goods (£3.1 billion), and telecommunications services (£1.2 billion).

Table 29.15: Computer Services Sales by Service Type, Great Britain, 2000 *£ million*

IT consultancy	7,687
Facilities management	5,407
Systems integration	4,190
Software maintenance	3,403
Packaged applications	3,402
Custom applications	2,875
Information services	1,789
Hardware maintenance	1,758
Non-applications	1,071
Disaster recovery	317
Other	53
Total	**31,951**

Source: Office for National Statistics

OTHER BUSINESS ACTIVITIES

In December 2000 a total of 182,000 employee jobs in Great Britain were in market research, business and management consultancy activities, and turnover in 2000 amounted to £145.8 billion, 5.0% higher than in 1999 (see box on p. 510 for legal services and accountancy).

Market Research

According to the British Market Research Association (*www.bmra.org.uk*), members' turnover grew by 7.1% in 2000 to an estimated £1.07 billion, following growth of 9.3% in 1999. UK-owned market research companies—600 are operating now—include the largest international customised market research specialists. The top ten companies by turnover are shown in Table 29.16 below.

Table 29.16: Top Ten UK Market Research Companies by Turnover *£ million*

Company	1999	2000
Taylor Nelson Sofres	101.7	110.1
NOP Research Group	70.3	68.1
Research International	60.4	64.7
Millward Brown International	58.4	64.5
NFO Worldgroup	38.8	43.4
BMRB International	36.0	39.5
Ipsos-RSL	34.3	39.3
Information Resources	24.7	30.9
MORI	21.2	26.9
Maritz TRBI	24.1	24.8

Source: British Market Research Association

Management Consultancy

The UK's 40,000 management consultants supply technical assistance and advice to business and government clients. In 2000 revenues for the industry were estimated at over £7 billion, with exports in excess of £1 billion. The 40 members of the Management Consultancies Association (*www.mca.org.uk*), which accounts for over half of UK revenues, earned a record income of £3,721 million, 21% higher than in 1999 (see Table 29.17).

Advertising and Public Relations

The UK is a major centre for creative advertising, and multinational corporations often use advertising created in the UK for marketing their products globally. British agencies have strong foreign links through overseas ownership and associate networks. According to the Advertising Association (*www.adassoc.org.uk*), advertising expenditure in the UK increased by 10.4% to £17 billion in 2000. The press accounted for 50.6% of the total, television for 27.3%, direct mail for 12.1%, and posters, transport, commercial radio, cinema and the Internet for the rest.

Table 29.17: Management Consultancy Income *£ million*

	1999	2000
UK fee income	**2,498**	**3,207**
of which:		
Outsourcing	871	797
Strategy	325	490
IT systems development	316	469
IT consultancy	285	465
Financial systems	210	389
Production management	151	218
Human resources	72	151
Project management	172	119
Marketing	56	61
Economic/environmental	40	48
Overseas fee income	**578**	**514**
TOTAL	**3,076**	**3,721**

Source: Management Consultancies Association

Table 29.18: Top Ten Advertisers in the UK in 2000

Advertiser	Total expenditure (£ million)
Procter & Gamble	121.2
British Telecom	107.5
COI Communications	102.7
Renault	70.7
L'Oréal	59.8
Vauxhall Motors	57.1
Ford Motor Company	55.8
Van den Bergh Foods	51.7
British Sky Broadcasting	47.9
Vodafone	47.8

Source: *Advertising Statistics Yearbook 2001—ACNielsen-MMS*

The largest advertising expenditure is on food, household durables, cosmetics, office equipment, motor vehicles and financial services. The top ten spenders in 2000 are shown in Table 29.18. British television advertising receives many international awards.

Campaigns are planned by around 1,600 advertising agencies. In addition to their creative, production and media-buying roles, some agencies offer integrated marketing services, including consumer research and public relations. Many agencies have sponsorship departments, which arrange for businesses to sponsor products and events, including artistic, sporting and charitable events.

Government advertising campaigns—on crime prevention, health promotion, armed services recruitment and so on—are often organised by COI Communications (see p. 543), an executive agency of the Government.

The UK's public relations industry has developed rapidly, and there are now many small specialist firms as well as some quite large ones. The Public Relations Consultants Association (*www.prca.org.uk*) represents 80% of the UK sector, with over 160 member firms, employing 6,500 people, and generates over £350 million a year in net fee income.

Business Support Services

One of the major growth areas in the services sector is in support services, reflecting the trend among more and more firms to 'outsource' non-core operations. Initially, operating areas that were outsourced or contracted out were in cleaning, security and catering. However, firms are now outsourcing other activities, such as IT and personnel support services.

Further Reading

Competition in UK Banking: A Report to the Chancellor of the Exchequer. HM Treasury. The Stationery Office, 2000.
Modern Markets: Confident Consumers. Cm 4410. The Stationery Office, 1999.
Bank of England Annual Report. Bank of England.
Financial Services Authority Annual Report. FSA.

E-commerce

Electronic commerce ('e-commerce') can cover trading in any electronic form, but is particularly used to cover sales and transactions using the Internet. The impact of the Internet and e-commerce has been acknowledged to be considerable, particularly for the long term, but until recently it has been difficult to assess its impact accurately as statistics have been relatively limited. However, the Office for National Statistics is now producing statistics on the use of, and access to, the Internet (see below and p. 286) and in May 2001 issued the first national statistics on e-commerce by UK business. The latter were compiled from a survey of 9,000 businesses with ten or more employees, and covered a representative sample of most of the UK economy.

The results of this first survey indicated that in 2000 there were nearly £57 billion of sales in the UK made over the Internet, representing 2% of total sales by the sectors surveyed. When all electronic networks (including electronic data interchange and other computer systems) were taken into account, sales were almost £162 billion, 5.8% of sales. The finance and insurance sector had the largest value of e-commerce sales (an estimated £43.7 billion),[1] followed by the wholesale, retail, catering and travel sector (£7.6 billion). Most sales over the Internet were 'business to business', with less than one-fifth of e-commerce sales being to households.

The survey found that 92% of UK businesses use personal computers, workstations or terminals and 63% have access to the Internet, ranging from 94% of the largest businesses with over 1,000 employees to 59% of firms with 10 to 49 employees. Of businesses with Internet access, 57% gain access through ordinary 'dial-up' telephone connections, 39% enter through high-speed digital (ISDN) lines and 10% through broadband connections.[2]

The National Statistics Omnibus Survey, conducted in July 2001, found that 51% of adults in Great Britain have accessed the Internet (see p. 286). Among the activities undertaken by adults for personal use were finding information about goods or services (74% of users); buying or ordering tickets, goods or services (35%); and personal banking, financial or investment activities (27%).

The Government is keen to ensure that the UK benefits fully from the growth of the Internet and e-commerce. Its e-commerce strategy, being taken forward by the Office of the e-Envoy (within the Cabinet Office), aims to make the UK a leading e-commerce nation, ensure universal access to the Internet within the UK by 2005 and provide all government services online by the same date; some 40% were online in February 2001. As part of this strategy, the Government's website has been expanded and was officially relaunched in February 2001. The site, *www.ukonline.gov.uk*, is a portal for more than 1,000 government department and agency websites, which together receive over 20 million 'hits' a week.

The Government is planning a new regulatory framework for the electronic communications sector (see chapter 17). It is also encouraging broadband access for both individuals and businesses, and in February 2001 announced a new £30 million fund over the next three years to support innovative schemes to meet local broadband requirements.

[1] As no sales data are held by ONS for much of the financial sector, 'turnover' from administrative sources was used to supplement the percentages supplied by business and produce the estimates. Accordingly, the estimates for e-commerce in the financial sector have to be treated with caution.

[2] As some businesses have more than one connection, these do not total 100%.

Appendix 1: Government Departments and Agencies

Below is an outline of the principal functions of the main government departments and a list of their executive agencies. An asterisk before a department's name shows that it is headed by a Cabinet minister. Executive agencies are normally listed under the relevant department, although in some cases they are included within the description of the department's responsibilities.

The main contact address, telephone number, fax number and website of each department are also given. The *Civil Service Year Book* contains more detailed information.

A new single point of entry to government information and services using the Internet went online in December 2000. The UK online Citizen Portal—www.ukonline.gov.uk—gives the public simple access to links to more than 1,000 official websites.

The work of many of the departments and agencies covers the United Kingdom as a whole and is indicated by (UK). Where this is not the case, the abbreviations used are (GB) for functions covering England, Wales and Scotland; (E, W & NI) for those covering England, Wales and Northern Ireland; (E & W) for those covering England and Wales; and (E) for those concerned with England only.

*Cabinet Office

70 Whitehall, London SW1A 2AS
Tel: 020 7270 3000 Fax: 020 7270 0618
Website: www.cabinet-office.gov.uk
The responsibilities of the Cabinet Office are described on p. 60.

Executive Agency

Government Car and Despatch Agency

*Prime Minister's Office

10 Downing Street, London SW1A 2AA
Tel: 020 7930 4433
Website: www.number-10.gov.uk
See p. 59 for further information.

UK TERRITORIAL DEPARTMENTS

*Northern Ireland Office

Castle Buildings, Stormont, Belfast BT4 3SG
Tel: 028 9052 0700 Fax: 028 9052 8473
11 Millbank, London SW1P 4QE
Tel: 020 7210 3000 Fax: 020 7210 8254
Website: www.nio.gov.uk

Through the Northern Ireland Office, the Secretary of State for Northern Ireland has direct responsibility for political and constitutional matters, law and order, security, and electoral matters.

Executive Agencies

Compensation Agency
Forensic Science Agency of Northern Ireland
Northern Ireland Prison Service

For the Northern Ireland Executive, see p. 543.

*Scotland Office

Dover House, Whitehall, London SW1A 2AU
Tel: 020 7270 6754 Fax: 020 7270 6812
Website: www.scottishsecretary.gov.uk
Represents Scottish interests within the UK Government in matters that are reserved to the UK Parliament under the terms of the Scotland Act 1998. Promotes the devolution settlement by encouraging cooperation, between both the parliaments and between the UK Government and the Scottish Executive, or otherwise intervenes as required by the Scotland Act.

For the Scottish Executive, see p. 545.

*Wales Office

Gwydyr House, Whitehall, London SW1A 2ER
Tel: 020 7270 0549 Fax: 020 7270 0568
Website: www.walesoffice.gov.uk

The Secretary of State for Wales is the member of the UK Cabinet who takes the lead in matters connected with the Government of Wales Act 1998. The Secretary of State is responsible for consulting the Assembly on the Government's legislative programme.

For the National Assembly for Wales, see p. 546.

ECONOMIC AFFAIRS

***Department of Trade and Industry**
1 Victoria Street, London SW1H 0ET
Tel: 020 7215 5000 Fax: 020 7222 0612
Website: www.dti.gov.uk
Competitiveness; enterprise, innovation and productivity; science, engineering and technology; markets; the legal and regulatory framework for business and consumers. Specific responsibilities include innovation policy; regional industrial policy and some aspects of the Regional Development Agencies (E); small business (E); spread of management best practice; business/education links (E); employment relations; international trade policy; energy policy; company law; insolvency; radio regulation; patents and copyright protection; import and export licensing; relations with specific business sectors.

Executive Agencies

Companies House
Employment Tribunals Service
Insolvency Service
National Weights and Measures Laboratory
Patent Office
Radiocommunications Agency
Small Business Service

British Trade International (see p. 421) is a body jointly funded by DTI and the Foreign & Commonwealth Office.

Office of Manpower Economics (OME)

Oxford House, 76 Oxford Street,
London W1N 9FD
Tel: 020 7467 7244 Fax: 020 7467 7248
Website: www.ome.uk.com
The Office of Manpower Economics is a non-statutory body providing a secretariat for the six public-sector Pay Review Bodies which deal with: school teachers; nurses; doctors and dentists; senior civil servants and the judiciary; the armed forces; and prison officers. It also serves the Police Negotiating Board and the Police Advisory Board, and carries out a range of studies into Civil Service pay levels and other related pay matters.

*HM Treasury

Parliament Street, London SW1P 3AG
Tel: 020 7270 5000 Fax: 020 7270 5653
Website: www.hm-treasury.gov.uk
Oversight of the framework for monetary policy; tax policy; planning and control of public spending; government accounting; the quality and cost-effectiveness of public services; increasing productivity and expanding economic and employment opportunities; promoting international financial stability and the UK's economic interests; the regime for supervision of financial services, management of central government debt and supply of notes and coins (UK).

HM Customs and Excise

New King's Beam House, 22 Upper Ground,
London SE1 9PJ
Tel: 020 7620 1313
Website: www.hmce.gov.uk
A department reporting to the Chancellor of the Exchequer. Responsible for collecting and accounting for Customs and Excise revenues, including VAT (value added tax); agency functions, including controlling certain imports and exports, policing prohibited goods, and compiling trade statistics (UK).

ECGD (Export Credits Guarantee Department)

PO Box 2200, 2 Exchange Tower, Harbour Exchange Square, London E14 9GS
Tel: 020 7512 7000 Fax: 020 7512 7649
Helpline: 020 7512 7887
Website: www.ecgd.gov.uk
A department reporting to the Secretary of State for Trade and Industry. Access to bank finance and provision of insurance for UK project and capital goods exporters against the risk of not being paid for goods and services; political risk insurance cover for UK investment overseas (UK).

Office of Fair Trading

Fleetbank House, 2–6 Salisbury Square,
London EC4Y 8JX
Tel: 020 7211 8000 Fax: 020 7211 8800
Website: www.oft.gov.uk
A non-ministerial department, headed by the Director General of Fair Trading. Administers a wide range of competition and consumer protection legislation, with the overall aim of protecting the economic welfare of consumers and enforcing UK competition policy (UK).

Regional Co-ordination Unit

Regional Co-ordination Unit (Operations)

2nd Floor, Riverwalk House, 157–161 Millbank, London SW1P 4RR
Tel: 020 7217 3595 Fax: 020 7217 3590
Website: www.rcu.gov.uk
Strategy development, corporate relations and business development for the nine Government Offices for the Regions (see p. 11). (E)

Inland Revenue

Somerset House, Strand, London WC2R 1LB
Tel: 020 7438 6622 Fax: 020 7438 6971
Website: www.inlandrevenue.gov.uk
A department reporting to the Chancellor of the Exchequer responsible for the administration and collection of direct taxes and valuation of property (GB).

Executive Agencies

National Insurance Contributions Office
Valuation Office

National Savings

Charles House, 375 Kensington High Street, London W14 8SD
Tel: 020 7605 9300 Fax: 020 7605 9438
Website: www.nationalsavings.co.uk
A department in its own right and an executive agency reporting to the Chancellor of the Exchequer. Aims to raise funds for the Government by selling a range of investments to personal savers (UK).

Royal Mint

Llantrisant, Pontyclun CF72 8YT
Tel: 01443 222111 Fax: 01443 623190
Website: www.royalmint.com
The Royal Mint is responsible for the production of coins for the United Kingdom and overseas customers. It also produces military and civilian decorations and medals, commemorative medals, and royal and official seals. The Mint manufactures special proof and uncirculated quality coins in gold, silver and other metals, as well as accessories such as paperweights and jewellery.

LEGAL AFFAIRS

***Lord Chancellor's Department**
Selborne House, 54–60 Victoria Street, London SW1E 6QW
Tel: 020 7210 8500 Website: www.lcd.gov.uk
Responsibility for procedure and administration of the Crown Court, the Supreme Court and county courts and a number of tribunals under the Court Service; overseeing the locally administered magistrates' courts; work relating to judicial appointments; overall responsibility for the Community Legal Service and criminal legal aid and for the promotion of general reforms in the civil law (E & W); policy on and funding for marriage and relationship support; sponsor department for the Children and Family Court Advisory and Support Service (CAFCASS); freedom of information and data protection; human rights issues; Royal, Church and hereditary issues and Lords Lieutenants and Crown Dependencies. The Lord Chancellor also has responsibility for the Northern Ireland Court Service.

Executive Agencies

Court Service
Public Guardianship Office

Two sister departments—HM Land Registry and the Public Record Office—fall under the Lord Chancellor's responsibility and are run on executive agency lines (see p. 543).

Legal Secretariat to the Law Officers

Attorney-General's Chambers, 9 Buckingham Gate, London SW1E 6JP
Tel: 020 7271 2400 Fax: 020 7271 2430
Website: www.lslo.gov.uk
Supporting the Law Officers of the Crown (Attorney-General and Solicitor-General) in their functions as the Government's principal legal advisers (E, W & NI).

Treasury Solicitor's Department

Queen Anne's Chambers, 28 Broadway, London SW1H 9JS
Tel: 020 7210 3000 Fax: 020 7210 3004
Website: www.treasury-solicitor.gov.uk
A department in its own right and an executive agency reporting to the Attorney-General. Provides legal services to most government departments, agencies, and public and quasi-public bodies. Services include litigation; giving general advice on interpreting and applying the law; instructing Parliamentary Counsel (part of the Cabinet Office) on Bills and drafting subordinate legislation; and providing conveyancing services and property-related legal work (E & W).

Crown Prosecution Service

50 Ludgate Hill, London EC4M 7EX
Tel: 020 7796 8000 Fax: 020 7796 8651
Website: www.cps.gov.uk
Responsible for deciding independently whether criminal proceedings begun by the police should be continued, and for prosecuting those cases it decides to continue (E & W). The CPS is headed by the Director of Public Prosecutions, who is accountable to Parliament through the Attorney-General.

Serious Fraud Office

Elm House, 10–16 Elm Street, London WC1X 0BJ
Tel: 020 7239 7272 Fax: 020 7837 1689
Website: www.sfo.gov.uk
Investigating and prosecuting serious and complex fraud. The Director of the SFO is accountable to Parliament through the Attorney-General. (E, W & NI).

The Crown Office and Procurator Fiscal Service (see p. 546).

EXTERNAL AFFAIRS AND DEFENCE

*Ministry of Defence

Main Building, Horseguards Avenue, London SW1A 2HB
Tel: 020 7218 9000 Fax: 020 7218 6460
Website: www.mod.uk
Defence policy and control and administration of the Armed Services (UK).

Defence Agencies

Armed Forces Personnel Administration
Army Base Repair Organisation
Army Personnel Centre
Army Training and Recruiting Agency
British Forces Post Office
Defence Analytical Services Agency
Defence Aviation Repair Agency
Defence Bills Agency
Defence Communication Services Agency
Defence Dental Agency
Defence Estates
Defence Geographic and Imagery Intelligence Agency
Defence Housing Executive
Defence Intelligence and Security Centre
Defence Medical Training Organisation
Defence Procurement Agency
Defence Science and Technology Laboratory
Defence Secondary Care Agency
Defence Storage and Distribution Agency
Defence Transport and Movements Agency
Defence Vetting Agency
Disposal Sales Agency
Duke of York's Royal Military School
Hydrographic Office
Logistics Information Systems Agency
Medical Supply Agency
Meteorological Office
Ministry of Defence Police
Naval Manning Agency
Naval Recruiting and Training Agency
Pay and Personnel Agency
Queen Victoria School
RAF Personnel Management Agency
RAF Training Group
Service Children's Education
War Pensions Agency
Warship Support Agency

*Foreign & Commonwealth Office

King Charles Street, London SW1A 2AH
Tel: 020 7270 3000
Website: www.fco.gov.uk
The Foreign & Commonwealth Office provides, through its staff in the UK and through its diplomatic missions abroad, the means of communication between the British Government and other governments and international governmental organisations on all matters falling within the field of international relations. It is responsible for alerting the British Government to the implications of developments overseas; for promoting British interests overseas; for protecting British citizens abroad; for explaining British policies to, and cultivating relationships with, governments overseas; for the discharge of British responsibilities to the Overseas Territories; for entry clearance (through the Joint Entry Clearance Unit, with the Home Office) and for promoting British business overseas (jointly with the Department of Trade and Industry through British Trade International).

Executive Agency

Wiston House Conference Centre (Wilton Park)

*Department for International Development

94 Victoria Street, London SW1E 5JL
Tel: 020 7917 7000 Fax: 020 7917 0019
(from January 2002: 1 Palace Street, London SW1E 5HE)
Website: www.dfid.gov.uk

Responsibility for promoting international development and the reduction of extreme poverty globally; managing the UK's programme of assistance to poorer countries and for ensuring that government policies which affect developing countries, including the environment, trade, investment and agricultural policies, take account of developing countries' issues.

SOCIAL AFFAIRS, THE ENVIRONMENT AND CULTURE

*Department for Culture, Media and Sport

2–4 Cockspur Street, London SW1Y 5DH
Tel: 020 7211 6200 Fax: 020 7211 6032
Website: www.culture.gov.uk
The Department has an overall interest in the arts, public libraries and archives, museums and galleries, tourism, sport and the built heritage in England—in Scotland, Wales and Northern Ireland these are the responsibility of the devolved administrations. The Department also has overall responsibility for the film industry and for alcohol and public entertainment licensing in England and Wales. The Department has UK-wide responsibility for broadcasting, press regulation, creative industries, public lending right, gambling and the National Lottery, censorship and video classification, and planning for the Queen's Golden Jubilee celebrations in 2002. However, the devolved administrations have some operational responsibilities in some of these areas.

Executive Agencies

Historic Royal Palaces
Royal Parks

*Department for Education and Skills

Sanctuary Buildings, Great Smith Street, London SW1P 3BT
Tel: 020 7925 5000 Fax: 020 7925 6000
Website: www.dfes.gov.uk
Overall responsibility for school, college and university education (E); student support (E & W); youth and adult training policy and programmes (E).

*Department for Environment, Food and Rural Affairs

Nobel House, 17 Smith Square, London SW1P 3JR
Tel: 020 7270 3000
Website: www.defra.gov.uk
Responsible for government policies on sustainable development and the environment; agriculture, horticulture, fisheries and food; rural development; the countryside; animal welfare and hunting.

Executive Agencies

Central Science Laboratory
Centre for Environment, Fisheries and Aquaculture Science
Pesticides Safety Directorate
Rural Payments Agency
Veterinary Laboratories Agency
Veterinary Medicines Directorate

*Department for Transport, Local Government and the Regions

Eland House, Bressenden Place, London SW1E 5DU
Tel: 020 7944 3000
Website: www.dtlr.gov.uk
Policies for planning; housing; regeneration; local and regional government; roads; local transport (E); shipping (E); railways (GB); aviation, including the Civil Aviation Authority (UK); and the fire service.

Executive Agencies

Driver and Vehicle Licensing Agency
Driving Standards Agency
Fire Service College
Health and Safety Executive and Commission
Highways Agency
Maritime and Coastguard Agency
Planning Inspectorate
Queen Elizabeth II Conference Centre
Rent Service
Vehicle Certification Agency
Vehicle Inspectorate

*Department of Health

Richmond House, 79 Whitehall, London SW1A 2NL
Tel: 020 7210 3000 Fax: 020 7210 5661
Website: www.doh.gov.uk
National Health Service; personal social services provided by local authorities; and all other health issues, including public health matters and the health consequences of environmental and food issues (E). Represents UK health policy interests in the EU and the World Health Organisation.

Executive Agencies

Medical Devices Agency
Medicines Control Agency

NHS Estates
NHS Pensions Agency
NHS Purchasing and Supplies Agency

*Home Office

50 Queen Anne's Gate, London SW1H 9AT
Tel: 020 7273 4000 Fax: 020 7273 2190
Website: www.homeoffice.gov.uk
Administration of justice; criminal law; treatment of offenders, including probation and the prison service; the police; crime prevention; regulation of firearms and dangerous drugs; the UK Anti-Drugs Co-ordination Unit; the voluntary sector; electoral law; work permits; passports, immigration and nationality; race relations; responsibilities relating to the Channel Islands and the Isle of Man.

Executive Agencies

Forensic Science Service
HM Prison Service
United Kingdom Passport Agency

*Department for Work and Pensions

Richmond House, 79 Whitehall,
London SW1A 2NS
Tel: 020 7238 3000 Fax: 020 7238 0831
Website: www.dwp.gov.uk
Responsible for welfare and pensions; employment and disability issues (GB).

Executive Agencies

Benefits Agency
Child Support Agency
Jobcentre Plus (from October 2001—see p. 153)

REGULATORY BODIES

Financial Services Authority

25 The North Colonnade, Canary Wharf,
London E14 5HS
Tel: 020 7676 1000 Fax: 020 7676 1099
Website: www.fsa.gov.uk
Regulatory body for the whole of the financial services industry (see p. 510) (UK).

National Lottery Commission

Ashley House, 2 Monck Street,
London SW1P 2BQ
Tel: 020 7227 2000 Fax: 020 7227 2005
Website: www.natlotcomm.gov.uk
See p. 123 .

Office of Gas and Electricity Markets (Ofgem)

9 Millbank, London SW1P 3GE
Tel: 020 7901 7000 Fax: 020 7901 7066
Website: www.ofgem.gov.uk
Ofgem regulates the gas and electricity industries in England, Scotland and Wales (see p. 500).

Strategic Rail Authority (SRA)

55 Victoria Street, London SW1H 0EU
Tel: 020 7654 6000 Fax: 020 7654 6010
Website: www.sra.gov.uk
See p. 368.

Office of the Rail Regulator (ORR)

1 Waterhouse Square, 138–142 Holborn,
London EC1N 2TQ
Tel: 020 7282 2000 Fax: 020 7282 2040
Website: www.rail-reg.gov.uk
See p. 368.

Office for Standards in Education (OFSTED)

Alexandra House, 33 Kingsway,
London WC2B 6SE
Tel: 020 7421 6800 Fax: 020 7421 6707
Website: www.ofsted.gov.uk
See p. 134.

Office of Telecommunications (OFTEL)

50 Ludgate Hill, London EC4M 7JJ
Tel: 020 7634 8700 Fax: 020 7634 8943
Website: www.oftel.gov.uk
OFTEL is the independent regulator for the UK telecommunications industry (see p. 285).

Office of Water Services (OFWAT)

Centre City Tower, 7 Hill Street,
Birmingham B5 4UA
Tel: 0121 625 1300 Fax: 0121 625 1400
Website: www.ofwat.gov.uk
See p. 507.

OTHER OFFICES AND AGENCIES

COI Communications

Hercules Road, London SE1 7DU
Tel: 020 7928 2345 Fax: 020 7928 5037
Website: www.coi.gov.uk

A department in its own right and an executive agency reporting to the Minister for the Cabinet Office. Main responsibilities are procuring publicity material and other information services on behalf of government departments, agencies and other public sector clients (UK).

Information Commissioner's Office

Wycliffe House, Water Lane, Wilmslow, Cheshire SK9 5AF
Tel: 01625 545745 Fax: 01625 524510
Website: www.dataprotection.gov.uk
The Data Protection Act 1998 sets rules for processing personal information and applies to some paper records as well as those held on computers. It is the Commissioner's duty to compile and maintain the register of data controllers and provide facilities for members of the public to examine the register; promote observance of the data protection principles; and disseminate information to the public about the Act. The Commissioner also has the power to produce codes of practice and is responsible for freedom of information.

HM Land Registry

32 Lincoln's Inn Fields, London WC2A 3PH
Tel: 020 7917 8888 Fax: 020 7955 0110
Website: www.landreg.gov.uk
An executive agency responsible to the Lord Chancellor. Main purpose is to register title to land in England and Wales, and to record dealings once the land is registered. It grants guaranteed title to interests in land for 18 million registered titles, providing a system for the transfer and mortgage of land and access to up-to-date and authoritative information (E & W).

Office for National Statistics

1 Drummond Gate, London SW1V 2QQ
Tel: 020 7533 5888 Fax: 01633 652747
Website: www.statistics.gov.uk
A government department and an executive agency accountable to the Chancellor of the Exchequer. The Director is National Statistician and Registrar General for England and Wales (see p. 63).

Ordnance Survey

Romsey Road, Southampton SO16 4GU
Tel: 023 8079 2000 Fax: 023 8079 2615
Customer helpline: 08456 05 05 05
Website: www.ordsvy.gov.uk
An executive agency, which reports to the Secretary of State for Transport, Local Government and the Regions, providing official surveying, mapping and associated scientific work covering Great Britain and some overseas countries (GB).

Public Record Office

Ruskin Avenue, Kew, Richmond, Surrey TW9 4DU
Tel: 020 8876 3444 Fax: 020 8878 8905
Website: www.pro.gov.uk
The National Archives: a government department reporting to the Lord Chancellor. Responsible for the records of the central government and courts of law dating from the 11th century. Advises government departments on the selection of records for preservation and makes records available to the public (UK).

NORTHERN IRELAND EXECUTIVE

Website: www.northernireland.gov.uk

Office of the First Minister and Deputy First Minister

Castle Buildings, Stormont, Belfast BT4 3SR
Tel: 028 9052 8400
Economic policy; equality; human rights; executive secretariat; liaison with the North/South Ministerial Council, British-Irish Council, British-Irish Intergovernmental Conference and Civic Forum. Liaison with the Northern Ireland Office on excepted and reserved matters. European affairs; international matters; liaison with the International Fund for Ireland; the Executive Information Service; community relations; Programme for Government; public appointments policy; honours; freedom of information; victims; Nolan standards; women's issues; policy innovation; public service improvement.

Department of Agriculture and Rural Development

Dundonald House, Upper Newtownards Road, Belfast BT4 3SB
Tel: 028 9052 0100
Food; farming and environment policy; agri-food development; veterinary matters; Science Service; rural development; forestry; sea fisheries; rivers.

Executive Agencies

Forest Service
Rivers Agency

Department of Culture, Arts and Leisure

Interpoint, 20–24 York Street, Belfast BT15 1AQ
Tel: 028 9025 8825
Arts and culture; sport and leisure; libraries and museums, Armagh Planetarium; Ulster Historical Foundation; inland waterways; inland fisheries; Ordnance Survey; Public Record Office; language policy; Lottery matters; visitor amenities.

Department of Education

Rathgael House, Balloo Road, Bangor, County Down BT19 7PR
Tel: 028 9127 9279
Control of the five education and library boards and education from nursery to secondary education; youth services; and the development of community relations within and between schools.

Department for Employment and Learning

39–49 Adelaide House, Adelaide Street, Belfast BT2 8FD
Tel: 028 9025 7777
Higher education; further education; vocational training; employment services; employment law and labour relations; teacher training and teacher education; student support and postgraduate awards; training grants.

Executive Agency

Training and Employment Agency

Department of Enterprise, Trade and Investment

Netherleigh House, Massey Avenue, Belfast BT4 2JP
Tel: 028 9052 9900
Economic development policy; industry, Industrial Development Board and Local Enterprise Development Unit; research and development, tourism; Health and Safety Executive; Employment Medical Advisory Service; company regulation; consumer affairs; energy policy; Minerals and Petroleum Unit; NICO; company training grants schemes, Company Development Programme and Explorers.

Executive Agency

Industrial Research and Technology Unit

Department of the Environment

Clarence Court, 10–18 Adelaide Street, Belfast BT2 8GB
Tel: 028 9054 0540
Most of the Department's functions are carried out by executive agencies. These include: planning; protection and conservation of the natural and built environment; and driver and vehicle testing and licensing. Core departmental functions include: the improvement and promotion of road safety and supporting a system of local government which meets the needs of citizens and taxpayers.

Executive Agencies

Driver and Vehicle Licensing (Northern Ireland)
Driver and Vehicle Testing Agency
Environment and Heritage Service
Planning Service

Department of Finance and Personnel

Rathgael House, Balloo Road, Bangor, County Down BT19 7NA
Tel: 028 9127 9657
Control of public expenditure; personnel management of the Northern Ireland Civil Service; provision of central services and advice.

Executive Agencies

Business Development Service
Construction Service
Government Purchasing Agency
Land Registers of Northern Ireland
Northern Ireland Statistics and Research Agency
Rates Collection Agency
Valuation and Lands Agency

Department of Health, Social Services and Public Safety

Castle Buildings, Stormont, Belfast BT4 3SJ
Tel: 028 9052 0500
Health and personal social services; public health and public safety.

Executive Agencies

Health Estates Agency
Health Promotion Agency

Department for Regional Development

Clarence Court, 10–18 Adelaide Street, Belfast BT2 8GB
Tel: 028 9054 0540

Main functions include: strategic planning; transport strategy; transport policy and support, including rail and bus services, ports and airports policy; provision and maintenance of roads; and water and sewerage services.

Executive Agencies

Roads Service
Water Service

Department for Social Development

Churchill House, Victoria Square,
Belfast BT1 4SD
Tel: 028 9056 9100 Fax: 028 9056 9240
Departmental functions include: urban regeneration; voluntary and community sector; housing; social policy and legislation; social security; child support; state, occupational and personal pensions; policy and legislation.

Executive Agencies

Northern Ireland Child Support Agency
Northern Ireland Social Security Agency

SCOTTISH EXECUTIVE

The Scottish Executive

St Andrew's House, Edinburgh EH1 3DG
Tel: 0131 556 8400 Fax: 0131 244 8240 (for all departments)
Website: www.scotland.gov.uk
The Scottish ministers and Scottish Executive are responsible in Scotland for a wide range of statutory functions. These are administered by six main departments (see below). Along with Corporate Services, Finance and Central Services Department, and the Crown Office and Procurator Fiscal Service, these departments are collectively known as the Scottish Executive. In addition, there are a number of other Scottish departments for which Scottish ministers have some degree of responsibility: the department of the Registrar General for Scotland (the General Register Office), the National Archives of Scotland and the department of the Registers of Scotland. Other government departments with significant Scottish responsibilities have offices in Scotland and work closely with the Scottish Executive.

Scottish Executive Environment and Rural Affairs Department

Pentland House, 47 Robbs Loan,
Edinburgh EH14 1TY
Agriculture and food: safeguarding public food, plant and animal health and welfare; land use and forestry; livestock subsidies and commodities. Coordination of the Executive's policy on the promotion of rural development and overall responsibility for land reform. Environment, including environmental protection, nature conservation and the countryside; water and sewerage services; sustainable development. Fisheries and aquaculture; protection of the marine environment. Funding of the agricultural and biological science base.

Executive Agencies

Scottish Agricultural Science Agency
Scottish Fisheries Protection Agency
Fisheries Research Service

Scottish Executive Development Department

Victoria Quay, Edinburgh EH6 6QQ
Housing and area regeneration, social justice (including equality, voluntary and social inclusion issues); transport and local roads, National Roads Directorate; land-use planning; building control.

Scottish Executive Education Department

Victoria Quay, Edinburgh EH6 6QQ
Administration of public education; science and technology; youth and community services; the arts; libraries; museums; galleries; Gaelic; broadcasting and sport. Protection and presentation to the public of historic buildings and ancient monuments. Also responsible for taking forward Executive policy on Modernising Government across the public sector in Scotland.

Executive Agencies

Historic Scotland
Scottish Public Pensions Agency
The Student Awards Agency for Scotland

Scottish Executive Enterprise and Lifelong Learning Department

Meridian Court, Cadogan Street, Glasgow G2 7AB and Europa Building, 450 Argyle Street,
Glasgow G2 8LG
Industrial and economic development: responsibility for selective financial and regional development grant assistance to industry; for the promotion of industrial development and for matters relating to energy policy; urban

regeneration and training policy. The Department is also responsible for policy in relation to Scottish Enterprise, Highlands and Islands Enterprise and the Scottish Tourist Board. Lifelong learning: further and higher education; student support; youth and adult training; transitions to work; development of the Scottish University for Industry (learndirect scotland) and individual learning accounts; science.

Scottish Executive Health Department

St Andrew's House, Regent Road,
Edinburgh EH1 3DG
Executive leadership of NHSScotland and the development and implementation of health and community care policy, in particular: improving, protecting and monitoring the health of the people of Scotland, implementing policies which address health inequalities, prevent disease, prolong life and promote and protect health; developing and delivering modern primary care and community care services; providing hospital and specialist services; encouraging collaboration and joint working between health and other partner organisations; and promoting and monitoring consistent standards of performance throughout NHSScotland.

Scottish Executive Justice Department

Saughton House, Broomhouse Drive,
Edinburgh EH11 3XD
Central administration of law and order (including police service, criminal justice and licensing, access to justice and legal aid, the Scottish Court Service and the Scottish Prison Service); civil law, fire, home defence and civil emergency services, judicial appointments and the European Convention on Human Rights.

Executive Agencies

Scottish Court Service
Scottish Prison Service

Corporate Services

16 Waterloo Place, Edinburgh EH1 3DN
Human resources including personnel policy, propriety, recruitment, staff appraisal and interchange, pay, employee relations, training and development, equal opportunities and welfare. estate management, accommodation services, internal communications, IT facilities and security matters. Organisational management and development and the Civil Service Reform agenda.

Finance and Central Services Department

Matters relating to powers and functions of the Scottish Parliament and Executive; constitutional policy, Scottish Parliament elections; local government; Europe and external relations; finance; analytical services; Information Directorate and the Office of the Solicitor to the Scottish Executive.

The Crown Office and Procurator Fiscal Service

25 Chambers Street, Edinburgh EH1 1LA
Tel: 0131 226 2626 Fax: 0131 226 6910
Website: www.crownoffice.gov.uk
The Crown Office and Procurator Fiscal Service provides Scotland's independent public prosecution and deaths investigation service. Although it is a Department of the Scottish Executive, the independent position of the Lord Advocate as head of the systems of criminal prosecution and investigation of deaths in Scotland is protected by the Scotland Act 1998.

NATIONAL ASSEMBLY FOR WALES

National Assembly for Wales Cynulliad Cenedlaethol Cymru

Cathays Park, Cardiff CF10 3NQ and Cardiff Bay, Cardiff CF99 1NA
Tel: 029 2082 5111 Fax: 029 2082 3807
Website: www.wales.gov.uk
www.cymru.gov.uk (yn Gymraeg).
The National Assembly for Wales (see p. 28) is responsible for many aspects of Welsh affairs, including agriculture, forestry and fisheries; education; health and personal social services; local government; Welsh language and culture, including the arts, museums and libraries. Also responsible for housing; water and sewerage; environmental protection; the countryside and nature conservation; sport; land use, including town and country planning; transport issues; tourism; training and enterprise; economic development, business support and regional selective assistance to industry. The Assembly is also responsible for over 50 public bodies which discharge functions in these areas in Wales.

Executive Agencies

Cadw: Welsh Historic Monuments
Wales European Funding Office

Appendix 2: Obituaries

Douglas Adams
Author
Born 1952, died May 2001

Sir Campbell Adamson
Director-General of the Confederation of British Industry, 1969–76; chairman of Abbey National, 1978–91
Born 1922, died August 2000

Jean Anderson
Actress
Born 1907, died April 2001

H. N. (Andy) Andrews, DFM and Bar
Wartime fighter pilot
Born 1920, died September 2000

Gertrude Elizabeth Margaret Anscombe
Professor of Philosophy, Cambridge, 1970–86
Born 1919, died January 2001

Duke of Argyll (Ian Campbell; 12th duke)
Chief of Clan Campbell and restorer of Inveraray Castle
Born 1937, died April 2001

Henry Wilfred (Bunny) Austin
Tennis player; last British player to reach men's singles final at Wimbledon (1938)
Born 1916, died August 2000

Joseph Bamford, CBE
Creator of the JCB digger
Born 1916, died March 2001

Rosa Beddington
Developmental biologist
Born 1956, died May 2001

John Bond, LVO
Horticulturist
Born 1932, died February 2001

Alan Boon
Publisher
Born 1913, died July 2000

Muriel Bowen
Journalist and horsewoman
Born 1926, died August 2000

Professor Sir Malcolm Bradbury
Novelist and critic
Born 1932, died November 2000

Baroness Brooke of Ystradfellte, DBE
(Barbara)
Joint vice-chairman of the Conservative Party, 1954–64
Born 1908, died September 2000

John Bury, OBE
Theatre designer
Born 1925, died November 2000

Ken Cameron, OBE
Sound engineer, responsible for Second World War film soundtracks; founding director, Anvil Films
Born 1915, died August 2000

George Carman, QC
Barrister
Born 1929, died January 2001

Lord Cledwyn of Penhros, CH
(Cledwyn Hughes)
Leader of Opposition in House of Lords, 1982–92
Born 1916, died February 2001

Lord Cocks of Hartcliffe
(Michael Francis Lovell)
Labour chief whip in House of Commons, 1976–85
Born 1929, died March 2001

Sir Colin Cole, KCB, KCVO
Garter Principal King of Arms, 1978–92
Born 1922, died February 2001

Russ Conway
Popular pianist
Born 1925, died November 2000

Professor Robert Manuel Cook, FBA
Classical archaeologist
Born 1909, died August 2000

John Cooper, CBE
Automobile engineer
Born 1923, died December 2000

Malcolm Cooper, OBE
Olympic rifle-shooting champion
Born 1947, died June 2001

Lord Cowdrey of Tonbridge, CBE (Colin)
Kent and England cricketer
Born 1932, died December 2000

Sir Julian Critchley
Journalist, author, former Conservative MP
Born 1930, died September 2000

Stanley Cullis
Footballer and former manager of Wolverhampton Wanderers
Born 1915, died February 2001

Paul Daneman
Actor
Born 1925, died April 2001

Baroness Denton of Wakefield, CBE
(Jean Moss)
Rally driver and former Conservative minister
Born 1935, died February 2001

Donald Dewar
First Minister of Scottish Executive, MP and MSP
Born 1937, died October 2000

John Diamond
Journalist and broadcaster
Born 1953, died March 2001

Sir Antony Duff, GCMG, DSO, DSC
Submarine commander and diplomat
Born 1920, died August 2000

Nancy Evans, OBE
Mezzo-soprano
Born 1915, died August 2000

Kenneth Fleet
Financial journalist
Born 1929, died August 2000

Sir Richard Foster
Director of National Museums and Galleries on Merseyside
Born 1941, died March 2001

Judy Fryd, CBE
Founder of Mencap
Born 1909, died October 2000

Nicholas Georgiadis, CBE
Stage designer
Born 1923, died March 2001

Sir Alistair Grant
Businessman and retailer
Born March 1937, died January 2001

Lord Greenhill of Harrow, GCMG, OBE
(Denis Arthur)
Head of Diplomatic Service, 1969–73
Born 1913, died November 2000

Bruce Gyngell
TV executive
Born 1929, died September 2000

Nicholas Geoffrey Lemprière Hammond, CBE, DSO, FBA
Classical scholar and authority on ancient Greece
Born 1907, died March 2001

Lord Harmar-Nicholls, Bt
(Sir Harmar Nicholls)
Former Conservative MP and MEP
Born 1912, died September 2000

Lord Harris of Greenwich (John Henry)
Liberal Democrat chief whip in House of Lords, 1994–2001
Born 1930, died April 2001

Lord Hartwell, MBE, TD (Michael Berry)
Proprietor of *Daily Telegraph*, 1954–85
Born 1911, died April 2001

Adrian Hastings
Theologian
Born 1929, died May 2001

Walter Hayes
Former newspaper editor, sports car enthusiast and chairman of Aston Martin
Born 1924, died December 2000

Ronnie Hilton
Popular singer
Born 1927, died February 2001

Ken Hughes
Film director
Born 1922, died April 2001

Rita Hunter
Operatic soprano
Born 1933, died April 2001

Air Vice-Marshal Johnnie Johnson, CB, CBE, DSO & two bars, DFC & bar
Fighter ace
Born 1915, died January 2001

Betty Kenward, MBE
Society columnist (*Jennifer's Diary*)
Born 1906, died January 2001

Professor Tom Kilburn, CBE, FRS
Computer pioneer
Born 1921, died January 2001

Peter Kilner
Arabist
Born 1928, died December 2000

Hyman Kreitzman
Retailing pioneer
Born 1914, died May 2001

Sir Denys Lasdun, CH, CBE
Architect
Born 1914, died January 2001

Sir Frederick Lawton, QC
Lord Justice of Appeal, 1972–86
Born 1911, died February 2001

Jimmy Logan, OBE
Comedian, actor and impresario
Born 1928, died April 2001

Sir Patrick Lowry, CBE
Industrial relations expert
Born 1920, died May 2001

Professor Henry Royston Loyn, FSA, FBA
Historian
Born 1922, died November 2000

Fr Herbert McCabe, OP
Theologian
Born 1926, died June 2001

Kirsty MacColl
Singer and songwriter
Born 1959, died December 2000

Lord Mackay of Ardbrecknish
(John Jackson Mackay)
Deputy Leader of Opposition in House of Lords
Born 1938, died February 2001

Professor Sir Leslie Martin, RA
Architect
Born 1908, died July 2000

Eric Morley
Impresario
Born 1918, died November 2000

Jack Morpurgo
Professor of American Literature, Leeds University, 1969–83; publisher and author
Born 1918, died October 2000

Lord Morris of Castle Morris
(Brian Robert)
Academic, writer and editor
Born 1930, died April 2001

Frank Newby
Engineer
Born 1926, died May 2001

Lord Onslow of Woking
(Cranley Gordon Douglas)
Conservative MP and chairman of 1922 Committee, 1984–92
Born 1926, died March 2001

Hugh Paddick
Actor
Born 1915, died November 2000

Gilbert Parkhouse
Glamorgan and England cricketer
Born 1925, died August 2000

Rt Rev. Simon Phipps, MC
Bishop of Lincoln, 1974–86
Born 1921, died January 2001

Sir Antony Pilkington
Glassmaker
Born 1935, died September 2000

Lady Plowden, DBE (Bridget Horatia)
Chairman, Independent Broadcasting Authority, 1975–80; Chairman, Central Advisory Council for Education, England (1963–66)
Born 1910, died September 2000

Lord Plowden (Edwin Noel)
Economic adviser
Born 1907, died February 2001

Sir Fred Pontin
Founder of Pontin's holiday camps
Born 1906, died September 2000

Nyree Dawn Porter, OBE
Actress
Born 1940, died April 2001

Pat Pottle
Anti-war campaigner
Born 1938, died October 2000

Lord Prentice (Reg)
Former Labour cabinet minister who switched to the Conservatives in 1977 and served as Minister for the Disabled, 1979–81
Born 1923, died January 2001

Dame Ruth Railton, DBE
Founder of National Youth Orchestra of Great Britain
Born 1915, died February 2001

Sarah Raphael
Painter
Born 1960, died January 2001

Simon Raven
Author
Born 1927, died May 2001

Sir Harold Ridley, FRS
Ophthalmic surgeon
Born 1906, died May 2001

Professor Edward Calverley Riley
Hispanist and expert on Cervantes
Born 1923, died March 2001

Alan Ross
Editor of the *London Magazine*
Born 1922, died February 2001

Hon. Sir Steven Runciman, CH, FBA
Scholar, linguist, Byzantinist
Born 1903, died November 2000

Baroness Ryder of Warsaw, CMG, OBE (Sue)
Charity worker and organiser; founder of Sue Ryder homes
Born 1923, died November 2000

Lorna Sage
Literary critic and scholar
Born 1943, died January 2001

Peggie Scriven (Margaret Vivian)
Tennis player
Born 1912, died January 2001

Sir Harry Secombe, CBE
Comedian, singer and writer
Born 1921, died April 2001

Sir Jimmy Shand, MBE
Scottish country bandleader
Born 1908, died December 2000

Lord Sieff of Brimpton, OBE
(Marcus Joseph)
Former chairman of Marks & Spencer
Born 1913, died February 2001

Joan Sims
Actress
Born 1930, died June 2001

Stan Smith
Artist
Born 1929, died January 2001

Sebastian Snow
Explorer of South America
Born 1929, died April 2001

Sir Richard Southern, FBA
Historian; formerly Chichele Professor of Medieval History at Oxford
Born 1912, died February 2001

Sir David Spedding, KCMG, CVO, OBE
Chief of Secret Intelligence Service, 1994–99
Born 1943, died June 2001

Anthony Steel
Actor
Born 1920, died March 2001

Alec Stock
Football manager
Born 1917, died April 2001

Anthony Storr
Psychiatrist and writer
Born 1920, died March 2001

Catherine Storr
Author
Born 1913, died January 2001

Sidney Sutcliffe
Oboist
Born 1918, died July 2001

Duke of Sutherland, TD
(John Sutherland Egerton; 6th duke)
Landowner and art collector
Born 1915, died September 2000

David Sylvester, CBE
Art critic
Born 1924, died June 2001

Godfrey Talbot, CVO, OBE
Broadcaster and royal correspondent
Born 1908, died September 2000

Rev. Ronald Stuart Thomas
Poet
Born 1913, died September 2000

Kathleen Tillotson
Literary critic, editor and academic
Born 1906, died June 2001

Joan Trimble
Pianist
Born 1915, died August 2000

Brian Trubshaw, CBE, MVO
Test pilot
Born 1924, died March 2001

Sir Anthony Tuke
Banker
Born 1920, died March 2001

Alan Tyson, CBE
Musicologist, psychoanalyst and translator
Born 1926, died November 2000

Dame Ninette de Valois, OM, CH, DBE
(Edris Stannus, Mrs Connell)
Founder and director of the Royal Ballet
Born 1898, died March 2001

Kyra Vayne
Operatic soprano
Born 1916, died January 2001

Bernard Venables, MBE
Angler and writer
Born 1907, died April 2001

Rosemary Verey
Plantswoman, gardener, writer
Born 1918, died May 2001

Lewis Edgar Waddilove, CBE
Former Director of Joseph Rowntree Memorial Trust (1946–79), the UK's largest independent social policy charity
Born 1914, died August 2000

Jack Walker
Businessman and owner of Blackburn Rovers Football Club
Born 1929, died August 2000

Jack Watling
Actor
Born 1923, died May 2001

Colin Watson
Obituaries editor, *The Times*, 1956–82
Born 1919, died January 2001

Auberon Waugh
Journalist and author
Born 1939, died January 2001

Iain West
Forensic pathologist
Born 1944, died July 2001

Desmond Wilcox
Broadcaster and TV and film producer
Born 1931, died September 2000

Michael Williams
Actor
Born 1935, died January 2001

Thomas Winning
Cardinal Archbishop of Glasgow
Born 1925, died June 2001

Howard Winstone, MBE
Boxer
Born 1939, died September 2000

Audrey Wise, MP
Labour MP
Born 1935, died September 2000

Martin Wright
Biomedical engineer—inventor of the breathalyser
Born 1912, died March 2001

Ted Wright, MBE
Archaeologist
Born 1918, died May 2001

Paula Yates
TV presenter
Born 1959, died September 2000

Gavin Young
Foreign correspondent
Born 1928, died January 2001

Muriel Young
TV presenter and producer
Born 1928, died March 2001

Desmond Zwemmer
Publisher and bookseller
Born 1919, died September 2000

Appendix 3: Principal Abbreviations

ACAS: Advisory, Conciliation and Arbitration Service

ACE: Arts Council of England

ACW: Arts Council of Wales

AIDS: Acquired Immune Deficiency Syndrome

AONB: Area of Outstanding Natural Beauty

ASA: Advertising Standards Authority

ASEM: Asia-Europe Meeting

ASSI: Area of Special Scientific Interest

ATMs: Automated teller machines

BAFTA: British Academy of Film and Television Arts

BBC: British Broadcasting Corporation

BBSRC: Biotechnology and Biological Sciences Research Council

bfi: British Film Institute

BL: British Library

BNFL: British Nuclear Fuels

BSC: Broadcasting Standards Commission

BSE: Bovine spongiform encephalopathy

BT: British Telecom

CAA: Civil Aviation Authority

CAF: Charities Aid Foundation

CAP: Common Agricultural Policy

CBI: Confederation of British Industry

CCGT: Combined cycle gas turbine

CCLRC: Council for the Central Laboratory of the Research Councils

CCW: Countryside Council for Wales

CFCs: Chlorofluorocarbons

CFP: Common Fisheries Policy

CFSP: Common Foreign and Security Policy

CHD: Coronary heart disease

CHP: Combined heat and power

CITES: Convention on International Trade in Endangered Species of Wild Fauna and Flora

CJD: Creutzfeldt-Jakob disease (sometimes vCJD—variant Creutzfeldt-Jakob disease)

CO: Carbon monoxide

CO_2: Carbon dioxide

CPS: Crown Prosecution Service

CRE: Commission for Racial Equality

CSA: Child Support Agency

DARD: Department of Agriculture and Rural Development (Northern Ireland)

DCAL: Department of Culture, Arts and Leisure (Northern Ireland)

DCMS: Department for Culture, Media and Sport

DEFRA: Department for Environment, Food and Rural Affairs

DEL: Department for Employment and Learning (Northern Ireland)

DERA: Defence Evaluation and Research Agency

DETI: Department of Enterprise, Trade and Investment (Northern Ireland)

DfES: Department for Education and Skills

DFID: Department for International Development

DH: Department of Health

DNA: Deoxyribonucleic acid

DOE: Department of the Environment (Northern Ireland)

DPP: Director of Public Prosecutions

DRD: Department for Regional Development (Northern Ireland)

DSD: Department for Social Development (Northern Ireland)

DTI: Department of Trade and Industry

DTLR: Department for Transport, Local Government and the Regions

DWP: Department for Work and Pensions

EC: European Community

ECGD: Export Credits Guarantee Department

EEA: European Economic Area

EEBPP: Energy Efficiency Best Practice Programme

EHS: Environment and Heritage Service (Northern Ireland)

EMU: Economic and monetary union

EOC: Equal Opportunities Commission

EP: English Partnerships

EPSRC: Engineering and Physical Sciences Research Council

ERDF: European Regional Development Fund

ERDP: England Rural Development Programme

ESA: Environmentally sensitive area; European Space Agency

ESRC: Economic and Social Research Council

EU: European Union

EUROPOL: European Police Office

FA: Football Association

FCO: Foreign & Commonwealth Office

FSA: Financial Services Authority; Food Standards Agency

G7: Group of seven leading industrial countries

G8: Group of eight leading industrial countries (the G7 members plus Russia)

GCE: General Certificate of Education

GCSE: General Certificate of Secondary Education

GDP: Gross Domestic Product

GLA: Greater London Authority

GM: Genetically modified

GMOs: Genetically modified organisms

GNP: Gross National Product

GNVQ: General National Vocational Qualification

GOs: Government Offices (for the Regions)

GP: General Practitioner

HIV: Human Immuno-deficiency Virus

HSC: Health and Safety Commission

HSE: Health and Safety Executive

ICT: Information and communications technology

IEA: International Energy Agency

ILO: International Labour Organisation

IMF: International Monetary Fund

IPC: Integrated Pollution Control

IPPC: Integrated Pollution Prevention and Control

ISA: Individual Savings Account

ISO: International Organisation for Standardisation

ISP: Internet Service Provider

IT: Information technology

ITC: Independent Television Commission

JNCC: Joint Nature Conservation Committee

JSA: Jobseeker's Allowance

km/h: Kilometres per hour

kW: Kilowatt

LEA: Local education authority

LEC: Local enterprise company

LFS: Labour Force Survey

LIFFE: London International Financial Futures and Options Exchange

LPG: Liquefied petroleum gas

LTPs: Local Transport Plans

m (mm, km): Metre (millimetre, kilometre)

MEP: Member of the European Parliament

Ml: Megalitre

MoD: Ministry of Defence

MP: Member of Parliament

mph: Miles per hour

MRC: Medical Research Council

MSP: Member of the Scottish Parliament

mtc: Million tonnes of carbon

MW: Megawatt

NATO: North Atlantic Treaty Organisation

NATS: National Air Traffic Services Ltd

NAW: National Assembly for Wales

NDPBs: Non-departmental public bodies

NERC: Natural Environment Research Council

NETA: New electricity trading arrangements

NFFO: Non-fossil fuel obligation

NGC: National Grid (Company)

NGLs: Natural gas liquids

NHS: National Health Service

NI: Northern Ireland; National Insurance

NICE: National Institute for Clinical Excellence

NIE: Northern Ireland Electricity

NIHE: Northern Ireland Housing Executive

NO_x: Oxides of nitrogen

NSF: National Service Framework

NTOs: National Training Organisations

NVQ: National Vocational Qualification

OECD: Organisation for Economic Co-operation and Development

OFSTED: Office for Standards in Education

OFTEL: Office of Telecommunications

ONS: Office for National Statistics

OSCE: Organisation for Security and Co-operation in Europe

OST: Office of Science and Technology

OTs: Overseas Territories

PEP: Personal Equity Plan

PFI: Private finance initiative

plc: Public limited company

PM_{10}: Particulate matter

PPARC: Particle Physics and Astronomy Research Council

PPC: Pollution Prevention and Control

PPG: Planning Policy Guidance

PPP: Public-Private Partnership

PSA: Public Service Agreement

R&D: Research and development

RAF: Royal Air Force

RDAs: Regional Development Agencies

RECs: Regional electricity companies

RNT: Royal National Theatre

RPG: Regional Planning Guidance

RPI: Retail Prices Index

RPI(X): Retail Prices Index (*ex*cluding mortgage interest payments)

RSC: Royal Shakespeare Company

RSL: Registered social landlord

RSPB: Royal Society for the Protection of Birds

RUC: Royal Ulster Constabulary

SAC: Scottish Agricultural College; Scottish Arts Council

SBS: Small Business Service

SE: Scottish Executive

SEERAD: Scottish Executive Environment and Rural Affairs Department

SEN: Special educational needs

SEPA: Scottish Environment Protection Agency

SERPS: State earnings-related pension scheme

SET: Science, engineering and technology

SIC: Standard Industrial Classification

SIP: Social Inclusion Partnership

SMEs: Small and medium-sized enterprises

SNH: Scottish Natural Heritage

SO_2: Sulphur dioxide

sq km: Square kilometre

SRA: Strategic Rail Authority

SRB: Single Regeneration Budget

SSSI: Site of Special Scientific Interest

SVQ: Scottish Vocational Qualification

TA: Territorial Army

TAC: Total allowable catch

TB: Tuberculosis

TOCs: Train Operating Companies

TUC: Trades Union Congress

UDP: Unitary development plan

UK: United Kingdom of Great Britain and Northern Ireland

UKCS: United Kingdom Continental Shelf

UKSI: United Kingdom Sports Institute

UN: United Nations

US: United States

VAT: Value added tax

V&A: Victoria and Albert Museum

VED: Vehicle excise duty

VOCs: Volatile organic compounds

WDA: Welsh Development Agency

WEU: Western European Union

WFTC: Working Families' Tax Credit

WTO: World Trade Organisation

Appendix 4: Public Holidays, 2002

Tuesday 1 January	New Year Holiday	UK
Wednesday 2 January	Bank Holiday	Scotland only
Monday 18 March	St Patrick's Day	Northern Ireland only
Friday 29 March	Good Friday	UK
Monday 1 April	Easter Monday	England, Wales and Northern Ireland
Monday 6 May	Early May Bank Holiday	UK
Monday 3 June	Golden Jubilee Bank Holiday[1]	UK
Tuesday 4 June	Spring Bank Holiday	UK
Friday 12 July	Orangemen's Day	Northern Ireland only
Monday 5 August	Summer Bank Holiday	Scotland only
Monday 26 August	Summer Bank Holiday	England, Wales and Northern Ireland
Wednesday 25 December	Christmas Day	UK
Thursday 26 December	Boxing Day	UK

[1] Special commemorative holiday for 2002 only.

Note: In addition, there are various traditional local holidays in Scotland which are determined by local authorities there.

Index

A

Aberdeen 4, 22, 68, 140, 264, 343, 375, 533
Aberystwyth 33, 254
Abortion 208
Accidents 210
Accounts Commission for Scotland 70
Acid rain 333–4
Action Teams (employment) 156
Acts of Parliament *see* Legislation
ADAS 464
Adoption of children 164, 171
Adult and Community Learning Fund 144
Adult education 143–4
Advertising 277, 283, 534–5
Advertising Standards Authority 283
Advisory, Conciliation and Arbitration Service 162
Advisory Committee on Business and the Environment 337
Advocate General for Scotland 59, 232
Advocates *see* Legal profession
Aerospace industry 486–7
Africa 88
African, Caribbean and Pacific (ACP) countries 418, 419
Agricultural shows 453–4
Agriculture 88, 152, 446–61
see also Fishing industry; Food; Forestry
Agriculture and Environment Biotechnology Commission 426
Agri-industrial materials 452
Aid *see* Development aid
AIDS 185, 203, 424
Air Force *see* Royal Air Force
Air quality and emissions 330–4, 491, 503
Aircraft and aviation 374–7, 408, 437
see also Aerospace industry; Royal Air Force
Alcohol *see* Drink
Alcohol Concern 204
Aldeburgh 254
Ambulance services 190, 206
Amsterdam Treaty 82, 84, 85
Ancient monuments 322
Anglesey 1
Anglican Churches 238
see also Church of England
Angling 300
Anglo-Irish Agreement (1985) 16
Anguilla 79, 80
Animal welfare 459–61
Anti-social behaviour order 227, 335
Appeals (law) 45, 228, 229, 231
Arable Area Payments Scheme 450
Archbishops' Council 241
Architects and architecture 345
Area Museum Councils 253
Areas of Outstanding Natural Beauty 12, 32, 313, 315
Areas of Special Scientific Interest 319
Armagh 4, 344
Armed forces 99–107
defence agencies 540
Armenian Church 239
Arms control 90–1, 420
Army 101–7
agencies 540
Arrest and detention 220
Art 2001 261
Arts 21, 27, 33, 245, 247–68
Arts & Business 252–3
Arts Councils 248, 249, 250, 251, 252, 253, 254, 262, 264, 265
Artsmark 264
Arvon Foundation 253
Ascension 80
Asia, Central 85–6
Asia-Europe Meeting 87
Asia-Pacific region 87
Assemblies of God 239
Assisted Areas 391
Associated British Ports 373
Associated Northern Ireland Newspapers 282
Association of:
British Insurers 518
British Travel Agents 530
Exhibition Organisers 533
Independent Research and Technology Organisations 443
Investment Trust Companies 521
Unit Trusts and Investment Funds 520
Astronomy *see* Space science and equipment
Asylum 113–14, 182
Athletics 290, 300
Atomic energy *see* Nuclear power
Attendance Allowance 180
Attorney-General 59, 222, 539
Auction houses 261
Audit Commission 70, 223
Aviation *see* Aircraft and aviation

B

BAA 375, 376
Back to Work Bonus 176–7
Badminton 300
BAE SYSTEMS 486, 487
Bahá'i movement 241
Bail 224, 229
Balance of payments 410–15
Ballet *see* Dance
Baltic Exchange 523
Banff 261
Bangor 4
Bank of England 386, 509, 512–13
Banking services 288, 509, 511, 513–18
Bankruptcy 397
Baptist Church 238–9, 243
Bar Council 215
Barbican Centre 253, 256
Barcelona Declaration 87
Barristers *see* Legal profession
Basel Convention 326
Basic Skills Agency 144
Basketball 290, 300–1
Bath 4, 296
Bathing waters 329
BBC *see* British Broadcasting Corporation
Beef *see* Livestock and livestock products
Belfast 4, 13, 17, 233, 264, 271, 322, 358, 374, 375, 376, 454, 533
see also Good Friday Agreement
Belize 101
Benefit Fraud Inspectorate 173
Benefits, social security 117–18, 174–83
Benefits Agency 156, 173, 321, 542
Bereavement benefits 179
Bermuda 79, 80
Berwick upon Tweed 261
Betting 277, 299, 408
see also National Lottery
bfi see British Film Institute
Bibliographical Society 262
Billiards 309
Bills, Parliamentary *see* Legislation
Bio Products Laboratory 205
Biodiversity 312, 318, 320, 438

Biological weapons 90
Biotechnology 424, 478
Biotechnology and Biological Sciences Research Council 424, 434, 464
Birds 318, 321
Birmingham 4, 115, 264, 265, 271, 375, 376, 533
Birth rates 108–9, 111
Bisham Abbey 296
Black Rod 45
Blackpool 531
Blood transfusion services 205
Board of Deputies of British Jews 242
Bodleian Library 263
Books 262–4, 475–6
Bosnia and Herzegovina 89
Boston Spa 264
Botanic gardens 320, 438, 444, 464
Boulby 504
Bovine spongiform encephalopathy *see* BSE
Bowls 301
Boxing 290, 301
Bradford 4, 259
Brewing industry 471
Brighton & Hove 4
Bristol 4, 247, 255, 265, 271, 372
Britain Abroad Task Force 96
Britannia Royal Naval College, Dartmouth 106
British Academy 262, 441
British Airways 374–5
British Antarctic Survey 80, 424, 433
British Antarctic Territory 80
British Association for the Advancement of Science 430, 444
British Board of Film Classification 251
British Broadcasting Corporation 96, 258, 269, 270, 271–3, 275, 276, 277, 278
British Cattle Movement Service 459
British Chambers of Commerce 397
British Council 47, 96, 97–8, 251, 442
British Crime Survey 186, 216
British Dental Association 194
British Farm Standard 453
British Film Institute 250–1, 253, 263
British Franchise Association 525
British Geological Survey 433
British Humanist Association 238
British Incoming Tour Operators Association 530
British Indian Ocean Territory 80, 321
British-Irish Council 16–17, 18
British-Irish Intergovernmental Conference 17, 19
British Library 248, 262, 263–4, 283, 401
British Medical Association 194
British Museum 259
British National Space Centre 439, 440, 487
British Nuclear Fuels 502–3
British Olympic Association 294, 298
British Paralympic Association 295
British Satellite News 96
British Screen Finance 253
British Society of Magazine Editors 282
British Sports Trust 294
British Standards Institution 391
British Telecom *see* BT
British Tourist Authority 96, 532
British Trade International 96, 421, 538
British Trust for Ornithology 318
British Virgin Islands 79, 80, 321
British Waterways 372
Broadcasters' Audience Research Board 278
Broadcasting 33, 51, 52, 269–79, 283–4, 292
  see also British Broadcasting Corporation; Radio; Television
Broadcasting Standards Commission 276, 278
Brunei 101
BSE 438, 446, 458, 460
  see also Creutzfeldt-Jakob disease
BT (British Telecom) 284
Buckingham University 141
Buddhism 240, 242
Budget 11, 193, 379, 385, 387–8, 399–400, 404, 407
Building *see* Construction
Building materials 479
Building societies 515
Buildings, listed 321–3
Builth Wells 453, 454
Burrell Collection 27
Bus services 366–7
Business:
  Connect 389
  Development Service 544
  e-commerce 536
  and education 137
  environmental practice 337–8
  finance 389–90
  Links 389, 390, 437
  rates 409
  regulation 397
  structure 383–4
  support services 388–9, 535
  see also Companies; Small business; Sponsorship

C

Cabinet 17, 59–60, 120–1
Cabinet Office 60, 62, 66, 118, 121, 354, 397, 425, 536, 537
Cable services 269, 270, 275–7
Cadw: Welsh Historic Monuments 321, 322, 546
Cambridge 4, 140, 263, 264, 424, 433
Cambridge-MIT Institute 429
Canada 87–8
Canals and waterways 372
Cancer 184–5, 191, 200–1, 433, 443
Canterbury 4, 241
  Archbishop of 44
Capital gains tax 404, 406–7
Capital Modernisation Fund 400
Carbon trust 492
Cardiff 4, 28, 33, 254, 265, 271, 295, 296, 322, 373, 375, 510, 533
CARDS 85
Care Standards Inspectorate for Wales 211
Career development loans 142
Careers 137
Caribbean 87
Carlisle 4
Carnivals 247
Cars *see* Motor vehicles
Catering trade 529
Cattle *see* Livestock
Cayman Islands 80, 321
Census of Population 34–6, 237, 435
Central Arbitration Committee 160
Central Council of Physical Recreation 294
Central Europe *see* Europe, Central and Eastern
Central School of Ballet 265
Central School of Speech and Drama 265
Central Science Laboratory 464, 541
Centre for:
  Ecology and Hydrology 433
  Environment, Fisheries and Aquaculture Science 464, 541
  Genome Research 424
  Polar Observation Modelling 440
Ceramics 479
CERN 441
Certification Officer 161, 162
Chairman of Ways and Means 46
Chancellor of the Duchy of Lancaster 41, 59, 60
Chancellor of the Exchequer 387
Channel Islands 1–2, 18, 40, 42, 43
Channel Navigation Information Service 373
Channel Tunnel 2, 370–1, 531
Channel Tunnel Rail Link 370, 403
Charismatic Movement 239
Charities 121–3, 245–6, 314, 443
Charter Mark 63, 64
Chartered Institute of Patent Agents 215
Chemical weapons 90
Chemicals industry 326, 476–8
Chess 302
Chester 4
Chichester 4
Chief of the Defence Staff 107
Chief Scientific Adviser 425, 428
Chilbolton Observatory 436
Child Benefit 177
Child safety order 227
Child Support Agency 173, 178, 542
Children
  abuse 169
  adoption 164, 171
  childcare 168
  fostering 170
  health and welfare 206–7
  in care 118, 169
  teenage pregnancy 208
  see also Families; Schools

Children's Hearings 169, 231, 232
Children's Tax Credit 405
China 87
Choral music 256–7
Christadelphians 241
Christian Brethren 239
Christian community 238–40
Christian Scientists 241
Church Commissioners 241
Church in Wales 237
Church of England 9, 40, 237, 238, 240, 241, 242–3, 245
Church of Scientology 241
Church of Scotland 237, 241, 243, 246
Church Urban Fund 245–6
Church-state relations 237
Churches Conservation Trust 243
Churches Together in Britain and Ireland 239, 246
Cinema and film 250–1, 253, 254, 258–9, 263, 265, 266
CITES 321, 420
Citizens Advice Bureaux 236, 528
Citizenship 114–15, 401
City Academies 130
City Technology Colleges 130
Civil Aircraft Research and Technology Demonstration Programme 437
Civil Aviation Authority 374, 376–7
Civil Justice Council 229
Civil justice proceedings 228–9, 231–2
Civil law 213
Civil List 41
Civil Procedure Rule Committee 222
Civil Service 60, 65–7
CJD *see* Creutzfeldt-Jakob disease
Classical Swine Fever 460–1
Clergy 242–3
Clerk of the House of Lords/Commons 45, 46
Climate 2–3, 331–3
climate change levy 334, 408–9, 491
Clinical Sciences Centre 432
Clothing industry 473–4
Coach services 367
Coaching, sports 297
Coal industry 490, 498–9
Coasts 12, 32, 117, 329
Cohabitation 110
Cohesion Fund 83, 84
COI Communications 542–3
Combined Cycle Gas Turbines 501
Combined Heat and Power 502
Commando Training Centre, Lympstone 106
Commercial policy 388–96
Commission for Health Improvement 188
Commission for Racial Equality 116–17
Commissioner for Complaints (Northern Ireland) 71
Commissioner for Public Appointments 65
Committee on:
the Medical Aspects of Food and Nutritional Policy 209
the Public Understanding of Science 430
Standards in Public Life 49, 52, 64–5
Commodities (international trade in) 411–12, 413
Common Agricultural Policy 83, 450, 457–8
Common Fisheries Policy 83, 462–3
Common Foreign and Security Policy 81, 82, 84
Common law 213–14
Common Travel Area 182
Commons, House of *see* Parliament
Commonwealth 40, 42, 47, 75–6, 145; map 78
Commonwealth Games 290, 294, 295
Commonwealth of Learning 95
Communicable Disease Surveillance Centre 203
Communications 124, 276, 284–8, 483
Communities Scotland 345, 351, 352, 357
Community Forests 316
Community Learning Scotland 146
Community Legal Service 114, 235, 236
Community Paediatric Service 207
Community sentences 226–7, 231
Companies 396–8
see also Business
Companies House 538
Compensation Agency 537
Competition Commission 284, 395, 513
Competition policy 388, 393–6
Comprehensive Test Ban Treaty 90
Comptroller and Auditor General 402
Computers and computing 124, 482, 533–4
see also Information and communications technology
Confederation of British Industry 162, 397
Conference centres 532–3
Connexions Service 137
Conservation 32, 312–23, 495
see also Sustainable development
Consignia 287–8
Consolidation Bills 56
Constitution 37–8
see also Devolution
Construction 152, 468, 488–9
Construction Service 544
Consumer expenditure 266, 381–2
Consumer protection 527–9
Consumers and the environment 337–8
Consumers' Association 529
Contingencies Fund 57
Conventional Armed Forces in Europe Treaty 90–1
Co-operative Movement 523
Coptic Orthodox Church 239
Copyright 251
Corby 355
Coredeal 522
Cornwall 11, 393
Cornwall, Duchy of 41
Coronary heart disease 185, 201–2
Coroners' courts 228
Corporation tax 404, 405
COST programme 441
Costume, Museum of 260
Council for:
the Central Laboratory of the Research Councils 436
Nature Conservation and the Countryside 315, 319
Professions Supplementary to Medicine 195
Science and Technology 425–6
Council of:
Christians and Jews 246
Europe 79, 92, 279
Science and Technology Institutes 443
Council housing
see social housing
Council tax 70, 404, 409
Council tax benefit 181
Country parks 12, 315
Countryside Agency 11, 12, 312, 313, 315, 316, 356, 367
Countryside Council for Wales 313, 314, 315, 317, 319
Countryside Stewardship 455, 456
County courts 222, 228–9, 233
Couriers, private 288
Court of Appeal 45, 215, 222, 228, 229, 231, 232, 233
Court of Session 215, 231–2
Court Service 222, 539
Courtauld Institute Galleries 260
Courts 27, 217, 223–33
Coventry 4
Crafts 261–2
Creative Industries Task Force 249
Credit cards *see* Plastic cards
Credit unions 516
Creutzfeldt-Jakob disease 210–11
see also BSE
Cricket 289, 290, 298, 302
Crime
international action against 92–3
racially motivated 116
reduction 216–17, 354
statistics 215–16
victims and witnesses 226
wildlife 318–19
see also Drugs misuse and trafficking; Terrorism
Criminal Cases Review Commission 228
Criminal Defence Service 235
Criminal Injuries Compensation Scheme 226
Criminal Justice Consultative Committee 223
Criminal justice proceedings 223–8, 229–31, 233
Criminal law 213
Crofts 448
Crops 450, 451, 452–3
Crown *see* Monarchy
Crown Agent 230
Crown Counsel 230

Crown Court 215, 222, 224–5, 228, 229, 232, 233
Crown Office 230, 546
Crown Prosecution Service 222, 223–4, 540
Croydon Tramlink 371
Crystal Palace 296
Culham 145, 503
Cultural Heritage National Training Organisation 250
Culture 12, 21, 27, 33, 247–68
see also British Council
Culture, Media and Sport, Department for 62, 248–9, 264, 265, 269, 291, 321, 323, 531, 541
Cumbrae 296
Curfew order 227
Curriculum *see under* Schools
Customs and Excise 222, 404, 538
see also Taxes and duties
Cycling 289, 302–3, 365
Cyprus 88, 101

D

Dance 258, 265
Daresbury Laboratory 436
Darwin Initiative 321, 438
Data Assimilation Research Centre 440
Dean Gallery 261
Debit cards *see* Plastic cards
Debt 94, 246, 403
Defence 99–107
see also Aerospace industry; Arms control; North Atlantic Treaty Organisation
Defence, Ministry of 62, 97, 107, 437–8, 540
agencies 540
Defence Science and Technology Laboratory 438, 540
Delegated legislation 52, 54
Dentists and dental treatment 193–4, 198
Derby 4
Design 96, 266, 311, 390
Design, Build, Finance and Operate 363
Detention and training order 227
Development aid 93–6, 418–19
Development plans and control 343–5
Devolution 1, 13, 16–17, 22, 23–5, 28–31, 38, 43
Diet 208–9
Digital broadcasting 270–1, 272, 276, 277
Diplomatic Service 66, 96
Director General of:
Fair Trading 283, 394, 395, 527, 528
Telecommunications 285
Water Services 507
Director of Public Prosecutions 222, 233
Disability Rights Commission 159, 167
Disabled people
and the arts 248
benefits 180–1
employment 155, 159
social services 166–7
and sport 294–5
Discrimination *see* Equality
Diseases 185, 202–3
see also AIDS; Cancer; Creutzfeldt-Jakob disease; Livestock
District courts 230, 231
District judges 215, 225
Divorce 111
DNA analysis 220, 318
Docklands Light Railway 371
Doctors 193–4, 198
Dog fouling 327
Domestic appliances 482
Dounreay 503
Dover 374, 531
Downing Street Declaration 16
Drama 253–4, 255–6, 265, 266
Drigg 336
Drink
alcohol consumption 185–6, 203–4, 217–18, 472
excise duties 408
manufacturing industry 26, 468–72
see also Public houses
Drinking Water Inspectorate 507
Driver and Vehicle Licensing Agency 359, 541
Driver and Vehicle Licensing (Northern Ireland) 544
Driver and Vehicle Testing Agency 364, 544
Driving Standards Agency 363–4, 541
Drugs misuse and trafficking 27, 92–3, 103, 186, 204–5, 217–18, 227, 234, 298
Drugs Prevention Advisory Service 218
Duke of Edinburgh's Award scheme 146
Dundee 4, 22, 68, 220, 254
Durham 264
Bishop of 44
Duxford 260

E

e-commerce 390, 536
e-science 432
Early English Text Society 262
Early Years Directorate 168
Earnings *see* Pay
East England 11, 12, 117, 148
East Midlands 12, 375, 468
Eastern Europe *see* Europe, Central and Eastern
Eco-Management and Audit Scheme 337
Ecolabelling 337–8
Economic and monetary union 82, 385
Economic and Social Research Council 435
Economy 11, 20–1, 25–6, 32, 117–18, 379–98
Edinburgh 4, 22, 25, 27, 68, 140, 230, 231, 254, 256, 258, 260, 264, 265, 320, 322, 343, 375, 424, 430, 444, 453, 464, 510, 533
Education 21, 27, 95, 126–47, 245, 264–7, 272, 399–400, 442–3
see also Training
Education Action Zones 130
Education and library boards 126, 128
Education and Skills, Department for 62, 70, 127, 264, 265, 354, 426, 541
Education Maintenance Allowance 138
Elections
European Parliament 9, 17, 25, 31, 73–4
local government 9, 10, 68–9
National Assembly for Wales 30–1
Northern Ireland Assembly 16
Scottish Parliament 24
Westminster Parliament 9, 17, 37, 45, 46–8, 49, 50
Electoral Commission 46, 49, 50, 51
Electrical and optical equipment 482–3
Electricity supply 499–503
Electronics 26, 482–3
Elim Pentecostal Church 239
Ely 4
Embryology 208
Emigration 111
Employers' organisations 162
Employment 20, 26, 32, 70, 119, 148–63, 193, 379, 385, 446, 468, 471, 509
see also Pay; Training; Welfare-to-Work programme
Employment agencies 156–7
Employment Direct 154
Employment Opportunities Fund 154
Employment Service 153, 156
Employment Tribunals Service 160, 538
Employment Zones 155–6
Endangered species 321, 420
Energy 333, 334, 490–508
see also coal, electricity, gas and other types of energy
Energy Efficiency Best Practice Programme 337, 492–3
Energy Saving Trust 493
Engineering 423–45
Engineering and Physical Sciences Research Council 432–3, 441
Engineering Council 443
England 7–12; maps 8, 10
England Rural Development Programme 455
English Association 262
English Heritage 243, 321, 322
English Institute of Sport 296
English National Ballet 258, 265
English National Opera 257
English Nature 312, 313, 314, 317, 319
English Partnerships 341, 354, 355

English Sports Council *see* Sport England
English Tourism Council 532
Enterprise Fund 389
Enterprise Grant scheme 392
Enterprise Insight 398
Environment 11–12, 32–3, 95–6, 456–7, 495
see also Conservation; Countryside; Environmental protection; Planning; Pollution control; Sustainable development
Environment, Food and Rural Affairs, Department for 62, 312, 317, 319, 323, 333, 334, 338, 354, 372, 438, 446, 452, 454, 459, 464, 493, 541
Environment Agency 317, 323, 324, 325, 328, 336, 339
Environment and Heritage Service 314, 322, 323, 328, 339, 544
Environmental:
health 209–11
labelling 337–8
management 337
Pollution, Royal Commission on 324
protection 312–39
research 338–9
Technology Best Practice Programme 337
Environmentally Sensitive Areas 12, 33, 455, 456
Equal Opportunities Commission 121
Equality 19, 66, 115–17, 121, 159, 167
Equestrianism 303
Estate Action 351
Estate Partnership 352
Estyn 134
Ethnic groups 114–17, 221, 247, 281
see also under Religion
Euratom 503
EUREKA 441
Euro, the 82, 385
Euro-Atlantic Partnership Council 85, 100
Euromarket 510, 522
Europe, Central and Eastern 85–6
European Agricultural Guidance and Guarantee Fund 83
European Bank for Reconstruction and Development 79, 85
European Bioinformatics Institute 441
European Central Bank 82
European Community *see* European Union
European Community Youth Orchestra 265
European Convention on Human Rights 19, 79, 92, 214
European Economic Area 83, 112, 211
European Investment Bank 84
European Laboratory for Particle Physics 441
European Meteorological Satellite Organisation 439
European Molecular Biology Laboratory 441
European Patent Convention 431
European Regional Development Fund 83, 393
European Science Foundation 441
European Security and Defence Policy 84–5, 100
European Social Fund 83
European Southern Observatory 442
European Space Agency 439, 440, 487
European Trade Union Confederation 162
European Union
and Africa 88
agriculture 83, 450, 457–8
arms exports 91
ASEM process 87
broadcasting 278–9
budget 83
and Central and Eastern Europe and Central Asia 85–6, 419
citizenship 81
communications 286
consumer protection 528
Council of the European Union 73, 82
Court of Auditors 74
Court of First Instance 74
defence and security 81, 82, 84–5, 100
economic and monetary union 82, 385
economic reform 84
education programmes 144–5
employment and social affairs 82, 84, 158
energy 491–2, 503
enlargement 82–3
environment 33, 319, 321, 324, 326, 327, 329, 331, 333, 495
European Commission 73, 82
European Council 73
European Court of Justice 74, 82, 214
European Parliament 9, 17, 25, 29, 73, 74, 82
fisheries 83, 461, 462–3
justice and home affairs 81, 85
and Latin America 88, 419
law and legislation 72–4, 213, 214, 396
map 77
and Mediterranean 87, 419
membership 75, 81
regional policy and aid 11, 20, 83–4, 354, 356, 393, 423, 457
research and development 423, 440–1, 491
single European market 83, 395, 417–18
social protection 183
and South Africa 88
trade 417–18
treaties 81–2
and UK Government 72–3
water 507
EUROPOL 85, 93, 219
Evangelical Alliance 240
Examinations *see* Qualifications, educational
Excellence in Cities scheme 130
Excise *see* Customs and Excise
Executive agencies 66–7
Exercise and fitness 208–9, 303
Exeter 4
Exhibition and conference centres 532–3
Export Credits Guarantee Department 85, 422, 538
Exports *see* Trade, international
Eye services 194–5

F

Factoring companies 518
Faculty of Advocates 215
Falkland Islands 80, 81, 101, 114
Families 109–11, 168, 177–9
see also Children; Households
Family Health Services 198–9
Faraday Partnerships 429
Farm holdings 446–7
Farm Woodland Premium Scheme 455, 456–7, 466
Farming *see* Agriculture
Federation of Small Businesses 398
Felixstowe 373, 374
Ferries 373
Festivals 27, 33, 244, 254–5, 257
Field sports 303
Film Council 250–1, 253, 265
Finance and Leasing Association 518
Financial Action Task Force 93
Financial Instrument of Fisheries Guidance 83
Financial services 26, 79, 509–23
Financial Services Authority 349, 510–11, 542
Financial Services Compensation Scheme 511, 517
Financial Stability Forum 386, 512
Fines 227
Fire Service College 541
Fire services 68
Firearms 220–1
First Lord of the Treasury *see* Prime Minister
Fiscal policy 386–7
Fish farming 462
Fisheries Research Service 439, 464, 545
Fishing (angling) *see* Angling
Fishing industry 26, 83, 461–4
Flight, Museum of 260
Flooding 342, 446
Folk music 257
Folkestone 371
Food
eating habits 208–9
exports 453
genetic modification 452–3
manufacturing and processing 468–72
safety 210, 453
see also Catering trade; Output
Food from Britain 453
Food Standards Agency 210, 426, 453
Foot-and-mouth disease 299, 316, 446, 460, 530

Football 33, 124, 289, 290, 292–3, 303–4
Footwear industry 474–5
Foreign & Commonwealth Office 79, 96, 145, 251, 271, 540
Foreign exchange market 509, 522
Foreign Press Association 282
Forensic Science Service 219–20, 222, 542
Northern Ireland 537
Foresight Programme 427–8
Forests and forestry bodies 12, 25, 26, 315, 316, 464–7
Forth 374
Fostering children 170
Foundation for Sport and the Arts 253, 299
Fraud 173
see also Serious Fraud Office
Free Christians 239
Free churches 238, 239–40
Freedom of information 63
Freight transport 366, 370, 372–3
Fresh Start initiative 134
Freshwater fisheries 464
Friendly societies 517
Fringe benefits 157
Fuel *see* Energy
Further education 31, 137–40
see also Vocational education
Futures and options, financial 522–3

G

Gaelic Books Council 262
Gaelic Broadcasting Committee 275
Gaelic Games 304
Gaelic language 27, 134, 270
Gambling *see* Betting
Gas industry 26, 490, 493–8
Gateshead 296
Gatsby Charitable Foundation 429
Gatwick 375, 376, 531
General Certificate of Education 138
General Certificate of Secondary Education 133
General Dental Council 194
General Insurance Standards Council 519
General Medical Council 193–4
General National Vocational Qualification 133, 138
General Optical Council 194
General Register Office for Scotland 34
General Social Care Council 165
General Teaching Councils 136–7
Genetics 424, 434, 452–3
see also Biotechnology; DNA analysis
Genomics Co-ordinating Group 432
Gibraltar 80, 81, 101, 114
Gilt-edged stock 403
Girl Guides 146
Glasgow 4, 22, 27, 68, 140, 217, 230, 231, 247, 256, 264, 265, 271, 343, 357, 371, 375, 510, 533
Glass 478–9
Glenmore Lodge 296
Globe Theatre, South Bank 256
Gloucester 4
Glyndebourne 257
GNVQs
see General National Vocational Qualification
Goldsmiths College of Art 266
Golf 289, 304
Good Friday Agreement (April 1998) 13, 16, 38
Gothenburg Protocol 334
Government
departments and agencies 61, 62, 537–46
HM Government 37, 48, 58–60
ministers 59, 60
modernisation 63–5
origins 38
and pressure groups 72
resignation 57
see also Cabinet; Civil Service; Constitution; Devolution; Local government; Monarchy; Parliament
Government Car and Despatch Agency 537
Government Offices for the Regions 9, 11, 60, 61, 340, 343, 354
Government Purchasing Agency 544
GPs *see* Doctors
Great Ormond Street Hospital 200
Great Seal of the Realm 42
Greater London Authority 1, 9–10, 61, 250, 342, 354
Greater Manchester *see* Manchester
Greek Orthodox Church 239
Green Belts 343
Green Papers 53
Greenhouse effect 331–3, 491
Greyhound racing 304–5
Grimsby and Immingham 373, 374
Grocery trade 524–5
Gross domestic product 11, 20, 22, 32, 117, 266, 379, 380, 382, 383, 399, 425, 468, 509
Group of Seven/Eight 76, 512
Guardian's Allowance 177–8
Guildhall School of Music and Drama 253, 265
Gymnastics 305

H

Habeas corpus 220
Hadley Centre 332, 339
Hansard 46, 52, 56
Harmonised index of consumer prices 384, 385
Harwell 503
Harwich 373
Hatfield 369
Hay-on-Wye 255
Hazardous waste 326–7
Health 95, 184–212
see also Diseases; Medicine; Mental health; National Health Service; Public health; Sickness benefits
Health, Department of 188, 201, 438, 541
Health Action Zones 197, 354
Health and safety at work 162–3
Health and Safety Commission 163, 541
Health and Safety Executive 163, 336, 496, 503, 541
Health and Well-being Partnership Council 190
Health Development Agency 189
Health Education Board for Scotland 190
Health Estates Agency 544
Health Improvement Programmes 190
Health professions 193–5
Health Promotion Agency for Northern Ireland 191, 544
Health Promotion England 189, 207
Health Service Commissioners 196
Health Technology Board for Scotland 191
Health visitors 194, 198–9
Heathrow 375, 376, 531
Heavily Indebted Poor Countries Initiative 94
Hebrides 1, 27
Helicopters 487
Hereford 4
Heritage Coast 12, 32, 317
Heritage Lottery Fund 243, 252, 253, 320, 322
High Court 215, 222, 228, 229, 232, 233
High Court of Justiciary 45, 215, 230–1, 232
Higher education 140–1, 442–3
Higher education funding councils 31, 127, 139, 428, 439
Higher Education Innovation Fund 426
Highland Games 305
Highlands and Islands 393, 448
Highlands and Islands Enterprise 26, 142, 357, 389, 392, 439
Highways Agency 362–3, 541
Hill farming 455, 456
Hindu community 240, 242, 243
Historic Buildings Council 322
Historic Chapels Trust 243
Historic Monuments Council 322
Historic Royal Palaces 323, 541
Historic Scotland 321, 322, 323, 545
Historical Manuscripts Commission 264
History 7, 9, 13–16, 22–3, 28
HIV/AIDS *see* AIDS
Hockey 290, 305
Holidays 124–5, 555
Holme Pierrepont 296
Home Energy Efficiency Scheme 493
Home improvement 351–2
Home Office 62, 116, 216, 542
Home ownership 346–9
Home Secretary 219, 222, 234
Home shopping 527
Home Zones 356, 366
Homelessness 353–4

Hong Kong 87, 114
Honours 41
Horse racing 289, 305–6
Horticulture 450, 452
Horticulture Research International 464
Hospices 206
Hospitals and specialist health services 199–211
Hotels 529
House of Commons/Lords *see* Parliament
Households 11, 109–11, 117–18, 266, 381–2, 513
Housing 341, 345–54, 488
Housing Action Trusts 351
Housing Benefit 181
Housing Corporation 345, 346, 352, 353
Housing Revenue Account 350
HPSSnet 198
Hull 4, 373
Human Fertilisation and Embryology Authority 208
Human Genetics Commission 426
Human Genome Project 424
Human rights 19, 79, 91–2, 94, 214
Humanitarian assistance 96
Hybrid Bills 54

I

Ice hockey 290, 306
Ice skating 306
Immigration 111–14
Immunisation 202–3
Imperial War Museum 260
Imports *see* Trade, international
Improvement and Development Agency 341
Incapacity Benefit 155, 180
Income and expenditure
  household 11, 117–18, 381–2
  taxes on 25, 405–6, 407–9
Income Support 155, 177
Independent Television Commission 269, 273, 276, 277, 278, 283
Individual learning accounts 143
Individual Savings Accounts 405, 521, 522
Industrial associations 397–8
Industrial Development Board 20, 393
Industrial heritage 323
Industrial Injuries Disablement Benefit 181
Industrial policy 388–96
Industrial pollution control 324
Industrial relations 158–62
Industrial research *see* Research and development
Industrial Research and Technology Unit 393, 436, 544
Inflation 379, 380, 384–5
INFORM 241
Information Commissioner's Office 543
Information and communications technology 124, 151, 390
  see also Computers; Internet
Inheritance tax 404, 407
Inland Revenue 222, 404, 539
Inner Cities Religious Council 246
Insolvency Service 397, 538
Institute of:
  Arable Crops Research 424
  Contemporary Arts 254
  Directors 397–8
  Legal Executives 215
  Sports Sponsorship 298
Instrumentation and control equipment 483
Insurance 408, 422, 510, 518–20
Integrated Administration and Control System 458
Intellectual property 251, 431
Inter Faith Network for the United Kingdom 246
Interest rates 386, 512
International Confederation of Free Trade Unions 162
International Criminal Court 92
International Criminal Tribunal 89, 90
International Development, Department for 79, 94–6, 97, 145, 418–19, 438–9, 540–1
International Energy Agency 491
International Financial Services London 510
International Fund for Ireland 20, 358
International Labour Organisation 148
International Monetary Fund 79, 97
International Musical Eisteddfod 33
International Petroleum Exchange 523
International Underwriting Association of London 519
Internet 124, 136, 143, 169, 196, 197, 248, 272, 286–7, 514, 536
INTERPOL 93, 219
Invalid Care Allowance 155
Inverclyde 296
Inverness 4
Invest UK 421–2
Invest to Save 401
Investment 20, 26, 32, 87–8, 369, 382–3, 410–22, 520–1
Investment banks 515
Investment Northern Ireland 393
Investment trusts 520–1
Investors in People 158
Ipswich 373
Iraq 86, 88, 102
Ireland, Northern *see* Northern Ireland
Irish language 21
Irish Republic 16, 18, 47
Ironbridge Gorge 261, 323

J

Jainism 241
Jazz 257, 265
Jehovah's Witnesses 241
Jerwood Foundation 253
Jewish community 240, 242, 243
Job Transition Service 156, 391
Jobcentre Plus 153, 173, 542
Jobseeker's Allowance 149, 153, 176
Joint Infrastructure Fund 428–9
Joint Nature Conservation Committee 312, 314, 318, 330
Joint Research Equipment Initiative 428
Joint Services Command and Staff College 106
Journalists 282
Judges 214–15, 231, 232
Judicial Committee of the Privy Council 42, 215, 232
Judo 306
Juries 225, 226, 230, 232
Justices of the peace 215, 225, 231

K

Keep fit *see* Exercise and fitness
Kew 264, 320, 438, 444
Kittochside 27
Kosovo 89–90, 103
Kyoto Protocol 332–3

L

Laboratory of Molecular Biology 424, 432
Laboratory of the Government Chemist 437
Labour *see* Employment
Labour Force Survey 148, 161
Labour Relations Agency 162
Lancaster 4, 424
Lancaster, Duchy of 41
Land
  access to 316–17
  agricultural 446–8
  pollution control 324–5
  see also Planning
Land Court 232
Land Registers of Northern Ireland 544
Land Registry 539, 543
Landfill tax 325, 408
Landlords and tenants 345, 346, 347, 349–53, 447
Landmines 91
Lands Tribunal 232
Lantra 459
Larne 374
Latin America 88, 419
Law 159, 160, 213–36, 282–3, 396
  see also Legal
Law Commission 223
Law societies 215, 236
learndirect 143
Learned societies 443–4
Learning and Skills Council 127, 137, 138, 144

Learning & Teaching Scotland 136
Learning difficulties, people with 167
Leasing companies 518
Leeds 4, 255, 260, 264, 372, 510
Legal advice and assistance 114, 235–6
Legal profession 215
Legal Secretariat to the Law Officers 539
Legal Services Commission 235
Legal Services Ombudsman 215
Legal systems:
 England and Wales 9, 222–9
 Northern Ireland 20, 232–3
 Scotland 26, 229–32
Legislation 43, 52–4, 55, 56, 213, 229, 232
Leicester 4, 115
Leisure 123–5, 530–2
Libraries 250, 262–4
Lichfield 4
Life expectancy 108, 184
Life imprisonment 226
Lifelong learning 143
Lilleshall 296
Lincoln 4
LINK scheme 428
Literacy 133
Literary societies 262
Literature 262–4
Litter control 327
Liverpool 4, 259, 262, 355, 374, 510
Livestock and livestock products 448–50, 459–61
 see also BSE; Classical Swine Fever; Foot-and-mouth disease
Living standards 117
Llanarthne 444
Llanberis 33, 261
Llangollen 33
Lloyd's 509, 511, 518, 519
Lobby correspondents 63
Lobbying, parliamentary 72
Local Economic Forums 392
Local Enterprise Companies 357, 392
Local Enterprise Development Unit 389, 393
Local government 9–10, 15, 17, 23, 30, 31, 67–71, 250
Local Government Boundary Commissions 49, 69
Local Government Commission 67, 69
Local Government Ombudsmen 71
Local Health Boards 189
Local Health Councils 191
Local Nature Reserves 12
Local Regeneration Fund 356–7
Local Transport Capital Settlement 361
Locate in Scotland 26
London 4, 7, 11, 115, 117, 200, 219, 322, 343, 444, 454, 468, 533
 arts and culture 12, 255, 257, 258, 259–60, 265, 266, 271
 financial markets 509–23
 local government 1, 9–10, 67, 68, 342
 transport and communications 11, 331, 360, 365, 368, 371, 374, 375, 531
London, Bishop of 44
London, Corporation of 219, 253
London, Lord Mayor of 9
London, Museum of 253, 260
London, Tower of 260
London Academy of Music and Dramatic Art 265
London bullion market 523
London Clearing House 523
London Contemporary Dance School 265
London Development Agency 9
London Fire and Emergency Planning Authority 9
London International Film School 265
London International Financial Futures and Options Exchange 522–3
London Market 519
London Metal Exchange 523
London Radio Service 96
London School of Economics 264
London Stock Exchange 509, 511, 520, 521
London Transport Museum 260
London University 264, 266
Londonderry/Derry 4, 233, 344, 358, 374
Lone parents 155
Lord Advocate 230, 232
Lord Chamberlain 41, 42
Lord Chancellor 42, 45, 51, 58, 59, 222, 233
Lord Chancellor's Department 62, 222, 539
Lord Chief Justice 222, 233
Lord Privy Seal 59
Lord Provost 68
Lords, House of *see* Parliament
Lorries *see* Road haulage
Lottery *see* National Lottery
Lowry, The 260
Lutheran Church 239
Luton 375

M

Maastricht Treaty 81, 82, 85
Macedonia 90
Machinery and equipment 480–2
Magistrates 215, 225
Magistrates' courts 224–5, 229, 233
Mail order 527
Man, Isle of 1–2, 18, 40, 42, 43
Management consultancy 510, 534
Manchester 4, 7, 67, 115, 264, 265, 295, 296, 343, 355, 371, 372, 375, 376, 510
Manorial Documents Register 264
Manpower *see* Employment
Manufacturing 20, 26, 32, 152, 468–87
Manufacturing Advisory Service 391
Manuscripts, historical 264
Marine engineering 484–5
Marine environment 330
Maritime and Coastguard Agency 330, 373, 541
Maritime heritage 323
Maritime Trust 323
Market research 534
Marriage 110–11, 244
Martial arts 306
Maternity rights 159, 177
Measurement standards 391, 437
Meat Hygiene Service 453
Media *see* Broadcasting; Press
Medical Devices Agency 542
Medical equipment 483
Medical Research Council 424, 433, 441
Medicine
 complementary 212
 private 211
 safety 211
 sports 294, 297
 see also Health
Medicines Control Agency 197, 541
Mediterranean 87, 419
Mental health 167–8, 185, 202
MEPs *see* European Union: European Parliament
Mergers 395
Merseyside 7, 11, 67, 343, 393
Metal products 479–80
Meteorological Office 332, 339, 540
Methodist Church 238, 240, 243
Metropolitan Police Authority 9, 219
Metropolitan Police Service 219
Middle East 86
Midwives 194, 198–9
Migration 111–14
Milford Haven 374
Millennium Greens 313
Millennium Link 372
Millennium Seed Bank project 320, 444
Minerals (non-energy) 504, 506; map 505
Minimum Income Guarantee 177
Ministers, government *see* Government
Mobile communications 124, 244, 285
Modern Apprenticeships 142
Modernisation Agency 188
Monarchy 7, 37, 39–42, 237
Monetary policy 385–6, 512
Monopolies 395
Montreal Protocol 332, 333
Montserrat 79, 80
Monuments 321–3
Moorfields Eye Hospital 200
Mormon Church 241
Mortality 109, 244
Mortgage loans 348–9
Motor sports 306–7
Motor vehicles
 emissions 331
 excise duties 331, 407–8
 industry 483–4, 485
 licensing and standards 363–4
 ownership 11, 124
 retailing 525–6

see also Roads
Mountaineering 296, 307
MPs *see* Parliament
MSPs *see* Scottish Parliament
Museums and galleries 27, 248, 249, 250, 253, 259–61, 445
Music 33, 256–8, 265, 266
Music Standards Fund 264
Muslim community 240, 242, 243

N

National Air Quality Archive 331
National Air Traffic Services 360, 376, 403
National Archives of Scotland 264
National Army Museum 260
National Art Collections Fund 253
National Assembly for Wales 1, 28–31, 38, 43, 69, 120, 127, 166, 187, 189–90, 204, 249, 252, 271, 312, 316, 317, 323, 340, 342, 344, 345, 353, 354, 357, 361, 392, 454, 531, 546
National Asylum Support Service 114
National Audit Office 403
National Biodiversity Network 320
National Cancer Research Institute 201, 433
National Care Standards Commission 165, 166, 170, 211
National Childcare Strategy 128–9
National Clinical Assessment Authority 194
National College for School Leadership 136
National Consumer Council 528
National Council for:
Education and Training for Wales 127, 137, 139, 144
Hospices and Specialist Palliative Care Services 206
Voluntary Youth Services 145
National Crime Squad 219
National Criminal Intelligence Service 93, 219
National Curriculum 132–3, 221, 264, 401
National Cycle Network 365
National Endowment for Science, Technology and the Arts 252
National Engineering Laboratory 437
National Film and Television School 265
National Forest 467
National Forest Company 312
National Foundation for Youth Music 264
National Galleries of Scotland 27, 249, 261
National Gallery 259
National Grid for Learning 135–6, 263
National Health Service 187–212, 399, 438
National Heritage Memorial Fund 322
National Hospital for Neurology and Neurosurgery 200
National identity 114–17
National Institute for Clinical Excellence 188, 201
National Institute for Medical Research 433
National Institute of Adult Continuing Education 144
National Insurance 173–4, 404
National Insurance Contributions Office 539
National Insurance Fund 174
National Land Use Database 341
National Learning Targets 144
National Library of Scotland 263
National Library of Wales 33, 248, 263
National Lottery 123, 192, 252, 277, 291, 294, 297, 298, 299, 322, 408, 430
National Lottery Commission 123, 542
National Maritime Museum 260
National Measurement System 391, 437
National minimum wage 157
National Monuments Record Centre 322
National Museum of Photography, Film and Television 259
National Museum of Science and Industry 259
National Museums and Galleries of Northern Ireland 261
National Museums and Galleries of Wales 33, 261
National Museums and Galleries on Merseyside 260
National Museums of Scotland 27, 249, 260
National Nature Reserves 12, 32, 314
National Parks 12, 32, 314–15, 343
National Physical Laboratory 437
National Portrait Gallery 259
National Qualifications 134, 139
National Radiological Protection Board 336
National Railway Museum 259
National Register of Archives 264
National Savings 517, 539
National Scenic Areas 315
National Science Week 430
National Secular Society 238
National Service Frameworks 166, 195
National Sports Centres 293, 295, 296
National Sports Medicine Institute 297
National Statistics 63–4, 536
National Trails 316
National Traineeships 142
National Training Organisations 142–3, 265, 459
National Trust 314, 317
National Trust for Scotland 314, 317
National Vocational Qualifications 138
National Weights and Measures Laboratory 437, 538
National Youth Agency 145
National Youth Theatre 265
NATO *see* North Atlantic Treaty Organisation
Natura 2000 321
Natural disasters 95
Natural Environment Research Council 338, 424, 433–4, 441, 464
Natural History Museum 259, 261, 339, 445
Natural resources 490–508
Navy *see* Royal Navy
Neighbourhood Renewal National Strategy Action Plan 118–19
Netball 307
New Deals 152, 154–5
New Opportunities Fund 192, 263, 291
New Technology Institutes 143, 391
Newcastle upon Tyne 4, 375
Newport 28, 373
News agencies 282
Newspaper Publishers Association 282
Newspaper Society 282
Newspapers, national and regional 279–81
NHS *see* National Health Service
NHS Boards 190–1
NHS Direct 196–7
NHS Estates 542
NHS Pensions Agency 542
NHS Purchasing and Supplies Agency 542
NHS Trusts 189, 190, 200
NHS Walk-in Centres 197
NHSnet 197–8
Nice Treaty 82, 83
Nitrate Vulnerable Zones 329
Nobel Prizes 423
Noise pollution 334–6, 376
Non-departmental public bodies 61–2
North America 87–8
North Atlantic Treaty Organisation 75, 76, 85, 99, 100–1, 102, 105
North East England 11, 12, 117
North Sea *see* Gas industry; Oil Industry
North/South Implementation Bodies 16, 18
North/South Ministerial Council 16, 18, 191
North West England 11
Northern Ireland 13–21, 101–2; map 15
Northern Ireland, Secretary of State for 16, 17, 219, 233, 234
Northern Ireland Assembly 1, 13, 16, 17–18, 38, 43, 120, 271, 531
Northern Ireland Child Support Agency 178, 545
Northern Ireland Civil Service 66
Northern Ireland Committee of the Irish Congress of Trade Unions 162
Northern Ireland Co-ownership Housing Association 348, 351

Northern Ireland Electricity 500
Northern Ireland Executive 13, 16, 17–18, 116, 121, 191, 312, 345, 508
 departments 18, 127, 155, 188, 203, 250, 252, 315, 317, 323, 325, 340, 357, 362, 454, 459, 543–5
Northern Ireland Film Commission 251
Northern Ireland Forest Service 315, 465, 467, 543
Northern Ireland Grand Committee 55
Northern Ireland Health and Personal Social Services 198
Northern Ireland Health and Safety Executive 163
Northern Ireland Housing Executive 345, 351, 352
Northern Ireland Human Rights Commission 18
Northern Ireland Network for Education 136
Northern Ireland Office 537
Northern Ireland Police Service 13, 19–20, 219
Northern Ireland Prison Service 233–4, 537
Northern Ireland Railways 370
Northern Ireland Social Security Agency 545
Northern Ireland Sports Forum 294
Northern Ireland Statistics and Research Agency 34, 544
Northern Ireland Transport Holding Company 367
Northern School of Contemporary Dance 265
Norwich 4
Notting Hill Carnival 247
Nottingham 4, 371
Nuclear power 490, 502–3
Nuclear waste 336–7
Nuclear weapons 90, 103
Numeracy 133
Nurses 194, 198–9
Nursing homes *see* Residential care homes
Nutrition *see* Diet
NVQs *see* National Vocational Qualification

O

Obituaries 547–51
Occupational pensions 176
Occupations *see* Employment
Ofex 522
Office for National Statistics 34, 64, 119, 148, 401, 435, 536, 543
Office for Standards in Education 61, 134–5, 140, 168, 542
Office of:
 Communications 276
 Fair Trading 284, 394, 515, 538
 Gas and Electricity Markets 395, 497, 500, 542
 Government Commerce 402
 Manpower Economics 538
 Science and Technology 425, 426, 431
 Telecommunications 276, 285–6, 542
 the e-Envoy 390, 536
 the Rail Regulator 368, 542
 Water Services 507, 542
Oil industry 26, 490, 493–8
Older people 164, 165–6
Olympic Games 289, 290, 294
OM London 522
Ombudsmen 57–8, 71, 176, 215, 234, 510, 511–12
ONE 156
Open Skies Treaty 91
Open University 141, 272
Opera 257–8
Opposition, official 48
Optical equipment 482–3
Opticians 194–5
Orchestras 33, 256, 265
Orders in Council 42
Ordnance Survey 341, 543
Organ transplants 205
Organic farming 455, 456
Organisation for Economic Co-operation and Development 79, 414
Organisation for Security and Co-operation in Europe 76, 92
Organisation for the Prohibition of Chemical Weapons 90
Orkney Islands 1, 374
Orthodox Church 239
OSPAR 336, 496
Ottawa Convention 91
Output 379–81, 448–53
Overseas Territories 40, 42, 79–81, 99, 101, 114, 321; map 78
Oxford 4, 140, 263, 264
Ozone layer 333

P

Pacific region 87
Paper industry 475
Parades Commission 19
Paralympic Games 285
Parenting order 227
Parents *see* Children; Families; Lone parents
Parks *see under types of parks*
Parliament
 broadcasting 52, 271, 278
 committees 52, 54–6, 402
 duration and sessions 44
 and the EU 55, 56
 finance, control of 57
 functions 43–4
 law lords 42, 45, 215, 228, 229
 law-making and legislation 43, 52–4, 55, 56, 213
 Lords 44–5, 46, 52, 53–4, 242
 modernisation and reform 51
 MPs 9, 17, 25, 29, 45–6, 47, 50, 52, 116, 120
 Officers 45, 46
 origins 42–3
 party system in 48–9, 56
 powers 43
 and pressure groups 72
 privilege 58
 procedure 51
 public access 52
 Queen's Speech 52
 scrutiny of government policy 56–8
 Speakers 45, 46, 51
 whips 49
 see also Devolution; Elections; Monarchy
Parliamentary Boundary Commissions 45, 46, 49
Parliamentary Commissioner for Administration 57–8
Parliamentary Commissioner for Standards 52
Particle Physics and Astronomy Research Council 435, 440, 441
Parties, political *see* Political parties
Partners, New Deal for 155
Partnership for Peace 85, 100
Partnership Fund 158, 160
Partnerships UK 403
Part-time working 149
Patent Office 431, 538
Paternity leave 159
Patients 196
Pay 46, 59, 70, 117, 120, 121, 157–8, 159
Paymaster General 59
Payment systems, banks 515
Peacekeeping 88–90
Peerages 44–5
Pension funds 520
Pension Service 173
Pensions 172, 175–6, 179, 181
Pentecostalism 239
Periodical press 281–2
Periodical Publishers Association 282
Pesticides Safety Directorate 450, 541
Pet Travel Scheme 461
Peterborough 4
Petroleum *see* Oil
Petroleum revenue tax 404
PHARE 85, 503
Pharmaceuticals 477–8
Pharmacists 194
Philological societies 262
Phoenix Fund 355, 389
Pigs *see* Livestock
PILOT 495
Pipelines, oil and gas 495
Pitcairn, Ducie, Henderson and Oeno 79, 80
Planning 340–5
 see also Rural development; Urban regeneration
Planning Appeals Commission 344
Planning Inspectorate 344, 541
Planning Service 340, 341, 344, 544
Plas Menai 296
Plas y Brenin 296
Plastic cards 516–17
Plastics 478

Plymouth 4
Plymouth Marine Laboratory 434
Poet Laureate 36
Poetry Society 262
Police Complaints Authority 221
Police Ombudsman 20, 221
Police service 13, 19–20, 219–21, 401
Political parties 9, 10, 17, 24, 25, 29, 37, 45, 48–51, 56, 278
Pollution control 323–37, 491
Pop and rock music 257, 266
Population 3–4, 7, 12, 13, 14, 22, 23, 24, 29, 108–9
see also Census
Port Talbot 373
Ports 373–4
Portsmouth 4, 260, 323
Postal services and Post Offices 287–8, 514
Poultry *see* Livestock
Power *see* Energy
Premium Bonds 517
Presbyterian churches 238, 239
Prescriptions, medical 192–3
President of the Council 59
Press 33, 279–84
Press Association 282
Press Complaints Commission 282–3
Pressure groups 71–2
Prestwick 376
Primary Care Groups and Trusts 189, 198
Prime Minister 58–9, 66
Prime Minister's Office 59, 60, 537
Prince's Trust 146
Printing industry 475–6
Prison Service 222, 233–4, 542
Prisons Ombudsman 234
Private Bills 52, 54
Private Finance Initiative 192, 200, 234, 352, 403, 489
Private Members' Bills 52, 54
Privy Council 42
Privy Purse 41
Probation 234–5
Procurator fiscal 230, 546
Production *see* Output
Professional institutions, scientific 443–4
Prosecution 223–8, 229–31
Protein Fractionation Centre 205
Proudman Oceanographic Laboratory 434
Public Accounts Committee 402
Public Bills 52–4, 55
Public finance and expenditure 20, 25, 31, 70–1, 106, 119, 127, 154, 171, 172, 174, 251–2, 399–409, 426–7, 436
Public Guardianship Office 539
Public health 184–7
Public Health Laboratory Service 202–3
Public houses 529
Public Lending Right scheme 263
Public life, standards in 49, 52, 64–5
Public-Private Partnerships 360, 371, 376, 403, 489, 517
Public Record Office 264, 401, 543
Public relations 534–5
Public Service Agreements 63, 402
Publishing 262, 475–6

Q

QinetiQ 437, 438
Qualifications, educational 133, 134, 138, 139, 140–1
Qualifications and Curriculum Authority 133, 138
Quality and standards 390–1
Queen Margaret University College 265
Queen *see* Monarchy
Queen Elizabeth II Conference Centre 533, 541
Queen's Awards 338, 390

R

Race relations 115–17, 221
Radio
BBC 96, 258, 270, 272–3
digital services 270, 272
independent 258, 270, 275, 277
listening time 124
media ownership 276, 283–4
sports coverage 292
see also Broadcasting
Radio Authority 269, 275, 276, 277, 278, 283
Radio Joint Audience Research 278
Radioactivity and pollution 336–7
Radiocommunications Agency 276, 538
RAF *see* Royal Air Force
Railtrack 368
Railway equipment 485–6
Railways 323, 368–72
Rambert Dance Company 258
Ramsar Convention 33, 321
Rastafarianism 241
Rates Collection Agency 544
Recreation *see* Leisure; Sport
Recruitment 153–7
Recycling 325–6
Redundancy 159
Refineries 496
Reformed Church 239
Refugees 113–14
Regeneration *see* Planning; Rural development; Urban regeneration
Regional Co-ordination Unit 11, 60, 61, 539
Regional Development Agencies 10–11, 61, 354, 355, 390, 391, 392
see also Government Offices for the Regions
Regional Innovation Fund 392, 427
Regional Planning Guidance 342
Regional Selective Assistance 391
Regional Venture Capital Funds 390, 391
Registered social landlords *see* Landlords and tenants
Registers of Scotland 545
Registrar of Companies 396
Rehabilitation services 206
Religion 237–46
Religious education 133, 134, 245
Religious Society of Friends 239
Renewable energy sources 503–4
Rent Service Agency 541
Rental services 533
Rented housing 347, 349–53
Research and development 338–9, 423–45, 464, 477–8, 491, 503
Research and Technology Organisations 443
Research Councils 426, 428, 431–6, 441, 442
Reserve Forces (defence) 106
Residential care homes 165, 166
Resource: the Council of Museums, Archives and Libraries 250, 253
Restaurants 529
Retail banks 513–15
Retail Prices Index 384
Retail trade 524–7
Retirement pension 175–6
Rights of way 316–17
Ripon 4
Rivers Agency 543
Road haulage 366, 484
Roads 210, 362–8
see also Motor vehicles
Roads Service 363, 545
Roman Catholic Church 238, 241–2, 243
Rome Treaty 81, 214
Roslin Institute 424
Rowing 307–8
Royal Academy of Arts 260
Royal Academy of Dramatic Art 265
Royal Academy of Engineering 426, 443–4
Royal Academy of Music 265
Royal Air Force 101–7
agencies 540
Royal Air Force College, Cranwell 106
Royal Air Force Museum 260
Royal Armouries 260
Royal Assent 40, 53
Royal Ballet 258, 265
Royal Botanic Gardens 320, 438, 444, 464
Royal College of Art 265, 266
Royal College of Music 265
Royal Commissions 223
Royal Family *see* Monarchy
Royal Institution 430, 444
Royal Jubilee Trust 146
Royal Mail 287
Royal Military Academy, Sandhurst 106
Royal Mint 539
Royal Museum 260
Royal National Eisteddfod 33
Royal National Lifeboat Institution 373

Royal National Theatre 255, 265
Royal Navy 101–7
agencies 540
Royal Northern College of Music 265
Royal Opera House 257, 258
Royal Parks Agency 323, 541
Royal Pharmaceutical Society of Great Britain 194
Royal Scottish Academy of Music and Drama 265
Royal Shakespeare Company 256
Royal Society 426, 427, 430, 441, 443
Royal Society for the Protection of Birds 320
Royal Society of Arts 444
Royal Society of Edinburgh 444
Royal Society of Literature 262
Royal Ulster Constabulary *see* Northern Ireland Police Service
Rubber industry 478
Rugby football 33, 289, 290, 308
Rural Development Commission 11
Rural Development Programmes 392, 454, 455–6
Rural housing 353
Rural Payments Agency 541
Rural regeneration 356
Rural Transport Partnership 367
Russia 85, 86
Rutherford Appleton Laboratory 436

S

Safety
food 210, 453
health and, at work 162–3, 496
medicines 211
nuclear 503
radioactivity 336
sports grounds 292
transport 364, 369, 373, 376–7
Sailing 308–9
St Albans 4
St David's 4
St Fagans 33, 261
St Helena and dependencies 79, 80
St Ives 259
Salaries *see* Pay
Salford 4, 260
Salisbury 4
Salmon 464
Salvation Army 239, 245
Sanger Centre 423–4
Satellite broadcasting 269–70, 277
Satellite equipment 439–40
Scholarship schemes 96, 145
Schools
admissions 131
Beacon 131
broadcasting for 272
business links with 137
City Academies 130
City Technology Colleges 130
class sizes 129
community 127
controlled (Northern Ireland) 128
curriculum and assessment 132–4, 221, 264, 265
European schools 145
foundation 127
governing bodies 131, 132
independent 128, 131
information and communications technology 135–6
inspection and performance 134–5
integrated (Northern Ireland) 128
management 131–2
nursery/pre-school 128–9
parents' involvement 132
physical education 291
primary 128, 129
pupil numbers 128
secondary 128, 129–31
special educational needs 128, 135
specialist 130
voluntary 128
see also Teachers
Science, sports 298
Science and technology 423–45
Science Budget 426
Science centres 430, 445
Science Enterprise Challenge 429
Science festivals 430
Science Parks 442–3
Science Research Investment Fund 426, 429
Science Year initiative 430
Scientific museums 259, 445
Scilly Isles 1, 11, 393
Scotland 22–7; map 23
Scotland, Museum of 27, 260
Scotland, Secretary of State for 25, 38
Scotland Office 537
Scottish Agricultural and Biological Research Institutes 439, 464
Scottish Agricultural College 439, 459, 464
Scottish Agricultural Museum 260
Scottish Agricultural Science Agency 545
Scottish Arts Council *see* Arts Councils
Scottish Ballet 258, 265
Scottish Centre for Infection and Environmental Health 203
Scottish Commission for the Regulation of Care 169
Scottish Council on Alcohol 204
Scottish Country Life, Museum of 27
Scottish Court Service 232, 546
Scottish Crime Squad 219
Scottish Crime Survey 216
Scottish Criminal Cases Review Commission 231
Scottish Daily Newspaper Society 282
Scottish Drug Enforcement Agency 218
Scottish Enterprise 26, 357, 389, 392, 439
Scottish Environment Protection Agency 323, 324, 325, 328, 336, 339
Scottish Executive 22, 23–5, 27, 38, 121, 127, 187, 188, 190–1, 197, 204, 214, 217, 232, 249, 264, 312, 317, 334, 340, 342, 344, 345, 350, 354, 357, 362, 372, 392, 403, 439, 448, 454, 455, 508, 545–6
Scottish Fisheries Protection Agency 545
Scottish Grand Committee 55
Scottish Health Plan 190, 191, 202
Scottish Homes *see* Communities Scotland
Scottish Institute of Sport 296
Scottish Legal Aid Board 236
Scottish Legal Services Ombudsman 215
Scottish National Gallery of Modern Art 27, 261
Scottish National Portrait Gallery 261
Scottish National War Museum 260
Scottish Natural Heritage 313, 314, 316, 317, 319
Scottish Newspaper Publishers Association 282
Scottish Opera 257
Scottish Parliament 1, 22, 23–5, 38, 43, 120, 213, 214, 229, 232, 271, 531
Scottish Parliamentary Commissioner for Administration 58
Scottish Partnership Agency for Palliative and Cancer Care 206
Scottish Poetry Library 262
Scottish Prison Service 233–4, 545
Scottish Public Pensions Agency 545
Scottish Qualifications Authority 134, 140
Scottish Rural Development Programme 455
Scottish Screen 251
Scottish Sports Aid Foundation 298
Scottish Sports Association 294
Scottish Sports Council *see* sportscotland
Scottish Trades Union Congress 161
Scottish University for Industry 143
Scottish Wildlife Trust 320
Scottish Youth Theatre 265
Scouts 146
SCRAN 248
Sea *see* Marine; Shipping
Sea Fish Industry Authority 461
Security policy (Northern Ireland) 19–20
Select committees (Parliament) 52, 55-6, 402
Self-employment 151
Sellafield 336, 503
Sentencing 226–8, 231
Serious Fraud Office 222, 224, 540
Serjeant at Arms 46
SERPS 172, 176
Service industries 148, 151, 509–35
Seventh-Day Adventists 241
Severe Disablement Allowance 155, 180
Sex education 133, 134
Sexual health 207–8
Sgrîn 251
Share ownership 521
Sheep *see* Livestock
Sheffield 4, 296, 355
Sheriff courts 230, 231, 232

Shetland Islands 1
Shipbuilding 484–5
Shipping 372–4
Shopping facilities 526–7
Sickness benefits 180
Sierra Leone 89
Sikh community 240–1, 242
single European currency *see* Euro, the
single European market 83, 395, 417–18
Single Regeneration Budget 351, 355, 392
Sites of Special Scientific Interest 12, 32, 313, 319, 320
Skiing 309
Skill Build 142
Skill Force 401
Skills Development Fund 392
Skills for Life 144
Skills Investment Fund 265
Skillseekers 142
Skillset 265
Slade School of Art 266
Small Business Council 389
Small Business Gateway 389, 392
Small Business Investment Taskforce 390
Small Business Research Initiative 427
Small Business Service 355, 389, 390, 391, 436, 437, 538
Small Firms Loan Guarantee Scheme 389
Small Firms Training Loans 142
Smallholdings 447–8
'Smart' cards *see* Plastic cards
Smart scheme 437
Smoking 186, 204
Snooker 309
Soccer *see* Football
Social Care Institute for Excellence 165
Social exclusion 118–19
Social Exclusion Unit 60, 208, 354
Social Fund 179
Social housing 350–1
Social Inclusion Partnership 197, 357
Social security 171–83, 399
see also Welfare-to-Work programme
Social services, personal 164–71
Social trends 119–25
Society for Education through Art 266
Society of Editors 282
Solicitor-General 59, 222, 539
Solicitor-General for Scotland 230, 232
Solicitors *see* Legal Profession
Solvent misuse 205
Somerset House 260
South Africa 88
South Bank Centre 254, 262
South East England 7, 11, 12, 115, 117, 148
South Georgia and South Sandwich Islands 80
South Pacific Commission 87
South West England 7, 12
South Yorkshire 7, 11, 67, 371, 393
Southampton 4, 373, 374
Southampton Oceanography Centre 433
Space for Sport and Arts 264, 291
Space science and equipment 424, 435, 439–40, 487
Special Areas of Conservation 32, 321
Special Educational Needs 128, 135
Special Protection Areas 33, 321
Specialist Sports Colleges 291
Spiritualists 241
Sponsorship 252–3, 277, 298
Sport 33, 289–310
Sport Action Zones 291
Sport England 291, 293, 296, 297, 298
sports coach UK 297, 298
Sports Councils 293, 294, 296, 297, 298
SportsAid 298
sportscotland 293, 296, 298
Sportsmatch 298
Squash 309
Stabilisation and Association Agreements 86, 419
Stadiums, sports 292–3, 295, 296
Stakeholder pensions 172
Stamp duty 409
Standing committees (Parliament) 55
Standing Orders 51
Stansted 375, 376
State Second Pension 172
State Veterinary Service 459
Statistical service *see* National Statistics
Statute law *see* Legislation
Statutory instruments 54
Statutory Maternity Pay 159, 177
Statutory Sick Pay 180
Steel industry 32, 479–80
Stock Exchange *see* London Stock Exchange
Stoke-on-Trent 4, 261
Stoneleigh 453
Strategic Defence Review 99
Strategic Rail Authority 360, 368, 542
Structural Funds 20, 83–4, 354, 393, 457
Student Awards Agency for Scotland 545
Students 140, 141, 145
Styal 261
Sullom Voe 374
Sunderland 4
Supermarkets 524
Sure Start 129, 159, 177, 354
Sustainable development 337, 378
Swansea 4, 28, 261, 373
Swanwick 376
Swimming 309–10
Swindon 322

T

Table tennis 310
TACIS 85, 503
Tate (art galleries) 259
Taxes and duties 25, 83, 70, 117–18, 182, 299, 325, 331, 334, 404–9, 491, 493–4
Taxi services 368
TCS 436
Teachers 136–7
see also Schools
Technology *see* Science and technology
Teenagers *see* Children
Tees and Hartlepool 374
Telecommunications 124, 284–6, 483, 533–4
Teletext 275
Television
audience share 270, 278
awards 258
BBC 258, 269, 271–2, 273
cable and satellite 269–70, 275–7
digital services 33, 270–1
exports 273
independent 269, 273–5, 276, 277
international agreements 278–9
media ownership 276, 283–4
sports coverage 292
teletext 275
viewing time 123, 258
see also Broadcasting
Teleworking 151
Temporary employment 151
Tenants *see* Landlords and tenants; Rented housing
Tennis 289, 290, 310
Territorial Army 106
Terrorism 19, 92–3, 218, 233
Textile industry 473–4
Thamesport 373
The Appeals Service (TAS) 173
Theatre *see* Drama
Tidy Britain Group 327, 329
Tir Gofal 33, 455
Tobacco industry 472–3
excise duties 408
see also Advertising; Smoking; Sponsorship
Tollymore 297
Tourism 11, 26, 124–5, 529–32
Trade, international 20, 87, 383, 410–22, 453, 496–7
controls on 91, 419–20
see also World Trade Organisation
Trade and Industry, Department of 62, 97, 269, 333, 354, 388, 391, 415–16, 420, 425, 428, 436–7, 496, 503, 538
Trade associations 398
Trade Partners UK 421
Trade unions 160, 161–2, 282
Trades Union Congress 161
Traffic *see* Roads
Training 142–3, 264–6
see also Adult education; Lifelong learning; Vocational education
Training and Employment Agency 544
Tramways 371
Transcendental Meditation movement 241
Transplant surgery 205

Transport 11, 118, 152, 341–2, 359–77
  see also under types of transport
Transport, Local Government and the Regions, Department for 62, 67, 246, 336, 340, 341, 344, 345, 353, 354, 362, 365, 377, 438, 541
Transport for London 9, 360, 366, 371
Travel 124, 359, 529–30, 531
Treasury, HM 60, 79, 97, 385, 387, 402, 403, 512, 538
Treasury Solicitor's Department 539
Tree preservation and planting 315–16
Trials 225–6, 230–1
Tribunals 161
Trinity College of Music 265
Tristan da Cunha 80
Truro 4
Tuberculosis 185, 203, 459
Turks and Caicos islands 79, 80, 321
Tyndall Centre for Climate Change Research 3, 434
Tyne and Wear 67, 371

U

UK Accreditation Service 391
UK Anti-Drugs Co-ordination Unit 291
UK Atomic Energy Authority 503
UK Central Council for Nursing, Midwifery and Health Visiting 194
UK Debt Management Office 403
UK High Technology Fund 390
UK Online Centres 143, 400
UK Passport Agency 542
UK Publishing Media 282
UK Sports Council (UK Sport) 293, 298
UK Sports Institute 295–7
UK Transplant 205
Ukraine 85, 86
Ulster *see* Northern Ireland
Ulster museums 261
Ulster Sports and Recreation Trust 298–9
Ulster Youth Drama Theatre 265
Unemployment 20, 26, 32, 115, 148–9, 154–5, 176–7, 385
Unification Church 241
Union Learning Fund 143
Union of Industrial and Employers' Confederations of Europe 397
Union of Welsh Independents 239
Unit trusts 520
Unitarians 239
Unitary authorities *see* Local government
United Nations 75
  drug control programme 93
  human rights 92
  and Iraq 86, 88
  peacekeeping 88–9
  refugees convention 113
  register of arms transfers 91
  Security Council 75
  terrorism convention 93
United Reformed Church 239, 240, 243
United States 87, 93
Universal Declaration of Human Rights 92
Universities 140–1, 263, 264, 266, 442–3
University Challenge Fund 429
University Innovation Centres 391
Urban regeneration 354–8
Urban Task Force 355
Utilities, privatised 395

V

Valuation and Lands Agency 544
Valuation Office 539
Value added tax 83, 404, 407
Vehicle Certification Agency 364, 541
Vehicle Inspectorate 331, 364, 541
Vehicles *see* Motor vehicles
Venture capital 517–18
Veterinary Laboratories Agency 459, 464, 541
Veterinary Medicines Directorate 461, 541
Veterinary Products Committee 461
Victim Support 226
Victims of Violence Commission (Northern Ireland) 19
Victoria and Albert Museum 259
Vienna Document 91
virt-x 522, 523
Visiting Arts Office of Great Britain and Northern Ireland 251
Vocational education 137–40
Voluntary organisations 121–3, 146, 297, 314
  see also Charities
Voters and voting *see* Elections

W

Wages *see* Pay
Wakefield 4
Wakehurst Place 320, 444
Wales 28–33; map 30
  see also Welsh
Wales, Prince of 41
Wales, Secretary of State for 31, 38
Wales European Funding Office 546
Wales Office 537–8
Wales Rural Development Plan 455
Walking 289, 365–6
  see also Rights of way
Wallace Collection 260
Walsall 260
War pensions 181–2
Warm Front Team 493
Warrenpoint 374
Waste disposal 325–7, 336–7
Water Service 545
Water sports 296
Water supply 504, 506–8
  pollution control 328–30
Waterways 372
Weald and Downland Museum 261
Wealth distribution 117–18
Weapons *see* Arms control; Firearms
Weather *see* Climate
Welfare-to-Work programme 138, 154–5
Wellcome Trust 424, 426, 428, 429, 443, 444
Wells 4
Welsh Academy 262
Welsh Administration Ombudsman 58
Welsh Assembly *see* National Assembly for Wales
Welsh Book Council 262
Welsh College of Music and Drama 265
Welsh Development Agency 31, 32, 357, 392–3
Welsh Fourth Channel Authority 274
Welsh Grand Committee 55
Welsh Institute of Sport 296
Welsh language 32, 249, 270, 274
Welsh League of Youth 146
Welsh Life, Museum of 33, 261
Welsh Mental Health Strategy 167
Welsh National Opera 33, 257
Welsh Slate Museum 33
Welsh Sports Association 294
Welsh Youth Agency 145
West Drayton 376
West Midlands 7, 11, 67, 343, 468
West Wales and the Valleys 356–7, 393
West Yorkshire 7, 67, 115
Western European Union 84
Westminster 4
Westminster, Palace of 45
Westminster Abbey 40
Wetlands 33, 321
Whisky industry 26, 471–2
White Papers 53
Wholesaling 523–4
Widows' benefits 179
Wight, Isle of 1
Wildlife and Countryside Directorate 312
Wildlife protection 33, 314, 317–21, 495
Wildlife Trusts 320
Wilton Park International Conference Centre 96, 540
Wimbledon 289, 295
Winchester 4
  Bishop of 44
Wind power 504
Windscale 503
Winfrith 503
Winter sports 309
Witness Service 226
Wolfson Foundation 427, 430
Wolverhampton 115
Women
  in the Civil Service 66
  clergy 243

in developing countries 94–5
employment and income 119–20, 149
equal opportunities 121
in Parliament and Government 45, 120–1
in science 431
see also Children; Families
Women's National Commission 121
Women's Sports Foundation 294
Woodland Grant Scheme 316, 455, 466
Woodland Trust 316
Woods *see* Forests
Worcester 25
Work and Pensions, Department for 62, 152–3, 164, 167, 173, 542
Workers' Educational Association 143
Workforce *see* Employment
Working Families' Tax Credit 178–9, 405
Working hours 157–8
WORKSTEP 167
World Bank 79
World Class Events Programme 292
World Class Performance Programme 292
World Conservation Union 321
World Heritage Sites 80, 323
World Trade Organisation 79, 418
Wytch Farm 494

Y

Yachting *see* Sailing
York 241, 259
Archbishop of 44
Yorkshire and the Humber 12
Young people
and the arts 264–6
in care 118, 170–1
offenders 225, 227–8, 231
training and employment 149, 154
youth service 145–6
see also Children; Education
Youth Council for Northern Ireland 146
Youth courts 225
Youth Justice Board 222, 291
Yugoslavia, Federal Republic of 89–90

Z

Zoological gardens 444
Zoroastrians 241

Gas and Oil Production in the UK

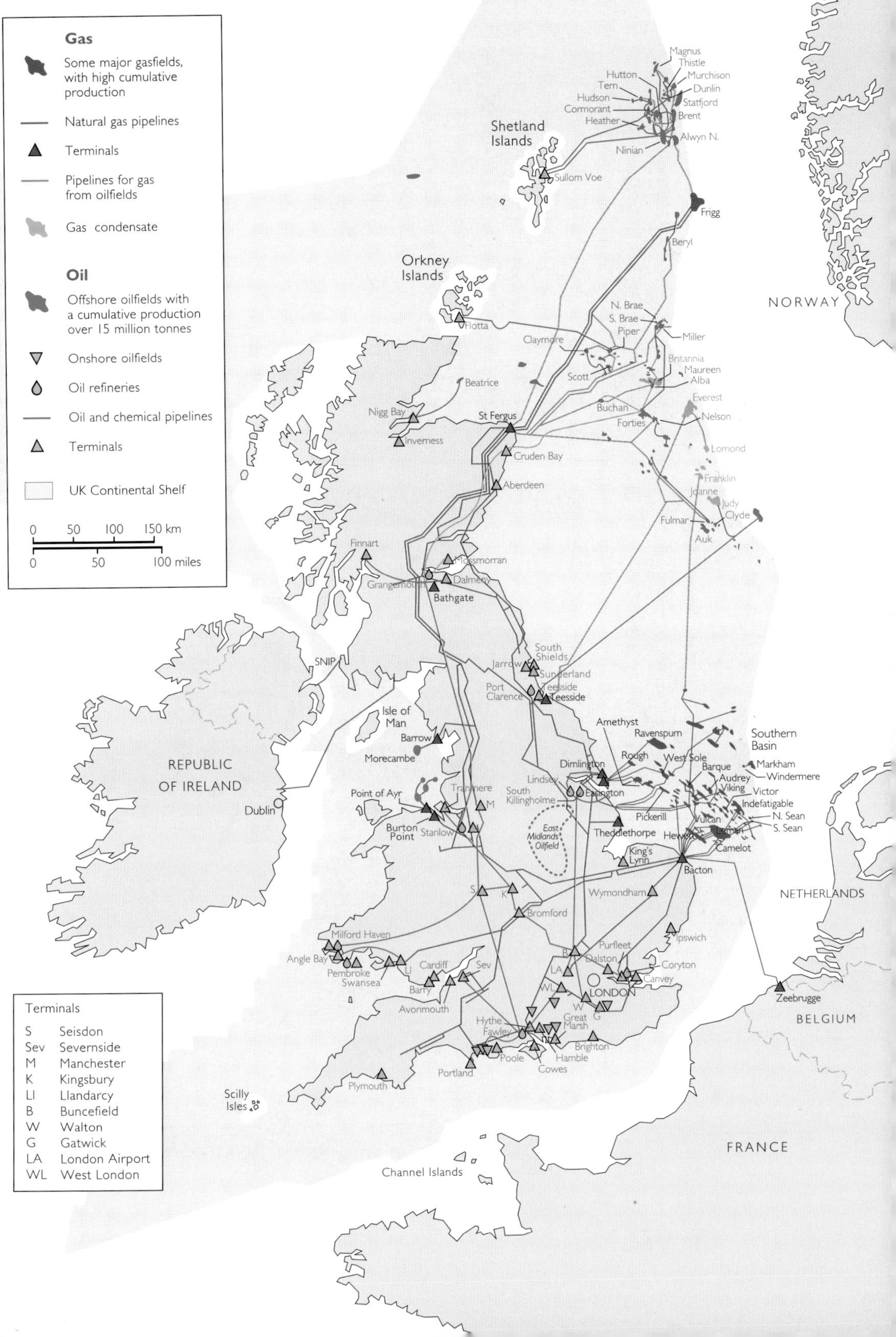
Gas
Some major gasfields, with high cumulative production
Natural gas pipelines
Terminals
Pipelines for gas from oilfields
Gas condensate
Oil
Offshore oilfields with a cumulative production over 15 million tonnes
Onshore oilfields
Oil refineries
Oil and chemical pipelines
Terminals
UK Continental Shelf
0 50 100 150 km
0 50 100 miles
Terminals
S Seisdon
Sev Severnside
M Manchester
K Kingsbury
Ll Llandarcy
B Buncefield
W Walton
G Gatwick
LA London Airport
WL West London
Shetland Islands
Sullom Voe
Magnus
Thistle
Murchison
Hutton
Tern
Dunlin
Hudson
Statfjord
Cormorant
Brent
Heather
Alwyn N.
Ninian
Frigg
Beryl
Orkney Islands
Flotta
NORWAY
N. Brae
S. Brae
Piper
Miller
Claymore
Britannia
Maureen
Alba
Scott
Beatrice
Everest
Buchan
Nelson
Forties
Nigg Bay
Inverness
St Fergus
Cruden Bay
Lomond
Aberdeen
Franklin
Joanne
Judy
Clyde
Fulmar
Auk
Finnart
Mossmorran
Grangemouth
Dalmeny
Bathgate
SNIP
South Shields
Jarrow
Sunderland
Teesside
Port Clarence
Teesside
Isle of Man
Amethyst
Ravenspurn
Southern Basin
Barrow
Morecambe
Rough
West Sole
Markham
Windermere
Dimlington
Barque
Audrey
Viking
Victor
REPUBLIC OF IRELAND
Lindsey
Tranmere
South Killingholme
Easington
Indefatigable
Point of Ayr
M
Pickerill
N. Sean
S. Sean
Dublin
Burton Point
Stanlow
East Midlands Oilfield
Theddlethorpe
Hewett
Vulcan
Leman
Camelot
King's Lynn
Bacton
S
K
Wymondham
NETHERLANDS
Bromford
Milford Haven
Ipswich
Angle Bay
Pembroke
Swansea
Ll
Cardiff
Sev
B
Purfleet
Dalston
LA
Coryton
Canvey
Barry
WL
LONDON
W
G
Zeebrugge
Avonmouth
BELGIUM
Hythe
Fawley
Great Marsh
Brighton
Poole
Hamble
Cowes
Portland
Plymouth
Scilly Isles
FRANCE
Channel Islands

Passenger Railway Network in the UK

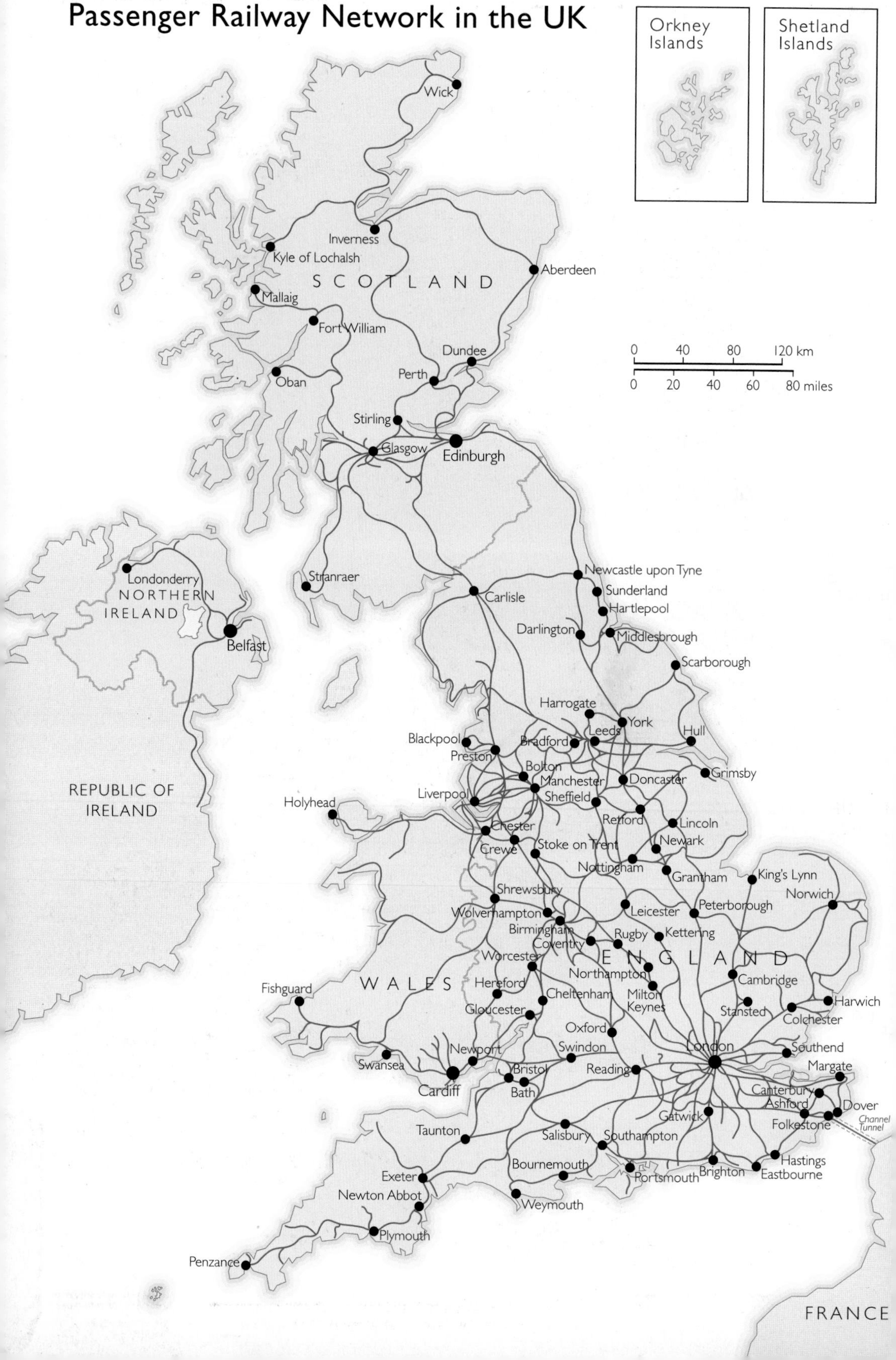

Orkney Islands
Shetland Islands
0 40 80 120 km
0 20 40 60 80 miles
SCOTLAND
Wick
Inverness
Kyle of Lochalsh
Aberdeen
Mallaig
Fort William
Dundee
Perth
Oban
Stirling
Glasgow
Edinburgh
Stranraer
Londonderry
NORTHERN IRELAND
Belfast
REPUBLIC OF IRELAND
Newcastle upon Tyne
Sunderland
Hartlepool
Carlisle
Darlington
Middlesbrough
Scarborough
Harrogate
York
Leeds
Hull
Blackpool
Bradford
Preston
Bolton
Grimsby
Manchester
Doncaster
Liverpool
Sheffield
Holyhead
Retford
Lincoln
Chester
Crewe
Stoke on Trent
Newark
Nottingham
Grantham
King's Lynn
Shrewsbury
Norwich
Wolverhampton
Leicester
Peterborough
Birmingham
Rugby
Kettering
Coventry
Worcester
ENGLAND
Northampton
Cambridge
Fishguard
WALES
Hereford
Cheltenham
Milton Keynes
Harwich
Gloucester
Stansted
Colchester
Oxford
London
Southend
Swindon
Newport
Swansea
Bristol
Reading
Margate
Cardiff
Bath
Canterbury
Ashford
Dover
Gatwick
Channel Tunnel
Folkestone
Taunton
Salisbury
Southampton
Hastings
Bournemouth
Portsmouth
Brighton
Eastbourne
Exeter
Newton Abbot
Weymouth
Plymouth
Penzance
FRANCE